# PEOPLES, NATIONS AND CULTURES

# PEOPLES, NATIONS AND CULTURES

## AN A–Z OF THE PEOPLES OF THE WORLD, PAST AND PRESENT

GENERAL EDITOR
PROFESSOR JOHN M. MACKENZIE

WEIDENFELD & NICOLSON

This edition first published in the UK 2005 by
Weidenfeld & Nicolson
Wellington House, 125 Strand, London WC2R 0BB

10  9  8  7  6  5  4  3  2  1

**British Library Cataloguing-in-Publication Data**
A catalogue entry for this book is available from the British Library

ISBN 0-304-36550-5

Printed and bound in Finland by WS Bookwell Ltd.


Produced by John Haywood and Simon Hall
Designed by Darren Bennett
Edited by Lisa Isenman, Mark Hawkins Dady and Jonathan Dore
Maps by John Haywood and Darren Bennett
Contributing authors: Nigel Dalziel, John Haywood, Antony Jack,
Colin Penny and John Swift

**... a Haywood & Hall production for Weidenfeld & Nicolson**

# Contents

# Editors and advisors

**Professor Hermann Hiery,** University of Bayreuth, Germany (Oceania)

**Professor Victor King,** University of Hull, UK (Asia)

**Professor John M. MacKenzie,** University of St Andrews, UK (Africa)

**Professor David MacNab,** Trent University, Canada (The Americas)

**Professor Jeffrey Richards,** University of Lancaster, UK (Europe)

**Dr Jane Samson,** University of Edmonton, Canada (Australasia)

**Professor Sergei Savoskul,** University of Moscow, Russia (Asia)

**Dr Deborah Sutton,** University of Lancaster, UK (Asia)

**Dr Alan Wood,** University of Lancaster, UK (Europe)

# Introduction

In the 21st century, human beings seem to be such an extraordinarily diverse, dominant and prolific species. But it was not always so. The great explosion in human populations around the globe has mainly occurred since 1750, and it is only in comparatively recent times that human societies have come fully to dominate their environments. The age-old checks of disease, war, natural disaster and famine still inhibit human numbers, reducing opportunities for satisfactory subsistence and increasing the dangers of early mortality, particularly among children, in some parts of the globe. But for many people in the world, these checks have largely been banished. While some populations are under real threat, for example in a few parts of Africa, most have passed through a period of unsurpassed, and some would argue unsustainable, growth. While the global human population grew from approximately 5 million to 10 million people 10,000 years ago (obviously a highly tentative estimate), then to some 800 million in 1750, it had ballooned to 5 billion by 1990. Some predict that it will have reached 9 billion by 2050.

With this great growth in numbers, there seem to have been two contrary trends. On the one hand, human societies, which in the early Stone Age era were strikingly similar, have apparently become ever more complex and differentiated. On the five continents that sustain human existence, peoples and cultures appear to be very different in terms of language, spiritual values and social formations, in ideas encompassing the environment, in concepts of past and future, and in representations of all of these in myth, literatures and artistic forms. Yet the biological and physical differences among peoples are actually very slight. Modern techniques like blood-typing and DNA analysis reveal a much closer affinity among peoples than was suspected in the past, for example during the 19th century in Europe and America. But despite this apparent diversity, the world also appears to have become victim to a homogenizing global culture, in which media, communications, transport, urbanization, consumption and international markets have produced recognizable similarities in lifestyles in all the continents.

But cultures remain resistant to these trends. When peoples and cultures are placed under threat, whether by the encroachments and power-play of dominant nations or through processes of internal or global change, they have a tendency to rediscover and re-imagine what it is that makes them different. As the archaeological record shows, environmental factors have had, perhaps, an even greater capacity to threaten the survival and autonomy of societies than was formerly recognized; but even here, survivors often re-establish themselves through efforts to recreate past traditions and forms. Looking at the peoples of the world, it is the dynamic survival of cultures rather than their decline and disappearance that is most striking. That is not to say that all such peoples have survived. There are some notable exceptions, of whom the Caribs and the Tasmanians (the manner in which they are named neatly represents their dispossession and destruction) are among the best known.

In the 19th century, many Europeans and Americans saw such 'extinctions' as representing an iron law of evolution. They expected many other peoples, including Native Americans, Canadian First Nations (to use modern terminology), some Africans, Australian Aborigines, Maoris, Pacific Islanders and many of the Asian so-called 'tribals' (that is, subordinate groups, appearing to be survivals of earlier peoples) to 'go the wall'. This did not happen, and many peoples revealed themselves to be more resilient and resistant than Westerners had often supposed. They still passed through very difficult times, in which their survival techniques were tested to the limit, but the peoples who died out remained relatively few in number. Despite this, it has to be said that some peoples remain under threat to this day.

## Hominids and early humans

These considerations, in respect of the history of human cultures, represent a very shallow time-span. If we turn to the much deeper history of humans on this planet, the story is not only much more complex, but also considerably more obscure. Early hominids, the predecessors of *Homo sapiens*, can be identified in the archaeological and geological record as emerging over 3 million years ago. Remains of such hominids have been found in Africa, Europe and Asia. Forms known as *Homo erectus* (because an upright gait had already been adopted) and *Homo habilis* (because of the evidence of tool-using) are generally accepted as being the ancestors of *Homo sapiens*, who probably developed towards the end of the Middle Pleistocene era, some 100,000 to 250,000 years ago (although some suggest that this transition may have taken place even earlier). The early hominids disappeared, and some, like the Neanderthals, were evolutionary dead-ends. *Homo sapiens* is generally defined as those humans with an upright stance, a brain capacity averaging roughly 1350 cubic centimetres, a high forehead and smaller teeth than the earlier hominids, a well-defined chin on a flatter face, and the ability to make and use tools and to conceptualize symbols that represent the development of language and even of aesthetic sensibilities.

### *Homo sapiens* and global expansion

It is now generally accepted that modern *Homo sapiens* first emerged in eastern Africa. It may be that this was because of a very favourable climate and a landscape well filled with faunal resources for food. Glaciation further north and south on the globe would have made many regions much less habitable. But from eastern Africa, the dispersal of *Homo sapiens* seems to have been fairly rapid, first into Europe and western Asia, then across the Asian continent. Remarkably, the ancestors of Australian aborigines may have reached the southern continent as long as 60,000 years ago. To do this, they must have crossed the sea from Southeast Asia to New Guinea and may be among the earliest navigators. The Americas were reached by a land bridge across the modern Bering Strait towards the end of the Ice Age about 12,000 years ago. North and South America were populated fairly rapidly by hunting peoples, although there remains a debate about the precise ways in which this happened. Thus far, *Homo sapiens* had travelled largely (but not exclusively) overland, often using land bridges that no longer exist; but the final peopling of the globe took place in the Pacific Ocean, when people who are now identified as Micronesians, Melanesians and Polynesians embarked on truly heroic voyages in search of land that lay well over their visible horizons. These movements probably started about 4000 years ago and culminated with the arrival of the Polynesian Maoris in New Zealand.

It should not be thought, however, that this peopling of the world by *Homo sapiens* occurred as a result of a set of simple and linear migrations. The reality was probably a good deal more complex than that, with populations emerging, mingling, dispersing and re-forming in many different parts of the globe. Not only did many and varied cultures, languages and social formations develop as a result of these processes, but soon larger-scale societies began to appear. Evidence for central political and spiritual authority, together with widely held belief-systems, can be found well back in the archaeological record. In the millennia before the Christian era, the great centralized civilizations of the Indus Valley (in modern Pakistan), of Mesopotamia (the modern Iraq), Egypt, Persia (Iran), Greece, Rome, Southeast Asia, and later those of Central and South America, together with some in other parts of the world, had emerged, leaving a rich archaeological and artistic heritage. But such civilizations collapse as well as rise, and in the debris of their demise new cultures, often mingling elements from the past and from neighbours as well as creating new forms, emerge.

Another characteristic of dominant cultures is that they tend to set up waves of migrations of peoples. Sometimes such migrations result from the movement of refugees as a result of wars, occasionally from an elite's desire to 'pacify' or otherwise dominate outer regions by settling their own people there, and often from the need for labour or additional recruits for military service. Such migrations can be identified in many past eras, such as the movement of Aryans into western and South Asia or the dispersal of Greeks and Persians. At times such movements of people involve the spread of religions, such as Buddhism, Hinduism and Islam into Southeast Asia or Islam in the Mediterranean or African worlds. The latter saw the spread of Arabic-speaking peoples from the Middle East throughout North Africa, into parts of Europe, and also into East Africa.

## Modern migrations

The past few centuries have seen an acceleration of such migrations. White people have moved in large numbers from Europe to North and South America, to Australasia and to some parts of Africa. European Russians migrated to many parts of Asia. Africans (perhaps more than 10 million of them) were transported through slavery across the Atlantic to the Americas, the Caribbean, and also to the Indian-Ocean and Middle-Eastern worlds. Groups of such black peoples have now moved to Europe. Chinese people constituted key labour forces in Southeast Asia, North and South America and even Australasia. Indians became indentured labourers in the Caribbean, Indian Ocean islands and East Africa. In a smaller-scale migration, people from the Levant and the Mediterranean worlds appeared in West Africa and elsewhere. More recently, some Indo-Chinese (from Vietnam and Cambodia) have moved to Australasia. Sometimes, such migrations establish new cultures or nations; at other times they create ethnic minorities within different cultures and peoples.

## Dominant cultures

One of the striking aspects of dominant human cultures is that they tend to view themselves as unique, central civilizations to which all other peoples are inferior and sometimes tributary. This was the case with the great dynastic civilizations of China, which tended to categorize other peoples as 'barbarians' beyond the pale of the central culture. It was also true of the successive Mediterranean societies and of many others in the world. This was often reflected in the manner in which the globe was conceptualized by such people, with the major culture at the centre of the known world and all other peoples represented as beyond the boundaries. In the era of cartography, this was incorporated into the making of maps. Some of the earliest maps that are still extant placed Jerusalem at the centre of the known world.

These attitudes were recreated in modern times by the western European empires. The maps of the Spanish and Portuguese, later of the British, empires placed Europe at the centre of the globe, with colonies fanning out east and west and south. In the British case, this way of looking at the world was emphasized by the notion that the Greenwich meridian of zero longitude ran through the outskirts of London, while the projection of the 16th-century Flemish cartographer Mercator (turning the circular globe into a flat projection) could be conveniently used to place Europe at the centre. All of this is important because it illustrates the manner in which cultures have a tendency to form distinctive mutual conceptions of each other, both in a global 'imperial' sense and in terms of regional groupings on the various continents. Hence definitions of, and attitudes towards, 'peoples, nations, cultures' (see below) invariably emerge from patterns of political dominance and subordination.

## Identities

Identities are made up of at least two elements. One is the way in which people view themselves. They may imagine themselves as a small kin-grouping, a 'band', as they might well have done in the Stone and early Iron ages. They may, further, conceive of this group as belonging to a wider society with which they share many characteristics, and might indeed inter-marry. These forms of localized and wider imagining of a sense of community span many centuries, and even millennia, of human development. Once more centralized political forms emerge, people may well identify with the structure that supposedly gives them protection and organizes multifarious aspects of their lives. Then, a political or spiritual elite might have an interest in propagating notions of shared identity among a wide range of people or peoples sometimes inhabiting a considerable geographical area. In this situation, identities may well be formed out of an interaction of ideas and shared experience between the dominant elite and the people themselves. But around the fringes of such a formation, identities are always going to be weaker and will invariably be prepared to, or be forced into, maintaining or developing a different identity, not least by their relations with neighbouring peoples not fully integrated into the dominant culture.

The second way in which identities are formed is by a process often known as 'othering'. This is the manner in which people invariably create a self-definition of their characteristics by contrasting themselves, usually favourably, with neighbouring peoples. Once again, this is an interactive process. The people who act as the comparators often have cultural features projected upon them and sometimes they acknowledge these as acceptable stereotypes (for example, that they are warlike or eager to trade). The terminology of identifying and naming people is closely bound up with these processes. Sometimes the name of a people actually has a derogatory ring to it, having been coined by their neighbours or by a conquering empire. Such names are sometimes based on a major geographical, demographic or cultural misconception. Some of these names have survived into modern times, and a few have only recently been changed (North American 'Indians' to 'Native Americans' is one example).

The compilation of a work of reference of this sort is fraught with these problems of identity, definition, naming and stereotype. The entries on the peoples, nations and cultures that follow try to make clear the manner in which a degree of critical scepticism has to be brought to bear on the ways in which humans are divided up into groups with supposedly shared characteristics. Yet such divisions and sub-divisions are part of the fabric of everyday communication, of every sort, across the globe. They are also a means to the understanding of many of the major and minor conflicts of world history, so often based on differences in ethnicities. It is a tragic fact that pogroms and genocide, the 'ethnic cleansing' of more recent years, have been based upon these perceptions of difference, real and imagined.

But there are also positive reasons for understanding these differences. The range of its peoples is a source of rich cultural diversity without which our planet would be a less interesting and exciting place. It is therefore vitally important to clarify the vast range of names and terms used to identify peoples, both in historic contexts and in respect of the shared cultural features that these peoples, individually and collectively, display.

**Organization and terminology**
In order to achieve the kind of perspective described above, this volume sets out to be a manageable, but reasonably comprehensive listing. To explain the present, there is a three-fold focus on prehistorical, historical, as well as current, peoples and cultures. This reveals the manner in which some cultures have disappeared, some have fed into others and yet others have formed the basis for the ethnic identities, cultures and nationalities that we see in the world today.

The book is organized into five sections corresponding to the large regions of the world, with peoples listed alphabetically within those geographical (often continental) sections. Cross-references to the other topics in the book are used liberally within entries. In the great majority of cases, these are to peoples and cultures within the same section of the book, for that is simply a reflection of the way in which, historically, identities have been formed: *vis-à-vis* neighbouring peoples and cultures, often by way of competition, conquest and defeat, as well as processes of cooperation and assimilation. A complete alphabetical Index of Entries is included at the end of the book to aid the reader in locating peoples and cultures in other sections.

Many historic and current alternative names for peoples or cultures are included, both within entries and as cross-referencing headings to aid the reader find the subject he or she is looking for. Such variations themselves reveal the manner in which many peoples have been through complex naming processes reflecting the ways in which they have been identified, both by themselves and by others. The relationships between major groups (such as the ancient Celts or the Mongols) and sub-groups of peoples are often tackled, either in the main text of entries or by the means of boxes. Maps are also included to aid geographical identification and to relay, visually, the historical or current diffusion of a people or civilization – or, in some cases, to convey visually more detailed information on historical events of key importance in the identity of such a group. And a sprinkling of quotations, giving a flavour of the insights – sometimes prejudices – that historical encounters with other cultures aroused, feature in the book's margins.

Standard information included in each entry covers population levels – from the recent census information of modern states to those people, current and historical, whose extent must remain a matter of conjecture or estimate – languages spoken and predominant religious beliefs. As the readers will discover, the peoples considered here vary in scale from small, almost-extinct Siberian or Amazonian groups, numbering in the mere hundreds or a few thousand, to the present-day Indians and Chinese, who together account for two-fifths of the global population. Such differences in scale, added to the differences in our knowledge-levels when it comes to ancient or otherwise relatively obscure peoples, mean that beyond the core elements, described above, the entries range widely in attempting to describe salient characteristics, the constituents of identities.

Nomenclature is a problematic topic, not just in respect of the names used to identify different peoples, but also in the very words used to describe collective groups of humans. Various words will be found here – 'band', 'kin', 'clan', 'tribe', 'people', 'culture', 'civilization', 'nation', 'state'. These are seldom amenable to precise definition and some are regarded as having ideological overtones that render them more acceptable in one period rather than another. Some definitions of these are offered below:

**Kin** – often the word used to describe a group of related family members, more often an extended rather than a nuclear family.

**Band** – a social group made up of a large extended family or of several families, probably the major unit of social organization among Stone Age people, but also in more modern decentralized societies.

**Clan** – generally a clan is a grouping of extended families who trace their origins back to a single ancestor. Thus, the term contains within it a notion of history based on ancestry. Anthropologists have used the concept of the clan throughout the world, although it is very familiar as an extended grouping of people bearing the same name within Scottish – and therefore worldwide migrant – society.

**Tribe** – this was a unit that was so used and abused in the imperial period that it has fallen into disfavour in modern times. In theory, a tribe was a group of clans owing allegiance to some form of reasonably centralized political leadership. The problem is that such groups can be highly amorphous. Colonial rulers found some administrative comfort in identifying tribes, and in doing so often attempted to freeze what was essentially a highly dynamic situation. The words 'tribe' and its adjective 'tribal' also came to epitomize the primitive, contrasting with supposedly civilized peoples who would more likely be categorized as nations. Where these words do appear in the pages that follow, they therefore relate to eras that pre-date the great European imperialism of the 19th century, where their use can have a more neutral hue.

**People** – this word has often been used of human groups who share identifiable characteristics (for example language), which may well transcend, or cross over, so-called national boundaries. Examples might be the Celts, the Slavs, or the Arabs. Some are categorized as ethno-linguistic groupings. A good example here is the Bantu-speaking peoples of Africa, a very large group sub-divided into many different sub-groups. A number of other language groupings in the world can be seen to transcend more local ethnicities – Semitic or Aryan would come into this category.

**Culture** – This word is used to define peoples who clearly share cultural characteristics, not just in respect of language, but also in economic, religious and aesthetic matters such as ways of achieving subsistence, belief systems, architecture, ceramics, tools, weapons, and so on. A culture may embrace a number of different ethnicities and it may also represent central political or spiritual authority, which causes the common cultural forms to be spread and to become identifiers of shared experience and identity.

**Civilization** – In its technical rather than in its normal, everyday usage, this word is often used in historical and archaeological contexts to identify a notable culture which rose to prominence in a specific era and location, and which can be identified by many common characteristics. Civilizations have a high degree of social and economic complexity. They can be defined by settlement in cities, the creation and concentration of surpluses, full-time specialization of labour, class structure and state organization. These are invariably combined with public works, often of a monumental sort and incorporating unique forms of artwork, long-distance trade, writing (though not universally), and some comprehension of numerical systems, applied to efforts to understand geometry and astronomy.

**Nation** – At one time, it used to be perfectly clear what this word meant. It referred to peoples who had come together to form a particular nation state, within identifiable boundaries and owing shared allegiance to a common ruling system, whether a monarchy, a republic or some other form of central political or spiritual authority. In theory, all the peoples embraced within a nation shared the same language, ethnic origins and culture. In reality, this was seldom the case. Some nations, like the United States, Brazil, Spain, the United Kingdom, or India embrace many different peoples, languages and cultures. In reality, very few such states conform to the pure ideal of the nation, which is now seen as an attempted construct of the 19th and early 20th centuries. In modern times, the word has come to be used more widely. Thus, indigenous peoples in Canada and the United States now like to be thought of as nations, although aboriginal peoples in Australia do not. Thus, 'nation' is, by and large, a matter of self-definition, in some cases an attempt to escape the pejorative categories of the past, such as 'tribal'.

**State** – This is the classic political grouping of modern times, states being those peoples, and their boundaries, recognized in international law as representing the political authorities through which peoples can deal with each other. Generally, they are represented at the United Nations. But it is important to recognize once more that peoples and states are not coterminous. A good example is the Kurds, who are divided up, by modern boundaries, among several Middle Eastern states. In this book, both the inhabitants of states themselves, formerly seen as constituting nationalities, and a people like the Kurds, receive entries. There are many other examples across the globe.

Still, the questions of definition and of nomenclature remain so complex that consistency is almost impossible. These difficulties arise precisely from the manner in which peoples (perhaps the most useful general word) have been defined, partly by themselves, partly by others, partly from above (in terms of political power), partly from below, partly by history and partly by anthropology and other disciplines founded in the modern era. When it comes to defining and categorizing human societies, nothing is set in stone. The situation has always been essentially one of fluidity representing a whole range of dynamic forces. That has always been the nature of the human condition. This volume is designed to provide clarification of the situation in the early 21st century.

John M. MacKenzie
2004

# List of maps

# The
# Americas

# ABENAKI

A Native North American nation of northern New England and southern maritime Canada. Their name means 'people of the dawn', but they call themselves *Alnabal*, meaning 'men'. Seasonally mobile within their territory as farmers, fishers, hunters and gatherers, they speak Algonquian dialects. They established a loose confederacy around 1670 and were long involved in the fur trade with the French. In the 17th and 18th centuries they were involved in a series of wars with the English and their allies. As a result, Abenaki lands were whittled away, and warfare and diseases had a disastrous impact on their numbers and strength.

During the American Revolution they were divided in their loyalties. Those siding with the British generally withdrew to Canada. Those siding with the Americans were left without federal recognition by the USA, and the separate sub-groups were forced to come to terms with the various states as best they could. For most, the result was the loss of their lands and self-sufficiency and a still-continuing struggle for federal recognition. They established a tribal council in 1976 to pursue their national interests and reverse the fragmentation resulting from their history. In 1995 they numbered nearly 12,000.

# ABIPÓN

A Native South American nation of Argentina's Gran Chaco. Seasonally mobile within their territory as hunters, gatherers, fishers and to a limited extent farmers, they spoke a Guaykuruan language. In the 1640s they began to acquire horses and abandoned farming for raiding. They became feared by their neighbours and the Spanish, from whom they stole over 100,000 horses and even threatened major cities. Even Abipón women were reputedly aggressive and held considerable power in their people's religious rites.

From 1710 a major military effort by the Spanish began gradually to impose authority. By 1750 Jesuit missions had been established among the Abipón, and they had been forced to become sedentary. By 1768, when the Jesuits were expelled by the government, over half of the Abipón had succumbed to disease. When they attempted to resume their former lifestyles they found their traditional lands occupied by settlers and other nations. Within fifty years, disease and warfare had destroyed them as a nation, with the remnants assimilated into the general Argentinian population.

# ACADIANS

A Canadian people of French descent, found in Nova Scotia, New Brunswick and Cape Breton Island. The original colony was established by the French in 1604, and subsequently disputed by England and France. The British eventually secured the territory in 1710. By then, however, the Acadians were prosperous farmers and developing their own distinctive culture and French patois. They were also independent-minded and suspicious of outsiders, offering little cooperation with British authorities and refusing the oath of allegiance. Initially the British tolerated this independent spirit, but in 1755, with war looming in Europe, they deemed the Acadian lack of allegiance unacceptable and deported thousands them.

Some fled to Quebec, while others ended up in Louisiana, becoming the CAJUNS. All were left embittered. They were allowed to return in 1764, but their lands had been confiscated and they were permitted only to live in the small settlements that were already occupied. Acadian culture, however, survived and flourished. The Acadians developed their own media, university, flag and national anthem. In 1997 300,000 people spoke the Acadian language.

# ACHAGUA

A Native South American nation of eastern Colombia. Sedentary hunters and gatherers who practised limited agriculture, they spoke an Arawakan language. Deemed by their neighbours to be warlike, they used poisoned arrows and collected human trophies, but were in turn subject to raids by the CHIBCHA. By 1994, when their population had been reduced to about 400, their entire culture was in danger of destruction from the environmental damage done by extensive cattle-herding.

**Abenaki: sub-groups**

Amaseconti
Androscoggin
Becancour
Kennebec
Maliseet
Ouarastegoniak
Paksuiket
Passamaquoddy
Pennacook
Penobscot
Pigwacket
Rocameca
Sokoni
St Francis
Wewenoc

*" Abenakis painted their faces the colors of death ... when they went on the warpath. "*

R.P.T. Collins, 1947

## ACHAR

A Native South American nation of the Ecuadorian and Peruvian Amazon. Sedentary farmers, hunters and gatherers, they spoke Jivaro. Largely isolated until the 1970s, they quickly learned to deal with outsiders attempting to exploit their land. In 1997 three Americans surveying for oil trespassed on their territory and attempted to deceive the Achar about their purpose. The Achar kidnapped them and demanded a $2 million ransom. In 1995 they numbered about 5500 and were developing ecotourism.

## ACHUMAWI

A Native North American nation of northeast California. Their name means 'river people' and they are sometimes called Pit River Indians for their practice of using pit traps for hunting. Semi-sedentary hunters and gatherers who spoke a Hokan language, they relied heavily on fish and waterfowl for subsistence. They were often the victims of slave raids by neighbouring Native American nations and proved helpless to resist the invasion of prospectors and settlers, accompanied by violence and disease, in the 1849 gold rush. Their lands were rapidly stolen and their numbers greatly reduced. In 2000 there were perhaps 1500 Achumawi, heavily acculturated, with only a few speaking their own language.

## ADENA CULTURE

A former Native North American nation of the Ohio area. They were sedentary farmers, traders, hunters and gatherers, and their culture reached its height between 500 and 100 BC. They had a wide-ranging trading network stretching from Mexico to the Great Lakes, and built ceremonial and funeral mounds as well as elaborate earthworks. The cause of their disappearance is unclear, but environmental damage from unsustainable farming practices, leaving later generations reliant on hunting and gathering, is a likely explanation.

## AFRICAN AMERICANS

A culture of the USA having its origins in racial exploitation. The first African Americans arrived from Africa as slaves in Jamestown in 1619. Denied basic human rights from the beginning, their population in the southern states grew slowly, until the 19th century cotton boom led to a huge increase. The existence and future of slavery was the central issue that led to the Civil War (1861–5).

Although the Civil War ended with the abolition of slavery and with amendments to the constitution providing African Americans with citizenship and equal legal rights, it did not end their exploitation. Very soon after the military occupation of the southern states ended in 1877, state legislatures enacted a series of 'Jim Crow' laws, disenfranchising African Americans by various indirect means and institutionalizing racial segregation. Behind this, the organized racism of the Ku Klux Klan and lynch law ensured that protest was silenced, while the federal government remained indifferent. African Americans found employment mainly as sharecroppers or minimally paid labourers, and exploitation remained as rife as ever.

In the 20th century a mass migration of African Americans to northern cities occurred, but still employment opportunities and access to housing, education and social services remained limited, and racism was also common. Self-help through their own political institutions, such as the National Association for the Advancement of Colored People (NAACP, founded 1909), and their own churches developed in the 1950s into the Civil Rights Movement, which defeated legal discrimination. The cultural enrichment of the USA, for example through African-American music, has been recognized. Since the 1960s, African Americans have enjoyed a greater degree of social mobility, But unemployment, poverty and social problems remain the plight of many. In 2000 they numbered nearly 34 million.

## AHTENA

A Native North American nation of Alaska, whose name means 'ice people'. They are also called Copper River Indians. Originally nomadic fishers, hunters and gatherers, they spoke an ATHABASKAN language. Considered warlike by their neighbours, they would raid for women, and were allegedly responsible for massacring a Russian party who tried to enter their territory, bent on rape and robbery, during the 19th century. The Ahtena remained isolated, mostly seeing only traders, until the late 19th century. They were unable to expel heavily armed groups of prospectors, and their traditional culture was rapidly eroded. Of a population estimated at 3000 in 2001, there were few native-language speakers, though there is a growing interest in cultural preservation.

## AIZUARE

A Native South American nation of Brazil's Amazonia. Sedentary farmers, hunters and gatherers, they spoke Omagua, a nearly extinct language. In 1990 they numbered 157, but a further, uncontacted group of about 60 is suspected to exist.

## ALABAMA

A Native North American nation, originally of the Alabama area, now of Southeast Texas, whose name perhaps means 'here we rest'. Sedentary hunters (especially of bear meat) and gatherers, they farmed as a secondary form of subsistence and spoke a Muskogean language. By the mid-17th century they had been brought into the CREEK confederation by conquest. They were initially friendly with the English, but abuses by settlers and traders had driven the Alabama into an alliance with the French by 1763. The French defeat in America left them in a highly vulnerable position. Some remained with the Creek and were eventually removed to Oklahoma, while others joined the SEMINOLE, but the main group migrated, arriving in Texas in 1805. Here they joined with the KOASATI, becoming the Alabama-Coushatta.

In 1854 they were awarded their present reservation as a reward for neutrality during the Texan War of Independence. Their territory, however, soon came under pressure from settlers, costing them hunting and fishing resources and

reducing them to a poverty that persisted well into the 20th century. The Alabama-Coushatta numbered approximately 1100 in 1999.

## ALACALUT

A Native South American nation of the southern coast and islands of Chile. Nomadic hunters, gatherers and fishers, they spoke Alacalufan. They lived in small groups unable to come together for more than brief ceremonies due to lack of resources. Never numbering more than a few thousand, and with little experience of warfare, they could offer little resistance to the encroachment of settlers in the 19th century. Disease and theft of resources virtually destroyed them. Most survivors became assimilated, and only 20 native-language speakers survived in 1996.

## ALEUT

See ALUTIIQ.

## ALGONKIN

An Aboriginal nation of Quebec and Ontario, whose name means 'at the place of spearing fish'. Seasonally moving through their territory as traders, hunters, gatherers and fishers, they speak Algonquian. Divided into several sub-groups, including the Iroquet, Kichesipirini and Kinounchepirini, many became wealthy through trade. In the 17th century they entered the fur trade and became allies of France. This earned them the enmity of the IROQUOIS, who defeated and drove them from their lands in the 1640s. The OTTAWA absorbed some, but many returned to their lands at the end of the century. In 1721 the French persuaded them to join with some of their traditional Iroquois enemies, and they remained valuable allies until 1760, when the British forced them to accept a treaty guaranteeing their lands in return for neutrality. After the American Revolution, however, American loyalists stole much of their territory in Ontario, and many Algonkin were nearly landless by the mid-19th century. In 1999 they numbered nearly 8000 and had been in negotiations to recover their unceded lands since the 1970s.

## ALSEA

A Native North American nation of the Oregon coast. Sedentary hunters, fishers, gatherers and traders, they travelled widely by cedar dugout canoes. In 1855 miners encroached on their territory and massacred several, beginning the Rogue River War. The Alsea were defeated in 1856 after hard fighting and forced onto a reservation. Starvation, disease and alcoholism rapidly reduced their numbers, giving the US government the excuse to close their reservation and move them to the SILETZ reservation. Their descendants can still be found among the Confederated Siletz Indians of Oregon.

## ALUTIIQ or Aleut

A Native North American nation of coastal Alaska and its islands. They call themselves *Unanga*, which means 'the people'. Sedentary fishers, hunters (especially of sea mammals) and gatherers, they speak an Eskaleut language. In the late 18th century contact with Russian fur traders proved disastrous. The Russians wanted the Alutiiq to hunt sea otters, and reacted brutally to resistance. Children were taken hostage to force the Alutiiq to serve, and parties were forced to hunt as far as California. Only the Russian Orthodox Church offered any protection, though it was still determined to eradicate traditional religious practices. Normal subsistence of the Alutiiq and much of their traditional culture was destroyed, and disease, starvation, brutal treatment and suicide caused a catastrophic loss of population. The USA's purchase of Alaska in 1867 changed little. The government neglected the Alutiiq, allowing abuse to continue. From around 1900 schools were established among the Alutiiq, but their primary aim was to destroy the language. Only in 1973 were steps taken to preserve it. In 2000 they numbered nearly 17,000 and were attempting to preserve their culture and protect an extremely fragile environment.

## AMANYÉ

A Native South American nation of Brazil's Amazonia. Sedentary farmers, hunters and gatherers,

they speak TUPÍ. They frequently relocate villages as their soil becomes exhausted, and possibly also to avoid their enemies. First contacted in 1755, they tended to avoid all whites except missionaries. Despite this, most disappeared into the MESTIZO population in the 20th century. A group numbering up to 66 remained in 1995.

## AMERICANS

Generally used to mean citizens of the USA. The origins of the Americans can be traced back to the foundation of the English colonies at Jamestown, Virginia, in 1606, and Plymouth, New England, in 1620. The Virginia colony was conceived as a commercial venture. It developed a society dominated by an upper class of 'gentlemen planters' with an underclass of poor white indentured servants and increasing numbers of African slaves. The New England colony was founded by more middle-class Puritans whose primary motive was to practise their religion in freedom. These settlers had characteristics that have become central to American self-identity: a strong sense of social cohesion, a commitment to self reliance and an unshakable conviction that they were doing God's work. The annual Thanksgiving celebrations, which commemorate the survival of the Plymouth colony, are a measure of the extent to which the Puritan settlers, rather than the earlier Virginia planters, have come to be seen popularly as the true founders of America.

In the 18th century, the predominantly English composition of the colonists began to be diluted by the arrival of substantial numbers of Scots, ULSTER SCOTS (or Scots-Irish) and Germans. The most influential of these immigrants were the Ulster Scots. As Presbyterians, the Ulster Scots reinforced the religious values introduced by the 17th-century Puritan settlers and they brought with them a ready-made frontier mentality. Differences between American English and British English also emerged, partly because colonists adopted Native American words into their vocabulary. However, the main differences between American and British English emerged only after US independence and then mainly because changes in British English were not adopted in the USA. The conservativeness of

*a*

"When asked by an anthropoligist what the Indians called America before the white man came, an Indian said simply, 'Ours'."

Vine Deloria, Jnr, commenting wryly on the colonial origins of most Americans

American English operates both grammatically (for example, the continuing use of inflections that British English has dropped, such as 'gotten') and tonally (for example in the US predilection for euphemism).

In the absence of strong control from Britain, political liberties and democratic representation flourished in the colonies. When the British government attempted to recoup some of the costs of the French and Indian War (1756–63) by taxing the colonists without their consent, a major crisis quickly occurred. Although an American national identity was still incompletely formed, the colonials had already ceased to regard themselves as simply transplanted Britons, and they had ample cause to be confident of their ability to govern themselves. The American Revolution (1775–83) established the United States of America as an independent state. The US constitution was essentially a codified version of England's constitutional arrangements with what were felt to be their worst defects, not least the inherited power of the aristocracy and monarch, removed. Although the American Revolution was in many ways socially conservative – the colonial elite effectively became the new governing elite – its democratic ideals have proved to be immensely and powerfully influential throughout the world. It was during the Revolutionary War that Americans (specifically New Englanders to begin with) were first nicknamed Yankees. The origins of the term are uncertain but it may be derived from Dutch diminutive Janke ('Johnny').

### National unity

Independence did not at first bring national unity. The social and economic differences between north and south remained wide and the constitution did not settle the relationship between the federal government and the states of the union. In the first half of the 19th century the issue of slavery became symbolic of these divisions. The north was strongly abolitionist, but the southern states believed that they had the right to decide the issue for themselves and they finally seceded from the Union in 1861. The north's victory in the Civil War (1861–5) united the nation by force, ended slavery and opened the way for the creation of the relatively homogenous national identity shared by modern Americans. However, it left unsettled the extent to which the federal government had the right to interfere in the affairs of individual states. Faced with violent opposition by the white supremacist Ku Klux Klan, the federal government did not persevere with attempts in the Reconstruction period (1865–76) to force the southern states to give equal rights to AFRICAN-AMERICANS. By the 1890s the discriminatory 'Jim Crow' laws had left African-Americans in the south largely disenfranchised and segregated from the white population. African-Americans finally achieved equal rights only in the 1960s, but racism remains pervasive, especially in the south. This is despite the fact that American culture's popular appeal in the rest of the world is in part based on African-American music, particularly jazz, rhythm and blues (from which rock 'n' roll developed), and more recently rap and hip hop.

### A society built on immigration

Since independence, vast waves of immigrants have arrived from every corner of the world: primarily from Ireland and Germany before the Civil War; Italy, Eastern Europe and Russia between the Civil War and World War I; and Latin America, the West Indies and Asia in the later 20th century. Though a desire to escape from political or religious oppression was a factor for some immigrants, the vast majority, whatever their origins, came in search of improved living standards. Idealists conceived of America as a 'melting pot' where all immigrants would be assimilated to a common American identity, but the appeal of nativism, which prompted those already established to resent the arrival of newcomers as 'foreign' and often suspect, was very strong. In the 1840s, for example, Irish Catholic immigrants were stereotyped as impoverished, diseased and drunk. These suspicions of newcomers persist; today, for example, Hispanic immigrants are stereotyped as unwilling to learn English. Despite this, the USA has, by any measure, been remarkably successful in assimilating its immigrants, although the initial resentment they met persuaded many consciously to retain aspects of their original national identities. This has led to the unusual

*"I know of no country in which there is so little independence of mind and real freedom of discussion as in America."*

Alexis de Tocqueville, *Democracy in America*, 1840

phenomenon of 'hyphenated Americans', for example IRISH-AMERICANS or ITALIAN-AMERICANS. Although long reduced to minority status by immigration from the rest of the world, white Anglo-Saxon Protestants – WASPs for short – are still among the most privileged and wealthy sections of the American population.

### The appeal of the frontier

One of the revolutionaries' grievances against British rule had been Britain's attempt to avoid conflict with NATIVE AMERICANS by setting a western limit on European settlement. Following independence, the frontier was pushed steadily westwards. Many Americans believed it was their divinely ordained 'Manifest Destiny' to conquer and settle the whole continent. Despite their occasionally fierce resistance, Native Americans were herded onto reservations, where they have since struggled to maintain their national identities. Although the real frontier ceased to exist in the 1890s, it retains a powerful hold on the American imagination as a symbol of the nation's rugged individualism and enterprising spirit. Most Americans now live in cities and suburbs, for which reason small town life, with its strong community spirit and neighbourliness, is idealized.

An important expression of rugged individualism is the idea of the 'American Dream'. In the 19th century, American society was highly mobile and it was assumed that anybody with ambition, ability and willingness to work could follow the example of entrepreneurs such as the steel magnate Andrew Carnegie and become a multi-millionaire. America was, it was held, a land of unlimited opportunity, and this has led to a tolerance for huge disparities in wealth. For the same reason, America has never developed a comprehensive welfare state; many believe it would encourage a dependency culture and undermine personal initiative and responsibility. Polling suggests that faith in the American Dream is declining and, in fact, social mobility in the USA today is comparable to that of other developed nations like the United Kingdom – and much less, for example, than that of the high-tax, high-welfare, Scandinavian countries.

Americans have a willingness to stand up for their rights; for example, the constitutional right to bear arms is vigorously defended despite clear evidence that the ready availability of guns feeds violent crime. As a result they are a litigious people, which unsurprisingly has created an enormous class of lawyers.

### A world power

After many years of isolationism, the USA emerged as a world power in the 20th century and took up the mantle of leadership of the 'free world' during the Cold War. American influence was spread not only through its economic and military power but also by exporting its popular culture. Of particular importance in this respect is the Hollywood film industry, which has presented to the world an idealized view of America's history and an often exaggerated view of its achievements. Coca Cola and fast food outlets such as McDonalds have also helped to Americanize the diet of much of the world. Americans are keenly aware of the massive power of their nation, and are confident that this is a power generally used to the benefit of humankind. Believing themselves to be the most free nation on earth, they tend to question the legitimacy of any criticism, foreign or domestic. Those domestic critics whose values are deemed to be un-American, such as communists, tend to be rejected as aliens. The pressure on Americans to conform is in fact extremely strong. This is particularly apparent in politics. Only two mass political parties have established themselves, the Republicans and the Democrats, and both are, in European terms, parties of the Right, although the Democrats have more liberal instincts than the Republicans. The most potent symbol of American identity is the US flag. There are clear rules defining how it is to be handled and folded, and any misuse is deeply resented – which is why anti-American demonstrators make such a point of doing so.

While the US constitution separates church and state, strong Christian beliefs remain widespread among modern Americans. In 2003 over 40% of Americans claimed to have had a 'born again' experience and a similar percentage believed the Biblical account of the creation to be literally true. Religious faith is an important factor in the nation's high level of charitable giving. The conservative Christian right has emerged as a potent force in American politics and played an important role in the Republican victories in the presidential elections of 2000 and 2004. In these elections the Republicans swept the south and centre of the country, while Democrats held New England, the Great Lakes and the west coast, creating the superficial impression of a politically deeply polarized nation. The reality is somewhat different: in no Republican state did the Democrat vote fall below 43%, with Republican support being comparably high in Democrat states. Despite this, issues such as abortion, same-sex marriage, the teaching of evolution and human stem cell research are the subjects of bitter controversy.

Following defeat in the Vietnam war (1964–73) and the Watergate scandal (1974), Americans experienced a brief period of uncertainty and self-doubt. Politicians attempted to lead them out of this by appealing to their sense of moral superiority. By criticizing the failures of others over human rights (for example over the mistreatment of dissidents), politicians worked to reclaim America's moral leadership of the world and reinvigorate national pride. Certainly American self-confidence made a rapid recovery in the 1980s, and the end of the Cold War and the collapse of the USSR in 1991 left the USA as the unchallenged global superpower. Insulated by oceans to east and west, Americans felt invulnerable on their own territory. This sense of security was shattered by the al-Qaeda terrorist attacks on New York and Washington DC on 11 September 2001, which left over 3000 people dead. It is too early to say what the long-term consequences of these events will be. In 2000 the Americans numbered about 275 million.

## AMHUACA

A Native South American people of the Peruvian and Brazilian Amazonia. Sedentary farmers, hunters and gatherers, they speak a Panoan language and reputedly practised endocannibalism – the ritual cannibalism of deceased relatives. Isolated until the 18th century, they are currently under threat from the ecological devastation, disease and violence brought by oil extractors and illegal loggers. In 1998 they numbered about 520.

## AMOIPIRA

A Native South American nation of Brazil's Amazonia. Sedentary farmers, hunters and gatherers, they spoke a TUPÍ language. A sub-group of the TUPINA, they relocated their palisaded villages as the soil became exhausted, and allegedly practised ceremonial cannibalism. By the late 20th century their language was extinct and they had ceased to exist as a nation.

## AMUESHA

See YANESHA.

## ANASAZI CULTURE

A former Native North American culture of the southwest USA. Their name comes from the NAVAJO and means 'ancient enemy', though the HOPI, who claim descent from them, call them *Hisatsomin*, meaning 'people of long ago'. By about AD 500 they had adopted farming, and hunting and gathering had become secondary occupations. Their culture became more complex, as reflected in the developments in ceramics and architecture – by AD 700 they were building pueblos (large compounds and ceremonial centres of stone buildings). The culture peaked between about 1050 and 1300, centred around the town at Chaco Canyon, the hub of a great trading network. Thereafter their pueblos were abandoned for more defensible sites, which were in turn abandoned within a couple of generations, and the culture simply vanished. Navajo and APACHE raids may have been one cause of this. However a period of prolonged drought coupled with the environmental stress of unsustainable farming techniques could simply have made their lifestyle untenable and forced them to revert to hunting and gathering.

## ANGUILLANS

Inhabitants of colonial origin of the British Caribbean dependency of Anguilla, east of Puerto Rico. The Spanish annihilated the island's CARIB population in the 16th century, leaving it open to English colonization in 1650. In 1688 an IRISH group first attacked and then

**Apache:
main
sub-groups**

Chirichaua
Cibecue
Coyotero
Jicarilla
Lipan
Mescalero
Northern
  Tonto
Southern
  Tonto
White
  Mountains

joined the colony. A plantation economy was developed, which introduced very strong African influences into the culture. The abolition of slavery allowed the development of a poor, but independent, peasantry. From 1824 they were administered by St Kitts, which they increasingly resented, but repeated demands for separation were rejected. In 1967, to show their determination, they disarmed and expelled the St Kitts police. This led in 1969 to a British military intervention, which, since the Anguillans knew it meant their case had been heard, was warmly welcomed and named 'the Bay of Piglets'. In 1971 the Anguillans gained their separation from St Kitts. Economic problems, however, remain, with employment heavily dependent on tourism, and emigration common.

# APACHE

A Native North American nation of Arizona, New Mexico and Oklahoma. Their name comes from the ZUÑI and means 'enemy', but they call themselves *Diné*, meaning 'people'. They were nomadic hunters and gatherers and spoke ATHABASKAN dialects. Inhabitants of the Great Plains, they moved southwards between the 14th and 16th centuries. They lost their hunting grounds when their enemies, the COMANCHE, acquired horses in the early 18th century, and they were driven into New Mexico. There, denied access to the bison herds, they raided PUEBLO and Spanish settlements for subsistence.

The Spanish, like the Mexicans and Americans later, were frustrated by the independence of each Apache group: it was impossible to treat the Apache as a nation. The Spanish allied with the Comanche in 1786, and used them as well as the NAVAJO to hunt down Apache groups. A bounty of 20 pesos was offered for an Apache scalp; all under eight years old were to be enslaved and all older were to be killed as untameable. A more successful policy was established where bands were offered a choice between death or residing peacefully at Spanish missions, with a guarantee of a generous subsistence. Mexicans and Americans, however, did not follow this policy, and by the mid-19th century, Apache raiding had begun anew. The Mexicans reintroduced the scalp bounty in

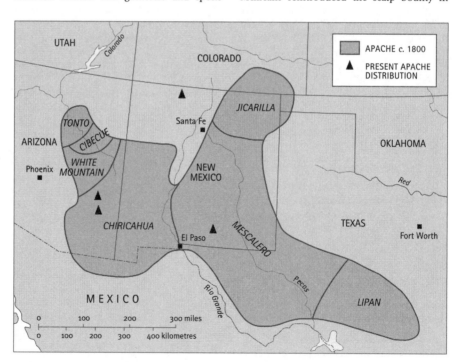

Apache

response to devastating raids. The Americans used the army to force the Apache onto reservations. Apache resistance and repeated escapes turned this into a frustrating and costly endeavour. The great Apache hero Geronimo escaped three times. In his final act of defiance in 1886, his band of 16 men, 12 women and 6 children were pursued by one-quarter of the US Army, as well as thousands of Mexican troops. They were then removed to Fort Marion in Florida, and only allowed to return much later, when they were placed on reservations.

Reservation life for the Apache was marked by intense poverty and determined American efforts to destroy their culture, for example by sending children to distant residential schools to be educated in white culture. Their language and religion have survived, however, and cattle-ranching, logging and tourism provide some employment, though levels of unemployment and poverty remain very high. In 1990 they numbered over 50,000.

## APALACHEE

A Native North American nation of northwest Florida, whose name perhaps means 'people on the other side'. Sedentary farmers and traders, they hunted and gathered as secondary means of subsistence. They spoke a Muskogean language and built temple and ceremonial mounds. During the 17th century the Spanish established missions among them, leading to the suppression of much of their culture, and devastating epidemics. In 1703 the English, seeking to disrupt Spanish power, assisted the CREEK in attacking the Apalachee, killing and enslaving large numbers. This was followed by new epidemics. The survivors migrated to Louisiana, where, by the end of the 18th century, they were assumed to be extinct as a nation. In the 1990s, however, a group of Apalachee descendants in Louisiana were seeking official recognition, claiming to have maintained a functioning community throughout their settlement in the state.

## APALACHICOLA

A Native North American nation of coastal northwest Florida, whose name perhaps means 'land of the friendly people'. Sedentary farmers, hunters and gatherers, they spoke a Muskogean language. In 1823, wanting to develop a port in their territory, the USA persuaded them to take a reservation. Promises to protect them from slave raids and provide annuities were often broken. Poverty and population loss led the remnants to join the CREEK. By 1840 they were generally considered extinct. There still exists, however, the Apalachicola Band of Creek Indians, who in 1996 began to campaign for federal recognition.

## APALAI

A native nation of Brazil's Amazonia. They were sedentary slash-and-burn farmers, necessitating periodic relocation as soil became exhausted, but also hunters and gatherers. They spoke a Carib language and in the 20th century their subsistence shifted towards artisan work as they attempted to adapt to modern Brazil. In 1993 they numbered 450.

## APANTO

A former Native South American nation of coastal Guyana. Sedentary subsistence farmers using slash-and-burn methods, they were also hunters and gatherers and practised fishing using poison. They spoke Waiwai and had friendly relations from the late 16th century with the British and Dutch, with whom they traded and sometimes joined in raids on the Spanish. They became heavily acculturated, lost their language and disappeared as a nation.

## APOLISTA

A Native South American nation of western Bolivia. Sedentary farmers, hunters, gatherers and fishers, they spoke an Arawakan language now gravely endangered, if not extinct. From 1713 they were gathered at a variety of missions with other nations, and rapidly lost their traditional culture to the point that a realistic census count is no longer possible.

## ARAPAHO

A Native North American nation of the western

and southern Great Plains of North America. Their name perhaps comes from the CROW and means 'people of many tattoos'. Nomadic hunters, gatherers and traders, they spoke an Algonquian language. Acquiring European horses in the 1730s, they prospered as traders and hunters. In the 19th century, however, wagon trains began to disrupt bison migration and deplete their resources. The Southern Arapaho followed a conciliatory path, but, with the CHEYENNE, were victims of the Sand Creek Massacre (1864). After three years of warfare, disease and starvation so weakened them that they were forced onto a reservation in Oklahoma with the Cheyenne. The Northern Arapaho resisted until 1878, when they were driven onto the SHOSHONE reservation in Wyoming. Both were subject to an intense deculturation policy and were defrauded of lands. They numbered about 7000 in 1990, when cultural preservation and economic development were major concerns.

## ARÁRA

A Native South American nation of Brazil's Amazonia. Sedentary hunters and gatherers, they spoke a Carib language. They had a warlike tradition and were reputedly headhunters, though they tended to shun contact with whites and by the 1940s were assumed to be extinct. Contact was reopened in 1982 when the Transam road was built through their territory. The immediate result was a fatal influenza epidemic. Another result has been repeated and blatant illegal logging, which is steadily depleting their environment. In 1982 they numbered 205.

## ARAUCANIANS

See MAPUCHE.

## ARAWAK

A Native South American nation of Brazil, Colombia, Venezuela and the Caribbean. Sedentary farmers, hunters, fishers and gatherers, they speak an Arawakan language. A peaceful nation, they were already being driven from the Caribbean by the CARIBS when the Spanish arrived in the early 16th century. Many were

quickly exterminated through disease, starvation and slavery. The rest survive, and in 2000 numbered about 3 million, in various communities seeking greater autonomy.

## ARCHAIC CULTURES

The cultures succeeding those of the first Native Americans, the Paleoindians, who had arrived on the continent by about 12,000 years ago. These were nomadic hunters and gatherers who roamed freely, mainly hunting large game such as mammoths, wild ponies and camels, which were abundant and produced a large amount of food per kill. From about 8000 BC a warming climate reduced plant cover, and herds declined drastically. Continued hunting drove many prey species to extinction. The Archaic cultures then emerged, adapting to new conditions, exploiting a wider range of resources that were harder to procure and process, such as hickory nuts and fish. Movement became seasonally prescribed within more specific territories, and groups became more specialized, particularly after about 1000 BC, when the first casual cultivation of food plants such as maize began. This period of adaptation is held to have ended by around the time of Christ. More sedentary and complex societies developed, giving rise to such cultures as the HOHOKAM and ANASAZI.

## ARGENTINIANS

Citizens of Argentina, a nation of colonial origins; the name comes from the Latin and means 'land of silver'. The first European settlers were the Spanish in 1527, who conquered and largely acculturated the mostly nomadic native peoples. Argentina was part of the Viceroyalty of Rio de la Plata, which declared independence from Spain in 1816, but by 1828 Paraguay, Bolivia and Uruguay had broken away. The dominance of Buenos Aires was a source of resentment and political instability. This in turn gave the military a considerable role in politics and frequently led to military dictatorship, such as Juan Perón's (1943–55). From the 1850s onwards more than 4.5 million immigrants were attracted from across Europe, especially Italy, producing a more heterogeneous, but still largely Catholic, culture.

> " A friendly, hospitable people. "
>
> E. Bancroft, referring to the Arawak, 1769

As in neighbouring states, an obsession with sport, especially football, has promoted stars like Diego Maradona to iconic status. Argentina was indeed a nation with immense resources, and in the early 20th century it was the largest exporter of corn and meat in the world. This, however, was not reflected in the living standards of many Argentinians, among whom widespread poverty was a further source of political instability. Economic mismanagement also caused bursts of great inflation, compounding the nation's problems even further. The disparity between the nation's resources and the scale of its poverty enrages Argentinians, and indeed in 2002 popular fury at massive foreign debts, which caused even greater impoverishment – leading to violent crime – threatened to become revolutionary. Argentinians aspire to be a regional power, and have considerable territorial claims, covering a great deal of Antarctica and the Falkland Islands, the latter of which led to a brief, inglorious war with Britain in 1982. Defeat was particularly galling, as the defeat of two British armies in 1806 and 1807 had been a source of immense national pride. It led to the overthrow of the Leopoldo Galtieri dictatorship, but no cure for severe economic problems. In 2001 Argentinians numbered over 37 million.

## ARIKARA

A Native North American nation of North Dakota, whose name means 'people'. Seasonally mobile within their territory as farmers, hunters, gatherers and traders, they spoke a Caddoan language. Close allies of the MANDAN and HIDATSA by 1700, they were decimated by epidemics and, by the 1830s, driven by LAKOTA pressure into Nebraska, where the three peoples coalesced. They were forced onto Fort Berthold reservation, North Dakota, in 1870 and formally became a single nation, the Three Affiliated Tribes, in 1934. Subsequent uncompensated land loss to damming caused great poverty. In 1980 they numbered over 1500.

## ARUAKI

A Native South American nation of the Guianas (Guyana, Suriname and French Guiana), who call themselves *Locono*, meaning 'the people'. Sedentary slash-and-burn farmers, they were also hunters, fishers using poison, and gatherers. They spoke an Arawakan language and had a perhaps undeserved reputation as fierce warriors and, allegedly, cannibals. This has not saved them from logging corporations, who have been accused of genocide for their treatment of the Aruaki. In 1990 they numbered 15,000, though their population includes many MESTIZOS.

## ARUBANS

A Caribbean nation largely of colonial origin. Initially settled by Arawaks, the islands were claimed by the DUTCH in 1636, but were not seriously developed until the 19th century. Lacking the necessary water supply, a plantation economy was never developed. The culture therefore combined ARAWAK and European elements, with very little African influence. Initially federated with the Dutch Antilles, in 1986 they seceded, but Arubans have shown no interest in seeking complete independence, being content with autonomy under the Dutch Crown. In 2003 they numbered over 70,000.

## ARUPAI

A former Native American nation of Brazil's Amazonia, whose name means 'persons'. They were sedentary slash-and-burn farmers, but also hunters and gatherers, and spoke a Tupi language. No direct European contact was ever made with them; they appear to have been terrified of the rumours they heard about white settlers. They are thought to have been destroyed in warfare with other native Brazilian nations in the 19th century.

## ASPERO TRADITION

A former Native American culture of northeast coastal Peru. A pre-ceramic culture that flourished from about 2800 to 1800 BC, its people were sedentary fishers, farmers, hunters and gatherers and built ceremonial mounds. The mesh bags of stone used in their construction of these mounds suggest a standard contribution (a form of taxation on households or individuals), a large population and complex social structure. The cause of the culture's decline is unclear.

## ASSINIBOINE

A Native American nation of the northern Great Plains. Their name means 'stone', but they call themselves *Nakota*, meaning 'allies'. Nomadic hunters, gatherers and traders, they spoke a Siouan language. Once part of the NAKOTA, they broke away in the mid-17th century, and subsequently the two tribes became bitter enemies. Warfare and disease reduced the Assiniboine, and in 1851 they were forced to cede their Minnesota territory for new lands in Montana. They were soon confined to two reservations. Some bands in Canada accepted a land settlement there in 1870, which did not protect them from a massacre by US whiskey-traders at Cypress Hills (1873). By then the disappearance of the bison had reduced them to utter dependence on government supplies. Severe poverty marked their subsequent existence, relieved only slightly by tourism. They numbered over 6500 in 1996, when their attempts at cultural revival included keeping a bison herd.

## ATACAMEÑOS

A Native South American nation of the Atacama desert of Chile and Peru. Sedentary farmers where water was available, as well as hunters and gatherers, they spoke a language, now extinct, which was never classified. Living in small communities near scarce water sources, they were strongly influenced by their INCA neighbours, who never saw their territory as worth conquering. They were, however, vulnerable to white settlers stealing their water rights, and most were scattered and acculturated by the late 20th century. Only a few groups remain, still seeking some security in their water and land rights.

## ATHABASKAN or Athapascan

A Native North American group of speakers of related languages also called Athabaskan. They are thought to have arrived in America across the Bering Land Bridge about 10,000 years ago. Initially they were seasonally mobile in their own territories, following the caribou herds upon which they depended entirely for survival. As they fragmented, some travelled to Alaska and Canada, such as the HARE, TANANA, TANAINA and DOGRIB. Others sought a less harsh climate to the south, and migrated to the Great Plains and eventually to the southwestern USA. These include the APACHE and NAVAJO.

## ATSEGUWA

A Native North American nation of central California. Semi-sedentary hunters and gatherers who spoke a Hokan language, they relied heavily on fishing for subsistence. They were willing to fight to protect their territory from aggressive neighbours, such as the MAIDU. But in 1856 settlers, soon protected by the US Army, began encroaching into their territory. The Atseguwa were finally forced onto the Round Valley reservation, where their culture began to disintegrate. In 2000 they numbered perhaps 50. They were attempting to revive their culture, but their language survives only in ethnographers' records.

## ATSINA

An aboriginal nation of Montana, Alberta and Saskatchewan, whose name is from the BLACKFOOT meaning 'hungry'. The French called both the Atsina and the HIDATSA *Gros Ventres*, meaning 'big bellies'. Nomadic hunters and gatherers, they speak an Algonquian language, now nearly extinct. Splitting from the ARAPAHO in the 17th century, they survived the hostility of the CREE, ASSINIBOINE and white traders only through the protection of the Blackfoot. Reduced by diseases and the destruction of the bison herds, they were forced by starvation onto the Fort Belknap reservation, Montana, with their traditional enemies the Assiniboine, in 1878. Mainly farmers and ranchers, there were about 2800 Atsina in 1990.

## AUAKÉ

A Native South American nation of the Amazonia of Venezuela and Brazil. They were sedentary slash-and-burn farmers, which requires periodic relocation as soil becomes exhausted, and were also hunters, fishers and gatherers and spoke

Arutani. Heavily influenced culturally by the CARIB, they adopted agriculture sometime after the 16th century, and further acculturation followed white contact. In 1998 they numbered just 30 in Venezuela and 22 native-language speakers in Brazil.

## AYMARA

A Native South American nation of the Peruvian, Bolivian and Chilean Andes. Sedentary farmers, herders, hunters, gatherers and fishers, they spoke Aymara Altiplaco. Conquest by the INCA around 1430 was followed by severe acculturation but also several revolts; the Aymara were then enslaved by the Spanish from 1535. They continued to be rebellious, especially after 1780, which led to savage reprisals. In the early 19th century, their lands were contested by Bolivia and Peru, leading to further poverty and the erosion of their traditional culture, though many adopted Christianity only superficially. In 2000 the Aymara numbered over 1.3 million, and were demanding an apology as well as compensation from their governments.

## AZTEC

A Native North American nation of Mexico. Originally nomadic hunters and gatherers who spoke an Uto-Aztecan language, they built a great empire when they migrated from northwest to central Mexico and adopted intensive agriculture. They founded the city of Tenochtitlán (on the site of today's Mexico City) around 1345 and in the 15th century began to expand by conquest, believing they were chosen by the sun and war god Huitzilopochtli (one of perhaps 1000 of their gods) to conquer the world. They were detested as rulers, however, and held their empire together by force, practising large-scale human sacrifice. When the Spanish arrived in 1519 they quickly gathered allies only too eager to destroy the Aztec empire, which they achieved in two years. Thereafter the Aztec were enslaved; their traditional culture was banned and they soon disappeared as a distinct nation.

## BACAIRI

A Native South American nation of Brazil's Amazonia, whose name means 'sons of the sun'.

**❝** We shall establish ourselves ... and we shall conquer all the people of the universe. **❞**

**Aztec legend**

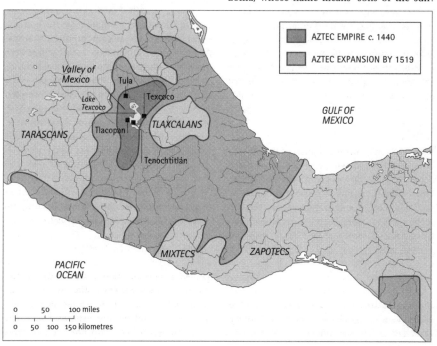

Aztec

Sedentary slash-and-burn farmers, they were also hunters, fishers and gatherers. They spoke a CARIB language, but a long history of murder, slavery and forced integration at white hands has destroyed their traditional culture. The Bacairi have retained their identity as a nation, however, and in 2001 were campaigning for better health care. In 1999 they numbered up to 900.

## BAFFIN ISLAND ESKIMO

See INUIT.

## BAHAMIANS

A Caribbean people of colonial origins who live on the Bahamas, southeast of Florida. The Spanish exterminated the original ARAWAK population by 1520, leaving the island group, which had poor soil and few resources, as a haunt for pirates. They were joined in 1648 by Puritans from Bermuda, and after the American Revolution by loyalists and their slaves, and a culture combining European and African elements developed. For most, economic opportunities were very limited; poverty was endemic. Economic recovery occurred when American tourists evading prohibition arrived in the 1920s. Tourism, with illegal drugs and immigrant transshipment, became the main sources of subsistence. Independent since 1973, the Bahamian population numbered nearly 300,000 in 2001.

## BANNOCK

A Native North American nation of the western Great Plains. Nomadic hunters, gatherers and fishers, they spoke an Uto-Aztecan language. Originally of Oregon, they acquired European horses in the 17th century and began to follow the bison herds. They became close allies of the Northern SHOSHONE, and by 1840 the two had amalgamated.

## BARBACOA

A former Native South American nation of coastal Colombia. Sedentary farmers, hunters, gatherers and fishers, they spoke Barbacoan.

They were early victims of 16th-century Spanish colonialism, and their nation did not long survive its diseases and exploitation.

## BARBADIANS

A Caribbean people of colonial origin who live on the island state of Barbados, northeast of Venezuela. When the ENGLISH established a colony in 1627, the Spanish had already exterminated the original CARIB inhabitants. A plantation economy developed, dependent at first on indentured labour or transported criminals, then from the 1640s on imported African slaves, who eventually made up 90% of the population. The Africans had a great impact on the developing culture, although cricket remains a national obsession. In the 20th century poverty and unemployment caused much emigration. Tourism and industry provided alternative forms of subsistence after independence in 1966. Unemployment still plagued the population of over 275,000 in 2001.

## BASKETMAKER CULTURE

A term that describes more a stage in the prehistory of the Utah area than a specific culture, which lasted from perhaps 200 BC to AD 700. Basketmakers were hunters and gatherers who grew dependent on agriculture. They became increasingly sedentary, ultimately building villages of pit houses and developing a complex society. The basketry for which they were named was used for gathering and storage. They were succeeded by even more complex cultures such as the HOHOKAM and MOGOLLON.

## BEAR RIVER INDIANS

A Native North American nation of northwest California. Sedentary hunters and gatherers who spoke an ATHABASKAN language, they called themselves *Mattole Niekeni*. During the 1850s they were driven from much of their lands by settlers, and could only survive by stealing cattle. The settlers responded by massacring many during a dance at Blue Lake. The survivors were forced onto Smith River reservation, whereupon their culture began to disintegrate and they largely dispersed as a nation. In 1997, however, 14 still maintained a federally recognized nation at Rohnerville *rancheria* (settlement).

## BEAVER

A Native North American nation of northeast British Columbia and Alberta. They refer to themselves as *Dunne-za*, meaning 'our people'. Originally nomadic hunters, they also gathered and fished (but only in times of great hardship). They speak an ATHABASKAN language. Their original territory was further east and south, but the CREE drove them out in the 18th century. They joined the fur trade and acquired horses in the 19th century. In the 20th, however, settler pressure made their lives increasingly impossible. Of approximately 600 in 1991, about half still spoke the Beaver language.

## BELLA BELLA or Heiltsuk

A Native North American nation of coastal British Columbia. Sedentary hunters, gatherers and fishers, they speak a Wakashan language. They entered the fur trade in the late 18th century until fur-bearing species became depleted. In the 1850s growing tensions with settlers led to raiding and indiscriminate reprisals. Forced onto a reservation in 1880, they found their traditional culture under sustained attack, with their potlatches banned and residential schools destroying their language. In the 1990s, cultural revival, and a bitter dispute with the provincial government over rights to control fishing and logging on Bella Bella lands were major issues. In 1998 they numbered about 1840.

## BELLA COOLA

A Native North American nation of British Columbia. They call themselves *Nuxalk*. Sedentary hunters, gatherers and fishers, they speak a Salishan language. In the late 19th century, settlers (primarily Norwegians), prospectors and trappers decimated them through starvation and disease, while their culture was under attack through residential schools and the banning of potlatches. A cultural revival is underway, and in the 1990s they were increasingly vocal in

defending their fishing rights and in opposing commercial logging of their traditional lands. In 1991 they numbered 980.

## BEOTHUK

A former aboriginal nation of Newfoundland, whose name means 'red skins' – a reference to their body paint. Seasonally mobile within their territory as hunters, gatherers and fishers, they spoke an Algonquian language. Possibly descendants of the DORSET CULTURE, they had early contacts with European fishermen at least since the 16th century. The scraps of metal these fishermen left were much prized by the Beothuk for tools, and, not comprehending the concept of private property, they scavenged what they could before the fishermen left. Irritation at such 'thievery' led to reprisals. The MICMAC were reputedly offered bounties for Beothuk scalps, and British and French settlers shot them for sport and for the bounties offered by the British government. Denied the food resources of the coast, most who escaped murder starved. The last known Beothuk was thought to have died in 1829, but modern research suggests this is incorrect. Micmac people reported seeing some Boethuk in the interior in 1889, and the anthropologist Frank Speck reported meeting one at his summer residence north of Boston in the early 20th century. They evaded total genocide by continuing to intermarry with their aboriginal neighbours and by crossing to Labrador and joining the INNU or the Micmac on the western and southern coasts of Newfoundland.

**❝** The poor Beothuk, armed only with his bow and arrow. **❞**

**J.P. Howley, 1915**

*b*

## BERMUDIANS

A North Atlantic people of colonial origin who live on the island of Bermuda, east of North Carolina. The island was uninhabited until English settlers en route to Virginia were shipwrecked in 1609 and soon developed an economy based on piracy, whaling and tobacco. African slaves were imported, and they eventually made up three-fifths of the population, which had a great impact on the developing culture. In the 19th century American tourists escaping severe winters laid the foundations of prosperity. Luxury tourism gives Bermudians a very high per-capita income. This wealth and an easing of racial tensions have undermined movements towards independence, and Bermuda is still a British colony. In 2001 Bermudians numbered nearly 64,000.

## BILOXI

A Native North American nation originally of Mississippi, whose name perhaps means 'first people'. Sedentary farmers, hunters and gatherers, they spoke a Siouan language. War and diseases brought by settlers drove them to the brink of extinction in the 18th century. Some joined the CHOCTAW or CHITIMACHA, but most moved to Louisiana, though some subsequently split away and went to Texas. Eventually the survivors merged with the TUNICA, becoming the Tunica-Biloxi, which received federal recognition in the 1980s. In 1991 they numbered 430, and were seeking to rescue fragments of their culture through the repatriation of ceremonial artefacts, often pilfered from graves.

## BLACKFOOT

A Native North American nation of Montana and Alberta. Nomadic hunters, gatherers and traders, they spoke an Algonquian language and called themselves *Siksika* ('black feet'). They were long hostile to the SHOSHONE, and the acquisition of European horses by 1750 made them formidable. They nearly destroyed the Shoshone as they expanded their territory. At the same time they were being undermined by epidemics. Initially hostile to settlers, whom they regarded as thieves, they fought a number of skirmishes from 1865. But a massacre on Marias River in 1870, when the US army attacked a peaceful Blackfoot camp 'by mistake', convinced them of the hopelessness of resistance. They accepted a reservation in Montana in 1874 and two in Alberta in 1877. The extinction of the bison reduced them to complete dependence on government supplies, and when these were not delivered in Montana in 1883, nearly half the Balckfoot starved. They numbered about 25,000 in 1996, and were attempting to preserve a badly undermined traditional culture. (See also PIE-GAN.)

> " The Blackfoot is a sworn and determined enemy of all white men. "
>
> J. Townsend, 1834

## BLOOD or Northern Piegan

An Aboriginal nation of Alberta, who call themselves *Kainai*, which perhaps means 'many chiefs'. Seasonally mobile as hunters and gatherers, they speak an Algonquian language. Part of the BLACKFOOT confederation, they attempted to save their nomadic lifestyle by retreating from the northern plains of the USA to Canada in 1874, but the destruction of the bison caused famine, and they became dependent on government supplies. By 1995 they numbered about 7500 and were seeking economic development through a large-scale irrigation project.

## BOLIVIANS

A South American people partly of colonial origin who inhabit the nation of Bolivia, named after Simon Bolívar (1783–1830). When the Spanish arrived in 1532 most of the AYMARA population were under INCA rule. A brutal colonial rule was established, which eventually led to the War of Liberation (1809–39). The republic proved highly unstable, with nine constitutions proclaimed and violated by 1869. The CREOLE and CHOLO elite proved self-serving and oppressive against the estranged Aymara majority, whose lives were unchanged by independence.

Nation-building was a slow and difficult process. It was achieved, however, largely through a series of national humiliations, beginning with the War of the Pacific (1879–84), which Bolivian dictator Hilarión Daza needlessly provoked. Even with Peru as an ally, the Bolivians were defeated by Chile and lost their mineral-rich coastal provinces, making the country landlocked. Subsequently they were forced to cede territory to Argentina, Brazil and Peru. The loss of the coast remained a major source of national anguish, and in 1932, when it was clear that the League of Nations would not help recover it, Bolivia provoked the Chaco War (1932–5) against Paraguay. The larger, better-equipped Bolivian army suffered yet a further humiliation, and more territory was lost.

This defeat, more than any other factor, brought Bolivia into modernity. A new government proclaimed, but did not enforce, land reform, giving rise to new revolutionary political parties. In 1952 they achieved a national revolution which effected land reforms and the nationalization of industries. Counter-revolution followed in 1964, and Bolivia entered a period of seemingly endless political crises, fed by inflation, corruption and mass poverty.

Despite severe problems of poverty, this largely Native American and Mestizo people had, by the 20th century, developed a distinct culture combining Native American and European elements. With 70% living in poverty, however, a sense of rage against politicians is widespread. A US-sponsored coca eradication programme led to intense anti-Americanism. In 2001 there were some 8.3 million Bolivians.

## BORORÓ

A Native South American nation of the Amazonia of Bolivia and Brazil, whose name means 'village court'. Sedentary slash-and-burn farmers, they were also hunters and gatherers, and they spoke a Gê language. From the late 19th century the western Bororó came under intense pressure from settlers. They became heavily acculturated and by the 1960s had all but disappeared as a nation. The eastern Bororó had fought a 50-year losing war against encroachment after a road was built through their territory in the mid-19th century. Missionaries attempted to suppress their language. They survived, but are limited to six tiny demarked territories whose environment is badly degraded. In 1997 they numbered 1024, living in poverty due to loss of resources, made worse in 2001 by severe drought.

## BOTOCUDO

A Native South American nation of Brazil's Amazonia. They were hunters and gatherers, and also practised slash-and-burn agriculture. They spoke a Gê language and resisted white encroachment until 1914. Subsequently their interests were largely ignored. They protested in 1997 when damming flooded their farmlands and they were left uncompensated. Protests that needless delays in demarking their lands was allowing timber companies to pillage their environment led to allegations of police brutality in 2001. In 1986 they numbered 634.

## BRAZILIANS

A South American people of mainly colonial origin who inhabit the nation of Brazil, the name of which possibly means 'red-dye-wood land'. The first Portuguese colonists arrived in 1531 and immediately began enslaving the Native American peoples, later importing Africans to support a plantation economy. Soon claiming vast stretches of the Amazon rainforest, Brazilians assumed they were destined for greatness. In this vast land Catholicism and the Portuguese language provided the unifying forces needed to overcome local interests. This Catholic nation does possess a second religion – football – and defeat of the national team regularly causes a spate of suicides, such is the passion the game arouses.

In 1822 they proclaimed themselves an independent empire. This was overthrown in 1889, and a republic under military rule or military controlled civilian regimes provided stability if not democracy. In 1888 slavery had been abolished, which encouraged large-scale immigration, especially from Italy, to work on the coffee estates. The culture became progressively more cosmopolitan. Poverty affected each group, and therefore racial tensions were rarely a problem, except for the Native Americans. Indeed, Brazilians were noted for their good-natured casualness and sense of moderation. In the 20th century, however, a more literate population, with new forms of mass media, were less prepared to suffer poverty with their customary resignation. The collapse of the coffee market in 1929 began a mass migration of rural poor to the cities, where *favelas*, or shantytowns, grew to house huge populations. Brazilian cities eventually became among the largest in the world.

The collapse of the coffee market also had more immediate effects. In 1930 the military installed as dictator Getúlio Dornelles Vargas, who promised much in terms of social welfare, education and health. He also suggested that it was time for Brazil to grasp the great destiny that it had so often been promised. Under Vargas and his successors a period of great, dramatic projects began that captured the Brazilian imagination but benefited the elite at the expense of the poor. Hydroelectric projects, a

**b**

**"You cannot disillusion a Brazilian."**

Peter Fleming, 1933

nuclear power station (known as the 'glow worm' for the feeble amount of energy it produces), and a new capital at Brasilia all failed to deliver the promised transformation of Brazil. For the poor, benefits in education and health were soon negated by population growth.

In the 1980s the foreign credit that made these projects possible dried up. Poverty and crime persist amidst great wealth. The international outcry at the destruction of the rainforest is resented: Brazilians want to exploit their resources and find the prosperity others know. In 2001 Brazilians numbered over 174 million.

# BROTHERTOWN

A Native North American nation of Wisconsin. Sedentary farmers, they spoke an Algonquian language. The nation was formed in the 1770s after a religious movement in New England that led a number of MOHEGAN, NARRAGANSETT and PEQUOT to adopt Christianity and European culture. In an effort to escape settler pressure and the influence of alcohol, two communities were formed: Brothertown on ONEIDA land, and Stockbridge. The Brothertown were relocated to Wisconsin, but the pressure was soon renewed. In an effort to avoid forced relocation to Kansas, they agreed to allot their lands to individuals, abandon their sovereignty and accept US citizenship. By the 20th century this had resulted for many in growing impoverishment, marginalization and fragmentation. In an effort to reverse this trend, the Brothertown, who numbered over 2200 in 2001, are still campaigning to regain their sovereignty through federal recognition.

# BUBURE

A Native South American nation of Brazil's Amazonia. Sedentary slash-and-burn farmers, they were also hunters and gatherers. They spoke a Gê language and in 1986 numbered about 50.

# CADDO

A Native North American nation of Louisiana, whose name perhaps means 'the real chiefs'. A confederation of Caddoan-speaking tribes, they referred to each other as *Tayshes*, meaning 'allies'.

They were possibly descended from the mound-builders of the region. Sedentary farmers and traders, they hunted, fished and gathered as secondary activities. In the 18th century they entered the fur trade and prospered initially, but warfare and diseases associated with the trade reduced their numbers and they came under pressure from settlers. In the 1830s they were forced off their lands. Some merged with the CHOCTAW or the HASINAI, while others moved to Texas, where they were forced onto a reservation in 1854. Local settlers were so violently opposed to their presence, however, that they were moved to Oklahoma to avoid a massacre. There they remained, temporarily fleeing to Kansas during the Civil War, and merged with the WICHITA. In 1992 the Wichita-Caddo numbered 3371.

# CAHOKIA

A Native North American Nation of southwestern Illinois. Sedentary farmers, hunters, gatherers and fishers, they spoke an Algonquian language. Once part of the ILLINOIS confederation, they entered the fur trade and became French allies in the 18th century. As a result of this alliance they suffered repeated and ultimately disastrous wars. The FOX destroyed their main village in 1752, and subsequently their lands were whittled away by settlers. In 1832 they joined the PEORIA in Kansas, and the combined group was moved to Oklahoma in 1867, where their descendants are found.

# CAHTO

A Native North American nation of northern California. Sedentary hunters and gatherers who spoke an ATHABASKAN language, their name means 'lake people'. They depended heavily on fish and acorns for subsistence. In the 1840s they began a bitter war against the YUKI. This ended in 1856 when settlers began to steal Cahto lands. Forced to survive by cattle-stealing, many were massacred by vengeful settlers in 1859. Of the survivors, some were removed to Round Valley reservation, where their descendants still exist. Others were granted Laytonville *rancheria* (settlement) in 1908, where, in 1997, 142 maintained a distinct nation.

## CAHUILLA

A Native North American nation of southern California. Probably semi-sedentary, they were hunters, fishers, gatherers and skilled basket-makers who spoke an Uto-Aztecan language. Their name means 'masters' or 'powerful ones'. By 1800 Spanish missions had made contact with them, but they vigorously defended their independence and culture. Even those converted to Catholicism still maintained some traditional religious practices. The 1849 gold rush was disastrous for them, as their lands were stolen and numbers reduced by murder and disease. Even when they were forced onto reservations, land thefts continued. Energetic government attempts to suppress their language and culture followed. In 2001, however, about 290 still maintained their nation and much of their culture. They remain determined to defend their nation from legal challenges to jurisdiction over Americans living in their territory.

## CAINGANG

A Native South American nation of Brazil's Amazonia. Sedentary hunters and gatherers, they adopted farming as a secondary activity in the 20th century. They speak a Gê language and were considered hostile by settlers, who preferred to avoid their rather poor lands. Only in the 20th century has land encroachment been a real problem. In 1996 some Caingang took government representatives hostage to force the government to act on this issue, and the Caingang were again active in demanding the return of stolen lands in 2002. Other problems have arisen; in 1999 they protested against the pillaging of their plant resources by pharmaceutical companies. In 1997 they numbered about 22,000.

## CAJUN

A culture of the USA of colonial origin. The original Cajun were ACADIANS, French colonists expelled from Nova Scotia by the British in the 18th century. They settled in small communities of farmers in Louisiana and spoke their own patois. Their culture, distinct especially in its cuisine and music, has tended to merge with that of the

CREOLES. In 1996 they formed Action Cadienne to preserve it. In 1990 nearly 600,000 people claimed Cajun ancestry.

## CALUSA

A former Native North American nation of southwest Florida, whose name perhaps means 'people on the other side'. Sedentary fishers, hunters and gatherers, they farmed as a secondary activity and spoke a Muskogean language. They maintained temple mounds, which early archaeologists assumed they used for human sacrifice (by analogy with the Maya and Aztec pyramids), but which were in fact spiritual centres and places for burying the dead. A powerful nation, they conquered and exacted tribute from their neighbours. Initially hostile to the Spanish, they came to see raiding by the CREEK and English as a greater threat and became Spanish allies. Constant warfare and epidemics caused their population to collapse during the 17th century. By the time Spain lost Florida in 1763 only remnants remained. The SEMINOLE absorbed some, while others went to Cuba, where they soon vanished as a nation.

## CAMARACOTÓ

A Native South American nation of the Amazonia of Guyana and Venezuela. Sedentary slash-and-burn farmers, which requires periodic relocation as soil becomes exhausted, they were also hunters and gatherers and practised fishing with poison. They spoke a CARIB language and originally lived nearer the coast. In 1727, however, presumably in response to white pressure, they burned their villages and moved inland. In 1990 they numbered over 5000.

## CAMPA

A Native South American nation of northeast Peru. Sedentary hunters and gatherers of the Amazon rainforest, they fought Spanish rule for 300 years and were only defeated in the late 19th century. By the end of the rubber boom in 1913, however, 80% had been exterminated by settlers, who systematically destroyed their settlements and stole their land. From 1984 the Campa have been caught in the middle of the Sendero Luminoso (Shining Path) guerrilla war and many have been driven from their lands, which were subsequently seized by coca-growers. In 1999 they numbered 55,000 and were attempting to recover their lands, but it was unclear if they could survive as a nation.

## CANADIANS

The people of the nation state of Canada, in North America. Largely of colonial origin, Canadians also include 542 native Aboriginal, MÉTIS and INUIT nations. Canadians have a diverse and industrialized economy and are officially bilingual in English and French (though the QUÉBÉCOIS have discriminatory laws restricting the use of all non-French languages). Originally the homeland of many Aboriginal nations, Canada became a French colony, then passed to Britain in 1763. From the founding of Quebec in 1608, however, colonial governments were primarily concerned with attracting immigrants to settle and control their vast lands.

Canadians have their origins in a variety of nations, but most think of themselves as primarily Canadian. The modern nation of Canada was formed in 1867, when the British, fearing that the United States would invade, confederated the colonies of Nova Scotia, New Brunswick, Quebec and Ontario into the Dominion of Canada. Britain retained only nominal control over foreign policy until 1931. British Columbia, on the west coast, joined Canada in 1871, and the Canadian Pacific Railway, intended to unite the new country's far-flung provinces, was completed in 1885. In 1982 Canada's constitution was fully patriated from Westminster under Prime Minister Pierre Trudeau, along with a Charter of Rights and Freedoms, which recognized the founding nations of Canada as the Aboriginal ('First Nations'), Inuit, Métis, British and French. This was the first written constitution in the world that recognized aboriginal nations.

Modern Canadians generally enjoy prosperity brought by a great wealth of natural resources and have developed distinct, diverse and rich Aboriginal and non-Aboriginal cultures. However, this diversity has perhaps hindered the development of a Canadian national identity. Provincial loyalties have tended to take precedence. Though steadfastly loyal to Britain in the 20th century, Canadians have their own political concerns. The most pressing of these is the troubled relationship between the Québécois and other Canadians. A tendency on the part of many English-speakers to dismiss French language and cultural claims as trivial infuriates the Québécois. Anglophone Canadians are divided between Québécois-sympathizers and those who see an independent Quebec as a way to rid themselves of a tiresome problem. Canadians also have a fear of domination by the USA, and the further west one goes in the prairies (though not in British Columbia), the more similar the two cultures are. Americans have also long tended to assume that Canada's entry into the Union is inevitable. Though they are part of a continental economy, maintaining political independence remains a strong concern for most Canadians. Occasional upsurges of anti-Americanism have marked Canadian politics. In 2002 there were over 31 million Canadians.

## CANAMARI

A Native South American nation of Brazil's Amazonia. They were sedentary slash-and-burn farmers, which requires periodic relocation, and also hunters and gatherers. They spoke Katukinan and had a rich culture, remaining isolated until 1940. Subsequently rubber companies introduced alcohol as a means of control, and over 50 years their traditional culture greatly deteriorated. In 1999 they numbered 643.

## CAPANAWA

A Native South American nation of Peru's Amazonia. Sedentary slash-and-burn farmers, they were also hunters and gatherers and spoke a Panoan language. Attempts to evangelize them in 1817 failed when they fled to escape diseases. Thereafter they appear to have been subject to raiding by neighbouring nations. In the 20th century contacts with modern Peruvian culture grew, and by 1998, when they numbered up to 400, their language was considered endangered as the young generally failed to learn it.

C

## CAPE BRETON HIGHLANDERS

A Canadian culture of Scottish colonial origin, found on Cape Breton Island, Nova Scotia. First arriving in 1802 from the Scottish Highlands and islands, the Cape Breton Highlander population grew rapidly as the Scottish agricultural economy and kelp industry went into decline. Their own lairds (landowners) encouraged, or forced, many Scots to emigrate.

Often depicted as subsistence farmers with no interest in material wealth, the Cape Breton Highlanders were in fact reasonably prosperous. Proud of their heritage, many were Gaelic-speakers. But the need for education and employment led to English generally becoming their first language, though Gaelic Highland culture, such as the ceilidh (a social gathering with traditional music, dancing and storytelling) is still strong. Their economy is based on farming, fishing and tourism, but limited economic opportunities have led many to leave. In 1996 the population of Cape Breton Island was over 48,000.

## CAQUETIO

A former sub-group of the ARAWAK of the Caribbean island of Bonaire, now part of the Netherlands Antilles. They were sedentary hunters, fishers, farmers and gatherers. When the Spanish arrived in the 16th century, they had already been driven away by the CARIB, leaving behind little but petroglyphs (rock inscriptions). A few possibly fled to coastal Venezuela, but they rapidly disappeared thereafter.

## CARAJÁ

A Native South American nation of Brazil's Amazonia, on Ilha do Bananal, the world's largest inland river island (20,000 sq. km/7700 sq. miles). Sedentary hunters and gatherers and especially fishers, they spoke a Gê language. Their tattoos, body paint and ornate dress made them a notably colourful nation. They were first contacted in 1673, but it was only in the late 20th century that improved communications began seriously to undermine their culture. Development of the waterways threatens many species crucial to Carajá fishers, and in 1998

there were complaints that buyers of fish, skins and turtles were exploiting them through supplying alcohol in order virtually to enslave them. In 1998 they numbered 1725.

## CARIB

A Native Central/South American nation of the Caribbean area. Sedentary farmers, fishers, hunters, gatherers and expert navigators, they spoke a Carib language. The Spanish who encountered them in the 16th century described them as ferociously warlike and cannibalistic, possibly to justify their ill treatment. Conquest, epidemics and enslavement had all but exterminated them by the 17th century. A few Carib descendants survive in Dominica (about 1500 in 1988) and Guatemala, and a few other groups in the region claim Carib descent.

## CARIBOU ESKIMO

See INUIT.

## CARIJONA

A Native South American nation of Colombia's Amazonia. Sedentary slash-and-burn farmers, they were also fishers, hunters and gatherers. They spoke Peba and were once a huge nation that dominated an area including parts of Peru, Colombia, Ecuador and Brazil. Portuguese slave raiders and European diseases, however, decimated their numbers. In Brazil the remnants were absorbed into the MESTIZO population. In Peru missions were established but proved an easy target for slavers. In 1993 there were only 140 native-language speakers. In 1999 they met with other nations in an attempt to end exploitation such as the pillaging of their plant life by pharmaceutical companies.

## CARIRÍ

A Native South American nation of Brazil's Amazonia. They were sedentary slash-and-burn farmers, hunters and gatherers. They spoke a Gê language and came under missionary and then government control from the late 19th century. The government, however, declared them extinct

C

in the early 20th century and they became land-less beggars, clinging to a tiny corner of their lands, which they deem sacred and vital to their identity. In the 1970s they became politically active and in 1994 some of their lands were returned. However, when local farmers threat-ened to massacre them, the government would do nothing to protect them. In 2001 they num-bered perhaps 2000.

## CARRIER

A Native North American nation of northern British Columbia. They call themselves *Dekelh-ne*, meaning 'people who go on water' or perhaps 'people of the earth'. Seasonally moving through their territory as traders, hunters, gath-erers and fishers, they speak an ATHABASKAN language. The fur trade brought both prosperity and epidemics in the 19th century. From 1876, however, they were forced onto reservations, where their traditional culture was largely destroyed. In 1979 they formed the Carrier-SEKANI Tribal Council to protect their interests, including resisting provincial attempts to regu-late their resources. The question of logging rights, for example, led to their suspension of treaty talks with British Columbia in 2000 and the referral of their case to the Inter-American Commission on Human Rights. In 1995 they numbered about 7000.

## CASTANOAN

A Native North American nation of central coastal California who spoke dialects of Cas-tanoan. They were sedentary hunters, fishers and gatherers who once controlled a highly lucrative and extensive trade network. In the 18th century the Spanish forced them onto missions, where disease and poor conditions reduced an original population of about 20,000 by 90% by 1834. The Mexican government then broke up the mis-sions, leaving them landless and destitute. The traditional Castanoan culture had almost entirely disappeared. Between 1850 and 1870 many were massacred or enslaved by Americans. Many others were dispersed among the general population, and by the 20th century they were widely thought to be extinct as a nation. Several

thousand descendants did survive, however, and in 2002 about 500 were members of the Ohlone/Castanoan Esselen Nation, which was campaigning for federal recognition as a nation, as well as compensation for stolen lands.

## CATAWBA

A Native North American nation of the Caro-linas, whose name means 'river people'. Seasonally mobile within their territory as farm-ers as well as hunters and gatherers, they spoke a Siouan language. Early allies of the English, they were, however, alienated by the depredations of settlers and traders, and fought in the Yamasee War (1715–16). Though defeated, they absorbed other more decimated nations and remained powerful, and were awarded a considerable reservation in 1763. They fought for the USA in the American Revolution, but were nevertheless swindled out of their lands and hunting and fishing rights in the 1840s. Many converted to Mormonism in the 1880s. They suffered reli-gious intolerance along with racism (they were denied the vote in state elections until 1944) and desperate poverty. Half moved to Mormon communities in Colorado. The remainder, under government pressure, disbanded as a nation in 1962, and only regained federal recog-nition in 1993, when they numbered over 1400.

## CATUKINA

A Native South American nation of Brazil's Ama-zonia. Sedentary farmers, hunters and gatherers, they spoke Katukinan, a language all but extinct by 1976. During the 20th century, miners, log-gers and rubber extractors exploited them as cheap labour, causing malnutrition and disease as well as the degradation of their traditional culture. In 2000 they numbered just 306.

## CAYABI

A Native South American nation of Brazil's Ama-zonia. Sedentary slash-and-burn farmers, they were also hunters and gatherers and spoke a TUPÍ language. They were first contacted by settlers in 1848, and subsequent exploitation by rubber extractors led to violence and in 1910 a punitive expedition that killed many. Peaceful contacts only resumed in 1936. In the 1990s, however, their lands became increasingly attractive to gold-seekers and loggers, and the Cayabi became more vocal in protecting their lands from invasion. In 1990 they numbered 1028.

## CAYAPÓ

A Native South American nation of Brazil's Amazonia, who practised slash-and-burn farming, hunting and gathering, and spoke a Gê language. Noted for their colourful head-dresses and body paint, many still wear distinctive lip discs. From the 18th century they fought colonization and slave raids. By the 20th century they were widely deemed extinct, but several groups were later contacted, the last in 1975. Adept at relations with the outside world, they recruited the popular musician Sting to publicize their cause, especially the destruction of their environment after a gold rush into their territory in 1982. However, they were also willing to exploit their environment and in 2000 prevented government representatives from halting logging operations, when they needed the revenue. In 1993 they numbered about 4000. Some sources place their numers at around 5000 in 2000.

## CAYMAN ISLANDERS

The inhabitants of the Cayman Islands, a British dependency between Cuba and Honduras in the Caribbean Sea. It was first settled from Jamaica in the 18th century, and its population includes a mixture of African and European elements. Its lack of fresh water sources and arable land made fishing the primary means of subsistence until the 20th century, leaving most islanders in deep poverty. Thereafter, offshore banking and tourism provided relatively high living standards, undermining calls for independence. In 2001 they numbered over 35,000.

## CAYUGA

A Native North American nation of New York state, whose name means 'where the boats are taken out'. Sedentary farmers, hunters, gatherers and fishers, they spoke an Iroquoian language.

Part of the IROQUOIS Confederacy, they were powerful and feared allies of the British. This proved their undoing during the American Revolution, when several of their villages were destroyed. Some fled to Ontario, while others joined with the SENECA and were forcibly moved to Oklahoma in 1831. Those who tried to cling to their lands were defrauded between 1795 and 1807, which the US government chose to ignore. Scattered and impoverished, they still strove to maintain their culture and pursue compensation. In 1980 the award of cash and public lands aroused racist protests, but the final settlement in 2000 of nearly $250 million is probably the largest on record. In 1973 they numbered 2500.

## CAYUSE

A Native North American nation of northeast Oregon and southeast Washington. Their name comes from the French and means 'people of the stones', but in their Penutian language they called themselves *Waiilatpu*, meaning 'we the people'. Hunters, gatherers and traders, they adopted a semi-sedentary lifestyle with the acquisition of horses in the mid-18th century and became noted horse-breeders. They were a warlike nation and enemies of the SHOSHONE. Initially they welcomed settlers for the trade they offered, but grew alarmed at their rapidly rising numbers and the diseases they brought. In 1847 the murder of missionaries started the Cayuse War, in which they were defeated by 1849. In 1855 they were forced to cede their lands and most entered the UMATILLA reservation, finding there only disease, poverty and hunger. Reservation lands were whittled away and dams destroyed their traditional fishing grounds in the mid-20th century, causing economic problems. They are now part of the Cayuse, Umatilla and WALLA WALLA Confederation.

## CENÚ

A Native South American nation of Colombia's Amazonia. Sedentary intensive farmers, fishers, hunters and gatherers, they lived in large, palisaded villages that they successfully defended from Spanish attacks in the 16th century. Their land, however, was particularly fertile and was beleieved to contain gold. Despite their poison arrows, they could not withstand continuous pressure, and disappeared as a nation by the 19th century. Many still claim Cenú descent, however, even if the language is extinct. These descendants have been caught in the middle of Colombia's civil war, which along with environmental destruction threatens their survival.

## CERO DE LAS MESAS CULTURE

A former Native Central American culture of Mexico. Sedentary hunters, gatherers, farmers, fishers and traders, its people were perhaps part of the OLMEC, in whose former territory they developed. Some of their sculptures gave rise in the 1970s to controversial speculation of an African origin, while an enormous hoard of jade recovered from the site remains unexplained. The culture flourished from about AD 300 to 600, and was strongly influenced by the TEOTI-HUACÁN. The cause of their disappearance is unclear.

## CHACHI

A Native South American nation of Ecuador's Amazonia. Sedentary fishers, hunters and gatherers, they spoke Che'palaachi and might be related to the CHIBCHA. In isolated communities along the rivers, they lost much of their traditional culture through missionary activity. In 2002 they numbered about 7000 and were seeking to end severe poverty but still protect their environment.

## CHANA

A Native South American nation of the Amazonia of Paraguay, Uruguay and Brazil. Sedentary farmers, hunters and gatherers, they spoke an Arawakan language. Evangelized in the 17th century in Paraguay, they became largely acculturated, though there were up to 600 speakers in 1991. In Uruguay and Brazil settlers apparently exterminated them.

## CHARRÚA

A Native South American nation of Uruguay. Nomadic hunters and gatherers, they spoke Charruan. They were hostile from their first meeting with the Spanish in the 16th century, and by acquiring horses became formidable enough to protect themselves until the early 19th century. They were then were overwhelmed by large-scale BRAZILIAN and ARGENTINIAN immigration into their lands, which were valuable for cattle ranching. Genocide and disease rapidly destroyed them as a nation, though many URUGUAYAN gauchos are their descendants.

## CHASTACOSTA

A Native North American nation of the southwest Oregon coast. Their name is possibly a corruption of *Shista Kwutsa*, perhaps their name for themselves. Sedentary hunters (especially of sea mammals), fishers and gatherers, they spoke an ATHABASKAN language. Initially happy to trade with visiting ships, they were provoked by the settlers' diseases and land thefts to fight in the Rogue River War (1855–6). The defeated survivors were forced onto the SILETZ reservation, where their descendants can now be found.

## CHAVÍN CULTURE

A former Native South American culture of the northern and central Peruvian coast. Its people were sedentary farmers, hunters, gatherers and traders. Their first settlements appeared around 1300 BC, and they flourished at their main centre at Chavín de Huantar from about 900 BC, disappearing about 200 BC. They are credited with giving the region much of its material culture, in textiles, ceramics and architecture, though much of this may have been inherited from earlier cultures. The spread of Chavín iconography and material culture suggests a high degree of social and political integration, but little is known of them. It is unclear whether Chavín de Huantar was the centre of an empire or simply a centre of pilgrimage. The cause of the culture's disappearance is also unclear, but there is evidence of declining trade and fortification construction, so external pressure is plausible.

## CHEHALIS

A Native North American nation of western Washington state. Their name means 'sand' (it was originally the name of a single village, later applied to the entire nation). Hunters, fishers, gatherers and traders (especially of salmon), they also practised agriculture and spoke a Salishan language. They became wealthy through the fur trade with Europeans from the 1820s, and individuals acquired slaves as status symbols. From 1846, however, settlers brought disastrous epidemics. In 1864 they were unable to resist pressure to enter two reservations in Washington, where they numbered about 550 in 1997.

## CHELAN

A Native North American nation of the Lake Chelan area, Washington state, whose name means 'big water' or 'beautiful water'. They were hunters, fishers and gatherers, and spoke a Salishan language.

In 1855 they were forced to sign the YAKIMA Treaty, but took no part in the Yakima War the treaty provoked. Despite promises, their fisheries at Wanatchee were stolen and settlers invaded their land. In 1872 an earthquake that destroyed their village effectively ended their existence as a separate nation. Most were subsequently moved onto the COLVILLE reservation, where their descendants can be found today.

## CHEMEHUEVI

A Native North American nation of northern California and southern Nevada. Semi-sedentary hunters and gatherers who practised some agriculture by the 18th century, they spoke an Uto-Aztecan language. They called themselves *Nuwu*, meaning 'people'. Once part of the PAIUTE, they broke away in the 18th century. In subsequent years they allied with the MOHAVE in resisting Spanish slave raiders and in the mid-19th century attacked settlers and prospectors intruding into their territory. Though these attacks were suppressed, they refused to share a reservation with another nation and clung to what they could of their lands. Only in 1907 did they receive their own reservation, but not by act

of Congress, which raises doubts about their legal title to it.

In 1930 the Parker Dam created Lake Havasu, drowning much of their reservation, forcing many to leave. Ironically, by the end of the 20th century, tourists attracted by the lake did provide a modicum of prosperity to the Chemehuevi, of whom there were over 500 in 2002.

## CHERAW

A Native North American nation of South Carolina who spoke a Siouan language. Sedentary farmers, hunters and gatherers, they moved to the borders of Virginia in the late 17th century and became allies of the English in the Tuscarora War (1711–13). Owing to the abuses of the settlers, however, the Cheraw fought against them in the Yamasee War (1715–16). Defeat, followed by epidemics, left them impoverished and fragmented, and they were generally regarded as an extinct nation by the end of the 18th century. Some moved to North Carolina and, joining with the remnants of other Siouan nations, formed the LUMBEE. In the 1990s the Lumbee Tribe of Cheraw Indians, who then numbered over 48,000, were seeking federal recognition. This has proved to be a long and drawn-out quest, which is still proceeding.

## CHEROKEE

A Native North American Nation whose lands once stretched from Alabama to West Virginia. They called themselves *Ani'-Yun'wiya*, meaning 'the real people'. Sedentary farmers, hunters, gatherers and fishers, they spoke an Iroquoian language.

The largest of the so-called FIVE CIVILIZED TRIBES, the Cherokee became heavily involved in the fur trade in the 18th century. They also undertook a remarkable transformation from the 1790s, adopting white culture wholesale in their religion, agriculture and education. They developed their own written language and had their own press. Their relative prosperity, however, highlighted the value of their lands to settlers, who called for them to be dispossessed.

In 1830 President Andrew Jackson approved the Indian Removal Act, which he administered by military force, despite the Cherokees' successful challenge to its legality in the US Supreme Court. Some managed to hide in North Carolina, where their descendants remain. Most were forced on a brutal death march, known as the 'Trail of Tears', to Oklahoma. They re-established their nation and again prospered, though they lost further lands when some sided with the Confederacy during the Civil War. Efforts were also made to eradicate surviving elements of their traditional culture.

In 1906, as Oklahoma became a state, the US government arbitrarily dissolved the Cherokee nation and made the Cherokee US citizens. Only in the 1970s was a Cherokee nation reformed. In 1990 they numbered over 300,000 and were the largest Native American nation in the USA.

> **66** Colorado soldiers have again covered themselves with glory. **99**
>
> *Rocky Mountain News* report of the Sand Creek Massacre of the Cheyenne (1864)

## CHEYENNE

A Native North American nation of the northern and central Great Plains. Their name comes from the SIOUX and means 'people who are alike', though they call themselves *Tsitsitas*, meaning 'our people'. The Northern Cheyenne acquired European horses by 1800 and adopted a nomadic hunting and gathering lifestyle, while the Southern Cheyenne remained more sedentary and practised agriculture. They spoke an Algonquian language.

By the 1840s streams of settlers crossing their territory were increasingly disruptive, and agreements reached with the US government proved to provide no protection. The Cheyenne fought a sporadic war from 1857 to 1879, which included the Sand Creek Massacre, when howitzers were used against their fleeing women and children. The Southern Cheyenne were pushed onto a reservation in Oklahoma in 1867. The Northern Cheyenne, after fighting in the battle of the Little Bighorn (1876), were likewise moved to Oklahoma, but found conditions so terrible that they fled towards the old lands, pursued by 13,000 soldiers. Caught in Nebraska, many perished due to ill treatment. They were given a new reservation in Montana, though within a few years the bison disappeared.

> **66** The great and powerful Chikazas. **99**
>
> D. Coxe, 1722, referring to the Chicasaw

In 2002 the Cheyenne numbered nearly 11,000. They were trying to preserve a language and traditional culture severely harmed by deliberate government deculturation policies, and to achieve economic self-sufficiency.

## CHIBCHA

A former Native South American nation of Venezuela. Sedentary farmers, hunters and gatherers, they spoke Chibchan. Relatively isolated, they traded, especially in the gold, copper and emeralds, and had towns connected by stone roads. From about AD 1000 they were driven from their coastal areas by CARIB invaders. They offered little resistance to Spanish conquest, completed between 1536 and 1541, and rapid acculturation followed. Those not enslaved were driven into sub-marginal lands unable to support a large population, where their descendants remain. Their nation was quickly destroyed.

## CHICASAW

A Native North American nation of northeast Mississippi, whose name might mean 'they left not so long ago', though this is disputed. They were seasonally mobile within their territory as fishers, hunters and gatherers, and farming was a secondary activity, generally performed by women and slaves. An offshoot of the CHOCTAW, they spoke a Muskogean language and were one of the FIVE CIVILIZED TRIBES. Deemed by their neighbours warlike and formidable, they maintained a warrior culture often likened to the SPARTANS. As such they were valuable allies to the British in the 18th century, who armed them generously. Warfare and epidemics proved disastrous, decimating their population. Supporting Britain during the American Revolution cost them their lands, and in the 1830s they were forced along the 'Trail of Tears' to Oklahoma. Despite losses on the journey, renewed epidemics and starvation from ruined government rations, the Chickasaw eventually prospered, largely through cattle and oil. They supported the Confederacy during the Civil war, and were the last Confederate force to surrender.

In 1906 the US government forced them to dissolve their nation and divide its lands between individuals. Most of the land fell into white hands, and many Chicasaw moved away. Federal recognition was only restored in 1983.

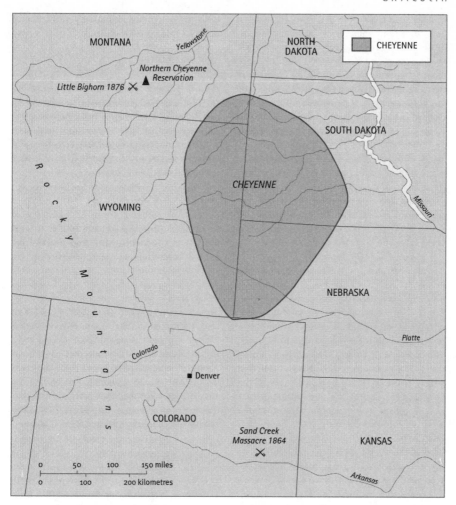

Since then the Chickasaw have been interested in preserving their culture and defending their sovereignty. In 1995, for example, they successfully challenged the right of Oklahoma to impose state taxes in their territory. At that time they numbered over 20,000.

## CHICKAHOMINY

A Native North American nation of coastal Virginia, whose name means 'coarse-ground corn people'. Sedentary farmers, hunters, gatherers and fishers, they spoke an Algonquian language. They were early enemies of English settlers, and from 1616 warfare, epidemics, fragmentation, land loss and famine had a disastrous impact. By 1705 they had all but ceased to exist. They struggled to survive as a nation for two centuries, losing their language and much of their culture. In the 20th century, however, they were seeking federal recognition, and in 2002 held the first powwow of all six state-recognized tribes since the 17th century. They number around 1200.

## CHILCOTIN

A Native North American nation of sub-arctic British Columbia. Originally nomadic hunters, gatherers and fishers, they speak an Athabaskan language. They entered the fur trade in the 1820s, but the construction of a road through their territory and abusive behaviour towards them, along with the threat to spread smallpox, led to an incident in 1864 in which a Chilcotin group massacred a party of road builders; five Chilcotin were subsequently hanged. Forced to accept a more sedentary lifestyle, the population of about 1800 in 1982 was becoming more assertive in defending its sovereignty and traditional culture, such as asserting hunting rights. In addition, in cooperation with other nations, they have demanded environmental and cultural protection and economic development.

## CHILEANS

A South American people of colonial origin who inhabit the nation of Chile. Divided between the INCA and MAPUCHE when the Spanish arrived in the 16th century, much of the land was conquered quickly, though Mapuche resistance was not broken until 1885. Independent in 1817, the Chileans were a relatively homogeneous, largely MESTIZO population and culture, though a largely white aristocracy owned most of the land. For the rest of the population intense poverty, with all its attendant social evils, was the norm. In foreign relations it was a highly successful nation, defeating Bolivia and Peru in the War of the Pacific of 1879 and conquering Bolivia's mineral-rich coastal provinces – a constant source of tension between the two nations thereafter. They have also put forward a territorial claim in Antarctica, which, like all other such claims, has been in abeyance since the Antarctic Protocol of 1991. Domestically they were less successful. Constitutionalism remained strong, but even reforming governments never dared tackle the serious but politically dangerous issue of land reform. However, the majority of the population is urbanized, allowing them to become one of the best-educated nations of Latin America.

In the early 20th century, as the collapse of the nitrates market caused them immense economic problems, growing labour unrest and a growing Communist party led to rising political coalescence, turbulence, and the intrusion of the military into politics. Politically the nation split between a reactionary countryside, where landowners controlled votes, and a radical urban population. This culminated, after the election of Salvador Allende's left-wing government in 1970, in the American-backed military coup by Augusto Pinochet in 1973, followed by many years of rule by terrorism. Democracy was only restored in 1990. The nation has since sought to contain its political divisions and address its great social problems. In 2001 they numbered over 15 million.

## CHILULA

A Native North American nation of northwest California, whose name means 'people of the bald hills', although they call themselves *Hoil'kut*. Sedentary hunters and gatherers, they were closely allied with the HUPA, and spoke an ATHABASKAN language. In the 1850s gold miners and settlers encroached on their territory. When they attempted to defend themselves, settlers formed militias to exterminate them. In 1859 the US Army invited them to peace talks, but about 160 were seized and sent to a distant reservation. They escaped and tried to return, but were massacred by the LASSIK. The survivors were absorbed by the Hupa, although in 2002 a few families still identified themselves as Chilula.

## CHIMARIKO

A Native North American nation of northern California. Sedentary hunters, fishers and gatherers who spoke a Hokan language, they lived in villages along the Trinity River and were ruled by hereditary headmen. They enjoyed relatively peaceful contact with Europeans until gold was found on their lands in the 1850s. When they resisted US encroachment in the mid-1860s, the miners responded savagely. Some found refuge with other nations and were absorbed. The rest were hunted almost to extinction.

## CHIMÚ

A former Native South American nation of Peru. Sedentary farmers, hunters and gatherers, they were descendants of the TIWANAKU. Their first settlements appeared about AD 800, but in the early 11th century they began to expand their territory, possibly because of the destruction of farmlands from flooding. They were ceremonial-mound builders and constructed vast irrigation works, as well as Chan Chan, the largest adobe city in the world. The INCA, who conquered them in 1466, possibly adopted their class and administration system. They shared the fate of the Inca at SPANISH hands.

## CHINCHOROS TRADITION

A former Native South American culture of the coast of southern Peru and northern Chile. Sedentary hunters, gatherers and very sophisticated fishers, from about 5000 BC they began embalming their dead and became the only South American culture to practise mummification. They flourished particularly between 3000 and 500 BC, adopting ceramics around 1200 BC, but subsequently disappeared for no clearly understood reason.

## CHINOOK

A Native North American nation of Oregon and western Washington state, who spoke a Penutian language. Sedentary hunters, fishers and gatherers (with much of this work done by slaves), they also controlled a great trade network, and their language became the regional trade language. They assisted the first European explorers with information and food and in the early 19th century prospered through the fur trade; but they also suffered serious losses through European epidemics.

In the mid-19th century they were forcibly combined with other nations on several reservations, where their culture began to disintegrate. A long battle for federal recognition and compensation ensued and was finally won in 2001. In 1990 they numbered about 1700.

## CHIPEWYAN

A Native North American nation of northern Canada. Their name comes from the CREE and means 'pointed skins', but they call themselves *Dene*, meaning 'the people'. Residing on the tundra and primarily hunters, they also foraged and fished. They speak an ATHABASKAN language. Entering the fur trade in the 17th century, they proved particularly vulnerable to its associated diseases, and their population declined drastically. The Canadian government negotiated

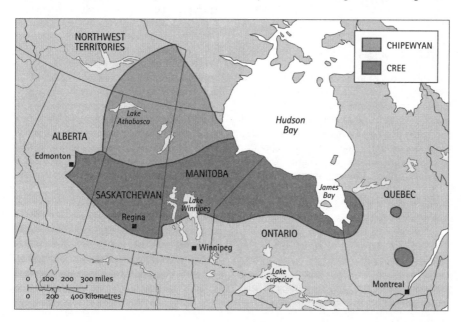

Chipewyan and Cree

questionable treaties with them, stripping them of their lands and subsequently ignoring their interests. During the late 20th century, furthermore, trapping became increasingly unviable as a form of subsistence.

From the 1960s the Chipewyan became politically active, campaigning to protect their environment, receive education in their own language and control their own resources through the federal government's claims process. Unemployment also remains a great concern; many can rely only on lumbering, fishing and seasonal fire-fighting for employment. In 1991 they numbered nearly 10,000. (For map of the Chipewyan, see page 53.)

## CHIQUITO

A Native South American nation of Bolivia's Amazonia. Sedentary farmers, hunters and gatherers, they spoke a Gê language. They lived in autonomous villages protected by thorn hedges and poisoned caltrops. They were evangelized in the late 17th century, which undermined their traditional culture, but they still numbered up to 42,000 in 1991.

## CHIRICHAUA

See APACHE.

## CHIRIGUANO

A Native South American nation of Argentina, Paraguay and Bolivia's Amazonia. Nomadic hunters and gatherers, they spoke a TUPÍ language. Once part of the GUARANÍ, they separated at the start of the 16th century and began raiding into INCA territory. The SPANISH attempted to evangelize them from 1690, although early attempts failed. Cultural degradation still occurred, and in 1994, when they numbered nearly 37,000, UNESCO deemed their language potentially endangered.

## CHITIMACHA

A Native North American nation of coastal Louisiana. Sedentary farmers, traders, fishers, hunters and gatherers, they spoke Chitimachan,

a now extinct language. Once powerful, they offered an obstacle to FRENCH plans to dominate the region. The French therefore stirred up neighbouring nations against the Chitimacha in 1699, burning villages and enslaving captives. They were driven into remote areas and their population was decimated, so they were unable to resist settlers overrunning their lands in the 18th century. Heavily acculturated, they became French-speaking Catholics who gained federal recognition and a tiny reservation only in 1919. In 1977 they numbered about 300.

## CHOCÓ

A Native South American nation of Panama and northwest Colombia. Seasonally mobile within their territory as farmers, hunters and gatherers, they spoke a Chocó language. Using poisoned blowgun darts, throughout the 16th century they resisted the SPANISH, who gave them an undeserved reputation for ferocity. Thereafter the Chocó remained, and still remain, rather isolated and suspicious of outsiders. They tend to ignore governments, despite being threatened by civil war in Colombia in the 1990s. They numbered perhaps 29,000 in 1990.

## CHOCTAW

A Native North American nation from Mississippi. Sedentary farmers, hunters and gatherers, they spoke an Algonquian language. One of the FIVE CIVILIZED TRIBES, they were early allies of the FRENCH, and helped them destroy the NATCHEZ in 1701. Later the Choctaw supported the USA in its early wars, although they received little thanks. Large-scale land seizures followed and in the 1830s they were forced along the 'Trail of Tears' across the Mississippi. They founded a new republic and briefly prospered. After supporting the Confederacy during the Civil War, however, they lost more land and were soon driven into Oklahoma, where land was allotted to individuals and their nation dissolved. Most were impoverished until a new nation was formed in 1981. By 2001 they were beginning a new period of prosperity as investment poured in. In 1990 they numbered over 82,000.

> **"** The least polished, i.e. the least corrupted of all the Indian nations. **"**
>
> J. Wesley, referring to the Choctaw, 1736

# CHOLOS

See BOLIVIANS and PERUVIANS.

# CHONO

A former Native South American nation of southern Chile's coast and islands. They were nomadic hunters, gatherers and fishers. Seafood, especially shellfish, was a staple in an environment too cold and rainy to supply much plant food. They never numbered more than a few hundred, and appear to have avoided contact with Europeans until the 18th century. Thereafter they rapidly disappeared, perhaps by absorption by neighbouring nations. The last report of them was in 1875.

# CHONTAL

A Native Central American nation of the Yucatan peninsula, Mexico. They are sedentary farmers, hunters and gatherers who speak a Mayan language (see MAYA). Perhaps descendants of the TOLTEC, they had a strong stonemasonry and sculpture tradition that flourished up to the end of the 17th century. Thereafter SPANISH conquest, slavery and diseases reduced them rapidly. In 1990 there were 3600 Chontal language speakers who were seeking to improve their economic, political and social conditions through the Zapatista revolutionary movement, which took up arms in 1994 against a state that tolerated such desperate poverty and inequality.

# CHOROTI

A Native South American nation of the Gran Chaco plain of Argentina, Bolivia and Paraguay. Nomadic hunters and gatherers, they speak a MATACO language. Divided into autonomous bands until the introduction of the horse, and until Spanish aggression encouraged unity, they fought fiercely against the Spanish until their final subjugation. Intense poverty followed, but in the late 20th century they began to take common action with other nations to protect their environment. In 1991 they numbered over 2800, mostly in Argentina.

# CHORRERA CULTURE

A former Native South American nation of southern Ecuador. Sedentary farmers, hunters, gatherers and fishers, they flourished from 1200 to 300 BC. They had a wide-ranging trade network, importing metals and exotic stones, and made much use of obsidian in their tools. Their ceramics were imitated throughout the region, especially by the CHAVÍN. The cause of their disappearance is unclear.

# CHORTI

A Native Central American nation of Honduras and Guatemala. Sedentary farmers, hunters and gatherers, they are descended from the MAYA, although their language is nearly extinct. From the SPANISH conquest of the 16th century, they have been victims of exploitation, discrimination and determined attacks on their traditional culture – policies still being vigorously pursued. Poverty and unemployment remain rife: despite the tourists attracted by MAYAN sites, Chorti claims to a share of tourist revenues remain ignored. As late as 2000 four leaders were murdered after pressing land claims against a landowning family. Cultural survival remains a high priority. There were 31,500 Chorti in 1990.

# CHUMASH

A Native North American nation of southern California. Semi-sedentary hunters (especially of sea mammals), fishers, gatherers and traders, their name means 'beadmakers' or 'shell people'. Their name for themselves meant 'first people'. They used plank boats like those of the POLYNESIANS, which have prompted romantic but unconvincing theories of a Pacific origin. In the 1760s the SPANISH forced them onto missions, where their traditional culture was destroyed. In 1834 the missions were closed and the Chumash were left landless and destitute. A tiny area was set aside for them in 1855 at Santa Yuma mission, where a few survived in poverty, but most dispersed into the general population. The Somala band of Chumash are one of several trying to gain federal recognition. The overall Chumash population is unknown.

## CIBONEY

A Native American nation originally of Cuba, whose name comes from the ARAWAK word meaning 'cavemen'. Arriving in the area from about 1000 BC from either Venezuela or Florida, they had a simple nomadic, hunting, gathering and farming culture. By AD 200 they were being displaced by the Arawak, and from the 15th century enslaved by the CARIB. They initially welcomed the SPANISH, but when the Ciboney began killing cattle they were subject to genocidal attacks. They were all but exterminated by 1800, and are widely viewed as extinct. In 1998, however, a group claiming descent formed the Ciboney tribe of Florida and sought recognition.

## CIMMARONES

A former Caribbean culture of colonial origin, whose name comes from the Spanish, meaning 'wild'. Largely formed by runaway slaves of African descent in the Spanish colonies, subsisting as best they could as farmers, hunters and gatherers, they were depicted as dangerous murderers and thieves. Some groups were certainly formidable: in Jamaica they fought the British to a standstill in two wars in the 18th century, and won a peace treaty recognizing their autonomy. Subsequently, however, they became subsumed within the dominant cultures.

## CLATSOP

A Native North American nation of northern Oregon and southern Washington state. They spoke a Penutian language and were related to the CHINOOK. Sedentary hunters, fishers and gatherers, they were considered hard bargainers by Europeans. In the 19th century the fur trade brought them prosperity, but it also brought diseases that almost exterminated them. As a result they merged with the Chinook, among whom about 200 claimed Clatsop descent in 1995.

## CLOVIS CULTURE

One of the Paleoindian cultures of North America and Mexico, characterized by fluted spear points, which gave them very effective and portable tools. They were nomadic gatherers and hunters, especially of large game such as bison. They appeared around 10,000 BC and vanished around 8500 BC, as large game animals began to disappear. Their origins are mysterious, as there is no evidence of their technology crossing from Asia. This has led to speculation of their descent from Ice Age Europeans crossing to America by boat (Clovis points are similar to SOLUTREAN points of about 13,000 BC from southern France). The theory has traditionally been dismissed, but it has been supported by recent research into OJIBWA DNA, which contains a component that may have originated in Europe at a time contemporary with Solutrean points.

## COAHUILTEC

A Native North American nation of southeast Texas and northeast Mexico. Nomadic hunters and gatherers, they possibly spoke a now extinct ATHABASKAN language. Their autonomous groups could offer little resistance when outsiders (APACHE from the north and SPANISH from the south) began to encroach on their territory during the 16th century. As Spanish cattle devoured the vegetation on which they depended, and stealing livestock resulted in vicious reprisals, they were steadily driven into extinction. Some were absorbed by other nations while others sought refuge in Spanish missions or were assimilated into the general population. Very few can now claim Coahuiltec descent.

## COCAMA

A Native South American nation of Peru's Amazonia. Sedentary slash-and-burn farmers, they were also hunters and gatherers and spoke a TUPÍ language, now seriously endangered. By the late 20th century the rapidly growing nearby city of Iquitos provided opportunities in commercial fishing and charcoal-burning, but also threatened catastrophic damage to their environment. In 1981 they numbered up to 18,000.

## COCHIMI

A Native North American nation of Baja California, Mexico. Semi-sedentary hunters, fishers and gatherers, they survived a harsh environment by such expedients as drying their own faeces after feasting on the pitahaya cactus fruit, and sifting out the seeds in hard times. They numbered about 25,000 in 1697 when the SPANISH established the first missions among them. Having already suffered European slave-raiding, they were reputedly willing converts, losing their traditional culture in return for the protection the missions offered. Diseases and inadequate diets, however, reduced their population until they were believed to be extinct by the 1860s.

## COCOPAH

A Native North American nation of Baja California, Mexico, and southern Arizona, perhaps descended from the HOHOKAM. Semi-sedentary agriculturalists who also hunted, fished and gathered, they spoke a Yuman language, and their name might mean 'proud people'. They were dependent on the Colorado River, which placed an international frontier across their territory. Those in Mexico suffered disaster in 1935 with the damming of the river by the USA, which deprived them of irrigation water, and most dispersed, leaving just 30 families in 1997. In the USA the Somerton reservation (Arizona) was established in 1917 and enlarged in 1985. In 1999 there were 941 people on the reservation, subsisting on agriculture and tourism, and attempting to preserve as much of their traditional culture as possible.

## COEUR D'ALENE

A Native North American nation of Idaho. There name is French and means 'heart of an awl', a reference to their hard bargaining, but they called themselves *Skitswish*, meaning 'those who are found here'. Seasonally mobile within their territory as hunters, gatherers and fishers, they spoke a Salishan language. Not excessively aggressive, they had no wish for contact with whites. In 1858 a US force entered their lands and was destroyed at Pine Creek. A much larger force soon followed and took grim revenge, executing leaders, killing horses and destroying supplies. Forced onto a reservation in 1873, where they were joined by the SPOKAN, they lost

much more land when it was allotted to individuals. Economic development and cultural preservation were major issues to the population of nearly 1800 in 2002.

## COFAN

A Native South American nation of the Amazonia of Ecuador and Colombia. Sedentary farmers, hunters and gatherers, they spoke Chibchan. Conquered by the SPANISH and evangelized by the early 17th century, they were decimated by exploitation and disease. Real disaster struck in the 1960s, however, when oil companies destroyed their environment. In 1972 a road through their territory brought in hordes of land-hungry settlers. Although the Cofan became more active in defence of their rights as a result, in 2001, when they numbered about 1300, they could not prevent AMERICAN anti-drug programmes from spraying their crops with pesticides, causing hunger and illness.

## COHARIE

A Native North American nation of North Carolina. They were sedentary farmers, and hunting and gathering were secondary activities. They probably spoke an Iroquoian language. By the early 18th century they had been incorporated into the TUSCARORA, but when the Tuscarora were driven from the area, the Coharie reasserted their independence and remained. They suffered racial discrimination and became heavily acculturated, but maintained an identity and ran their own affairs. In 2001 they numbered 2185 and had achieved state but not federal recognition.

## COLOMBIANS

The people of the South American Republic of Colombia, the majority of MESTIZO descent. Originally much of the land was under CHIBCHA control, but SPANISH conquest began in 1525. The modern nation emerged in 1830, after the expulsion of Spanish rulers and the breakaway of Venezuela and Ecuador from Gran Colombia. The new nation developed a remarkable culture. Bogotá, for example, became known as the 'Athens of America' for its literary tradition.

C

*"* We occupy the centre of the universe and border upon every nation. *"*

Simón Bolívar, on Gran Colombia, 1822 (see Colombians)

Politically, however, there were severe problems. Power and wealth remained in the hands of an aristocratic oligarchy, which consigned the bulk of the population to destitution and ignorance.

Class enmities simmered continuously – indeed class divisions were so sharp that racial tensions were hardly seen. Class conflict often led to unrest and dictatorships, but a Colombian national identity still emerged. The nation's isolation ended in the 20th century, and the patriarchal society began to change and modernize, although African and Native American influences remain strong in the culture, especially in their dance and music. A sense of great national destiny developed. But in 1903 the nation suffered its greatest humiliation ever, when the USA fomented separatist rebellion in Panama (then part of Colombia) in order to create a client state that would grant favourable terms for building the Panama Canal. Twice, in 1909 and 1921, massive protests brought down presidents who discussed recognizing Panama. Internal conflicts, however, were to dominate the nation. In 1930, after severe unrest brought about by the Depression, there was a peaceful transfer of power from Conservative oligarchs to a progressive Liberal regime. Unfortunately it was unable to answer the social problems of rapid urbanization and economic change, not least from a thriving oil industry. In 1948 an explosion of fury in Bogotá signalled that growing class inequalities were no longer tolerable. Thereafter political violence became the norm.

In 2003 a civil war of 40 years was still raging, with left- and right-wing guerrillas despoiling the countryside, and cocaine and heroin producers inflicting their own reigns of terror. Although negotiations began between the guerrillas and the government, Colombians cannot look forward to peace in the near future. In 2002 they numbered more than 41 million.

## COLORADO

See TSACHILA.

## COLUMBIA

A Native North American nation of northeast Washington state. Hunters, fishers, gatherers and traders, they spoke a Salishan language. In the 18th century they acquired horses and began an annual hunt on the Great Plains, which brought them into regular battle with the BLACKFOOT. As settlers began to flood their lands, they joined the YAKIMA War (1855–6). Defeat and subsequent internal divisions left them split among the Yakima, UMATILLA and COLVILLE reservations.

## COLVILLE

A Native North American nation of northeast Washington state. Possibly nomadic originally, they became sedentary hunters, fishers and gatherers, and spoke a Salishan language. Angered by the depredations of settlers in the 1850s, they nevertheless refused to join the YAKIMA War (1855–6), which they believed would be defeated. In 1872 a reservation was established for them, but the land was desirable and they were moved. Subsequently their lands were whittled away, and in 1941 even more was lost from the flooding of the Grand Coulee Dam, which led to decades of litigation against the AMERICAN government. Dwindling land holdings did not stop the government from using the reservation as a dumping ground for other nations, and by 2000 the Confederated Tribes of the Colville Reservation numbered some 8700 from 12 nations.

## COMANCHE

A Native North American nation of the southern Great Plains. Their name comes from the UTE and means 'those who are against us', although they call themselves *Nemene*, meaning 'our people'. Nomadic hunters and gatherers, they spoke an Uto-Aztecan language. Originally part of the SHOSHONE, they acquired European horses at the beginning of the 18th century and began to split away. They became feared by all their neighbours as raiders who kidnapped women and children for the slave trade or for ransom. They also stole horses and cattle on a massive scale, necessitating the establishment of the Texas Rangers to halt them. The annexation of Texas by the USA in 1848 and the flood of AMERICAN settlers that followed this began their downfall. From 1858 a series of campaigns, interrupted by the Civil War, ground them down. In 1874, weakened by the destruction of bison herds, they were defeated in the Red River War. In 1998 they numbered about 8000 and were troubled by high unemployment and poverty levels as well as racial discrimination.

## COMECHINGÓN

A Native South American nation of northern Argentina. Sedentary farmers, herders, hunters and gatherers of the Andean lowlands, they perhaps numbered 15,000 in 300 autonomous villages when the SPANISH arrived in the 16th century. Conquest and acculturation were rapid, and although large numbers of descendants are known to exist, no reliable census is possible.

## COMOX

A Native North American nation of Vancouver Island and coastal British Columbia, whose name means 'place of abundance'. Sedentary hunters, gatherers and fishers, they spoke a Salishan language (the last speaker died in 1995). Forced onto reservations in 1877, they faced determined efforts to destroy their culture. From the 1960s, in cooperation with other nations, they became active in defence of their rights and culture. In 1995 they numbered perhaps 950.

## CONCHO

A former Native North American nation of Florida, Texas and northern Mexico. They called themselves *Yolli*, probably meaning 'people'. Sedentary hunters and gatherers, they probably also practised farming and possibly spoke an Uto-Aztecan language. In the late 16th century the SPANISH entered their territory, bringing epidemics and raiding for slaves. Some bands of Concho were evangelized, but repeated attacks left them either enslaved or dispersed. Some fought alongside the JUMANO, who probably absorbed their remnants. During the 18th century the Concho ceased to exist as a nation.

## COOS

A Native North American nation of coastal Ore-

gon, whose name means perhaps 'on the south' or possibly 'place of pines'. Semi-sedentary hunters (especially of sea mammals), fishers and gatherers, they spoke Penutian dialects. After years of good relations with European fur-traders, the encroachment of settlers precipitated violence in 1851. Several Coos villages were destroyed, persuading them to keep out of the YAKIMA War (1855–6). They were forced onto the SILETZ reservation, where half had starved by 1875. Subsequent attempts to gain compensation for stolen lands were rejected, leaving their economic position parlous. In 1997, 27% lived in poverty and there was little hope of economic development. They numbered 720 in 2002.

## COQUILLE

A Native North American nation of southwest Oregon whose name is French for 'shell', although it is perhaps a French corruption of their original name. Sedentary hunters, fishers and gatherers, they spoke an ATHABASKAN language, which is now nearly extinct. The epidemics and violence brought by encroaching settlers nearly destroyed the Coquille. In a treaty of 1855, they were promised their own reservation, but the treaty was never ratified. They were rounded up and eventually dumped at the SILETZ reservation. They lost federal recognition in 1954, but regained it in 1989. They have also made efforts to preserve as much of their culture as possible; in 1985 they celebrated their sacred salmon ritual for the first time in 30 years, and in 1997 celebrated the first potlatch (ceremonial feast) in 150 years. In 1996 they numbered 650.

## COSTA RICANS

The population of the Central American Republic of Costa Rica, situated between Nicaragua and Panama. The vast majority are of white or MESTIZO descent. From the 1560s SPANISH colonists began to dispossess Native Americans in Costa Rica. The settlers remained poor and isolated until coffee-growing began in 1808. Thereafter, their new-found wealth brought independence, but also introduced growing class tensions between poor peasants and a rich landowning elite who were suspicious of democratic ideas and involved in internal power struggles that often led to periods of military rule. A brief civil war in the 1940s brought a democratic constitution that provided political stability. But in the 1980s economic crises forced severe austerity measures on the government. The population numbered nearly 3.8 million in 2001, and environmental degradation, corruption and poverty remained major concerns.

## COWLITZ

A Native North American nation of southwest Washington state, whose name means 'seeker' or 'capturing the medicine spirit'. Sedentary traders, fishers, hunters and gatherers, they spoke a Salishan language. Deemed a warlike nation by their neighbours, they raided by dugout canoes as far as Vancouver Island for slaves. Epidemics in the 19th century were disastrous, killing three-quarters of them in 1829–30 alone. During the YAKIMA War (1855–6) they were interned by the US Army, which allowed settlers to steal their lands. A promised reservation was not delivered. Most were forced onto the CHEHALIS reservation. After years of effort they finally gained federal recognition in 2002, and could legitimately claim compensation and protection of their fishing rights. They numbered about 1480 in 2002.

## CREE

An aboriginal nation of northern Canada residing in Quebec, Ontario, the prairie provinces, British Columbia and the Yukon Territory. Traders, hunters, gatherers and fishers, they speak an Algonquian language. Subsisting in both woodlands and plains environments, they became briefly wealthy through the fur trade from the 17th century, resulting in heavy acculturation. The ravages of diseases and depleted fur stocks drove increasing numbers of woodland Cree to join their plains-dwelling relatives and to depend on the bison. Those who remained in the woodlands were persuaded by questionable means to cede most of their lands. Those on the plains faced disaster by the 1870s with the destruction of the bison. They sought government aid to transform their various and diverse modes of subsistence to agriculture. They

> **" The Cricks [Creek] ... are a very powerful confederacy. "**
>
> W. Bartram, 1789

were unaware, however, that Canada had no intention of allowing them to compete with white farmers, and the assistance the Cree received was deliberately inadequate. When many began to prosper anyway, new regulations were imposed to ensure they could only make a bare subsistence from their lands at best. Accompanying this was a determined effort to destroy their traditional culture through residential schools. In 1885 some joined the savagely suppressed MÉTIS rebellion in desperation.

By the late 20th century the Cree had become increasingly politicized and determined to protect their rights. The degradation of their environment and discrimination in employment became major issues. The Cree of northern Quebec have proven especially politically adept: in 1996 they took their case for greater self-determination to the United Nations Commission on Human Rights. They complained to the same body in 1995 when, during the referendum for Quebec independence, it became clear that the QUÉBÉCOIS had no intention of involving them in deciding their own nationality. In 1996 they numbered over 200,000.

## CREEK

A Native North American nation of Georgia and Alabama. Sedentary farmers, hunters, gatherers and fishers, they spoke a Muskogean language. One of the FIVE CIVILIZED TRIBES, they are descendants of the MISSISSIPPIAN TEMPLE MOUND CULTURE. Some supported the British during the AMERICAN Revolution, for which they suffered large-scale land seizures. Like the CHEROKEE, they were successful in adopting Western culture and had a highly democratic government. Their success threatened to prevent further white settlement, and from the 1820s Georgia adopted a policy of expulsion. The federal government threatened to intervene, but when it was defied it decided the issue was not worthy of a confrontation. By 1836, under the Indian Removal Act, most Cherokee were forced to move to Oklahoma, although a few remained in Alabama. By the Civil War they began to enjoy prosperity, but as some supported the Confederacy, half of their lands were seized. In 1898, ignoring Creek protests, the USA arbitrarily abolished their government. They recovered their sovereignty only in 1971. In 1990 they numbered over 43,000.

## CREOLES

An American culture of colonial French origin, concentrated in former colonies such as Louisiana. The term was originally used in the 17th century by the French to denote a colonist born in the New World. From the 18th century they began to merge with the CAJUN, although their cultures are still distinct.

## CREYE

A Native South American nation of Brazil's Amazonia. Probably sedentary farmers, hunters and gatherers, they spoke a Gê language. In 1995 only 30 native language-speakers could be found, all scattered far from their original lands. They had in effect ceased to exist as a nation.

## CROW

A Native North American nation of Montana, who call themselves *Absaroka*, meaning 'children of the long-beaked bird'. Nomadic hunters, gatherers and traders, they spoke a Siouan language.

Originally part of the HIDATSA, they split off in the early 17th century. They built a very large horse herd, often by theft – horse-stealing was a source of prestige, and stealing a tethered horse from another camp was a considerable coup. This, however, earned them the enmity of other nations and in the late 19th century they allied with the US Army in its wars in the Plains. They received little reward, being confined to a reservation, but this action perhaps prevented the LAKOTA exterminating them. They suffered determined attempts to destroy their traditional culture, but in the late 20th century greater self-government allowed a cultural revival. In 1991 they numbered over 8000.

## CUBANS

The population of the Caribbean island Republic of Cuba, south of Florida. Spanish settlement began in 1509, and the Native American population was soon driven to the brink of extinction.

The importation of slaves introduced a large African population and a culture combining African and European elements, for example in cuisine and music. A plantation economy based on sugar provided prosperity for landowners in the 18th and 19th centuries.

An anti-racist revolutionary movement was first established in 1868. In 1898, as Spanish forces laid the island waste attempting to suppress revolt, the USA intervened, defeated the Spanish and provided independence in 1902, under US supervision. Concerned with protecting their own investments, the AMERICANS proved indifferent to the rise of brutal dictators in Cuba.

In 1959 the revolutionary forces of Fidel Castro swept to power. Castro's regime introduced long-needed reforms, but his anti-American rhetoric (popular in Cuba) and nationalization of American property alienated the USA, which made determined efforts to bring him down. Poor relations culminated, in 1962, in the Cuban Missile Crisis, perhaps the closest the world has come to nuclear war. Castro's regime survived, but earned the undying hostility of the USA and permanent economic sanctions.

In 2001 the Cubans numbered over 11 million, and severe economic crises, coupled with a fear of the future after Castro's death, remain issues. There is a sizeable and vocal anti-Castro Cuban exile community in the USA, a powerful grouping among the HISPANICS of Florida.

## CUBEO

A Native South American nation of the Amazonia of Colombia and Brazil. They called themselves *Pamiwa*, meaning 'first people'. Sedentary slash-and-burn farmers, they were also hunters, fishers with poison and gatherers, and spoke a Tucanoan language. They resisted evangelization until the 1880s, but exploitation, mainly from rubber-extractors, reduced their population; in 1986 they numbered just 300.

## CUNAS

A Native South American nation of Panama, who call themselves *Tule*, meaning simply 'men'. Concentrated on the west coast and many offshore islands, they are sedentary farmers (the

*“ Cuba, forcibly disjoined from its own unnatural connection with Spain, and incapable of self-support, can gravitate only towards the North American Union. ”*

John Quincy Adams, 1823

coconut crop is an economic mainstay) and fishers, and speak a CARIB language. Relative isolation allowed them to preserve much of their traditional culture. In the late 19th century they rebelled and established a short-lived Republic of Tule, and they still aspire to independence. Attacks by outsiders provoked a new revolt in 1925 that gained them a measure of autonomy. In 1999 they numbered about 20,000, and were increasingly protective of their political rights, traditional culture and natural resources.

## CUPEÑO

A Native North American nation of southern California. Semi-sedentary hunters, fishers and gatherers, the Cupeño people's name is a Spanish corruption of their own name for themselves, *Kuupangaxwichen*, meaning 'people who slept here'. They spoke an Uto-Aztecan language, which only nine people still spoke in 1990.

They survived being reduced to servile labourers by the SPANISH and later by AMERICAN settlers. Their greatest catastrophe struck in 1903: a former governor of California acquired title to their lands at Warner Springs and quickly realized its potential as a health spa. Deciding the venture would be more profitable without the Cupeño, he used the courts to evict them.

To this day they still strive to recover their traditional lands and to maintain as much of their culture as possible. In 2000, for example, they tried to prevent their sacred site at Gregory Canyon from being used for landfill. In 2000 they numbered about 200.

## CUSABO

A former Native North American nation of coastal South Carolina, whose name perhaps means 'river people'. Sedentary farmers, fishers, hunters and gatherers, they spoke a Muskogean language. In the 17th century they were severely weakened by YUCHI attacks, and were unable to resist effectively the English colony founded in 1670. Poor relations led to the Coosa War in 1671 and renewed fighting in 1674, but defeat left many enslaved and most of their lands lost. They did support the colonists in the TUSCARORA war (1711–13) and were granted Patawana

Island as a reward. But in 1738, for no clearly understood reason, they disappeared from the island, and within a few years had entirely vanished as a nation. Their descendants may be found among the CREEK, CATAWBA and EDISTO.

## DAKOTA

A Native North American nation of the eastern Great Plains, and a sub-group of the SIOUX. Their name means 'allies'. Seasonally mobile within their territory as farmers, hunters and gatherers, they spoke a Siouan language. On their expulsion from the Great Lakes area by the OJIBWA in the 18th century, they settled in Minnesota. In a series of treaties from the early 19th century, they ceded most of their lands and suffered attempts to suppress their traditional culture. In 1862 the US government's failure to deliver promised supplies provoked a brief but bloody war. In reprisal the Dakota were expelled from Minnesota and ended up scattered across reservations stretching from Canada to Nebraska, in severe poverty. They numbered about 20,000 in 2001, and were involved in defending their sovereignty and campaigning for the return of their Minnesota lands.

## DELAWARE

A Native North American nation, once of the northeast United States, now of Oklahoma and Ontario. They call themselves *Lenni Lenape*, meaning 'original people'. Sedentary farmers, hunters, gatherers and fishers, they speak an Algonquian language. They traditionally had great prestige among their neighbours as peacemakers. In the 17th century they initially welcomed Europeans, many of whom could not have survived without Delaware help. In return they were repeatedly robbed, abused and defrauded of their lands, and by the 20th century some groups had been forcibly relocated twenty times. Some fled to Ontario, where they now have a reserve of their own, while others ended up in Oklahoma, landless among the CHEROKEE, winning federal recognition only in 1996. In 1990 they numbered 9800.

66 If you give us the best place in the world, it is not as good as this. This is our home. We cannot live anywhere else; we were born here, and our fathers are buried here. 99

Cupeño chief
Agua Caliente
(1902)

**C**

**Dakota: main sub-groups**

Mdwekanton
Sisseton
Wahpekute
Wahpeton

## DESANA

A Native South American people of the Amazonia regions of Brazil and Colombia. Sedentary farmers, hunters and gatherers, they speak a Tucanoan language and exercise strict population control to preserve their very limited resources. In 1995 they numbered nearly 1800.

## DIAGUITA

A Native South American people of the Chilean and Argentinian Andes. Sedentary farmers, herders, hunters and gatherers, they lived in autonomous villages and were under the cultural influence of the INCA, but had successfully withstood Inca conquest. From the 16th century they fought a long and bitter war against the SPANISH, but, weakened by diseases, they were overwhelmed during the next century. Those who escaped slavery in Spanish mines or in forced re-settlement far away were evangelized and largely acculturated. Their descendants on their original lands still suffer severe poverty.

## DJAPAS

A Native South American nation of Brazil's Amazonia. Nomadic hunters and gatherers, they were contacted in 2001 when it was claimed that they had been enslaved by the CANAMARI for seven years. Then they numbered only 25.

## DOGRIB

An aboriginal nation of the Northwest Territories. Their name refers to their creation myth in which they were descended from a being part dog and part man. They call themselves *Dene*, meaning 'men'. Nomadic hunters, gatherers and fishers, they speak an ATHABASKAN language. In the 19th century fur traders and missionaries began to degrade their culture. This process was accelerated by the Canadian government, who pressed them into becoming sedentary, and sent their children to residential schools. The results included social disintegration and intense poverty. In 2001, when they numbered 3400, they were working to reverse these problems through winning greater self-determination.

## DOMINICAN REPUBLICANS

A Caribbean people of largely colonial origin who inhabit the Dominican Republic (the eastern two-thirds of the island of Hispaniola), which they share with Haiti. The SPANISH arrived in the 16th century, destroyed the Native American populations and introduced African slaves, who made a major cultural impact, especially in music and dance. The wealth of the AZTEC and INCA empires, however, attracted settlers away and Hispaniola became a backwater. Declaring independence in 1821, the country was rapidly invaded by HAITIANS, and it won real independence only in 1844. Thereafter the populace was ruled by a series of dictators, and political instability became the norm, twice leading to US intervention in the 20th century. Free elections were held in 1996, but the great disparity between rich and poor remains a problem for the 8.5 million people.

## DOMINICANS

The people of mainly colonial origin who inhabit the island state of Dominica, between Puerto Rico and Trinidad and Tobago. Owing to furious CARIB resistance, the FRENCH settled the island only in the 18th century, thereafter importing African slaves. Although reduced by disease and warfare, the Carib survived and are today the only significant Carib community in the area. In 1763 the BRITISH took control; Dominica became a colony in 1805 and achieved independence in 1978. Democracy was established after some years of corrupt government. English is the official language, but most Dominicans use French patois. An agricultural economy developed, dependent on bananas. Unemployment and poverty remained major problems for the 70,000 Dominicans in 2003.

## DORSET CULTURE

A now vanished native culture of the North American Arctic, emerging around 500 BC. The people were seasonally mobile within their territory mainly as hunters and fishers. Their tools were better suited to their harsh environment than their less successful predecessors, although

**"** Look to a Delaware ... for a warrior! **"**

J.F. Cooper

d

they did not seem to use the bow and arrow like earlier cultures. They had largely disappeared by about AD 1000, when the THULE CULTURE arrived. The reason for this disappearance is unclear, although perhaps climate change affected their food supply. Their remnants might have been absorbed by the Thule to become ancestral to the INUIT.

## DUTCH ANTILLEANS

The people of the autonomous Caribbean states of the Netherlands Antilles. Claimed by the DUTCH in the 1640s, the islands became a centre of the Caribbean slave trade, with African cultural influences apparent, especially in the northern islands. Local ARAWAKS were not exterminated and they contributed to the developing culture. Poor soil means that tourism and industry offer the main sources of subsistence, although there is heavy dependence on remittances from migrant workers. In 2003 the population numbered over 216,000; they remain content with their autonomous status under the Dutch Crown.

## DUWAMISH

A Native North American nation of the Lake Washington area, Washington state, whose name means 'inside the bay people'. Sedentary hunters, fishers and gatherers, they spoke a Salishan language. Had it not been for Duwamish assistance, the first settlers at Seattle would not have survived their first winter; but relations soured very quickly and in 1855 most Duwamish were forced onto reservations with other nations. Some attempted to remain on their traditional lands, but settlers burned them out. In 1925 the Duwamish began to seek federal recognition. This was finally granted in 2001; however, in a particularly cruel blow, recognition was revoked within months because of irregularities by government officials. In 2002 the Duwamish numbered 560.

## EASTERN CREE

See CREE.

**❝** We have a revolution here every Thursday afternoon at half-past-two. **❞**

Ludwig Bemelmans on Ecuador, 1947

## ECUADOREANS

The population of the South American Republic of Ecuador. Lightly settled by the SPANISH in the 16th century, the population and culture remained overwhelmingly Native American (40%) and MESTIZO (40%), but with political power and the land firmly in the hands of a white elite (10%). With independence in 1830, government remained oligarchic and little changed from colonial days. Only in 1888 did the Ecuadoreans gain a liberal, progressive government; the countryside, however, remained essentially feudal.

During the 20th century a growing awareness of social problems caused greater, usually left-wing and anti-AMERICAN radicalism. The result was considerable political instability, rapid government changes, military coups and right-wing political terrorism against growing communist influence. In 1952 the resumption of a border war with Peru, temporarily halted in 1942 after nearly 100 years of sporadic fighting, did help to whip up considerable nationalist enthusiasm. However, the nation's enormous social problems remained unanswered and perhaps unanswerable, despite an oil boom in the 1970s.

The nation remains deeply divided between liberals, conservatives and communists over its future progress. Radical land reform has never been carried out, leaving the vast majority of people in desperate poverty, leading to their alienation – few take active part in constitutional political processes, while the potential for political violence is always high. The collapse of the banking system in 1999 provoked a coup in 2000. However, there are signs that the poor are no longer willing to accept government indifference to their plight. A national revolution, if not civil war, might yet decide the nation's fate. In 2001 Ecuadoreans over 13 million.

## EDISTO

A Native North American nation of South Carolina, named after the river in their territory. They called themselves *Kusso*. Sedentary farmers, hunters and gatherers, they spoke a Muskogean language. An unsuccessful French attempt to establish a colony in their territory prompted the

SPANISH to establish a mission and a fort there in 1566. The Edisto destroyed both ten years later, and while the Spanish rebuilt them, they had abandoned the area by 1587. The ENGLISH arrived in 1670 and succeeded in establishing a permanent settlement. This proved disastrous to the Edisto; epidemics and continual warfare with their neighbours reduced them, and in the 18th century the English assumed they were extinct. Joined in 1747 by about 40 NATCHEZ, fleeing genocide by the French, a Kusso-Natchez nation survived on their traditional lands. In 1975 they officially adopted the name Edisto to end confusion over their identity. They won state recognition in 1986 and were seeking federal recognition in the early 21st century. In 2002 they numbered about 780.

## EL PARAISO CULTURE

A former Native South American culture of north coastal Peru. A sedentary people, they were primarily fishers, but also farmers (although not of maize), hunters and gatherers. They flourished from about 2000 to 1600 BC and built ceremonial platforms of bags of stones, the uniformity of which suggests a form of labour tax, and which were the largest pre-ceramic monumental structures in the Americas. Why the culture disappeared is unclear.

## ENCABELLADO

A Native South American nation of the Amazonia regions of Peru, Ecuador and Brazil. Sedentary farmers, hunters and gatherers, they spoke a Tucanoan language. In Brazil, slave-raiders exterminated them in the 17th century. Evangelization in Peru and Ecuador began a process of acculturation that came close to destroying them as a nation by the mid-19th century. Although their language was nearly extinct, they survived to mount a legal campaign in the 1990s to make oil companies responsible for their environmental destruction. There were some 140 Encabellado in Peru in 1981 and about 350 in Ecuador in 2000.

## ERIE

A former Native North American nation of southern Michigan and northern Ohio, whose name means 'people of the panther'. Sedentary farmers, hunters, gatherers and fishers, they spoke an Iroquoian language.

They were indirectly victims of European expansionism. Allied to the HURON and the NEUTRAL, they were enemies of the IROQUOIS, who saw them as formidable foes. They controlled fur-producing territory when the Iroquois' own fur resources were becoming depleted. Warfare broke out in 1648, ostensibly over Erie acceptance of refugees from the newly defeated Huron and Neutral, but really over fur stocks. Lacking guns, and despite bitter resistance, the Erie were defeated in 1656. Some were absorbed by other nations, and while a few fought on for several years, their nation had ceased to exist.

## ESKIMO

See INUIT.

## ESSELEN

A Native North American nation of northern California. Semi-sedentary hunters and gatherers, they spoke a Hokan language. Their name is derived from *Ex'seien*, meaning 'the rock'. By the mid-19th century, evangelization and mistreatment had largely destroyed them as a nation. In 1996, however, about 260 descendants were seeking federal recognition as part of the Ohlone/Castanoan Esselen Nation.

## ETOWAH

A former Native North American nation of northwest Georgia, whose name comes from the CREEK, and means 'town' or 'tribe'. Sedentary farmers and traders, they also fished, hunted and gathered. Possibly descended from the MISSISSIPPIAN TEMPLE MOUND CULTURE, they built elaborate temple mounds and dominated the region from the 13th century. Through a combination of disease, environmental misuse, crop failure and warfare (later villages were fortified), their sites were abandoned by the early 18th century.

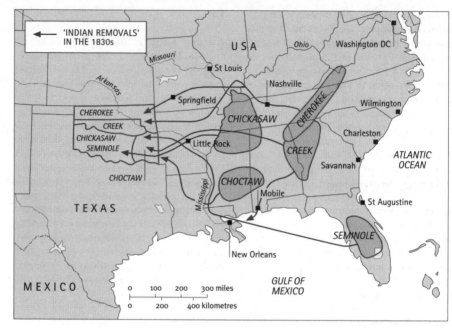

'INDIAN REMOVALS' IN THE 1830s

USA
Ohio    Washington DC
Missouri
St Louis
Nashville
Springfield
CHICKASAW    CHEROKEE    Wilmington
CHEROKEE
CREEK
CHICKASAW    Little Rock    Charleston
SEMINOLE    CREEK
CHOCTAW    Savannah    ATLANTIC OCEAN
CHOCTAW
Mobile
TEXAS    Mississippi    St Augustine
New Orleans    SEMINOLE

MEXICO    GULF OF MEXICO

0    100    200    300 miles
0    200    400 kilometres

## EYAK

A Native North American nation of Alaska. They call themselves *Daxuhya*, meaning 'human beings'. Nomadic hunters, gatherers and fishers, they speak an ATHABASKAN language.

They offered determined resistance to Russian attempts to exploit their territory from the 1790s, but were subsequently reduced by epidemics and were unable to resist large-scale AMERICAN exploitation of their resources, destruction of their culture and land thefts from the 1880s. Protecting their environment became a major issue for the Eyak, especially after the damage wrought by the *Exxon Valdez* oil spill in 1986. In 1999 they numbered 580.

## FALKLAND ISLANDERS

The inhabitants of a BRITISH dependency in the southern Atlantic Ocean, known in neighbouring Argentina as the *Islas Malvinas*. The islands passed through English, French, SPANISH and ARGENTINIAN hands before the British expelled the Argentinians in 1833 and established a colony. By the end of the 19th century the Falk-

land Islanders had become self-sufficient through fishing and sheep-herding. They established essentially a transplanted British culture, and remained insular and isolated. In 1982 Argentina invaded the Falkland Islands, leading to Britain's last, brief, colonial war. The islanders still cling tenaciously to their British identity. In 2001 they numbered nearly 3000.

## FIVE CIVILIZED TRIBES

A name collectively given by settlers to the CHEROKEE, CHICKASAW, CHOCTAW, CREEK and SEMINOLE nations. They were so named for their ability and willingness to adopt European culture and institutions. They were also prosperous. The USA, however, preferred to regard them as 'savages' whom they could 'legitimately' dispossess, and were wary of other tribes emulating them and thus limiting opportunities for settler expansion. In the 1830s, therefore, under the Indian Removal Act, most of these tribes were forcibly marched to Oklahoma.

They were promised that their sovereignty and land tenure were secure in this new location. But after the Civil War, the AMERICAN government

*"All preceding experiments for the improvement of the Indians have failed. It seems now to be an established fact that they cannot live in contact with a civilized community and prosper."*

President Andrew Jackson (1835), expressing the views that led to the Indian Removal Act claimed that the tribes had supported the Confederacy and so restricted their lands. Nothing was done to stem the mass incursion of new settlers, and in 1906 the last governments of the Five Civilized Tribes were abolished. From the 20th century, however, they have made progress in reclaiming sovereignty.

## FLATHEAD

See SALISH.

## FOLSOM CULTURE

The last Paleoindian culture of North America. It was a successor to the CLOVIS CULTURE, but better adapted to a warmer climate, and the people hunted large prey such as bison more cooperatively, using thinner and smaller fluted points. The culture flourished 9000–8000 BC, before vanishing for no clearly understood cause.

## FORT ANCIENT CULTURE

A former Native North American culture of the Kentucky area. Sedentary farmers, hunters and gatherers, they were contemporaries of the MISSISSIPPIAN TEMPLE MOUND CULTURE, and existed from about AD 1000 to 1700. They built small burial mounds, and their communities grew in size and complexity, but not to the level of their contemporaries. As with the others, however, a combination of over-population and resource exhaustion probably caused their demise.

## FOX

A Native North American nation of Michigan and Wisconsin. They call themselves *Mesquakie*, meaning 'people of the red earth'. Seasonally mobile as farmers, hunters, gatherers and fishers, they spoke an Algonquian language. Friendly to the English and IROQUOIS, they controlled the Fox River, and their tolls aggravated the FRENCH, leading to intermittent war from 1712 to 1737. To the French, this became a war of extermination, but their ILLINOIS allies were unwilling to commit genocide. The survivors of the Fox found sanctuary among the SAUK and withdrew to Illinois. In 1830, however, the US Army

moved them to Iowa to make room for settlers. Their attempt to return led to the Black Hawk War, in which many were slaughtered under a truce flag as they attempted to cross the Mississippi. Returning to Iowa, many were later moved to Kansas and then again to Oklahoma. They became increasingly fragmented and suffered attempts to destroy their traditional culture. In 1997 they numbered over 5300, mainly in Oklahoma and Iowa, where they are attempting to preserve their sovereignty and culture.

## FREMONT CULTURE

A former Native North American culture of the Colorado area. Like the related ANASAZI culture, the Fremont material culture featured pit houses and ceramics. The people became sedentary farmers, hunters and gatherers by AD 750, and their society became increasingly complex, but like the Anasazi they had vanished by 1500, probably for the same reasons: prolonged drought coupled with unsustainable agriculture.

## FUEGIANS

See ALACALUT, ONA and YAHGAN.

## GABRILENO

A Native North American nation of southern coastal California. Semi-sedentary hunters, fishers, gatherers and traders, they spoke an Uto-Aztecan language. Named after the San Gabrileno mission, where disease and mistreatment reduced their numbers, the Gold Rush completed their destruction as a nation. In 2001, however, over 300 descendants were seeking federal recognition under their chosen name, *Tongva*, which means 'people of the earth'.

## GARIFUNA

A Native Central American and African-descended people of Nicaragua, Belize, Honduras and Guatemala. Sedentary farmers and fishers, they spoke an Arawakan language. They originated on the island of St Vincent when, in the 17th century, two ships carrying African slaves ran aground, and the survivors

Garifuna

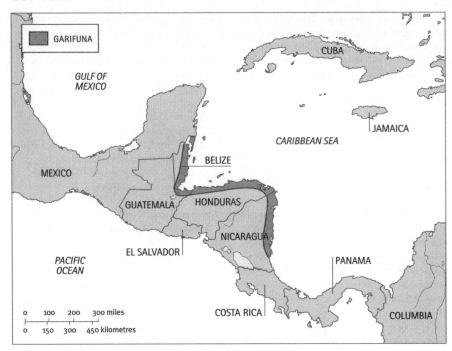

GARIFUNA

GULF OF
MEXICO

CUBA

JAMAICA

CARIBBEAN SEA

MEXICO

BELIZE

GUATEMALA    HONDURAS

NICARAGUA

EL SALVADOR

PACIFIC
OCEAN

PANAMA

| 0 | 100 | 200 | 300 miles |
| 0 | 150 | 300 | 450 kilometres |

COSTA RICA

COLUMBIA

inter-married with the native ARAWAKS. Their off-spring stubbornly resisted colonization, and in 1797 the exasperated British administrators deported them to the mainland. There, despite discrimination, they prospered and their culture, combining African, Native American and European elements, survived. In the 20th century, however, economic problems forced many into wage-labour, and large-scale migration occurred, leading to cultural erosion, especially linguistic. Furthermore, in 1998 changes to Honduran law, allowing outsiders to purchase their traditional lands, were passed despite their vocal opposition. Their numbers are uncertain, but there were about 90,000 native language-speakers in 1999; cultural preservation is a major issue..

## GISPIRA

See KOLLA.

## GITXSAN

A Native North American nation of northwest British Columbia, whose name means 'people of the river mist'. Sedentary hunters, gatherers and fishers, they speak a Penutian language. The late 19th century saw increasing disruption of their lifestyle as prospectors spread epidemics and commercial canneries offered new economic opportunities. In the 1960s they formed the 'Ksan Association to protect their culture and promote ethnic pride. Demands to control the resources on their own territory led to a bitter dispute with the provincial government, and Gitxsan and police accused each other of unprovoked violence during demonstrations. In 1993 the United Nations Human Rights Commission (UNHRC) concluded that the provincial government was acting wrongly in dismissing Gitxsan land claims, but subsequent negotiations broke down. They won their court case against the provincial and federal governments in 1997. They numbered about 10,000 in 2001.

## GOAIIRO

A Native South American nation of northern Venezuela and Colombia. Mostly nomadic hunters, gatherers and traders, they practised limited agriculture and spoke an Arawakan language. From the 16th century they began to acquire cattle from the SPANISH, and cattle ownership became the basis of a hereditary class system. In the late 20th century they numbered around 127,000.

## GOSHUTE

A Native North American nation of Utah, whose name perhaps comes from the SHOSHONE for 'desert people'. Nomadic hunters and gatherers, they spoke an Uto-Aztecan language. Their harsh environment limited contact with whites until the mid-19th century, when wagon trains crossed their territory and Mormons settled there, competing for scarce food and water. Goshute attempts to defend their territory led to great loss of life, and they were forced to cede their lands in 1863. They refused to enter a reservation with another nation and had to abandon subsistence for wage labour. By 1914 they had two reservations, in which hazardous-waste storage, under strict environmental controls, provided some funds for economic development. In 1997 they numbered around 410.

## GREENLANDERS

The people of Greenland, an autonomous island province of Denmark. They are largely of INUIT and Danish origin. An independent NORSE colony was established in modern Greenland in AD 986, but had vanished by 1530. NORWEGIAN sovereignty was established in 1261, but transferred to Denmark in 1398 via the Union of Kalmar. The DANES returned in 1721 and reasserted their sovereignty. The THULE CULTURE, from whom the Inuit are descended, arrived in the 12th century. The Danes closed Greenland to foreigners, and the Greenlanders remained isolated, with much inter-marriage between the two populations, and the gradual erosion of traditional Inuit culture. After coming under AMERICAN protection in the 1940s, the island became an integral part of Denmark in 1953 but was granted home rule in 1979. This, however, has not resolved many concerns of the Greenlanders. They remain dependent on Denmark for most government income, and Danes control much of the economy. Inuit-speaking teachers are scarce, and the Inuit language has suffered in consequence, although Inuit culture remains very strong. Employment opportunities remain limited, and the USA has failed to remove military bases, showing the limits of autonomy. In 2000 there were over 56,000 Greenlanders.

## GRENADANS

A Caribbean people of colonial origin who inhabit the state of Grenada, a small island north of Trinidad and Tobago. The original CARIB population resisted colonization until the mid-17th century, but were gradually ground down by the FRENCH, and the last survivors committed suicide. The BRITISH gained control in 1763 and imported African slaves, establishing a plantation economy. French influence in Grenadan culture, especially in language, is still evident.

Grenadans achieved independence in 1974. In 1979 a bloodless coup established a left-wing regime, which the USA overthrew in 1983 on the pretext that it was CUBAN-controlled.

In 2001 Grenadans numbered over 89,000, and despite the growth of the tourist industry, unemployment and poverty remain serious problems, exacerbated by a davastating hurricane in 2004.

## GROS VENTRE

See ATSINA.

## GUACHICHIL

A former Native North American nation of northern Mexico. Nomadic hunters and gatherers, they spoke an Uto-Aztecan language. They were contacted by SPANISH missionaries in the 1530s, and the discovery of silver on their lands caused a great inrush of settlers and four decades of desperate resistance. They gained a reputation for cunning and for terrifying brutality to prisoners; the Spanish claimed that they were cannibals. With the aid of TLAXCALAN allies, the Spanish wore down their resistance and forced them to become sedentary farmers. Thereafter their traditional culture died out, and they became extinct as a nation in the 17th century.

## GUADELOUPIANS

The inhabitants of the French Caribbean dependency of Guadeloupe, an archipelago of nine inhabited islands southeast of Puerto Rico. The area was colonized in 1635 by the FRENCH, who imported African slaves and established a plantation economy. In 1794 revolutionary France abolished slavery, but it was reinstated in 1802 despite determined resistance, to be abolished finally in 1848. Race relations remained poor and Asian labour was imported, which added a further influence to Guadeloupian culture. In 1946 Guadeloupe became an Overseas Department of France (legally part of metropolitan France), although greater autonomy was awarded in 1982. In 2001 Guadeloupians numbered over 430,000, and calls for independence were muted by dependence on French subsidies.

## GUAHIBO

A Native South American nation of the Amazonia regions of Colombia and Venezuela. Nomadic fishers, hunters and gatherers who practised some animal husbandry, they travelled in small bands and tended to avoid contact with more powerful peoples. In 1994 they numbered about 20,000 and were seeking greater safeguards to their rights.

## GUAICURA

A former Native North American nation of Baja California, Mexico. Nomadic hunters and gatherers, they greeted the first SPANISH visitors with calls of *guaxoro*, meaning 'friend', which the Spanish mistook for their name. Evangelized by the Spanish, they were decimated by disease to such an extent that when their mission was closed in 1823, they were unable to recover from the destruction of their culture and they rapidly disappeared as a distinct nation.

## GUAJÁ

A Native South American nation of Brazil's Amazonia. Nomadic hunters and gatherers, they spoke Tupa-Guaraní. They were hardly contacted until the 1950s, when road-builders,

ranchers and logging companies began to invade their lands. They found little protection from the government, and in 1966 they fled a planned massacre by ranchers. In 1990 gunmen were hired by logging companies to intimidate them. In 1995 they were estimated at 370, but some groups had yet to be contacted.

## GUALE

A former Native North American nation of coastal Georgia, South Carolina and Florida, whose name possibly meant 'south'. Sedentary farmers, fishers, and hunter-gatherers, they spoke a Muskogean language. Initial friendly relations with SPANISH missionaries who arrived in the 1560s were strained by attempts to destroy their traditions and regulate their lives. The killing of a missionary in 1597 led to terrible reprisals as the Spanish destroyed crops and enslaved large numbers. War, disease, and English-backed slave raids reduced their population by 95% by 1684, when the survivors relocated to Amelia island, Florida. An English attack in 1702 completed their destruction, and the remnants were absorbed by the CREEK, YAMASEE and others.

## GUAMO

A former Native South American nation of Venezuelan Amazonia. Sedentary fishers, hunters and gatherers, they also farmed, at least after being evangelized in the 18th century. They were possibly CARIB-speakers. After the expulsion of the Jesuits in 1767, Franciscan missionaries allowed Guamo resources, especially turtle oil, to be over-exploited. After the mission economy collapsed, the Guamo scattered and their culture had disappeared by the early 19th century. The Guamontey people were a sub-group.

## GUAMONTEY

See GUAMO.

## GUARANÍ

A Native South American nation of the Amazonia regions of Paraguay, Uruguay, Argentina, Bolivia and Brazil. They called themselves *Abá*, 'men'. Sedentary slash-and-burn farmers (which necessitates periodic relocation as the soil becomes exhausted), they were also hunter-gatherers and spoke Tupí-Guaraní. Although SPANISH settlers used the name rather indiscriminately, the Guaraní probably numbered about 400,000 when Europeans arrived. The Spanish evangelized and decimated them with disease, and the PORTUGUESE used slavery to the same result. The Guaraní have since suffered further land theft, poverty, acculturation and attacks from ranchers. The Guaraní are still campaigning for recognition of their land rights. In 1996 they numbered about 80,000.

The Cainagua and Caracara are sub-groups of the Guaraní.

## GUATEMALANS

The population of the Central American country of Guatemala. The area was claimed by Spain in 1523. SPANISH conquest still left an overwhelmingly MAYA and Ladino (MESTIZO) population, whose influence on the culture remains very strong. Independent in 1821, the country was often subsequently ruled by military governments who ignored grinding poverty to attract foreign investment. In 1950 a democratic government undertook land reforms that harmed AMERICAN commercial interests. In response the US Central Intelligence Agency (CIA) engineered the government's overthrow in 1954 and reversed the reforms. By 1960 popular resentment exploded into a savage civil war in which government death squads countered left-wing guerrillas. Only in 1996, after 100,000 deaths, did the war end. In 2001 Guatemalans numbered nearly 13 million and were attempting to recover from the ravages of civil war, in one of the poorest countries in the western hemisphere.

## GUATÓ

A Native South American nation of Brazil's Amazonia. Nomadic fishers, hunters and gatherers, they had a river-based subsistence economy. They fought PORTUGUESE slavers and settlers from their first contact in about 1543, but were gradually ground down by genocide, slavery and smallpox. By 1901 fewer than 50 were found, and ranchers soon dispossessed them. In the 1950s they were declared extinct, but many had migrated to the cities. In the 1980s they began to reorganize and seek the return of their lands. In

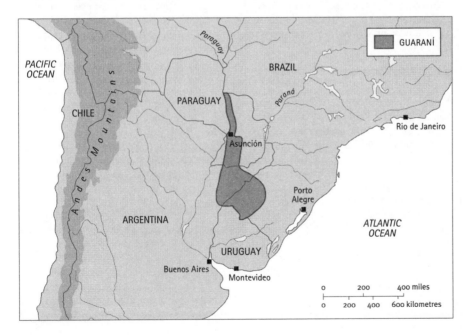

Guaraní

1992 the courts awarded them Insua Island on the border with Bolivia, but the BRAZILIAN military refused to evacuate a security area there. In 1994 a few families reoccupied the island, and the army agreed to let them stay. In 1999 the Guató numbered about 120.

## GUAYAKI

A Native South American nation of Paraguay's Amazonia who spoke Tupí-Guaraní. They were originally sedentary farmers, but after the 16th century pressure from settlers and the GUARANÍ forced them to adopt a nomadic, hunting-and-gathering subsistence economy. Thereafter they avoided white contact as far as possible and remained one of the least acculturated nations on the continent. In the 1990s they did attempt some sustainable exploitation of their resources, for example by marketing their yerba maté tea. In 1995 they numbered about 900.

## GUAYANA

A Native South American nation of Suriname, Guyana and French Guiana. Sedentary slash-and-burn farmers, they were also hunters and gatherers; they spoke a CARIB language. Pressure from settlers and poverty have forced many into Brazil and Venezuela. In 1979 they numbered about 750.

## GUAYMIES

A Native Central American nation of western Panama. Sedentary farmers, hunters and gatherers, they spoke a Chibchan language. They put up determined resistance to SPANISH encroachment, and even forced a (later broken) treaty upon them. They maintained their independence and clung to their traditional culture, but by the end of the 20th century they were slowly being acculturated. In 1986 they numbered 2500, and in 2000 they sought to address serious problems of poverty by marketing their coffee in the European market as 'humanely grown'.

## GUYANANS

The population of the South American country of Guyana; the name means 'land of many waters'. The land was contested for centuries by Spain, France, the Netherlands and England, before the ENGLISH secured it in the 17th century. A plantation economy based on African slaves was established, but with the abolition of slavery in 1833 indentured labour was imported from India; now South Asians and people of African descent constitute the largest ethnic groups. There are Native American, European and CHINESE minorities. Guyanese culture is a colourful blend of all these influences, although politically and racially there have been South Asian–African tensions. Independent since 1966, after some unrest, Guyana is a heavily indebted, deeply impoverished nation, and claims of electoral fraud have been rife. In 2001 the Guyanese numbered nearly 700,000.

## GWICH'IN

A Native North American nation of Alaska and the Yukon Territory, whose name comes from the CHIPEWYAN and means 'squint eyed'. They originally called themselves *Dijiezu*, but have adopted the name *Gwich'in*, meaning 'people of the caribou'. Nomadic hunters (heavily dependent on caribou), they also gathered and fished. They speak an ATHABASKAN language.

In the 19th century contacts with traders and missionaries spread epidemics and led to some cultural erosion, with some adopting a sedentary lifestyle. Caribou, however, remained central to their existence, and when in the late 20th century commercial exploitation of their lands began, they organized to protect themselves. They remain bitterly opposed to oil extraction in the Arctic National Wildlife Refuge, fearing that it will destroy the caribou and cause their own extinction, and in 1999 referred the matter to the United Nations Human Rights Commission. In 2001, the AMERICAN government proceeded with measures to extract oil from their territory, although the move was defeated in the Senate. They then numbered over 7500.

## HAIDA

A Native North American nation of the Queen Charlotte Islands in British Columbia and

> " They stamped out the plains Indians when they killed the buffalo. They can't do it to us. "
>
> Faith Gemmill, Gwich'in spokesperson (2001)

Prince of Wales Island in southern Alaska. Sedentary traders, hunters, gatherers and fishers, they speak the Haida language. Accomplished seamen, they were widely travelled traders as well as feared sea-raiders, attacking European ships in the 18th century. Growing contacts with whites in the 19th century began to destroy their traditional culture. Missionaries destroyed the totem poles for which the Haida are famed, and potlatches were banned. The Haida also suffered a disastrous population fall through epidemics.

In the 20th century they united with the TLINGIT to protect their sovereign rights. This union promises considerable success. In 2002, for example, after several decades of failed negotiations, they appeared set to win a land claim for the Queen Charlotte Islands. As the area is oil-rich, vast wealth is at stake. In 1996 the Haida numbered approximately 3400.

## HAISLA

A Native North American nation of northern British Columbia, whose name means 'those living at the river mouth'. Sedentary hunters, gatherers and fishers, they speak a Wakashan language. They entered the fur trade in the early 19th century, and its associated diseases decimated them. Missionaries, residential schools and the banning of potlatches eroded their traditional religion, while commercial fishing undermined their traditional economy.

In 2001, however, they erected their first totem pole in 125 years as part of a cultural revival. This revival has included the repatriation of artefacts, including a mortuary totem pole erected to the victims of a smallpox epidemic, removed in 1929 and sent to the Stockholm Museum of Ethnography. In 2001 they numbered around 1200.

## HAITIANS

The population of the Caribbean Republic of Haiti, who share the western third of the island of Hispaniola with the DOMINICAN REPUBLICANS. The Spanish destroyed the native ARAWAK population, but did not themselves settle extensively, allowing the FRENCH to conquer in the mid-17th century and establish a plantation economy. A

large African slave population grew, and a distinctive culture developed, principally famed for voodoo practices. Today, 95% of Haitians are of African origin; most speak Haitian Creole, while the official language is French.

In 1804 Haitians won independence, but subsequently experienced difficulties in establishing a stable government. Political violence became the norm, culminating in the brutal dictatorship of the Duvalier family (1957–86). In the 1990s there were moves towards democracy, but political turmoil continued with the ousting of President Aristide in 2004. Nevertheless, for most of the nearly 7 million Haitians (2001), desperate poverty, alongside serious crime and violence, malnutrition, malaria, tetanus, AIDS and the effects of natural disasters remain the more pressing concerns.

## HALCHIDHOMA

A Native North American nation of southern California. Sedentary hunters and farmers, they spoke a Hokan language and were noted as expert traders who travelled along the Colorado River. Their aggressive and powerful MOHAVE neighbours drove them to merge with the MARICOPA in the mid-19th century.

## HALYIKWAMAI

A former Native North American nation of Arizona. Sedentary farmers, hunters and gatherers, they spoke a Hokan language. In the late 18th century they came under severe pressure because of wars between the neighbouring MARICOPA and the PIMA and APACHE. At the beginning of the 19th century they began abandoning their territory, seeking sanctuary among the Maricopa, who rapidly assimilated them.

## HAN

A Native North American nation of the Alaska–Yukon Territory border area, whose name means perhaps 'people of the river', or just 'house'. They call themselves Tr'ondek Hwech'in. Seasonally mobile as hunters, gatherers and fishers, they spoke an ATHABASKAN language. Little-known in the mid-19th century, their

*66* When a Haida Indian wishes to obtain a fair wind, he ... shoots a raven. *99*

J.G. Frazer, 1890

interests were ignored during the Alaska Purchase (1867), allowing trappers, traders, and later gold prospectors to flood into their territory. By 1900 they were acculturated, dependent on the cash economy and much reduced by diseases. In 2001 they numbered about 550.

## HARE

A Native North American nation of Yukon and the Northwest Territories. They speak an ATHABASKAN language. Originally nomadic hunters, they were isolated and led a very precarious existence. They were widely believed to practise cannibalism on their own elders during times of famine. They entered the fur trade in the 19th century, which led to a more sedentary lifestyle, but also brought diseases and cultural erosion and failed to relieve periodic famines. In 1991 they numbered nearly 1200.

## HASINAI

A Native North American nation of eastern Texas, whose name perhaps means 'our own fold'. Sedentary farmers, they hunted and gathered as secondary activities and spoke a Caddoan language. They built ceremonial and burial mounds and possibly practised ceremonial cannibalism on war captives. Contact with settlers and traders in the 17th century brought epidemics that began to destroy them. By 1839 their lands were lost, and along with the CADDO they moved to the Fort Worth area, only to be removed to Oklahoma in 1859. By 1874 they had united with the Caddo into a single nation.

## HAVASUPAI

A Native North American nation of Arizona's Grand Canyon area, whose name perhaps means 'people of the blue green water'. Sedentary farmers and traders, they also hunted and gathered. They spoke a Yuman language and lived in a nearly inaccessible area, which was still, however, coveted by cattle-ranchers. In 1880 they were confined to a small reservation on their traditional territory, later reduced by mining interests, and they suffered disastrous epidemics. In the 1960s they lost federal recog-

nition, and there were attempts to relocate them. In 1974 they regained recognition and some land, but remained dependent on federal aid, with tourism offering limited economic opportunities. In 1998 they numbered about 640.

## HET

A former Native South American nation of Argentina. Probably sedentary farmers, hunters and gatherers, they spoke Cecehet, a now extinct language. They might have been a sub-group of the TEHUELCHE or the QUERANDI, but it is clear that as a nation they did not long survive contact with the Spanish. As many as 5% of ARGENTINIANS, however, could be descendants of the Het.

## HIDATSA

A Native North American nation of North Dakota, whose name comes from the MANDAN and means 'they crossed the river'. Sedentary farmers, hunters and gatherers, they spoke a Siouan language. From the late 18th century a series of epidemics, as well as pressure from the LAKOTA, caused them to unite with the Mandan and by 1862 with the ARIKARA. They formed a single nation, the Three Affiliated Tribes, in 1934. Forced onto a reservation in 1870, they found the land barren and poorly wooded. They refused relocation to better land in Oklahoma, however, fearing to lose their attachment to their traditional territory. They still maintain much of their traditional culture, but social and economic problems were exacerbated in 1950 with uncompensated land losses through damming. In 1980 they numbered over 1500.

## HISPANICS

An AMERICAN culture, based on a cultural and/or ancestral background in the PORTUGUESE and SPANISH colonization of the New World. Some consider the term 'Hispanics' offensive and use the term 'Latinos'. Hispanic presence began in the USA after territory was taken from Mexico in 1848. Their numbers grew in the 20th century, through legal and illegal immigration, including from Mexico and Cuba; in 2001 they numbered about 35 million, the USA's largest minority.

> **"** Owing partly to the nature of their habitat, dreary steppes which are the home of starvation ... they retained their practice of abandoning and even eating the old and infirm in times of scarcity. **"**
>
> Description of the Hare, *Catholic Encyclopedia* (1910)

> **"** Some of the Hidatsa Indians explain the phenomena of gradual death ... by supposing that man has four souls. **"**
>
> J.G. Frazer, 1890

Originally concentrated in the south, especially in former Spanish colonies such as Texas and California, Hispanics are now spread throughout the nation. Their contribution to American culture, through music and cuisine for example, has been extensive. However, they have suffered severely from prejudice and poverty, and different national origins hampered collective political action to combat them. By the late 20th century, however, they had made considerable progress, even if serious social problems remained. While they generally see themselves as Americans, they often maintain a distinct cultural identity. Many are bilingual in Spanish and English, but in many areas their specific language-needs have received official recognition.

## HITCHITI

A former Native North American nation of Georgia, whose name means 'to look upstream'. Sedentary farmers, hunters and gatherers, they spoke a Muskogean language. Contacts with settlers from the 1670s began their destruction through disease and warfare. By 1738, they were reduced to some 60 warriors; most were absorbed by the CREEK, while others joined with the SEMINOLE in Florida.

## HOH

A Native North American nation of coastal Washington state. Sedentary hunters (especially of sea mammals), fishers and gatherers, they spoke a Chimakuan language.

In 1855 the Hoh were forced to cede their lands and were moved onto the QUINAULT reservation, receiving their own reservation only in 1893. Their relative isolation causes unemployment, and fishing is a primary means of subsistence. This has caused problems with sports fishers, who claim that the Hoh use their rights to fish for 'ceremonial purposes' as an excuse to deplete fish-stocks on a commercial basis. In 1990 they numbered almost 160.

## HOHOKAM CULTURE

A former Native North American culture of the Arizona area, arising in about 300 BC and

disappearing by AD 1450. The people became sedentary farmers, hunters and gatherers, with an extensive trade network, and constructed an elaborate irrigation canal system, parts of which were renovated and in use in the 20th century. They were a complex society, with distinctive ceramics and ball games, and there is little evidence of their involvement in warfare.

It is unclear why they disappeared, but overpopulation perhaps coupled with drought seems a probable explanation. The PIMA and TOHONO O'ODHAM claim to be their descendants.

## HONDURANS

The population of the Republic of Honduras in Central America, most of whom are MESTIZO. The area was originally inhabited by the MAYA, but SPANISH conquest beginning in 1524 decimated them through massacre, disease and slavery. The Spanish population remained small, however, and the Mestizo came to dominate, blending Native American and European elements in the culture. The Hondurans declared independence in 1838, but were subsequently dominated by Guatemala and later Nicaragua.

In the 20th century military dictatorships and extreme poverty caused unrest, which led to AMERICAN military interventions. In the 1970s there were land reforms (which benefited only a few), and in 1982 a civilian government returned. Left-wing guerrillas, however, still exist, having grievances such as mass illiteracy and malnutrition. In 2001 Hondurans numbered over 6.4 million. Minorities include the GARIFUNA and MOSQUITO.

## HOPEWELL CULTURE

A former Native North American culture of the Ohio area. The people are possibly descendants of the ADENA, but their ceremonial and burial mounds are larger, and their artwork more refined. Sedentary farmers, they still relied heavily on hunting and gathering, and also had an extensive trade network. They appeared about 100 BC, reached their peak about AD 300 and had disappeared by 750. The causes of their disappearance are unclear, but there is evidence of rising warfare, either internally because of depleted resources, or as a result of invaders. Their successors were the MISSISSIPPI TEMPLE MOUND CULTURE.

## HOPI

A Native North American nation of northeast Arizona, whose name means 'peaceful people'. Sedentary farmers, they hunted and gathered as secondary activities. They speak an Uto-Aztecan language and are pueblo-dwellers. Living on their lands since the 6th century AD, they claim to have the longest history of occupancy in the USA of any group still extant.

Being an isolated and closed community with a complex religion, from 1629 they were able to resist attempts by the SPANISH to convert them, continuing their religion in secret. Between 1680 and 1700 they succeeded in driving out the Spanish, but NAVAJO encroachment had begun, and proved more troublesome. In 1882 they accepted a reservation in an effort to end this, but Navajo settlement continued and the AMERICAN government took no action until 1974, when about half the disputed lands were returned to them. This issue was still being disputed in the early 21st century. The 20th century saw a developing rift between traditionalists and progressives (who see some degree of compromising with modern American culture as essential for the survival and prosperity of the nation). Only three out of twelve villages agreed to form Western-style forms of government. In 1990 the Hopi numbered about 7300.

## HOUMA

A Native North American nation of southeast Louisiana. Sedentary farmers, hunters, fishers and gatherers, they spoke a Muskogean language. In the 17th century they were friendly with the FRENCH and suffered English attacks in consequence, forcing them to migrate south from their original territory.

In 1814 the AMERICAN government (who have never recognized them) dismissed their land claims, and settler pressure forced them into less desirable marshlands. Their lands were still whittled away, especially after oil was discovered there in 1901. Government neglect has caused

serious problems, denying them state education until 1963. In 1994 their application for federal recognition was rejected on the grounds that they could not prove their continuous existence as a nation since white contact. In 1995 they claimed a population of about 17,000.

## HUANCA

A former Native South American nation of Peru. Sedentary farmers, herders, hunters and gatherers, they spoke a Quechuan language. Once in scattered hilltop villages, they dispersed and disunited to resist INCA conquest in 1476. The Inca re-settled them in more concentrated valley communities to keep them under control. The Huanca helped the SPANISH conquer the Inca in the 1530s, but then shared the Inca's fate. By the end of the century the vast majority had died from disease, famine and war, and the remnants became assimilated in the general population.

## HUANCAVILCA

A Native South American nation of the Ecuadorean coast. Sedentary farmers, hunters, gatherers, fishers and traders, they were foremost a wide-ranging maritime nation and spoke a Quechuan language, now apparently extinct. They flourished from the 8th to the 14th centuries AD, after which the INCA conquered them.

In the 1530s they were conquered by the SPANISH, and thereafter suffered great exploitation and acculturation, but survived as a nation. In combination with the MANTEÑO, with whom they are closely associated, they numbered nearly 66,000 in 2001. Then they were struggling to combat racism and to secure land rights.

## HUAORANI

A Native South American nation of Ecuador's Amazonia, whose name means 'the people'. Seasonally mobile within their territory as hunters and gatherers who practised limited agriculture, they were contacted only in the 1950s; some bands have still not been contacted. They have a reputation for their fierce independence, and have attacked oil-company employees. In 1995 they attracted international attention by occupying oil wells in protest against the destruction of their environment and society. In 2002 they numbered about 1600.

## HUARI (Brazil)

A former Native South American nation of Brazil's Amazonia. Probably sedentary, they were farmers, hunters and gatherers and spoke a Gê language. Disease, acculturation and perhaps genocidal attacks destroyed them as a nation by the mid-20th century.

## HUARI (Peru)

A former Native South American nation of northern Peru. Sedentary farmers, hunters and gatherers, they first emerged around 300 BC. They built a great city at Pikillaqta, and came under the cultural influence of the TIWANAKU. It is unclear, however, whether or not relations between the two were peaceful. From around AD 600 to 1000 the Huari began to expand by conquest, building a powerful empire. At the end of that period they abruptly collapsed, possibly because of climate change, although this has not been proven. Their culture and religion influenced successor nations, including the INCA.

## HUARPA

A Native South American nation of the Peruvian Andes. They were sedentary farmers, hunters and gatherers, and their ceramics suggest some links with the NAZCA. They lacked cities, but small villages and towns had well-developed terracing and irrigation systems, suggesting a complex social system. They flourished from about AD 200 until a severe drought between 562 and 594 caused their collapse. They were perhaps predecessors of the HUARI of Peru or the TIWANAKU.

## HUASTEC

A Native North American nation of eastern Mexico. Sedentary hunters and gatherers, whose sophisticated environmental management techniques could be described as agriculture, they spoke a Mayan language. They were conquered by the AZTEC in the 15th century, and a rebellion

in 1487 led to their near extermination. They therefore saw the SPANISH as liberators, but soon found they had swapped one brutal conqueror for another. Ignorance, poverty and exploitation became their lot, and are still major concerns of the approximately 80,000 Huastec in 1998.

## HUCHNOM

A former Native North American nation of northern California. Sedentary hunters and gatherers, they spoke a Yukian language. In the mid-19th century settlers stole their lands and they were decimated by disease and murder. Some were transplanted to the Round Valley reservation. Those who refused to go tried to subsist on settlers' cattle and were exterminated. The last known Huchnom died in the 1970s.

## HUICHOLE

A Native North American nation of western Mexico. Sedentary farmers and herders, they speak an Uto-Aztecan language. Their very rugged terrain kept them isolated, and the SPANISH conquered them only after 1722. Even then, isolation allowed them considerable autonomy and made Spanish cultural influence minimal. By the 1860s MESTIZO land thefts led some to join insurrections, but most avoided conflict. In 2000 they numbered about 15,100, the vast majority still animists and self-sufficient, if poor.

## HUILICHE

See MAPUCHE.

## HUPA

A Native North American nation of northwest California. Semi-sedentary hunters and gatherers, the Hupa spoke an ATHABASKAN language and used dugouts and weirs for fishing. Once a powerful nation, they met disaster in the 1850s when gold was discovered on their lands and a flood of miners brought disease and murder. By 1864 they were confined to the Hoopa Valley reservation, and as their numbers declined this was used as a dumping ground for other nations, which caused further conflict.

h

Eventually a combination of ranching, farming and lumbering brought some prosperity and assisted their efforts to preserve their culture. In 1996 they even succeeded in regaining some land that had been fraudulently removed from the reservation by corrupt surveyors in 1875. In 1990 there were about 2450 Hupa.

## HURON

A Native North American nation of Ontario. Their name comes from the French and means 'ruffian', but they call themselves *Wyandot*, meaning 'island people'. Sedentary traders, farmers, hunters, gatherers and fishers, they spoke an Iroquoian language.

In the 17th century they became allies of the FRENCH and acted as middlemen in French trade with the Great Lakes area. This alliance caused IROQUOIS hostility and resulted in disastrous wars and land loss by 1649. Many Huron scattered and were absorbed by other nations. Some moved south to Ohio and Michigan before being moved by the AMERICAN government to Kansas and Oklahoma.

Others moved to Quebec, where they eventually found some prosperity through traditional handicrafts and have a small reserve at Wendake near Quebec City. In 1995 they numbered about 1900 and have been seeking to reaffirm the unity of their scattered groups, revitalize their culture and regain some of their traditional lands. From 2000 many have gathered annually in their original homeland near Ste Marie among the Hurons in southern Ontario.

## ICA

A Native South American nation of Peru. Seasonally mobile within their territory as farmers, hunters and gatherers, they spoke a Chibchan language. They were defeated by the SPANISH around 1600, and large numbers fled to less accessible mountainous areas in Colombia.

This enabled their traditional culture to survive, although they expelled missionaries in the 1980s for trying to suppress their language and religion. A greater threat came from the encroachment of COLOMBIAN farmers, and civil war on their lands. Their territory is also the source of Ica stones, hand-etched rocks apparently showing men hunting dinosaurs, beloved of ufologists, but clearly frauds. In 2001 they numbered about 18,000.

## ILLINOIS

A Native North American confederation of the Illinois area. Sedentary farmers, hunters, gatherers and fishers, they spoke an Algonquian language. Trading partners and allies of the FRENCH from the 17th century, they suffered severely from IROQUOIS attacks. Disaster, however, struck in 1769, when one of them murdered the OTTAWA leader Pontiac. The FOX, KICKAPOO and other Great Lakes nations joined in a war of revenge. Withdrawing eventually to Kansas, they were driven from there in the 1860s by illegal taxes levied on their lands.

They were re-settled in Oklahoma, where most of their lands were again fraudulently removed. Their traditional culture and language were largely lost. By 1868 they had merged with the remnants of other nations to form the PEORIA, who in 2001 numbered about 2640.

## INCA

A Native American nation of western South America, whose lands stretched from Ecuador to central Chile. Sedentary farmers, hunters and gatherers, they spoke a Quechuan language, and their name means 'prince', a reference to their military caste. They were empire builders and assimilated their conquests. Their ruler, the Inca, was believed to be a descendant of their sun god, Inti. Their government was a despotic theocracy, which occasionally practised human sacrifice.

Inca expansion began about 1438, and had reached its greatest extent when the Spanish arrived in 1532, but they had been weakened by civil war and by the European diseases that had arrived before the Spanish. The Spanish kidnapped the Inca, Atahualpa, and subsequently murdered him. They ruled at first through a puppet Inca, but the provinces rebelled, and it took 40 years of savage fighting before all Inca forces had been crushed. The population was enslaved. Their material culture was despoiled and largely destroyed.

66 The Hurons ... believe that the souls of the departed turn into turtle-doves. 99

A.H. Sayce, 1880

66 A numerous nation of Indians who were destitute of the cruelty of savages. 99

J.M. Peck on the Illinois, 1834

66 [Incas] have a Jewish cast of feature, speak gutterally and are much given to unnatural vice. 99

Augustín de Zárate, c. 1555

The last major revolt was led by Tupac Amaru in 1572, who was brutally killed, although the fighting did not end until the Spanish issued a general pardon. In 1824 Inca lands were distributed to individuals by Simon Bolívar , but they Inca were subsequently defrauded of much of it. Poverty remains the lot of many in a population of about 6 million (1999).

# INGALIK

A Native North American nation of Alaska, whose name comes from the INUIT and means 'having many nits'. Seasonally mobile within their territory as hunters, gatherers and fishers, they speak an ATHABASKAN language. Probably driven into their territory by the CREE in the 12th century, they adopted much of the lifestyle and culture of the Inuit despite their mutual hostility. They were little noticed until after the AMERICAN purchase of Alaska in 1867, when missionaries and trappers brought diseases and acculturation. In 1996 they numbered about 300, one-third of whom maintain their language.

# INNU

A North American aboriginal nation of Quebec and Labrador. Their name means 'human beings', but the French called them *Montagnais* or *Naskapi*. Nomadic hunters, gatherers and fishers, they speak an Algonquian language.

Entering the fur trade by the early 17th century, the small autonomous Innu bands could neither resist the acculturation that followed nor enter treaty relations with settlers. Commercial exploitation of their lands damaged their environment and depleted their food sources.

In the 20th century determined efforts were made to force them onto fixed settlements. The results for the Innu have been disastrous. Massive unemployment, substance abuse, violence and despair have had a corrosive social impact. By 1999 they had the highest suicide rate in the world. Canadian indifference to the plight of the Innu led, in that year, to international protests as well as condemnation by the United Nations. In 2000 the Innu were campaigning to win Canadian recognition of their sovereignty as part of

their efforts to survive as a nation. In 1997 they numbered over 16,000.

# INUIT

An aboriginal nation of Arctic Greenland, Canada, Alaska and Siberia, whose name means 'people'. They are often called Eskimos. Seasonally mobile within their territory, they subsist almost entirely as hunters and fishers. Most Inuit live on the coast and hunt marine mammals, but some groups, notably the Caribou, live inland and hunt caribou. The Inuit speak many dialects of an Eskaleut language, operate in independent but highly cooperative groups and are well

**"** We were once Warriors. Now we are lost. **"**

Graffiti in an Innu village (2002)

Inca

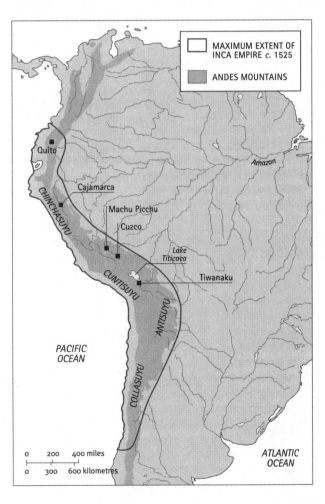

MAXIMUM EXTENT OF INCA EMPIRE c. 1525

ANDES MOUNTAINS

Quito

Amazon

Cajamarca

CHINCHASUYU

Machu Picchu

Cuzco

Lake Titicaca

Tiwanaku

CUNTISUYU

ANTISUYU

PACIFIC OCEAN

COLLASUYU

0    200    400 miles
0    300    600 kilometres

ATLANTIC OCEAN

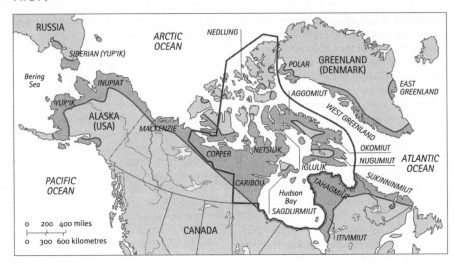

adapted to an extremely harsh environment. The snow houses for which the Inuit are popularly known are temporary structures, used for hunting camps. Until recently coastal Inuit lived in well-insulated, partly subterranean huts built of turf, stone and driftwood; those living inland relied on tents. The Inuit practised an animistic religion and shamans acted as a link between humans and animal spirits. Several groups had no contact with the outside world until the 20th century, but their traditional culture has been steadily eroded since then. Snowmobiles and outboards have largely replaced the traditional dogsleds and skin boats (both the single-cockpit kayaks, used by men for hunting, and the larger open umiaks, used by women) that were used by nearly all Inuit, while rifles are used for hunting. Mineral extraction, commercial fishing, whaling, military bases and global warming have all combined to degrade their environment.

The great influenza pandemic of 1918–19 killed one-third of the Inuit population. Attempts to forcibly settle the Inuit included the slaughter of their dog teams. As a consequence, various groups have been formed to protect Inuit interests and address the severe social problems they face. Erosion of their traditional lifestyle, scarcity of employment opportunities, limited access to higher education or recreation have contributed to isolation and boredom and a very high suicide rate among the young.

In 1999 Canada finally addressed Inuit demands and established a new territory – Nunavut ('our land'). It was hoped greater autonomy might empower the Inuit.

In 2000 the Inuit population was estimated at 22,000 in Canada, 40,000 in Greenland and 25,000 in Alaska.

## INUPIAT

An aboriginal INUIT nation of northern Alaska. Seasonally mobile as hunters, fishers and whalers, they speak an Eskaleut language. They were greatly reduced in the mid-19th century by disease and famine, and lost most of their best lands after the 1867 Alaska Purchase, although they regained part in the 1960s. In the 1990s, facing high unemployment, they sought to protect their subsistence lifestyle and gain economic opportunities by considering oil exploitation combined with assurances of environmental protection. In 1997 they unsuccessfully sought exemption from the worldwide ban on whaling. In 1994 they numbered about 12,000.

## IOWA

A Native North American nation now of Oklahoma and the Kansas–Nebraska border. They call themselves *Bah-kho-je*, meaning 'grey snow', a reference to their winter dwellings. Seasonally

" Formerly, they ... looked upon Europeans as upon dogs, giving them the appellation Kablunets, that is, Barbarians. "

B. La Trobe, 1774, referring to the Inuit

mobile within their territory as farmers, hunters, gatherers and fishers, they spoke a Siouan language. Originally of Iowa, they were moved to Kansas after ceding their lands in 1824. The lands they received were inadequate, and in the 1870s they split into two groups in their present location. By 1997, when they numbered over 2000, they were struggling to revive a traditional culture in decline. They were also at the forefront of the campaign to repatriate human remains and funerary objects excavated by archaeologists, acting as agents for 21 other nations in dealings with the University of Missouri.

## IPURINÁ

A Native South American nation of Brazil's Amazonia. Sedentary farmers, fishers with traps, hunters and gatherers, they spoke an Arawakan language. After first encountering settlers, they suffered 500 years of genocide, exploitation, land theft and the destruction of their environment. In 2000 they numbered about 2000, and were still suffering the theft of resources, especially plants by pharmaceutical companies.

## IRISH AMERICANS

An AMERICAN culture of colonial origin. IRISH migrants began crossing the Atlantic in the 1640s, but around 1840 overpopulation, poverty and soon famine in Ireland caused mass migration to begin. The first group to challenge ENGLISH cultural dominance in the USA, they were subject to prejudice and employment discrimination, which only very slowly declined. Their communities tended to be concentrated and tightly knit until the 20th century.

Their culture preserves many traditional Irish elements, and they maintain an affection for a highly idealized image of Ireland that has made them a valuable source of support to various Irish nationalist movements. Elements of their culture have been more generally adopted by other Americans. St Patrick's Day is widely celebrated, for example. Their numbers are uncertain, but they are largely concentrated in the urban northeast.

Ironically it was the Ulster Protestants (see NORTHERN IRISH) who had a much greater impact

on American values in the 18th century. They were part of the political and moneyed elite, allowing them to become thoroughly integrated into US society. The Catholic Irish immigrants, generally lacking skills and often desperately poor, tended to cling together for mutual support. This encouraged introspection and offered a barrier to integration. Conscious of their low social standing, they tended to be indifferent to the interests of other groups. Relatively few, for example, fought for the Union in the Civil War (1861–5) as they feared the end of slavery would expose them to greater competition in the labour market. Their unity, however, gave them political influence, and they came to dominate local politics in places such as Chicago. Prejudice persisted, however, and it was not until 1960 that one of their number, John F. Kennedy, could overcome the disadvantage of his origins to be elected president of the USA.

## IROQUOIS

A Native North American confederation comprising the MOHAWK, ONEIDA, CAYUGA, SENECA, ONONDAGA and later the TUSCARORA. Originally of New York state, now also of Wisconsin and Ontario, they called themselves *Handenosaunee*, meaning 'people of the longhouse'. Sedentary farmers, hunters, gatherers and fishers, they spoke an Iroquoian language. The confederacy ha been formed by the beginning of the 17th century to end the inter-tribal wars that left them vulnerable to attack by the surrounding Algonquian-speaking nations. Political unity and a military training system sometimes compared to that of the SPARTANS, alongside the fur trade and alliance with England, made them militarily formidable, but constant warfare and disease weakened them.

In the 18th century Iroquois political unity began to weaken, and they were fatally divided in their alliances during the American Revolution. By the 19th century many had been driven from their lands and the rest had become fragmented, though they clung to their culture. In 1995 they numbered nearly 75,000. They regard themselves not only as a sovereign nation, but also as the oldest participatory democracy on Earth. (See map, page 76.)

**Inuit: main sub-groups**

Aggomiut
Caribou
Copper
Greenland
Iglulik
Inupiat
Itivimiut
Mackenzie
Netsilik
Nugumiut
Okomiut
Polar
Sagdlirmiut
Siberian
 (Yup'ik)
Sukinninmiut
Tahagmiut
Yup'ik

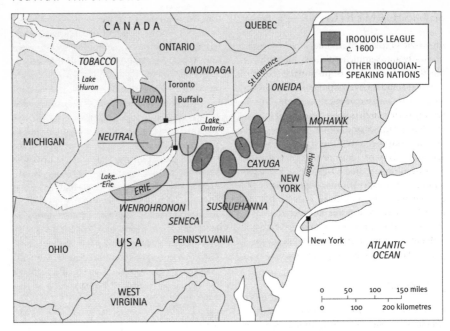

**Iroquois**

## ITALIAN AMERICANS

An AMERICAN culture of colonial origin. Italians crossed the Atlantic in great numbers after 1890, seeking to escape overpopulation and spreading industrial capitalism that was undermining traditional agricultural and craft economies, all of which spread poverty. Ironically the very capitalism that forced them from their homes was to provide them with new opportunities.

Initially, as in Italy, they identified with their regions rather than their national identity, but the achievements of Mussolini encouraged a pride in and identification with Italy. They were, however, steadfastly loyal to the USA in wartime and after – in 1948 a government-organized letter-writing campaign by Italian Americans to relatives in Italy did much to defeat a communist-led coalition in Italian elections. They faced considerable discrimination, often (with the Mafia-gangster subculture) being stereotyped as criminals, not least in Hollywood films.

In 1990 there were nearly 15 million Italian Americans, mainly concentrated on the east coast. Politically their cohesiveness has given them influence, although acculturation threatens to undermine this. Culturally their impact has been significant, not least in their wines and cuisine.

## JAMAICANS

the population of the Caribbean island state of Jamaica, south of Cuba. The SPANISH, arriving in 1494, destroyed the original ARAWAK inhabitants, but the island remained a backwater until the ENGLISH seized it in 1655. Thereafter it became a base for privateering, although a plantation economy soon developed. African slaves and their descendants had a massive effect on the culture, especially in its cuisine and music. The abolition of slavery in 1833 allowed an independent peasant economy to develop. However, the economy, dependent on agriculture, suffered repeated crises and violent unrest in the 1930s and the 1970s, despite independence in 1962. Severe poverty remains a continuing problem for the over 2.6 million Jamaicans in 2001, and was the cause of considerable illicit cannabis cultivation and its associated criminality.

# JEWISH AMERICANS

An AMERICAN culture of colonial origins. With no obviously anti-Semitic traditions, and with visible alternative victims of prejudice in AFRICAN AMERICANS and NATIVE AMERICANS, the USA was attractive to Jewish communities. From the 19th century their numbers grew steadily, often western European, cosmopolitan and appearing secular. From about 1881 much poorer, Yiddish-speaking eastern European Jews fleeing repression joined them. This did increase discrimination, especially in education and employment, which declined only from 1945. In 1990 Jewish Americans numbered about 6 million, and had become a large, wealthy and influential community, with an enormously powerful political lobby supporting the ISRAELIS.

# JICAQUE

A Native Central American nation of northern Honduras. Sedentary farmers, hunters and gatherers, they speak a language that is probably Hokan. In the 16th century the SPANISH found them formidable opponents, and claimed they were cannibals. Disease, warfare and slavery reduced them and left the remainder vulnerable to continuing exploitation. In 1999 Amnesty International highlighted official collaboration in murder and intimidation of the Jicaque over land claims. In 1990 they numbered nearly 600.

# JIVARO

A Native South American nation of the Amazonia of Peru and Ecuador. Sedentary slash-and-burn farmers, requiring periodic relocation as soil became exhausted, they were also fishers and hunter-gatherers, and spoke Jivaroan. One of the most feared nations on the continent, they are best known for their practice of shrinking the heads of their enemies killed in battle, in the belief that they have magic properties. By 1559 the SPANISH had established a strong presence in their territory, with a community 20,000 strong. They were, however, demanding rulers who were determined to extract every ounce of gold from the land. In a carefully planned operation, the Jivaro then attacked and massacred the Spanish,

perhaps taking some younger women captive. The Spanish were never able to re-conquer them. In the late 20th century, however, diseases were causing serious concern. In 1981 they numbered up to 34,000 in Ecuador and in 1998 over 52,000 were counted in Peru.

# JUMANO

A Native North American nation of Texas, New Mexico and Northern Mexico, who were perhaps descendants of the MOGOLLON CULTURE. Seasonally mobile within their territory as farmers, hunters and gatherers, they were also widely travelled traders. They possibly spoke a Tanoan language. From the 16th century they came under increasing pressure from the APACHE, losing access to hunting grounds on the Great Plains and vital trade routes. Appeals for help to the Spanish went unanswered. By the mid-18th century they had disappeared from the record. It may be that with their trade system destroyed, they were absorbed by the Apache and others, and perhaps formed the nucleus of the KIOWA.

In 1996, however, a group in western Texas, claiming descent from Jumano who migrated in the mid-17th century, applied for federal recognition, which has not yet been granted.

# KADIWEU

See MBAYA.

# KALAPUYA

A Native North American nation of Oregon. Semi-sedentary hunters and gatherers (especially of camas roots), they spoke a Penutian language. They used controlled fires to manage their environment, eliminating vegetation that restricted their food sources. Ploughing by European settlers caused starvation, and the epidemics they introduced reduced a Kalapuya population of up to 20,000 to near extinction in the 19th century. A reservation was promised them by treaty in 1851, but it was never delivered.

Some descendants are on the Grand Ronde reservation in Oregon. Perhaps 2000 Kalapuya are assimilated into the general population.

# KALISPEL

A Native North American nation of Idaho. They were seasonally mobile within their territory as hunters, fishers and gatherers, and spoke a Salishan language. In 1855 the Upper Kalispel were forced to cede their lands and move to a reservation in Montana. The Lower Kalispel refused to sign a treaty, which left them without legal protection when settlers occupied their lands. They gained a reservation in 1914, but it was steeply sloped, leading to a flood plain – almost useless for any form of economic development. They numbered about 240 in 1997, and poverty remained a serious problem.

# KALLAWAYA

A Native South American people of the Lake Titicaca area of Bolivia. Farmers and herders, they are also itinerant healers who see themselves as the guardians of INCA culture and learning. Their numbers are uncertain.

# KANSA or Kaw

A Native North American nation once of Illinois, now of Oklahoma, whose name means 'people of the south wind'. Seasonally mobile within their territory as farmers, hunters, gatherers and fishers, they spoke a Siouan language. By the 18th century they had moved to Kansas, but in the 19th century pressure from settlers pushed them further west, until they accepted a reservation in Oklahoma in 1873. The following year they participated in the last great bison hunt. Thereafter they became more dependent on agriculture and suffered from poverty. In 2002 they numbered over 2400 and were making efforts to preserve their culture. This will be no easy task: in 1998 only one academic spoke their language.

# KARANKAWA

A former Native North American nation of coastal Texas, whose name perhaps means 'dog lovers'. Seasonally mobile within their territory as hunters, fishers and gatherers, they comprised numerous autonomous groups sharing a common language and culture. From the 1680s the FRENCH and SPANISH competed for control over their territory with little success. Their numbers were drastically reduced by epidemics, loss of resources and COMANCHE raids, and in the 1790s they began to accept Spanish missionaries.

Real disaster, however, struck from the 1820s, with a large-scale influx of AMERICAN settlers. Not recognizing the concept of private property, the Karankawa raided livestock to survive, and were seen as dirty, dangerous savages and cannibals by the Texans, who launched a campaign of extermination in 1825. After supporting Mexico in the Texan War of Independence (1835–6), surviving Karankawa fled to Mexico. After the massacre of a group returning to their traditional lands in 1858, they ceased to exist as a nation.

# KAROK

A Native North American nation of northwest California, whose name means 'upriver people'. Sedentary traders, fishers, hunters and gatherers, they spoke a Hokan language. Initial contacts with Europeans were friendly, but in the 1850s gold prospectors flooded into their lands. There were no real wars, but disease, mass-murder and the destruction of their environment, all caused by settlers, nearly destroyed them. Most joined the HUPA and their culture began to disintegrate.

In 1994, however, they gained federal recognition and soon afterwards recovered their sacred site at Katamin. Also in 1994 they revived their world-renewal ceremony for the first time in 99 years. They view cultural renewal and the repair of the damage of 150 years of mining and logging on their traditional lands as crucial in addressing the severe problems of poverty, unemployment and welfare dependence.

# KASKA

A Native North American nation of northern British Columbia and southern Yukon. Originally nomadic hunters, gatherers and fishers, they speak an ATHABASKAN language. Entering the fur trade in the late 19th century, they became steadily acculturated, especially after the Alaska Highway opened in 1942. This has led to growing welfare dependence and alcohol abuse, spurring political activism and demands for greater sovereignty and control over their own resources. In 2001 negotiations over land led to a bitter political dispute in the Yukon parliament. In 1977 they numbered 750.

## KASKASKIA

A Native North American nation, once of Illinois, whose name might mean 'hide scraper'. Seasonally mobile within their territory as farmers, hunters, gatherers and fishers, they spoke an Algonquian language. They were once the leaders of the ILLINOIS confederacy and allies of the FRENCH, but diseases and constant warfare badly weakened them. The murder of OTTAWA leader Pontiac led to a war of extermination in 1769. The survivors fled to Kansas before being moved to Oklahoma in 1867, where they merged with the PEORIA, who numbered over 2600 in 2000.

## KAW

See KANSA.

## KAWAIISU

A Native North American nation of central California. Semi-sedentary hunters and gatherers, they called themselves *Niwiwi*, meaning 'people'. They spoke an Uto-Aztecan language, which they were attempting to preserve in 2000. In the 19th century SPANISH slave-raiding was followed by the great influx of the Gold Rush, which destroyed much of their culture. With their lands lost, they attempted to survive by stealing cattle, which led to a massacre of 35 Kawaiisu in 1863. Some settled on the Tule River reservation, but they have long been denied federal recognition and land. In 2000 they numbered about 50.

## KICKAPOO

A Native North American nation originally of Ohio, now three separate groups in Oklahoma, Texas and Kansas. They were once part of the SHAWNEE, and their name means 'he moves about'. Seasonally mobile within their territory as farmers, hunters, gatherers and fishers, they spoke an Algonquian language. In the 17th century they entered the fur trade with the FRENCH,

but were intensely suspicious of all Europeans. In 1832 they were moved onto a reservation in Kansas, but they split, with many moving to Mexico to serve as mercenaries against the APACHE and COMANCHE, where they also raided across the frontier. In 1873 the US Army entered Mexico, attacked their village and took several hostages, forcing most to settle in Oklahoma. Others later established themselves in Texas.

They have maintained their language, religion and traditional culture better than most Native American nations, but at the price of generally shunning AMERICAN education, which has resulted in very limited employment opportunities and widespread poverty. Their numbers are equivocal, but there were perhaps 3500 in 1990.

## KILIWA

A Native North American nation of Baja California, Mexico. They were semi-nomadic hunters and gatherers, and spoke a Yuman language, which is nearly extinct. The harsh local climate and the hostility of the Kiliwa prevented the Spanish from establishing missions on their territory, although raids and reprisals became regular. By the 20th century they subsisted on desert farming and ranching as well as wage labour. Many, however, had scattered, and only about eight households survived on their traditional lands by 1990.

## KILLKE CULTURE

A former Native South American culture of the Peruvian Andes. Identified by its style of ceramics, it is unclear if this culture, which combined HUARI and other elements, was a predecessor to the INCA, or if it was the Inca culture itself in its pre-imperial development. First appearing around 1200, the Killke lived almost entirely in small villages and certainly lacked the complex organization of the later Inca.

## KIOWA or Plains Apache

A Native North American nation of Montana, now of Oklahoma. Nomadic hunters and gatherers, they spoke a Tanoan language. In the 17th century they acquired horses and allied with the

k

KIOWA-APACHE as they moved to the Texas area. They have been credited with delaying the building of a railway to the Pacific for many years because of the ferocity of their resistance. They were only fully subdued and forced onto a reservation in 1875, when the bison were disappearing and the army destroyed most of their horses. Poverty and unemployment followed. In 1968 they formed the Kiowa Tribal Council to gain political influence and reverse the erosion of their language and culture. In 2000 they numbered about 11,500.

> " The Kioway loves the pale-face, and gives him warning. "
>
> A.F. Ruxton, 1849

## KIOWA-APACHE

A Native North American nation originally of the northern Great Plains, now of Oklahoma, who call themselves *Na-i-shan-Dene*, meaning 'our people'. Nomadic hunters and gatherers, they spoke an ATHABASKAN language. Possibly once an APACHE sub-group, they have been associated with the KIOWA from at least 1700. They communicate with the Kiowa via sign language and have largely adopted their culture. In 1997 they numbered about 1400.

## KITANEMUK

A Native North American nation of southern-central California. Semi-sedentary hunters and gatherers, they spoke an Uto-Aztecan language. Their culture had already been eroded by the SPANISH when the AMERICANS pushed them onto the Fort Tejon reservation in the 1850s. The reservation was subsequently reduced and finally confiscated in the early 20th century. About 500 were active in trying to preserve as much of their culture as possible in 2000. At that time they were bitterly opposed to oil drilling on their traditional lands, which threatened to destroy the evidence of their past.

## KITTITIANS AND NEVISIANS

The population of the Caribbean nation of St Kitts and Nevis, two islands between Puerto Rico and Trinidad and Tobago. They are mostly African-descended. In the 1620s both French and English colonies were established on the islands and cooperated in the destruction of the native CARIB population. There followed generations of rivalry between the two for control; the ENGLISH finally triumphed in 1782. By then a plantation economy had introduced a very strong African element into the developing culture. Britain granted the islands autonomy in 1967, and they united with Anguilla, but the latter broke away after a brief revolt in 1971. St Kitts and Nevis became independent under the BRITISH Crown in 1983. Relations between the two groups of islanders have not always been harmonious however, and there has often been considerable rivalry, especially over cricket. In the 1990s alleged government corruption sparked off an independence campaign on Nevis, but in 1998 a referendum on independence did not gain the two-thirds majority needed to succeed. In 2001 the Kittitians and Nevisians numbered nearly 39,000.

## KLALLAM

A Native North American nation of north coastal Washington state. Sedentary whalers, hunters, fishers and gatherers, they spoke a Salishan language. Seen as aggressive by their neighbours, they resisted pressure to enter a reservation with the SKOKOMISH in 1855, and were left as squatters on their own lands, and frequently displaced. There were repeated government attempts to suppress their culture, such as banning the potlatch – a traditional feasting and gift-giving ceremony. In the late 20th century they became more politically active in campaigning for fishing and hunting rights as well as for land acquisition, while high unemployment remains a key issue to them. In 1995 they numbered nearly 2000, although with only five speakers their language was nearly extinct.

## KLAMATH

A Native North American nation of northern California and southern Oregon. They call themselves *Maklaks*, meaning 'people'. Semi-sedentary fishers, hunters and gatherers, they spoke a Penutian language. They were relatively aggressive, raiding others for slaves to trade for horses. The violence of European settlers provoked war in the Rogue River area from 1848, but resistance weakened as food resources were destroyed and disease decimated the Klamath. In 1864 they were forced onto the Upper Klamath Lake reservation in Oregon, although some fought in the MODOC War (1872–3).

The Klamath survived and by the late 1970s numbered about 2000. A severe drought in 2001–2 caused neighbours to resent the water reserved for the endangered fish species vital to the Klamath. Racial tensions led to a shooting incident described by the press as a 'water war'.

## KLICKITAT

A Native North American nation of western Washington state, whose name comes from the CHINOOK, meaning 'robber'. They called themselves *Xwalxwaypan*. Semi-sedentary hunters, fishers and gatherers, they spoke a Sahaptian language. Mountaineers and warriors, they often acted as mercenaries for the Chinook against the SHOSHONE. As epidemics from the 1820s reduced their neighbours, the Klickitat expanded their territory before suffering themselves. A treaty of 1855 required them to leave their territory, and many fought in the YAKIMA War (1855–6). As a result they were forced onto the Yakima reservation, where their descendants can be found.

## KOASATI

A Native North American nation originally of Tennessee, whose name means 'white cane'. Sedentary farmers, hunters, fishers and gatherers, they spoke a Muskogean language. They were never a large nation, and epidemics nearly exterminated them in the 17th century, forcing the survivors to flee. Most settled in Texas, where they united with the ALABAMA. Of the Alabama-Coushatta tribe, perhaps 500 are of Koasati descent, and nearly all maintain their language.

## KOGI

A Native South American nation of the slopes of the Sierra Nevada de Santa Maria, in northern Colombia. Sedentary farmers who use the differing altitudes to grow suitable crops, they frequently know hunger, as centuries of slash-and-burn agriculture have degraded the soil.

They speak a Chibchan language and in 1996 numbered up to 6000.

## KOHUANA

A Native North American nation of Arizona. Sedentary farmers, hunters and gatherers, they spoke a Hokan language. They lived in stockaded pueblo-like villages, but conflicts with neighbouring nations forced their frequent relocation, and by the early 19th century they began to disintegrate as a nation. Some merged with other nations such as the MARICOPA, YUMA and MOHAVE. Some perhaps migrated to Mexico, and three communities in California and Arizona have inhabitants claiming Kohuana descent.

## KOLLA

A Native South American nation of northern Argentina. Sedentary farmers, herders, hunters and gatherers, they spoke a Quechuan language, now extinct. Conquered by the INCA in the 15th century, they were then conquered by the SPANISH in the 16th. Exploitation, acculturation and poverty followed, most Kolla surviving through subsistence farming. They did, however, retain their identity. In 1998 they succeeded, at least temporarily, in halting a gas pipeline crossing their lands on environmental grounds. By 2001 severe recession had driven many to desperation, and they protested vocally. They numbered about 170,000 in 2000. The Gispira, Omaguaca and Zenta are Kolla sub-groups.

## KOOTENAI

A Native North American nation of British Columbia, Alberta, Washington state, Idaho and Montana, who may have originally called themselves *Ksunka*, meaning 'people of the standing arrow'. Generally seasonally mobile within their territory as hunters, gatherers and fishers, they speak Kootenai. They occupied some of the richest hunting and gathering lands in North America, and settlers were quick to dispossess them. Those Kootenai in Canada were forced onto a number of small reservations, and while a treaty of 1855 promised those in the USA their own reservation, they were instead forced onto

k

the SALISH reservation. They continued to keep much of their traditional culture alive and to defend their interests. In 1975, for example, after years of frustration, they formally declared war on the USA to embarrass the government into fulfilling the 1855 treaty. In 2001 they numbered around 6800.

> " The Cootenais are the remnants of a once brave and powerful nation. "
>
> R. Cox, 1831

## KOYUKON

A Native North American nation of northern Alaska. They call themselves *Dene*, meaning 'people'. Originally nomadic hunters, gatherers and fishers, they speak an ATHABASKAN language, which, with 300 speakers out of a population of 2300 in 1995, is nearly extinct. The fur trade in the mid-19th century brought epidemics, worsened by the Gold Rush in 1897. The Koyukon attempted to maintain their traditional culture and subsistence during the 20th century, opposing oil extraction while seeking economic self-sufficiency. However, unemployment and alcohol abuse remain problems.

## KUIKURO–KALAPALO

A Native South American people of Brazil's Mato Grosso. Slash-and-burn CARIB-speaking farmers, they numbered under 500 in 1997.

## KUITSH

A Native North American nation of coastal Oregon. Sedentary hunters, fishers and gatherers, they spoke a Siuslawan language, which is now nearly extinct. In 1855, seriously reduced by epidemics and environmental destruction caused by settlers, they were unable to resist pressure to cede their lands in a treaty that was never honoured. They were forced onto the ALSEA reservation, where they suffered desperate poverty. Under settler pressure they were moved again in 1875. Many refused to go to the SILETZ reservation, and joined the SIUSLAW instead, where they largely vanished as a distinct nation; only 33 people claimed Kuitish identity in 1968. Their descendants can mostly be found among the Confederated Tribes of COOS, Lower Umpqua and Siuslaw. Along with the Siuslaw, their descendants have pursued compensation

for lost lands through the courts, without success to date, even although their case has reached the United Nations.

## KUMEYAAY

A Native North American nation of Baja California (Mexico) and southern California (USA). Semi-sedentary hunters and gatherers, with some groups practising agriculture, they spoke a Yuman language. They were a collection of autonomous groups more than a nation, but they still put up a stubborn resistance to SPANISH attempts to subjugate them. The disease and violence caused by the 1849 Gold Rush finally broke their resistance to settlers, and by 1875 they had lost their traditional lands. In 2000 over 2200 lived in the USA and about 1000 lived in Mexico, although they claim a much larger population, and they are striving to preserve their culture.

## KUTCHIN

See GWICH'IN.

## KWAKIUTL

A Native North American nation of coastal British Columbia, whose name probably means 'beach at the north side of the river'. Sedentary hunters, fishers and gatherers, they speak a Wakashan language. Seen as warlike by their neighbours, they practised blood feuds, head-hunting and slave-raiding. Rapid acculturation as well as diseases, however, followed large-scale contacts with whites from the early 19th century. Commercial fishing and logging became the main forms of subsistence. They established their own district council in 1974 to protect their interests, and in 1997 reached a final settlement of outstanding land claims with the provincial government. In 1991 they numbered over 4000.

## KWALHIOQUA

A former Native North American nation of southwest Washington state, whose name comes from the CHINOOK, meaning 'lonely place in the wood'. Probably semi-sedentary hunters, fishers and gatherers, they spoke an ATHABASKAN language. Never numerous, the epidemics brought by settlers nearly exterminated them. Only 15 Kwalhioqua remained in 1853, and they soon disappeared. Some may have joined other nations such as the Chinook.

## LACANDON MAYA

A Native Central American nation of south Mexico, who call themselves *Hachwinik*, meaning 'true people'. Sedentary farmers, hunters and gatherers, they spoke a Mayan language. Probably descended from the MAYA who fled into the rainforests to avoid SPANISH rule from the 17th century, they lived in small communities to avoid detection. Almost totally isolated until the mid-20th century, they were then driven almost to cultural disintegration from heavy frontier settlement, which destroyed half of their rainforest to 1993. In 1996 they numbered up to 500.

## LADINO

See MESTIZO.

## LAKE

A Native North American nation of western Washington state. They were named by the French, but called themselves *Senijextee*. Semi-sedentary hunters, fishers and gatherers, they spoke a Salishan language. Never numerous and much reduced by epidemics, in 1872 they were forced to enter the COLVILLE reservation, and their descendants are to be found among the Confederated Tribes of the Colville reservation.

## LAKOTA

A Native North American SIOUX nation of the northern Great Plains, whose name means 'allies'. Nomadic hunters and gatherers, they spoke a Siouan language.

The Lakota were driven from the Great Lakes area by the OJIBWA in the 18th century and adopted a fully nomadic lifestyle. They became completely dependent upon the bison and established a spiritual centre in the Black Hills of South Dakota. Initial encounters from 1816 with

the AMERICANS were friendly, and they ceded considerable territory, but by 1862 continued settler land encroachment caused conflict, and their 38-year resistance was the bloodiest of all the Indian Wars. Despite a number of victories, such as the Battle of the Little Bighorn (1876), the weight of US numbers and the slaughter of the bison herds doomed the Lakota.

The last gasp of resistance came in the Ghost Dance religious movement of 1890, but at Wounded Knee in the same year a group that had already surrendered was massacred. Thereafter they were confined to the poverty of reservations, mostly in South Dakota, dependent upon government supplies to survive and subject to determined government efforts to destroy their traditional culture.

In the late 20th century, however, the Lakota experienced a cultural revival and began to campaign for true sovereignty. Central to their aims is regaining the Black Hills. In 1980 US courts awarded over $100 million in compensation for this territory, but despite their desperate economic needs, the Lakota rejected this money, determined to repossess the Black Hills. In 1999 they numbered about 60,000.

## LAS VEGAS CULTURE

An ARCHAIC hunting and gathering culture that flourished on the Santa Elena peninsula of Ecuador between 10,000 and 6600 BC. The culture is known from over 30 seasonal camps and settlements.

Typically, Las Vegas people lived in small circular huts around 2 m (6.5 ft) across, with walls of cane plastered with mud. In the culture's early stages, the Las Vegas people primarily hunted land mammals, especially deer, and collected plant foods. Later, there was a gradual shift towards greater exploitation of marine resources, such as fish and shellfish from mangrove swamps, and possibly cultivated plants, such as gourds (which may have been grown mainly to make floats for fishing nets).

## LASSIK

A former Native North American nation of northwest California. Sedentary hunters, fishers

---

**Lakota: main sub-groups**

Hunkpapa
Itazipacola
Miniconjou
Oglala
Oohempa
Sicanjou
Sihasapa

---

"Lakota people have not yet developed a ritual to forgive the white man for what he did."

Lakota spokesperson Alex White Plume (1993)

and gatherers, they used controlled burning to manage their environment, and spoke an ATHABASKAN language. In the 1850s they came under great pressure from settlers and miners because of the Gold Rush. They attempted to defend their territory from interlopers and massacred a large group of CHILULA who were trying to escape captivity. They were, nevertheless, rapidly reduced, and the few survivors were absorbed by other groups.

## LATGAWA

A Native North American nation of Oregon, whose name means 'living on the uplands'. Semi-sedentary traders, hunters, fishers and gatherers, they spoke a Takilman language, which is now extinct. A small nation, much reduced by diseases, they were reduced further when they fought in the Rogue River Wars of the 1850s. The survivors were forced onto the Grand Ronde and SILETZ reservations. Most descendants are found among the Confederated Tribes of Grand Ronde.

## LATIN AMERICANS

A collective term for all the people who inhabit those modern countries of the New World settled by colonists from the Iberian peninsula, and particularly the descendants of colonists. These areas comprise all of South and Central America (with the exception of the Guianas), much of the Caribbean and Mexico. In the USA, the substantial Latin American minority is generally known as HISPANICS.

The conquest began in 1494, and the first colonists were attracted by the fabulous wealth to be won. Some did gain wealth and formed an extremely rich landowning class. The majority remained a transplanted peasantry. In various areas, depending on the size and power of their respective populations, Latin American culture was influenced by Native American elements (in cuisine, music and clothing, for example), although Catholicism remained the norm.

In the early 19th century most colonies won independence, but political fragmentation into several states resulted. Indeed, social and economic paralysis and political upheaval often led

to dictatorships as the landowning elites tried to keep their grip on power through violence and intimidation. Poverty, illiteracy and resort to revolution were the lot of the lower classes.

By 1900 a degree of prosperity and stability was secured, but it was accompanied by the growing domination of, and occasional intervention by, the USA. This has been deeply resented even while AMERICAN wealth and freedom is envied. Radical or revolutionary movements, therefore, often tended to be anti-American in character. This in turn prompted the USA to support (and sometimes install) repressive but subservient regimes, further fuelling resentments. Rates of poverty and illiteracy tend to be high, even crushing, while economic mismanagement has saddled many Latin American states with huge international debts and recurrent economic and political crises. In 2000 there were at least 500 million Latin Americans; poverty and lack of educational opportunities and political freedoms remain concerns for many of them.

## LENCA

A Native Central American nation of Honduras and El Salvador. Sedentary farmers, hunters and gatherers, they probably spoke a Chibchan language that is nearly extinct. In the 16th century they were fierce opponents of the SPANISH, and their hot and humid rainforest, which was difficult to settle, provided some protection until the 20th century. By the late 20th century, however, they faced growing incursions and in Honduras lost legal protection for their lands. Assertions of intimidation of Lenca over land claims, with official connivance, are widespread. The Lenca numbered about 140,000 in 1999 and were as concerned about economic as much as cultural survival.

## LILLOOET

A Native North American nation of southwest British Columbia, whose name means 'wild onion'. They call themselves *St'at'imc*, meaning 'traders'. Seasonally mobile within their territory, primarily as hunters, fishers and gatherers, they speak a Salishan language.

Historically divided into autonomous villages, they had difficulty dealing with the land thefts and destruction of their traditional culture that began in the mid-19th century. By 1911 they had come together to protect their interests and demand that the Canadian government address their land claims, and later protect their environment. Little progress was made, and at one point they applied for United Nations membership. By 2000 they were engaged in a campaign of civil disobedience, blockading roads to halt logging, and occupying land to stop development. In 1979 they numbered over 2500.

## LIPE

See ATACAMEÑOS.

## LUISEÑO

A Native North American nation of southern coastal California. Semi-sedentary hunters, fishers and gatherers, they spoke Uto-Aztecan dialects and lived in about 50 autonomous villages. Villages would fight their neighbours over trespassing or blood-feuds, and while SPANISH missionaries evangelized some, others resisted Christianization successfully. Their rapid decline began in the 1850s with the diseases and violence of the Gold Rush. In 1990 they numbered about 1800. In 2000 they were campaigning for a site in San Diego to honour their culture and, like the CUPEÑO, trying to protect their sacred site at Gregory Canyon from use as a landfill site.

## LULE

Two former Native South American nations of Argentina, both given the same name, meaning 'inhabitants', by invading MATACO. One, calling themselves *Cacana*, meaning 'mountaineer', lived in the Andean foothills. The other, calling themselves *Pelé*, meaning 'men', lived in the Gran Chaco. Both, however, were forced onto missions by the SPANISH, where diseases rapidly reduced their numbers. In 1692 the remnants of the Cacana fled their mission after an earthquake, and in 1767 the Pelés' mission was closed. Both peoples rapidly disappeared among the other nations of the area.

## LUMBEE

A Native North American nation of North Carolina. Sedentary farmers, they spoke a Siouan language. They were formed in the 18th century by the merger of surviving CHERAW and other Siouan-speakers, including a group claiming to be descendants of the first failed ENGLISH colony at Roanoke. By that time they had largely absorbed white culture, and developed their own unique English dialect.

In the 19th century they suffered racial discrimination and land theft. Labour conscription during the AMERICAN Civil War led them to launch a guerrilla war against the Confederacy in 1865. They became more assertive of their rights, winning state recognition in 1885, and applying for federal recognition in 1889, which was still not granted in 2002, allegedly because of the high degree of mixed blood in their nation. In 1958 they famously drove off at gunpoint an attempted rally by the Ku Klux Klan on their lands. In 1992 they numbered over 40,000.

## LUMMI

A Native North American nation of coastal Washington state, whose name means 'facing one another'. They called themselves *Nuglummi*, meaning 'people'. Sedentary hunters, fishers and gatherers, they spoke a Salishan language.

In the 1820s the Lummi entered the fur trade, which brought epidemics that were so severe that by 1850 they had abandoned their islands on Puget Sound in favour of the mainland. In 1859 the Lummi reservation was established and they were ordered to stay there and become farmers. They were not allowed to enter the commercial fishing industry until a court decision of 1974 defined their rights. Thereafter, they gained responsibility for over one-quarter of Washington's salmon catch. In 1998 they numbered about 4440.

## MACKENZIE ESKIMO

See INUIT.

## MACÚ

A native American nation of the Amazonia regions of Colombia and Brazil. They find the name 'Macú' offensive, and call themselves *Jupdá*, meaning 'people'. Mostly sedentary farmers, hunters and gatherers, they originally spoke a Tucanoan language. Often dominated by their neighbours, they have assimilated considerable CARIB and ARAWAK cultural elements. In 1995 they numbered about 1360.

## MACUSI

A Native South American nation of Guyana and neighbouring countries. Sedentary farmers, hunters and gatherers, they spoke a CARIB language. Once considered by their neighbours to be poisoners, they had lost much of their traditional culture by the 20th century as they entered the cash economy. In 1989 human-rights organizations protested when a road was constructed across Macusi territory, destroying fields and threatening them with starvation. In 1990 they numbered up to 13,000.

## MAHICAN

A Native North American nation of New York, whose name means 'people of the great river'. Sedentary farmers, hunters, gatherers and fishers, they spoke an Algonquian language.

Once a large and powerful confederacy, they eagerly entered the fur trade in the 17th century, but the resulting wars and epidemics nearly exterminated them. From about 1730 the remnants became increasingly fragmented. Some joined the ONEIDA; others re-settled in Pennsylvania and Wisconsin. One group became the STOCKBRIDGE.

They served the USA faithfully in its early wars, but received little gratitude, and only narrowly avoided forced relocation to Oklahoma in the 1830s. Closely related to the MOHEGAN, they constantly battle the popular perception, erroneously taken from J. Fennimore Cooper's book *The Last of the Mohecans*, that they are extinct. In 1996 they numbered nearly 1500 and were struggling to protect their environment, culture and their sacred sites.

## MAIDU

A Native North American nation of northern and central California whose name means simply 'people'. Sedentary hunters, fishers and gatherers, they spoke Penutian dialects and were relatively isolated because of their rugged terrain. In 1849, however, miners seeking gold attacked a Maidu village and raped several women, beginning an escalating cycle of violence and retaliation and the destruction of the Maidu's environment.

In 1863 they were forced to march at gunpoint along their own 'trail of tears' to Round Valley reservation, about one-third of them dying along the road. Even there land encroachment and vigilante killings continued, while the government attempted to destroy their culture by compulsory residential education.

In 1994 they numbered 2500 and were trying to recover their traditional culture, even regaining a small section of their traditional lands in 2002.

## MAKAH

A Native North American nation of Washington state's Olympic peninsula, whose name means 'generous with food', although they called themselves *Kwah-dich-ahtx*, meaning 'people of the rocks and seagulls'. Sedentary traders, fishers, hunters (especially of whales, which provided 80% of their diet) and gatherers, they spoke a Wakashan language.

In 1855 they were forced to cede their lands in return for guaranteed rights of fishing and whaling. Whaling, however, came to an end in the 1920s because of near extinction of grey whale stocks. But in 1999, hoping to improve their diet, and hoping that a revival of their traditional culture would help overcome the serious problems of unemployment, crime and substance abuse among their young, they exercised their treaty rights to resume limited whaling. This was done in spite of mass protests and vilification by conservationists. In 1998 they numbered approximately 1800.

## MALISEET or Malecite

A North American aboriginal nation of Quebec, New Brunswick and Maine. Their name comes from the MICMAC and means 'lazy talkers', although they call themselves *Wula'stegwi'ak*, meaning 'good river people'. Sedentary hunters, gatherers and fishers, they practised some agriculture and speak an Algonquian language.

Entering the fur trade with the FRENCH, they became embroiled in France's wars with the BRITISH in the 18th century. After their defeat in the American Revolution, the British forced most Maliseet from their lands to make room for loyalists fleeing the USA. Subsequently the Maliseet experienced a high level of acculturation. In the late 20th century they became increasingly politicized and determined to revive their traditional culture and defend their rights. This has caused problems: in 1999, when they numbered over 3000, the Maliseet, together with the Micmac, were involved in violent confrontations with whites after winning unlimited fishing rights. (See map on page 93.)

## MANDAN

A Native North American nation of North Dakota. Sedentary farmers, traders, hunters and gatherers, they spoke a Siouan language. From the late 18th century white visitors found them hospitable and eager to trade. Some found their conduct too 'civilized' for Native Americans, and romantic but implausible theories of a European origin developed (such as descent from the legendary 12th-century WELSH prince, Madoc, or from VIKING settlers). Their hospitality, however, was their undoing: close contacts made them more vulnerable to epidemics. In 1837 smallpox almost annihilated them. The survivors joined with the HIDATSA and ARIKARA, to form the Three Affiliated Tribes nation. Forced onto a reservation in 1870, most of their traditional sites were flooded because of damming in the 1950s. The survival of their traditional culture was of great importance to the population of over 1500 in 1980.

## MANHATTAN

A former Native North American nation of New York, whose name perhaps means 'place of great drunkenness'. Seasonally mobile within their territory as farmers, hunters, gatherers and fishers, they spoke an Algonquian language. A sub-group of the DELAWARE, they were famed for selling Manhattan island to the DUTCH for a few trinkets – although they probably thought they were agreeing to share it. Violence committed against 'trespassers', disease and alcohol had destroyed them as a nation by 1700. The DELAWARE and MAHICAN absorbed the remnants.

## MANSO

A former Native North American nation of New Mexico. They were nomadic hunters and gatherers, with a language perhaps Uto-Aztecan or ATHABASKAN, and they were possibly descendants of the MOGOLLON culture. In 1659 the SPANISH established a mission in their territory, with the effect of reducing them through epidemics; and the Spanish also tried to erase their culture. They resisted and, merging with the APACHE in the 17th century, lost their identity as a nation. By the 1770s they were officially extinct, although survivors were reported near El Paso in the 1880s.

## MANTEÑO

A Native South American nation of coastal Ecuador. Sedentary farmers, hunters, gatherers, fishers and traders, they were foremost a wide-ranging maritime nation, and spoke a Quechuan language, now apparently extinct. Inhabiting a confederation of trading towns, with cottage industries producing trade goods, they flourished from the 6th to the 14th centuries AD, after which the INCA conquered them. In the 1530s they were conquered by the SPANISH, and thereafter suffered exploitation and acculturation, but survived as a nation. In combination with the HUANCAVILCA, with whom they are closely associated, they numbered nearly 66,000 in 2001, and were struggling against racism and to secure land rights.

**"** In intelligence and in the arts of life the Mandans were in advance of all their kindred tribes. **"**

L.H. Morgan, 1877

# MAPUCHE

A Native South American nation of southern Chile and Argentina, whose name means 'people of the land'. Some sedentary farmers, others nomadic hunters and gatherers, they spoke Mapu-dugun. They had their own metalworking and ceramic traditions, but they are more noted for not only successfully resisting INCA invasion, but also fighting off SPANISH, and later ARGENTINIAN and CHILEAN conquest for 350 years. Adapting rapidly to the horse, they proved formidable opponents. In 1541 they burned down Santiago and cost the Spanish more lives and money than any of the Spaniards' other Native American opponents.

By 1860, however, the Mapuche were under growing pressure from the rapidly growing and land-hungry populations of Chile and Argentina, who were seizing territory and committing genocidal attacks. In desperation they formed the kingdom of Araucania and Patagonia, with a written constitution, and sought international recognition, which was denied. Their king was kidnapped and deported, although a successor still exists. In 1885 a joint Chilean and Argentinian campaign broke their last resistance. Poverty and deculturation followed, but they still hope to regain their stolen lands. In 1992 they numbered nearly 1 million.

The Huiliche, Moluche and Pehuenche are sub-groups of the Mapuche.

# MARACA CULTURE

A former Native South American culture of Brazil. Sedentary farmers, hunters, gatherers and fishers, they lived on the river-banks near the mouth of the Amazon. Their agricultural techniques were notable for their ability to improve the notoriously limited fertility of the rainforest soil. They were also noted for polychromatic ceramics, especially funerary urns.

# MARAJO CULTURE

A former Native South American culture centred on Marajo island on the Amazon. Perhaps flourishing between AD 1000 and 1400, the culture, which included ceremonial mound building and fine ceramics, appears alien to the area. Possibly the people migrated from Peru, but their origins, like the cause of their disappearance, remain a matter of speculation.

# MARICOPA

A Native North American nation of Arizona. Sedentary farmers, hunters and gatherers, they spoke a Yuman language. They called themselves *Xalychidon Piipaash*, meaning 'people who live towards the water'.

In the early 19th century they formed a close alliance with the PIMA against raiding APACHE and YUMA. They were friendly towards the USA because of this, assisting in combating marauding Apache warriors in the 1840s, and rescuing Northern troops during the American Civil War. This assistance was quickly forgotten. Settlers subsequently stole much of their lands, and even worse, diverted the Gila River to irrigate their crops, leaving Maricopa lands desolate.

In the late 20th century they campaigned vigorously to regain land and water rights, hoping to address severe social problems of poverty, unemployment, crime and alcoholism. In 2001 the Pima-Maricopa Indian Community numbered over 7000.

# MAROONS

See CIMMARONES.

# MARTINIQUAIS

Inhabitants of the Caribbean island Martinique, a dependency of France. A FRENCH colony was established in Martinique in 1635, and African slaves were imported. With the original CARIB population largely destroyed, the culture was thus predominantly European and African.

Martinique was made an Overseas Department of France (legally part of metropolitan France) after 1945, but the islanders suffered severely from unemployment and poverty. The French government encouraged emigration, which, combined with a low birth rate, resulted in one of the slowest population growths in the region. Despite heavy aid-dependency, there have been demands for independence, which the French have completely rejected. In 2003 the Martiniquais numbered nearly 426,000.

## MASSACHUSETT

A Native North American nation of eastern Massachusetts, whose name means 'at the range of hills'. Seasonally mobile within their territory as farmers, hunters, gatherers and fishers, they spoke an Algonquian language. When the *Mayflower* settlers arrived in 1620, European epidemics had already decimated the Massachusett. Intensive missionary work converted the remnants to Puritanism and they were joined by converts from other nations and became known as Praying Indians.

During King Philip's War (1675–6) some joined in the attacks on settlers; the rest narrowly avoided massacre in reprisal. Thereafter their numbers steadily declined. They never entirely vanished, however, and an uncertain number of descendants are attempting to reorganize as a nation in 1999.

## MATACO

A Native South American language and cultural identity of the Chaco plain of Argentina and Bolivia. The culture comprised some 12 nations, generally seasonally mobile within their territories as hunters and gatherers who practised limited agriculture. Most have been heavily acculturated, but 30,000 people still use the Mataco language.

## MATTAPONI

A Native North American nation of eastern Virginia. Sedentary farmers, hunters, gatherers and fishers, they spoke an Algonquian language. Once part of the POWHATAN confederacy, they fled their lands in the 1640s to avoid settler attacks, and when they returned in 1658 they accepted a reservation – one of the oldest in America. Despite strong pressure to assimilate, much of their traditional culture has been maintained, as has their sovereignty. They are currently fighting a planned reservoir that threatens their environment and indispensable fisheries, claiming it would breach their treaty of

1658. Because of the case, they are also pursuing federal recognition. In 2002 they numbered approximately 450.

## MAUÉ

A Native South American nation of Brazil's Amazonia. Sedentary farmers, fishers, hunters and gatherers, and spoke a TUPÍ language. First contacted by Jesuits in 1669, they established generally friendly contacts with missionaries, but not with other PORTUGUESE visitors. Violence became common, and punitive campaigns and trade embargoes designed to starve them into submission all failed. In the 20th century, however, despite renewed fighting from 1916, rubber-extractors stole much of their land and devastated much of their environment, forcing them to abandon a large part of their agricultural activity. Some became urbanized, living in desperate poverty, but 14 villages containing about 9000 people survived in 1994.

## MAWACA

A Native South American nation of Venezuela's Amazonia. Sedentary farmers, hunters and gatherers, they spoke a Panoan language. Little contacted until the 19th century, they became victims of rubber-extractors from 1875, particularly Tomas Funes, who by the time he was murdered in 1921 had all but exterminated them through enslavement, murder and the destruction of their means of subsistence. They recovered somewhat, and numbered perhaps 3000 in 1995, but by then pipeline and road construction again threatened their survival.

## MAYA

A Native Central American nation stretching from southern Mexico to Honduras. Sedentary farmers, hunters, gatherers and traders, they spoke dialects of Mayan. The Maya developed a series of city states with a complex social structure and highly developed architecture and ceramics, for example. Their civilization reached its peak around AD 250 but began to go into decline about 850, apparently because of diminishing food resources, probably caused by

**Maya**

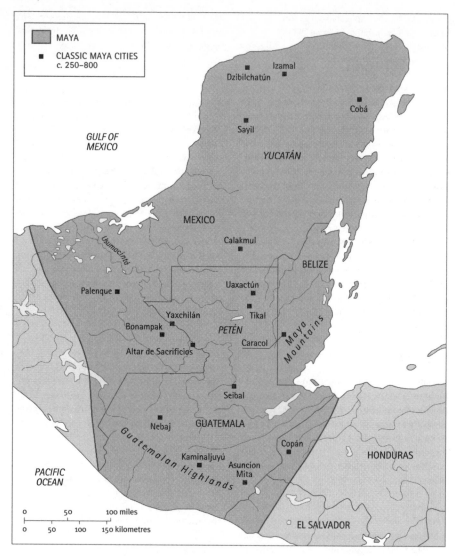

MAYA

CLASSIC MAYA CITIES
c. 250–800

*GULF OF MEXICO*

Izamal

Dzibilchatún

Cobá

Sayil

*YUCATÁN*

MEXICO

Calakmul

BELIZE

*Usumacinta*

Uaxactún

Palenque

Yaxchilán

Tikal

*Maya Mountains*

Bonampak

*PETÉN*

Caracol

Altar de Sacrificios

Seibal

Nebaj

GUATEMALA

*Guatemalan Highlands*

Copán

HONDURAS

Kaminaljuyú

Asunción Mita

*PACIFIC OCEAN*

EL SALVADOR

| 0 | 50 | 100 miles |
| 0 | 50 | 100 | 150 kilometres |

climate change. Several great cities were abandoned. When the SPANISH arrived in the early 16th century, however, the Maya were still strong enough to repel the invaders for many years, remaining undefeated until 1546.

Even after this they launched numerous rebellions against the abuses and exploitation they suffered. Between 1847 and 1901 they fought a savage war with Mexico, with atrocities committed by both sides, and were still left unsubdued. Even in the 1990s, in southern Mexico, there was another resistance movement.

Economic development and cultural preservation are serious concerns to the Maya: the repatriation of cultural artefacts is currently being pursued actively. Autonomy is another concern: a pan-Mayan movement is emerging to further the aims of the Maya in several central American countries. In 1994 they numbered over 7 million.

## MAYO

A Native North American nation of southern Sonora and northern Sinaloa, in northwest Mexico. Sedentary farmers, hunters and gatherers, they speak an Uto-Aztecan language. They welcomed the SPANISH in 1600 for aid against their traditional enemies the YAQUI and willingly accepted missionaries, which led to intense acculturation. Relations soured after silver was found on their lands, and many were conscripted to work the mines. In 1740, perhaps encouraged by Spanish officials jealous of missionary influence, they allied with the Yaqui in a war against the Spanish. More wars followed, especially in the 19th century when settlers encroached on their lands. It took decades before they were fully subjugated by Mexico. In 1982 they numbered about 30,000. At the end of the 20th century they were attempting to regain their traditional culture, although poverty and lack of education were more immediate concerns to many.

## MBAYA

A Native South American nation of the frontier of Brazil and Paraguay, whose name comes from the GUARANÍ and means 'savage'. Nomadic fishers, hunters and gatherers, they spoke a Guaycuran language. They constantly raided the Guaraní, who in 1542 allied with the SPANISH and inflicted a major defeat on them. The Mbaya soon acquired horses, however, and raiding continued until the mid-18th century when peace was agreed. Missionaries subsequently persuaded some to become sedentary farmers. Others clung to a precarious lifestyle as their lands were whittled away. In 1995 they numbered up to 1800. The Kadiweu are a sub-group of the Mbaya.

## MEHERRIN

A Native North American nation of coastal Virginia and North Carolina, whose name means 'people of the muddy water'. Sedentary farmers, hunters, fishers and gatherers, they spoke an Iroquoian language. In the mid-17th century they entered the fur trade and in 1677 signed a treaty

with Virginia. As their lands came under pressure from settlers, relations soured and during the TUSCARORA War (1711–13) they provided guns and shelter, and many merged with the Tuscarora. They won a new treaty and a reservation in 1718, but soon their lands were stolen again. Several stayed in their traditional territory and in 1986 they won recognition from North Carolina, but in 2002 still sought federal recognition. In 1998 they numbered about 600.

## MENOMINEE

A Native North American nation of Wisconsin, whose name means 'good seed' or 'wild rice gatherers'. Sedentary farmers, hunters, gatherers and fishers, they spoke an Algonquian language. Entering the fur trade and an alliance with the French in the 18th century, they suffered disastrous wars and epidemics as a result. In 1854, after a series of treaties, they accepted a reservation but resisted attempts to force them to farm. Instead they took to selling their timber commercially, and became known for their forestry. Subsequently they resisted repeated attempts to defraud them of their forest-lands. In 1909 the government supplied a modern sawmill, but refused to allow the Menominee to manage it themselves. In order to gain control, they accepted de-recognition in 1954. This proved financially disastrous, and they regained recognition in 1973. In 1993 they numbered about 3500 and were engaged in protecting their environment, especially from mining.

## MESCALERO

See APACHE.

## MESTIZO

A term generally used in South and Central America for those of mixed European and Native American ancestry. They form a large, sometimes majority, proportion of the population of several Latin American countries. Usually they are subsumed within the dominant cultures. The term 'mestizo' can have social and cultural connotations, and is also used to refer to any Native American who adopts a dominant culture. In

Guatemala, the Mestizo are known as Ladino.

No meaningful population estimate across the American continent is possible, as only recently have any countries counted them separately in official censuses.

## MÉTIS

A nation of western Canada and along the Canadian–US border, whose name comes from the French and means 'to mix'. They are descendants of Native North Americans (often CREE and OJIBWA) and Europeans, generally SCOTTISH and FRENCH. They speak a language combining those elements. Emerging in the 17th century, they found themselves increasingly marginalized by settler society; communities drifted westwards in the late-19th century and adopted a nomadic plains lifestyle as traders, hunters, gatherers and fishers. Their great problems came from the refusal of the Canadian government to treat them as a nation and accept their land and treaty rights. The Métis fought to defend their lands 1869–70 and in 1885. The government offered them scrip, exchangeable for land or cash, to settle their claims, but many sold them to speculators at a fraction of their value and were left with only poverty and discrimination. Although they became active in defending their rights, for example by launching lawsuits in 2002 over lands promised but never delivered, they still face the problem of agreeing with the authorities on a definition of 'Métis'. Their own definition, which is based on mixed descent, self-identification and acceptance by their own communities, has yet to win wide acceptance in Canada. In 2001 they numbered nearly 300,000.

In 2003, the Canadian Supreme Court reached a landmark decision. By accepting that the Métis had a constitutional right to hunt and fish for subsistence, they recognized that the Métis had equality under the law to the INUIT and other native Canadian peoples. This will enable them to defend their rights and freedoms far more vigorously in the future.

## MEXICANS

The population of Mexico, officially the United Mexican States, a country that straddles North and Central America. Once home to several highly developed nations, Mexico came fully under SPANISH rule by the 1540s, winning independence only in 1821. Today its people are mostly MESTIZO and Spanish-speaking, with about 7% retaining Native American languages.

With a culture influenced by European and Native American elements, Mexico's politics have been dominated by the gulf between rich and poor. In the 19th century Mexico was notably revolution-prone, and was humiliated in wars with Texas (1836) and the USA (1846–8), and further by AMERICAN military interventions (1914 and 1916–17), suppressing radicals who threatened US commercial interests. These defeats, as well as continued economic domination by its powerful northern neighbour, have been the source of burning resentment. Indeed, rapid economic growth has in no degree matched massive population growth. Mexicans numbered nearly 102 million in 2001, two-thirds of whom were urban-dwellers. For too many, unemployment, poverty and the lack of opportunities were the norm, with the USA often blamed. The recent NAFTA (the North American Free Trade Agreement) with the USA and Canada remains controversial.

For the Native American population conditions have been generally worse than for the rest of Mexicans, prompting the Zapatista revolution in 1994: then, the government, willing to tolerate such suffering, confronted the armed challenge from Native Americans, who attracted worldwide attention and sympathy.

## MIAMI

A Native North American nation originally of the Michigan area, whose name means 'peninsula dwellers'. Sedentary farmers, hunters, gatherers and fishers, they spoke an Algonquian language. Originally part of the ILLINOIS confederacy, they split off around the beginning of the 18th century on account of religious disputes and moved to Ohio, where they became powerful allies of the FRENCH. Alarmed at settler pressure, they aided the BRITISH during the American Revolution, and were subdued only after three campaigns, culminating in the Battle of Fallen Timbers in 1794. After being defrauded of

*m*

" [We salute you for] the long struggle of your Miccosukee Nation and the perseverance and courage of your indomitable and freedom-loving people... "

Fidel Castro (1959)

their remaining lands, most moved to Indiana, but many were forcibly re-settled in Kansas in the 1820s, only to be moved to Oklahoma in the 1870s. In 2000, after a failed land claim, they resorted to suing individual white farmers for illegally taken lands, which the farmers denounced as a land-grab. In 1993 they numbered over 4000, mainly in Oklahoma and Indiana.

## MICCOSUKEE

A Native North American nation of Florida's everglades, who chose this name in 1962. Sedentary farmers, hunters, fishers and gatherers, they spoke a Muskogean language. Originally part of the SEMINOLE, they avoided removal under the 1830 Act by retreating deep into the everglades. Agriculture was difficult and they came to rely on trade. In 1947, when the creation of Everglades National Park banned hunting and fishing in many of their traditional lands, they sought federal recognition, winning it in 1958. The following year they became the only Native American nation to win international recognition through a treaty with Cuba, to the fury of the AMERICAN government. In 2000 they claimed a population of about 650, but the census of that year failed to record a single Miccosukee. This led to widespread outrage and demands for a recount (the census results being used to calculate federal funding).

Maliseet, Micmac

## MICMAC

An aboriginal nation of eastern Canada, whose name perhaps means 'allies'. Seasonally mobile within their territory as traders, hunters, gatherers and fishers, they practised limited agriculture and speak an Algonquian language. Allies of the FRENCH from the early 17th century, they were responsible for the survival of early French colonies. The fur trade made them wealthy and allowed them to expand their territory, even as it undermined them through disease. After the American Revolution, needing land to re-settle displaced loyalists, the BRITISH whittled away the Micmac's land, leaving them in poverty and increasingly dependent on the wage economy, most notably in high-rise construction. In the late 20th century they became more politicized in defence of their rights. In the 1990s they blockaded roads to protest against damage to their environment, especially their fisheries. This led, in 1999, to violent confrontations with whites angered by their new-won rights to fish without the usual restrictions. During these confrontations the Micmac complained that the police were failing to protect them. In 2001 they were estimated to number over 19,000 in Canada, with several thousand more in the USA. (See also MALISEET, and the map on page 93.)

## MIMBRES

A former Native North American culture of the New Mexico area. Sedentary farmers, hunters and gatherers, the people produced fine ceramic art, typically depicting human and animal figures on white vessels, and are sometimes associated with the MOGOLLON. First appearing about AD 200, their communities became larger and more complex, but suddenly, around 1150, they abandoned their large sites. A few communities survived for several generations. The cause of their collapse is unclear; there is no evidence of warfare. Overpopulation, unsustainable farm techniques and drought are all possible causes.

## MINNESOTA SWEDES

An AMERICAN culture of European origin. A wave of SWEDISH immigrants, seeking to escape from economic stagnation, peaked in the 1880s. Many were attracted to Minnesota, where land suitable to their traditional farming methods was available. Families and friends joined them, and a considerable community developed (although not as large as that in California). Often stereotyped as heavy-drinking and simple, they still prospered. In the 20th century they were also making strenuous efforts to preserve Swedish culture in the USA. In 1990 they numbered nearly 540,000.

## MISSION INDIANS

A collective name for the Native Americans, largely of California, including the GABRILENO and CASTANOAN, whom the Spanish managed to confine on missions between 1769 and 1823. These missions were intended to be 'civilizing agencies' that would spread Catholicism and produce useful serfs for landowners. Disease rapidly reduced their populations, destroyed much of their cultures and made them dependent. When the missions were closed in 1834 the Mission Indians were rapidly robbed of their lands, and the violence and diseases ushered in by the Gold Rush drove them to near-extinction. In 1990 over 2000 identified themselves as Mission Indians, but the number of descendants is a matter of speculation.

## MISSISSIPPIAN TEMPLE MOUND CULTURE

A former Native North American culture that stretched at least from Alabama to Illinois. Sedentary farmers, hunters and gatherers, the people had a very extensive trade network, as well as a complex social system and religion, which seems to have involved human sacrifice. The last temple mound culture historically, it arose around AD 700 and built great cities, such as Cahokia, Illinois (with a population of perhaps 20,000). From around 1200 it began to decline, possibly from overpopulation coupled with climate change. In the 16th century the first European epidemics decimated the survivors, and the FRENCH completed the destruction by exterminating the NATCHEZ. Descendants might be found among the CREEK and CHEROKEE.

# MISSOURI

A Native North American nation originally of Missouri, whose name means 'people with dugout canoes', although they call themselves *Niutachi*, 'people of the river mouth'. Seasonally mobile as farmers, hunters, gatherers and fishers, they spoke a Siouan language.

The Missouri were closely related to the OTO, but the two split in the 17th century over the seduction of a leader's daughter. This left both peoples vulnerable to attack, with epidemics and warfare rapidly reducing them, and thus they reunited around 1829. In 1854 they were forced to cede their lands and accept a reservation in Nebraska, before being relocated to Oklahoma in the 1880s. In 1953 they became the first Native American nation to win a land claim against the USA. In 1993 the Oto-Missouri numbered over 1400 and were trying to reverse severe cultural erosion. The last fluent language-speaker died in 1996.

# MIWOK

A Native North American nation of central California, whose name means 'people'. Mostly sedentary hunters, fishers and gatherers, they spoke a Penutian language, which has all but disappeared. They were generally peaceful and little able to resist the attacks of Mexican settlers from the 1820s, and the hordes attracted by the 1849 Gold Rush. Those who survived could only marginally subsist as labourers. There are several bands of Miwok with a combined population of about 3380 in 1990, but only two bands were federally recognized. The other bands were seeking such recognition in 2000, hoping it would help recover both traditional lands and culture.

# MIXE

A Native Central American nation of southern Mexico. Sedentary farmers, hunters and gatherers, they speak Mixe-Zoque. Descended from the OLMEC, they maintained their independence from the AZTEC and ZAPOTEC. The SPANISH conquered their territory in 1521 but never truly subdued them. Rather, the Mixe gave the appearance of conformity while clinging to their

traditional culture, for example by burying their idols beneath Christian altars. Stereotyped as stupid and suspicious by the Spanish, they were in fact aloof and deeply conservative culturally. In 1993 they numbered over 100,000.

# MIXTEC

A Native Central American nation of central Mexico. Mainly farmers who hunted and gathered as a secondary occupation, they spoke Mixteco. Descendants of the OLMEC, in about AD 900 they conquered territory from the ZAPOTEC, with whom they enjoyed considerable cultural fusion. In 1497 they together defeated the AZTEC, but were conquered by the SPANISH after 1521, subsequently losing 80% of their population to exploitation and disease. In the 20th century soil erosion and poverty forced many to become often-exploited migrant workers, especially in the USA. In 1995 they numbered over 300,000.

# MOBILE

A former Native North American nation of Alabama and eastern Mississippi, whose name might come from the CHOCTAW and means 'to paddle'. Sedentary farmers, hunters, fishers and gatherers, they spoke a Muskogean language. They built ceremonial and burial mounds and stockaded towns. They fought the SPANISH from the 16th century and became FRENCH allies. Epidemics and constant warfare caused their destruction. By 1763 they had vanished, and the Choctaw probably absorbed the remnants.

# MOCHICA

A former Native South American nation of northern coastal Peru. Sedentary irrigation farmers, fishers, hunters and gatherers, they were a complex society, producing textiles, ceramics and metalwork as well as being seafarers and traders. Successors to the CHAVÍN, they emerged as a culture about 100 BC. They expanded by conquest until about AD 500. They were overthrown by the HUARI by 800. Some of their ceramics suggest either Oriental or African features, leading to romantic but unproven theories of a migratory origin.

## MOCOVÍ

A Native South American nation of Argentina's Gran Chaco. Nomadic hunters and gatherers, they spoke a Waikwan language. Acquiring horses in the late 16th century, they put up a ferocious resistance to SPANISH conquest, destroying major towns and massacring their populations, acquiring a fearsome reputation for atrocities. In 1710 the Spanish launched a major offensive against them, and conquered some of their territory. In 1743 Jesuits established a mission among them and the process of forcible settlement and acculturation began. The Spanish expelled the Jesuits in 1767, however, and most Mocoví returned to their traditional lifestyles. By the 19th century warfare and diseases were reducing them, and in 1904 Argentina inflicted a final defeat on them, massacring many and trying their own forcible acculturation policies. In 1984 they established a centre to resist this pressure, reverse the decline of their language, and seek international support in pursuit of land rights. In 1993 they numbered about 60,000.

## MODOC

A Native North American nation of the California and Oregon border area, whose name comes from the KLAMATH and means 'southerners'. Semi-sedentary hunters, fishers and gatherers, they spoke a Penutian language. From the 1840s settlers heading towards Oregon began to drive through their territory, destroying game and spreading diseases. Frequent skirmishes, epidemics and starvation forced them to accept a treaty in 1864, confining them to the Klamath reservation in Oregon and the QUAPAW reservation in Oklahoma. In 1870 hunger and poverty led Modoc leader Kintpuash ('Captain Jack') to lead a band back to their traditional lands. They ignored the settlers, who still clamoured for their removal, which the US Army achieved after pursuing them for about a year. When some were eventually allowed to return to their traditional lands, they found they had been stolen, and they shared the Klamath reservation. In 1990 they numbered about 500.

## MOGOLLON

A former Native North American culture of the Arizona area. Usually seasonally mobile within their territory as farmers, hunters and gatherers, the people flourished between about 200 BC to AD 1400. Developing a highly stylized art in their ceramics and petroglyphs (rock inscriptions) they eventually became strongly influenced by the ANASAZI. In the 13th century the culture suddenly disappeared for no clearly understood reason. There might be descendants among the HOPI and ZUÑI.

## MOHAVE or Mojave

A Native North American nation of southern California and southwest Arizona who spoke a Yuman language. Semi-sedentary farmers as well as hunters, fishers and gatherers, their name means 'going wrong', a reference to their creation myth. They were warlike, and fought white encroachment fiercely from the 1820s. After defeat by the US Army in 1859 they were located on the Colorado River reservation in Arizona, where poverty and disease, alongside largely successful government efforts to destroy their culture, turned most into urban wage-earners. In the late 20th century they were trying to promote their sovereignty and economic self-reliance as well as protect their environment. In 1996 they numbered about 1500.

## MOHAWK

A Native North American nation originally of New York, now also of Quebec and Ontario. They call themselves *Kanien'kehake*, meaning 'people of the flint'. Sedentary farmers, hunters, gatherers and fishers, they spoke an Iroquoian language. Once part of the IROQUOIS league, its demise in the late 18th century caused many to seek refuge in Canada. They continue, however, to disregard the international frontier dividing their nation, and have proven militant in protecting their heritage. In 1990 they were involved in a major confrontation with Canadian authorities at Oka (Kanesahtake) over municipal plans to expand a golf course over a sacred site. In 1997 they numbered about 10,000.

# MOHEGAN

A Native North American nation of Connecticut, whose name perhaps means 'wolf'. Seasonally mobile within their territory as farmers, hunters, gatherers and fishers, they spoke an Algonquian language. Once part of the PEQUOT, they split off over a dynastic dispute in the 1630s and became allies of the ENGLISH. The wars and epidemics of the fur trade seriously reduced them in subsequent decades, and they became fragmented. Some became the BROTHERTOWN. Others remained in Connecticut, but were robbed of their lands in 1861 – a legal case concerning this is currently unresolved.

Much of the Mohegan traditional culture has been lost, although attempts were made in the 20th century to rebuild and preserve it. One result of this has been a very bitter legal battle over which of several groups claiming Mohegan descent has the right to use the name. Consequently their numbers are highly debatable, although the main group numbered nearly 1500 in 2002. (See also MAHICAN.)

# MOJO

A Native South American nation of Bolivia's Amazonia. Nomadic hunters, gatherers and fishers, they spoke an Arawakan language. They lived in autonomous bands, which often fought each other, and the INCA only temporarily subdued them in 1460. The SPANISH claimed the Mojo were cannibals and drunkards, but others noted their skill in boat-building, pottery and music. From 1674 many Mojo were gathered onto missions, but they became targeted by PORTUGUESE slave-raiders, and, suffering also diseases, they were drastically reduced. Those who avoided the missions adopted extensive animal husbandry, and by 1990 they were involved in territorial and environmental disputes with the BOLIVIAN government. They numbered about 30,000 in 1990, a threefold increase since 1970.

# MOLUCHE

See MAPUCHE.

# MOMPOX

A former Native South American nation of the Bolivian and Colombian rainforests. Sedentary in large palisaded villages, they were intensive farmers, as well as hunter-gatherers, and spoke a Chocoan language (now extinct). In a relatively complex society, they had hereditary leadership and were noted for the construction of great liana bridges. They do not appear to have survived long as a nation after white contact.

# MONACAN

A Native North American nation of West Virginia, whose name perhaps comes from the POWHATAN and means 'sword'. Sedentary farmers, hunters, gatherers, fishers and traders (especially of the copper they mined), they spoke a Siouan language. Once a confederation, the sub-groups merged into a nation as land loss and warfare reduced them by the late 18th century. Their subsequent experiences were of severe racial discrimination, and they subsisted largely through sharecropping or wage labour, which had a dire impact on their traditional culture. Finally gaining state recognition in 1989, their foremost aim is to regain land, notably their sacred site at Bear Mountain. In 2002 they numbered about 1400.

# MONO

A Native North American nation of eastern California. Semi-sedentary hunters and gatherers, they spoke an Uto-Aztecan language. In the 1850s the hordes attracted by the Gold Rush rapidly stole their lands. Most Mono were reduced to wage-labourers, plagued by unemployment and poverty. In 2001 there were 375 (probably a fraction of Mono descendants) on three California *rancherias* (settlements).

# MONTAGNAIS

See INNU.

# MONTAUK

A Native North American nation of Long Island, New York, whose name perhaps means 'hilly land'. Sedentary farmers, hunters, gatherers, whalers and fishers, they spoke an Algonquian language.

In the mid-17th century the Montauk became allies of the ENGLISH against local DUTCH settlers, and in 1702, not understanding the concept of owning land, ceded territory in return for continuing subsistence rights within it. Many subsequently joined the BROTHERTOWN as growing pressure from settlers made subsistence increasingly difficult. The remainder lost their last lands by very dubious means, when a land speculator, Arthur Benson, persuaded many to sign away their rights for as little as $10 in 1879. In 1910, during a legal attempt to reclaim their treaty rights, a State Supreme Court judge decided that they were extinct as a nation. In 2002, however, they numbered over 300 and were still trying to regain recognition.

## MONTSERRATIANS

Inhabitants of the BRITISH dependency of Montserrat, a Caribbean island southeast of Puerto Rico. The Spanish destroyed the original ARAWAK population, paving the way for colonization by the ENGLISH in 1632; English settlers were soon joined by IRISH refugees from Oliver Cromwell's regime in the 1650s. A plantation economy was established and African slaves were imported, having a profound impact on the culture of the colony.

In the 1960s independence entered the Montserratian political agenda, but fears for their economic prospects deterred a majority from ever voting for it. In 1997, when they numbered about 12,000, catastrophe struck with the eruption of the Souffriere Hills volcano. This forced half the population to flee and destroyed half of the island, rendering the Montserratians even more aid-dependent.

## MOSQUITO or Miskito

A Native Central American nation of the Atlantic coast of Honduras and Nicaragua. Sedentary farmers, hunters, fishers and gatherers, they spoke a Chibchan language. Their inhospitable terrain allowed them to resist SPANISH conquest. They accepted runaway African slaves and had

**"** They [the Mosquito] are very ingenious at throwing the lance, ... harpoon, or any manner of dart, being bred to it from their infancy. **"**

William Dampier, 1697

warm relations with European pirates, both of whom strongly influenced their culture. Under BRITISH protection in the 18th century, they were abandoned to Honduras and Nicaragua by 1860. In the 20th century they were drawn into the cash economy, but managed a degree of autonomy until the Sandanista revolution in Nicaragua (1979). Thereafter unwise Sandanista policies drove them to support the AMERICAN-backed Contras, and turned their territory into a war zone. In 1987, however, they won limited autonomy, but major concerns such as resource piracy and unexploded ordnance remained unsolved. In 1993 they numbered over 183,000.

## MOUNTAIN

An aboriginal nation of the Canadian sub-Arctic, whose name is a translation of their name for themselves: *Sihta Gotine*. Nomadic hunters, gatherers and fishers, they speak an ATHABASKAN language. The harsh environment occupied by the Mountain often caused starvation and kept their numbers low. Both the fur trade in the 19th century – which they exploited through very large, moose-hide-covered boats – and a gold rush in 1898 reduced them further by diseases. By then, most Mountain had become sedentary. In 1995 they numbered up to 150.

## MOVIMA

A Native South American nation of Bolivia's Amazonia. They were seasonally mobile within their territory as farmers (at least after they were evangelized in the 18th century), hunters and gatherers, and spoke Movima, a language now nearly extinct. They were under constant threat of massacre and land theft from MESTIZO settlers, and in the 20th century their survival was uncertain. Probably numbering about 1000 in 1976, they were subsequently victims of AMERICAN efforts to eliminate coca-growing, which undermined their subsistence further.

## MUCKLESHOOT

A Native North American nation of coastal Washington state. Sedentary hunters, fishers and gatherers, they spoke a Salishan language. They joined with others to resist the flood of settlers entering the region in the Puget Sound Indian War (1855–6). Defeat left them confined to a small reservation, where they were forced to absorb the remnants of other nations. In 1974, after a series of protests known as the 'fish wars', they were awarded half of the salmon catch on their traditional lands. In 2002 the extent of those lands was still the subject of litigation, when the Muckleshoot numbered some 3000.

# MUNDURUCÚ

A Native South American nation of Brazil's Amazonia. They call themselves *Weidyenye*, meaning 'our own'. Sedentary farmers, hunters and gatherers, they spoke a TUPÍ language. Willing to trade with settlers, they came under increasing land pressure, and participated in the Cabanos War (1832–40) against landowners. Their resistance continued until its final tragic phase in the 'Mundurukania revolt' of 1938, when defeat was followed by wholesale slaughter. In 1996 their lands were again threatened by gold-seekers, and in 1997 by road construction. Their spirit of resistance resurfaced as they threatened to kill invaders. In 1999 they numbered over 7000.

# MUNSEE

A Native North American nation of Ohio, whose name means 'people of the stony country'. Sedentary farmers, hunter-gatherers and fishers, they spoke an Algonquian language. Once part of the DELAWARE, they became a separate nation in 1805, when they accepted a treaty ceding vast territories south of Lake Erie. Settlers pushed them further west, and the Munsee divided after Moravian missionaries converted many. From the mid-19th century there was a STOCKBRIDGE-Munsee settlement in Wisconsin, and Moravian Munsee communities in Kansas and southern Ontario. They numbered about 1400 in 1996.

# MURA

A Native South American nation of Brazil's Amazonia. Sedentary slash-and-burn farmers, thus requiring periodic relocation as soil became exhausted, they were also fishers, hunters and gatherers and probably spoke a TUPÍ language. From the early 18th century, because of the depredations of PORTUGUESE slavers, they repeatedly attacked travellers, traders and settlers. They also expanded at the expense of other nations weakened by the same depredations and disease. Punitive expeditions and calls for their extermination failed, and they were finally defeated only in the 1830s. Considerable acculturation and decline through diseases followed. So did environmental destruction, and in 1996 illegal loggers murdered several Mura who were attempting to defend their lands, while the government did little to protect them. In 1990 they numbered about 1600. The Mura-Pirahã are a sub-group of the Mura, isolated until recently and numbering about 150 in 1990.

# NAHUA

A Native South American nation of Peru's Amazonia. Seasonally mobile within their territory as fishers and hunter-gatherers, they spoke a Panoan language. In the late 19th century they fell victim to rubber-extractors, who brought enslavement, disease and murder. Survivors fled into the rainforest and remained isolated, apart from occasional raids by miners and loggers, until 1984. Disease brought by illegal loggers decimated them again, and oil explorers later continued their depletion. In 2000 they numbered about 250.

# NAKIPA

A former Native North American nation of Baja California, Mexico. Nomadic hunters, fishers and gatherers, they spoke a Yuman language. Highly suspicious of the SPANISH, they were persuaded to settle at missions only with great difficulty, and there diseases decimated their numbers. With the closure of the missions in 1823 the remnants of the Nakipa scattered and disappeared among the general population.

# NAKOTA

A Native North American nation of the northern Great Plains, whose name means 'allies'. Sedentary farmers, hunters and gatherers, they spoke a

| Nakota: main sub-groups |
| --- |
| Yankton |
| Yanktonai |

Siouan language. Their major sub-groups include the Yankton and the Yanktonai. Part of the sioux, they were driven from the Great Lakes area by the ojibwa in the 18th century. Unlike the lakota and dakota, they were determined to avoid conflict with americans and ceded vast territories in the 1850s, receiving little in return. Now scattered in reservations in the Dakotas and Montana, their traditional culture was eroded, and the promised economic self-sufficiency never arrived. Poverty became endemic. In the late 20th century they attempted to revive their traditional culture, including the sacred pipe ritual. In 1997 they numbered about 10,000.

## NAMBICUARA

A Native South American nation of Brazil's Amazonia, whose name perhaps comes from the tupí and means 'pierced-ear'. Nomadic fishers and hunters-gatherers, they probably spoke a Gê language. Their autonomous bands were usually hostile to settlers, and they were relatively isolated until the 1970s. Epidemics, land theft and starvation then killed many. In the 1990s they were granted legally defined lands, but heavily armed illegal loggers continued to violate their territory. In 1983 they numbered about 1025.

## NANAIMO

A Native North American nation of Vancouver Island, British Columbia. They call themselves *Snuneymuxw*, 'big, strong nation'. Sedentary hunter-gatherers and fishers, they speak a Salishan language. Longhouse dwellers, they had a strong oral tradition that was severely eroded on contact with settlers in the mid-19th century. They never received all the lands promised in a treaty of 1854 and later faced a determined effort via residential schools to erase their traditional culture. In the early 21st century they were negotiating a new treaty, seeking compensation, sovereignty and economic self-sufficiency. In 1995 they numbered around 1200.

## NANSEMOND

A Native North American nation of Virginia whose name means 'one who goes to fish'.

Sedentary farmers, hunters, gatherers and fishers, they spoke an Algonquian language, now extinct. In 1609 they expelled colonists from Jamestown who attempted to encroach on their lands, but thereafter were willing to trade food with them. They became the colony's granary, and remained peaceful during the powhatan War in 1622. Driven from their lands anyway, they fought back in the Second Virginia War of 1644–6. They suffered generations of racial prejudice, and while they gained a reservation in 1677, it proved unviable and was sold in 1786, after which they began to fragment.

In the 20th century they attempted to revive a traditional culture and gained state recognition. There was, however, much opposition to federal recognition in 2002, from fear that they would introduce casinos. In 1997 they numbered about 300.

## NANTICOKE

A Native North American nation of Maryland, whose name means 'seashore dwellers'. Sedentary farmers, traders, hunters, gatherers and fishers, they spoke an Algonquian language. Their early contacts with colonists in the 1640s were violent, when livestock wandering into their fields was killed, leading to reprisals.

Between 1668 and 1742 they accepted five treaties, but none stopped the encroachment and violence of squatters. In the 1740s most Nanticoke quit their remaining lands. Some joined the delaware, while others continued to Canada. Those who remained were assimilated, but they retained still an identity, and in 2000 a federation of clergymen apologised on behalf of the white man for the atrocities they had suffered. Their current numbers are uncertain.

## NARRAGANSETT

A Native North American nation of the Rhode Island area. Seasonally mobile within their territory as farmers, hunters, gatherers and fishers, they spoke an Algonquian language. They supported the English in the pequot War of 1636–7 and were promised a share of the lands conquered. Instead they lost land, and as a result stood neutral in King Philip's War (1675–6).

When they refused to surrender WAMPANOAG refugees to the colonists, they were attacked. Large numbers were massacred in the Great Swamp Fight, and many survivors were sold as slaves. They were awarded a reservation, but in 1880 Rhode Island unilaterally terminated it, and the federal government refused to intervene despite the state's illegal conduct.

The Narragansett only gained redress in 1978. In 1990 they numbered over 2500 and were campaigning to recover some of their ancestral lands.

## NASKAPI

See INNU.

## NATCHEZ

A former Native North American nation of southwest Mississippi. They called themselves *Theloel*, its meaning uncertain. Sedentary farmers, hunters, fishers and gatherers, they probably spoke a Muskogean language. Living in nine villages under the absolute rule of a religious and political leader, the Great Sun, they built temple mounds and worshipped the sun.

The FRENCH established a trading post among them in 1713, followed by colonists. Abuse and violence turned the Natchez against the French. In 1729 the French ordered the evacuation of the main Natchez village in order to make room for a tobacco plantation, provoking a war. The Natchez fled a French attack and built a stronghold on Sicily Island, where the French captured most of the population in 1731. Those (including the Great Sun) not burned at the stake were sold as slaves in the West Indies. Some fled and joined other nations. Many claim Natchez descent among the EDISTO.

## NATIVE AMERICANS

A term to describe all of the native nations of the New World, although often more specifically the native peoples of North America. (The term s 'First Nations' or 'aboriginal' are often used in Canada, while 'Amerindians' retains currency in parts of Central and South America.) 'Indians' and even 'American Indians' are now considered obsolete and even insulting terms for Native Americans, resting as they do on a geographical and historical misunderstanding.

Their experiences, cultures and subsistence patterns are in fact highly diverse. Although they are often romanticized as a wise people living in harmony with their environment, they exploited it, as all peoples do, and as the disappearance of several cultures such as the ANASAZI shows, occasionally misused it disastrously.

Native Americans have in common a record of catastrophe from the arrival of white colonists. Diseases against which they had no immunity swept the continent, killing vast numbers. In North America these were spread repeatedly when whites introduced the fur trade. Game depletion caused territorial wars, made bloodier by guns and horses. Generally having no concept of private land ownership, they were easily cheated of their lands. Some groups such as the LAKOTA attempted to resist, while others, such as the FIVE CIVILIZED TRIBES, tried to assimilate. The AMERICAN government, however, claimed a Manifest Destiny to conquer and settle the entire continent, and swept them aside.

Popular Social Darwinist theories convinced many whites that the extinction of the Native Americans was inevitable. Common white practice was to confine them in reservations until they died out or were assimilated. When, at the end of the 19th century, many groups survived, reservation lands were allotted to individuals, in order to undermine the unity of the nations and to allow most remaining land to be expropriated. Intense efforts were made to use education as a means of undermining traditional cultures.

Many Native American nations survived, however, and in the 20th century they became more vocal and politically active in their own defence. In 2000 their combined populations in North America numbered nearly 2.5 million. Poverty, lack of sovereignty and cultural survival still, however, remain major issues to most of them. While many have come to terms with the USA and Canada, and identify themselves with these states, there remains a bitter sense of grievance at past and present injustices. To many of these nations only true sovereignty and an adequate economic base could reconcile them with the modern states they inhabit.

*n*

**"** The utmost good faith shall always be observed towards the Indians; their lands and property shall never be taken from them without their consent. **"**

Northwest Ordinance, enacted by the US Congress, 1787

## NAVAJO

A Native North American nation of Arizona, Utah and New Mexico, who call themselves *Diné*, which means 'people'. Sedentary farmers, hunters, herders and gatherers, they spoke an ATHABASKAN language.

They had established their territory by the 13th century, and adopted much of the culture of the neighbouring PUEBLO peoples, including farming. By 1775, however, pressure from the SPANISH and COMANCHE forced them further west to the area of Canyon de Chelly. The Navajo were not excessively warlike, but were willing to raid in reprisal for slaver attacks, or if crops failed. This caused problems in their dealings with the AMERICAN government, which found it impossible to establish a treaty binding all the autonomous groups. In response, the US army undertook a campaign to suppress Navajo independence, destroying villages, crops and livestock in the mid-19th century.

In 1864, about half the Navajo were forced on a 300-mile march to Bosue Redondo. Stragglers were simply killed or left for slavers; disease and starvation killed more when they arrived. A reservation on their own lands was established in 1868, but the land was arid and the Navajo lacked the means to re-establish themselves. There were soon bitter complaints of Navajo encroachmnt on HOPI land, beginning a dispute that continued into the 21st century. Coal found on their lands did provide much-needed funds in the 20th century, but strip-mining has caused environmental problems, not least in depleting aquifer water resources. They numbered over 220,000 in 1998, most of whom retained their traditional language.

## NAZCA CULTURE

A former Native South American culture of southern coastal Peru. Sedentary farmers, hunters and gatherers, the culture, perhaps originating with the PARACAS, had developed by the 2nd century BC and lasted until about the 7th century AD, when the HUARI apparently overthrew the Nazca. They produced notably fine textile and polychromatic ceramics, which influenced successor cultures in the region. Their most noteworthy achievement, however, was the Nazca Lines, patterns drawn on the desert floor, in a climate ideally suited to preserve them. These patterns, including accurate geometrical shapes and creatures, some several kilometres long, serve no known purpose, and could not even be viewed except from a great height. They have been the source of a great array of romantic speculation, not least from ufologists. Perhaps the Nazca drew them simply because they could.

## NEUTRAL

A former Native North American nation of New York state, whose name was given by the French. Sedentary farmers, hunters, gatherers and fishers, they spoke an Iroquoian language. They were a militarist society, but living between the HURON and IROQUOIS they allowed raiding parties to cross their territory as long as they were peaceful while there. After the destruction of the Huron nation in 1649, however, many Huron took refuge among the Neutral, which provoked an Iroquois assault that broke Neutral resistance in 1651. The SENECA absorbed some; the rest dispersed, ceasing to exist as a nation.

## NEWFOUNDLANDERS

An eastern Canadian culture of primarily FRENCH, ENGLISH and IRISH origin, based on the large island of Newfoundland. Initially valued only for its offshore fishing grounds, Newfoundland remained sparsely populated by settlers until the 19th century, by which time the original BEOTHUK population had been almost exterminated, although the MICMAC, who also originally resided there, remained strong.

In 1832 an elected assembly was formed, largely dominated by a Protestant middle class. The largely Catholic working class remained utterly dependent on the cod industry. Collapsing fish stocks and prices led to an economic crisis and political unrest in the 1930s. The autonomy of Newfoundland was suspended by Britain, and it joined with Canada in 1949.

The relative isolation of the Newfoundlanders still allowed the survival of a culture distinct in its dialects, folklore and music. Their insularity, however, has led other

Canadians to scorn them and use them as the butt of ethnic jokes. In 1991 they numbered nearly 570,000.

## NEZ PERCÉ

A Native North American nation of the northwest Great Plains. Their name comes from the French and means 'pierced-nosed', but they call themselves *Nimipu*, meaning 'our people'. Sedentary hunters, fishers and gatherers, they spoke a Penutian language. Their early contacts with white traders were friendly and they avoided conflict with rising numbers of settlers, signing a treaty ceding some lands in 1855 and remaining peaceful when it was violated. But gold was discovered on their lands and in 1863 the AMERICAN government fraudulently secured a few signatures to the so-called 'Thief Treaty', securing 90% of their land. Outraged, the Nez Percé refused to honour its terms, and in 1877 an impatient US government decided to force them to do so. The great Nez Percé leader Chief Joseph chose to flee to Canada. His followers fought 14 battles and evaded pursuit for four months before they were trapped a few miles from the frontier and sent to Colville reservation, in Washington state. One small band did reach Canada and remained there. The rest were confined to a reservation in Idaho.

In the 21st century, cultural revival, economic security and the return of land remain important issues. The 'Thief Treaty' is still resented, and those at Colville still see themselves as exiles. In 1996 they numbered about 4000.

## NICARAGUANS

The mostly MESTIZO and Spanish-speaking populace of Nicaragua, in Central America. Minority Native Americans, such as MOSQUITO, live in the Caribbean coastal areas. The original inhabitants of Nicaragua were conquered by the SPANISH in the 1520s, and a culture combining European, African and strong Native American elements developed. Nicaragua won full independence in 1838. Subsequently it suffered repeated AMERICAN interference in its affairs, culminating in 1934 with the establishment of the long and brutal dictatorship of the Somoza family.

Nicaraguan fury that aid received after a devastating earthquake in 1972 was stolen by the Somozas culminated in a revolution in 1979, which installed the Sandanista regime. However, the new regime earned the bitter enmity of the USA, which backed the so-called 'Contra' guerrillas in a savage and exhausting civil war. Much of Nicaragua's cultural heritage was destroyed in this war. Elections in 1990, held under the clear threat of continued civil war if the Sandanistas won, installed a regime acceptable to the USA. Desperate poverty and economic crises remain, denying the country stability. In 2001 the population was nearly 5 million.

## NIPISSING

An aboriginal nation of northern Ontario, whose name means 'people of the little water'. Traders, hunters, gatherers and fishers, they possibly practised some farming, and speak an Algonquian language. In the 17th century the fur trade brought them prosperity, but also diseases. As furs became depleted, the Nipissing also faced increasing warfare with the IROQUOIS and steady land loss. In the 20th century they became part of the Union of Ontario Indians to protect their interests. In 1991 over 500 lived on their reservation adjacent to Lake Nipissing.

## NIPMUC

A Native North American nation of central New England; their name means 'fresh water people'. Sedentary farmers, traders, hunter-gatherers and fishers, they spoke an Algonquian language. They were seriously reduced by epidemics in the 17th century, and few survived participation in King Philip's War (1675–6). Many survivors scattered as far afield as Canada. Three groups – two in Massachusetts and one in Connecticut – remained, and in the 20th century they began to re-emerge as a distinct nation and recover their traditional culture, including a noted wood carving tradition. They won federal recognition in 2001, only to have it revoked within months, on the grounds that they could not prove that they had maintained a continuous community, political entity or descent from an historical nation. In 1998 they numbered about 1400.

## NISKA

A Native North American nation of northwest British Columbia. Sedentary hunters, fishers and gatherers, they speak a Penutian language. In the 1830s they entered the fur trade and suffered badly from its associated epidemics. This was followed by land thefts and acculturation. A determined campaign during the 20th century to recover their traditional lands and to control their own resources, especially its timber and fish, led to a favourable new treaty in 2000 – despite white opposition and claims of endangerment to their property and voting rights. In 1996 the Niska numbered about 6000.

## NISQUALLY

A Native North American nation of coastal Washington state, whose name means 'tall grasses'. Sedentary hunters, fishers and gatherers, they spoke a Salishan language. They fought in the Puget Sound Indian War (1855–6), and defeat left them confined to a reservation where the disease, poverty, alcoholism and poor diet reduced their numbers steadily. In 1918 the AMERICAN government seized two-thirds of the reservation for military use, motivating the Nisqually to organize. In 1999 they went to the US Supreme Court to secure their right to gather shellfish on private beaches, much to the outrage of some property-owners and shellfish-farmers. In 1985 they numbered about 1725.

## NOMLAKI

A Native North American nation of northern California. Semi-sedentary hunters and gatherers, they spoke a Penutian language. The diseases, violence and slave-raiding of the 1849 Gold Rush were disastrous for them, killing three-quarters of their number. They were moved to Nome Lackee reservation in 1854, where the depredations continued, and settler pressure forced their removal to the Round Valley reservation. They won their own *rancheria* (settlement) in 1920, but federal recognition was withdrawn in 1961. It was restored in 1994. In 1990 there were about 330 Nomlaki.

## NONGATL

A former Native North American nation of northwest California. Semi-sedentary hunters, gatherers and traders, they spoke an ATHABASKAN language which has now disappeared. Their nation was destroyed during the Gold Rush in the 1850s, being moved onto reservations where terrible conditions left few survivors, who disappeared into the general population.

## NOOKSACK

A Native North American nation of coastal Washington state. Sedentary traders, hunters, fishers and gatherers, they spoke a Salishan language. Unable to attend the Point Elliot treaty negotiations because of bad weather, they never had a treaty with the USA. Their lands were simply stolen and many were driven to seek work in white settlements. They finally achieved federal recognition and gained a reservation in 1971. Other issues, such as the question of the right to hunt out of season on any public lands, rather than on just their own traditional lands, remain outstanding. In 1995 they numbered about 750.

## NOOTKA

A Native North American nation of Vancouver Island, British Columbia. Originally they were autonomous groups with a shared culture, officially united as a nation only in 1958, naming themselves the West Coast Allied Tribes, or alternatively *Nuuchahnulth*, meaning 'all along the mountains'. Seasonally mobile within their territory primarily as hunters, gatherers, fishers and whalers, they speak a Wakashan language. Originally having no concept of private property, they were quick to see the advantages of the fur trade, which began increasingly bloody strife over resources as well as bringing epidemics. During the 19th century settlers encroached on Nootka lands and brutally repressed any resistance. By the 20th century acculturation was widespread, although far from complete, and commercial fishing, sealing and logging were the main forms of Nootka subsistence. In 1991 the Nootka population was over 4300.

**n**

> ❝ The Nootkas are less than medium height ... but rather strongly built. ❞
>
> H.H. Babcroft, 1875

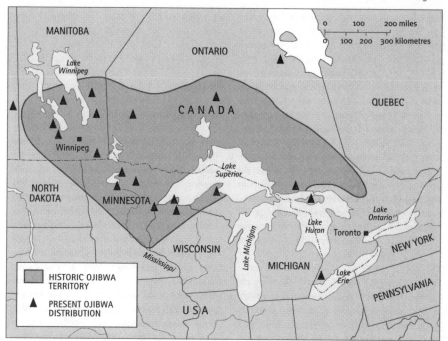

HISTORIC OJIBWA
TERRITORY

PRESENT OJIBWA
DISTRIBUTION

O

## NUKAK

A Native South American nation of Colombia's Amazonia. They are semi-sedentary hunters and gatherers, but now mostly farmers, and speak Maku. They were largely isolated until the 1980s, when extensive contacts with settlers brought epidemics and violence that drove them near to extinction. A reserve was established for them in 1997, when they numbered up to 1000.

## OJIBWA

An aboriginal nation originally of the Great Lakes area, now scattered across Canada and the USA. They call themselves *Anishinabek*, meaning 'spontaneously created people'. Seasonally mobile as farmers, hunters, gatherers and fishers, they speak an Algonquian language. Entering the fur trade in the 17th century, they acquired guns and expanded their territory at SIOUX expense, and their language became the trade language of the region. But the depletion of furs and IRO-QUOIS pressure forced them west in turn. Initially allies of the FRENCH, and then of the BRITISH, they

were left vulnerable by British defeat in the American Revolution. Forced onto reservations that were steadily whittled away, many were reduced to poverty. Diseases compounded their misery. The US Indian Removal Act of 1830 drove many to flee to Canada. The rest became fragmented and pushed steadily west and south. In 1898 a skirmish between the Ojibwa and the US army at the Leech Lake reservation, Minnesota, was officially the last battle of the Indian Wars. In the 20th century the Ojibwa were active in attempts to regain their sovereignty and their hunting and fishing rights, and to preserve their culture, enjoying some success. In 1995 they numbered 104,000, comprising 130 Canadian groups, as well as 22 federally recognized and several other unrecognized groups in the USA.

## OKANAGAN

A Native North American nation of Washington state and southern British Columbia. They call themselves *Isondva'ili*, 'our people'. Seasonally mobile in their territory mainly as hunters, fishers and gatherers, they speak a Salishan language. In 1848 they were divided by the US–Canadian frontier. The Okanagan in the USA agreed to sell their lands to the AMERICAN government in 1891, but were never paid. They received some compensation 100 years later.

In Canada many Okanagan sought to adopt white culture and became initially prosperous sedentary farmers. Over the years, however, settlers and miners stole their lands, and the government failed to protect them. With landholdings becoming increasingly unviable, poorly paid wage labour could not prevent growing poverty and social crisis. Attempts to negotiate a treaty with Canada broke down in 2000 when the provincial government insisted on imposing its own taxes on Okanangan land. In 1990 they numbered over 4200.

## OLMEC

A former Native Central American nation of west coastal Mexico. Sedentary hunters and gatherers, but mainly farmers, their language is unknown. The first complex culture of Mesoamerica, it exerted a strong influence on all of its successors. Arising about 1200 BC, the Olmec were notable for their invention of writing, advances in astronomy and mathematics, and architecture – they were pyramid builders and perhaps included human sacrifice in their religion. They also had an extensive trading empire. The most striking surviving examples of their sculpture are the widely dispersed colossal carved stone heads, up to 2 m /6.5 ft in diameter. About 500 BC the culture vanished for no clearly understood reason.

## OMAGUA

A Native South American nation of the Amazonia of Peru, Brazil and Ecuador. Sedentary slash-and-burn farmers, they were also fishers, hunters and gatherers, and spoke a Peba language, now nearly extinct. Once a powerful nation dominating much of the area, they resisted a SPANISH invasion in 1560. By the start of the 18th century, however, they had been greatly reduced by PORTUGUESE slavers and by the diseases of Spanish missions. Absorbed into the MESTIZO population, they largely disappeared as

a nation: in 1976 at most 100 existed in Peru; just 140 claimed to be Omagua in Colombia.

## OMAGUACA

See KOLLA.

## OMAHA

A Native North American nation of northeast Nebraska, whose name means 'those going against the wind'. Seasonally mobile within their territory as farmers, hunters, gatherers and fishers, they spoke a Siouan language. Separating from the PONCA in the 1650s, they prospered until losing 90% of their population between 1780 and 1802 through warfare and epidemics. Thereafter they were under constant pressure from settlers and neighbouring nations. Forced to accept a reservation in 1854, their lands were further whittled away. They have managed to preserve much of their traditional culture, especially a strong musical tradition. In the 1990s they numbered over 4100 and were concerned with promoting education, economic development and the repatriation of ancestral remains, even as they were dealing with allegations of corrupt government by 2001.

## ONA

A Native South American nation of Tierra del Fuego, at the southern continental tip. Nomadic hunters, gatherers and fishers, they spoke an Araucanian language. Their isolated and inhospitable terrain protected them from colonization for many centuries. Until the 1880s the only whites they saw were shipwrecked sailors. Thereafter their extermination began. Settlers introduced sheep-farming, and finding the Ona an inconvenience began a program of genocide. Given the diseases they introduced, this was hardly necessary.

In 1889 a group of Ona were kidnapped and displayed in a cage in Europe as 'cannibals'. Their numbers plummeted, and by the mid-20th century they had disappeared as a nation, although descendants still exist. The last full-blooded Ona was reported to have died in 1999.

O

“ We are the unconquered aboriginal peoples of this land, our mother; ... We will survive and continue to govern our mother and her resources for the good of all for all time. ”

Okanagan Nation
Declaration

# ONEIDA

A Native North American nation of the New York state area, whose name means 'people of the stone set up'. Sedentary farmers, hunters, gatherers and fishers, they spoke an Iroquoian language.

Part of the IROQUOIS league, the Oneida lost much of their land after its collapse and were forced to move to Wisconsin. They suffered further illegal land-loss, however, and several moved to southern Ontario, where they still reside on their own reserve. Their traditional religion was modified by Christian elements, but they resisted assimilation.

In the 20th century the Oneida sought redress for their lost lands in the USA and began to exercise hunting and fishing rights, much to the outrage of local landowners. This was part of a desire to gain federal recognition as a nation, which led them in the late 1990s to refuse further federal funding. The population may be about 5000, although their numbers are disputed.

# ONONDAGA

A Native North American nation of the New York area, whose name means 'people of the hills'. Sedentary farmers, hunters, gatherers and fishers, they spoke an Iroquoian language. Part of the IROQUOIS league, they continue traditional practices such as keeping the great council fire lit and holding the wampum-belt records of meetings, in which the patterns on the strings of shell beads are used to record important agreements.

When the league broke up during the American Revolution, the Onondaga backed Britain and lost most of their territory. In 1788 many were confined to a reservation; their lands were further whittled away, forcing them into wage labour. Others fled to Canada, especially to the Six Nations Territory on the Grand River, where they now reside in southern Ontario.

In the 20th century the Onondaga became active in asserting their sovereignty, refusing to accept government grants or levy state taxes on their lands. They also pursued a vast land claim that included large stretches of New York state and much of the city of Syracuse. In the 1990s

they sued several individual landowners as squatters, which was widely regarded as a ploy to force concessions from the state.

# OPATA

A Native North American nation of Arizona as well as northwest Sonora and Chihuahua provinces, Mexico. Their name comes from the PIMA and means 'hostile people'. Sedentary farmers, hunters and gatherers, they spoke an Uto-Aztecan language, which by 1993 was spoken by only 15 people. Pueblo-dwellers, they were friendly with the SPANISH when they arrived in the 17th century, allying with them against the APACHE and accepting missionaries, so becoming thoroughly acculturated. The Opata fought for Spain during the Mexican Revolution and joined the YAQUI in continued resistance to Mexico (1832–3). They were left with arid lands and insecure water rights, causing intense poverty. As the Opata are no longer recognized as a nation, no census data is available, but they probably number several thousand.

# OROTINA

A Native Central American nation of northern Costa Rica. Sedentary farmers, hunters and gatherers, they spoke an Oto-Manguan language. A complex culture, whose characteristics in dress, music and cuisine were adopted by much of the area, they perhaps practised human sacrifice and ritual cannibalism in their religion. In the 16th century they were conquered and enslaved by the SPANISH, and they rapidly disappeared as a nation. Descendants remain in the general population of Costa Rica, Honduras and El Salvador.

# OSAGE

A Native North American nation of the Missouri area. They call themselves *Nukonska*, meaning 'little ones of the middle waters'. Seasonally mobile within their territory as farmers, hunters, gatherers and fishers, they spoke a Siouan language. They separated from the Sioux in the 17th century. With a reputation for ferocity among their neighbours, they won much territory, but came under pressure from settlers in the 19th century. In 1865 they were forced to accept a reservation in Kansas, which was already being over-run by squatters. In 1870, therefore, they purchased land in Oklahoma confiscated from the CHEROKEE, which turned out to be above vast oil reserves. In the 1920s they became the richest nation *per capita* in the world. Naturally the unscrupulous attempted to defraud them, and several were murdered.

In 2000 the Osage sued the US government for $2.5 billion in oil royalties they claim were unpaid. In 2001 they numbered over 18,000, and were attempting to use their wealth to secure the long-term future of the nation.

## OTAVALANOS

A Native South American nation of the Equadorean highlands. Sedentary farmers and craftsmen, they speak a Quechuan language. Their handicrafts have not only provided them with prosperity, but also allowed them to preserve a considerable amount of their traditional culture. In 1996 they numbered about 40,000.

## OTO

A Native North American nation of Missouri. Their name means 'lechers', a reference to the Oto leader's son's seduction of a Missouri leader's daughter that caused the Oto to split from the MISSOURI. Seasonally mobile within their territory as farmers, hunters, gatherers and fishers, they spoke a Siouan language.

Moving to Nebraska after their split from the Missouri, they joined many OSAGE raids on settlers despite a series of treaties with the USA between 1817 and 1841. In 1829 they reunited with the Missouri and in 1854 they were forced to accept a reservation in Oklahoma, where, because of lack of numbers and the need to enter wage labour, much of their traditional culture was lost. In the mid-1990s they numbered 1550.

## OTOMI

A Native North-Central American nation of central Mexico. They called themselves *Ñañhu*, 'the people'. Sedentary farmers, hunters and gatherers, they speak an Oto-Manguan language.

Perhaps migrating from the south, they were dominated by, and adopted the culture of, the TOLTEC and later the AZTEC. In the 1520s they joined with the SPANISH in destroying the Aztec empire. This allegiance did not save them, however, from epidemics and exploitation. Their high-altitude homeland kept them isolated enough to limit acculturation until the 20th century, when became a major source of concern for the population of 324,000 in 1999.

## OTTAWA

A Native North American nation of Ohio, Michigan and Ontario. They called themselves *Neshinabek*, meaning 'people'. Seasonally mobile within their territory as farmers, hunters, gatherers and fishers, they spoke an Algonquian language.

In 1763 the Ottawa joined Pontiac's war against the ENGLISH, who, it is claimed, used germ warfare by deliberately spreading smallpox. After the Battle of the Fallen Timbers (1794), they lost their Ohio lands to the USA and were pushed into Kansas and southern Ontario, where they still reside at the Walpole Island and Wikwemikong reserves, among other places. In the USA they were defrauded of their new lands and began to fragment.

In 2001 there were five Ottawa groups in Canada and seven in the USA, with a total population of 10,400 in 1993. Despite signing 24 treaties, most groups remain unrecognized, including the United Michigan Ottawa, which, with 9000 members, is the largest unrecognized Native American group in the USA.

## OYANA

A Native South American nation of the Amazonia regions of Suriname and Brazil. Sedentary slash-and-burn farmers, they were also fishers, hunters and gatherers and spoke a CARIB language. By the late 20th century heavily armed miners, with the permission of the Suriname government, were causing serious pollution to their water supply. The Oyana are probably wrongly thought to have killed some miners in Brazil in 1998. In 1980 the Oyana numbered about 750.

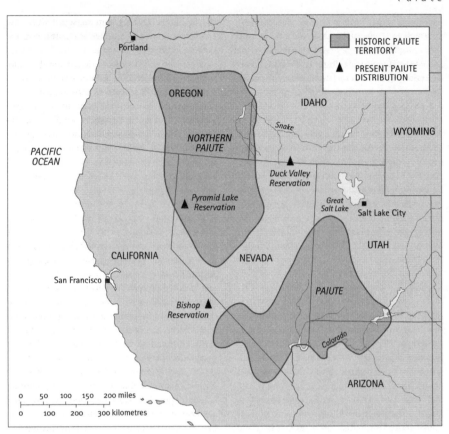

HISTORIC PAIUTE TERRITORY

PRESENT PAIUTE DISTRIBUTION

Portland

OREGON

IDAHO

WYOMING

Snake

PACIFIC
OCEAN

NORTHERN
PAIUTE

Duck Valley
Reservation

Pyramid Lake
Reservation

Great
Salt Lake    Salt Lake City

CALIFORNIA

NEVADA

UTAH

San Francisco

PAIUTE

Bishop
Reservation

Colorado

ARIZONA

0    50   100   150   200 miles

0    100   200   300 kilometres

# PAIPAI

A Native North American nation of Baja California (Mexico) and southern California (USA).
Semi-sedentary hunters and gatherers, they
spoke a Yuman language. Evangelized by the
SPANISH in the 18th century, they were much
reduced by diseases, and further depleted in
attempts to resist MEXICAN settlers in the 1840s.

In 2002 efforts were made to reunite the
nation divided by the US–Mexican frontier. Several Paipai living in Mexico were allowed to visit
California, where they could help their northern
kin revive their culture, in return receiving help
to relieve their desperate poverty.

The Paipai numbered about 350 in 2000.

# PAIUTE

A native North American nation of several
southwestern US states, whose name means 'true
Ute'. Originally nomadic fishers, hunters and
gatherers, some groups did become sedentary
farmers. They spoke an Uto-Aztecan language. In
the 1840s Mormons settled on their territory.
They tried to avoid antagonizing the Paiute, and
perhaps protected them from the worst depredations of slavers and the wagon trains of the
California Gold Rush. However, the Mormons
took the most productive land and water; they
also introduced diseases.

Pressure from settlers caused the Paiute War
(1860) and the Snake War (1866). Thereafter
many bands were forced onto reservations,
while others established settlements on the outskirts of AMERICAN cities and entered the wage

economy. Most have federal recognition, although in 1989 one band signed a treaty with the NAVAJO (the first between Native American nations in 160 years), gaining land of their own, and entitling them to increased federal funding.

## PALENQUE

A former Native Central American culture of southern Mexico. It was the most westerly centre of the MAYA culture. First occupied around AD 500, the Palenque city was noted for its unique four-storey palace and fine jade-work. Under the rule of Pacal (ruled AD 615–83), it became the predominant city of the region, and seems frequently to have been ruled by women. It was abandoned after AD 800 for no clearly understood reason.

## PALOUSE

A Native North American nation of Washington state, who called themselves *Na-ha-um*, meaning 'people of the river'. Semi-sedentary hunters, fishers and gatherers, they spoke a Penutian language. Although a small nation, they were noted horsemen who fought in the CAYUSE War (1847), the YAKIMA War (1855–6) and the NEZ PERCÉ War (1876). The US Army killed hundreds of their horses in 1858 to crush their resistance. Final defeat left them scattered and absorbed by other nations. Some descendants are found among the COLVILLE and Nez Percé.

## PAMLICO

A Native North American nation of North Carolina. Sedentary farmers, hunters and gatherers as well as traders, they spoke an Algonquian language. In the late 16th century they began trading with the ENGLISH, gaining guns, but also diseases. By the TUSCARORA War of 1711–13, they were reduced to just 75, and they did not survive as a nation. Remnants were absorbed by other nations, possibly including the Tuscarora.

## PAMUNKEY

A Native North American nation of Virginia. Sedentary farmers, hunter-gatherers and fishers,

they spoke an Algonquian language. Part of the POWHATAN confederation, following the Second Powhatan War (1644–6) they were confined to a reservation in 1658 and subsequently became fragmented. During the 19th century they narrowly avoided attempts to use racist laws to classify them as 'coloured', which would have enabled them to be defrauded of their lands. Their numbers are disputed, but a minimum figure of 75 was suggested in 2001. For some years they have been trying to protect their fish hatchery (the oldest in the USA) from destruction by proposed damming.

## PANAMANIANS

The inhabitants of the Central American Republic of Panama. Those of MESTIZO and European-African lineage constitute about 70%. The area was conquered in the 16th century by the SPANISH, who later imported African slaves, and a culture combining European, Native American and African elements, noted for its exuberant music and dance, developed. About 5% of the population are Native Americans.

Occupying the narrowest point of the Central American isthmus, Panama was a valuable transshipment point between the Atlantic and Pacific, a strategic location that was to shape the history of the Panamanians. They were absorbed by Colombia in 1821, and three subsequent attempts to secede were defeated. When the USA became interested in building a canal to connect the oceans and COLOMBIANS objected, however, the USA openly supported the independence movement, which triumphed in 1903. A treaty ceding sovereignty over the canal (built by 1914) and a surrounding zone to the AMERICANS was the cause of intense resentment. Frequent anti-American riots led to no less than 13 US military interventions, notably to topple the corrupt General Noriega from power (1990). In 1999 the removal of US forces and return of sovereignty over the canal to Panama eased hostility. In 2001 there were 2.9 million Panamanians.

## PAPAGO

See TOHONO O'ODHAM.

66 The Republic of Panama grants to the United States the rights, power and authority within the zone ... which the United States would possess and excercise if it were the sovereign of the territory. 99

Panama Canal Convention, 1903

## PARACAS CULTURE

A former Native South American culture of southern coastal Peru. Sedentary farmers, hunters and gatherers, they were strongly influenced culturally by the preceding CHAVÍN. They appeared about 1000 BC, reached the height of their civilization around 500 BC and disappeared about 200 BC, for no clearly understood reason. Their rich burial and ceremonial sites, ceramics, and particularly fine textiles influenced the succeeding NAZCA.

## PARAGUAYANS

The population of the South American Republic of Paraguay. The first SPANISH settlement was founded in modern Paraguay in 1537, on lands originally inhabited by the GUARANÍ (whose language is still widely used), although the MESTIZO population eventually became predominant (95%). Thereafter much of the colony consisted of Jesuit missions, which controlled trade with the Guaraní and held much of a highly productive and pleasant land. A culture combining European and very strong Native American elements emerged, most notably seen in their handicrafts, such as *nanduti* lace.

In 1767 the Jesuits were expelled, allowing a land-owning elite to assume political control and declare independence in 1811. Despotic and often incompetent dictators followed, one of whom needlessly provoked the War of the Triple Alliance (1865–70) against Brazil, Uruguay and Argentina. The consequences of this, the bloodiest war in South American history, were catastrophic for Paraguay. Over half of the population died, the economy was left in ruins and the nation was under military occupation until 1878. Paraguay escaped partition only because Argentina and Brazil could not agree on terms. Both nations confiscated territory, however, which was a deeply felt humiliation and a major factor determining Paraguyan national identity.

A constitution was agreed in 1870, but it proved utterly ineffective. Despotic rulers continued to ignore the terrible health and education needs of the poor, while the economy stagnated. The nation remained very isolated, but it did provide a refuge for persecuted foreign groups, such as the Mennonites. The Chaco War (1932–5) against Bolivia, however, aroused passionate enthusiasm. As the Paraguayan army advanced victoriously, the humiliations of the War of the Triple Alliance were eased. However, the armistice, when it came, was greeted with deep disappointment – Paraguayans wanted to advance on to La Paz, the Bolivian capital, and the victorious president was soon overthrown.

An economic boom followed the war, but at the cost of growing economic penetration from Argentina. The benefits spread only slowly, and dictatorships repressing rumbling discontent remained the norm, with thousands of political exiles fleeing oppression. Paraguay remains the poorest and most oppressed nation in South America. It has mounting international debts, economic stagnation and severe problems of corruption. As part of the seemingly endless political crisis, the assassination of the vice president in 1999 led to the closure of the frontiers. In 2001, Paraguayans numbered 5.7 million.

## PARINTINTIN

A Native South American nation of Brazil's Amazonia, who called themselves *Cawahib*, perhaps meaning 'wasp people'. Sedentary slash-and-burn farmers, they were also fishers, hunters and gatherers and spoke a TUPÍ language. Little-known before the 19th century, they fought a constant guerrilla war against white encroachment until the 1920s. Greater contacts thereafter reduced them through diseases. In 1996 loggers, miners and squatters invaded their lands, but their protests to the government were ignored. In 1990 they numbered a little over 100.

## PASSAMAQUODDY

A Native North American nation of coastal Maine and New Brunswick, whose name means 'pollock-spearing place'. Seasonally mobile within their territory as hunters, gatherers and fishers, they spoke an Algonquian language. The Passamaquoddy were allies of the FRENCH in the 17th century, but were decimated by warfare and disease, and in 1794 the AMERICAN government forced them onto a reservation. Until the late 20th century they experienced severe poverty, but gained compensation for stolen lands in 1980, which allowed them to re-acquire land. This included the island on Big Lake, where smallpox victims went to die to protect the rest of the nation. In 2002 they numbered over 2500 and were involved in a bitter legal wrangle with state authorities over their sovereign rights.

## PATAGONIAN WELSH

An ARGENTINIAN culture of colonial origin. It became established in 1865 through the work of Michael Jones, a nonconformist minister. Facing eviction from their land in Wales, it was natural for his community to look to new lands in the Americas. They were aware that emigrating to the USA risked rapid and complete assimilation, which they were determined to resist. They purchased land in Patagonia, which was thought to be fertile, for a new community. After considerable difficulties they prospered, and others followed the original 163 settlers.

The Patagonian Welsh still maintain their traditions. The Eisteddfod (cultural festival) is still celebrated, and with some help from the Welsh Assembly the decline in their language appears to have been reversed, although Spanish and English terms have crept into its usage. In 1998 they may have numbered up to 25,000.

## PATÁNGORO

A Native South American nation of the Colombian Andes. Sedentary slash-and-burn farmers, undertaking periodic relocation as soil became exhausted, they were also fishers, hunters and gatherers, and probably spoke a CARIB language. They were allegedly cannibals who regarded human flesh as an essential food, and supposedly pursued warfare as a form of hunting. By the late 16th century they were extinct, probably at the hands of the SPANISH.

## PATAYAN CULTURE

A former Native North American culture, or perhaps a group of similar cultures, of the Arizona area. Sedentary farmers and hunter-gatherers, they prospered from *c.* AD 500 until *c.* 1500. They used generally plain ceramics and very few

ornaments and so are little understood. Possibly undermined by drought and environmental stress, they may have been forebears of the YUMA.

## PATWIN

A Native North American nation of northern California. Semi-sedentary hunters, fishers, gatherers and traders, they spoke a Wintun language which now appears to be extinct. Spanish evangelization, followed by the ravages of the Gold Rush, destroyed most of their autonomous bands. Survivors mostly merged with the WINTUN and POMO in the late 19th century.

## PAUGUSSETT

A Native North American nation of southwest Connecticut, whose name means 'where the narrow waters open'. Seasonally mobile within their territory as farmers, hunters, gatherers and fishers, they spoke an Algonquian language.

In the 1650s the Paugussett were unceremoniously stripped of their lands and confined in a small reservation, which was immediately whittled away by squatters, while their woodlands were illegally logged. Their repeated complaints to the courts were ignored. In 1801 Connecticut authorities decided that because the Paugussett were supporting themselves through handicrafts, they did not need land, and they lost even more. Further robbery by state officials left them landless by 1849, and most Paugussett became scattered, urbanized and impoverished.

In 1999 they sought federal recognition, already denied three times on the grounds that they could not prove descent from a historical nation. They also pursued a land claim affecting one-third of the state and 1 million property-owners. They numbered some 100 in 2000.

## PAWNEE

A Native North American nation of the southern Great Plains. Sedentary farmers, hunters and gatherers, they spoke a Caddoan language.

In the 17th century, until they acquired guns from FRENCH traders, they lost so many people to APACHE slave raids that their name became synonymous with 'slave'. Perhaps because of this, they maintained friendly relations with the USA and provided scouts vital to US Army campaigns. Despite this, they were stripped of their lands by 1875 and moved to an Oklahoma reservation. In 2002 they numbered over 2500, and were attempting to counter serious poverty, protect burial grounds and repatriate remains.

## PAYA

A Native Central American nation of the eastern coast and offshore islands of Honduras. Sedentary hunters and gatherers who traded for farm produce, they were artisans, especially noted for their jade work, and spoke a Chibchan language. From the early 16th century they were raided by the SPANISH for slaves and exterminated in the islands. From 1638 they enjoyed the protection of the ENGLISH, until their territory was ceded to Honduras in 1859. Their inaccessible lands allowed them a degree of protection against acculturation, but by 1993, the nearly 2,600 population were deeply concerned with preserving a language in danger of extinction.

## PEDEE

A Native North American nation of coastal South Carolina, whose name possibly comes from the CATAWBA and means 'good' or 'capable'. Seasonally mobile as farmers, hunters and gatherers, they probably spoke a Siouan language. In 1744 they joined the NATCHEZ in attacking the Catawba. Defeat forced many Pedee to join the Catawba, although three groups remained on their traditional lands, subsequently losing both their language and their traditional culture.

After 50 Pedee fought for the rebels in the American Revolution, they received land grants, where many descendants still live. With federal recognition (2001), they numbered about 1600.

## PEHUENCHE

See MAPUCHE.

## PENNACOOK

A Native North American nation of New Hampshire, whose name means 'at the crooked place'.

Sedentary farmers, hunters, gatherers and fishers, they spoke an Algonquian language. They first encountered ENGLISH settlers in 1614; their great leader Passaconway adopted a policy of friendship, and in 1630 they officially submitted to English authority. In 1662 they accepted a reservation. As the settlers became more numerous, however, they also became more demanding and arrogant, and persuaded the MOHAWK to attack the Pennacook. A hurried alliance with the French could not save the Pennacook, and by 1713 most had scattered, some to Canada, and they ceased to exist as a nation. There is, however, a Cowasuck band of the Pennacook-Abenaki people extant in Quebec.

## PENOBSCOT

A Native North American nation of Maine, whose name means 'many stones'. Sedentary farmers, hunters, gatherers and fishers, they spoke an Algonquian language. Entering the fur trade and an alliance with France in the 17th century, they suffered severely from warfare and epidemics. They sided with the rebels during the American Revolution, but their lands were still stolen and state authorities sold logging rights without regard to them. Most were forced into wage labour, and their traditions were eroded.

The Penobscot won compensation and federal recognition, and even a seat in the Maine legislature in 1980. However, this caused a bitter legal dispute when, in 2002, state authorities insisted that the settlement reduce its reservation to the status of a municipality. In 1996 the Penobscot numbered nearly 2100.

## PEORIA

A Native North American nation of Illinois, whose name means 'he comes carrying a pack on his back'. Sedentary farmers, hunters, gatherers and fishers, they spoke an Algonquian language. Once part of the ILLINOIS confederacy, they were nearly annihilated in the 1769 war following the murder of Ottawa chief Pontiac in 1769. Driven to Missouri, they were moved to Kansas in 1832, and again to Oklahoma in 1854. They numbered over 2600 in 2001, but their language and traditional culture had largely been lost.

## PEQUOT

A Native North American nation of coastal Connecticut, whose name, perhaps taken from their enemies, may mean 'destroyers'. Sedentary farmers, hunters, gatherers and fishers, they spoke an Algonquian language. Entering the fur trade after 1614, they became wealthy, but ENGLISH settlers soon resented their control of trade. On a flimsy pretext, the English attacked the Pequot stronghold at Mystic fort and massacred the inhabitants. The rest were hunted to the brink of extinction. Some were enslaved by the MOHEGAN and NARRAGANSETT but were later released after resisting assimilation. The largest group was renamed Manshantucket.

Severe poverty meant that the Pequot had all but disappeared as a nation by the 1970s, but a land-claim settlement and federal recognition reversed their fortunes, and they became wealthy through building the largest casino in the USA. They numbered some 1600 in 2002.

> " Pequod ... was the name of a celebrated tribe ... now extinct as the ancient Medes. "
>
> H. Melville, 1851

## PERUVIANS

The people of the South American Republic of Peru. The original inhabitants included the INCA and AYMARA, whose languages (notably Quechua) are still widely used. Today, the combined MESTIZO and Native American population accounts for 90% of the total; most of the remainder are of European descent.

The SPANISH conquest began in 1533, but Native American and Mestizo influences remained very strong among the poor, and even influenced Catholic practices. Peru achieved independence in 1821, and in the first 40 years of nationhood had over a dozen constitutions, none of which was observed. This was a symptom of deep divisions, both political and class-based, within the nation. The economy was firmly in the grip of a CREOLE aristocratic oligarchy. A middle class emerged only very slowly, while the vast majority lived in severe poverty. Indeed, the Inca and Aymara played almost no role in national life; many were in servitude, and Peru as a country meant little to them.

A national identity did begin to appear with the trauma and humiliation of defeat by Chile in the Pacific War (1879–83), and the consequent loss of mineral-rich territory. There was a growing challenge to the oligarchy, but few cared for the sufferings of the poor. Education and land reform were slowly introduced from the start of the 20th century, but too few benefited. Political violence and coups were regular, and dictators ruled for much of the century. Only slowly did Western influences have an impact on the Native American population. Arguably the most important of these was revolutionary ideology.

In the late 20th century two revolutionary movements, the Sendero Luminoso (Shining Path, a Maoist grouping) and Tupac Amaru (named after the last Inca ruler), convulsed the nation. In 2001 the Peruvians numbered over 27 million, and Peru was still plagued with poverty and political violence.

## PIANKSHAW

See MIAMI.

## PIEGAN or Pikuni

An North American aboriginal nation of Montana and Alberta, part of the BLACKFOOT confederacy (see also BLOOD), whose name means 'small robes'. Nomadic hunters, gatherers and fishers, they speak an Algonquian language.

The Piegan attempted to avoid conflict with the USA, but in 1870 the US Army deliberately attacked their unprotected camp, which was under safe conduct. Many were massacred, and the survivors were left to starve. Forced onto a reservation, they suffered further starvation. The Piegan nation survived, however, and numbered some 18,000 in 1996, when they were attempting to preserve their culture and protect their lands from commercial exploitation.

## PIMA

A Native North American nation of Arizona and Mexico. They call themselves *Akimel O'Odham*, meaning 'river people' (see also TOHONO O'ODHAM). Sedentary farmers, hunters and gatherers, they spoke an Uto-Aztecan language. Remote and peaceful, they suffered raiding by the APACHE and YUMA, but had little contact with whites until the mid-19th century. Despite supplying the US Army with scouts against the Apache, and being willing to trade food with travellers, the Pima were overrun by settlers who diverted their water supplies, causing repeated famine. Pima agriculture became profitable only in the 1960s.

For many decades the Pima have been contributing to diabetes research, which suggests that Native Americans possess a 'thrifty gene' that allows them to store fat to survive droughts. This, combined with the sugar-rich modern US diet, is suspected of being the cause of widespread health problems among native peoples. In 1990 they numbered over 14,400.

## PISCATAWAY

A Native North American nation of Maryland. Sedentary traders, farmers, hunters, gatherers and fishers, they spoke an Algonquian language.

Their fertile, accessible land was coveted by several of their neighbours, and in the 17th century, unable to acquire guns, they were conquered by the IROQUOIS. Thereafter the nation dispersed and had disappeared by the end of the 18th century. A national organization is still active in Maryland for Piscataway descendants, which is seeking federal recognition and attempting to protect sacred sites.

## PLAINS CREE

See CREE.

## PLAINS GROS VENTRE

See HIDATSA.

## PLAQUEMINE CULTURE

A former Native North American culture of the lower Mississippi valley. Sedentary farmers, hunter-gatherers and traders, they were neighbours of the CADDO, who adopted much of their culture. They built ceremonial mounds and earthworks, and their burial goods included pottery and stone weapon points. The culture arose about AD 1000 and peaked by 1200; it disappeared by about 1700, European diseases probably accounting for the final collapse. Descendants may include some of the NATCHEZ.

## PODUNK

A former Native North American nation of Connecticut, whose name means 'where you sink in the mire'. Sedentary farmers, hunters, gatherers and fishers, they spoke an Algonquian language. They were probably defeated by the PEQUOT in the early 17th century, and reputedly responded by inviting ENGLISH colonists to settle among them. This involved them in local wars and exposed them to European diseases. As a result they had disappeared by 1760.

## POLAR ESKIMO

See INUIT.

## POLISH AMERICANS

An AMERICAN culture of European origin. Poles crossed the Atlantic in large numbers from the 1850s, driven not only by poverty, but also by oppressive foreign rule. Generally urban, they made Chicago the second-largest Polish city after Warsaw. They maintained close communities and preserved their traditional culture. They were, however, the victims of discrimination, and regularly stereotyped as stupid. By the late 20th century numerous cultural, religious and historical institutions had been founded to combat such defamation, to encourage pride in their achievements, and to increase their influence. In 1998 they numbered about 10 million.

## POMO

A designation for several Native North American nations of northern California. Usually semi-sedentary hunters, fishers and gatherers, they spoke dialects of Hokan. In the early 19th century the RUSSIANS enslaved many, and murder and disease reduced them sharply. The 1849 Gold Rush completed their destruction: settlers hunted them for sport or for rape and committed a number of massacres.

By 1867 most of the Pomo were forced onto reservations, and despite their efforts to resist assimilation, their religion and culture died. Their subsequent history has been marked by attempts not only to regain an adequate land base, but also to keep possession of it. In 1995 they numbered 4900.

## PONCA

A Native North American nation of Nebraska. Sedentary farmers, hunters and gatherers, they spoke a Siouan language. Weakened by epidemics and LAKOTA attacks, they signed a treaty ceding their lands in 1868, but a mistake by the government resulted in their relocation to Lakota lands, which led to bloodshed. In 1877 the US Army forcibly moved them to Oklahoma, where many starved. One leader, Standing Bear, decided to return home, but was arrested. A sympathetic lawyer applied for and secured a writ of *habeas corpus*, establishing for the first time that Native Americans had legal rights. Standing Bear also received a new reservation in Nebraska. In 2002 there were over 2500 Ponca in Oklahoma and over 2000 in Nebraska, who were trying to rediscover and preserve their history and traditional culture and protect their environment.

## POTAWATOMI

A Native North American nation of Michigan and Ontario. Their name means 'fire nation', since they were the firekeepers, or most prestigious nation and arbiters of the Three Fires Confederacy, which also included the OJIBWA and OTTAWA. They call themselves *Nishnabe'k*, meaning 'true people'. Sedentary farmers, hunters, gatherers and fishers, they spoke an Algonquian language. They became allies of the FRENCH by the 1670s and were able to force the IROQUOIS off their lands. Allied to the BRITISH during the American Revolution, they faced rapid land encroachment. Between 1795 and 1837 they signed 38 treaties with the USA, and lost most of their lands. Over the next 30 years they were removed to Kansas, where they fought the CHEYENNE and SHAWNEE over limited resources. They became much dispersed, and many met intense poverty.

The Potawatomi numbered about 17,000 in 1998, and were struggling against apathy to preserve their language. They were also defending their sovereignty, refusing to levy Kansas state taxes, claiming they receive nothing in return. In

the 19th century they also moved north and east into Ontario, where they still reside on reserves.

## POTIGUARA

A Native South American nation of Brazil's Amazonia. Sedentary slash-and-burn farmers, they were also fishers, hunters and gatherers and spoke a TUPÍ language. Originally a large, coastal nation, they were driven inland by the PORTUGUESE in the 16th century. They were allied with the DUTCH until the mid-17th century, but thereafter became increasingly impoverished and acculturated. By the late 20th century, their language was extinct, their environment was highly polluted, poverty was endemic and they were in the process of disintegration. But political mobilization began to try to reverse this. In 1995 they numbered over 6000.

## POVERTY POINT CULTURE

A former Native North American culture of the Mississippi area. They were sedentary hunters, fishers and gatherers. The oldest ceremonial mound-building culture in North America, they were unique among such cultures in not practising farming. Their earthworks were large-scale and their trading networks far-flung. Perhaps originating in Mexico, possibly from the OLMEC, they flourished from about 1730 to 1350 BC. Why they disappeared is unclear: there is no evidence of their demise through warfare.

## POWHATAN

A Native North American nation of coastal Virginia. They called themselves *Renape*, meaning 'human beings'. Sedentary farmers, hunters, gatherers and fishers, they spoke an Algonquian language. They led a confederacy, also called Powhatan, which was formed as a response to ENGLISH settlements. War against the English broke out in 1622. Interspersed with temporary truces arising from mutual exhaustion and hunger, this war dragged on for about a decade before ending indecisively. A Second Powhatan War (1644–6) saw the destruction of the confederacy, whose lands were flooded with settlers. Most eventually settled in Oklahoma or Canada.

In 1990, nearly 800 people in the USA claimed Powhatan descent. They actively oppose the stereotyping of their nation and the inaccuracies of the Pocahontas legend associated with them.

## PUEBLO

A Native North American nation of Arizona and New Mexico, whose name comes from the Spanish and means 'village'. Their distinctive settlements, sometimes built from sandstone, more often from adobe, have given them their name. Sedentary farmers, hunters and gatherers, they speak several languages, and consist of numerous independent nations sharing a common lifestyle. Cultural descendants of the ANASAZI and MOGOLLON, they have dwelt in their territory since c. 300 BC. The various nations only began to work together after the SPANISH began to establish permanent settlements in their territories and impose Catholicism in the late 16th century. New-found unity and the emergence of a new leader, Po'pay, led eventually to a major coordinated attack in 1680 (the Pueblo Revolt), which drove the Spanish away. Unfortunately this left many Pueblo vulnerable to APACHE and NAVAJO raids, allowing the Spanish gradually to re-assert their authority. Spanish, MEXICAN and, from 1848, AMERICAN attempts to suppress their religions fostered a sense of unity and drove religious practices underground.

The Pueblo achieved some success during the 20th century in protecting their ancestral lands and water rights. They have also seen success in gaining the repatriation for reburial of ancestral remains unearthed by archaeologists. In 1999 the remains of 2000 Native Americans were repatriated. In the mid-1990s they numbered nearly 69,000.

## PUELCHE

A Native South American nation of the Argentinian Pampas. The name was applied collectively to a number of nomadic hunting-and-gathering groups that probably shared a common language. From the 17th century they acquired horses and gained a reputation as formidable warriors. They were never very numerous, however, and were severely weakened by disease and war with the Spanish. During the 18th century they were absorbed and assimilated by the MAPUCHE.

## PUERTO RICANS

The inhabitants of the US Caribbean dependency of Puerto Rico. Settled by the SPANISH in 1508, Puerto Rico remained a backwater until the 1830s, when immigrants from newly independent LATIN AMERICAN states established a plantation economy. This entailed importing a limited number of African slaves, whose impact on the largely European culture was likewise limited. By the end of the 19th century an increasingly brutal colonial regime was facing growing resistance, and in 1897 Puerto Ricans won a degree of autonomy, which was terminated with US occupation in 1898. Thereafter their relationship with the USA was unusual. Puerto Ricans resented attempts to Americanize them, but accepted the advantages of their position. In 1917, for example, they became US citizens of an AMERICAN commonwealth. This meant they had limited self- government, could not vote in federal elections and paid no federal taxes. Incomes remained low, and in many fields, not least welfare, their standards were lower than in the USA but higher than in most of Latin America.

An independence movement launched a sporadic terrorist campaign in the 1970s, but in a referendum in 1993, few voted for independence; the issue was between US statehood and retaining the status quo, the latter of which won by a narrow majority.

In 2001 they numbered nearly 4 million. In addition, a sizeable expatriate community exists among the HISPANICS of the US mainland.

## PUKARA CULTURE

A former Native South American nation of the Peruvian Andes, near Lake Titicaca. Sedentary terrace-farmers and herders, the Pukara people also produced fine textiles and ceramics. They had a far-flung trading network, importing jaguar pelts and hallucinogenic coca leaves from Amazonia. They were also known for their carved stone statues. For no clearly understood

| Pueblo: main sub-goups |
| --- |
| Acoma |
| Cochiti |
| Isleta |
| Jemez |
| Keres |
| Laguna |
| Nambé |
| Pecos |
| Picuris |
| Piro |
| Pojoaque |
| San Felipe |
| San Ildefonso |
| San Juan |
| Sandia |
| Santa Ana |
| Santa Clara |
| Santo Domingo |
| Tano |
| Taos |
| Tesuque |
| Tewa |
| Tompiro |
| Towa |
| Yselta del Sur |
| Zia |

reason, their towns were occupied only for the brief period between about 200 BC and AD 100.

## PURÍ

A Native South American nation of Brazil's Amazonia. Nomadic fishers, hunters and gatherers, they spoke a Gê language, now extinct. From the 18th century they skirmished with white interlopers and raided their farms. As a result, except for a few isolated groups now largely absorbed into the MESTIZO population, they were mainly exterminated during the 19th century.

## PURUPECHA

A Native American nation of Central America. Sedentary farmers, hunters and gatherers, they spoke dialects of Purepecha. A powerful empire from about AD 1100, they resisted AZTEC conquest, and their culture had a wide impact, especially in its music. When the SPANISH arrived in the 1520s, however, the destruction of the AZTEC had impressed upon them that resistance would be suicidal. They submitted and allowed their temples to be destroyed. The Spanish called them *Tarascans*, which was an error; it was the Purupecha name for the Spanish and meant 'in-laws', an ironic reference to the Spanish habit of raping women. The protection by missionaries allowed the Purupecha to retain some of their lands, and their traditional culture survived relatively intact, a matter of great national pride. They numbered about 200,000 in 1999.

## PUYALLUP

A Native North American nation of coastal Washington state, whose name means perhaps 'shadow' or possibly 'the mouth of the river'. Semi-sedentary hunters, fishers and gatherers, they spoke a Salishan language. In 1854 they ceded their lands to the USA, but feeling cheated they joined in the YAKIMA War (1855–6). Subsequently they were robbed of their remaining lands and became impoverished and largely acculturated. They formed a government in 1936 to protect their interests, which in 2001 faced allegations of misusing funds and of ignoring pressing social needs. Armed but non-violent

occupations in 1976 and 1980 did regain them a hospital closed in 1959. In 2001 they numbered about 2600.

## Q'EROS

A Native South American nation of the Peruvian Andes. Sedentary farmers, herders and weavers, they speak a Quechuan language. A long history of exploitation by foreigners has given them a tradition of deep distrust of outsiders. In 1995 they numbered under 1000.

## QUAPAW

A Native North American nation, now of Oklahoma. Their name means 'downstream people', although they call themselves *Ugakhpa*. Sedentary farmers, hunters and gatherers, they spoke a Siouan language. Originally of the Ohio river valley, the IROQUOIS pushed them south to the Arkansas River by the late 17th century. In 1818 they signed a treaty ceding most of their lands, but squatters invaded what they retained and in 1824 they were forced into a new treaty, leading to their own 'trail of tears' to the CADDO reservation in Texas. Unwelcome, they attempted to return to their ancestral lands, but settlers found their presence intolerable, and in 1833 they were moved to Oklahoma. Subsequent fragmentation accelerated acculturation. The discovery of lead on their lands benefited only a few, and the gravel-like chat thrown up by mining was heavily polluted and caused a serious health problem. This chat was potentially valuable for road construction, but until 2002 they were forbidden to sell it, as the government feared health lawsuits. In 1995 they numbered approximately 2600 and were seeking cultural revival alongside economic development.

## QUÉBÉCOIS

A CANADIAN FRENCH culture. The first French colony in Quebec was founded in 1608, but was conquered by the BRITISH by 1763. The French settlers, however, rejected acculturation, and Catholicism and the French language became central to their culture.In defence of their identity they have proven far more culturally

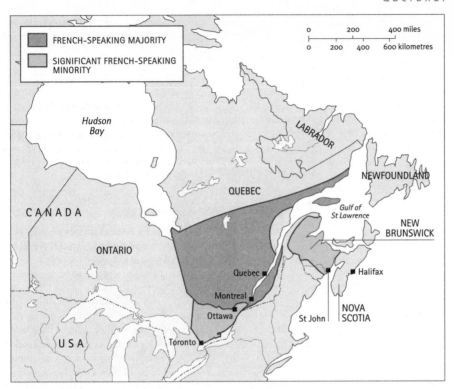

FRENCH-SPEAKING MAJORITY

SIGNIFICANT FRENCH-SPEAKING MINORITY

0    200    400 miles
0    200    400    600 kilometres

Hudson Bay

LABRADOR

NEWFOUNDLAND

QUEBEC

CANADA

Gulf of St Lawrence

NEW BRUNSWICK

ONTARIO

Quebec ■    ■ Halifax

Montreal ■

Ottawa ■    St John | NOVA SCOTIA

USA    Toronto ■

q

conservative and devout than their cousins in France. Justified complaints of discrimination politicized the Québécois, who blamed their grievances entirely on Anglicization and seethed when other Canadians dismissed their grievances as trivial. The Québécois have an international reputation for inhospitality to English-speakers, exacerbated by certain legal restrictions on the use of any language in the province other than French.

In 1995 a plebiscite on independence was defeated by a narrow margin; sufficient numbers were anxious at the economic consequences of independence, and possible exclusion from the North American Free Trade Area, to swing the vote. The plebiscite was deeply divisive, with the CREE and the INUIT outraged that they were offered no choice over their nationality, and little support for independence among recent immigrants from overseas. Few separatists are eager to see the plebiscite repeated unless they are certain of victory. In the long term, however,

the Québécois population is in relative decline. Some three-quarters of Quebec's 7.4 million people claimed solely French descent in 2001, a decline of 3% in five years.

## QUECHUA

A South American language and cultural group. Quechua was widely used in the Andes area and was the language of the INCA. Although the Spanish tried to suppress its use, and it continues to have a low social prestige, Quechua is still spoken by a quarter of the population of the ECUADOREAN, BOLIVIAN and PERUVIAN Andes, and also by others in Argentina, Brazil and Chile. The Quechua-speakers numbered over 8 million in 1987. (See map on page 120.)

## QUERANDI

A Native South American nation of Argentina's pampas. The Querandi were seasonally mobile

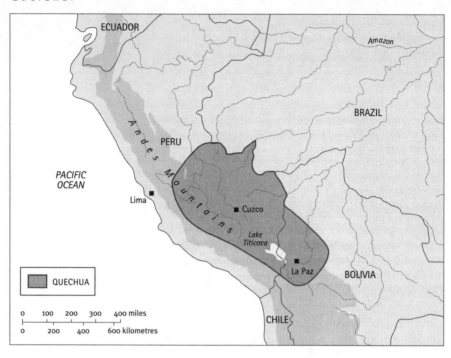

ECUADOR

Amazon

BRAZIL

Andes Mountains

PERU

PACIFIC
OCEAN

Lima

Cuzco

Lake
Titicaca

La Paz    BOLIVIA

CHILE

QUECHUA

0    100   200   300   400 miles
0       200    400    600 kilometres

within their territory as hunters, gatherers and fishers, and their autonomous groups were prepared to fight to protect their lands. In 1535 a SPANISH force attempted to extort food from them and were almost annihilated when bolas brought down their horses. The Querandi became more formidable after they themselves acquired horses in about 1580; allied with the CHARRÚA and TEMBÉ, and later joined by MAPUCHE refugees, they regularly raided Spanish settlements. They also contributed to war in the pampas by taking slaves from other nations for the European market. They were finally defeated only in 1883, their lands were overrun and their traditional culture all but destroyed. There are descendants of the Querandi among the agricultural population of the Argentinian pampas, especially among the traditional cattle-herders, the *gauchos*.

## QUILEUTE

A Native North American nation of coastal Washington state. Semi-sedentary hunters (and especially of sea mammals), fishers and gatherers, they spoke a Chimakum language. Regarded by their neighbours as warlike, they fought nearly every other nation in the area. They began to move from a fishing- to a whaling-based subsistence economy in the mid-19th century, just as settlers began entering their territory in numbers. They agreed to enter a reservation, but conflicts with settlers persisted, including the burning of Quileute houses. In 2002 their fishing rights were still resented by their white neighbours. Discrimination, sovereignty and economic development were central issues in an agreement they reached with Washington state in 1999. In 1995 they numbered almost 740.

## QUIMBAYA

A former Native South American nation of western Colombia. Sedentary farmers, fishers, hunters and gatherers, they produced fine gold work and ceramics. They rose around the first century AD, reached their height by about 1000, thereafter declining rapidly. When the SPANISH arrived in the 16th century they found only a small nation which might have been direct descendants, but which disappeared quickly.

## QUINAULT

A Native North American nation of coastal Washington state. Sedentary hunters, fishers and gatherers, they spoke a Salishan language, which only six people could speak in 1990. In 1855, already devastated by epidemics, they ceded their lands for a reservation. Determined efforts were made to destroy their culture. Even worse, their traditional enemies, the CHINOOK, were dumped onto their reservation by the US government. The Quinault have, in fact, persistently opposed federal recognition for the Chinook from fear they would secure Quinault lands and fishing grounds. Protecting their environment from commercial over-fishing and over-logging are also continuing concerns. In 1994 the Quinault numbered approximately 2500.

## QUITU

A Native South American nation of the Ecuadorean Andes. Sedentary farmers, hunters and gatherers, they spoke an AYMARAN language. In the late 15th century, after long, bitter fighting, the INCA conquered them. As the SPANISH conquered the Inca, however, the Quitu regained their independence, and the Spanish had to fight hard to impose dominance. Many Quitu leaders thereafter adopted Spanish culture and became part of the urbanized elite supporting Spanish rule. Most of the rest became urbanized, acculturated and impoverished by the 19th century.

## RAMAS

A Native Central American nation of Nicaragua's Atlantic coast. Sedentary farmers, fishers, hunters and gatherers, they spoke a Chibchan language, now nearly extinct. Seen by their neighbours as warlike, they raided for slaves, but could offer little resistance to SPANISH conquest in the 16th century. Much of their culture was suppressed, and only a few communities living near the MOSQUITO retained their identity. In the mid-1990s it is thought they numbered up to

1500 in Nicaragua and Costa Rica, and they were seeking self-determination.

## RAPPAHANNOCK

A Native North American nation of Virginia, whose name means 'where the tide ebbs and flows'. Seasonally mobile within their territory as farmers, hunters, gatherers and fishers, they spoke an Algonquian language. Not an overly militaristic nation, they fled their lands during the POWHATAN wars (1622–c. 1632 and 1644–6), and when they returned, ENGLISH settlers had occupied them. An attempt to regain them, known as Bacon's Rebellion (1675–7), was brutally suppressed, and by 1705 they had been confined to a reservation. Many were forced into wage labour, and, facing severe racial prejudice, they often concealed their background. In the 20th century they began to revive their traditional culture, and in 2002, when they numbered about 2700, they hosted the first joint powwow with other Virginia nations in centuries, in pursuit of federal recognition.

## REMOJADAS CULTURE

A former Native Central American culture of Mexico's Gulf coast. Part of the VERACRUZ CULTURE, lasting from AD 300 to 900, it borrowed elements of OLMEC and MAYA culture. Sedentary hunters, gatherers and farmers, the people were noted for their terracotta and smiling pottery figurines, perhaps depicting victims drugged for human sacrifice.

## SAC

See SAUK.

## ST LAWRENCE ISLAND ESKIMO

See INUIT.

## ST LUCIANS

The people, mostly of African origin, who inhabit the Caribbean island state of St Lucia, north of Trinidad and Tobago. The English first

**S**

attempted to colonize the island in 1605, but were driven off by the native CARIBS. The FRENCH finally succeeded in 1746. The BRITISH were persistent in their ambitions, however, and in 1814, after numerous attempts, they finally gained possession (the British monarch remains head of state.) By this time a (slave) plantation economy had brought a strong African element to the culture, which was officially English-speaking, although French patois was widespread. Independent in 1979, they found their agricultural economy vulnerable to world conditions. Unemployment remained high, and rapid population growth exacerbated their problems, leading to some unrest in the 1990s. In 2001 they numbered over 158,000.

*" [The Salish] speak a language remarkable for its sweetness and simplicity. "*

W.A. Ferris, 1831

## ST VINCENTIANS or Vincentians

The inhabitants of the multi-island Caribbean state of St Vincent and the Grenadines. Africans who had survived the shipwrecks of slavers augmented the original CARIB population in 1675. They prevented colonization until the FRENCH arrived in the early 18th century. The BRITISH, however, won the islands by 1763.

In 1773 the Caribs agreed to a British settlement, but disputes arose, leading to war (1795–6). The British deported most Caribs to Nicaragua (where they joined the SUNOS) and established a plantation economy: today, nearly 80% of the population is of African descent The culture became officially English-speaking, although French patois remained widespread. Later, Asian indentured labourers added yet another element to the mix. The islands became independent in 1979; but since then unemployment remained a great burden to the nearly 116,000 population in 2001.

## SALINAN

A Native North American nation of central coastal California. Semi-sedentary hunters, fishers, gatherers and traders, they spoke a Hokan language. From the late 18th century the Spanish evangelized them, and diseases reduced their numbers sharply. When the missions closed the Salinan were left landless and forced to subsist

by wage labour. They are trying to regain some of their cultural identity but have never gained federal recognition or tribal lands despite their efforts. They protested vehemently when the federal government proposed using some of their traditional lands for a bombing range in 2001. In 1990 some 279 claimed Salinan descent.

## SALISH

A Native North American nation of Montana. Sometimes called 'Flathead' (from the practice of binding flat boards against the foreheads of babies to flatten them as they grow), their name means 'we are the people'. Nomadic hunters and gatherers, they spoke a Salishan language. Despite their reputation for bravery and honesty, they were steadily weakened by epidemics and a series of wars with the BLACKFOOT from the 18th century. In 1855 they were forced to cede their lands, and in 1871 agreed, in a perhaps forged treaty, to move to a reservation, the boundaries of which are still contested. They refused to move onto it until forced to do so by the US Army in 1891. Some moved to Canada instead.

In 1936 they formally confederated with the KOOTENAI and have spent much of the late 20th century seeking greater sovereignty and economic security, especially through logging and tourism, as well as preserving an endangered language. In 1990 they numbered over 10,000.

## SALVADORANS

The population of the Central American Republic of El Salvador. Conquered by Spain in the 16th century, the large Native American population nevertheless had a great influence on the developing culture of the colony. Today the country is over 90% MESTIZO. El Salvador became independent from Spain in 1821, and left the Central American Federation in 1839. Since that time it has known little but political turmoil. With 14 families controlling the economy, and most people living in abject poverty, brutal oppression was used to crush any sign of dissent. In 1932, for example, a revolt was suppressed, leaving 30,000 dead. By the 1970s poverty was fuelling the ranks of left-wing guerrillas, who were confronted by government-backed death squads, leading to a severe refugee crisis. The success of the Sandanistas in Nicaragua in 1979 inspired fresh revolt, again suppressed with AMERICAN aid.

Poverty remains a major burden, and dysentery and malaria are endemic in many areas. The population was over 6.2 million in 2001.

# SAMISH

A native American nation of coastal Washington state. Sedentary hunters, fishers and gatherers, they spoke a Salishan language. In 1855 their name was omitted from the Point Elliot treaty, but others supposedly signed for them. This left their status uncertain. They never received their own reservation, being forced to live among the LUMMI and SWINOMISH.

In 1969 the Samish were again omitted from the list of federally recognized nations, and in 1979 the government declared them extinct as a nation. In 1996 they regained federal recognition but not treaty rights, such as a share in the salmon harvest. Litigation over stolen treaty rights continues. In 2001 they numbered 900.

# SAN AUGUSTIN CULTURE

A former Native South American culture of the Colombian Andes. Sedentary farmers, hunters and gatherers, the people appeared in the 6th century BC, began constructing earth mounds around the time of Christ, and disappeared after AD 500. The culture was noted for massive anthropomorphic statuary, some with carvings similar to NORSE runes, prompting romantic but unproven speculation of contacts between the two cultures.

# SANPOIL

A Native North American nation of Washington state. Semi-sedentary hunters, fishers and gatherers, they spoke a Salishan language. They were reputedly a highly pacific nation, which left them vulnerable to raids by their neighbours. Much reduced by epidemics, they were even more vulnerable to settlers. Having quickly lost their lands, they endured a reservation life of poverty, dependence and loss of culture. Most of

their descendants are found on the COLVILLE reservation.

# SANTARÉM CULTURE

A former Native South American culture of Brazil's Amazonia. The people were sedentary farmers, fishers, hunters and gatherers who produced fine, flamboyant ceramics. They were also territorially expansionist and were engaged in wars of conquest when the PORTUGUESE arrived in the 16th century and subjugated them. Thereafter slavery, disease and acculturation caused their rapid disappearance.

# SANTEE

A Native North American nation of South Carolina, whose name means 'river people'. Sedentary farmers, fishers, hunters and gatherers, they spoke a Siouan language. Although they were early allies of the English, mistreatment by settlers drove the Santee to join against them in the YAMASEE War (1715–16). Defeat, slave-raiding and CREEK attacks drove most to join the CATAWBA. Some, however, stayed on their traditional lands, and from the 1960s their descendants have been seeking state and federal recognition. In 2000 their number was estimated at 6000.

# SAPONI

A Native North American nation of Virginia, whose name means 'shallow water', although they call themselves *Yesah*, meaning 'the people'. Sedentary farmers, hunters, gatherers and fishers, they spoke a Siouan language.

From the 1650s the Saponi were increasingly caught up in regional wars and suffered severely from epidemics. The IROQUOIS drove them into North Carolina (where many remained); the Saponi returned around 1740, only to be attacked again. They became increasingly splintered, with many being absorbed by other nations, notably the CAYUGA and TUSCARORA, and their descendants are found as far afield as Canada. They participated in the first joint powwow of all Virginia's nations in 2002 in pursuit of federal recognition. Their numbers are today

S

uncertain, but were estimated to be at over 3000 in 1990.

## SARAMAKA

A South American nation of African descent in Suriname's rainforest. Originally escaped slaves, they prospered despite difficult conditions and attempts to destroy them. As most men were required to be migrant workers, they developed a matrilineal society, and speak an English-based Creole language. In 1995 they numbered about 23,000.

## SARSI

A North American aboriginal nation of Alberta and Montana, who call themselves *Tsuu T'ina*, meaning 'many people'. Nomadic hunters, gatherers and fishers, they speak an ATHABASKAN language. Once part of the BEAVER, they separated from them in the 18th century, traditionally because of a feud over the killing of a dog. In the 19th century they became part of the BLACKFOOT confederacy. They were forced onto a reservation near Calgary in 1877, resulting in heavy acculturation.

In 1997 the Sarsi numbered about 1100. Attempts to preserve their culture were supported by their victory in a 100-year-old land claim.

## SAUK or Sac

A Native North American nation of Michigan, who call themselves *Asakwaki*, meaning 'people of the yellow earth'. Sedentary farmers, hunters, gatherers and fishers, they spoke an Algonquian language.

The Sauk were driven by the OTTAWA into Wisconsin, where they accepted the remnants of the FOX in 1734 to protect them from genocide, and became the Sauk and Fox. By 1804, under pressure from settlers, a single band signed a treaty ceding all Sauk lands, and they were forced into Iowa. In 1828, while they were away on their winter hunt, the AMERICAN government simply sold their lands, and when they attempted to return across the Mississippi, many were slaughtered in the Blackhawk War (1832–3). The

remainder were moved to Kansas in 1842 and then to Oklahoma in 1867. On the reservation they resisted determined government attempts to destroy their traditional culture. In 1997, when they numbered about 3700, they won important litigation to protect their environment, forcing a power company to provide clean water and rectify decades of pollution.

## SCHAGHTICOKE

A Native North American nation of western Connecticut, whose name means 'at the confluence of two rivers'. Sedentary farmers, hunters, gatherers and fishers, they spoke an Algonquian language. Originally established in 1743 by Moravian missionaries as a refuge for Native Americans fleeing the wars to the east, especially MAHICAN and PEQUOT, Schaghticoke developed a distinct identity and became the name of a new nation. They suffered major land thefts in the 18th century, leading to severe poverty, as well as efforts to destroy their culture and identity lasting into the 20th century.

The Schaghticoke have had land claims rejected by the federal government, and the state government was still opposing their bid for federal recognition in the early 21st century, on the grounds that they were not descended from a historic nation. They claimed that the state has dealt with them as a nation for 250 years. They numbered about 300 in 2001.

## SECHELT

A Native North American nation of southwest British Columbia. Their name perhaps means 'land between two waters'. They are sedentary hunters, fishers and gatherers, and speak a Salishan language.

Seriously reduced by epidemics caused by diseases bought by fur traders in the 19th century, the Sechelt scattered into small villages. Only in the late 20th century did they become outspoken in defending their rights. They are currently engaged in a bitter dispute with the provincial government over logging rights. They are also opposing CANADIAN plans to allow US nuclear submarines to use waters next to their lands. In 1998 they numbered about 900.

# SEKANI

A Native North American nation of British Columbia's sub-Arctic, whose name might mean 'people of the earth'. Originally nomadic hunters, fishers and gatherers, they speak an ATHABASKAN language. They entered the fur trade in 1804, and missionaries and gold-seekers further disrupted their traditional culture and reduced them through diseases. During the 20th century, many were impoverished, and the damming of the Peace River in 1968 lost them much of their lands. In 1979 they formed the CARRIER Sekani Tribal Council to protect their rights, and it pursued cases of ex-servicemen's entitlements and of the sexual abuse of children in residential schools. It also sought control of their land's resources, especially logging and fishing. In 2000 the Inter-American Commission on Human Rights took up their case concerning the allocation of timber rights. In 1982 they numbered over 600.

# SEMINOLE

A Native North American nation of Florida and Oklahoma. Their name means perhaps 'wild one' or 'people who live at a distance'. Sedentary farmers, fishers, hunters and gatherers, they spoke a Muskogean language. One of the FIVE CIVILIZED TRIBES, they were originally part of the CREEK nation. When their ENGLISH allies encouraged them to attack other Native Americans in Florida under SPANISH rule, the Seminole broke away and settled their newly conquered lands.

Difficulties arose when Spain ceded Florida to the USA. Settlers flooded in, and soon they coveted Seminole lands and began slave raids. The government attempted to move the Seminole to Oklahoma in 1833. Most went, although unwillingly, while others fled as far as Texas and Mexico. Some, however, decided to stay, leading in 1835 to the USA's first guerrilla war, which was long and costly, in lives and money. The Seminole were not defeated then or in two subsequent wars.

The two independent Seminole groups in Florida and Oklahoma remain proud of their traditional culture and seek to preserve it, although their language is now in danger of extinction. In 1990 the Seminole numbered perhaps 14,000.

# SENECA

A Native North American nation of the New York area, now also of Oklahoma and Ontario, whose name means 'keepers of the western door'. Sedentary farmers, hunters, gatherers and fishers, they spoke an Iroquoian language and were part of the IROQUOIS league. When it went into decline they supported Britain in the American Revolution. Some fled to Canada, and those who stayed lost much of their land as punishment. They were defrauded of most of the remainder in 1838. Dependent on wage labour, they became largely assimilated culturally, but retained their identity.

In 1997 the Seneca were involved in a series of land claims, which involved the city of Buffalo and part of the city of New York. They also defended their sovereignty by successfully resisting attempts to force them to levy state taxes. In 1990 they numbered about 8500.

# SERI

A Native North American nation of Sonora, Mexico. They call themselves *Comcáac*, meaning 'the people'. Nomadic fishers, hunters and gatherers, they spoke a Hokan language. Spanish attempts to evangelize and settle them failed, and the Seri were therefore deemed barbaric, which might explain unproven accusations of cannibalism. Settlers feared them for the poisoned arrows they used, but the Seri remained reclusive, only entering the cash economy in the 20th century through wood-carving for tourists. They have no organized government, but in 2001 were estimated to number 800.

# SERRANO

A Native North American nation of southern California. Semi-sedentary hunters and gatherers, their name is Spanish for 'mountaineer', but they call themselves *Yuharetum*, meaning 'people of the pines'. In 1819 the SPANISH forced them onto a mission, which was closed in the 1830s, leaving them landless and destitute. The 1849

Gold Rush reduced them further. In 1866, after the death of three settlers, militias were formed to exterminate the Serrano. They received only the San Manuel reservation in 1891, where 295 lived in 1990.

## SHACRIABA

A Native South American nation of the Amazonia regions of Peru and Brazil. Sedentary farmers, fishers, hunters and gatherers, they spoke a Gê language, now extinct. After centuries of discrimination, land theft, acculturation, epidemics and murder, they managed in 1977 to gain one of the few convictions for murder of Native Americans in Brazilian history. They numbered over 5000 in 2001.

## SHASTA

A Native North American nation of northern California and southern Oregon. Semi-sedentary hunters, fishers, gatherers and traders, they called themselves *Ka'hosadi*, 'true speakers'.

In 1851 the Shasta negotiated a treaty with the USA, which was never ratified or honoured. Shasta legend claims that the food prepared for them to celebrate the treaty was poisoned, killing scores. Although there is apparently no documentary evidence of this, it remains central to their oral history. Settlers and gold miners quickly flooded their lands and destroyed entire villages, causing the Rogue River Wars (1850–7). The survivors were moved onto reservations in Oregon, where their lands were further reduced.

In 1995 they numbered about 1400 and were attempting to preserve their culture and protect sacred sites, although federal recognition was still being denied in 2002.

## SHAWNEE

A Native North American nation of South Carolina, Kentucky, West Virginia and Tennessee, whose name means 'southern people'. Nomadic hunters and gatherers, they spoke an Algonquian language. Seen by their neighbours as a warlike nation, they were willing to enter the fur trade after 1670, but remained hostile to settlers. They fought the ENGLISH from 1754 and after the

American Revolution fought the USA. Defeat at the Battle of Fallen Timbers (1794) forced them to cede a vast area, although their great leader, Tecumseh, spent the rest of his life trying to forge an alliance to defeat the AMERICANS. They became fragmented after defeat, forming groups such as the Absentee, the Eastern, and the Loyal (united with the CHEROKEE in the 1860s). Most were moved to Kansas and Oklahoma in the mid 19th century. There is also the Remnant Band in Ohio, descendants of Tecumseh's followers, who enjoy state, but not federal, recognition.

Prolonged recent litigation was attempting to recover lands confiscated for munitions works in Kansas. All Shawnee are trying to preserve their culture. In 2001 they numbered over 14,000.

## SHINNECOCK

A Native North American nation of Long Island, New York. Seasonally mobile within their territory as hunters, gatherers and especially fishers, they employed limited agriculture and spoke an Algonquian language.

Exploited by settlers in the 17th century as whalers, they quickly grew distrustful and insular. In 1703 they won a lease on their lands for an annual payment of one ear of corn, but in 1859 they were pressured, by, they claim, illegal means, into accepting smaller territory. The real-state surrounding their territory is owned by millionaires, and the Shinnecock are constantly alert to attempts by wealthy landowners to defraud them of their lands. By 2000 a younger generation were more vocal in their resentment of living in poverty surrounded by opulence, and are seeking federal recognition as a move towards pressing a massive land claim. They numbered around 350 in 1995, and had done much to protect their traditional culture, even if their language is nearly extinct.

## SHOSHONE

A Native North American nation of the northwest Great Plains, who call themselves *Newe* or *Nomo*, meaning 'people'. Mostly nomadic hunters and gatherers, they spoke an Uto-Aztecan language. Their harsh environment kept settlers out until the mid-19th century. There

> *"How can we have confidence in the white people? When Jesus Christ came upon the earth, you killed him, the son of your own God, you nailed him up! You thought he was dead, but you were mistaken. And only after you thought you killed him did you worship him, and start killing those who would not worship him. What kind of people is this for us to trust?"*
>
> Speech ascribed to Shawnee leader Tecumseh (1810)

was a brief resistance, but the Bear River massacre convinced the Northern Shoshone to enter a reservation in 1863, and in 1872 one-third of the reservation was removed by a 'surveyor's error'. The Eastern Shoshone aided the US Army against the LAKOTA and felt betrayed when forced onto a reservation themselves; the Western Shoshone were gradually pushed onto reservations by the early 20th century.

Scattered across 18 reservations in four states, often shared with traditional enemies, the Shoshone have been striving to reclaim their traditional lands. They resisted government pressure to accept cash compensation, and took their case to the United Nations in 2001. In 2002 the Organization of American States condemned the USA for violating the human rights of the Shoshone by denying them their ancestral lands. In 1990 they numbered over 9000.

# SHUAR

See JIVARO.

# SHUSWAP

A Native North American nation of British Columbia. They call themselves *Secwepemc*. Seasonally mobile primarily as hunters, fishers and gatherers, they speak a Salishan language.

Their neighbours considered the Shuswap aggressive and they were frequently involved in warfare. By the mid-19th century, wars and epidemics had weakened them, and they were unable to resist the theft by settlers of their mineral-rich lands. In the late 20th century they began to re-assert their rights, winning in 1974 half the salmon catch in their traditional territory, but campaigns to protect their environment have brought them into confrontation with the courts, which they accuse of corruption. In 2000 they numbered about 7500.

# SILETZ

Originally a Native North American nation of coastal Oregon, whose name means 'crooked river'. Sedentary hunters, fishers and gatherers, they spoke a Salishan language. They were drastically reduced by epidemics, and the discovery of gold on their territory doomed them. By 1855 only 21 remained. This offered the AMERICAN government the opportunity to use their reservation as a dumping ground for similarly depleted nations from California, Oregon and Washington. They were expected to die out quickly, but instead the Confederated Tribes of Siletz Indians, from 27 nations and 5 linguistic stocks, survived. In 2000 they numbered about 3300.

# SINABO

An uncontacted Native South American nation thought to exist in Bolivia's Amazonia. They are probably nomadic hunters and gatherers, numbering perhaps over 200.

# SINKYONE

A Native North American nation of central coastal California. Semi-sedentary hunters and gatherers, they spoke an ATHABASKAN language. Settlers massacred most in the mid-19th century, and many survivors were absorbed by other nations. Their descendants were still active enough to protest against being described as a 'vanished people' in the 1970s. There are no official population figures, but they are still trying to preserve some traditional culture and land.

# SIONA-SECOYA

A Native South American nation of the Amazonia of Colombia, Peru and Ecuador. Seasonally mobile within their territory as fishers, hunters and gatherers, they spoke a Tucano language. Originally two separate nations with close language and cultural links, they came under great pressure from rubber extractors from the late 19th century and began to merge, and by the 1970s were seen as a single nation.

In the 20th century they became vocal in defence of their interests. In the 1990s, for example, they were litigating against an oil company for damage to their environment, and complaining of coercion to grant further oil concessions. In 1993 they numbered about 1250.

S

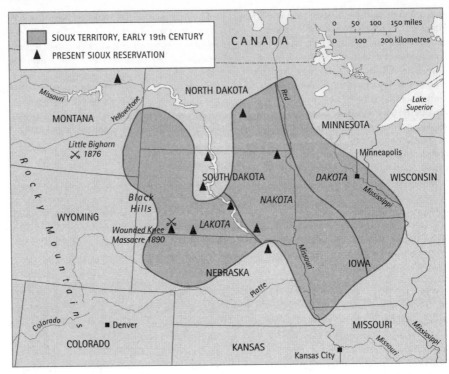

SIOUX TERRITORY, EARLY 19th CENTURY
▲ PRESENT SIOUX RESERVATION

# SIOUX

A Native North American nation of the northern Great Plains. Their name comes from the OJIBWA and means 'enemy', but they call themselves NAKOTA, DAKOTA and LAKOTA, meaning 'allies'. Mainly nomadic hunters and gatherers, they spoke a Siouan language.

Forced from the Great Lakes area in the 18th century, the Sioux acquired European horses and most adopted a nomadic lifestyle. The three groups began to diverge, although they saw themselves as a single federation. They continued to share a common culture, involving the sun dance (which involved self-torture as a form of religious sacrifice) and belief in a single creator, Watan Tanka. From the mid-19th century they were gradually forced onto various reservations, mainly in South Dakota, generally after bitter and bloody resistance. Thereafter they experienced intense poverty and government policies determined to destroy their traditional culture.

In the late 20th century the Sioux have proven more assertive of their rights and governments have become more sympathetic. A cultural renaissance emerged, but economic conditions remain dire. In 1998 they numbered over 100,000.

# SIRIONO

A Native South American nation of Bolivia's Amazonia. Nomadic fishers, hunters and gatherers, they spoke a TUPÍ language. Contacted in 1693, they steadfastly resisted efforts by missionaries to settle them. In 1937, however, some were settled forcibly, but disease and ill treatment killed many. The lived at bare subsistence, levels and reputedly ate alone to avoid envying others. In 1995 they numbered about 500.

# SIUSLAW

A Native North American nation of coastal Oregon. They were semi-sedentary hunters, fishers and gatherers, and spoke their own Siuslawan language. Although they suffered from settler encroachment and from epidemics, the Siuslaw remained neutral in the Rogue River War (1855). They were still forced to leave their traditional lands, and became part of the COOS Lower Umpqua and Siuslaw Tribe, which numbered about 670 in 1999. Repeated lawsuits against the AMERICAN government have failed to win them compensation for stolen lands. They are also seeking to take over lands from the US Forestry Service, hoping this will bring them economic self-sufficiency.

## SKAGIT

A Native North American nation of coastal Washington state. They refer to themselves as *Bastúlekw*, meaning 'people of the river'. Sedentary hunters, fishers and gatherers, they spoke a Salishan language. Entering the fur trade in the late 18th century, they were soon decimated by the diseases it brought. In the mid-19th century, under pressure from settlers, they avoided signing treaties, and instead retreated inland seeking isolation. Because they lacked a reservation, many ended among the SWINOMISH. They gained federal recognition only in 1974 and a reservation in 1983, and with the reservation some control over their traditional fishing grounds. In 1995 they numbered about 500.

## SKOKOMISH

A Native American nation of Washington's Puget Sound, whose name means 'people of the river'. They called themselves *Tuwa'duxq*. Sedentary hunters, fishers and gatherers, they spoke a Salishan language. In 1855, much reduced by diseases brought by the fur trade, they were forced to accept a reservation, which was enlarged in 1874; but cash compensation promised was paid only in 1966. In the 1920s the AMERICAN government and the city of Tacoma were indifferent to their interests when damming the Skokomish River, destroying their salmon run. By 1999 silting had made it the most flood-prone river in the USA, and the Skokomish were litigating for huge damages. In 1995 they numbered about 1350.

## SLAVE

A Native North American nation of the North-western Territories, British Columbia and Alberta. Their name is a translation of the CREE name for them, *Awokanak*. Originally nomadic hunters, fishers and gatherers, they speak an ATHABASKAN language and call themselves *Dene*, meaning 'people'. Driven from further east by the better-armed Cree in the 18th century, they were too isolated to have much contact with whites until the 1890s. In 1899 they agreed to cede their lands for reservations, annuities and services, but most of their more productive lands were subsequently seized. From the late 20th century they have been attempting to protect their environment and preserve their language. In 1982 they numbered about 5000.

## SNOHOMISH

A Native North American nation of northwest Washington state. Semi-sedentary hunters, fishers and gatherers, they spoke a Salishan language. Joining the fur trade in the early 18th century, they were much reduced by its associated diseases. In 1855 they were forced to cede their lands in exchange for two reservations, but only received a shared one at Tulalip.

In 1913 the Snohomish established the Northwest Federation of American Indians to fight for their rights and help preserve their culture. In 1998 they were outspoken in protests over plans to build over a Snohomish cemetery, and in 2002 sued the US government for failing to protect endangered fish stocks. In 1998 they numbered about 3370.

## SNOQUALMIE

A Native North American nation of Washington's Puget Sound. Sedentary hunters, fishers and gatherers, they spoke a Salishan language. In 1855 they were forced to cede their lands. Some moved to the Tulalip reservation with the SNOHOMISH, while others remained on their traditional lands, entering wage employment in logging and farming. This division, with two groups claiming to be the true successors of the Snoqualmie, caused great problems in their

S

quest for federal recognition, which was only gained in 2000. In 2001 they numbered around 1000.

## SOBAIPURI

A Native South American nation of Arizona, originally an offshoot of the 'Akimel O'Odham' (PIMA). Sedentary farmers, hunters and gatherers, they spoke an Uto-Aztecan language. At the end of the 17th century they came under attack from the APACHE, and subsequently were decimated by epidemics. By the mid-19th century, they ceased to exist as a separate nation, and the remnants were re-absorbed by the Pima.

## SONGHEES

A Native North American nation of Vancouver Island and coastal British Columbia. Their name perhaps means 'people gathered from scattered places', although they call themselves *Lkungen*. Seasonally mobile within their territory primarily as hunters, fishers and gatherers, they speak a Salishan language. They entered the fur trade in the 18th century and ceded their lands in a treaty in 1849 (without understanding its meaning). Subsequently settlers stole their best remaining lands, bringing intense poverty. Disease reduced them to just 171 in 1910, and they were expected to become extinct within a generation. They survived, however, and numbered about 2000 in 2001, when they were pressing a land claim and attempting to revive their traditional culture.

## SPOKAN

A Native North American nation of western Washington state, whose name means 'children of the sun'. Semi-sedentary hunters, fishers and gatherers, they spoke a Salishan language. They may have their origins in the fusion of several bands, although this is uncertain. In the 18th century they acquired horses and began annual bison hunts on the Great Plains, earning the enmity of the BLACKFOOT and alliance with the SALISH. In 1858 they joined the COEUR D'ALENE in resisting settlers. Defeat cost them their lands. Some received their own reservation in 1881,

while others were divided among the Salish, Coeur d'Alene and COLVILLE. Having lost considerable lands because of the Grand Coulee dam, they have pursued land and water claims against the AMERICAN government with some success. These successes, especially over water, have caused tensions with their neighbours; there were complaints of racist attacks in nearby towns in 2001. In 1990 they numbered about 2120.

## SQUAMISH

A Native North American nation of mainland British Columbia and once also of Vancouver Island. Seasonally mobile within their territory primarily as hunters (especially of sea mammals), fishers and gatherers, they speak a Salishan language. Originally in 16 sub-groups, they entered the fur trade in the early 19th century and were pushed onto 28 scattered reserves, where their best lands were stolen. In the 1870s the provincial government unilaterally denied their title to their lands and went on to try to destroy their traditional culture. They numbered 2910 in 2001 and were making progress in pressing land claims and asserting their sovereignty over their own resources after nearly 100 years of campaigning.

## SQUAXIN ISLAND

A Native North American nation of coastal Washington state. Sedentary hunters, fishers and gatherers, with a limited amount of agriculture, they spoke a Salishan language. Entering the fur trade in the 18th century, their numbers were much depleted by the associated diseases. In 1855 they were forced to cede their lands. During the Puget Sound Indian War (1855–6), they were confined to Squaxin Island, although some were subsequently moved to live among the SKOKOMISH and QUINAULT. In 1999 they numbered about 650.

## STEILACOOM

A Native North American nation of western Washington state, whose name is an Anglicization of *Scht'ileqwen*, originally the name of a single village. Sedentary hunters and gatherers, they spoke a Salishan language. In 1846 the US army established a fort on their territory, making it attractive to settlers. They were promised a reservation in a treaty of 1854, but the promise was broken because of the opposition of settlers. The Steilacoom were scattered among other nations, such as the PUYALLUP and NISQUALLY, or remained landless on their traditional territory. Cultural erosion resulted. They spent the 20th century seeking redress through the courts, but , numbering nearly 700, they suffered a devastating blow in 2000 when the US government decided they were extinct as a nation.

## STILLAGUAMISH

A Native North American nation of western Washington state, whose name means 'river people'. Sedentary hunters, fishers and gatherers, they spoke a Salishan language. In the 19th century they entered the fur trade and suffered severely from the resulting epidemics. After the Puget Sound Indian War (1855–6), they lost their lands and in 1863 were forced onto the Tulalip reservation with the SNOQUALMIE. They spent the 20th century unsuccessfully seeking federal recognition, and pressing a land claim with partial success. In 2000 they numbered about 150. In 2001 they were involved in disputes over plans to develop lands they considered sacred.

## STOCKBRIDGE

A Native North American nation of Wisconsin. Sedentary farmers, they spoke an Algonquian language. The nation comprised mainly MAHICANS who had chosen to embrace white culture fully, establishing Stockbridge, Massachusetts, as a mission town in 1734. Warfare and epidemics still did not leave them unscathed, and one-third died fighting for the rebels during the American Revolution. Despite their sacrifice for the country they were pushed off their lands by settlers and moved among the ONEIDA until they were again expelled. Eventually, in 1856, they settled in Wisconsin. In 2001 they numbered about 1500.

## SUMA

A former Native North American nation of northern Chihuahua, Mexico, and western Texas. Probably sedentary farmers, hunters and gatherers, they spoke an unknown language. In the mid-17th century the Spanish evangelized them. The resulting epidemics, rebellions and APACHE raiding destroyed them as a nation by the 19th century. The Apache, PUEBLO and the general population of Mexico probably absorbed the remnants.

## SUNOS

A Native Central American nation of the Caribbean coast of Nicaragua and Honduras. Sedentary farmers, hunters and gatherers, they spoke a CARIB language. Subject to Spanish slave raids in the 16th century, their unwelcoming terrain and the guns traded from buccaneers allowed them to retain their independence. They also strengthened their numbers by accepting escaped African slaves, and, in the 1790s, those expelled by the BRITISH from their island possessions. This gave a strong African influence to their culture.

In the 20th century acculturation became a serious concern for the Sunos, who numbered about 7400 in 1982 in Nicaragua and El Salvador.

## SUQUAMISH

A Native North American nation of western Washington. Sedentary hunters, fishers and gatherers, they spoke a Salishan language. In the 1830s they entered the fur trade, suffering seriously from its associated epidemics. They became famous for the powerful speech reputedly given by their great leader Chief Seattle in defence of their land and their connection to it. They were still forced to accept a reservation at Port Madison. In the 1870s, as part of the policy to undermine Native American culture, their communal and spiritual centre was destroyed. Suquamish culture did survive, and repeated challenges to their sovereignty, including over their right to impose their laws on non-Suquamish within the reservation, have been

*" When the last Red Man shall have perished, and the memory of my tribe shall have become a myth among the white man, these shores will swarm with the invisible dead of my tribe, and when your children's children think themselves alone in the field, the store, the shop, or in the silence of the pathless woods, they will not be alone ... The White Men will never be alone. "*

ascribed to
Chief Seattle of the
Suquamish, *c.* 1855

resisted. They have also defended their treaty rights – in 1995 the courts affirmed their right to gather shellfish on their traditional territory. These victories have caused tensions with their neighbours. In 2001 Chief Seattle's grave was vandalized, perhaps a racially motivated offence. In 2000 they numbered about 800.

## SURINAME CREOLES

A South American culture of Suriname. The term is generally used to refer to those of mixed European and African birth, with African elements are very strong in the culture. Often poor, the Suriname Creoles comprised nearly one-third of the national population and became very politically active in the late 20th century in defence of their interests. As the main supporters of the Suriname National Party in the 1950s and 1960s, they were at the forefront of the independence movement. In 1996 they numbered over 100,000, about one-quarter of whom spoke an ENGLISH-based Creole language.

## SUSQUEHANNOCK

A Native North American nation of Pennsylvania, whose name means 'people of the muddy water'. Sedentary farmers, hunters, gatherers and fishers, they spoke an Iroquoian language.

Regarded by their neighbours as warlike, the Susquehannock dominated their area and controlled trade with the DUTCH from the 1620s by terror. The fur trade provided them with at least one cannon. The POWHATAN claimed they were cannibals. They were powerful enough to hold the IROQUOIS at bay for many years in a major war (1649–75). At the same time, settlers were increasingly encroaching on their lands, and the Maryland colony also attacked the Susquehannock (1642–52) before they became allies against the IROQUOIS. Exhausted, the surviving Susquehannock moved into the Maryland colony. However, a white militia attacked their town, apparently by mistake, and the remnants fled and surrendered to the Iroquois.

The Susquehannock returned, much reduced, in 1706 to their traditional lands, where they became peaceful Christians. In 1763, when war broke out again, a vigilante group called the Paxton Boys, who went unpunished despite the horror of most colonists, finally massacred them. The Appalachian American Indians of West Virginia do, however, claim to be their descendants.

## SWINOMISH

A Native North American nation of northwest Washington state. Sedentary hunters, fishers and gatherers, they spoke a Salishan language.

In the 1830s the Swinomish entered the fur trade and were much reduced by its associated diseases. In 1855 they were forced to accept a reservation, which was also used for other nations. They lost access to their traditional fishing grounds until the late 20th century, which caused great poverty. In 2002 the extent of these fishing grounds was being legally challenged by the MUCKLESHOOT. That year the Swinomish were also becoming anxious at the levels of toxic pollutants in the shellfish, which were basic to their diet. In 1990 they numbered around 715.

## TAGISH

A Native North American nation of the Yukon Territory. Their name comes from the TLINGIT and means 'the spring ice is breaking up'. Originally nomadic hunters, fishers and gatherers, they speak an ATHABASKAN language, which in 1995 had just two speakers out of a population of about 400. In the 19th century, Tlingit control of the area's fur trade allowed them to dominate the Tagish. In the 1890s floods of gold-seekers depleted game, polluted streams and spread epidemics. Determined CANADIAN attempts to destroy the traditional Tagish culture followed, leading to intense poverty. Negotiations for land rights with the provincial government from the 1990s have proven frustratingly slow.

## TAHLTAN

A Native North American nation of northern British Columbia. Their name perhaps means 'something heavy in the water'. Originally nomadic hunters, fishers and gatherers, they speak an ATHABASKAN language. During the 19th

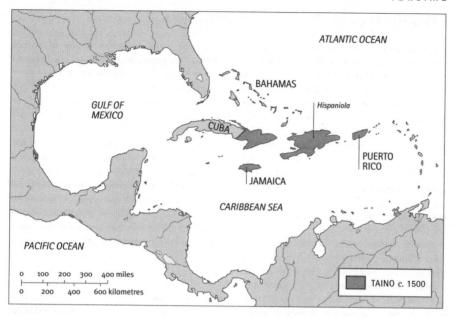

century TLINGIT control of the fur trade allowed them to culturally dominate the Tahltan. The Klondike Gold Rush brought further cultural erosion and diseases into their territory in the 1890s. Increasing dependence on the wage economy, and poverty, followed. In 2000, when they numbered about 650, they reached an agreement with the provincial government over protecting their environment, limiting logging and protecting wildlife.

## TAINO

A Native Caribbean nation of the island of Hispaniola (now comprising Haiti and the Dominican Republic) and the Greater Antilles. Sedentary farmers, hunters and gatherers, they spoke an Arawakan language. In the 1490s they welcomed the SPANISH at Hispaniola, and agreed to pay tribute. But the Spanish turned on them in 1503, and within 20 years had all but annihilated them. The only significant community to survive was in Puerto Rico.

In 2000 the Taino numbered over 13,000, and were not only trying to preserve their culture, but also, as a matter of national self-esteem, sought the revocation of the papal bull of 1493 that called for Native Americans to be subjugated by a Christian empire.

## TAKELMA

A Native North American nation of southern coastal Oregon, whose name means 'those living along the river'. Sedentary hunters, fishers and gatherers, they spoke a Penutian language that is now extinct. The fur trade and its associated epidemics had already decimated them by the 1850s, when settlers began to encroach on their lands. Perhaps half of their population died in that decade from disease and murder, and more were to follow. Eventually, after the Rogue River War (1855–6), the US army forced them on their own 'trail of tears' to SILETZ and Grand Ronde reservations. There, they ceased to exist as a distinct nation; the 1910 US census counted just one. Some, however, remained on their traditional lands, and in 1997, their descendants, along with some SHASTA and others, formed the Rogue-Table Rock group, seeking federal recognition; they numbered over 120.

## TAMAULIPEC

A former Native North American nation of central Mexico. Sedentary farmers (at least after the SPANISH arrived in the 16th century) and hunters and gatherers, they perhaps spoke a Coahuiltecan language, only traces of which survive. Divided into more than 24 autonomous groups, they could offer little resistance to the Spanish, who confined them onto missions that destroyed their traditional culture and identity as a nation. No reliable population estimates of their descendants are available.

## TAMOYA

A former Native South American nation of coastal Brazil. Sedentary farmers, fishers, hunters and gatherers, they initially welcomed the PORTUGUESE at the beginning of the 16th century. Exploitation and abuse, however, soon provoked what became a brutal war of resistance. Supported occasionally by the FRENCH, they proved formidable enemies, even taking ships, and battles were followed by wholesale massacres. Their strength, however, was gradually ground down. They were finally defeated in 1597. Those not slaughtered were enslaved, and their nation was destroyed.

## TANAINA

A Native North American nation of southwest Alaska. They call themselves *Dena'ina*, meaning 'people'. Seasonally mobile within their territory primarily as hunters, fishers and gatherers, they speak an ATHABASKAN language. In 1784 RUSSIANS brought the fur trade, as well as its associated diseases, to the Tanaina, and although Russian attempts to reduce them to serfdom were resisted, their cultural impact can be seen in Tanaina traditional stories and spirit-house designs. The 1867 purchase of Alaska by the USA was disastrous for the Tanaina, as commercial fishing and monopoly control of the fur trade undermined their economy. Much of their traditional culture has, however, been carefully preserved. In 1995 they numbered nearly 500.

## TANANA

A Native North American nation of central Alaska. Originally nomadic traders, hunters, fishers and gatherers, they speak an ATHABASKAN language. Comprising several autonomous groups, they were eager to join the fur trade in the 19th century and were willing to fight any nation attempting to block their access to it. The epidemics and territorial losses that followed seriously weakened them. In 1962, however, they came together to protect their interests, pursuing successful land claims and protecting the fishing rights they see as vital to the survival of their culture. By 2000, when they numbered around 14,000, they had won control of their own welfare programme.

## TAPIRAPÉ

A Native South American nation of Brazil's Amazonia. They were sedentary slash-and-burn farmers, fishers, hunters and gatherers and spoke a TUPÍ language. Possibly migrants from the coast fleeing European settlements, they had little contact with the outside world until the 20th century. By the late 1990s, however, the environmental damage threatened by a government waterways project, coupled with severe drought, threatened their survival. In 1990 they numbered 210.

## TARAHUMARA

A Native North American nation of northern Mexico, who called themselves *Raramuri*, meaning 'foot runners', a skill for which they were renowned. Seasonally migratory within their territory as farmers, hunters and gatherers, they spoke an Uto-Aztecan language.

In the early 17th century, the SPANISH established missions among them and were welcomed. But in 1638 the discovery of silver brought in a great influx of settlers, and abuses multiplied. This led to war in 1648, which lasted until 1700. Thereafter they were left isolated until 1856, when new MEXICAN land laws allowed them to be dispossessed and impoverished. In 2000 the Tarahumara numbered about 60,000 and were striving to protect their culture.

Many were barely surviving on subsistence agriculture, while others were forced to seek migratory employment.

# TARAIRIU

A Native South American nation of Brazil's Amazonia. Probably nomadic fishers, hunters and gatherers, they spoke a Gê language. In the 17th century they fought a merciless war against PORTUGUESE encroachment. In 1692 they achieved a peace treaty, but it was soon violated by ranchers and gold-seekers. By the early 18th century they had been destroyed by slavery and genocide.

# TARAPACÁ

A Native South American nation of Chile. Sedentary farmers, hunters and gatherers, they spoke an AYMARAN language. Originally of the inland valleys, they were conquered by the INCA in the late 15th century and forcibly relocated to the Atacama area to be under closer supervision. Their new terrain was harsh, with limited resources, and agriculture was possible only near oases and rivers. The main effects of conquest by the SPANISH in the 16th century were the loss of their language and the adoption of Catholicism. Economic hardship, however, forced so many to migrate that their cultural cohesion and identity as a nation was gradually undermined. No realistic census count is possible.

# TARASCAN

See PURUPECHA.

# TATAVIUM

A Native North American nation of southern California, whose name comes from the SHOSHONE and means 'people facing the sun'. Semi-sedentary hunters and gatherers, they spoke an Uto-Aztecan language. From 1797 the Spanish evangelized them and disease reduced their numbers rapidly. By the mid-19th century their language was extinct and they had scattered. The last known Tatavium died in 1921, although descendants can still be found in other groups, especially among the KAWAIISU.

# TAWAKONI

A Native North American nation of Kansas, whose name probably means 'neck of land in the water', a reference to the location of their village. Originally a WICHITA sub-group, they migrated from Kansas to Oklahoma and Texas by the early 18th century. Sedentary farmers, hunters and gatherers, they spoke a Caddoan language. In alliance with the HASINAI they fought SPANISH and later AMERICAN settlers. In 1859, however, they were forced to move to the Wichita reservation in Oklahoma, where they were re-absorbed.

# TEHUELCHE

A Native South American nation of southern coastal Chile and Argentinian Patagonia. Seasonally mobile within their territory as hunters and gatherers, they called themselves *Ahonicanka* or *Tchonek*. In the 17th century they acquired horses and began to trade with, as well as raid, Spanish settlements. Alongside their MAPUCHE neighbours they managed to maintain their independence, although in the north many were under such pressure that they joined the Mapuche. In 1883 they were finally overrun, and their lands and traditional culture were lost. In 1983 they numbered about 1500, but only about 35 still spoke their language. The Téuesh are a sub-group of the Tehuelche.

# TEMBÉ

A Native South American nation of Brazil's Amazonia, whose name perhaps means 'flat nose'. They were sedentary slash-and-burn farmers, fishers, hunters and gatherers and spoke a TUPÍ language. In 1861 violence erupted because of the abuses of traders seeking copal oil. The Tembé fled into the interior, and were hardly contacted until the 1960s, when land encroachment became a serious problem. They received demarked territories, but illegal logging and squatters were not removed. In 1993 they burned the homes of about 200 squatters, but problems still persist. In 1999 they numbered up to 14,000.

## TENINO

A Native North American nation of Oregon. Semi-sedentary hunters, fishers and gatherers, they spoke a Sahaptian language. In 1848, some sided with the CAYUSE in their war with settlers. In 1855 they were forced to accept a treaty ceding their lands and were moved to the Warm Springs reservation along with the WASCO and Northern PAIUTE. They became the Confederated Tribes of the Warm Springs reservation, which numbered about 3000 in 2001.

## TEOTIHUACÁN CULTURE

A Native North American culture of central Mexico. Sedentary farmers, hunters, gatherers and traders, the Teotihuacán people flourished from AD 200 to 650. They built Mexico's first great city, after which their culture is named (it lies some 40 km / 25 miles northeast of Mexico City), which was, with an estimated population of 200,000 at its height, one of the largest in the world. Their great pyramid (the Pyramid of the Sun) is the world's third-largest. They controlled a great trade network stretching to Guatemala.

The decline of Teotihuacán, for which there is no satisfactory explanation, was rapid after AD 650. Around 750 their city, virtually abandoned, was deliberately burned. However, they greatly influenced all the cultures that followed them; indeed the AZTECS claimed that it was at this spot that the sun and the moon were created, such was the impact of the Teotihuacán culture's legacy.

## TEPEHUAN

A Native Central American nation of Durango, Mexico. Sedentary farmers, hunters and gatherers, they spoke an Uto-Aztecan language. From the mid-16th century they fought against SPANISH attempts to evangelize them, but gradually their resistance was ground down and many of them became acculturated. In 1860 some joined a revolt against Mexico for an independent republic. In 2000 they numbered about 20,000, of whom three-quarters spoke their language. They were also one of the nations that the Zapatista revolutionaries, who took up arms in 1994

against government complicity in Native American poverty, claimed to represent.

## TEREMEMBÉ

A Native South American nation of the northern Brazilian coast. Probably nomadic fishers, hunters and gatherers, they spoke Teremembé. Initially friendly towards the PORTUGUESE, they were swept aside in the late 17th century as ranchers stole their lands. Their descendants are acculturated, and their language is assumed to be extinct.

## TÉUESH

See TEHUELCHE.

## THOMPSON

A Native North American nation of British Columbia, named after their residence in the territory of the Thompson River, although they call themselves *Ntlakapamux*. Seasonally mobile within their territory primarily as hunters, fishers and gatherers, they speak a Salishan language. They were feared by their neighbours for slave-raiding. However, they were unable to resist the flood of gold-prospectors into their territory during the 1850s and the ensuing confiscation of their lands by the provincial government.

In 1996, when they numbered about 4000, they still had not received satisfaction for their land claims, but had perhaps greater hope in winning some assistance towards their economic and social problems and greater autonomy from the CANADIAN government.

## THULE CULTURE

A former INUIT culture that emerged in the 10th century AD in northern Alaska and had spread across Canada and Greenland by the 13th century. It displaced, possibly by acculturation, the DORSET CULTURE. Seasonally mobile within their territory, especially as whalers and also as hunters, gatherers and fishers, the people spoke an Eskaleut language. They invented all the tools traditionally used by their Inuit successors, who are more diverse and generally have a less aquatic subsistence. Their culture began to disappear by the 15th century, a possible result of climate change leading to sparser resources.

## TIAHUANACO CULTURE

See TIWANAKU CULTURE.

## TILLAMMOOK

A Native North American nation of coastal Oregon, whose name perhaps means 'land of many waters'. Semi-sedentary traders, hunters, fishers and gatherers, they spoke a Salishan language. An isolated, loose-knit nation, they offered little resistance to settler diseases, murder and land theft. They signed a treaty in 1851, but it was neither ratified nor honoured. A few were persuaded to enter Grand Ronde reservation, while others scattered. In 1946 some descendants sued the AMERICAN government over their stolen lands, winning compensation in 1953. By then, however, they had ceased to exist as a nation.

## TIMBIRA

A Native South American nation of Brazil's Amazonia. Originally nomadic hunter-gatherers, they had become sedentary and practised limited farming by the 19th century. They spoke a Gê language and were prepared to fight to keep BRAZILIAN settlers off their lands, but were protected more by their relatively unattractive terrain. In 1995 they numbered about 950.

## TIMOTE

A Native South American nation of Venezuela's Amazonia. Sedentary irrigation farmers, fishers, hunters and gatherers, they spoke Timote. Their prosperous lands were coveted by the SPANISH in the 16th century, and despite their fierce resistance, they were soon conquered. Over time they became absorbed into the MESTIZO population. At least one village, however, numbering possibly over 200 in 1996, maintained a Timote identity, although only a few remnants of their traditional language and culture survive.

## TIMUCUA

A Native North American nation of coastal Florida and Georgia, whose name might mean 'chief' or even 'my enemy'. Sedentary farmers, fishers, hunters and gatherers, they spoke dialects of Timucuan. As the Timucua comprised mutually hostile autonomous groups, the SPANISH were able to establish control over them in the 16th century, using missions that rapidly reduced them through epidemics. From 1661 the English armed nations such as the YAMASEE to attack the Spanish in order to break their rule. Forbidden arms by the Spanish, the Timucua were nearly destroyed by war and slave raids. By the time Spain lost Florida in 1763 only a handful remained, who were evacuated to Cuba. Possibly some descendants remain among the SEMINOLE, while others remaining in Florida, along with the descendants of other nations, have formed the Taino Nation Timucua Tribal Council, seeking state recognition in the early 21st century.

## TIWANAKU CULTURE

A former Native South American culture of western Bolivia. Sedentary farmers, herders and fishers, the culture appeared around 1600 BC, reached its height between AD 300 and 900, and disappeared around 1200. The people built stepped pyramids, mostly of crude stones, although some massive masonry blocks were moved several kilometres by unknown means. They had a wide-ranging trading network and built a theocratic empire that had a political and cultural impact throughout the region. They may have been the ancestors of the INCA (there are similarities in their ceramics), but there is no conclusive evidence of this. The city of Tiwanaku, which once housed several thousand people, appears to have declined as the waters of Lake Titicaca receded, and it ceased to be a port. The decline of the city in turn appears to have undermined the entire empire by 1100.

## TLAXCALAN

A former Native North American nation of central Mexico. Sedentary farmers, hunters and gatherers, they perhaps spoke a Nahuatl language. They were bitter enemies of the AZTEC, and although their small mountainous territory was not easily conquered, they were subject to Aztec attacks in search of victims for human sacrifice. They became eager allies of the SPANISH in 1519 and were crucial in the destruction of the Aztec. This gave them a favoured status, but it did not protect them from epidemics, nor did Spanish gratitude last long. They were soon exploited as ruthlessly as their neighbours and became increasingly fragmented. Within a few generations they had ceased to exist as a nation.

## TLINGIT

A Native North American nation of coastal Alaska and British Columbia. Their name means 'human beings'. Sedentary traders, hunters, fishers and gatherers, they speak Tlingit.

After some conflict, the RUSSIANS established a profitable fur trade with the Tlingit in the 18th century. However, as the Russians became more aggressive in trying to control jealously guarded trade routes, they provoked a war in 1802. There-

after the Tlingit fought Russian and then AMERICAN attempts to dominate them, being fully suppressed only in 1882. As early as 1912, however, they had turned to political activism through the Alaskan Native Brotherhood, fighting and winning land claims, fishing disputes, and discrimination cases, as well as reviving their traditional culture.

A measure of their political power can be seen in their success in 2001 in winning the repatriation of cultural artefacts (including totem poles) from American museums, and their successful litigation against the high-handed manner in which the British Columbian government granted mining concessions without recognizing Tlingit sovereignty (2002). In 1999 they numbered about 17,000.

## TOBA

A Native South American nation of the Gran Chaco of Paraguay, Bolivia and Argentina. Nomadic hunters and gatherers, they spoke a Guaycuran language.

Often allies of the MOCOVÍ, the Toba fought a long and bitter war against SPANISH colonization. Largely subdued in the 18th century, they still remained relatively isolated. Around 1900, however, a century of land theft began, and they were almost driven out of Bolivia. The PARAGUAYAN government moved to re-settle them. In Argentina, which had the largest Toba population, their land claims were, however, ignored. Overgrazing reduced their lands to semi-desert, and it was not until 1993 that their protests were heard. But official promises were undelivered, and in 1996 they occupied a partly-built bridge linking Argentina and Paraguay, which finally forced the government to grant land titles and environmental restoration. In 2001 they numbered about 25,000.

## TOBACCO

An Aboriginal nation of Ontario, who called themselves *Khionontateronon*, meaning 'where the mountain rises'. Sedentary farmers, traders, hunters, gatherers and fishers, they perhaps spoke an Iroquoian language. They grew plentiful tobacco for trade, had warm relations with

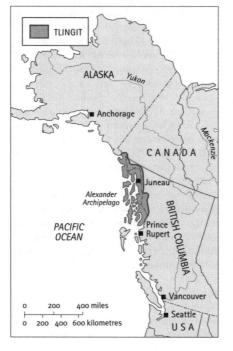

Tlingit

the HURON, and entered the fur trade with the FRENCH. This was enough to earn them the hostility of the IROQUOIS, who destroyed their village in 1649. The survivors were absorbed by the Iroquois, ILLINOIS and Huron, but in 1980 over 1000 still claimed Tobacco descent in the USA.

## TOHONO O'ODHAM

A Native North American nation of Sonora, Mexico, and Arizona, whose name means 'desert people'. They are also called Papago, and are closely related to the PIMA. Sedentary farmers, hunters and gatherers, they speak an Uto-Aztecan language. On the fringes of SPANISH and later MEXICAN power, they escaped enslavement even when there were continual encroachments into their territory by miners. In 1853, however, the Gadsden Purchase split their territory between Mexico and the USA. Despite helping the US Army against the APACHE, the Tohono O'Odham lost most of their lands.

Of the 24,000 population in 2001, about 7000 lacked AMERICAN birth certificates, meaning that even veterans were denied benefits they were due. In 2001 an Act was sent to Congress to rectify this. The Tohono O'Odham have also been active in patrolling their stretch of the frontier, forming a border patrol, the Shadow Wolves, which has impressed international observers.

## TOLOWA

A Native North American nation of northwest California whose name comes from the YUROK and might mean 'I speak Athabaskan'. They call themselves *Hush*, meaning 'people'. Semi-sedentary hunters, fishers, gatherers and traders, they spoke an ATHABASKAN language.

In 1853, during the Gold Rush, they were subjected to calculated genocidal attacks by white militias; 600 were slaughtered during a religious ceremony at Burnt Ranch. Some found refuge among other nations, and in 1906 they received two *rancherias* (settlements) on their original territory. They numbered 451 in 1990. Although only five spoke their native language in 1997, the survival of their culture is of great importance to them.

## TOLTEC

A Native North American nation of central Mexico. Sedentary farmers, traders, hunters and gatherers, they spoke a Nahuatl language. The successors to, and possibly destroyers of, the TEOTIHUACÁN CULTURE, they were a militaristic culture that expanded rapidly in the 10th century AD. Skilled architects and among the first skilled metalworkers in the region, they were able to create a great empire by about AD 950, reaching into Yucatan and Guatemala. Their decline, from about 1150, was equally rapid. Perhaps drought and famine, coupled with internal divisions (possibly because of constant immigration) and invasion are the explanation for this. By about 1170 their great city of Tollán (which once housed perhaps 30,000) had been destroyed, although their Yucatan centre at Chichén Itza survived until 1221. The survivors scattered and were absorbed by other nations.

*" The Toltecs were well instructed in agriculture. "*

**W.H. Prescott, 1843**

## TOLÚ

A Native South American nation of Colombia's Caribbean coast. Sedentary farmers, fishers, hunters and gatherers, they spoke a Choco language. A socially stratified culture, they also traded gold, which made them an early target of SPANISH greed in the 16th century. Thereafter they rapidly disappeared as a nation.

## TONKAWA

A Native North American nation of eastern Texas, whose name might mean 'people of the wolf'. They call themselves *Titskan-watich*, meaning 'most human of people'. Nomadic hunters and gatherers, they spoke Tomkawan. Their neighbours saw them as warlike and apparently believed they were cannibals. The Tonkawa resisted SPANISH attempts to convert them but were willing to ally with Texas against the COMANCHE although they continued raiding settlements. In 1855 the AMERICAN government tried to settle the Tonkawa on a reservation in Texas, but settler hostility forced their relocation to Oklahoma. During the Civil War neighbouring nations attacked and all but destroyed them. In 1995 they were estimated to number 1300.

*" Tonkawa ... have no land ... but are always moving. "*

**J. Sibley, 1806**

## TOTONAC

A Native North American nation of Mexico's Caribbean coast. Sedentary farmers, hunters and gatherers, they spoke a Zoquean language. When the SPANISH arrived in 1519 the Totonac had been subjugated by the AZTEC for 25 years, burdened with very heavy tribute. They were therefore only too eager to ally against them, providing 50,000 warriors. Their rewards were epidemics, the systematic destruction of their traditional culture, especially their religion, and the theft of their lands. Left impoverished, they nevertheless retained their national identity, and in the 1990s were amidst a cultural revitalization. They were also more vocal in the defence of their rights, and enacted a non-violent seizure of government offices in 1995. In 1990 they numbered about 260,000, although fewer than one-quarter of those spoke their language.

## TRINIDADIANS AND TOBAGONIANS

The population of the Caribbean Republic of Trinidad and Tobago, an island country northeast of Venezuela; the overwhelming majority live on Trinidad. It was first settled by the SPANISH in 1592, and they destroyed the native ARAWAK population. The islands were then sought after by several European powers. The BRITISH secured the territory in 1802, by which time a plantation economy had introduced strong African influences into the culture. (Those of African descent now form about 43% of the population.) Tobago was claimed by Britain in 1763, but made a ward of Trinidad in 1889 after the colony became bankrupt. After slavery was abolished in 1833, there were large-scale arrivals of South Asian indentured labourers, and now 41% of the people are of this extraction.

Culturally, the islanders are known as the inventors of steel-drum calypso music and the holders of a boisterous and popular carnival, to whom cricket is nearly a religion. Independent since 1962, the islands experienced an oil boom in the 1970s, providing relief from poverty. Yet political tensions remained, and in 1990 the Muslim minority attempted a *coup d'état*. In 2001 the population was nearly 1.2 million.

## TRIÓ

A Native South American nation of the Amazonia of Suriname and Brazil. Seasonally mobile within their territory as fishers, hunters and gatherers, they spoke a CARIB language. Despite the depredations of gold-seekers and the destruction of their environment, they have succeeded in preserving much of their traditional culture and language. In 2001 conservationists helped them map their territory to enable them to claim legal title to it. In 1995 they numbered about 330 in Brazil, and in 198 about 820 in Suriname.

## TSACHILA

A Native South American nation of Ecuador, whose name means 'true people'. Sedentary farmers, hunters and gatherers, they speak a Baracoan language, and were once widely called *Colorado*, because of their red body paint. Until the 1950s they remained almost completely isolated, but when a road was built through their territory, they became a popular tourist attraction. The result was rapid assimilation, and their traditional culture and language are seriously endangered. In 1999 they numbered 2100.

## TSETSAUT

A former Native North American nation of the Alaska–British Columbia border area. Their name comes from the NISKA and means 'people of the interior'. Probably nomadic hunters, fishers and gatherers, they spoke an ATHABASKAN language. Given to raiding their neighbours for women, they became so troublesome during the mid-19th century that the TAHLTAN drove them from their traditional lands into TLINGIT and TSIMSHIAN territory. The ensuing warfare was so severe that the Tsetsaut were almost exterminated by 1865, and they soon disappeared as a nation. The last language-speaker died *c.* 1930.

## TSIMSHIAN

A Native North American nation of northwest British Columbia and later of Anette Island, Alaska. Sedentary traders, hunters, fishers and gatherers, they speak Tsimshian. Considered warlike by their neighbours, they possibly practised ritual cannibalism on their enemies. They have a strong trading tradition, particularly in their dazzling art works. At the end of the 18th century the fur trade brought them both greater prosperity and diseases. In 1857 an Anglican mission was established among them. The missionaries moved with part of the nation to Anette Island in 1887, in an attempt to draw them away from traditional practices such as the potlatch.

Land claims and the defence of their resources and traditional culture made the Tsimshian politically active in the 20th century, often in alliance with the TLINGIT. In 1990 they numbered nearly 7000, but with around only 320 Tsimshian language-speakers, they were undertaking a language preservation project.

## TSOYAHA YUCHI

See YUCHI.

## TÜBATULABAL

A Native North American nation of eastern California, whose name means 'pine-nut eaters'. Semi-sedentary hunters and gatherers, they spoke an Uto-Aztecan language and were once part of the SHOSHONE. In the 1850s they joined with the PAIUTE in resisting the encroachment of settlers and miners, and in 1863 the US Army massacred about 40 Tübatulabal. Epidemics reduced their numbers further, and they were allotted land near their traditional territory only in 1893. In 1995 they numbered about 900 and were still trying to preserve their culture and attain federal recognition.

## TUNICA

A Native North American nation of Mississippi, whose name means 'the people'. Sedentary farmers and traders who hunted and gathered as secondary forms of subsistence, they spoke Tunican. They lived in walled towns and built temple mounds. In the 17th and 18th centuries epidemics and warfare, especially with the CHICKASAW and NATCHEZ, greatly reduced them

and forced a series of migrations. By 1790 they were in their current location in Louisiana. In the early 19th century they merged with the BILOXI, becoming the Tunica-Biloxi, who won federal recognition only in 1981. Numbering about 180 in 1990, they were deeply concerned with preserving what remained of their culture.

## TUPÍ

A term denoting a culture and language group found in much of Brazil, Paraguay, Peru, Bolivia and French Guiana. Depending on their environment, Tupí people were often sedentary slash-and-burn farmers, which required periodic relocation as soil became exhausted; they were also fishers, hunters and gatherers, and they spoke Tupí dialects. Generally territorially expansionist and often practising ceremonial cannibalism on their enemies, they had reached the Brazilian coast, perhaps originating in Paraguay, by the late 15th century. Shortly afterward SPANISH and PORTUGUESE aggression began the destruction of many groups, but in 1998 the Tupí still numbered nearly 5 million.

## TUPINA

A former Native South American nation of coastal Brazil. They were sedentary slash-and-burn farmers, fishers, hunters and gatherers, and spoke a TUPÍ language. They had palisaded villages and practised ceremonial cannibalism on their enemies. Driven inland by the TUPINAMBA when Europeans arrived in the 16th century, they subsequently vanished as a nation.

## TUPINAMBA

A Native South American nation of coastal Brazil. Sedentary slash-and-burn farmers, they were also fishers, hunters and gatherers, and spoke a TUPÍ language. Having driven out the TUPINA in the 15th century, they subsequently battled PORTUGUESE encroachment. With large canoes they were willing to fight on the open sea, and practised ceremonial cannibalism on their enemies, most notably Brazil's first bishop. With FRENCH allies they withstood Portuguese pressure until the end of the 16th century, before

*" although all of [the Tupí] confess human flesh to be wonderfully good and delicate, nonetheless it is more out of vengeance than for the taste. "*

Jean de Léry, 1578

*" In appearance they [the Tupinamba] are dark, somewhat reddish, with good faces and good noses, well shaped. "*

Pedro Vaz de Caminha, 1500

**Tupinamba,
Tupinikin**

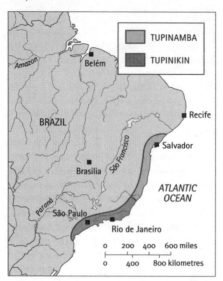

being driven inland after great bloodshed. Some scattered groups still survive, but have generally become heavily acculturated, making a census count impossible.

## TUPINIKIN

A Native South American nation of coastal Brazil. They practised slash-and-burn farming, fishing, hunting and gathering, and spoke a TUPÍ language. Initially welcoming PORTUGUESE settlers, who wanted to evangelize them, they accepted demarcated lands in 1610. Exploitation and impoverishment followed, much worsened in 1940 when most of their land was confiscated. Extreme hunger and poverty drove the Tupinikin to launch an international campaign to regain their land in 1996, when they numbered about 1300.

## TURKS AND CAICOS ISLANDERS

The inhabitants of a BRITISH Caribbean dependency of two island groups, north of Haiti. By the mid-16th century the SPANISH had exterminated the native TAINO population, leaving the islands the subject of conflict among European powers. Settled by English from Bermuda in 1678, the islands became a base for buccaneers in the 18th century. After the American Revolution, loyalists from the former colonies attempted to establish a plantation economy, and although this failed, it introduced strong African influences into the developing culture. Living standards were low and unemployment often high. The islands were governed first from Jamaica and then from the Bahamas until 1973, when they became a Crown Colony. They were promised independence in the 1980s, but corruption scandals removed independence from the political agenda until 1996.

The country today is of mostly African descent. There is also a fairly large HAITIAN expatriate community there. In 2001 the inhabitants numbered over 18,000.

## TUSCARORA

A Native North American nation originally of North Carolina, now of New York state and Ontario. Sedentary farmers, hunters, gatherers and fishers, they spoke an Iroquoian language. A numerous and powerful tribe when first encountered by Europeans, they were quickly reduced by epidemics and warfare. By 1711 repeated slave-raiding and land thefts provoked a war, which by 1713 saw the majority of Tuscarora killed or enslaved. Fewer than 2000 survivors fled to New York, where they joined the IROQUOIS league. Their decision to support the rebels during the Revolution contributed to the decline of the league. Despite their loyalty the Tuscarora were forced to cede their lands and moved among the SENECA. Four scattered groups in North Carolina joined to seek federal recognition and the restoration of ancestral lands in 2001. There were about 1200 Tuscarora in total in the USA in 1996.

## TUTCHONE

A Native North American nation of the Yukon Territory. Originally nomadic hunters, fishers and gatherers, they speak an ATHABASKAN language. In the 1840s they entered the fur trade, suffering diseases in consequence. Serious cultural destruction followed the Klondike Gold Rush in 1898, when the Tutchone lost most of their lands. Measures to preserve their language were part of treaty negotiations with the provincial government in 1998. This was followed in 2001 with an offer of funds for a re-forestation programme. In 1982 they numbers were estimated at about 1500.

## TUTELO

A Native North American nation of Virginia who called themselves *Yesah*, meaning 'the people'. Sedentary farmers, hunters, gatherers and fishers, they spoke a Siouan language. Part of the MONACAN Confederation, they were under constant IROQUOIS attack between 1671 and 1722, when they took refuge on Roanoke Island. They made peace by 1740, and moved to Pennsylvania under Iroquois protection, and in 1753 they were formally adopted into the CAYUGA.

The descendants of the Tutelo reside mostly in Ontario, but there is a Tutelo-Occaneechi band in North Carolina claiming descent and seeking federal recognition.

## TUTUTNI

A Native North American nation of southwest Oregon, whose name means 'people close to the river'. They possibly called themselves *Tunne* meaning 'people'. Sedentary hunters, fishers and gatherers, they spoke an ATHABASKAN language, which only two speakers maintained in 2002. In 1851 they agreed a treaty ceding their lands, but still suffered attacks from settlers. In 1858 they were forcibly relocated to the SILETZ reservation, where their culture disintegrated and they seemed to be nearing extinction as a nation. In 2002, however, there were over 100 descendants in Oregon. Indeed, one group, who call themselves the United Chetco-Tututni Tribe and number just 27, was seeking federal recognition in 1998.

## TWANA

A Native North American nation of Washington state's Puget Sound, whose name means 'people from below'. Sedentary hunters, fishers and gatherers, they spoke a Salishan language. In the 19th century they entered the fur trade, suffering severely from its associated epidemics, and in

1855 were forced to accept a treaty ceding their lands. They moved to the SKOKOMISH reservation, where they were rapidly acculturated and nearly disappeared as a distinct nation. Their descendants are seeking to recover some of their culture and preserve their language.

## UMATILLA

A Native North American nation of northeast Oregon, whose name means 'many rocks' and was initially the name of a single village. Semi-sedentary hunters, fishers and gatherers, they spoke a Penutian language. In the early 18th century they acquired horses and undertook annual bison hunts. Growing numbers of settlers began to alarm them in the 1840s, and in 1848 the Umatilla joined in the CAYUSE War. Conflicts with settlers continued and in 1855 the Umatilla were forced to accept a treaty ceding their lands for a reservation, where they were joined by the WALLA WALLA and Cayuse.

These nations became the Confederated Tribes of the Umatilla Nation Reservation, who numbered about 2315 in 2000. Their lands were steadily reduced until little was left, and the damming of their rivers destroyed their salmon runs. From the 1970s they became more militant in exercising their treaty rights, and in 1994 they achieved the return of the salmon. Water rights are still a cause of friction with their neighbours.

## URUGUAYANS

The population, largely of European descent, of the South American Republic of Uruguay. The original inhabitants were the CHARRÚA, but white settlers rapidly displaced them in the 17th century. Thereafter the territory was contested between first Portugal and Spain, and then Brazil and Argentina. In 1828 Britain intervened to restore stability to an important trading area, and Uruguay became an independent buffer zone between the ARGENTINIANS and BRAZILIANS.

Initially the new state was chaotic, with a 40-year power struggle between conservative land-owning and liberal-urban elites. In 1872 a power-sharing arrangement provided stability. Commercial ranching and agricultural exports thereafter provided prosperity and attracted

Ute

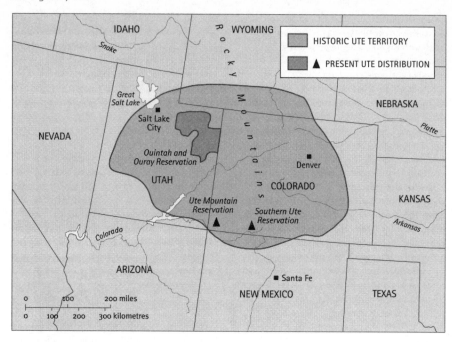

HISTORIC UTE TERRITORY

▲ PRESENT UTE DISTRIBUTION

IDAHO

WYOMING

NEBRASKA

Snake

Rocky

Platte

Great
Salt Lake

NEVADA

Mountains

Salt Lake
City

Ouintah and
Ouray Reservation

Denver

UTAH

COLORADO

KANSAS

Ute Mountain
Reservation

Southern Ute
Reservation

Arkansas

Colorado

▲

▲

ARIZONA

Santa Fe

NEW MEXICO

TEXAS

0      100      200 miles

0   100   200   300 kilometres

u

immigrants, and the SPANISH and ITALIANS came to dominate the culture. Football became a national obsession (they have won the World Cup twice). Valuable social reforms also followed. At the start of the 20th century Uruguay became the best-educated nation in South America. Uruguayans also achieved the first welfare state on the continent, even if the resources supporting it were limited. They were by then a model of stability in a deeply troubled region. Periods of severe economic crisis, however, put that stability to the test. In 1933, with exports collapsing, Uruguay entered a brief period of military rule, but the constitution was soon restored.

In the 1960s, when prosperity again declined and the government was widely seen as corrupt, a group of urban revolutionaries, the Tupamaros, emerged. The result was a coup and an extended period of military rule (1973–84). Constitutional restoration did not disguise the divisions in Uruguayan society, and the fact that its stability could be fragile. In 2001 Uruguayans numbered over 3.3 million.

# URUPA

A former Native South American nation of the Amazonia regions of Bolivia and Brazil. Little is known of their culture, but they were possibly sedentary slash-and-burn farmers, fishers, hunters and gatherers, and they spoke Urupa. Decimated by European diseases, they ceased to exist as a nation by the early 20th century.

# UTE

A Native American nation of Utah and Colorado. Their name means 'land of the sun, although they call themselves *Noochew*, meaning 'the people'. Nomadic hunters and gatherers, they spoke an Uto-Aztecan language. From the 17th century the various independent bands began to acquire European horses and herd cattle and sheep gained through raiding. In 1868 they were forced to cede much of their land, but retained much of western Colorado. They stubbornly resisted government efforts to force them to become sedentary farmers, and an attempt by a government agent to plough up their race track caused a brief war in 1880. Colorado voters had already been campaigning for their removal, and this war was an adequate pretext to do so. Many Ute were forced into Utah reservations. In 2000 they were awarded the largest land restoration in history. Much of it, however, needed decontaminating of nuclear waste. In 1990 they numbered over 7200.

## U'WA

A Native South American nation of Colombia's Amazonia. Once seasonally mobile within their territory as farmers, fishers, hunters and gatherers, they were more sedentary by the 20th century. They consider themselves guardians of the rainforest and bitterly oppose oil drilling. In 1997 they threatened to commit mass suicide if planned drilling occurred on their lands, an act one community committed in the 17th century to avoid SPANISH conquest. An international outcry was raised at the alleged violence and threats used to intimidate them. In 2002 U'wa spiritual leaders prayed that the oil would be hidden from test drilling, and much to the amusement of international observers, no oil was found. They numbered about 5000 in 2000.

## VALDIVA TRADITION

A former Native South American culture of the Andes. One of the first cultures of the area, it appeared in the late fourth millennium BC in coastal Ecuador, and probably had a marine-based subsistence. It developed, without any apparent antecedents, fine ceramics, which by about 1400 BC had some similarities to contemporary Japanese work. This led to romantic but unproven theories of trans-Pacific contacts.

## VENEZUELANS

The inhabitants of the South American Republic of Venezuela. The first spanish settlers arrived in 1521 and had to combat Native American resistance, as they pressed inland in their quest for the supposed El Dorado. A largely MESTIZO population and culture developed, combining African, European and Native American elements, distinctive especially in its music. Independent

from Spain in 1821 and separated from Colombia and Ecuador in 1830, the Venezuelans experienced severe economic and political instability. For 150 years they endured the autocratic rule of dictators, or *caudillos*, who protected the wealth and privileges of a property-owning elite. Indeed, the only effective political institution was the army. Economic development benefited few; the poverty and illiteracy of the majority were ignored.

The 20th century saw increasingly brutal and venal dictators, such as Cipriano Castro (1899–1908). The economy deteriorated because of corruption. Default on foreign debts and mistreatment of foreign citizens twice (in 1903 and 1908) led to European powers blockading Venezuelan ports and bombarding fortresses. Only AMERICAN influence saved Venezuela from complete humiliation, but the population rallied to their ruler. A national identity containing a strong element of xenophobia and a heroic self-image of a small state successfully defying great powers developed. The discovery of oil only provided dictators with the resources to secure their rule. When Castro was overthrown there were riotous public celebrations, but he was soon replaced. Anti-Americanism grew as the USA was blamed for sustaining dictators in order to control the oil. In 1958 US Vice President Richard Nixon was nearly lynched by an enraged mob, and a coup attempt in 2002 was automatically assumed in Venezuela to be American-backed.

From the 1960s democratically elected governments, with mildly reformist programmes, became the norm, although economic mismanagement has still left severe social problems. After so much history of repression, however, Venezuelans have become more assertive and demanding politically, and less likely to tolerate dictatorships. In 2001 the size of the population approached nearly 24 million.

## VERACRUZ CULTURE

A former Native North American culture of Mexico's Gulf coast. Sedentary farmers, traders, hunters and gatherers, the people flourished from about AD 300 until about 1200. They borrowed much of their culture, especially

V

architecture, from the MAYA, although there has also been speculation about cultural links with the TOTONAC and OLMEC. The Veracruz cities were great trading centres, with pyramids and platforms with ornately decorated stonework. The culture might also have invented a ball-game that had a deep religious significance.

The cause of their decline in the 12th century is unclear, although environmental collapse because of over-exploitation is likely. Invasion is also a possibility – the main city of El Tajin was destroyed by fire.

## VINCENTIANS

See ST VINCENTIANS.

## VIRGIN ISLANDERS

The inhabitants, mostly of African descent, of a Caribbean island group, dependencies of Britain and the USA. Between 1672 and 1733 the islands were settled by the ENGLISH and Danish; the original inhabitants had already vanished. Plantation economies were established, producing a culture combining European and African elements. The abolition of slavery in the 19th century led them into economic decline, and the DANES sold their islands to the USA in 1917, adding a new AMERICAN element to the culture. Remaining dependencies with considerable autonomy, they gained relative prosperity through US tourism, especially after the embargo on Cuba from the 1960s, which has muted any discussion of independence. In 2001 Virgin islanders numbered over 143,000.

## WACCAMAW

A Native North American nation of South Carolina, who called themselves *Wap-ka'-hare*, meaning 'people of the fallen star'. Sedentary farmers, hunters and gatherers, they spoke a Siouan language. In the 18th century they fought a series of disastrous wars against the BRITISH and their CHEROKEE and NATCHEZ neighbours. Many merged with the CATAWBA. Others fled to the swamps of North Carolina, where they remain as the state-recognized Waccamaw Siouan Tribe. Others who remained on their ancestral lands

were named the Chicora-Waccamaw Indian People and numbered about 1800 in 1997. By 2001 this latter group had failed to win either state recognition or the repatriation of ancestral remains.

## WAICA

A Native South American nation of Brazil's Amazonia. Once nomadic fishers, hunters and gatherers, from the 17th century they became more sedentary slash-and-burn farmers. They spoke a Yanoman language, and were seen as aggressive by their neighbours. As the PORTUGUESE population of the coast grew, they tended to withdraw inland. They are commonly counted as part of the YANOMAMI, to whom they are related.

## WAILAKI

A Native North American nation of northern California, whose name comes from the WINTUN and means 'north language'. Sedentary hunters, fishers and gatherers, they spoke an ATHABASKAN language that is now extinct.

A warlike nation who were reputedly headhunters, they were involved in a war with the CAHTO in the 1850s. This ended when settler militias undertook a war of extermination against them in 1861. Even when confined on the Round Valley reservation they were still attacked by squatters. With unemployment driving many to leave the reservation, they complained bitterly of police harassment and racism in the 1990s. In 2000 they numbered about 1000.

## WAIWAI

A Native South American nation of Brazil's Amazonia. Sedentary slash-and-burn farmers, they were also fishers, hunters and gatherers and spoke a CARIB language. Although they were relatively isolated, and many migrated to Guyana in the 19th century, they had become heavily acculturated by the 20th century. In 1995 they numbered about 1350.

# WALAPAI

A Native North American nation of northwest Arizona and Mexico, whose name means 'pine tree people'. The call themselves *Pa*, meaning 'people'. Seasonally moving as farmers, hunters and gatherers, they spoke a Yuman language. In the 1850s settlers and prospectors began to flood into their territory, leading to war. They were defeated in 1869, more by dysentery and whooping cough than by the army and its MOHAVE allies. Forced onto a lowland reservation where further epidemics broke out, they escaped in 1875 only to find their traditional lands lost. They were pushed onto their current reservation in 1883. In 1995 the Walapai numbered about 1900, living largely by cattle-ranching, timber and tourism, and were seeking to keep their traditional culture alive.

# WALLA WALLA

A Native North American nation of southeast Washington state, whose name means 'many waters'. Sedentary traders, hunters, fishers and gatherers, they spoke a Sahaptian language. In the 18th century they acquired horses, becoming highly skilled horse-breeders. In 1855 they were forced to agree to a treaty ceding their lands, but they chose to fight back. They were defeated by 1858, and the following year they were driven to the UMATILLA reservation and told they would be shot if they left. There they still remain. By the end of the 20th century they were seeking to revive their culture and gain the repatriation of the remains of their ancestors held by American museums. In 2000 there were possibly about 300 of Walla Walla descent on the reservation.

# WAMPANOAG

A Native North American nation of Rhode Island and coastal Massachusetts, whose name means 'people of the first light'. Sedentary farmers, hunters, gatherers and fishers, they spoke an Algonquian language. In 1621, devastated by disease and under MICMAC and NARRAGANSETT attack, they allied with the struggling ENGLISH Massachusetts colony. Repeated land thefts, however, provoked King Philip's War (1675–6),

in which militias attempted to exterminate or enslave the Wampanoag. Forced onto reservations, the survivors had to subsist from wage labour. Their language fell into disuse in the 19th century, and they began to organize and preserve their traditional culture only in the 20th century. One group alone, which numbered 550 in 1996, has received federal recognition.

# WAPPINGER

A former Native North American nation of New York state, whose name means 'easterner'. Sedentary farmers, hunters, gatherers and fishers, they spoke an Algonquian language. In the 17th century they entered the fur trade with the DUTCH, but relations were never easy. In 1643 the massacre of a group of Wappinger at Pavonia started a war; the Dutch hired English mercenaries who massacred up to 700 in an attack on a Wappinger fortress. The murder of a woman for picking peaches started a new war in 1655 (the Peach War).

As the settler population increased, the Wappinger population decreased through disease, war and land theft. The most notorious example of the last was perpetrated by the ENGLISH in 1683, and 60 years later the Wappinger were still refused redress. By the end of the 18th century the Wappinger had disappeared, many being absorbed into the MUNSEE and MAHICAN.

# WAPPO

A Native North American nation of northern California whose name comes from the Spanish *guapo*, which means 'brave'. Sedentary hunters, fishers and gatherers, they spoke a Yukian language, which by 2002 was seriously endangered. After great resistance, they were evangelized by the SPANISH in the early 19th century. When the MEXICANS sold off mission property in 1834, the new owners regarded the Wappo as servile labourers. The Gold Rush brought them genocidal attacks and expulsion from their lands. Alexander Valley *rancheria* (settlement) was eventually allotted to them, but federal recognition was withdrawn in 1958. In 2000 they numbered about 250 and were still trying to regain that recognition.

" God has prospered us so that wee had driven the Wampanoogs with Philip out of his countrie. "

R. Williams, 1676

## WARRAU

A Native South American nation of the Amazonia regions of Guyana and Venezuela. Sedentary traders, fishers, hunters and gatherers, they spoke Warrau, although some adopted ARAWAKAN culture, including farming, from the 16th century. Although generally friendly towards SPANISH settlers, they still tended to migrate inland as the Spanish population grew. In 1996 there were about 18,500 native language-speakers.

## WASCO

A Native North American nation of Washington state, whose name means 'those who have the cup', referring to a distinctive rock near their main village. Sedentary traders, hunters, fishers and gatherers, they spoke a Penutian language, maintained by only five elderly speakers in 1999. In the early 19th century they entered the fur trade, suffering severely from its associated epidemics. In 1855, under growing settler pressure, they were moved to the Warm Springs reservation along with the TENINO and Northern PAIUTE, where they remain as part of the Confederated Tribes of Warm Springs.

## WASHOE

A Native North American nation of Nevada, whose name means 'person'. Seasonally mobile within their territory as fishers, hunters and gatherers, they spoke a Hokan language. Always a small nation, they may have been vassals of their PAIUTE neighbours when settlers and miners began to flood into their lands in the 1850s. They were simply brushed aside onto marginal lands and reduced to desperate poverty. Their plight was ignored until they were awarded a small tract of land in 1917. They still experienced racial discrimination; some towns would not permit them to stay overnight until the 1970s. Since then, the Washoe have been more vocal in defending their rights and protecting their environment. In 1997 they sought to prevent rock-climbers from defacing their sacred site at Cave Rock with bolts. In 1994 they numbered over 1500.

## WENATCHEE

A Native North American nation of Washington state's Columbia River area who spoke a Salishan language. Traditionally sedentary hunters, fishers and gatherers, they acquired horses around 1730 and adopted annual bison hunts on the Great Plains. Fishing, however, remained vital to their subsistence. In 1855 they accepted a treaty ceding lands in return for a reservation including their vital fishery at Wenatchapman. They believed that their title to the land was secure, but it had not been surveyed. A survey was begun in 1893, but it was soon halted; corrupt US government officials, realizing the value of the land, through which a railway ran, chose to rob the Wenatchee. Although aware of its obligations, the government did not stop the fraud, and later obstructed all efforts by the Wenatchee to gain redress. Some Wenatchee went to the COLVILLE reservation, while others scattered. In 1977 there were perhaps 500 Wenatchee. They were still seeking restitution in 2002, when the television documentary *False Promises* gained widespread publicity for their predicament

## WENROHRONON

A Native North American nation of New York, whose name means 'people of the place of floating scum'. Sedentary farmers, hunters, gatherers and fishers, they spoke an Iroquoian language. They were affiliated with the NEUTRAL, whose protection allowed them to maintain their territory alongside IROQUOIS lands. In 1639, however, they lost that protection and joined the Neutral and HURON. By 1651, both these nations had been destroyed by the Iroquois. Some descendants might be found among the SENECA and the Huron.

## WEST INDIANS

The inhabitants of all the Caribbean islands, including 23 political entities, who have much in common in their historical experience, ethnic mix, culture and current concerns. The definition can stretch to include those coastal peoples of the South American mainland with cultural connections (the GUYANESE). The West Indies

were so called by default because, after Columbus, it was realized that these lands did not relate
to the (East) Indian subcontinent. Today, given
the fact that the term 'Indian' in relation to the
Americas is essentially a misnomer, the region is
often known simply as 'the Caribbean'.

From the 16th century most of the original
inhabitants (the ARAWAK and CARIB) were exterminated through disease and slavery. The islands
were colonized by Europeans, particularly the
ENGLISH, FRENCH and SPANISH. In the late 17th
century they began establishing slave-based
plantation economies, which introduced the
African elements into the islands cultures that
would become very marked, particularly in cuisine, music and dance. In terms of ethnicity, the
majority of West Indians are of African descent,
and today are often referred to as 'Afro-
Caribbeans'.

The abolition of slavery turned most of the
islands into economic backwaters, with much of
the population limited to farming on smallhold-
ings, and suffering sometimes-severe poverty.
Many were forced into migratory labour, especially to the USA, until immigration restrictions
prevented this in the 20th century. Many of the
islands – particularly the BRITISH colonies – also
saw the introduction of South Asian (sometimes
called East Indian) influences into their cultures
with the arrival of indentured labour, post-slav-
ery; an African-Asian cultural mix is common in
parts of the region today.

In the late 20th century most of the West
Indies became independent. This did not solve
economic problems, however, which often led to
political instability and emigration. Indeed the
scale of emigration, especially to the former
colonial European powers, has amounted to
something of a diaspora, and despite facing
often-harsh discrimination, West Indians have
had a great cultural impact on the recipient
countries. In 1998 West Indians probably numbered over 24 million in total.

## WESTERN MEXICAN TOMB CULTURE

A former Native North American culture of west-
coast and central Mexico. Sedentary farmers,
hunters and gatherers, the people flourished

between 300 BC and AD 300. They were noted
for their tombs, often carved into rock and furnished with symbolic ceramic funerary goods.

## WHILKUT

A Native North American nation of northwest
California whose name probably comes from
the HUPA, meaning 'the givers'. They are also
called Redwood Indians. Semi-sedentary
hunters, fishers and gatherers, they spoke an
athabaskan language. The gold rush brought disease, land theft and the genocidal attacks of
white militias. In 1856 they were forcibly
removed from their territory, most settling on
the Hoopa Valley reservation, despite their poor
relations with the Hupa. In 2000 they numbered
about 100.

## WICHITA

A Native North American nation of Texas and
Oklahoma, whose name means 'big platform'. A
confederation of nations, they call themselves
*Kitikitish* meaning 'the people' or perhaps 'rac-
coon eyes', a reference to male tattoos. Sedentary
farmers, traders, hunters and gatherers, they
spoke a Caddoan language.

An offspring of the CADDO, the Wichita
acquired horses in the 18th century and became
widely travelled traders. Allied to the FRENCH,
they attacked the SPANISH in the 18th century,
and they continued fighting after the French
defeat of 1763. Decimated by epidemics, the
confederated nations began to merge, but they
were unable to resist confinement on the Brazos
reservation, Texas, in 1836. The hostility of
neighbouring settlers, and an unprovoked attack
in 1858 by the US Army, which claimed to have
mistaken them for COMANCHE, forced their relocation to Oklahoma in 1859 to prevent their
extermination. They were coerced into ceding
most of their remaining lands in 1894.

In 2001 the Wichita numbered about 1900
and they were attempting to rediscover and preserve their traditional culture and language
(although there were only ten Caddoan speakers
left in 1998).

| Wichita: main sub-groups |
| --- |
| Kichai |
| Taovayas |
| Tawakoni |
| Tawehash |
| Waco |
| Yscani |

# WINNEBAGO

A native American nation of Wisconsin, whose name means 'people of the filthy waters'. They called themselves *Hotcangara*, which perhaps means 'trout nation'. Sedentary farmers, hunters, gatherers and fishers, they spoke a Siouan language. Entering the fur trade in the 17th century, they were all but destroyed by epidemics and war with the ILLINOIS, and were forced to move westwards. In 1832 the AMERICAN government forced them to move to Iowa. Fort Atkinson was built to prevent their attempted return to Wisconsin, but not entirely successfully. By 1862 they had been moved again, to Nebraska. They numbered about 7000 in 1990, and were struggling to revive a traditional culture much damaged by repeated removals and dispersion.

# WINTUN

A Native North American nation of northern California. Semi-sedentary hunters, fishers, gatherers and traders, they spoke a Penutian language. In 1844 the MEXICAN government granted their lands to AMERICAN settlers, whose livestock consumed the vegetation the Wintun relied on for subsistence. Hostilities soon followed. The 1849 Gold Rush brought far greater destruction to their environment and the kidnapping of their children by slavers. Deliberate massacres intended to drive the Wintun from their lands, known as the Wintun War, escalated in 1858. During the 1860s the Wintun were gradually hunted down and forced onto reservations; the landholdings of these were later reduced. Cultural preservation and economic development are now their major concerns, with profits from their casino vital to both. In 2002 they numbered about 2500.

# WISHRAM

A Native North American nation of Washington state's Columbia River area, who called themselves *Ilaxluit*. Sedentary traders, hunters, fishers and gatherers, they spoke a Chinookan language. They were noted for their rock art – one petroglyph called *Tsagiglalal* ('she who watches') is the most famous in the USA. The Wishram

acquired horses in the mid-18th century, widening their trade activities and fighting more wars, especially against the PAIUTE. They were, however, hostile to fur-traders, trying unsuccessfully to avoid the diseases they brought. Seriously weakened, in 1855 they were forced to agree to a treaty that required them to reside on the YAKIMA reservation. Acculturation was accelerated by poverty and a falling population. By 1962 only ten people identified themselves as Wishram, and they are now officially part of the Yakima nation.

# WITOTO

A Native South American nation of Colombia's Amazonia. Sedentary fishers, hunters and gatherers, they practised limited agriculture and spoke Witotoan. Little-contacted until the late 19th century, the encroachment and depredations of rubber-extractors thereafter proved disastrous. Driven from their traditional lands, they lost much of their culture, and by the 1940s they were thought to be on the verge of extinction. Colombia's civil war added to their suffering. Currently only one-third of them speak their language, which is classed as endangered. In 1995 they numbered perhaps 4700.

# WIYOT

A Native North American nation of northwest California. Semi-sedentary hunters, fishers and gatherers, they spoke an Algonquian language.

Settlers began encroaching on their territory in the 1850s, soon leaving them with no other food source but the cattle the settlers brought. Violence erupted, culminating in the particularly vicious massacre of up to 250 Wiyot as they celebrated a religious festival at their sacred site on Indian Island. All but exterminated, the Wiyot were removed to the miserable conditions of Klamath reservation. Eventually they returned to three *rancherias* (settlements) on their traditional lands, but their ceremonies and language fell into disuse, and the last language-speaker died in 1962.

In 2000, however, the Wiyot finally regained access to Indian Island, and, as part of their efforts to resurrect their language and culture,

**"** They were all killed with the exception of some few who hid themselves during the massacre. No resistance was made, it is said, to the butchers who did the work, but as they ran or huddled together for protection like sheep, they were struck down with hatchets. **"**

Report of the Indian Island massacre of the Wiyot, *The Northern Californian* (1860)

celebrated their first festival there since 1860. They had over 300 enrolled members in 1995.

## WYANDOT

See HURON.

## XAVANTE

A Native South American nation of Brazil's Amazonia. Sedentary farmers, fishers, hunters and gatherers, they spoke a Gê language. A proud people, they resisted subjugation, and had little contact with the outside world until the 1950s. They have resisted acculturation, but land encroachment and the environmental destruction caused by illegal logging became serious threats by 2000. In 2002 some leaders received death threats after they took legal action against landowners reputedly involved in the logging. In 2002 they numbered over 10,000.

## XIKRIN

A Native South American nation of Brazil's Amazonia. Sedentary farmers, hunters and gatherers, they speak a Gê language. Often victims of exploitation by settlers, they long shunned contacts with outsiders, but the violence and epidemics brought by loggers and traders have threatened their existence. They now seek to survive alongside BRAZILIAN society. In 1986 they numbered about 470.

## XINCA

A Native Central American nation of eastern Guatemala. Sedentary farmers, hunters and gatherers, they appear to have borrowed much of their culture from the MAYA and spoke Xinca, a language isolate that is now almost extinct. They were conquered by the SPANISH in the early 16th century and suffered brutal exploitation and epidemics alongside forced acculturation. By 1995, when right-wing death squads in Guatemala's civil war had murdered thousands, the Xinca were rapidly approaching extinction as a distinct nation, although a human-rights pact with the government might possibly reverse this. There are no census figures available for them.

Yahgan

## YAGUA

A Native South American nation of Peru's Amazonia. They subsisted by sedentary slash-and-burn farming, fishing, hunting and gathering, and spoke Yaguan. By the late 20th century tourism was a major source of subsistence, but traditional dress was only worn for the benefit of tourists. Acculturation continues to be a growing problem. In 1998 they numbered up to 6000.

## YAHGAN

A Native South American nation of Tierra del Fuego, at the continent's southern tip. Seasonally migratory within their territory as hunters, gatherers and especially fishers, they spoke a language similar to that of the MAPUCHE.

Until 1832 the Yahgan's inaccessible lands kept them isolated from white contacts. Thereafter, although whalers and settlers provoked the occasional skirmish it was the diseases they brought that caused real catastrophe. Once several thousand strong, by the 1950s, combined with the ALACALUT, the Yahgan were reduced to about 200 people. Although descendants exist among the general population of the region, only one full-blooded Yahgan was known to be surviving in 1991.

## YAHI

A former Native North American nation of northern California, whose name simply means 'people'. Semi-sedentary hunters, fishers and gatherers, they spoke a Hokan language. Genocide began in the 1840s as settlers passing through their territory destroyed their food sources. To survive, the Yahi stole cattle, which led to massacres by settlers and demands for their extermination. By the end of the 19th century they were believed to be extinct as a nation.

In 1911, however, a man called Ishi was discovered, who was widely believed (perhaps incorrectly) to be Yahi. When he died in 1916 the Yahi were proclaimed finally extinct. In a bizarre footnote to this, the Smithsonian Institution admitted in 1999 that, in violation of Ishi's wishes and religious beliefs, his brain had been removed and preserved. Nine people came forward claiming Yahi descent and demanded its repatriation so that Ishi could be reburied whole. This repatriation was achieved in 2000.

## YAKIMA

A Native North American nation of south-central Washington state, who called themselves *Waptailmin*, meaning 'people of the gap', officially adopting the name Yakima only in the 1990s. Semi-sedentary hunters, fishers and gatherers, they spoke a Penutian language. Around 1730 they acquired horses and began annual bison hunts on the Great Plains. Early in the 19th century they entered the fur trade and suffered severely from the resulting epidemics.

In the 1850s they came under pressure to cede their lands, accept a reservation and adopt farming. Eventually they agreed to a treaty, but its meaning was not made clear. When their lands were declared open to settlers they felt cheated and began the Yakima War (1855–6). Along with the WALLA WALLA, UMATILLA and CAYUSE, they inflicted early defeats on the US Army, in a war fought with great savagery. They were eventually defeated, but they were awarded

a larger reservation. Incursions, especially by prospectors, led to renewed war and a second defeat in 1858.

In the 20th century the Yakima were involved in repeated disputes over water rights and access to traditional fishing grounds as promised in their treaty. In 2000 they attempted to ban the possession and sale of alcohol on the reservation, but their right to impose the ban on non-Yakima was challenged, setting the scene for an extended legal battle. In 2000 they numbered approximately 9000.

## YAMASEE

A Native North American nation of South Carolina, Georgia and northern Florida. Sedentary farmers, hunters and gatherers, they spoke a Muskogean language. They fled to South Carolina after a war with Spain provoked by slave-raiding. They proved valuable allies to the ENGLISH, particularly during the TUSCARORA War (1711–13). Subsequently, however, they were defrauded of their lands and subjected to English slave-raids, which the colonial government proved unable to prevent. In alliance with the CATAWBA and APALACHEE they launched the Yamasee War (1715). Defeated, they withdrew back to Florida and, in alliance with the SPANISH, raided English colonies. In 1727 a surprise punitive raid by the English on their village all but exterminated them. The remnants joined the SEMINOLE, whose Oklawa Band probably contains Yamasee descendants.

## YANA

A Native North American nation of northern California, whose name means 'people'. Semi-sedentary hunters and gatherers, they spoke a Hokan language. In 1844 the MEXICAN government began to grant their lands to settlers. As their food resources were reduced, the Yana stole cattle, leading to genocidal attacks by white militias. In 1863 some Yana were removed and most of the remainder were exterminated the following year. The 1930 census counted just nine Yani, and they are now officially deemed extinct. There are, however, several dozen descendants on Redding *rancheria* (settlement).

## YANESHA

A Native South American nation of Peruvian Amazonia. Sedentary farmers, hunters and gatherers, they speak an Arawakan language. In the 1630s they fought SPANISH colonization. In the 1670s missions were established among them, but they killed the priests in retaliation for the misdeeds of other Spaniards. Thereafter they remained relatively isolated until the rubber boom in the 20th century. From the 1960s repeated complaints that the government was failing to protect their lands from settler incursion were ignored. A reservation was established only in 1988, but the Yanesha are still under pressure from multinational concerns seeking to exploit their valuable mineral and timber resources. In 1998 they numbered up to 10,000.

## YANOMAMI

A Native South American nation of Brazil's Amazonia. Sedentary fishers, hunters and gatherers, they practised limited agriculture and spoke Yanomami. From the 1980s, when a gold rush brought tuberculosis and malaria into their territory, killing about one-fifth of their population, their plight has aroused considerable international concern. Mining and illegal logging have caused great damage to their environment. They have also brought violence: in 1993 a group of miners was convicted for genocide against 73 Yanomami. Up to 2000 Yanomami have been murdered since encroachments began, and alcohol has been introduced to cause dependency. In 2000 it was claimed that an American geneticist deliberately spread measles, killing hundreds, as part of an experiment. The Brazilian government has also been criticized for its treatment of the Yanomami, attempting to reduce their reserved lands and health budget, and doing little to protect them. In 2001 the United Nations High Commission on Human Rights expressed concern for their future. In 2002 they numbered about 26,000.

## YAQUI

A Native North American nation of southwest Arizona and northern Mexico. The Yaqui were sedentary farmers, hunters, gatherers and later herders, who spoke an Uto-Aztecan language. They are noted as the only Native American nation to have had constant contact with whites, and yet never to have been fully subjugated. Although missions were established among them from 1610, and most Yaqui accepted Catholicism, they never hesitated in fighting against settlers, who began to encroach on their lands from about 1740. A resulting series of wars did not end until the 20th century. The MEXICAN government deported thousands to the south to weaken them in 1907, but 20 years later renewed warfare broke out. In 1993 they numbered about 16,000 in Mexico, and over 9000 in the USA in 1997, where they had only just gained federal recognition.

## YAQUINA

A former Native North American nation of central coastal Oregon, whose name comes from an ALSEA name for their territory. Sedentary hunters, fishers and gatherers, they spoke a Yokonan language. The Yaquina joined the fur trade in the 19th century and suffered severely from its associated epidemics. In the 1850s they came under pressure from settlers, but did not initially take part in the wars of their neighbours. Nonetheless, settlers demanded they be brought under AMERICAN control, and in 1854 the Yaquina were forced to accept a treaty confining them to the SILETZ reservation. Conditions were so poor that they joined the Rogue River War (1855–6). After returning to the Siletz reservation, their culture deteriorated and they ceased to exist as a distinct nation.

## YARURO

A Native South American nation of Venezuela's Amazonia. Seasonally mobile within their territory as farmers, fishers, hunters and gatherers, they relied heavily on river resources. By the late 20th century their environment had been badly degraded by the encroachment of cattle ranchers, and in 1998 the Yaruro complained that these incursions were spreading diseases. The possibility of violent confrontation was very high. In 1990 the Yaruro numbered nearly 4000.

## YAVIERO

A Native South American nation of Venezuela's Amazonia. Probably sedentary farmers, fishers, hunters and gatherers, they spoke an Arawakan language. From the 17th century they were badly weakened by the depredations of PORTUGUESE slavers. Catastrophe came, however, with the rubber boom from the late 19th century, during which rubber-extractors all but annihilated the Yaviero. The last known native language-speaker died in 1984.

## YAYA-MAMA TRADITION

A former Native South American culture of Bolivia. Based around Lake Titicaca, the people were sedentary farmers, hunters and gatherers. The culture developed by 800 BC, and particularly flourished between 600 and 400 BC. Ceremonial mound-builders, the Yaya-Mama became the centre of a religious ideology that spread throughout the area. Many features of their culture became common in succeeding civilizations, such as the PUKARA.

## YAZOO

A Native North American nation of Mississippi. They were sedentary farmers, hunters and gatherers and spoke a Tunican language. Allied to the ENGLISH, they attacked the FRENCH in 1702, and again in 1729 in alliance with the NATCHEZ; in the latter war, both they and the Natchez were destroyed as nations. The CHICKASAW and CHOCTAW, among whom their descendants still survive, absorbed the remnants.

## YELLOWKNIFE

A Native North American nation of the Northwest Territories, named after the copper tools they used. They call themselves *Dene*, meaning 'people'. Originally nomadic hunters, fishers and gatherers, they spoke an ATHABASKAN language. Entering the fur trade in 1784, they acquired guns and attempted to expand their territory and fur resources. In 1823, however, a war with the DOGRIB closed their trade outlets. The effects of disease, warfare and starvation rapidly reduced

the Yellowknife population, and the CHIPEWYANS absorbed the survivors.

## YOKUTS

A Native North American nation of central California who lived in up to 50 autonomous bands. Semi-sedentary hunters, fishers and gatherers, they spoke Penutian dialects. In the 14th century they began to expand their territory, and by the 18th century they numbered up to 50,000. In 1772 the SPANISH began to evangelize them, which decimated their numbers through disease. Those resisting the missions raided for horses, leading to brutal reprisals. The Gold Rush of 1849 doomed the Yokuts. After massacres and land theft they agreed to a treaty in 1851 (which was neither ratified nor honoured) ceding their lands for a reservation. That year the US Army established Fort Miller by burning a Yokuts village and conscripting its inhabitants as a workforce. The Yokuts were left destitute and landless, and local employers reduced them to economic slavery. Three federally recognized *rancherias* (settlements) were eventually established, but most Yokuts were scattered, and much of their culture seems to have been lost. In 1990 they numbered over 2800.

## YUCHI

A Native North American nation of South Carolina, whose name, 'Tsoyaha Yuchi' in full, means 'children of the sun from far away'. Mound-building sedentary farmers, hunters and gatherers, they spoke a Siouan language. Hostile to ENGLISH settlers, they were much reduced by disease and warfare in the 17th century. In 1714 the CHEROKEE stormed their village and most Yuchi committed suicide to avoid capture. Most of the survivors were absorbed by the Muscogee CREEK nation. They numbered around 1500 in 1995, and were making a last-ditch effort to preserve their traditional culture and language (there were only five speakers in 2000). In a bizarre footnote, the discovery of the Bat Creek Stone in 1889 in one of their mounds, which was supposedly inscribed with Hebrew characters, caused romantic speculation about their being a 'lost tribe of Israel'. Although the Bat

> 66 To this day among the Yumas I have never seen anger expressed. 99
>
> A.W. Whipple, 1849

Creek Stone is generally dismissed as fraudulent, it still generates controversy.

## YUKI

A Native North American nation of northeast California whose name comes from the WINTUN, and means 'enemy' or 'thief'. They called themselves *Uk-um-nom*, meaning 'in the valley'. Semi-sedentary hunters, fishers and gatherers, they spoke a Yukian language. In the 1850s they were subject to slave-raids and massacres. In 1855 the AMERICAN government decided to establish the Round Valley reservation for them and six other nations, but squatters occupied the land and refused to move. Concentrated in the Round Valley, the Yuki became even more vulnerable to slavers and reprisals by settlers, whose cattle they stole to survive. By the 1870s over half of the Yuki were said to be suffering from syphilis because of rape, and they appeared to be approaching extinction. Many of their traditions and much of their culture were destroyed.

Only six people spoke the Yuki language in 1990, and they had a population of approximately 100 at the end of the 20th century.

## YUMA

A Native North American nation of southwest Arizona, who call themselves *Quechan*, meaning 'those who descend', a reference to their creation myth. Sedentary farmers, fishers, hunters and gatherers, they spoke Yuman. In the 1770s the SPANISH established settlements among them, but cordial relations soon broke down as the Yuma lands were stolen, and the Spanish were expelled in 1781.

In the mid-19th century their monopoly of river crossings led to a very profitable business in helping settlers and prospectors across the Colorado River. Fort Yuma was established in 1852, however, breaking this monopoly. Soon their lands were flooded with settlers. In 1893 most Yuma land was confiscated, leading to poverty and their forced entry into the wage economy. Acculturation followed, even though much of the land was recovered in the 20th century. Land claims, water rights, cultural preservation and the exclusion of archaeologists from their sacred sites are still important issues to the estimated 3900 Yuma in the 21st century.

## YUP'IK

A Native North American nation of southwest Alaska. They are a branch of the INUIT, and their name means 'real people'. Seasonally mobile within their territory, primarily as traders, hunters, fishers and gatherers, they speak an Eskaleut language. Entering the RUSSIAN fur trade in the 18th century, they were rapidly diminished by diseases, allowing the Russians to reduce them to serfdom. Forced to hunt furs while their families starved, they were reduced further. After the Alaska Purchase of 1867, the AMERICANS tried to destroy what was left of their traditional culture. Numbering about 25,000 in 1995, they were attempting to preserve their environment and revive their traditional culture.

## YUROK

A Native North American nation of northern coastal California, whose name comes from the KAROK and means 'down river'. Sedentary hunters, fishers and gatherers, they spoke an Algonquian language. They had over 30 settlements, some of which were evangelized by the SPANISH in the early 19th century. The 1850s brought throngs of settlers onto their territory, willing to use any pretext to deprive them of their lands. Many Yurok scattered, often joining other nations such as the WIYOT. Some were located on a Yurok reservation. Much of their traditional culture was subsequently lost.

In 1998, intending to improve their lives, they began the difficult task of cleaning up the hazardous waste that had been dumped illegally on their lands. By then they numbered perhaps around 3500.

## ZACATEC

A former Native North American nation of northern Mexico. They were mostly nomadic hunters and gatherers, although some groups were sedentary and primarily farmers. They perhaps spoke an Oto-Manguan language that is now extinct. Feared by their neighbours as

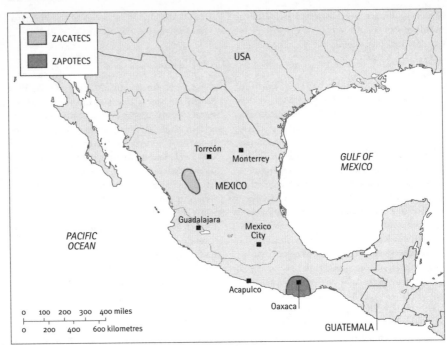

ZACATECS

ZAPOTECS

USA

Torreón
Monterrey

GULF OF
MEXICO

MEXICO

Guadalajara

PACIFIC
OCEAN

Mexico
City

Acapulco

Oaxaca

GUATEMALA

| 0 | 100 | 200 | 300 | 400 miles |

| 0 | 200 | 400 | 600 kilometres |

raiders, they resisted AZTEC attempts to subdue them, and became even more formidable when they acquired horses in the 16th century. When silver was found on their lands in 1546, SPANISH prospectors swarmed into it, provoking a protracted and bitter war. In 1585 the Spanish sought to end this indecisive war by offering land, supplies and implements for them all to adopt a sedentary, farming lifestyle. This proved more effective and began the process of acculturation that eventually saw their disappearance as a distinct nation.

## ZAMUCO

A Native South American nation of the Bolivian Chaco. Seasonally mobile within their territory as farmers, hunters and gatherers, they lived in large autonomous bands united in a common Zamucoan language. Although they resisted SPANISH colonization and most bands maintained their independence, by the mid-18th century the majority of them had been Christianized. In the 20th century, however, disease and deforestation, coupled with the aggressive

deculturation policies of the American-backed New Tribes Mission, greatly threatened their chances of surviving as a nation. In 1995 they numbered up to 1500.

## ZAPOTEC

A Native Central American nation of southern Mexico, who called themselves *Vinizza*, meaning 'cloud people'. Sedentary farmers, hunters and gatherers, they spoke an Oto-Manguan language. By about 500 BC they had established a great city at Monte Albán and began to create an empire. A decline began about AD 700 for no clearly understood reason. They subsequently suffered MIXTEC incursions, and in the 15th century AZTEC invasion, which they overthrew in 1497 in alliance with the Mixtec. A few years later, however, most Zapotec were reduced to slavery by the SPANISH and half died in epidemics within 50 years. Nevertheless, they determinedly resisted acculturation and retained their national identity.

By the last decade of the 20th century the Zapotec numbered over 750,000, and were enjoying a cultural resurgence. They also had an active political movement protesting against human rights abuses, which has led to the murder of some of their leaders.

## ZENTA

See KOLLA.

## ZOQUE

A Native Central American nation of southern Mexico. Sedentary farmers, hunters and gatherers, they spoke Mixe-Zoque and were a long-established nation, with the ruins of some settlements over 1000 years old when the SPANISH conquered them in the 16th century. The Spanish described them as cannibals, possibly to justify their treatment of them. The Zoque were exploited and reduced to a degree of poverty that they still suffer.

In 1990 the Zoque numbered some 45,000, and in years since severe drought and forest fires have continued to take a toll.

## ZUÑI

A Native North American nation of northwest New Mexico, who call themselves A'shiwi, meaning 'the flesh'. Sedentary farmers, traders, hunters and gatherers, who occupy the largest pueblo in America, they speak Zuñian. The SPANISH established control over their territory in the 17th century. Although the Zuñi were able to expel the Spanish in 1680, APACHE pressure forced them to accept Spanish authority once more in 1692. But they had very little contact with outsiders until the 1880s, when an influx of settlers stripped them of their most productive irrigated lands. Subsequently their traditional craft of jewellery-making became an economic mainstay.

Despite Spanish, MEXICAN and AMERICAN efforts to the contrary, the Zuñi have clung tenaciously to their traditional culture and religion since the 17th century, when they killed some over-intrusive missionaries. They have been equally determined to defend their sacred sites from strip-mining, winning a crucial legal case in 2002. In 1996 they numbered about 8000.

Z

# Africa

# ABAHA

See HA.

# ABALUYIA

See LUYIA.

# ABYSSINIANS

See ETHIOPIANS.

# ACHEWA

See CHEWA.

# ACHOLI or Acoli

NILOTES of the Acholi district of northern Uganda. They are also heavily settled in the towns of Gulu and Lira. They are mainly descended from LUO migrants who arrived in the mid-2nd millennium AD and were traditionally organized into loose chieftainships. They depend on cattle and sheep but also farm, hunt and fish.

The BRITISH government regarded the Acholi as a martial people and recruited many into the colonial police and army; as UGANDANS they were persecuted under president Idi Amin (governed 1971–9) partly for this reason.

As a result of droughts in the 1980s and 1990s, they have experienced considerable hardship and have suffered from disease and raiding. Since the 1990s they have also suffered attacks from the Lord's Resistance Army, based in Sudan. Their population in the late 20th century was estimated at around 850,000.

# ACILOWE

See LOMWE.

# AFAR

Nomads of northeastern Ethiopia, Eritrea and Djibouti in the Horn of Africa. They are also known as the Danakil after the desert region they inhabit and where they have to endure some of the hottest temperatures on the planet.

There are over half a million Afar in the 'Afar triangle' spanning the borders of these three countries. Originally they were pastoralists of the southeast Ethiopian highlands who largely adopted a nomadic existence in their new home, herding cattle, sheep, goats and camels. Consequently, grazing rights and access to water have always been of supreme importance and a source of friction within Afar society. Their respective governments have tried to force them to adopt a sedentary agricultural lifestyle but they are strongly attached to their culture's traditional ways, so this has not met with much success. Since the 19th century, however, the Afar have successfully adapted to the market economy and have supplied increasing quantities of animal food and products to Djibouti and other urban centres.

The Afar are organized into patrilineal family groups (among which traditional blood feuds are still to some extent pursued) within several sultanates comprising federated tribes. The role of their chiefs has essentially been to act as mediators in inter-tribal and inter-family disputes.

The Afar speak Saho, an Eastern Cushitic branch of the Afro-Asiatic family of languages, and are predominantly Muslim. They form roughly one-third of the population of Djibouti, where they are traditional rivals of the dominant Somali ISSA. Their prosperity and freedom of access to traditional grazing lands have suffered in recent decades from the hostilities between Ethiopians and Eritreans; they have also been badly affected by the severe droughts that have plagued much of sub-Saharan Africa.

# AFRIKANERS or Boers

Descendants of the original DUTCH settlers in South Africa who went to the Cape of Good Hope in the decades after the first settlement in 1652. They constitute about 55% of the white population of more than 2.2 million in South Africa. They became known as Afrikaners ('Africans' in Dutch) about 300 years ago when it became clear that they constituted a permanent settlement. In the late 17th and early 18th centuries they were joined by French and German Protestants who were escaping from religious persecution in Europe.

The Afrikaners came to be distinguished by their language, Taal or Afrikaans, a local form of Dutch with some loan words from African languages, Arabic and Portuguese. This language only came to be written in the late 19th century when it became part of the literary and cultural identity-formation of the Afrikaners. Their other distinguishing characteristic is adherence to the Dutch Reformed Church. In modern times, the Afrikaners became notorious as the instigators of the system of apartheid, or separateness, which kept the races apart and underpinned the South African state from the election victory of the Afrikaner Nationalist Party in 1948 until the modern South African 'rainbow nation' was formed in 1994.

### Early history

The original intention of the Dutch East India Company (Vereenigde Ostindische Compagnie or VOC) was that the party of Dutch colonists who landed at the Cape would constitute nothing more than a 'refreshment station' to aid the passage of ships sailing to the Dutch East Indies. The excellent climate and disease-free conditions of the Cape helped rapid population growth, and social, environmental and economic pressures sent the Afrikaners into the interior in search of more land. They established an informal and formidable militia known as the commando (a word later taken into the English language). Having overcome resistance from the indigenous KHOIKHOI and SAN peoples, the Afrikaners expanded rapidly. By the end of the 18th century they had reached some 600 km / 375 miles into the interior and come into conflict with the Bantu-speaking Southern NGUNI of what later became the eastern Cape. In this migration the Trekboers (as they were later known) travelled mainly north and east, avoiding the deserts to the west. Whereas at the Cape the Afrikaners had been primarily arable farmers and growers of vines, the Trekboers were pastoralists, seeking land upon which to run their animals, mainly sheep. They were a classic frontier people: individualists who hunted and raided, maintaining connections with the colony only through trade and the church. This sense of expansive land-holding became part of the Afrikaner myth of the interior.

The VOC found these settlers difficult to control, particularly as the power of the company was waning in the later 18th century. The British first seized the Cape from the Dutch in 1795 and took it permanently in 1806. It was eventually confirmed as a British possession at the end of the Napoleonic wars. The Afrikaners then commenced a long period of conflict with the British colonial power, and with British missionaries, in respect of differences over law, language, the abolition of slavery, the acquisition of land and conflict with Africans. In the years after 1835, large numbers of Afrikaners left the Cape and headed for the interior to settle in what became known as the Orange Free State and the Transvaal (or South African Republic). They also settled in Natal, but most left again when the British annexed it in 1843. This movement was known as the Great Trek and its participants as Voortrekkers. They were frequently involved in fierce conflicts with African peoples such as the SOTHO/TSWANA and NGUNI, forcing further migrations (as with the NDEBELE) and encouraging defensive state formation (as in Lesotho), among many other transformations of African societies. The Voortrekkers also broke up the GRIQUA statelets. By the later 19th century the Afrikaners had expanded right up to the Limpopo river and were casting covetous eyes upon lands in Mozambique and what later became Southern Rhodesia. These areas, however, were infested with the tsetse fly, fatal to the Afrikaner horses and cattle.

### The modern Afrikaners

The Afrikaners, or Boers (the Dutch word for farmers, so called by the British), came to international prominence during the South African wars with the British colonial power (1877–81 and 1899–1902). In the first of these wars, the British annexed the Transvaal and the Orange Free State, but once ZULU power had been broken in 1879, ceasing to threaten the Boer settlements, the Afrikaners began to resist and defeated the British at the Battle of Majuba Hill in 1881. The Afrikaner desire to simply farm had already been disrupted by the discovery of diamonds in Griqualand West, just beyond the Cape frontier, from 1869. The British soon annexed the area, and farmers like Nicolaas and

"God put us here, we have a duty to stay here and civilize this place."

Afrikaner Freedom Front spokesman, March 2002

Diederick de Beer, who unwittingly gave their name to the greatest of the diamond companies, left the area to avoid the diggings of the miners. From 1886, the greatest gold reserves in the world were discovered on the Witwatersrand near modern Johannesburg, and the Afrikaners could no longer keep the modern world at bay. Their colonies, particularly the South African Republic, became extremely rich, and a major urban and transport infrastructure was laid down. Large numbers of Europeans were sucked in to work on the mines and associated

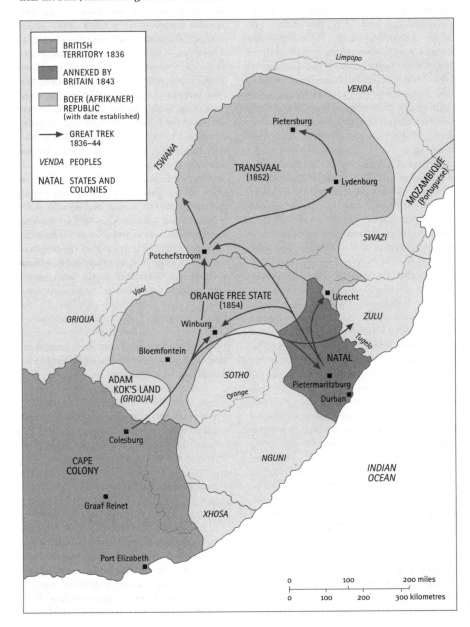

**Afrikaners**

*The 'Great Trek' of Afrikaners from the British-ruled Cape Colony and Natal to establish their own short-lived states became a foundation myth for the Afrikaners.*

Map legend:
- BRITISH TERRITORY 1836
- ANNEXED BY BRITAIN 1843
- BOER (AFRIKANER) REPUBLIC (with date established)
- GREAT TREK 1836–44
- *VENDA* PEOPLES
- NATAL STATES AND COLONIES

Limpopo
*VENDA*
MOZAMBIQUE (Portuguese)
Pietersburg
*TSWANA*
TRANSVAAL (1852)
Lydenburg
*SWAZI*
Potchefstroom
Vaal
ORANGE FREE STATE (1854)
Utrecht
*ZULU*
Winburg
*GRIQUA*
Bloemfontein
Tugela
NATAL
*SOTHO*
ADAM KOK'S LAND (GRIQUA)
Orange
Pietermaritzburg
Durban
Colesburg
CAPE COLONY
*NGUNI*
INDIAN OCEAN
Graaf Reinet
*XHOSA*
Port Elizabeth

0       100      200 miles
0    100   200   300 kilometres

industries, while Africans from all over southern Africa became the principal labour power of the mines. The non-Afrikaner whites became known as 'Uitlanders', or people from outside.

The second Boer or South African War (1899–1902), which many historians view as the first modern war, was fought by the British allegedly to protect the civil rights of these 'Uitlanders', although many have noted wider strategic and economic motives. President Paul Kruger of the South African Republic (governed 1883–1900) became an iconic figure of resistance, although he later went into exile in the Netherlands. In the conventional stage of the war, the Afrikaners had many successes, and laid siege to the British settlements of Kimberley, Mafeking and Ladysmith. After their own capital, Pretoria, had been seized, they conducted a very effective guerrilla campaign. The tradition of the Boer commandos, constantly on horseback and using their guns, stood them in good stead in this imperial war. Their fierce resistance joined the Great Trek and conflict with the Zulus as central aspects of the Afrikaner historical identity.

In the aftermath of this war, the British hoped to encourage emigration from Britain in order to create an English-speaking majority that would electorally overwhelm the Afrikaners (as the English speakers had done in the case of the Québecois in Canada, a common analogy). This did not happen, however, and when the Union of South Africa, bringing together four separate provinces, was formed in 1910, it was immediately dominated by the Afrikaners. Celebrated Boer generals of the war, such as Louis Botha and Jan Christian Smuts, rose to power. They represented a moderate group, generally loyal to the British, and the Afrikaners, though with some fierce dissent, joined World Wars I and II on the Allied side. Economic depression, however, ensured that the forces of Afrikaner nationalism became increasingly powerful between the wars and, after the victory in 1948, held power for over 40 years.

The policy of apartheid attempted a total separation among the races, with all South Africans classified as either Whites, Indians, 'Coloureds' (see CAPE COLOUREDS) or Blacks. Legislation created segregation in every area of life, including

residence, employment, government, transport, sex and marriage, as well as all social services and recreational activities. Africans were all ascribed to so-called 'homelands', in which they would be under the theoretical control of their own authorities. These homelands were on the poorest land and were hopelessly over-populated. As workers in white South Africa, where most of them in fact resided, they were regarded as temporary migrants. By the 1990s, international and regional developments, sanctions, and economic difficulties, as well as the internal absurdities of the system, placed the apartheid government under considerable pressure. The last Afrikaner president, F. W. de Klerk, in an astonishing turnaround, decided to release Nelson Mandela and other detainees, allowing the development of opposition politics. This paved the way for a transfer to majority rule. The Afrikaners, however, retain their identity within modern South Africa, expressed through their language, their church, a number of cultural organizations and sporting activities such as rugby (which they learned from the British). Some have even tried to establish their own small separate 'homeland', in some ways reversing the situation that obtained under apartheid.

## AFRO-ASIAN

A linguistic classification relating to peoples of Africa and southwestern Asia who speak Afro-Asiatic, formerly Hamito-Semitic, languages (see HAMITES). This is a group of more than 200 languages spoken by upwards of 200 million people today and, apart from ancient Egyptian, which is extinct, includes Cushitic (in Ethiopia), Berber (in northwest Africa), Chadic (in parts of Chad and Nigeria) and Semitic, the main subgroup, in Asia. The latter includes Arabic, Hebrew, Amharic and Tigrinya.

## AGAW or Agau or Agew

A Cushitic-speaking people concentrated in central and northern Ethiopia (see ETHIOPIANS). They are mostly subsistence farmers and are thought to be the original people of the region, with whom the incoming Semitic groups intermarried. This process continues with the closely-related AMHARA and TIGRAY so that Agaw cultural distinctiveness has been eroded, though less so among sub-groups such as the FALASHA and BILIN. The Agaw are a mixed Christian and Muslim people and number possibly as many as 300,000.

## AKA or Baka

PYGMIES of Central Africa comprising two separate groups. Members of the Eastern cluster include the Pygmies of the northwestern Ituri forest of Congo (Kinshasa). With the Sua and Efe they are collectively known as the Mbuti or Bambuti, and number as many as 40,000. Members of the Western cluster number upwards of 5000 and are concentrated in the Central African Republic. They have adopted local languages and live symbiotically with their farming neighbours, although they remain nomadic hunters and gatherers. Music is central to their cultural life.

## AKAN

An ethnolinguistic grouping of peoples of the West African coast. Akan languages include ANYI, BAULÉ (Tano), ASANTE and FANTE, which belong to the KWA branch of the Niger-Congo family. The Akan established several highly developed kingdoms, notably among the Fante and Asante (Ashanti) in modern-day Ghana, where most Akan now live. They are also present in Burkina Faso, Togo and the Ivory Coast. Gold and kola nuts were major products of their forest region, and the basis of their wealth. Planting of maize and manioc from America led to further development and large population growth in the 16th and 17th centuries. Today, yams are the staple food, with palm oil and cocoa the major commercial crops, helping to support a population of around 5 million. The Akan of the northern savannah have traditionally concentrated more on cattle herding. Their social structure is based on matrilineal descent, although traditional social organization and culture have been eroded by increasing migration to the cities in recent years.

## AKSUMITES or Axumites

An early African civilization of the southern Red Sea coast and northern Ethiopian Highlands, which became the foundation of the future Christian kingdom of Ethiopia (see ETHIOPIANS). The Aksumite state developed from the 5th century BC in the area between Aksum and the port of Adulis. These Cushitic peoples (see CUSHITES) were heavily influenced by south Arabian, or SABAEAN, culture, probably a result of inward migration as well as trade. The population adopted the same south Arabian language, that developed into Ge'ez, the root of later Ethiopian languages including Amharic. They also worshipped the same gods, including Mahrem, god of war and monarchy. Religion was used to legitimize the ruler and the power of the state, a role that Christianity continued to fulfil after its adoption in the reign of King Ezana (ruled around AD 320–50).

South Arabian influence greatly declined by the 1st century AD. A powerful and sophisticated state had developed in Aksum, whose people were advanced technologically, especially in iron-making. The healthy climate favoured pastoralism and the cultivation of a wide variety of crops, including cereals grown with the aid of the ox-drawn plough. Major achievements were the use of irrigation and terracing. Not surprisingly, Aksum has been described as one of the foremost cradles of agriculture in Africa. It has been suggested that the control of irrigated land in times of drought created a small, powerful landholding group, which encouraged social stratification.

### Trade and culture

Although agriculture remained the foundation of economic life, international trade became very important. It further encouraged the development of a wealthy and powerful monarchy and elite group ruling over a small middle class and the mass of peasants and slaves. It also contributed to the process of urbanization. Aksum dominated the Red Sea trade and the commercial network that connected the Indian Ocean and Mediterranean worlds with tropical Africa, particularly the powerful Nubian civilization of the KUSHITES (within the territory of the modern

*"* The forest is our home; when we leave the forest, or if the forest dies, we shall die. *"*

**Moke, Mbuti spokesman, 2003 (see Aka)**

Sudanese Republic). A system of coinage was introduced in the 3rd century AD, the first in tropical Africa, which lasted for several centuries. It was based on the coinage of Byzantium (see BYZANTINES), whose political and cultural influence was strengthened following Aksum's conversion to Christianity.

At its height Aksumite dominion extended over many tributary states and peoples, as far as northern Somaliland, and to Yemen until the Persian invasion of southern Arabia in the late 6th century AD. In AD 320 the emperor Ezana invaded and comprehensively ravaged Kush and its capital at Meroe. The cities of Aksum still display the impressive ruins of temples, tombs and complex palaces that testify to the culture's extraordinary development. The city of Aksum itself is best known for its monumental stelae, tall carved granite monuments, of which the largest is 33 m / 108 ft long. It is possibly the largest stone ever quarried and sited in the ancient world.

The Aksumite people flourished for several more centuries, but their state declined after AD 700 for reasons that remain unclear – but included population pressure, deforestation and soil erosion. There was extensive conflict on its borders, including with new Muslim states to the north and east along the Somali coast in the 7th and 8th centuries, which disrupted trade with the Mediterranean world. Aksum was finally destroyed in the late 10th century by the Ethiopian chieftainess Gudit. The Christian Ethiopian people became much more withdrawn and defensive, and the focus of power came to be located much further to the south among the AGAW. Modern Ethiopia developed in this mountain stronghold.

## AKWAMU

An AKAN people who established one of several important kingdoms on the Gold Coast around 1600. Known historically as Aquamboes and Oquies, they currently live in eastern Ghana.

The Akwamu kingdom grew wealthy on the sale of local gold, adopted flintlock muskets and extended its power over the GA-ADANGME, FANTE and EWE, mainly through enslaving and trading. By the early 18th century it extended across the central Gold Coast into Dahomey. It was finally defeated by the state of Akim in 1730, in turn conquered by the ASANTE, the most powerful Akan state, in 1740–1, which was made a British colony in 1874. Most modern Akwamu are small farmers and labourers with some professional and business people.

## ALGERIANS

People of the Democratic and Popular Republic of Algeria, nearly all of whom are of ARAB (some 80%) or BERBER (20%) origin. The KABYLE are the major Berber group.

The country, which is the second largest in Africa after Sudan, includes fertile coastal plains bordering the Mediterranean, an area that is home to more than 90% of the population, now numbering around 31 million. It also extends southwards into the Atlas mountains and the arid Sahara, which has been used as a highway since ancient times to link the Mediterranean world and sub-Saharan West Africa.

The territory of modern-day Algeria was conquered by many peoples from classical times onwards, notably the Arabs who brought Islam to the region between the 8th and 11th centuries AD. The population today is overwhelmingly Sunni Muslim. The Turks gained control from the 16th century, although the port of Algiers, now the country's capital city, became the independent base of the feared Algerine pirates, one of a number of corsair bases on the Barbary Coast of North Africa. France ruled the country from 1830 until it was overthrown in the Algerian war of liberation (1954–62).

Algeria subsequently became a socialist Islamic republic and began to play a prominent part in the non-aligned Third World bloc in international relations. Under pressure from inside the country, both its economy and its society became more open. In 1989 Algeria introduced multi-party democratic elections, which led to the success of the Islamic Salvation Front in 1992. However, the elections were declared null and void by the secularist and conservative establishment and the army. The result has been an ongoing insurrection by militant Islamic groups. Elections since then have excluded Islamic parties. Liberalization has

a

improved the economy, which is supported by large oil and gas revenues, although unemployment has grown considerably in recent years.

## ALOMWE

See LOMWE.

## ALUR

NILOTES of western Uganda and northeastern Congo (Brazzaville), East-Central Africa. They number more than 500,000. They have traditionally been organized around numerous small chiefdoms occupying rich farmland that has been efficiently exploited using crop rotation techniques. The chiefs also have a religious function, mediating with ancestor spirits to ensure rains and other advantages.

## AMERICO-LIBERIANS

Emancipated black slaves from the USA who were resettled on the Grain Coast of West Africa by American philanthropic societies, notably at Christopolis, later Monrovia, founded by the American Colonization Society in 1822. Most arrived before slavery was abolished in the USA in 1865. The term also refers to their descendants, who speak English, Liberia's official language, and form only around 5% of the population. Their identity has been diluted through inter-marriage but they continued to form the ruling elite until a military coup in 1980 and subsequent civil war (see LIBERIANS).

## AMHARA

ETHIOPIANS of the central highlands, forming Ethiopia's second-largest ethnolinguistic group after the OROMO (Galla), more than one-third of the total population. Mainly subsistence farmers, they keep cattle, grow coffee as a cash crop and produce cereals and oil plants. The Amhara probably emerged from a union of incoming Semitic peoples from Arabia and the indigenous AGAW early in the Christian era. They provided Ethiopia's ruling dynasties from 1270 until the 1975 revolution, and remain its dominant culture. They speak Amharic, a Semitic language of the AFRO-ASIAN family, the official language of Ethiopia, and adhere to the Ethiopian Orthodox Church. Traditional tensions exist with the closely related northerly TIGRAY people.

## AMRATIAN CULTURE

A predynastic phase of ancient Egypt, also known as Naqadah I culture, dating from around 3600 BC, based on the area of Abydos, Upper Egypt. It succeeded BADARIAN CULTURE and is named after the type-site of al-'Amirah (El Amrah). It was one of several cultures that developed in the Nile Valley between *c.* 5000 BC and *c.* 3100 BC based on cultivation and animal husbandry in the development of the first great agricultural civilization in Africa. The Amratian culture also made growing use of copper, exhibited advanced craft and building techniques in towns and developed hieroglyphics, the first African system of writing. It was succeeded by Naqadah II, known as GERZEAN, and Naqadah III culture (see EGYPTIANS).

## ANGOLANS

Inhabitants of the People's Republic of Angola, capital Luanda, formerly a Portuguese colony that achieved independence in 1975. Some Angolans also inhabit the Cabinda enclave, which is separated from Angola by a strip of Congo (Kinshasa). The name is derived from the *ngola*, or king, of the NDONGO who ruled the region when the PORTUGUESE arrived in the 15th century. The modern country is composed almost entirely of BANTU peoples; the largest ethnolinguistic group is the OVIMBUNDU.

The Ovimbundu dominate the capital. The population of the country is probably about 10.5 million, and the official language is Portuguese. Many Angolans are Christian, mainly Roman Catholic, although animist beliefs are strong. There are a large number of people who adhere to Afro-Christian syncretic religions. The country is rich in oil and could be the second largest producer in sub-Saharan Africa, after Nigeria, but Angola's infrastructure and economic and cultural life were much damaged by the struggle for independence and the subsequent civil war.

*"* The liberated slaves of Freetown and Monrovia had great contempt for the indigenous Africans ... *"*

J.C. Anene, referring to the Liberians, 'Slavery and the Slave Trade' in *Africa in the Nineteenth and Twentieth Centuries*, 1996

Although the Portuguese were powerful in the region for several centuries, the modern boundaries were only established during the partition of Africa in 1891. The Portuguese maintained a tight grip during the 20th century, attempting to suppress the literary and intellectual activity of the educated Creoles of the coastal towns. At Angolan independence, only 10–15% of the population were literate.

The independence campaign, led by MPLA (Movimento Popular de la Libertação de Angola) lasted from 1961 to 1975, when the Portuguese withdrew. Subsequently the MPLA adhered to Marxism/Leninism and aligned itself with the Soviet Union and Cuba. Cuban troops arrived in the country to help suppress the southern revolt of UNITA (União Nacional para a Independencia Total de Angola), which was supported by apartheid South Africa. Great suffering and dislocation accompanied this civil war, which continued until the death of the UNITA leader Jonas Savimbi (1934–2002). However, Cuban troops withdrew in 1989 and the MPLA abandoned Marxism/Leninism as a political philosophy soon after.

Angola has now adopted a form of constitutional democracy, with guaranteed civil rights. Political parties have to demonstrate that they have support across the country and among its ethnic groups before they can participate in elections. Many museum and cultural collections dispersed during the independence struggle and the civil war are now being rebuilt. Football is a national passion and helps to promote a national identity.

## ANGOLARES

Descendants of 16th-century African slaves shipwrecked on the island of São Tomé in the Gulf of Guinea off the coast of Equatorial Africa. Their name refers to mainland Angola where many slaves originated. Until the late 19th century the Angolares were restricted to the southern part of the island but are now more widespread. They were BANTU-speakers but have become assimilated into the main population of the islands and speak the Portuguese creole *lingua franca*.

## ANKOLE or Nkole or Nyankole or Nyankore

A BANTU-speaking people of southwestern Uganda. Their territory lies between lakes Edward and George and the area straddling the River Kagera, which forms the current border with Tanzania. Around the beginning of the 16th century improved forms of state organization emerged in the lake region of modern Uganda, initially in the developing kingdom of Bunyoro-Kitara (see NYORO). Its new rulers, members of the Bito dynasty who claimed descent from the former Chwezi kings, attacked and assimilated neighbouring territories. They were resisted by the Hima, who retreated southwards and established other kingdoms, including Ankole, which was led by Ruhinda, founder of the Hinda line of kings.

Ankole society was stratified and divided between the pastoralist Hima 'citizenry' and the iru underclass of cultivators, blacksmiths, potters and craftspeople. Below them were a smaller number of *abahuku*, or 'slaves', mostly captives in war. The system was based on mutual dependence similar in some respects to medieval European feudalism and vassalage. The king (*omugabe*) demanded war service and cattle, or tribute, from the Hima who were bound to him by an oath of fealty. The Hima formed perhaps 10% of the overall population. They farmed out their cattle to the Iru cultivators, who in return were given protection from enemies by a warrior class substantially freed from the demands of food production. The cattle supplied manure, which increased the production of crops, notably millet, leading to plentiful food supplies and a growing population that strengthened the state. The Iru also paid tribute to the king, which was collected by local village headmen. Today the Iru also grow coffee, cotton and tea for cash.

### The modern Ankole

By 1600 a number of kingdoms in modern-day western Uganda had grown powerful as a result of these developments. Bunyoro was the largest and most successful, but by the 18th century had overreached itself and subsequently declined. Conflict led to its military defeat by Ankole and other states, particularly the GANDA kingdom of

Buganda, which supplanted it as the pre-eminent state of the region. Ankole suffered in turn from its attacks, but also raids from the RWANDANS.

From the mid-1890s the UGANDANS belonging to the kingdoms of Buganda, Bunyoro, Toro, Busoga and Ankole came under British protection through treaty agreements. British rule was maintained through traditional hierarchies and institutions. The previously despotic power of kings, however, was modified partly through the creation of quasi-parliamentary systems. The assembly created in Ankole was known as the *Eishengyero*. The Ankole were subsumed into Uganda at independence in 1962.

Although inter-marriage between Hima and Iru has traditionally been banned, the social divide has become less rigid. Both groups are Bantu-speakers with a cultural affinity whose distinctions have tended to diminish since the 19th century. This has been encouraged by the spread of the tsetse fly, which has forced the population to abandon cattle-rearing in favour of cultivation. Both societies are also polygynous and divided into patrilineal sub-groups. The population of Ankole in the late 20th century has been estimated at 1.5 million, and about 2% are Muslims. The Hima tended to become Protestants and the Iru Roman Catholics, although many of the latter remain loyal to traditional religious forms. During Idi Amin's rule of Uganda, 1971–9, the Ankole were persecuted, and they actively supported the Tanzanian invasion that overthrew Amin. Many have now migrated to Ugandan towns in pursuit of employment.

# ANTIMERINA

See MERINA.

# ANUAK

NILOTES living in the border region and along the Blue Nile in southeastern Sudan and adjoining Ethiopia. The Anuak were pastoralists who migrated from southern Sudan and northwestern Uganda before AD 1500, part of the movement of SHILLUK peoples that took place at that time. They were strongly opposed to British

rule in the Sudan and waged a guerrilla campaign, which lasted until the 1920s. They have continued to oppose control from Khartoum.

In contrast to the Sudanese Anuak, the Ethiopian element of the population live in the higher lands and more settled villages undisturbed by the annual savannah floods. This has encouraged more sedentary agriculture, unusual among pastoral peoples of the region, and a more centralized society headed by a king and royal clan. Anuak society comprises clans settled singly or together in villages.

# ANYANJA

See NYANJA.

# ANYI or Agni

Inhabitants of Ghana and the eastern Ivory Coast, who are closely related to the BAULÉ. They speak Anyi, a language that belongs to the AKAN sub-group of the KWA branch of the Niger-Congo family. Historically they were organized into princely states, but were displaced by the powerful ASANTE people in the mid-18th century when many migrated westwards. Typically cultivators living in matrilineal societies, in scattered homesteads led by village chiefs, they practise a system of shifting agriculture and keep livestock. The Anyi are predominantly Christian but retain an attachment to their traditional animist faith, sometimes in the form of syncretic beliefs.

# ASANTE or Ashanti

Twi-speaking AKAN people who inhabit southern Ghana and adjacent Togo and Ivory Coast. They are renowned for their development of a powerful and sophisticated state in the region during the 18th and 19th centuries. Although a significant number live and work in urban centres today, most remain agriculturists practising cultivation and stock-keeping and inhabiting villages governed by headmen assisted by councils of elders. Traditionally, villages were grouped into divisions under paramount chiefs subject to a king, the *Asantahene*, in the capital, Kumasi. Today, chiefs continue to hold administrative positions as agents of local government

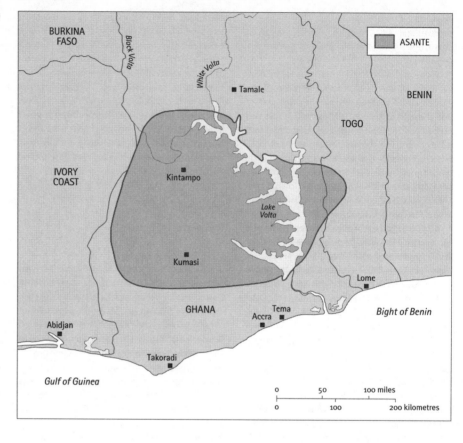

BURKINA FASO

Black Volta

White Volta

■ Tamale

BENIN

TOGO

IVORY COAST

■ Kintampo

Lake Volta

Kumasi ■

Lome ■

GHANA

Tema ■

Accra ■

Bight of Benin

Abidjan ■

Takoradi ■

Gulf of Guinea

ASANTE

| 0 | 50 | 100 miles |
| 0 | 100 | 200 kilometres |

> **❝** With the Golden Stool was bound their souls, their honour, their power, their welfare, and if it were ever destroyed or captured, they would perish. **❞**
>
> **Asante legend**

but their functions are no longer mainly religious or military.

Asante family groups are based on descent from a common female ancestor, and local matrilineages comprise the component clans of Asante society. These individual lineages act as self-governing cooperatives, separate from village administration and providing common assistance to members in farming activities, house-building, funerals and other ways. Senior members of the lineage, both men and women, choose its (male) head whose role is to maintain harmony between its members and with other lineages. He also has a quasi-religious function as keeper of the lineage stools, the embodiment of ancestral spirits linking past and present generations. There is still widespread belief in spirits and the traditional pantheon of gods, and only a small number have converted to Christianity

and Islam, although various syncretic beliefs have also emerged. Some traditional religious festivals formerly involved human sacrifice.

### The Asante empire

The Asante empire developed following the accession of Osei Tutu to the chieftainship of Kumasi in the 1670s. He sought to overthrow the Denkyira suzerainty, which he achieved in 1701 by uniting the smaller Asante chiefdoms and undertaking a series of successful conquests of neighbouring peoples. These were mostly former subjects of Denkyira. Osei Tutu was influenced by the more advanced AKWAMU state organization, which he developed further, but he also used religion to buttress both royal and state power with the introduction of the state cult of the Golden Stool. This venerated object, on which Asante kings were enthroned, said to have been bestowed by heaven, symbolized the authority of the *Asantehene* and the unifying bond between all Asante people. Osei Tutu was installed as the first *Asantehene* of the most powerful of the Akan states, extending to over 250,000 sq. km / 155,000 sq. miles at its peak around 1820. A later *Asantehene*, Osei Bonsu, was responsible for the conquest of the FANTE territory in modern-day southern Ghana in 1807, a move that led to the first conflict with British forces based at Cape Coast castle.

The strongly militaristic Asante empire exacted tax and tribute, including slaves, from outlying conquered peoples such as the Gonja and Dagomba, and was ruthless in its exploitation of weaker peoples and in its suppression of revolt and dissent. The Asante empire was also rich in agriculture and minerals, especially gold, making it commercially powerful. The state maintained a theoretical monopoly on trade through a Company of State Traders, although private dealings also took place and were later encouraged. A system of death duties exploited successful private enterprise for the benefit of the state. The Asante empire was also geographically well-placed to control the main trade routes between the savannah and the coast, where gold, ivory and slaves were in great demand. In return, firearms were acquired, which reinforced Asante power. A major reason for the success of the Asante was the well-balanced state organization headed by the king and council, the *Asanteman-hyiamu*, composed of chiefs chosen by the Queen Mother (or sister of the king) and senior leaders, which largely eliminated succession disputes. To a large extent the Asante government was a meritocracy. These developments, and others such as a fine road system, were the work of many leaders over a long time.

The conservative and expansionist Asante clashed with British interests in West Africa; they were especially hostile to the abolition of the slave trade, missionary activity and any form of European influence. The Asante were regarded as too powerful and a considerable threat to British interests. The Asante defeated British forces in 1824 but made peace in 1831. In 1874 Sir Garnet Wolseley's expeditionary force sacked Kumasi, which began the disintegration of the Asante empire. The southern territories of the empire, incorporating Fante and GA-ADANGME lands, became the colony of the Gold Coast, and in the north various subject peoples revolted against Asante rule. Sharp divisions appeared in Asante society, which led to a series of coups. The Asante homeland was annexed in 1896 and formally declared a British Crown Colony at the start of 1902, its former northern territories becoming a separate protectorate. During the 1920s British authority was applied informally, with British officials acting through indigenous rulers. Within this process the office of *Asantehene*, abolished by Britain, was restored in the 1930s. Asante became part of the modern Republic of Ghana at independence in 1957 (see GHANAIANS).

The Asante have become increasingly westernized in recent years but maintain their distinctive identity and outlook, regarding themselves as more sophisticated than, and superior to, many of their neighbours. The rich Asante culture has incorporated elements of dance, music and other features from subject peoples. Brass gold weights and scales are characteristic and refined examples of their material culture.

## ATERIAN CULTURE

A society based on the stone age tool tradition named after the type-site of Bir el-Ater in Tunisia and associated with Neanderthal hominids. It appeared in the Middle and Late Palaeolithic period, perhaps as early as *c.* 30,000 BC in Morocco, and spread throughout North Africa, possibly into Iberia. It was distinguished by the production of advanced stone tools, particularly bifacial leaf-shaped arrowheads and spearheads with tanged points, made using the sophisticated pressure-chipping, or flaking, technique. Their distribution throughout the Maghreb and Sahara suggests they were used by desert hunters. The Aterian culture was succeeded by the Oranian and CAPSIAN traditions.

## ATESO

See TESO.

## AZANDE or Zande

An agricultural people found in the southwest of the Sudanese Republic, Congo (Kinshasa) and the Central African Republic, who speak an Adamawa-UBANGI language of the Niger-Congo classification. They live in scattered homesteads and number around 4 million. They are noted for their crafts, especially weapons and shields which in the 18th century enabled the Ambomu (NGBANDI) people to conquer the region to the south and east of the Mbomu River and create a series of powerful Zande kingdoms. These were characterized by a rigid social hierarchy, which still lingers. In religion, the Azande adhere to traditional ancestor worship and beliefs in magic, ritual, divination and the infallibility of the oracle of the chief of the traditional ruling Avongara clan.

## BADARIAN CULTURE

A forerunner of AMRATIAN CULTURE in pre-dynastic Egypt in the late 5th millennium BC, named after the type-site of al-Badari beside the Nile in the Asyut region, Upper Egypt. It appears to have been a peasant society without centralized political authority, possibly succeeding the local Tasian culture, whose agricultural and pastoral practices they shared. Their innovative artistic and craft skills are reflected in their grave goods, notably luxury slate palettes used to grind cosmetics, and finely-made decorated black-topped pottery.

## BAGGARA

A Muslim BEDOUIN people (*Baqqarah* in Arabic, meaning 'cattlemen'), also known as Rashaida, Humr and by several other names. They are a sub-group of the numerous Juhayna Arabs and live in the west of the Sudanese Republic and Chad, moving north or south with their herds of cattle according to the seasonal rains and the need for pasture. Grazings are communal but they also grow food and cash crops on individually owned ground. The Baggara are known for their manufacture of basketry and leather goods.

## BAKA

See AKA.

## BALANTA or Balanta-Brassa or Balente

A people of the Republic of Guinea-Bissau who form the country's largest ethnic group, perhaps 30% of the population. They are notable for their farming of commercial rice, an agricultural speciality suited to their marshy territory. Over several centuries they built earthen dikes to exclude sea-water and reclaim coastal land. They also produced sea salt. In their social organization the Balanta are traditionally egalitarian, and in religion largely animist.

## BALILI

See LALI.

## BAMANA

See SENE.

## BAMBARA

A people inhabiting the Upper Niger region of Mali, as well as Guinea-Bissau and some northern areas of the Ivory Coast. They speak Bambara (Bamana) of the MANDE branch of the Niger-Congo languages and use the N'ko alphabet, reading from right to left. They are organized into small chiefdoms, each led by a *fama* (chief), without any overall centralized authority. For environmental reasons relating to the heavy soil of their area, they have a communal agricultural system in which every member of the community is involved. Historically, they founded two important states based on the towns of Segu (*c.* 1650) and Kaarta (*c.* 1753) respectively, which were conquered by the Muslim TUKULOR in the mid-19th century. Subsequently, French imperial rule set about destroying the Bambara warrior elite, and a growth in trade facilitated the spread of Islam. Revived resistance to the French after World War II continued to take Islamic forms. Traditional animist beliefs and practices, related to their sophisticated system of cosmology and metaphysics, have partly suffered as a result of the growth of Islam. The Bambara are still admired for their religious sculptures in both metal and wood. During the 1980s and 1990s they were badly affected by drought, famine and disease, including AIDS, and today they number around 2.5 million.

## BAMILEKE

The largest ethnic group in Cameroon, with a population of more than 2.2 million. They are a BANTU-speaking group and include the TIKAR people. They are traditionally cultivators but many have migrated to urban centres, especially the capital Yaounde, where they have developed business and professional skills. Historically they were divided into more than 90 chiefdoms, but opposition to French colonial control and nationalist sentiment have tended to encourage Bamileke unity. In politics many of them still support the nationalist Union des Populations du Cameroun party. In religion they mostly practise ancestor worship.

## BAMUM or Bamoum

A people who occupy the high grasslands of Cameroon, where they cultivate food and cash crops. They are an offshoot of the TIKAR, from whom they separated around 1750, part of the large BAMILEKE ethnic group. A syncretic religion has taken root among the Bamum, combining traditional beliefs involving the worship of the god Yorubang, Christianity and Islam, although 80% of the population of around 140,000 are nominally Muslim.

## BANANA

See MASSA.

## BANDA

The largest ethnic group in the Central African Republic. They also live in Congo (Kinshasa), Cameroon and Sudan. The Banda number around 1.3 million, one-third of the total population of the Central African Republic, and migrated from the mountainous Sudanese

province of Darfur in the 19th century. They speak a Ubangian language of the Adamawa-UBANGI branch of the Niger-Congo group, like their neighbours the GBAYA and NGBANDI, agricultural peoples with whom they have much in common socially, politically and culturally. Women generally grow crops and gather wild foods while the men hunt and fish. The Banda appointed war leaders who were key figures during their migration to their present homeland, where conflicts with indigenous peoples continued until the French and Belgians took control at the end of the 19th century. Banda craftsmen are renowned wood-carvers, particularly noted for their fine slit drums.

## BANDJABI

See NZABI.

## BANTU

A linguistic classification identifying the 60 million or so people occupying almost the whole southern projection of Africa, or roughly one third of the entire continent. These areas were previously mostly the preserve of the PYGMY people and the Khoisan (SAN). Owing to the vast regions the Bantu (the word means simply 'people') came to occupy, they are extremely diverse in political organization, religious beliefs and agricultural practices. They speak 500 different Bantu languages and dialects, which form the Bantoid sub-group of the Benue-Congo branch of the Niger-Congo language family. All Bantu languages appear to have originated in the region of the modern-day Cameroon–Nigeria borderlands, identifying this area as the homeland of Bantu peoples.

The pattern of Bantu expansion, itself probably resulting from the exploitation of new food crops, has been the source of much speculation. The consensus view based on linguistic evidence is that the Bantu divided into Eastern and Western groups around 3000 BC. The Eastern Bantu gradually penetrated eastward along the edge of the Equatorial rainforest to southern Sudan and then south to the Great Lakes region of East Africa and beyond. The Western Bantu eventually moved southward from Cameroon into the

*b*

*" Unplanned education creates many problems, disrupts the communal life of the Bantu and endangers the communal life of the European. "*

Hendrik Verwoerd, 1954

*Bantu-speaking peoples spread through most of southern Africa from about 3000 BC, with the Eastern Bantu reaching modern South Africa by about AD 1000.*

b

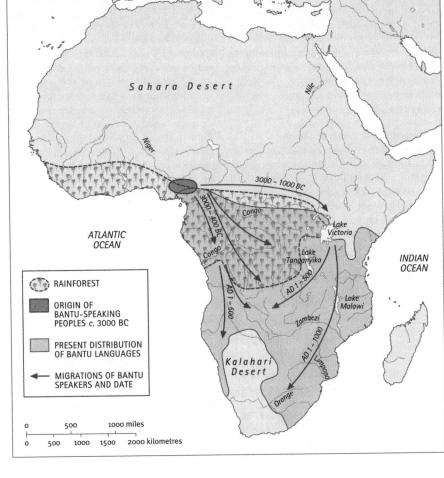

lower Congo River area by around 400 BC, and then further south as far as the Kalahari. Elements of this Western group diverged and also headed east towards Lake Tanganyika and the central Zambezi River.

### Expansion and settlement

The Eastern Bantu reached Lake Victoria by 1000 BC, where they practised mixed agriculture, adopting sorghum and millet from Nilo-Saharan-speaking farmers of the savannah; and cattle-keeping possibly from pastoralist NILO-SAHARANS or CUSHITES of the Upper Nile. There is also evidence of newly acquired skills in iron-working and smelting. From here they spread to

the East African coast (where the Bantu SWAHILI language later developed) and southwards to KwaZulu/Natal in South Africa by the 3rd century AD, exploiting the fishing resources of the coast en route. They reached the Eastern Cape late in the 1st millennium. Other Bantu took a route south from Lake Nyasa via the central Zambezi River to the high veld of Zimbabwe and North Transvaal by the 4th century AD. Because of the high altitude, cattle were unaffected by tsetse fly, and mixed agriculture flourished. Descendants of the Eastern Bantu include the ZULU, SWAZI, XHOSA and SHONA.

The Western Bantu, who expanded southward from Cameroon to the edge of the

Kalahari, exploited different food sources along the coast, river valleys and on the forest margins, namely fish, shellfish, goats, cowpeas, yams, oil palms and possibly plantains. By AD 1000 they had colonized most of the region. Iron-working, evident in Gabon and Congo (Kinshasa) by the 3rd century AD and probably diffused southward from Nigeria, stimulated trade, which eventually formed part of the interaction with the Eastern Bantu. From this source the Western Bantu probably obtained the cereals, cattle and sheep that became an important part of the economy of the savannah regions in southern Angola and western Zambia. The Bantu adapted to their varied environments and formed distinctive ethnic groups and polities that emerged during the course of the 2nd millennium, including the HEREROS and TONGA.

## BASOTHO

See SOTHO.

## BASSA

A BANTU-speaking people of southern Cameroon who are mostly village-dwelling subsistence farmers, numbering about 380,000. In recent decades many have migrated to nearby urban centres, where they work as labourers, artisans and businessmen. They are closely related to the neighbouring Babimbi and Bakoko, who were displaced from the coast by the powerful DUALA people following the arrival of European traders. The Bassa and their related groups opposed German and later colonial control, and retain a strong sense of identity. They are distinct from the kwa-speaking Basa, or Bassa, a people who are mainly small farmers in Liberia.

## BATEKE

See TEKE.

## BATORO

See TORO.

## BATSWANA

See TSWANA.

## BATWA

See TWA.

## BAULÉ or Baoulé

A major ethnic group of the Ivory Coast, numbering more than 1.5 million. They ruled a large part of the area of the modern-day state until the late 19th century, and are still an influential element in Ivoirean national society who regard themselves as perhaps more sophisticated and westernized than other compatriot groups. Although closely related to the ANYI, they are descended from a group of ASANTE who moved into the area around 1750 and absorbed various local peoples. They are predominantly agriculturists who also keep livestock and commonly live in village family compounds. Coffee and cocoa cash crops are important in their economy. They speak Tano, one of the AKAN group of KWA languages. Many are Christians, though animism and ancestor worship are the basis of their surviving religion, which makes use of carved ritual statuettes and masks, for which the Baulé are noted.

## BAVENDA

See VENDA.

## BAVILI

See VILI.

## BAYA

See GBAYA.

## BEDOUIN

Ethnic Arabs of northeastern Africa. Historically they migrated from Arabia through Egypt and across North Africa – many as part of the Islamic conquest – into the Sudan, where they are represented today, for example, by the BAGGARA. They

*b*

**"** We must be as the shifting sands, as God intended. **"**

**Bedouin saying**

are traditionally nomadic or semi-nomadic, herding camels, horses, donkeys, cattle and other livestock in winter and undertaking simple cultivation in summer. Many have now settled permanently. They generally form independent patrilineal, patriarchal and patrilocal tribal groups led by sheikhs and tribal elders.

## BEJA or Bega

Pastoral nomadic tribes of the Nubian desert, extending southeast from Aswan in Egypt, through Sudan to Eritrea and the Red Sea coast of northeastern Africa. They keep camels and sheep; further south they have cattle. Some are settled agriculturists. They are Cushitic-speakers who have occupied this region from before 4000 BC and were known as the Blemmyes, warlike nomads partly responsible for the fall of the kingdom of the KUSHITES in the 4th century AD. Some became settled NUBIANS of the Christian kingdoms of the Nile Valley, but later adopted Islam, although they also adhere to traditional religious beliefs. Severe droughts have reduced the numbers of their herds, and many have settled in more permanent communities. War in Eritrea forced many Beja across the borders into Sudan, where some have demanded a degree of political autonomy for 'Bejaland'. Today they number around 1.9 million, some speaking their native Bedawiye, others TIGRE and Arabic.

## BELLA or Bellah or Ikelan

A group who originated as slaves, serfs or servants of the dominant TUAREG, nomadic pastoralists of the central Sahara and northern Sahel region of North and West Africa. Traditionally they were the sedentary slaves who looked after the property, lands and livestock of their nomadic masters. Today the Bella work as nomadic herdsmen and are concentrated in Burkina Faso and Niger. They have always been at the bottom of the strictly hierarchical Tuareg social order.

## BEMBA

The dominant ethnic group in Zambia, where they number more than 4 million; they inhabit the northeastern plateau of the country and adjoining areas of Congo (Kinshasa) and Zimbabwe. Bemba country, or Lubemba, was never very fertile or suitable for cattle rearing due to the tsetse fly, and the people still practise a traditional form of shifting cultivation to produce their main subsistence crop, finger millet. They also produce maize and, occasionally, cotton as a cash crop. The area's transport links are undeveloped and its people have remained poor, many men seeking employment in the mines of the central copperbelt. By coming into widespread use in the economic heart of Zambia their BANTU language, Bemba, has now become the country's *lingua franca*.

Historically, the poverty of the country encouraged Bemba expansion, which eventually led to the creation of a large and powerful empire. The process began towards the end of the 17th century when members of the LUBA Ngandu clan led by Chiti Maluba, also named Chitimakulu, arrived from the west across the Luapala River and settled among the Bemba. Through war and other means they combined a group of small chiefdoms into the core of the Bemba empire. They began to raid their neighbours, especially the cattle-rearing Lungu, Mambwe and Iwa, who also paid tribute in livestock. The Bemba also exploited their favourable geographical location to trade salt, iron goods and ivory, which in due course were exchanged with the NYAMWEZI and SWAHILI on the East African coast.

The Bemba were a cohesive people, but throughout the 18th century they remained a collection of chiefdoms rather than a centralized kingdom. The paramountcy revolved between the various senior chiefs, who all belonged to the same royal clan, but the role of the king (the *Chitimakulu*, the praise-title of the founder) was primarily religious. In the early 19th century, however, this system changed. One of the royal lineages gained control of the succession, concentrated power among close relatives, and developed a more centralized political system on the classic Luba-Lunda model (see LUNDA). Their power was consolidated by new conquests including several Bisa chiefdoms to the south in 1829–31. Expansion was further encouraged by the growth of the slave trade to the East coast.

**"** Life is a constant journey, towards Lesa, the high god. **"**

Bemba saying

The Bemba became even more warlike to protect themselves and their trade and to supply the necessary numbers of slaves who were obtained by constantly raiding peoples such as the NSENGA. They were powerful enough to beat off NGONI attacks in 1856. Increasingly they bought guns from the coast and conquered territory to the south and west from the Bisa, Lungu and Tabwa under the famous warrior Chitimakulu Chitapankwa. Lubemba power was broken by the British South Africa Company at the end of the 19th century, when it was incorporated into Northern Rhodesia.

The Bemba move their hut villages every four to five years, when the soil becomes exhausted. The scrub and forest are then cleared or cut back and the vegetation burned to provide soil-enriching ash in fields, whose cultivation is generally undertaken by women. This is known as *citemene* cultivation. In some places, the adoption of crop-rotation practices and fertilizers has permitted the Bemba to settle more permanently. The villages are uxorilocal, where husbands come to live in the wife's village, in which the women are all kindred and related to the headman. Polygyny is also common. Bemba society as a whole comprises 40 matrilineal clans whose members are widely dispersed. In religion they are mostly Christian but retain some traditional beliefs and ceremonies relating to initiation and burial.

# BENINOIS

The inhabitants of the coastal Republic of Benin, adjoining the Bight of Benin, in West Africa, where they number around 6.5 million. The republic comprises a number of formerly warring principalities, notably the FON kingdom of Dahomey and the YORUBA kingdom of Oyo. These two peoples remain the largest ethnic groups in what was formerly the French colony of Dahomey, which achieved independence in 1960. The capital is at Porto-Novo, although Cotonou is the largest city and port. The country was renamed Benin (after the Bight of Benin) in 1975, but it should not to be confused with the ancient EDO kingdom of Benin in southern Nigeria. A small number of Beninois are descendants of Portuguese settlers as well as slaves who

returned from Portuguese plantations in South America in the 19th century.

The history of the country in pre-colonial times is unclear. Dahomey emerged in the early 17th century, and under its first notable ruler, Wegbaja, defeated a rival chief known as Dan. Wegbaja's royal palace compound was built on the grave of Dan, which gave rise to the name Dahomey (meaning 'on the belly of Dan'). Under a succession of able and aggressive rulers, and through the conquests of the EWE kingdom of Allada and its former tributary Ouidah (Whydah) in the 1720s, Dahomey became the most powerful kingdom in the region. Extensive slave raids were made on the neighbouring Yoruba territories, and Dahomey became a chief supplier of slaves to the coast for export to the New World. Around 1830, however, it was attacked and defeated by the kingdom of Oyo and became a tributary state, only regaining its independence by war in 1823. It then began a gradual decline, suffering in its attacks on the Nigerian state of Abeokuta and from European policies to end the transatlantic slave trade. The FRENCH, who had had commercial interests in the region from the 17th century, began extending their authority from the coast, driven by rivalry with Britain and the commercial possibilities of the new trade in palm oil. The coastal kingdom of Porto-Novo was made a protectorate in the 1860s, re-established in 1882; and Dahomey itself was brought under French control following the campaigns of 1892–4.

## French colony to modern state

The peoples conquered by the Fon had been successfully incorporated into the kingdom of Dahomey. They became part of a centralized militaristic state with a highly successful standing army (including a corps of royal wives) buttressed by a state religion in the form of a royal ancestor cult, which also involved human sacrifice. The French adopted the name Dahomey in 1894 and applied it to all the territories brought under the control of the region's strongest and most coherent indigenous state. Colonial rule did little to reduce the differences between the component parts of the country, and ethnic divisions remain pronounced despite government attempts since independence to

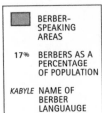

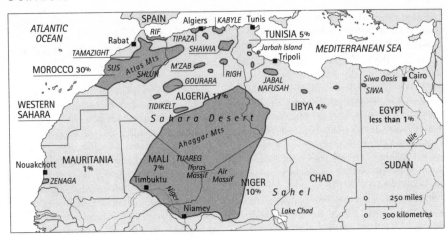

| | |
|---|---|
| ▨ | BERBER-SPEAKING AREAS |
| 17% | BERBERS AS A PERCENTAGE OF POPULATION |
| *KABYLE* | NAME OF BERBER LANGUAUGE |

Berbers

instill a greater sense of national identity. French is the official language and medium of instruction, and has been important in this process. Nevertheless, indigenous languages are still in common use. Religion also emphasizes differences, for although most Beninois follow traditional animist and voodoo beliefs, more than 10% of northern peoples are Muslim and 20% of the population, mostly southerners, are Christians. Culturally, the Beninois have strong traditions in music, dance, craft and other skills, which include wood-carving (their masks are particularly admired) and bronze casting.

The country has suffered a turbulent and unstable political life since independence, including numerous military interventions and constitutional revisions, and Marxist rule under the earlier regimes of Mathieu Kérékou (1972–90). Multiparty democracy was introduced in 1990. The majority of the population is still engaged in agriculture.

## BERBERS

A people descended from the pre-ARAB inhabitants of North Africa, including the NUMIDIANS. They call themselves *Amazigh* (plural *Amazighen*, meaning 'free men'). The name Berber is derived from the Roman word for barbarian, hence the 'Barbary Coast' of North Africa. Today they number more than 15 million, extending from Egypt westwards to Morocco (which has the largest concentration) and Mauritania southwards into the Sahel region of West Africa, mainly Mali and Niger. They are divided into hundreds of tribes and their constituent families, clans and communities, including the KABYLE of Algeria and the more widespread, transnational TUAREG. Many Berbers have been assimilated into Arab society and speak Arabic, although around 11 million still speak the various Berber (Berbero-Libyan) languages of the Afro-Asian group.

### History and culture

The Berbers opposed the Arab invasion of North Africa from the 7th century AD but eventually adopted Islam and participated in the conquest of Spain in the 8th century. Between the 11th and 13th centuries they combined in military federations known as the Almoravids and later Almohads, which extended their power from Spain to sub-Saharan West Africa. Invasions of Arab BEDOUIN from the 12th century ruined the settled coastal agricultural economies of many Berbers, who became nomads in the harsh desert and mountains of the interior, where they have enjoyed a natural freedom. Here effective control by the coastal states has only been possible since the 19th century, especially following the extension of European power. The French invasion of Algeria in 1830, for example, ended with the capture of the Berber stronghold of Kabylia in 1857. Moroccan Berbers were defeated by French and Spanish forces in the Rif War (1919–26), although colonial control was only slowly established.

Berber economies and lifestyles are diverse, encompassing settled, semi-nomadic and nomadic ways of life. Most are sedentary farmers living in villages, who grow a wide variety of crops and fruit as well as herd livestock. Other tribes are transhumant, cultivating lower ground in winter and moving to upland and mountain pastures in summer. Political structures reflect these lifestyles as well as the longstanding communal and egalitarian attitudes of the Berbers. Leaders tend to be elected, sometimes for only a single migrating season in the case of semi-nomadic tribes, and for longer periods in fully nomadic tribes. Because they are so widely scattered and diverse, the Berber people never developed highly centralized political systems, except perhaps for the Republic of the Rif in the 1920s. Berber women are less heavily circumscribed in their personal lives than their neighbouring Muslim Arabs.

Today, increasing numbers of Berber men are migrant workers in southern Europe and in urban centres within their respective countries. As minority peoples they have felt politically excluded and subject to economic and cultural discrimination, which caused serious unrest in Algeria, Niger and Mali in the 1990s, and to a lesser extent in Morocco. Growing transnational awareness has become a feature of political life in the North and West African countries with significant Berber populations.

## BERGDAMA

See DAMARA.

## BILIN or Bilen or Bogo

A branch of the ancient Cushitic-speaking AGAW people whose traditional homeland lies in the Keren region of Eritrea and the adjoining northern TIGRAY province of Ethiopia (see ERITREANS and ETHIOPIANS). They number around 65,000, up to half now scattered throughout Eritrea due to drought and war in recent decades. They practise mixed cultivation and stock-farming. Traditional society is divided into territorial lineages within hereditary chiefdoms, and around 66% of the population is Muslim, the rest Christian. Many adhere to Roman Catholicism,

encouraged during the Italian occupation in the 1930s, when the colonial army attracted many Bilin recruits.

## BINI

See EDO.

## BOA

A people of Congo (Kinshasa). They are mainly farmers and herdsmen living in simple patrilineal groups. They comprise only a small part of the country's population (roughly 2.5%) but are generally well-educated and have become prominent in the professions and in government and business administration. They are concentrated around Kisingani in northeastern Congo, and in the urban centres.

## BOBO

An ethnic group concentrated in northwestern Burkina Faso with some in adjoining Mali. They speak a SENUFO language of GUR (Voltaic) and are settled agriculturists whose food stocks are supplemented by livestock-rearing, hunting, fishing and gathering. Lineages are grouped into locally dominant clans, although villages are autonomous. Bobo society is polygynous and comparatively egalitarian, although craftworkers form a despised caste. Animist beliefs prevail, but more than a fifth of the population of 230,000 is Muslim, a faith spread by DYULA traders who settled among the Bobo.

## BOERS

See AFRIKANERS.

## BOGO

See BILIN.

## BORNU or Borno

See KANURI.

## BOZO or Boza

A people belonging to the large MANDE-speaking community of West Africa. They are concentrated in Mali, where they number nearly 100,000 people, but are also present in Niger. Their economy is based on commercial fishing along the Niger and Bani rivers, which they travel and exploit seasonally. The Bozo are overwhelmingly Muslim.

## BUBI

Inhabitants of the island of Bioko (Fernando Po) off the coast of Equatorial Guinea. Their BANTU-speaking ancestors migrated from the mainland, probably from the area of Cameroon, and although their numbers declined into the early 20th century they now form 10% of the population (roughly 50,000 people). Their society is matrilineal and based on yam cultivation. The Bubi rebelled against Spanish power in 1907, but they have bridled at the domination of the majority FANG since independence. Political repression has led to the growth of a separatist movement in recent times. The Bubi are mostly Roman Catholic, but follow some ancient customs, notably reverence for the sacred Moka Mountain.

## BUNYORO

See NYORO.

## BURKINABE

Inhabitants of Burkina Faso, a republic in sub-Saharan West Africa, formerly the French territory of Upper Volta. It is located in a harsh environment of desert and savannah, and has suffered from prolonged droughts since the 1970s. The population of around 12 million, largely subsistence farmers and herders, remains desperately poor. It is primarily composed of two ethnolinguistic groups: the GUR or Voltaic, who include the MOSSI, BOBO and SENUFO and comprise about half the population; and the MANDE, who include the DYULA people. There are also HAUSA and FULANI herders, as well as the settled BELLA who are associated with the TUAREG.

At the heart of Burkina Faso is the former complex of powerful Mossi kingdoms established following the arrival of the Mossi and Gurma in the 14th century. The territory was conquered by France towards the end of the 19th century. The only densely populated region is the Mossi territory in the centre and east of the country, where there are numerous villages situated away from the river valleys where it is easy to contract malaria and river blindness.

The capital Ouagadougou (Wagadugu), centre of the main historic Mossi kingdom, is also located in the centre of the country, although urban residents of Burkina Faso form only around 10% of the total population. The country became independent in 1960 and was re-named Burkina Faso in 1984. It has been subject to a series of military coups since then, but progress has recently been made towards the establishment of full democracy.

In religion, traditional ancestor worship and animist beliefs are strong, but around 40% of the population is Muslim.

## BURUNDIANS

People of the small Republic of Burundi in Central Africa, capital Bujumbura, which emerged as a significant kingdom during the 17th century. Today 6 million people live in one of the poorest and most densely populated countries in Africa, embroiled in conflict between the TUTSI (14% of the population) and HUTU (85%).

Historically, as in Rwanda (see RWANDANS), Tutsi pastoralists infiltrated the valleys between the Hutu-occupied uplands and established chiefdoms that gradually coalesced into the kingdom of Burundi. A certain cultural alignment took place between the two peoples. The founder of the Tutsi royal line was Ntare Rushatsi, whose origins have been variously attributed to Rwanda and Buha (see HA). The kingdom greatly increased in size from the late 18th century, aided by population growth and improved agriculture, but it was also unstable, and civil war was endemic. The ruling Tutsi also increased the amount that they exacted in tribute from the agricultural population, while subservience and exploitation were at the root of Hutu antipathy.

> " Their language depends so much on gesture that they cannot talk it to each other in the dark. "
>
> Mary Kingsley, 1897, on the Bubi

**Burkinabe: main ethnic groups**

Bella
Bobo
Dyola
Fulani
Hausa
Lobi
Mande
Mossi
Senufo

German explorers entered the country in the 1890s as forerunners to the conquest of 1903. Belgium assumed colonial authority in the country during World War I, and afterwards administered it as part of the League of Nations-mandated territory of Ruanda-Urundi. Political development was complicated by the Belgian encouragement of representative democracy, which naturally favoured the majority Hutu, and which increased tension between the two peoples. There was also rivalry between ruling dynasties and within the ruling Bezi royal line, focused particularly on Crown Prince Rwagasore who, in opposition to the wishes of his father, the *Mwambutsa* (king), sought to follow a more inclusive and populist policy. He was assassinated in 1961. The *Mwambutsa* ignored the election results of 1965, which favoured the Hutu, and the political tensions this provoked led to an attempted Hutu-led military coup. The Hutu prime minister Pierre Ngendandumwe was also assassinated. The *Mwambutsa* was unable to maintain control and resolve the competing demands of the Hutu and Tutsi communities, and a Republic based on the capital at Bujumbura was declared in 1966. The hatred between the two communities continued and led to an outbreak of genocidal killing of up to 150,000 Hutu in 1972.

The history of Burundi since 1972 has remained turbulent, involving a military coup in 1976, a new constitution promulgated in 1981, and a further coup in 1987. The Hutu finally won electoral power in 1993, leading to a further bout of civil war between the Tutsi-dominated army and Hutu rebel forces, involving (by 2000) the death of more than 200,000 people and imprisonment of hundreds of thousands more in concentration ('regroupment') camps.

Religion has also been part of the endemic inter-ethnic tension. Tutsi authorities regard the Roman Catholic Church as a focus for Hutu political aspirations and subversion of Tutsi authority. Catholicism is the faith of 60% of the population and is still regarded with suspicion by the Tutsi community.

The official languages are French and Rundi (Kirundi), a language of BANTU origin. In the cultural sphere the Tutsi were highly developed in the arts of music and dance, much of this involving the praise or celebration of the *Mwambutsa*. Some of these practices have declined in popularity since the post-independence violence and the worsening relations between the communities. Dance, however, remains very popular and dancers in the tradition of the *intore*, the royal court dancers, still preserve important elements of national folklore. Drumming is also widely pursued, as are crafts, notably basketry and beadwork. Sport and shared cultural activities have been promoted as a way of reconciling the communities, but much of this work is in abeyance.

## BURUNGI

Pastoralists of the central highlands of Tanzania (see TANZANIANS). Their Cushitic Burungi language (Mbulunge) suggests they are a 'remnant', like their closely-related neighbours the IRAQW, of the population that occupied the region before the arrival of the BANTU in East Africa. They are known for being shy and self-sufficient, and number little more than 30,000.

## BUSHMEN

See SAN.

## BWAKA

See MBAKA.

## CADAU

See DOGON.

## CALABAR

See KALABARI.

## CAMEROONIANS

Inhabitants of the republic of Cameroon, whose capital is Yaounde. The country is inhabited by the DUALA, BAMUM, BAMILEKE (the largest BANTU-speaking group) and the related TIKAR. The Muslim FULANI are also prominent, particularly in the north of the country, where they arrived only in the 18th and 19th centuries. In the late

**Cameroonians: main ethnic groups**

Bamilekes
Bamum
Duala
Fang
Fulani
Tikar

1990s Cameroon had a population of more than 15.5 million.

Cameroon had early trading contacts with Europeans, initially with the Portuguese, who arrived in the 1470s and subsequently established a profitable trade in sugar and slaves. The trade endured in West Africa for several centuries until suppressed in the 19th century largely through the efforts of the British government and the Royal Navy, which was based on the island of Fernando Po.

During the intense European rivalry for territory and influence in Africa in the late 19th century, the region became the German protectorate of Kamerun, in 1884. It was divided between Britain and France in 1919 under mandates authorized by the League of Nations. The French territory opted for independence in 1960 and was joined by the southern area of the British territory in 1961, but the northern region of the British territory chose union with Nigeria.

Despite their common history and heritage friction continues between Anglophone and Francophone communities within the country, and the Southern Cameroon National Council has recently been active in pursuing separatist aspirations. The people of Cameroon lived in an authoritarian one-party state from independence until multiparty elections were introduced under President Paul Biya (who has governed since 1982), although his ruling RDPC party has been accused of electoral fraud to maintain power.

The northern Cameroon grassland peoples have a distinguished sculpture tradition and brass-casting skills. The Bamileke and Tikar are known for their expressive and fluid sculptural techniques, the tradition historically associated with the exaltation of kings and chiefs in traditional societies. Craft skills vary according to the particular ethnic group; the Fulani for example are accomplished in leather-working. Cameroonians have also excelled in the fields of literature, cinema and, increasingly, football.

## CANARY ISLANDERS

The Canary Islanders are mostly the descendants of Spanish settlers who colonized the archipelago after it was claimed by Spain in 1479. At the time of the Spanish occupation there was a small aboriginal population, thought to be related to the Imraquen people of Western Sahara (see MOORS). These inhabitants were swamped by the settlers, but some aspects of the culture have survived, such as aspects of the islanders' cuisine, and their language has contributed words to the local Spanish dialect. These non-Spanish aspects of their culture has helped nurture a strong sense of local Canarian identity.

Canarians have often seen themselves as having a colonial relationship with Spain, and there was a shortlived independence movement at the end of the 19th century.

## CAPE COLOUREDS

A people of South Africa who are genetically a product of much inter-racial mixing. They are the descendants of whites and a variety of other peoples, for example of relationships between AFRIKANERS and slaves, who were transported to the Cape mainly from Madagascar and Angola from the 17th century. Some have Malay ancestors, brought to the Cape by the Dutch East India Company, while others are the inheritors of the KHOIKHOI and the GRIQUA. They live mainly around Cape Town, and there is also a community in Port Elizabeth. Some are farm workers in rural areas, while others work in service industries in the towns. Since majority rule in South Africa, they have seized opportunities to work throughout the country.

Cape Coloureds were a focus of anxiety and tension to the Afrikaners: a reminder of past inter-racial mixing and a source of fear that the 'poor whites', the Afrikaner rural poor, might ultimately fuse with them. During the period of apartheid they were classified in a specific racial and census category and were required to live in designated areas and to intermarry only among themselves. This served to enhance their sense of community.

Most Cape Coloureds are Christians, but some have maintained a Muslim identity and coalesce socially around their mosques. Under a Cape franchise which was demarcated by property, many Coloureds had the vote earlier in the 20th century, but under apartheid this was removed from them, to be restored in the 1990s.

> 66 We wish to have your laws in our towns. We want to have every fashion altered. 99
>
> Letter to Queen Victoria, from a number of chiefs, requesting a British protectorate over Cameroon, 1880

> 66 We must adopt a system of despotism such as works so well in India, in our relations with the barbarians of South Africa. 99
>
> Cecil Rhodes's opinion of the Cape Coloureds, 1887

## CAPE VERDEANS

Inhabitants of the Cape Verde island group, which lies in the Atlantic 500 km / 310 miles west of Dakar, Senegal. The islands were uninhabited until colonized by Portugal from 1462, and they subsequently prospered from the slave trade and shipping. The islands have formed an independent republic since 1975 with a population of around 400,000 (1997), two-thirds Creole (mulatto) and the rest black African and European, mostly Portuguese. The official language is Portuguese although the *lingua franca* is the Portuguese dialect Crioulo. The population is mostly Roman Catholic but animist customs are strong. The economy is largely based on agriculture (which is dependent on irrigation), tourism and service industries.

## CAPRIVIANS or Caprivis

A Namibian people, linguistically and culturally related to the BANTU-speaking LOZI of Zambia. They number around 50,000. Caprivi territory was part of the Lozi empire until 1890, when Britain allowed Germany to incorporate the 'Caprivi strip' into German South-West Africa. This gave them access to the Zambezi River, but this was useless as a waterway so the partition of Lozi territory was wholly unnecessary.

## CAPSIAN CULTURE

A stone-tool tradition of North African hunter-gatherers which developed contemporaneously with the European Mesolithic, or Middle Stone Age. It is named after the type-site at al-Maqta near Qafsah (Capsa) in southern Tunisia and succeeded the ATERIAN CULTURE. Capsian culture influenced the Oranian (Ibero-Maurusian) culture as it spread along the North African coast from 9000 to 5000 BC. The Capsian flint-working tool tradition of the Maghrib continued alongside the developing agricultural and pastoral economy of the Neolithic, to the 1st millennium BC; this is why the culture is sometimes called Neolithic-of-Capsian. Capsian peoples are ancestors of the LIBYANS.

## CARTHAGINIANS

Inhabitants of the city of Carthage ('New City'), now a suburb of Tunis, and its extensive territories bordering the North African coast. The city was established by the PHOENICIANS from Lebanon, the pre-eminent traders of the ancient world. They colonized the western Mediterranean from the late 2nd millennium BC aiming to capture the region's trade. Carthage was their main settlement, established soon after its traditional foundation date of 814 BC.

> *The superiority of their constitution is proved by the fact that the common people remain loyal to it. The Carthaginians have never had any rebellion worth speaking of.*
>
> Aristotle *c.* 340 BC

C

Carthaginians

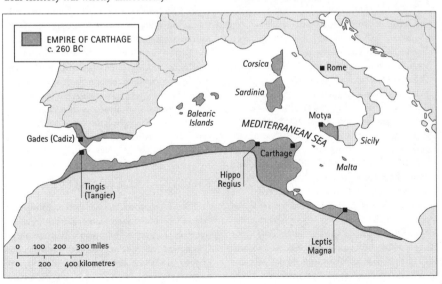

EMPIRE OF CARTHAGE
c. 260 BC

Corsica
Rome
Sardinia
Balearic Islands
Motya
MEDITERRANEAN SEA
Gades (Cadiz)
Carthage
Sicily
Malta
Tingis (Tangier)
Hippo Regius
Leptis Magna

0  100  200  300 miles
0  200  400 kilometres

During the 6th century BC the Carthaginians expanded from their limited coastal enclave as far as 200 km / 125 miles inland. This fertile territory, in what is now northern and eastern Tunisia, became the centre of large agricultural estates renowned for their wheat and olives. They were probably worked by indigenous subject BERBERS (NUMIDIANS) who were either slaves or subject to some form of tied or forced labour. Sources refer to 'slave risings' and 'slave estates'. The Punic (Phoenician language) heartland extended from Sfax in central Tunisia to Bone in eastern Algeria and the Mediterranean. Outside this area Carthaginian power progressively weakened, although it was exerted through local Berber rulers.

**Rise and fall**

Carthaginians introduced iron-working to North Africa, which assisted agricultural development. It is impossible to say if this knowledge was disseminated across the barrier of the Sahara to sub-tropical Africa. Certainly indirect trade contacts were developed through peoples such as the Garamantes of the Fezzan, who supplied slaves and precious stones. Carthage remained a maritime power, however, focused on Mediterranean trade and the various ports it came to control. Its main effect was to help incorporate North Africa into the Mediterranean world both economically and culturally. Its trade and communication network disseminated Hellenic and Phoenician culture to the western Mediterranean. The origin of Berber script lies in Phoenician, for example, although the Berbers influenced the Phoenicians as well.

Carthaginian commercial dominance was challenged by the rising power of Rome, which won the first Punic War (264–241 BC) and the Carthaginian islands of Sicily and Sardinia. In response Carthage consolidated its control of North Africa and exacted more tax, tribute and labour. The reaction of Berbers and the tributary states was fierce. The Numidians from the coastal plains west of the city, under their leader Masinissa, helped the Romans to eventual victory over the Carthaginians in the Second Punic War (218–201 BC) which had followed Hannibal's campaign from Spain to the gates of Rome itself. Carthage was forced to surrender all its overseas possessions and became a client state. The third war lasted only three years and ended with the total destruction of the city, and power, of Carthage in 146 BC.

The ROMANS then colonized Carthaginian territory and exploited the productive wheat and olive estates using tributary and tied labour much as the Carthaginians had done. The city of Carthage was re-founded in 29 BC, restored as the capital of the invading VANDALS in AD 439–533 and destroyed by the ARABS in AD 698.

# CENTRAL AFRICANS

Inhabitants of the Central African Republic, formerly part of French Equatorial Africa prior to independence in 1960. Around 80 ethnic groups make up the population of the modern state. French is the official language, although Sango is widely spoken. Around half the population are Christian, mainly Roman Catholics. The country was briefly renamed the Central African Empire (1976–9) by its then despotic ruler, Jean-Bédel Bokassa.

# CHADIANS

Inhabitants of the Republic of Chad, capital N'Djamena. The population of around 7.5 million people comprises around 200 ethnic groups speaking more than 200 languages and dialects, including TAMA, SANGA and FUR, although the official languages are Arabic and French. Chad was part of French Equatorial Africa until independence in 1960. Since then the population and largely agricultural economy have suffered because of civil war, LIBYAN invasion (prompting French intervention in the south) and natural disasters. More than half the population is Muslim, mostly concentrated in the north, and one-third Christian.

# CHEWA or Cewa or Achewa

An ethnic group living in Zambia, Zimbabwe and Malawi. Like their neighbouring offshoot the NSENGA, they speak Nyanja (Chinyanja or Chichewa), the *lingua franca* of Zambia and Malawi. They are the largest of a cluster of BANTU-speaking peoples known as the MARAVI, and are culturally related to the BEMBA, sharing features such as matrilineal descent and polygyny. They commonly live in stockaded villages, grow crops such as maize, beans and rice, and hunt and fish. In the 19th century they were regularly raided by the YAO for slaves. The NGONI also settled among them, adopting the Chewa language and culture. The Chewa population is around 2.5 million, and most are small farmers and Christian in religion.

## CHOKWE

An ethnic group occupying parts of Congo (Kinshasa), Angola and Zambia. These matrilineal Chokwe-speaking BANTU comprise aboriginal and LUNDA peoples who in the north are given more to hunting, and in the south to hoe cultivation and cattle-rearing. They live in village groups under chiefs or other autonomous political structures and they number around 1.3 million. They are accomplished craftspeople renowned for their wood carvings and masks (worn especially at initiation ceremonies) and ironwork. Many have become labour migrants to the Shaba copper mines.

In the 19th century their conquests and sale of slaves, ivory and forest products made the Chokwe wealthy, but their expansion was checked by the establishment of colonial rule in Zambia. Their numbers were increased by incorporating female slaves into their own society.

## COMORANS

Inhabitants of the Comoros Islands, formerly ruled by France, which lie in the northern Mozambique Channel in the Indian Ocean and form the Federal Islamic Republic of the Comoros. The population of around 600,000 Comorans is almost entirely Sunni Muslim and ethnically the product of a mixture of BANTU, MALAGASY, ARABS, MALAYS, INDONESIANS and INDIANS who participated in the Indian Ocean trade network via the SWAHILI Coast of East Africa over many centuries. The official languages of the Comoros are French, Comoros and Arabic.

Comoran culture is an interesting blend of indigenous and outside influences, for example in contemporary music, and football is widely

followed. Traditional craft skills have developed in wood-carving, basketwork, jewellery-making and embroidery. The people of the islands are some of the world's poorest, most making a living from subsistence agriculture and livestock husbandry, which remain the basis of the national economy. The environment is fragile, the crops susceptible to climatic fluctuation, and unemployment is common, so that foreign aid is very important to the islands.

## CONGOE

West Africans who were originally liberated from slave ships by the US Navy after the international trade in slaves became illegal in America in 1807. The captives were re-settled on the coast of Liberia (see LIBERIANS) and were known as the Congoe, or Congoe Recaptives, after the origin of many in the Congo River basin. The distinct identity of this population has become blurred, although it is still apparent in their coastal settlements.

## CONGOLESE (BRAZZAVILLE)

Inhabitants of a republic that lies on the coast of west-central Africa, officially the Republic of Congo, capital Brazzaville. It is often referred to as Congo (Brazzaville) to distinguish it from the Democratic Republic of Congo, or Congo (Kinshasa). The territory formed part of French Equatorial Africa until independence in 1960, but it became Africa's first Marxist state in 1968 following a military coup. French is the official language.

The largest ethnic groups are the KONGO, forming half the population, SANGA and TEKE. They are overwhelmingly employed in agriculture and forestry. Roughly half the population of 3 million are Christian, mostly Roman Catholic, and the rest still follow traditional beliefs.

## CONGOLESE (KINSHASA)

Inhabitants of a republic that encompasses almost the entire vast region of the Congo River basin in equatorial Africa, officially the Democratic Republic of Congo, capital Kinshasa. It is often referred to as Congo (Kinshasa) to distin-

C

| Congolese: main ethnic groups |
| --- |
| Azande |
| Banda |
| Bemba |
| Boa |
| Chokwe |
| Hum |
| Kongo |
| Luba |
| Lugbara |
| Lunda |
| Mongo |
| Ngale |
| Ngbandi |
| Rundi |
| Rwandans |
| Sanga |
| Teke |

guish it from the Republic of Congo, or Congo (Brazzaville). Kinshasa is the largest city in central Africa, and its name originates from the KONGO people who occupied the coastal territory of the country when the Portuguese arrived in 1482. Between 1971 and 1997 the republic was known as Zaire after the River Zaire, an historic alternative name for the River Congo, at the instigation of the notorious Mobutu Sese Seko (governed 1965–97). It has now reverted to the name adopted at independence in 1960.

The population of more than 49 million consists of more than 200 ethnic groups, mostly of BANTU origin. The main ethnic groups are shown in the box on p. 183. They speak a bewildering variety of languages, including English and French, the *lingua franca*, and are predominantly subsistence farmers and Christians.

In the 1870s the expeditions of Henry Morton Stanley brought the territory to the attention of King Leopold II of Belgium, whose personal fiefdom it became as the Congo Free State. Between 1885 and 1908 its natural resources, especially ivory and rubber, and its population were ruthlessly exploited. Atrocities were committed against villages and individuals failing to produce required quantities of rubber. The international opprobrium was such that Leopold was obliged to relinquish control of the Congo to the Belgian parliament.

Improvements in what was now known as the Belgian Congo were marked, including an efficient health care system (although sleeping sickness became a major problem in the territory), improved housing, relative economic prosperity and a state primary school system that led to the highest literacy rates in Africa by 1960. The Belgians, however, were reluctant to cede control of the Congo and suppressed the growing nationalist movement. There was no official policy to encourage indigenous recruitment to the higher civil service, the professions or the government.

In response to intense popular pressure, elections were hurriedly called in 1960, leading to political paralysis, army mutiny, the attempted secession by the province of Katanga and to civil war. United Nations forces helped restore order, which was consolidated by General (later President) Mobutu.

> **"** The carnage against the ancient Coptic community is one of the least reported assaults on a minority anywhere in the world. **"**
>
> UK Member of Parliament David Alton, 1994

Mobutu maintained power until 1995, but in 1997 Laurent Kabila seized power with Rwandan support to establish the Democratic Republic of Congo. Since then, Uganda and several other African states have become involved in the vicious and convoluted civil war that has reignited many ethnic tensions in the country.

The Congolese have suffered severely from famine and economic dislocation, and it is estimated that since 1998, some 4.7 million have died from war, disease and hunger, the highest death toll in any conflict since World War II.

## COPTS

Christian followers of the ancient church that dominated Egypt before the Arab Muslim invasion of North Africa in the 7th century. They described themselves in Greek as *Aigyptos*, which was translated as *Qibt* in Arabic, hence Copt in English. The Coptic Orthodox Church is the main Christian church in Egypt today, although the number of Copts has dwindled to 10 million out of the total population of around 65 million EGYPTIANS. The Coptic language, descended directly from ancient Egyptian (SEE AFRO-ASIAN), was superseded by Arabic, which came into widespread use in the 7th century, and although some Coptic remains in limited use in church rites, it is essentially extinct as a living language.

In terms of everyday life, modern Egyptian Copts are indistinguishable from their Muslim compatriots, although centuries of marrying within their own community has preserved a physical appearance more akin to their ancient Egyptian ancestors of the Pharaonic period. This is especially true in the remoter rural areas. Many Copts live in the towns and cities, especially in the middle Nile Valley, and perhaps 25% in Cairo itself, where they have been associated particularly with employment in the civil service and in the financial sector. However, they continue to suffer discrimination at the hands of the Egyptian authorities.

Christianity first arrived in Egypt at the port of Alexandria, certainly by the early 2nd century. It soon gained many adherents in both Upper and Lower Egypt, and despite early Roman persecution, by AD 400 around 90% of Egyptians were Christian. Numerous bishoprics were

C

established, and the Bible itself was translated into Coptic, which was ancient Egyptian written in Greek script. It has been suggested that the church's development of disciplined religious communities and elaborate charity were inherited from ancient Egypt.

As elsewhere in North Africa, Christianity evolved from a religion of protest to the official faith of the ROMAN and BYZANTINE empires. In AD 451 the Council of Chalcedon laid the foundations for the schism of 536 in which the Egyptian Church refused to abandon its Monophysite beliefs (that Christ had only one nature) and even proselytized successfully among the NUBIANS. Byzantine persecution of what was regarded as an heretical church weakened the Christian opposition to Muslim invasion in 639, but the Copts, led by the Patriarch of Alexandria, became protected tributaries, allowed to practise their beliefs in exchange for taxes. They were also important functionaries in the administration of the country. The pressure to convert to Islam, however, was compelling by the 8th century and by the 14th century the proportion of Copts in the population fell to less than 10%.

The Coptic Church has been democratically governed since the 1890s and its leader, the Patriarch of Alexandria, who is now based in Cairo, is chosen by an electoral college. The church also operates its own schools and other institutions. The other main Egyptian Christian denomination is the Coptic Catholic Church, which emerged in 1741 when a Monophysite bishop became Roman Catholic.

## CREOLES (Sierra Leone)

See KRIO.

## CUSHITES

Cushitic-speaking people of northeast Africa concentrated in Ethiopia and the Red Sea coast. They are part of the same Afro-Asiatic language group as the BEJA, OROMO, SOMALI and Chadic peoples, the last pastoralists who migrated westward along the Sahel corridor after 3000 BC. Other Cushitic speakers moved from the Sudan plains southward to the Lake Turkana area of northern Kenya and southern Ethiopia around

2500 BC, then down the Rift Valley to Tanzania. Later BANTU expansion absorbed many Cushitic speakers in East Africa, but those who survive include the BURUNGI and IRAQW of Tanzania. Indigenous Cushites (not to be confused with KUSHITES) helped to create the kingdom of the AKSUMITES in northern Ethiopia around 500 BC.

## DAGOMBA or Dogamba

The main ethnic group in the northern Ghanaian chiefdom of Dagbon (see GHANAIANS). They number around 500,000 and are one of the larger GUR-speaking peoples of West Africa; their language is Dagbani.

The ancestors of the Dagomba are thought to have invaded the region from the north in late medieval times, ruling over a number of local peoples and forcing others into Togo. Their extensive kingdom was reduced in size by the GUANG of Gonja in the mid-17th century, and soon after, Dagbon became subject to the powerful ASANTE kingdom. Their annual tribute of slaves continued until 1874, when Britain extended its control over the region.

Most Dagomba live in nucleated villages occupied by related patrilineal groups divided into mostly small-scale farming families. Some hunting and fishing is undertaken.

Ancestor worship, along with an earth cult, are the main features of Dagomba religion. The lineage heads, as custodians of ancestral shrines, exercise a continuing authority in a traditionally hierarchical chief-based society whose leaders are subject to a paramount chief known as the *Ya-na*. Most Dagomba are now Muslim.

## DAHOMEYESE

See FON.

## DAMARA or Dama or Bergdama

A people of Namibia. Today they number around 100,000 and speak a NAMA Khoikhoi language or HERERO.

The Damara were nomadic hunters and pastoralists, but today are farmers. They were also skilled in copper-smelting.

> *"The Dagomba warriors, having been defeated in battle, were at some stage under the control of Asante and had to pay tribute by giving captured slaves."*
>
> Kwadze Senano, 2003

d

'Damaraland' was the name applied to north-central Namibia by early European settlers, although it was territory from which the Damara had been expelled by the Khoisan Nama and the Herero. They were further persecuted by European settlers in the 20th century.

## DANAKIL

See AFAR.

## DINKA

Pastoralists living in a vast area of the savannah in the Nile basin of southern Sudan. They are NILOTES like the NUER with whom they have much in common: they speak a similar language (but with many dialects), and raise cattle, which are central to their culture. They move to higher ground in the rainy season, avoiding the flooding of the Nile, and then often grow millet at their villages. They are proud and warlike and live in independent groups, lacking centralized authority and recognizing only certain priest-chiefs. Historically the Dinka have opposed the imposition of outside rule and interference in traditional society. They have been part of the southern Sudanese opposition to the Islamic government in Khartoum in the long-running civil war following the colonial period. Their population at the end of the 20th century was nearly 3 million.

## DIOLA or Diula

See JOLA.

## DJERMA

See ZERMA.

## DJIBOUTIANS

People of the small former French colonial enclave of Djibouti, a port on the Gulf of Aden at the entrance to the Red Sea. It was created from the colony of French Somaliland in 1896, largely at the instigation of the territory's first governor, Léonce Lagarde. Djibouti is now a major entrepôt and railhead for the Djibouti-Addis Ababa

> **"** These days the choice is that either you have food without a wife, or you have a wife without food. **"**
>
> A Dinka account of the impact of civil war, 1997

railway. It became the independent Republic of Djibouti in 1977, although still retains a significant French garrison and has recently become an American military outpost.

The main ethnic groups are the ISSAS and SOMALIS, among whom the AFARS predominate. The current population of around 650,000 is mostly Sunni Muslim. Drought and war among neighbouring ETHIOPIANS, ERITREANS and Somalis have caused economic problems and a refugee influx in recent decades. The policy of strict neutrality in the conflicts of its neighbours has enabled the Djiboutians to preserve the internal harmony of its population and survive as an independent state. Opposition parties were banned in 1981 and overt traditional ethnic rivalry between the Issa and Afar has been restricted, although the Issa predominate in the armed forces, government administration and the ruling party, the Rassemblement Populaire pour le Progrés (RPP). The potential for conflict remains, however, due to the influx of large numbers of people from the rural areas to the city itself. The government has struggled to improve the living conditions of growing numbers of migrants from rural areas to the large shanty towns such as Balbala on the outskirts, and within the city itself. Incomes of urban residents also continue to diverge.

## DOGON or Habé or Cadau

Inhabitants of the upland plateau region centred on Bandiagara in Mali, West Africa. They number more than 600,000 and have developed a fascinating culture, largely due to their isolation from much of the outside world. There has also been limited interaction between the Dogon peoples themselves, which explains the several distinct dialects of the Dogon language.

Most Dogon are simple cultivators who live in patrilineal extended families under headmen. They have no centralized system of government, although there is an overall *hogon*, or spiritual leader. Their unique religion is based on a creation myth involving the visit of amphibious beings from the star Sirius, a belief which has strongly influenced the development of their culture and social organization.

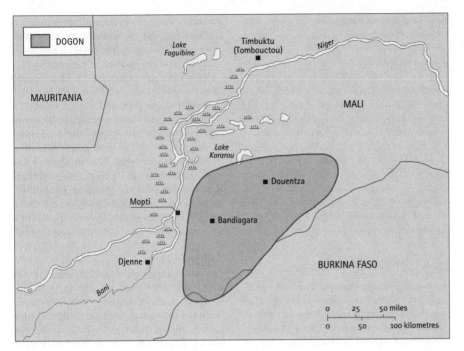

## DUALA or Douala

A people of the coastal forest region of Cameroon, who live in nucleated settlements adjoining the Wouri River estuary. They exploited early trade with the Europeans, which encouraged the growth of populous towns and chiefdoms; these developed into the 19th-century kingdoms of Bell and Akwa, whose power faded from the 1880s. Their traditional chiefs remain, although they have only a residual and declining authority. The Duala are mostly Christian, although still strongly attached to their indigenous beliefs involving a creator god, witchcraft, magic and ancestor spirits. Many Duala are now urban dwellers, though most remain predominantly agricultural, and also exploit the coastal fishing.

## DYULA or Diula or Jula

MANDE-speaking Muslims who emerged as traders in Ghana and flourished in the Mali empire, migrating throughout West Africa by the 14th century. They carried Islam throughout West Africa, particularly the savannah territories, where it is still important. Much of their associated Arab-inspired architecture and material culture was also disseminated at the same time. The Dyula are an offshoot of the SONINKE, to whom the word *dyula* means 'trader', but they also incorporated other peoples. Dyula is an important trade language in the Ivory Coast and Burkina Faso, where it is spoken by more than 4 million people. Many are settled agriculturists, but most remain active traders or travelling tinkers, at least seasonally.

## EDO or Bini

An agricultural people occupying mostly the state of Edo, southern Nigeria (see NIGERIANS). Their state capital is Benin City, former centre of the powerful kingdom of Benin founded in the 13th century and ruled by an *oba*, an omnipotent sacred priest-king. They provided large numbers of slaves to the Portuguese. Benin's decline culminated in the British conquest of 1897. The Edo are noted for religious observances that included human sacrifice and for their exquisite brass and bronze artefacts. They currently number around 4 million.

## EFIK

An offshoot of the IBIBIO people who inhabit the lower Cross River region of Nigeria, an area known to Europeans as Old Calabar. They lived by canoe fishing and trading from their arrival in the 17th century, later selling slaves and palm oil to the Europeans on the coast. Many are now cultivators. The Efik were led by the appointed chief of the *ekpe* secret society responsible for all tribal and religious affairs, a role now largely assumed by the state. They speak Efik-Ibibio of the Niger-Congo language family.

## EGYPTIANS

The people of Egypt. Modern Egypt is the product of a flourishing civilization along the River Nile, fundamental to the country's existence. With its large population of around 65 million, its historical importance in the Muslim world, and its advanced economic and cultural development, it is regarded in many ways as the leading Arab state. Its geographical location, where the continent of Africa meets the Middle East, reinforces this status.

Almost all Egyptians live in the well-watered and fertile Nile Valley and Delta region leading to the Mediterranean. Ethnically, most are descended from ancient Egyptian peoples (see AFRO-ASIAN) and, since the 7th century, ARABS, although there have been many invading peoples over the centuries who have contributed to this mixture, including PERSIANS, ROMANS, GREEKS and TURKS, as well as desert nomads who have settled in the towns and cultivated lands along the Nile. The nomadic BEJA have occupied the southeastern desert and adjoining areas of the Sudan and Eritrea for thousands of years, and their forbears, together with ancestral NUBA people, contributed to the settled populations of the Nile Valley that emerged from the decline of the Kushite kingdom in the 4th century AD (see KUSHITES). Many of the nomadic BEDOUIN arrived from Arabia following the Muslim conquest and have subsequently assimilated with the established population, including the

> **" Their strength is to sit still. "**
>
> The Bible,
> Isaiah 30:7,
> on the Egyptians

BERBERS of the Western Desert. The Bedouin of the Eastern Desert and Sinai are of a purer Arab stock who arrived in comparatively recent times and have not intermarried to the same extent. Today many nomads have become sedentary or semi-nomadic.

The settled population of Upper (southern) Egypt differ slightly in their physical characteristics from those of Lower Egypt and the deserts, notably in having darker skin, which is even more pronounced in the NUBIANS south of the First Cataract at Aswan. Trade and the institution of slavery also led to many Sudanic, Nubian and sub-Saharan Africans becoming incorporated into the Egyptian population over a period of several millennia.

### Ancient Egypt

Egyptian civilization is one of the oldest in the world and the earliest to develop in Africa, although whether it influenced cultures south of the Sahara is open to doubt. It certainly had a profound effect on Greek civilization, and the development of other cultures that have formed the modern world. Egyptian origins lie in the migration of early peoples into the Nile Valley following the desiccation of the Sahara. They came to rely on agriculture, introduced around 5000 BC. Various early Neolithic cultures developed, notably the BADARIAN CULTURE of the late 5th millennium BC, leading into the important AMRATIAN CULTURE and GERZEAN cultures, which flourished prior to the start of the dynastic period around 3100 BC.

This political unification of Egypt under the rule of a single king, accompanied by an even greater cultural efflorescence, marks the founding of the Egyptian state and its extensive empire. A total of 31 dynasties (including those of the HYKSOS and KUSHITES) succeeded through the Old, Middle and New Kingdoms down to the invasion of Alexander the Great in 332 BC and the establishment of the Ptolemaic line. Egyptian social and cultural developments were remarkable, in the royal pyramids beginning in the Old Kingdom, as well as in religion, sculpture, bureaucratic organization, literacy, agricultural development and many other ways. Also remarkable was Egypt's continuity, which was the product of a deeply conservative society.

The Ptolemaic period ended with ROMAN conquest from 30 BC, which later saw the growth of Christianity and eventual control from Christian Byzantium. In the period after AD 313 the Egyptian Church became very influential in North Africa, and to this day it has preserved the later Coptic form of the ancient Egyptian language (see COPTS).

Christianity gradually withered following the Muslim Arab conquest of Egypt, and BYZANTINE forces were evacuated in AD 642, the year the Egyptian capital Cairo was founded as El Fustat. Islam became the dominant religion and remains so today (although there are still nearly 10 million Coptic Christians). Arabic became and remains the language of the country, although there are many dialects in use.

A succession of caliphates was established during the early Arab period, including that of the Mameluks between 1250 and 1517. A political and cultural decline followed under the OTTOMANS, when Egypt became an imperial province ruled from Istanbul. The Franco–British world conflict led to Napoleon's short-lived French occupation in 1798–1801, but Egypt really began to interest European powers because of its strategic importance on the route to India and East Asia. Britain was particularly keen to safeguard its imperial lines of communication and trade, even more so following the opening of the Suez Canal in 1869. Britain occupied Egypt in 1882 following the political problems left by the acquisitiveness and expansionist policies of the Ottoman viceroy, Muhammad Ali (governed 1805–48).

**Modern Egyptian culture**

In 1922 the country became a constitutional monarchy and nominally independent of Britain, although Egyptian nationalism was only fully asserted in 1952 with the overthrow of King Farouk in a military coup which included Gamal Abdel Nasser (1918–70), prime minister from 1954 and the first president of the Republic of Egypt, 1956–70. His nationalization of the Suez Canal led to a failed invasion by Britain, France and Israel in 1956. Further wars with Israel took place in 1967 and 1973, in which the Sinai was occupied by the Israelis but returned in 1982 as part of a bilateral peace agreement.

The Egyptian republic has also been influenced by wider Arab nationalism, which led to the political union of Egypt and Syria as the United Arab Republic from 1958–61, and to the Confederation of Arab Republics from 1971–9. Both unions fell apart. In 1971 a new constitution was adopted following a plebiscite, which declared the Arab Republic of Egypt to be a democratic socialist state with normal democratic freedoms. Since 1960 effective local democratic government has also given people control over important aspects of their daily lives.

Around half of Egyptians live in the countryside and desert areas, the rest in urban areas and

**Egyptians**

*The empire of ancient Egypt reached its greatest extent in the New Kingdom, around 1500 BC.*

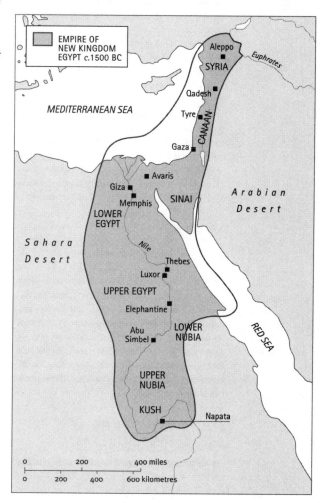

especially the Cairo conurbation, which forms the largest city in Africa (with a population of around 10 million). Agriculture provides around one third of national income, and was greatly helped by the building of the Aswan High Dam ,completed in 1970, which has assisted in the irrigation of cultivated lands along the Nile as well as electricity generation for industrial purposes. Tourism is also a major source of income, but it has been badly affected by the security scares and US-led wars with Iraq since 1991. Militant Islamic groups have also caused periodic worry, notably in the assassination of President Anwar Sadat (1918–81). Their influence has also aggrieved the Coptic community, who are generally subject to discrimination by the Egyptian authorities.

Culturally, Egyptians have succeeded in embracing a wide variety of influences from the Arab world and the West. These have contributed to a flourishing tradition in music, the visual arts, theatre and film-making, often inspired by Egyptian history, folklore, urban life and the countryside. There are also strong folk-art and dance traditions, which are actively supported by the state. The government has recently established the Biblioteca Alexandrina, a conscious revival of the library that flourished in Hellenic Alexandria from the 3rd century BC.

## EMBU

BANTU-speaking KENYANS who occupy the fertile central Rift highlands in East Africa. They are closely related to the MERU and KIKUYU. They were originally a hunter-gatherer people but became agriculturists and stock-keepers, although elephant-hunting remained important through the 19th century in order to supply ivory to traders on the SWAHILI coast. The town of Embu was established on tribal territory by the British colonial authorities in 1906. They number around 180,000.

## EQUATOGUINEANS or Equatorial Guineans

Inhabitants of the coastal Republic of Equatorial Guinea. It was the colony of Spanish Guinea until 1968 and includes a number of islands,

notably Bioko (Fernando Po), home of the BUBI, and the capital Malabo. The country is dominated by the FANG, who make up 83% of the country's mostly agricultural BANTU population of around 480,000. There are also coastal tribes, known as the *playero*, who are partly the result of indigenous and European inter-marriage; Fernandinos, descendants of freed slaves; and *crioulos* from São Tomé and Príncipe (see SÃO TOMÉANS). Spanish is the official language, although a pidgin English is in use, especially on Bioko. French is also becoming more widespread due to commercial links with Francophone West Africa. Agriculture has been the traditional basis of economic life.

The Portuguese were the first Europeans to visit the region, in the 15th century, before the arrival of the ancestors of the main Fang and Bubi population of today. The vast seaboard territory including Guinea and Bioko was ceded to the Spanish in the late 18th century, although Bioko was later administered and occupied by British naval forces attempting to stop the slave trade. The mainland (Rio Muni) was only effectively brought under control by the Spanish in the 1920s. Under colonial rule, the economic resources of the territory were exploited – in particular its timber and cocoa – although little attempt was made to develop the indigenous communities.

At independence in 1968 there were few professional and educated Guineans, and the economy was underdeveloped. There followed an economic crisis and political repression under the regime of the dictatorial President Macias Nguema, overthrown in 1979. The Fernandinos, who formed a significant bourgeoisie under Spanish rule, lost much of their influence to the majority Fang, who had been the main proponents of the nationalist struggle. Another result of independence was increased friction between the Bubi of Bioko and the Fang, many of whom moved to the island capital for employment and to be close to the centre of power. They still dominate the island.

The post-independence political dysfunction has continued, and only limited democratic government is permitted. More recent events have improved the fortunes of Equatorial Guineans, notably the exploitation of oil and gas discovered in the Gulf of Guinea off Bioko in 1991, although it is believed that some of this wealth has been diverted to the family of President Teodoro Obiang Nguema and their allies. His semi-dictatorial regime has recently been responsible for the brutal suppression, involving human rights abuses, of Bubi Bioko separatists who are engaged in an active military campaign. The legacy of Spanish colonial rule is still evident in the appearance and culture of the country, especially on Bioko, and Roman Catholicism is the faith of around 80% of Guineans today. Traditional beliefs are strong, especially among the Fang of the mainland, and are often held conjointly or in a syncretic mix, evident in the Mbwiti cult. Folklore and traditional religion have undergone a resurgence since independence.

# ERITREANS

Inhabitants of the state of Eritrea, in the Horn of Africa. The name Eritrea derives from the Italianized Latin *Mare Erythraeum* (Red Sea). The Eritreans are descended from the area's original Cushitic inhabitants and from Semitic SABAEAN immigrants who arrived from Arabia in the 1st millennium BC. Eritrea's location on the Red Sea bestowed a commercial and strategic importance, contributing to the development of the kingdom of Aksum (see AKSUMITES) in the 1st century BC, one of the earliest states of sub-Saharan Africa.

Maritime trade links with the Middle East led to the introduction of Christianity in the 4th century and Islam in the 7th century. After the fall of the Aksumite kingdom in the 5th century, Eritrea came under the control of a succession of imperial powers: Ethiopia in the Middle Ages, the OTTOMAN empire in the 16th century, Egypt in the 19th century and Italy in 1885. Eritrea was occupied by British forces in 1941 and was federated with Ethiopia in 1952, although in an unsuccessful attempt to forestall growing nationalist sentiment it was directly incorporated into the Ethiopian empire ten years later. A war of liberation ensued, led by the Eritrean People's Liberation Front, which resulted in independence in 1993. Friction with Ethiopia remains (see ETHIOPIANS).

The Eritreans are a diverse nation: religious and ethnic differences remain divisive issues. Eastern Orthodox Christianity remains the religion of half the Eritrean population today, especially among the Tigrinya-speaking TIGRAY people in the highlands bordering Ethiopia. Most of the population speaks Tigrinya and Tigre (spoken by the TIGRE people of northwestern Eritrea), both of Semitic origin. Other ethnic minorities have their own cultures and languages and include the nomadic AFARS of the Danakil (the southeast desert region); the Nilotic NARA and KUNAMA; SAHO and BEJA pastoralists; and the BILIN, whose language is of Cushitic origin. The population of Eritrea was estimated at 3.84 million in 1998, mostly peasant farmers and pastoralists. The civil war and persistent drought have brought death and destruction to many. High mortality rates and limited educational opportunities are major problems. The farming and livestock sectors of the economy are slowly recovering, including the irrigated plantation sector, which was a legacy of ITALIAN rule.

# ETHIOPIANS

People of the Federal Democratic Republic of Ethiopia, capital Addis Ababa. Formerly called Abyssinia, it is one of the world's oldest countries, surviving in various forms for the past 2000 years. It was also the first Christian country in Africa, giving rise to the ancient Ethiopian Orthodox Church, which has been fundamental to Ethiopian culture and still predominates today. The rival AMHARA and TIGRAY peoples, the 'Abyssinians' who together form roughly half of today's population of around 64 million, are ethnically and culturally similar and have been largely responsible for maintaining Ethiopia's historical identity and independence. Tensions between them, however, led to active Tigray opposition to Amhara dominance in the former Mengistu regime and in the current government, and helped to fuel the secession of the coastal province of Eritrea in 1993 (see ERITREANS).

## Peoples and culture

The large Amhara population is concentrated in the southern Ethiopian plateau, with the smaller

*" It should be possible to accelerate development of the Eritrean people together with their kith and kin in the rest of Ethiopia. "*

Haile Selassie, 1962

*" Abyssinia is a place to teach patience to a man who lacks it, and take it away from him who has it. "*

Anon, 19th century

Tigray population to the north. Both are Semitic-speaking peoples who are descended from the indigenous AGAW and SEMITES from Arabia. From this union early in the 1st millennium AD emerged the AKSUMITES and their powerful and sophisticated highland kingdom, which straddled the modern-day Ethiopian and Eritrean border and benefited from extensive trade and advanced agricultural techniques. These peoples have traditionally been dominated by landed aristocracies.

Approximately equal to the Amhara in numbers are the Cushitic OROMO (Galla) of southern Ethiopia, who expanded into the Christian heartland from the 16th century and adopted Christianity or Islam, generally merging into the local populations and becoming subject to the Amhara ascendancy. Traditionally they were nomadic pastoralists but many have now adapted to a settled agricultural existence. Both the Amhara and the Tigray practise mixed cultivation and livestock farming.

In the lower and hotter regions to the south are the GURAGE, Ometo and Kafa-Sidamo peoples. Coffee, native to Ethiopia and widely grown in the region, probably derives its name from the Kafa. Other significant groups are the traditionally pastoral nomadic AFAR of the hot and arid eastern regions and the SOMALI, both Muslim peoples with large compatriot groups in neighbouring countries, contributing to cross-border tensions in recent decades. In their own societies they are clannish and prone to feuding, more characteristic of nomadic societies.

Rivalries persist among such a diversity of peoples and cultures, which makes it even more remarkable that Ethiopia has survived as a unitary state over such a long period. Languages reflect this diversity, for apart from the *lingua franca*, Amharic, there are around 100 languages in total. Oromo is widely spoken. The Semitic Ge'ez was spoken in the ancient Aksumite empire but is now restricted to use in the rites of the Ethiopian Orthodox Church. Apart from the Semitic, Cushitic and Omotic languages, Nilotic is spoken in the western regions of the country by the KUNAMA and others.

The cultural heritage of the Ethiopian people is a product of their many and diverse constituent ethnic and religious groups. Christianity is the religion of around half of Ethiopians, and the church has been very important as the mainspring of the Ethiopian literary and artistic traditions. Byzantine and Coptic art and architecture are recognizable formative influences. Since the end of the old imperial regime, the importance of the church in national affairs has declined, and Islam, followed by a quarter to one-third of the population, has been given greater recognition. There is also a sizeable minority of animists.

In terms of social interaction, Ethiopians generally place a high value on respect for old age, refinement of speech and manners, and the common courtesies, especially hospitality. On the other hand, they have traditionally despised craftworkers, including the FALASHA metalworkers and potters, and labourers such as the Gurage. Employment in trade was also considered degrading, especially in the Christian communities traditionally dominated by landed aristocracies, although this attitude was less evident among Muslim peoples and has recently changed.

**Development of the state**

The Amhara and Tigray occupy the agriculturally productive highland region of Ethiopia, whose physical geography provided a large measure of protection to its people and an environment conducive to the development of the state and their respective cultures.

Aksum, the forerunner of Ethiopia, was Christianized from the 4th century AD, but its trade and power were undermined by growing Arab Muslim control of the area near the Red Sea. The Aksumites withdrew into the country's hinterland and extended their power there, while the more southerly Agaw people, in the form of the Zagwe dynasty, eventually assumed power in the Ethiopian empire, the political expression of the new amalgam of peoples and cultures. The Zagwe emperor Lalibela (ruled *c.* 1185–1225) was responsible for the triumph of medieval Christian architecture in the form of churches hewn out of the living rock at Roha.

From the late 13th century the Amhara Solomonid dynasty, claiming descent through the Aksumite kings from King Solomon and the Queen of Sheba, responded aggressively to

Islamic encroachment on the eastern and southern borders of Ethiopia. They had strong church support, and a new form of militant Christianity emerged that severely repressed non-orthodox belief, including the Jewish Falasha (Beta Israel).

From the 1520s, however, Ahmad ibn Ibrahim al-Ghazi (Ahmad Gran) launched an Islamic jihad that almost succeeded in conquering the Ethiopian state before he was defeated and killed in 1543 by a well-organized Ethiopian army trained by the Portuguese.

Ethiopia was again threatened by foreign powers, first in the short British Abyssinian campaign against the Emperor Tewodros (Theodore) II in 1867, in which many important cultural monuments were looted or destroyed; and more seriously by the imperial designs of the ITALIAN state, whose forces, based in Eritrea, were comprehensively defeated at the important Battle of Adowa in 1896. Ethiopia's independence was internationally recognized when it joined the League of Nations in 1923. Ethiopian economic development, helped by coffee exports, continued steadily through the period up to 1935–6, when Italy again invaded and occupied the country, before being ejected by British and Ethiopian forces in 1941.

After the war, greater social discontent developed and with it opposition to the rule of Emperor Haile Selassie (ruled 1930–74). Eritrea, federated with Ethiopia in 1952, revolted in 1960, leading to the long insurrection up to independence in 1993 and subsequent hostilities. Somalis also rebelled in the Ogaden in 1963, which brought clashes with the newly-independent Somalia. Drought, famine and economic weakness contributed to the hostility against the imperial elite, and in 1974 a successful army coup took place, which brought Major Mengistu Haile Mariam, head of the revolutionary committee, known as the Derg, to power. He increasingly relied on Soviet military assistance, and mass arrests and executions of opponents took place in 1977–8. His Marxist regime's ill-judged policies, particularly relating to land reform, worsened the endemic problems of drought and famine that seriously affected the Ethiopian people during the 1970s and 1980s. War and internal strife increased, involving Eritrea, local revolts, the brief Somali invasion of the Ogaden in 1977 and the growing threat of the respective Tigray and Oromo People's Liberation Fronts. Mengistu was forced from power in 1991. The transitional government introduced a new democratic constitution in 1995, which relied on a federal union of states reflecting Ethiopia's main ethnic groups. A peace treaty in 2000 ended the war with Eritrea, but economic weakness and drought remain serious problems.

## EUONDO or Ewondo

See YAOUNDE.

## EWE

Agricultural and fishing peoples originating in Oyo, western Nigeria. They are now present in southeastern Ghana, southern Benin and Togo, where they are influential in politics, administration and trade (see TOGOLESE). They grow maize, manioc, millet, and plantains, and occasionally the cash crops rice and cocoa. They are mainly Christian. The Ewe kingdom of Allada was the strongest in the region in the 16th and 17th centuries until succeeded by FON Dahomey. Since then, the Ewe have lived in autonomous chiefdoms, avoiding centralization, and have formed complex alliances. They speak Ewe dialects of KWA and have strong trading and craft traditions in textiles, metalwork and pottery. Their traditional belief in ancestor spirits was carried to the New World by slaves and is represented in the voodoo religious cult of Haiti (see HAITIANS).

## FALASHA or Felasha

Jewish ETHIOPIANS who call themselves House of Israel (Beta Israel). Falasha means 'Black Jews'. Their language is mainly Amharic, though they are descended from AGAW people who converted to Judaism around the start of the Christian era. Persecuted under the Christian AKSUMITES and later Ethiopian rulers, they consolidated around Lake Tana, northern Ethiopia. They were traditionally a farming people with skills as potters, ironsmiths and weavers. A mass emigration of 45,000 Falasha to Israel took place 1980–92, leaving only a small number in Ethiopia.

**❝** We are direct descendants from the family of Abraham. **❞**

Falasha belief

# FANG or Fãn or Fang–Pahouin

Diverse BANTU-speaking peoples of southern Cameroon, Equatorial Guinea and northern Gabon (see CAMEROONIANS, EQUATOGUINEANS and GABONESE) in west-central Africa, numbering roughly 3.3 million. The generic Fang comprise the Bulu and Beti tribal groups, including the MAKA and YAOUNDE, as well as the Fang proper, who predominate in the south of the region, all of them having a fearsome reputation as warriors, hunters and cannibals. Attracted by the trade wealth of the coastal forest regions, and mobilized by the FULANI jihad, they migrated westwards in the early 19th century, which led to widespread conflict. In modern times cocoa farming and widespread educational advancement have bestowed economic benefits and political influence. In religion they combine Christian and animistic beliefs. Storytelling and music played on traditional instruments are important cultural legacies.

## FANTE or Fanti

AKAN people who occupy modern-day southern Ghana. They are matrilineal and in religion a mix of Christian, Muslim and animist, though these are often combined in syncretic beliefs. They established several kingdoms on the coast, largely west of Accra, by the late 15th century, and became middlemen in the lucrative trade in gold, slaves and firearms between the inland ASANTE and the European forts on the coast. They were conquered by the Asante in 1806–24 and were frequently allied with British forces against their conquerors during the 19th century, before they became part of Britain's Gold Coast Crown Colony in 1874. Today they continue to be fishermen, cultivators and pastoralists, and have become increasingly Westernized. Their population is estimated to number around 2 million.

## FAURESMITH CULTURE

A Palaeolithic culture of the south and east African grassland and steppe in the late Pleistocene era, between 130,000 and 10,000 years ago, associated with the Neanderthal-like 'Rhodesioid' hominids. It was contemporaneous with the SANGOAN CULTURE, which, like the Fauresmith, developed from the late Acheulian culture, known for its characteristic hand-axes. Fauresmith remains have been found in sites such as Saldanha in Cape Province, South Africa.

## FON or Dahomeyese

Southern BENINOIS coastal people, also present in adjoining Togo. They are traditionally agricultural and speak a dialect of EWE. The Republic of Benin was formerly named Dahomey after the powerful kingdom which expanded in the late 17th century and grew rich on the supply of slaves for the New World. It was devastated by YORUBA cavalry in the 1720s, revived in the early 19th century, and was annexed by France in 1883. Annual sacrifice of prisoners took place to ensure the goodwill of royal ancestors, and ancestor worship remains important. The Fon are important in contemporary Beninois government and business. They number more than 3 million.

## FORROS

People of the islands of São Tomé and Príncipe (see SÃO TOMÉANS) in the Gulf of Guinea, western Africa. They are mixed-race descendants of slaves from the mainland, imported to work on the plantations, and Europeans, mostly Portuguese, and speak a Portuguese Creole. Mostly Roman Catholic, they form a majority of the population, which also includes ANGOLANS, CAPE VERDEANS, MOZAMBICANS and ANGOLARES.

## FULANI or Fulbe or Fula or Peul

A predominantly Muslim people originating in modern-day Senegal and now widely dispersed across the Sahel region of West Africa as far east as Lake Chad and Cameroon. They speak Fulfulde, a language of the West Atlantic branch of Niger-Congo. The Fulani are cattle and other livestock pastoralists (the largest such group in the world) but many have now adopted settled agriculture and town life among other peoples and become acculturated and socially diverse. In

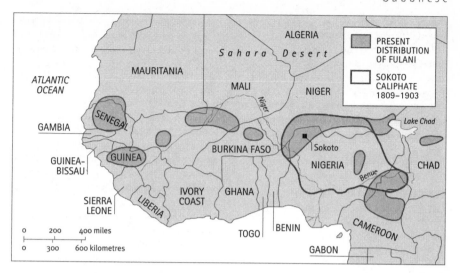

*The Fulani are now dispersed across West Africa, but established a powerful theocratic Muslim caliphate around Sokoto in northern Nigeria in the 19th century.*

northern Nigeria, where they established the theocratic Sokoto Caliphate in the early 19th century, around half of the Fulani have adopted HAUSA culture and language.

## FUNJ or Fungor

An agricultural NUBA people from the area of the White Nile in northern Sudan bordering Ethiopia. They grow cotton, sorghum and peanuts in the Nuba mountains. Arab Islamic forces finally conquered the Christian NUBIANS with the fall of the kingdom of Alwa in the late 15th century, and the Funj, in alliance with Arab tribes, took control here in 1504. They established the Sultanate of Sennar and soon adopted Islam, by the 17th century ruling much of Nubia. Internal conflict and the Egyptian invasion of 1821 led to the collapse of the sultanate and to Egypto-Turkish rule until 1885.

## FUR

A NILO-SAHARAN-speaking people occupying the highlands of Sudan. They give their name to the western province of Darfur (see SUDANESE). During the 16th century the Fur retreated from the Nile corridor and plains into the mountains in the face of Arab penetration, where they developed terraced farming in addition to cattle-rearing. They soon adopted Islam and a

Fur sultanate. Their hierarchical society is divided into chiefs and wealthy landowners (often polygynous and of Arab descent), village headmen, serfs and artisans.

## FUTANKOBE

See TUKULOR.

## GA-ADANGME or Ga-Adangbe

The closely related Ga and Adangme tribal groups who occupy the coast of Ghana and the Volta River valley, West Africa. They number around 1.5 million, and speak Ga-Adangme languages. Their ancestors migrated south from the Niger Valley in about the 16th century.

Both peoples are cultivators and traders but the Ga concentrate on coastal fishing and trade, the latter generally the preserve of women, who possess a large degree of financial independence as well as inheritance and other rights. Many Ga-Adangme are Christian, but local ancestral cults, gods and festivals are widely celebrated.

## GABONESE

People of the coastal Democratic Gabonese Republic (commonly called Gabon). Its capital Libreville was established by France as a settlement for freed slaves in 1849, and it remained part of the French empire until independence in 1960. The country came to incorporate around 40 BANTU-speaking peoples, including the FANG, TEKE and NKOMI, as well as a small number of PYGMIES. Most are Christians. FRENCH is the official language and is the sole language of educational instruction. France also dominates the economy and cultural life of the country, although there is strong interest in indigenous Bantu culture and history.

## GALLA

See OROMO.

## GALLINAS

See VAI.

## GALOA or Galwa

A Myene-speaking people of Gabon. They number only several thousand, but are influential in the administrative and commercial life of the country. In the 19th century they were subject to other Myenes and were part of a wider movement down the Ogooué River valley to the Atlantic coast of western Gabon, where they cooperated with European traders and French colonizers. The Galoa adopted Christianity and exploited the educational opportunities brought by colonialism.

## GAMBIANS

Inhabitants of the Republic of the Gambia. The country is the product of 19th-century Franco–British colonial rivalry. Its narrow territory extends 480 km / 300 miles eastwards from the Atlantic coast, enclosing the lower River Gambia, and is entirely surrounded by formerly French Senegal, its natural hinterland. This divided political control meant that the river, one of the continent's finest waterways, has never achieved its full potential as an artery for trade and communication with a large area of the western Sudan. Furthermore, it imposed political divisions on peoples indigenous to both Gambia and Senegal.

The Gambia River basin provided an attractive home and a natural refuge from the wars and political turmoil in the western Sudan from at least the 12th century. Numerically, the MALINKE are the largest group in the Gambia, forming perhaps 40% of the national population of around 1.4 million, although the WOLOF predominate in the capital Banjul (formerly Bathurst). The JOLA also inhabit western Gambia. Up-river are the nomadic FULANI and SONINKE. Gambians are primarily farmers, whose main cash crop is peanuts, which is also the country's staple export. Government aid has helped to develop particular sectors of agriculture such as large-scale palm-oil production, rice cultivation and livestock-rearing, as well as forestry and the Atlantic fisheries.

The first Europeans to visit the Gambia were the Portuguese in 1455. They traded with local individuals and chiefs such as the *mansa* (king) of Kasa, in what is now the Casamance region southwest of the river in Senegal. Slave-trading became important, and the British established fortified trading posts on the river in the 17th century. In the early 19th century British involvement centred on the elimination of the slave trade from the Gambia, and the territory became a British Crown Colony in 1843, although the transition from slave-trading to legitimate trade and agriculture was difficult. Gambia became independent in 1965, and elections for the first time allowed the rural inland peoples to predominate over the traditional urban coastal elite that had emerged under colonial rule. Recognizing their common interests and cultural links, the Gambia joined with Senegal in 1982 to form the Senegambian Federation, though this split in 1989. English remains the official language. Around 95% of the population is Muslim and 4% Christian.

## GANDA or Baganda

A people from the territory of Buganda on the northern shores of Lake Victoria, East Africa. The kingdom formed the core of the modern country of Uganda, created in the British colonial period, from which it takes its name (see UGANDANS). The Ganda speak Kiganda and are one of the

> *" Notwithstanding the country of Gambo [Gambia] is so unhealthy, yet the people of that place live very long. "*
>
> Samuel Pepys, 1662

---

**Gambians: main ethnic groups**

Fulani
Jola
Malinke
Soninke
Wolof

---

main ethnic groups of Uganda, exhibiting a high standard of education, which has allowed them to dominate the government and professions.

During the 15th century Buganda was one of several kingdoms of BANTU-speaking peoples subordinate to Bunyoro under the Chwezi rulers (see NYORO), and it continued after 1500 as part of the Bito empire of Bunyoro-Kitara. It developed as a well-organized and centralized kingdom to become the most powerful state in the region by the early 19th century. It was led by a series of able *kabakas* (kings) who originated as leaders of a confederacy of patrilineal clans. They defeated Bito armies and aggressively expanded the Bugandan kingdom, largely at the expense of Bunyoro.

### From Buganda to Uganda

The Ganda were greatly assisted by favourable geographical and climatic conditions which allowed the cropping of food-bananas all year round, still important today. There was also limited dependence on cattle, both factors freeing manpower for military service more effectively than in neighbouring states. The *kabakas* also extended their authority over the important *batokas* (sub-chiefs); appointed their own agents to govern newly conquered peoples; designated a prince regent, which avoided damaging succession disputes following the death of each king; and used tribute and the control of trade to reward followers and distribute patronage. They also reorganized and strengthened the army, creating a militaristic and despotic state living by war. Conquest supplied the livestock, slaves and ivory that were essential for growing trade. Iron-producing territories were incorporated into Buganda, assisting trade and boosting Buganda's power. From the 1840s SWAHILI traders seeking ivory and slaves also brought modern firearms, further destabilizing the politics of the region and aggravating the rivalry of Bunyoro and Buganda.

European and Egyptian-SUDANESE agents were increasingly drawn into local politics as rulers sought protection from, or advantage over, their enemies. British-American explorer Henry Morton Stanley, who visited in 1875, admired Buganda and persuaded the British government to support the kingdom against Bunyoro. From 1877 Christian missionaries began to arrive, and their influence led to the creation of rival politico-religious factions and civil war. European imperial rivalry led to German interest in Buganda, but from 1890 it came into the BRITISH sphere of influence. In 1894 Buganda was made an official British government protectorate, reinforced in the Buganda Agreement of 1900, and the Ganda were used as agents of British rule throughout Uganda. The kingdom became an autonomous part of an independent Uganda in 1962. Concern to maintain this position led to conflict between Kabaka Mutesa II (ruled Buganda 1939–53 and 1955–66) and the government of Milton Obote (prime minister 1962–70 and president 1966–71 and 1980–85), who abolished the kingdoms of Uganda in 1967. The kingdom of Buganda was restored in 1993. Today around 60% of Bugandans are Christian, 20% animists according to traditional beliefs, and 20% Muslim, a faith originally introduced by the Swahili.

## GAZA

See SHANGANE.

## GBANDI

See NGBANDI.

## GBAYA or Baya

A people who originated in northern Nigeria but were displaced by the Muslim FULANI in the early 19th century. They now occupy areas of the adjoining states of Cameroon, Congo (Kinshasa) and the Central African Republic and number more than 1.2 million. The Gbaya also comprise sub-groups descended from peoples they conquered during their migration. They operated under village chiefs, but they never developed a centralized state structure, only appointing war leaders in times of need. Society is based on age grades and patrilineal clan identity. The Gbaya are mostly agriculturists, hunters and fishers and speak a Ubangian language of the Adamawa-UBANGI branch of the Niger-Congo.

# GERZEAN CULTURE or Naqadah II culture

The most important pre-dynastic culture of ancient Egypt (see EGYPTIANS), which thrived at the type-sites al-Girza (or Gerzeh) in the Fayum and at Naqada in Upper Egypt. Gerzean developed from AMRATIAN CULTURE, also called Naqadah I, and became widespread throughout Egypt by the Late Gerzean, also termed Naqadah III. There was a growing differentiation in wealth and status in a much richer material culture influenced by trade with Mesopotamia. The use of mud brick was an important architectural development, and cities also became much larger. Most importantly, writing was brought to a level of development that heralded the new level of civilization beginning with the dynastic period of around 3100 BC, effectively the foundation of the Egyptian state.

# GHANAIANS or Ghanans

People of the Republic of Ghana, capital Accra, whose ancestral population colonized the region from the north and east between 700 and 1000 years ago. The modern country was created from the union of the BRITISH Gold Coast and British Togoland, and in 1957 became the first of Britain's African colonies to achieve independence. It takes its name from the ancient empire of Ghana, which flourished until the 13th century in western Sudan, around 800 km / 500 miles to the northwest. The people of this empire were believed to have colonized the area of modern-day Ghana, although there is no evidence to confirm this. The population of 20 million comprises around 75 different peoples, identified on the basis of language, the most significant being the AKAN, GUR (Mole-Dagbane), EWE, GA-ADANGME, GUANG and GURMA.

Tensions exist between these many groups, especially in the north, but the country has had a good tradition of inter-communal cooperation prior to independence, helping to create a unified Ghanaian society. English is the common and official language.

The origins of modern-day Ghana were strongly influenced by contact with Europeans. The Portuguese, attracted by the easy availability of gold, arrived in 1471, giving rise to the name Gold Coast, by which Ghana was known until 1957. They established their first fortified trading post at Elmina in 1482, the forerunner of 40 such stations subsequently built by British, Dutch, Danish, Swedish and Prussian traders (today listed as World Heritage sites). Slaves became important in the 18th century to feed the growing demand on the American and Caribbean plantations.

New empires arose, aiming to control the new southerly trade to the coast. The first was the AKWAMU, followed by the ASANTE empire, which began to conquer the coast from the late 18th century. To protect trade, British merchants extended an informal protectorate over the FANTE in the 1830s, later assumed by the British government, which was also subject to missionary pressure to extend Christianity and end the slave trade. British forces attacked the Asante in 1874, and the Fante and Ga lands of southern Ghana were declared the Gold Coast Crown Colony, which absorbed the main Asante territories 1895–1901. After World War I the western part of former German Togoland was added to complete the main elements of modern-day Ghana.

Long contact with European trade, education and culture, and exclusion from power, put the Ghanaians of the Gold Coast in the forefront of the African independence movement. The whole country benefited from growing economic prosperity and investment by the 1920s, based on the widespread exploitation of cocoa, some gold mining, manganese and timber, which encouraged Ghanaians to demand control of their own affairs. But the economic advantages enjoyed by Ghana were squandered after independence; power was centralized and democracy was curtailed. The people of Ghana are still largely agricultural (the country is the world's largest producer of cocoa), but many are employed in mineral extraction and timber production.

Almost two-thirds of Ghanaians are Christian, although adherence to traditional ancestor worship and pantheism remains strong. There are also a significant number of Muslims, especially in the north of the country.

g

# GISU or Bagisu

A cluster of BANTU-speaking peoples in the Mount Elgon area of eastern Uganda. They include the Nyole and Samia and altogether number around 1 million. The Gisu cultivate good soils and produce coffee, cotton and other cash crops. Their society is patrilineal and predominantly Christian and animist, or a mixture of both.

# GOURMA

See GURMA.

# GREAT ZIMBABWE CULTURE

A culture and, it is thought, an associated state system located on the high plateau of what is now central Zimbabwe between the 12th and 15th centuries. Its central site, known as Great Zimbabwe, is a complex of stone-built enclosures, now ruined, which gave their name to the modern state of the ZIMBABWEANS.

The culture is known only from archaeology. It existed at a period too early to permit the survival of oral testimony, and the Portuguese only arrived in the area when the culture had collapsed, giving way to successors in the west (Butua or Butwa) and the north (Mwanamutapa). When Europeans arrived in the area in the second half of the 19th century, they attributed the 'buildings' to ancient, or possibly Islamic, invaders. They gave credence to the notion that this might be the fabled King Solomon's mines, tapping the gold resources of Central Africa. Some claimed to see later Islamic influence and speculated that Muslims from the East African coast or even Arabia had established a trading centre in Central Africa to facilitate their search for gold.

From the early 20th century, however, archaeologists came to the view that it was a medieval African site, noting the absence of ancient artefacts or inscriptions, as well as building styles that bore no relationship to the Middle East or the Islamic world. Pottery analysis and carbon 14 dating later confirmed this view, though the relationship between its inhabitants and today's inhabitants of the region remains unclear.

New Iron Age pottery types seem to have appeared in the region from the 12th century. These may reflect the migration of an invading people from the north or the arrival of fresh stylistic influences. By the 13th century, people were living in huts surrounded by granite walling in hill-top villages – the one at Great Zimbabwe being known in modern times as the 'Acropolis'. Later, at Great Zimbabwe, they began to build impressive stone structures on the valley floor below. A large elliptical enclosure may have acted as the palace walls, rising to a height of up to five or six metres, structurally strong and with some elaborate decoration. Within are further walls and an impressive conical tower. Many other smaller walls and enclosures run down the valley, indicating that this was a densely populated site. Many other smaller 'zimbabwes' (possibly meaning 'stone-built places') have been found throughout the high plateau of Zimbabwe, within the area where granite was available as a building material, and there are also some related sites in the northern Transvaal. Many of these are located on the characteristic granite *kopjes* or hills of southern Africa, although there is little evidence that they were intended to be defensive sites.

### Material culture

Great Zimbabwe was well positioned. It had a reasonable rainfall and was free of the tsetse fly, which is destructive to domestic cattle. It probably had good resources of trees in the period, was close to gold deposits and was strategically placed in relation to trade routes leading to the Indian Ocean coast. The people of Great Zimbabwe were cattle owners (large assemblages of cattle bones have been found at the site) and gold-miners who traded extensively, probably with visiting Muslims from the coast (a 15th-century coin of the East African trading town Kilwa has also been found there). Some gold artefacts have been found at the site, together with soapstone sculptures, including the famous Zimbabwean birds, now in the Cape Town Museum. Similarities in styles of building and of domestic and luxury artefacts have led to the notion that the peoples of the region were organized into a state structure, with Great Zimbabwe as its capital. Although there is no

*g*

*" ... an Arab slave trading outpost. "*

One of several, now disproved theories on the origins of Great Zimbabwe independent confirmation of this, there is no doubt that Great Zimbabwe and some of the other sites reveal evidence of the existence of a social elite. It has also been suggested that the principal sites had some religious significance, although this remains under speculation. The most likely theory for the rise of the culture remains its environmental advantages, enabling extensive cattle-keeping (a source of visible and accumulated wealth) as well as trade.

Great Zimbabwe seems to have been abandoned in the 15th century. This may have been because the dense population there placed too much strain upon resources. There may also have been a drought. Oral traditions in the north speak of the failure of salt supplies, which may be symbolic of environmental difficulties. Other cultures emerged, some of them also using stone structures. The Khami ruins near Bulawayo, together with other impressive structures at Naletale and Dhlo Dhlo may be connected with the successor Butwa, which was ruled by the Torwa dynasty, possibly connected to the SHONA sub-group known as the Kalanga. The Munhumatapa state to the north, nearer the Zambezi Valley, was known to the Portuguese and survived until the later 17th century. The people of both of these states were also involved in the gold trade.

## GRIQUA

A South African people of mixed race, mainly the product of unions between the DUTCH and the KHOIKHOI, though some are of SAN or slave descent. They emerged in the early 19th century, and groups left the Cape Colony to form minor independent polities just north of the Orange River. They were originally known as the Bastards, but missionaries renamed them. The Griqua spoke Dutch and were, in many respects, culturally related to the AFRIKANERS. However, in the conflicts of the frontier region, they aligned themselves politically with the British. They were also influenced by British missionaries.

The two principal Griqua communities were led by the Kok and Waterboer families. The group led by the Koks had a capital known as Philippolis, named after London Missionary Society Scottish missionary John Philip. Further

west, the Griqua led by Waterboer inhabited territory near to what was to become the diamond fields area around Kimberley. The Griqua had cattle, sheep, horses and firearms, and hunted and raided northwards into the lands of Bantu-speaking peoples. They traded ivory and other commodities and, for a time, established a very successful system, complete with political institutions and offices based on the Boer models.

After the Great Trek of the Boers, whites encroached increasingly upon their lands. In 1837 Adam Kok III succeeded to the leadership of the eastern Griqua. He subsequently sided with the British against the Boers and in 1848 his people were granted a degree of autonomy by the British. However, the Griqua could not resist the increasing tentacles of white power. The Orange Free State increased its pressure, and Boers settled among them. In 1861, Adam Kok abandoned the Griqua lands and led his people on a trek eastwards to an area to the south of the Drakensberg which became known as Griqualand East. The British, who had invited him to take this land, hoped that the Griqua would constitute a buffer against the African peoples of the eastern Cape frontier. In 1879 Griqualand East was annexed to the Cape Colony, became part of the Transkei and was later divided between the Cape and Natal.

The western Griqua, led by Nicholaas Waterboer, came under threat when diamonds were discovered in their area in 1867. The British annexed the territory in 1871 in order to frustrate the Boers, and many of the Griqua sold their farms to whites, often under pressure. Kimberley became the main centre of the diamond fields and few Griqua remained. Today the Griqua have become part of the CAPE COLOURED community of South Africa. There are said to be about 9000 Griqua left at present, including some in Zimbabwe.

## GUANG

One of the earliest peoples identified with the territory of modern-day Ghana. They form a large cluster of tribal groups numbering more than 600,000 people in total, scattered throughout eastern, central and northern parts of the country. They speak Guang, which is a GUR language of the Niger-Congo family. They established the Gonja trading state in the north in the 16th century, led by invading MANDE Muslim people, ancestors of the current ruling dynasty and local chiefs. Most adhere to Christian or local religious beliefs, but approximately 10% are Muslim.

## GUERZE

See KPELLE.

## GUINEA-BISSAUANS

People of the Republic of Guinea-Bissau, formerly Portuguese Guinea, capital Bissau. It was first visited by the Portuguese in 1446, but became a colony only in 1879, gaining independence in 1973. It incorporates a mix of different ethnic groups, notably the BALANTA, FULANI, MANJAKO and MALINKE, most of whom are Muslim, although one-third of the population of around 1.3 million still follows traditional beliefs. The economy is based on agricultural and pastoral pursuits. Portuguese is the official language but many local languages are spoken.

## GUINEANS

Inhabitants of the Republic of Guinea, capital Conakry. Guinea was a region within the medieval Mali empire and from 1849 to independence in 1958 it was colonized by France. French is the official language. The main ethnic groups among its population of around 7.5 million are the northern FULANI, who speak the Pular dialect of the Fula language; the MALINKE in Upper Guinea; and the coastal SUSU. The KPELLE and others inhabit the forest region.

Guineans are overwhelmingly reliant on agriculture, although mining (especially of bauxite) is a major industry and employs a significant number. Most Guineans (around 75%) are Muslim although traditional beliefs are still strong. There is a relatively small number of Christians and tension with the Muslim community has occasionally led to conflict. In recent years there has been serious trouble along the border with Liberia, where armed raids have taken place.

## GUR

A large linguistic group sometimes known as Voltaic due to its origins in the Upper Volta River basin, West Africa. There are known to be 85 Gur languages, which form a branch of Niger-Congo and are spoken by approximately 20 million people of the savannah region. The languages are found across the northern Ivory Coast, Ghana, Togo and Benin into southern Mali and throughout Burkina Faso, spoken by peoples across the region who are generally skilled farmers, traders and state-builders. Roughly a third of Gur-speakers are Muslim.

## GURAGE or Gerage or Gerawege

A Semitic-speaking but partly Cushitic people of southern Ethiopia (see ETHIOPIANS) who possess a complex linguistic and cultural identity as a result of outside influences over a long period. They number around 3 million and are settled in concentrated villages. Most are farmers of the staple ensete, the false banana, and coffee, but some grain is grown in the east and cattle rearing pursued where the terrain is suitable. Some Gurage work as labourers in Addis Ababa. Traditional animist beliefs are still followed by many, although Christianity is also common along with Islam, which was introduced to the Gurage in the 13th century.

## GURMA or Gourma

A GUR-speaking people of eastern Burkina Faso and northern Togo. Like the closely related MOSSI they originated in modern-day northeastern Ghana, where they also still live. The Gurma are millet cultivators and artisans working in pottery, basketry, textiles and other forms, although many men and women are migrant workers. They live in circular mud-brick house compounds in polygamous family groups forming clusters of patrilineal kin and clan groups. These can form sizeable villages. Gurma chiefs acknowledge the authority of the paramount chief, *Moro Naba*, at the main town of Fada Ngourma. Gurma religions include both Islam and Christianity.

*" We prefer poverty in liberty to riches in slavery. "*

Guinean nationalist Sékou Touré, 1958

# GUSII or Kisii or Kissi

> *We came from a place called Misri a long time ago. We do not know where this place is, but we do know that life there was hard, full of sickness and famine.*
>
> Gusii legend

BANTU-speakers of the region of Kenya lying between Lake Victoria and the border with Tanzania. They are notable for their very diverse economy, exploiting various crops including bananas as well as poultry, bees and livestock, tended by the Gusii men, who also hunt and fish. Most of the crop-tending is done by the Gusii women.

The Gusii number more than 1.5 million and live in dispersed family homesteads under chiefs who are part of the regional administration. They are closely related to the KIKUYU and LUYIA, and first emerged as a distinctive group in the 18th century.

# HA or Waha or Abaha

A BANTU-speaking people concentrated between lakes Tanganyika and Victoria in western Tanzania. The population of around 1.5 million are mostly agriculturists, particularly cultivating tobacco and gathering honey. Cattle and other livestock are reared on the good pasturelands of southwestern Buha ('Ha territory') and are important as a form of social currency. Like the HUTU of Rwanda and Burundi, they became subordinate to a small population of TUTSI pastoralists, who formed a ruling aristocracy, as recently as the 18th century. The Hutu/Tutsi tensions are absent here, however, as the Ha and Tutsi share a common language, culture and important elements of traditional belief. The Tutsi are also a much less numerous proportion of the total population (around 2%).

Traditionally, the Ha have lived in scattered homesteads within one of the six Ha kingdoms, whose political significance has declined since Tanzanian independence. Many Ha are migrant workers on plantations and farms outside Buha, but there is a strong attachment to their traditional lifestyle.

# HABE

See DOGON.

# HAMITES or Nilo-Hamites

Ham is identified in the Bible as the second son of Noah and the supposed progenitor of all the African peoples. His name has subsequently been applied as both an ethnic and (in modern times) a linguistic descriptor.

In the 1860s the term 'Hamito-Semitic' (or 'Semito-Hamitic') was adopted by the German philologist Karl Richard Lepsius to describe a group of languages spoken in northern Africa and southwestern Asia. These are now known as Afro-Asiatic languages (see AFRO-ASIAN), an alternative term proposed by the US historical linguist Joseph Greenberg in 1950 that better reflects the unity of these languages and eliminates the undue prominence given to 'Semitic' in the former term.

On the basis of the original flawed linguistic analysis, a formerly influential but now discredited theory – known as the Hamitic Myth – held that major developments in African civilization were due to the early migration of 'Hamitic'-speaking peoples into northeast Africa. These 'Hamites' were identified with the lighter-skinned North Africans, in contrast to the black-skinned sub-Saharan Africans, in a typically crude 19th-century correlation between cultural advancement and race.

In fact, subsequent linguistic analysis has shown that all the languages in question (except Semitic itself) had their origin in Africa, and the ancestral Afro-Asiatic language was possibly spoken in northeastern Africa as long ago as 13,000 BC. Furthermore, a number of Afro-Asiatic Chadic languages are spoken south of the Sahara by black African peoples.

This theory of Hamitic migration into northeast Africa should not be confused with the movement of Cushitic-speaking peoples into the rest of tropical Africa from the Ethiopian region. From around the start of the Christian era the CUSHITES were supplanted in much of East Africa by the NILOTES and BANTU-speaking peoples. Some of these peoples, whose languages were part of the NILO-SAHARAN language family, were also formerly described as Nilo-Hamitic.

# HAUSA

A large agglomeration of linguistically related people of West Africa, concentrated in the Muslim emirates of northern Nigeria (see NIGERIANS) and adjoining southern Niger. They speak (Arabic-influenced) Hausa, which is a Chadic language of the Afro-Asiatic family, and the official language of northern Nigeria. Its two most important dialects are spoken in the Nigerian cities of Kano and Sokoto. The Hausa can also be found in Benin, Chad, Ghana and the Sudan, and have been estimated to number more than 45 million. Because of their cultural diversity and inter-marriage with other peoples in West Africa it is difficult regard them all as a single ethnic group. For example, they are closely associated with the numerous FULANI people, with whom they historically coexisted, many of whom adopted Hausa language and culture but are more accurately described as Fulani-Hausa.

The origins of the Hausa are a mystery, although their linguistic roots suggest they migrated southwards from the Sahara region, probably due to its increasing desiccation. By the early 2nd millennium AD numerous small chiefdoms had emerged around sacred sites and iron-working centres, the foremost being the sizeable and sophisticated city of Kano. Regional and trans-Saharan trade began to assume greater importance in the 15th and 16th centuries, based on successful Hausa grain agriculture and Fulani pastoralism. Hausa traders eventually dispersed throughout West Africa and established an impressive commercial network, using the currencies of silver and cowrie shells, which improved on the DYULA trading system. Urban centres prospered, and economic and craft specializations emerged among the Hausa, along with other important social changes. A process of state-building occurred around this time, associated with the development of a powerful ruling aristocracy exploiting the new possibilities of cavalry warfare tested over several centuries in the continuous battles of the savannah states. This new mobility further encouraged

*" ... the civilised, commerce-loving, and industrious Hausas "*

**Sir George T. Goldie, 1898**

h

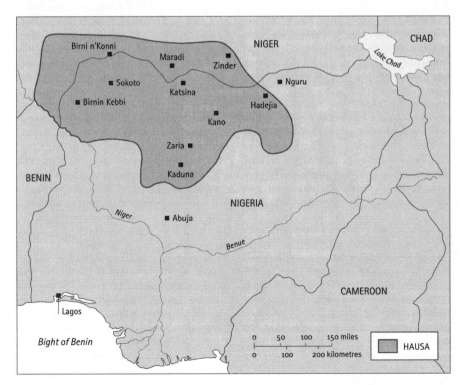

Hausa

slave-raiding among the Niger-Congo peoples to the south and helped pay for the heavy expenses of the equestrian ruling class. Slaves were taken in increasing numbers across the Sahara to North Africa and also used in the traditional servile and military roles, as well as new administrative positions in the several and increasingly sophisticated Hausa states.

### The impact of Islam

The major transformation was the adoption of Islam. Hausa aristocracies were first converted to the new faith, which arrived on the back of trade with North Africa and Mali, in the 14th century. It soon spread throughout Hausaland, although indigenous beliefs coexisted, and indeed some peoples, such as the small Hausa Maguzawa or Bunjawa, remained unconverted. Traditional herbal and spirit medicine also survived in the countryside, and in the cities among women in particular.

The fortunes of Hausaland were galvanized in 1804, however, by the jihad of the religious zealot Usuman dan Fodio (1754–1817) which created a unified caliphate out of its several kingdoms. It was one of the most important events in 19th-century West Africa. His revolt against the oppressive rulers of Gobir found a ready response in the other Hausa chiefdoms, whose subjects now established theocratic emirates united under an Islamic caliphate based on the new city of Sokoto. The majority Fulani assumed power in the new states, a process completed in 1809, but they were soon absorbed into the Hausa urban culture and lost their pastoral ways, many adopting the Hausa language. Islam and this cultural elision gave Hausaland society a stability absent from rival savannah states.

Further jihads, territorial expansion and the raiding of infidel neighbours for slaves continued to take place throughout the rest of the century. Aristocratic militarism and elitism went hand in hand with heavy taxes, but overall Hausaland prospered. Trade and the significant indigenous textile industry continued undiminished well into the 20th century. Agricultural estates worked by slaves assumed greater importance in a region that had always been sparsely populated, helping to boost food production and population growth.

British rule was extended over the Hausa following the invasion of 1900. Caliph Attahiru and his followers were killed at the Battle of Burmi in 1903, and the caliphate was abolished, although the emirs were subsequently co-opted in the imperial policy of indirect rule pioneered in Sokoto by Frederick Lugard. Concern to protect the position of indigenous rulers allowed a continuation of slavery until 1936, and of other policies favourable to the local aristocratic ruling class at the expense of their subjects, making Hausaland the world's last slave society (at least in institutional terms). Nevertheless, they managed to ride the forces of nationalism, and the emirs and their feudal organizations, which have tax-raising powers, still survive today. Their bureaucracies also continue to utilize the Arabic script adopted early on as the written form of Hausa, although Roman script is also in use.

Many other elements of historic Hausa society and economy remain. A large part of the population is still involved in trade based on the urban centres. Most Hausa are agriculturists and are involved in intensive grain production which still relies on livestock manure of the Fulani pastoralists. They continue to live in small patrilineal family farm compounds under the authority of headmen responsible to the emirs through various officials. Society remains extremely hierarchical, from commoners up to nobles, who dominate the administration and who possess territorial rights. Since the 19th century and the introduction of a more rigid interpretation of Islam, women further up the social and economic scale have been more likely to live in seclusion. Hausa craft skills, which historically developed on the basis of surplus agricultural production, remain an important part of the Hausa culture and economy.

## HAYA

A BANTU-speaking people of Buhaya, between Lake Victoria and the Kagera River in Tanzania (see TANZANIANS). Their land is fertile, and they grow bananas as a staple and coffee as a cash crop. They were possibly Hima people who moved south to Karagwe when the Bito took power in Bunyoro (see NYORO) in the 16th century, later founding other dynasties in Buhaya and ANKOLE. Haya society is divided between the pastoral Hima and the agricultural IRU. Numerous clans exist within the eight small former statelets, each led by a *mukama*, abolished in 1962. The Haya are largely Christian and are well-represented in economic and government posts, mainly because of their exposure to Western education in the colonial period. There are probably more than 1 million Haya today. They traditionally live in thatched, beehive-shaped huts.

## HEDAREB

A people occupying adjoining areas of Eritrea, Ethiopia and the Sudanese Republic. They form the majority of the Beni Amer, Muslim pastoralists who number around 300,000 today and are the major sub-group of the BEJA. The Hedareb are traditionally subservient to the 'true' Beni Amer, who form a small social and political elite in a highly stratified feudal society. They speak Hedareb, Tigre and other languages. Many Hedareb have migrated from Eritrea due to the conflicts with Ethiopia in recent decades.

## HEHE

A culturally and linguistically similar group of BANTU-speakers practising mixed cultivation and cattle-farming in the Iringa region of southern Tanzania. Numbering more than 600,000, they live in traditional scattered patrilineal clans and worship ancestral spirits, although many are Christians or Muslims.

The Hehe only became a single tribal grouping under their founding chief Muyugumba following NGONI invasions of the 1840s. From the Ngoni they borrowed military tactics and organization to oppose German conquest, but were defeated in 1898. The paramount chieftainship was abolished, but restored in 1924. The Hehe today are prominent in the Tanzanian police service.

## HEREROS or Ovahereros

A cluster of peoples forming a large ethnic group in southern Angola, Namibia and Botswana. They are traditionally nomadic or semi-nomadic pastoralists, but today many are settled farmers and urban labourers. The Herero rebellion of 1904–7 was crushed by German forces (see NAMIBIANS); many were killed and others fled to Botswana and the Transvaal. By 1911 only 15,000 were left in Namibia out of a population of around 80,000. Traditional ancestor worship has given way to Christianity. Herero women wear long Victorian-style dresses in the fashion of German missionary wives.

> **"** Let us die fighting. **"**
>
> Herero leader Samuel Maharero, 1904

## HIMA

See TUTSI and NYORO.

## HOTTENTOT

See KHOIKHOI.

## HOVA

See MERINA.

## HUM or Humbe

A people who are concentrated near the Kwango River in southwestern Congo (Kinshasa) and spread into northern Angola. They are traditionally traders, fishermen and cultivators, particularly known historically as members of the royal guard of the Kingdom of Kongo. They were enlisted in the 17th century, recruited from the Stanley Pool area of the Congo River and armed with muskets.

## HUMR

See BAGGARA.

## HUTU or Bahutu or Wahutu

The traditionally agricultural majority BANTU-speaking peoples of the republics of Rwanda and Burundi. They were dominated by the powerful TUTSI warrior-pastoralists of Nilotic origin (see NILOTES) from the 15th century until recent times. Culturally they have also coalesced, the Hutu adopting Tutsi-style kinship and clan organization, as well as their regard for cattle. They also acknowledge the same animist and

Christian beliefs. Severe ethnic tensions involving the Hutu (see BURUNDIANS and RWANDANS) remain following several pogroms in recent years, especially the 1994 genocidal killing of minority Tutsi in Rwanda.

## HYKSOS

Ancient Semitic-speaking nomads from Palestine who settled in northern Egypt during the 18th century BC. Their name has been variously translated as 'rulers of foreign lands' or 'princes from foreign parts'; their kings reigned over Egypt as the 15th dynasty (c. 1630–1521 BC), also known as the 'shepherd kings'. The theory that they were ancestors of the HEBREWS is now discounted. They introduced horse-drawn chariots to Egypt, used superior weapons and built improved fortifications. They were defeated by a Theban rebellion led by Pharaoh Ahmose I (ruled c. 1539–1514 BC), founder of the 18th dynasty and the Egyptian New Kingdom.

## IBANI or Ubani

A sub-group of the IJAW peoples occupying the Niger Delta of southern Nigeria. They are mostly subsistence farmers and fishermen concentrated in the Bonny area of Rivers State. Like other Ijaws in Calabar (see KALABARI) and elsewhere, the people of Bonny successfully exploited the slave and other trades with the Europeans after 1500. The modern-day town and port of Bonny was the capital of the Bonny Kingdom which grew rich as a major West African exporter of slaves for the transatlantic market during its heyday at the end of the 18th century.

## IBIBIO

A cluster of peoples of the Niger Delta area of southeastern Nigeria, who speak the EFIK-Ibibio dialects. Originally fishermen and traders, they became slave traders and producers of palm oil from the 18th century. All village, tribal and religious affairs were organized through *ekpe* (leopard) secret societies, which still exist for men and women. Today the Ibibio are primarily rainforest cultivators, and are also renowned as woodcarvers. Animist beliefs have largely given way to Christianity. They number around 3.5 million.

## IGBO or Ibo

An agricultural people whose ancient homeland is in southeastern Nigeria. They produced some of the earliest bronze art in West Africa. Most Igbo are still agriculturists, and continue to live in patrilineal groups in autonomous villages under elders chosen by merit. Historically, many Igbo were enslaved by the IBANI and others and transported by European traders well into the early 19th century. Since the British colonial period they have spread throughout Nigeria as long-distance traders, administrators and professionals.

The Igbo formed the putative secessionist state of Biafra, which led to the Nigerian civil war of 1967–70 and the widespread persecution and death of many Igbo throughout Nigeria. They now number more than 15 million and speak a language of the KWA branch of Niger-Congo.

## IJAW or Ijo

A people inhabiting the Niger Delta of Nigeria. Many, especially the KALABARI and IBANI, became middlemen supplying slaves and later palm oil to Europeans after 1500. Their several sub-groups also include the NEMBA. They developed trading and political institutions known as 'canoe houses', headed by wealthy merchants, their kin groups and dependants, which offered the possibility of promotion and in which even slaves reached high office. Wealthy traders living in autonomous groups governed in council under an hereditary king.

Today, groups of Ijaw live in village clusters subject to the authority of elders, and are occupied in agriculture, fishing and palm-oil collecting. Many now work in oil and gas extraction and related industries. Their numerous Ijoid languages, part of the Niger-Congo family, are spoken by around 2 million people, and through contact with Europeans Ijaw became one of the earliest Nigerian languages to acquire written form.

h

# IKELAN

See BELLA.

## ILA or Baila or Sukulumbwe

The most prominent of a cluster of a dozen BANTU-speaking peoples inhabiting the Southern Province west of Lusaka, capital of Zambia. They inhabit the Kafue Valley, a tributary of the Zambezi River, and are thought to have originated near Lake Tanganyika to the northeast. Together they are known as the Ila-TONGA peoples, and all speak closely related dialects. The Ila practise mixed cattle-farming and cultivation, the latter generally undertaken by women, and live in dispersed homesteads and villages under local chiefs (*mwami*) but without any overall ruler or centralized political structure. They were also known for their hunting skills and for fishing where possible to supplement their diet. Many Ila are Christian but traditionally worship ancestor spirits and the creation god Leza. Recently, the invasion of the tsetse fly has decreased their cattle herds.

## IRAQW

One of the 'remnant' Cushitic-speaking peoples of East Africa (see CUSHITES), numbering more that 500,000. They have avoided incorporation by the dominant BANTU by occupying the more marginal agricultural land of northern Tanzania. They are a largely agricultural people with a hunting tradition, but less given to aggression and warfare than their Nilotic pastoral neighbours. Traditionally they had no military organization or ethos and, possibly originating for defensive reasons, their characteristic home is a *tembe*, or pit dwelling, with a flat roof of mud and dung.

## IRU

A BANTU-speaking people of Uganda. They were historically subject to dominant Hima pastoralists in the kingdoms of the ANKOLE, TORO and NYORO. There has been a long period of association and inter-marriage, so that they can be regarded as a sub-group of the Hima. Although traditionally agriculturists, the Iru reared cattle on behalf of the Hima, which has become the mainstay of their economy. They number about 1 million and are mostly Roman Catholic.

## ISSA

A SOMALI people in Somalia, Ethiopia and Djibouti, where they are the largest ethnic group (see DJIBOUTIANS). Some are also found in Eritrea. They are Sunni Muslims like the AFARS with whom they have often been in conflict as equally proud and independent pastoralists who place great value on cattle-wealth and individual bravery. The traditional lifestyle of the Issa continues unaltered in rural areas. Many came to live in the coastal sultanates of Djibouti, and today they still dominate Djibouti City and the southeast of the country. Their egalitarian social organization centres on a highly developed nexus of clan and family ties. The Issa and Afar speak Eastern Cushitic languages, but they are mutually unintelligible.

## ITESO

See TESO.

## IVORIANS

Inhabitants of the Ivory Coast (officially Côte d'Ivoire), capital Yamoussoukro. It is home to more than 60 tribal peoples, all speakers of Niger-Congo languages. The most important groups are the KWA-speaking ANYI and BAULÉ (affiliated with the AKAN of Ghana) as well as the KRU of the forest regions; the Mande-speaking MALINKE and DYULA, and the GUR (Voltaic)-speaking SENUFO and BOBO peoples of the inland savannah. France had a longstanding commercial interest in the Ivory Coast, which was incorporated into the FRENCH empire from 1889, first as a protectorate and then as a full colony in 1893. The Baulé were particularly hostile to the French takeover and fought them almost village by village until 1911. The Anyi were also fierce in their opposition to forced labour and a head tax imposed by the French authorities. The final pacification came only in 1918, after further revolts caused by conscription for war service in

> " Fear drives [the Ila] to maintain a constant war against the hippopotomi which swarm in the river. "
>
> David Livingstone's diary, 20 December 1855

> " The land was so good, that we decided to remain. "
>
> Iraqw account of their arrival in their homeland

France. The inter-war period saw a considerable amount of investment in the national transport infrastructure, education and other services, as well as a concentrated exploitation of the country's natural resources. The cash crops of cocoa and coffee became widely cultivated. The country became independent in 1960 under its first president Félix Houphouët-Boigny, who was in power until 1993. Relations with France have remained close.

Agriculture, and cocoa production in particular, is still the basis of the national economy. The growth in the country's population since independence (now around 16 million) has encouraged both migration to the urban centres and progressive colonization of forest land for agriculture. Between 1958 and 1980 around 12 million ha / 30 million acres were cleared for subsistence agriculture and cash-crop cocoa and coffee plantations. Economic growth and foreign investment after independence were impressive, but from 1980 falling commodity prices led to an economic decline, which has brought serious political unrest in recent years. Traditional cultural activities of the Ivory Coast peoples remain strong, notably art and music. There is also a thriving literary tradition in French, the official language. Around 40% of the population is Muslim and 25% Christian, although animist and local religious beliefs remain widespread.

## JOLA or Jola or Dyola or Diula

A people concentrated in western Gambia, southwestern Senegal, Guinea-Bissau and elsewhere in West Africa. They are agriculturists who cultivate rice in the wetter lowland river areas and groundnuts elsewhere. The Jola are socially fragmented according to language and ethnicity, and also as a result of commercial influences in recent decades that have encouraged cultivation by individual families rather than as cooperative villages. Many have sought work in the region's urban centres. It is hard to assess the total size of their population but it is possibly around 1 million. More than half are estimated to be Muslim although traditional animistic beliefs remain strong and widespread. Their language has suf-

fered a decline under the influence of stronger local languages.

## JULA

See DYULA.

## KABIYE

A people living in the north of the Republic of Togo. They are mainly subsistence farmers who number around 60,000 and speak a language that is part of the Eastern Grusi sub-group of GUR. It is spoken as a second language by perhaps 6 million people across the region.

## KABYLE

The main BERBER people of Algeria. Numbering more than 2 million, they are agriculturists who herd goats and grow grain and olives on their terraced farms in their inland mountain home. The impenetrability of their environment has encouraged a strong Kabyle identity, which is also strongly Muslim. Social and political organization is centred on their villages which occupy high ground overlooking their fields, and are occupied by rival clans. Like many North African societies, the Kabyle are also divided into hierarchical castes, with artisans and manual labourers (many formerly slaves) at the bottom. They speak Kabyle, a Berber language also called Zouaouah or Zwawah.

## KALABARI or Calabar

One of the IJAW peoples of the Niger Delta of southern Nigeria. Like the other Ijaw, they were traditionally involved in trade, especially the slave trade with Europeans, who knew them as the Calabar. Today many Kalabari remain business people, civil servants and professionals. They are concentrated in Rivers State, where their language, also known as Kalabari, is the *lingua franca*. Like IBANI, it is one of the Eastern Ijaw languages. In former centuries it was taken to Guyana in South America by slaves and became the basis of the Dutch creole Berbice.

## KALENJIN

Southern NILOTES of the Rift Valley region of western Kenya, who are cattle pastoralists and small-scale farmers. They comprise a number of sub-groups, the most significant being the NANDI, and together are believed to number more than 2 million. They migrated to Kenya from the north, absorbing indigenous peoples along the way, and were militarily powerful, able to mobilize armed men on a large scale based on the age-set system (in which all males of roughly equivalent age assume the role of warriors for a considerable period of their early lives before assuming other community roles).

## KAMBA

One of the BANTU-speaking peoples who occupy the Central Rift highlands east of Nairobi, the capital of Kenya. They are one of the country's main ethnic groups, numbering more than 2 million, and some are also found in Tanzania. The Kamba are an agricultural people, although many have now migrated to cities. Historically, they controlled the inland trade route from Mombasa until it was wrested from them by coastal SWAHILI traders in the mid-19th century.

## KANURI or Bornu or Borno or Kanembu or Beriberi

The people of Bornu state in northeastern Nigeria. Some are present in Niger where they are known as Bornuans. The roughly 5 million Kanuri, many of whom are Sufis, speak NILO-SAHARAN and were converted to Islam from the 11th century onwards. Their social organization is highly stratified and their families polygynous. Early involvement in regional and trans-Saharan trade led to the creation of the important empire of Bornu, which peaked in the 16th century. Commerce remains important, along with mixed agriculture, craft production and fishing on Lake Chad. Their highly centralized political organization has also endured.

## KAONDE or Bakaonde

A BANTU-speaking people of northwestern Zambia, closely related to the LUBA. Traditionally they practised slash-and-burn cultivation, growing sorghum and maize, but they also hunt, fish and gather wild food according to the season, and have a strong belief in ancestor spirits. The Kaonde moved into their present homeland in the 16th and 17th centuries and were subject to the more northerly LUNDA people. Powerful autonomous chieftainships emerged in the 19th century, and they warred with the LOZI and raided the ILA for slaves. Many Kaonde now work in the Zambian copper-mining industry. They number more than 300,000.

## KARA

A people who live near Lake Victoria in northern Tanzania. They are renowned as skilled cultivators who use cattle to manure the poor highland soils of their region, their property unusually held in personal rather than communal or tribal ownership. Historically, the Kara formed the kingdom of Karagwe probably under the influence of the Hinda clan, said to have retreated southward when the Bito rulers took control of Bunyoro (see NYORO) in the 15th century. The Karagwe Hinda conquered the RWANDANS and spawned ruling dynasties elsewhere. They should not be confused with the Kara sub-group of the GBAYA of Chad and the Central African Republic.

## KARIMOJONG

Semi-nomadic cattle pastoralists of northeastern Uganda. They are the largest of a group of NILOTES, who include other UGANDANS and the TURKANA who arrived in Kenya around 1850. Cattle milk and blood form the basis of the Karimojong diet, although settled cultivation undertaken by their women (growing sorghum and millet) has become more common. Inter-tribal raiding, 19th-century exploitation by slave- and ivory-traders, and drought, famine and cattle diseases up to the 1990s have seriously affected their prosperity.

k

*" The old men have got tired. "*

The supposed meaning of the name Karimojong, reflecting a legend that they dropped out of a major migration

## KASANJE

Modern-day BANTU-speaking ANGOLANS of the upper Kwango River in southwestern Africa. Kasanje was an historic kingdom, its capital at Cassange on the eastern borders of Bakongo. It was founded around 1620 by emigrant LUNDA people known as the Imbangala, led by the eponymous Kasanje. They developed a thriving trade (especially in slaves) with the Portuguese coastal colony of Angola between the 1650s and 1850s. This was undermined by the appearance of the rival OVIMBUNDU people. The fiercely independent Kasanje blocked the Portuguese advance into the interior in the 19th century, but were finally incorporated into Angola around 1911.

## KAVIRONDO

See LUO.

## KEBU

A people of northern Uganda. They are subsistence cultivators and livestock farmers and are one of the country's few Sudanic-speaking peoples. They number around 250,000, half of whom are Christian while most of the remainder follow traditional beliefs. They should not be confused with the Kebu people of central Togo.

## KEDI

A BANTU-speaking people of eastern Uganda and western Kenya. Numbering more than 1 million, they are predominantly subsistence and cash-crop cultivators, and have historically been subject to the economic and cultural domination of the GISU people, who are numerous in the Mount Elgon area of Uganda. They are mostly Christian or followers of local beliefs, but around 10% are Muslim.

## KENYANS

People of the Republic of Kenya, which lies astride the equator on the coast of East Africa, and is named after the country's highest mountain. Kenya was a British colony until independence in 1963 under Jomo Kenyatta (governed 1963–78), remaining a stable and relatively prosperous state despite the arbitrary amalgam of many and diverse cultural and ethnic groups that make up its population.

The ethnolinguistic make-up of the country is complex. The territory of Kenya, especially the Rift Valley, shows evidence of very early occupation by hominids, and it has been subject to important waves of migration ever since. Most (around 98%) of the population today are indigenous Africans, some of ARAB descent along the SWAHILI coast, which was strongly bound into the Arab Indian Ocean trading network in the middle of the 1st millennium AD. The main result of this Arab-BANTU cultural fusion is the country's *lingua franca*, Swahili, which replaced English as Kenya's official language in 1974, although English continues to be widely spoken.

### Colonial rivalry

In the mid-19th century BRITISH interests in East Africa were particularly concerned with Zanzibar, whose Sultans claimed large stretches of coastal territory, and with suppression of the slave trade. Growing German interest in the region led to partition following the Berlin Conference of 1884–5, creating German Tanganyika (which became Tanzania after its independence and union with Zanzibar) and a British sphere of influence to the north run by the chartered British East Africa Company.

This British sphere included much of modern-day Kenya, and it was consolidated by military means from 1895, when it was taken under direct British government control as the East African Protectorate. In 1920 it was renamed Kenya Colony, and the coastal territories leased from Zanzibar became the Kenya Protectorate, combined at independence.

Under colonial rule a significant number of British and European settlers arrived, largely as farmers, but their numbers fell sharply at independence when many returned home or relocated to other colonies, fearful of black majority rule. Asians, who arrived as merchants and small traders, are still well represented in the main urban centres such as Mombasa and the capital, Nairobi.

> **"**This is a British Colony for better or worse... [and] Kenya and its people are for ever British.**"**
>
> Sir Philip Mitchell, British governor of Kenya, 1949

## The Kenyan people

The largest proportion (roughly 66%) of Kenya's African population are BANTU-speakers, concentrated in the south of the country, and include the EMBU, GUSII, KAMBA, KIKUYU and LUYIA. The Kikuyu played an important role in the independence movement, which crystallized in the Mau Mau uprising of 1952–6 (see KIKUYU), and they were favoured by Kenyatta's powers of patronage after independence.

A further 25% of Kenyans are NILOTES, most significantly the KALENJIN, LUO, MASAI, NANDI and TURKANA. They have traditionally pursued a pastoral way of life dominated by their herds of cattle and by cattle-raiding, and although many have adapted to settled agriculture, nomadic pastoralism is still common among the northern Turkana and southern Masai.

Cushitic-speaking Kenyans include the OROMO and SOMALI, largely pastoralists inhabiting the fragile eco-systems of the dry, semi-desert regions of the north and northeast.

## Economy and demography

Agriculture is still the most important sector of the Kenyan economy, particularly the tea and coffee cash crops vital for foreign-exchange earnings, and which benefited many small farmers after independence. Tourism, based on Kenya's well-developed network of national parks, game reserves and sanctuaries, has been a major source of foreign income. Since the early 1970s, however, the drastic oil-price increases, drought and an excessive rate of population growth have hindered Kenya's development, leading to wider unemployment and poverty. At the same time, as in many African countries, the middle and elite classes benefited disproportionately in their exploitation of the new state bureaucracies, political power and economic freedoms: by 1980 the richest 10% of households received 45% of household income, giving rise to marked social inequality. Despite setbacks, however, the mixed public–private economic system has served Kenyans reasonably well since independence. International aid and investment have also continued to flow, helped by Kenya's alignment with the West during the Cold War years, and partly in exchange for a return to multi-party elections in 1992.

The rate of population increase has also slowed recently. From a total of five million in 1948, the population now stands at approximately 30 million, the birth rate peaking in the late 1970s, helped by improved health and falling death rates. At this period each woman was bearing an average of eight children during her lifetime. Modern Kenyans are more aware of the costs of schooling, health care, food, housing, the excessive subdivision of land among too many sons and other factors.

## Culture and religion

Kenyans are a diverse nationality and much of their cultural heritage is specific to their own ethnicity and origins. The state has developed the usual range of institutions, such as libraries, archives and museums, to preserve aspects of traditional culture subject to the erosion of modern society. This is also a subject explored in important works of Kenyan literature, which flourishes in Swahili as well as English. Music and dance are an integral part of national and local life and fully utilized in religious ceremony, most commonly in the churches of the various Christian denominations, which have a widespread following in the country. Theatre is also popular, and used in part for educational and political purposes, for example for campaigning against the national culture of corruption in public and business life, which worsened under the presidency (1978–2002) of Daniel arap Moi. Such activities have become possible in the less repressive political environment prevalent since the election to power of the Rainbow Coalition in 2002 and the end of nearly 40 years of KANU party rule. The new government has also introduced free primary education, which has been hugely popular.

| Kenyans: main ethnic groups |
| --- |
| Embu |
| Gusii |
| Kalenjin |
| Kamba |
| Kikuyu |
| Luo |
| Luyia |
| Maasai |
| Nandi |
| Oromo |
| Somali |
| Turkana |

# KHASONKA

A MANDE-speaking people located predominantly in western Mali. Also known as Khassonkés, they are concentrated on the upper Senegal River and also live in eastern Senegal and southern Mauritania. Numbering more than 100,000, they are sedentary farmers and overwhelmingly Muslim. They believe they are descended from FULANI pastoralists.

# KHOIKHOI

A people, formerly known as Hottentots, who are important historically in South Africa, but barely exist today, except insofar as they have contributed genetically to the CAPE COLOURED population. A few survive in Namibia and South Africa, but they are difficult to distinguish from the SAN, and indeed the two peoples are so inter-related that they are often referred to as the Khoisan. The main sub-groups are the Nama and the Oorlams, each further sub-divided into smaller communities. Each was organized into a patriarchal group of related families.

The Khoikhoi were probably hunting and gathering people who added cattle and sheep to their economy as they migrated southwards. By the time of Portuguese and DUTCH shipwrecks on the southern coasts of Africa in the 16th and 17th centuries, they inhabited most regions of the Cape, and were also to be found on the beaches collecting sea foods. Dutch seafarers and, after 1652, settlers, traded with them, but the relationship soon turned to one of conflict.

The Dutch AFRIKANERS were able to assert their authority over them, but the greatest danger to the Khoikhoi came from smallpox epidemics, transmitted from passing ships, which ravaged them from 1713 onwards. 'Hottentots' were displayed as curiosities in Europe in the late 18th and early 19th centuries, and their name became synonymous with any supposedly 'uncivilized' or 'heathen' people.

A Moravian mission to the Khoikhoi attempted to proselytize among them in the early 18th century, but failed. The London Missionary Society brought Christianity in the early 19th century, and one or two of the missionaries inter-married with them, but by then they had almost ceased to exist as an independent people. However, their existence undermines the Afrikaner propaganda that they encountered an 'empty land' at the Cape. The demise of the Khoikhoi, as with that of the CARIBS or the TASMANIANS, has become emblematic of the destructiveness of European colonial settlement.

# KHOISAN

See KHOIKHOI and SAN.

# KIKUYU

A BANTU-speaking people who are the largest ethnic group in Kenya. Between the 17th and 19th centuries they slowly expanded from the northeast of present-day Kikuyuland into new clearings within the forested areas, becoming known as the settlers where the fig tree, *mukuyu*, grew – the origin of their name. They occupy the highlands of the south-central part of the country and number around 5 million, roughly one-sixth of the population.

Their society, similar to that of many other relatively peaceable agricultural Bantu peoples, operated without the need for any centralized political authority. Instead, disputes were settled according to shared custom.

The common organization of Kikuyu expansion was the *mbari*, or a colonizing group of young men who cleared a tract of land that was then shared out for farming. The Kikuyu have traditionally used hoe cultivation, especially involving millet (their staple crop), as well as some mixed farming involving livestock. Today's cash crops are primarily coffee and maize together with other fruit and vegetables. The Kikuyu properties were hereditary according to patrilineal descent, the townships remaining subject to *mbari* councils, which still regulate community affairs. Families followed the male pioneers and set up family homesteads, which included a hut for each wife in what was a polygamous society. Another important feature of Kikuyu society is the system of age-sets, the ruling group traditionally providing members for councils of elders. In religion they believe in ancestor spirits as well as the existence of a creator god, Ngai.

## Colonization and resistance

The upland forests and highlands of Kikuyuland were always useful for protection from enemies, notably the MAASAI who were one of the constraints on Kikuyu expansion toward the end of the 19th century. Although they lacked centralized political organization, the Kikuyu did appoint temporary war leaders as circumstances required. They remained vulnerable to raiding, however, although the threats from hostile neighbours were eliminated with the establishment of the British protectorate from 1895. Today, the rural Kikuyu mostly live in villages, a change brought about by British colonial policy, which sought to protect, concentrate and control the Kikuyu during the Mau Mau uprising, which began in 1952. This was the first rebellion in Kenya against British rule, sparked by discontent over a land policy that prevented Kikuyu expansion while reserving under-utilized land for white settlers.

The Mau Mau emergency ended in 1956 after a brutal guerrilla war that left 11,000 rebels dead. Well over 20,000 others were detained and pressured to abandon their nationalist beliefs. The Kikuyu went on to form the backbone of the independence movement, which led to Jomo Kenyatta, a Kikuyu, becoming Kenya's first prime minister and, later, president (1963–78). In office, however, he appointed a growing number of Kikuyu to posts in the government and administration. Other policies, notably land sales, also predominantly favoured the Kikuyu, which led to growing ethnic tensions during the period of his rule.

## KIMBU

A large and loosely defined BANTU group, like the NYAMWEZI and SUKUMA, of western-central Tanzania. They were displaced during the upheavals of slave-raiding in the late 19th century, and established small independent chiefdoms in their present territory for their own protection. They appear to have incorporated others similarly affected, as well as peripatetic farmers. Many are still semi-nomadic hunter-gatherers as well as agriculturists. They follow traditional religions as well as Christianity or Islam. The Kimbu number more than 75,000 today.

## KISALIAN CULTURE

A society in what is now Congo (Kinshasa), of the 8th–14th centuries AD, which later developed into the LUBA kingdom. The heartland of the Kisalian culture was the Upemba Depression, particularly the area around Lake Kisale on the upper Luapala River. The Early Kisalian period (8th–11th centuries) was followed by the Classic Kisalian (to the end of the 14th century).

This was succeeded by the intrusive Kabambian culture of Lubaland (to the early 19th century) and the modern era.

Social stratification emerged in the Kisalian culture, together with a sophisticated material culture involving fine pottery. Specialized craftspeople were skilled in metalworking in iron and copper, as well as in carving ivory and bone. Trade became increasingly important. A proto-state was formed during the Classic Kisalian period, precursor of the major Luba political reorganization at the start of the Kabambian era.

## KISII

See GUSII.

## KITARA

See NYORO.

## KOLOLO or Makololo

A people who live in Zambia and Botswana. They are a sub-group of the Western SOTHO, or TSWANA, from whom they broke away northwards, conquering what became the Barotse, or LOZI, kingdom of the Zambezi Valley around 1838. Their power and influence declined with the re-assertion of the former royal house in the 1860s, when many Kololo were killed or expelled.

From the early 1850s the great Scottish missionary and explorer David Livingstone recruited Kololo from Barotseland to help spread Christianity and open up the interior, where they became influential. They included some who were expelled from the Lozi kingdom and moved eastwards to the Lower Shire Valley in Malawi, where they became petty chiefs among the NYANJA. In the 19th century the Kololo became renowned for their cattle-raiding, and cattle remain an important part of their traditional economy.

## KONGO or Bakongo

Culturally related BANTU-speakers concentrated in the western Congo basin in central Africa. They are present in both republics of Congo, as

**k**

*" The influence of the Makololo over the tribes they subdued has been extraordinary. "*

François Coillard, 1878

well as northern Angola. The medieval Kongo kingdom developed an important trade network but was undermined by slave-raiding and Portuguese imperialism, fragmenting into warring chiefdoms in the 17th century. The Kongo remain socially fragmented, divided into many tribes, matrilineages and independent villages. Their fragmentation also assisted Portuguese and Belgian colonization, although this was actively resisted into the early 1900s. Ethnonationalism was bolstered by local religions, still important in Kongo society. The Kongo number around 10.5 million and are mainly agriculturists, but many live in cities and are active in all trades and professions. The LALA are an important sub-group.

> " In the management of a bargain I would back the Congoese native against Jew or Christian. "
>
> Henry Morton Stanley, 1885

## KOREKORE

The Northern sub-group of the SHONA people of Zimbabwe and Mozambique. They comprise several sub-groups, all primarily mixed cattle and crop farmers, who speak their own BANTU Korekore language and dialects. They number 1.3 million.

## KPELLE or Guerze

MANDE-speaking farming people of central Liberia and Guinea, from where they began to expand into adjoining territory during the 16th century. They now form Liberia's largest ethnic group, numbering about 1 million. They have strong oral traditions, through which they trace their origins to the great medieval empire of Mali. Traditional hut villages are the home of many polygamous family groups who acknowledge the authority of chiefs. Paramount chiefs act as government officials and perform traditional administrative and legal functions. The Kpelle are noted for their *poro* (male) and *sande* (female) secret societies, which have religious and social authority and perform a unifying role within Kpelle society. They are also responsible for the initiation of young people.

## KRIO or Creoles

A people of mixed racial origin living in Sierra Leone, concentrated in the capital, Freetown.

They speak Krio, or Creole, a pidgin language which has developed into their mother tongue, derived from English and a variety of local languages. It is now the country's *lingua franca*. Its development was a consequence of the creation of Freetown and coastal Sierra Leone as a home for the black poor of London and others from North America and the Caribbean from 1787. These groups formed the core of the Krio community, supplemented by an estimated 74,000 black Africans freed from slave ships by the Royal Navy. The Krio community became the willing agents of BRITISH imperialism and Christian evangelism in West Africa, and remained politically dominant in Sierra Leone until shortly before the country became independent in 1961.

Originally, the displaced black Africans resettled in Sierra Leone had lost their close cultural attachments, and they were more amenable than the region's indigenous population to European culture and the proselytizing work of the British missionaries who arrived from 1804. Christianity, especially the education brought by the churches, was eagerly adopted by the Krio and by 1868 one-sixth of the population attended school. The Krio regarded themselves as agents of modernization and civilization in Africa, and this helped define their nascent community. They also sought to profit from the British and European exploitation and transformation of West Africa. Many Krio were merchants as well as doctors, lawyers, teachers, parsons, government officials and other skilled workers, forming the coastal elite who dominated the country. In 1827 the Krio John Macauley Wilson became the first West African doctor with European qualifications to practise in the region.

Some Krio also returned to their original homelands in West Africa, notably ethnic YORUBA to Nigeria, where they acted as a modernizing element within traditional society. They promoted trade and Christianity and were followed by white missionaries from Sierra Leone. Generally the Krio played an important role in the development of the whole of British West Africa. Towards the end of the 19th century the British government extended its control of the interior, and the Krio became essential in its administration and control. Their aura of superi-

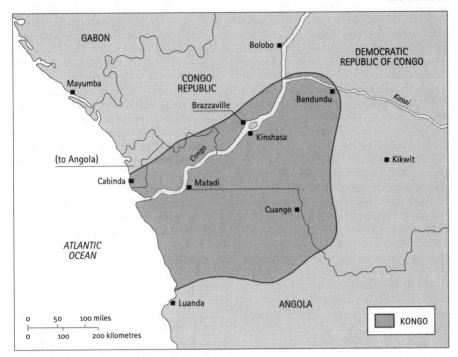

GABON

Bolobo ■

DEMOCRATIC
REPUBLIC OF CONGO

Mayumba ■

CONGO
REPUBLIC

Bandundu ■

Kasai

Brazzaville

Kinshasa ■

Congo

(to Angola)

■ Kikwit

Cabinda ●

■ Matadi

Cuango ■

ATLANTIC
OCEAN

| 0 | 50 | 100 miles |
| 0 | 100 | 200 kilometres |

■ Luanda

ANGOLA

KONGO

ority and disrespect for the beliefs and traditions of other Sierra Leonians, however, always provoked great hostility in the country. The division between the coastal Krio and up-country inhabitants was a significant feature of internal politics into the post-independence period.

## KRU

Peoples of southern Liberia and the Ivory Coast, also dispersed along the whole West African coast. The largest concentration today is in Monrovia, Liberia. Kru men are famous as stevedores, fishermen and seamen and were a common sight on British merchant ships in particular in the 19th and 20th centuries. Kru languages of the KWA branch of Niger-Congo are spoken by approximately 3 million, and include Seme in Burkina Faso, suggesting that the Kru moved south during the 15th–17th centuries to escape the MANDE invasion.

The Kru strongly resisted enslavement and involvement in the transatlantic slave trade. They were politically decentralized but clans formed autonomous sub-tribes based on townships. In the Ivory Coast they use secret societies to maintain their identity across a large forest region.

## KUNAMA or Kunema

Cattle pastoralists who occupy a region straddling the border of Eritrea and the Sudanese Republic. Numbering more than 100,000, they speak Kunama, an Eastern Sudanic language. Perhaps 30% are Roman Catholic due to European missionary activity during the Italian occupation of Eritrea before World War II.

## KUSHITES

The name originally used by the ancient EGYPTIANS to describe the NUBIANS of Kush (or Cush), the area from the second Nile cataract south to modern-day Khartoum in the SUDANESE Republic. Kushites (not to be confused with Cushites) were culturally influenced by, and often politically subject to, Egypt but from the 11th century

BC developed the rich and powerful Kushite state, reflected in the NAPATAN CULTURE. Its kings ruled Egypt as the 25th dynasty of pharaohs (751–668 BC) until expelled by the ASSYRIANS. The Kushites developed a stronger 'African' MEROITIC CULTURE from the 6th century BC, but a gradual decline ended with the invasion of the AKSUMITES from about AD 320.

## KWA

A branch of the Niger-Congo language family. Kwa- speaking peoples are estimated to number more than 20 million, and occupy a large area of West Africa. They are concentrated in southwestern Nigeria and adjoining southern Togo, Ghana and the Ivory Coast. Within the Kwa language family, the larger Nyo group of 35 languages includes ANYI, BAULÉ, GUANG and AKAN, spoken by around 7 million people including the ASANTE. A further ten 'left bank' languages are spoken east of the Volta River, notably EWE and GA-ADANGME.

## KWERE

A BANTU-speaking people who are hoe cultivators and livestock-rearers of the coastal lowlands of Tanzania. They are part of the ZARAMO cluster of peoples and live in the Muslim SWAHILI heartland, although they are relatively relaxed in their religious observance. Their territory was frequently raided for slaves during the 19th century, and in response the Kwere withdrew into protective stockaded villages, traditionally noted for their mud huts with distinctive high conical thatched roofs. Today the Kwere population is more dispersed in townships.

*" Among the Lango only the wizards eat snakes. "*

J.H. Driberg, 1923

## LALA

A people of central Zambia who originated in the Congo Basin and form an important sub-group of the KONGO. Environmental degradation in their Zambian homeland due to the increasing level of shifting agriculture and other practices has forced many off the land and into the towns to seek work.

The Lala are traditionally known for their craft skills in copper and iron. They number

around 250,000, and should not be confused with the ROBA of eastern Nigeria, who are sometimes called the Lala or Lalla.

## LALI or Lari or Balili

A major sub-group of the KONGO. They practise shifting agriculture in their homelands in the Congo (Kinshasa) and adjoining Angola, Zambia and the Central African Republic, although many have migrated to urban centres in recent decades. They are particularly strong around Brazzaville, the capital of the Republic of the Congo. Renowned metalworkers in copper and iron, they altogether number around 1 million. It is believed they are of ethnic TEKE origin.

## LALLA

See ROBA.

## LANGO or Langi

NILOTES of central-northern Uganda who speak a Western Nilotic language like the related ACHOLI. They were predominantly semi-nomadic cattle pastoralists until rinderpest epidemics ravaged their herds in the 19th century, which led to a greater concentration on the sedentary cultivation of a wide variety of crops. They are thought to number around 770,000 people.

## LENDU

A farming and fishing people of northeastern Congo (Kinshasa), who live on the western shores of Lake Albert, and also across the border in northern Uganda. They speak a Central Sudanic language and are related to the LUGBARA. The Lendu are numerous and have been active in the Congolese civil war from 1998. Since the Ugandan army withdrew from the Congo in May 2003, the Lendu militia has been vying for prominence against the smaller rival Hima, leading to several massacres in the province of Itari.

## LIBERIANS

Inhabitants of Liberia, Africa's oldest republic. The territory of Liberia was chosen by philanthropists in the USA as a home for liberated slaves, hence its name (which dates from 1824). A small colony was founded at Cape Mesurado under the auspices of the American Colonization Society in 1822. Liberia became a sovereign state in 1847, under Joseph Jenkins Roberts (1848–56), based on the capital, Monrovia.

Originally a group of coastal settlements, the new country set about expanding inland. American economic and strategic interests led to a strengthening relationship from the 1920s when the Firestone Tyre and Rubber Company obtained a lease of 1 million acres of land. Most Liberian peoples (95%) are indigenous, the rest descendants of re-settled black slaves from the USA, the Caribbean and elsewhere in West Africa (see AMERICO-LIBERIANS and CONGOE).

Americo-Liberians dominated the politics and administration of Liberia and were resented by the people of the interior of the country, until the True Whig Party was overthrown in the military coup led by Samuel Doe in 1980. This discontent was partly the result of serious economic problems. The government's failure to remedy these led to political unrest, civil war and associated human-rights abuses, which continued after Doe's murder (1990) under the next president and warlord, Charles Taylor.

There are many ethnic groups in the country: the northern MANDE-speaking and the southern KWA-speakers. The population in 1998 was 2.77 million, two-thirds dependent on subsistence agriculture. Most are Christian and about 15% are Muslim, but traditional beliefs are also strong.

# LIBYANS

The people of the oil-rich Libyan state, officially the Socialist People's Libyan Arab Jamahiriyah, in North Africa. The narrow coastal strip is home to the majority of the rapidly growing population (currently around 6.2 million), and the major towns include the capital, Tripoli. The rest of the country comprises inhospitable mountains and the Sahara desert. The ancient Greeks gave the name Libya to the area west of the Nile after a tribe living in Cyrenaica, although it only became the official name of the territory when it

was adopted by the Italian colonial authority in 1934. Among the many ancient occupiers of the region were the Phoenician CARTHAGINIANS, whose eastern province, Tripolitania, centred on Tunis; and the GREEKS in Cyrenaica to the east. They were followed by the ROMANS in the 1st century BC and ARABS from the 7th century AD, who established the primacy of Islam in North Africa, although some COPTS remain.

Most modern Libyans, perhaps 80% of the population, are mixed ARABS and BERBERS who are Sunni Muslims. They claim descent mostly from the Arab Banu Hilal and Banu Sulaym, pastoral tribal BEDOUIN from Arabia who arrived only in the 11th century; and the Berbers, the indigenous agricultural people of the region who have been generally assimilated into Arab society and culture. Although the Berber language is widely used among that community, Arabic is spoken by all Libyans and is the country's official language. Libya's ethnic mix also includes the descendants of Turkish occupiers, other Arab peoples and black slaves brought to North Africa from the Sudan and sub-Saharan regions up to the 20th century. Some TUAREG live in the southwest of the country. The remaining 20% are mostly foreign workers, especially from Egypt, Chad, Sudan and Europe.

## Modern Libya

The modern country assumed its territorial unity only under the OTTOMANS from the early 16th century, when they subdued the provinces of Fezzan, Tripolitania and Cyrenaica and controlled them from their administrative capital, Tripoli. Libyan autonomy after the Ottoman withdrawal was ended by ITALIAN invasion in 1911 and the imposition of colonial rule. Libyans regained power after World War II and the country became a fully independent kingdom in 1951.

A coup led by Colonel Muammar al-Gaddafi in 1969, however, led to the deposition of the king and the creation of the present Muslim republic, or *Jamahiriyah*, meaning government through the masses, espousing a form of Islamic socialism. Originally there was a strong emphasis on pan-Arabism and efforts at political union with the other Muslim countries of North

**"**The love of liberty brought us here. **"**

Motto on the Liberian coat of arms

**Liberians: main ethnic groups**

*Mande-speaking:*
Bandi
Dan
Kpelle
Ma
Malinke
Mende
Vai

*Kwa-speaking:*
Bassa
Bella
Kru

African and the Sudan, but these came to nothing. In recent years Libya's radical world view, involving support for foreign terrorist groups, liberation movements and others, has put it at odds with many countries in the region and further afield, particularly the USA. Sanctions were imposed on Libya following its implication in the bombing of an American civilian aircraft over Locherbie, Scotland. These were lifted in 2004 when a settlement was reached over compensation and responsibility, along with Libya's renunciation of so-called 'weapons of mass destruction'.

## LOMWE or Alomwe or Acilowe or Nguru

A people who occupy southern Tanzania, northern Mozambique and Malawi. The Lomwe are small-scale cultivators and migrant workers who today number more than 2 million and speak the BANTU Chilomwe language, similar to MAKUA. Both the Lomwe and Makua are part of the YAO cluster of peoples, with whom they share important aspects of social organization based on matrilineal descent. Inter-marriage is common.

## LOZI

A major grouping of about 25 BANTU-speaking peoples of western Zambia. They were originally known as the Aluyi, possibly a local name meaning 'foreigners'. After they were conquered by the KOLOLO in 1838 they became known as the Barotse, from which the name Lozi is derived. This refers to both the dominant Lozi tribe and its formerly subject peoples in Zambia, Angola and the Caprivi Strip (see CAPRIVIANS).

The origins of the Lozi kingdom are obscure. It was probably created out of several local chiefdoms after 1650 by the southward-moving LUNDA who settled in the land called Ngulu. Political authority was relatively centralized, divided between appointed chiefs who owed loyalty to the king (litunga) in the characteristic LUBA-Lunda system. The leading families were supported by the mass of Lozi as well as the conquered peoples, who all paid tribute to the wealthy ruling group. Failure to incorporate tributary peoples, who included the ILA and LUVALE,

into Lozi society as equals became a source of political weakness. There was also a political separation and longstanding rivalry between the Lozi of northern and southern Bulozi, where a second capital was usually occupied by a royal son or daughter.

The Lozi adapted well to the conditions of the upper Zambezi flood plain and created one of the most sophisticated and intensive agricultural systems in pre-colonial Africa, also supporting a high density of population. They dug drainage channels and canals for transport, built fish-weirs and dams, and occupied man-made mounds above the normal level of the floodwaters. During the annual floods they moved with their cattle to villages on even higher land at the edge of the river valley. When the floods subsided they returned to their usual homes in the flood plain, where the cattle pastures were refreshed and the soils newly fertilized. The king was traditionally transported in a great ceremonial canoe (the *nalikwanda*) during the annual migration from his capital at Lealui to Mangu in the eastern hills and later back again. This mixed-farming economy (in which fishing was also exploited) relied upon a high level of cooperation and centralized administration, which encouraged social cohesion. As an economic system it was also labour intensive and the Lozi made great use of serfs, or slaves, acquired in war and provided by tributary peoples.

### The Kololo conquest

In 1838 the Lozi were conquered by the migrating Kololo, a SOTHO people arriving from the south. The Kololo had themselves been displaced by the growing ZULU empire in South Africa. Harried by the NDEBELE, several thousand Kololo under Sebituane defeated the Aluyi, who were themselves weakened by a political power struggle. The Kololo consolidated their power through integration: cattle-clientage, inter-marriage, fair administration, the recognition of existing Lozi chiefs and an appeal to formerly excluded tributary peoples. Sebituane was also strengthened by success in war, defeating Ndebele raids on Bulozi. David Livingstone described him as 'the greatest warrior ever heard of beyond ... [Cape] Colony'.

Sebituane's successors after 1851 were much less able and conciliatory. Following an insurrection in 1864, and the massacre of the Kololo, who were relatively few in number, the old royal house was restored and the kingdom rebuilt under King Lewanika. His fear of the Ndebele and other outsiders, and of Lozi rivals for the throne, led him to accept a British protectorate ('Barotseland') toward the end of the 19th century. Under British colonial influence the system of servile labour was abolished and agricultural prosperity declined sharply. The monarchy survived and had an important influence in the creation of an independent Zambia, in which Barotseland was incorporated in 1964. The Lozi population of Zambia today is around 750,000.

## LUBA

BANTU-speaking peoples of southern Congo (Kinshasa). They are best known to history for their development of powerful, centralized and sophisticated kingdoms. The Luba, who appeared at the end of KISALIAN CULTURE in the 14th century, were instrumental in the forcible amalgamation of a number of smaller states into larger kingdoms, and in their political reorganization during the 15th century.

The new hierarchical system of government they created concentrated unprecedented political power on the king, bolstered by trade wealth and tribute paid by subject peoples, and by their semi-divine status. Luba chiefs were appointed for life by these kings, but owed their position and loyalty to an individual king. On his death they were forced to resign, and although some were re-appointed, the dispossessed contributed to political instability. Some led bands of warriors into neighbouring territories and created new kingdoms as Luba satellites.

Further development then occurred in the larger LUNDA empire, forming a complex of kingdoms known as the Luba-Lunda states, and among the MARAVI people south and west of Lake Nyasa. The Luba empire reached its fullest extent in the 18th century. Cultivation, food gathering and hunting are traditional pursuits, and trade, which became important as a foundation of political expansion and development, is still widely undertaken at a local level.

## LUGBARA

Agricultural people of northwestern Uganda and the adjoining area of the eastern Congo (Kinshasa) who largely practise shifting hoe cultivation. They are Central Sudanic speakers who in Uganda form only around 10% of the population. They traditionally acknowledge the authority of family heads (and rainmakers) but never adopted a centralized political structure, so for the purposes of administration and control chiefs have been appointed by the central government in Uganda. Many Lugbara are agricultural workers in Buganda. The Lugbara worship ancestor spirits and the creator god Adroa.

## LUHYA

See LUYIA.

## LUNDA

A BANTU-speaking people who, like the LUBA with whom they are closely associated, originated in the southern Congo (Kinshasa), central Africa. They successfully developed the Luba techniques of state organization to create the larger Lunda empire with its numerous satellite kingdoms. In this process new peoples emerged, including the LUVALE, CHOKWE and MBUNDU. Luba-Lunda culture and organization influenced political systems throughout central Africa. Traditionally the Lunda live in small compact villages and pursue hoe cultivation, food gathering and hunting, along with the rearing of livestock of various types. Trade is important locally. Indigenous religious beliefs centre on a supreme sky or earth god and ancestor worship.

### The Lunda empire

Ancestral Lunda territory is traditionally thought to have been invaded by a group of Luba warriors around 1600 under the leadership of Kibinda Ilunga. A new line of kings, known as Mwata Yamvo, successfully improved Luba methods of rule and absorbed new peoples, which made the state more cohesive. It is possible that the creation of the Lunda state could have been a local process, with borrowings from

> **"** I found this morning that the Barotse [Lozi] believe firmly in the metamorphosis of certain persons into alligators, lions, & hippopotomi. **"**
>
> David Livingstone's diary, 5 February 1854

the Luba. Either way, the result of Lunda development was the creation of a much larger and stronger empire occupying adjoining northern Zambia and northern and central Angola. It developed trade between central Africa and the west coast, forming important links with the Portuguese, who required slaves and ivory, and across to Zanzibar and the coast of East Africa.

> " Lovalé [are] ... reported to be harsh task-masters. "
>
> Verney Lovett Cameron, 1875, referring to the Luvale

The Lunda empire, like the Luba, had imprecise boundaries, formed around the central state and closely controlled inner provinces ringed by tribute-paying autonomous outer provinces. Further away were independent kingdoms linked by cultural ties, such as LOZI and the KASANJE, the latter founded by Lunda Imbangala warriors in Angola in the 17th century. The last major Lunda expansion took place in the early 18th century with the creation of the kingdom of Kazembe, centred on the Luapula Valley in northern Zambia. It reached the height of its power in the 1850s but was attacked by the Chokwe, the conquering Portuguese in Angola in the 1880s and Belgians in the Congo (Kinshasa) at the end of the century. Although the Lunda empire was destroyed, guerrilla resistance continued until 1909. Kazembe in Zambia was colonized by Britain.

## LUO or Lwo or Kavirondo

Kenya's third-largest ethnic group, comprising around 11% of the population. They are also present in adjoining Uganda and Tanzania and total around 3.5 million people. The Luo are NILOTES who arrived from the Sudan in the early 2nd millennium, settling east of Lake Victoria as cattle pastoralists and cultivators, supplementing their diet by hunting and fishing. The Luo intermingled with existing Nilotic and BANTU agriculturists to establish several loosely organized autonomous territories (*oganda*) ruled by local chiefs (*ruoths*) with political and religious power. They have traditionally lived in compounds defended with thorn-scrub hedges. Today the Luo are found scattered throughout East Africa, many having migrated to work in the urban centres of the region, notably Mombasa and Nairobi.

## LUVALE

BANTU-speaking farming, fishing and hunting people of northwestern Zambia and southeastern Angola. They also cultivated cassava, which they used to trade with the LOZI for cattle. They were involved in trading metals and ivory, although today many of the Luvale are migrant workers. The Luvale are possibly an offshoot of the neighbouring LUNDA of Katanga in Congo (Kinshasa), who by tradition were led to their new homeland by Chinyama. They have strong matrilineal and clan identities, which can be traced back to the 16th century, further than those of any other ZAMBIANS. Commoner lineage groups remain socially and politically important and operate independently of the several Luvale chiefdoms, which only developed from the early 18th century.

## LUYIA or Luhya or Abaluhya or Abaluyia

A group of BANTU-speaking agricultural peoples of western Kenya, the country's second-largest ethnic group by the 1980s. They number more than 2.5 million. The name is short for Abaluyia, roughly 'people of the same hearth', a term which was the creation of intellectuals who, from around 1930, saw the political advantages of uniting to pursue their interests under British colonial administration and eventually within an independent Kenya dominated by others. The Abaluyia can therefore be said to be an entirely invented tribe, or 'supertribe', although ethnolinguistically they are closely related. Their traditional social and political organization is characterized by autonomous patrilineages devoid of chiefs. They are dominated by 17 clans, and in recent times many of them have become labour migrants in the cities.

## LWO

See LUO.

## MAASAI or Masai

Traditionally nomadic pastoralists of the Rift Valley area of Kenya and Tanzania. They speak

Maa (or Maasai), a Nilotic or Eastern Sudanic language of the Nilo-Saharan family. They formed part of the slow drift of Nilotic peoples from southern Sudan into East Africa who reached as far south as Kilimanjaro by the early 2nd millennium AD (see NILOTES). They were the most powerful group and came to dominate the Rift Valley from the 17th century. Sub-groups include the Samburu who live near Lake Turkana in Kenya, and the semi-pastoral and agricultural Baraguyu and Arusha of Tanzania.

Cattle have always been central to the Maasai way of life. In small groups with their herds they constantly wander in search of fresh pastures and live almost entirely on the meat, milk and blood of their livestock. Their temporary villages of mud-dung huts are surrounded by thornbush to protect themselves and their herds. Cattle are also used as marriage dowries among the Maasai, who are polygynous. Male age-sets are an important feature of their society, in which circumcision marks the initiation of young men into adulthood. Each generational grouping

moves through a progression of grades within the respective clan starting as *morans*, young men between the ages of 15 and 30, who live in the bush and learn the necessary tribal knowledge and field and fighting skills as junior warriors. As senior elders they acquire a leadership role in an impressively egalitarian society which, because of its peripatetic lifestyle, never adopted a system of rule by chiefs. Wife-lending also takes place among men of the same age-set.

The pastoral Maasai have always been contemptuous of agriculturists, mixed farmers and even hunters. They coveted all cattle and routinely engaged in cattle-raiding among their neighbours and others they encountered in the course of their expansion.

The Maasai were also propelled southwards by a growing population and the need for more pasture land, which was much better in the south. They migrated along the river valleys and plains and began colonizing the flatlands of northern Tanzania until halted by the Gogo BANTU people in the 1830s. They also benefited

*"* [The Maasai are] marauders who generally lie in wait... for weak caravans. *"*

**H.M. Stanley, 1874**

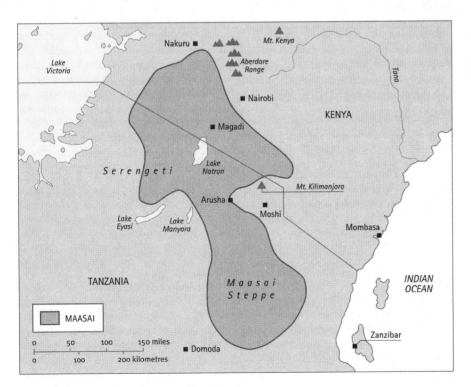

Maasai

from taxes that they levied on the caravans from the SWAHILI coast trading in ivory and slaves, which brought them highly prized cloth, beads, brass wire and other items used as personal adornment. In addition, they sold ivory obtained from neighbouring peoples such as the hunting Dorobo people.

When expansion ended in the mid-19th century, the Maasai began to fight among themselves for dominance, affording neighbouring rival peoples such as the NANDI an advantage. This led to the development of a more centralized Maasai political authority (but no king or chieftain) wielded by *laibons*, religious or ritual experts who had the task of achieving peace and unifying different groups in the face of threats from outside.

From the 1880s this threat was mainly from Germany and Britain, but Maasai opposition to European control was severely weakened by cattle disease and human epidemics. Colonial rule put an end to the traditional cattle-raiding of the Maasai, who were eventually incorporated into the modern states of East Africa. There has been constant pressure on the Maasai to give up their nomadic lifestyle in favour of sedentary agriculture, and a semi-nomadic way of life has become more common.

## MADAGASCANS

> ❝ The people subsist by trade and manufacture, and sell a vast number of elephants' teeth .... The principal food eaten at all seasons of the year is the flesh of camels. ❞
>
> Marco Polo, 1298, on the Madagascans

The people of the Democratic Republic of Madagascar, capital Antananarivo, off the coast of southeast Africa. The Madagascan economy is overwhelmingly agricultural. The majority of the population of around 15.3 million are ethnic MALAGASY. More than half are Christian and the rest adhere to traditional local beliefs or to Islam, which is common on the northwest coast and was brought by SWAHILI traders and by BANTU immigrants from the mainland from the 16th century.

European contact began with the Portuguese in the 16th century, but the island was made part of the French empire in 1885. The Madagascans rose against French rule in 1947, but the revolt was brutally suppressed. They finally achieved independence in 1960. Initially a one-party state, the country adopted democratic reforms in the 1990s.

## MAKA

An agricultural people who occupy southern Cameroon, Equatorial Guinea and northern Gabon. Historically they profited from the Atlantic slave trade in this area. Now numbering only around 150,000, they are a sub-group of the Beti, part of the FANG ethnic grouping. They are rivals of the larger neighbouring BAMILEKE people, and many are now Christian, although adherence to traditional beliefs is strong. Their BANTU language is closely related to Beti YAOUNDE.

## MAKONDE

A BANTU-speaking people inhabiting southeastern Tanzania and northern Mozambique. They are matrilineal and practise coastal farming, fishing and hunting. Like the related MAKUA, they are possibly a sub-group of the YAO. Traditionally, small clan and family units existed without any centralized political authority. Their territory stood astride the main southern slave-trade route inland from the port of Kilwa, and the Makonde used slaves to farm their land while they collected wild rubber for sale and export.

They are famous for their wood-carving skills, their designs often drawing on subjects in traditional folklore. The majority are Muslims, but there is a considerable Christian minority. Many have migrated to the towns of Malawi, Mozambique and Tanzania.

## MAKUA

One of the coastal peoples of southern Tanzania, East Africa. Like the MAKONDE, they are thought to be one of the YAO cluster of peoples. Some live in northern Mozambique and Malawi. They number up to 6 million and live in clan and family groups, without central authority, by farming, fishing and hunting.

The BANTU Makua language is closely related to LOMWE, and together they are spoken by about one third of the population of Mozambique. Most Makua are Muslim, the religion that spread with Arab and SWAHILI trade and culture.

# MALAGASY

A people who form the majority (99%) of the population of the island Republic of Madagascar off the southeast coast of Africa (see MADAGAS-CANS). They comprise around 50 ethnic groups including the SIHANAKA and are traditionally autonomous and without centralized political systems, except for the MERINA people of the north-central Highlands, whose kingdom was seized by the French in 1895. The origins of the Malagasy are complex and owe much to the ancient pattern of Indian Ocean trade and exploration, which brought INDONESIAN immigrants as well as BANTU and Muslim SWAHILI from the African mainland.

The Indonesian immigrants to Madagascar arrived around the start of the Christian era and are the primary ethnic origin of the Malagasy peoples. They brought the original Austronesian (Malayo-Polynesian) Malagasy language, which diverged into numerous dialects, although these are mutually intelligible. They incorporate Bantu, Arab, Swahili, Indian, French and English words. The Merina form of Malagasy (standardized in 1820) and French are the country's official languages. With limited ancestral, historical and cultural links with the African continent the Malagasy regard themselves as Indonesians more than Africans, although links have been developed with Francophone Africa.

**Unification and colonial rule**

Historically, the island of Madagascar was dominated by the Merina kingdom, which developed from the 15th century, insulated and protected in its highland territory. Irrigation was used to enlarge the area of paddy fields for rice production. The population grew, and a process of political expansion incorporated many smaller kingdoms on and around the central plateau. The Merina kingdom was fully centralized under King Nampoina, who ruled 1797–1810. This process of consolidation would inevitably have resulted in a single unified Malagasy state, but this was forestalled by the French at the end of the 19th century, who imposed a single colonial government instead.

The Malagasy are traditionally agriculturists. Their economy is based particularly on the culti-vation of rice but also on cattle and livestock-farming. Traditional beliefs associated with ancestor worship, pantheism, spirits and taboos remain strong. Half the Malagasy are now Protestant or Roman Catholic Christians due to missionary activity beginning in the early 19th century. The missionaries also introduced European education, and their schools were extremely well attended: by 1894, some 50,000 children regularly attended schools in the Merina highlands. Around 7% of the population are Muslim.

Early 19th-century processes of modernization and Westernization approved by the king were revived again in the 1860s. A creative indigenous cultural life also developed, probably assisted by the free time allowed by the widespread ownership of slaves.

# MALAWIANS or Malawi

People of the Republic of Malawi, capital Lilongwe, which occupies territory to the west and south of Lake Malawi (Lake Nyasa). The country's population of more than 10 million is overwhelmingly BANTU in origin, 60% composed of MARAVI peoples, notably the CHEWA, NYANJA, Lake TONGA and Tumbuka. The LOMWE and YAO are also numerous.

The country's origins lie in the development of the late-medieval Maravi confederacy, which combined various Bantu peoples in the central and southern territories of modern-day Malawi, and immigrants from the north and east. It developed a sophisticated political system that reached full maturity in the 17th century, as well as a rich oral and written culture, the latter influenced by contacts with the Portuguese in the Zambezi Valley and later the British. Agricultural production also improved.

This flourishing indigenous society was undermined by the growth of the slave trade in the 18th and 19th centuries to satisfy the demand on the SWAHILI coast, and the arrival of armed traders. From the 1830s the Yao were particularly prominent in slave-raiding, and exerted control over large areas. They were heavily influenced by the spread of Islam from the coast, which remains an important religion in Malawi, followed by around 20% of the population.

Other regions were dominated by the incoming NGONI, a small proportion of the Malawian population today, who were fleeing ZULU expansion to the south.

This period also saw the arrival of Christianity through the various missions that were established in the country. From 1859 David Livingstone – and other missionary societies from Scotland and elsewhere – became involved in local affairs, concerned to pacify the region and end the slave trade. They gained the support of the British government, which also had trade and strategic interests, and in 1891 it declared the Nyasaland Districts Protectorate, which became the colony of Nyasaland in 1907.

**Colonial rule**

Colonial control of Nyasaland was characterized by agricultural underdevelopment among the Malawians and by government policies that favoured British settlers and their developing cash-crop sector. Large agricultural estates still enjoy government backing and remain successful producers for export, especially in tea and tobacco, while most of the population remain poor and undernourished subsistence farmers in a country of food surpluses. Around 90% of people are employed in the agricultural sector.

The iniquities of colonial control led to a growing nationalist feeling that rejected the brief settler-inspired Federation of Rhodesia and Nyasaland, dissolved in 1963, and to full independence the following year under Hastings Kamuzu Banda. His leadership degenerated into one-party rule under the Malawi Congress Party, and he became President for life in 1971. In 1994, however, his rule ended in multi-party elections, though political difficulties remain. The government is still widely attacked for gerrymandering, political favouritism in public appointments, and corruption. The ordinary life of the Malawians, who mostly live in traditional villages, continues much the same. Their rich heritage of song, dance, arts and crafts remains intact within modern society. Malawi remains one of the most peaceful countries in Africa, which has encouraged foreign investment and growing success in the extraction of minerals and other natural resources.

**"** [The Malinke are] perfectly blacke, living a most idle life, except for two months of the yeare. **"**

Richard Jobson, 1625

# MALIANS

The people of the Republic of Mali. The so-called 'black' population of largely agricultural MANDE-speaking Malians includes the MALINKE, BAMBARA, DYULA, KHASONKA and SONINKE, who form the majority, as well as the SONGHAI, SENUFO, DOGON and BOBO. The 'white' population includes the nomadic BERBERS, MOORS and FULANI of the north. The social structure of the region remains traditionally hierarchical, and a mirror image of this has emerged in the new urban population, especially in the capital Bamako, comprising commercial, government, service and industrial workers. The population numbers around 11 million, of whom 90% are Muslim.

At independence in 1960 the republic, formerly French Sudan, adopted the name of Mali, the great Malinke trading empire that flourished on the upper and middle Niger from the 13th to the 16th centuries AD. This empire was an important route for the Islamization of much of West Africa before it was attacked by the TUAREG, WOLOF, MOSSI and others, leading to its collapse by 1550.

The region was conquered by the French in the late 19th century, and was briefly part of a federation with Senegal prior to independence. After 1960 Mali followed a Marxist policy and established a cultural revolution that led to popular discontent, a military coup and serious political tension, leading to democratic reforms in the 1990s.

## MALINKE or Mandingo or Manding

A people who mainly occupy the western Sudan. They speak Malinke forms of the MANDE branch of the Niger-Congo language family, and are divided into many autonomous groups under the authority of hereditary nobles. From the 7th century AD Kangaba was the nucleus and capital of the great Malinke empire of Mali after which the modern republic is named.

The Malinke are cultivators who keep cattle which are important as currency and for prestige. They commonly live in defended villages in patrilineal groups.

## MANDE or Mandija

A linguistic classification forming a branch of Niger-Congo that includes 40 languages spoken by more than 20 million related people in West Africa. Mande-speakers mainly occupy the savannah plateau and include the BAMBARA, BOZO, DYULA, MALINKE, SONINKE, SUSU and MENDE. Possibly independently, they developed a very early agricultural economy (3000–4000 BC), the foundation of a sophisticated society reflected in their medieval trading empires of Ghana and Mali. The Mande remain largely traders, cultivators and cattle-pastoralists within a pronounced hierarchical social structure. Many are Muslim, and polygyny is variably adopted.

## MANDINGO

See MALINKE.

## MANJAKO or Mandyako

One of the ethnic groups of the Gambia, Senegal and Guinea-Bissau, also known as Manjaco or Manjago. They number only around 115,000 and are generally employed in agriculture, as either farmers or labourers on the groundnut plantations. In Guinea-Bissau the Manjako form around 10% of the population. In the late 19th century they actively opposed Portuguese colonization. They speak one of the Niger-Congo languages and are mainly Christian or Muslim, though animism is still strong.

## MARAVI or Malawi

Several BANTU-speaking peoples of Malawi, Zambia and Mozambique. The most numerous are the CHEWA and NYANJA peoples. The Maravi clans originated in the Congo (Kinshasa), and around 1500 adopted a centralized LUBA-LUNDA system of royal government. The powerful Maravi confederacy, or empire, peaked in the 17th century. Much of its wealth was obtained from trading slaves, ivory and iron goods to the SWAHILI COAST and the Portuguese. They still engage in trade, farming, hunting and fishing, and ironwork. Their social organization is matrilineal and families are polygynous.

| Malians: main ethnic groups |
| --- |
| Bambara |
| Berbers |
| Bobo |
| Dogon |
| Dyula |
| Fulani |
| Khasonka |
| Moors |
| Senufo |
| Songhai |
| Soninke |

Malinke

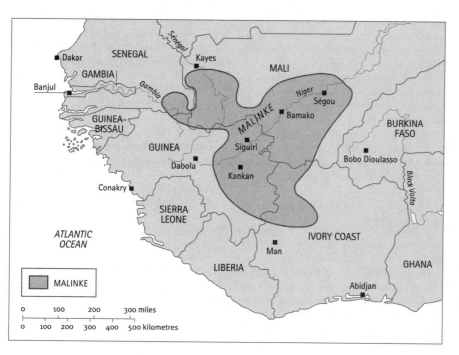

*"When the slave trade was brisk the Maravi made prisoners and kept them for sale, but now they kill all they can of the enemy."*

David Livingstone's diary, 24 March 1856

## MASSA or Banana

A farming people who live along the River Chari of southern Chad and northern Cameroon. They are Massa-speaking Nilotic immigrants to the region who arrived towards the end of the 18th century and today number around 200,000.

The Massa cultivate cotton and groundnuts as cash crops but also fish and raise livestock. Their distinguishing characteristics are their isolationism and animist religion, which in view of their arid environment, naturally centres on a rain god.

## MATABELE

See NDEBELE.

## MAURITANIANS

People of the Islamic Republic of Mauritania, a former FRENCH colony on the northwestern Atlantic coast of Africa. The chief ethnic groups are MOORS or Mauri (60%), the TUKULOR in the populous Senegal River valley, and the WOLOF, SONINKE and FULANI in the southern part of the country. Because Mauritania is mostly desert, roughly 25% of its people follow a nomadic lifestyle, and the population density is one of the lowest in Africa.

The official national language is French, and Arabic is also spoken in addition to Moorish Hassaniyah and other local languages. Most of the population relies on subsistence agriculture and pastoralism, although the country benefits from vast iron ore and other mineral reserves. Almost all Mauritanians are Muslim, though they adhere to several different religious orders and sects.

## MAURITIANS

Inhabitants of Mauritius, the Indian Ocean island republic of the Mascarene group. The island was known to Arab seafarers, visited by the Portuguese in the early 1500s then occupied by the Dutch in 1598, after whose governor, Maurice of Nassau, it was named. The French East India Company took possession in 1721, and as part of the French empire it was known as Île de France. Mauritius was captured by Britain in 1810 and became independent in 1968.

Its mixed population of Indo-Mauritians (two-thirds of the 1.2 million inhabitants), Africans, MALAGASY and others still speak the French creole, Morisyen, as well as English and an INDO-ARYAN (DRAVIDIAN) language. Around half the population are Hindu, a further 25% Roman Catholic and most of the remainder Muslim. Ancestors of most Mauritians were imported as indentured labourers to work the sugar and other plantations during the colonial period. The economy has been successfully diversified in recent decades so that tourism, manufacturing and general agriculture now employ many people, although sugar cultivation remains vitally important.

## MBAKA or Bwaka or Ngbaka

A people who inhabit northwestern Congo (Kinshasa) but are concentrated in the southwestern Lobaye region of the Central African Republic, where they have been influential in the country's development. They were the local administrative agents of colonial control in French Equatorial Africa and have provided many political leaders in recent years, including the infamous president Jean-Bédel Bokassa. Many Mbaka are fishermen along the River Ubangi. They currently number around 250,000.

## MBANZA or Mbanja

A people who are scattered throughout northwestern Congo (Kinshasa). They form one of the largest ethnic groups in the country, around 600,000 strong, and are mostly small farmers who speak BANDA, an Adamawa-UBANGI language of the Niger-Congo classification.

## MBUM

A BANTU-speaking ethnic group numbering around 800,000 in northern Cameroon, adjoining the Central African Republic, Congo (Kinshasa) and Chad. Historically they were more widespread, but they declined in the face of FULANI slave-raiding and active opposition to French and German colonization into the early

20th century. Today they are mostly small farmers and around half are Muslim.

## MBUNDU

A people comprising numerous groups who occupy north-central Angola. They number around 2.5 million, roughly a quarter of the country's population, and speak various forms of the BANTU Kimbundu language. They migrated to the present territory from the interior during the 16th century and formed several kingdoms with economies based on agriculture, trade and craft skills. They were incorporated into the Portuguese colony of Angola, and were later prominent in the struggle for independence, finally achieved in 1975.

## MBUTI

See PYGMIES.

## MENDE

The largest ethnic group in Sierra Leone. They inhabit the south and east of the country and are also present in Liberia. MANDE-speaking Mane soldiers moved into the region from Jenne in Mali via the modern-day coast of Ghana from the 15th century. Through inter-marriage, they formed the Mende people, now 35% of Sierra Leone's population (roughly 1.85 million). Their advance was halted in the northwest of the country by the susu, another branch of the Mande, so they predominate in the south.

The Mende are an agricultural people: 80% are small farmers who have traditionally practised shifting cultivation. This is organized on a cooperative basis by related family groups, and the process of cultivation is undertaken both by men, who are responsible for the heavy work, and women, who sow and weed. The drift of young men to the towns and cities of the region has led to some labour shortages in the rural areas in recent years.

Mende society is organized into patrilineal chiefdoms, each comprising sub-chiefdoms responsible for particular local areas. In Mende chiefdoms secret *poro* societies regulate social conduct, organize military training and undertake ritual observance and other tasks. The women's secret society, *sande*, initiates girls into womanhood. Traditional religion is complex and includes belief in ancestor spirits and witchcraft. Elaborate masks and stone carvings are a feature of Mende customs and ritual observance. Roughly one-third of the Mende are Muslim, however, and syncretic religions are common.

## MERINA or Antimerina or Hove or Hova

A people who live in the central plateau of the Indian Ocean island of Madagascar. This location gave rise to their name, Merina, meaning 'elevated people', and from the 16th century they formed the island's only powerful kingdom. The Merina are the country's largest group of ethnic MALAGASY, numbering more than 3 million, and comprise the Fotsy, descendants of free people, and the Mainty, whose ancestors formed a slave underclass. Education is important to the Merina and has promoted their domination of important areas of the country's life.

## MEROITIC CULTURE

A society based on a new capital of the KUSHITES created at Meroe on the Middle Nile after Napata (see NAPATAN CULTURE) was sacked by Egypt in 593 BC. The Meroitic was a more indigenous 'African' culture, less influenced by Egypt, which ended with invasion by the AKSUMITES from around AD 320. Kushite gods became more prominent, particularly the lion god Apedemak. A new Meroitic alphabet and script were developed from around 300 BC, and major advances were made in building, agriculture and ironwork. Trade and the production of gold were important pillars of Kushite wealth and power.

## MERU

A people who occupy an area of the Serengeti in Tanzania and central Kenya. Their Kenyan tribal centre is the town of Meru, 175 km / 110 miles northeast of the capital Nairobi, although they originated on the coast and moved inland only in the early 18th century. They are BANTU-speaking agriculturists and cattle-herders who exploit the fertile central Rift highlands, and they are also known for their skills as bee-keepers. The Meru are closely related to the EMBU and KIKUYU and number more than 700,000.

## MONGO

BANTU Mongo-speakers, also called Mongo-Nkundo, of Congo (Kinshasa). Their language is the *lingua franca* of the northwestern part of the country and is spoken by around 7 million people. The Mongo practise shifting agriculture in which the women are responsible for cultivation and the men for the work of clearing new forest and for hunting and fishing.

Inter-marriage is common with neighbouring PYGMIES, many of whom live in a symbiotic relationship with the Mongo. In religion, the Mongo maintain a strong belief in witchcraft and sorcery, practise ancestor-worship, and honour nature spirits to ensure fertility.

## MOORS

An ethnolinguistic group of northwest Africa, concentrated in Morocco, Mauritania, Senegal, Mali and Gambia, although the term is sometimes applied to Muslim groups further afield. The ROMANS used the Latin name *Mauri* to describe the subjects of the imperial province of Mauretania, extending across parts of modern-day Morocco and Algeria. It is still used to identify the people of today's Islamic Republic of Mauritania although this region is much further to the southwest. The name is also applied to those who speak the Moorish Hassaniyah dialect.

The ancestral Moors were largely a mixture of ARABS and BERBERS who were responsible for the Muslim conquest of the Iberian Peninsula in the 8th century AD. They intermingled with the local Spanish population and created an advanced civilization that was brought to an end by Castile and other Christian kingdoms in the Wars of Reconquest with the fall of Granada in 1492. A steadily increasing flow of Moorish refugees had crossed to North Africa, culminating in the expulsion of all Muslims from the dominions of Queen Isabella I of Castile and Aragon in 1502. The exodus continued from elsewhere in Spain until the early 17th century. Some 200,000 are known to have settled in the coastal regions of modern-day Tunisia and they brought with them more advanced techniques in agriculture and irrigation.

Today's population of Moors also includes a large proportion of black Africans, called the *Sudan*, whose ancestral origin lay mostly in sub-Saharan West Africa and the Sudanese region. They were originally incorporated into Moorish society as slaves and freed servants, and this role of servitude still lingers in North African societies where they are also a poor underclass in the urban centres, although in Mauritania they have managed to predominate in administration, largely through educational opportunities introduced in the French colonial period. The *Sudan* were, and are, the lowest caste in a strongly hierarchical society traditionally comprising vassals and artisans below noble castes of clerics and warriors drawn from the 'white' Moors, descended from Arab peoples.

The Moors number around 5 million, the largest population (2.5 million) in Morocco, followed by Mauritania (1.3 million), although accurate population figures are difficult to obtain. The Imraguen are an important sub-group living in Mauritania. In the desert areas Moors have a nomadic lifestyle, moving to new pastures as required by their camels, sheep, goats and cattle. Others cultivate crops in the oases where suitable land is inevitably limited. Many Moors also now live settled lives in the towns and cities.

## MOROCCANS

People of the Kingdom of Morocco, separated from Spain by the narrow Straits of Gibraltar. They have a distinctive sophisticated culture that emerged at the crossroads of the Mediterranean Sea and Atlantic Ocean, Europe and Africa. The country also has a proud history of independence, although it has been invaded many times during its eventful history and was subject to French and Spanish colonial occupation throughout the first half of the 20th century.

The country's founding people were the BERBERS, who established themselves in the region towards the end of the 2nd millennium

> *“* [The Moors are] a savage and superstitious people. *”*
>
> Edward Gibbon, 1776–88

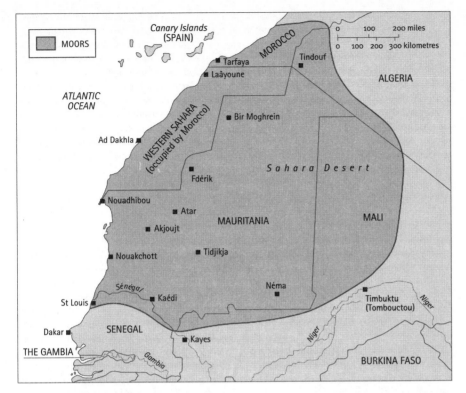

BC. It later became part of the ROMAN province of Mauretania. From the late 7th century AD north-west Africa was invaded by Muslim BEDOUIN ARABS and later Banu Hilal, both from the east, then by the gradual arrival of Arab (and Jewish) refugees from Spain, the re-conquest of which by the Christians was finally completed in 1492. Pre-Arab Berber Christianity gave way to (eventually Sunni) Islam, which remains the dominant faith.

Around 98% of today's Moroccan population of some 30 million is composed of ethnic Berbers and Arabs who have inter-married over many generations. There is still a core Berber population of around 10 million, the largest in North Africa, concentrated in the Rif and Atlas mountains, which rise to some 4000 m / 13,000 ft. The Berber language provides much of the distinctiveness of the Berber people, who are divided into the Rif, Shluh and Tamazight groups, although many also speak Arabic, the official and most widely spoken language in Morocco. Absorbed into this large Arab-Berber population are descendants of slaves and other migrants from sub-Saharan Africa. There has recently been renewed interest in Berber oral traditions and other aspects of culture as well as Moroccan contemporary literature in various languages and the visual arts. Otherwise the nature of daily and cultural life in the country is as varied and sophisticated as any of the other Mediterranean North African countries.

The early Muslim conquest of Morocco was fiercely opposed by the Berbers, who adhered to the separate Kharijite branch of Islam and continued to retain a measure of independence focused on their mountain strongholds. They were helped by their great geographical distance from the ruling Umayyad caliphs of Damascus and their successors, the Abbasids of Baghdad. From the 11th century the Berbers again took control of the country, initially under the confederation of the Almoravids, who were nomadic Sanhaja Berbers of southern Morocco and the western Sahara. They were responsible for introducing the refined Islamic culture of Muslim Spain, which they also controlled along with a vast swathe of territory to the east of Morocco as far as Algiers, paid for by control of the West African gold trade and by increasing agricultural development. One result of this cultural renaissance can still be seen in the sublime architecture of the city of Marrakesh, which became their new capital. This involvement and close proximity to Europe and one of the world's major maritime highways has continued to exert a lasting influence on Moroccan culture and development.

**Towards modern Morocco**

The Almoravids were succeeded by the rigorously Islamic Almohads, influenced by the sufi mystics, who became very influential and popular in Morocco from the late 12th century. The Almohads were succeeded in turn by the northern Marinids, before the political fragmentation of the country in the mid-15th century. Moroccans decisively repulsed both OTTOMAN and Christian attacks in the 1500s, and in the 16th century the Alawite dynasty of sharifs (exercising a combination of religious influence and secular authority) obtained power. Their descendants still rule Morocco today from the capital of Rabat.

During the late 19th century, Spain obtained additional territory to add to its enclaves on the coast, and in 1912 France declared a protectorate over the country, but Morocco regained its independence in 1956. The French and Spanish languages are still quite widely spoken.

Parliamentary democracy was introduced in the 1970s, although in this system of constitutional monarchy the king retains ultimate political power. Nevertheless, under the rule of King Hassan II, who died in 1999, liberal reforms took place together with a measure of political repression. He also pursued the widely supported policy of claiming the Western Sahara for Morocco, backed by military force, an issue that remains unresolved (see WESTERN SAHARANS). The radical Islamic opposition has been largely kept in check, though they staged a large-scale terrorist attack on Casablanca in 2003 and have been strongly antagonistic to the recent attempts by King Muhammad VI to introduce greater equality for women within marriage.

A large proportion of Moroccans live below the poverty line, and there are extensive slums in the larger cities. Despite universal schooling the literacy rate is only around 50%. The country's varied economy, largely based on farming, phosphate and other mineral extraction, industrial production, fishing and tourism has developed steadily in recent decades, but the rapid rate of population growth has reduced the benefits it could have bestowed. Today, continued drought, slow economic growth and large-scale unemployment are particularly serious problems.

## MOSSI

GUR Mole-speaking agriculturists of Burkina Faso. From the late 14th century invading horsemen from the area of modern-day Nigeria settled among the indigenous Gur inhabitants and founded several kingdoms, notably Ouagadougou, the capital of the feudal paramount chief known as the *Mogho Naba* (Lord of the World). They developed trade, especially in slaves sent to the coast, but this was curtailed by the French conquest of 1896. Large numbers of Mossi work in the Gold Coast cocoa and Senegalese and Gambian groundnut plantations. They number around 6 million, half the population of Burkina Faso, and roughly one-third are (Sunni) Muslims.

## MOZAMBICANS

People of the Republic of Mozambique. The modern population of around 20 million is largely BANTU, though there is a great deal of cultural and linguistic variation. The largest ethnic groups are the related MAKUA and LOMWE of the northeast, followed by the TSONGA (including the SHANGANE) south of the Save River, MALAWIANS, SHONA (who are concentrated in central Mozambique between the Zambezi and the Save rivers), YAO, SWAHILI and MAKONDE. Prior to independence in 1975, Mozambique was for many years a part of the PORTUGUESE empire, and Portuguese remains the official language, although the vast majority of Mozambicans speak their own languages, many of which are shared with people in adjoining Zimbabwe, Zambia, Malawi, Tanzania and South Africa. Swahili is the language of the northern coast and East Africa as far as the Banadir Coast of Somalia. A small number of Portuguese are still resident in the country, mainly in the capital Maputo, Quelimane and the major cities, where their language is more commonly spoken.

The vast majority of Mozambicans are agriculturists who observe a system of matrilineal descent to the south of the Zambezi river and patrilineal descent to the north. Most are part of a wider regional, transnational, ethnolinguistic group with their own distinctive cultural identities in terms of social organization and artistic, oral and musical traditions. These have been exploited to develop a vibrant modern culture in the visual arts and popular music. Literature also emerged strongly under 20th-century colonial rule and entered mainstream consciousness with the liberation movement, although a large part of the population remains illiterate. Since independence the national newspapers, radio and television stations have continued under government control.

The Mozambican government's early emphasis on socialism has given way since the late 1980s to a less prescriptive attitude in the process of state-building, which has accommodated the diversity of traditional beliefs and practices. The government's continued emphasis on the importance of African culture and achievements is partly reflected in the development of the museums and archives sector. The government has also allowed renewed religious freedom: almost half of the population follows traditional beliefs in natural and ancestral spirits, while the rest are mostly Christian or Muslim.

### Colonial and post-colonial history

Mozambique was subject to Portuguese economic and military influence from the end of the 15th century, particularly along the Zambezi River, as a way of gaining control of the gold trade. From the 18th century the slave trade became important, and many slaves were exported to South America, Arabia and the French Indian Ocean islands. Slaving also radically re-ordered traditional societies, helping to

lead to the creation of the NGONI state of Gaza in modern-day southern Mozambique in the early 19th century, which the Portuguese conquered in the 1890s. The country's boundaries were determined by the European scramble for territory, and Portugal's colony incorporated a random amalgam of peoples and cultures. The military campaigns to extend Portuguese authority across the territory continued until 1917, and the suppression of a revolt by the Shona Barwe people.

The country was systematically exploited by the Portuguese government and by private companies for its economic wealth. A major impetus behind colonial control was the hope of discovering rich gold and mineral deposits, as had occurred in South Africa. The imposition of taxation and other factors encouraged many tens of thousands of Mozambicans to become migrant labourers in the South African gold and diamond mines, and this practice has continued into modern times. The Portuguese also used compulsory labour on a large scale, and although the worst colonial abuses were modified after 1926, continued oppression, economic exploitation and the arrival of large numbers of favoured Portuguese settlers in the 1950s and 1960s led to a popular revolt in 1964 led by FRELIMO, the Mozambique Liberation Front, which won power in a one-party independent Mozambique in 1975.

Subsequent policy failures included centralized control of the agricultural sector and enforced 'villagization', also experienced by TANZANIANS, which antagonized many. FRELIMO's support for liberation movements in Rhodesia (now Zimbabwe) and South Africa also led to economic loss and to retribution, particularly in the form of sponsorship by the governments of those countries of the Mozambique National Resistance, RENAMO. The ensuing brutal civil war caused immeasurable dislocation and suffering throughout Mozambique, before a peace accord was signed in 1992. This successful reconciliation has allowed the development of a healthy democratic culture and moderately successful economy.

**Mozambicans: main ethnic groups**

Lomwe
Makonde
Makua
Maravi
Shangane
Shona
Tsonga
Swahili
Yao

# NAMA or Naman or Namaqua

The largest of the indigenous KHOIKHOI populations of the Kalahari Desert in southwest Africa. They are traditionally cattle-, sheep- and goat-pastoralists, and the hunter-gathering DAMARA were their clients in a mutually beneficial relationship. Their numbers seriously declined in the wars with the colonial authorities in German South-West Africa (now Namibia) in the late 19th and early 20th centuries; and in conflicts with the HERERO (see NAMIBIANS). A large number sought refuge in Botswana, where many still live, and their total population today is estimated at more than 200,000. There are also many who have mixed Herero and OVAMBO ancestry. The Nama speak Khoikhoi and their culture is indistinguishable from that of the KHOISAN generally. The Namaqualand region straddles the Namibia–South Africa border.

# NAMIBIANS

People of the Republic of Namibia, capital Windhoek. Namibia has a small population of around 1.9 million scattered across a largely arid and inhospitable region. This largely comprises the coastal Namib Desert, bounded by the Skeleton Coast to the west, and the eastern Kalahari Desert. The South African enclave of Walvis Bay on the central coast has been administered by Namibia since 1994. There is an eastern extension known as the Caprivi Strip giving access to the Zambezi River.

The early inhabitants of the region were the SAN, or Bushmen, who were pushed out of southern Namibia by the NAMA and associated DAMARA people. Further north, the OVAMBO formed several kingdoms, their economies based on mixed farming, while the pastoral HEREROS from central Africa formed a unified but unstable chiefdom.

European contacts were few until the 1860s, although trade in ivory, firearms and later cattle became significant and helped to upset the indigenous balance of military power. The Oorlam-Nama from Cape Province modelled their military organization on the mobile Boer commando and took power among the existing

Nama and Damara, creating a kingdom under Chief Jonker Afrikaner based near Windhoek, which led to friction with the Hereros. The territory was connected with GERMAN trading interests and was swept up in the European scramble for colonial possessions in Africa. From 1884 it was declared the German protectorate of South-West Africa, and resistance to colonial control was severely suppressed.

**British and South African rule**

During World War I, German South-West Africa was taken by British forces from South Africa, and from 1920 it was governed by the Dominion (later the Republic) of South Africa under a League of Nations mandate.

After World War II, South Africa declined to substitute United Nations trusteeship status for this mandate. Later, the South African government attempted to integrate South-West Africa into the nationalist republic. This was electorally significant because the white voters there, some of them still of German extraction, offered strong support to the Afrikaner nationalist government.

After 106 years of foreign occupation, the territory finally achieved independence from the South African Republic in 1990, after a long-standing war of liberation headed by the South-West Africa People's Organization. 'Namibia' was officially adopted as the name for South-West Africa in 1968, but only came into official use after independence, under the presidency of Sam Nujoma.

The vast majority of Namibians (85%) are black Africans, mainly the Ovambo (the largest group, forming half the population), Herero, Damara, Nama and CAPRIVIANS. The Kavango people, divided into several sub-groups and numbering around 100,000, work as small farmers. Most Namibians are engaged in livestock and agricultural production, fishing and some mining. Diamonds have been produced since 1908. Mixed-race Namibians form around 10% of the population and include CAPE COLOUREDS and REHOBOTHERS. A small proportion are whites of European descent, namely AFRIKANERS and GERMANS, and English is the country's official language. The vast majority of Namibians are Christian, mostly Lutheran.

**Namibians: main ethnic groups**

Caprivians
Damara
Herero
Kavango
Nama
Ovambo

# NANDI

KALENJIN-speakers of the Southern Nilotic language group, numbering around 450,000 (see NILOTES). These cattle pastoralists and cultivators, who were skilled warriors, occupied the western Kenyan highlands from before 1500. They later suffered cattle-raiding by the MAASAI, but after strengthening their loose tribal confederation around 1850 they expanded into Maasai territory, adopted tactics to neutralize the power of early firearms, and fended off SWAHILI trading expeditions. After ten years of fighting they finally submitted to British rule in 1905. Today, cash crops, including maize and tobacco, are more important than cattle, and many Nandi work in the urban centres.

# NAPATAN CULTURE

An African culture based on Napata (now Marawi) on the Dongola Reach of the Middle Nile, Sudan. It was formerly capital of the kingdom of the KUSHITES of Nubia, from around 900 BC. Napatan culture was influenced by Egypt, using the same hieroglyphic script and worshipping the same gods. The more strongly indigenous MEROITIC CULTURE developed after the Kushite capital moved south to Meroe following the sack of Napata by Egypt in 593 BC. Napata remained the religious centre of the Kushite state, the place of royal coronations and burials.

# NAQADAH I CULTURE

See AMRATIAN CULTURE.

# NAQADAH II CULTURE

See GERZEAN CULTURE.

# NARA

Semi-nomadic cattle pastoralists of northwestern Ethiopia and adjoining Eritrea. Many of the small population are also hoe cultivators. They speak the Eastern Sudanic language of the Chari-Nile branch of Nilo-Saharan, and are thought to number more than 100,000.

# NDEBELE

The second-largest ethnic group of Zimbabwe (formerly Rhodesia). Once known also as the Amandebele and the Matabele, they constitute some 20% of the population and are situated in the southwestern area of the country around Zimbabwe's second city, Bulawayo. A population of nearly 2 million Ndebele lives in Zimbabwe, while a few remain in the northern Transvaal and Botswana. Their language is Sindebele. They played a prominent part in the struggle for an independent Zimbabwe, but they have been persecuted under President Robert Mugabe (since 1980), who is a member of the rival SHONA people.

The Ndebele are a Northern NGUNI group who emerged out of the conflicts associated with the rise to prominence of the Zulu state. They left the Zulu heartland in the 1830s as part of the great dispersal of peoples known as the *Mfecane*, or crushing of peoples. Led by their king, Mzilikazi (1790–1868), they settled in the western Transvaal, where they later came into contact with AFRIKANER or Boer trekkers, the GRIQUA and British missionaries. Mzilikazi formed a relationship with the London Missionary Society missionary Robert Moffat, the father-in-law of David Livingstone.

Defeated by the Afrikaners, they moved on across the Limpopo River in 1838, travelling as far as the Zambezi before settling in southern Zimbabwe around their capital Gubulawayo. The Ndebele had incorporated many SOTHO-TSWANA and Shona peoples in the course of this migration. They brought with them Zulu fighting capacity and soon established their authority over many areas of central Zimbabwe, also coming into conflict with the TSWANA to the south and the LOZI to the north. They built up large cattle herds and also grew millet and maize. Their age regiments, characteristic of the northern Nguni people, repeatedly raided neighbours in order to maintain their power through tribute.

After Mzilikazi's death in 1868, one of his sons, Lobengula, ruled as king 1870–94 and became one of the most celebrated African leaders of the later 19th century. Lobengula's court became a honey pot for hunters, prospectors, traders, treaty makers and missionaries in the

Ndebele

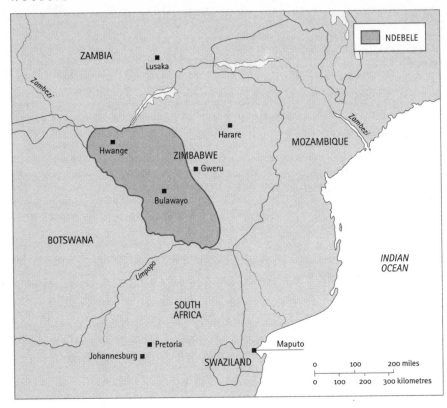

1870s and 1880s, all hoping to secure influence over the region he supposedly ruled.

### Colonial Rhodesia

It was the existence of Lobenguela's Ndebele state, with its alleged authority over the Shona, that enabled Cecil Rhodes to secure treaties and send his invading force of Europeans from Britain and the Cape into Mashonaland, the country of the Shona, in 1890. Between 1890 and 1893 these whites, settled among the 'vassal' Shona, maintained an uneasy peace with the Ndebele. But war broke out in 1893, largely because the Ndebele continued to raid the Shona, but also because the whites were spoiling for a fight in order to restore the fortunes of a stagnating colony.

The Ndebele were defeated and Lobengula died, probably of smallpox, at the end of the war. In its aftermath, much Ndebele land and most of their cattle herds were confiscated.

Unsuitable reserves were set aside by the victorious whites for Ndebele occupation.

The Ndebele, along with many Shona, participated in an uprising against the whites in 1896. In the peace settlement, Rhodes permitted their chieftaincies to remain, and they were active in labour migration throughout southern Africa. The Ndebele participated in exhibitions in Britain and elsewhere from the end of the 1890s, acting out their own conquest. One of Lobengula's sons, who appeared in these displays, married a white woman and settled in England, arousing predictable racial animosity. The Ndebele subsequently contributed much to political resistance and trade unionism in colonial Rhodesia.

## NDONGO

A sub-group of the MBUNDU people of Angola. The historical kingdom of Ndongo was based on the region inland from Luanda, Angola's capital, and established its independence from the KONGO kingdom at the Battle of Caxito in 1556. The Portuguese began the conquest of Ndongo territory in 1575, finally incorporating it into Angola in 1671. The eastern Ndongo retained some autonomy into the late 19th century.

## NDOWE

A group of peoples of Equatorial Guinea. They arrived in the country from the inland Ubangi River area in the 14th century. FANG expansion in the 19th century probably drove them towards the coast and their present homeland along the Rio Muni coastal plain, giving rise to their other name of *Los Playeros* (Beach People). They are agriculturists who speak the Kombe language, and are mostly Roman Catholic Christians.

## NEGROES

One of the main ethnic divisions of humanity. Negroid peoples originated in West Africa and now populate most of the African continent south of the Sahara. The trade in slaves also dispersed many to North and South America, the Caribbean and the Middle East. From Latin, via Portuguese and Spanish, 'Negro' simply means 'black' in reference to their skin colour. As an adaptation to the tropical environment this and other physical characteristics developed through a process of natural selection. PYGMIES of the Equatorial forest region are possibly a Negro sub-group. Most negroid peoples of West Africa speak Niger-Congo languages which began to develop around 6000 BC, of which BANTU is a branch. Others speak NILO-SAHARAN.

The term 'negro' became widely adopted in the USA for the descendants of slaves (see AFRICAN AMERICANS), but it has acquired a pejorative, racist sense today.

## NEMBA or Nembe

A sub-group of the IJAW people of southern Nigeria. Like other Ijaw people, they traditionally live by fishing and trade, and speak an Ijoid language that is part of the cluster known as Brass Ijo. Their town and port of Brass was one of the last of the region's slave depots to remain active. It remains an important agricultural and fishing centre.

## NGALE

See NGBANDI.

## NGBAKA

See MBAKA.

## NGBANDI or Gbandi

A people who live in the southern Central African Republic and northern Congo (Kinshasa). They speak a Ubangian language of the Adamawa-UBANGI branch of Niger-Congo similar to the neighbouring GBAYA and BANDA. It gave rise to the creole SANGA language. The Ngbandi are a martial people who originated in the Sudan, and in the 18th century a branch of the Ngbandi conquered ZANDE territory. Weapons such as spears and knives produced by their craftsmen have always been highly prized. They are agricultural, the women undertaking much of the cultivation and the men also hunting and fishing. Ancestor-worship is important in Ngbandi society, in which chiefs have an important priestly role.

## NGONI

One of several peoples displaced by the conflicts associated with the rise of the ZULU state, found today in Tanzania, Zambia, and Mozambique. They are patrilineal and retain some cultural characteristics of their Northern NGUNI parentage, but generally they inter-married with the people among whom they settled, and adopted local languages.

In the late 1820s and 1830s, at least four groups of Ngoni moved northwards from northern Natal. These were led by the chiefs of the Ndwandwe, one of the peoples defeated in the rise of the Zulu kingdom. After a brief sojourn in southern Mozambique – where the community known as the SHANGANE decided to stay and settle down – they headed deeper into Central Africa.

*n*

One group, led by Zwangendaba, crossed the Zambezi River during an eclipse of the sun in 1835. This group, including assimilated TSONGA and SHONA people, settled in southeastern Tanzania, and later further split, contributing Ngoni people to regions that later became northern Malawi, eastern Zambia and northern Mozambique.

Another Ngoni group travelled up the Indian Ocean coast and also entered southern Tanzania. Yet another moved into the KALOLO kingdom in what later became western Zambia, but were defeated and largely eliminated. Elsewhere Ngoni fighting techniques ensured that they dominated local peoples. In the 1890s, the Ngoni in Nyasaland (Malawi) and Northern Rhodesia (Zambia) were defeated by the British in short colonial campaigns. Generally, missionaries avoided them, preferring to settle with their supposedly subject peoples.

## NGUNI

The major BANTU-speaking people who inhabit the coastal regions of southeastern Africa. They have been a considerable source of labour migrants in South Africa in the late 19th and 20th centuries. As a result, they are now widely dispersed in urban areas in the country. Following the pre-colonial migrations of the 1830s, communities of Nguni, including the NDEBELE, NGONI and SHANGANE, are to be found in Zimbabwe, Mozambique, Malawi, Zambia and as far north as Tanzania. However, many of these groups adopted the languages of the peoples with whom they settled and were partially assimilated into their new areas.

In their original heartlands, the Northern Nguni include the SWAZI, most of whom inhabit Swaziland, and the ZULU, who captured the imagination of Europeans during the 19th century because of their military prowess, social organization and striking appearance. The Southern Nguni, separated from the Northern by a belt of territory in central Natal that came to be dominated by whites, include the important community of the XHOSA.

A striking contrast between the Northern and Southern groups is that the Northern formed centralized state systems in the late 18th and 19th centuries, while the Southern remained organized in multiple chieftaincies. The Nguni are mainly cattle-keepers and have been growing maize since the 16th century, soon after the Portuguese introduced it from South America.

The Nguni languages include 'clicks', a linguistic characteristic that connects them to the KHOISAN peoples.

Their history has been one of conflict with whites, in the 'Kaffir Wars' in the case of the Southern group (occurring intermittently between the 1770s and the 1870s) and in the Zulu Wars in the case of the Northern (in the 1830s and in 1879). In the late 19th century the Swazi became prey to white concession-seekers and others hoping to find wealth in their lands. Threatened by AFRIKANERS in the northern Transvaal, they succeeded in securing the protection of the British and surviving as a semi-independent state, though one much reduced in both land and economic circumstances. Today the Nguni, in a variety of ways, have come to dominate the politics of South Africa.

## NGURI

See LOMWE.

## NIANJA or Niassa

See NYANJA.

## NIGERIANS

Inhabitants of the Federal Republic of Nigeria, the pre-eminent state of West Africa, and in terms of population, wealth, development and influence, one of the foremost states of sub-Saharan Africa. This large country, capital Abuja, extends northwards from the tropical rainforests bordering the Gulf of Guinea to the dry savannah. Its Niger Delta is rich in oil and natural-gas reserves, which provide much of the country's wealth. These resources are also being exploited offshore.

Nigeria's population of around 120 million is the largest on the continent and reveals great ethnolinguistic variety. There are around 250 ethnic groups: the major groups are shown in the box opposite.

The northern HAUSA are the single most numerous ethnic group in Nigeria and they have integrated to a large extent with their Muslim co-religionists the FULANI, the two peoples together estimated to comprise around 32% of the population. The next largest are the YORUBA of the southwest, followed by the IGBO of the southeast, each with around 20%.

Languages also point to the complicated origins and historical development of this rich ethnic amalgam. Nigerians have incorporated AFRO-ASIAN, Niger-Congo and NILO-SAHARAN-speakers, over several thousand years. As a former BRITISH colony, English remains the official language and a unifying factor in national life, although Hausa is widely spoken due to their numbers and the post-independence political dominance of the Hausa-Fulani. Pidgin English is also in widespread use. Each of Nigeria's ethnic groups possesses its own cultural forms and institutions, although some, such as the *Ekpo* secret societies, are prevalent among various groups in the southeast of the country. Music and dance have traditionally played an important part in all societies, and the popularity of all traditional art forms has increased in recent years, supported by Nigerian government institutions. Western and Arabic influences have contributed to a lively modern cultural scene, especially in contemporary music.

## History of Nigeria

There is evidence of human occupation in the area of modern-day Nigeria from around 9000 BC, although the earliest recognizable organized and more cultivated society is the Nok culture (*c.* 500 BC–AD 200) of the east-central part of the country. The Nok artistic tradition was notably strong in wood sculpture and bronze-casting and is still evident in contemporary Igbo, Yoruba and other cultures.

During the Middle Ages, the KANURI, Hausa and Fulani peoples established a series of competing chiefdoms and empires that were gradually converted to Islam from the 13th century. Islam is still a powerful force in society. The nomadic Fulani also began to move south and settled in Hausaland where, in the early 19th century, they became rulers of several Hausa emirates and a growing empire.

Britain became directly involved in Nigeria with the aim of suppressing the slave trade and developing legitimate trade in palm oil and other products; these have continued to be of importance to the Nigerian economy. The Lagos district was annexed in 1861, developed into the Colony of Nigeria in 1886, and it later incorporated additional northern territories which held protectorate status. The amalgamated Colony and Protectorate of Nigeria was created in 1914 and gradually evolved into a federation of the different states and peoples in preparation for independence in 1960.

In 1963 Nigeria became a republic. Ethnic tensions soon became apparent, most noticeably in clashes between the Hausa and Igbo. The latter also declared their independence in 1967 as the Republic of Biafra, but were violently suppressed by Nigerian state forces in 1970.

## Religion and economy

Religious as well as ethnic tensions have remained an underlying problem for Nigerians. Around 45% of the country's people are Muslim, mostly in the north and in the southern states of Lagos, Oyo and Ogun. Around 35% are Christians, who predominate in the south. Relations between these two religious groups and the 20% of Nigerians who follow traditional religious beliefs have often been strained. One source of contention is the adoption of Muslim Shari'a law in northern regions, which many, especially non-Muslims living there, regard as draconian. The issue has recently led to rioting and deaths. Generally traditionalists are pantheistic but believe in a single supreme god, often mediated through rulers possessing both spiritual and temporal power, although less so today. Among all the Yoruba, the *oni* of Ife is the traditional spiritual leader.

A further obstacle to the cohesion and development of the Nigerian state has been rapid population growth (the largest in Africa) since the 1950s, placing a strain on economic and national development. It has contributed to the increase in economic migration within Nigeria, heightening the opportunity for friction between communities.

The economy has developed considerably since the 1960s, when oil and gas started to pro-

n

**Nigerians: major ethnic groups**

Edo
Hausa-Fulani
Ibibio
Igbo
Ijaw
Kanuri
Nupe
Tiv
Yoruba

vide the wealth that underlies Nigerian society. It has also led to urban development, industrialization and the growth of government, which has attracted many migrants into the towns and cities. The result of these developments, together with generally adverse international economic conditions in recent decades, has been the stagnation of the agricultural economy, which still employs the majority of Nigerians.

In the Niger Delta, the production of hydrocarbons has led to persistent protest by local people, who gain little by way of financial reward yet suffer from environmental pollution and disruption. Furthermore, corruption is rife in government and administrative circles, fed by oil revenues, although recent reforms have tried to address this issue. Much of the government's income also goes towards the repayment of international debts, depriving Nigerians of much of the benefit of the oil revenues. Since 1966 Nigerians have been ruled mostly by a succession of military regimes, but a return to civilian rule occurred following the elections of 1999, which installed the current government headed by President Olusegun Obasanjo.

## NIGERIENS

Inhabitants of Republic of Niger, on the southern fringe of the Sahara desert. The area was conquered by the FRENCH in 1883–99 and achieved independence in 1960. The name Niger derives from the phrase 'river among rivers' in the TUAREG Tamashek language. The chief ethnic groups are the HAUSA, who form more than half the population of more than 10 million, and the ZERMA, within whose territory lies the capital Niamey. French is widely spoken, and Islam predominates. The population is largely agricultural and pastoral, but has been affected by severe droughts since the 1970s.

## NILO-HAMITIC

See HAMITES.

## NILO-SAHARAN

One of the major surviving African language groups, along with AFRO-ASIAN, Khoisan and Niger-Congo. The proto-language was spoken by people of the central Nile Valley and Sudan region, who developed as pastoralists by the 6th millennium BC. They later adopted cultivation, and moved south and west into the Sahel corridor, reaching Lake Chad, the Niger Valley and the Rift Valley by around 1000 BC. Languages spoken in these regions today are descended from Nilo-Saharan, notably the Chari-Nile (Macro-Sudanic) branch, which includes KUNAMA, Berta, Central Sudanic and Eastern Sudanic. The last includes the Nilotic and Nubian sub-groups, and they are all spoken from southern Egypt and Ethiopia down to Kenya and Tanzania. The other branches of Nilo-Saharan are FUR, spoken in the central Sudan, Koma in Ethiopia–Sudan, Maba in Chad, Saharan in the Sudan and SONGHAI in West Africa.

## NILOTES

A cluster of peoples inhabiting western Kenya, northern Tanzania and Uganda, as well as southern Chad and modern southern Sudan, where they originated. The name refers to their place of origin in the region of the Upper Nile and its tributaries.

They speak related Nilotic, Eastern Sudanic languages of the NILO-SAHARAN family, carried with migrating peoples to a large area of eastern Africa where they intermingled with existing agriculturists to create new ethnic groups.

From the 1st millennium BC, Southern Nilotic pastoralists (also known as the Hill or Highland Nilotes), ancestors of the KALENJIN and NANDI, began drifting southward, followed by Eastern Nilotes (Plains Nilotes), forebears of the MAASAI, KARIMOJONG, TESO and TURKANA. Early in the 1st millennium AD they were followed by the Western Nilotes of the Sudan (River and Lake Nilotes). This group were cultivators as well as pastoralists, forming the SHILLUK, ANUAK, DINKA and NUER in southern Sudan, the LUO predominantly east of Lake Victoria in Kenya, and the ACHOLI, ALUR and LANGO in northern Uganda. The Luo Bito clan provided the ruling dynasties of the NYORO, GANDA and TORO in Uganda.

In the late 20th century the Nilotic peoples numbered around 7 million, and they remain predominantly pastoralists, with cattle central to

**❝** [The Nilotes are] essentially proud, aloof, tenacious of their old beliefs and ideas. **❞**

C.B. and B.Z. Seligman, 1932

their economy and culture. The cattle are carefully tended, protected and exploited for their milk rather than meat. They are a valuable currency, paid as bride-price for example, and reflect the importance and status of their owners. They are sometimes slaughtered for ritual purposes according to traditional beliefs, which centre on ancestor cults and a supreme god, often mediated by ritual experts. These experts have a wider role among those Nilotic peoples who are organized on more egalitarian lines (especially the Luo, Dinka and Nuer, who have no centralized political authority), by acting as peacemakers between the various elements in tribal society. Other Nilotic societies, especially the Shilluk, Acholi and Anuak, are noted for their centralized rule by chiefs, in which the chief also has a religious function to ensure the annual rains and the health and prosperity of the tribe.

Simple hoe cultivation has long been practised together with hunting, the gathering of wild food, and fishing where possible, which has helped to diversify food sources in hostile environments also subject to periodic extremes of weather. The Sudanese Anuak are more given to cultivation than most Nilotes, who are generally sedentary people, although some engage in transhumant or semi-nomadic herding and cultivation, notably the Nuer and Dinka.

## NKOLI

See ANKOLE.

## NKOMI

A people of Gabon, equatorial Africa, who number only several thousand and developed as small-scale traders, fishermen and cultivators. With the arrival of the Portuguese in the late 15th century, and other Europeans, they developed their role as middlemen in trade with the interior, supplying ivory, textiles, slaves and later rubber. They are generally well-educated and speak Myene, a language used by more than 30,000 people in Gabon.

## NSENGA

A BANTU-speaking people of Zambia, with some also living in Mozambique. They are an offshoot of the CHEWA people, with whom they share the Nyanja language. This is also spoken by the NGONI, who attacked and dominated them from the 1860s. Culturally, they also have much in common with other ZAMBIANS such as the BEMBA. The Nsenga were renowned hunters, especially for ivory, and continue to cultivate the fertile soils of the Luangwa River valley. Social structure is based on matrilineal descent and clan affinities within several chiefdoms. The Nsenga number around 330,000.

## NUBA

A people who inhabit the Nuba Hills of Kordofan Province in central Sudan. More than 100 distinct Nuba languages have been identified, all Eastern Sudanic forms of NILO-SAHARAN, although Arabic is the *lingua franca*. This diversity is explained by the Nuba's isolation and the periodic influx of diverse refugee groups over the centuries. Nuba nomads contributed to the downfall of the KUSHITES in the 4th century AD and settled in the Nile Valley. Their language is ancestral to modern Nubian (see NUBIANS). Today, the Nuba of Kordofan keep livestock but are largely hill cultivators.

Most Nuba are Muslim, a religion which gained many adherents in the 19th century through contact with Muslim traders and as an indigenous response to British colonial control, although many of the southern Nuba were converted to Christianity during the period. Traditional beliefs in ancestral spirits and priestly authority also remain strong. Personal adornment includes male body-painting and female scarification. Stick-fighting and wrestling are common sports. There is a Nuban nationalist movement that seeks self-determination despite the largely decentralized political administration of Sudan.

## NUBIANS

Inhabitants of the ancient region of Nubia in upper Egypt and the area of modern-day Khar-

> *"The liberality of the people [the Nsenga] is wonderful.*
>
> David Livingstone's diary, 4 February, 1856

Nuba, Nubians,
Nuer

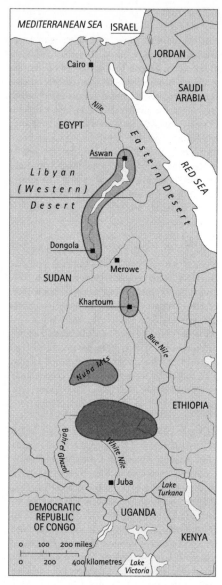

MEDITERRANEAN SEA   ISRAEL
JORDAN
Cairo ■
SAUDI
ARABIA
EGYPT
Nile
Eastern Desert
Aswan
RED SEA
Libyan
(Western)
Desert
Dongola
Merowe
SUDAN
Khartoum
Blue Nile
Nuba Mts
ETHIOPIA
Bahr el Ghazal
White Nile
Juba
Lake
Turkana
DEMOCRATIC
REPUBLIC
OF CONGO
UGANDA
KENYA
0   100   200 miles
0   200   400 kilometres   Lake
Victoria

NUBIANS
NUBA
NUER

n

also extended west into the Libyan Desert and across the Eastern Desert to the Red Sea. The territory from Aswan to the second cataract (Lower Nubia) was named Wawat by the ancient EGYPTIANS, and the area to the south (Upper Nubia) was named Kush, or Cush. The Nile corridor was the crossroads of tropical Africa, a highway for trade and conquest and a magnet for occupation. Many modern Nubians are active in the tourist industry, and they have a rich musical tradition. Most are Muslims, and the Nubian language has been declining in favour of Arabic.

The earliest inhabitants of this area were NILO-SAHARAN-speakers. By the end of the Neolithic period around 3000 BC their descendants had domesticated animals, begun cultivating wheat and barley and developed a prosperous and independent civilization strongly influenced by Egypt. It was the earliest recognizable state in tropical Africa. This so-called A-Group culture in Lower Nubia was destroyed by Egyptian invasion around 2950 BC under the First Dynasty. Egypt dominated Nubia, which it exploited for minerals and other natural resources. The population of Lower Nubia appears to have been decimated, many perhaps used in Egypt as slaves and soldiers, the latter a role in which Nubians have been highly regarded up to modern times. From around 2500 BC a new wave of immigrants arrived in the Nile Valley from the Libyan Desert, who amalgamated with the remaining population. They were probably impelled by the same desiccation that caused the famine and political upheaval in Egypt that is associated with the demise of the Old Kingdom.

Coinciding with this period of Egyptian weakness, the C-Group culture developed in Lower Nubia and the Kerma culture in Upper Nubia, the nascent kingdom of the KUSHITES, named after its capital south of the Third Cataract. Egyptian strength recovered with the creation of the Middle Kingdom in 1991 BC and their authority was again reimposed on Lower Nubia. Gold was mined in the Eastern Desert. Kushite power intensified and by 1650 BC it had occupied Nubia as far north as Aswan. Raids were made into Egypt, which coincided with the HYKSOS seizure of power. Many fine artefacts taken as booty have been found in the huge

toum in the SUDANESE Republic. Their modern population is over 1 million and, particularly since the construction of the dams at Aswan (the first in 1897, the High Dam in 1962), they have been relocated to towns and new villages. In some respects, this concentration has helped to develop their sense of identity. Historically, Nubia, like Egypt, is the gift of the River Nile, but royal tumulus-tombs at Kerma, along with scores of sacrificed retainers.

Egyptian power revived with the establishment of the New Kingdom, and Tuthmosis I (1506–1494 BC) was responsible for the destruction of Kerma and the conquest of Nubia far south beyond the Fifth Cataract. The population of Lower Nubia was fully Egyptianized, but Nubian culture and resistance continued further south. Egyptian weakness led to withdrawal from Nubia at the end of the New Kingdom (1070 BC), a vacuum filled by a revived Kingdom of Kush, based on Napata, around 900 BC (see NAPATAN CULTURE). Its kings managed to conquer Egypt itself and founded the 25th dynasty; they were finally expelled in 663 BC. Egyptian forces invaded Kush in turn and sacked Napata in 593 BC; the capital was then moved south to Meroe. Thereafter, reduced involvement with Egypt led to a more Africanized MEROITIC CULTURE.

The decline of the Kingdom of Kush took place from around AD 200 in the face of competition with the AKSUMITES, who provided an alternative artery of trade between tropical Africa, Egypt and the Mediterranean, and Arabia and the Indian Ocean world. It became increasingly difficult to protect the huge territory of the Kushites from attacks by desert nomads, such as the Blemmyes (BEJA) in the east and the Nobatae (NUBA) in the west. The intensive overgrazing of cattle, particularly in the south, is thought to have led to soil erosion and population dispersal. An Aksumite invasion between AD 320 and 350 was the *coup de grâce*. Kush was succeeded by a coalescent Nuba, Blemmye and remnant-Kushite X-Group culture, a new civilization that developed into the Christian kingdoms of the Nile Valley (Nobatia, Makuria and Alwa) and later the Islamic cultures of Sudan.

## NUER

NILOTES who live along the banks of the Nile in southern Sudan and adjoining Ethiopia. Like the DINKA, they move to higher ground in the rainy season with their cattle, which are central to their economy, culture and diet. They also fish and cultivate crops in autonomous communities characteristic of semi-nomadic pastoralists.

Socially they are polygynous and organized into patrilineal clans with territorial rights; feuding is common. They are animist in their religious beliefs. The different branches of the Nuer incorporated variably into the national SUDANESE economy and society following independence, but this has been even further retarded by the civil war of recent decades. They are thought to number around 1.75 million.

## NUMIDIANS

Ancestral BERBERS who occupied the whole region from western Libya (Tripolitana) to the Atlantic, herding livestock and cultivating the productive northern plains and hills. Numidia was the Roman name for the region of North Africa to the south and west of Carthage (see CARTHAGINIANS), corresponding with modern-day Algeria. Numidian religion was based on nature and fertility, although Christianity was strong before the Arab Muslim conquest in the 7th century. They were divided into lineages, clans and tribes and were egalitarian much like modern Berbers, producing strong political leaders only in times of need. The Numidian language is also known as ancient Libyan.

## NUPE

One of many peoples making up the major IGBO ethnic group of Nigeria. They mostly live along the Niger and Kaduna Rivers in the west-central part of the country, numbering around 600,000, and speak the KWA Nupe language. Islamic proselytization in the early 19th century prepared the way for FULANI conquest. Islam, and polygyny, remain strong among the elite of the traditionally hierarchical Nupe society. Christianity became more common among the rural population under British rule, but they remain attached to the traditional deity Soko. The Nupe were fishermen and river traders but have become grain cultivators and long-distance merchants.

## NYAMWEZI or Banyamwezi

A BANTU-speaking people who are distributed across a large area of western Tanzania, south of Lake Victoria. Some can also be found in Congo

*" ... the vagrant fierce Numidæans "*

A. Gorges, 1614

(Kinshasa). They arrived in the region early in the 2nd millennium AD and are particularly noted for their development of strong hierarchical *ntemi* chiefdoms in the 19th century in the face of NGONI raids, and for their participation in the slave and ivory trade to the SWAHILI coast, a large number of them working as porters. They also had a large slave population of their own.

The Nyamwezi speak Kinyamwezi and have a linguistic and cultural affinity with the SUKUMA, considered to be a Nyamwezi sub-group along with the Sumbwas, all of them together numbering more than 5 million. The Nyamwezi proper number around 1 million and are well known as merchants and traders, although they are largely cultivators who also keep some cattle, sheep and goats. They have been badly affected by droughts and soil erosion in recent years. Traditionally they lived in scattered homesteads, although in more recent times government policy has forced many to live in larger concentrated towns and villages (see TANZANIANS). Many are Muslims today, but traditional beliefs involving ancestor-worship and animism are still strong. Descent is matrilineal and polygyny is permitted.

## NYANJA or Nianja or Niassa or Anyanja or Wanyanja

The largest of the groups, along with the CHEWA, descended from the MARAVI clans centred on Malawi. The Chewa migrated from the area of modern-day Congo (Kinshasa), and the Nyanja separated from them in the 18th century, occupying the area adjoining lakes Malawi and Chilwa, where they are concentrated today. Their name means 'people of the lake'.

The Nyanja are strong in Zambia's Eastern Province, where their BANTU language, also Nyanja, a dialect of Chichewa, is the *lingua franca*. They are also numerous in the Zambian capital Lusaka, where many work in government offices. Many Nyanja in the countryside are still subsistence farmers.

## NYORO or Banyoro or Bunyoro or Kitara

UGANDANS of the ancient and powerful kingdom of Bunyoro east of Lake Albert in the Great Lakes region of East Africa. They became ethnically mixed over many centuries, and the pattern of migration and intermingling is by no means clear. In the early 2nd millennium AD the pastoral HIMA people produced their own lines of kings and ruled in a country populated by the much more numerous agricultural BANTU people, the IRU. This well-organized kingdom appears to have been at its height under the Chwezi rulers around 1400. Later in the century western Nilotic pastoralists, related to the LUO, moved southwards into the area of modern Uganda. One clan, the Bito, gained control and expelled the Chwezi.

Under the Bito, based on the old capital of Bigo, the kingdom expanded to the east and south, creating the empire of Kitara with its homeland in Bunyoro, the predominant state of the region. Bito princes appear to have been placed in charge of subordinate states such as Busoga and Buganda. The Bito of Bunyoro-Kitara provided all future kings, or *mukamas* (priest-kings), ruling over the Hima, who in turn dominated the Bantu-speaking cultivators, especially in the south. This pattern can be seen in other kingdoms of the Great Lakes, such as the ANKOLE. The exact pastoral–cultivator composition of the ruling class is unclear, but the amount of tribute they exacted increased by the 18th century. This possibly provoked discontent which, together with wars of succession, other internal disputes and over-expansion of the empire, led to its disintegration in the late 18th century. Several provinces broke away, notably the GANDA kingdom of Buganda, which became Bunyoro's chief rival.

### The creation of Uganda

Many peoples succumbed to the Bugandan onslaught, but towards 1850 Bunyoro was galvanized by *Mukama* Kamurasi, who bolstered his power by gaining control of trade routes north to the Sudan and east to the SWAHILI coast. His allies included the LANGO of northern Uganda, who assisted him in repelling Ganda attacks. Kabarega succeeded to the throne in 1869 and strengthened his army by purchasing modern firearms from the Zanzibaris and Sudanese traders. The army was also reorganized. His independent attitude and use of slave-trading

'Khartoumers' to reinforce his military strength alienated BRITISH support, which was directed towards Buganda instead. In 1894 Buganda was made a British protectorate, the defence of which led to a British military expedition against Bunyoro. Kabarega was defeated and finally captured and exiled to the Seychelles in the Indian Ocean. Bunyoro was incorporated into the Uganda Protectorate and ruled through Bito kings imposed by Britain. The Ugandan kingdoms were abolished in 1966 by Milton Obote.

Traditionally, Bunyoro power was assisted by its reserves of iron ore and the skills of its metalsmiths, now diminished. The Nyoro remain largely small-scale farmers producing millet, plantains, yams, cassava and numerous other subsistence crops. Tobacco and cotton are important cash crops. The Nyoro engaged in the large-scale hunting of elephants and game, initially restricted during the British colonial period and now further curtailed by the depredations that occurred during the political turmoil of the 1970s and 1980s in Uganda. Bunyoro territory includes the Murchison Falls (now Kabarega) National Park.

# NZABI or Nzebi or Njabi or Bandjabi

A people widely scattered across south-central Gabon and the northwestern Congo (Brazzaville). They were simple cultivators and hunters who were drawn into trade with the Europeans, including the supply of slaves, by the early 19th century, and actively resisted French colonial control in the early 20th century. A large number of Nzabi are Christians due to missionary work from that time.

# OLDOWAN CULTURE

The culture of the earliest humans so far discovered, named after the Olduvai Gorge in the Rift Valley of northern Tanzania. Their stone tools, typified by roughly worked pebble chopping tools, continued to be made and used by hominids for a million years. They are associated with the remains of *Homo habilis*, meat-eaters who lived there around 2 million years ago, although Australopithecines were also present at

the same site. Early hominids possibly spread such tools outside Africa.

# OROMO or Galla

Cushitic-speaking pastoralists of southeastern Ethiopia who constantly extended their territory in search of pasture for their cattle (see map on next page). They used cavalry in warfare to great effect in the 16th century, expanding into southern and central Ethiopia, Kenya and Somalia. The southern Oromo later suffered from attacks by the SOMALI, MAASAI and KAMBA.

In Ethiopia they remain, with the AMHARA, one of the largest ethnolinguistic groups, with a population of around 20 million. Through local adaptation they have lost much of their racial homogeneity and cultural unity. In the north they have adopted sedentary agriculture and Ethiopian Orthodox Christianity or Islam.

# OVAHEREROS

See HEREROS.

# OVAMBO or Ambo

A people comprising several sub-groups in southern Angola and northern Namibia. Their economy has long remained underdeveloped, not least because of the civil wars and independence struggles until very recent times. Many became refugees or struggled to make a living by cattle-herding and small-scale farming, and as migrant workers. Historically, the Ovambo formed several small states (the most powerful being Kwanyama) in Ovamboland, producing ivory, slaves, cattle, copper and iron ore in the 19th century. They were related to the similar Kavango people to the east.

# OVIMBUNDU

An agricultural BANTU-speaking people of the fertile Benguela Highlands of Angola. They are the largest ethnic group of ANGOLANS, numbering around 3.5 million. Ovimbundu women traditionally worked as cultivators, while the men hunted, raided neighbouring peoples and developed a trade network extending over much of

> ❝ They [the Oromo] are a fierce Nation, they make warre on their Neighours, and with all people, no more than onely to destroy them. ❞
>
> Don John Bermudez, 1625

Oromo

See previous page.

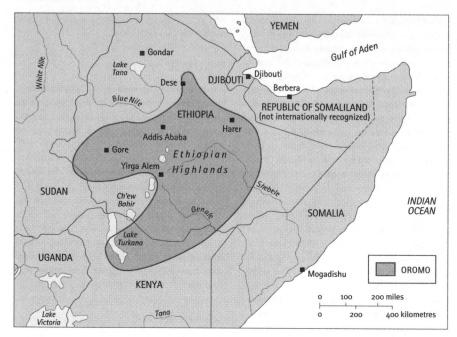

central Africa, supplying slaves to the Portuguese from the mid-17th century. Today, commercial maize production is important and many men are migrant workers. In the long-running Angolan civil war, which lasted until the end of the 20th century, many Ovimbundu supported the western-backed UNITA political movement led by Jonas Savimbi.

## PEDI or Bapedi

A sub-group of the SOTHO people who live in the northern Transvaal of South Africa and Swaziland. They speak a Sotho language and are polygynous, living in village communities and practising mixed farming under the authority of traditional chiefs. In the 19th century they were involved in trade and were a militarily powerful kingdom, but suffered at the hands of the NDEBELE, SWAZI and British forces. Under South African apartheid they were concentrated on the Lebowa homeland in Northern Transvaal, where many remain, while others have sought work as migrant labourers in the urban centres. They are thought to number around 4 million.

## PEPEL or Papel

A Senegalese and Gambian people of the Atlantic coast of West Africa. In the 15th century they emerged in the coastal regions of northern Guinea-Bissau, where they are prominent rice farmers. Their emergence was closely associated with the arrival of the PORTUGUESE, with whom they traded and inter-married. They were also influenced culturally, adopting Portuguese dress and the Crioulo trading language. They are one of the main ethnic groups of Guinea-Bissau and are estimated to number about 130,000, around 10% of the population. They have generally remained faithful to their traditional animist beliefs.

## PEUL

See FULANI.

## PYGMIES

People of small stature, full-grown males growing to an average of less than 1.5 m / 59 in. Central African pygmy groups include well over

200,000 individuals, and include the Western AKA; the Central or TWA (or Tswa) cluster; the Eastern Mbuti, who have an AKA sub-group; and the southeastern group, also known as TWA, of the Rift Valley. They are BANTU-speakers and were probably the earliest inhabitants of the equatorial rainforest. Traditionally pygmies are hunter-gatherers but live in economic symbiosis with non-pygmy neighbours, often working for them as seasonal agricultural labourers. Through acculturation they have lost much of their linguistic and cultural uniqueness.

## RASHAIDA

See BAGGARA.

## REHOBOTHERS or Rehoboth Basters

A unique ethnic group of Namibia. *Baster* is an Afrikaans word meaning 'bastard' or 'half-breed'. Originally the offspring mainly of KHOIKHOI women and Dutch men from the 18th century, they formed a new ethnic community strongly influenced by Christian missionaries and European culture and institutions. To escape the AFRIKANERS (Boers) many migrated into Namibia in the 1860s and established the settlement of Rehoboth, still the largest Baster community. Some are also descended from the German colonial officials and colonists of South-West Africa (see NAMIBIANS). Today they number more than 30,000, speak Afrikaans and are mostly subsistence farmers or migrant workers.

## RÉUNIONESE

The people of the Indian Ocean island of Réunion in the Mascarene group, east of Madagascar, a French colony until 1947 and now an overseas *département*. The uninhabited island was visited by the Portuguese in the early 16th century, and was later occupied by the French East India Company as a convenient base on the sea lanes to and from India. Like Mauritius (see MAURITIANS), the bulk of the population is descended from African slaves and indentured workers from East Africa, India, China and Indo-China brought to work the sugar and coffee plantations. Sugar and related industries still dominate the economy, which depends heavily

66 They be full grown at their third yere & at their seuen yere they be olde. 99

L. Andrews, c. 1520, referring to pygmy peoples

Pygmies

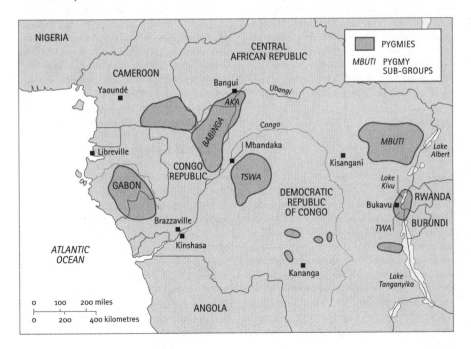

on trade with France, but there is also a strong tourism sector and some manufacturing. A FRENCH creole language is widely spoken that is related to Mauritian Morisyen, although French is the official language. Around 90% of the population of 700,000 are Roman Catholic, approximately 6% Muslim.

## ROBA or Lalla or Lala

A cluster of Adamawa-speaking people north of the Benue River in eastern Nigeria. Their territory lies along the mountainous border with Cameroon, where they live by agriculture and the rearing of sheep, goats and chickens. Historically, this terrain helped to protect them from raiding and conquest, but by the 20th century they were subordinate to the Yola emirate of the Muslim FULANI.

## ROZWI or Barozwi or Rozvi

A SHONA people of Zimbabwe. Their origins are unknown, but Urozwi, the land of the Rozwi, possibly emerged out of the disintegration of the empire of Mwanamutapa, led by kings whose title was *changamire*. These kings and their armies of deliberately brutalized young men successfully expelled the Portuguese from the Zambezi Valley in the 1690s and established a new kingdom, but were defeated and dispersed by NGUNI invasion in the early 1800s. Claim to Rozwi ancestry is still regarded as prestigious.

## RUNDI

See BURUNDIANS.

## RWANDANS

People of the Republic of Rwanda (or Ruanda), capital Kigali. It is a small, poor and densely populated country. In 1994 the country suffered one of the worst outbreaks of genocide in modern history with the government-inspired slaughter of up to 500,000 minority TUTSI (and others opposed to the government) at the hands of the dominant HUTU. Up to 2 million refugees fled to neighbouring countries, many of them Hutu fearing Tutsi revenge attacks. Today the Tutsi comprise 20% of the population of around 8 million. In addition to Hutu and Tutsi, there are a small number of TWA hunter-gatherers, possibly just 1% of the population of Rwanda, together with some SWAHILI-speakers from Tanzania and Congo (Kinshasa). Swahili is spoken more in towns and in trading communities but the official languages are the BANTU Kinyarwanda, closely related to Rundi (of Burundi), and French, adopted from the former colonial power, Belgium. Around 65% of Rwandans are Roman Catholic; others are Protestant and Muslim, and around 25% still adhere to traditional beliefs.

The pastoral Tutsi people moved into Rwanda in the 15th century, soon dominating the agricultural Hutu by military and other means, especially cattle-clientage. They established the kingdom of Rwanda, which gradually incorporated outlying Hutu communities into a centralized state that reached the fullest extent of its power at the end of the 19th century, when Germany assumed colonial control. It became part of German East Africa, but during World War I the Belgians occupied the territory and afterwards ruled it, along with Burundi, under a League of Nations mandate as the combined Territory of Ruanda-Urundi. The Belgian-inspired 'democratization' of Rwandan society encouraged the Hutu to exercise power within traditional society, but led to a civil war in 1959, which resulted in the overthrow of the long-standing Tutsi royal family and aristocracy. The *mwami* (king) Kigeri V and 300,000 Tutsis fled the country, which became independent in 1961.

The Tutsi population left in the country suffered further after a raid by exiles from Burundi in 1963. In 1990 another invasion was mounted, from Uganda, by the Tutsi-dominated Rwanda Patriotic Front (RPF), and the conflict ended with the Arusha Accords in 1993 which promised a system of power-sharing. The response of Hutu extremists in the government, army and within Hutu society (many of whom formed a widely feared militia) was the 1994 genocide of the minority Tutsi. The RPF resumed their military campaign and swiftly took power, imprisoning many thousands of Hutu suspects. The widespread nature of the crimes has led to crowded jails, with many prisoners waiting several years for trial.

Most of the refugees who fled the RPF advance have since returned to Rwanda, although the process of reconciliation remains difficult, and periodic outbreaks of violence have accompanied the post-genocide readjustment. The government is managing to maintain a system of ethnic power sharing, and foreign aid has helped in the process of reconstruction.

## SAHO

Nomadic and semi-nomadic pastoralists who live primarily on the coast of Eritrea and the eastern slopes of the Ethiopian plateau, with some in adjoining Ethiopia. They number around 175,000 and speak the Cushitic Saho language. Most are Muslim, although a main sub-group, the Erob, are Christian.

## SAN or Bushmen

A people who have traditionally been marginalized by stronger societies and who survive today in the deserts and marginal regions of Botswana and Namibia, sometimes as pastoralists (often as clients of BANTU-speaking Africans) and sometimes as traditional hunter-gatherers. It is estimated that there are perhaps 35,000 of them. Their marginal status is reflected in the fact that they are difficult to name. *San* was probably a

*❝ What a wonderful people the Bushmen are. Always merry and laughing, and never tell lies wantonly. ❞*

David Livingstone's diary, 6 May 1851

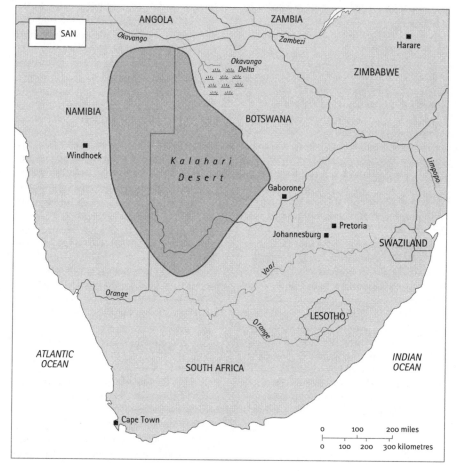

San

term of abuse used by the KHOIKHOI. The San were known as the Bushmen by the AFRIKANERS and British settlers in South Africa and were called the Sarwa by the TSWANA people. A subgroup has been known as the Twa.

Traditionally nomadic, the San prefer to move about in search of seasonal sources of wild foods, although postcolonial governments have often tried to settle them in permanent sites. The best-known communities in Botswana are the !Kung and the G/wi.

They speak a language distinguished by its 'click' sounds, and the existence of such clicks in the languages of some of the southern Bantu-speaking peoples indicates that there was probably inter-marriage in the past. The San have always interacted socially and economically with the Khoikhoi, and the two together are sometimes known as the Khoisan.

**San culture and society**

The San have an exceptionally rich oral culture, with many myths and stories relating to the environment. Although marginal today, they formerly inhabited areas throughout southern Africa. They were magnificent cave painters, and their complex and extensive paintings, illustrating the natural world as well as the position of humans within it, together with motifs that appear to have spiritual and philosophical significance, can be found throughout southern Africa. Iron Age people are sometimes depicted cutting down trees. They continued to paint until the arrival of whites, when they incorporated Europeans on horseback into their art.

The San have always lived in light, easily constructed shelters of branches and grass. They have few possessions and hunt with bows and poisoned arrows, snares, traps, and occasionally spears. They find wild fruits, nuts, vegetable matter, and insects. Game-meat was a key aspect of their diet until the game was largely shot out by other peoples possessing guns. The extreme simplicity of their lives, and their capacity to live at ease within the landscape, has caused them to be highly romanticized as representing the antithesis of advanced industrial society.

## SANDAWE

A people of the dry central highlands of Tanzania, numbering more than 100,000. They are thought to be the descendants of the ancient SAN-type hunter-gatherers who populated East Africa before the arrival of the CUSHITES and BANTU. They formerly lived by hunting, gathering wild fruits and food-plants, and fishing. Today they are mostly settled farmers although increasing numbers are wage-labourers in the urban centres of Tanzania.

## SANGA or Sango

An UBANGI people widely spread across central Africa. They number around 85,000 and are concentrated in the Ubangi River valley of the Central African Republic, Chad and a large part of the Congo (Kinshasa). Historically, they were traders along the river system. Sanga is a creole language of GBANDI and remains, along with French, the official language of the Central African Republic.

## SANGOAN CULTURE

A central African, sub-Saharan Palaeolithic culture associated with Neanderthal-type hominids. It derived from the late Acheulian and is characterized by its distinctive stone tool industry evidenced in sites at Sango Bay beside Lake Victoria, Uganda, where it was first identified in 1920, and in Angola, Kenya, Congo (Kinshasa) and Zambia. It dates from the late Pleistocene era (*c.* 130,000 to 10,000 years ago) and included new kinds of implements including picks, planes and other wood-working tools. Sangoan was contemporaneous with the FAURE-SMITH CULTURE of South Africa.

## SÃO TOMÉANS

Inhabitants of the islands of São Tomé and Príncipe in the Gulf of Guinea, equatorial Africa, which were Portuguese colonies from 1522 and became the independent Democratic Republic of São Tomé and Príncipe in 1975. São Tomé town is the capital. Their population of around 150,000 comprises the majority mixed-blood

S

African-European FORROS, CAPE VERDEANS (perhaps 10% of the total), ANGOLANS, MOZAMBICANS and ANGOLARES. The economy is largely agricultural, based on cacao production, which employs around 70% of the working population. The discovery of oil reserves around the islands at the beginning of the 21st century promises to transform the Republic's fortunes.

## SARA or Sar

A people found in southern CHAD (roughly one-third of the population) and northern Central African Republic. They comprise many sub-groups with strong clan loyalties and retain their traditional animist beliefs. Historically they suffered slave-raiding by Muslim Arab and FULANI peoples to the north, and this antipathy is still manifested in contemporary Chadic society and politics. The Sara are primarily farmers and fishermen on the Chari and Logone Rivers.

## SARWA

See SAN.

## SENE

See SENUFO.

## SENEGALESE

People of the Republic of Senegal, formerly a FRENCH territory. The name Senegambia is sometimes used to describe the region that includes the former British colony of Gambia, on the River Gambia, and Senegal which surrounds it except at the Atlantic coast. The Senegalese and GAMBIANS have much in common, but their development has diverged due to the accident of colonial history, despite the brief experiment of the Senegambian Confederation (1982–9). The Senegalese today are still largely subsistence farmers, overwhelmingly dependent on the production of groundnuts, which are well suited to Senegal's climate and light soils. French is the official language.

There are several important ethnic groups in the total population of more than 10 million, most of whom are Muslim. The largest group (36%) is the WOLOF, concentrated in the west of the country, whose West Atlantic language is the *lingua franca* of Senegal. A related language is spoken by the Serer (17%) who are mixed cattle- and crop-farmers in the southwest. The FULANI (18%) are traditionally nomadic pastoralists and are found scattered throughout Senegal, although many are now settled cultivators and town-dwellers. The strongly Islamic TUKULOR are concentrated on the middle Senegal River in the north, but are also found elsewhere, increasingly in the urban centres and particularly St Louis and the capital Dakar. The MANDE-speaking MALINKE and SONINKE are known for their trading skills, and like other peoples in Senegal and elsewhere in West Africa, the drought of recent decades has encouraged their drift to the cities. The MOORS (Mauri) in the north are also traders and rear livestock. In terms of social organization, many Senegalese societies traditionally lived within a strongly hierarchical system characteristic of savannah peoples, but these divisions have become less pronounced in recent times.

Islam began its slow domination of Senegal with the conversion of the Tukulor in the 11th century, although indigenous animistic beliefs are still followed. The slave trade in particular became important, following the Portuguese arrival in the mid-15th century, with many slaves supplied by the dominant Greater Jolof state of the Wolof people and their Serer subjects. Some, notably the JOLA in the southwest of the territory, refrained from participating in the trade. Successor Wolof kingdoms used armies of mounted slaves, *ceddo*, to maintain their power and the slaving system linked to the European traders on the coast.

These animist and mercantilist Wolof kingdoms fought with the growing power of Islam, which became stronger inland as clerics, called *marabouts*, gradually proselytized among the peasantry. Even emerging theocratic states, such as Futa Jalon, became involved in the slave trade, and their economies depended on large numbers of agricultural slaves.

The Europeans gained greater power on the coast, but it was only after 1817 that France established its authority there. The abolition of slavery in the French Empire in 1848 under-

| Senegalese: main ethnic groups |
| --- |
| Wolof |
| Serer |
| Fulani |
| Tukulor |
| Malinke |
| Soninke |
| Moors |

S

mined traditional rulers, traders and economies and perpetuated political instability, although groundnut production rapidly increased legitimate trade, which diverted the Wolof and others away from war and into agricultural development and colonization.

From the 1850s, under Governor Louis-Léon-César Faidherbe, the French also began to conquer more territory inland and establish a modern administration in Senegal. In 1895 Senegal became part of French West Africa, but obtained its independence under President Léopold Sédar Senghor in 1960, following a brief union with Mali (1959–60). Through democracy, the more conservative peoples of the inland regions were able to predominate over the coastal and urban elites. Economic and other difficulties have led to political repression, although this has lessened in recent years.

The creation of a national consciousness since independence has relied largely on Islam and the widespread Wolof language and culture. Oral traditions and poetry remain important features of Senegalese societies, and vibrant music and dance cultures have gained an international audience. France has continued to exercise an important influence on the country's cultural as well as national life.

## SENUFO or Sene or Siena or Bamana

A people whose homeland is the Middle Volta region in the West African states of the Ivory Coast, Mali and Burkina Faso. They are mostly subsistence farmers, although their lives have become increasingly commercialized.

The Senufo are subdivided into various Southern, Central (including the BOBO-DYULA) and Northern groups numbering more than 3 million, all speaking one of the numerous GUR (Voltaic) languages of Niger-Congo. In the past fifty years their individual identities have been eroded by the growth of the cash economy, the emergence of more virulent nationalism in their respective countries and the increasing adoption of Islam throughout the region.

> *"The Seychellois have a method of walling houses with the bark of the lathe palm."*
>
> F.A. Barkly, 1898

## SEYCHELLE ISLANDERS or Seychellois

People inhabiting the Indian Ocean island group north of Madagascar forming the democratic Republic of Seychelles. The 115 islands, scattered over 1300 sq. km / 530 sq. miles, were colonized by France in 1768, and today's islanders are descendants of these white settlers and the black slaves they imported from the African mainland. They speak a French creole, Seselwa, together with French and English. The islands were taken by Britain in 1794 and became independent in 1976. The Seychelles economy depends on cultivation, fishing, light industry and tourism.

## SHANGANE or Shangaans or Gaza

An NGUNI people who were displaced by the conflicts associated with the rise of the ZULU state and dispersed across the Zambezi River. They have lived in Mozambique since the late 1820s, settling among the TSONGA people. They adopted the Tsonga language and in many respects assimilated themselves into the Tsonga, becoming one of the major population groups of modern Mozambique. Their origins and migration lie in the violent circumstances of the rise of the Zulus. One of the Ngoni chiefs, from the defeated Ndwande, was Soshangane. For a period he survived as an independent raider to the north of the Zulu kingdom. But the Zulu king Shaka attacked him in 1828 and he withdrew across the Zambezi into Mozambique, where he established a state often known as the Gaza Kingdom.

This state remained a sufficiently formidable polity that the Shangane frequently attacked Portuguese trading settlements and threatened the southern part of the colony of Mozambique. They were notable as hunters, often setting aside hunting preserves for their rulers, and they were heavily involved in the ivory trade. The Portuguese were forced to acknowledge their authority, and traders paid tribute to them.

By the end of the 19th century, the Shangane had become celebrated labour migrants to the mines of South Africa. During the 1890s, they sometimes constituted two-thirds of the labour force of the Witwatersrand. They stayed for longer periods than other migrants, partly because the labour of the men was not traditionally required in their agricultural economy. Their deferred pay also became a very important aspect of the colonial Mozambiquan economy.

# SHILLUK

Southern Sudanese NILOTES occupying the region of the Blue and White Nile confluence south of Khartoum, northeastern Africa. They emerged from the same migratory movement that propelled the Eastern Sudanic LUO-speaking people southwards to Uganda and Kenya before 1500. There are several sub-groups, including the ANUAK and ACHOLI. Originally pastoralists, they are unusual because they became settled cultivators as well as herders of cattle, sheep and goats. Shilluk was founded as a centralized, tribal state by the legendary Nyikang. It was headed by a king (reth) with divine status and chosen from among the royal sons. The Shilluk today number around 500,000.

# SHIRAZI

A people who probably originated as a small group of migrants from Persia to the SWAHILI coast of East Africa, although not necessarily from the Persian city of Shiraz. There were strong trading connections in ancient times between these various regions at the edge of the Indian Ocean world. They arrived in East Africa between the 10th and 12th centuries by way of the Banadir Coast of Somalia. Ruling dynasties that claimed Shirazi origin (sometimes invented) were established in Kilwa, Malindi, Mombasa and elsewhere. In the Zanzibar islands (see ZANZIBARIS) they were absorbed by the indigenous BANTU, whose descendants still call themselves Shirazi. Many others are the descendants of former slaves who worked the Zanzibari plantations in the 19th century.

The name is reflected in the Afro-Shirazi Party, the political organization supported by the indigenous peasant farmers and small traders that was the main element in the revolutionary government that took power in Zanzibar in 1964. They are divided into the sub-groups

named after their island homes of Pemba, Hadimu and Tumbatu.

# SHONA or Mashona

The major ethnic group of Zimbabwe, constituting at least 75% of the people, up to 9 million in all. They inhabit almost every area of the country, including some in Matabeleland, the southwestern area of the country inhabited by the other major group, the NDEBELE. They have a common language and are all patrilineal, but they are divided into several sub-groups, including the Karangas, Kalangas, KOREKORE, Manhicas, Ndaus and Tembos, among others. These groups are often further sub-divided. There are also significant Shona populations in Botswana (Kalangas) and Mozambique (Manhicas and Ndaus), reflecting the often artificial nature of colonial boundaries.

Many Shona chieftaincies still exist, but the concept of a paramount chief or king seems to have died with the decline of the Shona states in the 17th century. They keep cattle and goats and grow millet, maize and vegetables. In religion, they have a strong ancestral cult, and unusually among African peoples they also have a concept of a single high god, whose priesthood works through oracular caves. The Ndebele may have been influenced by this religion when they arrived in the area.

Up to the end of the 19th century the Shona were notable iron-workers, using the abundant ores of Zimbabwe and often trading ironware over long distances. They also used elaborate hunting techniques to trap game animals to enhance their diet.

Their origin is, however, obscure. Some believe that they brought new Iron Age pottery styles to the area after the 1st millennium and that they were consequently the builders of GREAT ZIMBABWE, but there is no proof of this. However, it does seem to have been a Shona group that founded the Butwa or Butua state based on Khami, and it is possible that this resulted from the fall-out of the collapse of Great Zimbabwe. The Portuguese were well aware of them in the 16th and 17th centuries and became embroiled in some of the Shona dynastic disputes. Archaeologists believe they had a 'refuge'

**S**

" The Mashona ... are very fond of meat, but they hardly ever get it. "

**G.W.H. Knight-Bruce, 1895**

culture in the 18th and early 19th centuries – that is, a culture in defensive decline from its high points in previous centuries. But this notion of decline has, perhaps, been too common in colonial views of indigenous peoples of empire.

From the time that the Ndebele appeared in the area from 1838, the Shona became subject to raiding by this powerful northern NGUNI people. Some, close to the Ndebele heartland, became assimilated into the Ndebele social structure, inter-marrying and accepting aspects of Ndebele culture. Others became tributary peoples, offering tribute in iron and cattle, as well as boys for regiments and girls for marriage, in exchange for 'protection'. Others further to the north and northeast were raided occasionally by the Ndebele. More Shona were tied into the commercial patterns of the Portuguese and mixed-race traders of the Zambezi Valley. They were long involved in the ivory trade and disposed of ivory to Islamic traders from the East African coast and later to the Portuguese. They also traded gold, particularly towards the Zambezi Valley.

**The impact of colonization**

Scottish missionary and explorer David Livingstone (1813–73) became aware of the Shona when he travelled northwards from Botswana and visited Victoria Falls, and he encouraged missionaries to settle among them, although early missions were devastated by malaria. From the 1860s many prospectors, hunters and traders began to appear in Shona country, often permitted access by the Ndebele king Lobengula, who claimed a greater authority over the Shona than in fact he possessed. These whites turned out to be the precursors of the major invasion by Cecil Rhodes's British South Africa Company, the legitimacy of which was based on treaties with the Ndebele kingdom on the assumption that the Ndebele exercised a form of imperial power over the Shona.

In reality, that power was very limited, particularly in the more distant regions from the Ndebele heartland. Some of the Shona were employed as police and as soldiers and may have used their new-found power to score off their old enemies, the Ndebele. Nevertheless, in 1896, the Shona rose in revolt, together with the Nde-

bele, against the white settlers. They succeeded in killing a considerable proportion of them, although some Shona chieftaincies remained loyal to the new colonial rulers. This revolt, known as the *chimurenga*, was suppressed with considerable brutality. The revolt was largely led by the traditional political authorities, although it was lent legitimacy by the endorsement of spiritual leaders, such as the priesthoods of oracular caves and the spirit mediums who established contact with the ancestors.

The Shona were subsequently placed in reserves. Much of their best land was sold or granted to white farmers. They became labour migrants and worked in the mines and farms, as well as in the towns, of Southern Rhodesia. They also travelled to South Africa for work.

After World War I, they became involved in trade unions and new political parties, but white rule was consolidated. Missionaries of various denominations were active among the Shona in many parts of the country and, in some areas, there was an attempt to turn them away from communal life into individual small farmers.

After the white Rhodesians had illegally attempted to retain power throughout the 1960s and 1970s in the face of armed black insurgency and international disapproval, majority rule after 1980 effectively brought the Shona people, led by Robert Mugabe, to power in an independent Zimbabwe.

# SIENA

See SENUFO.

# SIERRA LEONEANS

Inhabitants of Republic of Sierra Leone. The country takes its name from Freetown's mountainous hinterland, named Serra Leão ('mountains of the lion') by Portuguese explorer Pedro de Sintra, who visited around 1460. The coast was also the scene of British slave-trading in the 18th century. The modern country developed from the original settlement beside the great natural harbour at the capital Freetown, founded by BRITISH philanthropists in 1787 as a home for the black poor of London, slaves who escaped or migrated from North America and the Caribbean, and others emancipated from slave ships captured by the Royal Navy.

The main ethnic groups of Sierra Leone, population 5.3 million, are the northern TEMNE and the MENDE in the south and east. The latter appeared in the early 16th century as all-conquering MANDE-speaking Mane warriors from the Niger Valley by way of Ghana. Their further expansion westwards was halted by the equally formidable Mande susu of northern Sierra Leone, who probably had similar military organization, tactics and weapons.

Numerous smaller ethnic groups include the coastal VAI and the FULANI and MALINKE (Mandingo) of the north and east. Generally, the country's ethnic groups have important features in common, notably patrilineal descent, rule by chiefs, secret societies and agriculture.

English is the official language, and Arabic is used by a small numbers of Muslims (especially in the north) and Lebanese traders. Local languages, among which Mande and Mel are predominant, are also spoken. Some of the population adheres to traditional pantheistic and animist beliefs and the belief in ancestral spirits. Around 60% are Muslim and 10% Christian.

Coastal Sierra Leone became a British Crown Colony in 1808, and Freetown was established as an important naval base during the war against France and in the fight against the slave trade. Anti-slavery patrols landed a cumulative total of 74,000 freed slaves at Freetown, the majority of the KRIO community that established itself as the governing elite of the coast, and later interior, of Sierra Leone under British rule. They also worked as willing agents of British imperial control, pursuing the commercial development and extension of European civilization and Christianity in British West Africa. They contributed to the aim of eradicating the slave trade in the region, which was also actively pursued by the British governors at Freetown.

The initial influence of Sierra Leone and its Krio population was felt largely on the coast, while traditional African civilizations inland were resistant to Christian and European influence. The Krio themselves were widely resented by neighbouring peoples. British influence, however, extended far into the interior, and the hinterland was declared a British Protectorate in 1896, bringing more people into the colony. The domination of the Krio was further entrenched, and the coast–hinterland division continued up to modern times. The introduction of democracy prior to independence led to the ousting of the Krio elite from power in the 1957 election, the so-called 'Green Revolution'.

Sierra Leone's other indigenous peoples were now able to demand the country's independence from Britain, which occurred in 1961. A one-party state was declared in 1978, and military rule has been a feature of Sierra Leonean politics ever since.

Large diamond reserves, discovered in the 1930s, provide a major source of government revenue (roughly 60% of exports by value), but have funded both blatant corruption and the ambitions of the rebel Revolutionary United Front (RUF) in the civil war that erupted in the 1990s. The Lomé agreement brought United Nations peacekeepers to the country in 1999, but the RUF reneged on its obligations to disarm. Renewed fighting and further rebel atrocities resulted in the intervention and continued presence of the British army in 2000. The economy has suffered and most of the population still relies on subsistence agriculture, although a measure of stability has returned.

| Sierra Leonians: main ethnic groups |
| --- |
| Fulani |
| Krio |
| Malinke |
| Mende |
| Temne |
| Vai |

## SIHANAKA

A MALAGASY people of the Indian Ocean island of Madagascar. Their name means 'people of the lake'. They are primarily rice-farmers and cattle-herders, but many fish along the coast of the eastern Tamatave Province, one of the most densely populated parts of Madagascar, where they are concentrated. They are neighbours of the MERINA and number more than 200,000.

## SMITHFIELD CULTURE

A Late Stone Age hunting-and-gathering culture of southern Africa, which ended with the introduction of farming and iron-working early in the 1st millennium AD. The excavated site at Kalambo Falls, south of Lake Tanganyika on the Zambia–Tanzania border, shows that it was active until the mid-4th century AD. The SAN are probably descended from the Smithfield people.

# SOMALI

A people who inhabit the Horn of Africa, divided among several states in the region because of colonial boundaries. They occupy the Ogaden of Ethiopia, northeastern Kenya and southern Djibouti as well as the Somali state, Somalia, with its capital at Mogadishu. Many are migrant workers in Arabia. They are one of the continent's largest homogeneous ethnic groups, and their strong supra-national identity and the refusal of many to accept the arbitrary established borders has contributed to regional tension and warfare in recent decades. Many hundreds of thousands of Somalis fled Ethiopia for Somalia and adjoining countries during the Ethiopia–Somalia Ogaden dispute 1977–8 and during Ethiopia's civil war 1974–91. The threat of border warfare has subsided now that the state of Somalia is without any effective central authority and its people are mostly living in conditions of extreme poverty, subject to the rule of local warlords and clan chiefs.

The largest number of Somali, perhaps around 7.5 million, live in Somalia itself. The country is composed almost entirely of ethnic Somali who have traditionally pursued a nomadic pastoral existence involving camels, sheep and goats. It has been estimated that this remains part of the livelihood of two-thirds of all ethnic Somali to a greater or lesser degree, although many have become settled agriculturists where suitable conditions prevail in this hot and arid region. Half of all Somalians are nomadic or semi-nomadic and the Somali generally remain an overwhelmingly rural people despite the migration of many young people to the towns and cities. They are Sunni Muslim and speak an Afro-Asian Cushitic language that, despite regional variations, is understood by all Somali. In Somalia, Arabic is the other official language and is spoken primarily on the coast due to the historic links and commercial ties with Arabia. Southern Somalians also speak SWAHILI, and Italian and English are still spoken largely as a consequence of colonial occupation.

## People and culture

The Somali are divided into numerous clans which, by patrilineal descent, can be traced back

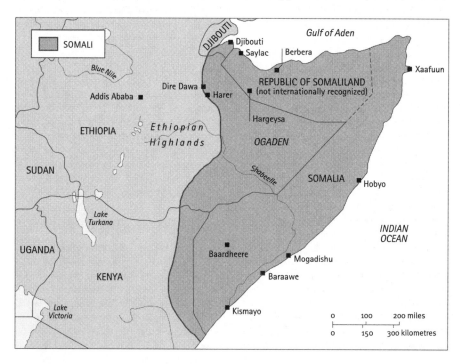

Somali

to the original founders. Individual clans and sub-clans in turn form tribal confederations within wider lineages. The Samale are the largest of these lineage groups, and they comprise 80% of the Somali population. Like most Somali they are proud of their history as warrior nomadic pastoralists, a livelihood and culture that has promoted a sense of independence and a desire for freedom that sits awkwardly with the demands of the modern nation-state.

The Samale Dir, concentrated in southern and northwestern Somalia, regard themselves as the original Somalis; the DJIBOUTI ISSA are a Dir sub-group. The other main clans are the Daarood, Hawiye and Digil-Mirifle.

In the southeast of the country there are a significant number of socially inferior Somalians of BANTU (mostly slave) descent, who are engaged largely in irrigated agriculture along the Juba and Shabelle rivers. Oral culture, including poetry, is very strong amongst the Somalians, whose language only acquired its written form comparatively recently, together with folk dancing and music. Otherwise, the national cultural infrastructure is as poorly developed as the physical infrastructure, due to the poverty of the country.

**Recent history**

Northern Somaliland was a British colonial territory when it became a protectorate in 1884, due to its strategic position opposite the important British staging post of Aden. Italy's territories in the region were incorporated in 1941 but reverted to Italy as a UN trust territory in 1950 before unification and independence as the Republic of Somalia in 1960.

A coup under Major General Muhammad Siad Barre in 1969 established the Somali Democratic Republic, a socialist state based largely on Islamic law. The disastrous attempt to conquer the ethnic Somali Ethiopian province of Ogaden in 1977 led to a mass displacement of Somali people. During the 1980s a growing rebellion by a number of Somali clans finally drove Siad Barre from power in 1991, which worsened conditions for most Somalians, this period of anarchy adding to the problems of drought, crop failure and widespread famine. In 1992 attempts were made by the USA and many other countries to assist in United Nations relief operations, but they encountered Somalian hostility and withdrew rapidly.

The unilateral declaration of a Republic of Somaliland in the north (not recognized internationally) has provided more stability there than in the conflict-riven south, which remains under the control of various clan militias. International attempts to establish a peace agreement have so far failed, and the people of Somalia remain in conditions of extreme hardship and vulnerability.

## SONGHAI

A formally nomadic pastoral people who are concentrated in Mali but are also present in Benin, Burkina Faso, Niger and Nigeria. Their language, also Songhai, belongs to the NILO-SAHARAN family, and the ZERMA are the most important of their several composite groups. They created a great Saharan trading empire centred on Timbuktu and the middle Niger which flourished in the 15th–16th centuries. They are still involved in the caravan trade although many men are migrant workers abroad.

Craft work is important to their culture and economy, and they undertake fishing, cultivation and cattle-rearing. The vast majority of the population still lives in the arid countryside of the region and they now number well in excess of 2 million. Their society is highly stratified, patrilineal and polygynous, and in religion the Songhai are overwhelmingly Muslim, generally being devout adherents of the Sunni branch.

## SONINKE

A MANDE-speaking people who created the first great West African trading empire of Ghana in the 7th–13th centuries AD. This sub-Saharan state was located in modern Mali and Mauritania but was destroyed by the Muslim Almoravids (BERBERS) from the 11th century. Soninke people are a mixture of MALINKE and FULANI and formed the nucleus of the multi-ethnic DYULA traders of West Africa. Today, most Soninke live as farmers in Senegal, and their social structure is typical of Mande peoples. They currently number around 1.5 million.

*" ... among the most inhospitable people I ever met "*

Heinrich Barth, 1858, on the Songhai

# SORKO

A fishing people of the Niger River in Niger and Mali. They comprise the Faran and Fono and form a part of the large SONGHAI group. They live scattered along the river-sides, although the Fono are concentrated in the lakes area south of Timbuktu in Mali.

# SOSO

See SUSU.

# SOTHO or Basotho

A BANTU Sesotho-speaking people occupying the high grasslands of southern Africa, where they are one of the largest ethnic groups. They are classified as Western Sotho or TSWANA of Botswana; Northern, or Transvaal, Sotho (who include the PEDI); and Southern Sotho, concentrated in the inland Kingdom of Lesotho, with its capital at Maseru. Smaller chiefdoms were amalgamated into the kingdom of Lesotho in the 1820s, and as British Basutoland from 1869 it provided a migrant labour pool for South

Africa which today employs around 25% of working Lesotho men, an important source of national income that also helps relieve serious overpopulation. Under apartheid in South Africa, some Southern Sotho peoples were designated part of the non-independent black state of Qwaqwa, which was reincorporated into the Orange Free State in 1994.

Most Sotho, who traditionally live in patrilineal and polygynous family groups, rely on mixed agriculture and animal husbandry. Women undertake much of the agricultural work. Although small scattered hamlets are widespread, the Sotho are best known for their large settlements of conical thatched huts, some built of stone, especially among the Tswana. Many Sotho migrant workers in South Africa live in large townships.

The Sotho were part of the Bantu colonization of southern Africa. They arrived in the region possibly early in the 2nd millennium as a mixed agricultural and cattle-keeping people, whose scattered clans became the nucleus of the modern-day Sotho chiefdoms, to which the Sotho remain loyal. They only coalesced in the 1820s during the great upheavals in southern

> " The old inhabitants, defended by their hills, have retained the largest measure of freedom. "
>
> James Bryce, referring to the Sotho, 1897

Sotho

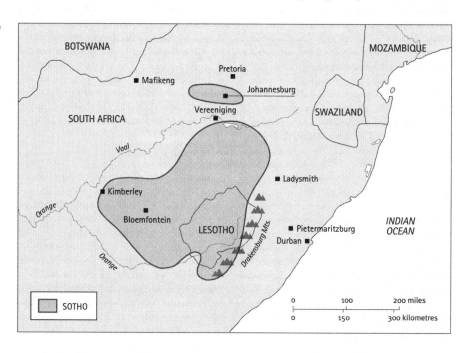

Africa known as the *difiqane* (crushing), in which smaller chiefdoms and peoples combined under able leaders, notably Moshoeshoe (1786–1870). He was responsible for repulsing attacks by the ZULU under Shaka and created the kingdom of Lesotho. In the face of Boer aggression he accepted a British protectorate in 1869 and Lesotho became Basutoland. The traditional elite retained their position throughout the colonial period and the independent kingdom of Lesotho re-emerged in 1966, although it was still dependent economically on South Africa. Under Chief Jonathan, Lesotho became increasingly autocratic, faced with South African hostility during the apartheid era and political opposition at home.

Despite political divisions among the wider Sotho people, they remain aware of their common nationhood and cultural unity, although outside influences and the fragmentation of traditional society are eroding tribal identity and traditional culture. Institutions such as the initiation schools, which inculcate traditional values, are no longer as significant, despite government support. Craft-work, particularly pottery and grass-weaving (notably of characteristic Lesotho hats) continue undiminished in rural areas. Traditional music and dance are also popular, and contemporary music incorporates influences brought from South Africa in particular. Sotho is a written language with a distinguished literary tradition, exemplified by the work of Thomas Mafolo and A. M. Sekese, an important strand of the canon reflecting Sotho pride in the genesis of the nation and the role of the Sotho in the evolution of modern southern Africa. Most Sotho are Christian, although traditional beliefs remain strong.

## SOUTH AFRICANS

The inhabitants of the Republic of South Africa who, since the dismantling of the apartheid system of segregation introduced by AFRIKANER nationalists, all have full citizen rights within their country. There are four groups within what Nelson Mandela (president 1994–9) and Archbishop Desmond Tutu called the 'rainbow nation', adding up to a population of around 43 million. By far the largest group are the BANTU-

speaking Africans, divided into the NGUNI (Northern – including the ZULU – and Southern), the SOTHO and the TSWANA ethnic communities. They constitute about 70% of the population. The next group by size are the whites, who make up 18%. The whites are divided (55% to 45%) into Afrikaans-speaking and English-speaking. The CAPE COLOURED community constitutes 9% of the population, while the Asian community (both Hindu and Muslim) makes up 3%. There are also tiny remnants of the former KHOISAN population.

The SAN and KHOIKHOI were the original inhabitants of the region, but, starting in the 17th century, they were almost eliminated by war, disease, famine and Afrikaner violence. The Bantu-speaking Africans began to reach southwards through the continent in the early centuries of the Christian era, but never reached the southern Cape area, partly because they had sufficient land, and partly because they did not like the climate. The Northern and Southern Nguni established themselves in the coastal regions of what later became the Eastern Cape, Natal, and Swaziland. The Sotho and the Tswana inhabited the higher lands of the interior, mainly suitable for pastoralism.

The white population has its origins with the first DUTCH settlement in 1652. The Dutch were joined by some French and German Protestants, and BRITISH settlers began to arrive during and after the Napoleonic Wars. A further infusion of whites came with the development of the diamond- and gold-mining industries, many of them coming from Eastern Europe and Germany.

The Cape Coloureds are the product of complex racial inter-mixing from the 17th century onwards. The Asians (mainly people from western India) were introduced into the country to work on the sugar plantations of Natal in the second half of the 19th century, but they soon performed other functions, particularly on the railways and as shopkeepers. M.K. Gandhi, known as the Mahatma, lived among the Asians of South Africa for some years before World War I. He fought for their rights and developed many of the techniques, such as *ashrams* (communities) and passive resistance, that became important in the struggle for Indian nationhood.

*" Fancy, a whole nation of lower middle-class Philistines! "*

Olive Schreiner, *c.* 1920, on her white South African compatriots

S

## Apartheid and after

By 1850, there were four separate colonies and states in what is now South Africa: the Cape and Natal under British control, and the Orange Free State and the Transvaal under Afrikaner. After the two South African Wars (1880–1 and 1899–1902), also known as the Anglo–Boer Wars, all four were brought together in the Union of South Africa, which was increasingly dominated by Afrikaner politicians. This domination became extreme after the Afrikaner National Party's victory in the election of 1948 and the institution of the apartheid ('separateness') system.

During this period, Africans were supposedly divided up into ethnic 'homelands' such as Transkei, Ciskei, Bophutatswana, Kwazulu, Gazankulu and a number of others. However, the system translated into greatly inferior conditions and a basic lack of rights for non-whites. After the emergence of majority rule in 1994, the apartheid system was dismantled. So many atrocities had been committed in the apartheid era that a Truth and Reconciliation Commission was established under the chairmanship of Archbishop Tutu to try to assuage the inter-racial bitterness of the era of white rule.

By and large, South African citizens now enjoy equal political rights, although the problems of poverty and landlessness remain serious for many citizens. AIDS constitutes a major threat to the health and survival of many South Africans, and the government is accused of not doing enough to take steps against this disease.

## SUDANESE

A term used for the people of a large area of northern Africa as well as for the population of the Sudanese Republic in the northeast of the continent that falls within this area. The name Sudan is derived from the Arabic *bilad al-Sudan*, 'the land of the blacks'. This term identified the black-African-populated area south of Egypt and the 5600-km / 3500-mile wide Sahara desert of North Africa from at least the 12th century. The Sudan, as a geographic definition, thus extends westwards and southwards across the savannah to the tropical forests of West Africa and the Congo, and is populated by the Negroid BANTU peoples as well as ARABS and BERBERS. Many are pastoralists and nomadic or semi-nomadic. The open plains have always permitted extensive trade links between the Mediterranean and subtropical Africa. In the west these trade links greatly influenced the development of states and civilizations such as ancient Ghana and Mali. The plains have also allowed population movement to the south and west, notably by the NILO-SAHARAN-speakers who now occupy this belt.

Chari-Nile (or Macro-Sudanic) languages are a branch of Nilo-Saharan and are spoken from Ethiopia to Chad and from southern Egypt to northern Tanzania and Kenya. The Eastern Sudanic sub-group includes NILOTIC and NUBIAN.

The name Sudan has come to be particularly associated with the large territory south of Egypt incorporating Nubia, now the northern part of the Republic of Sudan, Africa's largest country. Negroid Nilo-Saharan hunter-gatherers (30,000 –20,000 BC) were the original inhabitants of the Nile Valley and eventually adopted pastoralism and cultivation. Early attempts at state-building were hindered by Egyptian domination, but from the 11th century BC Nubian ambitions were realized in the powerful kingdom of the KUSHITES and its constituent NAPATAN and MEROITIC cultures.

Kushite power came to an end with the AKSUMITE invasion in the 4th century AD, but Kush was already weakened by attacks from the nomadic NUBA and Blemmye (BEJA). These desert peoples combined with the existing population to create three distinct kingdoms along the Middle Nile. They adopted Christianity from the 6th century AD and flourished for several centuries before succumbing to the movement of Arab Muslim nomads southward from Egypt between the 13th and 15th centuries. In 1504 this steady infiltration was halted by the FUNJ, whose power was based in the Gezira, the productive plains between the Blue and White Niles in the vicinity of Khartoum, central Sudan. They soon adopted and promoted Islam, spread throughout the country by itinerant *fekis*, non-orthodox teachers of religion who preached a simple faith that became a feature of Sudanic Islam. The northern and central Sudanese remain largely Arab and Muslim, in contrast to the black-African south of the country.

## Egyptian and British colonialism

In 1821 Muhammad Ali, ruler of Egypt, exploited the disintegration of the Funj confederacy and dispatched a military expedition to conquer the Sudan. Conquest was completed in 1874, but Egyptian-Turkish rule was a mixed blessing. Although the Sudanese gained from economic development (sugar, indigo and cotton became staples) they were subject to chaotic, arbitrary or ineffectual government. Private traders used modern firearms to further the slave trade in southern Sudan.

In 1863 Ismail Pasha, viceroy of Egypt, moved to suppress the slave trade through the agency of European Christians, notably the British general Charles Gordon. Gordon was made governor-general of the Sudan in 1877, but his zeal in trying to eradicate the trade in slaves incited the revolt of Muhammad Ahmed, the Mahdi ('the divinely guided one'), in 1881. The Mahdi was strongly supported by the BAG-GARA and other Bedouin peoples. Gordon was killed when the Mahdist forces captured Khartoum in 1885, and Britain and Egypt abandoned the country.

Indigenous theocratic rule in the Sudan lasted until 1898, when a British-Egyptian army under General Sir Horatio Kitchener defeated the Mahdist forces at Omdurman on 2 September. Later that month Kitchener faced down a French expedition at Fashoda (Kodok) further up the Nile, halting France's eastward expansion at the Nile watershed.

The Sudan became an Anglo-Egyptian condominium, but control rested with Britain, which attributed Mahdism to Egyptian oppression and poor administration of the Sudan. The administration of Sir Reginald Wingate (governor-general 1899–1916) did much to reconcile the Sudanese to British-Egyptian rule, although it was less readily accepted in the south.

In 1924 Ali Abd al-Latif formed the White Flag League, whose aim was the expulsion of Britain from Sudan. Britain adopted a policy of indirect rule through traditional tribal authorities, easier to adopt in the north than the south. This accentuated Sudanese ethnic and religious differences, which continue to hinder national unity today. From around 1925, British capital encouraged large-scale cotton-growing in the productive Gezira, now extensively irrigated and the centre of commercial agriculture in the Sudan. Cotton became the backbone of the Sudanese economy (and remains the largest cash-crop today, followed by groundnuts, sorghum and sesame) and permitted a major expansion of health and social services.

## The Republic of Sudan

Sudanese nationalism continued to grow throughout the 1940s, and an Anglo-Egyptian agreement was reached in 1953 allowing for Sudanese independence. The independent Republic of Sudan was proclaimed in 1956. Its politics have been turbulent and are the product of major divisions in Sudanese society. Foremost are religious and ethnic differences. There has been uneven economic development between towns, the more prosperous Gezira, and the rest of the generally remote country (Sudan has a territory of 2.8 million sq. km / 967,000 sq. miles). Divisions in outlook between the more prosperous townsfolk and Nile-side dwellers and the disadvantaged and conservative subsistence farmers have remained.

The imposition of Islamic law continues to be strongly opposed by southern peoples who are predominantly animist and Christian and who have ethnic affinities with Uganda and the Congo (Kinshasa). The imposition of northern administrators in 1955 led to demands for the secession of the southern provinces and, after 1963, open civil war. The Addis Ababa Agreement of 1972 provided for southern autonomy, but the conflict flared again from 1983.

In 1989 a repressive and strongly Islamic military government assumed power. The conflict has intensified and there have been widespread human rights violations. Armed Arab militia have been used against southern peoples such as the DINKA, and the number of refugees has swelled. United Nations sanctions were imposed in 1996 to attempt to force an end to the conflict. The war continues to hinder economic development and agricultural production and has contributed to endemic famine in the south since the 1980s. In Sudan generally the GNP is failing to keep pace with the growth in population, now over 35 million (compared with around 21.1 million in 1984).

*" These miserable people do not understand energy, and the Ramadan increases their incapacity. "*

**Sir Samuel Baker, 1874, expressing colonialist frustration at the Sudanese**

S

## SUKULUMBWE

See ILA.

## SUKUMA

The largest ethnic group of Tanzania, numbering more than 3 million. Their ancestors colonized the area of modern Tanzania south of Lake Victoria early in the 2nd millennium AD. They are BANTU-speakers, culturally similar to the neighbouring NYAMWEZI to the south. They are adapted to dry-land grain agriculture, but also keep cattle, used in the payment of marriage dowries. Polygyny is common. The Sukuma live in villages and are organized into small independent chiefdoms, although these were federated in 1946, and later became a unit of government.

## SUSU or Soso

A MANDE-speaking people concentrated in Guinea. Their Susu language is spoken by around 1.3 million people, especially in coastal Lower Guinea, where it has become the *lingua franca*. They originally ruled the MALINKE, who revolted and assumed power in 1230, establishing the Mali empire. The Susu migrated as refugees or followed in the wake of pioneering Mande hunters towards the Guinea coast. They are largely Muslim agriculturists, but some are also talented traders and blacksmiths.

## SWAHILI

"Every ... Sowhyly carries a sword."

W.F.W. Owen, 1833

A cluster of peoples belonging to the coast and islands of central East Africa, mainly modern-day Kenya and Tanzania. They speak Swahili, or Kiswahili, a BANTU language heavily influenced by Arabic. The name itself (Arabic *sawahili*) means 'of the coast' and is the product of centuries of maritime trade and interaction with Arabia to the north. The Swahili people are themselves an ethnic and cultural mix of Africans, ARABS and other peoples involved in trade around the Indian Ocean who have arrived on the coast since ancient times, settled and inter-married. Notable among them were the Omani Arabs (see OMANIS) and the SHIRAZI.

Settlements appeared on the coast around AD 700–900, and there is evidence of contact with the Persian Gulf, Arabia and northwest India, notably Daybul. Trade links were also established with China and Indonesia. The gradual adoption of Islam provided an important element in the creation of a distinctive Swahili culture. This outward-looking African-Muslim civilization flourished in the towns of the Banadir (Somali) Coast, Zanzibar and Pemba, and in independent 'city-states' as far south as Sofala in modern-day Mozambique. From around 1100 large stone-built mosques and forts were constructed, along with elaborately designed and embellished palaces for kings and merchants, who used ceramics from Persia and China, rich fabrics from India and other fine imported products. Coins were even minted in some towns.

This civilization and prosperity reached its height in the 15th century, prior to the arrival of the predatory Portuguese, who sought to control the commerce of the Indian Ocean. They ended up destroying much of the trade facilitated by the Swahili between Eastern countries and the African gold- and ivory-producing areas inland, where slaves were also obtained. Portuguese culture had a very limited influence on the Swahili during their two centuries of domination, but following the Portuguese departure in the early 18th century Swahili language, poetry and literature revived, though many towns did not.

The earliest preserved piece of Swahili writing, the heroic poem *Utendi wa Tambuka*, was composed in Pate and dates from 1728. It uses Arabic script, which had been adopted by the 16th century. Early poetry also used Arab verse styles. Arab influence on Swahili culture continued strongly through the period of Omani overlordship of the East African coast. The Omanis were successors to the Portuguese, whom they finally expelled with local help in 1729, and their dominion lasted until Britain and Germany carved up the region for their own benefit from the 1880s. The partly acculturated Sultan, Arab aristocracy and elite remained, centred on the island of Zanzibar (see ZANZIBARIS), but now only nominally led Swahili society.

There are around 15 Swahili dialects and other pidgin forms still in use. It became the language of commerce in East Africa, carried by the trade and slave caravans sent inland from the coast. Later the Germans used Swahili-coast men as their imperial agents and it became the language of administration in their colony of Tanganyika. Under British colonial administration the language was standardized for use throughout East Africa, based on the Kiunguja dialect of Zanzibar. It is now widespread and is spoken as a main language by 5 million people, in Tanzania, Kenya, Congo (Kinshasa) and Uganda, and is especially valued in administration, trade and education. It is the second language of many more people throughout East Africa.

## SWAZI

A Swazi- or siSwati-speaking BANTU people concentrated in the highland Kingdom of Swaziland, and also occupying adjoining areas of Mozambique and the Eastern Transvaal in South Africa. They number around 2 million people today and form part of the Southern NGUNI ethnolinguistic grouping, along with the ZULU and XHOSA. Their traditional economy was based on cattle-rearing, but now subsistence and commercial agriculture is more significant. Many Swazi work in the timber, sugar and mineral industries in Swaziland and South Africa.

The origins of the nation lie in the mass migrations of recent centuries. The Swazi, calling themselves the Emalangeni, moved south down the coast of Mozambique, and around 1770, under King Ngwane III, they struck inland to establish a new homeland around Nhlangano. The royal Dlamini clan formed the focus of the new people, comprising associated clans and local peoples. Under Sobhuza I they introduced a military reorganization based on Zulu discipline and age-grade regiments which, with their move further north into modern-day central Swaziland around 1820, ensured their security from the aggressive Zulu nation to the south. This process of assimilation, conquest and consolidation by the Swazi in their new territory was completed by 1860 under Mswati (or Mswazi) II (ruled 1848–68), who is immortalized in the name of the country. The subsequent combination of the arrival of European farmers and mineral prospectors, AFRIKANER expansion and British strategic interests made Swaziland an area of conflict and led to colonial control. It became a British High Commission Territory in 1903 and achieved independence again in 1968 as a constitutional monarchy. It had close links with the apartheid South African regime against internal opposition, and political instability remains.

The organization of Swazi society is complex. Today the nation comprises more than 70 clans divided into three major sub-groups: the Bemdzabukos, regarded as 'pure' Swazi, of which the Dlamini is the largest grouping; the Emafikamuvas, or 'latecomers' to Swaziland; and the Emakhandzambilis, SOTHO and Nguni clans whose ancestral peoples already lived in the territory when the Swazi arrived. Some Nguni also arrived with the Swazi. Clans and age-grades remain important in the national life of Swaziland, but local and national government is administered by a combination of semi-democracy and appointed individuals. In South Africa, Swazi tribal chiefdoms comprise regional administrative authorities. Royal villages housing the king's wives and children are scattered throughout the kingdom, helping to bind local peoples to royal authority exercised in all temporal and religious affairs. These powers are shared between the king and his mother or a substitute. The Swazi National Council advises the king on the uncodified National Law and Custom which governs all cultural and administrative affairs. Most of the country's land, alienated during the colonial period and a sensitive political issue to the Swazi, is now nominally held by the king in trust for the nation. Today, the population of Swaziland numbers around 1.1 million, 85% ethnic Swazi. 10% Zulu and the rest TSONGA and other groups.

## TAMA

A people who live in the mountainous border region of Chad and the Sudanese Republic. They comprise several ethnic groups including the Tama of eastern Chad, based on the historic Sultanate of Tama, which still exists today. The wider Tama people are livestock- and subsistence farmers living in traditional community compounds of circular huts. They number around 300,000 and speak the Tama language of the NILO-SAHARAN language family. Many are Muslim but elements of their traditional animistic religion survive.

# TANZANIANS

People of Tanzania, bordering the Indian Ocean. It comprises the former British colonial territories of Tanganyika and the islands of Zanzibar, whose names were combined to create 'Tanzania' when the territories became the United Republic of Tanzania in 1964. SWAHILI is the *lingua franca*, the national language understood throughout this diverse country and a unifying influence on all Tanzanians. English is the other official language.

Ethnically, the country is the most heterogeneous state in Africa, with more than 120 indigenous peoples plus INDIANS and a small number of Europeans comprising a population estimated at 35.3 million at the end of the 20th century. (The main ethnic groups are shown in the accompanying box.) None of these groups can be said to predominate either culturally or politically. Economically the vast majority of the population remain tied to the land and 80% of export earnings are derived from agriculture.

From before 1000 BC the CUSHITES, a primarily pastoral people represented today by the BURUNGI but also the agricultural IRAQW, began to settle among the SAN (Bushmen) who lived in the area of modern Tanzania by traditional hunting and gathering. They were followed by the BANTU-speaking agriculturists from whom most of Tanzania's population is descended. The Bantu were soon followed by Nilotic pastoralists from southern Sudan (see NILOTES), most notably the MAASAI.

The longstanding involvement of Persian Gulf, Arabian, South Asian and other peoples in Indian Ocean trade involving the East African coast has led to an even richer ethnic diversity. ARAB influence on the creation of the Swahili culture and people has been profound. OMANIS became more dominant from the 17th century with the expulsion of the Portuguese from the coast by the Sultan of Muscat and local forces. They dominated coastal society well into the

20th century, and Omani immigration has continued into modern times. INDIANS based on Zanzibar and the coastal towns became involved in inland trade under Omani auspices and their numbers increased sharply under British colonial administration. They came from Gujarat in particular, but also from Goa and the Punjab, and include ISMAILIS, SIKHS and Bohras. Their numbers, however, have declined since independence.

**The Tanzanian interior**

Little is known about the interior of East Africa before 1700. The bulk of the region supported a pastoral economy, and cattle were (and for many still are) the main form of wealth. In the 19th century the high demand for slaves, ivory and gold at the coast introduced new conflict and destabilized traditional societies.

The Anglo-German Agreement of 1886 partitioned the region and created a German sphere of influence, which was strongly opposed by peoples in the new territory, especially by those who benefited from traditional trade and now feared for their livelihoods. In 1888 there was an uprising on the coast which drew in at least 100,000 warriors, many from the various ethnic groups inland. It was suppressed, but armed opposition continued, culminating in the Maji Maji rising of 1905–7.

The territory was declared a protectorate in 1891, and a new exploitation began. Railways were built and new cash crops introduced, especially sisal, coffee, cotton and rubber, but this attempt to reorganize the agricultural economy and administration of German East Africa ended with World War I and its conquest by Britain. The campaign severely disrupted the economy and created hardship for many, but stability returned to Tanganyika under the British colonial administration, which adopted indirect rule through traditional chiefs and councils of headmen. In the process the British administrators consolidated some 'tribal' identities among peoples who were formerly only loosely associated.

The country continued to develop peacefully and without any strong tribal conflict up to Tanganyikan independence in 1961. The Tanganyika African National Union, formed in 1954, provided the necessary leadership and reflected the

> **“** The British Empire left us a country with 85 per cent illiterates, two engineers and 12 doctors. **”**
>
> Tanzanian president Julius Nyerere, 1998

**Tanzanians: main ethnic groups**

Chaga
Gogo
Ha
Haya
Hehe
Kimbu
Kwere
Maasai
Makonde
Nyakysa
Nyamwezi
Sukuma
Swahili
Yao

popular fear of settler domination. In the 1960s President Julius Nyerere introduced a policy of nationalization and 'African Democratic Socialism' as the preferred route to successful national development. Between 1969 and 1976 half the rural population was compulsorily 'villagized' – forced to move into villages to facilitate the provision of education, health and other services – and provided with land for communal farming for their own subsistence and as a way of boosting agricultural production and income for economic development.

**Modern Tanzania**

These policies were inefficient and unpopular. The rapid population growth, sharp international oil price rises in the 1970s, government inefficiency and indebtedness, a deteriorating transport system and other factors all served to undermine the economy, and Tanzania has found it difficult to recover. Recently new gold, mineral, oil and gas extraction projects have become more significant to the economy, which has been liberalized since 1986. In 1992 the country ceased to be a one-party state and became a pluralist democracy.

Culturally, Tanzania is richly diverse. In general, family ties are strong and geographical and ethnic identities are important to individual Tanzanians. In Zanzibar, where most of the population is Muslim, the Islamic tradition governs issues of inheritance, marriage and divorce. Traditional storytelling, music, dance and handicrafts continue to flourish, in particular Arab-inspired wood-carving in Zanzibar and on the coast, and among the MAKONDE in the southeast of Tanzania.

# TEBU

A central Saharan people living in northern Chad, Niger, the Sudanese Republic and Libya. They are fragmented linguistically, speaking variants of either Dazaga or Tebu within the NILO-SAHARAN language family. The Tebu are more culturally unified, however, and their society is based on patrilineal clans and overwhelming adherence to Islam. They number around 300,000 and are primarily nomadic pastoralists and oasis cultivators.

# TEGRE

See TIGRE.

# TEKE or Bateke

A BANTU-speaking people who live in eastern Gabon and adjoining areas of the Congo (Kinshasa). They arrived in the area many centuries ago from the northwest. They have been heavily influenced culturally by the long period of FRENCH rule prior to independence in 1960 and by their continuing attachment to Francophone culture. From the 17th century the Teke became important middlemen in trade with Europeans on the coast, especially supplying copper, palm-oil and slaves. They remain a hunting and agricultural people and now number more than 150,000.

# TEMNE or Temen or Timne or Timmanee

One of the two largest ethnic groups in Sierra Leone, comprising one-third of the population of about 5.3 million and dominating the area around Freetown. They speak Mel, a West African language belonging to the Niger-Congo family. They first arrived in the 15th century from Sudanic territory to the northeast, and developed a prosperous mixed farming economy. The Temne live in patrilineal and often polygynous family groups in villages under elected headmen within various independent chiefdoms. These became units of administration under the British colonial regime. *Poro* and other secret societies, often led by chiefs, exist to promote the health and prosperity of their communities through traditional religious and cultural beliefs. The women's society, *bundu*, prepares girls for marriage. Islam has made steady headway among the Temne since the 17th century and there is a constant tension between the *Poro* and Muslim traditions and their followers. Many Temne are skilled craftspeople.

# TESO or Iteso or Ateso

A people, probably numbering more than 2 million, who occupy an area of central Uganda and

*❝The Tebu [are] small active fellows, mounted on small horses, of great swiftness. ❞*

Dixon Denham, 1826

*❝[The Temne] file their teeth to a very sharp point and, by frequently keeping some particular vegetable matter ... in their mouths, they become quite Red ... particularly the females, who consider it a mark of unrivaled beauty. ❞*

Brian O'Beirne, 1821

speak an Eastern Sudanic language (see NILOTES). Towards the end of the 19th century they were conquered by the GANDA, and as UGANDANS their cultural and political distinctiveness has continued to be eroded. They are highly regarded as farmers and successfully developed cotton as a cash crop in the early 20th century under British colonial rule. Their belief in an indigenous pantheon of gods has been replaced by Christianity.

## THONGA

See TSONGA.

## TIGRAY or Tigrinya

A people of the Ethiopian Tigray Province and adjoining central Eritrea. They speak Tigrinya and constitute around 10% of ETHIOPIANS but almost half of ERITREANS. They are descended from Semitic immigrants (see SEMITES) and indigenous CUSHITES who were responsible for establishing the Kingdom of Aksum (see AKSUMITES), centred on the Tigray region, which was the basis of the subsequent Christian kingdom of Ethiopia. The Tigray are traditional rivals of the AMHARA, co-religionists in the Ethiopian Orthodox Church. They are a sedentary agricultural people, not to be confused with the TIGRE of Eritrea, who speak a related language.

## TIGRE or Tigray or Tigrai or Tegre

ERITREANS of the northern plateau and adjoining lowlands of Eritrea. They are predominantly Muslim nomadic herders and speak Tigre, the second-most important language in Eritrea after the related Tigrinya, spoken by the TIGRAY people. Both are Semitic languages descended from Ge'ez, the *lingua franca* of the AKSUMITES and the traditional language of the Ethiopian Orthodox Church, but they are mutually unintelligible. A large number of Tigre form a federation with the Beni Amer branch of the BEJA people, and in religion similarly adhere to the Mirghaniyah Muslim religious brotherhood of the eastern Sudan.

## TIGRINYA

See TIGRAY.

## TIKAR

An offshoot of the BAMILEKE, the largest ethnic group in Cameroon. The various Tikar sub-groups live in the northwestern highlands, where they cultivate a variety of food and cash crops, but they are better known for their sculpture tradition and craft skills in pottery, metal and other forms. The wider Tikar people number around 600,000 today, speak mutually unintelligible dialects and live in densely populated patrilineal settlements in traditionally highly centralized independent chiefdoms.

## TIMMANEE or Timne

See TEMME.

## TIV

A subsistence-farming people of Nigeria. They live together in patrilineal polygynous family groups in traditional villages. The males are organized into a complex system of age-grades and other cooperative institutions, and although historically without chiefs (elders predominated), a paramount ruler was appointed by the British colonial government in 1948. They have a warrior tradition and many have joined the Nigerian army. The Tiv speak a language of the Niger-Congo family and number more than 2.5 million.

## TOGOLESE

The people of the West African Republic of Togo, capital Lomé, numbering around 5.3 million and divided into numerous ethnic groups. Indigenous KWA are concentrated in the southwest of Togo but the most numerous are the EWE who migrated from the area of modern-day Nigeria by the 16th century, later joined by the GA-ADANGME, KPELLE and others from Ghana and the Ivory Coast. Other groups such as the MOSSI and GURMA came down from the north, notably the region of Burkina Faso. On the coast there is a small population of mixed European and Brazilian descent associated with the maritime trading communities that were established there, notably by the Portuguese.

The Togoland protectorate was declared by Germany in 1884, contributing to the political division of the Ewe into Togo, Benin and Ghana, where today they are the dominant national groups. From 1922 the territory was governed by France under a League of Nations mandate, and it gained independence in 1960. The official language remains French. The western, British-administered, half of the territory voted to join the Gold Coast (Ghana) in 1957 and reunification is still the aim of many Ewe. In religion, traditional beliefs still predominate, and in the south voodoo cults are strong.

# TONGA

BANTU-speaking agriculturists of southern Zambia. They are also known as the Valley Tonga (after the Zambezi Valley) to distinguish them from the unrelated Lake Tonga people in Malawi and the Tsonga (or Tonga) of Mozambique. Like the neighbouring ILA, they traditionally lived in matrilineal clans subdivided into lineages, but today live within chieftainships created in the British colonial period for administrative convenience. The Tonga are Zambia's second-largest tribal group, numbering around 1.5 million people. Traditional Tonga religion gives prominence to spirits associated with rainfall.

# TORO or Batoro

A people from the southwest of Uganda. The kingdom of Batoro was created from the empire of BUNYORO-Kitara following a secession led by Kaboyo around 1830, although a proto-state can be identified several centuries earlier. It was re-conquered by King Kabarega of Bunyoro in the 1880s, restored by Britain in the 1890s and finally incorporated into the Uganda protectorate in 1900. Although it remained a unit of government within the British colony, the kingdom was abolished with all the others in Uganda in 1966. The division of its population was similar to ANKOLE, comprising a Bito and Hima pastoralist overclass and a mass of IRU cul-

tivators. The Toro are also traditionally known as hunters. Toro territory includes the Ruwenzori National Park, and the population today numbers around 600,000.

# TSONGA or Thonga

A people spread across the southern coastal area of Mozambique, the South African Transvaal, Zimbabwe and Swaziland, and numbering around 5 million. They originally formed numerous independent groups under dominant patrilineages, but were conquered by the NGUNI in the early 19th century and adopted much of their culture. They are mixed agriculturists and pastoralists living in polygynous patrilineal village groups. The women undertake much of the cultivation, while many men are migrant labourers. Many Tsonga are Christian, but others follow traditional practices involving propitiation of ancestral spirits, witchcraft and sorcery.

# TSWANA or Batswana

A cluster of BANTU SOTHO-speaking peoples who occupy the temperate grassland and dry thorn-veld of the edge of the Kalahari Desert, the territory of the modern-day Republic of Botswana. Effectively indistinguishable from the Western Sotho or Khalagari, they numbered around 4 million at the end of the 20th century. Tswana are also present in the adjoining areas of Namibia and South Africa. In 1977 the South African apartheid government created a nominally independent Tswana Bantustan, or homeland, called Bophuthatswana; this was abolished in 1994. The singular of 'Tswana' is 'Motswana'.

The Sotho-Tswana were part of the Bantu colonization of southern Africa, probably early in the 2nd millennium AD, establishing large hut-settlements near water sources. These towns were the largest traditional urban centres in southern Africa and numbered up to 20,000 people by the time European Christian missionaries arrived in the 1820s. The Tswana prospered in livestock-herding and subsistence agriculture based on corn (maize) cultivation, which continues today. The increasing population led to constant sub-division and the creation of new

*t*

" [The Tswana] easily succumb before the white man and perhaps in future years the Sichuana Bible will ... [be] in a language which no mortal understands. "

David Livingstone's diary, 11 May 1855

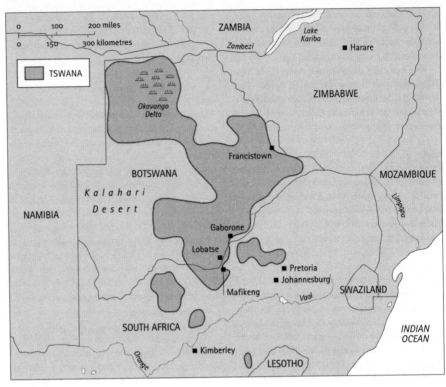

independent chiefdoms, which opposed 19th-century AFRIKANER expansion and the aggression of neighbouring African peoples such as the NDEBELE. These chiefdoms coalesced into the larger Tswana state.

To finance the acquisition of firearms to counter these threats, the Tswana chiefs used the SAN Sarwa hunting bands to exploit the wild produce of the Kalahari, transforming what had been a mutually beneficial relationship to one of authority and servitude. The chiefs were also receptive to missionaries, including David Livingstone, whom they saw as useful political allies. Christianity took root among the Tswana and remains strong, although traditional beliefs relating to ancestor-worship still predominate.

The Tswana territory, Bechuanaland, was given a measure of relief from its traditional enemies by becoming a British Protectorate in 1885, during the reign of Khama (1865–1923). The ruling elites continued in authority and managed eventually to ride nationalist sentiment to

form an independent Republic of Botswana in 1966. The country's bicameral political system includes a 15-member House of Chiefs representing the eight tribal states. The national capital is Gaborone.

The Tswana incorporated many peoples during the great political disruption of southern Africa in the 19th century and under colonial rule, such that ethnic Tswana form less than half Botswana's population today. While the Western Sotho of Botswana are indistinguishable from the Tswana, other ethnic elements retain their distinctiveness, including the Northern Sotho, western SHONA and HERERO, as well as the KHOISAN and other peoples from surrounding countries.

In terms of social organization, the Tswana (especially in Botswana) belong to patrilineal descent groups. Lineally related families, led by the senior family head, form town wards which are the basic social and administrative units of the country. Age-sets, or regiments, organized on a tribal basis, are an additional focus of loyalty. Tribes are still ruled by chiefs in conjunction with advisors and officials, but decisions are sanctioned by a more democratic general council of potentially all tribal adult males. The main languages are Setswana and English, and although Christianity is strong, most Tswana follow traditional religious beliefs. Many men work as migrant labourers in South Africa.

## TUAREG

A sub-group of the BERBERS of the central Sahara and northern Sahel of North and West Africa. They are traditionally nomadic pastoralists who range across parts of Libya, Algeria, Mauritania, Senegal, Chad, Mali, Niger, Burkina Faso and northern Nigeria in search of fresh pasture for their herds of goats, sheep and camels. The Tuareg are sub-divided into confederations, such as the Asban (Aïr Tuareg) in the southern Sahel zone and the Ahaggar and Azjer in the northern desert region. The southern Tuareg breed Zebu cattle as well as camels, which they sell to the northerners. Some Tuareg gather dates and cultivate small areas of desert oases. The overall population is estimated to approach 900,000, a large number having migrated to towns and cities for work during the prolonged drought from the 1970s to the 1990s, which devastated the traditional pastoral economy, especially in the south. The worst affected were the poorer farmers and pastoralists, especially descendants of emancipated slaves and servants of the Tuareg who had colonized the most marginal land during the 20th century.

The Tuareg speak Tamashek, an AFRO-ASIATIC language whose modern script is directly related to ancient Libyan (see NUMIDIANS). The Tuareg and other desert nomads were important in the trans-Sahara caravan trade in ancient times, and they were also feared for their plundering of caravans, travellers and other pastoralists to increase their herds of livestock and to take slaves. They were also one of the invading peoples who destroyed the wealthy and powerful SONGHAI empire in the Niger Valley in the late 17th and early 18th centuries. They remained fiercely independent under colonial rule and even took part in a major Islamic revolt against

the French in Niger in 1916–17, partly prompted by the threat to their trans-Sahara trade from railways built to take West African products south to the coast.

Tuareg men wear characteristic blue-coloured robes and bound head-dress, and they generally still live in their traditional red-dyed animal-skin tents with floors of woven grass matting, which they carry to each new settlement. Traditional society has always been feudal and highly stratified, much like that of the MOORS, and divided into several castes and related clans. At the top is an aristocratic class, itself divided into castes, descending to pastoral vassals and labourers or encampment servants (former slaves) known as the BELLA. The latter are also called the 'black' Tuareg, from their skin colour and origins in tropical West Africa, compared with the small caste of 'white' Tuareg, the nobility whose Berber ethnic origins were to the north and east. The clerics form a further group and are known as Ineslemen, whose upkeep rests on the voluntary contributions of other noble clans. The artisan class are despised, yet produce distinguished and characteristic metalwork and other items including traditional shields, swords, daggers and lances.

The Tuareg aristocracy employed members of these various castes in a range of integrated commercial activities. Resident servants and slaves looked after their property and, for commercial purposes, their own agents were installed in the urban centres. It was an effective system for exploiting the resources of a harsh environment and huge geographical region. This economic and social system has undergone important changes but its traditional structure remains.

## TUBU

See TEBU.

## TUKULOR or Futankobe

A FULANI people who originally settled in Futa Toro (ancient Takrur) in the Senegal Valley. They have also incorporated MOORS and SONINKE peoples, and Fulani Fulfulde (Fula) is their main language. They claim to be the first West Africans to convert to Islam, but they are best known for

**"** God has opened our mouths to put into them two things, either food to live or sand to die. **"**

**Tuareg saying**

the development of an austere form of the religion. In 1852 the Tukulor scholar Umar Tal established a religious brotherhood, the Tijaniyya, which soon grew in influence and inspired a Tukulor jihad against what they regarded as the pagan BAMBARA kingdoms. He died in 1864 and his warring sons added to the chaos in the region, a conflict that was only brought to an end by French conquest of the 1890s. After the Bambara Kingdom of Segu was overthrown by the French in 1890, 20,000 Tukulor were returned to Senegal. Traditional religion, involving a belief in witchcraft and spirits, has combined with Islam in a syncretic mix, which remains powerful today.

# TUNISIANS

People of the Democratic Republic of Tunisia, the homeland of the ancient CARTHAGINIANS. The population of around 9 million Tunisians are almost entirely Muslim BERBERS, although numerous invasions and waves of immigration have contributed a mixture of PHOENICIANS, ROMANS, VANDALS, JEWS, sub-Saharan Africans and TURKS as well as ARABS. In the 11th century Muslim refugees arrived in Tunisia from Sicily, and an estimated 200,000 Spanish Muslims (see MOORS) settled there following their expulsion from Spain between the 13th and early 17th centuries. The capital, Tunis, became notorious as a base for corsairs, or Barbary pirates.

Although Arabic is the official language, French is widely spoken due to colonial occupation by France between 1883 and 1956. Some Italian is spoken, but English is becoming more common as the language of commerce and the professions. Berber is spoken only by a tiny minority in the south of the country, which became completely Arabized in the medieval period. Arabic continues to be the language of Tunisian literature, which has a distinguished pedigree, and much of the arts, which are supported by a large and literate middle class. Annual theatre and music festivals have emerged, such as the Testour Maalouf Festival of traditional *malouf* music as well as more contemporary idioms. The course of Tunisia's history has contributed to the country's rich culture. More than half the population are now employed in industry, the service sector (notably tourism) and the exploitation of phosphates, oil and other minerals. Politically, the country has become more democratic and open in recent times.

# TURKANA

A strongly pastoralist people straddling the border of northeastern Uganda and northwestern Kenya as far as Lake Turkana (until 1979, Lake Rudolf). Some are also found in Ethiopia, and in total they are thought to number more than 400,000. They speak an Eastern Nilotic language and are closely related to the KARAMOJONG of northeastern Uganda, the Turkana homeland prior to their migration around 200 years ago. The Turkana live together in extended families and practise transhumant pastoralism, annually cultivating crops at winter homesteads (the responsibility of Turkana women). Cattle blood, milk and dairy products are central to their diet and culture.

# TUTSI or Batutsi or Watutsi

The traditionally dominant peoples of Rwanda and Burundi (though forming less than 10% and 15% of their national populations respectively), and among the HA of western Tanzania. The Tutsi comprise two large groups known as the Abanyaruguru and the Hima, each divided into numerous family lineages. The Hima should not be confused with the Hima sub-group of the Ugandan NYORO, ANKOLE and TORO peoples who have also undertaken a traditionally dominant role in their respective societies.

The Tutsi emerged in the region in approximately the 15th century as warrior-pastoralists of Nilotic origin, something that is apparent in their physical distinction from the indigenous agricultural HUTU people. Inter-marriage has since largely combined the physical characteristics of the muscular Hutu with the more lithe and paler-skinned Tutsi, whose average height approaches 1.83 m / 6 ft. They also adopted the BANTU Kinyarwanda language in Rwanda, and Kirundi in Burundi.

The Tutsi domination was achieved gradually through military power and by establishing a

> " The Tunisians are much more agriculturalists than their neighbours. "
>
> J.C. Loudon, 1825

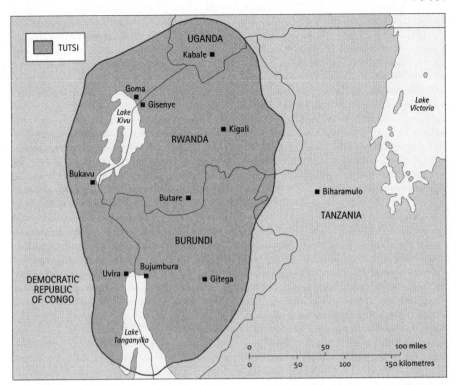

feudal-type system, in which the Hutu accepted Tutsi social and political superiority in return for the economic advantages of farming Tutsi cattle and land. The Tutsi became an aristocratic warrior class bound in turn to the semi-divine *mwami* (king) established in both countries. Like many pastoralists they viewed agriculturists as inherently inferior.

Belgian control of Rwanda (as part of the combined Ruanda-Urundi territory) following World War I, and encouragement of Hutu political ambitions, poisoned relations between the communities, which led to the expulsion of some Tutsis and the flight of others. This revanchist element contributed to the destabilization of the country following independence, which erupted in the 1994 genocide of mostly Tutsi RWANDANS. A largely Tutsi-dominated government has since been installed.

In Burundi the tensions remain, in a country whose Tutsi-dominated government has suppressed periodic Hutu revolts, notably in 1972 at a cost of 100,000 lives and in the early 1990s, when 700,000 people fled renewed civil strife.

Ironically, a process of cultural elision has taken place over the centuries. The Tutsi have adopted Hutu languages, while cattle have become central to the Hutu economy and way of life, and both groups acknowledge the same Christian and animist beliefs. The Tutsi clan and lineage structure also appears to have influenced the Hutu clan-based social organization. The Tutsi and Hutu both have a rich heritage of poetry, music and dance in particular, the more leisured life of the ruling Tutsi allowing them to cultivate the high arts to a greater extent. The Tutsi are skilled in decorative arts, especially in pottery and weaving of mats, screens, basketware and other items. Since the 1990s the government of Burundi has made efforts to reduce ethnic tensions by promoting the shared cultural heritage, including displays of craftwork and cooperative sports.

## TWA or Batwa

PYGMIES who inhabit the Great Lakes savannah region of east-central equatorial Africa. They live around Lake Kivu in Congo (Kinshasa) to the west, and Rwanda and Burundi to the east. Some remain wedded to their traditional hunter-gathering economy; others farm and herd cattle among the HUTU and TUTSI, with whom they have a close and mutually beneficial economic relationship. The Twa are BANTU-speakers like their neighbours and were probably the original inhabitants of the rainforest.

## UBANGI

A cluster of peoples living in the region of the Ubangi River, a major tributary of the River Congo in north and west-central Africa. It forms the border between modern-day Congo (Kinshasa) and the Central African Republic. They include the BANDA, NGBANDI, SANGA, GBAYA, Ngala and several others, all speaking Ubangian languages belonging to the Adamawa-Ubangi branch of the Niger-Congo family. A total of 40 Ubangian languages have been identified. The Ubangi people probably originated in the Sudan and migrated to their present territory from the 16th century.

## UBANI

See IBANI.

## UGANDANS

**❝** There is a tendency, wherever English authority is relaxed among them, to revert to their old terrible ways. **❞**

The *Daily Telegraph*, 1892, reflecting colonial beliefs about the Ugandans

People of the Republic of Uganda, capital Kampala. The former BRITISH protectorate of Uganda incorporated a wide range of ethnic groups, and achieved independence in 1962. The main ethnic divide is between the NILOTES in the north of the country and the more populous southern BANTU. The Bantu include the GANDA, the largest ethnic group, forming 20% of the country's total population, which is estimated at around 23 million at the end of the 20th century. Central Sudanic speakers, notably the KEBU and LUGBARA, are also found in the north but form only around 10% of the population, slightly less than the Nilotic groups. At least 32 languages are spoken in Uganda, but English is the sole official language. Ganda is widely spoken and SWAHILI has been promoted in order to assist regional integration with Kenya and Tanzania. A large number of South Asians lived in Uganda until most were expelled in 1972, although some have returned since the early 1990s.

Uganda occupies the region around the Great Lakes, having a more favourable geography and climate than the Sudan, its northern neighbour. North of Lake Victoria is lush and fertile, but there are harsher conditions in other parts of the country, notably the arid semi-desert in parts of the north. Uganda has high annual rainfall, and the tropical heat is tempered by the country's altitude of over 1065 m (3500 ft). Agriculture benefits from these conditions, and the history of Uganda involves constantly shifting groups of pastoralists and cultivators and their differential exploitation of food resources, which had important political consequences.

### Pre-colonial states

The pattern of ethnic migration and assimilation in the area of modern Uganda over many centuries is complex, but the result was the creation of a series of well-organized Bantu states, or kingdoms, incorporating southward-moving, predominantly pastoral Nilotes. Powerful chiefdoms emerged over time, such as the Atembuzi in northern Uganda after around 1300. Shortly afterwards the Hima kingdom in southern Uganda emerged as the most powerful regional state under the Chwezi kings. They appear to have been usurped by the LUO Bito dynasty of Bunyoro (see NYORO) in the early 16th century, who began to develop the empire of Kitara. As the power of Bunyoro-Kitara grew, a number of peripheral client kingdoms were created. These included Buganda, which from 18th century pursued its own expansion at the expense of Bunyoro-Kitara.

The characteristic form of western Ugandan political organization involved the rule of kings, chiefs and 'citizens' belonging to pastoral peoples over the more numerous cultivators. The former were stronger in warfare and offered protection to the farming population (who were also obliged to offer military service) in a sophisticated system of rights and responsibilities, seen for example in Ankole, Karagwe, Rwanda and Burundi. Other kingdoms were organized differently. Ruled by a series of able and aggressive *kabakas* (kings), Buganda became the most dynamic of all, dominating long-distance trade with the East African coast.

During the early 19th century, warfare supplied Buganda with slaves, livestock and ivory, which made it rich and powerful. Much of this was traded to the coast for the iron and skilled smiths the kingdom needed to maintain its agriculture and military power. SWAHILI and Egyptian-SUDANESE traders also introduced guns, which led to further warfare and disruption throughout the region. Rivalry became worse between Buganda and Bunyoro, whose ruler was determined to maintain his kingdom's independence.

**British rule and independence**

European involvement in local affairs deepened, impelled by a concern to eradicate the slave trade, as well as by religious zeal and great-power rivalry, and missionary involvement in politics further complicated affairs. In 1890, the region came under the influence of the Imperial British East Africa Company, and in 1894 the responsibilities of the IBEA Company were assumed by the British crown; Buganda became a British government protectorate.

A British military expedition invaded Bunyoro in 1894 and deposed its ruler, Kabarega. Treaties in 1896 incorporated Bunyoro, Batoro, Ankole, Busogo and northern territories into the British protectorate. Britain governed the Ugandan states through traditional tribal authorities, supplemented by a network of district councils.

Before 1914 British control extended further into the northern territories, whose 'martial' peoples supplied colonial police and army recruits. Southerners by contrast filled most other government and official posts. Agriculture was developed greatly, although the widespread settlement of white farmers was discouraged. Cotton was introduced in 1904 and coffee after World War I. Railways were built, and in 1931 Kampala was connected to the coast at Mombasa.

Ugandan independence was achieved in 1962, but sharp political divisions remained,

based largely on ethnic differences. Buganda continued to favour independence from the rest of Uganda despite a large measure of autonomy. In 1966, Milton Obote, the first prime minister, ordered the arrest of the Bugandan *kabaka*, Mutesa II, who escaped to Britain. A new republican constitution was declared, abolishing the kingdoms and the administrative division of Buganda. The reaction in the southwest of Uganda was hostile.

In 1971 Colonel Idi Amin assumed power in a coup, having consolidated his support within the army by recruiting large numbers of his own Kakwa people from the northwest. His rule lasted until 1979 and is notorious for the expulsion of all the non-citizen Asian community (which numbered over 50,000 in 1969) and economic collapse. Tanzanian invasion and several coups followed, and Obote returned to power between 1979 and 1985 before being ousted again. Economic confidence slowly recovered into the 1990s, helped by a new constitution adopted in 1995 and the rule of the new president, Yoweri Museveni.

The economy is now stable but still heavily dependent on agriculture, in which 80% of the population is employed. Exports of raw materials include copper and gold. The income of 66% of the population remains below the absolute poverty level (under $1 per day). Staple foods include plantain (matoke), sweet potatoes and cassava among a variety of vegetables. Ugandans have a rich oral culture and variety of traditional customs. Dance, music, theatre and film are popular, and football is widely followed.

## UPPER VOLTANS

See BURKINABE.

## VAI or Gallinas

A MANDE-speaking people of northwestern Liberia and adjoining Guinea and Sierra Leone. They share close cultural ties with the Mande people and are probably descended in part from MALINKE traders associated with the great Mali empire, established from the 13th century. Later they were heavily involved in trading slaves to the Portuguese and other Europeans on the

**Ugandans: main ethnic groups**

*Northern (Nilotes)*

Acholi
Alur
Kakwa
Karamojong
Kumaru
Lango
Padhola
Sebei
Teso

*Southern (Bantu)*

Amba
Ankole
Ganda
Gisu
Gwere
Kedi
Kiga
Nyole
Nyoro
Rwandans
Samia
Soga
Toro

coast. They are an agricultural and fishing people, highly skilled in craft-work (especially in textiles and gold), and largely Muslim, employing Arabic and their own syllabic script. Their numbers are small, estimated at about 200,000 in total.

## VENDA or Bavenda or Vhavenda

A BANTU-speaking people who number around 900,000 and live in the highlands of Northern Transvaal, South Africa. In origin they are a 'composite people', composed of different cultural groups who migrated to the region from the north in the early 18th century. They practise mixed farming and rear large herds of cattle and other livestock in a society led by traditional chiefs and headmen. Many are migrant workers. Both men and women belong to specific age-grades, which regulate their position in society. Under apartheid, in 1979, Venda became an independent Bantustan republic but was reincorporated into South Africa in 1994. Belief in ancestral spirits and animism remains strong.

## VILI or Bavili

A sub-group of the KONGO people of central Africa. They speak a related western BANTU language. Their oral traditions suggest an ancestral migration from inland regions, which reached the western Congo and coast of Gabon around the end of the 13th century. The Vili developed the sophisticated kingdom of Loango by the 1480s (contemporary with the powerful Kongo Kingdom), which benefited from ivory and slave-trading with the Portuguese to the west. This kingdom fractured and declined in importance from the early 18th century, although trade continued. The region was absorbed into French colonial territories in the late 19th century. Most of the Vili remained primarily hunters and small-scale farmers and fishermen along the Atlantic coast, but others continued their commercial activities as French company agents and porters.

## VOLTA

See GUR.

## WAHA

See HA.

## WANYANJA

See NYANJA.

## WATUTSI

See TUTSI.

## WESTERN SAHARANS

The indigenous inhabitants of the former Spanish colony of Western Sahara on the Atlantic coast of northwest Africa, known locally as Saharawis. They are MOORS and BERBERS and are largely nomadic, surviving mostly by animal husbandry. This desert country, rich in phosphate deposits and other minerals, was partitioned by Mauritania and Morocco when Spain decided to withdraw in 1975. It has been ruled by Morocco alone since 1979, in continuing defiance of the small indigenous population of perhaps 250,000. The Polisario Front, formerly aided by Algeria, has been fighting for independence for what they term the Democratic Saharan Republic.

## WOLOF

Cattle farmers and agriculturists of Senegal and Gambia. They speak variants of Wolof, which is related to FULANI Fula and is the national language of Senegal, estimated to be spoken by more than 13 million people in their native countries and in Mali, Mauritania and France. The Wolof became the first suppliers of black slaves to the Portuguese in the 15th century and developed a powerful empire between the 14th and 16th centuries. Wolof society was elaborately hierarchical, headed by a traditional ruling dynasty and aristocracy with a powerful equestrian tradition.

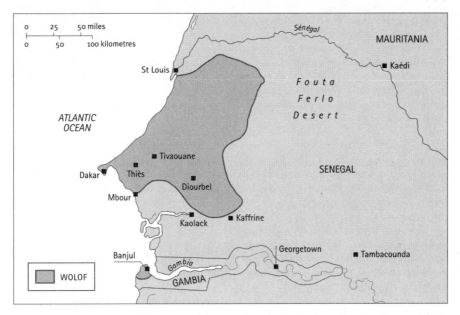

# XHOSA

A major community of Southern NGUNI who live in the Ciskei and Transkei regions of the eastern Cape (on each side of the Kei River) in South Africa. They have been highly significant in the history of black–white relations in South Africa. They number at least 600,000 today and are divided into several sub-groups. Their language is part of the Nguni group of the BANTU languages. Migrants into the area, such as the Thembu and the Mfengo, also came to speak the Xhosa language.

The Xhosa were the most southerly of the Bantu-speaking peoples and, in consequence, they were the first to encounter Boer expansionism (see AFRIKANERS) in the late 18th century. From the 1770s until the 1870s, a number of so-called Kaffir Wars were fought between the whites and the Xhosa and their allies. The Xhosa also became heavily involved in frontier trading and in the missions that the whites established among them. Nevertheless, they experienced periods of great economic distress. Economic and environmental pressures on the Xhosa were such that a prophetess induced them to kill all their cattle in 1856–7 in the hope of a better future. This led to considerable starvation and

suffering. Today many of the Xhosa are small farmers, still living under the authority of chiefs, but many others have migrated to the towns in search of employment, where many have obtained skilled or professional jobs. They have long been prominent in South African politics.

# YAO

A cluster of BANTU-speaking peoples inhabiting southern Tanzania, northern Mozambique and southern Malawi. Today they are agriculturists, mostly living in compact villages (traditionally stockaded for defence), who practise shifting cultivation supplemented by fishing where possible. In Malawi, tobacco is an important cash crop for the Yao. Historically, they are well known for their participation in the ivory and slave trades between the interior and the SWAHILI coast of East Africa, which reached their zenith during the late 19th century. As with the NYAMWEZI, this trade had a major influence on their social and political development.

The Yao became significant in northern Mozambique and southern Tanzania in the late 17th century. Partly at the expense of the MARAVI they extended their control over the main southern trade route from beyond Lake Malawi

*"Cattle is the foremost and practically the only subject of his care and occupation, in the possession of which he finds complete happiness."*

**Ludwig Alberti, 1811, on the typical Xhosa man**

(Nyasa) to the Indian-Ocean port of Kilwa which became the largest mainland slaving centre. From here countless thousands were shipped to the slave markets and plantations of Zanzibar. Yao control was further assured by 1850 with the purchase of guns, which increased their power to defend themselves and their trade and to capture more people to use and sell as slaves on the coast.

Faced with the threat of better-armed rivals, internal divisions, displacement by the warlike NGONI from the south, and defeat by the MAKUA in the 1850s, the Yao identified the need to strengthen their system of government. The various autonomous groups of Yao, including several who had migrated westwards to NYANJA territory in southern Malawi, combined into numerous territorial chiefdoms for the first time. Some grew from the extended families of individual traders and their large number of slave wives. They were led by men skilled in both trade and warfare and were essentially mercantilist. Their trading links to the coast also made them more open to outside influences, especially Arab-SWAHILI language and culture, also reflected in Yao building styles. Despite the work of the Scottish missions from the 1870s, inspired by David Livingstone, Islam was adopted by many of the traders and became widespread in Yao society. It was given added impetus as an indigenous response to European conquest and colonization, which prompted fierce armed resistance by Yao, who rightly feared an end to their traditional slave-owning and trading way of life. Today the majority of the total Yao population of more than 1 million are Muslims.

Annual initiation rites, involving circumcision for boys, are a feature of Yao society and were part of the traditional belief system associated with the worship of ancestor spirits. The Yao are still ruled by chiefs and headmen who succeed matrilineally, and married couples live in the wife's village.

## YAOUNDE or Yaunde or Jaunde or Ewondo or Euondo

A BANTU-speaking people who, together with the Eton, MAKA and others, make up the Beti people,

one of three sub-groups of the FANG of west-central Africa. The Yaounde live in the upland area of south-central Cameroon, concentrated around the capital city, also named Yaounde, where their dialect is the *lingua franca*. They number around 250,000 and are thought to have been among the last waves of Fang peoples driven down from the northeast, possibly under pressure from the FULANI. Yaounde has become the everyday language of much of the Fang population. Rural dwellers live in straggling hamlets and townships and grow a variety of crops with some livestock. The units of Yaounde society, which is essentially egalitarian, are patrilineal clans, which form individual tribes.

## YOLA

See JOLA.

## YORUBA

The third-largest ethnic group in Nigeria, where they are concentrated (see NIGERIANS). They dominate the western states of Oyo, Ondo, Ogun and Lagos and are also present in most of the other tropical West African territories, altogether numbering more than 20 million. This large ethnic group is divided into numerous sub-groups possessing different cultural identities and speaking various dialects of Yoruba, a KWA language of the Niger-Congo family. Standard written Yoruba, and an extensive literature, developed following the translation of the Bible into Yoruba by Bishop Samuel Crowther in 1884.

The Yoruba migrated to their present homeland west of the lower Niger River around 1000. They were probably Sudanic peoples from the east who, according to Yoruba tradition, conquered the indigenous forest-dwellers. They quickly established numerous towns that became the basis of a burgeoning number of autonomous kingdoms whose chiefs, hereditary kings or *obas*, were semi-divine religious as well as political leaders. Some towns coalesced into powerful cities, notably Ile-Ife, Oyo, Ibadan and others still flourishing in modern-day Nigeria. These powerful cities gave rise to the most urbanized societies of pre-colonial sub-Saharan

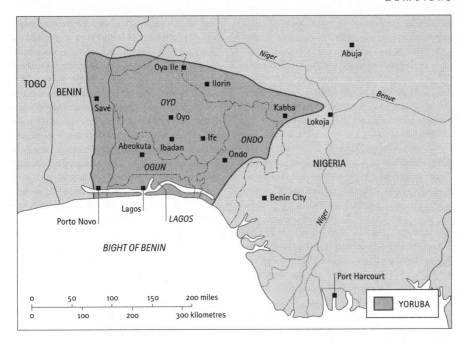

Africa, of which Ibadan was the largest. Although a single politically-centralized Yoruba state never developed, these kingdoms formed a powerful confederation. The most dominant of these city-states in the 17th–18th centuries was Oyo, but it declined in the early 19th century at a time of growing disputes among Yoruba rulers, and invasion by the FON of Dahomey and the Muslim FULANI of northern Nigeria. The individual kingdoms still exist, and although the state has assumed much of their political power, the *obas* and their councils of chiefs, who rule over constituent subordinate towns, still exercise limited local authority.

The Yoruba are a mostly agricultural people, the women specializing in the marketing of produce. Many are also urban workers, in all trades and professions. Their social organization is diverse, but patrilineal descent is widespread, members of the same patrilineage living in the same compounds under headmen. These compounds are commonly found surrounding the traditional walled urban palace compounds of the *obas* and chiefs. Each patrilineage has its own culture, land rights and religious observances, worshipping its own specific god, *orisha*, of which there are several hundred in the traditional Yoruba pantheon headed by the creator god Ifa. However, a large number of Yoruba are Muslims, a religion brought to the north by the Fulani and HAUSA, or Christians, especially in the south. Several self-help organizations are in operation assisting Yoruba welfare and commercial development. Historically, the Yoruba are renowned for their high level of craft skills, which found full expression in bronze casting during the 13th–14th centuries. Craftsmen also excelled as ironsmiths, carvers, weavers and workers in glass and leather, the women traditionally undertaking basketry, cotton-spinning and dyeing.

## ZAMBIANS

People of the Democratic Republic of Zambia. They are almost entirely BANTU-speaking and are traditionally agriculturists, although a large number now live in urban centres. Copper- and cobalt-mining are important industries in the copperbelt of the Western Province. The country was formerly Northern Rhodesia under British rule, a colony formed out of the 1890s protec-

*" [The Yoruba are] a race equally regardless of the past and reckless of the future. "*

Richard Burton, 1863

torates of Northeastern and Northwestern Rhodesia. Nationalist activity was much stimulated by its subordinate role in the Central African Federation, which was founded in 1953. When that federation broke up, Northern Rhodesia achieved independence as Zambia, under President Kenneth Kaunda, in 1964. Kaunda acceded to multiparty elections in 1991, and lost power.

Zambia is an amalgam of many cultures and peoples, speaking 80 different languages and dialects. English is the official language. The BEMBA dominate the north and are Zambia's largest people (roughly one-third of the population of 6.5 million). Other peoples are named in the accompanying box. They are predominantly Christian. The Zambian capital is Lusaka, founded as a planned colonial city in the 1930s. It replaced Livingstone, nearer the Zambezi, named after the missionary and explorer, who died at a village in northeastern Zambia in 1873 and inspired many of the Christian missionaries who settled in the territory. In the east, the Luangwa Valley is celebrated for its big game and for hunting.

## ZANDE

See AZANDE.

## ZANJ

An Arabic term denoting black Africans. It was applied to peoples of the East African coast by early Arab traders (see ZANZIBARIS). The geographer al-Masudi visited the region in AD 916 and described a powerful state and capital built by 'the Zanj' whose nascent SWAHILI language and culture he admired. Their chief export was ivory, but slaves were also traded to Arabia and the Persian Gulf. In 1331 Ibn Battuta recorded slave raiding among the Zanj of East Africa by the Sultan of Kilwa.

## ZANZIBARIS

People of the island and port-city of Zanzibar, now part of Tanzania. The island was originally named Unguja, but in the medieval period Arab traders applied the name Zanj-Bar, meaning 'the

coast of the ZANJ', a collective term for black Africans. Zanzibar has always been important as a juncture of Indian Ocean and world trade and cultures, the site of one of the earliest Muslim settlements, and an integral part of the development of SWAHILI language and culture, which fused African and Arab elements. Modern-day Swahili is largely derived from the classical Zanzibar dialect Kiunguja and is the principal language of Zanzibar, although Arabic is spoken by a large minority. Swahili and English are the two official languages of the TANZANIANS.

The population of Zanzibar, the main island of the small archipelago with an area of 1650 sq. km / 637 sq. miles, is diverse as a result of trading links throughout the Indian Ocean. Several different African groups reflect recent migration from the mainland, but the original BANTU peoples are the Hadimu and Tumbatu, sometimes known as SHIRAZI. They generally incorporated Arab and Persian settlers through intermarriage, although a distinct Arab minority, mainly OMANIS, developed especially from the early 18th century, under the rule of the sultans of Muscat and Zanzibar. More recent immigrants from Oman are known as Manga. There are also small groups of SOMALIS and COMORANS as well as Asians speaking Hindi, Gujarati, Urdu and Konkani, some descended from INDIANS who helped finance the trade and slave caravans into the interior of East Africa from the 18th century.

**The importance of trade**

There is evidence of coastal trade links between Zanzibar and Arabia, the Persian Gulf and the East from as early as the 7th century, which the prevailing trade winds did much to encourage. Various traditions suggest the 'Daybuli' people were among the earliest Arabs to arrive on the coast, probably from the seaport of Daybul in northwest India, captured by Muslim Arabs in AD 711. The PERSIANS arrived in the 10th century. By 1000 there were many Muslims resident in Zanzibar, where a stone mosque was built in 1107. Towns were increasingly Muslim and Swahili, with fine stone buildings and a rich material culture utilizing fine Chinese and Persian ceramics and Indian textiles.

The trade and civilization of the Swahili coast flourished along with the growth of strong independent outward-looking towns and city-states. Zanzibar was never a single town or polity but prospered as a diverse territory and base for traders. Soon after 1500 the Portuguese merchant Barbosa described the Zanzibaris as 'people ... who live in great luxury and comfort, dressing in good clothes of silk and cotton bought from Mombasa.'

The advent of the Portuguese after 1498 and their destructive attempts to control Indian Ocean trade led to two centuries of decline. Their expulsion was largely the work of the Omani Arabs (see OMANIS) who allied with local people and rulers to drive out the Portuguese from 1650 onwards. The Omanis established their own suzerainty over much of the coast, although they were resisted by many local people.

Trade and Swahili culture both revived in the early 18th century, leading to a new influx of Omanis. Indian merchants fleeing Portuguese oppression in Mozambique also relocated to Zanzibar in the 1780s and helped develop this growing trade in ivory and slaves.

### Omani domination

In 1832 the sultan of Muscat, Seyyid Said bin Sultan, made Zanzibar his political capital and began its transformation into the commercial centre of the coast and a lucrative plantation colony based on cloves. The Omanis exploited the labour of the indigenous Hadimu to clear land, develop clove plantations and build houses for the new Omani landowners. While trade prospered, the condition of the Hadimu, Tumbatu and other oppressed peoples worsened in the late 19th century as they were pushed off their land on the west side of the island onto the poorer land to the east. Slave labour was increasingly used to work the plantations and slaves formed roughly half of the island's population of 200,000 in the mid-19th century. Roughly 50,000 slaves were exported every year from the mid-19th century.

In 1861 Muscat and Oman became independent sultanates, but they were already part of Britain's informal empire in the region. Following the Zanzibar Treaty with Germany in 1890, Zanzibar became a British protectorate, and the sultan's East African dominions were divided between the two European powers. The separa-

tion of Zanzibar and its mainland possessions undermined the economy and encouraged the growth of the rival ports of Dar es Salaam and Mombasa.

Slavery was made illegal in 1897, although British concern to bolster the economy of Zanzibar and maintain the political position of its client sultans meant that most nominally free slaves were forced to remain on plantations as labour-tenants. Zanzibari society remained very undemocratic throughout the early 20th century. The divide between the African peasantry and Arab plantation-owning elite was reflected in their separate political aspirations after World War II.

The Sultanate of Zanzibar regained its independence in 1963, but the Arab ruling class was overthrown the following year in a revolution by the majority Africans. Zanzibar and Tanganyika signed a treaty of union, creating the modern United Republic of Tanzania. Land was also nationalized in 1964 and redistributed. Under the terms of the union with Tanganyika, Zanzibar retains its own autonomous government and constitution. Nevertheless, nationalist and separatist sentiment remains a current issue in both Zanzibar and Pemba.

The port of Zanzibar still exports large quantities of cloves (approximately 10% of world production), citrus fruits, coconuts and other produce. Fishing remains an important activity around the coast and employs around 10% of the population. Fertile soils provide rich crops of rice, yams, cassava and a variety of tropical fruit, helping to support a population estimated at around 600,000 in the late 20th century.

## ZARAMO

A cluster of SWAHILI peoples of the East African coast, which also includes the KWERE. The Zaramo proper live in Tanzania and are thought to have originated as the Kutu people in the Morogoro region, inland from the country's main city and port, Dar es Salaam. They developed through the incorporation of diverse peoples dislocated by the 19th-century slave trade, establishing fortified villages under headmen who had no wider overall political authority. Rural settlements became more dispersed in the 20th century, but Tanzanian government policy introduced around 1970 enforced a more concentrated settlement pattern once again. The Zaramo are mainly hoe cultivators and stock-keepers, although they are fishermen nearer the coast. Many have also migrated to the towns, especially Dar es Salaam, where they form the main ethnic group. They are united in their Muslim faith and Swahili language and culture, which influence such things as personal names and dress. They are known for their accomplished craft skills in ironsmithing and woodcarving, producing, for example, ornamental doors and latticework in the Arabic manner.

## ZERMA or Djerma

Inhabitants of the Sahel drylands of western Niger and adjoining Burkina Faso and Nigeria. They form a branch of the SONGHAI people and speak a related dialect. They are traditionally skilled in cavalry warfare, and horses remain an important currency of wealth and social prestige along with cattle, which are loaned to, and tended by, the FULANI or TUAREG. Crops are grown in the Niger Valley with the help of irrigation. The Zerma number around 1 million and many men travel south as migrant workers, especially to Ghana.

## ZIMBABWEANS

Inhabitants of the Republic of Zimbabwe, formerly Rhodesia, a country demarcated by Cecil Rhodes's British South Africa Company in the 1890s. The territory was named after the ruins of GREAT ZIMBABWE and the medieval culture associated with them.

The majority people of Zimbabwe are the SHONA, constituting about 75% of the population of around 11.5 million, but divided up into many sub-groups. They inhabit most areas of the country, with their power concentrated on the capital, Harare (formerly Salisbury). The other main group is the NDEBELE of Matabeleland in the southwest. There are also some whites (about 200,000), descendants of settlers and professionals of the colonial period. Many of the whites were farmers who acquired good land on the 'high veld', running cattle and growing maize. (They later became interested in the lower-lying areas of the country as well, because these were suitable for the cultivation of tobacco and sugar.) The languages of the country are Shona, Sindebele and English.

In 1953 Southern Rhodesia was swept up into the Central African Federation, a federal structure bringing together Southern Rhodesia (Zimbabwe), Northern Rhodesia (Zambia) and Nyasaland (Malawi). It seemed that white rule was well entrenched, but the federation collapsed in 1963 and independence under majority rule was granted to Zambia and Malawi.

In 1965, white settler politicians in Rhodesia rebelled against the imperial power through a 'Unilateral Declaration of Independence' and inaugurated a republic. This prompted the outbreak of the second *chimurenga*, in which armed guerrilla insurgency was based mainly in Zambia and Mozambique, and ultimately led to the Lancaster House agreements of 1980 and majority rule under Robert Mugabe.

The Shona now dominate Zimbabwe's politics, and Mugabe, president since independence in 1980, has suppressed the Ndebele and seized land from the white farmers. Land redistribution from whites to blacks was widely seen as necessary, but Mugabe's methods have largely destroyed the agricultural base of the country. Many of the blacks who took over 'white' farms had no interest in farming, having been selected on the basis of military service. Moreover, his policy coincided with a period of drought, a problem to which Zimbabwe has been frequently prone.

Under Mugabe's rule, infant mortality has risen, education (traditionally provided by missionaries) has declined, drought and economic failures have produced famine, and persistent decline in the Zimbabwean economy has become a regular feature. Adjacent states have, however, been disinclined to become involved in international concerns over his regime.

## ZULU

A Northern NGUNI people who live mainly in northern Natal, where their South African

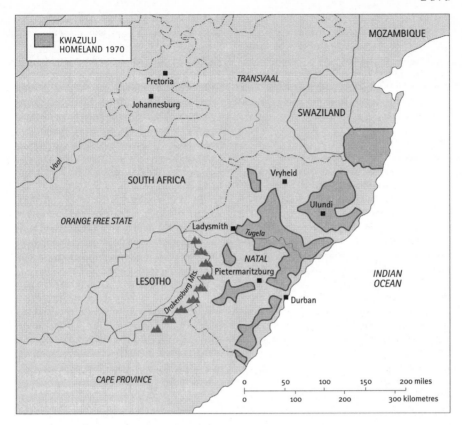

KWAZULU
HOMELAND 1970

MOZAMBIQUE

Pretoria

TRANSVAAL

Johannesburg

SWAZILAND

*Voal*

SOUTH AFRICA

Vryheid

*ORANGE FREE STATE*

Ulundi

Ladysmith

*Tugela*

NATAL

LESOTHO

Pietermaritzburg

*Drakensberg Mts*

INDIAN
OCEAN

Durban

*CAPE PROVINCE*

| 0 | 50 | 100 | 150 | 200 miles |
|---|---|---|---|---|
| 0 | 100 | 200 | 300 kilometres |

apartheid 'homeland' was known as KwaZulu (see SOUTH AFRICANS). They number over 5 million and practise a mixed agricultural economy combining the keeping of cattle, sheep and goats with the growing of millet, maize, peas and beans. Some Zulu are also labour migrants to South Africa's cities. They maintain a modified form of their traditional social and political structure, and still acknowledge a Zulu king.

In 1975 the political leader Mangosuthu Buthelezi revived a Zulu royalist movement of the 1920s, renaming it the Inkatha Freedom Party (IFP), intended as a rival to the African National Congress (ANC) of Nelson Mandela. As South Africa moved towards majority rule, the IFP attempted to secure a federal system for the new regime – or at least special privileges for the Zulu. The ANC, however, came to power and opposed these initiatives, though the province of Natal has been renamed KwaZulu-Natal.

## The Zulu state

In the early 19th century, the Zulu were only one small sub-group of the Northern Nguni. At the end of the 18th century, the Ndwandwe and the Mthethwa groups were notably more significant in forming state structures among the Nguni. Their chiefs Zwide and Dingiswayo began to create centralized and militarized systems, and started the process of conquering their neighbours. The Ndwandwe and Mthethwa eventually clashed in 1818–19, and a new chief, Shaka, rose to the leadership of the Zulu, who were at that time allied to the Mthethwa. Eventually he took over the entire northern Nguni kingdom and turned it into the most celebrated and feared African state of southern Africa.

The Zulu state may have been based on a new concept of centralized authority rooted in its revolutionary military techniques, but it may also have been stimulated by trading with Delagoa

Bay in the north, and possibly by population pressure on a deteriorating environment. In the 1820s and 1830s, the Zulu state attacked many neighbours and caused major African migrations in southern Africa. The movements of the NDEBELE, the SHANGANE and the NGONI into regions north of the Limpopo and Zambezi rivers were part of this process.

### British rule

When British traders began to settle at Port Natal, later Durban, in the 1830s, the Zulu were a major threat. Shaka's successor, Dingane, attacked Port Natal and tried to find means of keeping the whites under control. From 1837, he also faced incursions from parties of AFRIKANER trekkers who were seeking land concessions. He killed one group, led by Piet Retief, and attacked Boers encamped on the Tugela River, killing many of them, together with their KHOISAN servants. A village on the site of these events was named Weenen or 'weeping'. Dingane was subsequently defeated by a Boer commando led by Andries Pretorius at a battle known as Blood River (1838), because the river ran with the blood of the defeated Zulu. This became one of the mythic moments of Afrikaner history and continues to be commemorated to this day.

After the British annexation of Natal in 1843, the colonial authorities and the Zulu lived through several decades of uneasy peace. Natal's 'diplomatic agent to the native tribes' (1853–75), Sir Theophilus Shepstone, adopted a policy of 'indirect rule' towards the Northern Nguni, ruling them through their chiefs. In the late 1870s, however, the British feared that the Zulu king Cetshwayo threatened the Transvaal and Natal. British forces invaded Zululand in early 1879. They were defeated at Isandlhwana, and were nearly overwhelmed at Rorke's Drift, but later triumphed over the Zulu at Ulundi.

The Zulu were split up into 13 separate chieftaincies and their military power was brought under imperial control, with Cetshwayo in exile. Zulu warriors became performers at exhibitions and other Western entertainments. Much of their land was expropriated and settled by whites.

After the suppression of a tax revolt in 1906, the Zulu turned to more conventional political activity. But their reputation as a fierce and formidable foe remained in British popular culture. Their name was given to a North Sea fishing boat in the 1880s and to at least one warship in the mid-20th century, and they feature in late 20th-century films.

> " When the Zulus think how they were once a strong nation in the days of Chaka, and how other nations dreaded them so much that they could hardly swallow their food, and when they remember their kingdom which has fallen, tears well up in their eyes, and they say: 'They ferment, they curdle! Even great pools dry away!' "
>
> **Thomas Mofolo**
> **(1910)**

# Europe

# ABAZA

A Caucasian people of the Karachay-Cherkess autonomous republic, Russian Federation. They speak a North Caucasian language. Inhabiting the Caucasus Mountains since at least the 13th century, they mainly subsisted as herders of sheep, goats and horses. By the 16th century they had adopted Sunni Islam and had become powerful. Internal divisions, however, coupled with Russian and Turkish pressure, undermined them. Under RUSSIAN rule in the 19th century they proved rebellious, but Soviet rule, and collectivization in the 1930s, did much to crush nationalism. Subsequent education policy and Russification also undermined their traditional culture. Although they value their cultural identity, urbanization and migration threaten it. In 1989 they numbered nearly 45,000.

# ABODRITES

A SLAV tribe of the southern Baltic coast; their chief centre was Veligrad (modern Mecklenburg near Wismar in eastern Germany). They were conquered by the GERMANS in the 12th century.

# ACHAEANS

A name given to the ancient GREEKS by Homer and other ancient Greek poets; it is possibly the name the MYCENAEANS called themselves. The term also refers to the Ancient Greek population of Achaea, a region comprising southern Thessaly and the north coast of the Peloponnese. In the 7th and 8th centuries BC the Achaeans played an active role in the Greek colonization of southern Italy, founding the city of Kroton (Crotone) in 710 BC. The Achaeans lived in independent city-states, but in the 5th century BC they formed the federal Achaean League, which played an influential role in Greek politics in the 3rd century BC. Achaea became part of the ROMAN empire in 146 BC.

# ACHEULIAN CULTURE

A Palaeolithic culture named after an archaeological site at Saint-Acheul, near Amiens in France. The Acheulian culture was extremely widespread and long-lived, found across much of western and central Europe, the Middle East, India and Africa, and existed from around 1.65 million years ago to around 100,000 years ago. The characteristic tool of the Acheulian culture was the hand-axe, which was actually used for butchering. Although it is named after a European site, the culture originated in Africa and was spread by migrating early humans.

# ADYGHE

A Caucasian people of the Adyghea autonomous republic, formed in 1991 within the Russian Federation. They speak a North Caucasian language. One of the main branches of the CIRCASSIANS, the Adyghe are herders and farmers, and had converted to Sunni Islam by the 17th century, although some earlier religious practices persisted until recently. They have a long history of foreign domination, including by the GEORGIANS (12th century), MONGOLS (13th century), TURKS (17th century) and RUSSIANS (from the early 19th century). These last invaders were particularly detested and were bitterly resisted; many Adyghe migrated to Turkish territory to avoid Russian rule. Further emigration followed Soviet rule, with its policies of Russification and collectivization, and an autonomous *oblast* (region) established in 1922 was abolished in 1937. In 1993 they numbered 300,000, although they claim over 6 million descendants worldwide.

# AEDUI

A tribe of GAULS whose capital was at Mont Beuvray (now in Saône-et-Loire) in central France. The Aedui were longstanding allies of Rome, and it was their appeal for Roman protection against the HELVETII that gave Julius Caesar the pretext he needed to begin the conquest of Gaul in 58 BC. Aeduan aristocrats were the first Gauls to be allowed to become senators, during the reign of the emperor Claudius (41–54 BC). Under ROMAN rule, their capital was moved to Autun.

# AEOLIANS

An ancient GREEK people of the island of Lesbos and the coast of Anatolia, between Izmir and the

Dardanelles. The Aeolians settled the area early in the 1st millennium BC but were never politically united. Their ancestors came from Thessaly and Boeotia (see BOEOTIANS).

## AEQUI

An early Italian people who inhabited the upper Anio Valley in central Italy. With the VOLSCI, they were frequently at war with the ROMANS in the 4th and 5th century BC. They were conquered by the Romans in 304 BC and were massacred or enslaved. Little is known about their language.

## AESTI

A name used by ancient Greek and Roman writers to describe the BALTS.

## AGHUL

A Caucasian people of southeast Dagestan, Russian Federation, who speak a North Caucasian language. Mainly herders of sheep and cattle, they adopted Sunni Islam after being conquered by the ARABS in the the 8th century, although their oral traditions claim Jewish descent (see HEBREWS). They lived in 21 villages in four canyons so isolated that they were unable to form a unified state, and their lands were annexed by the RUSSIANS in 1813. Their isolation ended in 1936 with Soviet road construction. Collectivization and intense Russification followed. Education in Russian and official discouragement of Aghul religion and traditional dress and culture were imposed, but with limited success. In 2000 the Aghul numbered 19,000.

## AKHVAKH

A Caucasian people of northwest Dagestan, mostly in Akhvakh region, Russian Federation. Calling themselves *Ashvado*, they speak dialects of a North Caucasian language, but use Avar (see AVARS) as a written language. They are mainly herders of sheep, cattle and horses. A long history of internal feuding allowed their Avar neighbours to dominate them from the 15th to the 18th centuries. In the 19th century Russia

gradually established control over them. Soviet rule in the 1930s proved disastrous for the Akhvakh, with brutal collectivization and official attacks on their religious adherence to Sunni Islam. Subsequent Soviet education policies undermined their traditional culture among the young, and their language is in danger. In 1960, the last time they were officially counted as a separate people, they numbered about 4000.

## ALAMANNI

A confederation of Germanic tribes, first mentioned in history at the beginning of the 3rd century AD. Their mixed origins are reflected in their name, which means 'all men'. Alamannic attacks forced the ROMANS to abandon the territory between the Rhine and the Danube known as the Agri Decumates (roughly the Black Forest) in AD 261. As the Roman empire began to disintegrate in the 5th century, the Alamanni crossed the River Rhine, settling in Alsace and northern Switzerland. They were conquered by the FRANKS in the 6th century and gradually lost their identity in the Middle Ages. Their name, however, survives in the modern French name for the GERMANS: *Allemands*.

## ÅLANDERS

The Ålanders form part of Finland's Swedish-speaking minority and enjoy a considerable degree of political and cultural autonomy. Åland is an archipelago of over 6000 islands in the Gulf of Bothnia between Sweden and Finland. The present population is 23,000, around half of whom live in the islands' capital, Mariehamn. The economy is based on agriculture, tourism, fishing and shipping.

Åland was settled by SWEDES in prehistoric times and was part of the kingdom of Sweden until 1809, when it was annexed by Russia, which governed the islands as part of Finland. After Finland declared independence from Russia in 1917, the islands became the subject of a territorial dispute between Sweden and Finland. Although at a plebiscite in 1919 the population voted overwhelmingly in favour of reunion with Sweden, the League of Nations finally decided to award the islands to Finland in 1921, provided that the FINNS guaranteed the islanders' rights to use the Swedish language and to self-government. As a result, the Ålanders have their own parliament and are legislatively and administratively autonomous. They are also exempt from Finland's official bilingualism: Swedish is the only official language in the islands. Only native Ålanders have rights of residence and land ownership. Åland has had its own flag since 1954 and has issued its own postage stamps since 1984. It also has separate membership in the Nordic Council of SCANDINAVIAN nations.

Ålanders have a strong sense of Swedish identity and speak a dialect of Swedish that is closer to that spoken in the Stockholm metropolitan area than that of other SWEDISH-SPEAKING FINNS. Despite this strong sense of Swedish identity, the question of reunification with Sweden is not an important political issue in the islands.

## ALANS

A nomadic Iranian-speaking people who inhabited the Caspian steppes of southern Russia in the late Iron Age. The Alans were dispersed because of migration and conquest by other stronger peoples, gradually losing their identity in the Middle Ages. Their modern descendants

are the OSSETIANS. Also known as the Massagetae, the Alans were said to have derived their name from the Alanos Mountains.

The Alans were never one of the more powerful of the IRANIAN nomadic peoples and were frequently under the domination of the SARMATIANS, whose material culture they shared. According to the Greek historian Strabo, in the 1st century BC the Alans could muster around 20,000 warriors, compared to the Sarmatians' 200,000. Around the time of Christ, the Alans began to split up. One group tried to move into Iran but were repulsed by the PARTHIANS. The group then tried to move into Cappadocia but was again repulsed, this time by the ROMANS, before heading west into what is now Poland. In the 4th century AD, this group of Alans allied with two Germanic peoples, the VANDALS and the SUEBI, and in 406 successfully invaded the Western Roman empire, settling in the Iberian peninsula in 409. Their kingdom lasted only seven years before it was destroyed by the VISIGOTHS in alliance with the Romans. Those Alans who had remained on the steppes slowly migrated southeast, reaching the Caucasus in the 9th century. During the Middle Ages, the Alans were conquered by a succession of powerful nomadic peoples, including the HUNS and the

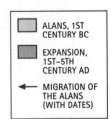

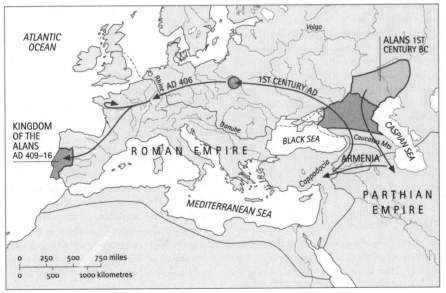

**Alans**

*The Alans migrated westward between the 1st century BC and the early 5th century AD, establishing a shortlived kingdom in the Iberian peninsula.*

ALANS, 1ST CENTURY BC

EXPANSION, 1ST–5TH CENTURY AD

MIGRATION OF THE ALANS (WITH DATES)

MONGOLS, and eventually disappeared as a distinct group in the 16th century.

## ALBANIANS

One of the major peoples of the Balkans. Of the estimated 7 million Albanians living in Europe, around 3.4 million live in the Republic of Albania, where they form more than 98% of the population. Outside Albania itself, the largest population of Albanians, around 2 million, lives in Kosovo, in the south of the Republic of Serbia, where they comprise over 85% of the population. Albanians comprise 20% of the population of the Republic of Macedonia and 6.5% of that of Montenegro. There are also small Albanian communities in Croatia, southern Italy and Greece. As a result of large-scale emigration in the 19th and early 20th centuries, more people of Albanian descent now live in North America and Australia than in Europe. Emerging from Enver Hoxha's Stalinist and isolationist regime (1949–85), Albanians have struggled to overcome poverty and civil strife, and many continue to look elsewhere for a better life. Most Albanians are Sunni Muslims.

Albanians are divided into two groups divided by the River Shkumbin: the Ghegs to its north and the Tosks to its south. The groups speak different, although mutually intelligible, dialects of the Albanian language. The Albanians regard themselves as the descendants of the ancient ILLYRIANS, a claim supported by linguistic evidence: although Albanian is an INDO-EUROPEAN language, it resembles more the few surviving records of the ancient Illyrian language than any modern Indo-European language. The Albanians first appear in the historical record in the 11th century AD when they called themselves *Arbëni*. Modern Albanians call themselves *Shqiptari*, deriving from *Shqipëri*, the Albanian name for Albania, meaning 'Eagles' Land', a reference to the country's mountainous landscape.

## ALLOBROGES

A tribe of GAULS that, in the last centuries BC, lived between the Alps, Lake Geneva and the Danube. Their name means 'the people who live in foreign places'. The Allobroges were conquered by the ROMANS in 121 BC and incorporated into the province of Gallia Narbonensis. Their chief towns were Vienne and Geneva.

## AMAZONS

A legendary race of female warriors, whose supposed habit of fighting with one breast exposed made them a popular subject for ancient Greek sculptors. The legend is probably based on the SCYTHIANS, an Indo-Iranian nomadic people whose women are known sometimes to have borne arms.

## ANDALUSIANS

The people of Andalusia, in southern Spain. In the Middle Ages Andalusia (*al-Andalus*) was the heartland of Moorish Spain. The last independent Muslim state there, the emirate of Granada, was conquered by Castile only in 1492. Andalusians believe that a history of inter-marriage between the native population and Moorish (see MOORS) and Jewish (see JEWS, EUROPEAN) immigrants during the Middle Ages has made them an ethnically distinct group within Spain. Andalusians speak a distinctive dialect of Spanish and have a distinctive regional cuisine, but their best-known contribution to SPANISH culture is flamenco music. Andalusians tend to consider themselves a part of the Atlantic rather than the Mediterranean community.

## ANDI

A Caucasian people of the mountains of Dagestan, Russian Federation, who speak a North Caucasian language. Livestock-breeders, with some terraced agriculture and orchards, they had close links with the AVARS, whose written language they use. Sunni Muslims, they were conquered by the MONGOLS, PERSIANS and TURKS, and finally, in the 19th century, by the RUSSIANS. Under Soviet rule there were determined efforts to destroy their traditional culture; collectivization in the 1930s was used to destroy any sign of resistance. The adoption of Russian culture is widespread, and from 1959 they were counted as Avars. In 1993 they numbered about 10,000.

**a**

# ANDORRANS

The population of the Pyrenean Principality of Andorra. The majority are CATALAN-speaking and Roman Catholic. Andorrans claim descent from the Andosians, an indigenous Iberian tribe, but most of the population are actually of SPANISH origin. There are about 45,000 Andorrans.

# ANGLES

An ANGLO-SAXON people whose original homeland was Angeln, at the neck of the Jutland peninsula, now part of Germany. The Angles first appeared in the 1st century AD, but they are rarely mentioned in contemporary writings before the early Middle Ages. In the 5th century they migrated to Britain. According to traditional accounts, the Angles settled mainly in East Anglia, the east Midlands and in eastern England north of the River Humber. The Angles have given their name to the ENGLISH.

# ANGLO-IRISH

A term which has been used in modern times to describe the descendants of medieval and later English settlers in Ireland, especially the landowning aristocracy of the period of Protestant ascendancy (18th century). The term is somewhat misleading, as the 'Anglo-Irish' generally identified themselves as English, even if they had been born in Ireland. Apart from their wealth and disproportionate political influence, they were distinguished by their Anglicanism, having rejected both the Catholicism of the Irish majority and the Presbyterianism of the north. The rise of Irish nationalism in the 19th century forced the Anglo-Irish to take sides, and their identity is now effectively extinct.

# ANGLO-NORMANS

A modern name given to the NORMAN and Angevin (from the County of Anjou in France) barons and knights who invaded and conquered much of Ireland 1169–72 and their ENGLISH, FLEMISH and WELSH followers.

# ANGLO-SAXONS

The population of England before the Norman Conquest of 1066. The Anglo-Saxons originated as a group of Germanic tribes that migrated from their homelands in north Germany and Jutland (in modern Denmark) and settled in eastern and southern Britain in the 5th century AD, following the end of Roman rule. Early written accounts of the Anglo-Saxon settlement, such as the Venerable Bede's *Ecclesiastical History of the English People*, identify these tribes as the ANGLES, SAXONS and JUTES. Archaeological evidence indicates that the settlers also included FRISIANS and probably FRANKS.

The term *Angli Saxones* was first coined by early medieval writers on the continent to distinguish the Germanic settlers from both the native BRITONS and the 'Old' Saxons who still lived in northern Germany. The term's first known use in England was by Alfred the Great (ruled 871–99) to symbolize the uniting of the Angles and Saxons under his leadership to fight the DANES. The growth of a common ENGLISH identity rendered the term obsolete in the 10th century, but it was revived by antiquarians in early modern times. Today, the French sometimes describe English-speaking peoples in general as Anglo-Saxons.

# ANTES

An early SLAV people who lived on the southern Ukrainian steppes between the Dniester and Dnieper rivers. They are first recorded in the 4th century AD; they disappeared after their conquest by the AVARS in 602. The name 'Antes' is not Slavic in origin and it is thought that they were originally an INDO-IRANIAN nomadic people who became assimilated by the Slavs after adopting a settled way of life.

# AORSI

A minor Iranian-speaking nomadic people who lived on the east European steppes in the early centuries AD. They were probably of SARMATIAN origin.

*❝ Not Angles but angels. ❞*

**Pope Gregory the Great (late 6th century AD), referring to novice monks of Anglo-Saxon origin**

*❝ A man does not become a horse just because he is born in a stable. ❞*

**The Irish-born Duke of Wellington on hearing himself described as an Irishman**

## AQUITANI

A group of Celtic peoples (see CELTS, ANCIENT) who, in ancient times, lived between the River Garonne and the Pyrenees. The Aquitani included the Eleusates, Sotiates, Tarbelli, Tarusates, Vocates and around half a dozen other tribes. Though generally considered GAULS, the Aquitani were also influenced by the IBERIANS. The Aquitani were conquered by the ROMANS 56–51 BC. Their name survives in the French region of Aquitaine.

## ARAGONESE

The SPANISH population of Aragon in north-central Spain. Aragon was an independent kingdom, founded in 1035, until its dynastic union with the larger neighbouring kingdom of Castile in 1516 created the kingdom of Spain. The medieval Aragonese spoke their own Romance language but it was similar to Castilian and has merged seamlessly into modern Spanish. The Aragonese identified closely with Spain, and it was not until the end of the 19th century that any sense of an Aragonese cultural identity re-emerged. For most Aragonese, however, this remains secondary to their sense of Spanish identity.

## ARCHI

A Caucasian people of Charondinskii region, southern Dagestan, Russian Federation. They speak a North Caucasian language, which they claim to be the most complicated in the world. Sunni Muslims since the 10th century, they are mainly herders of sheep, cattle and horses. Although they were under RUSSIAN rule by the 1870s, they remained relatively isolated until the 1930s, when collectivization began a concerted attack on their traditional culture. Road construction in the 1960s completed this process, with many young people adopting Russian ways. Classed by the Soviet state as AVARS from 1959, they have not been officially counted separately since. They were thought to number fewer than 900 in 1975.

## ARMINI

A minor Balkan people related to the ARUMANS and VLACHS.

## ARMORICANS or Aremorici

The tribes of GAULS who lived in Armorica (now Brittany, northern France) during the Iron Age and ROMAN period; they included the VENETI, Coriosolites, Namnetes, Redones, Unelli and Lexovii. Their name means 'the people who live facing the sea', and they had well-developed traditions of shipbuilding and seafaring. Several Armorican tribes played an important role as middlemen in the international trade in British tin. The Armoricans were conquered by Julius Caesar in 57–56 BC, but they were never fully assimilated into the Roman world, and, unlike most of the Gauls, they remained largely Celtic-speaking even in the 5th century AD. In the 5th and 6th centuries Armorica was settled by BRITONS from south Wales and southwest England who revitalized the region's Celtic culture and identity. From the fusion of the British settlers and the native Armoricans emerged the BRETON identity.

## ARUMANS

A Balkan people who speak a Romance language classified as Macedo-Romanian, derived ultimately from Latin. The Arumans first appeared in the early Middle Ages and several thousand still live in isolated mountain communities in Macedonia and northern Greece. The Arumans are thought to be descendants of the ancient DACIANS.

## ARVERNI

A tribe of GAULS whose territory was the Auvergne in central France. The main centre of the Arverni was Gergovia, a strongly fortified plateau southeast of Clermont-Ferrand. In 121 BC the Arverni allied with the ALLOBROGES to block ROMAN expansion into the Rhône Valley. Although defeated, the Arverni – unlike their allies – kept their independence and remained on friendly terms with Rome until Julius Caesar began his conquest of Gaul in 58 BC. Under their charismatic leader Vercingetorix, the Arverni led Gallic resistance to Caesar in 53 BC, but they were catastrophically defeated and submitted to Rome the following year. The Arverni were slow to become assimilated into Roman culture, and there were still pockets of Celtic-speakers in Auvergne in the 5th century AD.

## ASTURIANS

The inhabitants of the principality of Asturias in northern Spain, situated between the Bay of Biscay and the Cantabrian Mountains. The Asturians are SPANISH and speak a Castilian dialect, but the region's geographical isolation from the rest of Spain has led to the development of the strong local identity. The earliest known inhabitants of the region were the Astures, a CELTIBERIAN tribe who after long resistance were conquered by the ROMANS in 16 BC. The Astures were incompletely Romanized, however, and some elements of Celtic religious practice even survived the introduction of Christianity in the 4th century. The *xanas*, originally Celtic female nature spirits, continue to be venerated in local folklore and superstition. Asturias was one of the few parts of Spain not to be conquered by the MOORS, and it was the springboard from which the gradual Christian *Reconquista* (re-conquest) was launched. Asturias developed into a kingdom in the 8th century and later in the Middle Ages formed part of the kingdoms of León and Castile. Their important role in the formation of Spain enhances both the Asturians' local and Spanish identities. Asturias was granted limited autonomy in 1978, and Asturian traditions, such as bagpipe bands and the local dialect, are officially encouraged.

## ATHENIANS

The ancient GREEK population of the city-state of Athens. Athens originated as a citadel on the Acropolis during the MYCENAEAN period (around 1600–1200 BC) and it remained continuously inhabited through the Greek 'Dark Ages' (around 1200–800 BC). Because of this the Athenians believed that they were the original inhabitants of the area. In the late 6th century,

the Athenians entered a period of remarkable cultural, intellectual and political innovation, which saw the introduction of democracy in 509–507 BC, and which laid much of the foundation for later Western civilization. The Athenians took the lead in defeating the PERSIAN invasions of Greece in 490 and 480–79 BC and won control of most of the Aegean, using their strong navy and commercial power. Rivalry between the Athenians and the SPARTANS led to the outbreak of the Peloponnesian War in 431 BC. Athens never recovered its political pre-eminence after its defeat in 404 BC, but the Athenians continued to regard themselves as the moral leaders of Greece. Athens was incorporated into the ROMAN empire in 146 BC, but it remained an important centre of Greek culture until the 6th century AD.

## ATREBATES

A Belgic tribe (see BELGAE) whose main centre was at Nemetacum, now Arras in northeast France. The tribal name means 'settlers'. The Atrebates were conquered by Julius Caesar in 57–51 BC. The term also refers to a tribe of ancient BRITONS, whose territory lay south of the River Thames in Berkshire and adjoining parts of Surrey, Wiltshire and Hampshire. The tribal capital was at Calleva, now Silchester. There appears to have been a close relationship between the British Atrebates and their continental namesakes. After their defeat by Caesar, Commius, the king of the continental Atrebates, fled to Britain and was accepted as king by the British Atrebates. It was an appeal by Verica, last king of the Atrebates, to Rome for protection from the CATUVELLAUNI and TRINOVANTES that gave the pretext for the Claudian invasion of Britain in AD 43.

## ATTACOTTI

An ancient British tribe whose name means 'oldest inhabitants'. The Attacotti lived in northwest Britain, most probably in the Hebrides, or possibly in Ireland. They are first mentioned in the 4th century AD, initially as particularly savage pirates whose unsavoury habits included cannibalism. They were part of the 'barbarian conspiracy' that temporarily overran ROMAN

Britain in 367. Despite their reputation for savagery, or perhaps because of it, units of Attacotti were recruited into the Roman army, including the imperial bodyguard. The Attacotti were not heard of again after the 4th century.

## AURIGNACIAN CULTURE

An Upper Palaeolithic culture that originated in the Middle East and spread across most of southern, central and western Europe between 39,000 and 34,000 years ago; it survived until around 30,000 years ago. The Aurignacian succeeded the CHÂTELPERONIAN and was followed by the GRAVETTIAN culture. The Aurignacian culture is named after the rock-shelter of Aurignac in the Pyrenees. The earliest European cave art dates from the later part of the culture.

## AUSTRIANS

The people of the Republic of Austria. Austrians combine their national identity with strong local identities based on the country's nine *Bundesländer* (federal provinces). In Vienna, Burgenland and Lower Austria, national identity is much stronger than identification with the province; in Carinthia, Tyrol and Vorarlberg identification with the province is stronger; and in Upper Austria, Styria and Salzburg both identities are equally important. These differences are a result of the historical development of Austria. When Austria originated in 1156 as a duchy of the Holy Roman Empire it consisted of only Vienna and the provinces of Upper and Lower Austria. Before the early 19th century it was only the population of this region that was considered to be Austrian. The people in the rest of modern Austria were known after the names of their provinces: TYROLESE, BURGENLANDERS, CARINTHIANS, STYRIANS, and so on.

The Duchy of Austria was the heartland of the Habsburg dynasty, which dominated central Europe throughout the early modern period. As well as modern Austria, the dynasty came to rule Hungary, Bohemia, Moravia, Slovakia, Slovenia, Croatia and parts of modern Italy, Romania, Serbia, Poland and Ukraine. The Habsburgs also provided all but one of the Holy Roman emperors after 1438, making them the titular rulers of

Germany until the office was abolished in 1806. The rise of nationalism in the 19th century weakened the Austrian empire, and in 1867 it became the Austro-Hungarian empire after Hungary became an equal partner with Austria under the Habsburg dual monarchy. This concession left the aspirations of other ethnic groups unsatisfied, and in 1918 the Austro-Hungarian empire collapsed following its defeat in World War I, and the Habsburg dynasty was overthrown.

The borders of modern Austria were finally defined in 1922. The new Austrian republic was economically and politically unstable and it became a fascist dictatorship in 1933. In 1938 it was united with Nazi Germany by the *Anschluss* (union). Although the 99%-vote for the union was certainly rigged, there is no doubt that there was widespread support for it in Austria, highlighting another of the ambiguities of Austrian identity: its uneasy relationship to the GERMAN identity. Austrian independence was restored in 1945 and the country joined the European Union in 1995. At the end of the 20th century Turkish and other immigration into Austria caused a resurgence of far-right politics; Jörg Haider's neo-Nazi Freedom Party won 25% of the vote and joined the government in 1999.

The earliest known inhabitants of Austria were CELTS. They were conquered by the ROMANS in the 1st century BC, and in the 5th century AD the area was invaded and settled by Germanic tribes. Apart from small Serbo-Croat- and Hungarian-speaking minorities, modern Austrians are German-speaking. The majority speak a dialect related to Bavarian German but those in the western provinces speak a dialect more akin to Swiss German. About 80% of Austrians are nominally Catholic but fewer than 30% actively practise the religion.

## AUNJETITZ CULTURE

See ÚNETICE CULTURE.

## AVARS

A nomadic people of MONGOL origin, part of the JUAN-JUAN confederation that dominated the northeast Asian steppes between the 4th and 6th centuries AD. When the TURKS overthrew that confederation in 553, the Avars fled west across the entire breadth of Asia to reach the River Volga in 562. In just six years they conquered the remnants of the HUNS, the southern SLAVS and the GEPIDS, and chased the LOMBARDS into Italy. Further westward expansion was halted by the FRANKS. The Avars chose the former Lombard lands on the Hungarian plain as the centre of their khanate. In 580 war broke out between the Avars and the BYZANTINE empire. The Avars repeatedly raided the Balkans and in 626 they allied with the PERSIANS and laid siege to Constantinople, the Byzantine capital. Defeated, Avar power began a slow decline and much Avar territory was taken by another nomadic people, the BULGARS. The Avar khanate was finally destroyed by the Frankish king Charlemagne in 796. Communities of Avars survive in the northern Caucasus Mountains.

## AZOREANS

The people of the Azores, volcanic islands in the Atlantic about 1200 km / 740 miles west of Portugal. The Azores were uninhabited until they were discovered and settled by the Portuguese in the 15th century. The Azoreans are mostly of PORTUGUESE descent and speak a dialect of the Portuguese language. A shortlived separatist movement in the 1970s won little support.

## BAGVALAL

A Caucasian people of Tsumada and Akhvakh regions, northwest Dagestan, in the Russian Federation. They speak a North Caucasian language. Sunni Muslims by the 16th century, they were mainly herders of sheep and goats. Culturally similar to the AVARS, whose written language they use, they were conquered by the RUSSIANS in the 19th century. Cultural disaster, however, came with collectivization in the 1930s, which saw the destruction of the political and cultural elite. Russified education followed, further undermining traditional culture to the point that their language is now at risk. In 1962, the last time they were officially counted separately, they numbered about 5500. (See also AKHVAKH.)

## BALEARIC ISLANDERS

The population of the Balearic Islands archipelago off the east coast of mainland Spain. They are SPANISH and speak a dialect of CATALAN. Because of their strategic position in the western Mediterranean, the islands have a diverse history of settlement. The earliest inhabitants were IBERIANS, but the islands were successively colonized by PHOENICIANS, CARTHAGINIANS, ROMANS and MOORS before they were captured by King James I of Aragon in 1235.

## BALKARS

A Muslim Turkic-speaking people (see TURKS) of the northwest Caucasus region, to the east of Mount Elbruz, in the Russian Federation. Suspecting their disloyalty to the Soviet state, Stalin ordered the deportation of thousands of Balkars to Siberia during World War II; they were later permitted to return to their homeland. Around 70,000 Balkars now live in the Caucasus; about 8000 more live in other parts of Russia. Until the mid-20th century the Balkars were more usually known as Tauli ('mountain people').

## BALTS

A group of peoples who first settled on the southeastern shores of the Baltic in prehistoric times. The origins of the Balts, who speak INDO-EUROPEAN languages related to Slavic, can be traced back as far as *c.* 1800 BC. The term 'Balt' dates from only the 19th century; in ancient times they were known as the Aesti. The modern Balts are LITHUANIANS and LATVIANS (also known as Letts), but in the Middle Ages they also included the PRUSSIANS, Semigallians, Selonians, and CURONIANS. The Balts are notable for their stiff resistance to Christianity and were the last European peoples to abandon paganism; the Lithuanians did not convert until 1386.

## BANDKERAMIK CULTURE or Linear Pottery culture or Linearbandkeramik

The earliest Neolithic culture of central Europe. It developed in southern Hungary around 5600

BC and spread rapidly across an area extending from eastern France to the Ukraine. The culture is named for its distinctive decorated pottery; equally distinctive were its settlements of large rectangular longhouses, probably the largest freestanding structures in the world at the time. The Bandkeramik people lived by grain-farming and cattle-rearing. The culture died out around 5000 BC.

## BASHKIRS

A formerly nomadic Turkic-speaking people who are closely related to the TATARS. There are about 1.5 million Bashkirs, most of whom live in the southern Urals in Bashkortostan, an autonomous republic of the Russian Federation, where they make up about one-third of the population. The Bashkirs are Sunni Muslims and share the same oral literature and folk-song traditions as the Tatars.

## BASQUES

A people of the western Pyrenees Mountains. There are around 2 million Basques, all but 200,000 of whom live in the Spanish provinces of Vizcaya, Álava, Guipúzcoa and Navarra; the remainder live in the French districts of Labourd, Basse-Navarre and Soule. The English name for the Basques is derived from the French *basques*; the Spanish know them as *vascos* but the Basques call themselves *Euskaldunak*. The most important defining characteristic of the Basques is their language, Euskara, which is the only non-INDO-EUROPEAN language spoken in western Europe and has no demonstrable relationship to any known language group. The origins of Euskara are unknown, but it is certainly a very ancient language, possibly a lone survivor of a larger group of now-extinct languages spoken in Europe before the introduction of Indo-European in the 3rd or 2nd millennium BC. About 850,000 Basques, most of them rural, speak Euskara, but all also speak either Castilian Spanish or French. Although they are not physically distinguishable from neighbouring peoples, the Basques are also characterized by the lowest frequency of Rh-negative B and O blood groups in Europe, suggesting that they have been a separate and distinct population for a very long time. They have many distinctive customs, including energetic and athletic folk dances. They are strongly Roman Catholic.

The Basques were conquered with difficulty by the ROMANS and recovered their independence in the 5th century AD. They successfully resisted the VISIGOTHS, the MOORS and the FRANKS. The Basques were briefly united under a single government in the 11th century in the kingdom of Navarre, but the kingdom lost territory to Castile and Aragon, and in the early 16th century the Basque region was permanently divided between Spain and France. The Basques had a well-developed shipbuilding and seafaring tradition (for fishing and whaling rather than trade) and they were among the pioneers of Atlantic navigation.

The Spanish Basques were never reconciled to their loss of autonomy, and a nationalist movement developed in the 19th century. Although Basque nationalists were somewhat conservative and clericalist in their outlook, they allied with the leftist Republicans during the Spanish Civil War (1936–9) in return for a decree of local autonomy. The Nationalist victory, however, doomed this initiative, and under the dictatorship of Francisco Franco the use of the Basque language was outlawed. Repression bred violence and in 1959 the nationalist terrorist group ETA (Euzkadi Ta Azkatasuna, which means 'Basqueland and freedom') was founded with the aim of winning full independence from Spain. ETA targeted police and army officers as well as local politicians whom it considered 'collaborationists'. The democratic constitution introduced in 1978 gave autonomy to the Spanish Basques, but did not satisfy militant nationalists. Despite shortlived ceasefires, terrorism has continued, although with diminishing support among the majority of Basques.

ETA's campaign has received some active support from the French Basques, but as a political movement Basque nationalism is less important north of the Pyrenees.

## BASTARNAE or Peucini

An early GERMAN people who first appeared around 200 BC northwest of the Black Sea,

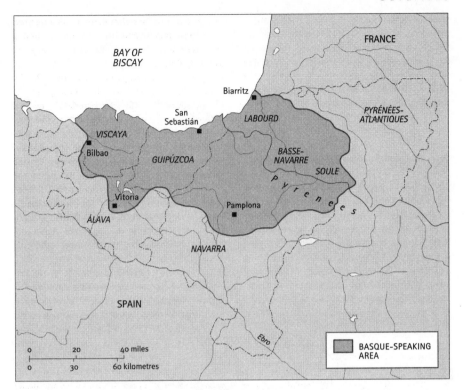

BASQUE-SPEAKING AREA

FRANCE

BAY OF BISCAY

Biarritz

San Sebastián

*LABOURD*

*PYRÉNÉES-ATLANTIQUES*

*VISCAYA*

Bilbao

*GUIPÚZCOA*

*BASSE-NAVARRE*

*SOULE*

*P y r e n e e s*

Vitoria

Pamplona

*ÁLAVA*

*NAVARRA*

SPAIN

*Ebro*

| 0 | 20 | 40 miles |
| 0 | 30 | 60 kilometres |

**b**

between the Danube delta and the Dniester. The Bastarnae raided the Greek cities around the Black Sea and served as mercenaries in the armies of Hellenistic rulers. They were pacified by the Romans in 29 BC and thereafter caused little trouble until they began raiding Roman territory in the 3rd century AD. They were transplanted *en masse* to Roman territory south of the Danube by the emperor Probus in 279–80 and then lost their distinct identity.

## BATAVI

A GERMAN people settled near the estuary of the Rhine. They originated as a breakaway faction of the CHATTI. The Batavi were conquered by the ROMANS in 12 BC and supplied recruits for the Roman army rather than pay taxes. They rebelled unsuccessfully in AD 69. The Batavi preserved their identity until the 4th or 5th century, when they were absorbed by the FRISIANS and FRANKS.

## BAVARIANS

A GERMAN people originating as an obscure tribe, or even a group of tribes, who settled in the area between the Danube and the Alps in what is now southern Germany in the 5th or 6th century AD. This area became known after them as Bavaria. Bavaria's modern borders as a German *Land* date only to the 19th century and include Swabia (see SWABIANS) and Franconia (see FRANCONIANS), whose inhabitants have their own distinct local identities. Only the inhabitants of the districts of Upper and Lower Bavaria actually consider themselves to be Bavarians. Historically, Bavaria has often had stronger cultural links with the Catholic south of Europe than the Protestant north, and it was a reluctant participant in the PRUSSIAN-led movement of German unification in the 19th century. As a result, Bavarians have perhaps the strongest sense of local identity of any of the German people. The stereotypical view of the Bavarians as *Lederhosen-*

wearing beer-drinkers derives from Bavaria's brewing tradition: it is home to two-thirds of Germany's breweries. The most important defining characteristic of the Bavarians is, however, their devotion to Catholicism. *Bairisch*, the Bavarian dialect of German, is still widely spoken and is similar to AUSTRIAN German.

## BELGAE

One of the three main groups of Iron Age Gaul; the others are the GAULS and the AQUITANI. In the 1st century BC the homeland of the Belgae lay between the North Sea, the Seine, the Marne and the Rhine. Around 100 BC some Belgae migrated to southern Britain, settling in what is today Berkshire and Hampshire. The Belgae believed that they had originally lived east of the Rhine and regarded themselves as being kin to the GERMANS even although they spoke a Celtic language. The Romans regarded the Belgae as the most warlike of the peoples of Gaul; the Belgae

put up fierce resistance to Caesar's legions before their final pacification in 51 BC. Modern Belgium is named after the Belgae.

## BELGIANS

The people of the Kingdom of Belgium. They are divided into two culturally and linguistically distinct peoples: the FLEMISH and the WALLOONS. The Flemish live in Flanders, in the north of Belgium, and speak a dialect of Dutch, while the Walloons live in the south ('Wallonia') and are French-speaking. The Flemish form about 60% of the population of Belgium, but historically it is the Walloons who have been politically and culturally dominant. As a result, relations between Belgium's two main peoples (there is actually also a small German minority) are frequently strained. Flemish resentment focuses on language issues, particularly the greater social and cultural prestige of French. This was embodied in the requirement that the Flemish learn

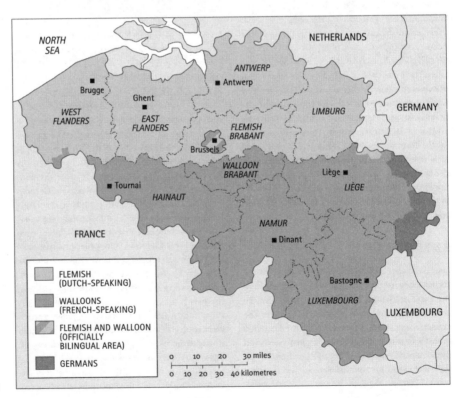

Belgians

French at school, while there was no reciprocal obligation to learn Dutch in French-speaking areas. The main cultural characteristic that unites the Flemish and Walloons is their Roman Catholicism.

An industrious people, the Belgians have a somewhat undeserved reputation for dullness and lack of imagination, perhaps in part due to the location of the headquarters of the labyrinthine bureaucracy of the European Commission in their capital, Brussels. They are frequently the butt of French jokes.

The origin of the Belgian identity goes back to the 16th century, when what is now Belgium was part of the Spanish Netherlands. When the northern Protestant DUTCH provinces rebelled against SPANISH rule and became independent, the Catholic Flemish and Walloons remained loyal. In 1713 the Spanish Netherlands passed under Austrian rule, then in 1794 under French rule. In 1815 the Congress of Vienna united Flanders and Wallonia with the Kingdom of the Netherlands, but neither the Flemish nor the Walloons were content with Dutch rule. In 1830 they rebelled, and the next year they elected prince Leopold of Saxe-Coburg-Gotha as King of the Belgians. The name of the new nation was taken from the BELGAE, a Celtic tribe which had dominated the area in the Iron Age, to give it an ancient history to stand comparison with its neighbours. Relations between the Flemish and Walloons began to deteriorate shortly before World War I and came to a head in the 1960s. In 1966 Belgium was divided into four official language regions, and in 1980 Flanders and Wallonia were granted local autonomy, turning Belgium, in effect, into a federation. The population was around 10.2 million in 1996.

## BELL BEAKER CULTURES

Late Neolithic and Chalcolithic ('Copper Age') cultures of western and central Europe. The cultures are associated with distinctive decorated pottery drinking vessels ('beakers') and other objects, such as copper and gold items and archery equipment, found in single burials under round barrows. The tradition emerged in the Rhineland around 2800 BC and spread to central Europe, Britain, France and Spain. The

cultures, which died out *c.* 1800 BC, are thought to mark the emergence of more hierarchical forms of society, with dominant social elites whose status was reflected in the special treatment of them after their deaths.

## BELORUSSIANS or White Russians

A SLAV people who constitute over 80% of the population of the Republic of Belarus. Belorussians speak a language that is closely related to Russian and Polish and traditionally practise Russian Orthodox Christianity. The name of the Belorussians is thought to derive either from their light blond hair, their white folk costumes or from the fact that their land remained unconquered by the MONGOLS in the 13th century.

Although they are recognizable as an ethnic group from as early as the 14th century, Belorussians have a weak sense of national identity and even in the 20th century described themselves simply as *tuteishiya* ('locals'). Before the break-up of the Soviet Union in 1991, the Belorussians had no experience of national independence, having always been under Soviet, RUSSIAN, LITHUANIAN or Polish (see POLES) rule. A national culture began to emerge in the later 19th and early 20th centuries but this was brutally suppressed by Soviet dictator Joseph Stalin. Of all the former Soviet republics, Belorussia remains the closest to Russia, and in 1997 the two countries signed a treaty committing them to gradual re-integration.

## BEZHTA

A Caucasian people of Tsunta region, Dagestan, Russian Federation. Primarily herders of sheep and cattle, they speak a North Caucasian language and have practised Sunni Islam since the 17th century. Close to the AVARS, whose written language they use, they came under Russian rule in the 19th century. They were little affected, however, until collectivization under Soviet rule, and subsequent policies to destroy their culture, for example through education, had a ruinous impact. In 1993 they numbered about 3000.

## BITURIGES

A tribe of GAULS. They were divided into two branches: the Vivisci, who lived around Bordeaux, and the Cubi, who lived around Bourges (which takes its name from them). The name Bituriges means 'kings of the world', and in the 6th century BC the Bituriges were counted as the most powerful of the CELTS. It was supposedly on the initiative of their king Ambigatus that the Gauls invaded Italy around 400 BC. The Bituriges were conquered by the ROMANS in 53–52 BC.

## BOEOTIANS

An ancient GREEK people of central Greece. They spoke an AEOLIAN dialect of Greek, and their chief cities were Thebes and Orchomenos. The Boeotians played no part in Greek expansion overseas and, perhaps as a consequence, were regarded as backward by other Greeks. A Boeotian Confederacy was founded in 447 BC under the leadership of Thebes, which survived until Greece was conquered by the ROMANS in the 2nd century BC.

## BOHEMIANS

For information on the Bohemians, see CZECHS. (The custom of describing people with unconventional and irregular lifestyles as Bohemians derives from a medieval French belief that Bohemia was the homeland of the GYPSIES.)

## BOII

A major Celtic people (see CELTS, ANCIENT) of central Europe. The territory of the Boii extended from what is now the Czech Republic eastwards into Hungary. Other groups of Boii migrated across the Alps c. 400 BC and settled in the lower part of the Po River valley in northern Italy. The Romans conquered the Boii in Italy in 191 BC; and the Boii were driven out of their lands in Hungary by the DACIANS around 60 BC. Thousands of refugees migrated west and were allowed to settle among the HELVETII. The remnants of the Boii were absorbed by the GERMANS around the time of Christ. Both Bohemia and the Italian city of Bologna are named after the Boii.

## BOIKOS

A RUTHENIAN people who live in the foothills of the Carpathian Mountains in Ukraine. Many Boikos reject their name, believing it to have derogatory overtones (although its origins are uncertain), and prefer to be called *Verkhovinsky* ('highlanders'). The present population tally of Boikos is uncertain, but thought to be over 300,000.

## BOSNIAN MUSLIMS

Descendants of CROATS and SERBS who converted to Sunni Islam while Bosnia-Herzegovina was part of the OTTOMAN empire (1463–1878). They speak Serbo-Croat. While they lived under Ottoman rule Bosnian Muslims had no sense of separate ethnic identity, identifying themselves as either Croat Muslims or Serb Muslims. After Bosnia-Herzegovina became part of the Austro-Hungarian empire in 1878, the Habsburg monarchy promoted the idea of Bosnian nationality (*bosanstvo*) to counter Serbian nationalism. The idea found no support among Bosnian Croats and Bosnian Serbs and very little support among Muslims until after the creation of Yugoslavia in 1918. The Bosnian Muslims were left exposed to persecution by their Serbian neighbours and many emigrated to Turkey.

During World War II, Bosnian Muslims were frequently massacred by the Chetniks, the Serbian nationalist resistance. Following the war, Bosnian Muslims became strong supporters of the Yugoslav unitarianism of Josip Tito's communist government, which seemed to offer a way to assuage ethnic tensions in Bosnia-Herzegovina. However, it was also the communist government that declared Bosnian Muslims to be a 'distinct nation' in 1971.

As the communist regime began to weaken after Tito's death in 1980, Bosnia's ethnic tensions escalated, encouraged by Serbian nationalist politicians such as Slobodan Milosevic. Bosnian Muslims reacted by becoming more politicized rather than by turning to religious fundamentalism – Bosnian Muslims are generally considered to be unobservant by other Sunni Muslims. When Bosnia declared itself independent from Yugoslavia in 1992, a three-sided civil war broke out between the Muslims, Croats and Serbs. The Bosnian Serbs enjoyed the support of the Yugoslav army, and the Muslims were 'ethnically cleansed' from large areas of eastern and northern Bosnia. Many thousands died in massacres, the most notorious of which was at Srebrenica in 1995, when Serbian forces killed around 10,000 Muslim prisoners. Before the civil war, Muslims made up over 39% of Bosnia's population and were a majority in about 25% of the country. Owing to 'ethnic cleansing' of Serbs from Bosnian Croat territories, at the end of the war in 1995 Muslims formed 49% of the country's population (3.6 million in 1996), but they controlled only 10% of the country, including the capital Sarajevo. Peace agreements provided for the return of refugees, but few have returned because of continuing fears for their safety.

## BOTLIKH

A Caucasian people of Botlikh region, southern Dagestan, Russian Federation. Primarily horti-culturalists, they were close to the AVARS, whose written language they use, and had adopted Sunni Islam by the 18th century. Although they were under RUSSIAN control during the 19th century, they proved rebellious under Soviet rule, and collectivization and attacks on their culture were brutal. From 1959 they were officially counted as Avars, but in 1999 they were, for a few weeks, at the centre of a rising against Russian authority. In 1962, the last time they were officially counted separately, they numbered about 3500.

## BRETONS

The inhabitants of Brittany, in northwest France. They are the descendants of the indigenous ARMORICANS and of BRITONS who immigrated in the 5th and 6th centuries AD. The Breton language is a Celtic language (see CELTS, ANCIENT), derived from ancient Gaulish and Brithonic. The number of modern Breton speakers is uncertain, but is thought to be around 660,000, which is slightly over 20% of the population of Brittany. Of these, fewer than 250,000 are thought to speak Breton as their first language, and their numbers are thought to be declining steadily. The first language of the majority of Bretons is now French.

Little is known about the period of British settlement. The leaders of the Britons were aristocrats with links to the royal family of Dumnonia (roughly Devon and Cornwall) who founded a number of independent principalities. Place-name evidence suggests that British settlement was most dense in the north of the peninsula. Because of the British settlement the peninsula became known as *Britannia Minor* ('Little Britain'), from which the name of Brittany is derived. In the 9th century the Bretons were united, and Brittany became a vassal kingdom of the Carolingian empire. By diplomacy and war, Breton rulers expanded Brittany eastwards, well beyond the Celtic-speaking area, which ended along a line extending from the mouth of the Loire in the south to Dol in the north. As a result, Brittany became permanently divided into two parts, *Bretagne Bretonnante* – Breton-speaking Brittany – and *Bretagne Gallo* – French-speaking Brittany. Although the new French-speaking territories enriched Brittany they also became an open door for French influences, which diluted the Celtic character of Breton culture. Brittany, however, had one enormously influential gift for medieval European civilization: the legends of King Arthur, which had such a seminal influence on the development of chivalry and courtly literature.

The kingdom of Brittany was destroyed by Viking attacks in the early 10th century and it subsequently became a feudal duchy under the nominal control of the French Crown. The Bretons maintained their independence until Brittany was annexed to France in 1491. Despite its loss of independence, Brittany remained legally distinct from the rest of France, retaining its own parliament with legislative autonomy. The French Revolution was a turning point, however. Brittany's established local identity and institutions were seen to be at odds with the new ideology of the indivisible republic. The Breton parliament was abolished and Brittany's administration was brought into line with that of the rest of the French republic. In 1794 instructions were issued to destroy the Breton language, which was seen as incompatible with republican unity. Laws establishing French as the sole language of education were not repealed until the 1950s, and the French government remains hostile towards any official recognition of Brittany's special identity, such as devolved regional government.

Despite the decline of their language, Bretons continue to maintain a non-French identity through their involvement in pan-Celtic cultural festivals, local customs such as the *fest-noz* harvest festival and *fêtes folkloriques*, and religious traditions such as the *pardons*, which involve processions in folk costume, religious and secular music, dancing and sports. Breton society is on the whole more conservative than FRENCH society, and Bretons are twice as likely to be regular (Roman Catholic) church-goers. Although the first Breton nationalist party was founded in 1932, there is no widespread support for outright independence from France.

# BRIGANTES

A tribe of ancient BRITONS whose territory covered most of northern England. The Brigantes originated as a federation of tribes, comprising the Carvetii, Setanti, Lopocares and Tectoverdi among others. Following the ROMAN invasion of Britain in AD 43, Cartimandua, the queen of the Brigantes, adopted a pro-Roman policy and kept her independence. However, the rebellion of Cartimandua's estranged husband Venutius in 69 sealed the fate of the Brigantes and they were conquered by the Romans in AD 71–73. The capital of the Brigantes may originally have been at present-day Almondsbury, near Huddersfield, but by the time of the Roman conquest it was at Aldborough, near Richmond, North Yorkshire.

# BRITISH

The legal identity of the population of the United Kingdom of Great Britain and Northern Ireland. The sense of Britishness is strongest in England, where a majority identify themselves as being British first and ENGLISH second. In Wales and Scotland Britishness is usually considered a secondary identity. Attitudes to Britishness are most polarized in Northern Ireland, where it is totally rejected by the large nationalist minority and often passionately espoused by the unionist majority.

The stiff upper lip and *sang froid*, among other stereotypical attributes of Britishness, were largely products of the Victorian public-school system which sought to inculcate the virtues (real or imagined) of the martial peoples of classical antiquity, such as the Romans and Spartans, and the medieval code of chivalry. These were the virtues thought essential for a race of empire-builders who felt confident that they were bringing the benefits of civilization to the lesser breeds of humanity. A gift for spontaneous organization, improvization and 'muddling through' have also been seen as British virtues. This is exemplified by the 'Dunkirk spirit', the extraordinary mood of popular resolution which prevailed after the fall of France in 1940, when Britain had hurriedly to prepare itself for the threat of a GERMAN invasion. In reality, however, there was little that was spontaneous about Britain's successful response to World War II: it was the result of the most efficient centralized government planning seen in any of the combatant nations. Today the 'Dunkirk spirit' is still regularly invoked, for troubles small and large: it stands for a sense of community and common purpose, which, except in occasional conditions of adversity, the British know they do not really now possess.

### British identity – origins

The origins of the modern British identity date to the Union of the Crowns of England and Scotland in 1603, when King James VI of Scotland also become King James I of England. James promoted the idea of Britishness as part of his campaign to persuade the English and Scottish parliaments to agree to a full political union. Although the SCOTS were willing, the English were not. By the time a political union was finally achieved in 1707, it was the English who were more in favour of it than the Scots. England's economy had leapt ahead during the 17th century, and it was apparent to most Scots that they were going to be junior partners in this relationship. The promotion of Britishness was an attempt to create a new identity that was neither English nor Scottish. However, England's dominance of the union meant that 'Great Britain' and 'England' became virtually synonymous, not only abroad but also in England. This made it impossible for Scots to identify themselves wholeheartedly as British. Britishness was also a challenge for the Welsh identity. As the descendants of the ancient BRITONS, the Welsh had always considered themselves to be 'the British', so these developments threatened an important part of their non-English identity. One response was that the Welsh increasingly identified themselves with the ancient CELTS.

In 1801 the IRISH parliament was dissolved and Ireland too became part of the United Kingdom. One of the motives behind the Act of Union of 1707 had been to guarantee a Protestant succession, and this guarantee was desired by all three peoples of Great Britain. Because of this, anti-Catholicism was an important part of the early British identity. Relaxation of anti-Catholic legislation came too late to persuade Irish Catholics that they were equal citizens. The British government's failure to provide relief during the Great Famine of the 1840s confirmed that they were not. The growth of the nationalist movement in the later 19th century showed that a majority of the Irish had emphatically rejected Britishness and, increasingly, British rule itself. However, Catholic domination of the nationalist movement alienated Irish Protestants and drove them to identify themselves increasingly as British, leading ultimately to the present division of Ireland.

### Britishness, empire and multiculturalism

The British identity was spread through Britain's empire by emigrants during the 19th century. Identification with Britain was naturally strongest in the white colonies of Canada, Australia and New Zealand, and it persisted even after those countries had been given their independence. The harsh experience of World War I affirmed the national identities of CANADIANS, AUSTRALIANS and NEW ZEALANDERS, and identification with Britain gradually declined thereafter, hastened in the later 20th century by increasing numbers of non-British immigrants to these countries. The British monarch is still head of state in Canada, Australia and New Zealand, but this is not so much a sign of continuing identification with Britain as of a lack of consensus about what might replace the monarchy. AFRO-CARIBBEANS in Britain's WEST INDIAN colonies also developed a close identification with Britishness in the first half of the 20th century as a result of an education system that emphasized British cultural values and loyalty to the Crown. Afro-Caribbeans who emigrated to Britain in the 1950s and 1960s were disillusioned to find that they were regarded as racially inferior aliens in what they had been taught to regard as their motherland. The impact of Britishness in Africa and Asia was more limited. There, British settlers were relatively few in numbers and were always a minority among native populations who continued to maintain their traditional cultures and values. The Asians who identified most closely with the British were those, mostly Indian Hindus, who left their own communities and emigrated to Uganda and Kenya as indentured labourers in the late 19th and early 20th centuries. Expelled from these countries in the post-colonial era, their descendants settled in Britain, where they have become the most prosperous and integrated of recent immigrant communities. Since the 1960s Britain has also experienced substantial immigration of Asians from India, Pakistan and Bangladesh. Although both British Afro-Caribbeans and British Asians have a sometimes problematic relationship with the British identity, their cultural impact, especially in music, fashion and cuisine, have been considerable: curry rather than roast beef is now Britain's most popular food.

In Great Britain, the prestige of being partners in the world's greatest empire made Britishness acceptable to the vast majority of the Scots and Welsh until after World War I. In fact, the Scots were arguably even more enthusiastic imperialists than the English. The postwar period saw the growth of Welsh and Scottish nationalism, calls for devolution and even independence, and an increasing rejection of any degree of British identity. Britain's membership of the EEC (now the European Union) took away some of the fear of independence, especially in Scotland, by offering an alternative economic safety net. The introduction of

*“May we be Brittains and down goe old ignominious names of Scotland and England.”*

George Mackenzie, Earl of Cromarty, 1707

devolved governments for Wales and Scotland in 1999 have led to more self-confident expressions of national identity there, which have not gone unnoticed by the English, some of whom have begun to re-assert their national and regional identities over their Britishness. In these developments some commentators have anticipated the beginning of the end of the British identity. Others argue that Britishness will continue to have value as a uniting civic identity in what is, because of Commonwealth and other overseas immigration, an increasingly multi-ethnic and multicultural society.

In the 2001 census the UK population was 58.8 million, of whom about 4.5 million were in non-white ethnic groups. In terms of religion, while Christianity predominates (about 77% of the population), almost 20% profess to no religion, while 3% are Muslims. English remains the official language, although where there are concentrations of minorities, in London and several other urban areas, South Asian and other languages are commonly used domestically and in local-government publications.

## BRITONS, ANCIENT

The inhabitants of Great Britain during the Iron Age and Roman periods. Although they never described themselves as such, the Britons are usually considered to be CELTS because of the close similarities in language (Brithonic), religion and material culture to the GAULS. These similarities may be due to exchanges of population between Britain and the Continent in prehistoric times, but there can be no doubt that the Britons were mainly the descendants of the original post-glacial settlers of Britain, as, in fact, the ancient Britons themselves believed. The name of the Britons is derived from *Pretanni*, meaning 'painted' or 'tattooed people'.

In the 1st century BC the Britons were divided into more than 30 separate tribes, representing a wide range of social development. The tribes of the southeast, such as the ATREBATES, CATUVELLAUNI and TRINOVANTES, were already well advanced along the road to statehood. Semi-urbanized tribal and trade centres, known as *oppida*, flourished at Colchester, St Albans, Canterbury, Silchester and

elsewhere. The economy was based on mixed arable and pastoral farming. Coinage and the Roman alphabet were coming into use and the social elite had adopted elements of a Romanized lifestyle, including drinking imported wine. Tribes were ruled by kings, power was centralized and society was rigidly hierarchical. In the far north of Britain a proliferation of family-sized fortifications show that very decentralized forms of society prevailed there. Transhumant pastoralism (seasonal movement of livestock) was the dominant way of life. The tribes between these two geographical and social extremes were ruled by chieftains from sometimes spectacular hillforts. Like other Celtic peoples, the Britons worshipped a wide range of deities, most of them specific to only a single tribe or place, and practised human sacrifice. The most distinctive aspect of the Britons' religion was the priestly class of druids, a phenomenon also known in contemporary Gaul.

Britain was famous in the Mediterranean world as a major source of tin, but it was still regarded as being beyond the known world when Caesar launched his famous but somewhat futile raids in 55 and 54 BC. The Romans returned in AD 43, but, although they quickly conquered the socially and economically advanced southeast, they were unable to subdue the whole island. In the 2nd century the Roman frontier finally stabilized along the Tyne–Solway isthmus, across which Roman emperor Hadrian built his wall to 'separate the Romans from the barbarians'. The Britons never became completely assimilated to Roman culture, and even the elite remained Celtic-speaking. The Romans introduced an administrative system which was based on tribal territories. After Roman rule ended in 410, many of the old tribal identities re-emerged to form the basis for new independent British kingdoms. These included the DUMNONII in Devon and Cornwall and the ORDOVICES in Gwynedd, north Wales.

Between the 5th and the 10th centuries the Britons lost control of most of Britain to the ANGLO-SAXONS and the SCOTS. The WELSH, and to a lesser extent the CORNISH, are the cultural and linguistic descendants of the Britons. However, much of the modern ENGLISH and Scottish populations are also probably descended from conquered Britons who were assimilated to Anglo-Saxon culture and language.

## BRUCTERI

An early GERMAN tribal group that lived in the late Iron Age, between the Lippe and Ems rivers, near modern Münster. In the 3rd century AD the Bructeri became one of the coalition of peoples that made up the FRANKS.

## BRUTTIANS

The Bruttians were an ancient ITALIAN people who lived in Calabria, the 'toe' of Italy. The Bruttians spoke the language of the OSCANS and had a culture that was Hellenized as a result of contact with GREEK colonies on the coast. In the 3rd century BC, the Bruttians vainly opposed ROMAN expansion into southern Italy and finally lost their independence after supporting the Carthaginians in the Second Punic War (218–201 BC).

## BULGARS

A Turkic nomadic people (see TURKS), who migrated onto the steppes of southeast Europe in the 6th century AD. The Bulgars divided into two branches in the middle of the 7th century. One branch crossed the River Danube and founded a khanate in the northeast Balkans *c.* 679; the other settled on the middle Volga. The Danube Bulgars were a minority military elite among a population of SLAVS. By the 9th century they had adopted the Slavic language of their subjects and in 864 they were converted to Orthodox Christianity. The Bulgars were the dominant power of the Balkans until they were conquered by the BYZANTINE empire in 1018. They regained their independence in the 12th century and built a second Balkan empire, but were conquered by the OTTOMANS in 1393. The modern state of Bulgaria is named after them.

The Volga Bulgars converted to Islam around 922 and were conquered by the MONGOLS in 1237, thereafter losing their distinct identity as a people.

## BULGARIANS

A SLAV people who form about 90% of the population of Bulgaria. Both they and their country take their name from the BULGARS, who conquered the area in the 7th century. After Bulgaria was in turn conquered by the OTTOMANS in 1393, Bulgarian traditions were preserved in monasteries and remote mountain villages, but it was not until the late 18th century that a sense of national identity began to be re-awakened. One of the first signs of this was the publication of a history of the Bulgarian people by the monk Paisii in 1762. The development of Bulgarian nationalism was encouraged by the RUSSIANS, who saw it as a potential tool to use against the Ottoman TURKS. The Turks were less hostile to Bulgarian nationalism than might be expected, especially after Greece became independent in 1835. Because they controlled much of Bulgaria's trade as well as the Bulgarian Church under the Greek Patriarch of Constantinople, Bulgarians were as antipathetic towards the GREEKS as the Turks. A Bulgarian school system was set up in 1835, a Bulgarian translation of the Bible was published in 1840, and an independent Bulgarian Orthodox Church was set up in 1870. Finally, following the Russo-Turkish War of 1877–8, Bulgaria became an autonomous state (full independence was internationally recognized in 1908).

### Bulgarians in the 20th century

In 1887 Bulgaria became a monarchy under the German prince Ferdinand of Saxe-Coburg-Gotha. Both Ferdinand and his Bulgarian subjects ardently aspired to recreate the medieval Bulgarian empire, inevitably bringing them into conflict with their Balkan neighbours Serbia, Montenegro and Greece. Fixing the western border of Bulgaria proved particularly difficult because there was no clear linguistic frontier between the Bulgarians, MACEDONIANS and SERBS. It took two Balkan Wars (1912 and 1913) and World War I, when Bulgaria was allied with Germany and Austria-Hungary, before the country's modern frontiers were defined. Bulgaria again allied with Germany in World War II, fell to Soviet occupation in 1944 and became a communist dictatorship in 1947. The commu-

*b*

❝ The Bulgars ... look hither and thither like men possessed: there is no joy among them but only sorrow and a terrible stench. ❞

**The Russian Primary Chronicle, 12th century**

nist regime was less unpopular in Bulgaria than in other Eastern Bloc countries, and the Communist Party survived the collapse of Soviet power 1989–91 and remains a major political force in the country. Because of their country's turbulent history since independence, Bulgarians idealize the medieval past and their struggle for independence. These preoccupations are reflected in Bulgarian literature, theatre and the country's school curriculum.

Most of the approximately 9 million Bulgarians belong to the Bulgarian Orthodox Church, but a minority, known as POMAKS, are Muslims, and Protestantism is increasing. About 9% of Bulgaria's population are ethnic Turks, who have often been the victims of persecution and attempts at forced assimilation, most recently in 1989 when some 300,000 fled to Turkey. Small Bulgarian minorities also live in Macedonia, Moldova and Ukraine.

## BURGENLANDERS

The population of the federal state of Burgenland, eastern Austria. The Burgenlanders have more diverse ethnic origins than other AUSTRIANS. Historically part of Hungary, Burgenland was settled by CROATS and German-speakers in the early modern period. Identification of Burgenlanders with Austria is strong, even among those with HUNGARIAN or Croat roots.

## BURGUNDIANS

An early GERMAN people. According to their own traditions, the Burgundians originated on the Danish island of Bornholm, which was formerly known as Borgundarholm. In the 2nd century AD the Burgundians lived between the Oder and Vistula rivers in Poland, but they had migrated to the Main-Neckar region of western Germany by 290. They invaded the ROMAN empire in 406–7 and seized lands around Worms, Speyer and Strasbourg. The Burgundians' catastrophic defeat at the hands of the HUNS in 436 forms the basis of the medieval German legend of the Nibelungen. The Romans settled the survivors as 'allies' in the Saône Valley and around lakes Geneva and Neuchâtel. At first the Burgundians kept to their side of the agreement, but as

Roman power began to fail in the 460s they gradually expanded to take over much of central Gaul, including Lyon, which became their capital. The Burgundian kings formed a close relationship with the Gallo-Roman aristocracy and their kingdom was prosperous and well-ordered, preserving a high level of cultural life.

Still pagan when they invaded the Roman empire, the Burgundians converted to Christianity in the early 5th century and were becoming integrated with the native population by the early 6th century. They were defeated by the FRANKS at Autun in 532 and lost their independence soon afterwards.

Despite this, the inhabitants of what had come to be called 'Burgundy' retained a distinctive local identity in medieval France. This was due largely to the region's prosperity, which permitted distinct local schools of architecture, sculpture and music to flourish. Particularly influential throughout Europe was the architecture of the 11th-century Benedictine monastery at Cluny. Burgundians also spoke their own Romance language called Burgonde.

Under the Valois dukes in the 14th and 15th centuries Burgundy became a major European cultural centre, and the court at Dijon was famous for its sacred and secular music. Attempts by the Valois dukes to have Burgundy recognized as a kingdom failed, and in 1477 it came under the direct control of the French monarchy. During the early modern period Burgundians were assimilated into the FRENCH culture; today Burgundy is known for wine, not separatism.

## BYELORUSSIANS

See BELORUSSIANS.

## BYZANTINES

The GREEK inhabitants of the medieval Byzantine empire. The name is an invention of modern historians and is derived from Byzantium, the ancient Greek name for Constantinople, the empire's capital. The Byzantines considered themselves to be Greeks and believed their empire to be, as it was legally if not culturally and linguistically, the continuation of the Eastern Roman empire, which survived the fall of the Western Roman empire in 476 by nearly 1000 years. Right up until the fall of their empire to the OTTOMANS in 1453, Byzantine emperors continued to describe themselves as Roman emperors and their empire as the Roman empire. The culture of the empire was Hellenistic and its religion was Orthodox Christian.

## CALEDONIANS

A confederation of almost a dozen tribes that inhabited Britain north of the Forth–Clyde isthmus in the first three centuries AD. Unlike their neighbours to the south, the Caledonians had no large-scale centralized power-structures, and their economy was based on transhumant pastoralism rather than settled farming. This helped them to resist conquest by the ROMANS in the 80s AD. The Caledonians are ancestral to the PICTS.

## CANTIACII

A confederation of four or more ancient British tribes, which took its name from Cantium (now Kent) in southeast England. The confederation is thought to have been an artificial creation of the ROMANS for governmental purposes following their conquest of the area in AD 43. The capital of the Cantiacii was at Canterbury, which had already become an important settlement before the Roman conquest.

## CARINTHIANS

The inhabitants of the region of Carinthia in southern Austria. Their AUSTRIAN nationality is combined with a strong sense of local identity. The Carinthians originally spoke Slovene, but they began to adopt Bavarian dialects of German in the early modern period. About 4% of Carinthians are still Slovene-speaking.

## CARNUTES

A tribe of GAULS. Their territory lay between the Loire and Seine rivers; their capital was Cenabum, modern Orléans. The territory of the Carnutes was considered to be the centre of Gaul and was the scene of an annual congress of Gaul-ish druids. The Carnutes were conquered by the ROMANS 54–51 BC. Their name survives in the French city of Chartres.

## CARVETII

Ancient BRITONS who lived in northern Cumbria. Their name means 'deer people'. At the time of the ROMAN conquest (1st century AD) they were subject to the BRIGANTES, but under Roman rule they were given their own self-governing *civitas* centred on Luguvalium (Carlisle). After the end of Roman rule in Britain, the Carvetii were the nucleus around which the Kingdom of Rheged formed. Rheged was conquered by the NORTHUMBRIANS in the 7th century.

## CASSUBIANS

See POMERANIANS.

## CASTILIANS

People of the SPANISH region of Castile, which extends from the Pyrenees and the Bay of Biscay in the north to the Sierra Morena in the south. Castile is a high, semi-arid plateau, interspersed with mountain ranges. This harsh environment has bred in Castilians a perception of themselves as an austere, hardy and spiritual people. The Castilians were the nucleus around which the modern Spanish identity crystallized and as a result their sense of local identity is relatively weak. The Castilian dialect has become accepted as 'standard' Spanish.

Castile emerged as a Christian kingdom in 1035 and came to play the leading role in the *reconquista*, the conquest of the Spanish MOORS. The marriage of Isabella of Castile and Ferdinand of Aragon in 1479 saw the two kingdoms united into the Kingdom of Spain in 1516. A revival of Castilian identity began, however, only after the devolution of regional government in 1978, following the fall of the Spanish dictator Francisco Franco in 1975. This revival has also led to the emergence of local identities within Castile itself, for example in Extremadura and Cantabria.

C

# CATACOMB GRAVE CULTURE

A pastoralist KURGAN CULTURE of the southern Russian and Ukrainian steppes between the Dnieper and Volga rivers, dating from the early Bronze Age, around 2200–1800 BC. The culture is named for its burial practices, in which the deceased, together with any grave offerings, were placed in a chamber dug in the side wall of a shaft. The shaft was then filled in and the burial covered with a burial mound or *kurgan*.

# CATALANS

A people of the Spanish autonomous region of Catalonia and of the districts of Roussillon and Cerdagne in the south of France. The most important defining characteristic of the Catalans is their language, Catalan (Català), a Romance language derived from Provençal. The language is understood by about 97% of native Catalans. Catalan is also spoken by the ANDORRANS, VALEN-CIANS and BALEARIC ISLANDERS. In the case of the last two, this is a legacy of the leading role that Catalans played in the medieval Spanish Kingdom of Aragon, which ruled a considerable Mediterranean empire. From this role Catalans, and especially those of Barcelona, the region's capital, derive their commercial and seafaring traditions and their perception of themselves as having a more 'European' outlook than other Spaniards. Other Spaniards, for their part, have tended to stereotype Catalans as hardworking but tightfisted.

The origins of Catalonia date to the early 9th century when Charlemagne, king of the FRANKS, captured Barcelona from the MOORS. Barcelona became the capital of an area that became independent when the Carolingian empire broke up later in the 9th century. In the 12th century the County of Barcelona united with the Kingdom of Aragon, becoming a major Mediterranean trading and naval power. Catalan literature and poetry flourished. Aragon declined after the opening up of the Atlantic trade routes in the 16th century. The concentration of political power at Madrid, following the union of Castile and Aragon, marginalized the Catalans for over two centuries. Resentment against Castile boiled over in two wars of independence in 1640–58

and 1705–15. The Catalonian economy recovered in the late 19th century thanks to the growth of the cotton industry, and many Castilian speakers migrated into the area.

Increasing prosperity led to a cultural revival and the development of a strong nationalist tradition during the 20th century. Regional autonomy was granted by the Republican government in 1932, but this was rescinded after the Nationalist victory in the Spanish Civil War. Franco banned the public use of the Catalan language and folk customs such as the *sardana*, the traditional dance of Catalonia. In 1980 Catalonia was granted local autonomy, and the Catalan language gained official status alongside Castilian. Catalans, especially younger ones, tend not to identify very strongly with Spain. These concessions, however, seem to have satisfied the political aspirations of most Catalans, and there is little support for outright separatism.

# CATUVELLAUNI

Ancient BRITONS whose core territory was the area of modern-day Hertfordshire, Buckinghamshire and Bedfordshire. Their name means 'good in battle'. Cassivellaunus, who led British resistance to Caesar's invasions in 55–54 BC, was probably an early chief or king of the Catuvellauni. Under their king Cunobelinus (died AD *c.* 40), the Catuvellauni expanded their territory, conquering the Ancalites, Bibroci, CANTIACII and TRINOVANTES. Cunobelinus' sons and joint successors, Caratacus and Togodumnus, were even more aggressive, but by attacking the ATREBATES, who were ROMAN allies, they gave the emperor Claudius the pretext to invade and begin the conquest of Britain. The main tribal centre of the Catuvellauni was Verulamium (St Albans).

# CELTIBERIANS

A group of Celtic-speaking peoples of Iron Age Spain, where they dominated the Meseta (the high central plateau) and the mountainous northwest. The origins of the Celtiberians are unclear, but it is generally thought that CELTS migrated into Spain from the north in the 6th or 7th centuries BC and assimilated with the indigenous peoples to produce a culture that was linguistically Celtic but which differed quite considerably in its material culture from the HALLSTATT and LA TÈNE cultures north of the Pyrenees. The Celtiberians originally lived in hillforts known as *castros*, but most of these were abandoned after about 400 BC. Those that remained inhabited gradually developed into pre-eminent semi-urbanized tribal centres like the *oppida* of the GAULS. The Celtiberians never developed a fully literate culture, but they adopted a version of the IBERIAN script for memorial inscriptions.

The Celtiberians came under CARTHAGINIAN influence in 237 BC and many served as mercenaries in Carthage's armies during the Second Punic War with Rome (219–201 BC). After defeating Carthage, the ROMANS occupied the Mediterranean coast of Spain and began a slow and costly conquest of the Celtiberians. The fall of the major Celtiberian stronghold of Numantia in the Ebro Valley in 133 BC secured Roman control over most of the Iberian peninsula, but the Cantabri, Astures and Gallaeci of the northwest were not pacified until as late as 16 BC. The Celtiberians never fully assimilated to Roman culture and retained much of their Celtic culture and language until they were converted to Christianity in the late 4th and 5th centuries AD.

## CELTS, ANCIENT

A group of peoples of Iron Age Europe. One of the most widespread groups of the time, at their greatest extent in the 3rd century BC they dominated a vast territory stretching from modern Hungary westwards across Austria, the Czech Republic and southern Germany to France, Belgium, Spain, Portugal, Britain and Ireland, with offshoots in Italy and Anatolia. Among the major Celtic peoples were the GAULS, BELGAE, ARMORICANS, CELTIBERIANS, ancient BRITONS and IRISH. Except for those living in Ireland and northern Britain, all of the Celtic peoples had been conquered by the ROMANS, GERMANS or DACIANS by the end of the 1st century AD.

The Celts first appear in history in the writings of Greek historians of the 5th and 6th centuries BC. In its earliest usage, the term 'Celt' (Greek *Keltoi*) was used specifically to describe the peoples who lived inland from the Greek colony of Massalia (modern Marseille, France).

Later the term was used virtually synonymously with the Greek word *Galatoi* (GALATIANS) and a related Latin word *Galli* (Gauls) to describe more generally the 'barbarian' peoples of central and western continental Europe. The origins and meanings of these terms are unknown, but they probably originated with the Celts themselves, as we find them used as elements in tribal, family and personal names (for example, 'Celtici' and 'Gallaeci').

Classical writers recognized cultural and linguistic similarities between the continental Celtic peoples and the inhabitants of Britain and Ireland, though they never actually described them as either Celts or Gauls. It is also clear that the ancient Britons did not consider themselves to be Celts or Gauls either, but a quite separate people. For this reason, some archaeologists are reluctant to use the terms 'Celt' and 'Celtic' in relation to the British and Irish Iron Age. Some historians and archaeologists go even further and argue that the concept of the Celts as a people, or group of peoples, is itself merely a modern construct. The Celts were divided into dozens of often mutually antagonistic independent peoples, so there is doubt as to what, if any, degree of common identity they actually shared. However, the more widely held view is that the term is made meaningful by the demonstrable similarities of material culture, religion and language across much of Iron Age Europe.

Written records of the Celts may begin only in the 6th century BC, but their origins lie at least 2000 years earlier. The Celtic languages, like most modern European languages, developed from Indo-European. This long-extinct language was introduced to Europe by migrating INDO-EUROPEANS sometime between 7000 and 4000 BC. Most linguists believe that Celtic developed in central Europe and was subsequently spread across western Europe by migrations. Because there is little material evidence to support this hypothesis, some archaeologists think it more likely that the Celtic languages evolved across much the same area where they were spoken at the beginning of historical times (around 500 BC), that is central Europe, France, Iberia and the British Isles.

Two forms of Celtic are recognized: q-Celtic, which included Hispano-Celtic and Goidelic

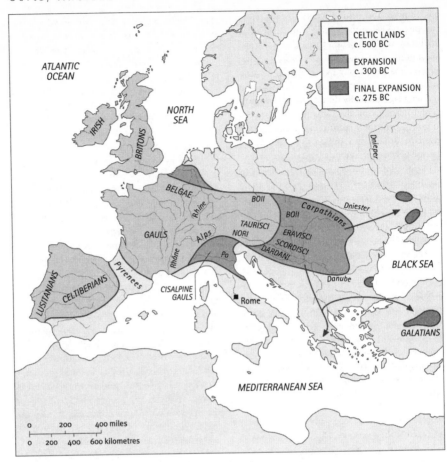

(the ancestor of modern Gaelic), and the more widespread p-Celtic, which included Gaulish and Brithonic (the ancestor of modern Welsh and Breton).

The earliest archaeologically recognizable material culture that can safely be identified as Celtic is the central European HALLSTATT CULTURE which flourished in the late Bronze Age and early Iron Age (*c.* 700–450 BC). These were the first Celts to come into contact with the literate Mediterranean civilizations. The Hallstatt was an aristocratic culture, whose elite displayed their status through the consumption of wine, which they imported via Massalia and the Rhône Valley. Hallstatt craftsmen adapted Mediterranean decorative motifs to create the first distinctively Celtic art style. Around 450 BC the Hallstatt cul-

ture was supplanted by the LA TÈNE CULTURE, which developed to the northwest, in the Rhineland and eastern France. The distinctive geometrical art-style of this culture was spread, mainly by trade in metalwork, throughout most of the Celtic-speaking world. The culture remained influential into the early Middle Ages in Britain and Ireland.

### Celtic history and Celtic image

Beginning *c.* 400 BC, the Celts began a series of migrations that carried them into northern Italy (sacking Rome in 390), the Balkans, Greece, and, in 278, Anatolia (modern Turkey). The Celts then began to come under pressure from their neighbours, the Germans, Dacians and, most of all, the Romans, who between them had conquered all of the Celtic peoples of continental Europe by 9 BC. Although the Romans invaded Britain in AD 43 they never completed the conquest of the island, nor did they invade Ireland, which remained largely free of Roman cultural influences too. Under Roman rule, Celtic culture and language gradually disappeared from continental Europe, and the Celts themselves were forgotten. But their culture and language survived in Britain and Ireland and re-asserted themselves strongly after the end of Roman rule in the 5th century, when it was re-exported to the Continent by British settlers (see BRETONS). However, it was not until the 18th century that the Celtic-speaking peoples of Britain and Ireland began to develop any sense of conscious Celtic identity (see CELTS, MODERN).

In modern conceptions, the ancient Celts have enjoyed a rather romantic and even otherworldly image, playing the noble savage to our materialistic and industrialized society. Antiquarians created this image in the 18th century, when they rediscovered classical writings about the Celts. Greek and Roman writers portrayed the Celts consistently as superstitious and irrational barbarians. Their warrior elite was violent and undisciplined, passionate, proud, hot-tempered and given to drunkenness, boasting and headhunting. They fought naked and showed reckless courage in a charge, but were easily discouraged if they were met by a stout defence. Celtic women were also fierce, proud and independent.

The Celtic priestly caste, the druids, practised human sacrifice, committed an enormous body of poetry, medical lore, astronomy and tribal law to memory, and conducted worship of their many gods in oak groves and other natural places. Bards and poets were highly respected. Hospitality was a sacred duty, but feasts could turn violent as guests disputed seating arrangements or the size of their portions (both of which were regarded as signs of status).

The Greeks and Romans did not mean to flatter the Celts, but this stereotyped view coincided with the values of the Romantic movement – itself a rebellion against Enlightenment rationalism and materialism – and it was accepted uncritically. It has since proved far too attractive and useful, to nationalists, tourist boards and marketing companies, to be allowed to fade from popular consciousness.

## The realities of Celtic life

In reality, the Celts were more like their neighbours than the Classical sources imply. Greek and Roman writers wanted to show that the Celts were inferior and savage in order to justify conquest by their own civilizations. Accordingly, they emphasized the differences and ignored the similarities. Portraying Celtic women as fiercely independent, for example, was guaranteed to appal Greek and Roman men, who expected their women to be demure and obedient. Celtic women did enjoy higher status than their Greek and Roman counterparts – Boudicca is only the most famous of several powerful Celtic women – but Celtic society was still male-dominated, and not, as some feminist historians claim, matriarchal. The Celts were warlike, but not because they were irrationally hot-tempered. They fought because success in battle was the surest route to wealth and status: Romans like Julius Caesar fought their wars for the same rational motives. There were few unique Celtic religious institutions other than the druids. As with the Greeks, Romans and early Germans, the Celts were polytheists who believed in a multitude of universal and local gods and goddesses. The Celtic reverence for natural places like springs and groves was also shared with these peoples. Human sacrifice, it is true, was practised, sometimes on an enormous scale: at one sanctuary dated to the 2nd century BC at Ribemont-sur-Ancre in France, the remains of nearly 1000 human sacrificial victims have been found. The image of druids worshipping in oak groves contrasts starkly with the formal rituals of Greek and Roman paganism, but the appearance of Celtic temples in France, Germany and southern Britain in the 2nd and 1st centuries BC suggests a clear move towards formal religion among the Celts too.

The Celts' way of life was also much less barbaric than Classical writers made out. On the eve of conquest by Rome, towns (*oppida*) were springing up across most of the Celtic world and a cash-based economy was developing. Literacy, based on the Greek and Roman alphabets, was spreading. The Celts were also technologically

C

innovative and the Romans copied the designs of their helmets, chainmail armour, wheels, barrels and ships. Celtic political institutions, such as monarchies and elected magistracies, were similar to those of the Mediterranean world, as was the system of clientship practised by the Celtic aristocracy. Whatever Greek and Roman writers may have said, the developed Celtic world was an increasingly civilized place, and it was this that made its conquest by Rome such an attractive proposition: it could be easily and profitably assimilated to the imperial system.

## CELTS, MODERN

Any definition of the modern Celts must be imprecise, because they are in reality as much a cultural phenomenon as a people. The Celtic League, an influential pan-Celtic organization, recognizes six Celtic regions – Brittany, Cornwall, the Isle of Man, Ireland, Scotland and Wales – on the grounds that Celtic languages are, or have in the recent past been, spoken there. However, it is far from being the case that all BRETONS, CORNISH, MANX, IRISH, SCOTS and WELSH would regard themselves as being Celtic. Few Northern Irish Protestants would describe themselves as Celts, for example, and neither would many Lowland Scots.

The modern Celtic identity originated in the early 18th century, when antiquarians rediscovered the history of the ancient Celts and began the methodical study of the surviving Celtic languages. Celtic-speakers in the British Isles and France subsequently began to describe themselves as Celts as a means of bolstering their non-ENGLISH or non-FRENCH identities. The Romantic movement popularized the ancient Celts, and in the 19th and 20th centuries the identity was adopted by people who, though they do not speak Celtic languages, claim descent from Celtic-speakers. In fact, most people who today claim a Celtic identity do not speak a Celtic language as their first language and are, apart from their espousal of Celtic identity, otherwise almost indistinguishable from their non-Celtic neighbours, sharing most of their material and popular culture, for example. Appeals to the Celtic past have had a powerful impact on nationalist movements in all of the

so-called Celtic countries but most especially in Ireland. A recent development is the adoption of Celtic identity by many GALICIANS as part of their efforts to preserve their non-SPANISH identity, even though Celtic languages have not been spoken in Spain for some 1500 years.

## CHAMALAL

A Caucasian people of Tsumadin region, southern Dagestan, Russian Federation, who speak dialects of a North Caucasian language. Primarily sedentary herders, they were strongly influenced by the AVARS, whose written language they use, and had adopted Sunni Islam by the 16th century. Under Soviet rule they resisted collectivization, and many were killed or deported. Education policies were imposed to destroy their traditional culture and identity, and they were officially counted as Avars. In 2001 there were an estimated 9000 Chamalal.

## CHAMAVI

An early GERMAN tribe. In the 1st century AD the Chamavi were settled on the east bank of the lower Rhine on what is now the Netherlands-German border. In the 3rd century the Chamavi became the nucleus around which the tribal confederation of the FRANKS formed.

## CHANNEL ISLANDERS

The people of the Channel Islands, in the English Channel off the coast of Normandy. Although many Channel Islanders are recent ENGLISH immigrants, the native population is of FRENCH descent. Formerly part of the medieval Duchy of Normandy, the islands are the last remnants of the English monarchy's once extensive French lands. Until the 20th century the main language in the islands was NORMAN French, but the main language is now English, with only about 5% of the population still French-speaking. Although the islands are not fully integrated into the United Kingdom, each island having its own autonomous government, there is a tradition of loyalty to the BRITISH state which remains strong, and which endured German occupation of World War II.

## CHÂTELPERRONIAN CULTURE

An Upper Palaeolithic culture of France, named after a cave site at Châtelperron in Allier, which developed from the MOUSTERIAN CULTURE about 40,000 years ago. The culture evolved from NEANDERTHALS emulating the AURIGNACIAN blade-tool technology used by modern human groups. The culture died out along with the Neanderthals around 30,000 years ago.

## CHATTI

An early GERMAN people who lived around the Lahn River in western Germany. They were conquered by the ROMANS in 10 BC, but in AD 9 they joined the CHERUSCI in their successful rebellion against Roman rule. The Chatti faded into obscurity after the 1st century AD.

## CHAUCI

An early GERMAN people who settled on the North Sea coast of Germany between the Ems and the Elbe rivers. In the 1st and 2nd centuries AD the Chauci were active pirates, often raiding the Roman empire. The Chauci disappeared as a distinct group in the 3rd century, assimilated into the SAXONS.

## CHECHENS

A Caucasian people of Chechen autonomous republic (Chechnya) and Dagestan who speak a North Caucasian language. Originally mountain herders who were part of the ALAN state, they descended to the north Caucasian plains and adopted agriculture by the 16th century. By the 18th century they had adopted Sunni Islam, and managed to maintain their independence from Russia until 1859. After fighting for independence in 1917, they suffered brutally during Soviet collectivization and were deported to Central Asia, where thousands died, for alleged collaboration with the Germans during World War II.

The exiles returned home in 1957, their national identity as strong as ever, and with the dissolutions of the USSR in 1991 Chechens declared their independence. They fought a bru-

tal war with the RUSSIANS to retain independence between 1994 and 1996 and forced humiliating terms on Moscow. However, renewed war, fought with great ferocity, allowed the Russians to impose a degree of control on their lands, although guerrilla warfare and terrorist attacks within Russia persisted. This has led to racist attacks against Chechens in Russia, where they are widely treated as criminal outcasts. Chechen resistance persisted, and in 2002 about 50 Chechen guerrillas took over 800 hostages in a Moscow theatre, threatening to kill them all unless Russian troops were withdrawn from their lands. All the guerrillas and over 100 hostages died when the theatre was stormed. This, and suicide-bombing attacks within Chechnya, convinced the Russian government to offer limited concessions, in an attempt to end the bloodshed. In 2003 a referendum was held in their republic on a new constitutional arrangement, which appeared to satisfy few. In 2004 a bomb explosion killed the newly elected pro-Moscow president of Chechnya, as the regional turmoil continued. To date, Chechen national aspirations remain unfulfilled.

In 1989 the Chechens numbered about 1 million, but with an estimated 100,000 killed in the civil war and possibly half the population refugees outside Chechnya, the present population can only be guessed at.

## CHERKESY

See CIRCASSIANS.

## CHERNOLES COMPLEX

A complex of early Iron Age culture (c. 750–500 BC) of Moldova, western Ukraine and southern Poland, which is often identified with the earliest SLAVS. The culture is named for a site in Moldova and is defined by its pottery styles. The complex disappeared following the arrival of SCYTHIAN nomads in the region.

## CHERUSCI

An early GERMAN people who were settled in the upper reaches of the valley of the River Weser around the beginning of the 1st millennium AD.

They were conquered and apparently pacified by the ROMANS 12–11 BC, but they rebelled in AD 2 and again in AD 9. During the second of these rebellions, their leader, Arminius, ambushed a force of three Roman legions in the Teutoburger Forest and annihilated them. This effectively ended Roman attempts to conquer Germany. After the death of Arminius in 21, the Cherusci were weakened by internal dissent and wars with their neighbours, the CHATTI. The tribe had broken up by the end of the 1st century AD.

## CIMBRI

An early GERMAN tribe from Jutland in Denmark. In company with the neighbouring TEUTONES and Ambrones, the Cimbri migrated out of Jutland around 120 BC and spent nearly 20 years traversing much of central and western Europe in search of a new homeland. After defeating a Roman army at Arausio (modern Orange in southern France) in 105 BC, they split up from the Teutones and Ambrones. The Cimbri invaded Spain, but were repulsed by the CELTIBERIANS. They later invaded Italy, where they were defeated and massacred by the ROMANS near Vercellae in 101 BC. Himmerland in Jutland probably gets its name from the Cimbri.

## CIMMERIANS

A nomadic Iranian-speaking people of the steppes north of the Black Sea and the Caucasus mountains. The Cimmerians are first recorded c. 900 BC but their main impact on history came around 700 BC when they were attacked by another nomadic people, the SCYTHIANS. Defeated, the Cimmerians crossed the Caucasus into Anatolia, destroying the kingdom of the PHRYGIANS and raiding Assyria, Urartu and the GREEK cities of the Aegean coast. Some Cimmerians settled in Cappadocia (east-central Turkey), while others migrated east into Iran, where they were assimilated by the MEDES.

## CIRCASSIANS or Cherkesy

A people of the northwest Caucasus Mountains. Their early history is obscure, but they were ruled by the GEORGIANS in the 12th century and then of the Crimean TATARS in 1234. The Circassians regained their independence in the 16th century, but were conquered by the RUSSIANS after 30 years of bitter warfare in 1864. More than 400,000 Circassians chose to go into exile in the OTTOMAN empire rather than live under Russian rule; they subsequently became widely dispersed across the Middle East. There are two main branches of Circassians still living in the Russian Caucasus: the ADYGHE and the KABARDIANS, numbering about 500,000 in all. About 150,000 Circassians live in Turkey, 35,000 in Syria, and smaller numbers in Jordan, Iraq, Iran and Israel. They are Sunni Muslims but until recent times they also continued to practise traditional cults associated with thunder and sacred groves.

## CONNACHTA

The inhabitants of Connacht in the west of Ireland during the late pre-Christian and early Christian times. Their name is derived from Old Irish cond ('head') meaning 'head tribe', but according to their own legends the 'Conn' part of their name was derived Conn Cétchathach ('Conn of the Hundred Battles'), a semi-legendary king of Connacht who may possibly have reigned in the 2nd century AD. Their chief ritual centre was at Cruachain, modern Rathcrogan in County Roscommon. In the Ulster Cycle of Irish myths, the Connachta were considered the traditional enemies of the ULAID.

## CONVERSOS

SPANISH JEWS who converted to Christianity in the 14th and 15th centuries as a result of anti-Semitic rioting and government hostility. As forced converts, Conversos were widely suspected, often rightly, of continuing to practise Judaism in secret. The Spanish Inquisition was founded in 1478, in part to root out secret observers of Judaism, and between 1480 and 1520 thousands of Conversos were executed. Conversos were often vilified by Christians as Marranos (pigs). Those Conversos who survived were assimilated into Spanish society in the course of the 16th century. The most famous Converso is probably St Theresa of Avila.

> **"** Scythia still retains traces of the Cimmerians; there are Cimmerian forts, a Cimmerian ferry, also a tract of land called Cimmeria and a Cimmerian Bosphorus. **"**
>
> Herodotus, 5th century BC

# CORD-IMPRESSED WARE CULTURE

See CORDED WARE CULTURE.

# CORDED WARE CULTURE or Cord-impressed Ware culture

A widespread culture of the late Neolithic period (c. 3000–2400 BC), which spread across Europe between the Meuse and Volga rivers. It is characterized by pottery beakers with cord-impressed decorations, stone battle-axes and burials under barrows. Compared to earlier Neolithic cultures, the Corded Ware culture showed a new emphasis on social hierarchy. It was the precursor of the western European BELL BEAKER CULTURES.

# CORITANI or Corieltauvi

A tribe of ancient BRITONS who inhabited Lincolnshire, Leicestershire and Nottinghamshire in the late Iron Age. The leadership of the tribe was divided between two kings or chiefs, who ruled from tribal centres at Old Sleaford in Lincolnshire and Leicester. The Coritani seem to have put up little resistance to the ROMANS and were conquered by AD 47.

# CORNISH

The native inhabitants of Cornwall, a county of southwest England. Cornwall is the only county of England where the inhabitants will not automatically identify themselves as ENGLISH. A recent survey of schoolchildren in the county showed that one-third saw themselves as being Cornish rather than English, and a tenth of the population of the county has signed a petition calling for the establishment of a Cornish assembly. While economic grievances, such as high unemployment caused by the decline of traditional industries such as tin mining and fishing, feed this nascent separatism, the Cornish identity has deep roots. In the late Iron Age Cornwall was inhabited by the CORNOVII ('people of the horn'), a Celtic-speaking British tribe. After the Roman conquest of Britain Cornwall formed part of the *civitas* of the DUMNONII, which, fol-

lowing the end of Roman rule, formed the core of the kingdom of Dumnonia. Cornwall was conquered by the ANGLO-SAXONS in the 9th century, but it remained a Celtic-speaking area throughout the Middle Ages. The Cornish language, which is related to WELSH and BRETON, began to give way to English in the early modern period. The last monoglot Cornish speaker died in 1777 and the language was extinct by the 20th century. Recent attempts at language revival have met with little success: it is estimated that fewer than 100 people have attained proficiency in Revived Cornish. Official recognition for Cornish, granted in 2002, is unlikely to change matters greatly. although it was founded in 1951, the Cornish nationalist party, Mebyon Kernow (The Party of Cornwall), has yet to make an electoral breakthrough, suggesting that, while devolution may be an important issue for many Cornish people, nationalism, so far, is not.

# CORNOVII

Three separate and, as far as is known, unrelated Celtic peoples (see CELTS, ANCIENT) of late Iron Age Britain. One Cornovii people lived in Cornwall, which is named for them, another in Shropshire in the West Midlands, and the third in Caithness in the far northeast of Scotland. The name Cornovii means 'people of the horn'. In the case of the Cornovii of Cornwall and Caithness, this could be a reference to the peninsulas in which they lived. Alternatively, the 'horn' could have belonged to a divinity, such as the horned god Cernunnos. This interpretation would certainly be more appropriate to the Cornovii of the Midlands.

# CORSICANS

The Corsicans are the inhabitants of the island of Corsica in the Mediterranean Sea. Although the Corsicans are now FRENCH citizens, their language and traditional culture betray their former links with Italy. Corsica was part of the maritime empire of of the CARTHAGINIANS in the 3rd century BC until it was occupied by the ROMANS in 238 BC. The island had a turbulent history in the Middle Ages and was invaded in turn by the VANDALS, LOMBARDS, MOORS and Pisans before it came under Genoese rule in the 14th century. The Corsicans rebelled against Genoese rule in 1729 and won their independence in 1755 under Pasquale Paoli, who worked to turn Corsica into modern political nation. He introduced a written constitution, elected legislature, Corsican currency and educational system. Corsican independence was short lived, however: the island was conquered by France in 1769. The British occupied Corsica in 1794 but French rule was restored in 1796 by the most famous of all Corsicans, Napoleon Bonaparte.

### The Corsicans and the French

Pride in Napoleon's achievements helped establish Corsican loyalty to France, although his popularity has declined in the postwar period as the separatist movement has grown. The roots of this separatism are a desire to preserve a Corsican Corsica in the face of increasing French cultural influence, and a lack of economic opportunities that has caused considerable emigration from the island in the last hundred years. Immigration from France, Italy and North Africa has offset these losses, but it has diluted Corsica's Corsican character. About 35% of the present total population of Corsica (about 250,000 people) were not born on the island. Many Corsicans who have emigrated to work in France eventually return home to retire. As a result the proportion of the Corsican population over 60 years of age is 25% higher than in the rest of France. It is clear that, while most native Corsicans do not feel French, neither do they desire full independence from France. However, there has been 40 years of sporadic violence from hardcore separatists. The Corsican National Liberation Front, founded in 1976, has conducted a bombing campaign against police stations, government offices and the property of non-Corsican immigrants. The government has offered limited concessions, including a degree of political devolution, in its attempts to bring an end to the violence.

The native language of Corsica is Corse, a Romance language derived from the Tuscan dialect of Italian. Most native Corsicans still speak Corse, but it is most often used as a private language among friends and family. French is increasingly used in public, especially by the younger generations and in towns. Corse existed as a completely unwritten language until the 19th century and it has no established literary tradition to sustain it. Most Corsicans are Roman Catholics and many of their distinctive folk customs are associated with religious festivals. Corsica was famous for banditry and for family blood feuds known as *vendetta* (vengeance). The tradition was encouraged by the weak and corrupt justice system of the Genoese administration and by the Corsican social structure, which was based on extended families and clans. Loyalty to family and clan was strong, and implacable codes of honour led easily to violence. These traditions are still not completely extinct. Corsicans are proud of their island's rugged landscape and they have resisted the kind of mass tourist development that has blighted much of the Mediterranean.

## COSSACKS

A paramilitary society that played an important role in the expansion of the Russian empire. Their name, derived from a Turkish word meaning 'adventurer' or 'vagabond', reflects their origins as a mix of RUSSIANS, POLES, TATARS and others who hired themselves out as mercenaries in Russian armies in return for land grants and tax privileges. Many of the original Cossacks were discontented peasants who fled their villages to the empty steppe lands around the Dnieper, Don and Ural rivers in modern Ukraine and Russia in the late Middle Ages to avoid the imposition of serfdom. These runaways were forced to band together for their own protection, and they developed into a potent cavalry force. Cossack social organization was modelled on the military hierarchy with officers (*hetmen*) forming an upper class. The Cossacks supplemented their military employment by arable and pastoral farming. Cossack society was rigidly patriarchal and there were clearly defined gender roles: for example, women worked the fields while men tended the livestock.

The Cossacks struggled against Polish expansion into the Ukraine in the 17th century and in 1653 they sought the protection of Russia. By the 18th century there were over a dozen Cossack cavalry regiments, serving mainly on

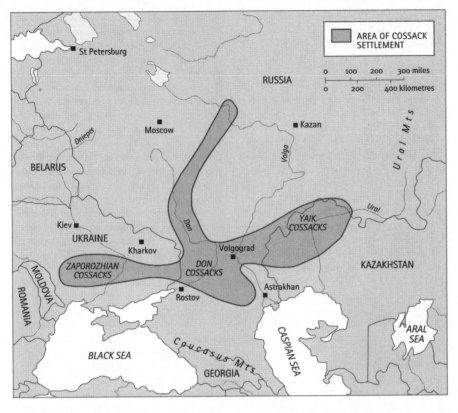

Russia's Asian frontiers. In the 19th century Cossack soldiers became instantly recognizable by their distinctive uniforms: tall Caucasian hats, long coats with bullet pouches and high riding boots. At the outbreak of World War I the Cossack population was 4.4 million, of whom about 285,000 were serving in the Russian army. The largest concentration of Cossacks was on the lower Don (see DON COSSACKS). When the Russian Revolution broke out in 1917, the Cossacks overwhelmingly sided with the Whites against the Bolsheviks and later opposed the collectivization of agriculture. They suffered starvation and deportation for this under Joseph Stalin. Today, about 3 million people claiming Cossack descent live in Ukraine and southern Russia.

## CROATS

A SLAV people of the Balkans who form the majority of the estimated 5-million-strong population of the Republic of Croatia and 17% of the population of neighbouring Bosnia-Herzegovina. The Croats describe their language as Croatian, but this is more of a political statement than a linguistic truth, born of a long rivalry with their neighbours the SERBS. Croats speak three distinct dialects of Serbo-Croat, a South Slavic language, the most important of which is Stokavski. This dialect was adopted by Croats, Serbs and BOSNIAN MUSLIMS as a standard literary language in the 19th century, a development that is now seen by many Croatian nationalists as having contributed to an undesirable blurring of the distinction between Croats and Serbs. The western and eastern variants of Stokavski spoken by Croats and Serbs are distinguished by small differences in vowel sounds and by differences in vocabulary reflecting the historical experiences of the two peoples. The vocabulary has a number of loan words from Italian, German and Hungarian, while Serbian is distinguished by loan words from Turkish and Russian. Different historical experiences have also produced differences in religion and outlook. The Croats are Roman Catholics and see themselves as western Europeans, in contrast to the Serbs who are Orthodox Christians and look to eastern Europe and, especially, Russia. The Croats use the Latin alphabet while Serbs use the Cyrillic.

The Croats were one of several Slavic peoples who migrated into the Balkans in the late 6th and early 7th centuries AD from the area of modern Ukraine. They settled most densely along the coast of Dalmatia and inland between the Sava and Drava rivers. Later in the 7th century the Croats were converted to Roman Catholicism. In the early Middle Ages, the Balkans were the scene of great-power competition between the FRANKS, AVARS and the BYZANTINE empire, but by the 9th century an independent Kingdom of Croatia had emerged. For a time it was a dominant naval power in the Adriatic. In 1097 Croatia came under HUNGARIAN rule, although much of the Dalmatian coast was subsequently conquered by the VENETIANS. Most of Croatia was conquered by the OTTOMANS after their crushing victory over the HUNGARIANS at Mohács in 1526. The small northern strip of Croatia to escape conquest was immediately annexed by the Austrian Habsburgs. The Ottomans altered the ethnic balance in Croatia by encouraging Serbian settlement in the Krajina district, and by bringing in GERMAN and Hungarian settlers. Croatia was reconquered by the Habsburgs in the 17th century, but Croats who had settled in Bosnia-Herzegovina remained under Ottoman rule until 1878, when they too came under Habsburg rule.

### Croatians in the modern era

The first stirrings of modern Croatian nationalism began during the Napoleonic Wars, when Dalmatia was briefly part of the FRENCH empire. During the 19th century the Illyrian movement promoted closer cultural links between the South Slavs (the Croats, Serbs, MONTENEGRINS and SLOVENES) or 'Yugoslavs'. This contributed to the development of a wider movement of political Yugoslavism. In 1915 the Yugoslav Committee began to call for the formal separation of Slovenia and Croatia from the Austro-Hungarian empire and union with Serbia. The defeat of the Austro-Hungarian empire in World War I was followed by the creation of an independent Yugoslav kingdom. Croats had believed they would enter the Yugoslav state as equals but they became disillusioned to find that it was in effect a Greater Serbia. When Yugoslavia was occupied by Germany during World War II, Croat resentment found expression in the 'independent' puppet state of Croatia under the pro-Nazi Ustase regime of Ante Pavelic. Large numbers of Croatian Serbs, JEWS and GYPSIES were murdered by the regime.

With integration into the federal Yugoslavia of Tito, the postwar communist regime cracked down hard on expressions of Croatian national identity, but this did nothing to lessen Croat resentment towards the Serbs. The first multiparty elections in Yugoslavia in 1990 brought the Croatian Democratic Union (CDU) to power in Croatia under Franjo Tudjman (1922–99). When Croatia declared independence in June 1991, the Serb-dominated Yugoslav army invaded and bitter fighting broke out. A ceasefire in 1992 ended the fighting, but large parts of the country remained under Serb control until 1996. In the process of restoring control of Krajina in 1995, the Croats expelled around 250,000 Serbs. Since independence, Croatians have worked to emphasize as much as possible the differences between themselves and the Serbs, for example by purging the Croatian language of its supposed Serbian influences.

## CRO-MAGNONS

A prehistoric people who were believed when first discovered to be the first fully modern human (*Homo sapiens sapiens*) inhabitants of Europe. They are named after a rock shelter in the Dordogne Valley in France, which was excavated in 1868. These excavations uncovered three human fossils dating to around 25,000 years ago. At the time, these were the earliest known fossils of modern humans discovered in Europe, although fossil evidence discovered since then places the arrival of modern humans in Europe at 38,000–40,000 years ago. The fossil evidence suggests that the Cro-Magnons were taller and had a more muscular build than modern Europeans, indicating that they were well nourished and had physically demanding lives.

## CUCUTENI-TRIPOLYE CULTURE

See TRIPOLYE-CUCUTENI culture.

## CUMANS

A nomadic Turkish people (see TURKS) who were the western-most wing of the KIPCHAQ confederation, which dominated the steppes from the Danube to Kazakhstan from the 11th century until the MONGOL invasion in 1237. The Cumans often served as mercenaries in the armies of the Russian princes. After the Kipchaqs were conquered by the Mongols, thousands of Cumans were allowed to settle in Hungary by King Béla IV, where they were slowly assimilated into HUNGARIAN culture and identity.

## CURONIANS

A Baltic people (see BALTS) who inhabited the Courland peninsula in Latvia during the Middle Ages. They were conquered by the GERMAN crusading order of the Livonian Knights in 1263 and forced to accept Christianity. The Curonians retained a distinct identity until the 18th century, before being assimilated by the LATVIANS, to whom they were culturally and linguistically closely related.

## CYPRIOTS

A people of INDO-EUROPEAN origin from the island of Cyprus. Today the islanders of Cyprus are known as Cypriots, although approximately half of all Cypriots reside in other countries – principally the United Kingdom, Canada and the United States.

Aboriginal Cypriots had established a flourishing Neolithic culture, now known as the KHIROKITIA CULTURE, by 6000 BC. This was succeeded, in about 4000 BC, by the Sotira culture. Owing to the island's excellent position within the eastern Mediterranean, however, both in military and trading terms, Cyprus has, for over

two millennia, been the focus of imperial interest. It was also one of the major sources of copper for the ancient world. As a result, PHOENICIANS, GREEKS, EGYPTIANS, ASSYRIANS, PERSIANS, ROMANS and BYZANTINES all established colonies or ruled the island as a province during the ancient period. Culturally, however, it was the establishment of Greek colonies on the island around 1100 BC that was to have the most profound effect, and much of the population of modern Cyprus is descended from these immigrants. Ancient Cypriots used the Cypro-Minoan writing script, which had its origins on the island of Crete (see MINOANS). From the medieval period to the late 19th century, the ENGLISH, Byzantines, Venetians and TURKS all in turn established political and economic dominance over the Cypriots. During the period of Turkish rule, over 20,000 Muslims were settled on the island, thus introducing a second major ethnic group to Cyprus, and sowing the seeds for later inter-necine strife.

Cyprus was governed by the British 1878–1960, and it was during this period that the notion of *enosis* (unification with Greece) became the focus of political activity amongst many Greek Cypriots. By the 1950s this activity had escalated into open violence, with terrorist attacks perpetrated against both British and Cypriot targets. These attacks were generally carried out by the National Organization of Cypriot Struggle (EOKA). Despite British attempts to prevent Cypriot independence, this was finally won in 1960.

### The two Cypruses

Though initial attempts were made to include Turkish Cypriots, the government of independent Cyprus has always been dominated by Greek Cypriots, the largest ethnic group. During the 1960s and 1970s ethnic clashes were not uncommon, and both communities have tended to look to the mainland powers for assistance. Certainly, the Turkish Cypriots have desired a republic independent of the Greek-dominated constitutional government, while many Greeks continue to desire unity with Greece. In 1974, President Makarios was deposed by a Greek Cypriot military coup, and this was followed swiftly by a Turkish invasion

*“ Almost every house has a garden, of which the Cypriots are most fond. ”*

*Penny Cyclopædia, 1836*

C

of northern Cyprus, which succeeded in taking about 37% of the island. This area continues to be controlled by Turkish Cypriots, who, in 1983, declared the Turkish Federated State of Cyprus to be an independent republic. However, its independence has not achieved international recognition. Since the 1974 invasion a UN peacekeeping force has patrolled a buffer zone between the two areas. In 2004 negotiations over the reunification of the island appeared to be making some headway.

The language of 80% of the population of Cyprus is Greek, although they use a dialect considerably different from that of mainland Greece, and 18% have Turkish as their first language. Farming remains the main occupation of many Cypriots. Most of the Greek-speaking population adheres to the Church of Cyprus, while the Turkish population is predominantly Sunni Muslim.

Perhaps not surprisingly, the culture of both communities has been heavily influenced by those mainland countries from which they derive. The imperialist powers who have at various times controlled the island have also left their own mark on local art and architecture.

Since 1974 there have been mass internal migrations, with Turkish Cypriots heading north and Greek Cypriots south; many also left the country at this time. Given these migrations, most of those living on Cyprus do not consider themselves to be first and foremost 'Cypriots'. It seems that ethnic identity, being 'Greek' or 'Turkish', has a much more important role to play in national identity than physical homeland.

## CZECHS

A SLAV people whose lands include the historic regions of Bohemia and Moravia, which today make up the Czech Republic. They form 95% of the 10.5-million-strong population of the Czech Republic and about 1% of the population of Slovakia. Although they are usually considered to be Czechs, some MORAVIANS regard themselves as being a distinct ethnic group in their own right. The Czechs are the western-most of the Slav peoples and, although the POLES and CROATS might disagree, they are arguably also the most western-European in outlook.

For most of their history the Czechs have lived in the shadow of, and frequently under the domination of, their GERMAN neighbours. The earliest historically recorded inhabitants of the Czech lands were the BOII, a Celtic tribe from whom Bohemia gets its name. The Boii were overrun by German tribes in the 1st century BC, and in the 6th century AD Slav tribes began to move into the area, the Czechs among them. After initial evangelization by the Orthodox Church, the Czechs converted to Catholicism in the 9th century. The first Czech state, the principality of Great Moravia, emerged in the later 9th century, but was destroyed by German and MAGYAR attacks in 905–8. In the 10th century Bohemia became a vassal kingdom within the German-dominated Holy Roman empire. German immigration, encouraged by Czech kings, stimulated urban development, trade and industry. In the 15th century the Czech preacher Jan Huss challenged papal authority with his proto-Protestant teachings. When he was burned for heresy in 1415, his many followers in Bohemia and Moravia staged a bloody uprising against the Holy Roman empire. This was put down with great difficulty only in 1436. The Hussite church survived underground to re-emerge during the Protestant Reformation.

The Kingdom of Bohemia came under the rule of the AUSTRIAN Habsburg dynasty in 1526 as a result of a dynastic marriage, although it remained technically independent of the Habsburg empire. Under the Habsburgs, Prague, the kingdom's capital, became a leading European cultural centre. Habsburg rule was not popular with the Czechs, not least because of its suppression of Protestantism. In 1618 the Bohemian estates declared the Habsburg Ferdinand II (1578–1637) deposed and elected Frederick V (1596–1632), a German Protestant, as king. The rebellion was crushed two years later at the Battle of White Mountain. The Protestant nobility was dispossessed of its lands, exiled or executed, and Catholicism became the only permitted religion. The German language was given equal official status with Czech and became the dominant language of administration and higher education. For the next three hundred years the Czechs struggled to maintain their culture and identity through the so-called 'time of darkness'.

### The struggle towards nationhood

Modern Czech nationalism began to develop in the 19th century and found expression in the arts, especially the music of composers Smetana (1824–84) and Dvořák (1841–1904). However, the Czech National Liberation movement made little political progress, and the introduction of the dual monarchy in 1867, which turned the Austrian empire into the Austro-Hungarian empire, decreased any form of national self-determination. Following the collapse of the Austria-Hungary at the end of World War I, the Czechs were united with the SLOVAKS in a federal state called Czechoslovakia. Neither people particularly desired the union, which was a product of the desire of the victorious allies to avoid creating a large number of small, weak ethnic states in central Europe. Czechoslavakia also included areas inhabited by RUTHENIANS, and, critically for the future, there was a large German population in the Sudetenland. In the 1930s the Nazis stirred up nationalistic feelings among the Sudetenland Germans who began to demand unity with Germany. With no European power prepared to risk war over the issue, Czechoslovakia had little choice but to sign the Munich Agreement in 1938 and cede the Sudetenland to Germany. In 1939 Bohemia and Moravia were completely annexed by Germany, and Slovakia became a German puppet state.

After World War II Czechoslovakia was restored (although losing its part of Ruthenia to the USSR). The 3 million Sudetenland Germans were all expelled. Czechoslovakia became a communist dictatorship in 1948 and, later, a member of the Warsaw Pact. The Czech-led attempt to introduce 'socialism with a human face' under Alexander Dubcek (1921–92) in the 'Prague Spring' of 1968 provoked a Warsaw Pact invasion. Dubcek's government was replaced by a hardline regime that was finally toppled peacefully by the 'Velvet Revolution' in 1989. The collapse of the communist government allowed differences of outlook between the Slovaks and Czechs to emerge. The Czechs were more eager to move towards a deregulated western capitalist economy than the Slovaks, who still wanted the state to play a major role in their less developed economy. The desire of Slovaks for national recognition and the recognition by Czechs that

their economy would only benefit by Slovakia becoming independent led to the 'Velvet Divorce' in 1992, by which Czechoslovakia was peacefully dissolved and the new states of Slovakia and the Czech Republic were created.

Since 1992, the economy of the Czech Republic has been the most successful of any in the former communist bloc. Czechs have shown their desire to be seen as western Europeans through membership of NATO (1998) and the European Union (2004). At the same time intolerance towards minority groups, especially GYPSIES, has increased. The communist government did its best to suppress religion, and most Czechs today do not subscribe to any organized religion. About 10% of Czechs are practising Roman Catholics and about 2% belong to the Hussite Czech National Church.

## DACIANS

An ancient people of the Carpathian Mountains and Transylvania, in what is now north-central and western Romania. The Dacians spoke a THRACIAN language and their culture was influenced by the ancient CELTS to the west and the SCYTHIANS to the east. They were primarily a farming people, but they also mined their homeland's rich deposits of silver, iron, and gold. The Dacians are first recorded in the 4th century BC, as slaves in Athens. They fought against Rome in 112, 109, and 75 BC. Originally a tribal people, the Dacians were unified c. 60–50 BC by King Burebista, who expanded his kingdom at the expense of the neighbouring Celtic peoples, such as the BOII. The Dacian kingdom broke up after Burebista was assassinated in 44 BC, but the Dacians continued to raid Roman territory south of the Danube.

The Dacians were reunited by King Decebalus c. AD 85. Decebalus invaded the ROMAN empire but was defeated in 89 by the emperor Domitian and was forced to acknowledge Roman overlordship. Decebalus refused to be pacified, however, prompting the emperor Trajan to conquer Dacia in two campaigns in 101–2 and 105–6. Trajan's Column in Rome preserves a pictorial record of these campaigns. The Dacian population suffered severe casualties in these wars and many dispersed into neighbouring territories. The mineral wealth of Dacia made this a profitable conquest for Rome, but the territory's exposed position north of the Danube and its lack of defined frontiers made it difficult to defend, and it was overrun by the GOTHS around 270. The subsequent fate of the Dacians is unclear but the ROMANIANS count them among their ancestors.

# DANES

The people of the Kingdom of Denmark, the most southerly of the SCANDINAVIAN nations. Danes also form 20% of the population of Greenland, a Danish colony, and a small minority in South Schleswig in north Germany, a legacy of medieval times when the Duchy of Schleswig-Holstein was subject to the Danish Crown. Until the 17th century the populations of Halland, Scania and Blekinge in southern Sweden were also Danish. Danes speak a North Germanic language descended from a common Scandinavian language that was known in the Viking Age as the *Dönsk tunga* ('Danish tongue'). Although they began to diverge a thousand years ago, the Danish, NORWEGIAN and Swedish languages are still mutually intelligible.

The Danish identity is one of the oldest in northern Europe and was already formed when Scandinavia entered the historical record around AD 800. The origins of the Danes is uncertain, but early medieval historians recorded the traditional belief that they came from Sweden.

In the 9th century, Danish Vikings raided the British Isles and the Frankish empire (see FRANKS), settling in eastern England (the 'Danelaw') and Normandy. These settlers were soon assimilated by the native populations. In the late 10th century the Danes were united into a single kingdom and their conversion to Christianity began.

Under Cnut (ruled 1018–35) Denmark was part of a North Sea empire that included England, Norway and Sweden. This empire broke up on Cnut's death, but Denmark remained the most powerful of the Scandinavian kingdoms throughout the Middle Ages; although it was the smallest of these, Denmark also had the highest proportion of good farmland. Queen Margrethe I (ruled 1375–1412) engineered a succession of dynastic unions, culminating in the Union of Kalmar in 1397, which brought Denmark control of Norway, Sweden, Iceland, the Faeroe Islands and Greenland. Danish power began to decline, however, in the 16th century, when the SWEDES rebelled and won their independence.

**From empire to welfare state**
By 1660 the Swedes had conquered the Danish provinces of Halland, Blekinge and Scania. The Swedes made great efforts to woo the Danish population there and by 1700 they had adopted Swedish identity. Denmark lost Norway to Sweden in 1815, the consequence of backing the losing side in the Napoleonic Wars, and Iceland became independent in 1918. The Faeroes (see FAEROESE) and Greenland remain Danish dependencies. More formative for the modern Danes than the loss of their Scandinavian empire was their defeat by Prussia in the war over the duchies of Schleswig-Holstein in 1864. Danes concluded that the technology of modern warfare made their country impossible to defend, and they have been at heart a pacifistic people ever since, making defence-spending a low priority. Denmark was occupied by GERMAN forces in 1940, becoming a 'protectorate' of the Third Reich. Campaigns of civil disobedience by the Danes forced the Nazi regime to introduce direct rule in 1943.

Postwar Denmark provided for its national security by joining NATO, but this remained a contentious issue until the end of the Cold War era, with a large minority of Danes always favouring neutrality. Dependence on British and German markets for its agricultural exports led Denmark to join the European Community (now European Union) in 1972, but Danes remain unenthusiastic Europeans. Denmark has secured so many opt-outs from EU treaties that it has been caricatured as 'the country that likes to say no', and in 2003 it was still outside the Eurozone. As a small nation (the population of Denmark is 5.3 million), Danes fear loss of identity in any future European superstate.

Unofficial annexation by Denmark's giant, and unloved, southern neighbour Germany is seen as a real possibility and there are, for example, laws to prevent Germans buying holiday homes in the country. English-language influence on the Danish language is also seen as a potential threat.

Nevertheless, Danes enjoy one of the highest standards of living in the world today as well as a relatively classless society, sexual equality, and high standards of state education, health care and welfare; taxes are correspondingly high. Right-wing pundits have long predicted an end to the social consensus that supports the welfare state, but there is a strong levelling tendency in Danish society, and these predictions show no sign of being fulfilled. Danes tend to believe that they have created a good society and regularly appear in surveys as being among the most contented people in the world. Danes have gained a reputation for easy-going tolerance, but this rests on the deep-rooted conformity of Danish society and a tendency not to push against accepted boundaries. This has, however, made it difficult for Danes to come to terms with increasing immigration from developing countries since the 1970s. Anti-immigration political parties have achieved some electoral success by advocating 'send them back' policies. The refusal of some immigrants – and Muslims are perceived as a particular problem – to integrate is widely seen as a threat to Denmark's social fabric. The Danes are not themselves a religious people; most are nominally Lutheran Christians, but church attendance is very low.

## DARDANIANS

An ancient people of the Balkans who inhabited Dardania, a region approximating to northern Macedonia and Kosovo. The exact affiliation of the Dardanians is uncertain, but it is thought that they were either ILLYRIANS or THRACIANS or a mixture of both. The Dardanians were frequently at war with the ancient MACEDONIANS in the 3rd and 4th centuries BC and they were allies of Rome in its wars with Macedonia in the 2nd century. The Dardanians continued to raid Macedonia after it became a Roman province in 146 BC, provoking the Romans to brutal retaliation. They finally submitted to ROMAN rule around 40–31 BC. The Dardanian identity survived until the end of the Roman period and was probably absorbed by SLAV immigrants in the 6th century AD. The Dardanians were known in

the Roman world for worshipping a snake god.

'Dardanians' was also a poetic name sometimes used by the ancient GREEKS to describe the Trojans, after Dardanus, the mythological founder of their race.

## DARGIN

A Caucasian people of Sergokola and Dakhadajev regions, central Dagestan, Russian Federation. Traditionally herders, especially of sheep, and noted goldsmiths, they adopted Sunni Islam in the 11th century and speak a North Caucasian language. Under RUSSIAN rule from the 19th century, they resisted assimilation until collectivization was brutally imposed under Soviet authority, although they successfully resisted efforts to relocate them to the lowlands. They clung tenaciously to their identity as a people, and since 1991 they have developed an increasingly vocal secessionist movement. In 2000 they numbered over 380,000.

## DÉISI

A number of IRISH communities in late pre-Christian and early Christian Ireland. Déisi means 'tenants' in Old Irish so it is thought that they were originally subordinate communities living under the domination of overlords. The main groups of Déisi were the Déisi Temro (Déisi of Tara) in Meath, the Déisi of Limerick and the Déisi of Waterford. A branch of the Limerick Déisi founded the kingdom of Dál Cais in Clare, whose most famous ruler was the high king Brian Boru (ruled 976–1014). Part of the Waterford Déisi migrated to Wales in the 5th century, founding the royal house of the WELSH kingdom of Dyfed (see also DEMETAE). The Waterford Déisi survived until the ANGLO-NORMAN conquest in the 12th century.

## DEMETAE

Ancient BRITONS of southwest Wales. The Demetae were brought peacefully under ROMAN rule around AD 50; it is likely that they welcomed the ROMANS as protectors against their hostile neighbours, the SILURES. The tribe was granted a self-governing *civitas* around AD 75, and they established their capital at Moridunum Demetarum (modern Carmarthen). After the end of Roman rule in the early 5th century, the Demetae formed the nucleus of the early WELSH kingdom of Dyfed (see also DÉISI).

## DEREVLIANS

See DREVLJANE.

## DIDO

A Caucasian people of Tsuntin region, southern Dagestan, Russian Federation, who speak a North Caucasian language. Similar to the AVARS, whose written language they use, they were primarily herders, especially of sheep, and adopted Sunni Islam in the 16th century. They were conquered by the RUSSIANS in the 19th century but proved rebellious until Soviet collectivization and cultural erosion undermined them. Since the 1960s they have officially been counted as Avars. In 1994 they numbered about 7000.

## DOBUNNI

Ancient BRITONS whose territory centred on the Cotswold Hills in Gloucestershire. By the time of the ROMAN invasion in AD 43 the Dobunni had established a kingdom that included neighbouring parts of modern Wiltshire, Oxfordshire, Worcestershire and Herefordshire. The kingdom was apparently divided into two sub-kingdoms, each with its own ruler. The main tribal centre was the fortified settlement at Bagendon, near Cirencester. The tribe was divided in its response to the Romans, with many seeing them as allies rather than enemies. The Dobunni were granted a self-governing *civitas* around AD 70, with a capital at Cirencester. The *civitas* of the Dobunni became one of the most prosperous farming areas of Britain during the 4th century, and many rich villas were built by local landowners.

The Dobunni still retained their tribal identity in the mid-6th century, but they probably did not survive for long after the ANGLO-SAXONS captured Cirencester in 577.

## DON COSSACKS

The largest group of COSSACKS; they settled on the steppes around the lower Don River in southwest Russia in the 16th century, where they lived as bandits, farmers and mercenaries. The Don Cossacks came under nominal RUSSIAN control in 1614 but remained effectively an autonomous paramilitary society under their elected leader, the *ataman*. Rebellions under Stenka Razin (1670–1) and Kondraty Bulavin (1707) were a pretext for the Russian government to bring the Don Cossacks under tighter control in the early 18th century. A Cossack and peasant rebellion against Catherine the Great, led by the Don Cossack Yemelian Pugachev in 1783, resulted in Cossack cavalry units being formally incorporated into the Russian army, where they could be controlled more easily. The Don Cossacks became some of the most loyal supporters of the tsarist regime, and they were frequently used to put down peasant uprisings and urban demonstrations. They fought for the White Russians during the civil war that followed the Bolshevik revolution in 1917. The Cossack way of life was, however, destroyed by the collectivization of agriculture in the 1930s.

## DORIANS

One of the two main ethnic groups of the ancient GREEKS; the other is the IONIANS. The Dorians were divided into the Hylleis, Dymanes and Pamphyloi. They migrated into Greece from the northwest during the ancient 'dark ages' (*c.* 1200–800 BC) that followed the fall of the MYCENAEAN civilization. Whether the Dorians played a direct role in that fall is unclear, but they certainly benefited by it, occupying most of the Peloponnese (especially Messenia, Argolid and Laconia), Crete and the coast of southwest Anatolia (modern Turkey). The Dorians spoke a distinct dialect of Greek, had a strong sense of common identity and saw themselves as a tough and austere people, while considering the Ionians decadent and effeminate. Their most important god was the sun-god Apollo, and they claimed descent from the sons of Hercules. Their name is derived from Doris in central Greece, which the Dorians believed was their homeland.

# DREGOVICHI

A SLAV people who lived to the west of the middle Dnieper River in the early Middle Ages. They became tributaries of the RUS and were ultimately assimilated with them.

# DREVLJANE or Derevlians

A SLAV people who lived between the headwaters of the Vistula and Dnieper rivers in the early Middle Ages. They became tributaries of the Kievan RUS around 910 but rebelled and killed the Rus king Igor in 945. They were soon reconquered by Igor's vengeful queen, Olga, and subsequently assimilated to the Rus identity.

# DUMNONII

Ancient BRITONS who inhabited the areas of modern Somerset, Devon and Cornwall during the late Iron Age. The Dumnonii were less advanced socially and economically than other southern British tribes. They issued no coinage and had no major hillforts or tribal centres, suggesting that they were a coalition of small tribes without any centralized leadership. Similarities in pottery styles indicate that the Dumnonii had close maritime links across the Channel with the ARMORICANS. The Dumnonii were brought under ROMAN control in the late 40s and 50s AD; there is little evidence that they put up much resistance. Under Roman rule, Isca (Exeter) became the tribal capital. The Dumnonii preserved their identity throughout the period of Roman rule. After the Romans left in AD 410, the territory of the Dumnonii became the Kingdom of Dumnonia. In the 5th and 6th centuries, Dumnonia played an important role in the British settlement of Brittany (see BRETONS). Devon and Somerset were conquered by the WEST SAXONS around 600, but Cornwall remained independent for another 200 years. Devon is named after Dumnonia.

# DUROTRIGES

Ancient BRITONS who inhabited Dorset and adjacent parts of Wiltshire and Somerset during the late Iron Age. They had several major hillforts,

the best known of which today is Maiden Castle, suggesting that they originated as a coalition of smaller tribes. In the early 1st century BC, the Durotriges were active partners in the trade routes along Europe's Atlantic coast; their port at Hengistbury Head, near Christchurch, had close connections with Brittany (see BRETONS). The Roman conquest of Gaul in 58–51 BC broke these trade routes, sending the Durotriges into relative decline. Nevertheless, they put up stiff resistance to the ROMANS in 44 BC: archaeological excavations have shown that hillforts at Maiden Castle, Hod Hill and South Cadbury all had to be taken by storm. Under Roman rule, Durnovaria (Dorchester), a few miles from Maiden Castle, became the tribal capital.

# DUTCH

The people of the Kingdom of the Netherlands. They compose 95% of the country's population (15.5 million in 1996); the remainder is of recent immigrant origin. The Dutch are the descendants of several Germanic peoples (see GERMANS), including the FRISIANS and FRANKS, who were settled around the mouths of the Rhine and adjacent parts of the North Sea coast in the Roman Iron Age and the early Middle Ages. The Dutch language, or Netherlandic, is a West Germanic language, which shares ancestry with the various dialects of Low German.

The Dutch identity began to coalesce in the 16th century. During the Middle Ages, the Low Countries (roughly the area of modern Belgium, the Netherlands and Luxembourg) were a patchwork of semi-autonomous feudal principalities within the Holy Roman empire. Through war and diplomatic marriages, these were united under the Valois dukes of Burgundy in the 15th century into a single principality, which later passed, via another diplomatic marriage, to the SPANISH Habsburgs. The Low Countries formed the richest and most urbanized region of northern Europe. Its strategic location gave it access to trade routes in the North Sea, the Atlantic and, via the Rhine, into the heart of Europe. Trade and manufacturing industries flourished.

During the Reformation, the independent-minded townspeople proved to be ready converts to the uncompromising Calvinist form of Protestantism. The Catholic Spanish king Philip II (ruled 1556–98) actively persecuted Protestants, introducing the Inquisition, and provoked wider discontent through his absolutist policies. In 1568 the Netherlands rebelled under Prince William of Orange. The overwhelmingly Catholic FLEMISH and WALLOONS in the south of the Low Countries were reconciled to Spanish rule, but the seven northern provinces (Holland, Zeeland, Utrecht, Gelderland, Groningen, Friesland and Overijssel) declared independence in 1581 as the republic of the United Provinces. Spain did not recognize the republic until 1648, ending a long war of independence. War with Spain did not prevent the Dutch from building an overseas trading empire and becoming Europe's leading maritime power until overshadowed by England later in the 17th century. Although Calvinists never became the majority religious group, they dominated the Dutch economy and the wealthy province of Holland, including the capital Amsterdam. Although they were morally austere, their civic virtues of religious toleration, press freedom and civil liberty have become ingrained in the Dutch nation.

### The creation of the Netherlands

The Dutch republic was brought to an end in 1795 when it was conquered by France. Following the end of the Napoleonic Wars in 1815, the former United Provinces were re-united with the southern provinces to form the Kingdom of the Netherlands under William I. William's rule antagonized the Flemish and Walloons of the south, and in 1830 they declared independence as the Kingdom of Belgium. From 1848, a series of gradual reforms turned the Netherlands into a democratic constitutional monarchy. Neutral in World War I, the Netherlands was occupied by Germany in World War II. Postwar, the Dutch experienced rapid industrialization and intensification of agriculture. Major land reclamation projects greatly increased the country's fertile acreage. Dutch living standards increased rapidly and are now among the highest in Europe.

Until the 1960s Dutch society was quite rigidly divided along religious lines, a phenomenon known as *verzuiling* ('columnization'). Catholics and Protestants sent their children to different schools, shopped at different stores, read different newspapers and voted for different political parties. As the Protestant majority was divided between several denominations, the large Catholic minority enjoyed a strong political voice. These divisions have become less important, and nearly 40% of Dutch people now say that they have no religious affiliation. As a wealthy and open country, and a former imperial power, the Netherlands has seen much immigration from developing countries in recent decades. This has become a political issue, as voiced by the party of the (assassinated) Pim Fortuyn which enjoyed spectacular, if brief, electoral success in 2002. The many regional identities that characterized the Netherlands in the 16th century had all but disappeared by the 19th century, and the Dutch identity is now a very homogeneous one. Only in Friesland, where a minority speak Frisian, is there a real sense of local distinctiveness.

## EAST SAXONS

The SAXONS in England who settled north of the Thames estuary in the 5th and 6th centuries AD. The East Saxons formed an independent kingdom, from which the English county of Essex gets its name. Never very powerful, the East Saxons were conquered by Wessex around 825.

## ELYMIANS

An ancient people of northwest Sicily. Their origins and language are unknown, but their own legendary traditions claimed descent from the Trojans. Their main city was Segesta. The Elymians were conquered by the ROMANS in the 3rd century BC.

## ENGLISH

The largest of the nations that make up the United Kingdom. Many English are descendants of the ANGLO-SAXONS, who invaded and settled Britain in the 5th and 6th centuries AD, and of conquered native BRITONS who were assimilated to Anglo-Saxon culture and identity. In later centuries the English successfully assimilated substantial numbers of immigrant DANES, NOR-

WEGIANS, NORMANS, FRENCH, FLEMISH and IRISH. Since the 18th century the English have seen their identity as being almost synonymous with the BRITISH identity. Amid political devolution and resurgent nationalism in Scotland and Wales, however, there are, at the beginning of the 21st century, signs that the English are beginning to re-assert their Englishness.

English identity is relatively homogeneous but there are pronounced regional identities, strongest in the northeast, the northwest, Yorkshire and the southwest.

### English beginnings

The Anglo-Saxons were not at first a politically united people – in the 7th century they were divided into seven kingdoms – but they shared a common culture and spoke closely related dialects of a West Germanic language which they called *Englisc*, and which linguists call Old English, a complex inflected language not easily understood by modern English-speakers. The modern English language is the product of gradual grammatical simplification and an enormously expanded vocabulary of words borrowed from dozens of different languages, the most important of which are Latin and French.

The earliest surviving expression of common English identity is Bede's *Ecclesiastical History of the English People*, written at the beginning of the 8th century. By about 850 Anglo-Saxons had come to describe themselves as the *Anglecynn* ('Englishkind'). This nascent English identity came close to being wiped out in the later 9th century by invasions of Danish and Norwegian VIKINGS, who conquered and settled large areas of the northwest, Yorkshire, the east Midlands and East Anglia, creating a number of small kingdoms. Alfred the Great's Kingdom of Wessex was the only Anglo-Saxon kingdom to survive these invasions with its territory intact, and he was able to appeal to their sense of common identity to unite all those English who were not under Viking rule.

By the mid-10th century Alfred's successors had conquered the Danish and Norwegian settlements and created a single 'Kingdom of the English', whose borders closely approximated those of modern England (from *Englaland*, 'land of the Angles'). The conquered settlers were not expelled, however, and by the 11th century they had come to regard themselves as English.

The Norman conquest of 1066 imposed on the English an alien ruling class whose language and culture were French. Yet the Normans came quickly to identify with the kingdom and people they had conquered. Soon after 1100 Normans born in England described themselves as English and were regarded as such in Normandy itself. These signs of assimilation were set back, however, when the Norman dynasty was replaced by the French Angevin dynasty in 1154, which revitalized the French cultural identity of the aristocracy. It was not until the late 14th century that English again became the language of the royal court.

Despite its lack of social prestige and aristocratic patronage, an English literary tradition survived and the language itself gained ground as a result of English conquests and settlement in Wales and Ireland. In retrospect, the Magna Carta of 1215, which curbed the arbitrary power of the monarch and guaranteed subjects' (at least the barons') rights under the law, came to be seen as the foundation of English liberty. The Hundred Years War (1337–1453), in which the kings of England tried to make good their claims to the throne of France, ended in defeat, but a string of spectacular victories won against heavy odds fed English pride and led to the beginning of a recognizably modern English nationalism. The end of serfdom, as much due to economic changes following the Black Death as the Peasants' Revolt of 1381, convinced the English that they were a uniquely free, and freedom loving, people, and they began to develop a strong tradition of economic individualism.

### Protestantism and a global empire

The Reformation initiated another formative period in the development of English identity. Henry VIII's break with Rome in 1533 left England without any important continental ally and embittered relations with its IRISH subjects, who clung resolutely to Catholicism. Diplomatic isolation and their successful resistance to Catholic Spain, the European superpower of the 16th century, confirmed the majority of the English in Protestantism, anti-Catholicism, and a firm belief that they were a race apart.

> " ... thank the goodness and the grace Which on my birth have smiled, And made me, in these Christian days, A happy English child. "
>
> Anne Taylor and Jane Taylor, *Hymns for Infant Minds* (1810)

The 17th century was one of the most turbulent in English history, seeing a dynastic union with the SCOTS in the Union of the Crowns (1603), a period of mid-century civil wars, the beheading of a king (Charles I), an unsuccessful experiment with republicanism under Oliver Cromwell, the deposition of a Catholic king (James II), the foundations of parliamentary government and a global colonial empire. England emerged as Europe's leading financial, commercial and naval power, as well as the leading exporter of population, all of which led to great colonial success. By 1700 England had 400,000 colonial subjects, most of them in North America and the West Indies, compared to a home population of 5 million. England's main colonial rival, France, with a home population of 20 million, had a mere 70,000 colonial subjects. This colonial success began the process by which English became the global language that it is today.

In 1707 England lost its political identity when the Act of Union with Scotland created the Kingdom of Great Britain. As the dominant partners in the union, the English were more enthusiastic about adopting the new BRITISH identity than the Scots or WELSH. For the English and indeed for foreigners, the English and British identities became almost identical. (It remains a source of considerable irritation to the Scots in particular when the English talk about 'England' when they are in fact actually referring to Great Britain.)

Between 1689 and 1815 England, then Great Britain, and France fought the 'Second Hundred Years War'. Although Britain lost its most populous North American colonies along the way, it emerged victorious to enjoy a century of unparalleled global dominance. It seemed to the English that God himself must be an Englishman. English ideas of representative government and the rule of law, party politics and loyal opposition were spread around the world, as were Anglicanism and team sports such as cricket, rugby and Association Football.

By the early 19th century England had been transformed into an urbanized and industrialized society. The long separation of most of the English population from the reality of food production has bred an intensely idealized attitude towards rural life not found in other European countries, where urban living is seen as the ideal. The Church of England was slow to adapt to this process of urbanization and in the 19th century the English began to lose the habit of churchgoing: they are now among the most agnostic of peoples.

**English identity after empire**

The costs, financial and otherwise, of fighting World War I ended Britain's global dominance, while those of World War II saw Britain relegated to a second-rank power in retreat from empire. Although Britain joined the European Economic Community (now European Union) in 1973, the English, unlike the Scots, have only reluctantly accepted the need for engagement with Europe. The English still feel close kinship with other English-speaking people,s and for many the Channel remains, psychologically, wider than the Atlantic Ocean. The English have also had to come to terms with rising nationalism in Scotland and Wales which is forcing them to redefine the relationship between Englishness and Britishness. Large-scale immigration, largely from the West Indies and South Asia, poses another challenge to English identity. As the wealthiest constituency of Great Britain, England has attracted a proportionately far higher number of immigrants than Scotland and Wales, and most major English cities are now multiethnic and multicultural communities. Racial tensions have several times exploded into violence, but overtly racist political parties have enjoyed little electoral success, and optimists point out that England has the highest rate of inter-racial marriage in the Western world. The English have in the past prided themselves on being a 'mongrel race' but it is not yet clear if they will learn to do so again.

The population of England in 2001 was just over 49 million, a figure which includes recent immigrants and residents from other parts of the United Kingdom.

# ERTEBØLLE CULTURE

A late MESOLITHIC culture (c. 6000–3500 BC) of Denmark and the western Baltic. The Ertebølle culture marks the beginning of the transition in northern Europe from the hunting, fishing and gathering way of life to farming. The culture is characterized by its microlithic tool industry, massive shell mounds at coastal sites, cemeteries with grave goods, and the adoption of pottery, polished stone axes and agricultural methods from farming peoples to the south.

# ERZYA

A FINNO-UGRIAN people of the Mordovian autonomous republic, Russian Federation. Russians classified them, along with the closely related MOKSHA, as Mordovians, but the Erzya retain a distinct identity. Under foreign domination since the OSTROGOTHS in the 3rd century AD, they adopted agriculture in the 12th century and were conquered by the RUSSIANS in 1552. Forcibly Christianized in the 17th century, they proved rebellious until the 19th. Soviet collectivization and assimilatory policies seriously undermined their traditional culture. In 1997 they claimed that such policies had so seriously endangered their language that they represented a violation of their human rights. In 2000, along with the Moksha, they numbered over 1 million.

# ESTONIANS

A FINNO-UGRIAN people who speak a language related to Finnish. They make up 65% of the Republic of Estonia's population of (in 2001) about 1.4 million; the remainder of the population is mainly of recent RUSSIAN immigrant origin. The Estonians have inhabited the region since prehistoric times. An essentially MESOLITHIC hunting, fishing and gathering way of life survived in this part of northern Europe until the 4th century AD, before giving way to settled farming. Throughout the Middle Ages Estonia was the subject of competition between the DANES, SWEDES, GERMANS and RUSSIANS. In the 13th century, the south of the country was conquered by the German Livonian knights, who began the conversion of the Estonians to Catholicism. At around the same time, the north of the country was conquered by the Danes, who built a castle at a place they called Reval but which the Estonians called Tallin ('Danes' castle'), now the capital of Estonia. After the

Reformation the Germans introduced Lutheranism, which remains the leading denomination in Estonia.

In the 17th century Estonia came under Swedish rule, a period generally viewed as a positive episode in Estonian history. The Swedes curbed the power of the German landowning classes. Following Sweden's defeat in the Great Northern War (1700–21), however, Estonia came under Russian rule. The privileges of the German landowning elite were restored and the peasantry was reduced to serfdom. Serfdom was ended by Alexander II in 1861 but was followed by the aggressive Russification programme of his reactionary son Alexander III, which made Russian the language of education.

**Defining the modern Estonian nation**

Estonian nationalism became a significant force in the first decade of the 20th century. The Russian Provisional Government granted Estonia autonomy after the February Revolution in 1917. The Estonians declared full independence in 1918, but the country was immediately occupied by Germany until the end of World War I. Estonia's independence was recognized by the Soviet government in 1920, but the Estonian government struggled to find stability. The Nazi-Soviet Pact of 1939 left Estonia firmly in the Soviet sphere of influence, and in 1940 the country became a republic of the USSR. Tens of thousands of Estonians were deported to labour camps. From 1941 to 1944 Estonia was under German occupation again. Many Estonians initially saw the Germans as liberators, but the Germans offered no support for Estonian national aspirations. 'Liberation' by the USSR was followed by more deportations, industrialization and an influx of Russian settlers intended to swamp the country's native population. Secretly watching Finnish television became an important way for Estonians to resist this new campaign of Russification. President Mikhail Gorbachev's policy of *perestroika* in the 1980s gave Estonians the opportunity to re-assert their national identity, and in 1990 they declared independence from the USSR. Newly independent Estonia implemented discriminatory laws against its large Russian minority, causing tensions with the Russian Federation. However, since independence the Estonian economy has fared better than the Russian Federation's. As a result, Estonia's Russians have not demanded reunification with their 'motherland' as was feared. Estonians have since then distanced themselves from Russia through membership of the European Union and NATO and by building links with the SCANDINAVIAN countries and their Baltic neighbours the LATVIANS and LITHUANIANS.

## ETRUSCANS

Etruscans

A pre-Roman Italian people whose homeland was Etruria, roughly equivalent to modern Tuscany. They also had colonies in the Po Valley and on the coast of Campania. The Etruscans spoke a non-Indo-European language that was unrelated

to any modern European language and which has yet to be fully deciphered. The origins of the Etruscans are not known, but they were most likely the descendants of peoples who had been living in Italy since the Stone Age. In archaeological terms, the immediate ancestors of the Etruscans were the people of the early Iron Age VILLANOVA CULTURE, which flourished in central Italy in the 8th and 9th centuries BC.

The Etruscans developed prosperous city-states, supported by agriculture, advanced bronze- and iron-working and a trading network that extended throughout the Mediterranean. The 12 most powerful cities were loosely federated in the Etruscan League, which met periodically at the sanctuary of Voltumna. Some cities were monarchies, while others were aristocratic republics. Roads, bridges, canals and city walls are testaments to their engineering and architectural abilities. Although they were commercial rivals, the Etruscans' art and religion was much influenced by the GREEKS, whose alphabet they adopted in a modified form. The Etruscans in turn had a pronounced influence on the development of early ROMAN civilization. No Etruscan literature has survived, and few of their cities have been excavated. Most of what we know about the Etruscans comes from the family tombs of their aristocracy. These were built in the style of houses and were elaborately furnished and decorated with wall paintings. They provide a vivid, and no doubt idealized, picture of a luxurious and leisured lifestyle. Almost nothing is known of the lives of the peasantry.

The Etruscans ultimately fell victim to the rising power of Rome, beginning with the ROMAN conquest of Veii in 396 BC. A Celtic (see CELTS) invasion of Italy around 400 BC had already weakened the Etruscans, ending their control of the Po Valley and causing great economic damage in Etruria. The last Etruscan city to fall to the Romans was Volsinii, in 264 BC. The Etruscans had assimilated to the Roman identity and had adopted the Latin language by the end of the 1st century BC.

## EUSKALDUNAK

See BASQUES.

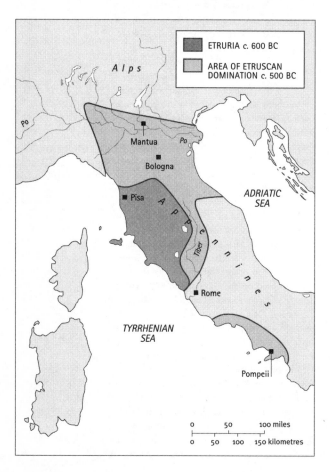

ETRURIA c. 600 BC

AREA OF ETRUSCAN DOMINATION c. 500 BC

Alps

Po

Mantua

Po

Bologna

Pisa

Apennines

Tiber

ADRIATIC SEA

Rome

TYRRHENIAN SEA

Pompeii

| 0 | 50 | 100 miles |

| 0 | 50 | 100 | 150 kilometres |

# FAEROESE

A SCANDINAVIAN people of the Faeroe Islands in the North Atlantic, a Danish dependency. Although they number fewer than 50,000, the Faeroese have a strong sense of national identity, fostered by isolation, language and resentment of their political link with Denmark.

The Faeroese are descendants of emigrants from western Norway who settled the then uninhabited islands in the 9th century. The islands came under Danish rule in 1380. Faeroese nationalism began to develop in the 19th century and demands for home rule grew in the early 20th century. The islands' *Løgting* (parliament) declared independence in 1946, but it was not recognized by Denmark. After negotiations the Faeroese were granted home rule within the Kingdom of Denmark in 1948. When the DANES joined the European Economic Community in 1972, the Faeroese chose to remain outside in order to protect the fishing grounds that are their most valuable economic resource.

Home rule has proved to be an imperfect solution to the difficult relationship between the Faeroes and Denmark. Most Faeroese aspire to independence but they are also reluctant to contemplate life without the substantial economic subsidies provided by the Danish government. When, in 2001, the Faeroese demanded that Denmark grant both independence and guarantee the continuation of its subsidies, the Danish government made it plain that independence meant independence.

The Faeroese language, which is closely related to Icelandic and the dialects of western Norway, has survived despite the imposition of Danish as the language of administration and the (Lutheran) Church in the 16th century. Faeroese now has equal status with Danish. Since the 19th century, Faeroese has developed a vigorous literary tradition.

The local custom for which the Faeroese are best known internationally is the *grindadráp*, the hunting and slaughter of pilot whales. Although its economic significance has decreased, the Faeroese continue to attach great importance to the *grindadráp*, believing it plays a vital role in reinforcing the bonds of their society. A successful hunt requires spontaneous organization and discipline, and the whole community shares in the meat and the celebrations afterwards, whether or not they were able to take part in the hunt itself.

# FALISCI

An ancient ITALIAN people, linguistically LATIN but sharing the same material culture as the ETRUSCANS, with whom they were often allied. The Falisci lived in the region between the River Tiber and Monti Cimini. Falerii (modern Civita Castellana) was their capital. The Falisci resisted ROMAN expansion from 437 BC until 241 BC when Falerii was razed to the ground. The Faliscan language was quite similar to Latin and is believed to have died out soon after the Roman conquest. Modern knowledge of the language is derived from a small number of inscriptions written in the Faliscan alphabet, which was derived from the Etruscan alphabet.

# FINNO-UGRIANS

A widespread group of peoples who speak Finno-Ugric languages, the major branch of the Uralic group of languages, which originated in the central Ural Mountains in distant prehistory. In the 1st millennium AD Finno-Ugric speakers were spread over a vast area extending from northern Norway eastwards to the Ob River basin in Siberia and south to the Danube in central Europe. Encroachment by the SLAVS in subsequent centuries greatly reduced their range and most are now confined to isolated enclaves within their former territories. Ugric-speakers include the HUNGARIANS, MANSI and KHANTY. Finnic-speakers include, in alphabetical order, the ESTONIANS, FINNS, INGRIANS, KARELIANS, KOMI-PERMYAKS, LIVS, LUDIANS, MORDVINS, SAAMI (Lapps), VEPS, and VOTYAKS (Udmurts).

# FINNS

A FINNO-UGRIAN people who make up 92% of the population of the Republic of Finland. They number around 5 million and speak a Finno-Ugric language similar to ESTONIAN but largely unrelated to those of their SLAV and SCANDINAVIAN neighbours.

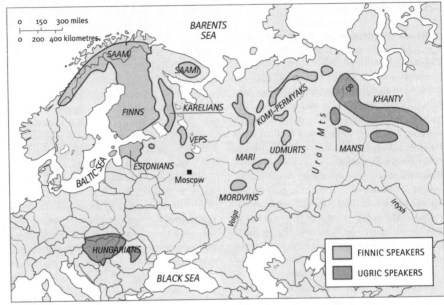

See previous page.

> There was a time when the Finns would offer wind for sale to traders who were detained on their coasts by offshore gales and when payment had been made would give them three magic knots ... When the first was untied they would have gentle breezes, when the second was unloosed the winds would stiffen and when they untied the third they would endure raging gales.
>
> Olaus Magnus
> (1555)

The Finns are believed to have originated in the Ural Mountains, spreading across northern Europe to modern Finland in the late Iron Age; their territory originally included large parts of northwest Russia. Although they had adopted agriculture, hunting remained an important activity throughout the Middle Ages, and furs were a major export.

Animals played a major role in pre-Christian Finnish religion; a bear cult was particularly important. The Finns were famous and sometimes feared by their neighbours for witchcraft and magic. Catholicism was introduced in the 11th century but it was several centuries before the Finns were fully Christian.

Between the 12th and 14th centuries the Finns were conquered by the SWEDES. There was substantial Swedish settlement in southwest Finland and about 7% of the population is still Swedish-speaking. Following the Reformation the Swedes introduced the Lutheran Church, which remains the main Christian denomination in modern Finland.

In the 18th century a Finnish separatist movement began to demand independence from Sweden, but its aspirations were thwarted when Finland was conquered by Russia in 1808–09. The Finns retained considerable

autonomy under RUSSIAN rule, but they also faced strong campaigns of Russification intended to undermine their national identity. However, this simply caused an intense nationalist reaction, manifested in the national epic, the *Kalevala*, published in 1835, and in the music of Jean Sibelius (1865–1957).

The outbreak of revolution in Russia in 1917 gave the Finns the opportunity to declare independence. Russian-backed communists who tried to seize control in 1918 were defeated in a civil war. Although they lost Karelia to the USSR, the Finns' heroic defence of their country against the Red Army in the Winter War of 1939–40 became the foundation of a patriotic legend. The Finns lost further territory to the USSR at the end of World War II, having allied with Germany in an attempt to recover Karelia. The Finns forestalled any further Soviet interventions in the Cold War period through a policy of strict neutrality, and though maintaining traditional cultural links with the Scandinavian countries via membership of the Nordic Council. The fall of the USSR made it possible for Finland to abandon its previous non-alignment and join the European Union in 1995. Modern Finnish society has much in common with the Scandinavian countries, having high standards of social welfare funded by high taxation. Rural life is idealized, but over 80% of Finns now live in cities. There are small Russian and SAAMI minorities in Finland, amounting to approximately 1% of the population.

## FLEMISH

The people of Flanders, the low-lying DUTCH-speaking northern province of Belgium. The Flemish are BELGIAN citizens but regard themselves as members of their own nation. Flanders was settled by Germanic tribes, including the FRANKS, in the 5th century, and for much of the Middle Ages was divided between France and the Holy Roman empire. In the 15th century Flanders was united with the rest of the Low Countries under the dukes of Burgundy. In the 16th century the Low Countries came under the control of the Spanish Habsburgs. SPANISH attempts to undermine local autonomy as well as their persecution of Protestants caused the Dutch to rebel in 1568. The Flemish at first joined the Dutch but unlike them they remained staunchly Catholic and were eventually reconciled with their rulers. While the Dutch became independent, the Flemish and their FRENCH-speaking southern neighbours, the WALLOONS, remained under Spanish rule. In the 18th century, the Spanish Low Countries passed under AUSTRIAN control before they were conquered by the French during the French Revolutionary Wars. After Napoleon's defeat in 1815, the former Spanish Low Countries were united with the Dutch, but the Flemish and Walloons rebelled in 1830 and declared the independent Kingdom of Belgium.

Although they constituted 60% of the Belgian population, the Flemish were from the start politically and culturally dominated by the Walloons; southern Belgium (Wallonia) was more industrialized and wealthy than the north in the 19th century. In the 20th century the Flemish Movement campaigned successfully for Dutch to be recognized as the official language in Flanders. The self-assertion of the Flemish was aided by the changing economic balance in postwar Belgium; as the heavy industries of Wallonia went into decline, Flanders emerged as the wealthiest region of the country. Calls by the

Flemish for cultural and administrative autonomy led to Belgium becoming a federal state, divided formally into Flemish- and French-speaking regions in 1980 (Brussels, the capital, is officially bilingual). This appears to have satisfied Flemish aspirations but, inevitably, some tensions with the Walloons remain. The Flemish presently number around 6 million.

## FRANCONIANS

The GERMAN population of the former Duchy of Franconia, which was centred on Frankfurt and the valley of the River Main. Most of the territory of the old duchy is now divided between the regions of Hesse and Bavaria. Franconians consider themselves to be the descendants of the Ripuarian FRANKS, who conquered and settled the area in the 6th century. In the 12th century Frankfurt became one of the main centres of the German Holy Roman empire, and as a result Franconians have long identified with both German unity and Roman Catholicism. In 1815 Frankfurt became the seat of the council of the German Confederation of states and the meeting place of the first national German assembly in 1848; the city remains Germany's main financial centre. Largely because it was the main dialect in Saxony when Luther translated the Bible into German in the1520s, the Franconian dialect has become the basis for modern standard German.

## FRANKS

A Germanic 'barbarian' people who successfully invaded the ROMAN empire in the 4th and 5th centuries. The name may mean 'bold' or 'fierce'. The Franks originated in the 3rd century as a confederation of tribes who lived in the area of western Germany bounded by the Rhine, Sieg and Ems rivers, including the Amsivari, BRUCTERI, CHAMAVI, Chattuari, CHATTI, Tencteri, Tubantes and Usipetes. Two main groups of Franks were recognized: the Salians and the Ripuarians.

The Salian Franks were allowed to settle in ROMAN territory on the west bank of the Rhine in the late 4th century in return for military service, an obligation which they fulfilled until the final collapse of Roman power in the west in the 460s–70s.

Under the kings of the Merovingian dynasty, the Franks began slowly to expand their territory, until in the reign of Clovis (AD 482–511) victories over the VISIGOTHS, ALAMANNI and the remaining independent Gallo-Roman warlords won them control of most of Gaul and much of western Germany. Much of this expansion was by political takeover, rather than folk movement. Frankish settlement was most dense in Franconia in Germany and in the area between the Rhine, Moselle and Somme rivers; it was very sparse south and west of the Seine.

The baptism of Clovis (c. 508) began the conversion of the Franks to Catholicism. In 534 the Franks won complete control of Gaul by conquering the BURGUNDIANS. The Franks practised partible inheritance and the kingdom was frequently divided. In course of the 7th century the Merovingian dynasty went into decline as a succession of shortlived kings allowed officials called 'Mayors of the Palace' to control the levers of power. In 751 the Carolingian mayor Pippin the Short overthrew the Merovingian dynasty and assumed the throne himself. Pippin's son Charlemagne (ruled 768–814) led another period of Frankish expansion, conquering the LOMBARDS of northern Italy, the SAXONS and the AVARS, and driving the MOORS out of northern Spain as far as the Ebro.

On the death of Charlemagne's son Louis the Pious in 840, a civil war broke as Louis's three sons fought over their inheritance. The dispute was settled by the Treaty of Verdun in 843, which divided the empire into three kingdoms. The empire was reunited under Charles the Fat 884–5, but on his death in 888 it broke up for good into the kingdoms of East and West Francia, Italy and Provence. East Francia developed into the Kingdom of Germany and West Francia into the Kingdom of France. By this time, the East and West Franks were already on culturally and linguistically divergent paths. In the east, the Franks had retained a Germanic cultural and linguistic identity: Charlemagne, whose capital was at Aachen in western Germany, spoke an early form of German. In the west, where they were a minority among a Romance-speaking population, the Franks had become assimilated to the

language and Romanized culture of their subjects, who for their part adopted the identity of their rulers. Although the Franks have an important role in the historical identity of the GERMANS (especially the FRANCONIANS), it is the FRENCH, whose name is derived from them, who see themselves as their main heirs. *Firanja* and *Firanji*, the Arabic words often used to describe Europe and Europeans, are also derived from the Franks, a telling sign of their importance.

# FRENCH

The people of the French Republic, and historically one of the most influential of European peoples. The country also contains three long-standing minorities, the BASQUES, BRETONS and CORSICANS, who have maintained non-French identities in the face of varying degrees of central-government hostility. Although the French identity is today a relatively homogeneous one, this is largely the result of the 'Parisianization' of France in the 19th century; the country is traditionally one of strong regional identities.

The French originated from the amalgamation of two ancient peoples, the Celtic GAULS and the Germanic FRANKS. Following the fall of the ROMAN empire in the 5th century, the Franks conquered Gaul (a region approximating to modern France), making it part of a vast kingdom that also included the Low Countries and Germany. The Franks settled densely only in the northeast of Gaul and nowhere were the native Gauls displaced. The culture of the Gauls was highly Romanized and Christian, and their languages, originally Celtic, were related local dialects of Latin. The Franks were non-Christians, and their pre-literate warrior culture was much less sophisticated than that of the people they had conquered. Once they had converted to Christianity around AD 500, the Franks were slowly assimilated into the culture and language of the Gallo-Romans, who for their part began to adopt the Frankish identity because of its political prestige. By the 8th century the term 'Gaul' had become archaic; Gaul was simply part of Francia.

Frankish power reached its peak under Charlemagne (ruled 768–814), who dominated western Europe. In 843 Charlemagne's empire was partitioned among his grandsons into three

**"** Their [the Franks'] eyes are faint and pale, with a glimmer of greyish-blue. Their faces are shaven all round and, instead of beards, they have thin moustaches which they run through with a comb. Close-fitting garments confine the long limbs of the men; they are drawn up so high as to expose the knees and a broad belt supports their narrow waists. **"**

Sidonius Apollinaris, 5th century.

kingdoms, one of which, West Francia, emerged as the kingdom of France after the empire broke up completely in 888. The early French kingdom was a highly decentralized collection of feudal principalities. The kings had direct control of little more than Paris, the surrounding Ile de France and Orléans, and they lacked the power to impose their authority on their mightier subjects, such as the dukes of Normandy and the counts of Anjou. Local identities at this time were often more important than the 'French' identity, which was predominant only in those areas directly controlled by the king. A line roughly from the Gironde to Lyon divided medieval France into two linguistic provinces, the northern *langue d'oïl*, where dialects of Old French were spoken, and the southern *langue d'oc*, where Occitan, or Provençal, was spoken (both areas are named for their words for 'yes'). This line also represented a cultural divide, with the south being an integral part of the Mediterranean world, with different customs to the more feudalized north.

## From monarchical control to revolution

In the course of the 12th and 13th centuries the Capetian monarchy finally began to assert its authority over the feudal nobility. Paris became the dominant administrative and cultural centre of France, raising the prestige of *Francien*, the dialect of the Ile de France, so that it began to replace other dialects, ultimately becoming the basis of modern standard French. The civilization of France in the 12th and 13th centuries was enormously influential. The French Gothic style of art and architecture spread throughout western Europe. Courtly literature and chivalry were essentially French innovations. The French also saw themselves, with some justification, as playing the leading role in the Crusading movement. The later Middle Ages were dominated by the Hundred Years War (1337–1453) with England. It was during this long struggle that a recognizably modern sense of French national identity began to emerge for the first time. Victory over the English allowed the French kings, notably Louis XI (ruled 1461–83), to complete the consolidation of centralized royal power.

The Reformation caused deep divisions in France. Catholics and Calvinist Huguenots each sought to control the Crown, leading to the Wars of Religion (1560–98). The wars were ended by the Edict of Nantes, which granted toleration to the Huguenots, but this was only a temporary solution. The 17th century saw the growth of royal absolutism, culminating in the reign of Louis XIV, the 'Sun King' (ruled 1643–1715), under whom France became the dominant European power. Louis revoked the Edict of Nantes, seeing religious diversity as a threat to the unity of the state. Persecution of Huguenots, many of whom emigrated, restored Catholicism to an unchallenged position in French religious life, which it still retains. Louis XIV cultivated a glittering court life at his palace of Versailles and was a lavish patron of the arts. French fashions in art, music, architecture, dress, cuisine and manners were widely imitated across Europe. French became the language of international diplomacy.

During the 17th century the French also built an important colonial empire in North America, the Caribbean and India. French emigrant populations were established in Quebec and Louisiana. Most of this empire was, however, lost to Great Britain in the Seven Years War (1756–63), but the descendants of the French settlers in Quebec still retain their French cultural and linguistic identity (see QUÉBECOIS).

The defining event in the creation of the modern French identity was the Revolution of 1789–1804. Economic crisis and rising taxes caused by the huge cost of France's wars with Britain led to increasing popular discontent in the 1780s. The writings of the Enlightenment philosophers such as Jean-Jacques Rousseau (1712–78), which were hostile to royal absolutism and religion, and the example of the American Revolution inspired calls for political reform. Popular dissent escalated and demands included the overthrow of the monarchy, aristocratic privilege and serfdom and the foundation of the French Republic in the name of 'Liberty, Equality and Fraternity'. The legacy of the Revolution was mixed. It brought to the fore concepts such as human rights, popular sovereignty and civil equality whose subsequent global influence is hard to overstate. On the other hand, the Revolution's descent into terror and dictatorship make it a prototype for the bloody revolutions of

the 20th century. Within France, the revolutionaries' anti-clericalism alienated conservative opinion and created divisions that still underlie the Left and Right in French political life. The Revolution also unleashed a fervent political nationalism. Harnessed by Napoleon, France seemed for a time to be on the brink of achieving dominion over continental Europe. But France never regained its political or cultural pre-eminence after his downfall in 1815.

### Centralization and La République

At the time of the Revolution, French identity was still strongly regional in character, and over one-fifth of French citizens did not speak French. The revolutionary government espoused the principle of the indivisibility of the French republic, a principle to which all subsequent French governments have strongly adhered. Since the Revolution a concerted effort has been made, mainly through the education system, to eliminate all regional dialects and languages and impose standard French on the whole country. Resentment towards this policy has bred movements dedicated to preserving minority languages, such as Breton, Basque, Occitan, Corse and Alsatian (a German dialect). So far, none has become extinct, but all declined rapidly in the 20th century, not only as a result of state language policies, but also through the influence of French-language mass media, national military service, internal migration and tourism, which have also helped to spread Parisian values throughout France. However, considerable regional variations in French pronunciation are still strongly in evidence. Members of the literary intelligentsia are now fearful that standard French itself faces a new threat in the form of Anglo-American borrowings. An academy exists to protect French from linguistic pollution, but its pronouncements are largely ignored by the population at large. The gulf between high culture and popular culture is a wide one in France.

Nineteenth-century political life saw temporary restoration of the monarchy, humiliating defeat in the Franco-PRUSSIAN War (1870–1), and bouts of civil strife. Through all this, French culture continued to exert global influence, and the French language was spread throughout the world in the expanding French territories of Africa and elsewhere. World War I established the GERMANS as the great national threat; and the subsequent, and swift, defeat and occupation of France by Nazi Germany would be the defining event of the 20th century. The contrast between a small but heroic resistance movement and Charles De Gaulle's Free French movement on the one hand, and the enthusiastically collaborationist Vichy government and business community on the other, continues to be a contrast that the French have struggled with. Spurred by a sense of national humiliation, postwar France strongly re-asserted its role on the world stage, taking a leading role in the European Economic Community (now the European Union), a spiky role in NATO and frequent recourse to l'exception français, the principle that France is exempt from the rules it expects everyone else to follow. The French continue to see themselves as an important nation and have overwhelmingly supported the attempts of their postwar governments to pursue an independent foreign policy. Part of this is expressed through the concept of La Francophonie, the French economic-cultural equivalent of the British Commonwealth; but whereas the latter is a diffuse arrangement, the former continues to ensure that France remains central to many of its former colonies.

The French also continue to show a commitment to culinary and cultural independence: refusing to eat fast food is a political statement, generous subsidies support Europe's most successful film industry, and the home-grown cartoon character Asterix the Gaul continues to hold his own against the legions of Disneyland. Nevertheless, the internationalization of English as the language of the computer age heralds a new threat. Also, after the homogenizing of the French identity in the 19th and 20th centuries, immigration, mainly from former French colonies in North and West Africa, is making France a more culturally diverse nation again. This has led to the sort of racial tensions familiar in other European countries. Racist violence was common in the 1960s and the racist National Front continues to be a significant force in French politics. Thus, while the population of France was almost 59 million in 1998, 7% were born outside the country. Thus, renewed attempts to enforce French secular values (such as the banning of religious emblems in schools in 2004) increasingly resemble a swimming against the tide.

## FRISIANS

An early GERMAN people who lived along the low-lying North Sea coast between the mouth of the Rhine and the River Ems and in the Frisian Islands off the German and Danish coasts. First recorded in the 1st century AD, they were a sea-faring people, active both as pirates and traders. They were known for cattle-rearing and built their settlements on artificial raised mounds called *terps* to protect them from flooding. Between the 7th and 10th centuries they played a leading role in trade between the Rhineland and countries around the North and Baltic seas.

The Frisians were conquered by the FRANKS in 734 and converted to Catholicism. For most of the Middle Ages, the Frisians were part of the Holy Roman empire, but they retained a considerable degree of autonomy. In the 16th century the western Frisians joined the DUTCH in their revolt against the SPANISH Habsburgs and became part of the Dutch United Provinces. The rest came under PRUSSIAN rule in the 18th and 19th centuries and are now part of Germany. The Frisians retained their separate identity until the later 19th century, but they are now largely assimilated to the Dutch and German identities.

The most important surviving element of the Frisians' identity is their language, a West Germanic language closely related to English. Although it has long been in decline, there has been a modest recovery in recent years in the Netherlands, where it is recognized as an official language. In the province of Friesland, Frisian is taught in schools and also used in law courts, but all Frisian-speakers also speak Dutch. In Germany Frisian has now been largely supplanted by German, but it is still spoken by around a thousand people in Saterland, near the Dutch border, and by around 8000 people on the west coast of Schleswig-Holstein. There are about 400,000 Frisian speakers in the Netherlands.

## FRIULIANS

A people who form about 60% of the population of the region of Friuli-Venezia Giulia in northeast Italy, bordering on Austria and Slovenia. The main characteristic distinguishing Friulians from ITALIANS is their language, Friulian (or *Furlan*), which is classified either as a Rhaetian language, distantly related to the Romansch spoken in Switzerland and the Ladin spoken in the Italian Adige, or as a variant of the VENETIAN dialect of Italian. Despite some encroachment by Italian, there are still around 700,000 Friulian speakers and the language has a healthy literary tradition. There is a Friulian separatist movement, the Moviment Friúl, which campaigns for local autonomy.

## FUNNEL-NECKED BEAKER CULTURE

The earliest Neolithic culture of northern Europe, flourishing *c.* 4200–*c.* 2800 BC. The culture is named for its distinctive pottery vessels, which have a globular body and an out-turned neck. There were distinct regional variants of the culture centred in the Netherlands, Germany, the Czech Republic, Poland and southern Scandinavia. The culture is associated with megalithic tombs in southern Scandinavia and with early copper-working in the Czech Republic. It is also known as the TRB culture from its German name *Trichterrandbecher*.

## GAELS

The inhabitants of Ireland, Scotland and the Isle of Man who speak Gaelic, part of the Celtic family of languages (see CELTS, ANCIENT and MODERN). 'Gael' is derived from *Gwyddel* ('savages'), the Welsh name for the Irish. The Irish began to use the word to describe themselves in the 7th century, and it eventually came to be used to describe all Gaelic-speakers. The numbers of Gaelic-speakers declined rapidly in the 19th and 20th centuries. Today there are only around 20,000 habitual Gaelic speakers in Ireland and 30,000 in Scotland, most of them in the Western Isles. Gaelic is extinct as a spoken language on the Isle of Man.

Gaels

See previous page.

50% OR MORE OF POPULATION HABITUAL GAELIC-SPEAKERS (2001)

Stornoway

Outer Hebrides

Skye

ATLANTIC OCEAN

Tiree

SCOTLAND

Edinburgh

NORTH SEA

Donegal

NORTHERN IRELAND

Belfast

UNITED KINGDOM

ISLE OF MAN

Galway

Aran Islands

REPUBLIC OF IRELAND

Dublin

ENGLAND

WALES

London

0   50   100 miles
0   50   100   150 kilometres

g

## GAGAUZ

A Turkic language-speaking people (see TURKS) who inhabit an autonomous region of southwest Moldova. Sedentary farmers and herders of Turkic descent, they were Christians who, in the late 18th century, began to migrate from Bulgaria into Russian territory, seeking escape from Turkish rule. While under RUSSIAN rule they resisted attempts to acculturate them by maintaining tightly knit communities and shunning contacts

with outsiders as far as possible. After World War II their territory was divided by the Soviet state between Ukraine and Moldavia (now Moldova). They were unhappy under Moldavian rule, and a movement for self-determination emerged in the 1980s. In 1990 separatists proclaimed their independence, beginning a five-year war, after which they went as far as to appeal in vain for Turkish protection. Fighting ended in 1995 after the Gagauz were offered autonomy, with their own flag and a national assembly. But they remain unsatisfied, and their independence movement is strong. There are currently around 175,000 Gagauz.

## GALICIANS

The people of Galicia, in far northwest Spain. Although they are citizens of Spain, Galicians regard themselves as a distinct nation and maintain a determinedly non-SPANISH identity. The Galicians claim descent from the Gallaeci, a CELTIBERIAN tribe that lived in the region during the Iron Age. Isolation and mountainous terrain allowed the Gallaeci to hold out against Roman conquest until the end of the 1st century BC. The Gallaeci never became fully Romanized, but by the 5th century AD their Celtic language was dying out and being replaced by a Romance dialect derived from Latin, from which Galego, the native Galician language, developed. Celtic paganism died out around this time too, replaced by Catholicism.

In the 5th century Galicia was conquered in quick succession by the SUEBI and the VISIGOTHS, two GERMAN peoples, but neither had much visible impact on its cultural development. The MOORS invaded Spain in the 8th century, destroying the Visigothic kingdom. The far north, however, held out and Galicia became part of the Christian kingdom of Asturias and Galicia and subsequently the kingdom of León and Castile. Galego was the language of the court of León and Castile until the 14th century, when it gave way to Castilian Spanish. Galego began to decline in prestige, ceasing to be a literary language and becoming confined to the lower social classes. The shrine of the apostle St James the Great at Santiago de Compostella brought pilgrims flocking to Galicia from all over Europe throughout the Middle Ages but, as the reconquest of the Muslim south proceeded, Galicia became a political and economic backwater. In the 19th century, poverty drove many Galicians to emigrate, mainly to Latin America, but also to the USA and even to Britain.

### Galician autonomy within Spain

Galician claims to a distinct identity finally received recognition when the Republican government of 1931–6 granted a statute of regional autonomy. Despite this, during the Spanish Civil War (1936–9) Galicians generally supported General Francisco Franco, who was born in Galicia. Nonetheless, Franco had no sympathy for Galician aspirations: after his victory he banned the public use of Galego in the name of national unity and abolished the region's autonomy.

Democracy was restored after Franco's death in 1975, and in 1978 Galicia again became an autonomous region. Teaching in Galego was permitted again, but by this time it was the first language of only about 36% of Galicians. Recovery has been slow to manifest itself. As both a national and international language, Spanish offers significant practical advantages and it continues to dominate both education and public life. Linguistic nationalism is a factor in Galician politics, but efforts by Galicians to maintain a non-Spanish identity have recently found a new outlet in a revival (some would say re-invention) of Celtic identity. Enthusiasts claim that Galician music, social values, folklore and building traditions are all Celtic in origin, but ethnographers are sceptical, and the Celtic Congress has so far turned down Galicia's application for membership. The population of Galicia is presently just under 3 million.

## GALLO-ROMANS

A term used by historians to describe the GAULS between their conquest by the ROMANS in the 1st century BC and subsequent conquest by the FRANKS, VISIGOTHS and BURGUNDIANS in the 5th century AD. The term comes from the Romanization of Gallic culture in this period.

## GASCONS

The inhabitants of Gascony, a historic region of southwest France. Their name is derived from *Vascones*, the Latin name for the BASQUES, who once inhabited all of Gascony, but who are now found only in the far south of the region by the Spanish border. With this exception, Gascons were assimilated into the FRENCH identity in the early modern period. Gascon, an Occitan dialect heavily influenced by the Basque language, is widely spoken in rural areas.

*g*

# GAULS

One of the major groups of ancient CELTS. The Gauls inhabited most of modern France and parts of Switzerland, southern Germany and northern Italy in the second half of the 1st millennium BC. They were progressively conquered by the ROMANS between 295 and 51 BC. The Gauls subsequently became highly Romanized in lifestyle, culture and language, but their separate identity survived the ROMAN empire, disappearing only in the early Middle Ages. The modern FRENCH consider themselves to be descendants of the Gauls.

The Gauls originated north of the Alps, in the area between the Garonne and the Rhine rivers. This remained their main area of settlement, but around 475 BC several tribes crossed the Alps, defeated the ETRUSCANS, and settled in the Po Valley and along the Adriatic coast. This area became known as Cisalpine Gaul ('Gaul this side of the Alps') to distinguish it from the main Gaulish area, Transalpine Gaul, or just plain Gaul. Around 390 BC the Gauls sacked Rome; the ROMANS never forgave them. Between 295 BC and 191 BC the Romans conquered Cisalpine Gaul and in about 123 BC they annexed the Mediterranean coast of Gaul proper. The rest of Gaul followed in 58–51 BC, conquered by Julius Caesar, who convinced the Roman senate, against the evidence, that the Gauls were still a threat to Rome.

Although Roman writers always presented the Gauls as barbarians, by 100 BC they were developing well-organized tribal states with urbanized capitals (*oppida*), a high-quality coinage and cash-using economy, and literacy using the Latin alphabet. The Gauls were governed by a variety of institutions. Most were monarchies, but the kings of some tribes, such as the Nervii, ruled in partnership with 'senates' of the leading noblemen. Elected magistrates called *vergobrets* ruled other tribes, such as the AEDUI and the HELVETII.

After their conquest by Rome, the Cisalpine Gauls were assimilated to Roman culture and lost their identity completely before the end of the 1st century BC. The Transalpine Gauls also adopted a Romanized lifestyle and by the 4th century AD most had become Latin-speakers.

Only among the ARMORICANS of the far northwest was Gaulish still widely spoken: they developed a strong identification with the Roman empire but they retained a dual identity, both Roman and Gaulish, and they continued to worship their Celtic gods until the 4th century, by which time most had become Christians.

In the 5th century Gaul was overrun by a succession of Germanic tribes until in the 6th century it came under the rule of the FRANKS. Over the next three centuries the two peoples became assimilated to one another as the Franks adopted Christianity and the Gauls' Romanized culture and local dialect of Latin, while the Gauls adopted the Frankish identity of their rulers. By the 8th century the term 'Gaul' had fallen out of use, replaced by 'Francia' (France). The names of the old Gaulish tribes were not entirely forgotten: they survive in the names of many of France's major cities, such as Paris, named for the PARISII, and Sens, named for the SENONES.

# GEPIDS

An early GERMAN people. They were first recorded in AD 260 when they invaded Dacia with the GOTHS. The Gepids and Goths went on to invade the Balkans but were defeated by the ROMANS in 269 in a battle at Naissus (Nis in Serbia). The Gepids never succeeded in creating a stable territory of their own, and it was perhaps for this reason that the Goths regarded them as lazy and lacking in initiative. In the early 5th century the Gepids were conquered by the HUNS and became loyal followers of their leader Attila. After Attila's death they rebelled with the SARMATIANS, RUGIANS and SUEBI, decisively defeating the Huns in 454 at the battle of Nedao, somewhere in western Hungary. The Gepids then settled around Sirmium (Belgrade) in territory that was claimed by the Byzantine empire. In 546 the BYZANTINES incited the LOMBARDS to attack the Gepids, who were finally and decisively defeated at the battle of Asfeld in 552. Their power broken, the Gepids were easily conquered by the AVARS in 567. The Gepids were last recorded participating in the Avar attack on Constantinople in 626. It is presumed that they were subsequently assimilated to the Avars.

Gauls

GAULS
*REMI* GAULISH TRIBES
MODERN BORDERS

NORTH SEA

NERVII
MENAPII
MORINI     ATREBATES
EBURONES
AMBIANI
CALETI     SUESSIONES
TREVERI
UNELLI
LEXOVII   AULERCI
REMI
MEDIOMATRICI
PARISII
CORIOSOLITES   REDONES   DIABLINTES   CARNUTES
LINGONES
VENETI
CENOMANI   SENONES
NAMNETES   ANDECAVI
TURONES
SEQUANI
BITURIGES   AEDUI
PICTONES
HELVETII
AMBARRI
LEMOVICES
SANTONES
ALLOBROGES
BAY OF
BISCAY
ARVERNI
VIVISCI   VOCONTI
CADURCI   VOLCAE
ELUSATES   SALUVII
TECTOSAGES

MEDITERRANEAN SEA

0     50     100 miles
0     100     200 kilometres

g

## GERMANS, EARLY

A major group of peoples of Iron Age and early
Medieval Europe who spoke Germanic languages. The earliest written references to the
Germans date to the end of the 2nd century BC,
when two tribes from Denmark, the CIMBRI and
TEUTONES, migrated southwards and threatened
the northern frontiers of the ROMAN empire. The

origins and meaning of the name 'German'
(Latin *Germanus*) are unknown, but it may have
been the name of a single tribe, only later
applied to peoples of similar language and culture. This was probably done by the Romans
rather than the Germans themselves, who did
not use this name (or indeed any other) to
describe themselves collectively. The Germans
are thought have emerged in northern Germany

and Scandinavia sometime between 2500 and 1000 BC. They spoke a common language known to linguists as proto-Germanic. By the early centuries AD this had already begun to develop into three distinct languages: Eastern Germanic, which is now extinct; Northern Germanic, from which the modern SCANDINAVIAN languages have developed; and Western Germanic, from which modern English, German and DUTCH have developed.

## Germanic expansion south

The migration of the Cimbri and Teutones was the first sign of general movement south and southeast, which by around AD 1 had brought Germanic tribes to the Rhine and the Danube, where they were halted by the Romans. One German tribe, the SUEBI, crossed the Rhine into Gaul in 58 BC and was quickly expelled by Caesar. The Roman emperor Augustus attempted the conquest of the Germans, but gave up after Arminius, a chieftain of the CHERUSCI, destroyed three legions in the Teutoburg Forest in AD 9. Subsequently, the Romans dealt with the Germans by subsidising friendly chieftains and leading punitive raids against troublemakers. Many Germans served as mercenaries in Roman armies. The Germans were still at this time a

DISTRIBUTION OF GERMAN TRIBES AD 100

---- NORTHERN BORDER OF ROMAN EMPIRE

*QUADI* GERMAN PEOPLES

GAULS NON-GERMAN PEOPLES

**Germans, Early**

decentralized tribal people who lived in small villages and dispersed farms; they had no towns. Most Germans were peasant farmers, whose labour supported a small warrior elite. The most important institution was the *comitatus*, the chieftain's personal retinue of household warriors who formed the core of the tribe's army in wartime. Small-scale warfare and cattle raiding were endemic – chiefs and warriors alike needed war as an arena in which to win status and wealth. They were polytheists who worshipped their gods in sacred groves. Three gods seem to have had universal importance among the tribes: Woden (Odin), Donar (Thor) and Ziu (Tiu).

Long contact with the Roman empire had profound effects on the structure of Germanic society. Power became increasingly centralized, and by the late 2nd and 3rd centuries tribal kingdoms were emerging and smaller tribes were joining to form confederations. In this way the CHAUCI, Reudingi and Aviones coalesced to form the SAXONS, for example. The Romans found that the Germans had become much more formidable enemies. When the MARCOMANNI invaded the empire in the late 2nd century they were defeated only with difficulty. In the 3rd century the GOTHS overran the Roman province of Dacia. They also expanded as far east as the Volga.

The arrival of the HUNS in eastern Europe in the late 4th century completely destabilized the Germanic world. To escape conquest, many peoples sought refuge in the Roman empire. The VISIGOTHS entered with Roman permission in 376, but rebelled when they were badly treated and went on to sack Rome itself in 410. Other tribes, such as the FRANKS, ALAMANNI, BURGUNDIANS, SUEBI and VANDALS invaded at the beginning of the 5th century, eventually overrunning the whole of the Western Roman empire and establishing kingdoms of their own; and ANGLES, Saxons and JUTES from north Germany and Denmark crossed the North Sea and settled in Britain.

# GERMANS, MODERN

The people of the Federal Republic of Germany. Numbering over 80 million, the Germans are, after the Russians, the most numerous of the European peoples. The German identity is now confined almost exclusively to Germany, but until World War II large German minorities were found in most eastern European countries, especially in Hungary, the former Czechoslovakia, Romania and Poland. This was a legacy of German expansionism in the Middle Ages. These minorities were expelled in the aftermath of the war. Small German minorities survive in Denmark, Belgium and the Netherlands.

Perhaps because they have historically been a widely dispersed people, shared language has traditionally been seen by Germans as the most important uniting element of their identity. However, German language is more widespread than German identity, as it is also the language of the AUSTRIANS and of the majority of the SWISS.

Despite the homogenizing effects since the 19th century of internal migration, military conscription and mass media, regional identities are still important to some German consituencies, such as the BAVARIANS and FRANCONIANS, and there is also something of an east–west divide, which is a legacy of Germany's postwar division.

### The origins of modern Germans

The modern Germans are descended from many different EARLY GERMAN peoples and from other peoples whom they conquered and assimilated in the later Iron Age and Middle Ages, including CELTS and SLAVS. The modern German identity began to develop in the 9th and 10th centuries, from the break-up of the Carolingian empire (see FRANKS). The Treaty of Verdun in 843 partitioned the empire into three kingdoms, the eastern-most of which, East Francia, comprised most of modern Germany. The main divisions of East Francia were the duchies of Bavaria, Saxony, Franconia and Swabia, each of which claimed a tribal origin (from the BAVARIANS, SAXONS, FRANKS and ALAMANNI respectively).

When the last Carolingian ruler of East Francia died in 911, the dukes of the tribal duchies elected one of their number, Conrad of Franconia, as the first king of Germany. In 919 the crown passed to Henry the Fowler, Duke of Saxony. Henry's son Otto I (ruled 936–73) defeated the Magyars, who had been raiding Germany for decades, conquered Italy and consciously revived Carolingian traditions by being crowned Holy Roman emperor in 962. Possession of Italy was at first a great advantage to the German kings, as it gave them the resources to dominate the powerful dukes. However, the Investiture Contest, a long dispute with the papacy which lasted from 1075 to 1122, severely undermined the power of the monarchy. While England and France were developing into politically centralized kingdoms, Germany underwent a process of gradual fragmentation, until by the end of the Middle Ages it was divided into hundreds of autonomous principalities owing allegiance to the Holy Roman emperor.

This state of affairs did not, however, prevent the Germans from dominating central Europe. During the 12th to 14th centuries Germanic Crusading orders, such as the Teutonic Knights, conquered the non-Christian SLAVS and BALTS of the southeast coasts of the Baltic Sea. Thousands of German settlers moved into the conquered lands. In the 14th and 15th centuries the Hanseatic League of German cities almost monopolized maritime trade around the North Sea and the Baltic. Almost every port in the region had its colony of German merchants. Eastern European rulers encouraged German settlers for the commercial opportunities they brought. These settlers tended not to assimilate with the host communities, retaining their linguistic and cultural identity.

As the homeland of Martin Luther, Germany was the cradle of the Reformation, but wars between Catholic and Protestant princes weakened the region and added religious divisions to its political divisions. Northern Germany became, and still remains, mainly Protestant (Lutheran or Calvinist), while the south stayed Catholic. The ambition of the Catholic Austrian Habsburg Holy Roman emperors to turn the empire into a centralized state led to the Thirty Years War (1618–48). This left Germany devastated and destroyed the last semblance of central authority.

A partial recovery in the 18th century led to a flourishing of Baroque art, architecture and music; there was no shortage of patrons among Germany's many princes who were keen to outdo their rivals with the cultural splendour of their courts. The leading German state was the Kingdom of Prussia. Its lack of readily-defendable borders made the PRUSSIANS feel constantly

vulnerable to attack by their neighbours and they developed a strong military, and militaristic, tradition. Despite this, Prussia could not prevent Napoleonic France from conquering the German lands in 1806. This final humiliation led to the beginnings of modern German nationalism.

### The emergence of the nation state

Napoleon simplified the map of Germany by abolishing most of the minor principalities and consolidating them into about three dozen larger states. After Napoleon's defeat in Russia in 1812, the Prussians took the lead in overthrowing French rule. German patriots hoped that the Congress of Vienna, which redrew the map of Europe in 1815, would help create a united Germany, but it simply joined the states Napoleon had created into a loose German Confederation under the domination of the Habsburg emperors of Austria. The first step towards unity was the establishment, under Prussian leadership, of the Zollverein, a customs union, in 1834. Liberal revolutions took place in many German states, and in 1848 a shortlived parliament, whose task was to bring about national unification, was established at Frankfurt. It failed because of the opposition of conservative Prussia.

Prussia finally took up the cause of German unification following the appointment of Otto von Bismarck as its prime minister in 1862. Not a nationalist in the liberal tradition, Bismarck believed in uniting Germany by 'blood and iron', provoking a succession of wars with Denmark, Austria and France that left other German states little option but to join a Prussian-led federation. Following the defeat of France in 1871, King Wilhelm I of Prussia was declared emperor (*Kaiser*) of Germany.

The Germany Bismarck had created was authoritarian and militaristic, and the tradition of liberalism that had inspired the early German nationalists was sidelined. Catholics and socialists were persecuted as enemies of the state, the latter with more success than the former. Economic development proceeded so rapidly that by 1900 Germany had overtaken Great Britain as the leading industrial power; its technical and scientific education were regarded as the best in the world.

Wilhelm II (ruled 1888–1918) refused to consider demands by working-class socialists and middle-class liberals for democratic reform. A constitutional crisis was headed off only by the outbreak of World War I, which was greeted with wild popular enthusiasm. Whatever they thought of their emperor's domestic policies, Germans agreed with him that their history of national disunity had cost Germany the chance of 'a place in the sun': an exotic colonial empire like Britain's or France's. Defeat in 1918 and humiliating peace terms at Versailles a year later left a legacy of bitterness. The democratic Weimar Republic struggled to cope with the difficult postwar economic conditions, a heavy burden of reparations, and political violence from Right and Left. The Depression of the early 1930s caused widespread disillusionment with democracy and paved the way for Adolf Hitler's National Socialist (Nazi) Party to seize power in 1933. Hitler's success in turning the German economy around in the 1930s greatly increased his popular following and persuaded millions of Germans who were not supporters of the Nazi Party to ignore the dark side of the regime. Using pseudo-Darwinian theories, the Nazis promoted the idea that the Germans represented the purest-blooded ARYANS and were a genetically superior master race destined to rule inferior races, such as the SLAVS. The most genetically impure peoples, such as the JEWS and the GYP-SIES, were to be exterminated. Popular prejudice against these peoples allowed the Nazis to carry out their policies virtually unopposed. Hitler also had popular support for his aim of bringing all German-speakers into the Third Reich. The annexations of Austria and the CZECH Sudeten-land, which had a German majority, were a consequence of this.

Hitler's invasion of Poland in 1939 led directly to the outbreak of World War II. Their spectacular early victories cemented the German reputation, largely inherited from the Prussians, for militarism and ruthless efficiency. This was far from being deserved – the German war effort was in reality very inefficiently managed. By the war's catastrophic end in 1945, much of Germany lay in ruins, and the country was divided into AMERICAN, BRITISH, FRENCH and Soviet occupation zones. In the Soviet zone, the Nazi dictatorship was replaced by communist dictatorship. This Soviet puppet state adopted the name 'German Democratic Republic' (East Germany). The US, British and French zones became the Federal Republic of Germany (West Germany): thus the German people were to find themselves on opposing sides in the Cold War. Despite postwar war-crimes trials and 'de-Nazification', the Nazi era was something Germans found difficult to live down; even today the memory of the Holocaust makes it hard for many Germans to feel pride in their nationality.

## Postwar divisions and reconstruction

West Germany's first postwar chancellor, Konrad Adenauer, saw economic prosperity as the essential prerequisite for rebuilding German society on liberal and democratic lines, which in turn would permit the 'normalizing' of German identity. In the 1950s and 1960s West Germany experienced an 'economic miracle' and developed into a stable social democracy that played a leading role in the establishment of the European Economic Community (now the European Union), whose main purpose was to try to make another war in Europe impossible. To meet labour shortages, West Germany began to admit 'guest workers' from Turkey and other Middle Eastern countries, millions of whom became permanent residents. In an attempt to create a separate national identity, the East German government tried to present their state as the heir to Germany's progressive and humanist traditions, the antithesis not only of the Nazi past but also of West Germany's consumerist and materialistic society. However, East Germans had little enthusiasm for a separate identity even before the dismal economic failure of the communist system became apparent. With the Soviet Union loosening its grip on its power bloc, formal reunification of Germany took place in 1990 to celebration on both sides of the former Iron Curtain. But re-integration of has proved more difficult than most Germans imagined. No economic miracle has transformed the former East Germany, and living standards there still lag behind those in the rest of the country. Disillusionment with reunification has sometimes found expression in neo-Nazi violence directed at immigrants and refugees; however, far-Right

> " From its rising to its setting the sun shall look upon a beautiful, free Germany, and on the borders of the daughter-lands, as on the frontiers of their mother, no downtrodden, unfree people shall dwell; the rays of German freedom and German gentleness shall light and warm the French and Cossacks, the Bushman and Chinese. "
>
> Richard Wagner
> 1848

politics have little appeal to the majority of post-war Germans, who have espoused the principles of democracy, international cooperation, and a continued rejection of militarism.

## GETAE

An ancient people of THRACIAN origin who inhabited the plains along both banks of the lower River Danube. When they were first recorded in the 6th century BC, they were subjects of the nomadic SCYTHIANS under whose influence they became expert mounted archers. The Getae were later influenced by the CELTS who migrated to the lower Danube in the 3rd century BC. In the 1st century BC the Getae were conquered by the DACIAN king Burebista, but they regained their independence when his shortlived empire fell apart. Conquered and dispersed by the ROMANS in the middle of the first century AD, the Getae disappeared soon afterwards. Later writers often confused the Getae with the Germanic GOTHS.

## GHODOBERI

A Caucasian people of Botlikh region, south Dagestan, Russian Federation. Similar to the AVARS, whose written language they use, they were primarily herders and had adopted Sunni Islam by the 16th century. They speak a North Caucasian language now considered endangered. Under Soviet rule their traditional culture and identity as a people were suppressed by collectivization and assimilatory education policies, to the point where both are now in danger. In 2002 they numbered about 2500.

## GIBRALTARIANS

The people of Gibraltar, a British dependency on the southern coast of Spain. The strategic importance of Gibraltar was first recognized by the MOORS, who captured it in 711 in the early stages of their conquest of Spain. Gibraltar has been an important fortress and naval base ever since. It was captured by the SPANISH in 1462, who held it until 1704 when it was taken by the BRITISH. Spain formally ceded Gibraltar to Britain in 1713 by the Treaty of Utrecht, but it has always aspired

to regain sovereignty of the territory. As the BRITISH developed as a major naval base, a trickle of MALTESE, Genoese, JEWISH and IRISH immigrants arrived seeking work. So many of these immigrants married women from the Spanish side of the border that Gibraltar remained a mainly Spanish-speaking, Roman Catholic, community, yet its people developed a distinct identity of their own and a strong sense of loyalty to Britain. With the break-up of the British empire after World War II, Gibraltar's military significance declined and Spain began to press its claim to sovereignty with increasing persistence. In a referendum in 1967, over 98% of Gibraltarians voted against accepting Spanish rule and in 1969 they were granted self-government by the British government. Spain retaliated by closing the border later that year, and even after it was reopened, in stages (1982–85), Gibraltarians faced frequent harassment by Spanish customs officers. This has only strengthened the Gibraltarian identity and induced an island mentality and a determination not to be bullied. In a 2002 referendum the Gibraltarians delivered a 97% vote against a proposal for joint British-Spanish sovereignty. The population of Gibraltar is currently around 30,000.

## GODODDIN

See VOTADINI.

## GÖTAR

A confederation of early SCANDINAVIAN peoples, first recorded in the 2nd century AD. The Götar lived in southern Sweden in two main groups: an eastern group living between Lake Vättern and the Baltic (Östergötland), and a western group, living between lakes Vättern and Vänern (Västergötland). The Götar appear in the Old English epic poem *Beowulf* as the 'Geats'. Very little is known of the history of the Götar. During the Viking era they were dominated by their northern neighbours, the SWEDES, with whom they shared their language and culture. This is probably the main reason why so little is known about them, as it is likely that to outsiders they were indistinguishable from the Swedes. Around 1000 the Swedes and Götar were united in a dynastic union under the Swedish king Olof Skötkonung. In the course of the Middle Ages the Götar were assimilated to the Swedish identity, a painless process given the similarity of the two peoples.

## GOTHS

An early GERMAN people who claimed to have originated in southern Scandinavia. At the time they are first mentioned in written sources, in the 1st century AD, the Goths were living along the River Vistula in modern Poland. By the 3rd century, the Goths had migrated southeast onto the Ukrainian steppes north of the Black Sea. The Goths coerced local sailors into helping them conduct large-scale pirate raids on ROMAN territory. These raids ceased before the end of the century, after new lands were opened up for Gothic settlement when the Romans evacuated the trans-Danubian province of Dacia (roughly modern Romania). The Goths who settled in this region came to be known as the VISIGOTHS (West Goths) while those who remained in the Ukraine were correspondingly known as the OSTROGOTHS (East Goths).

The Goths have nothing to do with the medieval Gothic style of art and architecture, which was given its name in the Renaissance by humanist scholars who wished to characterize it as barbaric and lacking merit.

## GRAVETTIAN CULTURE

An Upper Palaeolithic culture named after a site at La Gravette, Dordogne, France. It originated in central Europe before spreading to western Europe and Russia. The culture, which flourished between 28,000 and 23,000 years ago, was preceded by the AURIGNACIAN CULTURE and succeeded by the SOLUTREAN CULTURE. The Gravettian is defined by its stone tool technology, which included small pointed blades used for hunting big game, such as horse, bison, reindeer and mammoth. It is usual to divide the Gravettian into a western region, characterized by cave dwellings, and an eastern region, characterised by open sites, some with mammoth-bone houses. Examples of cave art, such as the famous 'Venus' figurines, were made by Gravett-

ian craftsmen. In France the Gravettian is sometimes known as the Upper Perigordian.

## GREEKS

The inhabitants of the Republic of Greece. Although the Greek state dates only from the mid-19th century, the Greek identity is one of the oldest in Europe, traceable to more than 3500 years. The word 'Greek' is derived from Latin *Graeci*, a name originally applied to just one specific tribe of Greeks, the Graia. By the Classical period the Greeks called themselves *Hellenes*, from *Hellas*, their name for their country. The enormous cultural achievements of the ancient Greeks form the basis of much of Western civilization: it is a legacy of which modern Greeks are justifiably proud, but it is also one that overshadows their own achievements. As well as forming 97% of the population of Greece, Greeks constitute 80% of the population of Cyprus (see CYPRIOTS) and 2% of the population of Albania. There is also a small, and declining, Greek community in Istanbul, in modern Turkey.

The earliest historically known Greeks were the MYCENAEANS or, as they probably called themselves, the ACHAEANS. Greek is an INDO-EUROPEAN language, and it is thought that the Mycenaeans were the descendants of people who entered Greece from the Balkans around 2000 BC. The Mycenaeans created a civilization based on small kingdoms ruled from fortified citadels. This civilization flourished around 1600–1200 BC, when it was violently destroyed by unknown invaders. A 400-year-long 'dark age' followed, during which another Greek-speaking people, the DORIANS, migrated into Greece (see also IONIANS). When Greece emerged from its dark age in the 9th century BC it had become a land of city-states, chief among which were Athens, Corinth and Sparta (see ATHENIANS and SPARTANS). Most city-states were at first ruled by kings, but by around 500 BC most had abolished their monarchies and were ruled by aristocratic oligarchies or popular dictators called 'tyrants'. One, Athens, had become a democracy. These cities dealt with their growing populations by forced emigration to colonies spread around most of the Mediterranean and

g

Black Sea coasts. Greek colonization was most dense in Sicily and southern Italy and on the Aegean coast of Anatolia (modern Turkey). These areas remained culturally and linguistically Greek into the Middle Ages and, in the case of Anatolia, into the 20th century. These colonies, each an independent city-state, greatly aided the diffusion of Greek culture throughout the Mediterranean world. The Greek city-states were frequently at war with one another, but though the first loyalty of Greeks was to their city, they recognized a shared Greek identity. As well as sharing a common language, Greeks worshipped a common pantheon of gods, who were ruled by Zeus from Mount Olympus. This common identity found its most important expression in pan-Hellenic religious festivals, such as the Olympic games. The Greeks would also unite in the face of common enemies, such as the Persians, who twice invaded Greece during the 5th century BC.

### From Roman rule to independence

Greece was formally incorporated into the ROMAN empire in 146 BC, but the Romans greatly respected the Greeks' cultural achievements and did not attack their identity. Many Romans were overt Hellenophiles, including the emperor Hadrian. For their part, Greeks became loyal subjects of the empire. When the Western Roman empire collapsed in the 5th century AD, the Greek-dominated Eastern empire survived and developed into the medieval BYZANTINE empire. Greeks were among the first non-Jews to convert to Christianity, beginning in the 1st century AD, and the majority of Greeks were Christian by the 4th century. Byzantine Greeks turned their backs on the legacy of Classical Greece because of its paganism – its preservation for posterity was largely the work of the Muslim ARABS. The Greek Orthodox Church remained suspicious of ancient Greek civilization well into the 20th century: for example, it opposed the use of pagan names such as Aristotle and Pericles as personal names.

The cultural divide between the Latin west and the Greek east that had existed throughout Roman times became a yawning gulf during the Middle Ages. This was primarily due to the Greek Orthodox Church's refusal to recognize the Pope as the supreme head of the Christian church. Mutual suspicion between Greek and Latin Christians became outright hostility in 1204, when Crusaders sacked the Byzantine capital, Constantinople. In the 15th century the Greeks came under the control of the OTTOMANS. Western Europe's refusal to help the waning Byzantine empire unless the Greek church recognized the supremacy of the Papacy left Greeks with feelings of hostility and suspicion that have not entirely dissipated, even today. Even though Greece has been a member of the European Union since 1981, the shared experience of centuries of Ottoman rule means that Greeks still have more in common with their Balkan neighbours, such as the SERBS, than with western Europeans. The Turkish influence is still very apparent in Greek cuisine.

Although the Orthodox Church was generally supportive of Ottoman rule, it was also instrumental in preserving a sense of Greek nationhood. Modern Greek nationalism began to develop in the late 18th century, expressed at first mainly in literature but quickly developing into a political movement. In 1821 a major rebellion broke out against the Ottomans. With help from the British, French and Russians, who were all motivated by respect for Greek civilization as much as by a desire to weaken the Ottomans, a small independent Greek state was created in 1830. In 1833 Athens, then merely a village amid spectacular ruins, became the country's capital, and a German prince was imported to found a monarchy.

Greece achieved its modern borders in stages between 1864 and 1947. This process involved three wars with the TURKS, in 1881, 1913 and 1922. In the last, an opportunistic attempt to seize territory in Anatolia ended in defeat and the expulsion to Greece of most of the long-established Greek population on Turkey's Aegean coast, amounting to 1.3 million people. Greece, a poor and mountainous country, was ill-equipped to cope with this influx; it had previously been a exporter of people, especially to the USA. Some 400,000 Turks were also expelled from Greece at this time. (About 100,000 Turkish Muslims remain in northeast Greece.)

Greece was occupied by the Axis during World War II. BULGARIAN forces proved particularly brutal, ethnically cleansing large areas of northern Greece. Memories of this have conditioned Greeks to see their northern SLAV neighbours as a potential threat. Resistance was led by communist partisans; but when they tried to seize power in 1945, civil war broke out between communists and royalists. The communists were defeated in 1949, but Greece remained politically unstable, culminating in the overthrow of the monarchy and a military coup in 1967. Popular opposition to the military junta helped bridge the divisions created by the civil war, and democratic government (although not the monarchy) was restored in 1974.

**Greeks and the wider world**

By 1948 the largest Greek community in the eastern Mediterranean outside Greece was in Cyprus. Although the CYPRIOT Greeks fought a guerrilla campaign for *enosis* (union) with Greece, this was unacceptable to the island's Turkish minority and to its British rulers. Cyprus became an independent state in 1959, but fears that Greece was preparing to annexe the island led to a Turkish invasion in 1974 and the partition of the island along ethnic lines. The situation remained unresolved in 2003; *enosis* is off the political agenda both in Greece and Cyprus, but relations with Turkey remain tense.

The most important issue to confront the Greek state in recent years has been the break-up of Yugoslavia in the 1990s. Greeks were justifiably concerned about the possibility that old territorial claims, particularly by the Bulgarians, might trigger a wider Balkan war. Greece's hostility towards the Former Yugoslavian Republic of Macedonia (see MACEDONIANS, MODERN) reflects the fear that Greece's own small population of Macedonian Slavs might develop separatist ambitions.

The Greeks' sometimes uncomfortable relationship to their past since their independence is clearly demonstrated by language issues. Modern Greek has changed relatively little since ancient times: ancient Greek stands in relation to modern Greek much as Chaucer's English does to modern English. Independence raised the question of what form the official national language should take. Some believed that every-

day spoken Greek (*Demotiké*) had become polluted during the years of Ottoman rule and wished to return to the ancient language. A compromise solution was chosen, with the introduction of *Katharévousa* ('purifying') Greek, a synthetic language combining elements of both the ancient and everyday languages. Only in 1976 did *Demotiké* become the official language of Greece and the language taught in schools.

## GREUTHUNGI

A clan of GOTHS who, with the TERVINGI, became the nucleus around which the VISIGOTHS formed in the 4th century AD.

## GYPSIES or Romany

Trader nomads who inhabit all European countries and also the Middle East, North Africa, North and South America and Australia. The name of the Gypsies derives from the belief, common in medieval Europe, that they originated in Egypt. The name that the Gypsies commonly use to describe themselves is *Rom*, though this strictly applies only to Gypsy peoples who migrated out of the Balkans in the 19th century. The basic vocabulary and grammatical structure of Romani, the Gypsy language, points to a North Indian origin for the Gypsies.

It is not known when, or indeed why, the Gypsies left India, but IRANIAN and ARMENIAN influences on Romani are a sign that that they spent a considerable time in the Middle East before they arrived in the Greek BYZANTINE empire in the 11th century.

For several centuries the Gypsies lived mainly in the Balkans. A pronounced ROMANIAN influence on the Gypsy language, including its name, is a legacy of this.

Following the conquest of the Balkans by the OTTOMANS in the 14th and 15th centuries, Gypsies began to disperse across western and eastern Europe, travelling and living in horse-drawn vehicles. Wherever they went they made a living in the same way, from horse-trading, metal-working, music and entertainments, healing, fortune-telling and conning alms from pious folk by pretending to be on pilgrimage. They

*g*

**POPULATION OF GYPSIES BY COUNTRY**

- 0–50,000
- 50,000–500,000
- 500,000 OR MORE

**Gypsies**

avoided wage labour, seeing it as representing a loss of independence.

The industrialization of Europe in the 19th and 20th centuries changed Gypsy lifestyles. Seasonal movements were no longer so important and Gypsies concentrated around the urban population centres; some became more or less permanently settled. Everywhere that Gypsies travelled they faced suspicion and hostility and in some countries, notably Spain and Hungary, forced settlement. Most hostile were the Nazis, who judged them an inferior race: during World War II Gypsies were systematically exterminated in all areas that came under German control: around 500,000 are believed to have died.

The Gypsy way of life came under more pressure after the war. In communist countries nomadism was forcibly suppressed as being incompatible with a centrally controlled economy. Persecution of Gypsies has continued in post-communist Romania and Slovakia. There was no such coercion in western Europe, but the intensification of land use for farming, industry,

housing and recreation drastically reduced the number of places where Gypsy camps were tolerated. Some countries, such as Britain, attempted to provide authorized sites, but these were often opposed by hostile local residents, who claimed that Gypsies would bring increased crime in their wake. At the same time, Gypsy families began living in caravans drawn by motor vehicles, although horse-trading remains an important activity for a minority.

Estimates for the present numbers of European Gypsies vary from about 3 million to a high of 8 million. This uncertainty reflects the difficulty of identifying Gypsies when so many are now sedentary. About two-thirds of Europe's Gypsies are believed to live in the Balkans and the republics of the former Soviet Union. In western Europe, Spain and France have the largest Gypsy populations, and the Gypsy population of Germany is increasing rapidly due to immigration of eastern European Gypsies.

It is remarkable that, although without a homeland of their own, the Gypsies have lived in Europe for at least 800 years without losing their separate identity. This is partly because their mobility has been a barrier to assimilation by the various sedentary host communities, but the values of Gypsy society are perhaps the most important factor. Traditionally, Gypsies have had codes of taboos and ritual purity relating to food, parts of the body, objects, relations between the sexes and even topics of conversation. Because they are ignorant of these codes, non-Gypsies (*gadjé*) are necessarily unclean. This acts as an almost insurmountable barrier between Gypsies and non-Gypsies, discouraging social intimacy and inter-marriage.

This does not mean, however, that there has been no assimilation between Gypsies and their various host communities. Gypsies usually adopt the language and religion of the country in which they live. Romani survives because of its usefulness as a secret language, indecipherable to potentially hostile non-Gypsies. There are many dialects of Romani, each influenced by the language of the host country.

Gypsy folklore and music are also usually strongly influenced by the local non-Gypsy community. Because of this partial assimilation of Gypsies, it is often difficult for non-Gypsies to distinguish them from other groups, such as the tinkers in Britain and Ireland and the *jenisch* in Germany, who have a similar lifestyle but different ethnic origins.

## HALLSTATT CULTURE

The earliest archaeologically identifiable Celtic culture (see CELTS, ANCIENT). The Hallstatt culture developed in the areas that are now Austria, southern Germany and the Czech Republic during the Bronze Age as a variant of the widespread URNFIELD CULTURE; but it was not until *c*. 600 BC, after the beginning of the Iron Age, that it developed the distinctive vegetal decorative styles for which it is famous. The Iron Age Hallstatt style was very influential and spread to most of western Europe and southern Britain by 500 BC. Iron Age Hallstatt society was aristocratic, its wealth derived from increasingly efficient agriculture and control of trade in wine and other prestige commodities with the GREEK port of Massalia (Marseille). Hallstatt chieftains ruled from hill-

forts and were buried in great splendour with offerings of jewellery, wine jugs, furniture, weapons and wagons. A change in patterns of long-distance trade around 450 BC led to the collapse of the Hallstatt chiefdoms and the subsequent centres of Celtic power, the LA TÈNE chiefdoms, developed to the north and west.

## HELVETII

A major tribe of GAULS, originating in what is now southwest Germany. Around 100 BC the Helvetii migrated south into northern Switzerland, but they soon found their new homeland too confined and began a second migration to southwest Gaul in 58 BC. This threatened to destabilize the whole of Gaul, and the Helvetii were defeated by Julius Caesar at Mont Beuvray and driven back to their Alpine homeland, much depleted in numbers. The circumstances of their migration show the Helvetii to have been a sophisticated, highly organized and at least partly literate people. The decision to migrate was reached by a tribal council, and when one of its members, Orgetorix, tried to set himself up as king, he was quickly imprisoned. Planning and preparation for the migration took three years and involved the compiling of a tribal census, written in the Greek alphabet. According to Caesar, who captured the documents, the Helvetii numbered more than 380,000. The Helvetii kept their identity under Roman rule, finally disappearing from the historical record in the 5th century AD, when their territory was overrun by the ALEMANNI.

## HERMUNDURI

See SUEBI.

## HERNICI

An Italic people of the Sacco River valley in central Italy. They were related to the SABINES and became allies of the ROMANS in 486. After rebelling against the Romans in 306, the Hernici were conquered and granted Roman citizenship, although without the right to vote.

# HERULS

A minor but enterprising and much-travelled early GERMAN tribe from northern Jutland (Denmark). In the 3rd century AD groups of Heruls migrated southeast to the north coast of the Black Sea where they joined the GOTHS in raiding the ROMAN empire by both land and sea. These raids ended after the Heruls were defeated by the Romans at the battle of Naissus in 268.

Although they lived successively under Gothic and HUN domination, these Heruls preserved their identity (and links with their homeland) and founded a kingdom on the middle Danube in the later 5th century. They became an important source of mercenaries for the armies of the Eastern Roman empire. The Herul kingdom was conquered by the LOMBARDS in the early 6th century.

Those Heruls who remained in Denmark became active as pirates toward the close of the 3rd century, raiding the coast of the Roman empire between the Rhine and northern Spain until the late 5th century. The Heruls disappeared after the 6th century, absorbed by the DANES.

# HINUKH

A Caucasian people of southern Dagestan, Russian Federation. They adopted Sunni Islam in the 16th century. Similar to the AVARS, whose written language they use, they were herders, and speak a North Caucasian language. Under Soviet rule collectivization and assimilatory education policies undermined their traditional culture and attacked their identity as a people. They were officially counted as Avars. With their language dying, they complained that Russification was still continuing in the early 21st century. In 1991 there were only around 200 Hinukh language-speakers.

# HOMO SAPIENS NEANDERTHALENSIS

See NEANDERTHALS.

# HUNGARIANS

A people who comprise over 92% of the population of the Republic of Hungary. They also form minority populations in Romania, Slovakia and Yugoslavia. The Hungarians are descended from the Magyars, a FINNO-UGRIAN-speaking nomadic people from Central Asia who migrated into eastern Europe in the 9th century AD. The Magyars' wide-ranging and terrifying raids on horseback into Germany, Italy and France led other Europeans to identify them with an earlier, and even more fearsome, nomad people, the HUNS, who are the origin of their name. The Hungarians have never used this name, having always called themselves Magyars, and their country Magyarország, after their ancestors.

Hungary contains the most westerly extension of the Eurasian steppe grasslands, and because of this it had previously been occupied by two other nomadic peoples, the Huns and AVARS, before the Magyars arrived in the area in about 896 AD. After their decisive defeat at the battle of Lechfeld by the German king Otto I in 955, the Magyars began to settle down. Conquered native peoples were assimilated, and by the end of the century the Kingdom of Hungary had emerged.

Under Stephen I (ruled 997–1038) the Hungarians converted to Roman Catholicism. Around 67% of Hungarians are still Roman Catholics and about 25% are Protestants (mainly Calvinists). The medieval kingdom was more than twice as large as the modern state and included those areas of neighbouring states in which Hungarian minorities live today. Hungarians, however, made up much less than half of the kingdom's total population. In 1526 the Hungarians were catastrophically defeated by the OTTOMANS at the Battle of Mohács, and their kingdom collapsed. The southeastern two-thirds became part of the Ottoman empire, and the northeastern third was seized by the AUSTRIAN Habsburg dynasty. Conditions under Ottoman rule were in some ways better than under Habsburg rule. There was, for example, greater religious tolerance, which allowed Protestantism to become established, and in Transylvania (now part of Romania) Hungarians enjoyed political autonomy.

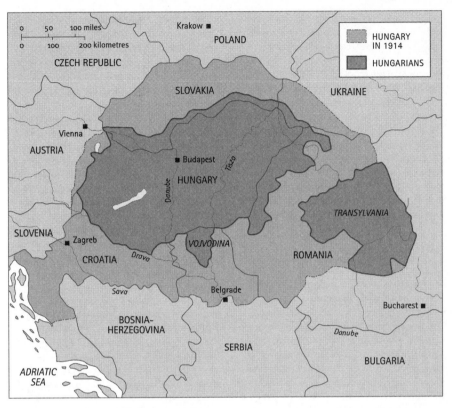

During the course of the 17th century the Habsburgs expelled the Ottomans from Hungary. At first Hungary retained its status as a separate kingdom under the Habsburg monarchy, but Hungarian dominance was diluted by encouraging German, Romanian and Serbian immigration. Finally, in the 1780s, Hungary was reduced to the status of a province, and a programme of Germanization was begun. This provoked a backlash from the Hungarians, who began to demand equal status with Austrians in the empire. In 1844 they achieved recognition of Magyar as the official language of Hungary. An attempted nationalist revolution in 1848 was crushed, but in 1867 the Habsburgs finally gave way and introduced the dual monarchy by which the Austrian empire became the Austro-Hungarian empire. The Hungarians then proceeded to treat non-Hungarians in their part of the empire much as the Austrians had treated them, via a programme of Hungarianization.

After the collapse of the Austro-Hungarian empire at the end of World War I, the Treaty of Trianon (1920) established Hungary's modern borders. Large areas of Hungary were lost to Czechoslovakia, Romania and Yugoslavia, and with them many ethnic Hungarians. Hungarians were left with a burning sense of resentment, a heavy burden of reparations and the problem of resettling half a million refugees who did not want to live under foreign governments. Economic difficulties during the inter-war years led to the collapse of democratic government, a Fascist dictatorship and anti-Semitism. In World War II Hungary allied with Germany and was rewarded with the return of Hungarian-populated areas of Yugoslavia, Czechoslovakia and Romania. Most Hungarian JEWS did not survive the war. Postwar Hungary returned to the Trianon borders and had a communist government imposed on it by its Soviet occupiers. A popular uprising in Budapest in 1956 was brutally crushed but helped sustain Hungarian national pride. Since the fall of the communist government in 1989, Hungary has become a stable democracy. One of the more successful economies of the former Soviet Bloc, it became a member of the European Union in 2004.

Hungarians see themselves as having a more western outlook than other eastern Europeans. The status of the 1.6 million Hungarians living in Transylvania was a source of tension with Romania during the 1990s. In 1996 Romania agreed to respect the rights of its Hungarian minority, but many issues remain unresolved, including education rights and demands for local autonomy.

## HUNS

A Turkic nomadic-pastoralist people (see TURKS) who originated from the steppes of Central Asia. During the 4th and 5th centuries AD, they built an impressive, but shortlived, European empire. The Huns were probably descended from the XIONGNU, who lived on the Mongolian steppes and migrated westward during the mid-4th century. Prevented from entering the Sassanian PERSIAN empire (where they were known as the Chionites), they continued west, crossing the River Don in about AD 372. They succeeded in destroying both the OSTROGOTHS and SARMATIANS, driving a number of other Germanic tribes, such as the VISIGOTHS, before them and over the frontier of the Roman empire. They subsequently attacked the ROMANS themselves in 376, and by the mid-5th century had conquered an area that stretched from the Alps to the Caspian Sea. Following the death of their leader Attila in 453, and plagued by internal wrangling, the Huns were defeated in 454 by a Germanic tribal confederation of the Ostrogoths, GEPIDS and HERULS, and their empire, which they had made little attempt to unify, rapidly disintegrated. Despite the relatively short life of their empire, it cannot be doubted that the Hunnic invasions were a primary factor in the collapse of the Western Roman empire.

Although no evidence exists of their language, the Huns probably spoke a Altaic-Turkic dialect. As a nomadic people, they were able to function as a highly mobile and unpredictable

fighting force, and were adept in the use of the composite bow, a weapon they introduced into eastern Europe, while mounted on horseback. It is thought that the Huns also introduced the stirrup to Europe. Prior to their entry into Europe, the Huns do not appear to have recognized any overall ruler, but by the early 5th century, perhaps because of the influx of wealth following their conquests, they had evolved a hereditary kingship. During the period of their European hegemony, the Huns retained their nomadic lifestyle. They also tended to assimilate conquered peoples into their own confederations as allies, which was a useful policy but often resulted in swamping their own cultural identity. Certainly, following their defeat in 454, many Huns were quickly assimilated into the cultures of those areas in which they found themselves, and they swiftly disappeared from history as a separate people.

As with a number of other nomadic tribes of the steppe regions, such as the SCYTHIANS, the Huns buried their dead in mounds (sometimes as horse burials), and many of these have been identified. A distinctive feature of Hunnic society was their tendency to bind the heads of their children tightly, resulting in a deformed skull, and providing a clear indication of Hunnic burials. Some burial sites bear witness to the wealth of the Hunnic aristocracy, with lavish burial goods of jewellery, horse furniture and textiles. The Huns were almost certainly related to the EPHTHALITES, AVARS and BULGARS; the Gujara (see GUJARATI) were also believed to have been of Hunnic descent, but this is now disputed.

## HUNZIB

A Caucasian people of Tsuntin region, southern Dagestan, Russian Federation. They had adopted Sunni Islam by the 16th century. Similar to the AVARS, whose written language they use, they were primarily herders, especially of sheep and goats, and speak a North Caucasian language now deemed endangered. Under Soviet rule collectivization and assimilatory education policies undermined their traditional culture and their identity as a people. They were officially counted as Avars. In 1995 they numbered about 2000.

> " The Companies or Armies of Huns, wandering up and down with most swift Horses, filled all things with slaughter and Terrour. "
>
> Edward Topsell, 1607

# HUTSULS

A RUTHENIAN people who live in the Zakarpattya province of southwest Ukraine. Their name is thought to be derived from a Romanian word meaning 'brigands'; for their part, the Hutsuls claim to be descended from aristocratic POLES who were exiled to this mountainous region in the 17th century. The numbers of Hutsuls is uncertain, as they are not counted separately from other UKRAINIANS for census purposes.

# IAPYGES

A group of related peoples of southern Italy including the Salentini, the MESSAPIANS, Peucetii and the Dauni. Conquered by the ROMANS in the 3rd century BC, they were traditionally believed to have originated in Illyria.

# IAZYGES

Along with the ROXOLANI, one of the two major branches of the SARMATIANS. The territory of the Iazyges bordered on the middle Danube and included parts of modern Hungary, Serbia, Romania and Ukraine. In the 2nd century AD the Iazyges became allies of the Germanic MARCOMANNI in their wars against Rome (168–79). They continued to raid ROMAN territory until crushingly defeated at the end of the 3rd century. Following this, they were dispersed and resettled across the eastern Roman provinces.

# IBERIANS

Ancient inhabitants of southern and eastern Spain. They spoke a so-far untranslated non-Indo-European language of unknown origin. It is possible that the Iberians were the direct descendants of the first modern human inhabitants settled in the Iberian peninsula around 30,000 years ago. Contacts with PHOENICIAN and GREEK traders and colonists in the first half of the 1st millennium BC led to the growth of towns, state-formation and the adoption of writing. The most important of the Iberian states was the kingdom of Tartessos, which was centred on Huelva on the Atlantic coast. Tartessos was also an important intermediary on the long-distance trade route linking Britain and Atlantic Europe and the sources of tin, copper and other metals to the eastern Mediterranean. The Iberians were conquered by the CARTHAGINIANS in the 3rd century BC and then passed under ROMAN rule after Carthage's defeat in the Second Punic War (218–202 BC). Under Roman rule the Iberians lost their distinctive identity. Their language died out, replaced by a local dialect of Latin.

# ICELANDERS

A SCANDINAVIAN people who inhabit the island Republic of Iceland. According to tradition, the settlement of the then uninhabited island was begun around AD 870 by emigrants from western Norway. They were joined by other Norse settlers from Ireland and Scotland who brought with them many IRISH slaves, who were later freed and assimilated with the Norse population. Because of their isolation, the settlers soon began to develop their own distinct identity. In 930 the Icelanders founded the Althing, an assembly that met annually to make laws and settle disputes. Often described as a democracy, the Althing was in reality an oligarchy: although all free men had the right to attend and speak, only the 36 leading chiefs had the right to vote.

Competition between the chiefs led to increasing disorder in the 13th century, and in 1263 the Icelanders agreed to accept NORWEGIAN rule to avoid a descent into anarchy. This loss of independence was followed by centuries of hardship. The Black Death ravaged the population, and the climatic deterioration of the late Middle Ages, known as the 'Little Ice Age', led to famines. Frequent volcanic eruptions caused further devastation to the island's agriculture. The transfer of sovereignty to Denmark in 1380 brought no relief. The DANES introduced an oppressive trade monopoly, which stifled the economy. In 1800 the Danish government abolished the Althing.

Modern Icelandic nationalism began to develop in the 19th century. The Danes restored the Althing in 1848 and granted domestic home rule in 1874. In 1918 Iceland became a sovereign state under the Danish Crown. After the German invasion of Denmark in 1940, Iceland was occupied by British forces. The Icelanders took advantage of this break with Denmark to declare Iceland a republic in 1944. Postwar development of the fishing industry has given Icelanders one of the world's highest standards of living, although this is now threatened by over-fishing.

Icelandic society is typically Scandinavian in its virtual classlessness, sexual equality, high standards of state education and health care, and high taxation. It is normal for everyone, including the republic's president, to be greeted on first-name terms. Despite this egalitarianism, Icelandic politics remains dominated by a small oligarchy of families, whose influence is so pervasive that it is popularly known as 'the octopus'. Icelanders are protective of their distinctive cultural identity.

The Icelandic language is derived from the dialects spoken in western Norway in Viking times and it has changed relatively little since. Great efforts are made to protect the language from 'outlandish' influences, and a committee coins Icelandic words for new concepts or inventions. Parents may not give their children non-Icelandic first names, and the Icelanders maintain the old Norse custom of deriving surnames from the father's first name and adding a suffix indicating the sex of the child. Thus Ólaf Magnússon's son would have the surname Ólafsson, his daughter Ólafsdottir.

Pride in their past is also evident in Icelanders' interest in genealogy – many can trace their descent back to the settlement period – and in their literary tradition, the greatest achievements of which are the gripping family sagas written in the 13th century. There are at present around 271,000 Icelanders.

## ICENI

A tribe of ancient BRITONS who lived in what is now the county of Norfolk in eastern England. After the emperor Claudius ordered the invasion of Britain in AD 43, Prasutagus, the king of the Iceni, became a ROMAN ally. When the Romans tried to take over the kingdom after Prasutagus' death, the Iceni and their neighbours the TRINO-VANTES rebelled under the leadership of his wife Boudicca. Although Colchester, London and St Albans were brutally sacked, the rebellion was quickly and decisively crushed by the Romans.

Boudicca committed suicide and the Iceni were subjugated to Roman rule.

## ILLYRIANS

A major but ill-defined group of tribes that inhabited the western Balkans in ancient times. The name was probably originally applied only to one tribe that lived in the region of Lake Shkodër on the present Albanian–Montenegrin border, but came to be used by the Greeks and Romans to describe other tribes who seemed to them to be related. By the 1st century AD these included the Autaries, Dardani, Enchelees, Daorsii, Dasaretii, Delmatae (Dalmatians), Liburnii, Paeonians, Pannonians, Perrhaebi, Scordisci and Triballi, although these were not all certainly Illyrians. In the 3rd century BC both the Scordisci and Triballi had contacts with migrating CELTS, who influenced their cultures. The Illyrians spoke an INDO-EUROPEAN language, although very few records of it have survived.

The Illyrians first appear in history in the 4th century BC when they began raiding the MACE-DONIANS and GREEKS. In the 3rd century BC those tribes who lived on the Adriatic coast, such as the Liburnii and Delmatae, were active as pirates. This provoked the ROMANS to invade and force the coastal tribes to submit in 228. A second Roman expedition in 219 BC began the subjugation of the inland tribes. The most powerful Illyrian ruler, Genthius, king of Scodra (Shkodër), surrendered to Rome in 168 BC, but it was not until 11 BC that the last Illyrian tribes were conquered. Even then the Romans faced a major rebellion, in AD 6–9. The Illyrians prospered under Roman rule and were an important source of recruits for the Roman army. Several Roman emperors were of Illyrian origin, including Diocletian and Constantine the Great. The Illyrians were mostly assimilated to the SLAVS who migrated into the Balkans in the 6th and 7th centuries; their only direct modern descendants are the ALBANIANS.

## IMPRESSED POTTERY CULTURES

The earliest Neolithic cultures of the western Mediterranean. The Impressed Pottery cultures originated in the western Balkans around 6000 BC and spread west along the coasts to Italy, southern France, Spain and across the Straits of Gibraltar to Morocco and Algeria. The cultures are named for their pottery, which was decorated by impressing patterns into the clay with sticks, combs, fingernails and shells. The most distinctive impressed ware is that decorated with the edge of a cockle shell (*cardium*), known as Cardial Ware, from southern France. The farming economy of the Impressed Pottery cultures was based on cereals, legumes and cattle- and sheep-rearing. The cultures had died out by around 4000 BC.

## INDO-EUROPEANS

A prehistoric people who spoke a language called proto-Indo-European, the ancestor of modern Indo-European languages. The Indo-European languages form the largest and most widespread of the world's language families; they are spoken on every continent and by about half the world's population in total. (For the surviving branches of Indo-European, see the box .) In addition, two extinct branches are known, Anatolian and Tocharian (see TOCHARIANS). No records of proto-Indo-European exist, but much of its grammar and vocabulary has been reconstructed by linguists from studies of the common elements in the modern Indo-European languages. Their vocabulary shows that the Indo-Europeans were a pastoral people (they had words for sheep, cow, horse, pig and dog) who knew of copper and bronze but not iron, and probably used wagons. They had no word for sea, suggesting that they lived inland.

Many attempts have been made to identify the Indo-European homeland. Most linguists believe this lay somewhere on the western Eurasian steppe, but some believe it was in Anatolia. The most credible of current hypotheses is that the Indo-Europeans are identified with the Yamnaya culture, which flourished on the steppes north of the Black Sea in the 4th millennium BC. The Yamnaya were the first people to combine wheeled vehicles and pastoralism, allowing them to adopt a migratory way of life. By around 2500 BC groups of Yamnaya people had spread east across the Ural Mountains into

Central Asia and west into southeast Europe. As the culture dispersed it developed into regionally distinctive cultures, including the KURGAN CULTURES and the CORDED WARE CULTURE.

## INGRIANS

FINNS who live to the south of the Gulf of Finland, between the Estonian border and St Petersburg in the Russian Federation. Descended from Finnish settlers who came under RUSSIAN rule in 1710, they maintained a distinct identity through their FINNO-UGRIAN language, which is related to KARELIAN, and Lutheranism. They resisted complete assimilation, and in the late 19th century there was a considerable upsurge in the traditional culture, which was further encouraged by the independence of Finland in 1917. This earned the Ingrians the suspicion of Joseph Stalin, who unleashed collectivization upon them with particular brutality. Thousands were murdered or deported while others fled. Their cultural life was destroyed and they were no longer deemed an indigenous people.

Since the collapse of the USSR many have left for Finland, only to meet discrimination there. Others either remained or returned, hoping to rebuild their own culture in their own territory. The Ingrian language is now close to extinction, with probably fewer than 1000 speakers. In 2002 the Ingrians numbered around 90,000.

## INGUSH

A Caucasian people of the Ingush autonomous republic, Russian Federation. Like the related CHECHENS, they were originally mountain-dwelling herders who migrated to the lowlands from the 16th century and became farmers. They speak a North Caucasian language. They adopted Sunni Islam by the 19th century, but came under RUSSIAN rule. Soviet rule later brought collectivization and attacks on their traditional culture. In 1943 many were deported to Central Asia for alleged collaboration with the Germans, and about half died in the process. Allowed to return in 1957, they greeted the collapse of the USSR with more caution than the Chechens, trying to steer a course between outright secession and reviving an eroding culture.

**Indo-Europeans: surviving branches of the Indo-European language**

Albanian

Armenian

*Baltic:*
Lithuanian
Latvian

*Celtic:*
Breton
Gaelic
Welsh

*Indo-Iranian:*
Bengali
Farsi (Persian)
Gujarati
Hindi
Kurdish
Nepali
Ossetic
Pashtun
Sinhalese
Urdu
Sanskrit
(*written only*)

*Germanic:*
Danish
Dutch
English
Faeroese
Frisian
German
Icelandic
Norwegian
Swedish

*continued over*

This has proved difficult as they openly sympathized with the Chechens in their war with Russia in 1994. In 1999 Moscow rejected their attempts to reintroduce traditional practices such as polygamy and carrying daggers. According to an estimate, which may or may not be reliable, there were nearly 213,000 Ingush in 2000.

# INSUBRES

A Celtic tribe (see CELTS, ANCIENT) of northern Italy. Their capital was at Mediolanum, modern Milan. In 225 BC the Insubres allied with the BOII against the ROMANS but were crushingly defeated at the battle of Telamon. Roman retribution was delayed by the oubreak of the Second Punic War with with the CARTHAGINIANS in 218 BC, during which the Insubres allied with Hannibal of Carthage. Carthage's defeat in 201 BC sealed the fate of the Insubres. The Romans captured Mediolanum in 196 BC, and the Insubres had been completely Romanized by the 1st century AD.

# IONIANS

The ancient GREEK population of Attica, Euboea, the Cycladic islands and the central part of the coast of Anatolia ('Ionia'). The Ionians spoke a distinct dialect of Greek and claimed descent from the Athenian hero Ion. Ionians considered themselves to be the most intelligent and creative of the Greeks. (See also DORIANS.)

# IRISH

The people of the island of Ireland. The modern Irish are divided into two communities based broadly on religion, ethnic origin and political allegiance. Around 90% of Irish are Roman Catholics; the balance are mainly Protestants, most of whom belong to various Presbyterian denominations, but a small minority of whom are Anglicans. Most Protestants are the descendants of Lowland SCOTS and ENGLISH immigrants; most Catholic Irish claim descent from Ireland's original Celtic inhabitants (see CELTS). Ireland is divided between the Irish Republic and the Province of Northern Ireland,

which is part of the United Kingdom. The majority of Irish Protestants live in Northern Ireland, where they form some 55% of the population. Northern Irish Protestants are overwhelmingly Loyalists who support the continuation of BRITISH rule in the Province. While the majority of Northern Irish Catholics are Nationalists who want to see a united Ireland, a significant minority are Loyalists.

Because of Ireland's long history of emigration, the exact number of Irish is unknown. The population of the Irish Republic is 3.55 million and Northern Ireland 1.5 million. Around a million Irish-born people live elsewhere in the UK, and tens of millions of people worldwide claim Irish descent as well. The Irish Republic recognizes English and Gaelic (a Celtic language; see GAELS) as official languages, but Gaelic has been in inexorable decline since the mid-19th century. Despite considerable government financial support and compulsory Gaelic teaching in schools, Gaelic is now spoken as a first language by fewer than 20,000 people. It is extinct as a spoken language in Northern Ireland.

**The early Irish**

The early Irish were a tribal people who had little sense of common identity before their conversion to Christianity in the 5th century AD. Around this time they adopted the name *Gaidel* (in modern Gaelic *Gaedheal*) from *Guoidel* or *Gwyddel* ('savages'), the BRITONS' name for the people of Ireland. Early Christian Ireland was divided into hundreds of local kingdoms and a smaller number of regional over-kingdoms (see DÉISI). The introduction of Christianity led to the development of a remarkable monastic civilization, which produced outstanding works of art and illuminated manuscripts, the most famous of which is the *Book of Kells*. The period is retrospectively viewed as a 'golden age'.

VIKING invasions in the 9th and 10th centuries brought an end to this civilization. The Vikings founded permanent raiding bases around the coast, one of which was Dublin, and these developed into Ireland's first towns. The Viking attacks began a process of political centralization, and in the 10th century the High Kingship of Ireland developed as a formal institution. However, Ireland was still a long way from political unity when the ANGLO-NORMANS invaded in 1169 and created the country's long and frequently unhappy link with England. The Anglo-Normans quickly conquered the south and east of the country, building castles and walled towns and encouraging English settlement. The rougher west and north resisted more successfully, and it was not until the beginning of the 17th century that the writ of the English government ran throughout Ireland. The English in Ireland tried to maintain their identity, but many adopted Irish ways.

### The colonial Irish

The Protestant Reformation of the 1530s created new divisions between Gaelic- and English-speakers. Protestantism failed to find acceptance among either the Irish or 'Old English' settlers. The government planned to make Ireland more Protestant by introducing a policy of plantation, that is, dispossessing Catholics of their lands and replacing them with Protestant New English and Lowland Scots settlers. The policy was less successful than expected because Ireland's reputation for rebellions discouraged settlers. Only in eastern Ulster was a Protestant majority established: these were the ULSTER SCOTS. Nonetheless, the policy caused great discontent, which boiled over into a major Catholic rebellion in 1641. Civil wars broke out in England and Scotland soon after, and it was not until 1649–52 that the Irish rebellion was put down by Oliver Cromwell.

This civil war period is probably the most glorified in Irish history, and it plays a key role in the historical consciousness of both Catholic and Protestant communities, which keenly remember (often with advantage) the atrocities perpetrated against them and conveniently ignore those which their own community committed. Cromwell's land settlement destroyed what was left of the Catholic land-owning class, and by the end of the 17th century, 90% of land was owned by a small class of ANGLO-IRISH Protestants, even though most of their tenants were Catholics.

The defeat of the exiled Catholic king James II by the Protestant William III at the Battle of the Boyne in 1690 confirmed this Protestant ascendancy. Celebrations of the anniversary of this battle provide the focus of the annual Loyalist 'marching season' in Northern Ireland.

Modern Irish nationalism began to develop in the late 18th century, and initially drew support equally from both Protestants and Catholics as Ireland lost its own parliament. However, as the movement developed in the 19th century it came increasingly to be dominated by Ireland's Catholic majority and its demands for Catholic emancipation, land reform and Home Rule. The British government's failure to provide adequate relief during the Great Famine of 1845–51 only heightened dissatisfaction with British rule. All too often the British government ignored Ireland's problems, acting only after Irish frustration had boiled over into violence. In this way the government undermined constitutional nationalism and, by showing that it got results, encouraged the tradition of political violence that has blighted Ireland. For their part, Nationalists blamed England for all of Ireland's problems and looked for the roots of true Irishness in an idealized Celtic, Catholic past. This identity made it increasingly hard for Protestants to be accepted as truly Irish. Their support for Unionism steadily increased, so that by the end of the 19th century most considered themselves to be British rather than Irish. This failure of nationalism to develop an inclusive Irish identity is a largely unacknowledged factor in the present division of Ireland. Irish Protestants feared, and continue to fear, that there could be no place for their cultural identity in a Catholic-dominated Ireland.

### Independence and compromise

The Republican Easter Rising in 1916, the pro-Republican Sinn Féin's party's victory in the 1918 general elections and the Anglo–Irish War that followed (1919–21) forced the British to accede to Nationalist demands for independence. However, fears that Protestant Unionists would obstruct a settlement by armed rebellion led the British government to partition Ireland in 1922. The bulk of the country became the independent Irish Free State (Republic of Ireland from 1948), while the six counties of Ulster that had a Protestant majority became the province of Northern Ireland within the UK. Most Nationalists have never accepted the legitimacy of the settlement, and it caused a civil war in the Free State in 1922–3.

After independence, the Republic of Ireland experienced decades of economic stagnation. Emigration, which had begun on a large scale in the 19th century, continued unabated. Northern Ireland was more industrialized than the south and enjoyed greater prosperity. The Catholic minority in the Province experienced systematic discrimination (as did the much smaller numbers of Protestants in the south). The Nationalist refusal to accept the legitimacy of Northern Ireland justified this discrimination in Protestant and Unionist eyes. The development of a Catholic civil-rights movement in the 1960s was met by Protestant mob violence, and in 1969 the descent into the long period of inter-communal terrorism known as the 'Troubles' began. The 1997 Good Friday Agreement, involving the British and Irish governments, provided a constitutional framework for the rival communities to resolve their differences. Despite the cessation of most of the violence, the implementation of the Agreement has been difficult: the history of mutual suspicion among both of Northern Ireland's communities is a strong one.

The outbreak of the Troubles was accompanied by the decline of Northern Ireland's traditional textile and shipbuilding industries. In contrast, the Irish Republic at last began to experience economic growth as a result of being a net recipient within the European Economic Community (now European Union) since 1973. This has turned the Irish into enthusiastic Europeans. Investment in hi-tech industries, such as computing, culminated in the booming 'Celtic Tiger' economy of the 1990s. Prosperity is bringing major social changes in its wake. The Republic is an increasingly secular society and the influence of the Catholic Church is rapidly declining. No longer an exporter of population, the republic is now experiencing immigration from the Third World and with it the growth of racism in what is still a very homogenous society. The Irish still like to project themselves as an easy-going and laid-back people who enjoy a pre-industrial pace of life, but this image is increasingly at odds with modern realities.

# ITALIANS

The people of the Republic of Italy. Since the fall of the Roman empire in the 5th century, Italy had been politically disunited and a frequent arena for great-power competition among LOMBARDS, FRANKS and BYZANTINES, NORMANS and GERMANS, FRENCH, SPANISH and AUSTRIANS. The term 'Italian' denoted an inhabitant of Italy, but there were few overtones of national identity about it. Italians showed great regional diversities of custom and dialect and reserved their strongest loyalties for their home towns and cities, many of which, such as Genoa, Florence, Milan and Venice, were independent sovereign states in their own right. A conscious sense of Italian nationhood began to develop only in the 19th century, largely under the influence of the spirit of Romantic nationalism unleashed by the French Revolution, giving rise to a movement for national unification known as the *Risorgimento* ('resurgence').

Among the first to work actively for unification were the Carbonari ('charcoal burners'), founded originally to fight a guerrilla war against the French during the Napoleonic Wars, and the Young Italy Movement. The liberal revolutions of 1848 affected every European region, Italy included. Republics were founded in Rome, Venice and Tuscany, and King Charles Albert of Sardinia-Piedmont declared war on Austria in the name of national liberation. Austria crushed the attempted revolution. Sardinia-Piedmont continued to play a leading role in the *Risorgimento* under Charles Albert's successor Victor Emmanuel II and his prime minister Camillo di Cavour. Having won the support of France and Britain, Cavour seized control of almost all of Italy north of Rome 1859–60. At the same time, Giuseppe Garibaldi's 'Red Shirts' led a revolution in the Kingdom of the Two Sicilies (Sicily and southern Italy), overthrew its Bourbon monarchy and then surrendered his conquest to Victor Emmanuel. In 1861 Victor Emmanuel was proclaimed king of Italy. With the acquisition of Venetia from Austria in 1866 and Rome from the Papacy in 1870, Italy had almost achieved its modern borders.

Post-unification governments struggled with Italians' strong regional loyalties and with the huge disparity of wealth between the prosperous, urbanized, industrialized north and the poor, agrarian south. Such poverty resulted in a considerable Italian diaspora, and there are notably large populations of Italian descent in the USA, Argentina, Australia and elsewhere. Disillusionment with the results of unification in the south allowed secret criminal societies such as the Cosa Nostra (Mafia) in Sicily and the Camorra in Calabria to corrupt the political system. These societies still plague Italy. The young state was persuaded to declare war on Germany and Austria in 1915, although it was quite unprepared and suffered heavy losses. When Italy was awarded only the Austrian South Tyrol and Trieste in the postwar peace settlement, there was a strong nationalist reaction, both against the Allies and against the government that had led the country to war. This played into the hands of extremist politicians on the Left and the Right, and helped bring the Fascist leader Benito Mussolini to power in 1922. Mussolini won a considerable degree of popular support for his public works programmes, creation of a sense of order (it is a cliché that he made the trains run on time) and aggressive foreign policy (including conquest of the ETHIOPIANS), which forced other European countries to treat Italy as a major power. But when Mussolini took Italy into World War II on the side of Germany in 1940, the country was no more prepared than it had been in 1915. Italy suffered humiliating defeats from the outset, helping to create a stereotype of Italians as un-military. When Anglo-American forces invaded Sicily in 1943, Mussolini was overthrown, and Italy surrendered and then changed sides. The Germans were occupying most of Italy and were expelled only with difficulty; Italian anti-Fascist partisans fought a heroic guerrilla campaign. Because of this experience as victims of occupation, Italians never engaged in the painful postwar self-examination that Germans did in the 1960s.

### Postwar reconstruction

Postwar Italy was rebuilt as a democratic welfare state. To prevent extremists from seizing power, a very pure form of proportional representation was introduced. This led to such a proliferation of political parties that stable governing coalitions proved impossible: between 1945 and 1991 Italy had 49 governments. Despite this, the Italian economy grew rapidly in the 1950s. Most Italians began to experience unprecedented affluence, although, as ever, the south lagged behind. As in other Western countries, this led to a social revolution, with changing attitudes to authority, religion, the family and sexuality. (The changing nature of Italian society was encapsulated most memorably in Federico Fellini's influential 1960 film *La Dolce Vita*). Although the vast majority of Italians are Roman Catholics, much of the Church's traditional teaching on morality is ignored, the prohibition on contraception so much so that at only 1.2 children per woman, Italy has the lowest birth rate in Europe. This has resulted in an ageing population, but Italians have so far proved reluctant to address the problems that this will eventually cause to the financing of pensions and the welfare state.

In the 1990s resentment about the economic backwardness of the south and the failure of the central government to root out Mafia corruption led to a political shake-up, which saw the disintegration of the dominant Christian Democrats (too tainted by allegations of Mafia collusion) and the development of the Lega Nord separatist movement in prosperous Lombardy. The movement draws on memories of the successful resistance of the Lombard League of cities to the medieval German emperors. Changes to the electoral system in the 1990s have produced greater government stability, but concerns about the effectiveness of Italian democracy remain. For many these concerns are manifested in the controversial figure of Silvio Berlusconi, a multi-millionaire who controls most of Italy's television stations and newspapers and has used his wealth to create his own political party, Forza Italia ('Come on Italy').

The current population of Italy is a little over 57 million, of whom about 6% are in minority groups. The most important of these are the SARDINIANS, FRIULIANS and the South TYROLESE (Italian-Austrians). There is also a small French-speaking population in the Val d'Aosta, Ladin-speaking communities elsewhere in the Italian Alps, small Slavic-speaking minorities in Venezia and Friuli, Greek-speaking communities in Calabria and Apulia, a legacy of GREEK colonization in ancient times. More recently, Italy has also seen large-scale legal and usually illegal immigration of ALBANIANS.

# JEWS, EUROPEAN

Jews are followers of Judaism, the religion of the Biblical HEBREWS. They became widespread in southern Europe in early Christian times following the Roman conquest of their homeland in Palestine and were living in most European countries by the 11th century. Historically the Jews have been both the most influential and most persecuted of Europe's stateless minorities.

In medieval Europe Jews were primarily a commercial class and their presence was welcomed and even encouraged by Christian rulers, who often offered them privileges and protection. It was probably their privileged status that first attracted the resentment of the host communities. Jews were also resented because they could not be assimilated into Christian European society: a Jew could not convert to Christianity without losing his identity; and as Judaism does not seek converts, so the Jews remained an essentially closed society. The Jewish laws of ritual purity also added a barrier between Jews and the host community, as non-Jews were considered impure. Christian anti-Semites could justify their prejudices in theological terms by casting the Jews in the role of the murderers of Christ. This was officially condemned by the Catholic Church in the strongest of terms, but to little effect. Wilder superstitions also flourished, including the belief that Jews sacrificed children. Easter week could be dangerous time for Jews, and the periods of Crusading enthusiasm that swept Europe were deadly for them. The killing of Jewish money-lenders and the destruction of their records shows that anti-Semitic rioters often had motives other than misplaced religious enthusiasm.

### The Ashkenazi and Sephardic traditions

It was in the Middle Ages that the two main branches of European Jewry originated. The Sephardi developed in Iberia and were influenced by both the Muslim and Christian intellectual traditions of the peninsula. The Ashkenazi developed in Germany and spread throughout northern and eastern Europe. Ashkenazi Jews now make up 80% of the world Jewish community. The later Middle Ages saw a general movement of Jews into eastern Europe in response to increasing persecution in the west: Jews were expelled from England in 1290, from France in the 14th century and from Spain, Portugal and much of Germany in the 15th century. Jewish immigration into Poland was so great that Jews made up 20% of the population in the 18th century. Many were coerced into serfdom by landowners in return for 'protection' and made up Europe's only Jewish peasantry. Poland was the birthplace of the mystical Hasidic sect of Judaism.

Increasing religious toleration from the 17th century onwards allowed Jews to return to most of the areas of western Europe from which they had been expelled in the Middle Ages (although not Spain and Portugal until the 20th century). Many also emigrated to North America, where today they form an influential community. By the 19th century Jews had equal rights with other citizens in the Netherlands, France, the UK and the USA, but discriminatory legislation remained in force in Germany and the Austrian empire. In the Russian empire Jews faced severe restrictions as to where they could live, and laws limited their access to certain occupations. Pogroms, often encouraged by the government, became more and more frequent, driving many Jews to emigrate to western Europe and the USA. Increasing toleration in the West met with a response from many Jews who wished to integrate themselves more closely with the host societies. Often well-educated and cosmopolitan in outlook, Jews were among the most influential cultural figures of the time, and included Karl Marx, Sigmund Freud, Marcel Proust and Gustav Mahler to name but four examples from politics, science, literature and music. However, the Dreyfus Affair in France, a scandal of injustice fuelled by anti-Semitism, showed that anti-Jewish feeling was still present in even the most officially tolerant countries. Similarly, not all Jews wanted to integrate, fearing dilution of their identity and abandonment of their religion. From these different approaches the three main strands of modern Judaism developed: the liberal, the united and the conservative (known in the USA as the reformed, the conservative and the orthodox). Another response was the Zionist movement to create a Jewish homeland in Palestine, which gained British approval for its plans in 1917 and culminated in the proclamation of the state of Israel in 1948.

## Holocaust and statehood

The first half of the 20th century saw a dramatic increase in organized and state-sponsored anti-Semitism in many European countries. In Germany this was justified by pseudo-Darwinian theories of racial superiority which placed Jews in the category of sub-humans. In Russia anti-Semitism was briefly banned after the 1917 Revolution, but was soon reinstated because of the Soviet government's official atheism. Their relative prosperity also made Jews targets of popular resentment during the economically difficult years after World War I. This was exploited by extremist politicians, especially Adolf Hitler's Nazi Party, which made Jews the scapegoat for the defeat of the GERMANS in the war. Immediately upon winning power in 1933 the Nazis disenfranchised Germany's Jews, excluded them from education and employment and subjected them to violence and public humiliation. Once World War II had begun, the Nazis decided to implement the 'final solution', that is, the complete extermination of European Jewry. In the Holocaust that followed, it is estimated that 6 million Jews – around one-third of the total Jewish population – were murdered, often in concentration camps. The long-established communities of Jews in Poland (over 90% of the country's 3.2 million Jews were exterminated), Germany, Austria, Czechoslovakia, Yugoslavia, Greece, Lithuania and the Netherlands were almost completely wiped out. Over a million Soviet Jews were killed. The collaborationist Vichy government deported around one-third of France's 280,000 Jews to the death camps and around half of Hungary's 400,000 Jews died. Under German pressure, Italy's fascist government introduced anti-Semitic laws. There was little popular anti-Semitism in the country, however, and most Italian Jews survived the war. The same was true in another German satellite, Romania. The fall of Nazi Germany in 1945 brought little respite for eastern Europe's surviving Jews. The remaining Polish Jews were subject to violent attacks that killed hundreds in the immediate postwar years and the Soviet government continued discriminatory policies until as late as 1987. Emigration to Israel since 1948 has further depleted the Jewish population of eastern Europe, but the French Jewish community was re-invigorated by immigrants from Algeria in the 1960s. One consequence of Nazi persecution was the resettling of Jewish refugees in Spain.

## The global Jewish community today

The largest Jewish communities in Europe today are in Russia, Ukraine and Belarus (about 2 million altogether), France (600,000) and Britain (350,000). By far the largest Jewish community in the world is in the USA (5 million), and there are now some 3 million ISRAELI Jews. The total world population of Jews now stands at over 14 million, but this is still nearly 4 million below its pre-Holocaust level. Recovery has been slowed by increasing secularization, which has seen many Jews give up the faith and marry outside the community. Europe's Jews are now closely integrated with their host communities and, although political sympathy with Israel is widespread, being Jewish is increasingly seen as a religious rather than ethnic identity. One obvious sign of this is the demise of Yiddish and Ladino, the traditional languages of European Jews (Yiddish is a Germanic language written in Hebrew characters; Ladino is a Romance language written in Arabic or Hebrew characters). Today the language of European Jews is the language of their country of residence.

## JUGOSLAVS

See YUGOSLAVS.

## JUTES

An early Germanic people who joined the ANGLES and SAXONS in their migrations to Britain in the 5th century AD. According to Bede, their main settlements were in Kent, the Isle of Wight and the New Forest area of Hampshire. Although some modern historians doubt the accuracy of Bede's account, the early ANGLO-SAXON kingdom in Kent did have several distinctive customs not found elsewhere in England, such as a system of partible inheritance, which may be a result of Jutish settlement. The Jutes were traditionally believed to have originated in the southern part of the Jutland peninsula in Denmark, though some modern researchers believe that they may actually have come from Frisia (a region now divided between the Netherlands and Germany; see FRISIANS).

## KABARDIANS

A Caucasian people mainly of the Kabardino-Balkar autonomous republic, in the Russian Federation. As one of the main CIRCASSIAN peoples, they are culturally similar to the ADYGHE, from whom they were separated by the 14th century. Primarily farmers and herders, they speak a North Caucasian language. They adopted Sunni Islam and came under RUSSIAN control in the 16th century. Assimilatory policies under both Russian and Soviet rule have been strong, but they have retained their identity as a people. In 1993 they numbered nearly 650,000.

## KARACHAY

A Caucasian people of Karachevo-Cherkess autonomous republic, Russian Federation. Similar to the ADYGHE, to whom they are related, they were primarily cattle herders. They adopted a Turkic language (see TURKS) after their conquest by Timur in the 1390s (see TIMURIDS) and adopted Sunni Islam in the 18th century. They were under RUSSIAN rule from the 19th century. Later, Soviet collectivization and assimilatory policies undermined their traditional culture. They were exiled to Central Asia in 1943–57 for alleged collaboration with the Germans in World War II. They are currently attempting to protect their culture and identity. In 1993 they numbered nearly 250,000.

## KARAIMS

A Turkic people (see TURKS) of the Crimea, Ukraine and Lithuania. Perhaps descendants of the KHAZARS, they adopted the non-Talmudic Jewish faith by the 13th century, and subsequently came under considerable RUSSIAN cultural influence. Traditionally farmers and traders, they became heavily urbanized by the 20th century. Long suffering from discrimination, they escaped extermination during the Holocaust only by persuading the Germans that they had no ethnic connection to other Jews. The steady fragmentation of communities has undermined their identity as a people, and their Turkic language is nearly extinct. In 2000 they numbered nearly 5000.

## KARAITES

A minor Finnic people considered to be a subgroup of the MORDVINS. They live only in three settlements in the Tatar Republic in Russia and also at Trakai near Vilnius in Lithuania. The Lithuanian Karaites, who number only about 200, are the descendants of a military garrison. The Karaites are now Tatar-speaking.

## KARATAS

A Caucasian people of Akhvakh region, northwest Dagestan, Russian Federation. Similar to the AVARS, whose written language they use, they had adopted Sunni Islam by the 16th century. They were primarily herders and speak a North Caucasian language. They were under RUSSIAN rule by the 1870s, and any residual spirit of resistance was crushed by Soviet collectivization and assimilatory education, which has left their identity as a people at risk. In 1962, the last time they were officially counted separately, they numbered about 6000.

## KARELIANS

A Finnic people (see FINNS) of Karelia, a region along Russia's border with Finland, stretching from Lake Ladoga north to the White Sea. The Karelians formerly also inhabited the Karelian isthmus north of St Petersburg. They settled this region in the late Iron Age and were converted to Orthodox Christianity by Russian missionaries in the 13th century. By the 14th century the region was ruled by the RUSSIAN principality of Novgorod, passing under the control of Moscow in 1478. In 1617 Sweden won control of all of Karelia, at which time many Karelians loyal to Russia resettled at Tver, northwest of Moscow, where there is still a large Karelian community. Russia regained control of Karelia in 1721. Karelians resisted complete assimilation, and in the late 19th century there was a considerable upsurge in the traditional culture. In the 20th century this earned them the suspicion of Stalin, who treated Karelians with particular brutality. Thousands were murdered or deported and others fled. Their culture was destroyed and they were no longer deemed an indigenous people.

Karelia remained under Russian rule until 1918 when it became part of Finland. Karelia was reconquered by the USSR in the 'Winter War' of 1939–40 and is now part of the Russian Federation. After the Winter War, around 400,000 Karelians were resettled in Finland, where they still retain their separate identity, although few now speak their language. About 130,000 Karelians still live in Russia.

Karelian culture shows strong Russian influences in domestic architecture and cuisine. The Karelian language has two main dialects: South Karelian, which includes many Russian loan words, and North Karelian, which is similar to Finnish. Other dialects, all of them in danger of extinction, are Votic, Liv and Ingrian. Karelian epic poems, collected and recorded by Elias Lönnrot in the 1830s, form the basis of the *Kalevala*, the Finnish national epic.

## KASHUBIANS

A west SLAV people who lived on Poland's Baltic coast between Gdansk and Lake Gardno. They spoke a language closely related to Polish. There were around 1 million Kashubians in the early 20th century, but they have now been assimilated to the Polish population (see POLES).

## KAZAN TATARS

See TATARS.

## KHAZARS

A Turkic-speaking people (see TURKS) from Central Asia who settled on the steppes north of the Caucasus Mountains in the 7th century AD. Their attempts to expand south of the Caucasus were blocked by the ARABS, but they came to dominate a huge area of the southern Russian steppes. They exacted tribute from the ALANS, BULGARS, MAGYARS and various SLAV tribes.

Around 740 the Khazar *khagan* (khan) and the ruling class converted to Judaism, but the khanate practised religious tolerance and traditional paganism; Christianity and Islam both flourished side by side with Judaism.

The Khazar capital was at Itil (Astrakhan), close to the mouth of the River Volga and the Caspian Sea. In the early Middle Ages Itil became a flourishing trade centre where VIKING and RUS merchants from the north met Arabs to trade furs, slaves, wax and honey for silver. Taxes levied on merchants were a major source of revenue for the *khagans*. The Khazars also controlled the lower Don River from their second city of Sarkel and taxed merchants from the north on their way down-river to the Black Sea and Constantinople.

Itil and Sarkel were both sacked in 964–5 by Svyatoslav I, the expansionist Rus ruler of Kiev. Khazar power never recovered, and by the 11th century they had declined as a political force and were gradually assimilated by other nomad peoples such as the PECHENEGS.

## KHIROKITIA CULTURE

A Neolithic culture of Cyprus dating to the 7th millennium BC. This shortlived town-based community used stone round houses and had trade contacts with an unknown foreign source of obsidian.

## KHVARSHI

A Caucasian people of Tsumadin region, eastern Dagestan, Russian Federation. Similar to the AVARS, with whom they were long associated, they were herders who adopted Sunni Islam in the 16th century. They speak a North Caucasian language. Under Russian rule by the 1870s, their culture and identity were eroded by Soviet collectivization and assimilatory education policies, and they were officially counted as Avars. The last time the Khvarshi were counted as a separate people, in 1962, they numbered perhaps 1800.

## KIPCHAQS

A Turkic-speaking (see TURKS) nomad confederation, which probably originated in east-central Asia. The Kipchaqs had migrated into Siberia by the 9th century before moving onto the steppes north of the Black Sea in the 11th century. They were involved in conflicts with most of their neighbours, including the RUSSIANS, BYZANTINES, HUNGARIANS and PECHENEGS.

The Kipchaqs suffered catastrophic defeat at the hands of the MONGOLS in 1237. Most of them were subsequently absorbed into the GOLDEN HORDE, but the western branch, known as the CUMANS or Polovtsy, took refuge in Hungary and was eventually assimilated with the native population there.

## KOMI-PERMYAKS

A FINNO-UGRIAN people of the Komi-Permyak national region, Russian Federation. Originally part of the UDMURTS, they split from them around AD 1 and divided from the KOMI-ZYRIANS around AD 500. By the 12th century they were increasingly under RUSSIAN domination and were adopting sedentary farming. Assimilation was steady and largely completed under Soviet rule through collectivization and subsequent education policies.

Komi-Permyak territory remained impoverished and deteriorated after the collapse of the USSR. Their Finno-Ugric language is endangered, as is their identity as a people, as large numbers migrate seeking employment. In 1989 they numbered over 106,000.

## KOMI-ZYRIANS

A FINNO-UGRIAN people of Komi autonomous republic, Russian Federation. Their culture and experiences are very similar to the KOMI-PERMYAK, although they live in a harsher climate further to the north, and were involved to a greater extent in reindeer-herding. Their Finno-Ugric language and identity as a people are similarly endangered, with the added problems of severe

environmental degradation. In 1993 they numbered nearly 350,000.

## KOSOVARS

ALBANIAN Muslims who form over 80% of the population of the Serbian and YUGOSLAVIAN province of Kosovo. Kosovo was at the heart of the medieval Serb empire, but it came under the rule of the OTTOMANS in 1389. Kosovo has had a mixed Albanian and SERB population since the early Middle Ages. Following the Ottoman conquest there was slow but steady emigration of Orthodox Serbs, which gradually altered the population balance in favour of the Albanians. By the early 20th century there were about equal numbers of Serbs and Albanians living in Kosovo. During the 19th century Kosovo had come to loom large in Serbian consciousness as a symbol of a national golden age. In the 1920s and 1930s the Serb-dominated Yugoslav government made unsuccessful attempts to re-establish a Serbian majority in Kosovo. During the German and Italian occupation of Yugoslavia in World War II, Kosovo was annexed by Albania, and Kosovo Albanians forcibly resisted reintegration with Yugoslavia at the end of the war. The Yugoslav government gave Kosovo administrative autonomy but suppressed expressions of Albanian identity until the 1960s. Serbs continued to migrate out of Kosovo until in 1980 they made up only 25% of the population.

Serbian resentment over the increasingly Albanian Kosovo was exploited by Slobodan Milosevic, who became president of Serbia in 1989. Milosevic abolished Kosovo's autonomy, dissolved its assembly, closed all Albanian-language schools and subjected the province to a virtual military occupation. This Serbian repression helped precipitate the break-up of Yugoslavia. Kosovar resistance to the Serbian government was at first non-violent. Kosovars set up their own system of Albanian-language schools and other organizations. Frustration with the lack of progress led to the foundation of the Kosovo Liberation Army (KLA) in 1996. In 1997 the KLA began attacks on Serbian police using arms smuggled from Albania. The Serbs retaliated with increasing brutality until a refugee crisis in 1999 led to the intervention of a

NATO force, the retreat of Serbian forces, and an exodus of many Serbs. In 2004 Kosovo was still occupied by NATO forces and its future to be finalized. Neighbouring states, especially Macedonia, which has a large Albanian minority, are unwilling to see an independent Kosovo, but there seems little prospect that Kosovars will agree to any solution that leaves them, however nominally, a part of Serbia.

## KRIVICHI

An East SLAV people who in proto-historic times lived in the region of Smolensk in western Russia. In the 9th or 10th century AD they came under the domination of the Kievan RUS and were subsequently assimilated to their identity. The Krivichi had highly distinctive burial customs. The dead were temporarily interred until the annual cremation season. The year's dead were then exhumed and cremated. The ashes were placed in cinerary urns, which were then buried together under long barrows. The Krivichi are sometimes considered to be ancestors of the BELORUSSIANS.

## KRYASHENS

A Turkic people of Tatarstan, Russian Federation. They are Christianized TATARS, but their identity as a people is a matter of great dispute. To Tatars they are the descendants of those who were bribed or forced into adopting Christianity, and are identified as a distinct people by the RUSSIAN government to divide and rule the Tatars, since this ensures that the Tatars remain a minority in Tatarstan. Kryashens, however, do regard themselves as a separate ethnic group, with a distinct culture and identity, and have sought their own autonomous republic. In 2002 they numbered about 300,000.

## KUMYKS

A Caucasian people of Kumyk autonomous republic, Russian Federation. Primarily farmers, Sunni Muslims and speakers of a Turkic language (see TURKS), they ruled an independent kingdom, the Tarkov Shamkalate, from the 15th century until 1867, when they were conquered by the RUSSIANS. Soviet collectivization and the forced relocation of other peoples into their territory did much to destroy their traditional culture. The collapse of the USSR and resulting economic problems resulted in a population drift, undermining their identity as a people further. In 2000 they numbered over 270,000.

## KURGAN CULTURES

Three successive pastoral cultures of the southern Russian and Ukrainian steppes. They take their name from the practice of covering graves with a *kurgan* (a Turkic and Russian word meaning 'barrow' or 'tumulus'). The earliest of the cultures is the late Neolithic-early Bronze Age Yamnaya or Pit Grave culture, which flourished around 3500–2200 BC. This culture is sometimes identified with the INDO-EUROPEANS. The second is the Bronze Age CATACOMB GRAVE CULTURE of around 2200–1800 BC. The third is the Srubnaya or Timber Grave culture of around 1800–1500 BC. While earlier steppe cultures had made use of wheeled vehicles, the presence of horse equipment in Srubnaya burials and the large quantities of horse bones in settlement middens suggest they had mastered the skill of riding on horseback.

## LAKS

A Caucasian people of the Lakskii and Kulinskii regions of Dagestan, Russian Federation. Primarily herders, they adopted Sunni Islam in the 13th century and speak a North Caucasian language. A long history of economic migration coupled with Soviet collectivization and assimilatory education policies have left them rather dispersed and increasingly urbanized, with many fully adopting Russian culture. In 2000 they numbered perhaps 130,000.

## LANGOBARDI

See LOMBARDS.

## LAPPS

See SAAMI.

## LA TÈNE CULTURE

An Iron Age Celtic culture (see CELTS, ANCIENT) famous for its art style, which was based on geometrically complex curvilinear patterns. The culture is named after a site on Lake Neuchâtel in Switzerland, first identified in the 19th century. The La Tène culture developed in the region between the middle Rhine and the Meuse rivers during the mid-5th century BC. A secondary centre developed in Bohemia shortly afterwards. From these centres the culture spread quickly across central Europe and western Europe north of the Pyrenees. Migrating Celtic tribes carried the culture with them into northern Italy around 400 BC, across eastern Europe as far as the River Dnieper around 300 BC and into Anatolia around 275 BC. The culture spread to Britain and Ireland after 300 BC, probably mainly through trade and social contacts, as both islands already had Celtic-speaking populations. Although much of Iberia was Celtic-speaking, La Tène culture had only limited influence there.

To judge by its many richly furnished warrior burials, the La Tène culture was aristocratic and warlike. Apart from weapons, including long slashing swords, burials often contained light and fast war-chariots. The art style for which the La Tène culture is so famous developed from a synthesis of the earlier Celtic HALLSTATT style and GREEK and ETRUSCAN vegetal-style ornaments. There were regional variations in La Tène art; vegetal ornaments were more important on the Continent, geometrical patterns more important in Britain and Ireland. It was an elite art form, for producing spectacular vessels, weapons, armour and jewellery for display at feasts and before battles. In continental Europe the culture died out in the 1st century BC, following the ROMAN conquest of Gaul. The style continued to flourish in Ireland and northern Britain, and it did not disappear entirely even from those areas of Britain that were conquered by Rome in the 1st century AD. Following the end of Roman rule in Britain (5th century AD), the style had a strong revival. Under the influence of the ANGLO-SAXONS it developed into the Hiberno-Saxon style in the 7th century, seen at its finest in illuminated Gospels, such as the *Book of Kells*.

## LATINS

An ancient Italic people of Latium Vetus ('Old Latium'), a region of central Italy roughly corresponding to the southern half of modern Lazio and including Rome. Although they lived in independent city-states, the Latins had a common language (Latin), common religious beliefs and a close sense of kinship, expressed in the myth that they were all descendants of Latinus, the father-in-law of Aeneas. Latinus was worshipped as Jupiter Latiaris on Mons Albanus (Monte Cavo) during an annual festival that was attended by all the Latins, including the ROMANS. The Latin states also extended common rights of residence and trade to one another. Rome's evident territorial ambitions united the Latins against it in 341 BC, but to no avail: the Latins were defeated in 338. Some of the Latin cities were incorporated into the Roman state, and their inhabitants were given full citizenship. Others became Roman allies and enjoyed certain privileges in their relationship with Rome. As Roman power spread in Italy, defeated enemies were granted the same 'Latin' rights. Gradually 'Latin' ceased to be used as an ethnic term, becoming instead a legal category.

## LATVIANS or Letts

A Baltic people who constitute about 52% of the Republic of Latvia's total population, which was about 2.5 million in 1996. The Latvians are the descendants of several Baltic-speaking tribes, including the Couronians, Latgalians, Selonians and Zemgalians, as well as Finnic-speaking tribes (see FINNS) such as the LIVS who were assimilated to Baltic language and culture. The names of some of these tribes are preserved in the names of modern Latvian districts: Kurzeme in the west, Latgale in the east and Zemgale in the south.

Despite trading contacts with the SCANDINAVIANS and RUSSIANS, the Latvians remained pagan until the 13th century, when GERMAN Crusaders established the bishopric of Livonia at Riga. Under the Teutonic Knights, the Latvians, Livs, ESTONIANS and PRUSSIANS were united into the Livonian Confederation. Their defeat by the POLES and LITHUANIANS at Tannenberg in 1410 began the decline of the Teutonic Knights. The order finally broke up during the Reformation after its Grand Master converted to Lutheranism. Most Latvians accepted Lutheranism, but Jesuit missionaries re-established Catholicism as a minority religion around 1600.

In the 1560s Livonia was partitioned between Poland-Lithuania and Sweden before coming under Russian rule in the 18th century. Under Russian rule the Latvians were reduced to the status of serfs. Serfdom was abolished in most of the country in 1817 following a peasant uprising, but it remained in Latgalia until its abolition throughout the Russian empire in 1861. Rising Latvian consciousness of their own language and culture in the later 19th century was met by an active Russification programme, which involved the deportation of intellectuals and suspected nationalists. By 1905, when the policy was relaxed, about 14% of the Latvian population had been deported.

Following the Bolshevik Revolution, Latvia declared independence in 1918, though it was 1920 before this was recognized by Russia. Latvia struggled to find economic and political stability in the inter-war years, and it became a fascist dictatorship in 1934.

In 1940 Latvia was annexed by the USSR, Russian became the official language and the tsarist policy of deportation was resumed. This was brought to a temporary end by German occupation in 1941. Over 65,000 Latvians fled to the West rather than stay to be liberated by the advancing Red Army in 1944. A small anti-Soviet resistance movement carried out guerrilla warfare until it was suppressed in 1952. Some 105,000 Latvians were deported to Siberia in 1945–6, and another 70,000 were deported in 1949 following the forced collectivization of agriculture. At the same time the Soviet government instituted a programme of rapid industrialization using a workforce brought from other parts of the USSR.

By the 1980s ethnic Latvians made up little more than half of the country's population. Expressions of Latvian nationality were suppressed until the *glasnost* era of President Gorbachev in the mid-1980s. Latvian nationalism found expression in public commemoration of victims of Soviet deportations and in calls for press freedom, independent political parties and an end to Russification. A national environmentalist movement, set up to protest against the pollution caused by Soviet industrialization,

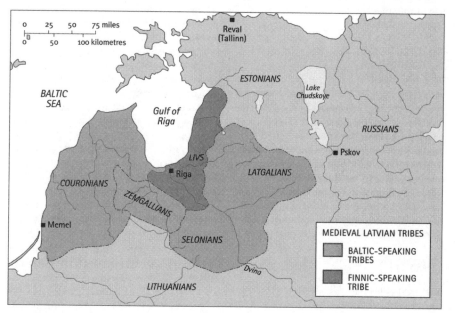

Latvians

*The modern Latvians are descended from both Baltic-speaking and Finnic-speaking medieval peoples.*

also became a focus for nationalist sentiments. In 1988 the Latvian Communist Party legalized the national flag and made Latvian the country's official language.

Massive public demonstrations in 1988 marked the founding of the Popular Front of Latvia (LTV), which united all of Latvia's nationalist groups. The non-violent character of Latvian nationalism meant that the growing demands for independence did not alienate the country's large Russian and BELORUSSIAN minorities. Latvia declared independence from the USSR in 1990, and this was formally recognized in 1991. Fearing that they might become a minority in their own country, the Latvians did not extend full citizenship rights to the large non-Latvian population, causing a certain amount of ethnic tension.

Despite some difficult years immediately after independence, Latvia has become one of the more prosperous of the former Soviet republics. This relative prosperity, with the extension of Latvian citizenship to non-Latvians and entry into the European Union (2004), seem to have eased ethnic tensions. Latvians have distanced themselves further from the former Soviet Bloc by their membership, in 2004, of NATO, and by building links with the Scandinavian countries and the other Baltic republics, Estonia and Lithuania.

## LAUSITZ CULTURE or Lusatian culture

A late Bronze Age–early Iron Age culture of Poland, Bohemia and eastern Germany. The culture was a development of the widespread URNFIELD CULTURE. The Lusatians buried their dead in Urnfield settlements and built fortified settlements that show clear signs of having been carefully planned. One of the best-known settlements at Biskupin, in Poland, contained over a hundred standardized houses built in parallel rows along streets paved with split logs. Cattle-ranching was the principal source of wealth.

## LEMKOS

A RUTHENIAN people originally from southeastern Poland. In the aftermath of World War II the Lemkos were deliberately dispersed by the Polish government. Many of the Lemkos consider themselves to be UKRAINIANS.

## LETTS

See LATVIANS.

## LIECHTENSTEINERS

The inhabitants of the tiny Alpine Principality of Liechtenstein. The Liechtensteiners, who numbered 27,700 in 1998, speak an Alemannic dialect of GERMAN similar to that spoken in neighbouring Switzerland. About 90% of Liechtensteiners are Roman Catholics.

The principality was formed in 1719 by the union of Vaduz and Schellenberg, two of the smaller duchies of the Holy Roman empire. In 1815 Liechtenstein became part of the German Confederation, which it left to become fully independent in 1866. The country became a constitutional monarchy in 1921, but in a referendum in 2003 the Liechtensteiners voted for the restoration of an absolute monarchy.

## LIGURIANS

An ancient people who lived on the Mediterranean coast between the mouths of the Arno and Rhône rivers. Their most important tribes were the Apuani and Ingauni. Classical writers also referred to Ligurian colonies in Corsica and Spain. Little is known about the Ligurian language, but it was probably non-Indo-European and unrelated to any modern language. Some Ligurian tribes, such as the SALLUVII, became Celtic by contacts with the GAULS.

Except for the Salluvii, who were conquered 50 years later, the Ligurians were conquered by the ROMANS between 238 and 170 BC. Under Roman rule the Ligurian language died out and was replaced by Latin. The Ligurian identity re-emerged as a strong regional identity in the Middle Ages, when Liguria was part of the wealthy and powerful Republic of Genoa. Modern Ligurians consider themselves to be ITALIANS first and foremost.

# LINGONES

A Gaulish tribe (see GAULS) that lived by the upper Marne River in modern France. Their chief settlement was Andemantunnum (Langres).

# LITHUANIANS

The native Baltic people of Lithuania. They constitute 83% of the total population of the country, which was around 3.7 million in 1996.

The ancestors of the Lithuanians were already living in the region roughly approximating to modern Lithuania in the late Iron Age. In the Middle Ages the Lithuanians fiercely resisted attempts by GERMAN Crusaders to conquer them and force them to convert to Christianity. The Lithuanians were united into a single state by Mindaugas (1236–63), who converted to Catholicism in 1253. But few Lithuanians followed Mindaugas' example, and the majority remained devoted to paganism.

Under the Grand Duke Gedminas in the mid-14th century, Lithuania began to extend its control into BELORUSSIAN territory. Lithuanians were soon outnumbered by their SLAV Orthodox Christian subjects. Vilnius emerged as the capital of the Grand Duchy. In 1386 Grand Duke Jogaila (Jagiello) converted to Catholicism, enabling him to marry Queen Jadwyga of the POLES and unite the two states. For the next 400 years Lithuania's history is inextricably tied up with Poland's.

Poland-Lithuania quickly emerged as a rival to Muscovy as the major power in eastern Europe. Much of the Ukraine was conquered in the 15th century after the German threat was finally ended by Poland-Lithuania's victory over the Teutonic Knights at Tannenberg in 1410. A consequence of the union with Poland for Lithuanians was that their culture and language lost prestige, and traditional paganism finally began to die out.

When, in the 18th century, the kingdom of Poland was partitioned among Austria, Prussia and Russia, Lithuania became part of the RUSSIAN empire. The Russians suppressed expressions of Lithuanian national identity. The Cyrillic alphabet was imposed, even for Lithuanian-language publications, and Catholics faced persecution. The cause of Lithuanian independence was kept alive mainly by émigrés in the United States of America.

### Lithuania in the 20th century

Lithuania was occupied by Germany during World War I. The Germans allowed the Lithuanians a considerable measure of autonomy, but the idea of inviting a German prince to become the leader of an independent Lithuanian state was seriously considered. Germany's defeat thwarted this plan, and when Lithuania declared independence in 1918 it was as a republic. Lithuanian self-confidence was badly damaged when the Poles annexed the capital Vilnius in 1920, and the country achieved political stability only through the establishment of a dictatorship in 1926. Vilnius was returned to Lithuania in 1939 after the USSR invaded Poland following the Nazi-Soviet Pact. The USSR annexed the whole country, however, in 1940. Lithuania was again occupied by Germany in 1941–5. The eventual re-establishment of Soviet control was followed by deportations of intellectuals and suspected nationalists as well as by a programme of rapid industrialization. Catholics were once again subject to persecution.

The Gorbachev era of *perestroika* (restructuring) and *glasnost* (openness) saw a powerful re-assertion of Lithuanian nationality. In 1988 Sajudis, a Lithuanian popular front, was set up, and in 1990 the Lithuanian parliament voted overwhelmingly in favour of a declaration of independence from the USSR. Lithuania, unlike the other Baltic republics Estonia and Latvia, had no large ethnic minorities to reconcile, but it was the late 1990s before the economy began to recover from the dislocations caused by the break-up of the USSR. As with the other Baltic republics, Lithuania, since 2004, is a member of both NATO and the European Union.

# LIUTIZIANS or Wilzians

A SLAV people who settled on the Baltic Sea coast of northern Germany between the Peene and Oder rivers in the 5th or 6th century AD. Their name means 'terrible people' or 'wolf people'. Contemporaries counted them among the WENDS. The Liutizians' main settlement, Jumne (also known as Jomsborg) near the mouth of the Oder, was a major European trading centre, which attracted merchants from as far away as Greece; in the 11th century it was reputed to be one of the largest cities in Europe. The Liutizians were conquered by the GERMANS and DANES in 1164–84 and assimilated into German culture.

## LIVS

A Finnic-speaking people (see FINNS) who lived between the mouths of Western Dvina and Gauja rivers in Latvia; they are probably now extinct. During the Middle Ages the Livs were a numerous people, and modern Latvia was at that time known after them as Livonia. The Livs were conquered and converted to Catholic Christianity in the 13th century by the GERMAN crusading Order of the Sword Brothers. Livonia came under RUSSIAN rule in the 16th century. Despite campaigns of Russification there were still 800 people who regarded themselves as Livs when Latvia became independent in 1918.

## LOMBARDS or Langobardi

An early Germanic tribe who probably originated as a branch of the SUEBI. The northern Italian province of Lombardy is named after them.

According to their own legendary traditions, the Lombards originated in Scandinavia, at which time they were called Winili. They believed that overpopulation had forced their migration to Germany. During the 1st century AD they were settled in northern Germany and it is from then that Roman writers regarded them as being part of the Suebi. By the 3rd or 4th century, when they began a migration south, the Lombards had developed a clearly separate identity. They arrived on the north bank of the Danube in modern Austria toward the end of the 5th century.

The Lombards adopted a form of social organization established on late ROMAN military institutions, with a hierarchy of dukes, counts, and others commanding warrior bands based on kinship groups. Around this time too the Lombards were converted to Arian Christianity. In 546 King Audoin allied with the BYZANTINES against the GEPIDS, eventually defeating them decisively at the battle of Asfeld in 552 and taking over their lands. However, the arrival in the area of the nomadic AVARS a decade later persuaded Audoin's son Alboin to lead the Lombards into Italy in 569.

Italy had been devastated in the wars between the Byzantines and the OSTROGOTHS, and within three years almost all of the Po Valley and Tuscany, as well as Spoleto and Benevento in the south, were in Lombard hands. This rapid advance ended when Alboin was murdered in 572 and the Lombard kingdom broke up into a collection of independent duchies. The Lombard monarchy was restored by Authari in 584, but it was effective only in the north; Benevento and Spoleto remained independent Lombard duchies.

The Lombards were only ever a minority in Italy, but their adherence to Arianism was an effective obstacle to their assimilation to their Catholic subjects. It was not until the reign of King Liutprand (712–44) that the Lombards felt secure enough to convert to Catholicism.

In the 8th century the Lombard kingdom was strong enough to begin encroaching on the remaining Byzantine territories in northern and central Italy, the Exarchate of Ravenna and the Duchy of Rome. This encroachment alarmed the Papacy and drove it to forge an alliance with the FRANKS, who forced the Lombards to withdraw. The Lombards did not give up their territorial ambitions, however. A move on Rome by the last Lombard king, Desiderius (756–74), brought the Frankish king Charlemagne over the Alps in 773. Charlemagne laid siege to Desiderius in his capital at Pavia, forcing his surrender in 774, and took the title 'King of the Lombards'; but there were no large-scale expulsions of Lombard landowners. Charlemagne also conquered the Lombard Duchy of Spoleto and forced Benevento to submit, but his power there was more nominal.

Lombard independence in southern Italy was finally ended by the NORMANS in the 11th century. Afterwards, the Lombards were gradually assimilated into the ITALIAN population, and their language, which had never developed a written form, died out.

### Lombards since the early modern period

The Lombard identity survived as a regional Italian identity. This came close to developing into a sense of nationhood during the 12th and 13th centuries, when the cities of northern Italy banded together in the Lombard League to resist the German Holy Roman emperors.

From the 16th century to the middle of the 19th Lombardy was under SPANISH and then AUSTRIAN domination. In 1859 the Austrians were expelled, and Lombardy was annexed to the kingdom of Piedmont-Sardinia, becoming part of the Kingdom of Italy in 1860–1.

Although a distinct Lombard dialect of Italian still survives, modern Lombards are not culturally distinct from other Italians. Lombardy is one of the most prosperous regions of Italy, and Lombards tend to see themselves as industrious and honest. Resentment at the idea that their taxes were being squandered by inefficient and venal bureaucrats in Rome or embezzled by the Mafia in the Italian south led to the rise of the Lega Nord (Northern League) in the 1990s, which consciously draws its inspiration from the medieval Lombard League. Initially a separatist party, the League now campaigns for Italy to become a federal state made up of self-governing regions.

## LUCANIANS

Inhabitants of Lucania, a mountainous area of southwest Italy to the south of Salerno. The Lucanians were the descendants of GREEKS who had settled the coastal areas around 700 BC and of the SABELLI, an Oscan-speaking people of central Italy who conquered the area around 420 BC. The OSCANS imposed their language, but the Lucanian culture became Hellenized from contacts with the Greeks.

The Lucanians had a long history of hostility toward Rome, and they were not finally subdued until granted ROMAN citizenship after the Social War (91–87 BC).

## LUDIANS

A FINNO-UGRIAN people of the Karelian autonomous republic, Russian Federation. Initially hunters, gatherers and slash-and-burn farmers, they speak a Finno-Ugric language now seriously endangered.

They were conquered by Novgorod in the 12th century and steadily Russified by large-scale RUSSIAN settlement of their lands. Now a small minority, they still maintain their identity as a people, expressed through such ethno-cultural organizations as the Lyydilainen Assembly. In 1989 they numbered perhaps 10,000

## LUSATIAN CULTURE

See LAUSITZ CULTURE.

## LUSATIANS

See SORBS.

## LUSITANIANS

An ancient Celtic-speaking people (see CELTS, ANCIENT), who lived in what is now central Portugal and western Spain.

For much of the 3rd century BC the Lusitanians successfully resisted the CARTHAGINIANS, who had conquered the IBERIAN peoples of south and east Spain. In 206 BC the ROMANS conquered Carthage's Spanish empire. Fearing Roman territorial expansion, the Lusitanians supported an unsuccessful Iberian rebellion in 197 BC, provoking Roman retaliation. A long series of wars with Rome followed; Lusitanian resistance was so stiff that the Romans lost over 15,000 soldiers between 155 and 153 BC alone.

By 150 BC Lusitanian resistance appeared to be broken, but when the Romans broke a peace treaty and massacred a group of unarmed Lusitanians, war broke out again.

By 147 BC leadership of the Lusitanians had fallen to Viriathus, a shepherd and outlaw who is still regarded as a national hero in Portugal. His background made him a natural guerrilla fighter and for years he ran rings around all the armies Rome sent against him. The Romans finally disposed of Viriathus by treachery, bribing one of his servants to murder him in 139 BC. Deprived of his inspirational leadership, Lusitanian resistance finally collapsed, and the Lusitanians were confined to the Roman province of Lusitania.

> " At first they [the Lombards] were Winili by their own proper name and parentage but their name was later changed into the common word Langobardi, on account of their profuse and always unshaven beards. "
>
> Codex Gothorum, c. 800

They rebelled again in 80 BC, but this time it was in support of a dissident Roman general called Sertorius, who was offering not independence but reformed Roman government. Sertorius' rebellion was defeated by Pompey in 73 BC. Lusitania subsequently became a peaceful and prosperous province. The Lusitanians themselves gradually became Romanized, and the Celtic language died out and was replaced by a local dialect of Latin before the end of the Roman rule in the 5th century AD. The POR-TUGUESE count the Lusitanians among their ancestors.

## LUXEMBOURGERS

The people of the Grand Duchy of Luxembourg, which had a population of 412,000 in 1996. Although Luxembourg has existed as a territorial unit since the 10th century, it was always subject to a foreign power – successively the Holy Roman empire, the Duchy of Burgundy, Spain, Austria and the Netherlands. It became an independent sovereign state only in 1830.

Luxembourgers' identity and culture has always been shaped by their position on the border between the FRENCH and GERMAN cultural worlds. French and German are both official languages in Luxembourg. French is the language of government and law, while German is the language of religion (95% of Luxembourgers are Catholics). Both languages are also used in schools, but the everyday spoken language is Letzeburgesch, a form of German with an intonation that has been influenced by DUTCH and a vocabulary influenced by French. The Luxembourgers combine their national identity with a strong commitment to the European Union.

## MACEDONIANS, ANCIENT

A GREEK-speaking people descended from a mixture of DORIAN Greeks, ILLYRIANS and THRACIANS whose ancient homeland encompassed northern Greece, the modern Republic of Macedonia and part of southwest Bulgaria.

Regarded by the Greeks as barbarians, the Macedonians became subject to Persia towards the end of the 6th century BC, and in the 5th century BC struggled to maintain their independence against the ATHENIANS and SPARTANS, as well as their Thracian neighbours. Under King Archelaus (died 399 BC), Macedonia emerged as a centralized kingdom. Archelaus invited Greek artists and scholars to his court, and Macedonian culture became Hellenized as a result. Under Philip II (ruled 359–336 BC) Macedonia emerged as a major military power. Philip's victory over Athens and Thebes at Chaeronea in 338 BC brought all of Greece except for Sparta under Macedonian control. Philip's son Alexander 'the Great' (ruled 336–323 BC) was a megalomaniac military genius who conquered the PERSIAN empire, extending the influence of Hellenistic civilization as far east as the River Indus in modern Pakistan.

After Alexander's death, the empire broke up into several successor kingdoms, but Macedonia remained dominant in Greece until it was conquered by the ROMANS in 168 BC and divided into four districts. After an unsuccessful rebellion in 146 BC, Macedonia became a province of the Roman empire. In the course of the 6th and 7th centuries AD Macedonia was occupied by migrating SLAV tribes, who transformed the ethnic and linguistic characteristics of the area's population.

## MACEDONIANS, MODERN

A SLAV people whose national identity developed in the 19th century. Macedonians constitute a little over two-thirds of the population of the Former Yugoslav Republic of Macedonia, whose population was around 2.17 million in 1996; there are also Macedonian minorities in Albania and the Greek region also named Macedonia. Macedonians speak a South Slavic language closely related to Bulgarian. Orthodox Christianity is the main religion but there is a small but increasing Sunni Muslim minority, known as POMAKS, Poturs or Torbeshes.

The historical region of Macedonia was settled by SLAV tribes in the 6th and 7th centuries AD. These tribes were conquered by a succession of empires: BYZANTINE, BULGARIAN, SERBIAN and OTTOMAN. It was in the declining years of Ottoman power in the 19th century that the Macedonian Slavs began to develop a national consciousness. Serbia, Greece and Bulgaria all had competing territorial claims to Macedonia, effectively forcing Macedonians to define their own identity. The GREEKS regarded the Macedonians as merely Slavophone Greeks, while neither the Bulgarians nor Serbs considered the Macedonians to be a distinct Slav nation.

The Macedonians identified themselves with the Slavs, especially the Bulgarians, rather than the Greeks and aspired to an autonomous, undivided Macedonia in a South Slavic federation with Serbia and Bulgaria. The Internal Macedonian Revolutionary Organization (IMRO) raised a rebellion against Ottoman rule in 1903 and declared Macedonian independence. The rebellion was quickly crushed, however, and when Macedonia was eventually freed from Ottoman rule in the Second Balkan War in 1913 it was divided three ways between Greece (Aegean Macedonia), Serbia (Vardar Macedonia) and Bulgaria (Pirin Macedonia). In 1918 Vardar Macedonia became part of the Kingdom of the Serbs, Croats and Slovenes, later known as Yugoslavia. Political identification with Bulgaria remained strong among Macedonians until World War II, when Bulgarian troops occupied Macedonia and, through a brutal programme, imposed Bulgarian culture.

After the war Josip Tito's communist government satisfied the nationalist aspirations of most Macedonians when it turned Vardar Macedonia into the autonomous YUGOSLAV Republic of Macedonia. Beginning in the 1920s, the Greek government Hellenized Aegean Macedonia by resettling tens of thousands of Greek refugees from Turkey in the area.

Serbs generally resented Tito's support for Macedonian nationality, which they saw as an attempt to undermine their identity. The rise of militant Serbian nationalism after Tito's death in 1980 was therefore seen as a serious threat by Macedonians. In 1992 Macedonia quickly followed Slovenia, Croatia and Bosnia in declaring independence from Yugoslavia.

Although full-scale civil war was avoided, independence has brought its own share of problems for the Macedonians. Macedonia is a poor country, and continuing instability in the Balkans is an effective brake on its economic development. Macedonia's large ALBANIAN minority has its own aspirations for autonomy or even unification with Albania, leading to sporadic violence. Greece at first refused to recognize Macedonia's independence and tried to block its entry to the United Nations unless it renounced the use of the name Macedonia. In 1994 Greece imposed an illegal economic blockade on the country. Greece claims to fear Macedonian revanchism, but Greek hostility is as much about what it sees as the Macedonian appropriation of the Hellenic past. This was the reason Greece pressured Macedonia to drop from its flag the star of Vergina, a symbol of the ancient Macedonian royal house that Greeks regard as a symbol of Hellenic culture.

## MADEIRANS

A PORTUGUESE people who inhabit the Madeira archipelago off Morocco. The islands of the Madeira group were uninhabited until the late 15th century, when they were settled by the Portuguese, who began cultivating sugar cane and vines. The islands, which have a population of around 265,000, are administered as an integral part of Portugal, but the islanders speak a distinct dialect of Portuguese.

## MAGDALENIAN CULTURE

The final cultural phase of the Upper Palaeolithic in western and central Europe. The Magdalenian culture flourished between around 17,000 and 11,000 years ago, during the final stages of the last Ice Age. The culture is named after a rock shelter at La Madeleine in the Dordogne Valley in France, which was excavated in the 1860s.

The Magdalenians specialized in hunting reindeer and ibex and also fished for salmon. The culture's stone tools are unremarkable, but they manufactured a wide range of finely made bone and antler harpoons, spear-throwers and other artefacts whose purpose is less clear, such as the *batons percés* (pierced batons), which may have been used for straightening spear shafts.

The culture represents the culmination of the cave-art traditions developed in earlier Palaeolithic cultures, such as the AURIGNACIAN and GRAVETTIAN. The impressive cave paintings at Lascaux and Altamira date to the Magdalenian period, which also produced many smaller, portable art works, such as ivory carvings. The culture died out along with the way of life of its people. As the climate warmed at the end of the Ice Age, the tundras that supported herds on which the Magdalenians depended gave way to a densely forested environment, which led to the emergence of the new survival strategies of the MESOLITHIC.

## MAGYARS

See HUNGARIANS.

## MALTESE

The people of the Mediterranean islands of Malta, Gozo and Comino. Because of their strategic position and deep-water harbours, the islands have seen a succession of occupiers and cultural influences over the centuries. Malta was first settled in prehistoric times by farming peoples from southern Italy; the temples they built at Tarxien around 3300 BC are among the oldest surviving stone buildings in the world. Malta became a PHOENICIAN colony early in the 1st millennium BC, then came under CARTHAGINIAN control around 600 BC. The locals helped the ROMANS expel the Carthaginians during the Second Punic War (218–201 BC).

On the fall of the Western Roman empire, Malta passed briefly to the VANDALS before becoming part of the BYZANTINE empire. It was captured by the ARABS in 870, who in turn were expelled in 1090 by the NORMANS, who incorporated Malta into the Kingdom of Sicily.

In 1530 the islands, by now under SPANISH rule, were granted to the Crusader Knights of St John. The Knights rebuilt the island's capital Valetta as a massive fortress city, which withstood a siege by the OTTOMANS in 1565. Napoleon expelled the Knights in 1798, but the FRENCH ruled for less than two years before the islands were occupied by the BRITISH.

The British developed Malta as their main Mediterranean naval base. Malta was heavily bombed by Axis forces during World War II, and the islanders were collectively awarded the George Cross for their resilience under attack. British rule was generally popular with the Mal-

tese, and in 1956 they voted in favour of full integration into the United Kingdom. However, negotiations broke down and the islanders became independent for the first time in their recorded history in 1964. At a referendum in 2003 the Maltese voted in favour of joining the European Union, effective in 2004.

The Maltese language is derived from a dialect of Arabic, but it has been much influenced by Sicilian. It has the distinction of being the only Semitic language to be written using the Latin alphabet. English is universally spoken and is, with Maltese, an official language. Maltese tradition holds that the islanders were converted to Christianity by St Paul, who was shipwrecked there in AD 60, and they remain a devout, mainly Catholic, people. The present Maltese population is around 370,000.

## MANX

The people of the Isle of Man, an autonomous possession of the British Crown in the middle of the Irish Sea. The population of the island was 69,600 in 1996. The Manx were originally a Celtic people (see CELTS), but a majority of the islanders today are of BRITISH origin, attracted from the mainland by the island's favourable tax regime.

The Isle of Man was first settled by hunter-gatherers in the Mesolithic period. The first historically known inhabitants were ancient BRITONS. The islanders were not conquered by the ROMANS, but there is evidence for trading contacts with the Roman empire. In the 5th century the island was conquered by the IRISH, who introduced Gaelic language and culture.

VIKING settlers arrived in the 9th or 10th century, and in the 11th century the Norse Kingdom of Man dominated the Irish Sea and the Hebrides. The Vikings founded the island's assembly, Tynwald, which, with a continuous history of nearly a thousand years, is arguably the oldest parliamentary institution in Europe (the Icelandic Althing is probably an earlier foundation but it was abolished for a period in the 19th century). Tynwald remains a source of national pride for the Manx.

The Vikings did not exterminate the native population, and slowly, through conversion to

**"** To honour her brave people I award the George Cross to the island fortress of Malta to bear witness to a heroism and devotion that will long be famous in history. **"**

King George VI of Britain

Christianity and inter-marriage, they became Gaelic. At the end of the 11th century the kings of Norway asserted their sovereignty over the Kingdom of Man, but it remained autonomous until 1266, when it passed briefly to Scotland and then to England.

Under English rule, the Manx retained their autonomous institutions and Gaelic culture. Rural poverty in the 19th century led many to emigrate, and Gaelic began to be replaced by English. The development of fast steamer links with Liverpool and other mainland ports led to the development of Man as a holiday resort later in the 19th century, and increasing numbers of English speakers began to settle on the island.

The last native speaker of Manx Gaelic died in 1974, and attempts to revive the language have had little success. Immigration to Man is now strictly controlled, but the economic and political life of the islands is dominated by new-comers. Celtic nationalism is an issue for a small minority of native Manx.

## MARCHLAND POLES

Ethnic POLES who live in Ukraine and Belarus. Also called 'borderland' Poles, they are a legacy of the union between Poland and Lithuania in the late 14th century.

In the course of the 15th and 16th centuries Poland-Lithuania expanded rapidly and won control of a vast area of eastern Europe, which included much of modern Belarus and the Ukraine. Polish nobles, and LITHUANIAN and RUTHENIAN nobles who had been assimilated to Polish culture and language, were granted estates in these newly conquered territories. They then brought in and settled communities of Polish peasants on the land.

After the partition of Poland in the 18th century, these Polish communities found them-selves living under RUSSIAN and AUSTRIAN rule. The Polish nobles kept their estates but lost their political influence, while the rise of Ukrainian and Belorussian nationalism in the 19th century perversely helped the Polish peasants retain their separate identity, even though they were not now associated with the ruling elite.

The newly independent Polish state took advantage of Russia's Civil War to annexe parts of Belarus and Ukraine (1918–20). Their March-land Polish populations briefly regained some of their former status. However, the re-occupa-tion of these areas by the USSR (1939) was followed by the deportation of around 2 million Marchland Poles to Siberia and elsewhere. At the end of World War II a further 2 million were expelled to Poland. Today, around a million Marchland Poles still live in Belarus and the Ukraine.

## MARCOMANNI

An early GERMAN people who originated on the north German plain but had migrated to the Main River valley around 100 BC. Shortly before the time of Christ, their king, Maroboduus, led the Marcomanni on a new migration to Bohemia. The Celtic BOII who already lived there were either displaced or assimilated. After a defeat in AD 19 by the CHERUSCI, the Marco-manni became dependants of the ROMAN empire.

Except for a period in the 90s, relations between the Marcomanni and the Romans remained peaceful until AD 166. While the empire was struggling to recover from an out-break of plague, the Marcomanni and the neighbouring QUADI invaded, reaching as far as northern Italy. The emperor, Marcus Aurelius, finally defeated the Marcomanni in 180, and many were resettled in Roman territory. The Marcomanni were never again a major power, but they were occasionally mentioned up to the 6th century when Bohemia was settled by SLAVS.

## MARI

A FINNO-UGRIAN people of Mari-El autonomous republic in the Russian Federation. With a long history of outside domination, the Mari came under RUSSIAN rule after a series of murderous wars in the 16th century. Subsequently they were pushed east to their present location by settler pressure. Though superficially Christianized in the 18th century, they proved adept in sustaining their animist and ancestor-worshipping religion, as well as their Finno-Ugric language, in secret into the 20th century. Soviet collectivization fol-lowed by assimilatory education policies and growing industrialization, however, caused a steep decline in both traditions, and since the collapse of the USSR the Mari have sought to reclaim them. Nonetheless, a recent attempt to build a new temple as part of this process failed because of a lack of interest among the young. In 1993 they numbered about 670,000.

## MASSAGETAE

See ALANS.

## MAZOVIANS

A West SLAV tribe that lived in the Masurian Lakes region of northern Poland. The Mazovians spoke a dialect of Polish. They were incorporated into the Kingdom of Poland in the 11th century and are considered to be among the ancestors of the modern POLES.

## MERCIANS

The people of the early ANGLO-SAXON Kingdom of Mercia, which comprised most of the Midlands of England. Mercia was founded around AD 600, probably from an amalgamation of smaller Anglo-Saxons kingdoms and chiefdoms. The Mercians were converted to Christianity in the second half of the 7th century, having earned a reputation for militant paganism under their king Penda (ruled c. 632–55).

Under King Offa (ruled 757–96) Mercia was the dominant Anglo-Saxon kingdom, but it declined after its defeat by Wessex in 825. The last independent ruler of the Mercians, Burgred, fled into exile in 874 after being defeated by the VIKINGS. In the course of the late 9th and early 10th centuries Mercia was absorbed into the Kingdom of Wessex.

The Mercians were traditionally regarded as being descended from the ANGLES.

## MESOLITHIC CULTURES

The prehistoric Europeans who lived during the Mesolithic or Middle Stone Age, the period between the end of the last glaciation of the Ice Age around 10,000 years ago and the adoption of farming at the beginning of the Neolithic or New Stone Age. The warmer climatic conditions brought major environmental changes to which prehistoric Europeans were forced to adapt. As the Ice Age tundras gave way to more forested conditions, the big-game-hunting way of life of the Upper Palaeolithic MAGDALENIAN culture became impossible. Hunter-gatherers had to adapt to conditions in which game was smaller (deer, wild boar) and harder to find, but other foods, such as berries, fungi and fish, were more abundant.

Different cultural traditions developed in different regions, depending on the nature of the environment and the character of the food sources. In richly diverse environments, such as areas of Britain and Scandinavia where marine, fresh-water and forest environments were in close proximity to one another, Mesolithic hunter-gatherers were able to adopt semi-sedentary life-styles. Mesolithic tool kits reflect the changed environment. The bow and arrow came into widespread use for the first time because of its usefulness in hunting small game and wildfowl. Fish traps were built, and wood-working tools such as axes and adzes appear: these were used to make, among other things, dug-out canoes. Microliths (small flakes of stone) were mounted in wood or antler shafts to construct composite tools, such as harpoons and knives. In southeast Europe the Mesolithic drew to a close around 6000 BC following the introduction of farming from the Middle East. Farming spread steadily across Europe thereafter reaching Britain and southern Scandinavia around 4000 BC. In parts of northern Europe an essentially Mesolithic way of life continued well into the Christian era.

## MESSAPIANS

An ancient people of Puglia (Apulia) in southern Italy. The Messapians were probably the descendants of ILLYRIANS who had crossed the Adriatic to Italy around 1000 BC. By around 500 BC the Messapians formed a loose confederation of city-states and had developed a literate culture using an adaptation of the Greek alphabet. They were conquered by the ROMANS in 266 BC but retained their own language until around 50 BC.

# MINOANS

Ancient inhabitants of Crete and the southern Aegean islands. Around 2000 BC the Minoans developed the first urbanized and literate civilization in Europe. They used a hieroglyphic script until around 1700 BC, when it was superseded by a syllabic script known as Linear A. Both scripts have defied translation, so the ethnic identity of the Minoans is unknown, but as they certainly did not speak an INDO-EUROPEAN language, they were not GREEKS. What the Minoans called themselves is also unknown; the name by which they are known today was coined in the early 20th century by the archaeologist Arthur Evans from Minos, a legendary king of Crete.

The basis of the Minoan civilization was intensive agriculture based on the 'Mediterranean triad' of wheat, olives and vines, as well as flocks of sheep kept on mountain pastures. Olive oil, wine, woollen textiles, pottery and decorative metalwork were exported to Egypt and the Middle East. Minoan society was ruled from four palaces at Knossos, Phaistos, Khania (Chania) and Mallia, which were probably the capitals of small kingdoms. The palaces

had vast storehouses for oil, wine and grain and acted as centres where produce collected as tax or tribute was gathered for redistribution as rations to craftsmen and officials or for export. Imported products, such as bronze ingots and other metals, were also stored at the palaces. Control over the distribution of valuable imports must have given the rulers great power.

The Minoans had a lively art style which was displayed in frescos and painted pottery. Sea creatures, boats and fishermen are common motifs, reflecting the importance of the sea to Minoan life. Other themes are probably associated with religion. Frescos at Knossos depict youths leaping over a bull's back in a ritual game, and stone bulls' horns were apparently important religious symbols. This symbol may have been the origin of the legend of the Minotaur, a half-human, half-bull monster, which lived in the labyrinth at Knossos. A Mother Goddess, who was adopted by the Greeks (who called her Artemis), was also important. Minoan palaces had cult rooms, but the most important religious sites were caves and mountain tops. The Minoans also practised human sacrifice.

Around 1700 war broke out between the palace kingdoms as they struggled with one

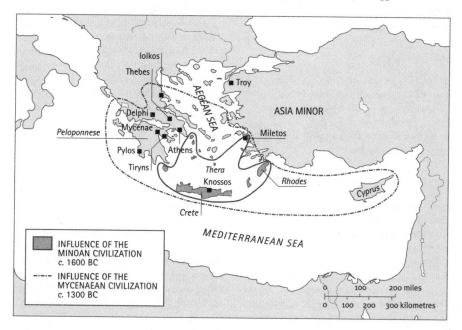

INFLUENCE OF THE MINOAN CIVILIZATION c. 1600 BC

INFLUENCE OF THE MYCENAEAN CIVILIZATION c. 1300 BC

Minoans, Mycenaeans

another for control of the island. Knossos emerged as the dominant centre and the other palaces became subordinate centres. The Minoans subsequently embarked on a period of expansion, establishing colonies on the Aegean islands of Kythera, Thera, Melos, Rhodes and Kea, and also at Avaris in Egypt. The cataclysmic eruption of the volcanic island of Thera, and its attendant earthquakes and ash falls, caused serious damage to the Minoan economy, but recovery was swift. Around 1450 BC, however, Crete was invaded and conquered by the MYCENAEAN Greeks who subordinated the Minoans and introduced new religious customs and art forms. Crete had been largely Hellenized by Classical times and the Minoan language (Eteocretan) had died out before the Christian era.

## MISHARS

A group of MORDVINS who are culturally Turkish and live in the middle Volga region of Russia. The Mishars were converted to Islam in the early Middle Ages through contacts with the Volga BULGARS and became Tatar-speaking after their conquest by the GOLDEN HORDE TATARS in the 13th century. The Mishars are now officially counted as TATARS for census purposes, but they remain a distinct community.

## MOESIANS

An ancient people of THRACIAN origin who inhabited Moesia, now northern Bulgaria. They were conquered by the ROMANS in 29 BC, but nevertheless subsequently they were able to retain their identity. Their homeland was settled by SLAVS in the 6th century AD.

## MOKSHA

A FINNO-UGRIAN people of the Mordovian autonomous republic, Russian Federation. RUSSIANS classified them as Mordovians, along with the closely related ERZYA, but the Moksha retain a distinct identity as a people, emphasized by differences in language and material culture. Under foreign domination since rule by the OSTROGOTHS in the 3rd century AD, they adopted agriculture in the 12th century and were con-

quered by the Russians in 1552. Forcibly Christianized in the 17th century, they proved rebellious until the 19th century. Soviet collectivization and assimilatory policies seriously undermined their traditional culture. In 1997 the Moksha claimed that assimilatory policies were seriously endangering their language, to the extent that they violated their human rights. In 1997 there was estimated to be around 1 million Moksha.

## MOLDOVANS or Moldavians

A ROMANIAN people who make up about two-thirds of the population of the Republic of Moldova, which was around 4.44 million in 1996. The medieval Principality of Moldavia was the first independent Romanian state, but it came under the domination of the OTTOMAN Turks in the 16th century. In 1812 the eastern Moldavia, known as Bessarabia, became part of the RUSSIAN empire. Romania seized control of Bessarabia in 1918 but had to cede it to the USSR in 1940. It was briefly re-occupied by Romania in 1941–44. Under Soviet rule, Bessarabia became the Moldavian Soviet Socialist Republic. This in turn became the independent Republic of Moldova in 1991.

Moldova's first year of independence was marked by fighting between government forces and the country's RUSSIAN and GAGAUZ minorities, who declared independent republics. The Moldovans were themselves divided into nationalist and pro-Romanian camps. The victory of the nationalists in the 1994 elections aided the peaceful conclusion of disputes with the Russian and Gagauz minorities, and these were granted internal autonomy.

The name for the Moldovan language is a cause of dispute. During the Soviet period Moldovan was written using the Cyrillic alphabet, and politically motivated Soviet linguists maintained that it was a separate language from Romanian. However, the differences between Romanian and Moldovan are so slight that many linguists maintain that they are not distinct languages and that Moldovan should really be called Romanian. The Cyrillic alphabet was replaced by the Roman alphabet in 1989.

# MOLOSSIANS

A Greek-speaking people of Epirus, in western Greece. Until at least the end of the 5th century BC they were regarded by other GREEKS as barbarians. The Molossians enjoyed a brief moment of glory under their king Pyrrhus (ruled 319–272 BC), whose kingdom encompassed much of western Greece and Albania. Pyrrhus campaigned in Italy to support the Greek city-states there against the ROMANS, but withdrew after sustaining heavy losses in his victory at Heraclea in 280 (the original 'pyrrhic victory'). The Molossians were conquered by the Romans in 167 BC.

# MONEGASQUES

The native inhabitants of the Mediterranean principality of Monaco, although they now make up only around 15% of its total population, which was 30,400 in 1996. The vast majority of Monaco's people are FRENCH. Monegasques speak a Romance dialect influenced by Provençal and the Genoese dialect of ITALIAN. Monaco has been an independent principality under the ruling Grimaldi dynasty since 1338, but, by a treaty of 1918, it will become a French territory if the dynasty ever becomes extinct.

# MONTENEGRINS

The people of the Republic of Montenegro, which together with Serbia forms what remains of the southeastern European nation of Yugoslavia. The Montenegrins are SERBS, but they are developing a separate national identity of their own.

Montenegro originated in the 11th century as the Serbian province of Duklja. When the medieval Serbian kingdom was conquered by the OTTOMANS in the 14th century, Montenegro (in Serbo-Croat, Crna Gora), although claimed by the Ottomans, remained autonomous under the rule of the *vladike*, the popularly elected Orthodox Christian prince-bishops.

Montenegro became a secular principality under the Petrovic dynasty in 1851 and a fully independent kingdom in 1910. Through these years Montenegrins continued to think of themselves as Serbs and aspired to recreate the medieval Serbian state. In 1918 the Montenegrin assembly deposed the Petrovic dynasty and voted to join the newly established Kingdom of the Serbs, Croats and Slovenes (Yugoslavia from 1929). Support for this union was not universal, and in the 1920s and 1930s Montenegrins were split into Whites, who favoured complete integration with the rest of the Serb people, and Greens, who wanted Yugoslavia to be re-organized on federal lines, as was finally realized by the postwar communist government.

The emergence of militant Serb nationalism under Slobodan Milosevic in the 1980s began what may become a permanent alienation of Montenegrins from their fellow Serbs. One of the first manifestations of this was a demand for the restoration of an autonomous Montenegrin Orthodox Church. Montenegro did not join Slovenia, Croatia, Bosnia and Macedonia in declaring independence from Yugoslavia 1991–2. However, as Milosevic's support for Serbian separatists in Croatia and Bosnia turned Yugoslavia into a pariah state, Montenegrins began to distance themselves from Serbia. This process has intensified since the 1999 NATO invasion of Kosovo.

Milosevic opposed any loosening of ties between Serbia and Montenegro, but his overthrow in 2000 opened the way for negotiations on the future of Montenegro. In 2001 Montenegrins voted to remain a part of Yugoslavia but with substantially increased autonomy. In 2000 the population of Montenegro was estimated to be around 680,000.

# MORAVIANS

A CZECH-speaking people who comprise around 14% of the population of the Czech Republic. They are descended from SLAVS who settled in Moravia in the early Middle Ages. The Moravians and Moravia both take their name from the River Morava, which flows through the region.

In the 9th century the Principality of Great Moravia was briefly a major power in central Europe until it was destroyed by Frankish (see FRANKS) and Magyar (see HUNGARIANS) attacks in 905–8. Since that time Moravia has always been a part of other states and the Moravian identity has been submerged. Today the Moravians are usually counted among the CZECHS. Many Moravians, however, consider that they are a distinct nationality, and Moravian separatist parties have achieved some electoral success since Czechoslovakia split into the Czech Republic and Slovakia in 1992.

## MORDVINS or Mordvinians

A FINNO-UGRIAN people who speak a Finnic language (see FINNS). They live mainly in the Mordovian autonomous republic and other parts of the middle Volga River region in Russia and are the most southerly of the Finnic peoples. Their name is thought to mean simply 'men'. The Mordvins have been recognized by outsiders as a separate people since at least the 6th century AD, but they have never developed a common identity for themselves. The Mordvins perceive themselves as two peoples, the ERZYA and MOKSHA, distinguished from one another by dialect and physical appearance (the Moksha are supposedly darker-skinned). A third group, the Teryukhan of Gorkiy, have lost their separate identity and now regard themselves as RUSSIANS.

The Mordvins were nominally converted to Orthodox Christianity in the Middle Ages, but pagan practices and beliefs survived into the 20th century. They have an extensive collection of traditional songs and poems, written using the Cyrillic alphabet, and much of it was concerned with national heroes, such as King Tushtyan, who was an ally of Ivan the Terrible. In the late 20th century there were around 740,000 Mordvins, about half of whom live in Mordovia, where they constitute 35% of the population.

## MORISCOS

Spanish Muslims who were forcibly converted to Christianity after the conquest of the Moorish Emirate of Granada by Castile and Aragon in 1492. Through the years of the Christian *reconquista* (12th–15th centuries), defeated MOORS were usually guaranteed freedom of religious worship, and substantial Muslim communities remained in Valencia and Aragon as well as in Granada. After a rebellion in 1502 the Muslims of Granada were required to accept baptism or to go into exile; the same requirement was imposed on the Muslims of Valencia and Aragon in 1526. Most chose to be baptised, but they retained their Arabic language and Muslim customs and continued to practise Islam in secret.

The Moriscos ('Little Moors') maintained covert contacts with Muslims in North Africa, which made their loyalty suspect in the eyes of the Spanish Crown. In 1566 Philip II forbade the Moriscos to speak Arabic, wear their traditional dress or practise any Muslim customs. After they rebelled in 1569–71, the Moriscos were dispersed throughout Spain, but they resisted assimilation with the established Christian population, prompting Philip III to order their expulsion in 1609. In all, around 300,000 Moriscos were expelled to Tunisia, Algeria and Morocco. Treated as outsiders at first, they were assimilated into the local populations within a few generations.

## MOUSTERIAN CULTURE

A Middle Palaeolithic tool culture of Europe, parts of western Asia and North Africa dating to between 150,000 and 40,000 years ago. The culture is named after a rock shelter at Le Moustier in the Dordogne Valley in France, where it was first identified in the 19th century. In Europe the culture is associated with the NEANDERTHALS (*Homo sapiens neanderthalensis*). The Mousterian culture is characterized by its distinctive stone tools, which were made from carefully prepared disc-shaped cores. Typical tools included hand-axes, flake tools and the earliest stone spear-heads, which were used for hunting large game. In Europe, the Mousterian was succeeded by the CHÂTELPERRONIAN CULTURE.

## MOZARABS

Christians who did not convert to Islam after the MOORS conquered most of Spain in the 8th century. The Mozarabs tried to preserve their Latin culture but became partially assimilated to Moorish language and culture. Mozarabic art is distinguishable from Arabic art only by its Christian content, and Ajami, the Mozarabic language, retained a Latin grammatical structure and pronunciation but had a vocabulary that was much influenced by Arabic.

Mozarabs were most numerous in Toledo, Seville and Córdoba where they formed self-governing communities that used the Visigothic law-code. The Mozarabs maintained their own Church and monasteries and translated the Bible into Arabic. In the 11th century Mozarabs suffered persecution, but at other times were tolerated, although with the usual financial disadvantages imposed on Christians in Muslim countries.

As the Christian reconquest of Spain gathered pace in the 12th and 13th centuries, Mozarabs were re-absorbed into Christian Spain. The Mozarabic rite, which is still practised in Toledo, is the most important surviving element of their culture.

# MYCENAEANS

A GREEK-speaking people, who migrated into Greece from the Balkans around 2000 BC. The Mycenaeans are named after the stronghold of Mycenae in the Peloponnese, which was excavated by Heinrich Schliemann in 1876. It is not known for certain what the Mycenaeans called themselves but it may have been ACHAEANS, Homer's name for the Greeks in his tales of the Trojan wars.

By around 1600 BC the Mycenaeans lived in a number of small kingdoms based on fortified towns. They had also adopted a system of writing known as Linear B, based on Linear A, a MINOAN syllabic script from Crete. Unlike its Cretan prototype, Linear B, which was used mainly for keeping accounts on clay tablets, has been translated.

Each Mycenaean state was ruled by a king with the support of a warrior aristocracy. The wealth of this ruling elite is made plain by a series of richly furnished shaft-graves at Mycenae, dating to between 1650 and 1550 BC, which contained bronze weapons and armour, gold and silver jewellery and tableware, and gold deathmasks. The craftsmen who produced these spectacular display objects worked under the control of the kings. The king of Pylos, for example, employed 400 bronzesmiths. The kings also owned hundreds of mainly female slaves.

According to traditions handed down to Homer, all the Mycenaean kingdoms theoreti-cally acknowledged the leadership of Mycenae. In Homer's *Iliad*, it was Agamemnon, King of Mycenae, who led the Greeks during the semi-legendary Trojan War.

Mycenaean cities were strongly fortified with walls built of massive stone blocks and bastioned gateways. After 1500 BC Mycenaean rulers were buried in stone vaulted *tholos* ('beehive') tombs, in which kingship rituals could be performed. The Mycenaeans already worshipped many of the gods familiar in Classical Greek mythology, including Zeus, Apollo, Athene and Poseidon.

**Forging an empire**

Around 1450 BC the Mycenaeans began a period of expansion, conquering the Minoans of Crete and founding settlements on the Aegean coast of Asia Minor and in Cyprus. They probably also launched plundering raids on the HITTITE empire and against Egypt. If there is a historical basis to the Trojan War, it probably dates to this period.

The Mycenaeans were accomplished seafarers who had trade links all around the eastern Mediterranean and as far west as Italy, Sicily and Malta. The Mycenaean civilization came to a sudden and violent end around 1200 BC. Most of the Mycenaean towns were sacked and abandoned, and writing fell out of use, plunging Greece into a 'dark age' that lasted for 400 years. The identity of the attackers is unknown, it may have been the mysterious SEA PEOPLES, who attacked Egypt and the Levant around this time, or the DORIANS, another Greek-speaking people who were settled in Greece by 1100 BC.

# NAVARRESE

The people of the autonomous Spanish region of Navarra, centred on Pamplona. They have a distinct communal identity, which developed in the Middle Ages.

The medieval Kingdom of Navarre developed in the 9th century and was briefly, under Sancho III (ruled 1000–35), the most powerful of Spain's Christian kingdoms. After Sancho's death Navarre declined, and it was eventually annexed to Castile in 1515. Navarre retained its own coinage, excise duties and legislature until 1841. The region still retains its own law-code, which not even the 20th-century dictatorship of Francisco Franco attempted to suppress. This remains a source of pride and a symbol of Navarrese identity.

Medieval Navarre had a mixed population of BASQUE-speakers in the north and Navarrese-speakers in the south. Navarrese is a Romance language similar to CASTILIAN Spanish, which is now spoken by all the population.

Church attendance is high and Navarre is a stronghold of the conservative Roman Catholic *Opus Dei* movement.

## NEANDERTHALS or Homo Sapiens Neanderthalensis

An extinct human species of Europe and the Middle East. The Neanderthals are named after the Neander Valley in Germany where their remains were first recognized in 1856.

The Neanderthals evolved around 200,000 years ago, probably from an earlier human species called *Homo heidelbergensis*. Slightly shorter than modern humans, the Neanderthals were stout and exceptionally robust. They had long low skulls with a prominent brow ridge and slightly larger brains than modern humans. Neanderthals had large bulbous noses, which would have been emphasized by their prognathous (jutting) faces and weak chins. It is thought that the large nose was an adaptation to the cold climate of Ice Age Europe as it would help warm air before it reached the lungs. Another possible adaptation to cold are the short distal segments of their forearms and lower legs, which are also found in modern humans such as the INUIT who live in very cold climates. This is known to help reduce heat loss from the extremities. Neanderthals inhabited caves and rock shelters when they could, but also inhabited open air sites and may have built shelters of mammoth bones.

Neanderthals are closely associated with the MOUSTERIAN stone-tool industry, which had a distinctive tool culture based on pre-prepared cores. They also made tools of bone, ivory and wood. There is evidence, much of it controversial, that the Neanderthals buried their dead and so may have had some kind of religious belief. It is not generally believed that the Neanderthals

had the same capacity for speech and language as modern humans.

Around 90,000 years ago modern humans (*Homo sapiens sapiens*) had moved into the Middle East, and then into Europe around 40,000 years ago. Modern humans and Neanderthals coexisted for over 10,000 years before the latter disappeared between 30,000 and 28,000 years ago. Their last strongholds were in the Balkans and Spain. Neanderthals appear to have adopted some tool-making techniques and body ornaments through contacts with modern humans (see CHÂTELPERRONIAN CULTURE).

The cause of the Neanderthals' extinction is uncertain. They may simply have been less efficient hunters and had less supportive social networks than modern humans and so would gradually have been forced into less favourable environments. They may even have been deliberately exterminated by modern humans.

Alternatively, some anthropologists believe that the Neanderthals may have been absorbed into the modern human population through inter-breeding. Advocates of this view cite the 24,000-year-old skeleton of boy from a cave in Lagar Velho in Portugal, which appears to have both modern and Neanderthal features. On the other hand, analysis of Neanderthal DNA suggests that they were not ancestral to modern Europeans.

## NOGAIS

A Caucasian people of north Dagestan and Stavropol, Russian Federation. Descended from the TATARS, they broke away from the GOLDEN HORDE and adopted Sunni Islam in the 14th century. Traditionally they were nomadic herders and speak a Turkic language (see TURKS).

In the 16th century the Nogais came under pressure from the RUSSIANS and Crimean Tatars. Those who came under Russian rule tended to become assimilated, settled farmers. Those who did not remained nomadic longer, and proved rebellious when Russia annexed their territory in the 19th century. Soviet collectivization undermined their traditional culture, but their identity as a people survived, despite their dispersal across several administrative units. In 2000 the Nogais were estimated to number between

73,000 and 86,000, with the higher figure the more likely.

## NORI

A Celtic people (see CELTS, ANCIENT) who lived in present-day eastern Austria. Originally a confederation of tribes, the Nori were united to form the kingdom of Noricum around 200 BC. The kingdom prospered from its control of trade routes across the Alpine passes, and it also exported iron and steel to the ROMAN empire. The royal centre of Noricum was the mountain-top stronghold of Virunum near Zollfeld. In 186 BC Noricum became an ally of the Roman empire. Through their trade and political contacts with the empire, the Nori became highly Romanized; there was no resistance when their kingdom was annexed by Rome around 15 BC.

## NORMANS

The Normans were a French-speaking people from Normandy, northern France. Their name comes from *Nordmanni* (Northmen), as the VIKINGS were usually known in continental Europe. Vikings, most of them of Danish origin, settled in the lower Seine River valley in the late 9th century. In 911 their leader, Rollo, made a peace treaty with the king of the FRANKS Charles the Simple. In return for homage, conversion to Christianity and agreement to defend the Seine against other Vikings, Charles appointed Rollo Count of Rouen. Rollo added Bayeux to his possessions in 924 and his son William Longsword gained the Cotentin peninsula in 933. In 1006 Longsword's grandson Richard II adopted the title 'Duke of Normandy' (from *Nordmannia*, 'Northmen's land').

Place-name evidence suggests that Viking settlement was fairly dense around Rouen, Caen, Fécamp and the Cotentin, but elsewhere in Normandy is was very sparse. The Vikings were certainly a minority in Normandy as a whole, and in the long term they had very little influence on its cultural development. Few Viking artefacts have been discovered in Normandy, suggesting that the settlers quickly adopted the material culture of their FRENCH subjects. Most settlers had accepted Christianity by the mid-

10th century and had become French-speaking by the early 11th century. Long before William the Conqueror invaded England in 1066, the Normans had become culturally and linguistically French, even though they identified more strongly with Normandy rather than with the Kingdom of France as a whole. One sign of this regional distinctiveness was the Norman variant of the Romanesque architectural style.

**Imperial ambitions**

The Norman nobility practised a system of strict primogeniture. This contributed to a period of Norman expansionism that lasted for about a hundred years, from roughly the mid-11th century to the mid-12th century. The younger sons of the nobility were given a good training in war but had no prospect of inheriting land and often sought service with other lords both in France and abroad. From the 1050s many Normans were recruited by the LOMBARD duchies of southern Italy to fight in their wars against the BYZANTINE empire. One of these Normans, Robert Guiscard, established himself as an independent ruler in Puglia (Apulia) and Calabria in 1059, and by 1076 he was master of southern Italy. His brother Roger I conquered Sicily from the ARABS in 1060–71. After Robert died in 1081, invading the Byzantine empire, Roger united Sicily and southern Italy into a single state that became the Kingdom of Sicily in 1139.

Normans played a prominent role in the early Crusades: the Crusader principalities of Antioch and Edessa were both founded by Norman lords. The most important of the Norman conquest was, however, England. As a result of it England became a feudal kingdom and ENGLISH culture and language were exposed to powerful French influences. England's high culture remained essentially French until the late 14th century. After the conquest of England, Norman lords conquered much of Wales, and in the 12th century they entered the service of Scottish and Irish kings. (See also ANGLO-NORMANS.)

The Norman conquest did not result in a permanent extension of the Norman identity. The Crusader principalities were reconquered by the Muslims in the 12th and 13th centuries. The Kingdom of Sicily came under German rule in the late 12th century, by which time the Nor-

> **"** They are a most astute people, eager to avenge injuries, looking rather to enrich themselves from others than by their native fields. They are eager and greedy for profit and power, hypercritical and deceitful about almost everything. **"**
>
> Geoffrey Malaterra *c.* 1090 (translation Elizabeth van Houts, *The Normans in Europe*)

mans were largely assimilated with the native population. The Norman dynasty in England came to an end in 1154 (to be replaced by the French Angevin dynasty), but as early as 1100 the Normans there had begun to identify themselves with the kingdom they had conquered. The final breach occurred in 1204, when Normandy was conquered by the French king Philip Augustus, breaking the link between the duchy and England that had been created by William the Conqueror. Normandy kept its own laws and provincial assembly (*Etats*) until the 17th century, but was thereafter fully absorbed into the increasingly centralized French state. In 1790 Normandy was divided into five *départments*, but collective consciousness of the region's historical identity remains strong today.

## NORSE or Norsemen

A name used to describe SCANDINAVIANS, and in particular the NORWEGIANS, of the VIKING era and the Middle Ages.

## NORTHUMBRIANS

The people of the ANGLO-SAXON Kingdom of Northumbria in England. At its peak under kings Edwin (ruled 633–41) and Oswy (ruled 641–70) Northumbria encompassed most of Britain between the River Humber in the south and the Firth of Forth in the north. The kingdom's main centres were at Bamburgh in Northumberland and at York. The kingdom developed around 600 from the union between two smaller kingdoms, Bernicia (approximately modern Lothian, Northumberland and County Durham) and Deira (Yorkshire).

In traditional accounts, the Northumbrians are described as ANGLES, but it is likely that the majority of them were actually the descendants of conquered BRITONS who had been assimilated to the language and culture of an Anglo-Saxon military elite. This is especially likely to have been true in Bernicia, where the evidence of pagan Anglo-Saxon settlement is very limited.

The Northumbrians were converted to Celtic Christianity in the 630s, but they had accepted the authority of the Roman Catholic Church before the end of the century. Early Christian

Northumbria developed an outstanding monastic culture. Its greatest achievements are the illuminated *Lindisfarne Gospels* and the works of the Venerable Bede. Bede's *Ecclesiastical History of the English People*, written around 731, played a significant role in the development of the ENGLISH identity.

Northumbrian power declined in the 8th century, and in 866 the DANES conquered and settled Deira, founding a kingdom at York and introducing distinctive Scandinavian legal customs. Bernicia remained independent until annexed by Wessex in 927. The conquest of the Kingdom of York in 954 completed the unification of England under the WEST SAXON dynasty. However, the Northumbrians retained a distinct identity until after the NORMAN conquest. The Northumbrian dialect of Old English formed the basis of the modern English dialects of northern England and Scotland.

## NORWEGIANS

A SCANDINAVIAN people who inhabit the Kingdom of Norway. The country is named for the 'North Way', an allusion to the sheltered sea route to the north through the Skerry Guard, a chain of coastal islands and reefs. The sea has always played an important role in Norwegian history. Norway's mountains made overland travel difficult and it was always quicker to sail across the long coastal fjords than to walk around them. This fostered an adventurous seafaring tradition and shipbuilding skills that in the VIKING Age allowed Norwegians to sail to Britain and Ireland, the Faeroe Islands, Iceland, Greenland and even Newfoundland. It also allowed Norway to develop the third-largest merchant fleet in the world in the 19th century.

Most of Norway is too high, wet and cold to support agriculture, and the shortage of good land was a factor in two periods of large-scale emigration from Norway. The first was during the Viking era, to Britain and Ireland, the Faeroe Islands and Iceland; the second was in the 19th century to the USA. Around 850,000 Norwegians emigrated in 1835–1935, a greater number proportionate to its population than any European country except Ireland. If Norway's land has been poor, the seas have been a source of wealth. Fishing was already a major industry in the Middle Ages, whaling was important in the 19th and 20th centuries, and in the last 30 years North Sea oil and gas have helped give Norwegians the highest living standards in Europe. The difficult terrain delayed the political unification of the Norwegians and has allowed them to retain a greater degree of regional identity than the other Scandinavian countries. Norway's regions traditionally have different outlooks. The southeast, centred on the capital Oslo, looks to Denmark, Sweden and the Baltic, while the west coast districts around Bergen and Trondheim have an Atlantic outlook. Because of its extensive maritime links, Bergen has always been a more cosmopolitan city than Oslo.

### Emergence of a nation state

When Viking pirates first began to raid western Europe around 800, the people of Norway were not distinguishable from other Scandinavians. The Anglo-Saxons, for example called all Scandinavians DANES, even when they knew that they came from Norway. Norwegians spoke several regional dialects of the common Old Scandinavian language, which was also spoken by the Danes and SWEDES: it was only during the Middle Ages that Norwegian emerged as a distinct language. The process of uniting the Norwegians into a single kingdom was begun by King Harald Fairhair around 900, but it was over 200 years before his achievement was secure. The first attempts to convert the Norwegians to Christianity were made in the 10th century, but paganism remained strong until the 11th century and even then was only eradicated by violent coercion by the Crown. In the 13th century Norway dominated the North Atlantic: Iceland, Greenland, the Faeroe, Shetland and Orkney Islands and the Isle of Man all acknowledged the overlordship of the Norwegian king.

Norway's power began to decline in the 14th century, and the Black Death ravaged its population. In 1380 Norway lost its independence through a dynastic union with Denmark. In 1536 the Danes imposed Lutheranism on the Norwegians and Danish became the main language of the church and government. In 1814 the Norwegians declared their independence, but Denmark had ceded Norway to Sweden as part of the peace settlement at the end of the Napoleonic Wars. The Swedes invaded and ended Norway's brief independence.

The Swedes ruled with a light hand, but although Norwegians enjoyed complete internal autonomy, the union was always unpopular. A rising tide of nationalist sentiment led the Norwegian Parliament to dissolve the union with Sweden in 1905. Language became an important issue in the years leading up to independence. Several regional dialects still survived, and the language of the southeast had become much influenced by Danish. Nationalist reformers sought to establish a standard Norwegian. One solution was an adaptation of Danish to the spoken Norwegian dialect of the southeast. This became known as Riksmål ('official' Norwegian) or Bokmål ('book' Norwegian). An alternative solution was a synthesis of west-coast dialects called Landsmål ('country' Norwegian) or Nynorsk (New Norwegian). Both languages were given official status in 1885, but Bokmål became the main language. Nynorsk is now the language of instruction in only about 15% of Norwegian schools.

During their years of political dominance the Swedes, and before them the Danes, developed a somewhat patronizing attitude to the Norwegians, which has not entirely died out even today. The experience of foreign rule has bred in Norwegians an assertive patriotism, marked by the adoption of high moral stances in international affairs and an unwillingness to accept criticism of their own conduct, such as their illegal resumption of commercial whaling in 1993.

Norway remained neutral in World War I, but it was invaded and occupied by Germany during World War II. The courage and daring of the Norwegian resistance during the occupation won the admiration of the free world and remains a source of considerable national pride. Since the war, Norwegian society has developed on much the same lines as the other Scandinavian countries into an advanced welfare state with high standards of education, health care and social security. Norway remains outside the European Union, and the majority of Norwegians are sceptical about the benefits of joining. Modern Norway has a very homogeneous population, which was around 4.34 million in 1996.

The only indigenous ethnic minority is the SAAMI (around 40,000) who live in the far north.

## ORCADIANS AND SHETLANDERS

The people of the Orkney and Shetland Islands to the north of Scotland. Although they are Scottish, they form distinct communities, which, for much of their history, have been more closely associated with Scandinavia than with the British Isles. The islands were settled in prehistory but the earliest historically known inhabitants of both archipelagos were PICTS, a Celtic people (see CELTS, ANCIENT). During the 9th century the islands were conquered and settled by VIKINGS from Norway, and they remained under SCANDINAVIAN rule for the next 600 years. The native Picts may have been largely wiped out by the invaders. Recent research into DNA indicates that the majority of the islands' populations are of NORWEGIAN origin. By the end of the 9th century the Orkney Islands were an independent earldom, while the Shetland islands were probably nominally part of the Kingdom of Norway. Norway asserted its sovereignty over Orkney at the end of the 11th century.

Both Orkney and Shetland came under Danish rule in 1380 until they were ceded to Scotland in 1469 in lieu of a dowry when Princess Margaret married King James III. The union with Scotland opened the islands to English-language influence, and the local Scandinavian dialect, called Norn, went into decline, dying out in Orkney in the 18th century and about a century later in Shetland. Many Norn words survive in the local English dialect however. Coming so late to Scotland, the Orcadians and Shetlanders played no part in the wars of independence against England, and the islanders are, at most, semi-detached SCOTS. Visitors to the islands may still be asked if they have come from 'Scotland'. In the 1990s islanders made a tongue-in-cheek request to the Danish government to resume sovereignty. Links with Scandinavia are strongest in Shetland, which has close maritime links with Norway and the Faeroe Islands. Lutheranism, the state religion of the Scandinavian countries, is strong in Shet-

land. The folklore and festivals of both archipelagos have a distinctly Nordic flavour, but the most famous of the islands' festivals, Up Helly Aa (a mid-winter fire festival that culminates in the burning of a replica Viking longship) is, for all its convincing Viking colour, a modern invention that dates back only a hundred years.

## ORDOVICES

Ancient BRITONS who inhabited present-day north Wales. Their name is thought to mean 'hammer warriors'. The Ordovices put up stiff resistance to the ROMANS for nearly 20 years until they were finally pacified by Agricola in AD 78. The Ordovices remained under military rule for the entire period of the Roman occupation of Britain. Then, in the early 5th century, the Ordovices came under attack by IRISH pirates who began to settle in the Lleyn peninsula. According to traditional accounts, the hardpressed Ordovices accepted Cunedda, a prince of the Gododdin (see VOTADINI), as their king. Under his leadership, they repelled the Irish invaders. The territory of the Ordovices formed the nucleus of the Kingdom of Gwynedd, which became the most powerful WELSH kingdom in the Middle Ages. However, the royal house of Gwynedd claimed descent from Cunedda rather than any local figure.

## OSCANS

See SABELLI.

## OSSETIANS or Ossetes

A people of the central Caucasus Mountains. They are descendants of the ALANS, an Indo-Iranian nomadic people, and speak an IRANIAN language. There are approximately 600,000 Ossetians, divided between the Russian Federation and Georgia. The largest concentration (335,000) is in the North Ossetia-Alania autonomous republic of Russia, where they constitute 53% of the total population. Around 230,000 Ossetians live in Georgia, and around 65,000 of them live in the South Ossetia region, where they form 66% of the total population. The dialect of the South Ossetians has been

heavily influenced by Georgian. The North Ossetians are divided into two dialect groups, the
Irons and the Digors.

The Ossetians were converted to Orthodox
Christianity in the 6th century, and this remains
the main religion, although some Digors are
Muslims. During the Soviet period South Ossetia had the status of an autonomous republic.
After Georgia became independent in 1990,
South Ossetians, fearing the impact of an
increasingly chauvinistic GEORGIAN nationalism,
declared an independent republic. The Georgian
government responded by formally revoking
South Ossetia's autonomy in 1991, which provoked a civil war with Ossetian separatists who
demanded union with North Ossetia-Alania.
Despite a ceasefire in 1992, the region's future
status has not yet been settled and it remains
outside the control of the Georgian government.

## OSTROGOTHS

A Germanic people who emerged, along with
the VISIGOTHS, from the break-up of the GOTHS in
the late 3rd century AD. The Ostrogoths ('East
Goths') settled on the River Dnieper and in the
4th century expanded east across the Ukraine as
far as the Don. During this period, the Ostrogoths were converted to the Arian sect of
Christianity by Ulfilas, who translated the Bible
into Gothic and devised a Gothic alphabet. In
370 the Ostrogoths were defeated and conquered by the nomadic HUNS; their king,
Ermanaric, committed suicide. After the collapse
of the Hunnish empire in 454 the Ostrogoths
moved west, crossing the Danube and settling in
present-day western Hungary and Serbia, where
they were reluctantly recognized as 'federates'
(allies) by the Eastern ROMAN empire.

In 489 the Eastern emperor commissioned
the Ostrogothic king Theodoric to invade Italy
and overthrow Odoacer, the Germanic merce-
nary who had ruled it since 476. By 483 Odoacer
was dead and Italy was theoretically under
Ostrogothic control; Theodoric (ruled 493–526)
governed it as a representative of the Eastern
emperor. The Ostrogoths were conscious of their
position as a minority among the native Italian
population. To resist integration, Theodoric
introduced a system of segregation. The native

Catholic Italians continued to live under ROMAN
law, while the Ostrogoths had their own parallel
Arian church and Germanic legal system. This
ensured that the Ostrogoths maintained their
separate identity, but it also prevented their subjects from developing a sense of loyalty toward
them. When the Eastern Roman emperor Justinian sent an army to take control of Italy in 536,
the Ostrogoths got little support from the local
population. Despite this, it was 17 years before
the last Ostrogothic resistance, north of the River
Po, was ended. The war had been extremely
destructive to Italy, and the Ostrogoths had suffered very heavy casualties and dispersal. Some
of the survivors went into exile in other Germanic kingdoms, while those who remained in
Italy were ultimately assimilated into the native
population.

## PAEONIANS

A people of mixed THRACIAN and ILLYRIAN origin
who inhabited the Vardar River valley and surrounding areas of present-day Greece,
Macedonia and western Bulgaria. They were
weakened by a Persian invasion in 490 BC, and
those living along the River Strymon (in western
Bulgaria) were conquered by the Thracians. The
Paeonians lost territory in 358 BC after they were
defeated by Philip II of Macedonia. The 3rd century Paeonian king Audoleon was important
enough to be given ATHENIAN citizenship and to
marry his daughter to King Pyrrhus of Epirus,
but the Paeonian kingdom lost more territory to
the MACEDONIANS in 219 BC. In the 180s and
170s BC the Macedonian king deported and dispersed much of the population of Paeonia,
replacing the natives with Thracians. Paeonia
was conquered by the ROMANS in 168 BC, and
the Paeonians subsequently lost their identity.

## PAINTED WARE CULTURES

The earliest farming cultures of Greece and the
Balkans (*c.* 7000–6000 BC), introduced from
Anatolia. The cultures are named for their
painted pottery and figurines. The people of the
Painted Ware cultures practised a mixed-farming
way of life, very similar to that of the contemporary Middle East. They bred cattle, pigs, sheep

and goats, and their main crops were barley, wheat, peas and lentils. They also gathered many wild plants and used mud bricks for building. Some houses had painted walls. As settlements remained on the same sites for centuries, domestic refuse and debris from old houses built up into mounds or 'tells', as happened across the Middle East.

## PARISI

Ancient BRITONS of East Yorkshire. Their main settlement was at Petuaria (today, Brough on Humber). The Parisi are associated with the Iron Age Arras culture, which is noted for its aristocratic chariot burials. These have close parallels with burial practices in northern Gaul and raise the possibility of some connection between the Parisi and the PARISII of the Seine Valley.

## PARISII

A tribe of GAULS who lived in the Seine River valley. Their main settlement was at Lutetia, now named after them as Paris.

## PECHENEGS or Patzinaks

A nomadic Turkic people (see TURKS) of Central Asian origin. The Pechenegs migrated onto the steppes of southern Russia and the Ukraine, defeating the BULGARS, MAGYARS and KHAZARS who occupied the area. The Pechenegs frequently attacked RUS traders travelling along the Don and Volga rivers and raided the BYZANTINE empire, earning a fearsome reputation for cruelty. Pecheneg power declined after they were defeated by the BYZANTINE emperor Alexius Comnenus in 1091. Soon afterwards they were conquered by another nomadic Turkic people, the CUMANS, and lost their identity as a people.

## PEUCINI

See BASTARNAE.

## PICTONES or Pictavi

An Iron Age tribe of GAULS who lived to the south of the lower reaches of the River Loire.

Their name survives in Poitiers, which was formerly known as Lemonum.

## PICTS

A Celtic people (see CELTS) who inhabited Britain north of the Forth-Clyde isthmus in the late Roman period and early Middle Ages. The earliest record of the Picts dates to AD 297, but they were descendants of the CALEDONIAN tribes who had inhabited the same area in the Iron Age. During the 4th century AD, the Picts frequently raided ROMAN Britain by both land and sea. After the end of Roman rule in 410, fear of the Picts led the BRITONS to recruit ANGLO-SAXON mercenaries to defend them.

The name of the Picts, which means 'painted people', is thought to have originated as a nickname among the Roman frontier garrisons, possibly because they painted or tattooed their bodies. The Picts were known to the BRITONS as *Prydyn* and to the IRISH as *Cruithin*, both names derived from the same Celtic word for Britain. Records of the Pictish language are limited mainly to place and personal names, but it is clear that they spoke a dialect of the Brithonic language spoken by the Britons. A few Pictish words that have defied translation may be survivors from a time before the development or introduction of Celtic languages.

Little is known about the Pictish religion, but like other pagan Celts the Picts are known to have practised human sacrifice. They are perhaps best known for their enigmatic sculpted symbol stones. The meanings of the symbols, which include a variety of animals, objects and abstract patterns, are unknown but they are not believed to be religious, as they continued in use after the Picts were converted to Christianity by British and Irish missionaries between the 5th and early 7th centuries. The Christian Picts used both the Latin and Irish ogham alphabets.

The Picts were divided into several small kingdoms or chiefdoms, but by the 7th century they recognized the kings of Fortriu (roughly modern Perthshire) as high kings of Pictavia ('Pictland').

The Picts lost Argyll to the SCOTS of the kingdom of Dál Riata (Dalriada) in northern Ireland around 500 but defeated an attempt by the

> ❝ The Picts were little more than pygmies in stature. They worked marvels in the morning and evening building towns, but at midday they completely lost their strength and lurked through fear in tiny underground houses. ❞
>
> Anonymous 12th-century writer

Anglo-Saxon NORTHUMBRIANS to conquer them at the battle of Nechtansmere in 685. Scottish influence on the Picts began to increase in the 8th century, and several of Pictish kings had Scottish origins. The Picts were weakened by VIKING raids in the early 9th century, giving the Scottish king Kenneth MacAlpin the opportunity to conquer them outright in 843. The use of Pictish symbols died out soon afterwards, and neither the Picts' language nor their separate identity survived long after around 900, when they were mentioned in contemporary documents for the last time. Later medieval writers spread the story, disproved by archaeological evidence, that the Picts were a race of pygmies who had lived underground.

## PIEDMONTESE

ITALIANS from the region of Piedmont (meaning 'foot of the hill') in northeast Italy, centred on the city of Turin and bordered in the east and north by the Alps. The Piedmontese feel a certain distinction in the leading role they played in the 19th century in the unification of Italy, but are not otherwise highly conscious of being different from other Italians.

During the Middle Ages Piedmont was part of the Duchy of Savoy, which straddled the Alps and was ruled by a French-speaking dynasty. Throughout the 16th, 17th and 18th centuries Savoy's independence was threatened by neighbouring France, but it retained a precarious independence. After occupation by France during the Napoleonic Wars, Savoy was united to the Kingdom of Sardinia. Because of Piedmont's dominant political and economic position, the new kingdom is usually described as Piedmont-Sardinia. The Piedmontese elite in this period was mainly French-speaking, while the majority spoke a distinctive dialect of Italian.

The Piedmontese developed a taste for radical politics, and exiles from other parts of Italy were welcomed. Piedmont-Sardinia fought a war (1848–9) to drive the AUSTRIANS out of Italy but was defeated. In 1858 Camillo di Cavour, Prime Minister of Piedmont, secured FRENCH help, and in 1859 the Austrians were finally driven out. Lombardy, Tuscany, Modena, Parma and most of the Papal States were annexed by Piedmont-Sardinia. In 1860 Giuseppe Garibaldi led an expedition of Piedmontese volunteers to overthrow the Bourbon Kingdom of Naples and then handed it over to Piedmont-Sardinia. The following year the Kingdom of Italy was proclaimed under the Piedmontese king Victor Emmanuel II.

After unification, the Piedmontese elite quickly adopted Italian as their language, but it is only since World War II that 'standard' Italian has become the language of the majority, mainly through the influence of radio and television.

The Piedmontese are nominally Roman Catholics but attendance at Mass is much lower than in most of Italy. Important minorities in Piedmont are the VALDAOSTANS and WALDENSIANS.

## POLABIANS

SLAVS who settled around the River Trave on Germany's Baltic Sea coast in the 5th or 6th century AD. Contemporaries counted them as belonging the WENDS. By the 10th century they had formed a confederation with their neighbours the WAGRIANS and ABODRITES under a single dynasty.

The chief town of the Polabians was Ratzeburg. The Polabians were conquered by the GERMANS in 1140–3 and were subsequently converted to Christianity and assimilated into German culture.

## POLJANI

An early SLAV people who lived on the lower Dnieper River in modern Ukraine. Their main settlement was at Kiev. The Poljani were conquered by the RUS in AD 840.

## POLES

The people of the Republic of Poland, and the most numerous of the West SLAV peoples. Their name is derived from the Polanie, an early Slavic tribe whose name meant 'people of the fields'. The area of Polish settlement has been in almost constant flux for the last thousand years, as the Poles have been buffeted by the greater powers that have generally surrounded them. Their struggle to survive as a nation has given them an assertive patriotism and a lingering hostility

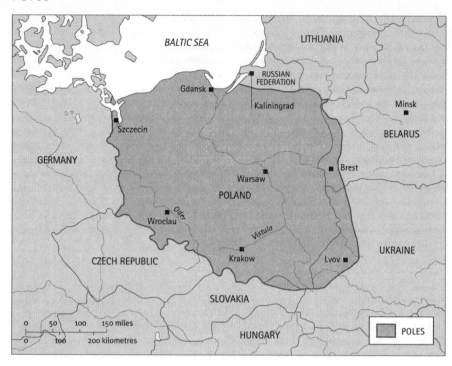

towards their one-time oppressors, the RUSSIANS and GERMANS.

The Poles emerged with the conversion to Catholic Christianity of the Polanian prince Mieszko I in 966. Mieszko's Principality of Poland was slightly smaller than modern Poland and lay entirely within its present borders. The Piast dynasty founded by Mieszko struggled to assert itself against the powerful nobility and was constantly threatened by German expansionism. The dynasty died out in 1370, and in 1386 Poland was united with Lithuania when its grand duke Jagiello married a Polish princess. Under the Jagiellonian dynasty, Poland expanded its territory into Belarus and Ukraine. Many Poles migrated east, some to form a landowning elite, others to found new peasant settlements. After the Jagiellonian dynasty died out in 1572, the Polish state was re-organized around an elective monarchy and a *sejm* (parliament) in which every noble had a vote. The rights of the nobility were paid for by the peasantry, who were reduced to serfdom. Religious toleration was officially practised, one result of

which was to attract large numbers of Jewish immigrants. Poland's days as a great European power came to an end in the second half of the 17th century, when it suffered repeated defeats at the hands of the Russians, COSSACKS and SWEDES. Finally, in partitions in 1772, 1775 and 1795, Poland was carved up between the Russians, PRUSSIANS and AUSTRIANS and disappeared from the map of Europe as a state. A new democratic constitution introduced in 1791, which ended serfdom, came too late to save the country.

A Polish state briefly re-emerged in 1807, when Napoleon created the Grand Duchy of Warsaw, but the partition of 1795 was restored by the Congress of Vienna in 1815. The circumstances of the Poles varied depending on which sector of Poland they inhabited. Those who lived in the Austrian sector fared best, enjoying considerable autonomy. In the Russian sector Tsar Alexander I established the Congress Kingdom of Poland, of which he was monarch. This failed to satisfy Polish national aspirations, and there were bloody but unsuccessful risings in 1830 and 1863. Poles in the Prussian (from 1870 the

German) sector faced systematic attempts to destroy their culture, especially under Chancellor Otto von Bismarck. Polish nationalists could not agree on how to restore their independence. Some saw the answer in pan-Slavism or an ethnic nationalism that leant towards anti-Semitism; others saw revolutionary socialism as the way ahead.

In the event it was the collapse of the German, Austro-Hungarian and Russian empires at the end of World War I that led to the restoration of Polish independence. A war with the Russian Bolsheviks in 1920 won very favourable boundaries for Poland, but these boundaries could hardly be justified on ethnic grounds as 60% of the population of the newly independent country were non-Polish (mainly BELORUSSIANS and UKRANIANS). In 1939, at the start of World War II, Poland was invaded by Germany and the Soviet Union and partitioned between them. The war was devastating for the country: around a quarter of Poland's population died during it. Around 3 million ethnic Poles died under the Germans, in concentration and labour camps, summary executions and uprisings. The Soviets deported around 2 million Poles and executed thousands of Polish POWs. In addition, some 3 million Polish JEWS were exterminated by the Germans, many of them betrayed by Polish anti-Semites. Even after the war, the few surviving Jews faced pogroms.

The postwar borders of Poland were redrawn by the victorious Allies. The Soviet Union kept much of the territory it had taken in 1939, but Poland was compensated with German territory in Silesia, Prussia and Pomerania. The German population was expelled from these territories and replaced with Polish refugees from the east. The impact of the Holocaust against the Jews, the border changes and population movements left postwar Poland an ethnically very homogeneous country. Ethnic Poles now make up 98% of the total Polish population, which was around 38.6 million in 1996. Approximately 1 million Poles, known as MARCHLAND POLES, still live in Belarus and Ukraine.

The end of World War II did not bring the Poles the freedom they sought: the country's Soviet 'liberators' imposed a communist dictatorship that never enjoyed popular support. As opposition political parties were illegal, the Roman Catholic Church emerged as the focus of opposition to the regime. Attending Mass became a patriotic statement. The election of the Polish Pope John Paul II in 1978 encouraged the rise of the Solidarity trade union movement. Under the leadership of Lech Walesa, Solidarity transformed itself in 1980 into a national democratic political movement. Solidarity's success caused consternation in the Soviet Bloc, and Poles feared Soviet military interference; the situation led general Wojciech Jaruzelski to take over leadership of the communist government in 1981 and impose martial law. Despite this, dissident activity continued underground. Mikhail Gorbachev's accession to the premiership in the USSR in 1985, along with his introduction of the policies of *glasnost* (openness) and *perestroika* (restructuring), led to a loosening of Soviet control. Jaruzelski entered negotiations with Solidarity which led in 1989 to elections and the fall of the communist government. Since then the Poles have shown their commitment to a Western orientation by joining NATO and, in 2004, the European Union.

## POLOVTSY

See CUMANS.

## POMAKS

Ethnic BULGARIANS and MACEDONIANS who converted to Islam during the period of OTTOMAN rule.

## POMERANIANS or Pomorzanie

SLAVS who settled the lowlands along the Baltic Sea coast between the rivers Oder and Vistula in the 5th century AD. Their name means 'those who live close to the sea'. Contemporaries counted them among the WENDS. Those Pomeranians who lived in the vicinity of Gdansk were later known as Pomerelians and Cassubians ('shaggy coat-men'). Mieszko I, Prince of Poland (died 992), conquered the Pomeranians, and his successor Boleslaw I founded a bishopric at Kolobrzeg. However, the Pomeranians soon recovered their independence and it was not until around 1127 that Christianity began to make any headway among them.

By the 11th century the chief centre of the Pomeranians was the town of Szczecin (Stettin), which was so strongly fortified that it was known to the DANES as Burstaborg ('Bristle-borough'). The town was at an important crossroads of sea and river routes and it became a prosperous trading centre. The *knes* (prince) of the Pomeranians lived further east at Bialogard, inland from Kolobrzeg. From the 1170s the Pomeranians came under attack from the Danes, whose raids devastated the countryside and reduced their townspeople to starvation. The year after the Danes had destroyed the joint LIUTIZIAN-Pomeranian fleet in 1184, Prince Bogislav submitted to them. The defeat opened Pomerania to settlement by GERMANS, Danes and SWEDES, and the Pomeranians gradually began to lose their identity as a people. By the end of the Middle Ages they had been assimilated to either German or Polish identity.

## PORTUGUESE

The people of the Republic of Portugal, which is one of the most ethnically homogeneous countries in modern Europe. Over 99.5% of the country's approximately 9.8 million inhabitants are ethnic Portuguese. The name of both the Portuguese and Portugal are derived from Portus Cale, the Roman name for the city of Oporto. The Portuguese emerged as a distinct people in the 12th and 13th centuries. Portugal itself has been continuously occupied by humans since Palaeolithic times. The earliest historically known inhabitants were IBERIANS, but by the 3rd century BC most of Portugal was occupied by the LUSITANIANS, a Celtic-speaking people. The Lusitanians were conquered by the ROMANS in the 2nd century BC and their culture and language became Romanized. In the 4th century AD Catholic Christianity displaced paganism as the popular religion. After the fall of the Roman empire, Lusitania came under the rule of the Germanic VISIGOTHS, whose kingdom encompassed all of the Iberian peninsula. In 711 the Visigothic kingdom was conquered by the Muslim MOORS, but Lusitania was not thoroughly

Islamized and there was little Moorish settlement north of the River Tagus. Much of what is distinctive about modern Portuguese cuisine, such as the popularity of cooking meat and fish with fruit, derives from Moorish influences.

In 997 Christian forces recaptured Oporto from the Moors, and the city became the capital of the county of Portucalense (Portugal), which comprised modern Portugal north of the River Douro. In 1095 King Alfonso VI of Castile and León appointed Henry of Burgundy as Count of Portugal. Henry's son Afonso (ruled 1112–85) broke free of the control of Castile and León and took the title 'King of Portugal' in 1139. Portugal was officially recognized as a kingdom by the Papacy in 1179. Afonso greatly expanded Portugal, capturing Lisbon in 1147 and Evora in 1165. With the conquest of the Algarve by Afonso III in 1249, Portugal had achieved more or less its modern borders. However, Portugal's independence from Castile and León was not finally secure until the battle of Aljubarrota in 1385.

**Imperial expansion and contraction**

The Portuguese identity was greatly advanced during the reign of King Dinis (ruled 1279–1325). Dinis introduced land reforms that benefited the peasantry, encouraged the development of a seafaring and shipbuilding tradition, founded the country's first university (in Lisbon) and made Portuguese the official language of the judiciary. Portuguese had by this time evolved with enough differences from Castilian to be considered a separate language.

Portuguese national identity was strengthened in the 15th and 16th centuries by the foundation of the first global maritime empire of any European power. In 1580 Portugal came under Spanish rule after its king was killed during a disastrous expedition to Morocco. An uprising in 1640 restored Portuguese independence – the day of the uprising, 1 December, is a national holiday – but lasting damage had been done to the economy, and the country never again played a major role in European history.

Signs of national recovery in the 18th century were snuffed out when Napoleon invaded Portugal in 1807 and forced the royal family to flee to Brazil, then a Portuguese colony. The royal family did not return until 1821, ending a period when Portugal had been an unofficial part of the BRITISH empire. The monarchy was overthrown in 1910 and Portugal became a republic. The republican government did little to address Portugal's economic backwardness and the country slid into a reactionary Catholic-corporatist dictatorship under António Salazar. Salazar involved Portugal in costly and bloody wars to hold on to its overseas colonies long after other European powers had abandoned their own. The wars crippled Portugal's economy and caused popular discontent. After Salazar's death in 1970 the dictatorship began to fall apart and was finally overthrown in a bloodless revolution in 1974. Portugal joined the European Community (now European Union) in 1986, but remains one of Western Europe's poorer countries, and millions of Portuguese are forced to work abroad. Although abortion was legalized in 1998, the Portuguese mostly remain devout Catholics.

## PROKHOROVKA CULTURE

A late Iron Age culture found across the steppes from the Urals to the Black Sea. It is usually associated with the SARMATIANS, an Indo-Iranian nomad people.

## PROVENÇALS

The inhabitants of the Provence region in southern France. Today, most Provençals regard themselves first and foremost as FRENCH, but for most of their history they have had a culturally and linguistically distinct identity. The earliest historical inhabitants of Provence were GAULS and LIGURIANS. In the 6th century BC GREEKS founded colonies along the coast, the most important of which was Massalia, now Marseille. From the Greeks, the native people learned how to cultivate vines and olives. Relations between the Greeks and the native people were often hostile, however. In 181 BC the Greeks appealed to the Romans for protection. In 121 BC the area was formally incorporated into the ROMAN empire as the province (*provincia*) of Gallia Narbonensis, known simply as 'the Province' for short, the origin of its modern name. With its Mediterranean farming economy and proximity to Italy, Provence soon became highly Roman-

ized in culture and language. Following the collapse of the Roman empire in the 5th century AD, Provence came under the rule of a succession of Germanic peoples – VISIGOTHS, BURGUNDIANS, OSTROGOTHS, and finally in 536 the FRANKS, none of whom had much influence on the local culture, which remained Romanized. The local dialect of Latin was by this time developing into Provençal or, as it is also known, the Occitan language. Provençal remained the main spoken and literary language not only of Provence but of southern France until the 19th century. The most important genre of Provençal literature is the courtly love poetry and songs of the medieval troubadours.

Following the break-up of the Frankish (Carolingian) empire in the 9th century, Provence became an independent kingdom for over a century before becoming part of the Holy Roman empire in 1032. Under the empire, Provence was ruled by a succession of semi-autonomous aristocratic dynasties until it passed to the Kingdom of France in 1481. Under French rule, Provence's distinctive laws and customs were gradually undermined. The full integration of Provence into France began in the late 18th century when the Revolutionary government abolished the country's remaining autonomous institutions. The advent of rail links to the north in the 1860s facilitated greater cultural integration. Military conscription, national newspapers, radio and television have completed the process. French has become the public language of Provence, although Provençal is not completely extinct in the countryside. Provençal folk music and dancing are flourishing, but traditional costumes are now worn only for the benefit of tourists.

## PRUSSIANS

A people who, by the 20th century, were seen as the archetypal efficient militaristic GERMANS, but who were originally BALTS (often called Old Prussians). By the early Middle Ages, they had settled on the Baltic Sea coast between the Vistula and Neman rivers in what is now Poland and the Kaliningrad enclave of the Russian Federation. The Old Prussians were a tribal people, who never became politically unified. Polish monks began the conversion of the Prussians to

Christianity around 1200, but progress was slow. Conversion was completed only after they had been conquered by the German crusading Order of the Teutonic Knights in a 50-year war, which ended in 1283. The Knights built castles and encouraged German peasant settlement, beginning the assimilation of the Prussians. Even before the Old Prussian language died out in the 17th century, the Prussians considered themselves to be Germans.

The Teutonic Order dissolved itself during the Reformation and Prussia became a secular duchy under the Hohenzollern dynasty. Prussians became strongly Lutheran. In 1611 the Duchy of Prussia was linked to Brandenburg in eastern Germany. Lacking defendable frontiers, Brandenburg-Prussia developed a strong military tradition, which made it a major European power by the time it became the Kingdom of Prussia in 1701.

In the 19th century Prussia became the driving force of German unification, and proved its military leadership in the humiliation of the FRENCH in the Franco-Prussian War (1870–1). On the proclamation of the German empire in 1871, King Wilhelm I of Prussia became Kaiser of Germany, and Prussia's capital, Berlin, became the capital of Germany. The Prussians cast Germany in their own militaristic image with ultimately disastrous consequences.

The fall of the Hohenzollern monarchy at the end of World War I ended Prussia's disproportionate influence on German politics and, following Germany's defeat in World War II, Prussia all but disappeared. All German territory east of the River Oder was lost, most of it going to Poland, except for Königsberg, which went to the USSR and was renamed Kaliningrad. Some 4 million Prussian Germans were expelled from these territories.

Now that it is completely dissociated from its original homeland, the Prussian identity is largely confined to older Germans.

## PRZEWORSK CULTURE

A late Iron Age culture of the Oder–Vistula region in Poland. The identity of the culture has been much debated between German and Polish archaeologists, the former claiming it as an early GERMAN culture, the latter as an early SLAV culture. Named after a site in southeast Poland, the culture is known mainly from its burials and is defined by its distinctive metalwork.

## QUADI

An early GERMAN people who originated as part of the SUEBI and were settled on the River Main when they first appeared in the historical record around 7 BC. Early in the 1st century AD the Quadi migrated to Moravia, where at first they enjoyed a close and friendly relationship with the ROMAN empire. In the 160s the Quadi allied with the MARCOMANNI, crossing the Danube and raiding as far south as northern Italy. After their defeat in 180 many Quadi were resettled in the Roman empire. The Quadi continued to raid Roman territory in the 3rd and 4th centuries. In the late 4th century the Quadi combined with the VANDALS.

## RADIMICHI

An early SLAV people who lived east of the middle Dnieper. They became subject to the RUS in the 9th century AD.

## RAETI

A Celtic people (see CELTS, ANCIENT) who lived in the Tyrol and Bavaria in the late Iron Age. The Raeti were conquered by the ROMANS in 16 BC. Related groups living in the same area included the Camunni, Venones and Vindelici.

## RANI

See RUGIANS.

## REMI

A Gaulish people (see GAULS) who lived in the area between the Aisne and Marne rivers. In 57 BC the Remi allied with Julius Caesar and remained loyal throughout the Gallic War. Their name survives in the city of Reims, formerly known as Durocortorum, which was their tribal capital.

# RHINELANDERS

The GERMAN population of the Rhineland (that is, roughly the modern *Länder* of Nordrhein-Westfalen and Rheinland-Pfalz) in western Germany. The Rhine's double role as frontier and major trade route gave the people who lived on its banks a distinct identity, which survived for centuries.

By 51 BC the Rhine had become a frontier of the ROMAN empire. On the east bank were unconquered GERMAN tribes, on the west a mixed population of GAULS, Germans and a large permanent military garrison of soldiers from all over the empire: this garrison became socially and economically closely integrated with the local population, which in turn became highly Romanized as a result. Even the Germans on the east bank underwent some degree of Romanization, and this ensured that when they finally overran the Rhine frontier in the 5th century the area kept its special character.

The Rhineland continued to be a frontier area, first between the FRANKS and the pagan SAXONS, and later between the German Holy Roman empire and France, bringing with it the advantages of trade and cultural diversity and the disadvantages of being frequently contested. The area became devoutly Catholic and remained so after the Reformation.

The Rhineland was awarded to Prussia at the end of the Napoleonic Wars in 1815, and in 1871 became part of the newly unified Germany.

After World War I the Rhineland was occupied by France. The FRENCH sought to capitalize on the Rhinelanders' strong sense of local identity to foment a separatist movement, hoping to detach the Rhineland from Germany and create a buffer state. Strong anti-PRUSSIAN and pro-Catholic feeling in the Rhineland seemed to provide a good basis for such a movement, but France's allies quickly quashed the plan.

In 1925 separatists declared a Rhineland Republic, but this collapsed in only a few weeks. French military occupation continued until 1930, by which time it was so thoroughly detested that separatism had given way to German nationalism. The Treaty of Versailles had decreed that the Rhineland should be a demilitarized zone, but when Hitler ordered German troops back into the region in 1936 there was general rejoicing.

After World War II the Rhineland became the economic and political heart of the new liberal and democratic Germany, and its inhabitants have largely lost their sense of separate identity.

# ROMANIANS

The people of the Republic of Romania. Ethnic Romanians make up around 90% of the population, which was around 22.65 million in 1996. There are also small numbers of Romanian-speakers in Ukraine and Yugoslavia, and the MOLDOVANS are also culturally and linguistically Romanian. The ARMINI, ARUMANS and VLACHS of Macedonia and northern Greece also speak Romanian dialects.

The origins of the Romanians are disputed. The earliest historical inhabitants of Romania were the DACIANS. The Dacians were conquered by the ROMANS in AD 105–6 and became Romanized to the extent that they adopted a Latin dialect, the basis of the Romanian language.

Around AD 270 Dacia was overrun by the GOTHS. There followed a succession of occupiers: HUNS in the 5th century, SLAVS in the 6th, BULGARS in the 7th, HUNGARIANS in the 9th, CUMANS in the 11th and MONGOLS in the 13th. What became of the original Dacian population in this 1000-year period is simply not known. It is possible that to escape the Goths many of the native population fled south of the Danube, where their Romanized language and culture was reinforced, their descendants drifting back across the river in later centuries. Others may have maintained their identity in the Transylvanian Mountains and gradually resettled the lowland areas of Wallachia and Moldavia, where the earliest Romanian states developed in the late Middle Ages.

This succession of occupations had its effects on the Romanian language. Although it retains the grammatical structure of a Romance language, almost 60% of its vocabulary is Slavonic in origin. Sometime in this period, too, the Romanians had been converted to the Slavonic form of Orthodox Christianity.

A conscious sense of Romanian identity first developed among the ruling aristocracies of

Moldavia and Wallachia, who took to describing themselves as 'Romans' in the 15th century. In the 16th century Moldavia and Wallachia came under the domination of the OTTOMANS but retained considerable local autonomy. As Ottoman power declined in the 19th century, the two provinces became independent and they united to form the Kingdom of Romania in 1862. The long experience of occupation gave Romanians an assertive and xenophobic nationalism, often expressed violently, especially against JEWS. Exceptions to this xenophobia were the adoption of FRENCH literary culture and, in the 20th century, of Italian-style pronunciation for the Romanian language. These measures were intended to heighten the distinction between Romanians and their Slav neighbours.

**Monarchy to democracy, via communism**

Romania achieved roughly its modern borders in 1918, when it acquired Banat and Transylvania from the collapsing Austro-Hungarian empire and Bessarabia (now Moldova; see MOLDOVANS) from Russia. All these areas had Romanian-speaking majorities, but Transylvania had a significant and vocal HUNGARIAN minority.

Romania's postwar democratic experiment soon failed, and the country became a royal fascist-leaning dictatorship, which exploited Romanian xenophobia. Bessarabia was occupied by the USSR in 1940 and re-occupied by Romania 1941–4 after it allied with Germany in World War II. Even before the war was over, the RUSSIANS had installed a communist puppet regime.

From the late 1950s, Romanian Communist Party leaders tried to assert a measure of independence from Moscow. After coming to power in 1965, Nicolae Ceausescu won the communist government a measure of popular support by pursuing openly nationalist policies, but by the 1980s his corrupt regime had reduced the country to poverty. In 1989, a short revolution brought the overthrow and execution of Ceausescu and the installation of a National Salvation Front government. Under pressure from violent street protests, the NSF finally introduced a multi-party constitution in 1991.

With no democratic tradition to build on, Romania has struggled with its economic problems, and ultra-nationalistic policies have alienated the country's GYPSY and Hungarian minorities, who remain the victims of systematic discrimination. Romania became a member of NATO in March 2004, but currently remains outside the European Union.

# ROMANS

The LATIN population of the Italian city of Rome. The Romans created the greatest empire of the ancient world. In the 5th century BC to be a Roman was simply to be a citizen of Rome, then an unexceptional Italian market town that had recently overthrown its monarchy and introduced a republic. In the centuries that followed the Romans conquered first their Italian neighbours and then the entire Mediterranean world, creating an empire that survived until the 5th century AD.

Although a fearsomely efficient military system won the Romans their empire, the reason the empire endured was its ability to assimilate conquered peoples to a Roman identity, turning them into loyal citizens who were proud to describe themselves as Romans.

According to their own legendary traditions, the Romans traced their ancestry to the Trojan hero Aeneas, who, with a band of followers, had escaped the sack of Troy. After long journeying Aeneas reached Italy and settled in Latium, where he married a Latin princess and founded a dynasty. Two of Aeneas's illegitimately born descendants, the twin brothers Romulus and Remus, were abandoned as babies on the banks of the River Tiber. They survived because they were suckled by a she-wolf, and they were eventually rescued and raised by shepherds. When they grew up the brothers founded a city on the spot where they had been abandoned. When the brothers fought over who should rule it, Romulus killed Remus and named the city Rome after himself. (The Romans dated this event to 753 BC, but the site of Rome was occupied several centuries earlier according to modern archaeological evidence.)

The Romans were then short of marriageable women so they invited their neighbours, the SABINES, for a feast at which the Roman men kidnapped the Sabine women. The war that broke out was stopped by the Sabine women, who placed themselves and their children between the combatants, and compromise was reached which placed Rome under the joint rule of Romulus and Titus Tatius, the Sabine leader.

**A large and polyglot empire**

This story exemplifies the way the Romans saw themselves. As their empire grew, the Romans assimilated a host of new peoples and cultural influences. The Romans were proud that they were a mixture of peoples and that they derived most of their culture from others (the GREEKS and ETRUSCANS being the most important influences). They celebrated their mixed origins in their foundation myths, because they rightly recognized that this was one of their strengths.

The Romans believed they had a genius for taking the ideas and technology of others and improving on them. During the First Punic War against the great sea-power of Carthage, the Romans were losing because they lacked a fleet. They captured a beached Carthaginian galley and copied it, built a fleet of their own and defeated the CARTHAGINIANS. The Romans invented neither the arch nor concrete, but no one in the ancient world came close to their mastery of both.

The Roman openness to new influences is clearest in their attitude to citizenship. While in the Greek city-states (see ATHENIANS and SPARTANS) citizenship was a jealously guarded privilege, open only to those born of citizens, Roman citizenship was based on residence and so was always open to new recruits. It was even possible for a freed slave eventually to become a Roman citizen.

As their empire expanded, the Romans offered citizenship, with all its legal privileges, to conquered provincials as a reward for their cooperation. By the 1st century BC all the free inhabitants of Italy were Roman citizens, and by AD 212 all free inhabitants of the empire were classed as citizens. After the foundation of the Principate by Augustus in 27 BC, it was not even necessary to be born in Rome to become emperor: among others, Hadrian was born in Spain, Septimius Severus in North Africa and Diocletian in the Balkans.

By the 4th century AD, Roman emperors rarely set foot in Rome and after the foundation

of Constantinople (Istanbul) in AD 330 it was no longer even the official imperial capital.

The assimilation of provincials to Roman identity was eased by the provision of the amenities of the Roman way of life, such as theatres, amphitheatres, race courses and bath houses. Romans had complete confidence that their ways were the best and they encouraged others to adopt them. Despite this, they were tolerant of other cultures and religions.

Until the official recognition of Christianity in the 4th century, it was necessary to sacrifice to the Roman state gods, but this was primarily a public display of loyalty to the empire; 'conversion' was neither required nor expected. Christians and JEWS were persecuted by the pagan emperors because their absolute beliefs threatened the empire's tolerant multiculturalism. Once Christianity became the official religion, the empire became a much more authoritarian state.

Romanization did not, however, mean the extinction of all local identities within the empire. Provincials were able to accommodate their local identities with their Roman identity. Thus the GAULS could be proud to be both Gaulish and Roman, while the self-consciously Greek inhabitants of Constantinople continued to call themselves Romans until their city fell to the TURKS in 1453.

**Today's Roman citizens**

The overthrow of the last Roman emperor in the west in AD 476 is generally accepted as marking the end of the Roman empire (although the eastern half survived as the increasingly Hellenistic BYZANTINE empire). Today, to be a Roman is again simply to be an inhabitant of Rome, although now the term has no ethnic overtones: Romans are ITALIANS. However, Roman influence lives on in innumerable ways.

The Roman language, Latin, was the international language of intellectual discourse until the 17th century, and the Roman alphabet is the most widely used in the world. The modern European Romance languages are all descended from Latin. Roman law is the basis of law in many European, Latin American and African countries. The administrative structure of the late Roman empire survives in the Roman

Catholic Church. The Roman republic was a representative form of government, which continues to influence modern democracies, while the tsars of Russia and Kaisers of Germany were, in their titles, paying homage to the Caesars of Rome's imperial age.

Because the Roman legacy to the modern world is so great, it is a common misconception that Romans were more modern in their outlook than they really were. The Romans were in reality highly superstitious and would undertake no course of action without seeking the approval of their gods first. Signs and omens were firmly believed, and Roman soldiers even had regulations about the reporting of dreams to their commanding officers in case they contained prophetic warnings. The Roman taste for gladiatorial combat was not, as it seems today, motivated solely by brutality and bloodlust. In those days of short life-expectancy, the Romans lived with death in a way modern people do not. The Romans saw themselves as a brave and martial people, and they found the spectacle of two gladiators fighting to the death, neither asking for nor expecting mercy, an edifying experience.

## ROMANY

See GYPSIES.

## ROXOLANI

A major SARMATIAN tribe who settled north of the Danube River estuary in the last centuries BC. After being defeated in two wars, the Roxolani became clients of the ROMAN empire in the 1st century AD. In the 3rd and 4th centuries they allied with the GOTHS to cross the empire's Danube frontier. The Roxolani disappeared by the 5th century, probably by assimilation with other peoples.

## RUGIANS or Rani

An early SLAV people who settled on the Baltic Sea coast of Germany between the Warnow and Peene rivers in the 6th century AD. Their main settlement was the clifftop stronghold of Arkona on the island of Rügen, an important trading centre for the whole Baltic region, which also

housed the principal shrine of their four-headed chief god Svantovit. The Rugians were conquered by the DANES in 1168–9. Arkona was sacked, the idol of Svantovit was destroyed and the Rugians were forcibly converted to Christianity. In the 13th century the Holy Roman empire took control of the Rugians, who were assimilated to the German identity.

## RUGII

An early GERMAN tribe, first recorded in the first century AD, who were settled on the Baltic coast between the Oder and the Vistula rivers. By the 3rd century AD they had migrated south to Slovakia. As ROMAN power collapsed in the second half of the 5th century, they crossed the River Danube and took over the province of Noricum (roughly today's Austria). By the end of the century they had been conquered by the OSTROGOTHS and soon afterwards lost their distinct identity as a people.

## RUS

A term used in the early Middle Ages to describe SCANDINAVIANS living in Russia, which is named after them. The name is thought to be derived from *Ruotsi*, the Finnish name for the SWEDES, the Scandinavians who were most active in eastern Europe during the VIKING era. An alternative interpretation is that the word is of GREEK origin and is derived from Rosomones (from *rusioi*, 'blondes'), a name for the HERULS, a Germanic tribe who raided the Eastern Roman empire between the 3rd and 6th centuries AD.

During the Soviet period many Russian historians claimed that the Rus were SLAVS, rather than Scandinavians; however, the archaeological, literary and linguistic evidence for their Scandinavian origin is overwhelming.

Scandinavian traders had been active on the east coast of the Baltic Sea since at least the 7th century, probably buying furs for the western European market. In the early 9th century they pressed inland along eastern Europe's great navigable rivers, carrying their boats across watersheds from one river system to another. By the 830s Rus merchants had travelled down the Dnieper and crossed the Black Sea to reach the

BYZANTINE capital Constantinople, and had reached the BULGAR and KHAZAR cities on the Volga to trade with ARAB merchants.

Later in the 9th century the Rus began to subjugate the native Slavs and force them to pay tribute in furs and slaves. By around 860 Novgorod, a former Slav settlement, had become the capital of a Rus state, supposedly founded by the semi-legendary Viking Rurik. Around 882 the capital was moved to Kiev, an event which is often seen as marking the foundation of the RUSSIAN state.

The Rus were only a minority among the native Slavs, and in the 10th century they became increasingly assimilated, worshipping Slav gods, such as Perun (the eastern Slavic god of thunder, lightening and warfare) inter-marrying with Slav families, and adopting Slav names and language. By the time Vladimir I converted to Orthodox Christianity in 988, the Rus had become entirely Slavic in character, and a new name, VARANGIANS, had come into use to describe visiting Scandinavians.

# RUSNAKS

See RUTHENIANS.

# RUSSIANS

The majority people of the Russian Federation, the world's largest Eurasian state, occupying territories stretching from the Baltic Sea to the Pacific Ocean. They take their name from the RUS, who founded the earliest Russian state at Kiev in the 9th century.

Although they are a SLAV people, and therefore Europeans, there has been much in their often tragic history to separate them from Europe. A relatively inefficient agricultural sector, suffering from limited productivity, meant they lagged behind western Europe economically. In the 17th century, to stop mass flight by impoverished peasants to newly conquered Siberian lands, serfdom was established in Russia just as the West was abandoning it.

The Russians were further separated from the West by the Mongol conquest of Russian lands in the course of the 13th century. Arbitrary government became standard. Unlike the West,

Russia never knew government based on the rule of law. Never part of the Roman empire, and adopting Christianity from the GREEK Church, Russians were never part of medieval Christendom, and were largely excluded from the cultural, economic and technological developments of the West by lack of the common language of intellectuals, Latin. Furthermore, the fall of Constantinople to the TURKS in 1453 arguably encouraged the Russians to see Muscovy as the only true Christian state in the world, and to see Moscow as the third Rome, or centre of Christianity (after Rome and Constantinople, both of which had fallen to 'barbarians').

The widespread belief that Russians must avoid contamination from heretical Westerners and their ideas was a major obstacle for rulers aware of Russia's backwardness, such as Peter the Great (ruled 1689–1725), who wanted to introduce Western innovations.

**The struggle against backwardness**

As time progressed, an increasingly radical Russian intelligentsia often saw their state system and institutions, especially serfdom, as painfully backward. Even in the 20th century, despite Soviet propaganda to the contrary, the struggle to match the West in technological and military power became an increasingly unsustainable burden to the national economy. Russian acknowledgement of the country's backwardness in many respects has been a painful experience, given a tradition of pride and fierce patriotism. Western invaders have been shocked at the ability of Russians to endure whatever suffering is necessary to triumph: an estimated 27 million dead as the price of victory over the GERMANS (1941–5) illustrates this.

The Russians are also a people given to long periods of political apathy, interspersed by periods of intense activism. As the imperial system failed in its foreign wars in the beginning of the 20th century, the challenge from revolutionaries and the demands of alienated peasants and workers became harder to contain. Major revolutionary upheavals in 1905–6 and 1917 swept imperial rule aside and established the Union of Soviet Socialist Republics (USSR). As this state was the product of their own revolution, Russians readily identified with it. Even dissidents of

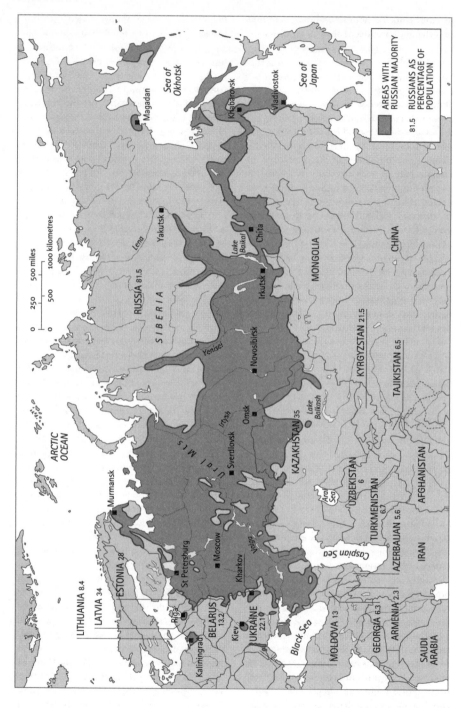

its latter years did not call for its dismantling, only that the government obey its own laws.

## Soviet Russia

Soviet-era Russians were proud to be a world power, despite the millions who died under Stalin's *dekulakization* (destruction of the rich peasants), collectivization of agriculture and subsequent famines, and brutal purges. By the 1980s, however, they were becoming disenchanted with the state's oppressiveness and its obvious failings, such as economic stagnation and environmental catastrophe caused by an unwinnable arms race with the USA. The last communist leader, Mikhail Gorbachev, removed the oppressive regime, but was unable to rebuild a failing economy.

The resulting collapse of Soviet power has left the Russians with the painful task of reconstructing a national identity. No longer Soviet citizens, they are struggling to come to terms with a much reduced world status, an economy seemingly beyond salvation, a lost empire, growing criminality and accelerating social disintegration. Some would prefer the certainties of a rebuilt USSR, while others look towards an extreme nationalist salvation. There is a growing perception that the democratic experiment has failed, but what the future holds is fraught with uncertainties. In 2002 the Russians numbered nearly 120 million.

## RUTHENIANS or Rusyns or Rusnaks

The East SLAV peoples who live in the Carpathian Mountains in the borderlands of Poland, Ukraine, Slovakia and Romania and in an isolated community in Vojvodina, Yugoslavia, established by immigrants in the 19th century. The term 'Ruthenian' was once used more broadly to include UKRAINIANS and BELORUSSIANS. Important Ruthenian sub-groups include the BOIKOS, HUTSULS and LEMKOS.

Defining the Ruthenians is difficult, as they have no unifying linguistic identity, and as a result their numbers are uncertain. Most Ruthenians speak either the majority language of their country or a Ruthenian dialect heavily influenced by the majority language. The Vojvodina Ruthenians have probably the clearest linguistic identity, because their Ruthenian dialect is still quite distinct from the Serbo-Croat spoken by the majority community of the region.

What Ruthenians do have in common is their religion: the majority are Uniate Catholics, that is Orthodox Christians who nonetheless accept the supremacy of the Papacy over the Church. The largest population of Ruthenians, nearly 1 million, live in the Transcarpathian province of the Ukraine. When Ukraine became independent in 1991, three-quarters of the population of this province voted for autonomy. When the Ukrainian government refused to grant autonomy, a token Ruthenian government in exile was set up in Moscow.

Around 130,000 Ruthenians live in Slovakia, 60,000 in Poland, 1000 in Romania and 30,000 in Yugoslavia.

## SAAMI or Sami or Sabme or Lapps

An aboriginal people of northern Europe; the Saami are the descendants of the first postglacial inhabitants of the region. Saami consider the name 'Lapp', given to them originally by the FINNS, to be derogatory.

Today, most Saami live north of the Arctic Circle in an area stretching from Russia's Kola peninsula through northern Finland, Sweden and Norway; but in the early Middle Ages they were more widespread, ranging as far south as lakes Ladoga and Onega in the east, and central Norway and Sweden in the west. In the 1990s around 30,000 Saami lived in Norway, 16,000 in Sweden, 4000 in Finland and 1600 in Russia.

The Saami are physically distinct from their Finnish and SCANDINAVIAN neighbours, being generally shorter, round-faced and darker. They speak a FINNO-UGRIAN language distantly related to Finnish. The language is divided into three main dialects, which are mutually unintelligible. However, almost all Saami are now bilingual, and some do not speak Saami at all. The decline of the language is partly the result of a lack of teaching opportunities in schools, although both school and adult education in Saami are now available, as are Saami newspapers and radio programmes. A further problem is that

S

Saami

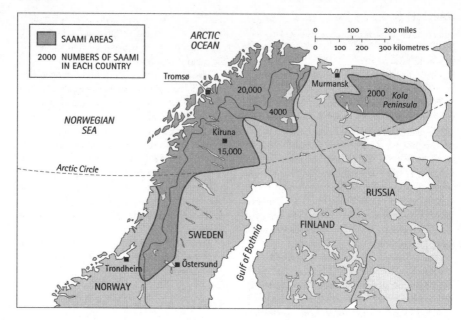

pure Saami lacks the vocabulary to deal with 21st-century life.

Traditionally the Saami followed a shamanistic religion that was based on a bear cult and holy mountains, and were believed by the Finns and Scandinavians to possess magical powers. Most Saami, however, converted to Christianity in the 18th century.

The Saami were originally a hunter-gatherer people who, because the climate of their land was so unfavourable to agriculture, preserved an essentially MESOLITHIC way of life into the Christian era. Trapping for furs was an important activity and reindeer were hunted for meat.

The nomadic reindeer-herding way of life, for which the Saami are now best known, developed in the Middle Ages. The Saami migrated up to 320 km / 200 miles between summer and winter pastures in groups of four or five families, living in tents and hunting and fishing to supplement their diets.

True nomadism has now died out. Reindeer still make seasonal migrations, but the herders, aided by modern technology like snowmobiles, accompany them alone; their families live in permanent modern homes. Reindeer are herded collectively, but each is individually owned.

Most Saami are now engaged in fishing, mining or forestry, rather than herding, which faces a bleak future because global warming threatens to destroy the tundra environment on which it depends.

A collective body, the Saami Parliament, campaigns for the rights of the Saami of Norway, Sweden and Finland.

## SABELLI

A Roman term for a group of peoples of central-southern Italy who spoke the Oscan language. Oscan was an Italic language related to Latin and Umbrian. The Sabelli included the Apuli, BRUTTIANS, LUCANIANS and SAMNITES. Other peoples who may have been included in the definition were the AEQUI, Marsi, Paeligni and Vestini.

The Sabelli were never politically united, so the term had mainly cultural significance. They were conquered by the Romans in the early 3rd century BC. The Oscan language began to be replaced by Latin in the 1st century BC, but did not die out completely until early in the Christian era.

# SABINES

An ancient ITALIAN people who lived in the central Apennines to the northeast of Rome. They probably spoke an Oscan dialect (see SABELLI). According to ROMAN legendary traditions, such as the story of the rape of the Sabine women, the population of early Rome was partly Sabine, and two of its kings were also Sabines. The Sabines were conquered by the Romans in 290 BC and given a limited form of Roman citizenship, upgraded to full citizenship in 268 BC. The Sabines were subsequently rapidly assimilated to Roman identity. Many Roman religious practices are thought to be Sabine in origin.

# SALLUVII

An ancient people of mixed Celtic (see CELTS, ANCIENT) and LIGURIAN origin, who lived between the River Rhône and the maritime Alps in the late Iron Age. After GREEK colonists founded the city of Massalia (Marseille) around 600 BC, the Salluvii adopted aspects of Hellenistic culture, including stone architecture and cultivation of vines and olives. The Salluvian capital at Entremont was destroyed in 122 BC, when the Salluvii were conquered by the ROMANS.

# SAMMARINESI

The native inhabitants of the tiny Apennine Republic of San Marino. They now make up less than half of the republic's population, which was around 25,600 in 1997; the majority are now ITALIANS. The state language is Italian, but a local dialect defined as Celto-Gallic, influenced by the Italian dialects of Romagna and Lombardy (see LOMBARDS), is also spoken.

# SAMNITES

An ancient Oscan-speaking people (see SABELLI) of south-central Italy, who regarded themselves as a branch of the SABINES. The Samnites were a warlike people who had a strong sense of common identity.

The four Samnite tribes, the Caraceni, Caudini, Hirpini and Pentri, formed a confederation to resist ROMAN expansion in three hard-fought but ultimately unsuccessful wars (343–341 BC, 326–304 BC, 298–290 BC). The Samnites were not easily reconciled to Roman rule and rebelled several times. They were only finally subdued in 82 BC, after which they became Romanized.

# SARDINIANS or Sards

The people of the Italian island of Sardinia, west of Italy in the Mediterranean Sea. The island has changed hands many times in its history but there has never been, in historical times at least, a true sense of Sardinian national identity.

Little is known about the origins of the earliest Sardinians, but they were a warlike society whose fortified towers (called *nuraghe*) are still prominent in the landscape. The Sherden, who joined the SEA PEOPLES in their raids on the Levant and Egypt in the 12th and 13th centuries BC, may have been Sardinians.

From the 9th century to the 6th century BC the coast of Sardinia was colonized by GREEKS and PHOENICIANS, and in the 3rd century BC the island became part of the ROMAN empire. Sardinia became closely integrated into Roman Italy, and after the fall of the Roman empire the Sardinian language developed from the local dialect of Latin.

The island was subsequently subjected to a variety of ARAB, SPANISH and ITALIAN influences, all of which left their mark on its culture. Until recently, the Tuscan and Genoese dialects of Italian, Arabic and Catalan, as well as Sardinian, were spoken in different regions of the island. Italian is now the main language.

Sardinia was for centuries notorious for lawlessness and rural brigandage, but this relative ungovernability has never been an expression of separatism. From the 18th century, Sardinia was linked to Piedmont in northern Italy to form the Kingdom of Piedmont-Sardinia (see PIEDMONTESE), which became the driving force behind Italian unification in the 19th century. For this reason the Sardinians have been an integral part of the Italian state, and thus of the modern Italian identity, since its inception.

S

# SARMATIANS

A nomadic INDO-IRANIAN people who, during the 6th and 5th centuries BC, migrated west from the Central Asian steppes. They settled on the steppes north of the Black Sea in the 3rd century BC, displacing the SCYTHIANS, to whom they were related. The Sarmatians absorbed them over the course of the next two centuries.

By the 1st century AD, the Sarmatians controlled an area that stretched from the middle Danube to the Volga. Their conquests brought them into contact with the borders of the ROMAN empire, and the Sarmatians periodically raided across the frontier. In the 3rd and 4th centuries AD the Sarmatians were overrun by the GOTHS. Many were assimilated into Gothic society while others were resettled in the Roman empire by Constantine the Great; the remainder were destroyed by the HUNS in AD 370. (For Sarmatian tribes, see the box). A closely related people were the ALANS.

Following their migration from Central Asia and subsequent wars of conquest, the traditional classless nomadic society of the Sarmatians began to give way to a more stratified form. The growth of an increasingly wealthy aristocracy is clearly evidenced in the finds from Sarmatian burial mounds. Their society and culture were very similar to those of the Scythians and Huns; for example, they were renowned for their horsemanship, and their art displays clear Scythian influence. Sarmatian jewellery and bronze reliefs were especially fine, and the latter influenced later Chinese forms. PARTHIAN influence is evidenced by the use of heavy armour worn by Sarmatian cavalry, but their use of the long sword was unique among similar nomadic peoples. Chief among the Sarmatian gods was a fire deity, to whom horse sacrifices were offered.

# SAVOYARDS

The FRENCH-speaking inhabitants of the historic County of Savoy in southeast France, between Lake Geneva and the Val d'Isère. Savoy was an autonomous county, later duchy, from *c*. 1000 until 1720, when it became part of the Kingdom of Sardinia-Piedmont. In 1860 the Savoyards voted in a plebiscite to be united to France.

# SAXONS

An early GERMAN people who lived in northern Germany between the River Ems and the neck of the Jutland peninsula. First recorded in the 2nd century AD, the Saxons probably originated as a confederation of tribes, including the Aviones, CHAUCI and Reudingi. Expert seafarers, they launched many pirate raids in the 3rd and 4th centuries on the coasts of Britain and Gaul, causing the ROMANS to set up a coastal defence command known as the Saxon Shore. In the 5th century Saxons played a major role in the ANGLO-SAXON settlement of Britain. The southern English kingdoms of Sussex (see SOUTH SAXONS), Essex (see EAST SAXONS) and Wessex (see WEST SAXONS) were traditionally regarded as having been founded by Saxon settlers. The relative proportion of Saxon and Anglian settlers is unclear: the modern ENGLISH take their name from the ANGLES, but the WELSH and Gaelic words for the English (*Saesneg, Sassenach*) are both derived from 'Saxon'.

Archaeological evidence shows that there was widespread abandonment of Saxon settlements along the North Sea coast in the 5th century, but the migrations to Britain did not involve the entire Saxon people. The continental Saxons, or Old Saxons as they were often called to distinguish them from the Saxons in Britain, remained a powerful people, expanding westwards into FRISIAN and FRANKISH territory. In 772 the Frankish king Charlemagne began the conquest of the Saxons. Charlemagne's strategy included attacks on their pagan sanctuaries and forced conversion to Christianity, with rewards for those who cooperated and brutal reprisals and deportation for those who did not. The Saxons were a tribal people, but they chose a common war-leader called Widukind, who led their resistance for many years. Only in 805 were the Saxons finally subdued, although they were left with a lasting rivalry with the Franks.

After the break-up of the Carolingian empire in the late 9th century, the Saxons retained a distinctive identity as one of the 'tribal' duchies of the Kingdom of Germany. Between 919 and 1024 the Saxon dukes were also kings of Germany and Holy Roman emperors. In the 12th century, Saxons spearheaded the *Drang nach*

*Osten* ('drive to the east'), the German colonization of the SLAV lands of eastern Europe. By the late 12th century the power of the duchy was becoming a serious threat to the German monarchy, and it was broken up into smaller principalities. Thus, the late medieval Duchy of Saxony was centred on lands in central Germany that were not traditionally Saxon. Present Lower Saxony, created in 1946, is a rough approximate of the old tribal duchy. A little of the Saxons' distinctive identity survives. Saxons are more likely to be Protestants than other Germans, and their dialect, Low German or *Plattdeutsch*, is the most distinctive German dialect still in common use.

## SCANDINAVIANS

A group of Northern European peoples who include the DANES, FAEROESE, ICELANDERS, NORWEGIANS and SWEDES, and who speak closely-related Germanic languages descended from a common ancestor called the *Dönsk tunga* (the 'Danish tongue') in the VIKING era. Scandinavians have a greater proportion of blue-eyed blondes than other European peoples and are believed to be the descendants of the first post-glacial inhabitants of the region. The FINNS are sometimes considered to be Scandinavians because of their close historical relationship with Sweden, but they do not speak a Germanic language. The Scandinavian countries all have relatively egalitarian societies with strong support for advanced social welfare and the high taxes needed to support it. Pan-Scandinavianism was influential for a whil in the mid-19th century, but Sweden's refusal to support Denmark when it was attacked by Prussia in 1864 effectively killed the movement. Today, cooperation among the Scandinavian countries is promoted by the Nordic Council, which also includes Finland.

## SCORDISCI

Ancient CELTS who, in the 3rd century BC, lived in the region around the River Sava in present-day Serbia. The Scordisci frequently raided Macedonia until they were conquered by the ROMANS around 12 BC.

## SCOTS

The people of Scotland, one of the four constituent nations of the United Kingdom. The majority of modern Scots are the descendants mainly of four different peoples, the Scots themselves, who, somewhat confusingly, were originally IRISH, the PICTS, the BRITONS and the ANGLES. There was also significant immigration from Scandinavia during the early Middle Ages. This mixed Anglo-Celtic background created deep divisions in Scottish society in the Middle Ages, and it was only in the 19th century that today's comparatively homogeneous Scottish identity finally emerged. Scots make up nearly 90% of Scotland's total population of just over 5 million (the ENGLISH being the largest minority) and more than 600,000 Scots live and work in other parts of the United Kingdom. The Scots are one of the few European peoples whose numbers are in decline. In addition there are millions of people in the USA, Canada, Australia and New Zealand who claim Scottish descent, which is the legacy of mass emigration between the late 18th and early 20th centuries.

Apart from some 30,000 people, most of them in the Hebrides, who speak Gaelic as a first language, the Scots are English-speaking. The English spoken by modern Scots is close to standard English, but its pronunciation and vocabulary are still very much influenced by Scots, the English dialect (some Scots would say it is a separate language) spoken in Lowland Scotland during the Middle Ages and early modern period and the language of the poems and songs of Robert Burns, Scotland's national poet. Scots developed from the NORTHUMBRIAN dialect of Old English, and so has a common origin with the dialects of northern England. The Scots dialect declined in the 19th century when schools began teaching in standard English so that Scottish people could compete on equal terms with the English.

### The nation and its southern neighbour

The Scots began to settle in what was then still 'Pictland' around AD 500, when King Fergus mac Erc of the northern Irish kingdom of Dál Riata (Dalriada) conquered Argyll. In the late 6th century Argyll broke away from its Irish

| Scandinavians: main ethnic groups |
|---|
| Danes |
| Faeroese |
| Icelanders |
| Norwegians |
| Swedes |

S

parent and became an independent Scots kingdom. In the 8th century Pictish power began to decline, and around 843 the Picts were conquered by the Scottish king Kenneth Mac Alpin. The Picts' culture, language and identity all disappeared within about 60 years as they were assimilated to the Scots' identity and their Gaelic language and culture.

By 900, Scots rulers were describing themselves as kings of Alba or Scotia ('Scotland'). However, Scotland in 900 comprised only the area between the Forth and the Spey rivers; the country's modern borders were achieved only by centuries of military and diplomatic expansionism. In the early 11th century Lothian, with its English-speaking population, was annexed, settling the Anglo–Scottish border on the Tweed. Around the same time the British Kingdom of Strathclyde was also annexed. The Hebrides were acquired from the NORWEGIANS in the 13th century and, finally, Orkney and Shetland were acquired from Denmark in the 15th century.

Genetically, the populations of these islands are among the most distinctive in Britain. While the mainland Scots are genetically indistinguishable from the English, the DNA of these islanders shows the clear legacy of VIKING-era NORSE settlement. While the Norse settlers in the Hebrides were assimilated to Gaelic culture and identity, the ORCADIANS AND SHETLANDERS still identify strongly with their Scandinavian roots.

### A Scottish identity

At the beginning of the 12th century, Scotland's peoples still had no common identity. The Britons of Strathclyde still thought of themselves as British, the Angles of Lothian still saw themselves as English and the Scots considered themselves to be Irish. This began to change during the reigns of David I (ruled 1124–53) and his successors.

Influenced by NORMAN England, David introduced feudal institutions and encouraged Norman and English settlers. This diluted the Celtic character of the Scottish kingdom. English became the language of the court (at a time when French was the language of the English court) and of the towns: it displaced Cumbric (a WELSH dialect) in Strathclyde and Gaelic in Fife and most of the northeast coast. These changes made the Scots aware of themselves as a separate people, and they began to distance themselves from their Irish origins.

This emergent identity was confirmed by the experience of the Wars of Independence against England (1296–1328); its most important expression was the Declaration of Arbroath, which asserted Scots nationhood in 1320. A determination not to be English has remained an important part of the Scots' mentality ever since.

### Highlanders and Lowlanders

The wars unified the Scots, but there remained a great fault line between the English-speaking Lowlands and the Gaelic-speaking Highlands. Lowlanders regarded the Highlanders as barbarian cattle thieves addicted to rebellion. The Reformation added a new layer of hostility to this relationship. In 1559 John Knox introduced the austere Protestantism of John Calvin from Geneva. Lowlanders were won over: Catholicism, however, remained strong in the Highlands.

It was not until a generation after the suppression of the Highland clan system, in the aftermath of the failure of the 1745 Jacobite Rising, that Lowlanders felt they could allow themselves the luxury of romanticizing the Highlander. The novelist Sir Walter Scott played a lead in this, almost single-handedly inventing the idea that the kilt and its accoutrements were the traditional dress of Scotland. Lowlanders seized on this Celticized Scottish identity: since the Act of Union in 1707 Lowlanders had felt increasingly vulnerable to assimilation by the far more numerous English and needed a way to strengthen their non-English identity.

This cultural unification, as well as the migration of Highlanders to Lowland cities after the Clearances (the eviction of farming tenants by landlords in the first half of the 19th century to make way for sheep pastures) and the spread of the English language into the Highlands, created today's homogeneous Scottish identity, with the CELTS once again achieving prominence. However, it is not the Irish but the Picts who are now considered the true, original Scots.

## The union, the empire, and nationalism

The unpopular Act of Union, which abolished the Scottish Parliament, was accepted only because it guaranteed Scotland's separate legal and educational systems and its Calvinist Presbyterian Church. While Scotland ceased to be an independent state, these guarantees ensured that Scots remained a nation, with their civil society intact.

Although there was no violent opposition to the union – the 1715 and 1745 Jacobite rebellions were not nationalist risings but attempts to restore the deposed Stuart line to the British throne – a significant minority of Scots have never been reconciled to it. However, political nationalism was a 20th century development. Support for the union was strongest in the 19th century, when Scots almost ran the BRITISH empire, and Scotland prospered through access to its global trading network.

The prominent role played by Scots in the empire was primarily a consequence of the country's fine educational system, which, in the 18th century, boasted four universities to England's two. Scots developed striking ethnic specialisms in the maritime, mercantile, military, medical and missionary spheres. The high standard of education also underlay the major role that Scots played in the Enlightenment and the foundation of new academic disciplines, such as political economy.

The decline of the British empire after World War II made being a part of Great Britain less prestigious, but doubts about the viability of Scotland's economy were a brake on nationalist politics until the discovery of vast oil reserves in the North Sea in the 1970s. Nationalism gained ground in the 1980s, during Margaret Thatcher's provocatively Anglocentric Conservative government, and by the 1990s the break-up of the United Kingdom seemed a real possibility. The creation of a devolved Scottish Parliament in 1999, with limited tax-raising powers and control over most of Scotland's internal affairs, was in large part an attempt to head off demands for full independence. The Parliament was given a proportional-representation system, a system which has been rejected for the United Kingdom as a whole, with the specific intention of ensuring a majority against full independence.

# SCYTHIANS

An INDO-IRANIAN people who originated in the Altai Mountains of Central Asia. They were closely related to the SAKA, SARMATIANS, YUE-QI and PARTHIANS. Their name is not their own, but one applied to them by ancient Greek writers.

During the 8th century BC, groups of Scythian tribes migrated westward, displacing the CIMMERIANS from a region north of the Black Sea – an area that later became known as 'Scythia'; some of the Cimmerians were subsequently absorbed, while others fled westwards, destroying the PHRYGIANS. Over the course of the next 200 years, these western Scythians succeeded in raiding as far as Palestine and the border with the EGYPTIANS. The Scythians were instrumental in the destruction of the ASSYRIANS (612 BC), and of the Anatolian URARTIANS (in about 600 BC). They were attacked, unsuccessfully, by the PERSIANS (c. 513 BC), but conquered by the ancient MACEDONIANS in 339 BC. The knock-out blow was delivered by the Sarmatians, however, who by the beginning of the 1st century BC had overrun Scythia; as in the case of the Cimmerians, those who stayed were absorbed by the victors, while others fled west and were absorbed by the DACIANS. The present-day OSSETIANS are said to be descended, in part, from Scythian nomads.

## Lifestyle and culture

Originally a nomadic people, the Scythians were highly regarded as horse-riders and breeders, and possibly invented the use of the stirrup. Following their conquests, traditional Scythian society began to erode. Many renounced a nomadic lifestyle in favour of sedentary arable crop production, and the inflow of booty also led to the concentration of a considerable amount of wealth in the hands of an emerging aristocracy. The ultimate result of this was the development of a hereditary monarchy, a phenomenon observed in a number of similar peoples, such as the Sarmatians.

Scythian burial rituals included embalming the corpse, human and animal sacrifice, and the inclusion of burial goods within a barrow tomb. They were famed for the exquisite quality of their arts and handicrafts, expressed in a range of materials. The most famous of these are their animal motifs rendered in precious metals. The Luristan Bronzes also date from this period. This style was extremely influential, and evidence of its influence can be seen in work produced in China, Bactria (through the KUSHANS), Mesopotamia and western Europe (through trading contacts with the GREEKS and PHOENICIANS); certainly, their influence is evident in the LA TÈNE CULTURE of Europe.

The Scythians themselves were heavily influenced in a number of areas by Hellenistic, Persian and Parthian cultures; for example, in military equipment, tactics and religion. In addition, grave goods are evidence of the trading contacts of the Scythians, which included the Chinese and Persians.

The Scythians spoke an INDO-IRANIAN language, but have left no written records.

## SENONES

A tribe of GAULS who lived in the region between the middle reaches of the Loire and Seine rivers. Their chief centre was Agedincum, now called Sens. In 57 BC the Senones allied with Julius Caesar against the BELGAE. By 53 BC they were disaffected with the ROMAN alliance, and the following year they joined the rebellion led by Vercingetorix of the ARVERNI. Their resistance was crushed within a few months. Another branch of the Senones migrated to northern Italy around 400 BC and settled in the hinterland of Rimini, Pesaro and Senigallia, an area known in the 3rd century BC as the Ager Gallicus ('Gaulish Fields'). Under their leader Brennus, the Senones sacked Rome in 390 BC, but the Romans defeated them in the Battle of Sentinum in 295 BC and conquered the Ager Gallicus. The Senones lost most of their lands in 232 BC when the Romans decided to divide the Ager Gallicus among the city's poor, and the Senones subsequently lost their identity.

## SEQUANI

A tribe of GAULS who inhabited the region between the Jura Mountains and the Rhône and Saône rivers. Their most important centre was Vesontio (modern Besançon). In 58 BC the Sequani unwittingly helped justify Julius Caesar's conquest of Gaul when they allied with the Germanic SUEBI against their rivals, the AEDUI, who were ROMAN allies. The Aedui appealed to Caesar for help and he quickly defeated both the Sequani and the Suebi.

The Sequani played little part in subsequent events. Under Roman rule they were granted a self governing *civitas*. Their tribal identity did not survive into the Middle Ages.

## SERBS

An eastern European people who, with the MONTENEGRINS, make up over 75% of the population of Yugoslavia and 32% of the population of Bosnia-Herzegovina (see SLAVS). Serbs were once a significant minority in Croatia, but most were expelled in the civil war that followed that country's declaration of independence from Yugoslavia. There are also small Serb communities in Hungary. The total population of Serbs is just over 9 million.

Serbs speak the Stokavski dialect of Serbo-Croat, a South Slavic language. This dialect was adopted by CROATS, Serbs and BOSNIAN MUSLIMS as a standard literary language in the 19th century. The eastern and western variants of Stokavski spoken by Serbs and Croats respectively are distinguished only by small differences in pronunciation and vocabulary that reflect the historical experiences of the two peoples. The Serbian vocabulary has loan words from Turkish and Russian, the Croatian has loan words from Italian, German and Hungarian.

Different historical experiences have also produced differences in religion and outlook. The Serbs are Orthodox Christians, who identify with eastern Europe and, especially, with Russia, while the Croats are Roman Catholics and see themselves as western Europeans. Serbs use the Cyrillic alphabet, while Croats use the Latin alphabet. Perhaps the most important historic trait of the Serbs is the sense of being a persecuted people. This stands in stark contrast to many outsiders' current perception of them, born of the Serbs' conduct in the Yugoslav civil wars of the 1990s, as being the persecutors of, in particular, Bosnian Muslims and KOSOVAR ALBANIANS.

In the 7th century the Serbs settled in the Balkans, where they later founded two principalities: Duklja, which developed into the Kingdom of Montenegro, and Raska, which became the core of the Kingdom of Serbia. Under Stefan Dusan in the 13th century, Serbia became the dominant power in the Balkans, expanding far outside its present borders. This 'Greater Serbia' became the inspiration for territorial claims of Serbian nationalists in the 19th and 20th centuries. The most important single event in Serbian history took place on 28 June 1389 when the OTTOMANS defeated the Serbs at Kosovo Polje and conquered Serbia. Under Ottoman rule, many Serbs emigrated to the AUSTRIAN empire, settling in the Vojna KrajinaI ('military frontier') in Croatia and Vojvodina, now part of Serbia but then part of Hungary.

The development of modern Serbian nationalism began with rebellions against Ottoman rule in 1804 and 1815. Serbia gained autonomy within the Ottoman empire in 1829 and was recognized as a fully independent kingdom by the Congress of Berlin in 1878.

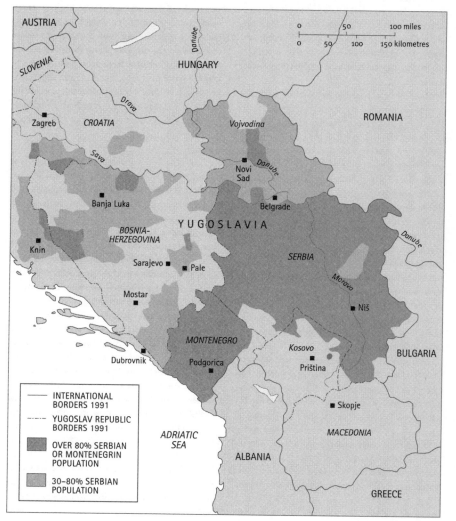

**Serbs**

*Serbian areas and major Serbian enclaves prior to the collapse of Yugoslavia in 1991.*

S

However, the nationalist dream of uniting all Serbs within a single state was thwarted when the Congress awarded Bosnia-Herzegovina to the Austro-Hungarian empire. Tension with the Austro-Hungarian empire came to a climax in 1914 when, on the anniversary of the Battle of Kosovo Polje, a Serbian nationalist assassinated the Austrian archduke Franz Ferdinand in Sarajevo. The killing dragged Europe into World War I and led, ultimately, to the fall of the Austro-Hungarian Empire.

After the war, Serbia became the dominant part of the Kingdom of the Serbs, Croats and Slovenes, known from 1929 as Yugoslavia. Serbian dominance of Yugoslavia led to a backlash when the country was occupied by Germany during World War II. Thousands of Serbs fell victim to genocide orchestrated by the Croat fascist *Ustasa*.

The Serbs continued to feel victimized by the postwar communist regime, whose leader, Josip Broz Tito, was a Croat. Any rapprochement with the Croats was made impossible by the Croats' conviction that it was the Serbs who were favoured by the communist regime. Serb resentment focused not only on the Croats but also on Muslim Bosnians, often dismissed as 'Turks', and Kosovar Albanians.

The Serb nationalist politician Slobodan Milosevic exploited these resentments in his rise to power in the late 1980s. Because of the historical significance of Kosovo for Serb identity, it was particularly hard for Serbs to stomach that Albanians were by now the largest ethnic group in Kosovo. Milosevic's decision to end the province's autonomy in 1989 was popular with Serbs, but it alarmed almost all of Yugoslavia's other ethnic groups.

Milosevic's support for Serbian separatists in Croatia and Bosnia-Herzegovina during the genocidal civil wars of the 1990s attracted international condemnation and made the Serbs the pariahs of Europe. This led the Montenegrins, who had always considered themselves to be Serbs, to distance themselves from their Serbian identity. However, Milosevic and his brand of extreme nationalism remained in control until Serbian repression of the Kosovar Albanians provoked a NATO intervention in 1999 and a change of regime.

Serbians are now trying to rebuild their country as a democracy, but many issues remain unresolved, particularly the status of Kosovo and Montenegro.

## SHETLAND ISLANDERS

See ORCADIANS AND SHETLANDERS.

## SICANI

An ancient people of western Sicily, thought to be of North African or IBERIAN origin. Their material culture was similar to that of their neighbours in the east of the island, the SICELS. After the GREEKS and PHOENICIANS founded colonies on the coast of Sicily from the 8th to the 6th centuries BC, the Sicani became increasingly Hellenized in culture, but remained independent until conquered by the ROMANS in the mid-3rd century. No records of their language have survived.

## SICELS or Siculi

An ancient people of eastern Sicily; it is for the Sicels that Sicily is named. The Sicels spoke an INDO-EUROPEAN language and are thought to have migrated to Sicily from the Italian mainland around 1250 BC. The indigenous SICANI were pushed into the western part of the island. After the GREEKS colonized the western coast of Sicily between the 8th and 6th centuries BC, the Sicels became increasingly Hellenized in culture, and by the 5th century they were speaking Greek. Around 460 BC the Sicels were united by Ducetius who led them in a war against the Greek colonists. After his defeat in 450, the Sicels lived under the domination of the Greeks until the 3rd century, when they were conquered by the ROMANS. The most impressive of the monuments left by the Sicels is the vast necropolis of Pantálica, where thousands of tombs were cut into the faces of sheer limestone cliffs.

## SICILIANS

The people of the Italian island of Sicily. For most of its very long recorded history Sicily has been ruled by foreigners. The earliest known inhabitants were the SICELS, SICANI and ELYMIANS. From the 8th century BC came PHOENICIANS, GREEKS, CARTHAGINIANS, ROMANS, VANDALS, OSTROGOTHS, BYZANTINES, ARABS, NORMANS, FRENCH, ARAGONESE and AUSTRIANS, until in 1734 it was conquered by the SPANISH Bourbon dynasty. In 1759 the Spanish king Charles III made his son Ferdinand King of Naples and Sicily (the Kingdom of the Two Sicilies). The Bourbons ruled until 1860, when they were overthrown by Garibaldi and Sicily was united with Italy.

This succession of invaders created the richly diverse culture of the island but also bred in Sicilians a sense of remoteness and disengagement from their rulers, which even unification with Italy has not eradicated. It was in the years after unification that the Mafia, originally an instrument of landlord oppression, took hold of Sicilian life. The all-pervasive corruption and fear that the Mafia created stunted the economic development of an already impoverished land. The failure of unification to bring tangible benefits convinced ordinary Sicilians that the Italian government cared little for them. In 1948 Sicily became one of only two regions of Italy to take the opportunity of local autonomy offered by the country's new constitution. In recent years progress has been made in eradicating the Mafia, and tourism has helped revive the economy. Through the influence of mass media, the Sicilians are becoming Italianized, but the distinctive local dialect is still spoken. The population of Sicily is around 5.25 million.

## SILURES

Ancient BRITONS of what is now southeast Wales. The Roman author Tacitus described the Silures as being swarthy and curly-haired and speculated that their ancestors had come from Spain. The Silures put up stiff resistance to the ROMANS, fighting a 13-year guerrilla campaign until finally subdued in AD 60. They remained under military government until the early 2nd century when they were granted a self-governing *civitas* with a capital at Venta Siluram (Caerwent). The territory of the Silures formed the basis of the early WELSH kingdom of Gwent, which takes its name from Caerwent.

## SKLAVENI

See SLAVS.

## SLAVS

The largest group of European peoples to share a common ethnic and linguistic origin. The principal modern Slav peoples are the BELORUSSIANS, BOSNIANS, BULGARIANS, CROATS, CZECHS, MACEDONIANS, MORAVIANS, POLES, RUSSIANS, RUTHENIANS, SERBS, SLOVAKS, SLOVENES, SORBS and UKRAINIANS.

The Slavic languages belong to the INDO-EUROPEAN family. Three main groups of Slavic languages are recognized: West Slavic, whose surviving representatives include Polish, Sorbian, Czech and Slovak; South Slavic, which includes Bulgarian, Serbo-Croatian, Slovenian and Macedonian; and East Slavic, which includes Russian, Belorussian and Ukrainian. In total, Slavic languages are spoken by around 285 million people.

Awareness of a common Slav identity emerged in the 19th century, but it has never overridden national identities, and the pan-Slavic movement of the 19th century foundered because of conflicting national interests.

The earliest certain records of the Slavs (*Sklaveni*) date only to the 6th century AD, when they began to migrate into the Balkans, Bohemia and eastern Germany. Place-name evidence indicates that the Slavs already inhabited a vast swathe of eastern Europe between the Vistula and Don rivers at this time, so it is clear that they were already an ancient people. However, the origins of the Slavs are extremely obscure. The ANTES, 'Scythian farmers' (an agricultural people living under the domination of the SCYTHIANS), Serboi and VENEDI – all eastern European peoples mentioned by Classical Greek and Roman writers – have all been plausibly identified as early Slavs, but historians are not unanimous about this, as it is uncertain what languages these peoples spoke. Unfortunately, archaeological evidence is also inconclusive because of the cultural disruptions caused by a succession of migrating Germanic and steppe nomad peoples. The early Iron Age CHERNOLES COMPLEX of the Dnieper region and the roughly contemporary LAUSITZ CULTURE of Poland have both been

S

described as proto-Slavic, but there is no certain link between either and the early Slavs. In all probability the Slavs emerged over a wide area of eastern Europe and from a range of different cultures. For most of their prehistory, the Slavs lived in turn under the domination of the Scythians, SARMATIANS, OSTROGOTHS, HUNS and AVARS. When Avar power declined in the 7th and 8th centuries, the Slavs finally emerged as the dominant peoples of eastern Europe. The most important cultural differences between the modern Slavs emerged in the early Middle Ages as a result of their conversion to different sects of Christianity. Under the influence of the BYZANTINE empire, the East Slavs, Serbs and Bulgarians converted to Orthodox Christianity. The West Slavs, Croats and Slovenes, who lived in closer proximity to the Holy Roman empire, converted to Roman Catholicism.

## SLOVAKS

A west SLAV people who inhabit the Republic of Slovakia. They have lived in their present homeland since the 7th or 8th century AD, but achieved statehood only in 1993, making them the newest of Europe's political nations. Most of the approximately 4.9 million Slovaks live in Slovakia, where they form around 85% of the population, while around 300,000 Slovaks live in the Czech Republic.

During the 9th century the Slovaks were converted to Orthodox Christianity while they were part of the MORAVIAN empire. In 1025 they were conquered by the HUNGARIANS under whose rule they became Catholics. The Slovaks remained under Hungarian, subsequently Austro-Hungarian rule, until 1918. Through this long period they retained both their identity and language, despite attempts to assimilate them to Hungarian culture and the imposition of a largely Hungarian land-owning class in the 18th and 19th centuries.

After the fall of the Austro-Hungarian empire in 1918, the Slovaks were united with the CZECHS and Moravians to form the Republic of Czechoslovakia. When the western part the republic was occupied by the Germans in 1938–9, Slovakia became a German puppet state. In 1945 Slovakia was restored to Czechoslovakia and industrial-

ized rapidly under the communist regime.

After the collapse of the regime in the 1989 'Velvet Revolution', the Slovaks were less enthusiastic than the Czechs to press ahead with free-market reforms, partly because of justified fears that their heavy industry would be unable to compete. This, and the desire that their nationhood be formally recognized, led Slovaks to vote for independence in 1992. Recognizing that Slovakia's independence would only benefit their own economy, the Czechs accepted and the peaceful 'Velvet Divorce' became effective on New Year's Day 1993.

Since independence, Slovakia's economy has struggled to adapt to the new conditions and there have been tensions with the country's Hungarian and Roma (GYPSY) minorities. Nevertheless, in 2004 Slovakians became members of both NATO and the European Union.

## SLOVENES

A SLAV people who inhabit the Republic of Slovenia, where they form about 90% of the population of around 1.93 million. There is also a small Slovenian population just over the border in northern Italy. Slovenian has just sufficient distinctiveness from Serbo-Croatian for it to be recognized as a separate language and not a dialect.

The Slovenes are descendants of Slavs who migrated into the eastern Alpine region in the 6th and 7th centuries AD. These tribes formed a loose federation called Carantia, from which the region of Carinthia (Kärnten), roughly corresponding to modern Slovenia and southeast Austria, was named. Carinthia was conquered by the BAVARIANS in the 8th century and subsequently became part of the Holy Roman empire. In the 16th century Carinthia became part of the crown lands of the AUSTRIAN Habsburg dynasty, remaining under Habsburg rule until 1918.

In the north of Carinthia the population became Germanized, while the south remained Slav-speaking, though lacking a clearly-defined sense of ethnic identity until Slovenian developed as a literary language in the 19th century.

Following the collapse of the Austro-Hungarian empire in 1918, the Slovenes became part of the SERB-dominated Kingdom of the Serbs,

**" After the fall of the tower of Babel and the confusion of tongues, the sons of Japhat occupied the countries of the west and north. From the descendants of Japhat came those who took the name of Slavs. "**

**The Russian Primary Chronicle, 12th century**

Croats and Slovenes, which became known as Yugoslavia in 1929. After World War II, Slovenia, under the communist regime, became the most prosperous republic of Yugoslavia.

It was resentment at having to subsidize the less prosperous republics, rather than hostility toward Serb political dominance, that led the Slovenes to declare their independence from Yugoslavia in 1991. A short war with the Federal Yugoslav army was followed by negotiations that led to international recognition of Slovenia's independence. Slovenia was fortunate in being the most ethnically homogeneous of the constituent republics of Yugoslavia in that it was able to avoid the horrors of civil war after its declaration of independence

## SOLUTREAN CULTURE or Solutrian culture

An Upper Palaeolithic tool culture that developed in the Rhône Valley approximately 20,000 years ago. The culture is named after an open-air site at Solutré in central France.

The Solutreans developed a pressure-flaking technique that enabled them to make fine bi-facially-worked tools, including leaf-shaped projectile points. The Solutreans lived during the cold glacial period and hunted large herd animals, such as horses and bison. Much cave art dates to the Solutrean period. The culture died out around 17,000 years ago and was succeeded by the MAGDALENIAN CULTURE.

## SORBS or Lusatians or Wends

A west SLAV people who live in the Lausitz (Lusatia) region of eastern Germany. The Sorbs are separated into two groups, the Upper Sorbs, who live around Bautzen near the CZECH border, and the Lower Sorbs, who live around Cottbus, near the Polish border. The two groups speak different dialects: the Upper Sorbs speak High Sorbian, which is influenced by Czech, and the Lower Sorbs speak Low Sorbian, which is influenced by Polish. The Upper Sorbs form the larger group, while the numbers of Lower Sorbs are declining, largely through assimilation to GERMAN language and identity. There are about 100,000–120,000 Sorbs in total, but only about half of them now speak the Sorbian language.

The Sorbs are the descendants of two tribes, the Luzici and Milcani, who settled in Lusatia in the 6th century AD. They were conquered by the Germans in 928 and forced to convert to Christianity. In 1002 Lusatia came under Polish rule but was reconquered by the Germans in 1038. German rule ended in the 14th century when Lusatia became part of Bohemia; this break from Germany probably saved the Sorbian identity. In 1635 Lusatia became part of Saxony until it was ceded to Prussia in 1815. After the unification of Germany in 1871, the Sorbs were again subjected to a campaign of Germanization. This led to a revival of Sorbian identity and the foundation of the nationalist organizations *Macica Serbska* in 1847 and *Domowina* ('Homeland') in 1912, to campaign for Sorbian rights. The Nazis suppressed all expressions of Sorbian identity, but the Sorbs were granted extensive minority rights by the communist government that ruled East Germany after 1945. The Sorbs have continued to enjoy these rights since German reunification in 1990, but the pressures to assimilate to German identity remain. The Sorbs are sometimes called 'Wends' by the Germans, a name that was once applied to a wider group of west Slav peoples (see WENDS) of whom they are the last survivors.

## SOUTH SAXONS

Inhabitants of the early ANGLO-SAXON kingdom of Sussex, which roughly approximated the modern English county of the same name. Traditionally, the kingdom was said to have been founded by the SAXON Aelle in AD 477, but Germanic settlement actually began much earlier in the century. Aelle was regarded as the most powerful Anglo-Saxon king of his day, but the South Saxons quickly faded into relative obscurity. From the late 7th century the WEST SAXONS and MERCIANS vied for dominance over the South Saxons, who were finally incorporated into the West Saxon kingdom around 825. The South Saxons were the last of the Anglo-Saxon peoples to accept Christianity; the work of conversion began only in the 680s.

S

# SPANISH

The people of the Kingdom of Spain, whose population in 1996 was around 39.7 million. Although Spain has existed as a unitary state for 500 years, the extent to which its inhabitants share the Spanish identity varies considerably from region to region. The Spanish identity is strongest among the CASTILIANS, ARAGONESE, NAVARRESE and ASTURIANS. The GALICIANS, BASQUES and CATALANS all maintain distinct non-Spanish identities and have strong separatist movements. The ANDALUSIANS, VALENCIANS, BALEARIC ISLANDERS and CANARY ISLANDERS have vibrant regional identities, but lack these separatist tendencies.

### Origins of the Spanish

People could be described as 'Spanish' (*Hispaniensus*) as long ago as Roman times, but the term signified geographical rather than ethnic origin – that is, someone who came from the Iberian peninsula. The early inhabitants of Iberia were a diverse mix of CELTIC and IBERIAN peoples. Between the 8th and 6th centuries BC GREEKS and PHOENICIANS founded colonies along the Mediterranean coast. Iberia was conquered piecemeal by the ROMANS between the 3rd and 1st centuries BC. Its population became Romanized and, by around AD 400, Christianized.

By this time all of the indigenous languages, with the exception of the ancestor of modern Basque, had been replaced by local Latin dialects. In the course of the Middle Ages these developed into separate Romance languages: Castilian and its close relatives Navarrese and Aragonese, Catalan, Galician and PORTUGUESE. This linguistic diversity lies at the root of Spain's many regional identities and also of the PORTUGUESE national identity, which began to develop separately in the 12th century.

As Roman power collapsed in the 5th century, Iberia was invaded by a succession of Germanic tribes, including the VANDALS, SUEBI, ALANS and VISIGOTHS. The Visigoths were the most successful, conquering all of Iberia and ruling it until 711, when the Islamic MOORS invaded from North Africa. The Visigothic kingdom collapsed and the Moors quickly overran the whole peninsula, except the mountainous north and

northwest, where small Christian kingdoms re-established themselves and gradually began to win back territory from the Moors. The experience of the wars of reconquest led the Spanish peoples to identify strongly with a militant Catholicism.

The Christian kingdoms have a complex history of mergers and separations for dynastic reasons. By the time the last Moorish state, Granada, was conquered in 1492, Spain was divided into three kingdoms: Castile, the largest, Aragon and Navarre. The marriage of Isabella of Castile and Ferdinand of Aragon in 1464 brought the two kingdoms together in a union of crowns in 1479, and with Ferdinand's annexation of Navarre in 1515 all of modern Spain was united under a single crown. The three kingdoms were formally unified as the kingdom of Spain by Ferdinand's grandson Charles V in 1517.

### Empire and identity

Following Columbus's accidental discovery of the New World in 1492, Spain built a vast American empire, whose inhabitants were forcibly converted to Christianity and frequently ruthlessly exploited. The mixing of native American and Spanish influences in this empire led to the development of the LATIN-AMERICAN identity.

The prestige of belonging to Europe's richest and most powerful kingdom helped cement the Spanish identity, but it was only partly successful in overriding older regional identities. Identification with Spain was easiest for the Castilians, as they were the dominant ethnic group of the kingdom, and the capital, Madrid, was in their province. Identification with Spain was also easy for speakers of Navarrese and Aragonese, but Catalans, Basques and Galicians retained their strong local identities based on language and separate historical experiences. Attempts to suppress non-Spanish regional identities peaked under the Franco dictatorship (1939–75), which cracked down particularly harshly on expressions of Basque and Catalan traditions. This repression served only to strengthen regionalist and separatist tendencies, however. After Franco's death and the restoration of democracy, the Spanish government recognized the strength of regionalist sentiments and has attempted,

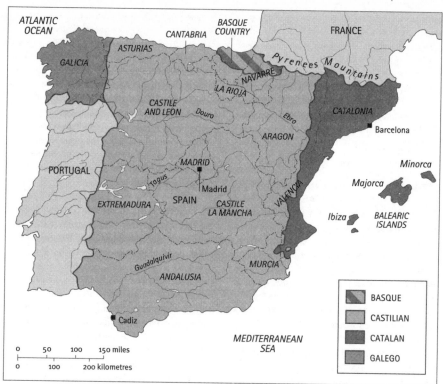

Map legend:
- BASQUE
- CASTILIAN
- CATALAN
- GALEGO

with considerable success, to satisfy them through the introduction of autonomous devolved regional governments. However, the Basque separatist organization ETA (see BASQUES) continues to wage an armed campaign against the Spanish authorities.

## SPARTANS

The descendants of DORIAN Greeks who settled in the Peloponnese in the 11th century BC. The city-state of Sparta developed from the amalgamation of four villages, a legacy of which may have been the city's unique double kingship. By the 8th century BC the Spartans had conquered all of Laconia (the southeast quarter of the Peloponnese) and had reduced its non-Dorian population to the status of helots or serfs. Other groups were given the status of *perioikoi* ('dwellers about'), who enjoyed self-government but no had no other political rights and had to serve in the Spartan army.

In the 7th century BC the Spartans conquered the Messenians (also Dorians) to gain control of the southwest Peloponnese. Sparta became the leading GREEK military power and played a principal role, in alliance with Athens, in defeating the PERSIAN invasion (480–479 BC). After the Persian War Spartans saw the rising power of the ATHENIANS as a threat to their own pre-eminence. In the Peloponnesian War (431–404 BC) Sparta decisively defeated Athens, but lost power after a defeat by Thebes in 371. Sparta had become a minor power by the time it was annexed by the ROMAN empire in 146 BC.

The need to control its resentful helot subjects turned Sparta into the most militarized society in ancient Greece. Boys were taken from their families at the age of seven and given an austere collective upbringing in state barracks, where they learned to become highly disciplined warriors. 'Spartan' has since become synonymous with severe austerity and simplicity. This collective upbringing almost eliminated all class

S

distinctions, creating a conformist, highly cohesive society, whose citizens called themselves *homoioi*, meaning 'the men who are equal'. Relieved of much of the burden of child-care, Spartan women were the freest in the Greek world. Spartan values went on to inspire, for better or worse, the Romans, the Nazis of Germany, and (less gravely) the headmasters of 19th-century ENGLISH public schools.

## SUEBI or Suevi

A major group of early GERMAN peoples. In the 1st century BC and 1st century AD the term 'Suebi' was used in a general sense to include a broad group of German peoples, including the Hermunduri, LOMBARDS, MARCOMANNI, Naristi, Nemetes, QUADI, Semnones, Triboci and Vangiones, who inhabited southern Germany and Bohemia. The Suebi were distinguished from other Germans by the hairstyles of their men, which involved tying their long hair into a knot on the side of their heads.

Originating in northern Germany, the Suebi had migrated south and west to reach the Rhine by around 100 BC and the Danube by around AD 1. Under their king Ariovistus, the Suebi invaded Gaul in 58 BC as allies of the SEQUANI in a war against the AEDUI. Caesar quickly intervened and drove them back across the Rhine. By the 3rd century AD many of the Suebian tribes, such as the Lombards and Marcomanni, had achieved distinct identities of their own and were no longer described as Suebi. Others were absorbed into new tribal confederations such as the ALEMANNI.

The Suebi came under pressure from the HUNS in the later 4th century. Allied with the VANDALS and ALANS, they crossed the Rhine in 406 and invaded Gaul. In 409 the Suebi entered Spain and settled in Galicia in the far northwest. Under their king Rechila, the Suebi had taken over the Roman provinces of Lusitania and Baetica by 447. While settled in Spain, the Suebi were converted to the Arian form of Christianity. In 456 the Suebi lost most of their kingdom to the VISIGOTHS, and what remained was annexed to the Visigothic kingdom in 585.

## SWABIANS

## SWABIANS

The people of the historic region of Swabia, which extends from the Black Forest south to the Swiss border in southwest Germany. The area gets its name from the SUEBI, an early GERMAN people who inhabited the area in the Roman period. The Swabians are descendants of the ALAMANNI, another Germanic people (who included elements of the Suebi) who lived in the area from the 3rd century AD until the 6th century, when they were conquered by the FRANKS, subsequently losing their identity.

After the break-up of the Frankish Carolingian empire in the late 9th century, Swabia emerged as one of the tribal duchies of medieval Germany. The Hohenstaufen dynasty, which ruled the Holy Roman empire 1138–1254, were also the dukes of Swabia. After the extinction of their line, Swabia fragmented into smaller principalities. During the Reformation, the Swabians became strongly Protestant – both Lutheran and Calvinist – and as a result Swabia was devastated by the Catholic Habsburg armies during the Thirty Years War (1618–48). Since 1945 Swabia has been part of Baden-Württemberg. Swabians are sometimes regarded by other Germans as being dour and mean, but they tend to see themselves as hard-working and good-humoured. The now nearly global custom of the Christmas tree is of Swabian origin, a Christianized survival of the pagan reverence for trees.

## SWEDES

The people of the SCANDINAVIAN Kingdom of Sweden. Numbering over 8 million, the Swedes are the most numerous of the Scandinavian peoples. They are probably also the people who come closest to the popular stereotype of the Scandinavian appearance, with nearly 70% of the population blue-eyed and blond-haired. Over 99% of Swedes live in Sweden; the ÅLANDERS share Swedish identity but are citizens of Finland. Finland also has a Swedish-speaking minority (see SWEDISH-SPEAKING FINNS), but they consider themselves FINNS.

The Swedes are a very homogeneous people, although Sweden is also home to small SAAMI and Finnish minorities. As with other European

**Their [the Spartans'] legislation is directed to a single aspect of virtue, the military virtue, which is a source of power.**

Aristotle, *Politics* (*c.* 330 BC)

countries, Sweden has also seen substantial immigration from the Middle East and beyond in the past 25 years.

Swedish society sets a high value on security and generally places the interests of the group above those of the individual. This is neatly encapsulated by the concept of *lagom*, which means 'just the right amount' and can be applied to almost anything, for example to wealth and freedom. Swedes are uncomfortable with straying too far from the average, and the social pressure to conform is considerable. A majority of Swedes claim to believe that social equality is more important than personal freedom. This conformism is the bedrock of the consensus and egalitarianism on which Sweden's advanced, and expensive, system of social welfare is built, but despite the apparent social liberalism of Swedish life it can also manifest itself as a relative intolerance of individualism. It also lies at the root of tensions with the recent immigrant population, many of whom have resisted integration into Swedish society.

**The roots of Swedish identity**

The Swedes take their name from the Svear people (Sweden – in Swedish, *Sverige* – means 'realm of the Svear'), who lived in the Lake Mälaren region in central Sweden. The founder of the Swedish kingdom is held to be King Olof Skötkonung (ruled *c.* 995–1020), who united the Svear and their southern neighbours, the GÖTAR, under his rule. During the Viking era the Swedes were primarily active in the Baltic and Russia, which gets its name from RUS, a corruption of the contemporary Finnish name for the Swedes.

The first attempts to convert the Swedes to Christianity were made in the 9th century, but paganism was not eliminated until the 13th century. In the 12th and 13th centuries the Swedes conquered the Finns, and there was substantial Swedish peasant settlement in the southeast of Finland. In 1397 Sweden was united with Denmark and Norway by the Union of Kalmar.

After a series of rebellions, Sweden regained its independence under the Vasa dynasty in 1523. During the Reformation Swedes adopted Lutheranism, which remains the country's official religion, although church attendance is low.

Under Gustav II Adolf ('Gustavus Adolphus') (ruled 1611–32) Sweden became the dominant power in northern Europe, but its defeat by Russia in the Great Northern War (1700–21) consigned it to the ranks of the minor powers.

Rising population and a shortage of good farmland led over 1.3 million Swedes to emigrate to the USA in the 19th century; Minnesota was a particularly popular destination. Emigration gradually declined as Sweden began to industrialize from the late 19th century onwards. The modern Swedish social model was introduced in 1932 when the Democratic Party came to power and began sweeping social and economic reforms.

Sweden was neutral in both of the 20th century's world wars and after 1945 its economy boomed, giving Swedes among the highest living standards in the world. Sweden's engineering-based industry, with its high labour and social costs, found it increasingly difficult to compete in the 1990s, and this led the country to join the European Union (EU) in 1995.

## SWEDISH-SPEAKING FINNS

A group of about 297,000 FINNS, or 5.9% of the population of Finland, who speak Swedish as their first language. They are descendants of Swedish immigrants during the long period of Swedish rule in Finland, from the 12th century until the RUSSIAN conquest of 1808–9.

Most Swedish-speaking Finns live close to the south and east coasts of Finland; they are mostly urbanized. Since Finland became independent in 1918 Swedish has been recognized as one of the country's official languages, and the right to use the language is enshrined in the constitution. The Swedish spoken in Finland is more conservative than that spoken in Sweden. Swedish-speaking Finns are guaranteed cultural autonomy: they have their own schools and a university (at Åbo), Swedish-language television and radio stations, newspapers and periodicals, a Swedish bishopric and even a Swedish army brigade. The Swedish People's Party represents the interests of Swedish-speakers in parliament. The Swedish-speaking ÅLANDERS are Finnish citizens, but they regard themselves as ethnic SWEDES.

# SWISS

The people of Switzerland, a federal republic. They combine considerable ethnic, linguistic, cultural and religious diversity with a strong commitment to their common national identity. Approximately 74% of the population of around 7.2 million are GERMAN in language and culture. Standard High German is used for writing but the spoken language, Schwyzerdütsch, is closer to the German dialects of Austria and Baden-Württemberg. About 17% of the population are French-speaking and about 8% speak Italian. About 1% of the population, living mainly in remote Alpine valleys in the southeast of the country, speak Romansch (or Rhaeto-Romanic), a Romance language related to Italian.

The Swiss are almost equally divided between Roman Catholics and Protestants (mainly Calvinists). Historically, religious divisions among the Swiss have been more significant than linguistic ones.

The Swiss state originated in 1291 when the three German-speaking cantons (provinces) of Schwyz (from which the country gets its name), Uri and Unterwalden declared independence from their AUSTRIAN Habsburg rulers and formed a confederation for mutual defence. In the 14th century four more cantons joined: Lucerne, Zurich, Bern and Glarus. The rugged mountainous terrain controlled by the cantons was easy to defend against Habsburg attacks and provided a secure base from which the confederation was able to expand further in the 15th century to include French- and Italian-speaking cantons.

By 1536 Switzerland had reached approximately its present borders, yet its independence was not formally recognized by the Habsburgs until 1648. This continuing external Habsburg threat was crucial to consolidating the Swiss national identity through the difficult years of the Reformation when religious tensions threatened to tear the confederation apart. Zurich and Geneva became major centres of the radical Protestant teaching of Ulrich Zwingli and John Calvin respectively.

The Swiss adopted a policy of neutrality in 1515 and have remained neutral in geopolitical affairs ever since, including through the two world wars. (Today, they are members of neither NATO nor the European Union.) This did not, however, protect Switzerland from French inva-

> " In Switzerland they had brotherly love, five hundred years of democracy and peace, and what did that produce ...? The cuckoo clock. "
>
> Orson Wells

Swiss

*Swiss national identity is strong despite the use of four major languages within Switzerland's borders.*

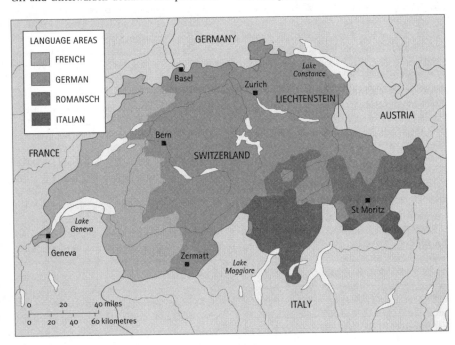

sion and occupation in 1797, when the country was renamed the Helvetic Republic, echoing the ROMAN name for the GAULS of the region, the HELVETII (Today, Swiss postage stamps retain the Latin 'Helvetica').

Although the confederation was restored in 1815, proposals to strengthen the federal government led to a three-week civil war in 1845 when seven Catholic cantons formed a league to oppose it. A liberal constitution introduced in 1874 widened participatory democracy and introduced the referendum as a way of dealing with national issues without vesting more powers in the federal government.

Switzerland changed greatly in the later 19th century through the introduction of railways, industrialization and the development of banking and tourism, but the Swiss have remained in many ways conservative. Women could vote in national elections only from 1971 and won equal rights in employment and marriage only in the 1980s. Although the Swiss may continue to look culturally to their linguistic 'fatherlands', there are no internal ethnic tensions that seem likely threaten the future of the confederation.

## TABASSARAN

A Caucasian people of Khiv and Tabassaran regions, southeast Dagestan, Russian Federation. Farmers and herders, they are Sunni Muslims who speak a North Caucasian language.

They were under RUSSIAN rule from the 19th century, and later Soviet collectivization and assimilatory education policies undermined both their culture and economy. Entire villages were forcibly relocated when the Soviet government decided to increase production in wine grapes, degrading their national identity further. Incursions into their territory by CHECHEN guerrillas were another source of concern in 1999. In 1996 they numbered nearly 96,000.

## TARTESIANS

An ancient IBERIAN people whose territory centred on the lower valley of the River Guadalquivir. They are named for Tartesos, their main settlement, which was probably at the modern Spanish port of Huelva. Famous for its mineral wealth, Tartesos (the Biblical Tarshish) attracted PHOENICIAN and GREEK merchants in the 7th century BC but was later overshadowed as a trading centre by the CARTHAGINIAN colony of Gades (Cadiz).

The culture of the Tartesians was much influenced by the Phoenicians, who introduced them to iron, the potter's wheel, vase painting and the alphabet.

## TATARS

A Turkic nation (see TURKS) centred on the Volga River area and the autonomous republic of Tatarstan in the Russian Federation, but also spread across the former USSR.

Originally nomadic herders from northeast Mongolia, the Tatars were combined with the MONGOLS by Ghengis Khan in the 13th century and sent to conquer the RUSSIAN lands. Renowned for their ferocity, they established the GOLDEN HORDE to rule their conquests and adopted Sunni Islam in the 14th century. They also became increasingly sedentary farmers and traders.

As the Golden Horde broke up into separate khanates, the Tatars became vulnerable to Russian aggression. The khanates of Astrakhan and Kazan (see KAZAN TARTARS) fell in the 16th century, the Crimea khanate in 1783. Attempts at Russification and forced baptism had only limited success and provoked many revolts. Soviet collectivization and assimilatory policies caused considerable hardship, but again failed to undermine Tatar national identity. In Tatarstan there is anger that KRYASHENS are treated as a separate people for political reasons, and that their own 1991 declaration of independence was not recognized.

The Crimean Tatars were deported to Central Asia in 1945 for alleged collaboration with the Germans. In 1999 many had returned, but found their homes and lands occupied, and were not even counted as UKRAINIAN citizens. In 1991 the Tatars numbered about 7 million.

## TAULI

See BALKARS

> ❝ They [the Tatars] are brave in battle, almost to desperation, setting too little value on their lives ... Their disposition is cruel ❞
>
> Marco Polo, 1298

# TECTOSAGES

See VOLCAE.

# TEPTIYARS

A Turkic language-speaking people (see TURKS) of Bashkiriya autonomous republic, Russian Federation. Descended from TATARS, along with UDMURT and MARI groups who fled east with the fall of the Kazan khanate in 1552, they took shelter among the BASHKIRS. They retained their identity as a people, but were heavily influenced by Bashkir culture. Under Soviet RUSSIAN rule they were not recognized as a separate people and were officially counted as Bashkirs or Tatars, whose subsequent experiences they shared. In 1980 there were still about 300,000 Teptiyar language-speakers.

# TERVINGI

A clan of GOTHS who, with the GREUTHUNGI, became the nucleus around which the VISIGOTHS formed in the 4th century.

# TEUTONES

Early GERMANS from Jutland in Denmark. Along with neighbouring tribes the CIMBRI and the Ambrones, the Teutones migrated out of Jutland around 120 BC and spent nearly 20 years traversing much of central and western Europe in search of a new homeland.

After defeating a Roman army at Arausio (Orange in southern France) in 105 BC, the Teutones, Ambrones and Cimbri split up. The Teutones and Ambrones headed north into the territory of the BELGAE, who forced them south again into the Rhône Valley, where they were defeated and annihilated by the ROMANS at Aix-en-Provence in 102 BC. The district of Thy in northern Jutland probably gets its name from the Teutones.

# THRACIANS

An ancient INDO-EUROPEAN-speaking people who inhabited Thrace, an area roughly approximating to modern Bulgaria. There were also scattered Thracian populations north of the River Danube and in Anatolia (modern Turkey and northern Syria).

The Thracians probably settled in the Balkans between 1600 and 1200 BC, but their original homeland is unknown. The earliest records of the Thracians are in ancient GREEK myths; the legendary musician Orpheus was a Thracian, for example.

The early Thracians were a tribal people, ruled by a warrior aristocracy who lived in fortified residences. They practised polygamy and the men tattooed their bodies. They were conquered by the PERSIANS in 516 BC, but recovered their independence in 476 BC and were united under King Teres of the Odrysae tribe. They were conquered again in the mid-4th century, this time by Philip II of Macedon (ruled 359–336 BC), and they remained under MACEDONIAN control until 168 BC, when western Thrace came under ROMAN control. Eastern Thrace became independent under a native dynasty until it too was annexed by the Romans in AD 48. The Thracians had lost their identity by the late Roman period. The y are best known for their spectacular metalwork, which shows the influence of Greek, SCYTHIAN and Persian art.

# THURINGIANS

A Germanic tribe who were settled around the confluence of the Saale and Elbe rivers in the 5th century AD. Thuringia in central Germany is named for them. The tribe probably formed in the 4th century, with the Hermunduri (part of the SUEBI) as its core. The Thuringians were conquered by the FRANKS around 530; some were absorbed by the BAVARIANS, while others joined the LOMBARDS.

# TINDI

A Caucasian people of western Dagestan, Russian Federation. They are closely related to the AVARS, whose history they largely share and whose written language they use. They are herders, Sunni Muslims and speakers of a North Caucasian language. Owing to Soviet collectivization and assimilatory policies, they are in danger of complete assimilation by the Avars. In

> **“** Each man among the Thracians has several wives and no sooner has a man died than a dispute breaks out among them as to which of them their husband loved the most dearly. **”**
>
> Herodotus
> 5th century BC

**Thracians: main tribes**

Crestonae
Getae
Odrysae
Thyni
Trausi
Triballi

1960, the last time they were officially counted separately, they numbered about 5000.

# TREVERI

A powerful Gaulish tribe of the Moselle Valley region who were renowned for their cavalry. The Treveri were conquered by Julius Caesar in 54–52 BC, but they rebelled against ROMAN rule in 28 BC, AD 21 and AD 70. They nevertheless became highly Romanized, and for a time in the 4th century their chief town, Augusta Trevorum (modern Trier in Germany), was the seat of the imperial Roman court.

# TRINOVANTES

A tribe of ancient BRITONS whose territory comprised modern Suffolk and Essex. Their main settlement and the seat of their kings was Camulodunum (Colchester). Under threat from neighbouring tribes, the Trinovantes became ROMAN allies following Julius Caesar's invasion of Britain in 54 BC.

Around AD 10 the Trinovantes were conquered by Cunobelinus, the king of the CATUVELLAUNI, who moved his capital to Camulodunum. After the Claudian invasion in AD 43 the city became the capital of the Roman province, but heavy demands for labour and taxes alienated the formerly pro-Roman Trinovantes and they rose in rebellion with the neighbouring ICENI in 60–1. After their defeat, the Trinovantes were granted a self-governing *civitas* and the Roman administration moved to London.

# TRIPOLYE-CUCUTENI CULTURE or Cucuteni-Tripolye culture

A late Neolithic culture of the west Ukrainian steppes, Moldova and Romania, dating to between 4200 and 3800 BC. The culture is named for two sites, Cucuteni in Romania and Tripolye in Ukraine.

The Tripolye-Cucuteni people lived in large villages on natural defensive sites or, where these were not available, surrounded by defensive ditches. Houses were built on platforms of tim-

ber and fired clay and often had plastered, painted walls. They made copper and gold artefacts and high-quality painted pottery, and were among the first peoples to domesticate horses.

# TUNGRI

A tribe of the BELGAE, whose chief settlement was Atuatuca, modern Tongres in Belgium. The Tungri prided themselves on their GERMAN ancestry, but by the time they were conquered by the ROMANS under Julius Caesar (58–51 BC) they had become completely Celtic in language and culture (see CELTS, ANCIENT).

# TURDETANI

An IBERIAN people of the Guadalquivir River valley in southern Spain. They were probably descended from the TARTESIANS and were brought under ROMAN rule in 197–195 BC.

# TYROLESE

Inhabitants of the Alpine Tyrol region, which is now divided roughly equally between Austria and Italy. The Tyrolese are AUSTRIANS, but their identification with their region is at least as strong as their identification with Austria. The division of the Tyrol between Austria and Italy dates to 1919. Following the fall of the Austro-Hungarian empire after its defeat in World War I, the South Tyrol was awarded to Italy as its reward for fighting on the Allied side during the war. After the Italian Fascists came to power in 1922, the German-speaking South Tyrolese were subjected to a campaign of Italianization and in 1939 were given a choice of emigration or, in effect, becoming ITALIANS. Most emigrated to Austria (then, following the *Anschluss* with Germany, part of the Third Reich). In 1945 most of those who had emigrated were given permission to return to their homes and given limited local autonomy, greatly extended in 1968.

# UBII

An early GERMAN tribe who had settled on the west bank of the middle Rhine shortly before the Roman conquest of Gaul. Threatened by the powerful SUEBI on the east bank of the Rhine, the Ubii adopted a pro-ROMAN policy, supporting Julius Caesar in his campaigns against the GAULS in the 50s BC and against other German tribes such as the Usipetes and Tencteri, and were rewarded with a territory around Cologne, founded in the 1st century AD as their tribal capital. They had lost their tribal identity, however, by the early Middle Ages.

## UBYKHS

A people who lived around the Black Sea resort of Sochi and the northwest Caucasus Mountains of southern Russia: they are now considered to be extinct. After they were conquered by the RUSSIANS in 1864 the Ubykhs migrated to the OTTOMAN Turkish empire, where they slowly became assimilated to the Turkish population. The Ubykh language, which died out in 1992, belonged to the Abkhazo-Adyghian group of the Caucasian languages and was closely related to ABKHAZIAN. It was notable for its very large number of distinct consonants (over 80) and small number of vowels.

## UDMURTS

A western Urals people of Udmurtia autonomous republic, Russian Federation. Largely sedentary farmers and herders, they speak a FINNO-UGRIAN language now endangered. Under RUSSIAN rule since the 16th century, many moved east to escape violently enforced Christianization, but Russification continued. Under Soviet rule collectivization and assimilatory education policies seriously weakened their traditional culture. The collapse of the USSR allowed attempts to preserve their language and culture, but also heralded severe economic decline. In 1998 they probably numbered around 715,000.

## UKRAINIANS

The people of the Slavic (see SLAVS) Republic of Ukraine. They are descendants of the RUS, whose capital Kiev was in fact the first Russian city-state. In the 10th and 11th centuries a loose confederation of city-states based on Kiev grew wealthy, but it fragmented and was easily conquered by the MONGOLS by 1241.

**Ukrainians**

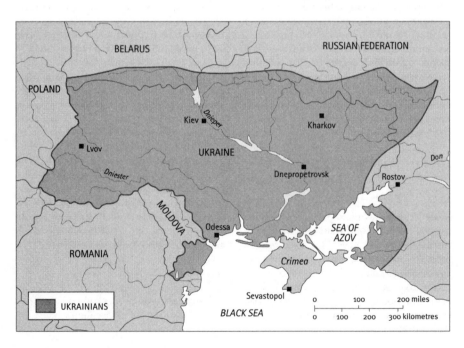

As the city-state of Moscow began the slow process of spreading its rule across the RUSSIAN people, Kiev and its people were being subjugated by LITHUANIANS from the 1360s. The Lithuanians in turn were increasingly dominated by the POLES, made official in the Union of Lublin (1596). For the Ukrainians this proved disastrous. Their nobility became thoroughly assimilated, the peasantry were brutally exploited and their Orthodox Church persecuted. For some, the opportunity of flight remained, especially for the COSSACKS, whose plain democratic ways, defiance of authority and daring raids made them the symbol of Ukrainian aspirations.

In 1648, under their great hero Bohdan Khmelnitsky, the Ukrainians launched a major war against Polish rule, and won considerable success, but failed to establish a stable nation. Peasants wanted Cossack freedoms, but landowners wanted subservient peasants. Lying between three powerful nations, the POLES, Crimean TATARS and the Russians, they were also unable to gain recognition of their independence. The Ukrainians turned to Moscow for aid, and a long war resulted in the partition of the Ukraine along the River Dnieper between Russia and Poland, through the Treaty of Andrusovo (1667).

**Russian and Polish domination**

The Ukrainians under Polish rule thereafter knew exploitation, poverty and forced assimilation, even after their lands passed to Austria in the partitions of Poland (1772–95). Under Russian rule they fared no better. Cossack freedoms were whittled away and Russian institutions such as serfdom were introduced. The Russians refused to accept, and never have accepted, that the centuries of separation have forged an entirely new nation. To them Ukrainians are simply 'little Russians', and their language merely Russian 'with a Polish accent'. Many Ukrainians see themselves as totally separate, with a more tolerant and distinct culture and much stronger traditions of personal liberty. Discrimination against their language and lack of education meant that the growth of a modern national consciousness was hampered until the late 19th century.

Only revolution in Russia (1917) and Germany (1918) allowed an attempt to forge an independent state and the spread of a national consciousness throughout all sections of society. By 1920, however, the independence movement was defeated, and the Ukrainian people were again partitioned among the USSR, Poland and Czechoslovakia. Those under Soviet rule suffered dreadfully through Stalin's deportation of richer peasants and forcible collectivization of agriculture, resulting in a famine that killed millions in the early 1930s. Millions more died under German occupation (1941–4), but the defeat of Germany allowed all Ukrainians to be brought into a single Soviet republic, with some trappings of nationhood, such as a separate seat in the United Nations. Ukrainian national aspirations, culture and language, however, were still suppressed.

When the USSR collapsed in 1991 the Ukrainians were quick to seize their independence. They are aware, however, that Russians do not accept this separation as permanent, and their relationship with their powerful neighbour remains uneasy. In addition, Ukrainians have struggled since 1991 with a corrupt and often gridlocked political system and a lack of democratic reforms, as well as severe economic problems. In 2002 Ukrainians numbered over 48 million.

# ULAID

An extended group of northern IRISH royal dynasties. In late pagan times the Ulaid ruled a confederation of kingdoms covering most of northern Ireland from their royal centre at Emain Macha near Armagh. Their wars with the CONNACHTA form the basis of the Ulster Cycle of early Irish myths.

In the mid-5th century AD the Ulaid lost control of Emain Macha and were confined to the area east of the River Bann (roughly County Antrim and County Down). The kingdom of the Ulaid was destroyed in 1177 by the ANGLO-NORMAN lord John de Courcy.

An important branch of the Ulaid was the Dál Riata (Dalriada) of Antrim who conquered Argyll around AD 500 and founded the first SCOTS kingdom.

# ULSTER SCOTS

A term used mainly in North America to describe the descendants of Lowland SCOTS Presbyterians who colonized Ulster during the early 17th century. The settlement was encouraged by King James VI & I of Scotland and England as a way of bringing rebellious Catholic Ireland more firmly under government control. Although Scots settled in all of the counties of Ulster, it was only in counties Down and Antrim that they formed a majority of the population.

The settlers were deeply resented by the native IRISH, whose lands had been expropriated, and they rebelled in 1640. Around 4000 of the settlers were massacred and thousands more died of disease, hunger and exposure after being driven from their homes. Although the Catholic rebellion was eventually defeated, the Ulster Protestants developed a siege mentality, which promoted social cohesiveness, self-reliance and the conviction that Catholicism was a standing threat to their identity and way of life. Presbyterianism has given their modern Unionist descendants in Northern Ireland a dour image and a tradition of plain-speaking that has set them at a public relations disadvantage when dealing with Nationalist negotiators in the modern peace process. The tendency of Unionists to say exactly what they mean is seen by outsiders as bigotry and intransigence – characteristics that they do not recognize in themselves.

Many thousands of Ulster Scots emigrated to North America during the 18th century, where their experience of living amid a hostile population made them ideal as frontier settlers. Ultimately, the contribution of the Ulster Scots to the founding values of the United States was second only to that of the ENGLISH. Many US presidents have been of Ulster Scots extraction. The distinctive Ulster Scots dialect, derived from the dialects of Lowland Scotland, is still widely spoken in Northern Ireland by both Protestants and Catholics.

# UMBRIANS

An ancient ITALIAN people who lived in north-central Italy between the Apennine Mountains and the Adriatic Sea. They spoke an Italic language related to Oscan (see SABELLI). The Umbrians were conquered by the ROMANS between 310 BC and 266 BC. Umbrian culture was much influenced by the ETRUSCANS.

# ÚNETICE CULTURE or Aunjetitz culture

The earliest Bronze Age culture of north-central Europe, centred on the Elbe and Oder river basins. The Únetice culture dates to between 2200 BC and 1800 BC and is named after a site near Prague. Bronze-working was probably an independent development of the Únetice culture, not an introduction from the Middle East, as its use here predates its adoption in southeast Europe by around 200 years. The Únetice culture is typical of the early Bronze Age cultures of temperate Europe in reflecting the development of a hierarchical society ruled by chiefs who commanded considerable resources and were buried with prestige goods under round barrows.

# URNFIELD CULTURES

A complex of Bronze Age cultures named after their distinctive burial practices. Bodies were cremated and the ashes placed in pottery funerary urns for burial in huge flat cemeteries containing hundreds or even thousands of graves. One of the largest Urnfield cemeteries, at Kelheim in southern Germany, contained over 10,000 graves. Urnfields first appeared around 1350 BC in modern Hungary, spreading from there into Poland, Germany, Austria, Switzerland, Belgium, France, Italy and Spain by 1000 BC.

The spread of the Urnfield cultures across western Europe is seen by some archaeologists as evidence of Celtic migrations from a hypothetical central European homeland (see CELTS, ANCIENT), but it has proved impossible to assign the Urnfield cultures to any particular ethnic group. They represent an ethnically and linguistically varied group of peoples, which probably included early Celtic-speaking peoples among them. The widespread nature of the Urnfield cultures is better explained by the social and economic circumstances of Bronze Age Europe. The geographically limited distribution of the copper and tin ores needed to make bronze meant that communities had to trade, often over long distances, if they wanted to obtain bronze weapons, tools and prestige display objects. These trade links also enabled new ideas to spread widely through Europe. By around 900 BC, the Urnfield cultures had diversified into a wide range of regionally distinctive cultures, such as the HALLSTATT and LAUSITZ cultures.

## URUM

A Hellenic people of the Donetsk region, southern Ukraine, and of Georgia. They were originally Anatolian GREEK farmers and miners who were invited by the RUSSIAN government to settle from the 18th century in order to weaken the newly conquered Crimean TATARS. They speak Turkish. They were never counted as a separate people and many became fully assimilated. Under Soviet rule they were collectivized and their culture and identity undermined. Since the collapse of the USSR many have migrated to Greece. In 1989 they numbered up to 60,000.

## VALDAOSTANS or Valdôtains

The inhabitants of the Val d'Aosta in the Italian Alps, bordering France and Switzerland. They speak both a Romance dialect called Harpeitanya and French. The ITALIAN Fascist government banned both Harpeitanya and French during the 1920s and 1930s, but the valley was given local autonomy in 1948 and is now officially bilingual, with both French and Italian being recognized. Preserving the Francophone character of the valley has been a live political issue since the 1970s; a large proportion of its 113,000 inhabitants are now Italian-speakers, attracted by the stunning mountain scenery.

## VALENCIANS

A CATALAN-speaking people of the Valencia region in southeast Spain. Valencians are anxious to distinguish themselves from the Catalans and maintain that *Valencià*, as they call their Catalan dialect, is actually an independent language, although few linguists agree. Valencia had only a brief period of independent statehood in

the Middle Ages, and Valencian nationalism has never found a popular following; on the whole Valencians, in contrast to the Catalans, are content to be SPANISH.

## VANDALS

A major early GERMAN people. They were first recorded living in what is now central Poland. By the 3rd century AD the Vandals had migrated further southeast into Hungary and divided into two groups, the Silings and the Asdings.

The arrival of the HUNS in eastern Europe in the late 4th century destabilized the whole Germanic world, and the Vandals, in alliance with the ALANS and the SUEBI, fled west toward the Rhine frontier of the ROMAN empire. On the last day of 406 this coalition crossed the Rhine, which was frozen hard, and invaded Gaul. In 409 they entered Spain, where the coalition broke up. The Asdings settled in Galicia and the Silings settled in Baetica in southern Spain. The Romans paid the VISIGOTHS to attack the Silings, and they were saved from extermination only when the Asdings moved south to join them.

The reunited Vandals were far from secure, and in 428 their king, Gaiseric, arranged for the whole nation, 80,000-strong according to contemporary accounts, to be transported to North Africa. Landing near Tangier, they moved east and in 439 captured Carthage in Tunisia, where they established their capital. They quickly took to the sea and launched pirate raids all around the Mediterranean. In 455 they sacked Rome itself: their name has been synonymous ever since with wanton destruction.

After entering the Roman empire, the Vandals converted to Arian Christianity and vigorously persecuted the native Catholic subjects of their African kingdom. The religious divide protected the Vandals from assimilation by the more numerous Romanized native population, but it also ensured that this population developed no sense of loyalty or identification with their Germanic rulers. When the Eastern Roman emperor Justinian sent an army to recapture Carthage in 533, the Vandal kingdom abruptly collapsed.

V

**Vandals**

*The long migration of the Vandals through the weakened Roman empire led to the establishment of a shortlived North African kingdom.*

# V

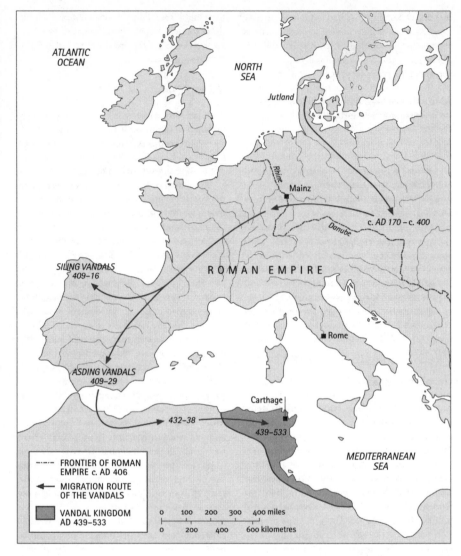

ATLANTIC OCEAN

NORTH SEA

Jutland

Rhine

Mainz

*c. AD 170 – c. 400*

*Danube*

ROMAN EMPIRE

*SILING VANDALS 409–16*

Rome

*ASDING VANDALS 409–29*

Carthage

*432–38*

*439–533*

MEDITERRANEAN SEA

----- FRONTIER OF ROMAN EMPIRE c. AD 406

← MIGRATION ROUTE OF THE VANDALS

▓ VANDAL KINGDOM AD 439–533

| 0 | 100 | 200 | 300 | 400 miles |
| 0 | 200 | 400 | 600 kilometres |

## VARANGIANS

A term used by GREEKS, ARABS and SLAVS from the mid-10th to the late 12th centuries to describe SCANDINAVIANS. Because of their Scandinavian origins, the RUS are sometimes described as Varangians, but by the time the term came into use they were becoming Slavic in language and culture, and the term was usually reserved for Scandinavian merchants and mercenaries newly arrived in the east from their homelands. The BYZANTINE emperor's elite bodyguard, the Varangian Guard, was recruited from Scandinavian and (after 1066) ENGLISH mercenaries. The name is thought to be derived from Old Norse *vár*, meaning 'pledge', probably because bands of Scandinavians customarily formed sworn fellowships.

# VASCOS

See BASQUES.

# VENDEL CULTURE

A Migration Period (AD 400-600) culture of central Sweden, associated with the development of the first SWEDISH royal dynasty in the 6th century AD. The culture is named after a pagan cemetery near Uppsala with richly furnished ship burials. The culture is defined by its distinctive style of animal ornament, a style that influenced cultures as far away as that of the ANGLO-SAXONS in England.

# VENEDI or Veneti

An ancient people of eastern Europe who are thought to have been early SLAVS. The Veneti are first recorded in the 1st century AD and disappeared from the historical record after the 6th century. The GERMAN name for the Slav tribes of the southern Baltic coast, WENDS, is derived from their name.

# VENETI (Brittany)

An ARMORICAN people of southeastern Brittany. The Veneti prospered in the late Iron Age by establishing themselves as key middlemen in the Atlantic tin trade, selling on CORNISH tin to merchants from the Mediterranean world. The Veneti were conquered by the ROMANS after Julius Caesar defeated their fleet in a naval battle in Quiberon Bay in 56 BC. Their name survives in the Breton city of Vannes.

# VENETI (Italy)

An ancient Italic-speaking people who settled on the Adriatic coast around the mouth of the Po River around 1000 BC. Venice is named after them. The Veneti held out against the GAULS, who invaded northern Italy around 400 BC, and repulsed a GREEK invasion in 302 BC. Their position made them natural allies of the ROMANS in their wars against the Gauls in 3rd and 4th centuries BC. The Romans founded the colony of Aquileia in 181 BC to protect the Veneti from

raids by Alpine tribes, and over the next century they were peacefully incorporated into the Roman empire. The Veneti were made full Roman citizens in 49 BC.

# VEPS

A FINNO-UGRIAN people who live south of Lake Onega in the KARELIAN autonomous republic, Russian Federation. The Veps are first recorded in the 11th century when they were active in the north European fur trade. They have been under RUSSIAN rule since the 15th century. Although the Veps were converted to Orthodox Christianity in the Middle Ages, belief in magic and spirits persisted into the 20th century.

The Veps are steadily being assimilated into the Russian identity. Numbering around 34,000 in the 1930s, their numbers had more than halved to fewer than 16,000 by the late 20th century, only 40% of whom could speak the Veps language.

# VERKHOVINSKY

See BOIKOS.

# VIATICHIANS

An East SLAV people who lived in central European Russia between the rivers Dniester and Don. They were conquered by the Kievan RUS in the late 10th century.

# VIKINGS

A term customarily used today to describe all early medieval SCANDINAVIANS, although it originally meant 'pirate' and had no ethnic overtones. To contemporaries, a *vikingr* was simply someone who went í *víking* – that is, plundering. Only a small minority of early medieval Scandinavians were, therefore, Vikings in the strict meaning of the word. The origins of the word are unclear but the earliest records of its use are from 8th-century England. There are several possible explanations of its derivation. One is that it is related to Viken in southern Norway and so means simply 'the men from Viken'. Another is that it comes from the Scandinavian

**V**

**❝** The Veneti [of Brittany] have the largest fleet of ships in which they trade with Britain; they excel all others in their knowledge and experience of navigation. **❞**

Julius Caesar, 1st century BC

word *vík* ('bay') and means 'men of the bays'. A third possibility is that it is derived from an Old English word *wic* ('port of trade') and so means the 'men who frequent (or attack) ports'. The term fell out of use around the 13th century and was revived with its current ethnic meaning by Scandinavian nationalists in the 19th century.

## VILLANOVA CULTURE

An early Iron Age culture (*c.* 900–700 BC) of the Po River valley, in the Tuscany and Campania regions of Italy. The culture is named after a site near Bologna. Influenced by the Bronze Age URNFIELD CULTURES, the Villanovans cremated their dead and buried their ashes in hut-shaped terracotta urns in vast cemeteries. This custom died out in the 8th century BC and was replaced by the burial of dead bodies. The larger Villanovan settlements developed into city-states around 700 BC, laying the foundations for the emergence of the ETRUSCAN civilization in the following century.

## VISIGOTHS

A Germanic people who emerged, along with the OSTROGOTHS, from the break-up of the GOTHS in the late 3rd century AD. The Visigoths ('West Goths') were formed of two main clans, the GREUTHUNGI and the TERVINGI, who settled in Dacia (Romania) in the late 3rd century.

The arrival of the HUNS in eastern Europe in 372 forced the Visigoths to seek refuge in the ROMAN empire in 376. The Romans allowed the Visigoths to settle in Thrace (modern Bulgaria), but treated them so badly that they rebelled, defeating and killing the emperor Valens at Adrianople (Edirne) in 378.

The Visigoths were pacified in 382, but they rebelled again in 395 when their king, Alaric, led them south into Greece. From there he led them through the Balkans and into northern Italy in 401. Alaric was seeking a permanent new homeland for his people, but the Romans proved intransigent. In 410 Alaric captured and sacked Rome itself, but, although the event sent shock waves around the empire, it did not bring the settlement he hoped for: Rome was no longer the capital of the empire – the emperor now ruled from Ravenna in northern Italy, and he refused to negotiate.

Alaric moved to southern Italy, preparing to invade Africa, but he died soon afterwards and his successor Athaulf took the Visigoths out of Italy into Gaul. After helping the Romans defeat the VANDALS, the Visigoths were finally granted a territory in Aquitaine. In 451 the Visigoths again supported the Romans, this time against the invasion of Attila the Hun. In 454 they suppressed peasant rebels in northern Spain and shortly afterwards attacked the SUEBI, who were settled in Lusitania.

The Visigoths abandoned their pro-Roman stance under Euric (ruled 466–84), who recognized the final collapse of Roman power and took advantage of it to conquer most of Spain and much of southern Gaul. In 506 the Visigoths were defeated by the FRANKS and driven out of Gaul. Except for the area around Narbonne, Visigothic power was then confined to Spain.

Spain remained prosperous under Visigothic rule. The Visigoths had become partially Romanized during their years of wandering in the empire and they maintained an efficient government and a cultured court. It is estimated that there were only between 100,000 and 200,000 Visigoths living in Spain among a native population that may have been 10 million. However, the Visigoths had converted to Arian Christianity and this was a barrier between them and their Catholic subjects, which helped them maintain their identity and avoid assimilation. Not surprisingly, their influence on SPANISH culture and identity was limited to Germanic place names and a few dozen Germanic loan words in SPANISH dialects. Even after the Visigoths converted to Catholicism in the late 6th century, their Spanish subjects never developed any great sense of loyalty to the kingdom, and it collapsed quickly after the MOORS invaded in 711.

## VIVISCI

See BITURIGES.

## VLACHS

A ROMANIAN-speaking minority of Macedonia, northern Greece, Bulgaria and Albania. The

**[The Vlachs] are as common and elusive as wolves.**

D. Seward & S. Mountgarret, *Byzantium, a journey and a guide* 1985 name is derived from *Volokh*, a word used by the SLAVS to describe Romance-speaking peoples in the Balkan region, including the ancestors of the Romanians. The early Romanian state of Wallachia ('land of the Vlachs') was named after the Vlachs. They are a dispersed people, living in the same villages as the majority populations but rarely inter-marrying with them. Although the MACEDONIAN Vlachs enjoy a measure of recognition, this is not the case for the GREEK Vlachs: no census of the Greek Vlach population has been carried out since 1951 (when their numbers were 40,000). It is estimated that the total Vlach population is now around 50,000, about 10,000 of whom live in Macedonia and perhaps 2000 in Bulgaria and Albania.

## VOLCAE

The major tribe of southwest Gaul. They were divided into two sub-tribes: the Arecomici, whose chief centre was Nemausus (modern Nîmes), and the Tectosages, whose chief centre was Tolosa (modern Toulouse). In the 3rd century BC a branch of the Tectosages migrated to eastern Europe and, with other GAULS, invaded Greece before settling in Anatolia (modern Turkey and northern Syria) in 278–277 BC, where, with the Trocmi and the Tolistobogii, they formed the GALATIANS. The Volcae were conquered by the ROMANS in 107–106 BC, after they had joined the CIMBRI and TEUTONES in invading Roman territory in southern Gaul. The Romans claimed to have carried off 100 tons of gold and silver when they captured the tribal cult centre at Tolosa, including treasures looted from Greece 170 years previously.

## VOLCI-TECTOSAGES

See VOLCAE.

## VOLSCI

An ancient ITALIAN people, probably originally from the central Apennines, who settled southern Latium (the region immediately south of Rome) in the 6th century BC. The Volsci were an Oscan-speaking people who were related to the SABELLI. The Volsci were involved in several con-

flicts with the ROMANS, but were finally conquered in 304 BC. Thereafter, the Volsci were rapidly Romanized and lost their identity.

## VORARLBERGERS

An Austrian people who inhabit the Vorarlberg, the most westerly Austrian *Land* (federal region). They speak a GERMAN dialect that is more closely related to that of the German-speaking SWISS than that of other AUSTRIANS. The Voralbergers' identification with their *Land* is among the strongest in Austria, in many cases their Austrian identity being secondary to their regional identity.

## VOTADINI

Ancient BRITONS who lived in the Lothian region of southeast Scotland. Except for short periods in the 1st and 2nd centuries AD, the Votadini were never brought under direct ROMAN rule, but they maintained a client relationship in return for subsidies. Substantial quantities of Roman silver and other artefacts have been discovered at the hillfort of Traprain Law, the tribe's main stronghold. In the 5th century the tribe formed the Kingdom of Gododdin and moved their capital to Edinburgh. Gododdin tried to halt ANGLO-SAXON expansion in the 6th century, but was crushingly defeated by the NORTHUMBRIANS at Catterick around 600. The battle is the subject of the Old WELSH epic poem *Y Gododdin* (The Gododdin), one of the oldest works of vernacular literature from the British Isles. The kingdom disappeared after the Northumbrians captured Edinburgh in 638.

## VOTES

A Finnish people (see FINNS) of Kingisepp region, Russian Federation. Similar to the related INGRIANS in culture and history, they became almost completely Russified by the 19th century. After 1926 they were counted as RUSSIANS, and by 1997 only 15 people, all of them aged 60 or over, had any knowledge of the Votic language, which is expected to become extinct by 2020.

> " Gododdin's [the Votadini's] host riding/ stallions with mailed harness/ and the colour of swans/ attacking in the van/ of the nation's army/ protecting the forests/ and the mead of Edin "
>
> Aneirin,
> *Y Gododdin*
> translated by
> S. Short

## VOTYAKS

An alternative name for the UDMURT, now considered offensive.

## WAGRIANS

The most westerly sub-group of the WENDS. They settled along the Baltic coast between Lübecker Bucht and Kieler Förde around the 6th century. Their chief settlement and religious cult centre was at Oldenburg. The Wagrians were conquered by the SAXONS in 1140–3 and forcibly converted to Christianity; they subsequently became Germanized.

## WALLACHIANS

See VLACHS.

## WALLOONS

FRENCH-speaking BELGIANS. The term Walloon is derived from an old German word used to describe the Romanized CELTS that is also the origin of the English word 'Welsh'. The majority of the 3 million Walloons live in southern Belgium (Wallonia or Wallonie). The Walloons trace their origins to the Celtic BELGAE, who dominated northern Gaul during the late Iron Age. Conquered by the Romans in the 1st century BC, the Belgae lost their Celtic language and identity and became Romance-speaking. In the 5th century Germanic tribes ancestral to the FLEMISH settled in Flanders, the northern part of modern Belgium, but Wallonia remained a Romance-(eventually French-) speaking area.

In the Middle Ages Wallonia was a collection of semi-autonomous feudal principalities, often contested by France and the Holy Roman empire until, in the 15th century, it was united with the rest of the Low Countries under the dukes of Burgundy. In the 16th century the Low Countries came under the control of the SPANISH Habsburgs. Attempts by the Spanish to undermine local autonomy and their persecution of Protestants caused the DUTCH to rebel in 1568 and, eventually, win their independence. The staunchly Catholic Walloons and Flemish remained under Spanish rule. In the 18th cen-

tury, the Spanish Low Countries passed under AUSTRIAN control before they were conquered by the French during the Revolutionary Wars. After Napoleon's defeat in 1815, the former Spanish Low Countries were united with the Dutch Kingdom of the Netherlands, but the Walloons and Flemish rebelled in 1830 and declared the independent Kingdom of Belgium.

Although they constituted only 40% of the population, the Walloons dominated Belgium, politically, economically and culturally. Wallonia industrialized quickly during the 19th century, and the region became one of the wealthiest in Europe. French was the language of government and high culture. Walloons resisted Flemish demands that Dutch should be the official language of Flanders well into the 20th century. The Walloons' dominance, however, has eroded rapidly since World War II. Because of a low birth rate, Walloons now make up only a third of the Belgian population, and the heavy industries, on which their prosperity was based, have collapsed. Because of their early political dominance, the Walloons had adopted the Belgian national identity more strongly than the Flemings and, as a result, their regional identity remained an ill-defined one. Walloon regionalist political parties were slow to form, and it was not until 1971 that the federalist *Rassemblement Wallon* won seats in the national parliament. It was therefore largely to satisfy Flemish aspirations for cultural and administrative autonomy that Belgium became a federal state, divided formally into Flemish- and French-speaking regions in 1980 (Brussels, the capital, is officially bilingual). Such unlooked-for regional autonomy has not led to a corresponding growth of self-conscious Walloon regionalism, and their identity still lacks sharp definition.

## WELSH

The people of Wales, one of the four constituent nations of the United Kingdom. The Welsh are the descendants of ancient BRITONS who successfully resisted conquest by the ANGLO-SAXONS during the early Middle Ages. Until the middle of the 19th century the majority of Welsh people spoke Welsh, a Celtic language that developed in the early Middle Ages from the Brithonic language spoken by the ancient Britons. The Welsh name for themselves is *Cymraeg*.

The number of Welsh speakers declined steadily from the 1850s until by 1991 only 591,000 people (22% of the population) claimed to have any knowledge of the language and only 326,000 claimed to speak it as their first language. The introduction of compulsory Welsh teaching in schools has led to a modest recovery so that by 2001 around 797,000 people (28% of the Welsh population) claimed to have some speaking knowledge of the language. The main strongholds of the Welsh language are in northwest and southwest Wales.

### Welsh identity

The Welsh identity formed in the 7th century when the remaining independent Britons began calling themselves *Cymry*, the people of *Cymru*, the British name for western Britain. The name 'Welsh' comes from Anglo-Saxon *waelisc*, meaning 'foreigners', which they used to describe the Romanized Britons. The Welsh continued to see themselves as the legitimate inhabitants of Britain for centuries after the Anglo-Saxon settlements. Even in the 12th century, the Welsh thought that they would one day drive the 'Saxons' (*Saesneg*), as they called the English, back into the sea and reclaim the country that they believed was theirs by right.

The Welsh were divided into small kingdoms which were occasionally united under able rulers such as Hywel the Good of Deheubarth (ruled *c.* 900–50) and Llywelyn the Great (ruled 1195–1240) of Gwynedd, although their achievements never outlived them. The last ruler to unite the Welsh was Llywelyn ap Gruffydd (ruled 1246–82), who forced the English king Henry III to recognize him as Prince of Wales in 1258. However, Llywelyn became too ambitious and provoked Henry's successor Edward I to undertake the conquest of Wales in 1282–4. English law was imposed, beginning the absorption of Wales into the Kingdom of England, a process that was completed with the Act of Union in 1536, by which Wales legally ceased to exist as a separate polity.

The Act of Union made English the language of law, education and administration, but it also placed local government in the hands of the native Welsh, ensuring that Wales did not become simply part of England. The Welsh gentry became anglicized in language and culture after the union, but Welsh survived as the language of the majority. This was due largely to the Reformation. The Welsh accepted Protestantism, and so translations of the Bible, the Prayer Book and other religious tracts into Welsh were quickly made available, so ensuring that Welsh remained the language of religion.

### Industrialization and resurgent nationalism

The 18th century saw a self-conscious revival of interest in Welsh language and literature that found expression in the revival of the medieval *eisteddfod*, a gathering of poets and musicians. The *eisteddfod* remains an important way of promoting and celebrating Welsh culture. This cultural revival did not lead to the development of political nationalism and much of its energy was dissipated later in the century into Methodism and other nonconformist churches. In the 19th century parts of Wales experienced rapid industrialization, which attracted large-scale ENGLISH, IRISH and CORNISH immigration to the coalfields of the south and northeast. Before the end of the century English-speakers far outnumbered Welsh-speakers. The decline of the language was hastened by Welsh-speaking parents who had their children educated in English to improve their job prospects. However, there was never, as nationalists often claim, any official policy to suppress the Welsh language. Some visionaries, fearing for the future of the language, founded Welsh-speaking communities overseas. Most soon failed, but one, founded in Patagonia in 1865, still survives.

It was primarily language issues that led to the foundation of the Welsh nationalist party, Plaid Cymru (the Party of Wales) in 1925. The party's campaigning won equal status for Welsh with English in 1967, and other measures supportive of the language have followed, including a Welsh-language television channel and compulsory instruction in the Welsh language in schools in Wales. Because of its close association with the Welsh language, political nationalism has not made a breakthrough in English-speaking parts of Wales. English-speaking Welsh people do not see language as central to their

Welsh identity and many parents regard compulsory Welsh-teaching as a politically-motivated waste of their children's time. Anglo-Welsh, the Welsh dialect of English, has its own distinctive idioms and lyrical qualities, which have lent themselves to some of the finest poetry in the language. Although the Welsh national identity remains a sharply defined one, independence from the United Kingdom is an issue only for a minority of committed nationalists. Even the limited regional autonomy introduced by the installation of the Welsh Assembly in 1999 was not greatly desired by the Welsh: barely half the electorate turned out for the referendum on the issue, and the vote in favour was a very narrow majority. The most passionate expressions of Welsh national identity are seen, or heard, at rugby matches, not at the ballot box.

## WENDS

The collective name given to the West SLAVS who, in the Middle Ages, were settled along the Baltic Sea coast between the River Vistula and the neck of the Jutland peninsula, as well as inland as far south as the middle Elbe. They included the ABODRITES, LIUTIZIANS, POLABIANS, POMERANIANS, RUGIANS, SORBS and WAGRIANS. The Wends had many prosperous trading towns, most of them close to the mouths of major navigable rivers. Large quantities of ARAB silver coins found around these towns show that they played an important role in the trade routes that led across eastern Europe to the Middle East. The Wends had a warlike aristocracy and were skilled at fortress-building. They learned shipbuilding from the DANES, and in the 11th and 12th centuries they launched Viking-style pirate raids on Scandinavia. The Wends were conquered and forced to convert to Christianity by GERMAN and Danish crusaders in the late 12th and early 13th centuries.

## WESSEX CULTURE

An early Bronze Age culture (*c.* 2000–*c.* 1400 BC) of Wiltshire and adjacent areas of southern England. The Wessex culture was characterized by elite burial traditions developed from the preceding BEAKER CULTURES. Wessex-culture cemeteries typically consist of groups of round barrows, each covering a single burial, with rich grave goods such as bronze daggers and axes, gold ornaments, and jet, amber and faience jewellery. These goods demonstrate contacts with central Europe and Brittany. Burying the dead

Wends

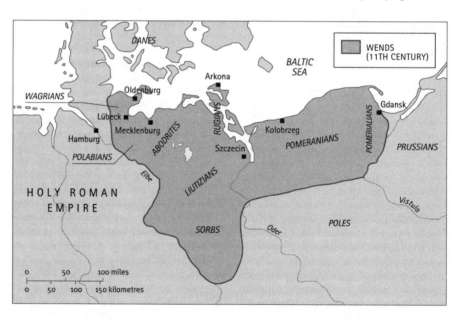

was normal in the early Wessex period, but the practice had given way to cremation before its end. The major building phase at Stonehenge, including the erection of the trilithon circle, is associated with the Wessex culture.

## WEST SAXONS

The inhabitants of the ANGLO-SAXON kingdom of Wessex, which, by the early 9th century AD, comprised most of England south of the Thames. The West Saxons were originally known as the Gewisse; the term 'West Saxon' only came into use in the 8th century.

The name of the founder of the West Saxon royal dynasty, Cerdic (died *c.* 534), is a corruption of the Celtic name *Caratacos*, suggesting that he may have been a Germanized BRITON. The base of the Gewisse was in the Thames Valley in Oxfordshire, from where they slowly extended their control over other SAXON groups in Hampshire and Wiltshire, the JUTES of the Isle of Wight and the BRITONS in the West Country by around 600. The West Saxons were dominated by the MERCIANS in the 8th century, but Wessex emerged as the most powerful of the Anglo-Saxon kingdoms in the 9th century.

Under Alfred the Great, Wessex was the only Anglo-Saxon kingdom successfully to resist the DANES in the later 9th century, and it was his successors in the 10th century who united England under their rule.

## WILZIANS or Wiltzites

See LIUTIZIANS.

## YUGOSLAVS

The people of the southeastern European nation of Yugoslavia, currently comprising Serbia and Montenegro. The Yugoslavs were and are the product of an unsuccessful 20th-century attempt at nation-building. Following the collapse of the Austro-Hungarian empire at the end of World War I, the SLOVENES and CROATS were united with the SERBS, MONTENEGRINS and MACEDONIAN SLAVS in the Kingdom of the Serbs, Croats and Slovenes, renamed Yugoslavia ('Land of the South Slavs') in 1929. The union was blighted from the start by the rivalry of the Serbs and Croats. Croats, who had believed that they would be treated as equals in Yugoslavia, deeply resented Serbian political dominance. Relations between the two peoples became more embittered during World War II, when the pro-Fascist Croat Ustasa committed acts of genocide against the Serbs and other minorities. In 1945 a communist government seized power under Josip Tito and re-organized Yugoslavia as a federal state. Tito stood up to Stalin, and unlike other communist states in eastern Europe, Yugoslavia did not fall under Soviet domination. A common desire not to afford the Soviets any pretext for intervention suppressed ethnic rivalries and kept Yugoslavs united. Beneath the surface, however, Serb–Croat rivalry remained as sharp as ever, each group harbouring the conviction that Tito's government favoured the other.

After Tito's death in 1980 the Yugoslav republics became more assertive and as separatist movements began to develop in Slovenia and Croatia. Serbian unease at these developments was exploited by the populist Slobodan Milosevic, who was elected president of Serbia in 1989. In 1990 he brought the autonomous province of Kosovo, which had an ALBANIAN majority, under direct Serbian rule and encouraged Serbian separatists living in Croatia and Bosnia to assert themselves. Fearing that this was a prelude to the recreation of Yugoslavia as Greater Serbia, Slovenia, Croatia and Macedonia declared independence in 1991; Bosnia-Herzegovina followed suit in 1992. Both Croatia and Bosnia-Herzegovina experienced bloody civil wars, ethnic cleansing and genocide in the aftermath. Kosovo, while still legally part of Yugoslavia, was occupied by NATO forces in 1999 after the Serbs began expelling its Albanian population. Its future status has yet to be determined.

Yugoslavia now consists only of Serbia and Montenegro, but even this union may not survive. Seeking to distance themselves from the atrocities committed by Serbian nationalists during the civil wars, Montenegrins have loosened their ties with Serbia and may seek outright independence.

# South and
# Central Asia
# and the
# Middle East

# ABDALIS (Afghanistan)

A PASHTUN people of Afghanistan. Ahmad Shah Durrani, one of the Abdalis, united Afghanistan in 1747 and went on to create an empire that included parts of Iran, Pakistan and northern India; the tribe subsequently became known as the Durrani. Although the empire disintegrated in 1818, the Durrani still form the social and political leadership of the Pashtun.

# ABDALIS (Yemen)

An ARAB tribe who occupied the region of Lahij in southern Yemen. Independent from 1728 to 1839, they subsequently fell under BRITISH domination as part of the Aden Protectorate. The Sultanate was eliminated in 1967, and the Abdalis now form part of the YEMENI people.

# ABKHAZIANS or Apswa

A Northwest Caucasian people, part of a group that also includes the CIRCASSIANS and the UBYKHS. There are presently around 600,000 Abkhazians, 94,000 of whom live in Abkhazia with most of the remainder living in Turkey. Although Abkhazia is legally part of Georgia, it has not been under the control of the GEORGIAN government since it declared independence in 1992. Most Abkhazians are Muslims.

The Abkhazians have inhabited the western Caucasus since ancient times. Contacts with the Byzantine empire led to the introduction of Christianity in 543–6 and, ultimately, to the formation of the kingdom of Abkhazia in the 8th century. In the 11th century Abkhazia became part of the Kingdom of Georgia but regained its independence under the Chachba dynasty after the MONGOL invasions of the 1240s. From the 15th century Abkhazia was under the influence of the OTTOMAN empire; an important consequence of this was the introduction of Islam.

In 1810 Abkhazia became a self-governing RUSSIAN protectorate, despite local resistance. After the Russian government took direct control in 1864, over 120,000 Abkhazians were expelled to the Ottoman empire, while Russian SLAVS were encouraged to settle in the region. These settlements were not successful because the Slavs lacked the experience to farm successfully in the mountainous terrain. It was under Russian rule that Abkhazian first became a written language, using an adapted version of the Cyrillic alphabet. In 1922 Abkhazia became a republic of the USSR, but in 1931 Soviet leader Joseph Stalin downgraded its status to that of an autonomous region of Georgia. In the 1930s and 1940s Lavrenti Beria, head of the NKVD (the secret police) and, like Stalin, a Georgian, headed a drive against 'nationalist deviationists' in the Caucasus. All publications in Abkhazian were banned and Georgian became the sole permitted language of education. At the same time, forced resettlement of MINGRELIANS made Abkhazians a minority in their own land. Stalin's death in 1953, which was followed by Beria's execution the same year, brought these discriminatory policies to an end, but they left a legacy of Abkhazian bitterness towards Georgia.

Abkhazians watched apprehensively as president Mikhail Gorbachev's policies of *glasnost* (openness) and *perestroika* (restructuring) encouraged the re-emergence of Georgian nationalism in the 1980s. In 1989 the Abkhazians joined with 16 other Caucasian peoples to form the Assembly (since 1991 the Confederation) of Mountain Peoples of the Caucasus to counter Georgian influence. After Georgia declared independence from the USSR in 1991, the Abkhazians attempted to negotiate a new federative union with Georgia that would protect their culture and language.

When Abkhazia declared independence the following year, Georgian forces occupied its capital, Sukhumi, but failed to suppress all resistance. With the support of Russia, which sought to exploit ethnic rivalries to re-assert some of its lost influence in the Caucasus and on the Confederation, the Abkhazians launched a successful counter-offensive in 1993 and recaptured Sukhumi. Russian pressure on both parties led to the declaration of a ceasefire in 1994. The presence of Russian peacekeepers has deterred any Georgian attempt at re-conquest, but Abkhazia's *de facto* independence is not recognized internationally. Until the status of their country is resolved, the Abkhazians will continue to live in a state of political and economic limbo.

# ADIVASI

A group of Hindu INDIAN tribes of Kerala who include the Dhodia, Komkan and Varli. The term means 'aboriginal', and today tends to refer to those tribes who have remained relatively isolated from the process of 'Sanskritization'. Feelings of discontent have increased significantly among the Adivasi in recent years. The migration of large numbers of non-tribal people into the traditional homelands of many Adivasi tribes, particularly in Kerala, linked with a concomitant loss of land ownership and climbing unemployment, has led to tensions between the Adivasi and both settlers and government. Mass demonstrations and violence have occurred, and the activities of some extremist groups have been met by government reprisals. Chief among the demands of the Adivasi are the provision of land for the landless and the creation of autonomous tribal regions. Conflicts have particularly centred on access and entitlement to natural resources, which have been restricted by the government, often subsequently awarded to private companies. The Adivasi population is nearly 2 million.

# ADZHARS or Adjars

Muslim GEORGIAN peoples comprising the majority of the population of the Autonomous Republic of Adzharia; their capital is Batumi. Although legally part of Georgia, Adzharia has been *de facto* independent since the collapse of the USSR in 1991.

# AFGHANS

The citizens of the modern Republic of Afghanistan (capital Kabul). The population was 28 million in 2004. Owing to its geographic location, Afghanistan has suffered many invasions and population movements throughout history, with the result that present-day Afghans are a very ethnically mixed people. In addition to indigenous elements, influences include PERSIAN, GREEK, ARAB, TURKIC and MONGOL. The term 'Afghan' is a modern coining; in the medieval period the region was identified as Khurasan.

Modern Afghans comprise four major ethnic groups: PASHTUNS (38%), TAJIKS (31%), UZBEKS

> 66 The Americans love Pepsi Cola. but we love death. 99
>
> Placard in Kabul, 2001

(5%) and HAZARAS (19%). Almost all are Muslim, with very small numbers of Hindus, JEWS and PARSIS. Of the 99% who are Muslim, 74% are Sunni and 15% Shi'ite. (Clashes between members of these two main branches of Islam have been frequent in recent years: for example, thousands of Shi'ites were massacred by the Sunni Taliban.)

Much of Afghanistan is very mountainous, and most Afghans live in rural settlements and practise agriculture; about 2.5 million still live a nomadic lifestyle. Cottage industries are widespread, with many families supplementing their income through carpet-making and other traditional handicrafts. Tribal society remains very strong and is predominantly patriarchal. In urban areas, however, restrictions on women are relaxing a little following the collapse of the fundamentalist Taliban regime. In many cases, tribal is more important than national identity, and inter-tribal tensions have been frequent during the 20th century. In the 1960s the Pashtuns agitated for the creation of an independent state – a movement that was violently crushed.

The Pashtun-based Taliban, who were politically dominant between 1995 and 2001, were defeated by a US-supported coalition of other Afghan groups, including the Uzbeks, Hazaras and Tajiks, who comprised the United Islamic Front for the Salvation of Afghanistan (or Northern Alliance). Many groups, such as the Uzbeks and Tajiks, also maintain close ties with their relatives across the borders of Afghanistan. The idea of a united Afghan people is therefore probably some way off, and although attempts are being made at reconciliation, some in-fighting continues to the present day: for example, remnants of Taliban forces, together with other extremist Islamic groups, continue to attack US and Afghan government troops and United Nations workers. Afghans have also tended to support the Pashtuns in Pakistan in their struggle for an independent state, and this has at times led to a considerable degree of tension between the two countries.

Most Afghans speak at least one of the official languages, Pashto and Duri, both of which are IRANIAN, but a number of other languages are in common use. Duri is the language of government, commerce and culture. Owing to close links with the USSR during much of the 20th century, and because of Afghanistan's geographical isolation, Western culture has had comparatively little impact on most Afghans, and traditional cultural forms predominate. Folk music, dance, traditional games and storytelling all remain popular pastimes. Economically, Afghanistan remains one of the world's poorest countries.

## AFRIDI

A PASHTUN people who live principally in the mountainous regions of northern Pakistan. They fought the British during the 19th century and were prominent in the INDIAN Red Shirt Movement during the 1930s. The Afridi are Muslim and fiercely independent. Most reject PAKISTANI status, seeking instead the establishment of an independent Pashtun state.

## AHHIYAWA

Inhabitants of an Anatolian kingdom, probably situated in the northwest of modern Turkey, which was contemporary with the HITTITES, and usually enjoyed friendly relations with their empire. Little is known of Ahhiyawa culture. They were traders and accomplished sailors, and can possibly be identified with the ACHAEANS, although this has been debated.

## AHL

See TODA.

## AHOM

A people of CHINESE origins who, from the 13th until the early 19th centuries, ruled the area of India now known as Assam. Their descendants have been thoroughly assimilated into ASSAMESE culture and society, and their native language has been lost.

## AKA

An Indo-Asiatic tribe who live in the region of Arunachal Pradesh in India. They are an agricultural people who live in an isolated area where their traditional tribal culture remains vital. They are a patriarchal society in which slavery is still practised and polygamous marriages are common. Although tribal identity is strong, it is common for the Aka to marry outside the tribal group. Traditional animistic religion remains popular, although both Buddhism and Hinduism are now winning converts. The Aka population is around 5500.

## AKHDAM

A YEMENI people comprising an ethnic mix of ARABS and Africans. They are regarded as socially inferior to other local tribes and tend to occupy low-status jobs.

## AKHLAME

An ancient nomadic Semitic people (see SEMITES) of northern Syria and Mesopotamia who regularly attacked the ASSYRIAN empire of the 14th to 12th centuries BC. By the late 11th century BC, however, they appear to have been overrun and absorbed by the ARAMAEANS. The term 'Akhlame' first appears in EGYPTIAN documents of the mid-14th century BC.

## AKKADIANS

A Semitic people (see SEMITES) originating in the Arabian peninsula. Little is known of their early history, but, having migrated northward, they were well established in southern Mesopotamia by the mid-3rd millennium BC. The Sumerian King List, written in Babylon around 1800 BC, dates the foundation of the first Akkadian royal dynasty to just after the Great Flood, and records a number of early conflicts with the SUMERIANS. In 2334 BC Sargon I (ruled 2334–2279 BC), following a palace *coup d'état*, founded a new royal Akkadian dynasty at the city of Kish. The name 'Akkadian' is derived from the city of Agade, which was constructed as a new capital by Sargon following a string of successful military enterprises. The term, however, is not an ancient one; rather, it was adopted in the 19th century as a means of identifying the thousands of clay tablets written in Akkadian cuneiform discovered by archaeologists, and of differentiating them from those written in other languages. Contemporaries knew the Akkadians simply as 'the people of Akkad'.

Sargon's military victories forged the largest empire the world had witnessed – stretching from the Persian Gulf to the Mediterranean Sea (and possibly including parts of modern Iran and Bahrain). It was the assimilation of the conquerors and the conquered that produced the people we refer to as the Akkadians; southern Mesopotamia subsequently became known as the 'land of Sumer and Akkad'. Although the site of Sargon's new capital remains to be discovered, it may have stood on the east bank of the Euphrates north of Babylon.

### Decline and influence

In contrast to the SUMERIAN period, Akkadian political control became increasingly secular: royal palaces dominated city landscapes at the expense of temples and priesthoods. Kings were also beginning to take on many god-like attributes, and they were increasingly viewed as intermediaries between the gods and humans. Despite its successes, however, the Akkadian empire lasted only a relatively short time. Many cities within the new empire retained a fierce desire for independence and, even at its height, the empire was beset by internal wars and rebellions. It also came under intense pressure from migrating AMORITES and GUTIANS. Indeed, within a century of Sargon's rule, the Gutians had sacked Akkad, and following the rebellion of the Sumerian city of Ur, in 2125 BC, Akkadian control over Mesopotamia disintegrated.

The influence of the Semitic Akkadian language, however, was far longer-lasting, and it remained the principal language of Mesopotamia until the 1st millennium BC. The languages of both the BABYLONIANS and the ASSYRIANS derived from Akkadian, and it was used by the ELAMITES, Gutians, Lullians and HURRIANS. It also became the standard international language throughout many regions of Western Asia, and the EGYPTIANS, HITTITES, SYRIANS, and PERSIANS used cuneiform in varying degrees. Similarly, Akkadian art was highly influential throughout Western Asia, and the Akkadians were particularly innovative in the areas of sculpture, relief-work and the decoration of cylinder seals.

## ALTAY

A western Siberian people centred on the Altay republic, in the Russian Federation. Formed between the 6th and 15th centuries through a merging of Turkic (see TURKS) and mongolian (MONGOL) groups, they speak a Turkic language.

Those Altay in the south were largely nomadic herders, while those in the north practised hunting and gathering to a greater extent. They were also noted metalworkers, their territory containing sizeable deposits of various ores.

Horsemen of considerable renown, they fought bitterly against RUSSIAN conquest for many years, but fell under Russian domination in the 18th century. Russian colonizers undermined their traditional shamanist beliefs and tried to force them to become sedentary, and they were successful during the 19th century, despite the tenacity with which the Altay clung to their traditional culture. This process was concluded under Soviet rule through collectivization, resulting in the destruction of much of the Altay educated elite.

In 1990 the Altay agitated for independence, hoping to preserve both a culture and an environment threatened by outside rule. They did gain a republic within the Russian Federation in 1991, but total only 30% (70,000 in 1993) of its population, regarding themselves as a still-exploited minority.

## ALUTOR

A northeastern Siberian people of the Kamchatka and Chukotka peninsulas, in the Russian Federation. Traditionally hunters, gatherers, fishers and reindeer-herders, they speak a Chukotko-Kamchatkan language. Conquered by the RUSSIANS in the late 17th century, they were brutally exploited, and collectivization under Soviet rule proved even more disastrous. Russification and attacks on their traditional shamanist religion were intensified. Following the collapse of the USSR and the withdrawal of state support, desperate poverty forced many to attempt to rebuild their traditional subsistence. Their very existence is now under threat. In 1997 they numbered about 2000.

# AMALEKITES

A Semitic (see SEMITES) nomadic people closely related to the EDOMITES, the CANAANITES, and the ISRAELITE tribe of Ephraim. They inhabited southwestern Palestine (Canaan and the Sinai peninsula), and are named after their leader, Amalek. Led by Moses, the Israelites, on their return from Egypt, forced their way through Amalekite territory, and a series of bitter wars ensued between the two peoples. The Amalekites were defeated heavily by King Saul in the 11th century BC, and by King David in 993 BC; these wars all but exterminated the tribe, and Hezekiah of Judah finally eradicated them in the 7th century BC. The word 'Amalekite' is still used by JEWS as a derogatory term to describe their enemies.

# AMMONITES

An ancient Semitic people (see SEMITES). In the Bible they are descended from Ben-Ammi (the son of Lot); they were also related to the MOABITES.

Although they were originally nomadic, the Ammonites had established themselves as a sedentary people by the 13th century BC, with a fortified capital at Rabbath Ammon (now Amman, in modern Jordan). They fought a number of wars against their neighbours, the ISRAELITES; King David sacked Rabbath Ammon in the 10th century BC, and Judas Maccabeus defeated them in the 2nd century BC. In the 1st century AD their territory was incorporated into the Roman empire, and there is very little historical evidence of a separate Ammonite people after the 3rd century AD; by this time they seem to have assimilated with a number of other ARAB tribes in the region.

Their capital, Rabbath Ammon, had been renamed Philadelphia as early as the Seleucid period (312–64 BC). Little is now known of Ammonite culture. The national god of the Ammonites was Milcom (also known as Molech or Moloch), a CANAANITE god of fire who was introduced, through Ammonite influence, into Judah. The Ammonite language was closely related to Hebrew.

# AMORITES

A CANAANITE tribe descended from a group of Semitic peoples (see SEMITES) who migrated from the Arabian peninsula (or possibly from modern Syria) into northeast Jordan around 2500 BC, and later into parts of Palestine. The term 'Amorite', meaning 'the high one', is obscure. In the Bible, the name 'Amorite' seems to be used interchangeably with 'Canaanite', which has led to some confusion regarding the area controlled by the tribe.

Although they were a nomadic tribe (known also as the Amurru), a number of Amorite kings were among the greatest empire-builders of the ancient world. Their raids into southern Mesopotamia during the 22nd century BC were one of the primary causes of the destruction of AKKADIAN domination in the region. A century later the Amorites helped bring down the SUMERIAN Third Dynasty of Ur. During the course of the next 200 years the Amorites continued to raid the area, founding a number of small city-states (for example, at Mari and Aleppo), until, in the 19th century BC, they overran much of northern and southern Mesopotamia.

After these successes, the Amorites abandoned their nomadic existence and founded new BABYLONIAN and ASSYRIAN dynasties. Having settled in the region, the invaders absorbed much of the indigenous culture of the MESOPOTAMIANS, and, over the course of the next few hundred years, gradually assimilated with the native peoples. As a result, the term 'Amorite' ceases to be used of them, being supplanted by 'Babylonian' or 'Assyrian'; in turn, the Amorite language disappeared from the region in favour of Akkadian and its offshoots. In Palestine, however, the Amorites and their language flourished until the 12th century BC.

The chief deity of the Amorites was Marduk, whom they introduced into Mesopotamia, and who remained the main god of the Babylonian region for over a thousand years (supplanting the Sumerian gods An and Enlil); indeed, the 6th-century restored Tower of Babel was, in fact, a seven-storey ziggurat-temple dedicated to Marduk (or Bel, as he was more commonly known by this time). The weather-god Adad also had Amorite origins.

*a*

> " We are digging up well-preserved Amorites who were buried naked and headless. "
>
> T.E. Lawrence, 1914

Thanks to a vigorous policy of imperial expansion, particularly under King Hammurabi (ruled 1792–1750 BC), Amorite Babylon had become, by the mid-18th century BC, the new religious and cultural centre of Mesopotamia. Although contributing comparatively little to the culture of Mesopotamia, the Amorites did introduce a far stricter law code to the area, with a new emphasis on the notion of 'an eye for an eye', and a more widespread use of the death penalty. This new empire was also far more centralized than previous imperial states; alongside codified laws, a well-organized system of taxation and military conscription was introduced. As in the Akkadian period, Amorite kings were believed to possess divine status.

The Babylonian dynasty founded by the Amorites survived until the HITTITE king Mursilis I invaded and sacked the city in about 1595 BC. Although he withdrew, a new KASSITE dynasty was subsequently established. In Assyria, the Amorite king Shamshi-Adad (ruled 1813–c. 1781 BC) established a new capital at Shubat-Enlil ('the dwelling place of Enlil'). Amorite Assyria, however, later fell to Hammurabi of Babylon, and then to the MITANNI. During the 13th century BC the Amorites defeated both the MOABITES and Hittites, but were finally defeated themselves by the ISRAELITES at Gibeon.

## AMURRU

See AMORITES.

## ANDAMAN ISLANDERS or Andamanese

A NEGRITO people who inhabit the Andaman and Nicobar islands in the Indian Ocean, now part of the Republic of India. It is possible that the forebears of the Andaman Islanders originated in Burma, Malaya or Sumatra, and they are first mentioned in outside sources by the CHINESE during the 7th century. The term 'Andaman' derives from the MALAY form of the Hindu monkey god, Hanuman (Handuman).

Until the late 18th century, the Andaman Islanders led a very isolated existence, little exposed to foreign political, social and cultural influences. As a result of this, their traditional

migratory hunter-gatherer lifestyle continued undisturbed. In the 19th century, for example, they subsisted without the deliberate use of fire. This isolation was propagated by their reputation for hostility toward outsiders and rumours of cannibalism. From the mid-19th century, however, the islands were subject to increasing European immigration, particularly following the foundation of a British penal colony at Port Blair. This led not only to the introduction of Western influences, but also to the demographic dilution of the Andamanese themselves. The islanders' tribal society and traditional culture were steadily eroded in he 20th century. Native Andamanese religion is animistic, with much magical ritual, and the Andamanese language was originally spoken throughout the islands, but with many differing dialects. Today, owing to immigration and inter-marriage, very few islanders are pure natives, and most do not adhere to traditional culture. In addition, most now live a settled agricultural lifestyle, and only the Jarawa and Onge are hunter-gatherers; the other two tribes, the Sentinelese and Great Andamanese, live lives that are much more akin to those of modern INDIANS.

## ANDHRAS

A people of central India, possibly descended from the DRAVIDIANS, who first appear in the historical record in about 1000 BC. They came to dominate the region of the north Deccan plateau during the 1st and 3rd centuries AD, are known to have clashed with the SAKAS and traded with the ROMANS. Their kings patronized Buddhism, and built lavishly, particularly at their capital, Amaravita. The magnificent sculptural work produced here, such as that displayed on the Great Stupa, later influenced SRI LANKAN and Southeast Asian art. The Andhra territories disintegrated during the 3rd century. During the post-Independence reorganization of the Indian Republic, Andhra Pradesh was created in 1958 as a state on the basis of the preponderance of the local TELUGU language.

## ANIZAH

An ARAB people, originally from central Arabia,

who migrated into the south of the peninsula during the early 18th century and whose descendants formed the nucleus of the KUWAITIS.

## APA TANI

An Indo-Asiatic tribe who inhabit the region of Arunachal Pradesh in the east of modern India. They are intensive rice farmers who use the irrigated 'paddy field' system of cultivation, as well as cattle-farmers and fishers. Hindu influence has remained relatively minimal, and their religion remains based on the worship of the sun and moon. They speak a Tibeto-Burman language. Their number is unknown.

## APARNI

See PARNI.

## APSWA

See ABKHAZIANS.

## ARABS

A Semitic people (see SEMITES) who originated in the Arabian peninsula but now comprise the ethnic majority in many West Asian and North African states. The term is first found in ASSYRIAN documents of the mid-9th century BC, but was not used by the Arabs until the 4th century AD.

The word 'Arab' means 'nomad' and was originally synonymous with BEDOUIN, the people who dominated the Arabian peninsula into the early modern period. It was the domestication of the camel, during the mid-2nd millennium BC, that made the nomadic lifestyle possible. Today the term Arab applies to all speakers of the Arabic language, regardless of lifestyle. However, ancient Arabian peoples such as the SABAEANS, QATABIANS and MINAEANS, who spoke Arabic dialects but were sedentary agriculturalists, are not usually described as Arabs.

In the 8th and 7th centuries BC, the Arabs fought frequent wars with the Assyrians, who deported many of them to Palestine. In contrast, they were often allied with the BABYLONIANS. Ancient Arab tribes included the Adbell, Badana, Marsimani, KINDAH and Thamud.

Although they were not initially a great trading nation themselves, the Arabs' nomadic skills and desert knowledge were employed by more settled peoples to trade across Arabia and into Mesopotamia, Africa and the Levant. Command of the great caravan routes brought considerable wealth to the Arab tribes and led to the rise of great trading cities such as Mecca and Medina, as well as to the development of significant social and cultural divisions between settled and nomadic Arabs, differences which led to some degree of tension.

Prior to the 7th century AD the Arabs were rarely a unified people, although occasional tribal confederations arose and harassed their neighbours. The most aggressive of these confederations was the Qedar. It was the rise of Islam during the 620s and 630s, however, that acted as the great unifying factor in Arab history, and the Bedouin tribes were at the forefront of the subsequent Islamic conquests. Prior to this, Arab religion had been polytheistic (initially animistic), although Zoroastrianism, Judaism and Christianity had made considerable inroads.

Warfare had always played a large part in Arab life: raiding rival tribes was an important way for warriors to win status and wealth. After unifying and converting the Arabs to Islam, Muhammad (c. 570–632) managed to suppress inter-tribal warfare (though the tradition soon re-asserted itself among the Bedouin). The caliphs ('successors') who followed Muhammad as religious and political leaders of the Arabs found an outlet for their martial tradition by attacking the neighbouring BYZANTINE and PERSIAN empires, which had only recently ended a mutually destructive war. By the death of the second caliph, Uthman, in 656, the Arabs had conquered the Persian empire and driven the Byzantines out of Syria, Palestine and Egypt.

By the early 8th century the Arab caliphate stretched from the Pyrenees to the Indus. Arab unity, however, was already strained. A disputed succession to the caliphate in 661 led Islam to split into its two main branches, the majority Sunnites and the minority Shi'ites. Political unity lasted until 750; when the Abbasid dynasty overthrew the Umayyad dynasty of caliphs, an Umayyad prince fled to Spain and set up an independent emirate. After this the

*a*

" The Arabs keep ... pledges more religiously than almost any other people. "

Herodotus, 5th century BC

political fragmentation of the Arab-Islamic world proceeded steadily and irreversibly. Nonetheless, the Abbasid caliphate (750-1256) was the period of the Arabs' greatest cultural achievements. Not least of these was the preservation of much of the philosophy and scientific knowledge of the Classical world at a time when it had been all but forgotten in Christian Europe.

The conquests enabled a great expansion of the Arab identity. Through conquest, large numbers of Arabs settled in Mesopotamia, Syria, the Levant, Egypt and northern Sudan, North Africa, Spain, Persia and northern India. With the sole exception of Spain, all of these areas became permanently Islamized. As translation of the Koran is forbidden, Islam became a powerful agent for spreading the Arabic language, and through it, Arab culture and identity. Most of the conquered peoples eventually became Arabized, the most notable exceptions being the Persians, MOORS and KURDS. Even in Spain, however, an Arab influence remains in evidence in language, architecture and cuisine.

### Arab nationalism

Many areas of Arab settlement later fell under the control of expansionist powers such as the SELJUKS, OTTOMANS, BRITISH and FRENCH. It was not until the late 19th and early 20th centuries that a resurgent Arab nationalism emerged, which culminated in the creation of independent Arab nationalities such as the LEBANESE, JORDANIANS, IRAQIS and (briefly) PALESTINIANS. This pan-Arabian nationalistic feeling perhaps reached its highest point with the formation of the Arab League in 1945, although the short-lived United Arab Republic (1958–61) can be seen as another expression of these sentiments. Ultimately, however, nationalism and unification have not always gone hand in hand, and many Arab nations have clashed over issues such as territorial rights, foreign policy, and the status of Israel.

There has also been tension between the traditional Arab monarchies and the newer Arab republics, and the sheer scale of Arab dispersal has made unity difficult. Most Arab nations, however, are united in their support of the Palestinians and their opposition to the ISRAELIS, and over the last 25 years Islamic fundamentalism

has grown into a new form of Pan-Arab nationalism. Culturally, Arabs remain united by Islam and the Arabic language.

In the ancient period the tribe and clan were the basis of Arab society, and in many regions this continues, particularly in rural areas and amongst the gradually decreasing numbers of Bedouin. Traditional Arab Islamic culture is very strong in many rural areas. There was also a great tradition of pre-Islamic poetry. Urban life, however, has led to both the disintegration of the tribal system and the exposure of many Arabs to Western culture. Many Arab states have introduced policies designed to counter these new influences and reinvigorate Arab/Islamic culture. A number of Arab/Islamic groups are hostile to Western powers such as the USA and the UK, which are perceived as being pro-Israeli. Arab–Western tensions have also risen in the wake of the 11 September 2001 attacks on the USA perpetrated by terrorists of the al-Qaeda network, which aims to end Western influence in the Arabian peninsula.

## ARAMAEANS

A Semitic tribe (see SEMITES) of nomads who migrated into the desert areas of Syria, Jordan and western Iraq around 1200 BC. During the course of the next 200 years they succeeded in overrunning considerable areas of Mesopotamia and the Levant, establishing a number of petty kingdoms, such as Aram Zobah and Aram Damascus to the north of modern Israel, and Aleppo and Hamath in Mesopotamia. Materially, little is known of these peoples, although some Aramaean sculpture has been discovered at Bit Bahyan (at the archaeological site Tell Halaf). The term 'Aramaean' was not one introduced by the people themselves, and there is more than one source for its origins. In Hebrew, *aram* means 'highland' – perhaps referring to the mountainous terrain of the area in which they settled. It could also, however, derive from Aram Naharain, meaning the 'field of the rivers' – describing the region they inhabited in northern Syria.

Generally, nomadic tribes such as the Aramaeans took advantage of internal weaknesses within much more powerful states and empires in order to encroach on their territory, and this was certainly the case during the Aramaean conquests of ASSYRIAN, BABYLONIAN and HITTITE lands. Following these victories, many Aramaeans gave up their nomadic existence in favour of a more sedentary lifestyle.

This change had two effects: first, they lost their tactical military advantage of mobility, and second, as with other tribes in similar circumstances like the AMORITES, they gradually assimilated with the native populations. Unusually, however, the Aramaeans succeeded in retaining some of their cultural heritage, and, between the 10th and the 5th centuries BC, their language and alphabet (Aramaic) gradually became the *lingua franca* for the whole of Western Asia, supplanting AKKADIAN; indeed, Aramaic texts have been found as far afield as Egypt and China.

This diffusion of the language throughout the region was certainly assisted by the expansionist successes of other Aramaic-speaking tribes, such as the CHALDEANS. The Assyrians also used many Aramaean prisoners as slave-labourers, and their descendants gradually assimilated with the native population. By the 8th century BC a number had advanced to high office within the Assyrian state.

The expansion of the Assyrians in the 8th century BC meant that many Aramaean enclaves in Western Asia were absorbed into their empire, which further facilitated the dissemination of Aramaean language. Aramaic remained the principal language of the area until the ARAB invasions, when Arabic finally replaced it.

# ARINS

A Siberian people, related to the KETIS, who were assimilated by the RUSSIANS or by neighbouring peoples and had disappeared as a distinct group by the mid-19th century.

# ARMENIANS

An INDO-EUROPEAN Caucasoid people. Modern Armenians are thought to descend from a mixture of native aborigines, URARTIANS, HAYASA, and Indo-Europeans; the latter migrated from the Balkans to the Caucasus during the late 2nd and early 1st millennia BC. Currently, there are approximately 3.3 million Armenians living in the Republic of Armenia (capital Yerevan) and the former USSR, with a further 5 million dispersed throughout the world (notably in the USA, France, Syria, Lebanon, Cyprus, Turkey, Jordan, Bulgaria and Ethiopia). Ancient Armenia, however, was over ten times larger than the modern republic, and included much of present-day Turkey and Iran.

The term 'Armenian' seems to stem from a misconception by classical Persian and Greek commentators that these people were in fact ARAMAEANS; however, there is no ethnic connection between the two. Indeed, the name does not appear in written sources until 521 BC, when the Persians refer to the incorporation of Armenia into their empire. Modern Armenians describe themselves as *Hayq* (singular *Hay*), and refer to their country as Hayastan – a term that recalls a mythological hero of the region, Hayk.

Despite relatively brief periods of independence, most notably between 331 and 62 BC, the Armenians have been invaded and annexed by nations as diverse as the ASSYRIANS, MEDES, PERSIANS, ROMANS, PARTHIANS, BYZANTINES, ARABS, MONGOLS, TURKS and RUSSIANS. Armenia has always been a region of great strategic importance and has also been a melting pot for the influences of both East and West, leading to the development of a distinctive Armenian culture – as displayed particularly in art and literature. The IRANIANS heavily influenced ancient Armenian religious practice, and Aramazd (Iranian Ahura-Mazda) was the chief deity. During the early 4th century, however, the Armenians were the first nation to be converted to Christianity, which has played a defining role in their cultural and historical development ever since. 'Popular' religion and folklore remain influential, however. The Armenians have always displayed great independence of thought and belief, and rejected the findings of the Council of Chalcedon, which asserted Catholic doctrine in 451, in favour of pursuing a more ancient apostolic tradition.

## Language and culture

The Armenian language developed following the Indo-European migrations of the late 2nd millennium BC; it was the product of assimilation between the languages of the invaders and the people they had conquered, mixed with the Aramaic, Greek and Persian. It was not, however, written down until after the arrival of Christianity, when St Mesrob-Mashtotz invented the Armenian alphabet and transcribed the Bible into Armenian in AD 404–406. Currently there are about 50 different spoken dialects of the Armenian language, and two principal written forms: Eastern and Western. Eastern is the official language, also known as Yerevan Armenian.

Despite pressure from by external invaders, the Armenians have always aggressively held on to their cultural identity through the preservation of their language, alphabet and religion. For example, they resisted Persian attempts during the mid-5th century AD to impose the Zoroastrian religion, and have likewise staunchly refused conversion to Islam. Indeed, it has often been during the worst periods of ethnic intolerance and persecution that Armenian art and literature have reached their greatest heights. While the vast majority of Armenians remain Christian and adhere either to the Armenian Apostolic Church or to the Armenian Catholic Church, there are a very small number of Russian Orthodox and Muslim practitioners living among them.

### Genocidal outbreaks

There have been a number of periods of mass Armenian persecution and emigration from the region. The first occurred following the SELJUK occupation of Armenia in the 12th century, when a new Armenian enclave was established in Cilicia.

More recently, during the late 19th and early 20th centuries, the Armenians have been the object of repression, massacre and genocide by the TURKS. A resurgence of Armenian nationalism during the late 19th century (supported by the Russians) was followed by anti-Armenian pogroms in various Turkish cities; for example, in 1895 the KURDISH population of Malatya was encouraged to turn on resident Armenians. During World War I, 90% of those Armenians living in Anatolia were either deported or massacred by Turkish forces, who regarded them as fifth-columnists within their empire. Those who survived the arduous forced marches were reset-tled in the Syrian desert, but over 750,000 Armenians may have died. In addition, between the end of World War I and 1925 over 1 million Armenians are thought to have left Turkish-controlled Asia Minor.

In 1922, a much-reduced Armenia was incorporated into the USSR, and in 1936 its status became that of an independent republic within the Union. Under Stalin, however, the USSR made an aggressive attempt to destroy its national identity and culture through the forced closure of Armenian schools and attacks on the Armenian Church.

Perhaps not surprisingly, the events of the late 19th and early 20th centuries have resulted in a mass migration of Armenians throughout the world. Many of the dispersed, however, remain proud of their ethnic roots, and consider themselves, above all else, to be Armenian. Two very important elements in this national identity remain their church and their language. In recent years the Armenian government has sought to strengthen ties with Armenians living abroad; in September 1999, a major conference was held in Yerevan attended by representatives of Armenian populations throughout the world.

In 1991, Armenia declared its independence from the Soviet Union, and the country is now a democratic republic. Since 1988, immigrants have been arriving into the country from neighbouring (Muslim) Azerbaijan, following border conflicts between the two nations over the autonomous Armenian-populated region of Nagorno-Karabakh – a conflict that has escalated ethnic and religious tensions within both countries. By 1995, these hostilities had left 20,000 dead and over 600,000 homeless (both Armenians and AZERIS). Due to these conflicts, the Azerbaijani government imposed a trade blockade of Armenia in 1988, which caused severe economic hardship for the country. The result was another period of migration: an estimated 750,000 left Armenia during the early 1990s. Friction still also exists with Turkey; in 1998, the Turkish government tried to impose a candidate as Patriarch of the Armenian Church in Istanbul. It was only following Armenian protests, and a refusal to accept the candidate, that the Turkish government backed down.

# ARYANS

An INDO-EUROPEAN semi-nomadic pastoral culture, possibly originating in Central Europe, which moved from Central Asia into Iran and northern India during the mid-2nd millennium BC. The term 'Aryan' is derived from the Sanskrit word for 'noble'.

It is unlikely that the Aryans were responsible for the destruction of the Indus Valley civilization (see HARAPPANS), though they seem to have absorbed some features of this culture. Following their arrival in northern India, the Aryans gradually moved both east and south, ultimately coming into contact with the DRAVIDIANS, whom they defeated. This cultural dichotomy provides one model for the development of the caste system in South Asia. The Dravidians became the servant class, while all higher social, economic and political positions were exclusive to the Aryans (priests, warriors, traders); intermarriage between Dravidians and Aryans was forbidden. This system has persisted into modern times and became the basis for erroneous 19th- and 20th-century theories of a superior Aryan 'master race'. By 700 BC the Aryans were dominant throughout the Indian sub-continent, forming a number of petty kingdoms and republics, some of which eventually united to form major powers, such as the Kingdom of Magadha (500 BC).

Despite their success, the Aryans had become culturally and ethnically assimilated with the indigenous INDIAN population by the mid-6th century BC. Both Sanskrit and Hindi are descended from the Aryan part of the Indo-European language group. The Aryans also composed the Vedic texts and introduced certain religious practices now designated as Hindu. By about 1000 BC they had (perhaps independently) mastered the production of iron. It is possible that the Aryans were related to the KASSITES.

# ARZAWA

An ancient Anatolian people after whom Asia is named. They lived to the west of the HITTITES, who frequently defeated but never wholly subdued them. The Arzawa spoke the LUWIAN language, but their culture was heavily influenced by the Hittites, whose language they used

for diplomacy. The kingdom disappeared following the invasion of the SEA PEOPLES. The area later became the centre of the LYDIAN empire.

# ASI

See YUE-QI.

# ASSAMESE

A group of Tibeto-MONGOL, INDO-IRANIAN and BURMESE peoples who inhabit the Indian state of Assam. Their principal language is Assamese, an INDO-ARYAN language, although Bengali is also widely spoken. 'Assam' probably derives from 'Ahom', the name of a SHAN dynasty who replaced the Kamarupa rulers and controlled the region between the 13th and early 19th centuries. The Assamese were dominated by the British 1826–1947, following their removal of the BURMESE, who invaded the area in 1817.

The region was never fully incorporated into the MUGHAL empire, and today the vast majority of the Assamese are Hindu. A significant number of Assamese, however, have converted to Islam. In addition, since the 1970s, large numbers of Muslim BANGLADESHIS have entered Assam as immigrant workers, and about 25% of the population of the region is now Islamic. Alongside these two religions, both traditional animism and Christianity prevail among the more isolated hill tribes. The migration of Bangladeshis into the region has caused significant ethnic and religious tensions, and violence against these newcomers was endemic during the 1980s. These events also coincided with the rise of an Assamese independence movement, centred on the United Liberation Front of Assam. Although this movement was disbanded in 1992, there is still support for an autonomous state, and violent clashes remain a feature of the region. A principal characteristic of recent attacks, for example a number perpetrated in late 2000, has been the targeting of non-Assamese BIHARI. Moreover, since Indian independence in 1947, some groups such as the BODO have agitated for autonomy and rejected Assamese status. The Assamese are predominantly an agricultural people, and tea-growing is a major economic activity.

> **❝**Though it be proved that there never was an Aryan race in the past, yet we desire that in the future there may be one.**❞**
>
> J. Lees, 1911

*a*

| Assamese: main ethnic groups |
| --- |
| Kacharis |
| Khasis |
| Mikirs |

# ASSYRIANS

A Semitic people (see SEMITES) who migrated into Mesopotamia perhaps during the 3rd millennium BC. Their origins are still subject to debate, but it is possible that they were related to the HURRIANS. The term 'Assyrian' is derived from the principal city, and god, of the people – Ashur (in modern Iraq). Their other main cities were Nineveh and, from the mid-13th century BC, Nimrud. Between the 10th and 7th centuries BC the Assyrians succeeded in creating one of the largest empires of the ancient world.

Between the late 3rd millennium and the mid-12th century BC, despite some short periods of imperial expansion, the Assyrians were conquered by the AKKADIANS, AMORITES, BABYLONIANS, KASSITES, Hurrians and MITANNI. Another, relatively short, period of imperial expansion followed, but this was halted by ARAMAEAN successes, which pushed the Assyrians back to their homeland around Ashur.

Despite these defeats, the Assyrians forged themselves into one of the most formidable fighting nations known to the ancient world, and by the late 12th century BC they were almost unstoppable; their heavy infantry and cavalry tactics were particularly effective. Perhaps what differentiated the Assyrians from their neighbours, however, was the sheer ruthlessness of their campaigns; whole cities would be put to the sword in order to facilitate the surrender of the surrounding country, and, later, entire populations would be deported to Assyria as slave labour. They were also at the forefront of Mesopotamian iron-working, and used their skills to increase their technical advantage over opponents. As a result, between the late 12th and mid-7th centuries BC, the Assyrians gradually built an empire that stretched from the Red Sea to the Taurus Mountains, the Levant and Egypt just south of Thebes. Unlike earlier empires, for example that of the Akkadians, the Assyrian empire, at least from the mid-8th century, was highly organized and centralized.

Ultimately, however, the over-stretched Assyrian armies found it impossible to beat off new attacks from the CIMMERIANS, SCYTHIANS and MEDES. During the late 7th century BC, occupied by civil war, they came under increasing pressure

from the Medes, who first expelled them from Media and then brought about the collapse of the Assyrian empire as a whole by taking Ashur (614 BC) and Nineveh (612 BC) – the latter was accomplished in league with the Babylonians, and these two peoples subsequently divided Assyria between themselves.

**Assyrian culture and science**

Culturally, in most fields, the Assyrians were not innovative. Chief among the deities of the Assyrian pantheon was Ashur, patron-god of the city that bore his name. Also of considerable importance, however, was the Akkadian Great Mother goddess Ishtar. Given that the Assyrians were a very warlike people, however, it is perhaps not surprising that they also considered Ishtar to be a goddess of war and hunting, and it is this personification that tends to be highlighted in Assyrian art; as in Babylon, the planet Venus (then thought to be a star) was associated with Ishtar. In other areas, Assyrian religious practice was much influenced by the Babylonians, and this was also true in the areas of law and social organization. Later, the Assyrians were one of the first peoples to adopt Christianity.

In the sciences, again, Babylonian influence was strong, but the Assyrians made some advances, notably, in astronomy and astrology. The Assyrians used the cuneiform system of writing, and their language was descended from Akkadian. By the 8th century BC, however, Aramaic was also a common language among the Assyrians.

It was in secular art that the Assyrians made their most notable contribution. Artistic tradition was strong in Assyrian aristocratic society, and some of the greatest surviving artworks from the ancient period were produced in Assyria between the 10th and 7th centuries BC. This period saw the construction of a series of magnificent new royal palaces, for example at Ashur, Nineveh, Dur Sharrukin and Calah, each decorated with sculptures, reliefs and paintings of unparalleled beauty and technical ability. The use of tin-glazed pottery was also an Assyrian innovation. Assyrian kings were eager to advertise their wealth and power, and also to have their conquests and achievements recorded for posterity and for their own self-aggrandisement.

Interestingly, Assyrian temples tended to be modest by comparison, thus emphasising the position of the king at the expense of the gods. Moreover, many kings commissioned great narrative friezes that displayed, among many themes, their armies, victories, spoils of war and the terrible penalties meted out to those who attempted to resist Assyrian domination. Hunting was also a popular theme. Unusually, these pieces also provide some insight into Assyrian society, as they depict everyday life in the military camp – their distinctive curled hairstyles, beards, dress, decoration and musical instruments. Possibly owing to Amorite influence, Assyrian laws and punishments were somewhat more draconian than in other areas of Mesopotamia, with the death penalty not uncommon.

In the modern world, the followers of the Church of the East (also known as Nestorians) are referred to as Assyrians, and are descended from the ancient people. Between the 1st and 12th centuries AD this church was very influential in Western Asia, but from the 14th century Islamic pressure and Arabization led to the conversion and assimilation of many Assyrians to native ARAB populations. Many of those who did not convert fled their native homelands and settled in the Hakkari Mountains in modern Turkey. Today, Assyrians form ethnic minorities in many West Asian countries, including Iraq, Syria, Armenia and Iran, as well as in Europe, Australia and the Americas. During World War I, the TURKS attacked and persecuted them in a similar manner to the ARMENIANS. Following the war, many settled in Iraq, where, in 1933, a major uprising by the Assyrians was brutally quashed by the newly independent Iraqi government. These events were a major contributor to the modern Assyrian diaspora, and to the present day many Assyrians continue to leave Iraq and Turkey in the face of ethnic tensions. There are currently around 3.5 million Assyrians worldwide who continue to speak the Neo-Aramaic language (also known as Syriac).

## AZERBAIJANIS

See AZERIS.

## AZERIS

Citizens of the modern Republic of Azerbaijan (capital Baku), and also of the Iranian province of the same name. The Azeri are also commonly referred to as Azerbaijani, although they have sometimes been erroneously termed TATARS. Today more than 80% of the 7.7 million people of the Azerbaijani republic are Azeri, with more than 10 million living in the Iranian province. The Azeri also form ethnic minorities in a number of countries, including Armenia, Georgia, Dagestan and Turkmenistan. Recently, however, increasing ethnic tensions between Azeris and ARMENIANS over the Nagorno-Karabakh region have led to large-scale migrations of both peoples to their native homelands.

The vast majority of the Azeri people are Shi'ite Muslims, and their culture has been heavily influenced by the IRANIANS and TURKS. More recently, however, RUSSIAN culture has also had a profound influence. The URARTIANS and later the MEDES originated from the area now known as Azerbaijan, and the present-day population has been formed from the mixing of the original indigenous population with those peoples who have dominated the region politically over the centuries – principally the PERSIANS, ARABS, MONGOLS, Turks and Russians – producing a very ethnically mixed population.

Following World War I, the Azeris experienced a brief period of independence, followed by incorporation into the USSR in 1920. After the collapse of the USSR, Azerbaijan became an independent republic in 1991. While the vast majority of the Azeris remain dependent on agriculture for their livelihood, many are employed in the industrial sector, particularly in oil and petroleum production. Azeri (an Altaic-Turkic language) is the official language, although due to Azerbaijan's former incorporation into the USSR, Russian is also frequently used.

## BABYLONIANS

A Semitic people (see SEMITES) whose capital lay at Babylon in Mesopotamia, in modern Iraq. The term 'Babylonian' came from their place of origin, Babylonia (Babili), meaning 'Gate of God'. They spoke a form of AKKADIAN, and wrote in the cuneiform script. Between the 18th and 6th centuries BC the Babylonians created one of the most advanced civilizations of the ancient world.

The site of Babylon was inhabited from the 5th millennium BC, and by the late 3rd millennium BC the city of Babylon had already grown into one of the foremost trading cities in ancient Mesopotamia. It was incorporated into the empires of both the SUMERIANS and the AKKADIANS. Following the collapse of the Third Dynasty of Ur, however, Babylon was captured by the AMORITES, who established a new dynasty in the city. The best-known Amorite king of Babylon was Hammurabi (ruled c.1792–1750 BC), who succeeded in creating an empire that stretched from the Persian Gulf to the Mediterranean Sea. The Amorite dynasty lasted until c. 1595 BC, when the HITTITES overran Babylonia; this left the capital unable to resist subsequent capture by the KASSITES. Babylon and its empire prospered under the Kassites, whose kings were considered equal in status to the EGYPTIAN pharaohs. Clashes with the ASSYRIANS and ELAMITES were not uncommon, however, and the latter eventually toppled the Kassite dynasty in about 1137 BC. The Babylonians were subsequently plunged into a dark age, losing most of their territory to invading Elamites and ARAMAEANS. From the 10th century BC Babylon became the prize coveted by both the expanding Assyrian empire and the nomadic CHALDEANS, the latter of whom succeeded in founding a new dynasty in the city during the 9th century. It was under the Chaldeans that Babylonian civilization reached its zenith. During this period in their history, the Babylonians were frequently referred to as Chaldeans.

Compared with that of their immediate neighbours the Assyrians, Babylonian culture was extremely advanced; they succeeded in producing some of the finest epic poetry, art and prose (including philosophical debate) known from the ancient world. In addition, the Babylonians were also extremely prolific in the areas of law codification (the Code of Hammurabi dates from the 18th century BC), civil administration, mathematics, science, astronomy and astrology. Much of this knowledge was firmly founded on the earlier works amassed by the Sumerians, but

the Babylonians, particularly under the Chaldean dynasty, went far beyond their predecessors in many areas, including mathematics, astrology and the sciences. Babylonian astronomical advances, their calendar, and system of weights and measures were also influential far beyond Babylonia; it is a testimony to Babylonian learning that an Assyrian king, Ashurbanipal, ordered the collection of a huge library of copied Babylonian texts to be housed in his new library at Nineveh. Moreover, Babylonian civilization was so successful that the Assyrians copied it almost in its entirety. A measure of the superiority of Babylonian culture over Assyrian can be seen in the fact that the Babylonian dialect of Akkadian far outpaced the Assyrian dialect of the same language, despite Assyrian imperial successes. By the 9th century BC, the Babylonian form was the major diplomatic language for the whole of Mesopotamia and the Levant, and remained so until supplanted by Aramaic in the 7th century BC. Babylonian civilization was also very influential on the HEBREWS and GREEKS.

### Babylonian religion

Under the Amorites and the Kassites, Babylon became the major religious and economic centre in Mesopotamia; the former imported their god Marduk into the region, but Ishtar (the Mesopotamian Great Mother goddess) was also extremely important in Babylonian religious practice. The Babylonian pantheon, however, remained heavily influenced by former Sumerian deities, spirits and angels, as did their religious rituals and beliefs concerning the heavens and after-life. Religion was, in all periods, very important in Babylonian daily life. The temple was an essential focal point in Babylonian towns and cities, and a number of the larger temples had imposing ziggurats within temple complexes. The temple priesthoods accumulated immense wealth and power, both through the exploitation of temple lands and through royal patronage, and, at times, were able to rival the kings themselves. Indeed, the priesthood of Marduk in Babylon was instrumental in bringing about the defeat of Nabonidus, the last Chaldean king, and actively encouraged the PERSIAN conquest. National dread would result if the king were not able to attend to the requisite New

**"The Babylonians have one most shameful custom. Every woman born in the country must once in her life go and sit down in the precinct of Venus, and there consort with a stranger."**

Herodotus,
5th century BC

Year rituals that culminated in a symbolic marriage, with the king taking the role of Marduk.

During the 8th century BC, the Chaldean dynasty at Babylon fought a series of wars against the Assyrians, with the city passing back and forth between the two rivals. These wars ultimately proved disastrous and culminated in the sack of Babylon by Sennacherib, (king of Assyria c. 705–681 BC), in 689 BC. Assyrian vassals frequently ruled Babylon during this period, some of whom were drawn from the Assyrian royal house. During the late 7th century BC, however, Assyrian power was undermined both by internal civil war and by external attack from the CIMMERIANS and MEDES. The Babylonians allied themselves with the latter, and assisted in the final destruction of the Assyrian capital Nineveh in 612 BC. The Babylonians then expanded their empire then to take in the whole of Mesopotamia, and from this period dates the great building project at Babylon that saw the construction of the Hanging Gardens, the great Tower of Babel (within the new temple of Marduk) and the Ishtar Gate. Many of these buildings were adorned with tin-glazed bricks – a process invented by the Babylonians. Other important Mesopotamian cities, such as Ur, were similarly embellished.

By 539 BC, however, the Persians had overrun Babylonia. Babylon itself was captured, and the whole area was annexed as part of the empire of Cyrus the Great. This conquest marked the beginning of the end for Babylon; Alexander the Great conquered the city in 330 BC, and in about 250 BC most of the population was moved to the new SELEUCID capital of Seleucia-on-the-Tigris. The region surrounding the former city of Babylon continued to be referred to as Babylonia, but by the time of the Islamic conquest in the 7th century AD Babylon, and the Babylonians, had almost ceased to exist.

## BACTRIANS

An INDO-EUROPEAN people originally of Bactria, situated in what is now modern Afghanistan, western Uzbekistan and Tajikistan. Several important trade routes from India and China (including the Silk Road) passed through Bactria and, as early as the Bronze Age, this had allowed the accumulation of vast amounts of wealth by the mostly nomadic population. The first proto-urban civilization in the area arose during the 2nd millennium BC. Control of these lucrative trade routes, however, attracted foreign interest, and in the 6th century BC the Bactrians were conquered by the PERSIANS, and in the 4th century BC by the MACEDONIANS. These conquests marked the end of Bactrian independence. From around 304 BC the area formed part of the SELEUCID empire, and from around 250 BC it was the centre of a Greco-Bactrian kingdom, ruled by the descendants of GREEKS who had settled there following the conquests of Alexander the Great. These people, also known as the Yavanas, worked in cooperation with the native Bactrian aristocracy. By the early 2nd century BC the Greco-Bactrians had created an impressive empire that stretched southwards to include northwest India. By about 135 BC, however, this kingdom had been overrun by invading YUE-QI tribes, an invasion that later brought about the rise of the powerful KUSHAN empire. From this point the Bactrians tend to disappear from the historical record, a disappearance made final by the ARAB invasion of the 8th century AD.

The Bactrians spoke a dialect of the INDO-IRANIAN language Bactrian, and the principal religion of the area, before the coming of Islam, was Zoroastrianism. It is believed that Zoroaster died in Bactria, and the country was regarded as the cradle of the religion. Buddhism, however, was also influential. Bactrian culture was heavily influenced by a number of very different traditions. In part this was due to its position along important East–West trade routes, but also to its incorporation into the Persian, Macedonian and Kushan empires. As a result, alongside native forms, the art of the Bactrians displayed Western influences, especially Greek and ROMAN, but also that of the CHINESE and INDIAN (especially Buddhist) cultures.

## BADAGAS

An INDIAN people of DRAVIDIAN origin. There is some dispute as to whether they are a tribe or caste; at present they are defined officially as an 'other backward caste'. Some Badagas are pressing to be recognized as a 'scheduled tribe'. The

> *"* The Bactrians were famous for their pithy, proverbial sayings. *"*
>
> H.G. Rawlinson, 1912

b

term 'Badaga' means 'northerner', and suggests that they migrated, during the 16th or 17th centuries, south to their present location in the Nilgiri Hills in the state of Tamil Nadu. They are a Hindu people, and have close social and economic ties with both the Kota and TODA. They speak a dialect of Kannada, a Dravidian language. The Badaga population is about 30,000.

## BAHRAINIS

An ARAB people living on the archipelago of Bahrain (capital Manama). In Arabic, *bahrain* means 'two seas'. Archaeological investigation has established that prehistoric settlements existed on the islands, and the AKKADIAN king Sargon the Great is thought to have traded with them (then known as Dilmun) during the late 3rd millennium BC; evidence for this is the discovery of SUMERIAN-style burial mounds. Dilmun also had trade connections with the Indus Valley civilization (see HARAPPANS). Sassanian PERSIANS conquered the islands in the 4th century AD, but it was the arrival of Islam in the 7th century that had the most profound political and cultural influence. The PORTUGUESE occupied the islands briefly in 1521–1602, and the Persians in 1602–1783, but since 1783 the al-Khalifah family have ruled as emirs. Bahrain was a British protectorate from 1861 to 1971.

The majority (about 70%) of the Bahrainis are Shi'ite Muslim, predominantly working-class. Most of the remainder (about 25%) are Sunnite and form the ruling and commercial classes. At times, particularly during the 1990s, this division has led to religious and class tensions; in recent years, the Bahrain Freedom Movement and the Islamic Front for the Freedom of Bahrain have been particularly active. Ethnic tension has also led to unrest; more than 60% of the workforce of Bahrain is drawn from foreign nationals, particularly INDIANS and PAKISTANIS, while the unemployment rate among the indigenous population is very high.

The oil and petroleum industries are the principal employers, and Arabic is the official language, although English, Urdu and Farsi are also common. Bahraini culture is Muslim-Arabic. Of the approximately 650,000 inhabitants of Bahrain only about half are Bahrainis.

## BAIKOTS

A Siberian people, related to the KETS, who were assimilated by the RUSSIANS or neighbouring peoples and had disappeared as a distinct group by the mid-19th century.

## BAKHTYARI or Bakhtar

A nomadic pastoralist IRANIAN people. Each of the two principal groupings, the Chahar Lang and the Haft Lang, has a chief, and overall leadership of the people alternates between these two individuals on a bi-annual basis; the other chief acts as second-in-command. In recent years, many Bakhtyari have relinquished their traditional nomadic lifestyles in favour of more settled living conditions and regular wages by finding alternative employment, principally in the oil industry. The Iranian government has also encouraged many to abandon nomadism. The Bakhtyari are Shi'ite Muslims, and speak the Luri dialect of Farsi. As in the case of other nomadic peoples such as the KURDS, Bakhtyari women enjoy more social freedom than many of their female co-religionists.

## BALOCHIS or Baluchis or Beluchis

A large group of mainly pastoral peoples who were originally IRANIAN and migrated to their present homeland around the 11th century AD. Many other ethnic influences have also been assimilated into the Balochis over the centuries. There are approximately 10 million Balochis worldwide, with the majority living in the historical region of Balochistan (capital Quetta), which now forms part of Pakistan, Iran and Afghanistan. About 70% of these live in Pakistan and a further 20% in Iran. Many Balochis have left their homeland, however, in order to seek work elsewhere, and significant numbers are found throughout the ARAB world. The Balochis are sub-divided into two principal groups: the Sulaimanis and the Makranis.

For much of their history the Balochi tribes were dominated by the Iranians, but from the late 19th century until 1947 most of Balochistan fell under British rule. Many Balochis reject current labels like PAKISTANI, Iranian or AFGHAN and support moves for an independent Balochistan. This has led to clashes with national governments, especially that of Pakistan.

Traditionally, the Balochis were a nomadic people. Although the vast majority still live a pastoral lifestyle, very few are now nomadic. Many have been assisted in the switch to a more sedentary existence by central governments wishing to encourage a more settled and stable population. As well as having a long tradition of rebellion against ruling powers, the Balochis were also frequently engaged in internecine strife. In recent years, they have become more culturally assimilated in their states of residence, and this has been particularly true of those who have left Balochistan to seek better-paid employment. Traditional culture remains important, however, particularly in storytelling and song; handcrafted Balochi rugs are prized throughout the world. Most Balochis continue to use the Balochi language and to practise Islam.

## BALTI

An Islamic people of the Kashmir mountains. They are culturally related to the peoples of Central Asia and speak a TIBETAN language. The Balti numbered 34,200 in the late 20th century.

## BANAS CULTURE

A society centred on the Banas River valley in India. It flourished c. 2200–1500 BC, continuing the traditions of the Indus Valley civilization (see HARAPPANS). Although it was destroyed after ARYAN migration into the region, the latter facilitated the spread of Banas black and red pottery throughout much of southern India.

## BANGLADESHIS

Citizens of Bangladesh, population (1998) 127 million. There are around 300 recognized ethnic groups in Bangladesh, most of which are very small, with populations numbering less than 5000. The large majority of Bangladeshis – around 70% – are Muslim Bengalis, from whom the country takes it name: until independence, after a short war in 1971, it was the PAKISTANI

province of East Bengal (for historical aspects, see BENGALIS). Around 15% of the population is made up of other Muslim peoples, including the Ansari, BIHARIS, Chittagonians and Sylhettis. Among the remainder of the population the most important religion is Hinduism. There are also significant numbers of Buddhists, mainly in the southeast of the country, and small numbers of Christians and followers of traditional religions. Bangladeshi politics has become more and more Islamized in recent years, and followers of minority religions are often discriminated against by the Muslim majority.

The largest concentration of ethnic minorities is found in the Chittagong Hill Tracts in the southeast of the country, where there are many tribal groups related to the peoples of neighbouring Burma (Myanmar). The most important of these are the CHAKMA, MARMA, Mro and Tripura. As the least densely settled part of Bangladesh, the hill tracts have attracted increasing numbers of Muslim Bengali settlers since the 1970s. Their arrival has been resisted by the indigenous peoples and there have been frequent outbreaks of inter-ethnic violence. Other tribal peoples of Bangladesh include the SANTAL, the KHASIS, the GARO and the Hajang. The majority of Bangladeshis, of all ethnic and religious backgrounds, speak Bengali.

## BANGNI

See DAFLA.

## BANJARI or Labhani or Indian Gypsies

A nomadic people who originate in the Indian province of Rajasthan, but now travel throughout Central India seeking temporary labour. They are related to the European GYPSIES.

## BANU ASAD

An Arabian BEDOUIN tribe. During the late 5th and early 6th centuries AD they were incorporated into the kingdom of the KINDAH and later came to dominate central Iraq through the Mazyadid dynasty, from the late 10th to the early 12th centuries.

# BARA-JANGAR

See BONDA.

# BARTANGS

A Pamir people of the southwest Gorno-Badakhshan autonomous *oblast*, Tajikistan, who speak an INDO-IRANIAN language. A long history of invasion culminated with the arrival of the RUSSIANS in the late 19th century. Little changed until the 1950s for this isolated people, who raised livestock such as sheep, goats and yaks, and follow Sunni Islam. Then two-thirds of the population were relocated to work on cotton plantations in the Vakhsh Valley, where they became acculturated with their new neighbours. Their population was reduced to about 1000, and only slowly recovered thereafter.

# BASMIL TURKS

A Turkic (see TURKS) nomadic people who, during the early 8th century AD, inhabited the southwestern steppes of Central Asia. They were defeated by CHINESE tribes in 720.

# BATS or Bacav

A people of the central Caucasus related to the CHECHENS and INGUSH. There are only around 5000 Bats, all of whom live around a single village in eastern Georgia. The Bat language is unwritten and appears destined for extinction as all Bats now also speak Georgian.

# BAYAD

A nomadic MONGOL people. They are not part of the KHALKHA people, and today constitute a small minority within the republic of Mongolia (less than 2% of the population). Most continue to live a nomadic pastoral lifestyle.

# BEDOUIN

Originally a nomadic people who inhabited the deserts of the Arabian peninsula, migrating with their herds between winter and summer pasturelands. The term 'Bedouin' derives from the Arabic word *bedawi*, meaning 'dwellers in the desert'. During the 2nd millennium BC, Bedouin tribes migrated from the Syrian Desert into Mesopotamia, and were instrumental in the later development of the civilizations based there; perhaps the most notable of these were the ARAMAEANS. Bedouins also infiltrated the Negev Desert of modern Israel. United for the first time under the banner of Islam, many Bedouin tribes were at the forefront of the Islamic conquest, forming the hub of the Muslim armies, and many ARAB ruling dynasties, particularly during the medieval period, were derived from Bedouin stock.

Traditionally, the Bedouin gained their livelihood in a number of ways; most common was livestock-herding, principally camels, horses, sheep, cattle and goats, but their knowledge of the desert also led to their control of the great caravan routes. Raiding and banditry also provided a lucrative income, particularly during more economically depressed times. These raids engendered a great deal of hostility and tension between settled communities and the Bedouin. The tensions, however, were also offset to a large degree by the cultural interactions brought about by commercial contacts.

**The modern Bedouin**

In the modern period, many Bedouin have abandoned a nomadic way of life in favour of a more sedentary lifestyle. There have been many reasons for these changes: contributing factors include the development of the oil industry, providing regular paid employment; the establishment of firmly-demarcated national borders, which cut across traditional Bedouin migration routes; government settlement policies (for example, in Saudi Arabia and Jordan); and the removal of grazing rights. As a result, less than 10% of Bedouin now live a permanently nomadic life, although many more are seasonal nomads. A measure of this process can be seen in the QATARI population, which is made up almost entirely of Bedouin, but with 92% now living in towns or cities. An effect of these changes has been the loss of tribal identity.

Social rank has always been of great importance to the Bedouin, and a well-defined class system has existed for centuries; traditionally,

> " [The Bedouin] will traverse burning sands barefooted, to receive the last breath of some kind of relation or friend. "
>
> Hester Stanhope, 1827

the camel-herders were regarded as the elite of Bedouin society. Ancestry has also played a key role, and the ability to trace ancestors back to either Qatan or his son Ishmael defines a 'noble' Bedouin, with all others considered ancestorless and socially inferior. Apart from these distinctions, however, there is very little class or economic stratification, although the marriage of individuals from differing classes is rare. Both the tribe and family unit are male-dominated, with the sheikh as tribal and family head.

During the pre-Islamic period, Bedouin poetry enjoyed a golden age, with much of it composed by the aristocracy. Of special note were the *qasida* (odes); these can be epic in proportion and give a detailed insight into Bedouin community, society and culture. Music and dance also continue to be very important.

## BENGALIS

An ethnically mixed people whose elements include ARYANS, ARABS and TURKS. Bengalis occupy historic Bengal, now divided between the Republic of Bangladesh ('Land of the Bengalis') and the INDIAN province of West Bengal. They speak an INDO-ARYAN language, Bengali or Bangla, and number over 200 million.

Traditionally an extremely rich area, Bengal was absorbed into the MUGHAL empire during the early 17th century. Western powers were also drawn to the region, notably the Portuguese and Dutch, but from 1765 until independence in 1947, the Bengalis were subject to BRITISH rule. Following the withdrawal of the British, they were divided between the new states of India and Pakistan – Hindus in the former, and Muslims in the latter, a division based broadly upon the demographic divisions of these two major religious communities.

Previously, tensions had existed between Hindus and Muslims; the Muslims were often regarded as having lower social status. In 1905 the region was divided between East and West Bengal in a deliberate attempt to exacerbate communal antagonisms as a means of diverting anti-British feeling in the area. Although revoked in 1911, the partition was reintroduced in 1947. Neither Hindus nor Muslims, however, would reject the label 'Bengali'.

From an early stage after Partition, Bengali language and culture provided a focus for a resistance to West Pakistani authority. Large numbers were unimpressed by the PAKISTANIS' attempts at nation-making, through the propagation of the URDU language, and many felt that the government of Pakistan was using income from Bengal to fund projects in the west of the country. The result of this disaffection was a growing desire throughout the 1950s and 1960s for Bengali independence. This was achieved in 1972 when the Republic of Bangladesh was formed, following a brief, though traumatic, war of independence.

Whether resident in India or Bangladesh, most Bengalis gain their livelihoods from agriculture, although millions also live in towns and cities, principally Calcutta in India and Dhaka in Bangladesh. Both Hindu and Muslim Bengalis acknowledge a shared cultural and artistic tradition; Bengali poetry and prose are particularly highly regarded. Since the 19th century, there

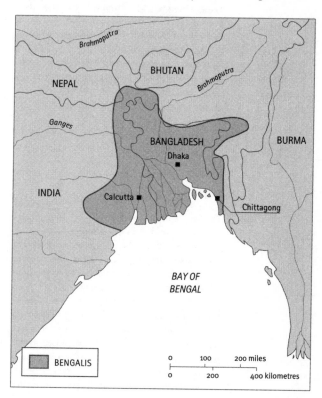

Bengalis

has been a resurgence of interest in this culture, but exposure to British rule for many years has also led to the influx of Western influences.

Following independence from Pakistan, the BIHARIS of Bangladesh were the subject of local reprisals and violence. In addition, migratory Bengalis in search of land have clashed with settled Buddhist peoples in the southeast of Bangladesh, most notably with the CHAKMA and MARMA in recent years.

## BHIL

An aboriginal INDIAN group of peoples who inhabit the upland areas of western India. Today they number around 5 million. They are fiercely independent and maintain a principally agricultural lifestyle. Their way of life has changed drastically over the last 150 years, however, mainly due to BRITISH influence. The Bhil were encouraged to abandon their traditional slash-and-burn cultivation in favour of more settled plough systems, and the result has been a much more sedentary existence for the vast majority. While some Bhil adhere to Hindu or Muslim beliefs, many continue to worship traditional local gods. Their native language is Bhili, a language related to INDO-ARYAN, but currently this is rarely used; most now speak the dominant language of the region in which they reside.

## BHOTIYA

See TAMANG.

## BHUTANESE

The people of the small Himalayan kingdom of Bhutan. Around 50% of Bhutanese are BHUTIA, 35% NEPALESE and 14% SHARCHOPS; there are also small numbers of LEPCHAS and SANTAL. Tibetan Buddhism is the majority religion (some 70%). Bhutan became independent from Tibet in 1630 under a rebel lama who made himself the *dharma raja* ('spiritual leader'). Later *dharma rajas* appointed *deb rajas* (temporal rulers), but power devolved to local chiefs. Bhutan was politically reunited in 1907 by Ugen Wangchuk, founder of the modern Bhutanese monarchy.

Though Bhutan was never part of Britain's

Indian empire, it was effectively a British protectorate from 1774 to 1947. Since 1949 Bhutan has been an Indian protectorate. In 1988 King Jigme Singye Wangchuk introduced a campaign to impose ethnic Bhutian culture, decreeing that all Bhutanese use the Bhutia language and wear Bhutia traditional dress. This alienated the large Nepalese minority, many of whom fled to India or Nepal. Others have turned to terrorism. Attempts by the government of Nepal to negotiate on behalf of Bhutan Nepalese have generally been frustrated by India's support for the royal government. In 1996 the population of Bhutan was 1.8 million.

## BHUTIA or Bhotia or Bhote or Ngalops

The largest ethnic group in the small Himalayan kingdom of Bhutan, an INDIAN protectorate where currently they comprise about half of the population of 1.8 million. They migrated to this area from Tibet during the 9th century AD. The Bhutia tend to live in eastern Bhutan, and significant numbers are also found in India (in Sikkim), Nepal and Tibet. Their name may be derived from 'Bod', an ancient term for Tibet. Around 200,000 Bhutia also live in India.

The ruling family of Bhutan and most of the other political, social and economic leaders of the country are Bhutia, therefore, more than any other people, it is the Bhutia who are identified as BHUTANESE. A dialect of the Bhutia known as Dzongkha, for example, has been imposed as the national language of Bhutan. Indeed, attempts at imposing Bhutian culture on the country since the 1980s have led to significant tensions between the Bhutia and the NEPALESE.

A mountain people, the vast majority of the Bhutia continue to live an agricultural lifestyle, mainly arable but with some animal-rearing, centred on small farms and villages. Most adhere to Tibetan Buddhism, often alongside ancient traditional animism. Bhutian women enjoy considerable social and economic freedom, and some of them have more than one husband, usually brothers.

The Bhutia are closely related to the SHERPA. In India, where many have become thoroughly assimilated into Indian culture, the Bhutia are also known as the Shouka, Marcha and Jad. Historically, these people traded with Tibet and became very prosperous as a result, many owning large landed estates. Since the inauguration of land reforms in the 1960s, however, much of this land has been lost, and many now farm their own much smaller estates, or have moved to cities in search of employment.

# BIHARIS

An INDO-ARYAN people whose original homeland was the region of Bihar, India. Following the Partition of India and Pakistan in 1947 many Muslim Biharis migrated to East Pakistan, where they subsequently settled. There are also significant numbers of Biharis living in Nepal. The Biharis are an ethnically mixed people: Bihar was the centre of both the Magadha and Mauyran empires and was later conquered by the MUGHALS during the 12th century. Subsequently falling under the hegemony of the kingdom of Delhi from 1497, the region then passed to British control from 1765 until independence in 1947.

Prior to the foundation of Bangladesh, many Biharis were content with PAKISTANI citizenship and openly opposed the BENGALIS' drive for autonomy. The tensions generated by these conflicting views developed into violent confrontation, particularly in the aftermath of BANGLADESHI independence, when many Biharis were attacked as enemies of the new state. During the later stages of the campaigns for independence a clear division became apparent between those Biharis who had migrated to East Pakistan, and desired Pakistani unity, and those who had been born after the migration and had become largely assimilated with the Bengali majority, and desired independence. Many of the former joined the Al-Shams pro-Pakistani militia and actively pursued pro-Bengali Biharis, some of whom fled to India and some of whom were placed in refugee camps.

In India, the vast majority (over 80%) of Biharis are Hindus, about 14% are Muslim, and there are also small numbers who adhere to Christianity or animism. Most rely on agriculture as a source of livelihood, although large numbers also work in the region's mining indus-

tries. Over 40 million people speak the Bihari language, which is sub-divided into three dialects – Bhojpuri, Maitili, and Magahi. Bihari is not recognized, however, as one of the 18 official Indian languages. Most Biharis also speak Hindi, which is the language of government and administration.

# BIRHOR

An aboriginal tribe that inhabits the jungle regions of the northeastern Deccan plateau, India. The tribe is divided into a number of totem groups that are identified with, for example, plants, animals or Hindu castes; the totem is regarded as a member of the tribe. The Birhor are a hunter-gatherer people and adhere to animistic beliefs. In the late 20th century there were 16,700 Birhor.

# BIROBIDZHANIS

A Jewish, Yiddish-speaking community of the Autonomous Region of Birobidzhan, southern Siberia, on the Chinese frontier of the Russian Federation. The region was established at Stalin's order in 1934 in answer to the international Zionist movement. It was presented as a homeland for the world's Jews, and received some financial support and a few of immigrants from Zionist organizations in Canada and the USA.

The reality, however, was far different from the claims of Soviet propaganda. Usually-urban Jewish settlers were expected to establish collective farms on swampy, mosquito-infested land with minimal support from the state. In fact only about 35,000 settlers ever arrived, and they remained a tiny minority among a largely Russian population. More did arrive after World War II, mostly survivors of German occupation. At this point Stalin was turning against Zionism, however, and he moved to suppress the identity of the community, disperse the population and ban religious education.

With the fall of the USSR, many Birobidzhanis left for Israel. Those who remained did, however, enjoy a cultural revival, even though they numbered only 6700, no more than 6% of the region's population, in 2000.

b

# BISHNOI

A people who inhabit the desert region of Rajasthan, northwestern India. They adhere to the Hindu religion and honour Vishnu, and are vegetarian, renowned for their respect for other living creatures and refusal to cut down trees. Bishnoi are prominent in the government and administration of Rajasthan, and their castes include the Jat Bishnoi, Bania Bishnoi, and Ahir Bishnoi. In the late 20th century there were 566,000 Bishnoi.

# BITHYNIANS

Ancient inhabitants of an area of northwest Asia Minor (now Turkey). The Bithyni were a Thracian tribe who migrated to the region during the later 2nd millennium BC. Between the mid-6th and early 3rd centuries BC, the Bithynians were dominated, in turn, by the LYDIANS, PERSIANS, MACEDONIANS and SELEUCIDS. Following two centuries of independence, and some prosperity, the region was bequeathed to Rome in 74 BC. Thereafter, the Bithynians never regained their independence, and disappeared as a people.

# BLACK KITAI

See KHITANS.

# BLACK SHEEP TURKS or Kara Koyunlu

A TURKMEN tribal confederation, which at its height, during the mid-15th century, controlled significant areas in what are now Azerbaijan and Iran. The confederation was eclipsed following its defeat and destruction by the WHITE SHEEP TURKS in 1467–9.

# BODO

An AUSTRO-ASIATIC tribal group, most of whom live in Assam (India) and Bangladesh. The majority derive their livelihood from sedentary agriculture. The Bodo now display a wide range of cultural influences. In many cases Bodo groups have become largely culturally assimilated with the ASSAMESE; for example, many, like the Dimasa Kachari, have adopted Hindu religious and social practices. In other areas, however, traditional culture remains strong, and animism is the dominant form of religious expression. Traditional Bodo culture and society are also extremely diverse; for example, Bodo practise both patrilineal and matrilineal succession. The Bodo language is Tibeto-Burman in origin. In recent years, the Bodo, who until the 1820s were the leading tribe in Assam, have been agitating for political autonomy from the Assamese, and significant tensions, frequently leading to violent confrontation, continue to exist between these two groups. About 1.7 million Bodo live in India, 36,500 in Bangladesh.

# BONDA

An AUSTRO-ASIATIC group of tribes who inhabit the hills and plains of northwest India; they are also known as Bondo but refer to themselves as *Remo* ('Men'). The Bonda are an agricultural people. Traditionally they practised slash-and-burn cultivation, but most now use sedentary terraced or ploughing systems. A few continue to use illegal transitory methods. Culturally, the Bonda are divided into two broad groups: hill-dwellers and plains-dwellers. The Bara-Jangar and Gabada, the hill-dwellers, have been relatively isolated from the rest of INDIAN society and largely maintain their traditional religious and social practices; for example, hill villages maintain a *sindibor* (a stone circle for the reverence of Mother Earth) and a shrine to Hundi. The plains-dwellers, however, have been far more culturally assimilated with their Hindu neighbours and have frequently abandoned their traditional gods, although a certain dualism in religious practice is evident. The hill and plains communities have grown increasingly apart, and there is now little contact between them. Marriage between plains and hill tribes is rare, even though the Bonda practise exogamous marriage. Bonda clans are totemic and principally based upon animals and plants. There is a great tradition of inter-tribal feuding among the Bonda, and tribes tend to view each other with a large degree of suspicion and mistrust. ORIYA culture has also heavily influenced the Bonda. The Bonda numbered about 12,000 in the 1990s.

---

**Bodo: main subgroups**

Cutiya
Dimasa
  Kachari
Galong
GARO
Koch
Mech
Moran
Rabha
Tippera

---

## BRAHUI

A group of 29 allied peoples, drawn from a number of disparate ethnic backgrounds, who reside in the historic region of Balochistan. Most are now PAKISTANIS, while a small number are AFGHANS. The core of the confederation (traditionally numbering eight tribes, and now comprising a small minority) is of DRAVIDIAN ancestry, and the Brahui still speak a Dravidian language. They are nomadic goat-herders, number around 1 million people and recognize the Khan of Kalat as their leader. Cultural and linguistic assimilation with other more dominant neighbouring peoples such as the PASHTUN and BALOCHI has led to the gradual dilution of Brahui culture. The Brahui language, for example, which has no written form and contains many loan words from other local languages, is gradually being supplanted. As a result, the Brahui are in danger of extinction as a distinctive cultural and ethnic group. The Brahui are predominantly Sunni Muslims.

## BUDUKHS

A Caucasian people of Kuba and Khachmas regions, Azerbaijan. Primarily herders of sheep and cattle and Sunni Muslim from the 14th century, they were strongly influenced by the AZERIS, whose written language they use. Under Soviet rule partly-successful efforts were made through collectivization and educational and cultural policies to destroy their identity as a people and forcibly assimilate them with the Azeris, with whom they were officially counted from 1959. In 1977 they numbered about 2000.

## BURGHER

A Christian Eurasian minority of Sri Lanka. The Burghers originated from the inter-marriage of male PORTUGUESE and DUTCH colonists with native women in the 17th and 18th centuries. The Burghers were originally divided into two groups. The Dutch Burghers spoke Dutch, were Protestants and could prove their European descent through the male line. The Portuguese Burghers, also called Mechanics, were Roman Catholic and Creole-speaking and had lower status than the Dutch Burghers because they could not prove their European descent. After Sri Lanka came under BRITISH rule in 1796, the Burghers gradually adopted English. They enjoyed a privileged position, playing a major role in the colonial administration. When Sri Lanka became independent in 1948, the Burghers lost this privileged status and their numbers have been in steady decline through emigration, principally to Australia, ever since. The Burghers currently number around 5800, most of whom live in the capital, Colombo.

## BURYATS

A Siberian people of the Buryatia autonomous republic, Russian Federation, and the surrounding region, who speak an Altaic language. Traditionally nomadic herders and shamanists, by the 12th century they lived around Lake Baikal, which they deemed a holy sea. Though they resisted conquest by the MONGOLS in the 13th century, they were driven further north. In the 17th century they adopted Buddhism (although traces of shamanism remained) and came under pressure from the RUSSIANS.

Buryat resistance to Russian conquest lasted over 100 years. Even when officially at peace, the Buryat would attack Russian settlers, travellers and especially tribute-collectors if the opportunity arose. In the course of this resistance, tribal differences were largely erased, and they became consolidated into a single people.

It was not until the 19th century that the Buryats were finally brought fully under Russian control, and gradually became sedentary farmers and herders. Even then they built houses resembling their traditional nomadic *yurts*. Under Soviet rule they were collectivized and the last traces of nomadism were suppressed. They became a minority in a land where the first steps towards urbanization and industrialization threatened what remained of their traditional culture. In 1990 they numbered over 420,000.

## BURUSHO or Hunzakuts

A people of the Hunza region in the Karakorum Mountains of northern Pakistan. The Burusho claim to be the descendants of soldiers who came to the region with Alexander the Great's army in the 4th century BC. Many Burusho do indeed have a strikingly European appearance. Their language, Burushaski, is unrelated to any other known language.

For centuries the Burusho raided or collected protection money from caravans crossing the mountains between China and India. From the 11th century until 1974, when Hunza was fully incorporated into Pakistan, the Burusho were ruled by the same family of *mirs* (rulers). In 1904 the Burusho converted to Islam, pledging allegiance to the Aga Khan and his ISMAILI sect. In the late 20th century they numbered approximately 60,000.

## BUYIDS or Buwayhids

A Shi'ite IRANIAN dynasty who created an impressive empire encompassing western Iran and Iraq between the early 10th and mid-11th centuries. The Buyids were great patrons of the arts and public works, but were defeated by the SELJUKS, who overran their empire during the mid-11th century. Buyid influence was most pronounced in the propagation of PERSIAN artistic styles throughout the region they controlled.

## CANAANITES

A people of mixed ethnic origin, comprising pre-Semitic, SEMITIC and MESOPOTAMIAN peoples, who lived in Palestine. Ethnically, they were probably identical with the PHOENICIANS. It is thought that 'Canaan' meant 'Land of Purple', and may have been derived from the fact that the coastal regions of the country were rich in murex shellfish, from which a highly prized purple dye was extracted. In the Bible, however, the people is said to have been descended from Canaan, a grandson of Noah. Although they were not an imperialist people, the Canaanites had a great effect on the later cultural development of Western Asia and Europe.

By the mid-2nd millennium BC, the Canaanites had developed into a highly-urbanized people, whose economy was based on the agricultural exploitation of the rich soils of the Levant. Their principal towns and cities included Jerusalem, Jericho, Meggido, Acre and Hebron.

An agricultural civilization had existed in Palestine as early as 8000 BC, centred on Jericho.

The original Canaanite population seems to have arrived in Palestine by the 5th millennium BC, but, over the next 3000 years, they never appear to have evolved a unified Canaanite state; rather, the region continued to be controlled by disparate city-states, leaving them somewhat vulnerable to external conquest. During the 2nd millennium BC, the Canaanites were the subject of migrations or attacks by peoples as diverse as the AMORITES, EGYPTIANS, HYKSOS, HURRIANS, HITTITES and PHILISTINES. They appear to have survived these invasions, at least in a material and cultural sense, relatively unscathed; the Amorites and Philistines, for example, were simply absorbed into Canaanite society.

However, the invasion of the ISRAELITES from the mid-13th century BC, culminating in the conquests of King David during the 10th century BC, destroyed the Canaanites as an independent people. Regarded initially as a second-class source of manual and slave labour, the Canaanites were assimilated, over a number of centuries, into the Israelite population.

**Cultural influences**
The Levant is, historically and geographically, one of the great crossing points of Western Asia. As a result, Canaanite civilization, particularly in the areas of art and literature, was heavily influenced by many of those peoples with whom they came into contact, both through trade and conquest; Egyptian, Hurrian, Mespotamian and MYCENAEAN influences, for example, can all be traced in Canaanite culture. Undoubtedly, however, the most important aspect of Canaanite civilization was their apparent invention of the alphabet. The Canaanite alphabet (named Proto-Byblian, and in use by the 16th century BC) has yet to be deciphered, but it seems to have been the precursor for later writing systems (for example, that of the PHOENICIANS), from which the GREEK and ROMAN alphabets were derived. For diplomacy, however, the Canaanites used the more familiar cuneiform script.

At the head of the Canaanite pantheon stood the god El, but probably the most popularly worshipped divinity in the region was Baal, god of fertility. The Canaanites were primarily an agricultural people, and one of the most important rituals in the sacred calendar was the symbolic marriage of Baal to his sister-bride – a ritual that had parallels across Mesopotamia, and which was designed to guarantee the coming harvest. These rituals, with their emphasis on sexual intercourse, were appealing to non-devotees, and the conversion of large numbers of Israelites caused serious rifts within the Israelite state. But other less contentious Canaanite festivals were adopted by the Israelites, and their religious practice has had a profound influence on Judaism, Christianity and Islam.

## CAPPADOCIANS

Inhabitants of the semi-Hellenized ancient kingdom of Cappadocia in northeast Asia Minor (eastern Turkey today). The area was incorporated within the PERSIAN empire, but later retained a considerable degree of autonomy from the MACEDONIANS and SELEUCIDS. Cappadocia was incorporated into the ROMAN empire in AD 17. By the time of BYZANTINE domination the region became sub-divided into a number of smaller provinces, and the term 'Cappadocian' gradually disappeared from use.

## CARIANS

A non-GREEK people who may have originated on the islands of the Aegean and were pushed eastwards, possibly during the 2nd millennium BC, to southwestern Anatolia – a migration occasioned by Greek expansion. By the early 1st millennium BC, the Carians had developed a characteristic culture, and are first recorded in the 7th century BC as mercenaries fighting for the EGYPTIANS. Even by this relatively early date, however, the Carians were already a heavily Hellenized people, a phenomenon stimulated both by trading contacts and the establishment of Greek colonies along the Carian coast.

For much of their history, the Carians were dominated by the LYDIANS, but were incorporated into the PERSIAN empire around 546 BC. By the time of the MACEDONIAN conquest of the region in 334 BC, the Carians had become so thoroughly Hellenized that they were culturally indistinguishable from their Greek neighbours.

As part of the SELEUCID empire, and later under the Pergamenes, Caria was divided between a number of disparate city-states and effectively ceased to exist as a unified region. By this period, the term 'Carian' disappears altogether. It is possible that the Carians, who spoke a Luwian dialect but used a Greek-influenced writing script, were related to the Lydians and MYSIANS.

## CHAGATAIDS

Subjects of the MONGOL Chagatai Khanate, named for the second son of Genghis Khan, to whom the region was allotted following his father's death. The khanate encompassed large tracts of the Central Asian steppes in northern Iran and southern Xinjiang. The vast area meant that many Mongol tribes continued to practise their traditional nomadic lifestyles and animistic beliefs, particularly in the eastern half of the region. This lifestyle frequently brought them into conflict with the increasingly sedentary Ilkhans.

Even within the Chagatai there were major social and economic divisions: the residents of the more urbanized and Muslim western regions, many of whom had converted to Islam by 1275 and were gradually losing their Mongol identity, frequently clashed with the much poorer nomadic easterners. The latter became known as the *Jete* ('robbers'), who continued to live in Mughalistan ('Land of the Mongols').

The TIMURIDS took advantage of these hostilities and succeeded in overrunning the western Chagatai during the late 14th century, followed by the UZBEKS. The nomadic easterners were able to withstand these raids, but the Chagataids were reduced to a much smaller area centred upon the city of Kashgar. Here they survived until the late 17th century, when they were incorporated into the MANCHU empire.

During the 17th and 18th centuries, the Chagataids were converted to Islam and gradually ceased to exist as a separate political and cultural entity.

The Chagataids spoke a Turkic language (Chagatai), which was used as a literary medium by a number of renowned Islamic poets under the Timurids and during the early modern period. Both the Uzbek and UIGHUR languages

C

> " Among the Carians ... they Sacrifice a Dog in stead of a Goate. "
>
> Edward Topsell, 1607

are related to Chagatai. The founder of the MUGHAL dynasty, Babur, was a western Chagatai prince who had been forced eastwards following the invasion of the Uzbeks.

## CHAHAR or Chakhar or Tsakhar

A MONGOL people who were overrun by the MANCHU in 1635 and today constitute one of the minority tribes of the Mongolian Autonomous Region of China. The last Great Khan, Ligdan (ruled 1604–34), was drawn from Chahar aristocracy.

## CHAKMA

A MONGOL-related people who form a minority population in Bangladesh and the adjoining regions of northeastern India. They are an agricultural people, and many still retain the nomadic slash-and-burn technique, although large numbers are now converting to settled plough-based production. Unlike their neighbours, the BENGALIS, the Chakma originally spoke a Tibeto-Burman language, but most residing in Bangladesh have now abandoned this in favour of Bengali. The vast majority of Chakma are Buddhists, although this is suffused with traditional animism and Hindu influences. Around 260,000 Chakma live in Bangladesh and 213,000 in India.

Over the last 20 years large numbers of Muslim Bengalis have been moving into the traditional Chakma homelands of the Chittagong Hills, and this has led to pressure on the resident population. Ethnic and religious tensions have frequently erupted into open violence. The Chakma are ethnically related to the ARAKANESE.

## CHALDEANS or Kaldu or Kashdu

ARAMAEANS who settled around the city of Ur, in southern Mesopotamia, around 900 BC, and were responsible for the final flowering of BABYLONIAN imperialism and civilization. They spoke Aramaic, and used the cuneiform system of writing. The Chaldeans are first mentioned in ASSYRIAN records in 878 BC. Over the next two-and-a-half centuries they made repeated inroads into the territory of the Babylonians, and fought a series of intermittent wars against the Assyrians for control of this area, culminating in the destruction of the city of Babylon in 689 BC. Taking advantage of growing Assyrian weakness, however, the Chaldeans were able to found a new dynasty at Babylon in 626 BC, and, alongside the CIMMERIANS and MEDES, they were instrumental in the final annihilation of Assyrian power in 612 BC.

Thereafter, the Chaldeans entered something of a golden age – an era known to history as the Neo-Babylonian Age – and by the 560s BC they had pushed their empire as far as the EGYPTIAN border. During this period, the Chaldean kings were responsible for some of the finest monumental constructions known from the ancient world – including the reconstructed Tower of Babel, the Processional Way and the Palace of Nebuchadnezzar, all situated in Babylon itself. Indeed, such was their influence that, in contemporary accounts, 'Chaldean' tends to replace 'Babylonian' as a term used to denote invaders from Babylonia. This new imperial age, however, was shortlived, and the year 562 BC really marked the beginning of the end for the Chaldean empire. Internal strife and foreign invasion following the death of Nebuchadnezzar led finally to the incorporation of Babylon, and the Chaldeans, into the PERSIAN empire of Cyrus the Great in 539 BC.

In addition to their achievements in architecture, the Chaldeans also became renowned for their astronomy, astrology and mathematics, and while these were founded on earlier SUMERIAN advances, Chaldean scholars continued to make considerable discoveries well into the period of Persian domination.

Today, members of the eastern-rite Nestorian church who accept Catholicism are referred to as Chaldeans, and are descended from those inhabitants of Mesopotamia who were not converted to Islam; there are significant numbers in Iraq, Iran, Syria and Lebanon. The spiritual home of the Chaldeans remains Chaldea (Babylon), which was one of the principal areas in which their belief in the distinct and separate divine and human natures originated, and they

**" The Chaldeans were most renowned in Astrologie that euer were anie. "**

**John Marbeck, 1581**

continue to use the Syriac language for their liturgy. At their height, prior to the 14th century, the Chaldeans had established churches across western Asia, and as far as China and India.

## CHARACENES

Inhabitants of a heavily Hellenized region in southern Mesopotamia, which formed a satrap of the SELEUCID empire. The region enjoyed a brief period of independence following the Seleucid collapse, but was swiftly brought under PARTHIAN control in about 121 BC. By the 2nd century AD the term 'Mesene' had replaced Characene as a designation for the area.

## CHENCHU

An aboriginal people of DRAVIDIAN origin who inhabit the region of Andhra Pradesh in the south of India. Traditionally they are hunter-gatherers, and considerable numbers still retain this lifestyle, little affected by Hindu culture and society. The push towards assimilation has been strong, however, and many have abandoned this way of life in favour of sedentary agriculture and Hindu religion.

The Chenchu language is a dialect of Dravidian Telugu (see TELUGU). Today, the Chenchu population is around 59,000.

## CHETRI

See PAHARI.

## CH'IANG or Qiang

A MONGOL people who reside in the steppe regions of northwestern China, related to the TIBETANS. Many have retained their traditional nomadic lifestyle, together with much of their original culture, and have been little influenced by the majority CHINESE. They are first mentioned in Chinese records in about 200 BC, and speak a Sino-Tibetan language.

## CHOLAS

A dynasty of TAMILS, of DRAVIDIAN origin, who were the dominant political power in southern India between the 10th and early 13th centuries AD. Their origins are unknown, but they are thought to have entered southern India in prehistoric times and by the 1st century AD established a kingdom in the region. Between the 6th and 9th centuries the Cholas fell under the suzerainty of the Pallava dynasty, but from the late 10th century they began their period of imperial expansion. Fighting a series of wars against their rival Pallava, Pandya, Calukya and Chera dynasties, the Cholas gained control of an impressive empire, which, by the mid-11th century, stretched north almost to the River Krishna, also including parts of Sri Lanka. They became the first southern people to raid as far as the Ganges region in 1022–3, transporting large jars of the sacred waters 2000 km / 1200 miles back to the Chola capital at Thanjavur (Tanjore). The accumulation of booty was one of the primary motivations for these conquests, but the Cholas were also a maritime trading power keen to dominate the trade routes that ran between Southeast Asia and the Arab countries to the west. This desire for dominance of trade routes in part explains their maritime expeditions against Sri Vijaya (on Sumatra) in 1025, and against the coastal regions of modern Malaya and Burma.

The Cholas were a Hindu people, and the period of their hegemony witnessed a great revival in Hinduism, as evidenced, for example, in much of the huge corpus of royally-patronized literature. They were also responsible for the construction of a number of magnificent temple-complexes, most notably that of Brhadisvara (c. 1010), which has the reputation of being the largest in India and was dedicated to Siva. Interestingly, the Cholas did not patronize only one Hindu deity; they also erected temples to Vishnu, and their rulers supported the popular *Bhakti* tradition, with its emphasis on the many Hindu saints. This policy may have been directed toward promulgating a greater sense of national unity.

Chola sculpture, painting and architecture are renowned as representing the summit of the South Indian style, and their bronze dancing Sivas are also famed for the realism of their movement. The Cholas spoke the Tamil language and have left very large numbers of

C

inscriptions and inscribed copper plates, which allow a detailed overview of Chola history and of their efficient bureaucratic system.

Chola supremacy was fairly shortlived. Sri Lanka was lost around 1070, and internal power struggles leading to the loss of control over many outlying regions marked much of the later 12th and early 13th centuries. The empire was finally destroyed in 1279, following attacks by both the resurgent Pandyas and the Hoysalas.

## CHUKOTS

See CHUKCHIS.

## CHULYMS

A Siberian people of the Chulym River area of the Russian Federation. Formed by the fusion of Turkic peoples (see TURKS) forced eastward by the Russian conquest of the Sibir Khanate in 1582, they speak a Turkic language and were nomadic hunters and gatherers.

Despite a fierce struggle, they were conquered by the RUSSIANS by the end of the 17th century. They were forcibly (though probably superficially) Christianized in 1720, and a road built through their territory in the 1760s brought large numbers of Russian settlers, further undermining their traditional culture. Many became assimilated by the Russians or the KHAKHASS, a process largely completed by collectivization, forced settlement and cultural erosion under Soviet rule. With the young educated only in Russian since the 1950s, their language is now considered seriously endangered. In 2000 they numbered some 12,000.

## CHUVASH

A Siberian people centred on the Chuvash Autonomous Republic of the Russian Federation, who speak a Turkic language (see TURKS), now endangered.

Formed from descendants of Bulgaria on the Volga (see BULGARS), after its destruction by the MONGOLS in the 13th century, they came under Russian rule in 1552. Assimilation followed, but in the late 19th century a cultural revival occurred. This was ended by collectivization and repression under Soviet rule. Only in 1989 did Moscow permit a new cultural centre and begin to address their environmental and economic problems. In 1999 they numbered 2 million.

## CILICIANS

Inhabitants of the ancient region of Cilicia in southern Asia Minor (in modern Turkey). The name is derived from Kilakku, a neo-HITTITE state formed following the destruction of the Hittite empire by the SEA PEOPLES.

By around 1000 BC large numbers of Greeks had immigrated into the region and founded a number of colonies along the coast. As a result of this colonization, the Cilicians became strongly Hellenized, a process that was accelerated when they became part of the SELEUCID empire between the 4th and 2nd centuries BC. The coastal Cilicians gained a considerable reputation as pirates, and were suppressed by the Romans in 67 BC. The region was subsequently incorporated into the Roman empire, and later fell under the sway of the BYZANTINES.

The ARABS conquered Cilicia during the 7th century AD, and the Byzantines retook the region in the 10th century. In 1080 large numbers of ARMENIANS arrived and founded the kingdom of Lesser Armenia. By this time, however, the term 'Cilician' had generally ceased to be used.

## CIMMERIANS

A nomadic people of possibly THRACIAN or IRANIAN stock, who by about 1200 BC dominated the southern regions of the Russian Steppes.

During the 8th century BC, SCYTHIAN pressure drove the Cimmerians into Anatolia, where they established a shortlived hegemony. Although the ASSYRIANS prevented their conquest of the URARTIANS (705 BC), the Cimmerians attacked the PHRYGIANS, and were responsible for the final destruction of their kingdom (Gordium, the capital, was sacked in 696–695 BC). In 652 BC, they also sacked the LYDIAN capital, Sardis (but failed to take the citadel) and destroyed Sinop, on the Black Sea.

The Cimmerians never established a centralized state in their newly-conquered areas, preferring to retain their nomadic lifestyle. Lydia survived, with Assyrian support, and destroyed the Cimmerian threat in 637 or 626 BC. Following this defeat, the Cimmerians probably settled in Cappadocia (whose Armenian name was 'Gamir', after the Cimmerians).

Culturally, the Cimmerians were very similar to the Scythians, and, like them, used their horse-riding skills to devastating effect during their conquests.

# CINGALESE

See SINHALESE.

# COLCHIANS

A people of uncertain ethnic origin who in ancient times inhabited the land of Colchis, in the Rioni River valley, inland from the Black Sea coast of modern Georgia. The ancient GREEKS, almost certainly incorrectly, believed the Colchians originated in Egypt because of their physical appearance and certain shared customs, such as circumcision.

Colchis was regarded as a land of fabulous wealth because of its alluvial gold deposits, and the legend of Jason and the Argonauts may be based on an early trading voyage to Colchis from Greece. Colchian linen was also renowned for its quality. Colchis became part of the ROMAN empire in the 1st century BC and remained under the rule of its successor, the BYZANTINE empire, until the 11th century AD. The modern GEORGIANS count the Colchians among their ancestors.

# DAFLA or Nissi or Bangni

An INDO-ASIATIC people who inhabit the hills of Bhutan and Arunachal Pradesh, India. At the end of the 20th century the Dafla numbered less than 1000. Relatively untouched by outside influences, they have retained their traditional animistic beliefs, and derive their food from slash-and-burn agriculture, linked with hunting and gathering.

The Dafla live in family-based communal longhouses, but there is little unity within the tribe, and neither social nor institutional organi-

zation within the village. Inter-tribal violence is frequent, but many arguments are resolved through a form of oratorical competition. The Dafla speak a Tibeto-Burman language.

# DAGHUR or Daghor or Dahur

A minority MONGOL people, most of whom reside in either the Mongolian Autonomous Region of China or the CHINESE province of Heilongjiang. They have remained a fairly isolated tribe, and, as a result, have retained many aspects of traditional Mongol culture. Many continue, for example, to live a nomadic lifestyle, and adhere to shamanistic animism (although a minority have converted to Buddhism). The Daghur speak an archaic Altaic dialect, which has been heavily influenced by the language of the MANCHUS.

# DANITES

A Hebrew sub-tribe (see JEWS), centred on the city of Dan. They disappeared after the ASSYRIAN conquest of Palestine in 721 BC.

# DARDS

An INDO-IRANIAN people who inhabit the Himalayan region of Dardistan, which occupies parts of northern Pakistan and Kashmir. They claim to be descendants of the ARYANS who migrated to India from central Asia in the 2nd millennium BC. They were first recorded by Herodotus in the 5th century BC.

Since the 14th century the Dards have been Muslims. They speak Gilgit but use the Iranian script. 'Dard' or 'Dardic' is a term also used by linguists to describe the group of Indo-Iranian languages which includes, among others, Gilgit and KASHMIRI.

# DARD SHIN

See SHINA.

# DHODIA

See ADIVASI.

**"The Colchians wore wooden helmets and carried small shields of raw hide, and spears."**

Herodotus, 5th century BC

*d*

## DIGARU

See MISHMI.

## DIMASA KACHARI

See BODO.

## DOGRAS

The ruling SIKH clans of Jammu and Kashmir between 1846 and 1947. Faced in 1947 with a widespread demand for Muslim integration with Pakistan, particularly among resident PASH-TUN tribes, the Dogra rulers consented to the union of Kashmir with India.

## DOLGAN

A Siberian people mostly of Taimyr region, within the Arctic Circle of the Russian Federation. Strongly influenced by the YAKUT and EVENKI, they were traditionally nomadic reindeer-herders, hunters and gatherers and speak a Turkic language (see TURKS).

In the 18th century, under Russian pressure, they moved north to their present location, displacing the NGANASANS, causing bitter enmity between them. Soviet rule, however, proved disastrous. They were forcibly collectivized and settled, and their traditional economy and culture were destroyed.

The collapse of the USSR left the Dolgan struggling to subsist in a polluted environment, forcing many to leave. In 1994 they numbered about 5000.

## DÖRBED

A minority MONGOL people, constituting less than 3% of the total population of Mongolia. The Dörbed were a key component in the OIRAT confederation.

## DRAS

See SHINA.

## DRAVIDIANS

A group of people who speak one of 22 Dravidian languages in southern India. These include the languages of the CHENCHU, Ghats, GOND, ORAONS, TAMILS and TODA. There are also important Dravidian peoples in Sumatra, Madagascar and Malaysia. The term 'Dravidian' is commonly used to refer to the aboriginal INDIAN peoples, although there is now much dispute over the accuracy of this usage. A surviving pocket of Dravidian-speakers in Balochistan (in modern Iran, Afghanistan and Pakistan) may indicate that the Dravidians actually migrated to the Indian sub-continent from this region.

It is possible that the Indus Valley civilization (see HARAPPANS) was Dravidian, but if so its people seem to have been transformed by the influence of ARYAN cultures during the 2nd millennium BC, and subsequently pushed into southern India, where most of their descendants reside to this day. Today's Dravidians are an ethnically mixed people, having inter-married over the last four millennia with, for example, Aryan, Greek, Kushan, Mongol and British peoples.

Traditional Dravidian religion was based on the worship of a serpent god (*naga*), mother goddess (*kala*), and various spirits. Many of these elements have been absorbed into the Hinduism that most Dravidians practise in the 21st century, although Dravidians tend to be of low caste. Despite the fact that many Dravidians have become heavily assimilated into mainstream Indian culture, there have been major attempts to foster a revival in traditional Dravidian culture since independence. In particular, Dravidians, especially the Tamils, have opposed the propagation of Hindi as the national language of India – for example, through the activities of the Dravidian Advancement Society, which were centred around an anti-northern-Hindi-Sanskrit manifesto.

Post-independence India has also seen movements for the revival of Dravidian music and literature, and there remain many Dravidian-speakers who do not identify themselves as 'Indian'.

# DRUZE

Members of a religious sect who live mainly in the mountains of Lebanon, Syria and Israel. Small numbers are also found in other countries of western Asia. There are about 350,000 Druze in total, but their tendency to assimilate with local cultures makes their exact numbers very difficult to calculate. Many belong to the TANUKH tribes. The Druze take their name from an early member of the sect, Muhammad al-Darazi, but call themselves as *Muwahhidun* (monotheists).

The Druze faith, which evolved from the Isma'ilite doctrine of Shi'ite Islam (see ISMAILIS), is centred on the belief that God has, on occasion, been made manifest in humans, the last such occurrence being in the early 11th century AD, in the figure of al-Hakim, sixth caliph of Fatimid Egypt (died or disappeared in 1021). The religion also reveals Jewish, Christian and Gnostic influences. Following the disappearance of al-Hakim, members of the sect were persecuted in Egypt; many migrated to Lebanon and Syria, where they established thriving agricultural communities, such as Jabal ad-Duruze. The Druze believe that al-Hakim will return to institute a new golden age.

The Druze have been very influential in the political history of western Asia; they fought the Crusaders , were almost autonomous under the OTTOMANS, and commanded a great deal of respect in 19th-century Lebanon.

> " Fierce, hardy, proud, in conscious freedom bold. "
>
> Reginald Heber, 1803, referring to the Druze

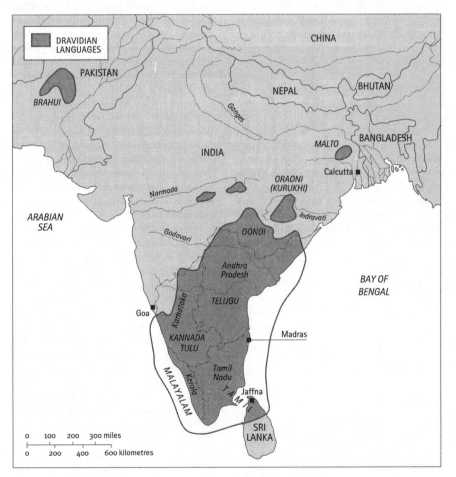

**Dravidians**

*The survival of a pocket of Dravidian-speakers in the Indus Valley suggests that the Dravidians may have migrated to the Indian subcontinent from the northwest.*

As a community, the Druze are very isola-tionist. Conversion either into or out of the religion is strictly forbidden, as is inter-marriage, and they avoid unbelievers as much as possible. However, as a response to persecution, particu-larly under the Mameluks during the 13th and 14th centuries, it is permissible for a member of the sect to deny his or her religion in order to escape death. In addition, when living as a minority amongst Christians or Muslims, the Druze will participate in the religious practices of their neighbours. The Druze are very loyal toward their religion, and toward other mem-bers of their sect, and among their core beliefs is a total acceptance of the will of God, and a strict moral and ethical code.

Religion aside, the Druze share the culture of other ARAB peoples, and the head of a Druze community is known as the sheikh.

## DURRANI

See ABDALIS.

## DZUNGARS or Jungars or Dsongars

A western MONGOL people who lived in the Ili River valley on the border of Kazakhstan and the Xinjiang province of China. The Dzungars got their name because they fought on the left wing (from *dson*, 'left', and *gar*, 'hand') of the Mongol army. They converted to Buddhism in the 17th century. The Dzungars were part of the OIRAT confederation.

## EASTERN CANAANITES

See AMORITES.

## EASTERN MONGOLS

See KHALKHAS.

## EDOMITES

A Semitic people (see SEMITES) who occupied southern Palestine between the 14th and 6th centuries BC. The important commercial cities of Ezion Geber (near modern Aqabah) and Petra were incorporated into their territory (Edom). The Edomites also benefited from the major trade route between Arabia and the Mediter-ranean that passed through their lands, and from their exploitation of significant iron and copper deposits.

Although they were ethnically related, hostil-ity was frequent between the Edomites and their neighbours the Israelites (see JEWS), who finally conquered them in the 10th century BC. Inde-pendent again by 843 BC, the Edomites were subsequently dominated by the EGYPTIANS and ASSYRIANS.

Following their incorporation into the BABY-LONIAN empire, and the subsequent Jewish exile, many Edomites migrated into Judaea; still more did so following the conquest of Edom by the NABATAEANS, who enforced their conversion to Judaism.

After the Babylonian conquest and their migrations to Judaea, the Edomites gradually disappeared. Their descendants are known as the Idumaeans.

## ELAMITES

An ancient people who inhabited the Khuzistan region, between the Zagros Mountains and the Persian Gulf, in what is now Iran. The Elamites were certainly present in the area by the 6th mil-lennium BC, and an early city-state civilization had evolved by the mid-4th millennium BC.

The earliest known Elamite kings date to about 2700 BC. They were frequently at war with the peoples of Mesopotamia (the SUMERIANS, AKKADIANS, BABYLONIANS and ASSYRIANS), and during the 12th century BC the Elamites briefly created an extensive empire, incorporating he lands of the KASSITES of Babylon in 1158 BC. Although they were frequently overwhelmed by their more powerful neighbours, the Elamites tended to exploit divisions between the Babylo-nians and Assyrians, particularly during the 8th century BC, but were finally crushed by the latter in 648 BC. Their capital, Susa, was destroyed, their land was contaminated with salt and much of their aristocracy was deported to Palestine.

Following the disintegration of Assyrian power, the Elamites were incorporated into the PERSIAN empire, and Susa became one of that empire's three principal cities. Many Elamites subsequently served in the celebrated Persian royal bodyguard (the Immortals).

Very little is known of Elamite culture; they worshipped Inshushinak, the bull-god of Susa, but they have left very few written records. The Elamites had devised a system of pictographic writing by the mid-4th millennium BC, but following their conquest by the AKKADIANS they began to use the cuneiform script. The Elamite language, however, was not related to INDO-EUROPEAN or Semitic types, and remains (for the most part) undeciphered. In many respects, Elamite culture was heavily influenced by that of the Babylonians (they are known to have looted Babylonian art), and Elamite art and architecture was highly derivative; in their turn the Elamites influenced the Persians.

The Elamites differed significantly from their Mesopotamian neighbours in their governmental structure, which was based on a system of power-sharing. The various city-states tended to recognize one overlord, who ruled from Susa. Alongside him, however, there was also a viceroy (the heir presumptive, and usually the overlord's brother), and another ruler known as the Prince of Susa (the overlord's son or nephew). Only when all the overlord's brothers were dead could the son succeed. Elamite law also demanded that an overlord's widow marry his oldest surviving brother (thus usually his heir). This system was extremely effective, allowing the Elamite state a degree of stability not shared by many of its contemporaries. The system remained in force until at least the 13th century BC.

Although the Elamite language continued in written use until the 4th century BC, and was probably spoken until the 10th century AD, the Elamites themselves tended to become assimilated with the Persians, and later with the ARABS.

# EMIRIANS

The citizens of a federation of the ARAB states of Abu Dhabi, 'Ajman, Dubai, Fujayrah, Ra's al Khaymah, Sharjah and Umm Al-Qaiwain (capital Abu Dhabi). In 2002 the population was approximately 2.7 million.

The United Arab Emirates were formed in 1971, following the withdrawal of the BRITISH

from the region. The British had dominated the area politically since the early 19th century.

Owing to very large oil deposits, the United Arab Emirates is one of the richest states in the world, and this has had a significant effect upon the lifestyle of its people. Prior to the discovery of oil in the late 1950s, agriculture, fishing, and pearl-diving were the principal sources of income, and many of the people followed the BEDOUIN nomad lifestyle. The coastal region had maintained important trading links since antiquity, but from the 16th century these were usually dominated by European powers, initially Portuguese and then British.

In recent years, the huge revenues accruing from the oil industry have led to large-scale urbanization and the eroding of traditional lifestyles. In addition, the native population was far too small to provide a sufficient workforce to exploit the country's natural resources, and this has led to major demographic changes. Today, only about 12% of the population of the United Arab Emirates are natives; the remaining 88% are foreign workers whose origins are diverse and include EGYPTIANS, SRI LANKANS, INDIANS, IRANIANS, PAKISTANIS, Europeans, BANGLADESHIS and FILIPINOS, among others. This has led to the creation of a very cosmopolitan society, with a considerable degree of Western influence.

Traditional Arab/Islamic culture remains important, however. Laws, both criminal and civil, are based on Islamic Shari'a law, and the central authorities rigorously advocate the official Arabic language. The majority of people are Sunni Muslim, although the minority Shi'ite sect has gained ground in recent years, and Islamic fundamentalism is on the rise.

In line with the other Arab and Islamic countries in the region, the United Arab Emirates has adopted a hostile attitude towards the ISRAELIS and has supported the claims of the PALESTINIANS. Although they supported the IRAQIS during the Iran–Iraq war, the Emirians subsequently joined the Allied coalition against Iraq in the first Gulf War of 1991.

Although the states are officially federated, tribal identities within the individual Emirates remain very strong, and each retains its hereditary emir who is a member of the ruling council of the federation. At times there has been friction within the federation, notably in 1978 when Abu Dhabi withdrew from the country's united defence force and subsequently pursued a separate military policy. Since Abu Dhabi controls by far the largest share of the federation's oil reserves, it has had a great influence on the development of the region.

## ENETS

A SAMOYED Siberian people of the Taimyr peninsula in the Russian Federation, who speak a Uralic language now verging on extinction. Traditionally semi-sedentary hunters and gatherers, and shamanists in religion, the Enets were superficially Christianized in the 18th century, but were otherwise largely ignored by the RUSSIANS. However, Soviet collectivization and forced settlement, along with compulsory boarding education, the industrialization of their lands and attendant pollution have eroded their culture probably beyond recovery.

## EPHTHALITES or White Huns

A group of nomadic peoples who possibly originated in the steppes of eastern Asia; to the Chinese they were known as the Hoa or Hoa-tun. During the 4th and 5th centuries AD, population pressures in their homeland drove the Ephthalites westward into Bactria and the Sassanid PERSIAN empire, and in 483 they inflicted a major defeat on the Sassanians. By 505 they were pouring into northwestern India, where they destroyed the Gupta empire (in India, they were known as the Hunas).

Ephthalite hegemony, however, was short-lived: they were defeated by the Indians in 528 and by the Sassanian king, Khosru I, during the mid-550s. An invasion of central Asia by the TURKS in the 560s delivered the *coup de grâce*, although they retained control of some areas of Afghanistan until the ARAB conquest of the mid-7th century. After their defeat, the Ephthalites ceased to exist as a separate people; those who were left tended to remain in the areas they had conquered, and in India their descendants comprised a number of Rajput tribes.

Nothing is known of their culture, although it may have been similar to that of the other nomadic HUNS; they had no system of writing, and their language remains unknown. Their invasions, however, tended to have a negative effect on the cultural and economic development of the regions they attacked – particularly in India. They were frequently allied with the JUAN-JUAN people, and the KUSHANS may also have been partly Ephthalite.

## ESKIMOSY

A Siberian people of the Chukchi peninsula in the Russian Federation. The Eskimosy share the language and culture of the YUP'IK people of Alsaka, to whom they are closely related, but for historical and geographical reasons they maintain a distinct identity. They are sedentary coastal-dwellers who hunt sea mammals and fish, and speak an Eskimo-Aleut language, and call themselves *Yuhyt*, meaning 'people'.

The early RUSSIAN invaders into their territory in the 17th century assumed they were a subgroup of the CHUKCHI, as both resisted conquest together. As a result, the Eskimosy were subsequently included administratively within Chukchi territory, where many became assimilated by the latter. Soviet collectivization and compulsory education in Russian further undermined their identity; their environment was looted of minerals while alcoholism spread among the young, making them heavily dependent on the Soviet state.

The collapse of the USSR left the Eskimosy with severe economic and social problems. Their environment is badly polluted and their language is endangered. They have taken the opportunity, however, to renew contacts with their Alaskan relatives in order jointly to protect their identity and interests. In 1989 they numbered about 1700.

## EVEN

A northeastern Siberian people mainly of the Magadan and Kamchatka *oblasts* (regions) in the Russian Federation. Similar to the EVENKI, of whom they were once considered a sub-group, they were traditionally semi-sedentary hunters, gatherers and reindeer-herders who maintained a shamanist religion and spoke a Tungus language. Contact with the RUSSIANS brought diseases and alcohol and a rapid decline in their population and culture. Soviet collectivization, assimilatory policies and industrialization furthered this, and drove many of the Even into marginal lands. Currently, they regard economic and environmental issues as more urgent than issues of national identity. In 1999 they numbered over 17,000.

## EVENKI

A southeastern Siberian people who have their own Evenki national *okrug* (district) in the Russian Federation, but are in fact spread across vast stretches of northeast and southeast Siberia, Mongolia and northern China. Nomadic hunters, gatherers and reindeer-herders, they speak a Tungus language, and were once named the Tungus.

Originally of the Lake Baikal area, the Evenki were forced north and east by the MONGOLS from the 13th century. From the 17th century, pressure from RUSSIAN settlers, diseases and demands for tribute pushed them still further east, as far as the Sakhalin peninsula. These migrations have left them one of the most scattered peoples of the whole Russian Federation.

They were superficially Christianized, but traditional shamanist practices survived at least until the 1930s, when many shamans were murdered at Stalin's order; traditional beliefs have resurfaced in the 1990s. There were some acts of armed resistance to Russian incursions, but the Evenki were unable to cling to much farmable land. This severely undermined a rich traditional culture, noted for its bone- and wood-carving and for the practice of *nimat*, or sharing the fruits of the hunt with the entire community. Some, however, especially in southern Siberia, did copy Russian sedentary farming as their traditional society began to fragment. Soviet collectivization, enforced settlement and compulsory boarding education furthered the destruction of their traditional economy and culture.

With families forcibly settled, adult men remained itinerant reindeer-herders, which resulted in long absences. A generation gap opened, as the young were taught to have different aspirations from the isolation, toil and

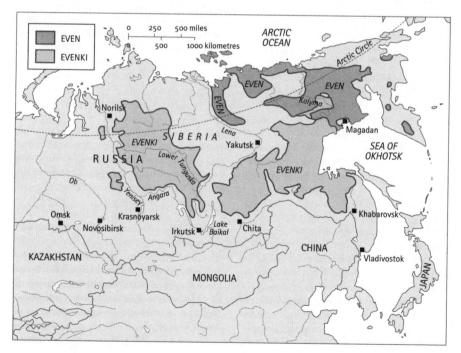

Even, Evenki

discomfort of reindeer-herding. Their language is in decline, alcoholism has become rife and the suicide rate is extremely high.

With fewer known mineral resources, the Evenki lands suffered somewhat less environmental destruction than others under Soviet rule, but still enough to cause severe difficulties for the inhabitants. The collapse of the USSR has worsened the Evenki plight, as the subsequent discovery of vast new oil reserves on their territory has brought an influx of oil workers and the threat of environmental catastrophe. The oil workers also brought a demand for fresh meat, which the younger Evenki proved willing to meet by selling their broad-backed reindeer, often in order to purchase alcohol. By 2002 the Evenki reindeer herd was severely depleted, and attempts were being made to purchase fresh breeding-stock from elsewhere. As older Evenki equate the survival of reindeer-herding with their own cultural survival, many face the future with intense pessimism. In 1997 they numbered perhaps 40,000.

> 66 The Garo apology for a robe does not reach half down the thigh. 99
>
> E.T. Dalton, 1872

## GABADA

See BONDA.

## GALATIANS

A Celtic people (see CELTS) who migrated into central Anatolia (modern Turkey and northern Syria) during the 270s BC, and who settled in an area that subsequently became known as Galatia (capital Ankara). The term *Galatae* (Galatians) was applied to them by contemporary Hellenistic commentators. The Galatians made frequent raids against the neighbouring Pergamenes until they were finally defeated by Attalus I during the 230s BC. Defeated by the ROMANS in 189 BC, they were subsequently ruled by vassal kings until they were finally absorbed into the Roman empire in 25 BC.

Initially, Galatian culture was identical to the cultures of other Celtic tribes, but four centuries of contact with Hellenistic peoples gradually led to their cultural assimilation with their neighbours; Celtic elements remained evident for some time, however, leading to their identification as 'Gallo-Graeci' (Gallo-Greeks) by some

> 66 O foolish Galatians, who hath bewitched you? 99
>
> The Bible, Galatians 3:1

classical authors. By the 2nd century AD, however, the Galatians had lost almost all of their Celtic cultural identity.

## GARO

A BODO sub-tribe who reside on the Shillong Plateau in the autonomous region of Meghalaya, in India. Significant numbers also live in Bangladesh. The Garo number just over 1 million.

Garo society is matrilineal, and marriages are frequently polygynous. Slash-and-burn agriculture was the traditional means of subsistence, and headhunting was practised until the late 19th century. Since the 1860s, however, the Garo have been exposed to a number of outside influences, principally BENGALI and BRITISH, and their Sino-Tibetan language has assimilated many loan words originating from these. In addition, large numbers of Garo have been converted to Christianity, and Hinduism is also profoundly influential. The INDIAN government has introduced policies designed to encourage a shift to sedentary agriculture.

Despite these influences, many Garo continue to adhere to traditional beliefs based on animism and reincarnation, but a relatively rapid dilution of traditional Garo culture has occurred over the last 150 years.

## GASGAS

See KASKAS.

## GENTOO

See TELUGU.

## GEORGIANS

A South Caucasian or KARTVELIAN people who officially make up around 70% of the population of the modern Republic of Georgia. However, this figure has been artificially inflated for political reasons by the practice, introduced in 1930, of counting MINGRELIANS and SVANS (both also Kartvelian peoples) as Georgians in census returns. The real figure is probably less than 60%. The name of the Georgians is derived from *Gorj*, the PERSIAN name for them. The Georgians call themselves *Kartveli* and their country *Sakartvelo*. As is often the case with mountain peoples, local loyalties are strong and there are great variations in dialect and customs from region to region.

The Georgians are the descendants of peoples who have inhabited the region since at least the Bronze Age, and perhaps earlier. The first Georgian states were Kolkhida (Colchis) on the Black Sea coast, founded before the 6th century BC, and Iberia in eastern Georgia, founded around the 4th century BC. These kingdoms were under loose ROMAN control from the 1st century BC until the 5th century AD. In 337 Christianity became the official religion of Iberia and was quickly adopted by all Georgians. The Georgian church is a branch of the Eastern Orthodox Church. The Georgian alphabet was devised around the time of the conversion, mainly for the dissemination of Christian literature.

The Georgians, Mingrelians and Svans were united into a single kingdom in 975 by Bagrat III. For over two centuries the kingdom of Georgia dominated the Caucasus, but it was conquered by the MONGOLS in 1221, beginning centuries of foreign domination.

**Foreign rule**
From the early the 16th century to the 18th the OTTOMAN Turks and the Persians competed for control of Georgia. As a result of their influence, a small number of Georgians, known as ADZHARS, converted to Islam. Most Muslim Georgians live in the province of Adzharia (capital Batumi), adjacent to the Turkish border. Georgian nationalists consider the practice of any religion other than Orthodox Christianity unpatriotic, and the present Georgian government has resisted calls by the Meshketians, a group of Georgian Muslims who were deported during the Stalin era, to be allowed to return. Georgia was annexed piecemeal by Russia between 1783 and 1804.

The tsarist government repressed Georgian language and culture, brought the Georgian church under control of the Russian Orthodox Church and pursued Russification campaigns which have left the Georgians with strongly anti-Russian attitudes.

After the 1917 revolutions, Georgia enjoyed three years of independence but was brought into the Soviet Union in 1921 by native Bolsheviks, including the USSR's future leader Joseph Stalin. Georgia fared relatively well under Stalin; living standards were higher than in the rest of the Soviet Union and expression of Georgian cultural identity was encouraged. (Stalin remains something of a hero in Georgia.) The non-Kartvelian population of Georgia, however, became victims of Georgian chauvinism, increasingly so as Soviet power began to wane in the late 1980s.

After Georgia became independent in 1991, civil wars broke out between the Georgians and the South OSSETIAN and ABKHAZIAN minorities., and in the early 21st century South Ossetia and Abkhazia remained outside the control of the Georgian government.

## GHASSANIDS

An ARAB tribal people from the northwest of the Arabian peninsula (their capital is Jabiyah, in Golan). During the 6th century AD, the Ghassanids were an important BYZANTINE vassal state and protected the empire from the Sassanid PERSIANS and the Bedouin LAKHMIDS. They adhered to the Christian Monophysite doctrine, central to which was the assertion that Christ remained entirely divine while living as a man. They were notable contributors to the religious schisms that affected Byzantine Christianity at this time, which led to Byzantine intervention, and persecution, on more than one occasion. As a result, the Ghassanids welcomed the ARAB Islamic conquest of 614 as an act of liberation, and were able to retain, at least in the short term, their Monophysite beliefs. Ultimately, however, Arabization led to the cultural and religious assimilation of the majority of the tribe.

Culturally, the Byzantines heavily influenced the Ghassanids, although Arab influence was also strong. During the 6th century there was something of a Ghassanid cultural golden age; their rulers funded significant building projects and patronized some of the greatest pre-Islamic poets, notably Nabighah adh-Dhubyani and Hassan ibn Thabit.

**Georgians: main ethnic groups**

Gurians
Imeretians
K'akhetians
Rach'ans

*"* The Georgians in general are by some travellers said to be the handsomest people in the world. *"*

Jedidiah Morse, 1796

# GHILZAI

Along with the Durrani (see ABDALIS) one of the two principal PASHTUN tribes, the majority of whom reside in Afghanistan. It is possible that they are of Turkic origin (see TURKS). They were originally nomadic, with many participating in the caravan trade between India and Afghanistan, but most now many live a more sedentary lifestyle. They have played a prominent role in the history of their region, founding dynasties in Afghanistan and Hindustan. During the 1880s they mounted a major, though unsuccessful, rebellion against the AFGHANS.

# GHUZZ

See OGUZ.

# GILYAKS

See NIVKHI.

# GOLDEN HORDE TATARS

The MONGOL-Turkic people who, between 1235 and 1241, created an extensive empire encompassing much of southern Russia, Poland, Hungary, Silesia and Siberia. The name 'Golden Horde' (Mongol, *Altan Ordu*) refers to both the people and the empire, and probably derives from a RUSSIAN reference to the colour of the tent used by Batu, first khan of the Golden Horde. Their capital was established by Batu Khan at Sarai Batu (Old Sarai), and subsequently rebuilt under his successor as Sarai Berke (New Sarai).

Although their leadership was undoubtedly MONGOL, the vast majority of the Golden Horde were Turkic (see TURKS), and it was the latter, along with trusted local rulers, who administered the empire; indeed, many resident Turks had joined forces with Batu on his invasion of southern Russia. By contrast, the Mongol population preferred to adhere to their traditional pastoral lifestyle in the eastern portions of their lands. This ethnic imbalance had a profound effect upon the cultural development of the Golden Horde. Gradually, Turkic culture superseded Mongol to the point where, in 1313, Khan Özbeg was converted to Islam, and from this date the Golden Horde are regarded as forming part of the Islamic world. In addition, the original language of the Mongol element was Chagatai (see CHAGATAIDS), but by 1280 this had been supplanted by Turkish (the Khwarezmian dialect). The Mongol assimilation was probably aided by the fact that the Golden Horde remained independent of other Mongol groups, leading to their cultural and political isolation. They fought a number of wars against related peoples, including the Ilkhans of Persia.

Culturally, following the initial devastation of their invasion, the Golden Horde appear to have had little effect upon the areas they invaded, and this was particularly the case in southern Russia. Ethnic tensions did exist, however, especially between the Islamic Turks and their Christian subjects, and rebellion was frequent. These tensions were further exacerbated by the Golden Horde's inability to unify their empire and their high rates of taxation.

## The decline of the Golden Horde

A number of factors led to the decline of the Golden Horde. The first was the Black Death of the mid-14th century, which spread to the region via the Silk Route. Weakened by the effects of the plague and internal power struggles, they were defeated by the Russians in 1380 and were subsequently overrun by the TIMURIDS (1389–95); the latter deported large numbers of artisans to Samarkand. Further Russian attacks led to the break-up of the empire into smaller khanates in 1438, and the Golden Horde were finally destroyed in 1502. The TATAR khanates, however, survived (Astrakhan, Kazan, Crimea, Sibir and Nogay), and the Crimea was not added to the Russian dominions until 1783. Many descendants of the Golden Horde continue to live in the region, including the TATARS, KAZAKHS, TURKMEN and UZBEKS.

# GOLDI

See NANAI.

# GOND

A group of aboriginal peoples of DRAVIDIAN origin, most of whom reside in Madhya Pradesh,

Bihar, Maharashtra, Orissa and Andhra Pradesh, central India. There are currently around 2 million Gond, and their tribes include the Muria, Bisonhorn Maria and Hill Maria. Historically, they are a fiercely independent people, successfully resisting the full incorporation of their homeland (Gondwana) into the MUGHAL empire, and were only conquered by the MARATHAS during the 18th century. In the course of the 19th century they gradually came under BRITISH control.

In recent years, however, there has been a marked decline in traditional Gond culture. The ancient Gond religion is animistic, and includes ancestor worship, but many have been exposed to strong Hindu influences, and large numbers have abandoned their ancient customs. Less than half, for example, now speak the Gondi language, which has no written form. Hindu influence has perhaps been rendered easier by the fact that the Gond have never been a fully unified people; many of the dialects of Gondi are mutually unintelligible and most Gond are now bilingual, speaking either Hindi or Marathi. Furthermore, while shifting agriculture was the traditional means of subsistence for many Gond, many are now turning to sedentary forms. The ruling clan, however, known as the Raj Gond, continues to be held in high regard by the Gond people, and are recognized as belonging to the warrior caste.

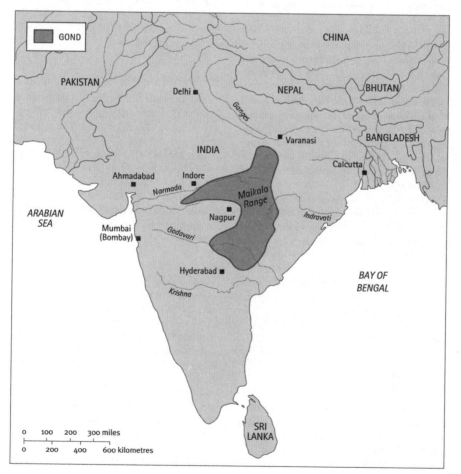

Gond

# GUJARATIS

An ethnically mixed people, most of whom reside in the INDIAN state of Gujarat, but with many others spread throughout the world, principally in Africa, Pakistan and Europe. The Gujarati language is of INDO-ARYAN descent, and there are currently over 40 million speakers in India alone; many Gujaratis also speak Hindi. Gujarati tribes and castes can be split into two main groups: Indic and DRAVIDIAN (see the accompanying box for a list of the major subgroups). The Gujaratis derive their name, and that of their state, from the Gujaras, a ruling dynasty of the 8th and 9th centuries.

Throughout their history, the Gujaratis have been exposed to a wide range of foreign influences. The region fell under Muslim domination in 1299, and during the 16th century it was conquered by the MUGHALS. Following a period of MARATHA rule from the mid-18th century, the Gujaratis fell increasingly under BRITISH domination until finally incorporated into Britain's Indian empire in 1857. The Gujaratis also have a long tradition of seafaring and trading enterprises, and the influence of this activity can be seen in the large number of foreign loan words that have been assimilated into the Gujarati language, including words of European, Persian and Turkish origin.

While the vast majority of the Gujarati people derive their livelihood from agriculture, over 30% are employed in the region's industrial sector. Traditional culture, expressed in poetry, prose, music and dancing, remains important, although modern Western forms have found a ready audience, particularly in large urban areas. Most Gujaratis are Hindu, while small numbers are Muslim, Jain and Zoroastrian. In recent years there have been increasing ethnic and religious tensions within the region.

# GURIANS

A MINGRELIAN people living in the Caucasus mountains in the Republic of Georgia. Their chief claim to fame in modern times is that Eduard Shevardnadze, former Soviet foreign minister and from 1992 to 2003 the president of Georgia, is a Gurian.

# GURKHAS

A former RAJASTHANI-speaking warrior dynasty that established itself in the region of Nepal centred on the town of Gorkha in the Middle Ages. They rose to dominate Nepal in the mid-18th century, following the collapse of the kingdom of Malla, and fought an unsuccessful war against the BRITISH in 1814–16. The British were very impressed with their fighting spirit and following this conflict large numbers of 'Gurkhas' were recruited into the British army, which, along with the Indian army, still retains some Gurkha units (these are drawn from a variety of NEPALESE ethnic groups).

Their close contact with the British has enabled the Gurkhas to combine Nepalese culture with Western culture. Gurkha soldiers are famed for their use of the *kukri* (a fighting knife with a curved blade).

# GURUNG

A NEPALESE people living mainly on the southern flanks of Mount Annapurna in Nepal. The term is also used as a general descriptor for Nepalese immigrants to Bhutan. The Gurung numbered around 200,000 in the late 20th century and speak a Tibeto-Burman language. Most Nepalese Gurung follow Tibetan Buddhism, but a minority are Hindus. The Gurung are primarily a farming people, but numbers of Gurung men are recruited into the GURKHA regiments of the British army.

# GUTIANS or Guti

A people originating from the hill country between the Tigris and the Zagros Mountains in southwest Asia. The Gutians launched frequent raids against the SUMERIANS and AKKADIANS, and were instrumental in bringing about the downfall of the Akkadian empire around 2200 BC. During this period they also dominated the ELAMITES.

It is believed that the Gutians controlled southern Mesopotamia, as far as Umma, for 50 to 100 years, but their power remained both tenuous and fragile; for example, they left the administration of their empire to trusted local governors, with no attempt at central control. They were eventually defeated by Utu-Khegal of Uruk (ruled *c.* 2120–*c.* 2112), and driven out of the region. Thereafter, they reverted to their former raids, which continued until they were absorbed into the ASSYRIAN empire during the 9th century BC. Following this defeat, the Gutians were assimilated into other peoples of the region, and lost their independent identity.

Almost nothing is known of Gutian culture, as they have left virtually no records. In line with many other invaders of Mesopotamia, they appear to have assimilated Sumerian/Akkadian culture, and it is known that they used the Akkadian language for administrative and religious purposes.

## HADRAMITES

The people of a prosperous ancient kingdom that occupied the region of Hadhramaut (capital Shabwah), in modern Yemen. Its wealth was based upon the production of frankincense and participation in international trade. Conquered by the AKSUMITES and then by the Sassanid PERSIANS, the Hadramites gradually disappeared as an independent force. The region was conquered by the armies of Islam during the AD 630s.

## HALAFIAN CULTURE

A Neolithic culture that flourished between about 6000 and 5400 BC, covering much of north and central Mesopotamia. The name is derived from the site at the ancient city of Tel Halaf, where many of the artefacts associated with the culture have been found.

The Halafian economy was based on mixed dry-farming, and quantities of votive objects – burnished and painted pottery (geometric designs predominate), woven cloth, bronze and copper ware and stone tools – have been discovered. Villages tended to be small, with clay-built huts, but the presence of imported obsidian suggests wide-ranging trade contacts.

Enough luxury items and storehouses have been unearthed to suggest that Halafian culture was socially divided, with a wealthy aristocratic elite at the head of the society.

## HARAPPANS or Indus Valley civilization

The first high civilization in South Asia, which at its greatest extent covered much of modern Pakistan and northern India.

Harappan prosperity was founded on the agricultural exploitation of the rich alluvial soils of the Indus Valley, with wheat and barley as the principal crops. This required the construction of large-scale irrigation works, and such huge engineering feats could only be accomplished through the formation of an organized state-based society. This development ran much along the lines of that achieved by the SUMERIANS in Mesopotamia, and there are striking similarities between these two civilizations. Harappan civilization reached its height between about 2600 and 1700 BC. The causes of its final destruction are unknown, but changes in the course and reductions in the flow of the rivers on which the civilization depended are thought to have been responsible.

The exact ethnic origins of the Harappans are unknown, but it is possible that they were related to the DRAVIDIANS. By the time of their demise, the Harappans had devised a pictographic writing script, which fell out of use under their successors and has yet to be successfully deciphered.

Large food surpluses allowed the foundation of urban centres, principally at Mohenjo-Daro and Harappa (both of which had populations in excess of 30,000 people). It is archaeological discoveries at Harappa that have given the Indus Valley civilization its alternative name.

While most towns and villages were much smaller, they contained many examples of advanced structures. Many were laid out using regular street-grids, and had buildings constructed from pressed or baked mud bricks, efficient drainage, large granaries, baths, cemeteries, citadels and perimeter-wall fortifications. These urban centres were the home to numerous artisans producing tools (in stone, bronze and copper), sculpture (in stone, terracotta and bronze), beads, ivory-ware, jewellery and pottery. Agricultural productivity was increased through the introduction of the plough. Fruits and vegetables were grown, pastoral farming was

*66* Bravest of the brave, most generous of the generous, never had a country more faithful friends than you. *99*

Sir Ralph Turner, British army officer, 1933, paying tribute to the Gurkhas

h

widespread, and food supplies were supplemented by hunting and gathering. Agricultural surpluses allowed the Harappans to trade extensively for valuable raw materials with India, the Arabian peninsula (in particular through the OMANIS and BAHRAINIS), and with Mesopotamia, where they established trade colonies. The MESOPOTAMIANS knew the region of Harappan settlement as 'Meluhha'. By the later Harappan period, a social hierarchy appears to have evolved, and this was no doubt stimulated by the economic opportunities available in the areas of agricultural production and trade.

Very little is known of Harappan religion. As yet no temples have been discovered, and it may have been the case that their religious ritual was not temple-based. It is probable, however, that they worshipped a Great Mother goddess, and some of their religious practices may have found their way into those of later Hinduism.

# h

## HASSUNA CULTURE

An ancient northern Mesopotamian culture that flourished *c.* 6500–5350 BC. It derives its name from the city of Hassuna in northern Iraq and is the oldest known mixed dry-farming culture of the region. Characteristic findings from the Hassuna period are painted pottery with innovative

**Hazara**

designs, clay-built houses, oval 'husking trays', large sunken clay jars used for grain storage, stamp seals, copperware and domed bread ovens. The Hassuna period was the precursor to both the HALAFIAN and the SAMARRAN cultures of Mesopotamia and overlapped with both.

## HATTI

A non-INDO-EUROPEAN people who inhabited central Anatolia (modern Turkey and northern Syria) prior to the arrival of the HITTITES. The settlement at Hattusha, for example, had been founded by the 3rd millennium BC. Their origins are obscure: virtually nothing is known of their culture or society, and their language has yet to be deciphered. The Hatti were overrun by the Hittites in about 1900 BC, and they were subsequently assimilated by their invaders.

## HAYASA

A vassal people of the HITTITE empire, whose rebellion during the mid-14th century BC was crushed by Mursilis II. Their society and culture appear to have been very similar to that of the Hittites.

## HAYQ

See ARMENIANS.

## HAZARA

A MONGOL people who inhabit the isolated mountainous regions of central Afghanistan, principally Hazarajat, with a further small number residing in Iran and Pakistan. In 2001, the Hazara accounted for about 19% of the population of Afghanistan (recently estimated at 28 million). The name 'Taimura' (or Timuri) is given by other AFGHANS to those isolated Hazara living on the border of Afghanistan and Iran.

The Hazara are culturally split between those in the west of Afghanistan who are Sunni Muslim and live nomadic or semi-nomadic lives, and those in the east who follow the Twelver doctrine of Shi'ism, whose central belief is the succession of twelve divinely inspired imams, and tend to be settled farmers. This cultural

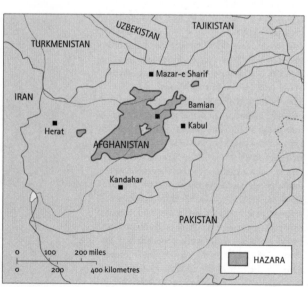

diversity has occasionally led to conflict, particularly in recent years, when the Shi'ite Hazara fought as part of the Northern Alliance against the Sunni Taliban. The Northern Alliance also included local TAJIKS, UZBEKS and TURKMEN.

Culturally, the Hazara have retained many Mongol traditions. They speak the Dari dialect of PERSIAN, which borrows from Turkic and Mongol languages; however, they also have their own dialect known as Hazaragi.

## HEBREWS

See JEWS.

## HEPHTHALITES

See EPHTHALITES.

## HIMYARITES or Homeritai or Hymr

A Semitic tribe (see SEMITES) who originated from the Dhu-Raydan region of southwest Arabia (modern Yemen); their traditional capital was the city of Zafar, but, from the fourth century AD, it lay further north at San'a. By 115 BC the Himyarites had conquered the SABAEANS, and, until AD 525, controlled an extensive empire that, at times, extended from the Persian Gulf to the Arabian Desert.

The Himyarites are first mentioned in Roman literature in the mid-1st century AD, but they were indistinguishable culturally and linguistically from the Sabaeans. The period of their hegemony, however, did witness a general rise in monotheism, and both Judaism and Christianity gained strong footholds in the Himyarite empire. Ultimately, their last king, known as Dhu Nuwas, converted to Judaism.

Local tensions between Jews and Christians reached a climax when Dhu Nuwas massacred the Christians. As many of those killed were foreign traders, these events prompted an invasion by ASKUM, and the Himyarites were defeated in AD 525.

After the region was annexed as part of the Persian empire in 575, and the last Persian governor converted to Islam in 628, the Himyarites became absorbed into the ARAB world. The Himyarite language is still spoken by a very small number of YEMENIS.

## HINDI

The most widely spoken language group in India. Today the majority of Hindi-speakers reside in northern Indian states such as Bihar, Haryana, Himachal Pradesh, Madhya Pradesh, Rajasthan and Uttar Pradesh. Significant numbers are also found throughout the remainder of India, as well as in South and East Africa, Mauritius, and western Asia. Many other Indians also possess Hindi as a second language.

Hindi is an INDO-ARYAN language, based on Sanskrit. In its earlier form it was known as Hindustani (see HINDI HINDUSTANI) or Hindi-Urdu, and is closely related to URDU; in its present form it contains a number of English loan words. About 40% of India's population of 1 billion people speak Hindi.

In the years immediately preceding Indian independence it was believed by many that Shudh Hindi ('pure' Hindi), a synthetic form of Hindi purged of Urdu influences, would be accepted as the official, national language of the new republic. Owing to a number of factors, including regional resistance to its imposition and the opposition of the first prime minister, Jawaharlal Nehru, this never happened. Today, Hindi is simply one of India's 18 officially recognized languages, but as the most widely spoken it remains one of the principal unifying features of the Indian state, and its dissemination has been strongly encouraged by the Indian government.

The growth of Hindi's popularity has led to the gradual abandonment of a number of traditional Indian languages, such as Kurukh and MUNDA. Nevertheless, significant numbers of people, especially the TAMILS of Tamil Nadu and the BENGALIS, continue to resist what they view as the imposition of the language. In addition, many within the Hindi-speaking areas, such as the HINDI CHHATTISGARHI, reject the notion that their languages are merely dialects of Hindi; they view these languages as independent entities.

*" With their superior technological skills, the Himyarites managed the precious water sources and controlled the ports in south-west Arabia and the rich trade from Egypt. "*

Penny Young, 1997

**Hindi**

*Some 400 million people speak Hindi, over a large area of northern and central India.*

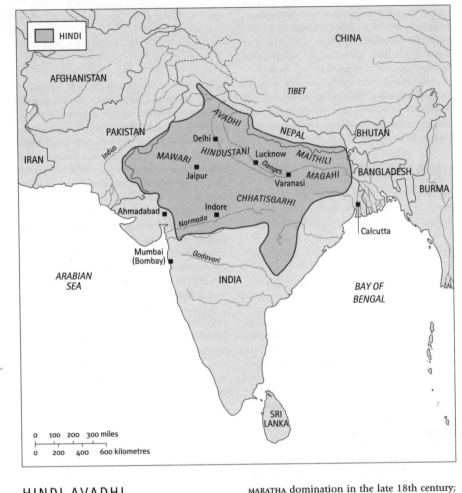

h

## HINDI AVADHI

An INDIAN people who speak the Avadhi dialect of HINDI. They tend to be concentrated in the Uttaranchal region of northern India, northeast of Delhi. This area was the site of the ancient kingdom of Korsala. As a result, the language, which has a long literary tradition, is also referred to as Korsali.

## HINDI CHHATTISGARHI

An INDO-ARYAN people who speak the Chhattis-garhi dialect of Eastern Hindi and live in the state of Madhya Pradesh. The term 'Chhattis-garhi' emerged only during the period of

**"** Trial by ordeal ... still keeps its place in the Hindostanee code. **"**

**W. Tennant, 1804**

MARATHA domination in the late 18th century; previously the region had been known as Dak-shin Kosala. It is believed that Chhattisgarhi is a corruption of 'Chedisgarth', which was the seat of the Chedis. During the 16th century the area fell to the MUGHALS, and, following the collapse of Maratha rule, was incorporated into the British empire in 1854. The Chhattisgarhi peo-ple are determinedly independent and have increasingly identified with their tribal back-ground and sought self-determination. This movement, evident from 19th and 20th century literature, has been in part stimulated by a large-scale migration of non-tribal peoples into their homeland. These population movements placed considerable pressure on available land resources, leading to some displacement of native peoples and labour exploitation. As a result, the Chhattisgarhi have fought a series of conflicts since the 18th century in pursuit of the recognition and establishment of their own region; this was finally won in November 2000. Despite the widespread influence of Hindi culture, their traditional culture remains important, and great efforts are made to preserve the Chhattisgarhi dialect.

## HINDI HINDUSTANI

Speakers of the INDO-ARYAN Hindustani language, also known as Hindu-Urdu, which developed during the 16th century in the region around Delhi. Promoted by the MUGHALS and used as a courtly language, later also by the British, it became particularly popular in the area now occupied by northern India, Pakistan and Afghanistan.

The term 'Hindustani' was coined by the British during the late 18th and early 19th centuries. During the years immediately preceding INDIAN independence, many hoped that Hindustani would become the official language of the new republic. With the Partition of India in 1947, however, the language diverged into two forms: Urdu, used by the PAKISTANIS, retained many PERSIAN loan words, whereas Hindi, used in India, remained much more influenced by Sanskrit, with some English loan words.

In recent years, there has been a great government-led drive to eliminate all Urdu elements from official usage within India in order to create a 'pure' Hindi with replacement Sanskrit words (known as Shudh Hindi). This has not been altogether successful, however, and Urdu remains much-used in everyday conversation and in some areas of popular culture, for example in Indian cinema.

## HINDI MAGAHI

A group of INDO-ARYAN tribes who reside in eastern areas of the Indian state of Bihar and speak the Hindi Magahi dialect of Bihari. Culturally, they are very similar to the BIHARI.

## HINDI MAITHILI

An INDO-ARYAN people of northern India who form one of the three major sub-groups of the BIHARIS. They are a very orthodox Hindu people who speak the oldest dialect of Hindi and remain centred on the ancient region of Mithila (capital Madhubani). The Maithili language is the only Bihari dialect to possess a written form, and has a literary tradition dating back to the early 15th century.

Since INDIAN independence there has been considerable growth in interest in the Maithili language and literary heritage. There is a strong artistic tradition among Maithili women, the themes of which are passed down from generation to generation, and they are renowned for the quality of their painting. Many works are produced for traditional Hindu festivals and important family occasions, and motifs range from gods and goddesses to representations of animals and flowers. These works are traditionally painted onto the walls of houses, on the ground, or on pottery and fans; more recently, some have been committed to paper as a means of ensuring their preservation.

## HINDI MARWARI

A northwestern INDIAN people who speak the Marwari dialect of RAJASTHANI. The term 'Marwari' is also used throughout India (mostly erroneously) as a means of identifying members of the emigrant Rajasthani business community.

## HITTITES

A term traditionally used to describe an ancient INDO-EUROPEAN people who inhabited the central plateau of Anatolia (modern Turkey and northern Syria), and who, by the 14th century BC, had created a substantial empire. The exact origins of these people are unknown, but many believe they migrated from somewhere north of Black Sea. It is certain that they had arrived in Anatolia by 1900 BC and quickly came to dominate the area politically and culturally. The name 'Hittite' originates from the Hebrew *Hittim*, which was used to refer to these people in the Old Testament. They referred to themselves, and

h

their language, however, as 'Nesian' or 'Nesite' – terms derived from the Anatolian city of Nesa.

On first entering Anatolia, the Hittites established a capital at Kussara, but from here they rapidly expanded across central Anatolia, and by the mid-17th century BC had overrun the entire area, establishing a new capital at Hattusha (Bogazköy). Further expansion into northern Syria followed, and by about 1595 BC they had overrun the BABYLONIANS and sacked their capital. During the 16th and 15th centuries BC the Hittites clashed with both the MITANNI and EGYPTIANS, and these wars, together with internal discord and frequent raids by the KASKAS, led to their temporary political eclipse. Their resurgence and expansion during the 13th century BC, particularly under King Suppiluliumas I (ruled *c.* 1344–1322 BC), saw them become one of the four major powers of western Asia (along with the Egyptians, ASSYRIANS and Babylonians), controlling an empire that included the Levant (Palestine), Armenia and northern Syria. With their victory over the Egyptians at the battle of Kadesh (*c.* 1285 BC), the Hittites reached the zenith of their influence.

### Decline of the Hittites

Within 100 years, however, the Hittites were swept aside by the invasions of the PHRYGIANS and SEA PEOPLES. Only a few city-states survived these onslaughts, for example Carchemish, Milid, Kummukhu and Khilakku. The population of these states, known to archaeologists as Neo-Hittite, was ethnically mixed, consisting of HATTI aborigines, refugee Hittites and previously subjected peoples (sometimes referred to as Syro-Hittites), and they never regained their former influence.

Some of these states were conquered by the ARAMAEANS in the 10th century BC, but the expanding Assyrian empire finally overran the whole area during the 8th century BC. As a result of this final conquest, the Hittites lost their ethnic and cultural identity and disappeared from the historical record (although the Assyrians continued to refer to the area as Hatti-land).

Comparatively little is known of Hittite government and culture, and a great deal of what has been discovered originates from the archives unearthed by archaeologists at Hattusha. The Hittites spoke the oldest form of Indo-European yet discovered. Ethnically, they were related to the LUWIANS, and at first they wrote using a hieroglyphic system. Following their initial imperial expansion, however, it appears that MESOPOTAMIAN scribes may have been deported to the Hittite homeland to devise a cuneiform system for the Hittite language.

From at least the mid-13th century BC, the Hittites were especially influenced by HURRIAN culture and used the Hurrian language, a phenomenon almost certainly prompted by the inter-marriage of Hittite and Hurrian royalty. For diplomatic and administrative purposes, however, the Hittites used the AKKADIAN language. During the Neo-Hittite era, Luwian was the principal language, and this was expressed in written form using hieroglyphs.

Hittite kings were very autocratic: they occupied the position of chief priest, took part in various religious festivals, and were believed to hold some form of divine right. Following their death, Hittite kings were deified and worshipped. Aristocratic women are known to have exercised great power; evidence exists of Hittite queens ruling alongside their husbands, and even remaining in power in their own right after the death of the king.

In line with many other ancient civilizations of Western Asia, Hittite administration was influenced by the Babylonians, especially in the areas of law and government; but Hittite punishments tended to be less draconian than those of their Babylonian contemporaries. Hittite society was based on agrarian feudalism.

In religious beliefs and ritual, the Hittites were heavily influenced by the Hurrians; their chief gods were the weather god Tarhum and his consort, the sun goddess Arinna. However, they also worshipped many other local deities, and a mother goddess was particularly important.

Their art, at least in the earlier period, was influenced by the Babylonians, but displayed some originality, best expressed in their exquisite metalwork, the colossal statues and rock-reliefs they carved for religious purposes (for example at Yazilikaya), and the design of their impressive temples, palaces and defensive structures (notably Hattusha). Neo-Hittite designs became reliant on Assyrian models.

The Hittites are reputed to have been the first civilization to master the technique of smelting iron, allowing then an important technical edge over their enemies. They were also accomplished horsemen and light-chariot drivers.

## HOMERITAI

See HIMYARITES.

## HSIUNG-NU

See XIONGNU.

## HUNAS

See EPHTHALITES.

## HUNZAKUTS

See BURUSHO.

## HURRIANS

A non-Semitic people who originated in the mountainous regions of Armenia and migrated into AMORITE areas of northern Mesopotamia during the late 3rd and early 2nd millennium BC. The area subsequently became known as Hurri, and here they established a number of autonomous Hurrian city-states.

From about 1700 BC, the Hurrians began a process of imperial expansion, and by the early 16th century BC had gained control of an impressive expanse of territory, generally at the expense of the ASSYRIANS, whom they conquered around 1680 BC. They moved into eastern Anatolia, coming into contact with the HITTITES, whose king Mursilis I inflicted a defeat upon them, and they also penetrated Syria and the Levant.

Their empire included the prosperous commercial and administrative centres at Nuzu and Aleppo. From around the early 18th century BC, however, the Hurrians were gradually infiltrated by INDO-IRANIAN migrants, who gradually supplanted the Hurrian ruling class and came to dominate them socially and politically. The kingdom and empire that emerged thereafter from about 1500 BC was the MITANNI.

The Hurrians did not impose a new culture on the areas in which they settled; rather, Mesopotamian culture heavily influenced Hurrian (and Mitannian) culture, and in turn they acted as important transmitters of this culture westward to the Hittites and, through them, to the Greeks. In religion, for example, the chief god of the Hurrian pantheon was the weather god Teshub, whose consort in many areas was Shauskha, goddess of love and war – a pairing that clearly mirrors Semitic-Mesopotamian types. As in Mesopotamia, the Hurrians also considered their sun and moon deities to be of great importance. Mesopotamian culture is also heavily in evidence in Hurrian art and their legal system. Much of the cultural interaction between Hittites and Hurrians was facilitated by the inter-marriage of their respective royal families.

The Hurrian language was related to URART-IAN and written in cuneiform from the early second millennium BC. Like most of the more important imperial powers of the period, the Hurrians used AKKADIAN as their governmental, religious and diplomatic language.

Following defeats of the Mitanni by the Hittites, Egyptians and Assyrians, the vast majority of the Hurrians were absorbed either into the culture of the conquerors or, as was the case in Canaan, into that of the indigenous population. As a result they tend to disappear as a separate people. A few Hurrian enclaves did survive, however, in the mountainous regions of Armenia (Hayasha). The Hurrians were almost certainly related to the Urartians and Subarians, and it is possible that Hurrian elements existed among the HYKSOS.

## IDUMAEANS

See EDOMITES.

## INDIAN GYPSIES

See BANJARI.

## INDIANS

A south Asian people who inhabit the nation of India, which, with a population of over 1 billion in 2003, is the world's largest democracy and second most populous state. The term India once referred to the entire subcontinent, also including Pakistan and Bangladesh. The Indian nation is ethnically and regionally diverse, but its culture is largely Hindu and distinct in its art, dance, music, architecture, martial traditions , film and cuisine.

The social structure of the subcontinent has been most often typified in descriptions of the 'caste' system. Caste combines ritual status with regional, cultural and occupational identities. Although the caste system has changed dramatically over the last 200 years, social divisions are deeply ingrained. Those without caste, the 'untouchables', redesignated *harijan* (children of god) by Gandhi and called *dalit* (oppressed) in Marathi by author and activist Jotirao Phule, still suffer severe discrimination.

### Early history

The first inhabitants of the subcontinent were probably DRAVIDIANS, who practised agriculture in the Indus Valley from the 7th millennium BC. The HARAPPANS, who had developed one of the world's oldest urban civilizations from the 3rd millennium BC, were probably related to the Dravidians.

This civilization collapsed early in the 2nd millennium BC, and around 1500 BC the ARYANS, an INDO-EUROPEAN-speaking people from Central Asia, invaded and occupied northern India. It was from their religious beliefs that Hinduism, the dominant religion of modern India, developed.

Northern Indian dynasties such as the Mauryans and Guptas, generally based in the Ganges Valley, were at times able to dominate most of the subcontinent, but political unity was usually fragile and transitory. Muslim invaders from around AD 1000 introduced a new layer of cultural diversity into the subcontinent.

BRITISH rule from the 18th century brought economic exploitation and a world-wide Indian diaspora as cheap labour was exported, but little in the way of national unity. Imperial rule in South Asia combined the directly ruled provinces of British India and the dependent states, ruled indirectly by Britain through the indigenous ruling dynasties.

*" With them, [Indians] all life seems to be sacred except human life. "*

Mark Twain, 1897

**Indians: main ethnic groups and historic cultures**

Assamese
Bhutia
Cholas
Dravidians
Gonds
Gujaratis
Hindi
Kashmiris
Kushans
Ladakhi
Marathas
Mughals
Oraon
Punjabis
Sakas
Sikhs
Sindis
Tamils

### A national identity

Forging a national identity was arguably accomplished in the creation of a pan-subcontinental movement that resisted imperial authority. In 1885 the first conscious steps in this process were taken with the formation of the Indian National Congress (INC). This body initially had moderate aims – simply a greater say in how India was governed. But a hesitant and grudging British response radicalized the nationalist movement.

The INC – and the cause of Indian freedom more generally – acquired its greatest leader in Mohandas Karamchand Gandhi. He and like-minded others such as Jawaharlal Nehru used civil disobedience as a tool to force concessions from the British. They also advocated an inclusive vision of the national identity, based on tolerance and incorporation. The social, ethnic and religious divisions, they held, could be incorporated into a unified India. An independent India would heal ethnic and religious strife and provide social justice to the impoverished and disadvantaged, especially the untouchables.

Political advocates of the Muslim minority, however, already fearful of Hindu domination, had formed their own national movement, the Muslim League, in 1906. Their aim was to protect their own cultural and religious identity, and in 1940 they announced they would settle for nothing less than an independent Pakistan. In 1947, therefore, independence was accompanied by partition. Despite the movement of up to 8 million people and the deaths of up to 2 million during the violence accompanying Partition, India still has over 100 million Muslim citizens, the second largest Muslim population in the world after Indonesia.

### Independent India

Independent India was created as a secular state. Although religion and cultural identity are inextricably intertwined, the government would be neutral. Many of Gandhi's dreams, however, were unfulfilled. Communal strife between Hindu and Muslim communities, often with political sponsorship, frequently escalates into bloody outbursts. In 2002, for example, around 2000 Muslims were killed in mob violence in Gujarat. The caste system survived all attempts to change or destroy it. The lowest orders in society still suffer discrimination and Hindu nationalism has greatly increased. This is seen in the rise of the Bharatiya Janata Party (BJP), which is widely supported by a rising middle class feeling threatened by the aspirations and demands from below.

The BJP entered government in 1998, expressing a more aggressive nationalism that very quickly saw a dangerous race in nuclear-weapons-testing with Pakistan, and a confrontation between the two over the disputed state of Kashmir that came perilously close to war. However, the BJP vision of a more disciplined Hindu society was brought into question by the surprise victory of the Congress Party in the 2004 elections under Sonia Gandhi, Italian-born widow of Rajiv Gandhi and representative of India's pre-eminent political dynasty. Her decision not to accept prime-ministerial office herself was a severe blow to her followers.

## INDO-ARYANS or Indics

Speakers of Indo-Aryan languages, who today number in excess of 800 million people, and who are principally concentrated in northern and central India. A sub-group of INDO-IRANIAN, the languages include HINDI, URDU, BENGALI and RAJASTHANI. The Indo-Aryans are descended from the ARYANS, a nomadic pastoral people who migrated from the Central Asian steppes into northern India during the mid-2nd millennium BC, and who were possibly responsible for the destruction of the HARAPPANS.

## INDO-IRANIANS

The peoples who spoke the eastern dialect of the INDO-EUROPEAN language. During the second and first millennia BC Indo-Iranian peoples migrated from the Central Asian steppes to many regions throughout southern and western Asia.

## INDUS VALLEY CIVILIZATION

See HARAPPANS.

## IRANIANS

The citizens of the modern Islamic Republic of Iran (capital Tehran), who numbered over 72 million in 2002. Historically, these people have always referred to themselves as 'Iranian' (meaning 'from the land of the ARYANS'), but until 1935 they were often referred to as PERSIANS by others. While the vast majority of Iranians live in the republic, significant numbers also reside in Qatar, the United Arab Emirates and in Scandinavia.

While it is certain that the area now encompassed by the modern Iranian state was inhabited by about 10,000 BC, with the exception of the ELAMITE civilization, the region remained dominated by Neolithic farming villages until well into the mid-2nd millennium BC. Some trading contact with Mesopotamian cultures, however, does appear to have been conducted through Elam. This apparent stagnation was ended by the migration of a group of INDO-IRANIAN Aryan tribes into the Iranian plateau from the steppes during the mid-2nd millennium BC. These groups lay at the heart of the political, economic and cultural advances of this region, and they were the ancestors of the dynamic MEDES and Persians. During the ancient period, following the collapse of the Persian empire, the Iranians were successively incorporated into the empires of the MACEDONIANS, SELEUCIDS and PARTHIANS.

Following the ARAB Muslim conquest of Iran in AD 641, the vast majority of the population was converted to Islam, and the religion has had a fundamental influence on the later development of Iranian civilization. In 945, the Iranians were conquered by the BUYIDS, a Shi'ite people, who promoted the growth of Shi'ism in the region. The Iranians were overrun by the SELJUKS during the mid-11th century, the MONGOLS during the 13th century, the TIMURIDS in 1393 and the TURKMEN in 1400. By 1501, however, a native dynasty, the Safavids, had been established.

Despite creating an impressive empire, which at its height encompassed northern India, Afghanistan, Armenia, Azerbaijan, Iraq and parts of Turkey, the Safavids were eventually defeated and toppled by an AFGHAN army in 1722. Subsequently, despite brief periods of

---

**Indo-Aryans: main language groups**

Bengali
Hindi
Rajasthani
Urdu

---

**Indo-Iranians: main ethnic groups**

Aryans
Cimmerians
Persians
Scythians

independence (notably under Nadir Shah), the Iranians were made subject to the political and economic aspirations of the TURKS, RUSSIANS and BRITISH, who all fought for control of the region.

## Modern Iran

From 1906, following increased nationalistic activity, a new independent Iranian constitutional monarchy was established, and this remained the form of government until the Islamic Revolution of 1979. The period of the monarchy was marked by significant efforts toward modernization and relatively close ties with the West, and Mohammed Reza Shah was the first Islamic ruler to recognize the state of Israel. The perceived Westernization of Iran led to clashes, at times bloody, between more conservative elements within Iranian society, notably the clergy, and the government. In addition, governmental reform programmes went hand-in-hand with increased despotism and a widening gap between the rich and poor, phenomena that further fuelled clerical and popular discontent. Opposition was frequently met by brutal repression, and these events culminated in the Islamic Revolution of 1979.

Since the Revolution, the Iranian system of government has been founded upon a theocracy, with a constitution based on Islamic law. The head of state is also the spiritual leader, or Ayatollah (a term used mainly in Iran). This period is marked by a rejection of Western culture and ideas, and by significant international tension, particularly between the USA and Iran.

During the 13th century Shi'ism grew to become the predominant Islamic doctrine of the Iranians, and, under the Safavids, it was acknowledged as the official creed. Today, 93% of the population of the republic is Shi'ite, with the vast majority of the remainder adhering to the Sunni doctrine (principally the KURDS and TURKMEN). A tiny number of Christians (mainly ARMENIANS and ASSYRIANS), Zoroastrians, and JEWS also live in Iran. A bare 50% of the population of Iran are descended from the Iranian tribes, and speak Farsi (PERSIAN). Other ethnic minorities are shown in the accompanying box. The official alphabet of Iran is Arabic.

Since the mid-7th century, Iranian culture has been very strongly influenced by Islam, and particularly Shi'ism, but has retained many independent features that are purely Iranian. Contact with other peoples has also introduced foreign influences such as European and Chinese. In the arts, Iranian architecture, particularly mosque construction, has been highly innovative, and Iranian literature displays many distinctive features. Iranian rugs and carpets have been prized for centuries, and this remains a very important Iranian industry and art form.

In contrast to many other Islamic countries, women are able to vote and enjoy an enhanced position within Iranian society. The period following the 1979 Revolution has witnessed an increased Islamization of society, and this has led to some tension within Iran, particularly between the government and ethnic minorities. Political parties are banned, and the law code is based upon Shari'a law, with draconian punishments, such as amputation, occasionally used. Those who admit to following the reformist doctrines of the Bahai faith are automatically subject to the death penalty.

The economy of Iran remains heavily dependent on the oil and petroleum industries, and slightly more than 60% of the population live in towns and cities.

## Ethnic tensions

Given the extremely diverse ethnic, cultural and linguistic composition of Iran, it is perhaps not surprising that tensions have occurred within Iranian society. Following World War II, both the Kurds and the Azeris, with Russian backing, proclaimed themselves independent of the Iranian government, but these movements were crushed in 1947. Again, following the 1979 revolution, the Azeris, Kurds and Arabs attempted, unsuccessfully, to gain independent status. Indeed, one of the motivating factors professed by the IRAQIS behind their invasion of Iran in 1980 was support of the Arabs of Khusestan. The ensuing war, which lasted nearly ten years, cost the lives of over 1 million people. Today, despite the flight of many Kurds to Iran following Iraqi attacks in the early 1990s, tensions still exist between the Kurds and the Iranian government, centred principally on the Kurds' desire to remain a culturally independent people.

> " The entire Iranian nation, which is proud to live under the holy banner of Islam, expresses its hatred of any yielding or recourse to foreigners. "
>
> Ayatollah Kashani, 1951

### Iranians: main ethnic groups

Arabs
Azeris
Bakhtar
Balochis
Dravidians
Farsi
Gilakis
Kurds
Lurs
Mazandaranis
Qashqa'is
Turkmen

# IRAQIS

The citizens of the republic of Iraq (capital Baghdad). The population stood at 24 million in 2002. Strictly speaking, the term 'Iraqi' should not be used to describe the people of this region prior to the foundation of the kingdom of Iraq in 1921.

The region of Mesopotamia now covered by Iraq has been described as the 'cradle of civilization'. It was in this area that the MESOPOTAMIANS, SUMERIANS, AKKADIANS, ASSYRIANS and BABYLONIANS cultivated their respective civilizations. Following the collapse of the Babylonians, the MACEDONIANS, SELEUCIDS, PARTHIANS and Sassanid PERSIANS all successively incorporated Mesopotamia into their empires. The ARAB invasions of AD 637–8 introduced Islam into the region, and for a time, under the Abbasid caliphate, Baghdad became the leading city in the Islamic world. Subsequently, however, the region again fell to foreign invaders, most notably the BUYIDS, SELJUKS, MONGOLS, TURKMEN, and IRANIANS. The OTTOMANS finally controlled the region from the 16th century until World War I.

After 1918, Mesopotamia fell under BRITISH control, which was deeply resented by the resident Arab population. The final years of Ottoman rule had witnessed a significant rise in Arab nationalistic feeling, and many Arabs were prompted to fight on the side of the Allies in the belief that, following victory, they would become free and independent Arab states. Their disappointment at the failure of this to happen and subsequent assignment of the region to British or French control led directly to another resurgence in Arab nationalism, with frequent rebellion and violence. This rise in nationalistic activity was much more a pan-Arab than an Iraqi movement. Even following the creation of the Kingdom of Iraq in 1921, many Iraqis continued to resent the continued presence of the British. Agitation for their withdrawal continued until their final departure in 1932, the year in which the Iraqis were finally recognized as an independent people by the League of Nations.

The majority of the Iraqi people, around 75%, are Arabs. About 20% are KURDS, and other smaller minorities include Turkmen, Iranians, SYRIANS and ARMENIANS. Given the state's relatively recent formation, the notion of Iraqi nationhood has taken some time to coalesce. As a result, in line with a number of other Arab states, to many the notion of being 'Arab' is just as important, if not more so, than the notion of being 'Iraqi'. Indeed, successive Iraqi governments have been at the forefront of promoting pan-Arabism, and this can be seen in Iraq's brief federation with Jordan (1958), its support of the PALESTINIANS, and its continued hostility towards the ISRAELIS.

## Internal tensions

Another obstacle to the unity and self-identity of the people of Iraq has been the significant numbers living within the frontiers of the republic who do not consider themselves to be Iraqi. Among these would certainly be the vast majority of the Kurdish population, who have agitated for many years for the formation of an independent state. These demands, and their rejection by Iraqi governments, have led to violence and civil war, for example in 1961–9, 1974, and most notably following the conclusion of the first Gulf War (1991) when thousands of Kurds were massacred by Iraqi troops, or died from disease or malnutrition. Following these events, a United Nations-sponsored security zone was created for the Kurds within northern Iraq, and they played an active role in the second Gulf War (2003). It is certain that, despite Iraqi attempts at assimilating them, most Kurds have no interest in Iraqi status.

The official language of the Iraqis is Arabic, although English and Turkish are also widely known. Their culture is predominantly Arab-Islamic, particularly in rural areas, although in the towns and cities Western culture has become very popular. Many desert and mountainous regions are still inhabited by the BEDOUIN, many of whom now live a semi-sedentary lifestyle, although significant numbers continue to adhere to traditional nomadism. There are a very small number of Christians, principally Nestorians, Chaldeans, Assyrians and Jacobites, living in Iraq. While tribal identity remains important, urban living has tended to have a detrimental effect on this aspect of traditional Arab society and culture.

The oil industry continues to be a major employer, from which the Iraqis derive most of their income, although agriculture remains important. Carpet-making is a traditional craft that is still practised. As is the case with many other Muslim nations, Islamic fundamentalism has increased amongst the Iraqi people in the last 30 years.

**The Gulf wars**

While 60% of the population of Iraq are Shi'ite Muslims, the majority of the ruling class under the Ba'athist regime (1968–2003) was drawn from Arab followers of the Sunni sect, who account for only 20% of the Iraqi people. This imbalance frequently led to sectarian and class tensions, with many Shi'ites looking for guidance to Tehran, rather than Baghdad. During the Iran–Iraq War (1980–8) tensions between the two communities ran high, and following the first Gulf War, a major Shi'ite rebellion around the southern city of Basra was brutally crushed by the Iraqi army.

Following the first Gulf War, Iraq experienced a period of considerable isolation from the international community, even from other Arab nations. The controversial US-led invasion of Iraq in 2003, the swift collapse of Saddam Hussein's regime and the troubled occupation of a country with a shattered infrastructure and continuing insurgency ensured that life for many Iraqis remained volatile in 2004.

The key to any future stability is likely to be whether the Sunnis, Shi'ites and Kurds manage to put in place a durable power-sharing agreement following the transfer of executive power back to an Iraqi government.

## ISHKASHMI

A Pamir people of the Gorno-Badakhshan autonomous *oblast* (region) in Tajikistan, and of Afghanistan. Primarily herders, and ISMAILI Muslims since the 11th century, they speak an East Iranian language. Their isolation meant that the Soviet impact was limited, but many were forced to resettle among the TAJIKS in the 1950s. They use Tajik as a written language, but their own language and traditions remain strong. In 1980 they numbered up to 2500.

## ISHMAELITES

See MIDIANITES.

## ISMAILIS

An Islamic religious sect, which developed from Shi'ism, whose devotees strive to get beyond the literal meanings of religious texts, such as the Koran, in order to discover the more important hidden meanings. In such groups the interpreter, or imam, rose to great prominence, and, despite attacks and persecution by Sunni Muslims, the movement gained popularity from the 8th century and fostered splinter groups such as the Carmarthians and DRUZE. The origins and name of the Ismailis derive from a religious schism in AD 765 that centred on the nomination of the seventh imam: those who became known as Ismailis favoured the designation of Ismail, son of the sixth imam, even though he had died before his father.

The Ismailis have, at times, played a prominent part in the history of western Asia. The Egyptian Fatimids, for example, were Ismaili. In Lebanon and northern Iran members of the sect became significant in the resistance to SELJUK rule; they formed a movement know as the Assassins, who believed it was their religious duty to propagate terror against their political enemies.

Today Ismailis, most of whom regard the Aga Khan as their imam, are found throughout the Asian continent. The TAJIKS, for example, are predominantly Ismaili, and within the sect there are two principal branches. The majority Khojas number around 20 million and recognize the Aga Khan as imam, while the minority Bohras, numbering around 1 million, are divided into two groups recognizing different leaders.

## ISRAELIS

Citizens of the Republic of Israel. The Israelis regard Jerusalem as their capital, but this is contested by the international community who regard Tel Aviv-Yafo as the legal capital. In 2002 the population was 6.3 million. The term 'Israelis' is only correct for the period after the formation of the state of Israel in 1948. Prior to this period, the terms Israelites, JUDAEANS, Hebrews and JEWS have all been used, from the ancient period to the mid 20th century. The region, and in particular the city of Jerusalem, is considered holy by three major religions – Judaism, Islam, and Christianity – and this has been a major cause of tensions.

The history of the Israelis has been dominated by their relations with their ARAB neighbours. The modern state was created, under British mandate (with United Nations approval), from lands in Palestine that had previously been peopled by Arabs, the descendants of whom have subsequently become known either as Israeli Arabs (who live within Israel proper) or PALESTINIANS (who live in the occupied territories). Large-scale Jewish immigration into this region from the late 19th century, and in particular during the 1920s and 1930s, has led to early clashes between Jews and Arabs, for example in 1921 and 1929. Moreover, the formation of the state of Israel in 1948 and Israeli encroachments on Palestinian regions provoked an almost immediate attack from the JORDANIANS, EGYPTIANS, IRAQIS, SYRIANS and LEBANESE – an attack that ended in utter failure and the acquisition of significant areas of Palestine by the Israelis. Since then, there have been frequent Arab–Israeli wars, most notably the Six Day War (1967) and the Yom Kippur War (1973). All of the major Arab–Israeli conflicts have proved Israeli victories and have led to the complete eradication of Palestine as a separate state, as well as the loss of territory for Jordan, Syria and Egypt.

Despite peace accords in recent years with Egypt and Jordan, Israeli–Palestinian relations have weighed heavily on the history and development of Israel as a nation. The foundation of the Palestinian Liberation Organization (PLO), terrorist attacks against Israeli targets and retaliatory missions by Israeli security forces have led to an almost continuous state of undeclared war between these two peoples. Indeed, the presence of PLO forces in Beirut led directly to an Israeli invasion of Lebanon in 1982, and it was not until 2000 that Israeli forces were finally withdrawn from that country.

Since the 1990s significant efforts have been made towards peace, but with limited success.

Dialogue has been established between the Israeli government and the PLO, and some Palestinian regions have been granted a degree of autonomy, but the emergence of a harder-line Likud government in the late 1990s resulted in a renewed *intifada* (low-level revolt) among the Palestinians. The USA, with which the Israel has a long history of friendship, embarked on a plan (the so-called 'Road Map' to peace) designed to bring peace to the area, together with the re-establishment of the Arab state of Palestine. Israeli moves to create a permanent border that effectively annexes large areas of the Palestinian territories brings into question Israel's commitment to such a solution. Tension and violence in the region continue, with Palestinian groups (many of whom are openly opposed to the more moderate line of the official Palestinian leadership, launching major terror campaigns against Israeli targets, and the Israelis retaliating with vigorous counter-attacks.

### Israeli society

Israeli society and culture are extremely diverse due to the disparate ethnic and cultural origins of many present-day citizens. The republic of Israel has an open policy of Jewish immigration, and as a result, millions of people, from all areas of the globe, have chosen to accept Israeli citizenship. Indeed, it has been the need to provide housing for new migrants in occupied Palestinian areas, which are not legally part of the state of Israel, that has at times provided the spark for Arab–Israeli tension. This need and consequent tension were particularly strong following a period of massive immigration from Eastern Europe in the late 20th century as a result of the collapse of the Soviet Union.

Within Israeli society, however, there are two major divisions: the Ashkenazim and the Sephardim (see JEWS, EUROPEAN). The former comprise immigrants of European extraction who follow the 'German rite' in synagogue worship and have a Yiddish tradition. Many Sephardim are also of European origin, but these are Iberian and retain Babylonian synagogue rituals together with Judaeo-Spanish (Ladino) culture. Large numbers of Sephardim also originate from North Africa. Although the two groups are approximately equal in number, the Ashkenazim tend to be more economically successful than their Sephardic compatriots. Two other groupings that are recognized within Israeli society are the *sabres* and non-*sabres*; that is, those who are born in Israel, and those who are not.

In addition to the Palestinians of the occupied territories, about 18% of the population of the state of Israel comprises Arabs who hold Israeli citizenship – a proportion that is growing steadily. These Israeli Arabs, while possessing the vote and an official political voice within the Israeli parliament, suffer considerable discrimination; for example, they are forbidden from marrying Arabs from the occupied territories.

The official languages of the Israelis are Hebrew and Arabic, although English, Ladino, Yiddish and Russian are widely spoken, and over 80 different languages or dialects are in use. While the majority of Israelis are Jews, the Arabs are principally Sunni Muslim, and there are very small numbers of Christians, DRUZE and Bahais. The desert areas of Galilee and Negev are also home to a number of BEDOUIN tribes.

Owing to the relatively recent creation of Israel and the vastly differing origins of many of its citizens, the formation of a distinctly 'Israeli' culture is still in an embryonic stage. Certainly, nationalistic feelings run high amongst many elements within Israeli society, particularly amongst the *sabres*. In addition, there have been energetic governmental efforts to promote the Hebrew language and culture, much of which is achieved through compulsory military service, and most Israelis have a common Jewish culture and tradition that acts as a strong unifying factor. Moreover, the very history of Israel since 1948, and in particular the wars with its Arab neighbours, has helped foster the unification of the Israeli people, despite internal political differences (many of which are centred around conflicts between and secular elements and Jewish fundamentalists).

## ISRAELITES

See JEWS.

## ITELMEN

A northeastern Siberian people of Tigil' region, Koriak national *okrug* (district), Russian Federation. Traditionally sedentary hunters, gatherers and fishers who practise shamanism, they speak a Chukotko-Kamchatkan language, now seriously endangered. From the late 17th century they fought bitterly against RUSSIANS demanding tribute, and for their pains were nearly annihilated in genocidal attacks. Those remaining were heavily assimilated – a policy continued under Soviet rule with compulsory boarding education. In the 1990s they began attempting to recover elements of their traditional culture. In 1991 they numbered about 1500.

## JADE

See TAMANG.

## JAINS

Followers of Jainism, an INDIAN religion resembling Hinduism and Buddhism, which takes its name from *ji* (Sanskrit, 'to conquer'). Currently there are around 3 million Jains living in India, principally in Gujarat, with small numbers also found in other countries throughout the English-speaking world.

Traditionally, Jainism is said to have been founded in 528 BC by Mahavira (599–527 BC), the first of the 24 Jain *tirthankaras* ('saints' – those who have broken free of the material world and consequent cycle of rebirth), who are venerated in Jain temples and homes. This is one way in which they differ from the majority Hindus. The Jains also have a far stricter code of non-violence (*ahimsa*), and in temples wear a cotton mask over their mouths in order to prevent the accidental inhalation of insects. In addition, they do not eat anything grown below ground level and reject the authority of the *Vedas*. Ideally, it is the goal of the Jain to reject the material world totally, cast off all accumulated negative *karma*, and ultimately break free of the constant cycle of earthly rebirth. In reality, the Jains are divided into two broad groups. The ascetics, many of whom are women and tend to live a nomadic lifestyle, are devoted entirely to a rejection of the body, the emotions and the material world, and concentrate solely on the spiritual life. These are divided amongst themselves between the *Svetambara* ('White-Clad'), who wear white robes, and the *Digambara* (who are naked – rejecting clothes as a 'possession'). This split seems to have occurred around AD 100 and is based upon significant differences in attitude towards ritual, textual authority and worship. The Lay-Jains, the second group, continue to function within the material world and have a duty of care towards the ascetics. Despite their need to conduct a secular lifestyle, it is believed that the latter group can inhibit the accumulation of negative *karma* both through care for the ascetics, and through the provision of Jain temples and sacred images, many of which are on a colossal scale. The most important of these sites is at Mount Abu (Rajasthan).

The need to provide funds for these enterprises has led the Jains to become one of the most successful and important groups within the Indian business and commercial sectors. Moreover, through their patronage of the arts, they have also had a disproportionate influence upon the development of Indian architecture, painting and sculpture. They were influenced by MUGHAL styles in the 15th century.

The Jains do not possess an official caste system but are divided into over 100 *jatis*, which are based on Hindu occupational castes. There has been very little tension between Hindus and Jains, as their differences in belief are not mutually offensive. In recent years, however, the latter have become much more aware of themselves as a separate cultural group, and this may account in part for the migration of some Jains to other English-speaking countries. In addition to the *tirthankaras*, the Jains also revere a number of Hindu deities, and marriage between the two groups is not forbidden, but requires the wife to abandon her former religion. Jainism has had a profound influence upon some key figures in Indian history, not least Mahatma Gandhi.

## JALAYIRIDS

A MONGOL tribe who ruled western Iran 1336–1410; their capital was Baghdad. They were generally successful in their wars with the GOLDEN HORDE TATARS, but were less so against the TIMURIDS, who defeated them in 1382. The BLACK SHEEP TURKS finally annihilated them in 1432.

## JEBUSITES

An ethnically mixed people, probably of mostly CANAANITE origin, described in the Bible as inhabiting Jerusalem at the time of King David's conquest around 1000 BC.

## JEU JEN

See JUAN-JUAN.

## JEWS

Jews are followers of Judaism and descendants of the Biblical Israelites. Their long history of statelessness and persecution has resulted in the Jews being a widely dispersed people: though of Middle Eastern origin, the majority of the world's 14 million Jews now live in Europe and North America. Around 4.7 million Jews live in Israel but, though most ISRAELIS are Jews, the two identities are not synonymous.

Religion is absolutely central to the Jewish identity, as a Jew cannot renounce Judaism without also ceasing to be a Jew. As the first of the world's monotheistic religions, Judaism was the main influence on the development of both Christianity and Islam, giving the Jews an importance in world history disproportionate to their relatively small numbers. Their religion has often made Jews the victims of persecution in Christian and Muslim countries, but it has also contributed to their survival in important ways. As an essentially tribal religion, Judaism does not actively seek converts but Jews believe that they have a special covenant with their god to spread his message to the world through their example and this has given them a sense of being a chosen people. An optimistic belief in the eventual coming of a Messiah has helped Jews keep the faith through times of persecution, when it might otherwise have seemed that their god had forsaken them. Just as important, but less often acknowledged, Judaism's emphasis on ritual purity has also helped Jews preserve their identity. By creating a barrier between Jews and non-believers, who are considered impure, this made it difficult for host communities to assimilate Jewish immigrants.

The Biblical Israelites were a Semitic nomad people (see SEMITES). Significantly, their alternative name, Hebrews (given also to the Israelites' language), comes from an AMORITE word meaning 'those who wander from place to place'. The Hebrew language had become extinct as a spoken tongue by the beginning of the Christian era, having been displaced by Aramaic, but it survived as a written language and has been successfully revived as an official language of modern Israel.

The Israelites settled in Palestine around 1200 BC, conquering the indigenous CANAANITES and warring frequently with the neighbouring PHILISTINES and ARAMAEANS. The Israelites were at this time divided into tribes ruled by chiefs known as 'judges', but around 1000 BC they were united into a kingdom by David, who made his capital at Jerusalem. David's son Solomon built the Temple in Jerusalem as the chief sanctuary of the Israelite religion in 928. Soon after Solomon's death in 928 BC the Israelite kingdom split into the two kingdoms of Israel and Judah.

### The Diaspora

In the 8th century BC Israel was conquered by the ASSYRIANS and its population was dispersed. Judah survived until c. 586 BC, when it was conquered by the BABYLONIANS, who destroyed the Temple and deported much of the population to Mesopotamia; others fled and settled in Egypt. It was during this period that the Israelites began to be known as Jews, after Judah.

Following his conquest of Babylon in 539 BC, the PERSIAN king Cyrus gave leave to the Jews to return to Jerusalem and rebuild the Temple. Many Jews had built prosperous lives in Mesopotamia and Egypt and they chose to remain, so beginning the world-wide dispersal of Jews known as the Diaspora.

After Alexander the Great conquered the Persian Empire in 334–330 BC, Judah came under Greek rule. When the Greeks tried to impose pagan worship in the Temple, a rebellion broke out in 168 BC. Judah, or Judaea as it was known

to the Greeks and Romans, finally became independent in 131 BC after years of bitter fighting.

In 63 BC Judaea was forced to become a ROMAN client state. High taxes made Roman rule unpopular, while the Jews' belief in the coming of a Messiah led to the formation of the Zealots and other radical groups dedicated to regaining independence. In AD 66 a major rebellion against Roman rule began. The Romans recaptured Jerusalem and destroyed the Temple in AD 70, but the last Zealot stronghold, at Masada, held out until 73. As a result of the rebellion thousands of Jews were sold into slavery and became scattered throughout the Roman empire. After another rebellion in 132, Jews were banned from Jerusalem and practising Judaism was, for a time, made a capital offence. The adoption of Christianity as the official religion of the Roman Empire in the 4th century led to further repression and the main centre of Judaism shifted east to the long-established community in Mesopotamia, then once again under Persian rule.

### Islamic rule

The ARAB conquest of the Middle East and North Africa brought perhaps as many as 90% of Jews under Islamic rule. As was the case in Christian Europe, Jews in the Islamic world were subject to discriminatory legislation. As *dhimmis* ('protected people'), Jews enjoyed physical protection and freedom of worship but paid special taxes, wore distinctive clothing and were banned from proselytising. Violence against Jews was rare until the 13th century, when the Islamic world, under threat from Christian crusaders and the MONGOLS, saw an increase in religious intolerance. The large and quite prosperous Jewish communities of Mesopotamia and Egypt went into decline as Jews migrated west to Morocco and Algeria, where attitudes were more tolerant.

However, the influx to these regions resulted in the growth of popular anti-semitism there too, and in the 15th century Moroccan Jews were segregated into *mellahs* (ghettos), ostensibly for their own protection, where they continued to live into the 20th century. In spite of this discrimination, the Islamic world received a new influx of Jews at the end of the 15th century, following their expulsion from Spain in 1492, most of them going either to Morocco or the Ottoman empire.

In general, however, the Jewish communities in the Islamic world continued to decline into the 20th century. Certainly by the 18th century, if not earlier, the majority of Jews lived in Europe (see EUROPEAN JEWS).

The Jewish communities in the Islamic world declined further as the result of emigration to Israel after its foundation in 1948 (see ISRAELIS). This emigration was often hastened by violent outbursts of both popular and state-sponsored anti-semitism in many Muslim countries opposed to Israel. Persecution of Jews was increased dramatically in Iran following the Islamic revolution in 1979 and many hundreds were executed for alleged Zionist activities.

By the end of the 20th century few Muslim countries were home to more than a hundred Jews: the only significant Jewish communities to survive in Muslim countries were in Turkey (about 25,000), Morocco (about 6500) and Tunisia (about 2500).

## JORDANIANS

An ARAB people who inhabit the modern country of Jordan (capital Amman). They numbered 5.2 million in 2002. The term is relatively modern, as the independent Jordanian state was only created in the mid-20th century.

During the ancient period, the area was inhabited by various peoples such as the AMMONITES, CANAANITES, AMORITES, EDOMITES, Gilead, Bashan and MOABITES; the region was conquered by the Israelites during the 11th century BC and was later controlled by the EGYPTIANS, ASSYRIANS, BABYLONIANS, PERSIANS, SELEUCIDS, ROMANS and BYZANTINES. Following the Arab invasion in AD 636 the region became part of the Islamic world, and from the early 16th to the early 20th centuries it was ruled as a part of the OTTOMAN empire. Following the conclusion of World War I, the region passed to the British, to be controlled by mandate, under the Sykes-Picot Agreement. In 1922, the name 'Transjordan' was applied, and nominal control was passed to a member of the Arabian Hashemite dynasty, who ruled as Abdullah I. From 1928 Transjordan became semi-autonomous, and in 1946 achieved independent status. In 1950, following its annexation of the West Bank, Transjordan became simply 'Jordan'.

Tensions with the neighbouring ISRAELIS have dominated modern Jordanian history. The two nations were at war in 1948 and in 1967, and during the latter conflict Jordan lost the West Bank. In addition to these major conflicts, however, frequent smaller-scale cross-border clashes have occurred, and anti-Israeli movements, such as the Palestine Liberation Organization and the Black September group, used Jordan as a haven from which to launch attacks against Israel until they were expelled. Moreover, Jordanians have also experienced difficult relations with the SYRIANS, EGYPTIANS and SAUDIS, sometimes because of their attempts to forge better relations with the militarily powerful Israelis. King Abdullah I was assassinated in 1951 by a Palestinian following his recognition of the Israeli state.

Conversely, the Jordanians have maintained close relations with the IRAQIS, from whom Jordan obtains most of its oil. This relationship led the Jordanians to support Iraq during the latter's war against Iran and – at least initially – following the Iraqi attack on the Kuwait. Following the Gulf War, the Jordanians tended to distance themselves from Iraq, and have attempted to forge better relations with other Arab states. To date, despite the 1994 peace agreement, significant tensions continue to exist between Jordan and Israel.

### Jordanian cultural identity

Most of the Jordanian population is actually comprised of PALESTINIANS who have migrated into the country since the late 1940s, many of whom have been granted citizenship. Doubts have to be raised as to whether a significant proportion of these people views itself as, above all else, 'Jordanian', and strains have been evident between the Jordanian government and the Palestinian political hierarchy. Traditionally, Jordan has presented itself as the protector of the Palestinians, but between 1974 and 1988 it relinquished this status in favour of the Palestinian Liberation Organization. Moreover, despite the government's closer relations with the USA after the 1991 Gulf War, much of the population continued to support Iraq.

The native population of the country comprises the descendants of some 20 BEDOUIN tribes and, although increasing numbers are deserting the traditional nomadic lifestyle, a significant number still retain a semi-nomadic existence. Minorities include ARMENIANS, TURKMEN and DRUZE.

Arab and Islamic cultures have heavily influenced the Jordanians, but Western culture has also had a significant impact on the 80% of the population exposed to the country's urban culture through media, sports, entertainment nd so on. Indeed, both kings Hussein and Abdullah II were educated in the West. For the 20% of the population that resides outside the towns, however, traditional Arabic-Islamic culture predominates. Over 95% of Jordanians are Sunni Muslims; most of the remaining 5% are Christians of varying traditions (Melchites, Byzantines, Armenians, Syrian Orthodox, and Greek Orthodox are some of the more popular forms). Small numbers of Bahai and CIRCASSIANS are also found in the country.

Most Jordanians speak a dialect of Arabic, but English is also widespread. Jordan produces very little oil and lost most of its agricultural land following the war with Israel in 1967. As a result, the Jordanians are heavily dependent on service industries for their income, and tourism has become a major industry. Large numbers of Jordanians, however, are choosing to live and work abroad.

## JUAN-JUAN or Jeu Jen or Jou Jan or Jwen Jwen

A group of nomadic MONGOL-dominated tribes, originating in the steppes of Central Asia, who forged an impressive empire in northern China around AD 400–552. The Blue Turks (a Turkic force) and the Wei CHINESE defeated them in 552, and they subsequently disappeared from history. One Juan Juan tribe, the AVARS, later conquered significant areas in eastern Europe. The Juan Juan were frequently allied with the EPHTHALITES. Culturally, they were identical with the Mongols.

## JUDAEANS

The inhabitants of the ancient kingdom of Judah, which was formed following the division of the territory of Israel in the late 10th century BC. They fought frequent wars against the Israelites (see JEWS), with whom they were ethnically and culturally identical, but were subsequently overrun by the EGYPTIANS, ASSYRIANS, and finally the BABYLONIANS, who destroyed the kingdom in 586 BC, deporting many Judaeans to Babylonia.

## JUNGARS

See DZUNGARS.

## KAFFIRS

A pejorative term, meaning 'infidel', of Arabic origin, used to describe the NURISTANI people of northeastern Afghanistan. Adopted by white South Africans (notably AFRIKANERS) in the colonial era, the term 'kaffir' was also used, again pejoratively, to describe any black African.

## KALDU

See CHALDEANS.

## KALKAS

see KHALKHAS.

## KALMYKS or Kalmucks or Torguts

A people of MONGOL origin who reside in the autonomous republic of Kalmykia (capital Elista) in the Russian Federation, and also in Central Asia and Siberia. They refer to themselves as the *Khal'mg*. They are descended from a group of OIRATS who, by the mid-17th century, had migrated west following prolonged competition with the CHINESE for control of the Beijing region, and who subsequently inter-married with the local population. Those who settled in what is now modern Kalmykia were initially made allies of the Russian tsars. Disillusioned, however, with conditions in the west, around

300,000 attempted to return to Central Asia in 1771. The difficulties of the journey, exacerbated by Russian and Turkic (see TURKS) attacks, prevented two-thirds from arriving at their destination. The Chinese had conquered those of their kinsmen who had remained in Central Asia by the mid-18th century.

Following the Russian Revolution, the Kalmyks were granted an autonomous district within the Soviet Union in 1920, and in 1935 they were granted the status of an autonomous republic. The republic was abolished 1943–57 following alleged collaboration with the Germans, and large numbers of Kalmyks were deported to Central Asia and Siberia. Since 1992, Kalmykia has been an autonomous republic within the new Russian state.

The Kalmyks are predominantly Buddhist, although the religion tended to be suppressed under Soviet rule. During the 20th century, significant efforts were made to assimilate the Kalmyks into Russian culture and society. In schools, Russian was taught at the expense of the Kalmyk language, and, in the 1930s, Kalmyk nomads were forcibly settled in agricultural collectives. Since 1992, however, traditional Kalmyk culture, religion and language (the Kalmyks use the Cyrillic alphabet for literary purposes) have enjoyed a revival. Nevertheless, Russification has had a profound influence on the development of Kalmyk culture – an influence that continues to the present day.

Ethnic Kalmyks comprise less than half the population of Kalmykia, and the second largest ethnic group is RUSSIAN. The Kalmyks remain principally a pastoral agricultural people.

## KAMAS

A southern Siberian people of Kansk region, Russian Federation. The descendants of NENETS, who were conquered and assimilated by Turkic invaders in the 5th century AD, they adopted a Turkic language. Primarily herders, under Russian and Soviet rule they became so thoroughly Russified that they are no longer counted as a separate people. In 1969 they numbered about 200.

## KANNADA or Kanarese

Speakers of Kannada, a DRAVIDIAN language of south India. They number around 40 million and are mainly concentrated in Karnataka on the southwest coast (capital Bangalore), which is an amalgam of Kannada-speaking territories based on the old state of Mysore.

The people of the region cultivate a variety of crops and exploit the extensive forest resources, but are becoming increasingly urbanized and educated. The Western-style culture in Bangalore, which has become India's Silicon Valley, is in marked contrast to that found in much of rural India.

The Kannada are predominantly Hindu, but the ancient ascetic JAIN religion, which influenced Kannada written records from as early as the 5th century AD, is still followed and is part of a rich cultural heritage.

## KARAGAS

See TOFALARS.

## KARDOUCHOI

An unknown mountain people who are documented as attacking the PERSIANS in 401 BC. They are perhaps to be identified with the KURDS.

## KARTVELIANS

A group of four peoples who speak South Caucasian languages. The GEORGIANS (the largest of the four), MINGRELIANS and SVANS live in the Republic of Georgia, the LAZ live mainly on the Black Sea coast in northeastern Turkey (see map, page 492).

## KASHDU

See CHALDEANS.

## KASHMIRIS

A diverse people of the region of Kashmir, divided between India, Pakistan and China, and located in the Himalayan mountain range in the extreme northwest of the Indian subcontinent.

Kashmir has been a source of international tension since its partition between India and Pakistan in 1947, arising from disputed claims to sovereignty and self-determination. Pakistan controls northern and western Kashmir, comprising Azad (Free) Kashmir (described in India as Pakistan Occupied Kashmir, commonly known as POK) and the Northern Areas provinces of Baltistan and Gilgit, while India administers the south and southeast regions which comprise the state of Jammu and Kashmir. China's long-standing territorial claims were satisfied with the military occupation of eastern Kashmir (northeast Ladakh) in 1962.

Kashmir is a place of widely different, even competing, ethnic, linguistic and cultural influences. Historically, the region was penetrated by European, Indian and Central Asian peoples, giving rise to various ethnic groups, notably the Kashmiri-speaking population of the Vale of Kashmir, the most densely-populated region and location of the state summer capital Srinagar (transferred to the city of Jammu in winter).

People here and in western Jammu are largely Muslim and mostly identify with their co-religionists in Pakistani Kashmir. In these areas they speak Urdu (the official language of Jammu and Kashmir) and Kashmiri, a language of disputed INDO-IRANIAN Dardic (see DARDS) or INDO-ARYAN origin. Indo-European Dardic-speaking peoples occupy northern Kashmir together with the Tibeto-Burman BALTI and LADAKHI. The people of

> **"** [The Kashmiris] are adepts beyond all others in the art of magic. **"**
>
> Marco Polo, 1298

eastern Jammu, who are Hindus, speak Dogri, HINDI and PUNJABI. They are closely related to the people of the Punjab to the south, but they are dominated by the Rajput Dogra clans (see DOGRAS). There is also a small population of SIKHS in the state.

### History and culture

Historically, the region flourished as a centre of Hinduism from the 9th century AD, but from 1346 Kashmir was ruled by Muslims who became the majority community. From the late 18th century Kashmir became subject to the Sikh kingdom of the Punjab and was annexed outright in 1819. The small Muslim state of Jammu also came under the control of the Sikhs in the late 1700s, and in 1820 Gulab Singh, founder of the Dogra dynasty, was made Raja of Jammu. He expanded his territory by conquering Baltistan and Ladakh.

After the First Sikh War (1845–6) Britain allowed Gulab Singh to gain control of Kashmir, and he became maharajah of a greatly enlarged but amorphous mountain kingdom under British protection, the basis of the modern Indian state of Jammu and Kashmir.

The large Muslim population has continued to resent the perpetuation of Hindu rule resulting from the then-ruling maharajah Hari Singh's decision to opt for union with India in 1947. This union is the cause of the current political disaffection and international tension and has led to war between India and Pakistan in 1962 and 1971 and to serious cross-border skirmishes from 1999.

The Kashmiris largely follow a traditional way of life tied to the land, which has meant adopting animal husbandry, often transhumant to take advantage of high-altitude summer grazing. Agriculture is practised in the valleys, where fruit and wild products are exploited, and forestry in the hills.

Since independence, a rapidly increasing population, now around 12 million (plus a significant refugee population in Pakistan), has put considerable pressure on the fragile mountain environment, leading among other problems to over-exploitation of the forests.

The traditional Kashmir (or 'Cashmere') shawl made from goat wool has been a characteristic product of the region for centuries and has been an important European fashion item since the 18th century, inspiring many copies and textile designs.

## KASKAS or Kashkus or Gasgas

A nomadic Anatolian people of unknown origin, who had occupied the northern mountainous regions of Anatolia (modern central Turkey) by the late 17th century BC.

The Kaskas were a constant enemy of the HITTITES and conducted raids into Hittite territory from about 1600 BC. These raids at times demanded almost annual counter-offensives by a succession of Hittite kings. Such was their success that in about 1300 BC, perhaps in league with a number of other tribes such as the Isuwa, the Kaskas sacked the Hittite capital, Hattusas.

The nomadic lifestyle of the Kaskas made it very difficult for the Hittite army to defeat them conclusively, and they remained a major threat until the final collapse of the Hittite empire – an event they may have had an active part in bringing about.

Following the fall of the Hittites, the Kaskas appear to have moved into central Anatolia, and are last mentioned, in about 700 BC, as enemies of the ASSYRIANS. It is possible that they were subsequently assimilated with the indigenous peoples of Anatolia.

Almost nothing is known of Kaskan society and culture. Certainly, they had no written language, but a number of archaeological finds have suggested that they were influenced by the Hittites. They are mentioned in contemporary sources as the producers of textiles and as pig farmers.

## KASSITES

An ancient INDO-EUROPEAN people who migrated from the Zagros Mountains into Mesopotamia. They are first mentioned by the ELAMITES in the late 2nd millennium BC, and had occupied northern Babylonia, where they gained control of a number of important cities, by the early 17th century BC. Although initially repulsed by the BABYLONIANS, they eventually succeeded in founding a new dynasty in about 1595 BC, following the HITTITE conquest of the city.

The Kassite kings raised the Babylonian empire to a status equal to that of the EGYPTIANS and ruled the city for over 400 years. In the 1220s, however, they were conquered by the ASSYRIANS under Tukulti-Ninurta I, and it was a much weakened power that the Elamites eventually destroyed around 1158 BC.

Very little is known of Kassite culture prior to their conquest of Babylon. Certainly, they spoke an Indo-European language, but no Kassite texts have survived. Following their conquest of Babylon, however, the Kassites became heavily influenced by Babylonian culture, and were almost completely assimilated, ethnically and culturally, with the native population. An example of this assimilation can be seen in the area of religion; although their chief deity was originally Shuqamuna, this god became quickly identified with the Babylonian Marduk, and it was the latter deity that the Kassites helped raise to a supreme position within Mesopotamia. In addition, they began using the Babylonian language and cuneiform script.

From about the late 15th century BC, the Kassite kings began to patronize the arts in earnest, and this period witnessed a high point in Babylonian art and literature, although very few Kassite words were introduced into the language. In addition, major architectural structures, usually of notably Babylonian type but with the introduction of moulded brick reliefs, were built at Ur and the new city of Dur Kurigalzu.

Kassite society was feudal in nature, and the king helped guarantee the loyalty of his nobles through grants of land which were recorded on boundary stones (*kudurru*). These stones, a Kassite innovation, were sometimes decorated with impressive reliefs, often with religious motifs, and inscribed with curses against trespassers.

The horse was greatly prized by the Kassites, and their mastery of the light chariot, a form of warfare they may have introduced into Babylonia, was instrumental in their military successes.

On the Macedonian conquest of the Zagros area, some Kassites were incorporated into the empire of Alexander the Great, and these people may have moved back to this region following their defeat by the Elamites. After gaining independence from the Macedonians, the Kassites disappeared from history as a distinct people.

> " ... the very
> warlike and
> turbulent
> mountain tribes
> of the Kasshi
> [Kassites]. "
>
> Z.A. Ragozin,
> 1888

## KAZAKHS

A central Asian people descended from nomadic pastoralists. They speak a Turkic language (see TURKS) and follow Sunni Islam. Around 1465 the Kazakhs broke away from the UZBEKS, who gave them their name, which means 'vagabond'. In the 15th and 16th centuries they established one of the world's last great nomadic empires. They developed a culture noted for its oral poetry, and *aqins* (bards) are still popular. They also invented *kökpar*, a precursor to polo.

Kazakh power began to decline from the 1680s from attacks by the OIRATS, who inflicted several defeats culminating in the 'Great Disaster' of 1723. This left them vulnerable to RUSSIAN expansion, and as they were edged out of the best water sources and pastures many were reduced to poverty, even those who adopted sedentary farming. A number of rebellions reduced their autonomy, but also allowed the easier adoption of new ideas like nationalism, and by the late 19th century a radical intelligentsia had emerged. This small but increasingly influential group began the process of developing a Kazakh national identity, for example through devising an alphabet, recording Kazakh history and founding a national organization, *Alash Orda*. Only the first steps had been taken, however, when revolution in 1917 brought chaos to Central Asia, and though *Alash Orda* initially attempted to establish an independent state before nation-building was complete, the Kazakhs submitted to Bolshevik rule in 1920.

They hoped to continue nation-building, but most of the intelligentsia were exterminated in Stalin's purges, while 1.5 million starved during collectivization and vast numbers fled the Soviet Union. These catastrophes, and the growing numbers of Russian settlers who made Kazakhs a minority in the own land, merely encouraged the spread of nationalist ideas. Environmental degradation through nuclear weapons tests and unsustainable agricultural practices were further unifying issues.

In 1991 Kazakhstan became independent, although relations with Moscow remained cordial and ethnic tensions appear to be contained. In 1996 the Kazakhs numbered about 9.2 million, with 6.6 million in Kazakhstan and the rest in China, Russia, Uzbekistan and Mongolia.

## KEREITS

A MONGOL people whose political cohesion was destroyed by Genghis Khan following the Mongol unification in the early 13th century. Thereafter the tribe was broken up. Culturally, they were identical to other Mongols.

## KEREKS

A northeastern Siberian people of Yakut Autonomous Republic, in the Russian Federation. They have a sea-based economy and speak a Chukotko-Kamchatkan language, which is now nearly extinct.

The Kereks had been brought under RUSSIAN control by the end of the 18th century, and assimilatory pressures reached a peak with Soviet collectivization and educational policies. The collapse of the USSR plunged them into serious poverty, but has allowed the Kereks to attempt to reclaim their identity as a people, provided they can survive. In 2002 they numbered about 100.

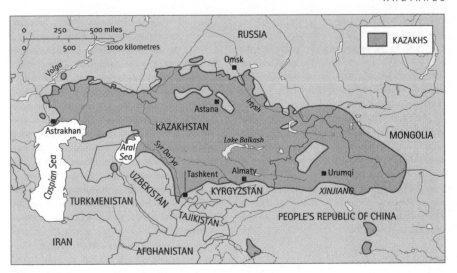

# KETIS

A northeastern Siberian people of Krasnoyarsk region, Russian Federation. Traditionally nomadic hunters, gatherers and reindeer-herders, they were conquered by the RUSSIANS in the early 17th century. Subsequently they were decimated by disease and famine.

Under Soviet rule, collectivization and compulsory boarding education undermined their traditional culture and language, while the collapse of the USSR left them impoverished. In the 1990s they began attempts to recover their identity as a people, with as yet uncertain results. In 1995 they numbered up to 1200.

# KHAKHASS

A southern Siberian people of Krasnoyar region, in the Russian Federation. Traditionally shamanists and nomadic herders who speak a Turkic language (see TURKS), they came under Russian rule in the early 17th century. They were exploited and forcibly Christianized in 1876. Under Soviet rule they faced collectivization, settlement, cultural erosion and prejudice, and became largely acculturated. In the 1990s some groups attempted to re-assert their identity, even forming militias and seeking independence, much to the alarm of their Russian neighbours. In 1993 they numbered around 80,000.

# KHALKHAS

A MONGOL people who constituted almost 80% of the population of modern Mongolia in 2002. Historically they are also known as the Eastern Mongols, and significant numbers are also found in the Uighur Autonomous Region of Xinjiang, China. Forming the predominant ethnic element of Mongolia, most Khalkhas would view themselves primarily as MONGOLS.

Under Genghis Khan the Khalkhas were united with other Mongol tribes for the first time, and they played a major role in the subsequent creation of the Mongol empire. Following the disintegration of the empire, however, the Mongol confederation dissolved, and a period of internecine strife began.

The Khalkhas enjoyed a period of political and military domination over significant areas of Mongolia from the late 15th to the early 17th centuries. Their own political eclipse by the MANCHU followed, and between the late 17th and mid-18th centuries they assisted the CHINESE in the destruction of their rivals, the OIRATS. Subsequent to these events, many of the Mongol tribes scattered throughout Mongolia, China and Eastern Europe. For the later history of the Khalkhas, see MONGOLS.

Like other Mongol peoples, the Khalkhas were traditionally a nomadic/pastoral people, but more than 50% now live in urban areas.

Originally, the tribe adhered to shamanist religions, but, by the mid-17th century, many had converted to TIBETAN Buddhism, and today this religion continues to predominate. A descendant of the Khalkha khans was proclaimed as the first reincarnation of the living Buddha under Altan Khan (1543–83).

Khalkha culture and society are Mongol, but, as is the case with with the other peoples in the region, both Chinese and Russian forms have also influenced them. The official dialect of Mongolian is that of the Khalkha, and the Cyrillic script is used; in recent years, however, there has also been a call for the return of the classical Mongolian script. The Khalkhas are closely related to the BURYATS.

<blockquote>
❝ It was a subject of pride among the Khalkha chiefs to have a ... regenerate Buddha among them. ❞

H.H. Howorth, 1876
</blockquote>

## KHANTY

A northwestern Siberian people of the Khanty-Mansi national *okrug* (district), in the Russian Federation. Nomadic hunters, gatherers and reindeer herders, they speak a Finno-Ugric language. Conquered by the RUSSIANS in the 16th century, they were forcibly (though superficially) Christianized and exploited. Under Soviet rule, collectivization, discrimination, assimilatory education and environmental destruction seriously undermined their culture. In the 1990s they began attempts to revive their language and culture and gain control of their natural resources, seeking a United Nations protected biosphere reserve on their lands. In 1994 they numbered about 21,000.

## KHASA

See PAHARI.

## KHASIS

One of many hill peoples of northeastern India, occupying the Khasis and Jaintia Hills region in the state of Meghalaya (from Assamese and meaning 'abode of the clouds'), capital Shillong, north of Bangladesh. Although the tribal Khasis were independent until conquered by Britain in the 1830s, the state was created in 1972 from Assamese territory following agitation for self-rule. The area has been described as the 'Scotland of the East' because of its scenic beauty and particularly high rainfall.

The origins of the Khasis are obscure, but it is thought that upwards of a million people speak Khasi or one of the several other Khasian languages, which together form the most westerly MON-KHMER group of AUSTRO-ASIATIC. These are the only Mon-Khmer languages outside Southeast Asia. The people are agriculturalists who primarily practise wet-rice and forest slash-and-burn cultivation, but they have increasingly turned to more productive sedentary farming.

Many Khasis were Christianized during the British colonial period, most notably by the presence of the most successful Welsh Overseas Mission in Asia. Christians in the region still maintain links with the Welsh Church. Hinduism is also strong and there are small populations of Muslims and Buddhists. The Khasis are traditionally divided into clans which, for the purposes of leadership and inheritance, are governed by a female line of descent, although men exercise power and ownership.

## KHINALUGS

A Caucasian people of Konakhkend region, northeast Azerbaijan. Sunni Muslims by the 18th century, they are traditionally herders and speak a North Caucasus language. They remained very isolated until the 20th century, when Soviet collectivization eroded their culture, and improved communications allowed the large-scale assimilation of Azerbaijani culture. Their identity as a people has been undermined as the young migrate for better economic opportunities. In 1976, when they were last counted, they numbered about 2500.

## KHITANS or Khitai

A Turko-Mongol tribal confederation that originated in the plains of Manchuria and whose principal tribe was the Yeh Lu. They controlled an impressive empire from the 10th to the 12th centuries, which encompassed, in addition to their homeland, parts of northern China, northern Korea and Mongolia. The term 'Cathay' is derived from 'Khitai', and the latter is still the Russian word for China.

The Khitans are first mentioned in the 5th century AD, following attacks against the northern CHINESE borders. Although initially repulsed, the Khitans succeeded in conquering significant portions of northern China and founded the Liao dynasty, which ruled 907–1125. By 926 the Khitans had also overrun parts of North Korea. They never succeeded in establishing a truly unified empire, and, following a number of rebellions during the later 11th century, their empire in China was destroyed by an alliance of the JUCHEN and Sung Chinese.

Following these defeats, many of the Khitans migrated west, where they overran the Muslim Karakhanids, defeated the SELJUKS (in 1141), and established a new shortlived Karakhitan ('Black Khitan') empire in Central Asia (modern Kazakhstan) – known to the Mongols as the Black Kitai or Western Liao. This new empire was destroyed in 1211 by the Khwarezm and NAIMANS and added to Mongol empire in 1218.

Originally a nomadic-pastoralist people, the Khitans retained a fierce pride in their ethnic and cultural identities. They devised a two-tier system for the administration of their empire: a traditional, Mongol system for the Khitans, and a Chinese-influenced system for the Chinese regions. The Khitans even invented a new script for their own language. At least initially, they were also debarred from wearing Chinese dress, and encouraged to adhere to their native language, traditions and culture; they spoke a Mongol language. Hence, the Khitan period is sometimes viewed as the formative stage of a culture and society that was to become known as 'Mongol'.

Attempts to resist assimilation were not entirely successful; the ruling Liao dynasty was itself increasingly culturally Chinese. The Liao patronized some impressive building projects (for example at Nanjing), which were heavily influenced by Chinese styles: octagonal pergolas were typical of this period. Khitan military tactics were also similarly influenced, and the population was increasingly converted to Chinese Buddhism. By the late 11th century many had been thoroughly assimilated into Chinese culture and society.

In contrast, the Khitans left very little cultural impact upon the Chinese. Many Khitans remained in northern China following the collapse of their empire and later allied with the Mongol invaders under Genghis Khan – some rising to positions of great authority. Outside China, native Khitan culture survived relatively unscathed, displaying continuing nomadic styles, but with noticeable SCYTHIAN and Islamic influences. The culture of the Khitans, and Karakhitan administrative practices, were to have a profound effect on the development of later Mongol equivalents. The Khitans were related to the KHALKHAS (Eastern Mongols).

## KHOJAS

See ISMAILIS.

## KHUFIS

A Pamir people of Gorno-Badakhshan autonomous *oblast* (region), Tajikistan. They have a culture and history very similar to that of the BARTANGS. When last counted in the 1960s they numbered around 1500.

## KINDAH

An ancient ARAB BEDOUIN tribe, which originated in the Hadhramaut region of modern Yemen. They gained a brief period of hegemony in the Arabian peninsula during the 5th and 6th centuries AD, when they headed an alliance of disparate Arab tribes. They were absorbed into the Islamic world during the early 630s.

## KIRGHIZ

See KYRGYZ.

## KOHISTANIS

A people of the Kohistan region of the North West Frontier Province, Pakistan, and adjoining Afghanistan. Their name loosely translates as 'highlanders' in Persian and Urdu. This rough mountainous region is inhabited by rugged, fiercely independent Muslim tribal peoples of Turko-Iranian origin.

In Pakistan they number around 40,000 and speak Kohistani and other closely related Dardic

k

languages generally classified with the INDO-IRANIAN family. They pursue a transhumant pastoral way of life, herding mainly sheep and goats, but they also cultivate crops on favourable terraced hillsides and in the fertile valleys. Logging is also important in this mountainous forested region and many are prosperous traders. The productive areas of Afghan Kohistan north and northeast of Kabul have traditionally been cultivated by TAJIKS.

## KONKANI

A southern Asian people who speak Konkani, an INDO-ARYAN language. Ethnically, Konkani-speakers are an admixture of Aryans originating in Central Asia and local peoples who emerged on the Konkan coastal plain of western India dominated by Bombay (Mumbai). They spread southwards and today are concentrated in the Ratnagiri and Sawantwadi districts of Maharashtra, Goa (where their presence can be dated from the 11th century), coastal Karnataka (particularly Mangalore) and Kerala.

Konkani is the official language of Goa, where many people are of part-PORTUGUESE descent and practise Roman Catholicism. Most Konkani-speakers are Hindu, although some are Muslim, the result of maritime trade contacts with Arabia. They are found working in a wide range of rural, urban and industrial activities.

## KOREISH

See QURAYSH.

## KORYAKS

A northeastern Siberian people of the Koryak national *okrug* (district), Russian Federation. Either sedentary fishers or nomadic reindeer-herders, they speak a Chukotka-Kamchatkan language. From the 1690s until the 1760s they fiercely resisted RUSSIAN conquest, facing genocidal attacks with reckless courage. Finally worn down and increasingly Russified, they were subject to collectivization and compulsory boarding education under Soviet rule that did much to destroy their traditional culture. With pollution from nuclear testing and a language in decline,

their survival as a people is in doubt. In 1997 they numbered about 7000.

## KRYZ

A Caucasian people of the Kuba and Khachmas regions, Azerbaijan. Traditionally herders and Sunni Muslims, they speak a North Caucasian language. They were steadily assimilated by the AZERIS, among whom they have been counted, since 1958. Then they numbered up to 6000. Soviet collectivization and educational policies hurried this process. Their identity as a people, like their language, is dying.

## KSHATRAPAS

See SAKAS.

## KURDS

An INDO-EUROPEAN people whose precise origins are unknown, but who probably migrated into the region sometimes referred to as Kurdistan during the 2nd millennium BC. They have been called Kurds since at least the 7th century AD. Kurdistan (meaning 'Land of the Kurds'), also known as the Kurdish Cultural Region, is not an officially recognized state, and the Kurds now form ethnic minorities in those countries that have partitioned the region since the World War I – namely, Iran, Iraq, Syria, Turkey and Armenia. Comparatively small numbers of Kurds also reside in Azerbaijan, Georgia, Kazakhstan, Lebanon and Western Europe.

Exact numbers are difficult to calculate, but it is estimated that there are some 16 million Kurdish people worldwide, and they comprise the world's largest ethnic minority without a state of its own. Currently some 8 million live in Turkey, where they form 20% of the country's total population; they also account for 20% of the population of Iraq, and 8% of that of Iran (where most inhabit the region of Khorasan).

The ARABS conquered the greater part of Kurdistan during the 7th century AD, after which the Kurds were converted to Islam. At times they have played a significant role in the political development of Western Asia. They founded a number of medieval dynasties in the region,

> 66 Although the wandering Koriaks treat their animals with kindness, their cruelty to women is proverbial. 99
>
> Harry de Windt, 1889

such as the Abbuyid dynasty (1177–1250), founded by Saladin. For much of the medieval period, however, the Kurds were dominated by the SELJUKS, and, between the 14th and early 20th centuries, they were subjects of the OTTOMAN empire.

In the aftermath of World War I, the un-ratified Treaty of Sèvres (1920) made provisions for the creation of a new Kurdish state, but this stipulation was ignored in later treaties, and the area was partitioned. As a result, the Kurds found themselves minorities in disparate countries, some of which have made aggressive attempts to assimilate them into the society and culture of the majority.

Most Kurds would not view themselves as anything other than Kurdish, and remain a fiercely independent people, with a great pride in their history, language and culture, and this unwillingness to assimilate has led to frequent clashes with the governments of Turkey, Iraq and Iran. In Turkey, for example, vigorous efforts have been made to eradicate even their separate ethnic identity, and the government has designated them 'Mountain Turks'. Not surprisingly, the vast majority of the Kurdish population have rejected such labels.

There have been sporadic Kurdish rebellions in Turkey since the 1920s, and throughout much of the 1990s the PKK (Kurdish Workers Party)

*" They [the Kurds] live under the commandment of the Great Turke, but with much freedome and libertie. "*

Edmund Scott, c. 1602

k

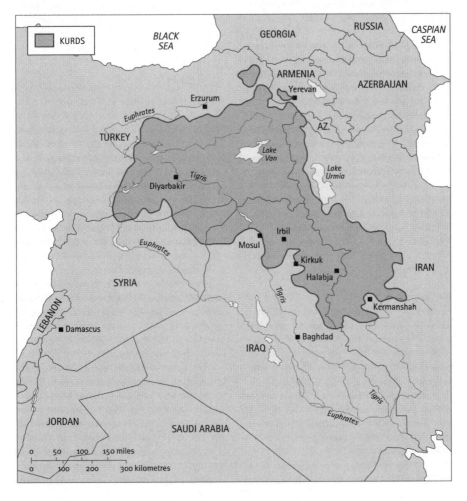

Kurds

conducted a series of guerrilla wars against the Turkish government, which have resulted in great loss of life.

Since the 1930s there have also been several Kurdish rebellions in Iraq, some of which have been extremely violent. Following a Kurdish uprising during the Iran–Iraq War (1980–88), and again following the first Gulf War (1991), the Iraqi government engaged in a genocidal policy of retribution against them.

In Iran, a Russian-backed attempt was made in 1946 to found an autonomous Kurdish enclave in Mahabad, a revolt that was crushed a year later. Another unsuccessful attempt was made following the Islamic Revolution, and since 1979 the Iranian government has tried to assimilate the Sunni Kurds into the majority Shi'ite state.

Some Kurdish efforts to gain independence, or at least political and cultural autonomy, have however met with success. The Khorasan region of Iran has enjoyed partial autonomy since 1961. In Turkey, the Kurds have enjoyed cultural concessions and some autonomy since 1993. In Iraq a semi-autonomous northern region has existed since 1974, and between the first and second Gulf Wars this was largely protected from Iraqi incursions by a UN military force. There are also ongoing efforts by the Kurds to win full independence. In Turkey the PKK has abandoned violent struggle and re-established itself as a political party, the Kurdistan Freedom and Democracy Congress. The redrawing of the political map of Iraq in 2003–4 offers the Kurds the prospect of increased influence there.

### Kurdish culture

Traditionally, the Kurds are a mountain-dwelling nomadic-pastoral people. Since the early 20th century, however, the foundation of new national boundaries has prevented many from pursuing a migratory lifestyle. Moreover, active government policies designed to eradicate nomadism and encourage a more sedentary lifestyle have also caused many Kurds to settle in agricultural villages. Modernization and industrialization have tempted many to start new lives in towns and cities.

These changes have led to a dilution of the traditional tribal structure upon which Kurdish society is based, although the effects have not been so drastic in the countryside, and the clan sheikh (or Aga) remains a figure of importance.

The Kurdish tradition of carpet- and rug-making remains an important source of income. Nonetheless, aggressive nationalistic policies, Arab settlement, mass deportations, cultural restrictions, suppression and Arabization have taken their toll on Kurdish identity.

The Kurdish language, known as Kurmanji, belongs to the West Iranian branch of Indo-European languages and is related to Farsi and Pashto. The vast majority of Kurds are Sunni Muslim, although Sufism and other forms of mysticism are common. In Turkey during the later 19th century there were frequent clashes between Kurds and Armenian Christians. The Kurds were a founder member of the Unrepresented Nations and Peoples Organization.

# KURUKHS

See ORAONS.

# KUSHANS

A nomadic people who originated in the steppes of Central Asia. Their exact ethnic origins are unknown, but they were probably related to the SCYTHIANS, and INDO-IRANIAN people.

The Kuei-Shuang-Wang were a sub-tribe of the YUE-QI who, by AD 25, had risen to prominence in Bactria, and who succeeded in uniting the disparate tribes of the region. It is from their name that we derive the term 'Kushan', which is used to describe both the newly united peoples and their subsequent empire. Over the course of the next hundred years they succeeded in amassing a large empire, which encompassed much of northern India, Afghanistan and Central Asia (their capital lay at Peshawar).

Little is known of their language, but their influence on the development of art and religion in Central and southern Asia cannot be overstated. The Kushans were a highly tolerant people, open to diverse cultural influences, and the Silk Route passed through their empire, exposing them to CHINESE and ROMAN cultures. In addition, the Kushans were highly influenced by INDIAN culture from an early stage in their control of northern India, and many, particularly among the aristocracy, had converted to Buddhism by the mid-2nd century (later rulers tended to be Hindu).

### Kushan culture
It was under the Kushans that the Mahayana doctrine of Buddhism originated, and their contacts with the Chinese almost certainly helped the spread of Buddhism into China by the 2nd century AD. The Kushans also propagated a form of ruler worship throughout their empire.

The Kushan rulers were great patrons of the arts, and the cultural centres at Gandhara and Mathura flourished during this period, with sculpture from the former displaying significant HELLENISTIC and native Indian influences. The Kushans also produced exquisite pieces of metalwork, some of which displays SARMATIAN and Scythian themes.

Kushan coinage was heavily influenced by Greco-Roman types, although the portraiture was Persian in style. The coins had representations of Persian, Hindu and Greek and gods inscriptions using the BACTRIAN language and Greek alphabet.

The Kushans founded or rebuilt a number of cities, including Taxila in India and Delbarjin in Afghanistan, which display the same cultural eclecticism. These multicultural influences can also be seen in the disparate titles claimed by the rulers of the empire, such as *maharaja* and *kaisara*, many of which were Roman, Greek, Persian or Indian in origin.

A significant weakness within the Kushan empire was the fact that it was never effectively centralized; the Kushans preferred to administer their realm through vassal kings. This left the area vulnerable to attack, and the western Kushan empire gradually declined with the rise of the Sassanian dynasty in Persia. The remaining eastern enclaves were finally destroyed by the EPHTHALITES, to whom they may have been related, during the mid-5th century AD. Following these defeats, the Kushans, already heavily assimilated into the native populations of their empire, disappeared from the historical record.

# KUWAITIS

The citizens of the modern state of Kuwait (capital Kuwait City). Although settlement in the area can be dated back to the 3rd millennium BC, modern Kuwait was founded only in AD 1710, following the migration of the ANIZAH, an ARAB tribe, into the area. The ruling emirs, members of the al-Sabah dynasty, have controlled the country since 1756. Initially, the region prospered due to its trading contacts with India, a control of important caravan routes, and the export of pearls farmed along the coast.

The name 'Kuwait' (and, therefore 'Kuwaiti') is derived from the Arabic *al-Kout* (fortified house), a feature common in the 18th century along the coastal region. For much of the 18th and 19th centuries, the Kuwaitis were loosely controlled by the OTTOMANS. Incursions by the militant Islamic fundamentalist Wahabbis, however, led to the establishment of a BRITISH protectorate over Kuwait. Although Kuwaiti independence was acknowledged in 1914, it was not until 1961 that the British relinquished their role in the country.

### Modern Kuwait
In 2002, the population of Kuwait stood at 2 million, but fewer than half of these were actually Kuwaiti citizens; most were foreign workers, drawn to the area by the petroleum industry, who do not qualify for citizenship. As a result, among others, large numbers of PAKISTANIS, EGYPTIANS, INDIANS and PALESTINIANS are found living in the country. In order to ensure the retention of a strong Kuwaiti national and ethnic identity, strict conditions are placed upon applications for citizenship, such as fluency in Arabic (the official language), literacy, adherence to Islam, and an ability to prove that one's ancestors lived in Kuwait prior to 1920.

The Kuwaitis are predominantly Sunni Muslim, although there are also significant numbers of Shi'ites. This has, at times, created tensions within the country, particularly following the Islamic Revolution in Iran (1979) and during the Iran–Iraq war, when Kuwait supported the IRAQIS. The latter, however, have also traditionally regarded Kuwait as part of their sphere of influence, and invaded the country in August

**k**

1990. Following the resultant first Gulf War, hundreds of thousands of PALESTINIANS and JOR-DANIANS were encouraged to leave the Kuwait because of their support for the invasion. Great hostility resulted between the Kuwaitis and Iraqi regime, as well as between those Kuwaitis who fled the Iraqi invasion and those who stayed and resisted the invaders.

As a result of events in the region since 1990, the Kuwaitis have close diplomatic and military ties with the USA and the UK. As in many other Islamic countries, religious fundamentalism has increased significantly during recent years, creating renewed tensions. The Kuwaiti government, for example, has supported America's 'war on terror', which has offended many resident Islamists. Nevertheless, Kuwait was the launching pad for the invasion of Iraq by US and British ground forces in the second Gulf War (2003). The Kuwaitis have, however, supported other Arab states in their opposition to the state of Israel, though they have not taken part in any of the past Arab–Israeli wars

**Islamic and Western influence**

The laws of Islam heavily influence those of Kuwait, and traditional Arabic-Islamic culture remains important. In the Kuwait's towns and cities, however, Western culture has also been influential, particularly in sports and leisure, and English is widely spoken as a second language. The wealth generated by the oil and petroleum industry, and subsequent urbanization and modernization, have seriously eroded the traditional BEDOUIN lifestyle of the region.

Class differences are not as pronounced as in a number of other countries in the Middle East, but there have been increasing calls for greater liberality within the political system. Though they occupy influential positions within the business and diplomatic communities, for example, women were only granted the electoral franchise, and ability to seek electoral office, in 1999. Political parties continue to be illegal.

**" The sail – in its shadow and from its bounties, the Kuwaitis live. "**

A. Rahini, 1930

# KYRGYZ or Kirghiz

A Central Asian people who are MONGOLOID in appearance and speak a Kipchaq Turkic language (see TURKS). There are about 2 million Kyrgyz, about 75% of whom live in the Republic of Kyrgyzstan, where they make up 53% of the population. The remainder live in adjacent areas of Tajikistan, Uzbekistan, Afghanistan and Xinjiang province in China. Though most are now sedentary, the Kyrgyz are traditionally nomadic pastoralists. Sunni Islam is the majority religion, but aspects of traditional shamanism survive in Kyrgyz folk customs.

The Kyrgyz originated in the region between the Yenisey and Irtysh rivers in Siberia, migrating to their present homeland between the 12th and 14th centuries, where their culture and language came under the influence of the local Turkic (see TURKS) and MONGOL tribes. The Kyrgyz lacked a hereditary ruling class, and authority was exercised by *manaps* (elders), whose status depended on their personal abilities and prestige.

In the 16th century the Kyrgyz were conquered by the OIRATS, and from the mid-18th century they lived under a CHINESE protectorate. In 1863 the Kyrgyz came under RUSSIAN rule, and much of their land was confiscated and given to ethnic Russian settlers.

The present borders of Kyrgyzstan were established in 1924 when the Soviet government created the Autonomous Region of Kara-Kirghiz. As well as including large numbers of Russian settlers, the autonomous region also incorporated large areas inhabited by UZBEKS, so that the Kyrgyz formed only a slim majority. In 1936 this autonomous region was renamed Kyrgyzstan and became a federated republic of the USSR. Forced collectivization of agriculture severely disrupted the traditional nomadic way of life of the Kyrgyz.

In 1991 Kyrgyzstan declared independence from the USSR. Since then, it has struggled – despite quite radical economic reforms – with economic problems, human rights abuses by the government of President Askar Akaev, and outbreaks of violence between the Kyrgyz and the Uzbek minority.

# LABHANI

See BANJARI.

# LADAKHIS

A Central Asian people who inhabit the sparsely populated region of Ladakh, also called 'Little Tibet', which lies in the Kashmiri Himalayas and includes the high Ladakh and Karakoram mountain ranges and the upper Indus River valley. It is an ancient kingdom (capital Leh) which, during the 20th century, was divided between India and Pakistan (since 1949) and China (1960s). The southern, Indian, portion forms part of Jammu and Kashmir state.

Ladakhis number around 115,000 and speak Tibeto-Burman Ladakhi and neighbouring languages. They are also predominantly Buddhist and historically divided by the Great Himalayan Range from Indian cultural and religious influences to the south, although the western population has largely adopted Islam. Herding is important at these high altitudes, but the Ladakhis also cultivate the terrace slopes and alluvial soils around their valley settlements to produce pulses, grains and root crops.

# LAKHMIDS

An ARAB tribal dynasty, prominent during the 5th and 6th centuries AD (capital Hira), and frequently in alliance with the Sassanid PERSIANS in their wars with the BYZANTINES and their allies the GHASSANIDS.

The Lakhmids were Christians from AD 580. The dynasty ended when the last Lakhmid king died in 602. The Lakhmids were great patrons of the arts and literature.

# LAZ

A KARTVELIAN people whose language is similar to MINGRELIAN but has no written tradition, making their numbers hard to estimate. Small numbers of Laz live in coastal areas of southern Georgia and in adjacent areas of Turkey.

In ancient times the Laz kingdom of Lazica was an important buffer state between the ROMAN and PERSIAN empires. Lazica became part of the Kingdom of Georgia in the 8th century.

# LEBANESE

The citizens of the modern Republic of Lebanon (capital Beirut). Lebanese also live in many other countries, including other ARAB states, western Europe, the United States, South America, Africa, Australia and the Caribbean. Inhabited since the Palaeolithic period, Lebanon has always been a great commercial and trading area, well placed to trade west via the Mediterranean Sea, south to Palestine and Egypt, and north and east to Syria and the great ancient MESOPOTAMIAN empires. As a result, the region was highly prized by numerous imperial powers. During the ancient period, the resident PHOENICIANS were conquered, in turn, by the AMORITES, EGYPTIANS, HYKSOS, ASSYRIANS, BABYLONIANS, PERSIANS, MACEDONIANS, Ptolomaic-EGYPTIANS, SELEUCIDS, ROMANS and BYZANTINES.

Christianity was introduced during the 4th century; two centuries later the MARONITES migrated into the region. The Islamic conquest in AD 635 had profound consequences for the area's political, social and cultural development, introducing a second major religion; power struggles between Christians and Muslims have dominated much of the subsequent history of the region. In the 11th century the DRUZE also migrated to the area of Mount Lebanon, adding a further religious dimension.

**Towards independence**

For much of the early medieval period the Fatimid Egyptians dominated the area. Between the late 11th and 13th centuries, however, the MARONITES achieved political dominance, aided by the establishment of the Crusader states. The Crusaders were succeeded by the Mameluks, and then, between the early 16th and mid 19th centuries, by the OTTOMANS. Under the nominal rule of the latter, local power swung between Druze and Christian dynasties, who frequently worked and lived in harmony. In 1861, however, following a period of political anarchy, civil war, and a massacre of Maronites by the Druze, the Christian regions were guaranteed autonomy after French intervention. A French protectorate from 1919 and created a republic in 1926, Lebanon finally gained full independence in 1946 following the withdrawal of French troops.

*❝ [The Laz are] tall, robust daredevils from the Black Sea coast ... each carries an abundant supply of daggers and revolvers. ❞*

*Daily Mail,* 1923

The Lebanese take their name from the Mount Lebanon range. Most of the present-day population is descended from a mixture of indigenous peoples and those who have conquered and settled in the area throughout history. The vast majority are Arabs, 12% are PALESTINIANS, 7% are Druze, and 6% ARMENIANS. In terms of religion, 21% are Sunni, 34% Shi'ite, 37% Christian and 7% Druze. While Arabic is the official language of Lebanon, French, English and Armenian are also spoken.

Lebanese culture reflects the cosmopolitan history of the area; traditional Arab/Islamic forms are common, particularly in country districts, and these have enjoyed something of a revival since the 1970s. Western culture is also very popular, particularly among the Christian population and in the towns and cities – 89% of Lebanese people live an urban lifestyle. Trading contacts have also led to the inflow of Western cultural styles, particularly in the areas of art and architecture. Some of the finest Arabic literature of the 19th and early 20th centuries was produced by Lebanese writers of Christian origin.

Ultimately, though, Lebanon is an artificial construct. The area was originally detached from Syria in order to facilitate French administrative control, and much of the country's post-independence history has been dominated by the differing political and religious aspirations of its citizens. Some have wanted reunification with Syria, thus negating the possibility that they see themselves as, primarily, Lebanese. Religious conflicts have also frequently undermined national unity. Certainly, until the mid-1970s, the minority Christian (Maronite) community tended to dominate the country both politically and economically, a legacy of French control, and much of this element would certainly consider itself to be 'Lebanese'. The Muslim community is much more divided: the Sunni, Shi'ite, Palestinian and Druze all have their own political agendas, in-fighting has been frequent, and many would reject the label 'Lebanese'. During the periods 1958–60 and 1975–90 civil war between Christians and Muslims, stimulated by economic inequalities as much as religious differences, severely hampered the political, social and economic development of the country. During the later conflict much of the banking and financial infrastructure of Lebanon was destroyed, crippling the country economically.

**Lebanese**

*Lebanon has long-established communities of Christians and both major branches of Islam, including the influential Druze.*

### Lebanon today

Today, the Christian, Muslim and Druze communities continue to occupy, for the most part, separate areas of the country. The terrain does not lend itself easily to integration. Traditionally, the Christians and Druze have dominated the Lebanon Mountains, while the Sunnis and Shi'ites have occupied the southern plain and the Bekaa Valley. Migrations since the civil wars have accentuated these divisions, and the city of Beirut remains largely split between Christian and Muslim areas. The Palestinians, who migrated into Lebanon in large numbers following the establishment of the state of Israel, have also used the region as a base of operations against the ISRAELIS. This led the latter to invade

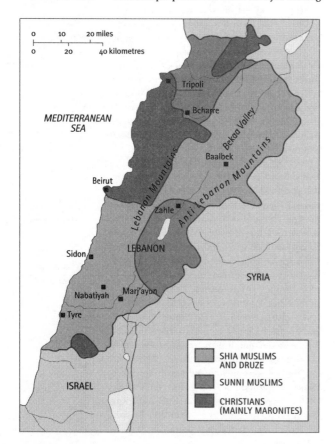

SHIA MUSLIMS AND DRUZE

SUNNI MUSLIMS

CHRISTIANS (MAINLY MARONITES)

and occupy large areas of Lebanon, most notably in 1982. In recent years, the IRANIAN-backed Hezbollah have also used Lebanese bases to attack Israel, stimulating Israeli counter-attacks, and they continue to dominate areas of the south. A United Nations force now patrols the Israeli–Lebanese border. The SYRIANS also invaded Lebanon during the civil wars, and a Syrian military presence remains today.

Since the 1990s, Lebanon has been a far more stable country internally, and the process of rebuilding continues. Under the present constitution (1990), the president must be Maronite, the prime minister Sunni, and the Speaker of the Assembly Shi'ite. It remains to be seen, however, if a fully unified Lebanese nation can be established; to date, there are no political parties, and religious factionalism remains the key element in political alignments.

## LEPCHAS or Rong

A Tibetan-speaking people regarded as the indigenous inhabitants of the north Indian Himalayan state of Sikkim and the Darjeeling area of West Bengal to the south. They are thought to number around 40,000, with a further 15,000 or so living in western Bhutan. They are organized into patrilineal clans and mostly pursue a mixed agricultural and pastoral existence in the mountain valleys. The Lepchas appear to have absorbed other early peoples of the region, but have been reduced to a minority by the BHUTIA from Tibet since the 14th century and by the current majority NEPALESE. The Bhutia were the agents of their conversion to Tibetan Buddhism, which overlies their ancient shamanic religion.

## LEZGIS

A Caucasian people of southeast Dagestan and northern Azerbaijan. Traditionally herders who speak a North Caucasian language, they adopted Sunni Islam by the 16th century. Soviet collectivization and educational policies undermined their traditional culture, and they faced very strong assimilatory pressures. Many were pressed to register as AZERIS. Since the USSR's collapse their partition has become a great issue.

They want unity to protect their cultural and political rights, and in 1990 they formed the political party Sadval (unity), to press for this. In response, the Russian and Azeri governments each sponsored their own political organizations, pressing for the Lezgis to come fully within their territory. In 1996 they numbered over 450,000.

## LULLUBIANS

An ancient nomadic people who inhabited the Zagros Mountains of western Iran. They are recorded as raiding, as well as trading with, the AKKADIAN empire. Nothing is known of their ethnic origins, language or culture. They were eventually overrun and absorbed by the ELAMITES.

## LURS

A nomadic mountain people of western Iran and eastern Iraq. The present day Lurs are probably descended from native peoples mixed with IRANIANS and ARABS. They speak Luri, a language closely related to Farsi (Persian). Occupying an area known traditionally as Luristan (Land of the Lurs), the native inhabitants of the region were incorporated into the area controlled by the ELAMITES, and later became subject to the MEDES, CIMMERIANS, SCYTHIANS, PERSIANS, MACEDONIANS, SELEUCIDS, PARTHIANS, and Sassanians. Their subsequent history parallels that of the Iranians, although some regions of Luristan were semi-autonomous, particularly between the 12th and 17th centuries. Although originally a nomadic people, many, encouraged by central governments, have chosen to adopt a more sedentary lifestyle since the beginning of the 20th century. Some, however, have remained nomadic or pursue a semi-nomadic existence similar to the BEDOUIN.

Lur culture mirrors that of other nomadic tribes in this region of Western Asia such as the KURDS and the BAKHTYARI, but much of their traditional culture has been eroded by the retreat from nomadism. Perhaps the most well-known artworks from the region are the Luristan Bronzes, which were produced around 1200–600 BC. Displaying a mixture of artistic influences, principally MESOPOTAMIAN and Iranian, these items have been found in nomadic burial sites and were perhaps produced by or for tribesmen migrating south from the Caucasus.

The Lurs are Shi'ite Muslims, and played an active role in the Islamic Revolution in Iran. In Iran, most would identify themselves as both Lur and Iranian. The relatively small number living in Sunni Iraq, however, share a position similar to that of the Kurds, and have resisted integration with the IRAQIS.

## LUSHAI

See MIZOS.

## LUWIANS

An INDO-EUROPEAN people of unknown origin who had migrated to southwestern Anatolia (modern Turkey), to an area known to the HITTITES as Arzawa, by the mid-18th century BC.

The Luwians are first mentioned by the Hittites, to whom they were related, in the 16th century BC, and it is probable that they played an active part in the destruction of the Hittite empire. Following this, many Luwians migrated eastwards, and were subsequently cut off from southwestern Anatolia by the arrival of the PHRYGIANS, who crossed into Anatolia from Thrace. The Luwians subsequently formed the principal political and cultural elements in the emergent Neo-Hittite city-states of southeastern Anatolia and northern Syria, for example at Carchemish, Milid, Aleppo and Hamath. The lack of political unity between these states, however, left them vulnerable to attack, and during the 10th century BC a number were overrun by the ARAMAEANS. Over the next two centuries, the region was frequently threatened by the expanding ASSYRIAN empire, and during the 8th century by the URARTIANS. By 708 BC, however, all the Neo-Hittite states had been absorbed by the Assyrians.

Prior to the 12th century BC, Luwian culture displays marked similarities with that of the Hittites and, through them, with that of the HURRIANS. For example, their gods were almost identical, their languages were from the same INDO-EUROPEAN group and Luwian hieroglyphs were used on Hittite seals as early as the 18th

century BC. Following the collapse of the Hittite empire, however, traditional Hittite forms were superseded by a number of disparate elements. For example, the new importance of the city of Carchemish led to the adoption of the local deity, Kubaba, as the principal god of the Neo-Hittite states. In addition, increased contact with the Aramaeans and Assyrians led to the mixing of their cultural influences with Luwian/Hittite forms, and the art produced by the Neo-Hittites was heavily influenced by MESOPOTAMIAN temporal forms. This is not to say that traditional Hittite culture was no longer important: local rulers appear to have remained attached to their Hittite inheritance and were frequently named after the more famous kings of the Hittite golden age. During the Neo-Hittite period, however, Luwian hieroglyphics became the principal medium for administrative and epigraphic purposes, and were used until the 8th century BC.

Following the collapse of the Neo-Hittite city-states, the Luwian language, writing system, and culture survived in southwestern Anatolia with the Lycians and western CILICIANS, who were descended from those Luwians who had not migrated eastwards following the collapse of the Hittite empire. It is possible to see Luwian influence in the linguistic development of the GREEKS. Certainly, both the Phrygian and LYDIAN languages were related to Luwian.

## LYDIANS

An INDO-EUROPEAN people who occupied the coastal area of southwestern Anatolia (modern Turkey), formerly known as Arzawa, and who briefly created an Anatolian empire that stretched to the River Halys. Their capital lay at the city of Sardis.

It is probable that the Lydians were the descendants of indigenous Anatolian peoples and HITTITES who migrated west following the destruction of their empire and subsequently gained control of the area. The Lydian language was related to the central Hittite dialect of the LUWIANS. The Lydians gained control of their empire between the 7th and mid-5th centuries BC, taking advantage of the destruction of the PHRYGIANS and the later collapse of the ASSYRIAN empire. They were only prevented from further eastward expansion by a clash with the growing Median empire (see MEDES), in 585 BC. A frontier was subsequently established on the River Halys. Further south, the Lydians gained hegemony over the Greek colonies of the Anatolian coast, including the PAMPHYLIANS and CARIANS. They were not, however, effective imperial administrators. Their rule was informal and the regions never fully unified. As a result their empire was shortlived and fell victim to PERSIAN expansion in 547 BC. They were subsequently controlled by the SELEUCIDS and ROMANS.

GREEK, Anatolian and MESOPOTAMIAN cultures all influenced the Lydians. The Lydian alphabet was partially derived from the Greek, and a number of Lydian kings are known to have honoured Greek shrines in Ephesus, Delphi and Miletus. The Lydians were highly regarded as a commercial people: they controlled a number of important trade routes and had extensive trade links with the Greek world and Mesopotamia. The Lydians are reputed to have been the first to coin money, in about 600 BC, and this innovation subsequently spread to the Greeks. The Ionian Greeks were also influenced by Lydian commerce and culture. Lydian kings were famed for their wealth, and this must have acted as a powerful stimulus to the Persians. Following the Persian conquest, the Lydians gradually lost their cultural and ethnic identity. It has been claimed that the ETRUSCANS were of Lydian descent, but this is unlikely.

## MAGARS or Mangars

A NEPALESE people of Central Asian origin who moved into Nepal via Assam and speak their own related Tibeto-Burman languages. They are one of the ethnic groups contributing to the GURKHA regiments of the British, Indian and Nepalese armies. They are concentrated in the western area of the Dhaulagiri Mountains in north-central Nepal, part of the great Himalayan range that has influenced the cultural development of the region to the extent that the northern Magars are predominantly Lama Buddhist and the southerners Hindu. They are largely an agricultural people and are estimated to number 1.8 million.

## MAHRA

An ARAB people of the southern Arabian peninsula, possibly of eastern, Australoid racial origin. They speak Mahri, or Mehri, of the South Arabian group of Semitic languages, although Arabic has become more common as a first language. The Mahra people are most numerous in the mountains and coastal plain of southeastern Yemen, including the island of Socotra, where they number around 300,000. Upwards of 100,000 live in adjoining Dhofar province of Oman and a further 20,000 in Saudi Arabia.

The Muslim Mahra are divided into numerous sub-tribal groups and as a people they remain strongly attached to their ancient customs, largely unaffected by modern society. Traditionally, men are noted for wearing a single large ring in the right ear and for their long curly hair; women for their face painting. In ancient times the Mahra were BEDOUINS associated with the trade in locally-produced frankincense transported as far as the Mediterranean by camel. The Mahra were famous for camel breeding, and camels are still an important element of their culture and economy. In the coastal areas in particular, Mahra villagers are occupied in limited agriculture, the rearing of livestock and fishing. The Mahra Sultanate of Quishn and Socotra was an important state before the arrival of Europeans and became a British protectorate from the 1880s until 1967, when it was incorporated into independent Yemen.

## MAHRATTAS

See MARATHAS.

## MALAYALI

A DRAVIDIAN Malayalam-speaking people of Kerala (until 1956 Travancore-Cochin, capital Trivandrum) on the Malabar coast of southwest India. Most of the Malayali are cultivators and live in the densely-populated countryside, especially along the coastal plain, numbering in the region of 30 million (1991), with another 10 million living predominately in southern India.

The now-predominant Hindu religion accompanied INDO-ARYAN migrants to the

*"The possibility ... that the predecessors of the Greeks were Luvians from western Asia Minor."*

L.R. Palmer, 1961, referring to the Luwians

Kingdom of Keralaputra from the late 1st millennium BC. Historically, various syncretic religious beliefs and faiths have coexisted harmoniously among the Malayali, including Islam, brought by Indian Ocean traders in the 8th century AD, and Christianity, first brought to Calicut (Kozhikode) by the Portuguese in 1498. These and later European influences have contributed to the rich Malayali architectural and cultural inheritance.

Malayalam has a long and distinguished literary and musical tradition dating from the early 13th century. Kerala enjoys exceptionally high levels of officially-measured literacy and is also noted for the matrilineal pattern of property inheritance among its Nayar community.

## MALDIVE ISLANDERS

The people of the Maldive Republic (capital, Male), an archipelago of more than 1300 islands and outcrops that lie in the Indian Ocean southwest of the Indian subcontinent. The inhabitants number around 300,000 and inhabit several hundred of these islands. Predominantly ethnically SINHALESE (from Sri Lanka) and DRAVIDIAN (from southern India), they speak an INDO-ARYAN language called Drivehi (or simply Maldivian). They appear to have settled in the islands as early as 2500 years ago. Their original Buddhist religion was superseded by Islam brought by Arab traders in the 12th century.

The Maldives have been an integral part of the Indian Ocean trading network over the centuries, and traders from many parts of the East – China, Indonesia, Malaya, Madagascar and East Africa – have alighted here, contributing to the islanders' ethnic mix. Originally the islands formed part of the Sultanate of the Maldives, ruled from time to time by sultanas as well as sultans in a society in which women have traditionally had greater freedom than elsewhere in the region. The Maldives became independent of Britain in 1965 and later became a republic. Their economy is based largely on fishing, related maritime services and tourism.

## MANIPURIS

See MEITHEIS.

*“The inhabitants of the Maldives are all Muslims, pious and upright ... they are unused to fighting and their armour is prayer.”*

Ibn Battuta,
14th century

## MANNAEANS

Inhabitants of the ancient kingdom of Mana, situated in northwestern Iran, who may have spoken a HURRIAN language. They are first mentioned by the ASSYRIANS during the mid-9th century BC. Attacked frequently by the Assyrians, they were finally destroyed and assimilated by Median (see MEDES) and SCYTHIAN peoples who migrated to the region during the 7th century BC. Almost nothing is known of their society, history or culture.

## MANSI

A northwestern Siberian people of the Khanty-Mansi national *okrug* (district). Their culture and experiences were very similar to the those of KHANTY. Soviet collectivization in the case of the Mansi was perhaps more brutal, but their dense marshlands provided some protection from outside interference until they were found to contain oil in the 1960s. The resulting exploitation had a shattering cultural impact and left their environment devastated. Their Finno-Ugric language and indeed their survival are now seriously endangered. In 1990 they numbered about 7000.

## MARATHAS or Mahrattas

A people of west-central India who inhabit the state of Maharashtra, created in 1960 based on the geographical spread of the Marathi-speaking people. The name of the capital, Bombay, was changed to Mumbai in 1998 on the insistence of the Shiv Sena, a regional militant Hindu political organization. The name Maharashtra was first recorded in the 7th century AD, and it is thought to derive from words describing a fighting force of charioteers. The state forms a triangular swathe of territory extending 725 km / 450 miles down the west coast and inland across a large area of the Deccan plateau. Pune (Poona) in the Western Ghats, formerly the seasonal resort and administrative centre of the Bombay Presidency, is the Maratha cultural capital.

Marathi is an INDO-ARYAN language associated with ancestral Marathas who migrated into the region from the north and absorbed both local peoples and later arrivals. The region was divided politically into various warring Hindu kingdoms which, from the 14th century, were ruled by Muslim dynasties. Their anarchy was ended by the Hindu champion Sivaji Bhonsle in the 17th century, who founded a centralized Maratha kingdom. The following century it expanded as a confederation of Maratha states and threatened to usurp the MUGHAL empire based at Delhi, which fell to the Marathas in 1785. Their policy of raids and exactions, however, and the activities of the plundering Pindari horsemen, created great hostility and an eventual clash with Britain in three wars (1775–82, 1803–5 and 1817–18) which led to the absorption of Maharashtra into the British Raj.

Historically, the region's farmers and peasantry have been regarded as warrior champions of Hinduism. The Maratha remain overwhelmingly Hindu, and around two-thirds are still cultivators, despite the high rate of industrialization and development in Maharashtra. Within the Maratha community the name itself can refer specifically to the dominant Maratha caste or the group of Maratha and Kunbi castes, which are sub-divided into regional groupings and their constituent clans.

The total Marathi-speaking population today is around 75 million. The language, which emerged by the 8th century AD from Maharastri Prakit, and was later influenced by court Persian, is now the official state language, spoken by more than 90% of the population of Maharashtra. Its literary tradition is a distinguished element of Maratha culture and has helped to nurture a wider Maratha identity that has been historically absent even in the period of political unification and empire in the 16th and 17th centuries. Maharashtra has a greater sense of cultural unity reflected in music, the performing arts, architecture and the visual arts, the early development of which can be seen in the sculpture and paintings of the rock-cut temples and caves of Ellora and Ajanta (early 1st millennium AD) and Elephanta Island near Bombay (8th–9th centuries AD).

## MARMA or Magh or Mogh

A MONGOLOID people of the Chittagong Hill Tracts of southeastern Bangladesh. The Marma numbered approximately 32,000 in the late 20th century. They are split into two groups: the Jhumia Marma, who have inhabited the region since early historical times, and the Rakhaing Marma, who migrated from Arakan in the 18th century after its conquest by the BURMESE.

Most of the Marma were assimilated to Bengali language and culture by the 20th century, but in areas close to the border with Burma (Myanmar) they speak a RAKHINE dialect of Burmese and are largely Burmese in culture. Rakhine-speaking Marma follow Buddhism and traditional animistic religions.

The Marma practice shifting cultivation and live in villages of up to around 50 households. Traditional Marma society was based on endogamous clans, but this system is in decline and clan chiefs do not exercise the same authority as they used to do.

## MARONITES

Adherents of a Christian sect that originated in northern Syria during the late 4th century AD. Their name is derived from St Maron, a 4th-century SYRIAN hermit, and St John Maron, a patriarch of Antioch (Antakya) who won their freedom from the BYZANTINES in 684. They are Roman Catholics but follow the Eastern rites of that church, and have, at times, played a very influential part in the political development of northern Syria and the Levant.

Today it is estimated that there are about 1.3 million Maronites worldwide, with many residing in Europe, the Americas, Israel and Cyprus. The Maronites were, initially, Monothelites, but were reconciled with the Church of Rome during the 12th century.

Following their persecution in northern Syria, many Maronites migrated to Mount Lebanon during the 7th century, and have retained a strong presence in the region to the present day. Most now see Lebanon as their homeland and have tenaciously held onto their religious and cultural heritage, despite living in a predominantly Islamic and ARAB region.

Subsequent to the foundation of the Crusader states in the 12th century, the Maronites played a leading part in the political history of the Levant. Later, under nominal OTTOMAN rule, they also provided a ruling dynasty for the region. For the most part they have tended to live in peace with their Islamic neighbours. During the late 1850s, however, serious conflicts broke out between the Maronites and the DRUZE, which culminated in the massacre of thousands of Maronites in 1860. Large numbers then emigrated from the region. In the wake of French intervention, an autonomous Maronite enclave was created, and since full LEBANESE independence in 1946, the Maronites have played a leading role in the government of Lebanon. They have frequently clashed with Lebanese and Palestinian Muslims, however, particularly during the civil wars of 1958–60 and 1975–90.

The Maronites are now an Arabic-speaking people, although for their religious liturgy they retain the West Syriac language. They were responsible for some of the finest Arabic literature produced during the 19th and early 20th centuries. After the Pope, the Maronites recognize the Patriarch of Antioch as their religious leader. In addition to their Maronite and Arabic cultural inheritance, many modern Maronites have been heavily influenced by Western cultural traditions, introduced through long-standing Mediterranean trading links as well as FRENCH influence in the Levant over the last 300 years.

## MATORS

A southern Siberian people of the Lake Baikal area. As RUSSIAN settlers flooded into their lands in the 18th century, they became increasingly assimilated, and disappeared as a distinct people by the 1840s.

## MAZANDARANIS

A people who inhabit the province of Mazdaran in northern Iran. Together with the Gilakis, they represent about 8% of the modern IRANIAN population. The present Mazandaranis are predominantly ethnically Iranian, but there are also a number of Mazandaranis descended from peoples who migrated to the region throughout history, including TURKMEN, AFGHANS, RUSSIANS, ARMENIANS, Qadikolahi, Palavi, Qajars, KURDS and BANGLADESHIS.

The Mazandaranis identify themselves as Iranians, and they speak their own dialect of Farsi (Persian). Although they are traditionally nomadic, many during the 20th century have abandoned this lifestyle in order to pursue farming, particularly following Iranian agricultural reforms since the 1970s. Many others have settled in towns in order to work in the major industrial enterprises that have grown in the region over the course of the last 40 years; this phenomenon has also led to an inflow of migrant workers into the area. Some, however, do adhere to a traditional nomadic BEDOUIN-like existence, and the Mazandaranis are still highly regarded for the quality of the horses they breed. The Mazandaranis are Shi'ite Muslims, and their culture is essentially Iranian and Islamic.

## MEDES

An INDO-IRANIAN people who migrated from Central Asia to the Zagros Mountains during the mid-2nd millennium BC and further west onto the Iranian plateau by the 9th century BC. The Median kings succeeded in creating an impressive empire that stretched from the Persian Gulf to the River Halys between the late 7th and mid-6th centuries BC. The Medes were closely related to the PERSIANS, and the aristocracy of these two peoples frequently inter-married.

On their arrival in the Zagros Mountains, the Medes were not a unified people; rather they comprised numerous disparate tribes, each following a recognized chief. The first mention of a people living in the Land of 'Mada' comes from records preserved from the reign of the ASSYRIAN king Shalmaneser III (ruled 858–824 BC); the people were henceforth referred to as Medes. The unification of the Median tribes was accomplished during the late 8th or early 7th century BC, and was almost certainly stimulated by successful attacks by the Assyrians, who may have feared the rapid spread of the Medes into western Iran. Following their unification, a new 'national' capital was founded at Ecbatana (Hamadan), and the Medes were more successful against the Assyrians, but were subsequently attacked by the SCYTHIANS. Under King Cyaxares (ruled 625–585 BC), however, the Medes were able to overcome the Scythians, extend their dominance over the Persians and MANNAEANS, and launch an offensive against the Assyrians, culminating in the destruction of Nineveh in 612 BC, achieved in alliance with the BABYLONIANS. Following their defeat of the Assyrians, the Medes extended their empire to the banks of the River Halys in eastern Anatolia (where they conquered the URARTIANS), a boundary established following a clash with the westward-expanding LYDIANS. The Median tribes, however, were never fully unified, and by the mid-6th century BC rifts were developing within the aristocracy. These, in part, facilitated the Persian conquest of Media by Cyrus the Great in 550 BC.

Almost nothing is known of Median culture, as they have left no written records, and comparatively little archaeological evidence has been uncovered. It is known that their art was essentially Assyrian in form, and that their religion was polytheistic. The Magi, a priestly caste, were highly regarded within Median society. Following their conquest by the Persians the term 'Mede' tended to be used interchangeably with 'Persian'. Although the term 'Median' faded from use, Medians continued to be employed in positions of great influence by the Persian kings, and Persian kingship was based on that of the Medes. Following the MACEDONIAN conquest, the Medes became fully assimilated into the wider Iranian population.

## MEITHEIS or Manipuris

A people of the northeast Indian state of Manipur (created 1972, capital Imphal), a name which means 'land of gems'. The Meitheis form between one half and two-thirds of the population, estimated at nearly 2 million in 1991. They are concentrated in the Manipur River valley and are overwhelmingly (high-caste) Hindu, a major distinction from neighbouring hill tribes such as the MIZO and NAGA with whom they share Indo-MONGOLOID ethnicity and related Tibeto-Burman languages. The Meithei language is known as Manipuri. The Meitheis, although they have absorbed adjoining hill peoples, also form a more coherent ethnic group, encouraged by exogamous marriage outside the numerous clans that form the basis of their society. The Meithei economy is based on rice-growing, and women have an important role in trading food and the products of cottage industries. The Meitheis' rich and varied culture has given rise to the Manipuri style of classical dance, and they have a particular liking for polo.

## MEOS

A PAKISTANI people concentrated in the northeast of the province of Punjab, not to be confused with the Chinese Meo, more commonly known as Miao or HMONG. They form a branch of the Mina people (also confusingly referred to as Meo or Mewati), claiming Rajput descent, who are found in the Indian provinces of Rajastan and Punjab. Whereas the Meos converted to Islam in the 11th century, the Mina have remained Hindu. Despite this major difference, they retain many similarities in terms of social organization, notably their division into clans, each under the leadership of a headman (*muqaddam*) and council (*panch*), and the tripartite class system of watchmen, farmers and landlords, which reflects their modern agricultural way of life, quite different from their martial, nomadic and pastoral origins. The Meos number upwards of 300,000, roughly a quarter of the size of the Mina population.

## MESOPOTAMIANS

A term commonly used to denote collectively the various ancient peoples who have lived in the geographical region of Mesopotamia, between the Tigris and Euphrates rivers in modern Iraq. These include the SUMERIANS, AKKADIANS, BABYLONIANS and ASSYRIANS. However, very few people (if any) throughout history would have considered themselves to be first and foremost 'Mesopotamian'.

## MIDIANITES or Ishmaelites

An ancient nomadic people who appear to have originated in the Arabian Desert and Transjordan; they are known only from passages in the Old Testament and Koran. They fought frequent wars with the Israelites (see JEWS), sometimes in league with other tribes such as the AMALEKITES. They are also known, however, to have forged marriage alliances with the Israelites, and the god Yahweh, later revered by the Israelites, was originally a Midianite deity.

## MINAEANS

The inhabitants of the ancient kingdom of Mina, in southern Arabia, which flourished between the 4th and 2nd centuries BC. Originally nomads, they became a trading and commercial people. They were ultimately destroyed by the SABAEANS and thereafter faded from history as a distinct people.

## MINGRELIANS

A KARTVELIAN people who live in the northwest of the Republic of Georgia. The size of the Mingrelian population is uncertain, as they are officially regarded as GEORGIANS, and not all Mingrelians actually speak the Mingrelian language. Most estimates are in the region of 1 million people. The majority of Mingrelians are Orthodox Christians.

## MISHMI

A tribal people of the northeast Indian state of Arunachal Pradesh, living in the high Mishmi Hills of the Himalayan mountain chain bordering Assam and Tibet. They are divided into three sub-tribes: the Idu, Digaru and Miju. The Mishmi are of Central Asian origin, number around 32,000 and speak Mishmi dialects of the Tibeto-Burman language family.

Historically, the Mishmi were part of the unsettled uplands where feuding, headhunting and slave capture were commonplace. They practise simple shifting agriculture on the terraced slopes and valley floors, raise cattle, hunt and fish and exploit other products of the region which form the basis of their extensive trading activities. They also possess a range of textile and craft-working skills.

The Mishmi live in family groups, without chiefs, and adhere to traditional Bon, Tibetan Buddhist and Hindu religious beliefs.

## MITANNI

The people of an ancient kingdom encompassing northern Mesopotamia and Syria, who supplanted the HURRIANS and established a substantial, but shortlived, empire during the late 15th century BC stretching from Nineveh to the Mediterranean coast. The majority of the population of Mitanni remained Hurrian, but they were ruled by a new INDO-IRANIAN aristocracy who had migrated into the region during the 17th century BC. It is probably these people who should be regarded as essentially Mitannian. Originally nomads from Central Asia, these new arrivals subsequently gained political and social ascendancy in the region, and reunited the Hurrians into an effective imperialist power under the leadership of a new warrior elite. The capital of the new kingdom lay at Washukanni. For a short time, the Mitanni were the political equals of the EGYPTIANS, with whom they forged marriage alliances, the HITTITES and the ASSYRIANS. Between the mid-14th and early 13th centuries BC, however, the empire of the Mitanni fell apart due to internal discord and Hittite aggression. The western portion fell to the Hittites, while the eastern portion was subsequently annexed by the Assyrians, around 1270 BC.

Very little is known of the culture of the Mitanni, as few of their records have survived. Certainly, their culture was heavily influenced by the Hurrians, and it is known that the social system was based on a form of feudalism. The position of their kingdom meant that they controlled a number of important trade routes, and the Mitannian aristocracy grew very wealthy. As a result, a number of kings were able to build impressive palaces designed to reflect their own magnificence. In addition to the Hurrian pantheon, the Indo-Iranians also introduced some of their own deities to the region: Varuna, Mitra and Indra, for example, were all worshipped by the Mitanni. As in other areas to which they migrated, they also introduced improved horse breeds, more effective cavalry and the lightweight chariot – innovations that influenced the development of Mesopotamian and Anatolian military tactics. Following their defeat, the Mitanni became fully assimilated with the populations of Mesopotamia, Syria and the Levant.

# MIZOS or Lushai

One of the many agricultural hill peoples of northeastern India, mostly inhabiting the state of Mizoram ('land of the highlanders', capital Aizawl) in the Mizo Hills (formerly Lushai Hills). They are estimated to number around 700,000 and, like the neighbouring Manipuris to the north (see MEITHEIS), exploit the extensive forests. The Mizos emerged from the assimilation of local peoples by tribes from the easterly Chin Hills who conquered the region in the century after 1750. Wars and feuds were endemic and accompanied by the practice of headhunting. War captives were reduced to the status of slaves in hierarchical village societies, of which there were several hundred, each independent and led by a hereditary chief.

The Mizos speak several Tibeto-Burman dialects, reflecting their varied ethnicity and development in different remote uplands. The area was brought under more peaceful BRITISH control during the late 19th century, and missionaries began work converting the largely Hindu population, so that 80% of the Mizos today are Christians (mostly Protestant). They were also very receptive to missionary education, and the Mizos remain highly literate. The state of Mizoram was created in 1987, following a guerrilla campaign, to satisfy Mizo nationalist sentiment.

# MOABITES

A Semitic people (see SEMITES) who settled in the highland regions east of the Dead Sea around the 14th century BC. Principal cities of this region, which now forms part of the modern Kingdom of Jordan, included Karak and Dhiban. The Moabites were closely related to both the AMMONITES and the Israelites (see JEWS), and their aristocracy is known to have inter-married with that of the Israelites. Their name is derived from Moab, the son of Lot, from whom the tribe was said to be descended.

The Old Testament mentions wars between the Moabites and the Israelites, and the two clashed frequently from the 13th century BC. The Moabites were certainly conquered by King David, becoming Israelite vassals. They regained

their independence, however, in 843 BC, after which they continued to attack their Hebrew neighbours. The Moabites lost their independence in the 8th century BC, when they were overrun by the ASSYRIANS. It was their conquest by the BABYLONIANS, however, in about 582 BC, and later by the PERSIANS, that appears to have led to the destruction of the Moabites' ethnic and cultural identities.

Comparatively little is known of Moabite culture, and very few written records have been recovered. Essentially, however, it was probably very similar to that of the Israelites, and their language was simply a different dialect of Hebrew. The Moabite Stone, produced in the 9th century BC, is the most important surviving text produced by this people, and is written using the CANNANITE alphabet. Their chief deity was Chemosh, and they are also known to have worshipped the sun god Moloch.

# MOGULS

See MUGHALS.

# MONGOLOIDS

A major group of culturally and linguistically diverse peoples which is thought to have originated in eastern Central Asia. The Mongoloids are defined by physical characteristics such as an epicanthic fold (a fold of the skin of the upper eyelid over the inner corner of the eye), straight black hair and a yellowish complexion. The Mongoloids are now the dominant peoples of east Central Asia, northeast Asia, East Asia and parts of Southeast Asia and include the CHINESE, JAPANESE, KOREANS, MONGOLS and TIBETANS.

The NATIVE AMERICANS and INUIT, who are ultimately of northeast Asian origin, are also often considered to be Mongoloids.

# MONGOLS or Mongolians

One of the principal ethnic groups of Central Asia. Today the overwhelming majority of Mongols reside in one of two regions – the Mongolian Autonomous Region of China (formerly known as Inner Mongolia) or the Republic of Mongolia (formerly known as Outer

> *"The Moabite worshipped the physically beautiful."*
>
> G. Matheson, 1903

Mongolia, capital Ulan Bator). There are currently about 5.5 million Mongols: 3 million in China and 2.5 million in Mongolia. The Mongols are first mentioned in Chinese texts dating to the Tang dynasty. Early Mongol peoples included the XIONGNU, HUNS and KHITANS. Traditionally, they were a nomadic pastoral people who migrated, along with their herds of horses, sheep and goats, from region to region in search of fresh pasturelands. Food supplies were augmented through hunting and gathering. Despite modern industrialization, urbanization and the propagation of sedentary agriculture, many Mongols continue to pursue a nomadic existence. In 2002, only 58% of the population of Mongolia lived in urban areas.

Mongol society was, and in many respects still is, tribal, and despite the practice of exogamous marriage, the nomadic lifestyle lent itself neither to pan-tribal unity nor to the promulgation of nationhood. Prior to the early 13th century, inter-tribal warfare was endemic, usually with the outcome that one tribe would gain a temporary political ascendancy over its neighbours, only to be later usurped by a rival clan.

The Mongol tribes were effectively united for the first time under Genghis Khan, in 1206, following a short period of warfare. Thereafter, they went on to conquer, in a relatively short period of time, the largest continuous land empire the world has ever known. At its height, the Mongol empire encompassed China, Central Asia, Mesopotamia, Iran, Tibet, and parts of Korea and Russia. The key to the Mongols' success was their incomparable command of cavalry warfare, speed of manoeuvre, devastating mounted archery and terrifying savagery.

Despite their initial success, however, the unity of the Mongol empire was compromised at a very early stage. Though many regions had efficient bureaucracies based on those of the Chinese and Khitans, the empire soon began to fragment. Following the death of Genghis Khan in 1227, the empire became divided among his successors. Smaller Mongol regions were created, and these became, in effect, entirely independent of the control of the Great Khan, whose domains were centred on China. The empires of the Ilkhans, CHAGATAIDS and GOLDEN HORDE TATARS were all formed during this period.

Moreover, Mongols tended to be gradually assimilated into the culture and society of subject peoples. For example, they converted to Islam in Persia, and to Buddhism in China. Finally, except in cases where geographic conditions allowed the Mongols to continue living a nomadic lifestyle, for instance on the Russian steppes, large numbers settled down in towns and cities or on farms. The result was the loss of the very skills that had allowed them to conquer such an extensive empire, and with this loss they soon began to suffer to military defeat. Both China and the Ilkhanate were lost in 1367.

**The post-imperial Mongols**

Following the collapse of their empire, the Mongols of Central Asia fell once more into disunity, notably among the KHALKHAS and OIRATS, and under the domination of both the RUSSIANS and Chinese. In 1911, Outer Mongolia proclaimed its independence from China, and the Communist People's Republic of Mongolia was formed in this region in 1924. Although technically independent, Mongolia fell under heavy Soviet influence from 1924 to 1991. During this period, the name of Genghis Khan was banned as espousing an outdated notion of nationalism. In addition, many abandoned the Buddhist faith, and today relatively few Mongols espouse any religious beliefs, despite a resurgence in monasticism since 1991. Shamanism may still be widely practised in more remote areas. Since the 19th century, many within the Mongol Autonomous Region of China have abandoned nomadism, and large numbers have assimilated with Chinese culture and society.

Some important Mongol tribes in existence today include the Khalkhas, BURYATS, Urat, Dariganga and DÖRBED. The population of the modern Republic of Mongolia also includes significant numbers of KAZAKHS and Russians, while the Autonomous Region has a large Chinese element. The official language of Mongolia is Mongolian, although Russian is widely known, and Chinese is commonly spoken in the Autonomous Region. The Mongolian language has a literary tradition dating back to the 11th century, and since the end of Russian domination there has been a re-awakening of interest in traditional Mongol culture within Mongolia.

> " [The Mongols] subsist entirely upon flesh and milk ... [they] eat flesh of every description, horses, camels, and even dogs, provided they are fat. "
>
> Marco Polo, 1298

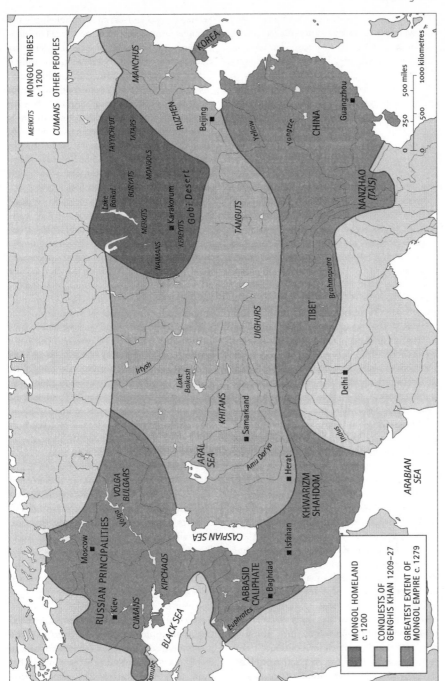

**MONGOL TRIBES c. 1200**

*MERKITS* MONGOL TRIBES
*CUMANS* OTHER PEOPLES

MANCHUS

KOREA

TAYYICHUT

TATARS

RUZHEN

Beijing

Yellow

CHINA

Guangzhou

BURYATS

MONGOLS

Lake
Baikal

MERKITS

■ Karakorum

Gobi Desert

Yangtze

NAIMANS

KEREYITS

Gobi Desert

TANGUTS

NANZHAO
(TAIS)

TIBET

Brahmaputra

Irtysh

UIGHURS

Lake
Balkash

Delhi

KHITANS

Samarkand

ARAL
SEA

Amu Darya

Indus

Herat

ARABIAN
SEA

VOLGA
BULGARS

KHWARIZM
SHAHDOM

Volga

CASPIAN SEA

RUSSIAN PRINCIPALITIES

Moscow

Isfahan

KIPCHAQS

ABBASID
CALIPHATE

■ Baghdad

Kiev

CUMANS

Euphrates

BLACK SEA

Danube

1000 kilometres

500 miles

250

500

0

**MONGOL HOMELAND
c. 1200**

**CONQUESTS OF
GENGHIS KHAN 1209–27**

**GREATEST EXTENT OF
MONGOL EMPIRE c. 1279**

**Mongols**

*At its greatest extent,
the Mongol empire
stretched from Korea to
Central Europe.*

Today, Mongolia remains, economically, one of Asia's poorer nations and is currently making the transition to a free-market economy. Genghis Khan remains a national hero: when the Mongolian government introduced surnames in 2004, 70% of the population chose 'Borjigin', the family name of Genghis Khan (thus rendering the whole exercise pointless).

## MUGHALS or Moghuls or Moguls

The Indian name, from Persian, for the Muslim conquerors of northern India in the early 16th century. The name denotes their Central Asian MONGOL origins which also included PERSIAN and Turkish elements (see TURKS). They combined with the existing Indian Muslim community, whose forebears had also arrived from the north over several centuries and established themselves as the ruling people in Hindustan. Persian remained the language of the court. At its height, the Mughal empire (1526–1857) dominated the Indian subcontinent, ruled from Delhi by a series of very able rulers whose energy and ability survived until the early 18th century. The dynasty was founded by Babur (ruled 1526–30), a dispossessed prince from north of the River Oxus (Amu Darya) descended on his maternal side from Chagatai Khan, second son of the great Mongol ruler Genghis Khan, and on his paternal side from the Turkic conqueror Timur Lang, or Tamerlane (see TIMURIDS), of Samarkand (now in Uzbekistan). The Mughals are sometimes described as Indo-Timurids.

At his death Babur's empire stretched across much of northern India, from the Indus to Bihar in the east, but it was his grandson Akbar (1556–1605), son of Humayun, who became the greatest of the Mughal rulers. He not only expanded the frontiers of the empire but also established a particularly efficient bureaucracy, military organization and political structure. Most of all, he obtained the loyalty of his numerically dominant Hindu subjects by a policy of religious toleration, which was continued by his son Jahangir (1605–27) and grandson Shah Jahan (1628–58). High-ranking Hindus were even taught in Persian-language Muslim schools. Under Aurangzeb (1658–1707) this policy was

reversed, resulting in war and rebellion and oppressive taxation, which contributed to political turmoil throughout the empire. The empire nevertheless reached its furthest geographical extent, incorporating 180 million people, then around 20% of the total world population. Its break-up followed under Muhammad Shah (1719–48) culminating in the capture of Delhi by MARATHA forces in 1785, then by the British in 1803. The ensuing titular emperors lived on in Delhi until the last, Bahadur Shah II (1837–57), was exiled to Burma (Myanmar) for his, largely passive, involvement in the Indian Mutiny.

Mughal wealth, which allowed cultural patronage on a large scale, was based on taxes levied on the Indian peasantry, but there was also growing commercial development and increasing contacts with the rest of the world in the 16th and 17th centuries. Mughal culture absorbed various influences but was essentially a fusion of INDIAN and Perso-Islamic elements, seen in Humayun's tomb built in the reign of Akbar and his new city of Fatehpur Sikri, which flourished 1569–1605. The cultural high point of the Mughal empire was the reign of Shah Jahan, renowned for commissioning the Taj Mahal (c.1634) and many other fine buildings including the Pearl Mosque at Agra and both the Great Mosque and the imperial palace in Delhi. Characteristic features were pierced panelling and *pietre-dure* inlay, which are still a feature of modern Indian decorative arts. Mughal culture is also particularly associated with painted miniatures in the Persian tradition, which often illustrated a remarkably wide-ranging Persian and Hindu literature. This fusion was also evident in crafts such as glass production and textiles, in music and in other aspects of Mughal life which remain an integral part of Indian cultural identity today.

## MUNDAS

A tribal hill people of east-central India. Their origins are unclear, though they were probably more widespread than their modern territory, in the Chota Nagpur plateau in southern Bihar (and adjacent West Bengal and Madhya Pradesh) and Orissa, suggests. This theory is partly supported by their affinity with the MON

> " It is said that the Mundas ... lived peacefully together until the Brahmins reached their country. "

H. Miller, 1854

people of Burma (Myanmar). The Munda were possibly pushed onto the less fertile, forested uplands by other immigrant peoples. They speak a number of Austro-asiatic languages including Santal, Mundari and Ho, but also Oriya and other Indian languages, especially for trade.

Traditionally, the aboriginal Munda hunted and practised a simple form of shifting cultivation, but they are now settled and increasingly employed outside agriculture. They now number more than the 9 million estimated in the late 20th century. They have become increasingly influenced by Hindu culture since Indian independence, but they retain many local religious beliefs, cultural traditions and languages.

## MURMI

See TAMANG.

## MUSHKI or Mushku

A confederation of INDO-EUROPEAN tribes, probably originating in Thrace, who were migrating into central Anatolia from around the Black Sea by the 12th century BC. Allied with the HURRIANS and KASKAS, they were defeated in Anatolia by the ASSYRIANS in 1115 BC and forced westwards. They were the ancestors of the PHRYGIANS and MYSIANS, although the former were frequently identified as Mushki by other peoples of western Asia. The Mushki were a nomadic people who left no records of their culture or society.

## MYSIANS

An INDO-EUROPEAN people, descended from the MUSHKI, who had settled in northwestern Anatolia (in modern Turkey) by the 8th century BC. During the 6th century BC they became subjects of the LYDIANS and were conquered in turn by the PERSIANS and MACEDONIANS. They were incorporated into the Kingdom of Pergamum during the 3rd century BC, and the term 'Mysian' was eventually replaced by 'Pergamene'. By the time of their annexation by the ROMANS in 133 BC, the Mysians had lost most of their cultural and ethnic identity. They were related to the CARIANS, PHRYGIANS and Lydians, with all of whom they shared a common culture.

## NABATAEANS

An ancient Semitic people (see SEMITES) who originated in the northern Hejaz in the Arabian peninsula. They are first recorded as living in this region by the ASSYRIANS. During the 7th century BC the Nabataeans migrated north and west into the land of Edom (in modern Jordan), displacing the EDOMITES, where they settled and established a new kingdom centred on a capital at Petra. By exploiting the valuable caravan routes between Arabia, the Levant and Egypt, the Nabataeans became a very wealthy commercial people. Between the 1st century BC and the 1st century AD they overran large areas north and west of Nabataea, including Lebanon, Damascus and Palestine to the Red Sea. During these conquests they defeated the MOABITES. They were in turn defeated by the ROMANS in 63 BC and subsequently became vassals of the Roman empire. The area was finally annexed by the emperor Trajan in AD 105, and the capital of the new Roman province was moved to Bostra. By the 3rd century AD the region's economic strength was being sapped by the rise of Palmyra. Following the Roman occupation, the Nabataeans faded from history and, by the time of the Islamic conquest in the 630s AD, they had lost their ethnic identity, having become part of the wider ARAB community. The last datable Nabataean text is from AD 356.

Very little is known of early Nabataean culture and society, but following their exploitation of the caravan routes they became prolific and impressive builders. No doubt owing to these trading contacts, but also because of the presence of Greek colonies in the region, a number of differing cultures influenced the Nabataeans, particularly those of the GREEKS, Romans and PARTHIANS. This influence is displayed in the fine art, architecture and pottery produced in the region, for example the designs on the rock-cut temples of Petra. In addition, the Nabataean pantheon was very Hellenistic in character; their chief deity was du-Shara (Ruda), but also important were al-'Uzza, equated with both Venus and Aphrodite, and Kutba (al-Aktab), a Nabataean version of Mercury. Although originally nomadic, the Nabataeans became very skilled agriculturists and converted large areas of the

n

Negev Desert into fertile land through terracing and improved water-storage techniques. The Nabataeans spoke the Aramaic language, and devised an alphabet based on that of the CANAANITES, which became the precursor of the Arabic alphabet of the Koran.

## NAGA

A diverse agricultural people who also fish and exploit the forests of the Naga Hills region of northeast India and neighbouring Burma (Myanmar). Most live in the Indian state of Nagaland (capital Kohima), established in 1963 in response to strong Naga demands for autonomy, but also in Manipur (see MEITHEIS) and elsewhere.

Though they are traditionally animists, two-thirds of the Naga are now Christian as a result of 19th-century British missionary activity and in the 20th-century links to North American Baptist Missions. Such was the strength and extent of Christianization in Nagaland that, after Indian independence in 1947, many Naga feared domination by Hindus. Armed nationalist Naga rebels remain active and Kohima is still under martial law.

The inaccessible mountain terrain of Nagaland has divided its people into more than 20 tribes, originally given to warring and headhunting until gradually pacified by Britain after 1826. Ethnically they are Indo-Mongoloid but they vary in appearance and custom. They also speak more than 60 main languages, or dialects, of the Tibeto-Burman group, and Nagamese (creolized Assamese), Hindi and English (the official state language) are employed for communication. Traditional administration varies from autocratic chieftainships to democratic councils in which women, who have a position of social equality, are also active. The *morung*, a communal decoratively carved house or dormitory for unmarried men, is a common feature of Naga villages. The population of Nagaland is around 3.5 million.

## NAIMANS

A MONGOL tribe defeated by Genghis Khan in the early 13th century and subsequently broken up.

Some escaped and established a shortlived hegemony over the Karakhitans (see KHITANS) until this too was ended by Genghis Khan. During this period they were converted to Buddhism.

## NANAI or Goldi

A southwestern Siberian people of Khabarovsk region in the Russian Federation, and of northwest China, whose name means 'people of this place'. They are traditionally shamanists and semi-sedentary hunters, fishers and gatherers, but many had adopted agriculture from the CHINESE by the time the RUSSIANS claimed their territory in 1858.

Soviet collectivization and forced settlement damaged their traditional culture, while industrial pollution damaged their environment. Attempts made to recover their culture, for example through theatre groups, have produced results of uncertain authenticity. Their Tungus language is in decline, and environmental degradation continues through potentially disastrous illegal logging. In 2002 they numbered about 13,500 in Russia and in 1990 over 4000 in China.

## NATUFIAN CULTURE

An Epipalaeolithic culture that arose in the Levant and Syria 10,500–8500 BC. Most of the evidence for this culture has been unearthed during excavations at Jericho, Enyan and 'Ain Mallaha. The term 'Natufian' is derived from finds made at Wadi an-Natuf. The Natufians appear to have migrated into the region from the north, and their culture displays humankind's first steps from a nomadic hunter-gatherer lifestyle towards a more sedentary, agricultural way of life. It appears that during this period the Natufians increasingly supplemented their animal-based diet with foodstuffs made from ground wild grains (emmer wheat). At the same time there was a tendency toward a partial abandonment of nomadism and the establishment of settled communities, such as that at Jericho, which was centred on a natural spring. Furthermore, the Natufians are known to have sown wild grains outside their natural habitat, thus creating an early farming culture. Excavations have revealed harvesting knives (with flint blades) and stone mortars and pestles, all bearing testimony to the agricultural activities of the Natufians.

While some Natufians lived in caves, others built small mud-brick round houses, and evidence of a local shrine has been uncovered at Jericho. Alongside a more sedentary lifestyle came the first indications of social stratification, evidenced by the varied quality of grave goods discovered at Natufian burial sites, mainly comprising carvings and ornaments made of stone and bone. Common artistic themes included the human head and animal motifs. It is possible that the Natufians later migrated to the Nile Delta, thus facilitating the spread of early agriculture to Egypt.

## NEGIDALS

A southern Siberian people of Khabarovsk region, Russian Federation; a few also live in North Korea. They call themselves *Elkan*, meaning 'true people'. They were probably EVENKI originally, and when RUSSIANS encountered them in the 17th century they were primarily semi-sedentary hunters, gatherers and herders who spoke a Tungus language.

Under Soviet rule collectivization and forced settlement seriously undermined their traditional culture, while Russian-language boarding education has left their language endangered. Perhaps even worse, in order to better control them, the Soviet authorities forcibly relocated them to mixed Negidal and Russian settlements, further undermining their identity as a distinct people. They are still, however, active in protesting against the environmental damage wrought by industrial pollution, although their long-term survival is doubtful. In 1989 they numbered 587.

## NENETS

A SAMOYED people of the Russian and Siberian Arctic, mainly living in the Nenets national *okrug* (district), in the Russian Federation. Nomadic reindeer-herders, they speak a Uralic language. Their isolation did not protect them from RUSSIAN domination, especially from the 17th century, but it did limit its effectiveness. Although many were forcibly baptized in 1824, they have a long history of risings against Russian rule. Soviet collectivization, assimilatory education policies and forced settlement finally crushed their resistance only in the 1950s. Large-

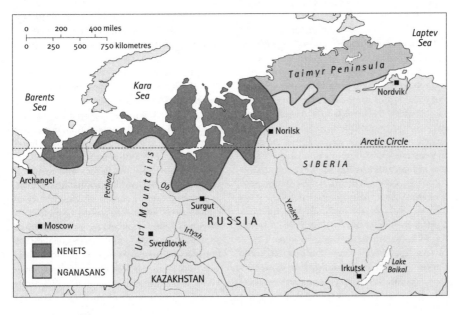

scale Russian immigration and environmental destruction through industrialization and nuclear tests have further undermined their identity and their language, though more so in European Russia than in Siberia. In 1994 they numbered about 27,000.

# NEPALESE

The people of the Kingdom of Nepal (capital Kathmandu), which lies on the southern slopes of the Himalayas between India and Tibetan China and is the world's only official Hindu state. It has been a cultural, ethnic and linguistic melting pot, combining dominant influences from the north and south. INDO-ARYAN peoples penetrating the area from northern India form the majority of the Nepalese population and are today represented by the Tarai, Tharus, NEWAR and the numerous PAHARI. They speak Nepali (Gorkhali), the country's official language, which is descended from Sanskrit, and related dialects. Other, Tibeto-Nepalese, peoples with links to MONGOLOID immigrants from Central Asia include the BHUTIA (and related highland SHERPAS of Nepal and Sikkim), GURUNG, Limbu, MAGARS, Rai, Sanwar and TAMANG. They generally speak a number of languages classified as Tibeto-Burman. Today the total population of Nepal is around 25 million.

Nepalese territory had strong links with the Gangetic Plain both politically and culturally in the 1st millennium BC, which led to the domination of the largely Buddhist country by Indo-Aryan Hindu kings and aristocrats. Their descendants still comprise the leading families of Nepal and the royal family. A unified kingdom emerged under the Licchavi dynasty from around AD 500 which benefited from the developing trade and communications between the Indian sub-continent and Tibet, China and Central Asia to the north. Its fragmentation into numerous small principalities from the 15th century was reversed by the Shah rulers of Gorkha (Gurkha), and in 1769 Prithi Narayan Shah finally unified the country by force. Nevertheless, parochial and familial interests flourished within the administration of the new state, and a fractious and conspiratorial political culture remained a feature of Nepali national life

> 66 In all matters of domestic policy the Nepalese brook no interference. 99
>
> *Encyclopædia Britannica*, 1884

until the mid 20th century. A version of this, in terms of its factionalism, remains with the democratic government system today.

## The modern Nepalese

From the late 18th century a series of expansionist border wars also took place, but with mixed results. British India came to exercise considerable influence over the Nepalese rulers, gaining the right to recruit highly-regarded Gurkha soldiers (from the Gurung, Magar and Rai) to the Indian army at a time when the loyalty of Indian troops was suspect. This recruitment continues into the British army, whose employment provides an additional form of foreign aid to local peoples in a country that remains one of the least developed anywhere in the world. This is partly the result of a policy of isolation, which was only reversed following a nationalist-backed coup in 1950 that restored royal authority and more recent, though faltering, democratization. Parts of Nepal have also been affected by violent Maoist insurgency. The overwhelming majority of the Nepalese still live in small villages and townships, where poverty is widespread. Bonded labour also existed until abolition in 2001, when 36,000 serfs were freed. These factors provided support for the Maoist insurrection, which began in 1996.

In 2001, in an extraordinary bloodbath, the ruling dynasty was shattered when Crown Prince Dipendra murdered nine members of the royal family, including his father King Birendra (ruled since 1972), before committing suicide. Birendra's brother Gyanendra took over the throne, and martial law was quickly introduced to prevent political chaos.

Over the centuries, Hindu influence on the Nepalese has gradually increased, and today approaching 90% of the population is Hindu. Around 8% are Buddhist in the country which is the birthplace of Buddha (Siddharta Gautama), at Lumbini in the south of the country. A remarkable cultural fusion has resulted from these two dominant religions, and the country's temples and material culture reflect their central importance in Nepalese society.

# NEWARS

A NEPALESE people who are small in numbers, with perhaps a population of 850,000, but are particularly prominent in the country's business community, concentrated in the capital, Kathmandu. Others are employed in government posts or farm in the Kathmandu (Nepal) Valley, their indigenous territory. They are the product of an ethnic and cultural mix, reflected in their INDO-ARYAN (north Indian) ancestry and Tibeto-Burman (Indo-European-influenced) Newari language. Most Newars are Hindus, but some are Buddhist, and for many centuries they have been prominent as architects, artists and craftsmen associated with the building of the area's many shrines and temples. Traditionally, craft specializations were the preserve of each of the 70 or so castes that comprise Newar society.

# NGALOPS

See BHUTIA.

# NGANASANS

The northernmost SAMOYED people of the Taimyr peninsula in Siberia, Russian Federation. Nomadic hunters, gatherers and reindeer-herders, they speak a Uralic language. In around 1610 the first RUSSIANS arrived, demanding tribute, but the Nganasans' remoteness protected them from much exploitation until the Soviet period. Under Soviet rule, however, collectivization, compulsory boarding education and forced settlement undermined their traditional culture and shamanist religion. Large-scale assimilation followed. Their reindeer herds were subsequently depleted and their environment suffered immense pollution. The collapse of the USSR left them suffering intense poverty on the fringes of a decaying economy. In 1994 they numbered up to 1300.

# NICOBARESE

The people of the Nicobar Islands in the Bay of Bengal, about 160 km / 100 miles north of the island of Sumatra. The Nicobar Islands came under British rule in 1869, and are now under

INDIAN sovereignty. The population in the late 1990s was around 39,000. The Nicobarese are the descendants of MALAY and BURMESE settlers and speak AUSTRO-ASIATIC languages, known collectively as Nicobarese. Burmese, English and Hindustani are also widely spoken in the islands. The majority of Nicobarese are Hindus, but there are significant Christian and Muslim minorities.

# NISSI

See DAFLA.

# NIVKHI

A southeastern Siberian people of Sakhalin and the Amur River area. Semi-sedentary shamanists and hunters, gatherers and fishers, they speak dialects of Nivkhi. They traded with the CHINESE, who influenced their material culture from the 12th century. Their lands were annexed by Russia in 1858, and they were subsequently (though superficially) Christianized.

Under Soviet collectivization they were forcibly settled and their traditional culture and economy were undermined. They were ordered to abandon fishing for lumbering and farming – a painful demand, as they believed that hurting the earth was monstrously sinful. They were also forced to gather in larger communities, and considerable assimilation followed.

Since the break-up of the USSR they have attempted to recover their traditional culture and revive their seriously endangered language, but their long-term prospects are uncertain. In 1996 they numbered nearly 5000.

# NIZARIS

A sub-sect of the ISMAILIS who formed the core of the Assassins, a movement in Lebanon and northern Iran that believed it was their religious duty to propagate terror against their political enemies. The Nizaris were named after Nizar, brother of the Fatimid caliph al-Mustansir, whom they considered the rightful successor to the caliphate in 1094. The sect continues to exist and is led by their imam, the Aga Khan.

66 The Newars ... worship the frog. 99

Sir James Frazer, 1911

66 The Nicobarese have all they want, yet they like very much to barter with foreigners. 99

F.A. De Roepstorff, 1875

## NURISTANIS

A people of whom the vast majority (about 65,000) live in the Hindu Kush mountains of southern Afghanistan; some 3000 live across the border in Pakistan. Most live in village communities, and gain their livelihood from agriculture (mostly undertaken by the women) and hunting (performed by the men). They speak Western Dardic, an INDO-ARYAN language (see DARDS) and are, at least officially, Sunni Muslims.

Originally known as the KAFFIRS, their name was changed by the AFGHANS following their forced conversion to the Islamic faith in 1895 (Nuristan means 'Land of the Enlightened'). Many Nuristanis would not use this term to describe themselves, nor would they consider themselves to be Afghans. They remain a fiercely independent people, and, despite attempts to assimilate them with the population of Afghanistan, many continue to adhere to their traditional culture and religion.

## OGUZ or Ghuzz

An early loose confederation of at least 24 Turkic tribes (see TURKS) whose homeland lay between the Caspian and Aral seas. During the early 11th century, following a prolonged period of inter-tribal warfare, the Oguz migrated west. Under SELJUK leadership, they subsequently created an impressive empire encompassing much of Iraq, Syria and Anatolia. They are first mentioned in the 8th-century Orhon inscription, the earliest known Turkish writings, discovered in Mongolia in the late 19th century. Today, speakers of the southwestern dialect of Turkic are still referred to as the Oguz.

## OIRATS or Oyrats

A MONGOL tribal confederation, which included the TORGUT, DÖRBED, Khoshut, Olot, DZUNGARS and Buzawa. They are also known as the Western Mongols and were enemies of Genghis Khan in the 13th century. Their name is derived from *dorben oirats*, meaning 'four allies'. More than any other single tribe within the confederation, it was the Dzungars who were usually dominant, and, in a political sense, were the Oirats.

Between the 13th and 18th centuries, the Oirats were frequently at war with the KHALKHAS, TIBETANS, KAZAKHS, CHINESE and MANCHU and, for a brief period in the mid-15th century, they were able to dominate trade through the capture of important trade routes through Tibet. During this period they succeeded in defeating the Chinese and even in capturing a Chinese emperor.

Despite some attempts at achieving cultural unity and nationhood, the Oirats were never successfully united, and this left them vulnerable to attack. They were finally destroyed in 1696 by a combined Manchu and Khalkha force. Following this conflict, many Oirats migrated west to the Volga, where they later became known as the KALMYKS. The remaining Oirats were finally defeated again by the Chinese in 1758, which resulted in their further disintegration, with many moving into Tibet and eastern Mongolia.

Today, members of the Oirats tribes live in southwestern Russia, northern China and the republic of Mongolia. Their culture is Mongol, although those living outside Mongolia have also absorbed many of the cultural aspects of the countries in which they reside. They speak the Oirats dialect of the Mongolian language, and, unlike the Khalkhas, use the traditional Mongolian vertical script. Like their Kalmyk relatives, they are Tibetan Buddhists. Though they are not as politically dominant as the Khalkhas, the Oirats living in the republic of Mongolia are not a separatist people.

## OMANIS

An ARAB people, the vast majority of whom live in the Sultanate of Oman (capital Muscat). Large numbers of people of Omani descent also live in East Africa (see especially the ZANZIBARIS) and Iraq (the descendants of the Azd tribe). A large number of immigrant foreign workers also live in Oman but are not considered Omani; these include PAKISTANIS (predominantly BALOCHIS), INDIANS, IRANIANS and Europeans, who together amount to over 25% of the population of the country.

There is evidence of human habitation in Oman from the 3rd millennium BC, and the Omanis are mentioned by SUMERIAN texts of this date. One of the key features of the success of the

Omanis throughout history, attested even by the Sumerians, has been their seafaring and commercial expertise, and from an early date their ships and caravans were trading with the MESOPOTAMIANS, Indians and INDONESIANS. These trading connections have acted as a strong 'pull-factor' on a number of peoples and nations who have sought to gain control of them. As a result, since the 6th century BC, the Omanis have, at various times, lost all or part of their territory (usually the coastal region) to the PERSIANS, Hinawis, Qarmatians, SELJUKS, PORTUGUESE, and IRANIANS. Between the late 17th and mid-19th centuries, however, the Omanis controlled a commercial empire in East Africa, based in Zanzibar – a region subsequently controlled by the BRITISH.

Following the expulsion of the Iranians from Oman in 1742, the region was ruled by the founder of the present dynasty, Imam Ahmed bin Said. The sultanate was created in 1861, and during the 19th century the British dominated the area.

**Omani culture**

The Omanis are a Muslim people and were amongst the first to convert to the Islamic faith (in AD 632). Their conversion began the process of tribal unification, but this was not finally accomplished until after the arrival of the Ibadites in mid-8th century. Today, most Omanis adhere to the Ibadite doctrine, closely related that of the Sunni, and the vast majority of the remainder are Sunni Muslims. Nonetheless, Oman suffers internal political and religious tensions.

The early Ibadite state was based on the election of an imam who exercised supreme authority over both secular and temporal matters. The modern sultanate, however, has been based on hereditary succession, and this has, at times, led to violent clashes between those loyal to the sultan and those who follow an elected imam, and who tend to live in the interior of the country. In 1895 and 1913–20, civil war resulted in the creation of an autonomous region for those opposed to the sultan. An armed attempt to gain full independence between 1954 and 1959 ended in disaster, following the intervention of British troops, and the autonomous region was abolished. Today, however, there remain significant numbers of Omanis who are discontented with the status quo, and as recently as 1994 hundreds of dissidents were arrested for anti-government activities. Moreover, significant numbers of people living in the mountainous Dhofar region, which was only incorporated into the sultanate in the 19th century, have strong ethnic and cultural links with southern Arabia, and in particular with the YEMENIS. Between 1964 and 1975 Chinese- and Yemeni-supported anti-government activity by Marxist movements was only overcome with the direct intervention of Iranian, Egyptian and Saudi troops.

There remain many in Oman who would not consider themselves Omanis, and who would prefer autonomy or Yemeni status. Following these disturbances, since the early 1980s, the Omani government has forged close political ties with the USA, and took part in the first Gulf War against Iraq in 1991.

As in many other Arab states, Western culture, particularly in the fields of sport and leisure, has strongly influenced the Omanis through political, trade and economic contacts – especially the more than 80% of the population who live in urban environments. Nevertheless, traditional Arab/Islamic culture remains important, and tribal culture remains strong. The government has inspired policies to retain traditional Omani culture during recent years, and foreign marriage is still regarded as undesirable. Arabic is the official language, although English and Urdu are also common. The Omani justice system is based on Islamic Shari'a law. Nonetheless, Omani women are relatively free, and since 1996 have been able to stand for election to the sultan's advisory council.

> **"** The Omány in all ages is celebrated in the songs of the Arabs as the fleetest. **"**
>
> J.R. Wellsted, 1838

# ORAONS or Kurukhs

An aboriginal people who migrated from central to northeastern India, now concentrated in the Chota Nagpur region of the state of Bihar. The DRAVIDIAN Oraon- or Kurukh-speakers number around 2 million, with a further small population of Oraons in Bangladesh to the east, many of whom now speak INDO-ARYAN Sadri. In Bihar a significant number of Oraons have also adopted the majority Hindi as their first language. There is no Oraon literary tradition.

Since the 19th century, many Oraons have been employed in mining for coal and other minerals or work in the industrial centres. Most, however, follow an agricultural way of life centred on the village, each operating under a headman, grouped into confederations run by representative bodies. Each settlement also has its own priest associated with traditional tribal religion involving ancestor worship, fertility rites, spirits and a pantheon led by a supreme god, Dharmes. There is a strong belief in reincarnation. The socialization and initiation of young people is pursued through the institution of dormitories for unmarried males and females, respectively, associated with each village. Traditional initiation ceremonies involved branding.

Christianity has been adopted by some better-educated and urbanized Oraon, but Hinduism and traditional tribal religion remain dominant. Oraon society is based on clans, which comprise numerous tribes in which endogamous marriages are preferred.

> " Oráon appears to have been assigned to them as a nickname, possibly with reference to their many migrations and proneness to roam. "
>
> E.T. Dalton, 1872

## ORIYAS

An INDO-ARYAN people who live mainly in the Indian state of Orissa (capital Bubaneshwar) in northeastern India, adjoining the Bay of Bengal. Oriya is the official language and a direct descendant of Magadhan, the language spoken in the Kingdom of Magadha which flourished from the mid-1st millennium AD in the Ganges Valley, in modern west-central Bihar.

Orissa was independent until the 16th century, when it was divided into numerous princely states. It re-emerged following Indian independence in 1947.

The Oriya-speaking people are preponderantly agricultural and number around 34 million, dominating the state, which also has Munda- and Dravidian-speakers (see MUNDAS and DRAVIDIANS). Emerging out of Orissa's complex and eventful history is a rich, broad culture closely allied to the Hindu religion. Surviving inscriptions date from as early as the 10th century, and literature from the 14th.

## OROCHI

A southeastern Siberian people of Sakhalin and the Amur River area, closely related to the NANAI. Originally from the coast of the Sea of Japan, they moved to their present territory at the beginning of the 20th century, seeking to escape warfare in the area. Semi-sedentary hunters, gatherers and fishers, they speak a Tungus language. Under Soviet rule they were forcibly settled and pushed into fishing collectives. A large-scale influx of RUSSIAN settlers left them a minority in their territory and increased assimilatory pressures, while industrialization has devastated their environment. Since the collapse of the USSR they have become more vocal in asserting their rights, but with fewer than 150 Orochi language-speakers out of a population of perhaps 700 in 1989, their cultural survival is doubtful.

## OROKI

A southeastern Siberian people of Sakhalin. Semi-sedentary reindeer-herders and sedentary fishers, they arrived in the 17th century from the Amur River area. Those under Soviet rule were forcibly settled and collectivized, which, coupled with compulsory boarding education, had a devastating impact on their traditional culture. Those under Japanese rule fled to Japan in 1946 when it became clear that Soviet authorities regarded them as collaborators. There they became fully assimilated. In 2000 there were fewer than 200 Oroki on Sakhalin, with only half speaking their Tungus language. Their survival as a culture is in doubt.

## OROSHORIS

A Pamir people of the Gorno-Badakhshan autonomous *oblast* (region) in Tajikistan. They have a culture and history very similar to those of the BARTANGS. They had a population of about 2000 in 1997.

## OTTOMANS

A ruling dynasty of TURKS, which derived its name from that of its founder, Osman I (died *c.*

1326). The Ottomans, who were Muslims, fought a number of successful wars of imperial expansion, and at its height the Ottoman empire included Anatolia, most of southeastern Europe (including Greece), much of North Africa, the Levant, Mesopotamia and parts of Arabia. The Ottoman conquest of Constantinople (subsequently renamed Istanbul) in 1453, which marked their emergence as a major power, also finally brought the ancient BYZANTINE empire to an end.

The Ottomans were great patrons of art, architecture and literature, particularly at the height of their power during the 15th and 16th centuries. From the 17th century onwards, however, the overstretched empire began a slow decline; between the mid-19th century and 1914 the Ottomans lost almost all of their European and North African possessions, and after World War I their domination of the Arabian peninsula and the Levant also came to an end. Their defeat as allies of the Central Powers during World War I finally ended Ottoman rule in Turkey itself, and in 1922 the modern Republic of Turkey was born under its charismatic leader Kemal Attatürk.

## PAHARI or Parbate or Khasa or Chetri

A people of mixed descent comprising mainly Hindus, Muslims and SIKHS. The majority are Hindu. Their name derives from HINDI and translates as 'of the mountains' or 'mountaineers'. The Pahari live in an area stretching from the lower regions of the Himalayas in Nepal in the east to the Chamba region of the Punjab in the west. They constitute approximately 60% of the NEPALESE population and are also found in a majority in the conjoining Indian Himalayan regions of Himachal Pradesh and northern Uttar Pradesh. The main occupation of the Pahari is agriculture.

Pahari, 'the language of the mountains', is a generic term denoting a series of languages or dialects that stem from the INDO-IRANIAN family of languages. The three main classifications of Pahari are Eastern Pahari (or Nepali, the national language of the NEPALESE), Central Pahari, (consisting of Garhwali and Kumaoni),

and Western Pahari. The various dialects of Pahari are the unifying factor for its peoples. Pahari dialects are spoken by some 17 to 20 million people.

Historically, the Pahari peoples date back to at least the 1st century AD. They are mentioned in the Hindu epic the *Mahabharata*, which would date them between 200 BC and AD 200. The Pahari may be distinguished from other peoples in the region by their ornamental attire: typically women wear silver ornaments such as *hasieri* (necklaces) and *chhalla* (rings). The Pahari are also famed for their miniature paintings and illustrations, first produced in the foothills of the Himalayas.

## PAINTED GREY WARE CULTURE

A Neolithic culture of Anatolia and the Balkans, named after its distinctive pottery. The culture was based on mixed farming, supplemented by hunting and gathering. Villages tended to consist of clusters of structures in mud-brick.

## PALESTINIANS

An ARAB people descended from a mixture of those who invaded Palestine during the Islamic conquest in AD 638 and other indigenous peoples. The name 'Palestine' is derived from PHILISTINE, and was used to refer to the inhabitants of the region since the ROMANS established a province of that name. The concept of being 'Palestinian', however, is really a 20th century phenomenon.

Between 1918 and 1947 large numbers of JEWS migrated to Palestine due to the growth and success of the Zionist movement, but also because of a promise made by the British in 1917 (the 'Balfour Declaration') that, on the conclusion of World War I, a Jewish state would be created in the area. Unfortunately, a similar promise had also been made to the Arabs of Palestine, and one result of large-scale Jewish immigration into the region was an increase in tensions between the two peoples. This tension developed into open violence, and since the early 1920s the two peoples have been in an almost perpetual state of conflict.

A result of this has been the development and consolidation of a national identity amongst both Palestinians and Jewish ISRAELIS. For the Palestinians, this has been particularly strong since the foundation of the state of Israel in 1948 when, following the first Arab–Israeli war, the Israelis seized control of all of Palestine except for the Gaza Strip and the West Bank. Israeli attacks on civilians caused hundreds of thousands of Palestinians to flee their homes, either to Gaza and the West Bank or to neighbouring Arab countries.

The Palestinian situation became even worse following the Six Day War in 1967 when Israel occupied Gaza and the West Bank, now usually referred to as the 'occupied territories'. Since that time, Jewish fundamentalists have founded hundreds of settlements in the occupied territories.

### The struggle for independence

Although there are approximately 7 million Palestinians worldwide, today only a minority live in Palestine. Around 2.7 million reside in the occupied territories and a further 150,000 in Israel itself. The remainder are spread over a number of countries, many living as refugees, principally in other Arab nations, South America (especially Chile and Brazil), Europe and the United States. The scattering of the Palestinians has in fact helped solidify and magnify Palestinian nationalism.

In 1974 the United Nations recognized the need for an independent state for the Palestinian nation. In 1987 the Palestinians began an uprising, the intifada ('shaking'), in the occupied territories. While the Israelis struggled to suppress the intifada, in 1988 Jordan relinquished its self-appointed position as overseers of Palestinian welfare. From this point onward the Palestine Liberation Organization (PLO) became the internationally-recognized mouthpiece for the Palestinians – an important step on the road to nationhood.

The 1993 Oslo accords began the first moves towards the establishment of a Palestinian state by granting the Palestinians limited autonomy over parts of the occupied territories and the establishment, in 1994, of a Palestinian Authority under PLO leader Yasser Arafat. Since that time the peace process has been set back for a number of reasons. The Israeli refusal to close Jewish settlements in the occupied territories seemed to offer Palestinians no hope that Israel was willing to concede a truly viable Palestinian state. The assassination by a Jewish extremist of the conciliatory Israeli prime minister Yikzhak Rabin (1995), and Yasser Arafat's refusal to sign up to a US-brokered deal with his successor, Ehud Barak, saw retrenchment in both camps and strengthened those who would not compromise. In Israel, the result was a succession of right-wing Likud governments, while the impasse allowed Palestinian Islamic terrorist organizations such as Hamas and Hezbollah effectively to take over from the PLO as the leaders of Palestinian resistance to the Israeli occupation. A new intifada began in 2000, accompanied by suicide bombings against Israeli civilians organized by these groups. The Israeli response has been to increase repression within the occupied territories, and there has been an escalation of violence on both sides.

While the PLO now officially recognizes Israel's right to exist, Hamas and Hezbollah are both dedicated to its destruction. Although these organizations do enjoy considerable public support, most Palestinians do not share either their Islamic fundamentalism or their publicly stated aims, and would willingly accept a settlement based on the 1967 borders.

Around 97% of Palestinians are Muslim, and the vast majority adhere to the Sunni doctrine; the remaining 3% are principally Eastern Orthodox Christians. There has been very little tension between the Muslim and Christian sections of the community, as most Palestinians consider themselves to be Arabs above all else. Arab and Islamic cultures dominate the community, although many who have remained in Palestine are familiar with the Hebrew language. Western influence is relatively slight. The Palestinians consider Jerusalem to be their capital, as do the Israelis – the city is holy to Muslims, Jews and Christians.

# PAMPHYLIANS

The inhabitants of the district of Pamphylia in southern Anatolia. By the 1st century BC they were a highly Hellenized people, using a variant of the Greek alphabet, who comprised native tribes mixed with migrant GREEKS and CILICIANS. Renowned as sailors and traders, the Pamphylians were conquered or dominated by the PHRYGIANS, LYDIANS, PERSIANS, MACEDONIANS, SELEUCIDS and ROMANS. They were eventually assimilated into the Roman empire.

## PARBATE

See PAHARI.

## PARNI or Aparni

A nomadic IRANIAN people who migrated south from the steppes of Central Asia into Parthia during the early 3rd century BC, where they established a capital at Abivard. They were quickly assimilated into the native population, but succeeded in establishing a new ruling dynasty. Although they were originally vassals of the SELEUCIDS, in 238 BC under Arsaces I (ruled *c.* 250–*c.* 211 BC) they proclaimed their independence and were responsible for the subsequent foundation of the PARTHIAN empire. They spoke an Iranian language, related to that of other Central Asian tribes such as the SCYTHIANS and MEDES, and were famed for their cavalry expertise.

## PARSIS

A South Asian people descended from PERSIAN Zoroastrians who fled south in the wake of Muslim persecution during the 7th century. They number around 150,000 in total; the majority live in India (chiefly in Bombay, now Mumbai), and small numbers are also found in Iran and Pakistan. Like the JAINS, the Indian Parsis have gained a considerable reputation as successful entrepreneurs, a success fostered during British rule. In many respects (outside religion) they have also assimilated many forms of INDIAN culture. They do not, however, possess a caste system, and remain proud of their cultural distinctiveness.

The Parsis are monotheists who worship Ahura Mazda, with fire veneration playing a key role in their religious ritual. Their sacred text is the *Avesta*. One of the Parsis' most distinctive religious practices is the disposal of their dead in funerary towers called *dakhma* ('towers of silence'), which contain grates on which corpses are exposed. After vultures have eaten the flesh, the bones fall through the grate into a pit below. This ritual fulfils the Zoroastrian injunction that a corpse must not come into contact with either earth or fire.

## PARTHIANS

A nomadic IRANIAN people who were related to the SCYTHIANS and MEDES. The Parthians are first mentioned in a Persian inscription of about 520 BC, and the name means 'exiled'. While very little is known of their early history, it is certain that they were made subject to the ASSYRIANS, MEDES, PERSIANS and MACEDONIANS. Between the mid-2nd century BC and early 3rd century AD, however, the Parthians were the foremost power in Iran and Mesopotamia.

The beginnings of Parthian expansionism are tied to the collapse of the Persian empire, following the invasion of the Macedonians, and the subsequent migration of the PARNI into Parthia. Although the latter were absorbed into the indigenous Parthian peoples, they succeeded in establishing a new dynasty, the Arsacids, who were responsible for gaining independence from the SELEUCIDS and establishing an empire that eventually stretched from the Euphrates to the Indus and the Indian Ocean, with a capital at Ctesiphon.

By the mid-1st century BC the Parthian empire was viewed as the successor to the Persian, and the Euphrates had been established as the frontier between the Parthians and the ROMANS. The ARMENIANS frequently acted as a buffer between the two empires.

To the east, the Parthian empire bordered that of the KUSHANS. The SAKAS, who invaded the empire during the mid-2nd century BC, were settled and ruled by Parthian aristocrats until their lands were annexed by the Kushans during the mid-1st century AD.

The Parthian empire was never fully united. Rather than administer areas directly, the Parthians generally preferred to rely on a series of semi-autonomous vassal states. A combination of internecine power struggles and frequent

Parthian–Roman wars threatened the empire. In addition, the Scythians made frequent attacks, and by the early 3rd century AD the Parthians had been fatally weakened.

In 226 AD the Persians rebelled, overthrew the Arsacids, and established a new dynasty – the Sassanians. Following this defeat, the terms 'Parthian' and 'Persian' were used interchangeably for a time, but 'Parthian' was eventually dropped altogether. The Parthians gradually lost their cultural identity and were assimilated with the other peoples of the Persian empire, particularly following the Islamic conquest.

**Parthian culture**
Following the collapse of the Seleucid empire, Parthian culture was greatly influenced by the GREEKS, and the empire was administered using established Greek institutions. Parthian coins, for example, continued to use Greek inscriptions, and the gods of the Greek pantheon were widely worshipped. Iranian culture was also very influential, particularly that of the Medes and Persians, and this came dominate particularly from the early 1st century AD; the increasingly frequent clashes with the Roman empire from the mid-1st century BC may, in part, explain the move away from Western influences. It would be true to say, however, that both culturally and politically, the Parthians were not a particularly innovative people.

Their control of the lucrative Silk Route led to an influx of wealth, which allowed the Parthian nobility to patronize the arts, and in particular to embark on a programme of spectacular building projects, particularly at Ctesiphon, Nisa and Hatra. Much of the architecture displayed in these programmes reveals both Persian and Mesopotamian influences, and was later to influence ARAB styles.

The Parthian aristocracy always remained in touch with the lower social classes, and this is reflected in Parthian art, which has been labelled 'popular' as opposed to the more elitist art produced by the Greeks. The Parthians were also renowned for their literature, in which heroic themes were very popular.

The Silk Route facilitated the passage of Eastern culture into the Parthian empire, although its influence seems to have been limited. The

Parthians were, however, responsible for the propagation of CHINESE Buddhism.

The Parthians were polytheists: local deities and members of the Greek pantheon were worshipped side-by-side. Zoroastrianism was also popular, and the growth of the empire helped its spread to more western regions. Parthian society was feudal in character, and hunting was widely favoured by the aristocracy, helping to hone the cavalry techniques for which they were famed. The Parthians spoke an Iranian language and used the Aramaic alphabet, though this was supplanted by a new cursive script better suited to the language.

# PASHTUN or Pakhtuns or Pathans or Pushtuns

A people of possibly ARYAN descent whose descendants now inhabit areas of Afghanistan and Pakistan. Until the creation of the modern state of Afghanistan, the Pashtun were the only people referred to as AFGHANS, although their exact ethnic origins are a matter of continuing debate. Today, they comprise 38% of the population of the modern republic.

Between the 13th and 16th centuries, significant numbers of Pashtun migrated to an area now incorporated into modern Pakistan, and around 14 million of their descendants still reside in the region. There are more than 50 separate Pashtun tribes, with the Durrani (see ABDALIS) traditionally forming the social and political leadership.

Pashto, an Eastern Iranian language known since the 16th century and now the national language of Afghanistan, is also the native language of the Pashtun, though for literary purposes they use an adapted form of the Arabic alphabet. Traditionally, however, the Pashtun are an intensely independent people, and during the late 1950s attempts to establish an independent Pashtun region were violently suppressed. Similarly, in regions now occupied by India and Pakistan, the Pashtun fought against the MUGHALS, SIKHS and British; the AFRIDI were particularly involved in the defence of the Khyber Pass.

More recently, since PAKISTANI independence in 1947, there have been frequent campaigns, such as that of the Red Shirt Movement, to establish an independent Pashtunsitan – campaigns at times supported by the Afghan government. Again, these actions have frequently led to violent clashes, but the Pashtun do now enjoy a limited amount of local tribal autonomy.

The Pashtun are predominantly an agricultural people, although comparatively small numbers have opted for an urban lifestyle. Traditionally nomadic, many are still pastoral, although significant numbers lead much more sedentary lives as settled agriculturists. Many also enlist in the military forces.

They are a Muslim people, and the vast majority follow the Sunni doctrine. Tribal society is still very strong, and traditional, Islamic, models of behaviour are firmly rooted. The tribal structure is patrilineal, and genealogies are carefully recorded for the purpose of inheritance and social ranking. The Pashtun believe they are all descended from one common ancestor. Internecine strife, however, has been a common feature of Pashtun history, and long-standing blood feuds between individuals, families and tribes are common. From the 17th century there developed a great tradition of Pashtun poetry, derived from PERSIAN originals.

The Taliban, who controlled significant areas of Afghanistan, including Kabul, from 1993 to 2002, are predominantly Pashtun. This resurgence in Pashtun power led to the formation of the Northern Alliance by those opposed to their hegemony, notably the UZBEKS, TAJIKS, TURKMEN and HAZARA; there were also clashes with the Shi'ite minority, which led to tension with the IRANIANS. Following the US and Northern Alliance defeat of the Taliban in 2002, the Pashtun no longer dominate the government of Afghanistan, and their future role in the development of the country is uncertain.

# PERSIANS

An INDO-IRANIAN people who migrated to the Iranian plateau around 1500 BC. Initially subject to the ELAMITES, they were later conquered by their close ethnic relatives, the MEDES. Under their king Cyrus the Great (ruled c. 600–529 BC), however, the Persians succeeded in subjugating the Medes in 550 BC, and over the course of the next 25 years, consolidated one of the

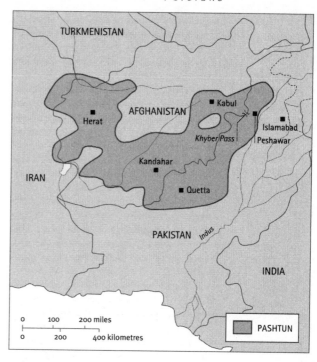

Pashtun

largest empires of the ancient world. At its greatest extent, the Persian empire stretched from Egypt to India, and involved the conquest of, among others, the BABYLONIANS (CHALDEANS), LYDIANS and EGYPTIANS.

The term 'Persian' was not one used by this people; historically, they have always referred to themselves as 'IRANIAN'. The Greeks derived this term from Persis (or Parsa), where the Persians originated, and the name remained in use for over two millennia. It was not until 1935, when the Shah of Iran officially requested that the outside world refer to his people as Iranian, that the term 'Persian' was eventually dropped.

Although originally a nomadic people, the Persians' rapid conquest of an extensive empire gave them access not only to vast sources of wealth, but also to artists from a hugely diverse range of traditions. As a result, the magnificent building programmes undertaken by the Persians, at cities such as Pasargadae and Persepolis, display influences from throughout the empire. The Persian culture was not entirely derivative, however, and their own Iranian traditions and artistic styles combined with all of these elements to forge an entirely new style: Imperial Persian. (Interestingly, Pasargadae was laid out using the ground plan of a traditional Iranian nomadic settlement.)

The Persians' willingness to fuse so many different influences with their own is simply one manifestation of the tolerance that dominated the Persian empire of this period. In almost all spheres, conquered peoples were simply allowed to carry on with their lives as before; local religious practice remained unaffected, and in many instances even rebels were allowed a second chance – often with disastrous results. The Persians themselves were polytheists, and the chief deity of their pantheon was Ahura Mazda. During the period of imperial greatness, however, Zoroastrianism also became very popular, particularly among the aristocracy, and the empire certainly encouraged its spread into more western regions. The Persians spoke a dialect of the Iranian language known as Old Persian, but possessed no means of writing this language down until around 520 BC, when a cuneiform script was devised. For administrative and epigraphic purposes, they also used Elamite, Assyrian or Aramaic.

### Rivalry with Greece and Rome

During the late 5th century BC, the Persians attempted to conquer the GREEKS, but were defeated in a series of battles between 490 and 479 BC. These events marked the beginning of a steady decline in Persian imperial fortune. Unfortunately, the very tolerance shown by the Persians was one of the endemic weaknesses of their empire. Complete unity was never accomplished, and rebellion and civil war were common during the 4th century BC. As a result, it was a much-weakened empire that the MACEDONIANS, commanded by Alexander the Great, defeated in 334–331 BC.

Following the death of Alexander in 323 BC, the Greek SELEUCIDS dominated the area, succeeded by the PARTHIANS, and Persian art and architecture became heavily influenced by Hellenistic forms. Beginning in the AD 220s, however, the Persians enjoyed a political revival under the Sassanian dynasty, destroying the Parthians in 226 and overrunning a considerable

empire. From this point until the ARAB conquest in the 7th century, the Persians were the foremost rivals of the ROMAN, and later the BYZANTINE, empires.

The Sassanians appear to have learned from some of the mistakes of the earlier Persian empire. Society remained feudal but was accompanied by rigorous absolutism, imperial centralization, a nationalistic revival of Persian culture (at the expense of Hellenistic styles) and the installation of Zoroastrianism as the state religion. As a result, other religions were systematically persecuted, especially the Christians during the 4th century when Christianity gradually became the state religion of the Roman and Byzantine empires.

While Zoroastrianism forbade the construction of temples and statues, Persian artistry flourished during this period, especially in the areas of metalwork (as seen in the Oxus Treasure), carpet and rug-making, and secular architecture. Despite periods of spectacular success, however, the Sassanians were debilitated by wars against the Byzantines and EPHTHALITES, and they were able to offer little resistance to the ARABS who overran their empire in 637–51. Following this defeat, while Zoroastrianism gradually declined in favour of Islam, Persian culture continued to influence later Arabic, Islamic and European forms.

## PHILISTINES

A non-Semitic people who invaded Egypt during the early 12th century BC. They were defeated and subsequently settled along the southwestern Levantine coast. By the EGYPTIANS they were known as the *Prst*, but are more commonly referred to as one of the SEA PEOPLES. They defeated the DANITES and the CANAANITES and established a number of confederated city-states, each with its own ruler. This area subsequently became known as Philistia. One longstanding legacy of these people is that the region they occupied is still known as Palestine, a derivative of Philistine.

During the 11th century BC they fought a number of campaigns against the Hebrews (see JEWS). Although initially successful, they were subsequently defeated in the 10th century BC and were reduced to vassal status. The wars against the Philistines were a major factor in the unification of the Hebrew tribes. The later division of the Israelite kingdom allowed the Philistines a brief period of independence, but they were overrun by the Egyptians in 924 BC. From the 8th century BC, the Philistines were conquered in turn by the Israelites, ASSYRIANS, Egyptians, BABYLONIANS, PERSIANS, GREEKS and ROMANS, and by the 1st century AD the term 'Philistine' had ceased to have any real meaning either politically or ethnically.

### Philistine culture

Very little is known of native Philistine culture, and even their origins are a matter of much debate. Historians have proposed Cyprus, Anatolia and especially Crete as their place of origin. Once they had settled in Canaan it appears that the Philistines were assimilated rapidly into the indigenous culture of the region. Certainly, no written examples of their language have survived, and their known gods, such as Dagan and Baalzebub, are Canaanite in origin. Although they may not have actually introduced ironworking into the region, the Philistines certainly advanced the levels of production in Canaan, and their skills allowed them a technical edge during their conquest of the area. They also introduced a new artistic style, displayed primarily in pottery, which exhibits Mycenaean, Egyptian and Canaanite influences. Other items, such as metalwork, votive objects and temple structures also display Aegean influence.

## PHOENICIANS

A people of mixed ethnic origins who were ethnically and culturally almost identical to the CANAANITES. The Phoenicians' homeland was the area of modern Lebanon, and they have won a deserved reputation as one of the greatest commercial people in world history. It is not known how they referred to themselves, and it is possible that they considered themselves to be Canaanites. 'Phoenicia' was a Greek term that came into usage during the 1st millennium BC.

Phoenicians had settled in the Levant by the end of the 4th millennium BC (their previous origins are unknown), and following their arrival a number of independent city-states evolved under the control of hereditary kings. The principal Phoenician cities included Byblos, Tyre, Sidon, Arvad and Ugarit, and usually one of these entities tended to dominate the others. As the Phoenicians were never unified, they were never truly a nation; for example the GREEKS and Hebrews (see JEWS) tended to identify them by the city from which they originated – Tyrians, Sidonians and so on.

For much of the period between the 18th and late 13th centuries BC, the Phoenicians were subject to EGYPTIAN rule. Following the invasion by the SEA PEOPLES, however, and subsequent withdrawal of Egyptian influence from the Levant, the Phoenicians embarked on a period of independence and self-determination. Despite suffering attacks from both the Sea Peoples and the ARAMAEANS, who destroyed a number of their cities, the Phoenicians began their rise as a great trading people during the 10th century BC. Their position on the Mediterranean coast allowed them to trade west to Cyprus, Greece, North Africa, Italy and Spain, where they founded a number of important trading colonies, such as Carthage. Many of these colonies, particularly in the western Mediterranean, subsequently gained their independence from the 9th century BC, and founded colonies of their own. The Phoenicians were also able to trade south with Egypt, with whom they had trading contacts from the 3rd millennium BC, east with Syria, Mesopotamia and Iran, and north with Anatolia.

### Phoenician culture

On account of their many disparate trading contacts, the Phoenicians displayed a very mixed range of cultural influences, and almost all of the regions with which they traded can be recognized in Phoenician goods. In addition to re-exporting items from their trading contacts in the east and west, the Phoenicians were famed for the quality of their jewellery, bronze ware, ivory-carving, textiles and inlay work. They are also credited with the invention of glass-blowing. Local raw materials included cedar and juniper wood, along with a highly prized purple dye. While little of the work produced by the Phoenicians was truly innovative, indigenous Canaanite culture remained important, and this helped produce a style that was essentially 'Phoenician'.

Because of their trading activities, the Phoenicians were also partly responsible for the dissemination of Eastern cultural influences and ideas to the western Mediterranean and vice versa, thus making them one of the most important engines of cultural change in world history. The Phoenicians were the foremost mariners of their day, and their ships were among the finest known to the ancient world.

The Egyptians influenced Phoenician polytheistic religious practice from the mid-2nd millennium BC, but traditional Canaanite gods such as Baal, Astarte (Phoenician, Tanit) and Dagon remained important, and these were the foremost deities worshipped in the region. Within Phoenician city life, the temple remained the central focus. During the 10th century BC, the Phoenicians maintained friendly relations with the Israelites and were responsible for the design and construction of the temple at Jerusalem, which was built to a traditional Canaanite/Phoenician plan.

During the 9th century BC, despite attempts at resistance, the Phoenicians were conquered by the ASSYRIANS, and remained vassals until the fall of Assyria in the late 7th century BC. They were subsequently conquered by the BABYLONIANS, PERSIANS (538 BC), MACEDONIANS (332 BC) and ROMANS (64 BC). From the 5th century BC, and especially following their incorporation into the SELEUCID empire, the Phoenician city-states, and the Phoenicians themselves, became increasingly Hellenized.

After its conquest by Pompey the Great, Phoenicia was absorbed into the Roman province of Syria, and from that date, at the latest, the term 'Phoenician' ceases to have any ethnic or political meaning. In North Africa, however, Phoenician culture continued, to a certain extent, through the CARTHAGINIANS and NUMIDIANS, and the Phoenician language remained in use in the region until at least the 5th century AD. Of more lasting importance, however, was the Phoenician system of writing. Although they originally wrote their SEMITIC language using AKKADIAN cuneiform, from about the 15th century BC the Phoenicians began using an alphabetic system based on that of the

Canaanites. Following their commercial expansion throughout the Mediterranean, they passed this system to the Greeks during the 8th century BC, and this subsequently became the basis of the Roman alphabet, which remains in use to the present day.

# PHRYGIANS

An INDO-EUROPEAN people whose exact geographical origins are unknown. During the later 2nd millennium BC they migrated into Anatolia (modern Turkey) and it is likely that they had previously formed a part of the population of Thrace (see THRACIANS). Known also as one of the SEA PEOPLES, they played a role in the destruction of the HITTITE empire before moving into central Anatolia.

Here they came into contact with the ASSYRIANS, who identified them as the MUSHKHI; they were defeated by Tiglath-Pileser I of Assyria in 1115 BC. The Phrygians later established a kingdom in central and western Anatolia and subsequently came to dominate most of the region; their capital lay at Gordium. The GREEKS referred to these people as the *Phryges* during the 1st millennium BC – the origin of the terms 'Phrygia' and 'Phrygian'.

The period of Phrygian domination in Anatolia was relatively shortlived. By the later 8th century BC they were at war with the expanding Assyrian empire, losing part of their eastern lands. The migratory CIMMERIANS destroyed the Phrygian kingdom, including Gordium, in about 695 BC. The region was subsequently incorporated into the LYDIAN empire, and was then subject, in succession, to the PERSIANS, MACEDONIANS, Pergamenes and ROMANS. The Romans divided Phrygia between the provinces of Asia and Galatia, and thereafter the term 'Phrygian' gradually lost all ethnic and cultural meaning.

The Phrygians spoke a language now unknown, but from the mid-8th century BC they adopted the Greek alphabet through their contacts with the Hellenized cities of western Anatolia. Although originally a nomadic mountain-dwelling people, they began to absorb native Anatolian culture. As a result, Hittite influences are very noticeable in early Phrygian

**"** For pheniciens were ye firste fynderes of lettres. **"**

John De Trevisa, 1387

art; later, Greek, LUWIAN, URARTIAN and Assyrian influences are evident.

The Phrygians became famed for the quality of their ivory-carving, bronze-working, wood-carving, carpets and textiles, and the Phrygian kings accumulated vast amounts of wealth; indeed, their last king, Midas (Mita), has become synonymous with affluence and avarice. The Phrygians were also great urban developers and produced a number of rock sculptures and carvings that have survived to the present day. Nevertheless, some aspects of their traditional nomadic lifestyle survived, and sheep-rearing and horse-breeding, alongside more sedentary agriculture, remained important factors in the Phrygian economy. Timber and marble were also important exports.

The principal deity in the Phrygian pantheon was Cybele, a mother goddess later adopted by the Romans. In the area of religious art, Greek prototypes appear to have been the inspiration behind much that was produced by the Phrygians. Certainly, from the 8th century BC, Phrygian culture became increasingly Hellenized, and King Midas is known to have sent offerings to the Oracle at Delphi.

## PUNJABIS

A people from the Punjab region of what is now northwest India and eastern Pakistan. Punjab means 'land of five rivers'; *pun* means 'five', and *aab* means 'waters'. The total number of Punjabis in the Punjab is now nearing 25 million. There are also many Punjabi speakers in other areas of India and Pakistan. The majority of Punjabis speak Punjabi, which has a distinct Gurmukhi script, the script associated with the SIKH Guru Granth Sahib. The Punjabi language is related to Sanskrit, from the INDO-ARYAN language family, and also incorporates Persian and Latin influences. The majority of Punjabis are Hindus, Muslims or Sikhs. Kurukshetra, the place where Krishna delivered his famous message found in the *Bhagavad-Gita*, was located in the Punjab.

The Punjabis are a heterogeneous people, as their history testifies. The Punjab was the cradle of the Indus Valley civilization (see HARAPPANS) in the 3rd millennium BC. Following the collapse of this civilization around 1700 BC, the ARYANS migrated into the area from Central Asia. The Punjab absorbed influences from many more migrations and invasions; among these were the GREEKS – under Alexander from 327 BC, the SCYTHIANS, PARTHIANS, KUSHANS, SAKAS and HUNS (4th–9th centuries AD), TURKS and MONGOLS (13th–16th centuries), AFGHANS and BRITISH (1849–1947). In the 11th century AD the Punjabis were first introduced to Islam by the invading armies of Mahmud of Ghazni. The 15th century saw the rise of Sikhism.

In the early 18th century the Punjabis were liberated by Banda Singh Bahadur from the Mughal empire. The following period saw great conflicts between the Sikhs and the Mughals and Afghans. However, the Sikhs established a power base, and under Ranjit Singh the Punjabis inhabited a large kingdom. Punjabi autonomy lasted until the establishment of British colonial rule in 1849.

In 1919 – with the rise of Indian nationalism – the Jallianwallah Bagh massacre took place at the Punjabi Sikh holy city of Amritsar. Conflicts continued in the Punjab region until, in 1947, the Punjab was divided between India and Pakistan. After 1947 the Punjab experienced mass ethnic and religious migrations and a spate of

Punjabis

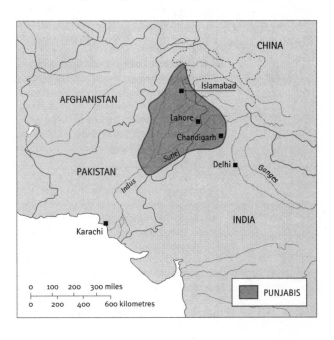

religious communal violence. Many Punjabis left the Punjab during and after this transition.

In 1955 the Pakistani part of the Punjab was incorporated into Pakistan, and one year later the Indian region of Punjab was officially enlarged by its inclusion into the Indian Patiala and East Punjab States Union (PEPSU). In 1966, after more campaigns for a separate state, the Punjab was divided further by language into a smaller Punjabi state and the Hindi state Haryana.

More recently, the Sikhs have mounted an unsuccessful campaign for an independent Punjabi state named Khalistan. As a result of Sikh militancy in the Punjab in 1984, prime minister Indira Gandhi was assassinated by Sikh bodyguards. Today, Punjabi are spread throughout Asia and the West. In 1986 The World Punjabi Congress met for the first time with the objective of promoting Punjabi culture and language.

## QASHQA'IS

A nomadic Turkic people (see TURKS) who inhabit the Fars region of Iran. They are renowned for their rug-making skills.

## QATABANIANS

The inhabitants of the ancient kingdom of Qataban (capital Timna), in modern Yemen. Relatively little is known of Qatabanian history or culture, although it seems that they fought wars against the SABAEANS, and for a short period may have enjoyed some sort of political supremacy in southern Arabia. Culturally, they appear to have shared many features with the Sabaeans, to whom the region fell during the 5th century BC.

## QATARIS

The citizens of the modern Emirate of Qatar (capital Doha). The region has been populated since the stone age. During the course of its history, despite long periods of independence, the local population has been subject to, or heavily influenced by, the AKKADIANS, Sassanid PERSIANS, BAHRAINIS, Portuguese, OTTOMANS and British. The British established a protectorate over Qatar

in 1916, which was not removed until they withdrew from Arabia in 1971, when the Qataris became fully independent.

Native inhabitants of the region, and therefore true 'Qataris', account for only about 20% of the population of the modern country, which in 2002 stood at 584,000. These are descended from BEDOUIN tribespeople who, until the exploitation of oil in the region from 1949, dominated the local population. The first steps toward unification and nationhood were only made during the 18th century. The Qataris were nomadic herders, and prior to the discovery of oil, they also gained income from pearl cultivation, fishing and trade. Over the last 50 years, however, the inflow of oil revenues has drastically changed the lifestyle of most of the population, and the vast majority now live in urban areas. Fewer than 10% live a rural lifestyle, and many of these are now sedentary farmers. About 40% of the indigenous population are members of the ruling al-Thani family. Many of the non-Qatari inhabitants of the Emirate are citizens of other ARAB nations, alongside large numbers of INDIANS and PAKISTANIS.

During the 7th century AD, Islamic armies overran the area, and today the vast majority of Qataris are Wahhabi Sunnis. Internal social and religious conflicts are rare, although there have been bloodless coups among the ruling Al-Thani family. Arabic is the official language, with English frequently used for business and governmental communication. Qatari culture displays the mix of traditional Arabic/Islamic and Western forms common in many oil producing Arab states. Western influences are particularly strong in the areas of sport and entertainment. Despite the application of Islamic Shari'a law, the secular courts are used more regularly in Qatar than in many other Arab nations, and women enjoy both suffrage and the right to stand for local office.

Since independence, the Qataris have tended to look to their neighbours the SAUDIS in matters of foreign policy, but have clashed occasionally with both the Saudis and Bahrainis over territorial matters. The Qataris have also played an influential part in Arab conflicts with the ISRAELIS. More recently, they supported the IRAQIS during the 1980s but cooperated with coalition forces during the Gulf Wars. The first of these conflicts led to considerable tensions with the JORDANIANS and PALESTINIANS.

## QURAYSH

An ARAB tribe, originally BEDOUIN, which had settled in the area of Mecca by the early 6th century AD, helping destroy the KINDAH. Over the course of the next 100 years, through their exploitation of the trade routes between the East and Mesopotamia and Africa, they forged the city into one of the major commercial centres of the Arabian peninsula. This commercial success also resulted in the disintegration of traditional Bedouin culture within the tribe, the growth of individualism, class divisions based on wealth, and a cosmopolitan outlook. The tribal name is derived from an early leader of the tribe whose personal name was Qusayy.

More than ten clans made up the Quraysh, who by the late 6th century AD were regarded as the leading tribe of the region. The prophet Muhammad belonged to the Hashim clan. Other clans included the Zuhra, Taim, 'Adi and Umayya. As well as an important trading centre, Mecca was also regarded as a significant religious focal point, and prior to the foundation of Islam the Quraysh worshipped a number of gods, including Allah, al-Lat, al-'Uzza and Manat. The Quraysh aristocracy initially rejected the teachings of Muhammad, believing that these would undermine their economic and social position. Although he was initially forced to flee, Muhammad conquered the Quraysh in 630, and the tribe was subsequently converted to Islam, and thereafter played a key role in the unification of the Arab people and the subsequent Islamic conquests. The writing of the Koran is based on the Quraysh dialect of Arabic.

The leaders of the Quraysh continued to amass considerable wealth following the Islamic conquests, and members of the tribe founded both the Ummayad and Abbasid dynasties. Early divisions within the Quraysh, centred on the succession to the caliphate, led to the split between the Sunni and Shi'ite doctrines of Islam.

## RAJASTHANIS

Speakers of the INDO-ARYAN Rajasthani language, most of whom live in the INDIAN state of Rajasthan. Unlike its geographical neighbours, Hindi and Gujarati, Rajasthani is not an official language of India, although over 56 million people currently use it either as a first or second language. Rajasthani comprises four principal linguistic groups, including HINDI MARWARI. The vast majority (over 85%) of Rajasthanis are Hindus, although there is also a significant minority of Muslims; an unusually large number are also members of smaller aboriginal tribes. The official language of Rajasthan, however, is HINDI, which is commonly used as the written script. Hindi is taught in Rajasthani schools, and since Indian independence significant numbers of Rajasthanis have been attracted by Hindi culture; as a result, the number of Rajasthani first-language speakers is declining. This phenomenon has caused some tension within the state. Other Rajasthani-speakers include the GURKHAS.

## RUTUL

A Caucasian people of Azerbaijan and Rutul region, southern Dagestan, Russian Federation. Similar to the LEZGIS, whose written language they use, they are herders who adopted Sunni Islam in the 11th century, and speak a North Caucasian language. Conquered by the RUSSIANS in 1844, they proved rebellious, but Soviet collectivization, attacks on their religious leaders and assimilatory education policies did much damage to their traditional culture. In 1989 they numbered over 20,000.

## SABAEANS

A Semitic people (see SEMITES) whose exact ethnic origins are unknown, but who migrated into the Arabian peninsula from the north, settling in an area now occupied by modern Yemen. Their capital was at Marib. In the Levant, the kingdom of the Sabaeans (Saba) was known as Sheba, but the first inscriptional evidence of their existence is found in an ASSYRIAN document dated to the 8th century BC. During the 1st millennium BC the Sabaeans became a wealthy people. This

**Quraysh:**

**clans**

'Adi
Hashim
Taim
Umayya
Zuhra

S

❝ Rajasthanis have settled down in all parts of the country without coming into conflict with the local people. ❞

A.B. Shah, 1975

prosperity was based on their domination of the trade in frankincense, myrrh and spices to Egypt, Mesopotamia and Africa. Their trade interests led to the foundation of a number of Sabaean colonies, most notably on the east African coast around 500 BC. These colonies later developed into the kingdom of Aksum (see AKSUMITES), which remained heavily influenced by Sabaean culture.

The economic success of the Sabaeans allowed them to invest in considerable feats of engineering, such as the Marib Dam at the Wadi Dhana, which facilitated the irrigation of surrounding land that otherwise would have been barren. In addition, they also adorned a number of cities with fine public buildings and temples. The Sabaeans were also noted for the exquisite quality of their jewellery, silverware and bronze reliefs. They were polytheists, and Tammuz, a MESOPOTAMIAN fertility god, was important in the region. The Sabaeans spoke an Arabic dialect and adopted an alphabet derived from proto-CANAANITE around 1000 BC – a writing system they later passed on to their African colonies.

The Sabaeans fought a number of territorial and trade wars against their neighbours, most notably the QATABANIANS, HADRAMITES and Aswan, but were later increasingly absorbed by the HIMYARITES from the 1st century BC to the 3rd century AD. The term 'king of Saba' remained in use for much of the Himyarite period, and their language into the 6th century AD. The Sabaeans disappeared from the historical record, however, following the PERSIAN and Islamic conquests.

## SAKAS or Shakas or Satraps or Kshatrapas

An originally nomadic Iranian steppe people who were a branch of the SCYTHIANS. (The name 'Saka' is a derivative of 'Scythian'.) The ruling Saka kings took the appellation *satrap*, which derives from Persian and Sanskrit and means 'King of Kings'; they also adopted the Indian title *maharaja*, 'Great King'.

In the 2nd century BC the nomadic Sakas were driven from their homeland by other nomadic tribes and the CHINESE. Migrating south, the Sakas split into two groups. One group passed east of the Hindu Kush to enter Kashmir and the Punjab around 140 BC; this group became known as the Northern Sakas or Northern Satraps. The second group passed east of the mountains into Afghanistan before over-running Sindh, Gujarat and Maharashtra in India between around 110 and 100 BC; this group became known as the Western Sakas or Western Satraps. In 75 BC the Northern Saka ruler, Manese, took Gandhara, and King Azez I expanded the kingdom to the east 55–50 BC. However, the Northern Saka kingdom was short-lived. In AD 50 it was conquered by the KUSHANS, and by AD 75 the Northern Sakas were assimilated into Indian culture as Ksatriyas (the warrior class).

The Western Saka kingdom endured much longer and became powerful and prosperous under its second dynasty, founded by King Chastana in AD 78. It is this period that is known as the 'era of Saka kings' in Indian history books. In AD 120 the Sakas lost power to the native ANDHRAS but quickly recovered it. Under the reign of the first great Saka king, Rudraman I (ruled from AD 130), revenge was taken: Saka power was re-established and fortified as the kingdom expanded westward into Ujjain. The Saka era lasted until around AD 397–410, when the Saka kingdom, ruled by King Rudrasimha III, was destroyed by Chandra Gupta II of the north Indian Gupta empire. By this time the Sakas had almost been completely assimilated by the indigenous Indian population.

## SAKHA

See YAKUTS.

## SAMARITANS

A people who originally inhabited the city of Samaria, Palestine. The city was founded during the early 9th century BC by King Omri as a new capital for the breakaway Kingdom of Israel. Many of the buildings in this new city displayed PHOENICIAN influence. The city was destroyed by the ASSYRIANS in 724 BC; much of the population was deported, and the city was repopulated by MESOPOTAMIANS. Over the course of the next few centuries these newcomers inter-married

S

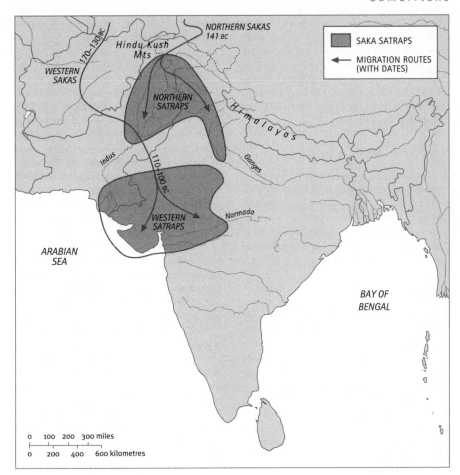

*Driven from Central Asia in the 2nd century BC, the Sakas established two states (satraps) in the Indian subcontinent. The Western Satraps played a formative role in early Indian history.*

S

with the remaining resident population and gradually absorbed much of the region's culture. As a result, when the JEWS returned from exile, following the PERSIAN conquest of the BABYLONI-ANS, the vast majority of those resident in Samaria had been thoroughly Judaized. Those who returned, however, refused to accept these 'foreigners', and tension continued to exist between the two communities for much of the remainder of the ancient period. This tension led to the Samaritans' rejection of the Temple cult and priesthood, and a complete break with the Jews occurred around 300 BC. Heavily Hellenized during the Roman occupation, the Samaritans were the focus of apostolic missions by St Peter, and significant numbers were con-

verted to Christianity; Gnosticism grew out of Samaritan Christianity. Following the collapse of BYZANTINE rule and the Islamic conquest of AD 636, the Samaritans were heavily influenced by the ARABS.

Today the Samaritans comprise a group of around 500 people who live around Mount Gerizim and in the nearby city of Holon, Israel. They constitute a sect of Judaism that recognizes only the Samaritan Pentateuch – the first five books of the Old Testament, but with all references to Jerusalem altered to signify Mount Gerizim. They reject other works such as the Talmud. They do not use the term 'Samaritan' for themselves, principally because they identify themselves as descendants of those not led into exile by the

Assyrians. They refer to themselves as 'Children of Israel' or 'Observant Ones'. Although they speak Arabic and have been heavily influenced by Arab culture, they use Hebrew as a liturgical language and in a wider context consider themselves to be ISRAELIS. They remain, however, a very insular people, and marriage is forbidden to anyone outside of the sect.

## SAMARRAN CULTURE

A Late Neolithic (stone age) culture of Mesopotamia that flourished in 6000–5500 BC and succeeded the HASSUNA CULTURE. The culture developed the first irrigation systems to increase crop yields and the availability of arable land. The pottery of this period bears human, animal and geometric swirling motifs.

## SAMOYEDS

A group of Asian peoples who speak Samoyedic languages, one of the two branches of the Uralic language family; the other is FINNO-UGRIAN. The Samoyeds include the NENETS, ENETS, NGANASANS and SELKUPS. Some KHANTY also speak Samoyedic. 'Samoyadj' are first recorded in RUSSIAN chronicles of the 12th century, but little is known of their history before modern times. They inhabit a vast area of forest and tundra in northern Siberia, in the Russian Federation, extending from the Kola peninsula in the west to the Taimyr peninsula in the east. The Samoyeds migrated to this area in the 1st millennium AD from an original homeland in the Sayan Mountains, to the north of Lake Baikal.

Traditionally, the Samoyeds are nomadic reindeer-herders, who move between the tundra in summers and the boreal pine forests in winter. They lived in tents of reindeer hide and wore hooded coats and boots made of reindeer hide with the fur turned outwards, and undergarments also of reindeer hide but with the fur turned inwards. Samoyed society was based on patriarchal clans, and their religion was animistic and shamanistic.

The Samoyeds' traditional way of life was severely disrupted by collectivization during the Soviet era. They have an Asiatic appearance, with yellowish skin, dark hair and high cheek-bones,

> " [The Samoyeds] have no houses, but only tents made of deers' skins, which they underprop with stakes and poles: their boats are made of deers' skins, and when they come on shore they carry their boats with them upon their backs ... "
>
> Stephen Burrough
> (1556)

and they are generally of short stature. They number around 50,000 in all.

## SANTAL

A nomadic tribal people who live in northeastern India, western Bangladesh and Nepal. They number around 4 million, the large majority of whom are in India. The name 'Santal' is possibly a derivative of 'Saotal' or 'Satar', both names used by the Santal themselves. Alternative names for the Santal are Santali, Sandal, Santhal(i), Hor, Har, Sandal and Sangtal. They speak Santali, the most widely spoken of the Munda languages of India, and the two most important Santali dialects are Karmali and Makli.

The Santal population consists largely of non-Hindu and aboriginal peoples. Their indigenous religion is called Sonaton Dharma. At its heart is Thakurji, a supreme omnipotent deity, with a number of sub-deities who are supplicated for daily needs.

The Santal, who are believed to be distantly related to the VEDDAS, are first recorded in central India, from where they migrated to west Bengal around the 2nd to 3rd centuries AD. Migration also occurred during BRITISH colonization, in the main through the search for employment opportunities. Because of colonization and Christian missionary activity, the Santal religion is now dying out.

## SASSANIANS

See PERSIANS.

## SAUDIS

Citizens of the modern state of Saudi Arabia (capital Riyadh). The population of this nation was about 22 million in 2002. The term 'Saudi' is relatively modern, and is useful only in referring to those who became citizens following the unification of Saudi Arabia in 1932. 'Saudi' is derived from the name of the Saud dynasty, which comprises the country's ruling family. Other peoples living in Saudi Arabia in significant numbers include YEMENIS, PAKISTANIS, PALESTINIANS, IRANIANS and Africans; foreign workers amount to about 5 million people.

While the vast majority of the population is now thoroughly urbanized, there remain large, although decreasing, numbers of nomadic BEDOUIN who continue to pursue a traditional lifestyle.

The region was originally the home of SEMITE peoples. It was subsequently under the influence of the MINAEANS and NABATAEANS during the 1st millennium BC. The unification of the ARAB Bedouin under Islam occurred during the 7th century AD. The region was under Mameluk influence from 1269 and OTTOMAN rule from the early 16th to the early 20th centuries. The nationalistic Islamic fundamentalist Wahhabi sect gained considerable power in the region during the 18th century and were at the forefront of efforts to unify the region under the Saud dynasty. Despite setbacks during the 19th century, this was finally accomplished 1902–32.

Saudi Arabia is by far the largest country in the Arabian peninsula, and contains both Mecca and Medina, two of the holiest cities in the Islamic world. As a result, millions of Muslims make pilgrimages to the country every year. Although more than 50% of the total land area is desert, Saudi Arabia has large oil-fields and is one of the largest producers of oil and petroleum in the world.

The Saudis are a Muslim people, and the vast majority adhere to the Wahhabi Sunni doctrine; about 3% are Shi'ite. Islamic Shari'a law forms the basis for Saudi government, which is an absolute monarchy, and is rigorously applied in the judicial system. Saudi religious leaders play a prominent role in the enforcement of this law. Traditional culture is encouraged, especially in the fields of art, architecture and calligraphy. Both theatres and cinemas are banned, as is the consumption of alcohol. However, the Saudi leadership has traditionally maintained close contact with a number of Western countries, in particular the United States, and Western culture has had considerable influence in some areas during recent decades, particularly in consumer items. Arabic is the national language, although English is commonly used for educational and business purposes. While allowed to participate in business, Saudi women remain under the authority of the family in many other areas of their lives.

**Political tensions**

Despite their participation in the Six Day War against the ISRAELIS in 1967 and ongoing friction between Israel and the Arab states, the Saudis are considered relatively moderate with regard to the Arab–Israeli conflict. However, the royal family's close economic and military ties with the USA – particularly in the wake of the Iranian Revolution of 1979 – together with Saudi economic divisions, have led to some degree of political tension within the country. In 1987 there were serious clashes between the Saudi police and Shi'ites, which resulted in the deaths of hundreds of people and tension with Iran. Moreover, following the First Gulf War, which led to the stationing of US troops in Saudi territory, attacks were made on US interests within the country by radical Islamic movements. The Saudi-born terrorist leader Osama bin Laden was deprived of his Saudi citizenship in 1994.

Since 1945, the Saudis have also clashed with the EGYPTIANS and YEMENIS, particularly following the Yemeni revolution in 1962. While initially supportive of the IRAQIS during their war against Iran, the Saudis subsequently played a leading role against them during the first Gulf War, an event that led to mass deportations of pro-Iraqi Yemenis and PALESTINIANS from the country. The Saudis did not play any significant part in the second Gulf conflict, and in recent years better relations have been fostered with both Yemen and Iran.

Since the 11 September 2001 terrorist attacks in the USA, however, the Saudi government has been under Western pressure to crack down on radical Islamist groups within the Kingdom. The country, and particularly its foreign workers, have witnessed several violent terrorist attacks and kidnappings, and the government has been forced to tighten its security measures.

## SEA PEOPLES

A group of peoples of mixed origin who migrated east to Anatolia and the Levant during the late 13th century BC. While their origins are the subject of much debate, it is possible that they included THRACIAN and GREEK (possibly CRETAN) elements. The term 'Sea Peoples' was introduced during the 19th century. At times

*" The ignorance and honesty of the Santal enabled the first adventurous traders from the plains to make rapid fortunes out of the hill-men. "*

J.H. Hutton, 1941

S

**Sea Peoples: main ethnic groups**

Ahhiyawa
Denyen
Lukka
Peleset
Shekelesh
Sherdana
Teresh
Tjeker
Weshesh

they were allied with settled peoples such as the LIBYANS and LYCIANS, and they were probably responsible for destroying the MYCENAEAN civilization. They succeeded in annihilating the HITTITE empire and badly damaging that of the PHOENICIANS, but were ultimately defeated by the EGYPTIANS. Following this defeat many settled in the southern Levant, becoming known to history as the PHRYGIANS and PHILISTINES.

## SELEUCIDS

A MACEDONIAN dynasty that gained control of large areas of West and Central Asia following the death of Alexander the Great in 323 BC. The dynasty is named after its founder, Seleucus I (c. 358–280 BC). While assimilating many features of the disparate peoples they ruled, particularly in government and administration, the Seleucids were responsible for spreading GREEK culture throughout their empire. By the mid-2nd century BC the Seleucid empire was in terminal decline, after PARTHIAN and ROMAN incursions, and in 64 BC the last vestiges of Seleucid territory became part of the Roman empire.

## SELJUKS or Seljuqs

A formerly nomadic Turkic people (see TURKS) from the Central Asian steppes, who formed the military elite of the OGUZ tribes. During the 11th century they migrated west and conquered an impressive but shortlived empire including much of modern Iran, Iraq, Syria, Anatolia and the Levant. The Seljuks were Sunni Muslims who were possibly converted by Islamic missionaries during the 10th century. They were zealous in their adherence to the Sunni faith and fought a number of wars against the Shi'ites, especially the BUYIDS and Fatimid EGYPTIANS, whom they regarded as heretics. They also fought the Christian BYZANTINES and later the Crusaders, to whom they lost their possessions in Palestine and Syria.

The Seljuks were a tolerant people, and their accumulation of enormous wealth through conquest and international trade allowed them to become great patrons of the arts, scholarship, law, architecture and urban development, in all of which they were heavily influenced by Islam. A true Seljuk style never really developed in the arts, but there was a degree of cultural unity throughout their empire, based on Islam, and this is witnessed by a great surge in the construction of mosques, monasteries and other religious edifices. Culturally, the Seljuks themselves were strongly influenced by the IRANIANS.

The Seljuk empire was never a very centralized or unified entity. In many cases local leaders continued to wield considerable power, and the empire was frequently divided. If a deceased ruler had more than one son, the empire would be split between them. Ultimately this proved to be a fatal weakness, as internecine strife and political fragmentation was a frequent result. By the early 13th century, the Seljuk domains had been reduced to the Anatolian Sultanate of Rum (the name of which, 'Rome', reflected its pre-Seljuk rulers, the BYZANTINES). Following Iranian and MONGOL attacks, this last enclave was finally destroyed in 1243.

Although they were ultimately assimilated into the OTTOMAN empire, the Seljuks' lasting legacy in Anatolia was the introduction of the Turkic people into a region that would ultimately become known as Turkey.

## SELKUPS

A SAMOYED Siberian people of the Yenisey River area, Russian Federation. They are similar to the KHANTY, from whom they split during the 16th century under pressure from RUSSIAN settlers. Traditionally nomadic reindeer-herders and shamanists, they speak a Uralic language. Soviet collectivization, forced settlement and assimilatory education policies seriously undermined their culture, while industrial pollution devastated their environment. In 1994 they numbered about 3600, but their survival as a people is in doubt.

## SEMITES

A group of ancient and modern peoples (see the accompanying box) who speak Semitic languages. The term was coined in the 18th century to denote people in the Bible descended from Shem, the eldest son of Noah. Their origins are uncertain, but they probably came from Arabia and had spread north to the Levant and

Mesopotamia by the dawn of urban civilization in the 4th millennium BC. Semitic peoples invented the alphabet, and were the source of Christianity, Islam and Judaism. The term 'Semite' is also used in the modern world to denote JEWS – mostly in the expression 'anti-Semitic' as a term for anti-Jewish and racist.

## SHARCHOPS or Sarchops

A people of Tibeto-Burman or Indo-Mongolian origin who are among the oldest peoples of Bhutan, and its second-largest ethnic group. The etymological meaning of their name is 'East-erner'. It is thought that they are tribes from northern Burma (Myanmar), northeastern India and Nepal who migrated to Bhutan sometime over the last thousand years. They inhabit the eastern provinces of Bhutan.

The Sharchops' language is of the Tibeto-Burman family and has several dialects including Sharchopkha, Kherig, Tsangla, Kurteop and Brokpa. Some Sharchops also speak HINDI and ASSAMESE. The majority are Buddhist, mainly belonging to the Tibetan Nyingmapa school of Mahayana Buddhism.

Exact demographic information restricted by the Bhutanese authorities, but it is reckoned that the Sharchops constitute approximately 14% of the BHUTANESE population of 1.8 million. They are denied all political, social and economic rights by the Bhutanese theocracy. In 1997 many Sharchops migrated to Arunachal Pradesh in India to escape political persecution following their support of the Druk Nat Congress party, which opposes theocratic rule in Bhutan.

## SHERPAS

A mountain people of Nepal and Sikkim state in India. Like the closely related BHUTIA, the Sherpas are of TIBETAN origin. They practise Tibetan Buddhism and speak a Tibetan dialect. The Sherpas are best known for their role as porters for Himalayan mountaineering expeditions. The first successful ascent of Mount Everest was made by a Sherpa, Tensing Norgay, with the New Zealand mountaineer Edmund Hillary in 1953. The Sherpas are mainly a farming people, but for centuries Sherpas have also traded with Tibet across the high Himalayan passes, to exchange rice from the lowlands for salt. The Sherpas number about 120,000.

## SHINA or Dard Shin or Dras or Sina or Shinaki

A group of peoples of Dardic origin (see DARDS) who speak the Shin language. They are ancient peoples thought to be of either INDO-ARYAN or INDO-EUROPEAN descent. They are mentioned by the Greek writer Herodotus and included in the Hindu Sanskrit *puranas* and epics, and are therefore at least as old as the 4th century BC. The Shina evolved in, and still inhabit, the Gurez Valley in what is known as Dardistan, a small area of land that borders northern Pakistan and northern India; their total population is around 25,000. The Shina adhere to Islam.

With recent plans to build a 330-megawatt hydro-electric power station that will dam the Gurez Valley, these ancient peoples are in severe danger of losing their homeland, heritage, language and culture.

## SHOR

A southern Siberian people centred on the Altai region in the Russian Federation. Traditionally shamanists and nomadic herders and traders, they speak a Turkic language (see TURKS). They were also famed metalworkers, and were known as 'Blacksmith Tatars' because of this skill. Despite determined resistance, they were conquered by the RUSSIANS in the 17th century. The Russians subsequently suppressed their metalworking, fearing they would produce weapons or rival them in trade. The Shor were also forcibly Christianized, though this was only a superficial conversion.

Soviet collectivization, forced settlement and assimilatory education policies seriously undermined their traditional culture, and exploitation of their mineral wealth led to large-scale immigration and environmental devastation. In the 1990s they began attempts to revive their culture. In 1979 they numbered about 16,000.

| Semites: main peoples |
| --- |
| *Ancient:* |
| Akkadians |
| Aramaeans |
| Assyrians |
| Babylonians |
| Canaanites |
| Chaldeans |
| Hebrews |
| Phoenicians |
| Sabaeans |
| *Modern:* |
| Arabs |
| Israelis |

S

## SHUGHNIS or Shugan

A people of Gorno-Badakhshan autonomous *oblast* (region) in Tajikistan, and of Afghanistan and China. They have a culture and historical experience very similar to the BARTANGS, and speak a similar language (called Shughni or Shughni-Rushan) of the Pamir family. In 1975 they numbered up to 60,000.

## SIBIR TATARS

See TATARS.

## SIKHS

People who adhere to the religion of Sikhism. The majority of Sikhs live or originate in the Punjab region of India and Pakistan; therefore most Sikhs are PUNJABIS. Sikhism is not, however, strictly an ethnic religion; any person may choose to become a Sikh. Sikhism is a monotheistic religion, and Sikhs follow the founding figure of Sikhism and the teachings of God as voiced through him. Indeed, the name Sikh means 'disciple'; a Sikh is a disciple of his or her teacher or Guru. For Sikhs, a Guru is one who has experienced God's voice and teaches his way; thus a Guru acts as temporal and spiritual

authority, and a Sikh is a disciple of God's way in accordance to the Guru's instruction.

The first Guru, the founder of the Sikh faith, was Guru Nanak (1469–1539). There were ten successive human Gurus, ending with Guru Gobind Singh (1666–1708), after which spiritual authority fell to the Guru Granth Sahib or the *Adi Granth* ('First Book') – the Sikh religious scripture – and temporal authority to the Guru Panth – the Sikh community. The Sikh house of worship is called a *gurdwara*.

The vast majority of Sikhs, around 13 million people, live within the Punjab. Of the remaining Sikh population, approximately 2 million live in regions of India, 450,000 in the UK, 200,000 in Canada, 150,000 in the USA, and 100,000 in the rest of the world.

The traditional language of the Sikhs is Punjabi, which is written using two alphabets: Lahnda, the indigenous alphabet, and Gurmukhi, which was devised by the second Guru, Guru Angad (ruled 1539–52) specifically for the Sikh scriptures.

Sikh history is inextricably bound up with the vicissitudes of the faith. However, as the majority of Sikhs are from the Punjab, the history of the Sikhs is also very much intertwined with the history of the Punjab from the 15th century AD onwards.

**Early Sikh history**

After the founding of the Sikh faith, efforts were made to unify the community by establishing teaching centres. The fourth Guru, Ram Das (1574–81), started the building of the Darbar Sahib – the Sikh 'Golden Temple' at Amritsar – their spiritual home of worship, on land given by Emperor Akbar the Great.

By 1601, during the reign of Guru Arjan Dev (1581–1606), the temple was complete. Arjan Dev attracted large numbers of converts to the faith in the Punjab region, and gradually the Sikh community emerged with its own distinctive identity. He also constructed the Akal Takht (God's Throne), which remains the centre of Sikh temporal power and socio-political decisions to the present day.

Before Guru Arjun was executed in Lahore by the MUGHAL emperor Jahangir, he sent a message to his 11-year-old son Guru Hargobind

Sikhs

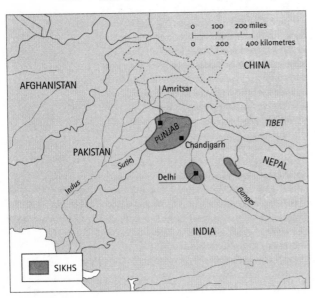

SIKHS

(1606–1664) to assemble an army and to wear two swords, as is now represented on the Sikh flag. One represents his spiritual leadership, the other his temporal leadership.

The ninth Guru, Tegh Bahadur, was executed by the Mughal emperor Aurangzeb for his efforts to stop prejudicial persecutions of KASHMIRI 'pundits' (from Sanskrit *pandit*, 'teachers').

### The consolidation of Sikh identity

One of the most significant events in Sikh history came during Guru Gobind Singh's reign (1675–1708). During this period there was growing unrest in the Punjab between the Sikhs, the Mughals, and Hindu royalty. In 1699, at Baisakhi, Guru Gobind Singh established the Khalsa (literally 'The Pure'), a body to further consolidate and emphasize Sikh identity. Practices initiated in the Khalsa include male Sikhs carrying the title of Singh, meaning 'lion', and female Sikhs bearing the name Kaur, meaning 'Princess' or 'lioness'. Further to their title, male Sikhs are identifiable by the 'Five Ks', the five marks of Khalsa identity, which include *kes* (uncut hair, usually carried inside a turban), *kangha* (a comb, to groom the beard and hair), *kirpan* (a sword), *kara* (a bracelet), and *kachh* (under shorts); each has a spiritual significance.

With the decline of the Mughal empire in the 18th century, Sikhs amassed much political power. In 1801 Ranjit Singh established a short-lived Kingdom of Lahore, but this was subsumed by the British empire in 1849.

An increase in religious confrontation between Hindus, Muslims and Sikhs occurred mainly as a response to the efforts of Christian missionaries during the late 19th century. The Sikh assemblies (Singh Sabha), headed by the Akali movement, ousted Hindu influences from their faith in an attempt to re-assert and 'purify' Sikh identity.

In 1947, despite opposition from the Akali Dal (the Akali movement's political wing), the Punjab was split when Pakistan and India were divided into independent nation-states. During the separation there was a mass transit of Hindus, Muslims, and Sikhs into their respective regions, and many were killed in riots. Sikhs also demanded their own Punjabi state (Khalistan), but all pleas were denied. In 1984, amidst the call for an independent state, a militant faction of the Akali, led by Sant Jarnail Singh Bhindranwale, decided on direct action. Indian troops entered the Darbar Sahib in order to evict armed militants who had occupied it. The result was thousands of deaths on both sides. As a response to the violence within the temple, Sikh bodyguards assassinated the INDIAN prime minister Indira Gandhi. The resulting riots, especially in New Delhi, led to massacres of both Hindus and Sikhs.

Between 1984 and 1993 an estimated 30,000 people were killed in the Punjab in violence between militants and the security forces, and between religious factions. The Akali Dal gained control in the Punjab Legislative Assembly elections in 1997. The campaign for an autonomous Sikh power base now continues peacefully.

## SINDHIS

The people of the state of Sindh (capital Karachi), now part of Pakistan. Technically the Sindhi peoples are those whose ethnic identity is defined by their Sindhi mother tongue and heritage, but the region's population includes URDUS, GUJARATIS, PUNJABIS and PASHTUN as well as Sindhis.

The Sindhi language is the second most widely spoken language in Pakistan, with between 12 and 16 million speakers; there are also some 2 million speakers in India. The Sindhi language is from the INDO-ARYAN family of languages, but also has strong influences from Arabic and Persian. The overwhelming majority of Sindhis adhere to Islam.

Historically the Sindhi people date back some 4000 years to the HARAPPANS and the Indus Valley civilization (c. 2600–1700 BC). The Sindhis were first influenced by the PERSIANS when King Darius I annexed the region in the 6th century BC. Two centuries later Alexander the Great conquered the area. After his death, Sindh came under the successive rule of the PARTHIAN, SCYTHIAN and KUSHAN empires, until the Persians retook it in the 3rd century AD. The Kushans introduced Buddhism to Sindh.

From the 6th to the 16th centuries Sindh was conquered by a succession of Muslim dynasties, culminating with the MUGHALS, and Islam became the dominant religion. After the end of Mughal rule in 1843, a number of independent Sindhi dynasties emerged, ruling until the BRITISH annexation. The British gave the Sindh region and its people the status of an independent state and province within the British Indian empire.

The India–Pakistan Partition of 1947 placed Sindh in Pakistan, and as a result many Indian Muslims of various ethnicities, including Urdus, settled in the Sindhi homeland. In 1970 the Sindhis were awarded separate provincial status within Pakistan.

One consequence of the ethnic mix in the Sindh, largely caused by the events of 1947, is the recent history of ethnic tensions, militant politics, and riots between the Sindhis and other groups such as Muhajirs and Urdus. At present a significant number of Sindhis live in Afghanistan, Malaysia, the United Arab Emirates, the USA and the UK.

# SINHALESE or Singhalese or Cingalese

The largest ethnic group of Sri Lanka, with a population of around 12.5 million, constituting approximately 77% of the SRI LANKAN population. They speak a language called Sinhala, part of the INDO-ARYAN family of languages, which is now the official language of Sri Lanka. The Pali language has also influenced Sinhala, especially since Buddhism was introduced to the country in the 3rd century AD.

Theravada Buddhism is the religion of 90% of the Sinhalese; the remaining 10% are largely Hindu, Christian or Muslim. Important places of pilgrimage for Sinhalese Buddhists include 'The Temple of the Tooth', a temple said to contain a tooth relic of the Buddha, and Samanala, a place that is said to contain his sacred footprints. Sinhalese identity is very much tied to their religion. The sizeable majority of Sinhalese reside in the south, southwest, and central regions of Sri Lanka.

### A history of conflict

The name 'Sinhalese' reflects the origins of the ethnic group. In the 3rd century BC the Indian Hindu prince Vijaya, son of King Sinha Bahu of Sinhapura, conquered the VEDDAS, the indigenous aboriginal peoples of Sri Lanka, and also possibly the TAMIL DRAVIDIANS. The *Mahavamsa* – the historical chronicle of Sri Lanka – confirms that the beginning of Sri Lankan civilization was in the 3rd century BC. When the prince landed on the island he planted a standard bearing a lion emblem, *sinha* or *singh*. The lion is still the official emblem of the Sinhalese and features on the Sri Lankan flag.

During the Vijaya dynasty, which lasted until around AD 65, Sinhalese civilization developed rapidly. The capital of the Vijaya kingdom was Anuradhapura, which remained the Sinhalese capital until the late 10th century, when it was abandoned in favour of Polonnaruwa. In the following centuries, the kingdom based on Polonnaruwa gradually broke up into smaller Sinhalese kingdoms.

From the 10th century, Sri Lanka was the subject of frequent attacks by the Tamils of southern India. In the 14th century the Tamils established a Hindu kingdom at Jaffna in northern Sri Lanka. These events led to a long history of Sinhalese–Tamil conflicts.

During the 12th and 13th centuries, the Sinhalese first came into contact with Islam. The descendants of the ARAB Muslims who settled in Sri Lanka are now referred to as 'Moors'.

The PORTUGUESE and the DUTCH arrived in the 16th and 17th centuries respectively. They controlled the coast, but never conquered the Sinhalese kingdoms. In 1796 the BRITISH arrived, and had brought the whole island under their control by 1815.

Colonization, subjugation and the centuries of conflict with other groups, most notably the Tamils, heightened fervour in post-colonial Sri Lanka for a separate Sinhalese identity, partly led by Sinhalese Buddhists. In 1956 the Sri Lankan government, dominated by the Sinhalese, passed legislation proclaiming Sinhalese the official language of Sri Lanka, and in 1972 Theravada Buddhism was formally decreed the state religion. Minority groups such as the Tamils were threatened by these developments, and further conflicts arose. Today many Sinhalese still aggressively assert their separate identity and regard it as more important than the Sri Lankan national identity.

# SINO-TIBETANS

People who speak any language belonging to the Sino-Tibetan language family, the world's second-largest linguistic family, consisting of some 300–360 languages and major dialects as well as a vast and complex array of minor dialects. There are three main branches: Sinitic (see CHINESE), TIBETAN and BURMESE. Sino-Tibetan-speakers live in China, Burma (Myanmar), Thailand, Laos, Vietnam, Tibet, Nepal, Bhutan, India and Bangladesh. The origin of Sino-Tibetan has been traced to the Himalayan plateau between 4000 and 7000 years ago. Research suggests that the earliest Sino-Tibetan-speakers may have been the Qiang (CH'IANG), of the Yellow River basin.

# SRI LANKANS

The people of the nation of Sri Lanka. The island of Sri Lanka was formerly known as Ceylon; 'Sri Lanka' is taken from the SINHALESE language and means 'resplendent land' or 'resplendent island'. The population of Sri Lanka is around 19.3 million. It is a matter of much contention as to what extent there is a Sri Lankan identity. The Sri Lankan ethnic composition is approximately 77% Sinhalese, 18% TAMIL, 7% Moor (that is, Muslims of Arabic descent) and 1% BURGHER, MALAY and VEDDA. Religion reflects these ethnic proportions: 69% are Buddhist, 15% are Hindu, 8% are Muslim and 8% are Christian. The ethnic and religious mix is far from a harmonious one. Rather, Sri Lanka is a nation with a long history of conflict, and indeed violence, between rival ethnic factions, a rivalry possibly as old as the arrival of the Sinhalese in Sri Lanka.

### History of Sri Lanka

The history of the Sri Lankans dates back to the INDO-ARYAN settlers, and possibly even to the pre-ARYAN and TAMIL DRAVIDIAN tribes. The original inhabitants of this island were probably the Veddas. During the 4th century BC, a number of Sinhalese kingdoms were established, most notably Anuradhapura. In the 3rd century BC Prince Mahinda, a Buddhist monk who was son of the famous Indian king Asoka, brought Buddhism to Sri Lanka, where it became the religion of the masses.

Over the subsequent centuries there were many Tamil invasions from southern India, and in the 14th century the Tamils established a kingdom in northern Sri Lanka. These events led to a long and bitter series of conflicts. During the 12th and 13th centuries ARAB traders also arrived in Sri Lanka. The PORTUGUESE and DUTCH arrived in the 16th and 17th centuries respectively, and also established coastal trading posts. In 1796 the BRITISH expelled the Dutch and by 1815 had won control of the whole island.

During their colonial rule, the British system of divide and rule reduced friction between the Sinhalese and the Tamils. After the British withdrew in 1948, Sri Lanka became an independent nation state and changed its name from Ceylon to Sri Lanka. In 1956 the predominantly Sinhalese socialist government declared Sinhalese the national language and established a predominant Sinhalese judicial process. These moves angered the Tamil minorities and increased ethnic and religious conflicts. The period up to 1972, when Sri Lanka became a republic and Buddhism was declared the state religion, was marred by violence, and violence continues today.

In 1983 open civil war broke out. Its main protagonists were the Liberation Tigers of Tamil Eelam (LTTE) and the majority Sinhalese government. As a direct consequence of the arrival of an Indian peacekeeping force to quell violence in Sri Lanka, Tamil agents assassinated the Indian prime minister Rajiv Gandhi in 1991. The same fate befell the Sri Lankan prime minister Ranasinghe Premadasa in 1993. The violence continued until the end of the year, when Norwegian officials brokered peace talks, resulting in a Tamil ceasefire and the lifting of a seven-year embargo on the LTTE.

Civil unrest, however, still continues. In the late 20th century over 66,000 Sri Lankan refugees, mostly Tamil, resided in India, with 40,000 on the Indian borders and a further 200,000 in the West.

# SUMERIANS

A mixture of Semitic (see SEMITES) and non-Semitic peoples who are credited with creating the world's first civilization. The Sumerians

> *"They be naked people all of them; yet many of them be good with their pieces which be Muskets. "*
>
> Ralph Fitch, 16th century, referring to the Sri Lankans

S

spoke a language unrelated to any other known language. Their origins remain a matter of conjecture, although Sumerian civilization was the successor to the UBAID CULTURE of Mesopotamia. The term 'Sumerian' is not an ancient one. They would have been identified by contemporaries as 'the people of Sumer' or 'the black-headed people'. The term 'Sumerian' was first coined by archaeologists following the rediscovery of their civilization in the 19th century.

Sumeria was situated in southern Mesopotamia, and by the mid-4th millennium BC a number of independent city-states had emerged that over the course of the next 1500 years frequently vied for political and economic supremacy. Chief amongst these were the cities of Kish, Uruk, Ur, Eridu and Lagash. The focal point of these early Sumerian cities was the temple, and the priesthood was responsible for many of the administrative, economic and executive advances necessary for the evolution of the city-state. These included the organization of workforces capable of building and maintaining irrigation works, the collection and storage of food surpluses and the propagation of early trade links. As a result, the priesthood gained considerable affluence and great political power. Social stratification was another feature of these developments.

### Political development

The growing competition between cities, however, together with attacks from other tribes such as the ELAMITES and GUTIANS, helped stimulate the development of kingship, as successful warrior leaders gained local political supremacy. Eventually the kings became more powerful than the priests and the king became known as the *lugal* or 'big man'.

Although the city-states would form confederations during times of external threat or unite under a single military conqueror, they were generally independent, and this left them susceptible to external invasion. Under Sargon the Great (ruled *c.* 2334–2279 BC), the AKKADIANS succeeded in overrunning all of Sumeria and incorporated the region into the world's first empire. Although following the death of Sargon the Sumerians recovered under the Third Dynasty of Ur (*c.* 2112–2004 BC), they were

finally defeated by the Elamites in 2004 BC. Following this catastrophe, and increasing AMORITE settlement in southern Mesopotamia, the Sumerians gradually lost their political and cultural identity.

One of the greatest legacies of the Sumerians was their invention of a writing system from which all later Western scripts are descended. This early form of writing was devised in order to facilitate the more efficient record-keeping needed for a developing city-state civilization. Originally pictographic in form (in use at Uruk by the mid-4th millennium BC), this system evolved into cuneiform by the early third millennium BC. The cuneiform system was later adopted by the Akkadians and spread by them and their political successors throughout much of western Asia.

The ability of the Sumerians to produce agricultural surpluses not only allowed the propagation of large urban centres, but also freed up many from the necessity of agricultural labour. This freedom allowed, among other things, the development of professional artisans, and the Sumerians became extremely proficient in the arts, particularly sculpture, relief work, bronze and copper work, pottery, and the carving of cylinder seals. The themes for much of this art were derived from religion, and much of it was used to adorn temple complexes or for liturgical purposes. Later kings also commissioned art to decorate their palaces, which were intended to rival the temples and to record their heroic deeds.

The Sumerians recognized a large number of gods, and each city-state had its own principal deity. In addition, all living things, including humans, were believed to have specific gods or spirits that governed their existence. Each person was also believed to have his or her own personal spirit, a kind of guardian angel. The Sumerians believed in an after-life, but it was merely a pale imitation of life on earth. Certain gods were revered above all others, such as Inanna (goddess of love), Sin (moon god) and Ninhursag (mother goddess). Sumerian religious practices drew heavily on divination and magic and were highly influential on the later religious practices of the BABYLONIANS, ASSYRIANS, HITTITES and HURRIANS.

The ziggurat temple-complex was a Sumerian innovation, as was the theory of kingship by divine right. Indeed, such was the reputation of the Sumerians in the field of religion that their language continued in use for religious purposes under the Babylonians and Assyrians, long after it had died out as a spoken tongue.

In addition to their religious influence, the Sumerians were also highly regarded in the fields of astronomy, law, medicine and mathematics, and many of the later advances in these fields, for example by the CHALDEANS, were founded on earlier Sumerian discoveries. The Sumerians also had a great reputation in the fields of music and poetry, and were responsible for the composition of the epic *Gilgamesh*, one of the finest pieces of pre-classical literature.

## SVAN

A minor KARTVELIAN people who are native to Svanetia in the Georgian Caucasus Mountains. The Svan number approximately 50,000, but they are officially counted as GEORGIANS.

## SYRIANS

The citizens of the modern Republic of Syria (capital Damascus). Significant numbers of Syrians also reside in neighbouring states, North and South America, the Caribbean and Europe. In 2002, the population of Syria was 17 million.

Some of the earliest civilizations, such as that of the CANAANITES, were formed in the region now known as Syria, and its geographical location, between Egypt and Mesopotamia and along the Mediterranean coast, has ensured its position as one of the world's most important trading areas – as evidenced by the success of the PHOENICIANS, and later by the cities of Antioch and Palmyra. It is also believed that both the AMORITES and HYKSOS may have originated in the Syrian desert.

The term 'Syrian' has no strict meaning until the formation of the Kingdom of Syria under Antiochus III (ruled 223–187 BC), which was a strongly Hellenized state derived from the SELEUCID empire. Before this, the region had been subject to incursions by the AKKADIANS, HITTITES, EGYPTIANS, ARAMAEANS, ASSYRIANS, BABYLONIANS,

PERSIANS and MACEDONIANS. The region had also formed the heartland of the kingdom of the MITANNI. Syrian independence, however, was extremely brief, and by 64 BC, following NABATAEAN encroachment, Syria was incorporated into the ROMAN empire. This annexation essentially marked the end of any Syrian self-determination until the mid-20th century.

Following the collapse of BYZANTINE rule in AD 636, the Syrians were incorporated into the ARAB caliphate, and the resident Christian population was influenced by Arab and Islamic culture. The Fatimid dynasty of Egypt gained suzerainty over the region during the late 9th century, but were succeeded, in turn, by the SELJUKS, Crusaders and Mameluks. The OTTOMANS controlled the region, with varying degrees of success, between 1516 and the conclusion of World War I. Following the end of Ottoman rule in 1918, Syria was governed as a French mandate until independence was finally achieved in 1946.

It was during the final years of Ottoman rule, and in particular under French political domination, that Syrian nationalism grew apace, with serious rebellions during the 1920s and 1930s. Nationalistic agitation continued until the final French withdrawal.

### Foreign relations

The Syrians were highly opposed to the foundation of the state of Israel, and since 1948 have been involved in frequent conflict with the ISRAELIS, most notably in the Arab–Israeli wars of 1948, 1967 and 1973. As a result of the Yom Kippur War of 1973, Syria lost the strategic Golan Heights to Israel.

The future of the region, together with the PALESTINIAN question, continues to be a source of tension between the two nations. The perceived pro-Israeli stance of the UK and the USA has also led to significant anti-Western feeling among many Syrians, while the UK and the USA have, at times, accused the Syrian government of sponsoring international terrorism. Syria's relations with other Arab states have not always been easy; in 1958 Syria and Egypt formed a new state, the United Arab Republic, but Syrian nationalism was a significant factor in the collapse of the new political entity in 1961.

S

The Ba'ath Arab Socialist Party came to power in a bloodless coup in 1970 under Hafez al-Assad, but relations with the Ba'athist regime of Saddam Hussein's Iraq (from 1979) were often hostile. Control passed to Assad's son Bashar in 2000.

During the 1980s, the Syrians were drawn increasingly into the LEBANESE civil war and were one of a minority of states that supported the IRANIANS during the Iran–Iraq war. During the first Gulf War, the Syrians joined the allied coalition against the IRAQIS, but were accused of aiding them during the second conflict.

**Religion and culture**

The vast majority of Syrians are Arabs. There are also, however, important KURDISH and ARMENIAN communities, as well as a very small number of TURKMEN and ASSYRIANS. Although there have been few ethnic clashes, there has been frequent internal political tension and a number of major coups since independence. During the late 1970s and early 1980s, a right-wing Islamic group known as the Muslim Brotherhood embarked on a series of attacks against the Syrian government, which culminated in a major rebellion at Hamah in 1982 that was crushed by pro-government forces. There remain certain Islamic elements that are dissatisfied with the political status quo.

Most Syrians are Sunni Muslim, but there are also numbers of Alawaites, ISMAILIS, Shi'ites and DRUZE, together with small Christian and Jewish populations. There have been no serious inter-religious tensions amongst Syrians since the 1860s. Culturally, the Syrians value their Arab/Islamic heritage, and efforts have been made to counter increased Western influences. Traditionally the Syrians have been renowned for the unsurpassed quality of their enamelled glassware.

## TAIMURA

See HAZARA.

## TAJIKS

A Central Asian people descended from INDO-IRANIAN peoples who settled the region of modern Tajikistan in the 1st millennium BC. They were sedentary farmers and craftsmen who were not unified into a single state, and their position on the great trade route connecting India, China and Persia led to repeated invasion. ARAB invasion during 7th century AD was followed by Turkic attacks, culminating in UZBEK and AFGHAN rule from the 15th century, and RUSSIAN rule from the 1860s. These influences made the Tajiks into Farsi-speaking Sunni Muslims, noted for their poetry and literature. Only as part of the USSR did a Tajik state appear, and a real national identity has been slow to develop.

In the 1970s the underground Islamic Renaissance Party was formed, but tribal-based divisions remained deep and were only contained by Soviet rule. The north was dominated by Leninabaders, the south by Kulyabis, the east by Garmis and the mountains by Pamiri groups. Following independence in 1991, a Kulyabi dominated government faced an immediate challenge from other groups claiming to stand for Islam or democracy. In the resulting civil war about 50,000 died, huge numbers fled, and the economy and infrastructure all but collapsed. Tajikistan became one of the world's poorest countries, and a United Nations-brokered peace deal in 1997 did not completely end the violence, while droughts in 2000 and 2001 threatened famine. There are 3.6 million Tajiks in Tajikistan, but 3.7 million are in Afghanistan, and over 1 million in Uzbekistan and China. A Tajik nation has not yet fully developed.

## TALYSH

A Caucasian people of south Azerbaijan and northwest Iran. They are Shi'ite Muslim farmers who speak an INDO-IRANIAN language. Mostly under RUSSIAN rule in the 19th century, they suffered Soviet collectivization and assimilation with the AZERIS, with whom they were officially counted in the census.

In 1993 the Talysh rebelled against Azerbaijan and proclaimed a Talysh-Mugan republic, but their rising was suppressed within three months. An exiled leadership was seeking international support for their cultural and political rights in 2000, at which point the Talysh numbered up to 2 million.

## TAMANG or Tamar or Murmi or Jade or Bhotiya

One of the original NEPALESE peoples. They live on the border of Nepal, south of the Himalayas. Their population is around 700,000, or around 3% of the Nepalese population of about 25 million people.

The Tamang language belongs to the Tibetan-Burman family. The vast majority of Tamang adhere to a form of Mahayana Buddhism heavily influenced by the Lama Buddhism of their neighbours, the TIBETANS.

Speculation places their origin as Mongolian, though almost nothing is recorded of their early history. One inscription, dating to the 13th century and possibly the earliest written account bearing the Tamang name, was found at Fort Lo Manthang in Tibet.

### Discrimination against the Tamang

Until about 250 years ago the Tamang were fairly autonomous; since then, however, they have lived under suppression and discrimination, and were even prohibited at times from descending from their mountainous abodes. The reason for such discrimination appears to be religious: the Tamang live in a country ruled by a Hindu monarchy and predominantly populated by Hindus. In 1846 rulers in the Nepalese capital Kathmandu prevented the Tamang from serving in the Indian or British armies, unlike the GURKHAS. To this day, despite the lifting of this restriction, few serve in these armies.

In 1854 legislation was passed classifying all Nepalese in accordance with the Hindu class (*Varna*) system. All non-Hindus were placed in the lowest class of *Sudra*, forced to work in menial jobs such as labourers and porters. Tamang land was also confiscated. The most famous Tamang porter was Sambhu Tamang, an 18-year-old who became the youngest person up to that time to climb Mount Everest when he worked for the Italian expedition of 1973.

Only in 1950 were the Tamang allowed to travel abroad for employment, and only recently did the Nepalese government allow the Tamang to use the Tamang name in the country's civil and legal rolls. Today the Tamang constitute the majority of the Himalayan work force and they still generally work in lower-paid and more menial jobs. Modernity has drawn the Tamang from their traditional environment in the hills to the cities where the majority can find employment, although many still work as poorly paid labourers. They continue to suffer political marginalization as well as economic and social discrimination. The population of 13,000 Tamang in India are afforded better treatment because of Indian tribal and caste rights.

## TAMILS

A people of DRAVIDIAN descent who live in southern India and Sri Lanka. They are unified by their native Tamil language, an ancient language belonging to the Dravidian family of INDIAN languages and currently an official language in both India and Sri Lanka. Tamil as a literary language is one of the oldest in Asia, dating back at least two millennia, with a very rich heritage. There are around 61.5 million Tamils in India and over 3 million in Sri Lanka, the latter constituting 18% of the SRI LANKAN population. Tamils are also found in Malaysia, South Africa, Burma (Myanmar), Indonesia and Singapore.

The vast majority of Indian Tamils reside in Tamil Nadu, southern India, where Tamil is the official language. The Tamil population of Sri Lanka is mainly found in the northern and eastern regions. Tamils are overwhelmingly Hindu, although there are some Christians, Muslims and a very few Buddhists. Tamil Hinduism is characterized by *bhakti*, 'devotion', and Tamil literature strongly reflects this. Hinduism is very much the core of Tamil culture.

### The Indian Tamils

The origin of the Tamils is thought to be traced to the Indus Valley civilization (see HARAPPANS). The first period of Tamil history, the Cangham ('academy') period, dates from around 100 BC to AD 300. Cangham refers to the period that provides the earliest evidence of a proliferation of Tamil literature, mainly that of heroic religious poetry. In this period Tamil culture flourished. Three kingdoms ruled over Tamil Nadu during this time: the Chera, Chola and Pandya; there were also many chieftains. Under the Kalabhra (AD 300–600), Buddhism and

Jainism prospered, and literature continued to flourish.

Perhaps the most important period of Tamil religious history was the Bhakti period (AD 600–1200). 'Bhakti' refers to an attitude of religious devotion, and it was during this period that many of the northern Brahminical religious influences were infused into the Tamil belief system. During the latter half of this period the great CHOLA empire ruled the Tamils.

A vast body of Tamil literature was written during the Bhakti period, in which the poet-saints, the *Alvars*, played a significant role. Two of the most influential Hindu religious schools also arose during this period: Advaita in the 8th century, and the Visistadvita school in the 11th and 12th centuries. The Saiva Siddhanta school flourished during the 13th and 14th centuries.

The Kingdom of Vijayanagar (of TELUGU origin), was also established during the 14th century, lasting over 200 years. It was this kingdom that officially patronized Sanskrit and placed a high value on its religious texts.

Roman Catholicism and Protestantism were introduced to the Tamils by the Portuguese and Dutch respectively in the 16th and 17th centuries. In 1639 the English East India Company established a base in Madras, and between that time and Indian independence in 1947 the whole region was known as the Madras Presidency, which became part of the British Raj from the 19th century until Indian independence in 1947.

In 1956 the Madras Presidency was split and Tamil Nadu and its people became an autonomous republic within India, as was Andhra Pradesh for the Telugu. Since that time, socio-political movements have sought to reinvigorate traditional Tamil cultural identity and to rid the state and its peoples of all Sanskrit and Hindi influence.

**The Sri Lankan Tamils**

The parallel history of the Sri Lankan Tamils is very different from that of their Indian relations, though both groups share the Hindu religion. Sri Lankan Tamils experienced conflict from the very beginning. The Dravidian Tamils migrated to Sri Lanka over a period spanning the early centuries AD to around AD 1300. At times the

north and east of the island were ruled by Indian Tamil kingdoms of the Pandyas and Cheras (up to the 3rd century), the Pallavas (5th–8th centuries) and finally the Cholas (9th–13th centuries). An independent Tamil kingdom was founded at Jaffna in the 14th century.

The majority of Tamils still reside in the areas previously dominated by these kingdoms. The settlement of these Tamils in Sri Lanka led to ongoing ethnic tensions with the Buddhist SINHALESE, who dominated most of the island until the European colonial period.

When the British took power in Sri Lanka in 1796–1815, they imported Tamils from India to work on tea plantations. These Indian Tamils (as they are still known) have a different caste system from that of the Sri Lankan Tamils and the two groups do not intermarry or live in the same areas. The British colonial policy of divide and rule greatly favoured the Sinhalese over both groups of Tamils in both economic and social terms. This further increased tensions between Tamils and Sinhalese.

After Sri Lankan independence in 1948, the government became majority Sinhalese. In 1956, Sinhalese became the official language and Sinhalese citizens were awarded greater social privileges. This led to calls from the Tamil minority for greater autonomy, resulting in rioting and demonstrations. The Tamil Federation Party spearheaded this campaign, and in 1958 the Tamil language was permitted for administrative purposes in Tamil regions. The Tamils were not satisfied with this gesture, however, while many fundamentalist Sinhalese felt that even this concession went too far. In 1972 Buddhism was declared the state religion, provoking further conflict. In 1977 Tamil became a national language and the Tamils were granted greater local autonomy, but violence continued to spiral.

Civil war broke out in 1983 after the Liberation Tigers of Tamil Eelam (LTTE) ambushed and killed a regiment of Sinhalese soldiers. The Sinhalese responded by killing thousands of Tamils. Mass internal migrations occurred, with Sinhalese in the north and east of the island fleeing south and west and Tamils in the opposite direction, while many Tamils also left as refugees for India.

Fearing invasion into Tamil Nadu, the Indian government, in co-operation with the Sri Lankan government, sent the Indian Peace Keeping Force (IPKF) to Sri Lanka to calm Tamil tensions in 1987. The Tamils felt betrayed by the Indian government and violence reached new heights. In 1991 Tamil agents assassinated the Indian prime minister Rajiv Gandhi, and the same fate befell the Sri Lankan prime minister Ranasinghe Premadasa soon afterwards. Violence continued until the end of 1993, when Norwegian officials brokered peace talks; the results of these talks were a ceasefire and the lifting of a seven-year outlawing of the LTTE.

In 1995 the LTTE broke the ceasefire. Retaliation occurred in Colombo, and the government responded in 1996 with Operation Sunshine, the military expulsion of the LTTE and Tamil peoples from the northern city of Jaffna, their most important stronghold. In 1998 Tamils attacked the sacred Sinhalese Buddhist temple, the so-called Temple of the Tooth. To date Tamil and Sinhalese ethnic relations are still fraught, despite renewed peace talks.

## TANGUTS

A TIBETAN people who originated in the highlands of western Sichuan (China). They spoke their own language, Tangut, which was heavily influenced by Chinese. The Tanguts practised a form of esoteric Mahayana Buddhism.

Prior to founding their own kingdom they formed a Chinese state under the Song dynasty (AD 960–1279). In the 9th century they helped the Song to put down a rebellion.

In the 10th century, the Tangut state gained independence, and in 1020 they moved their capital to Xingzhou, a move that afforded them control over a vital portion of the Silk Route and thus a role as middlemen in the trade activities between China and Central Asia. In 1038 the Tangut Li Yuanhao declared himself emperor and established the warlike Xixia (Hsi Hsia) dynastic kingdom. This kingdom lasted until 1227, when, after trade disputes with the MONGOLS, Genghis Khan crushed the Tanguts.

## TANUKH

An ARAB tribal confederation that migrated from southern Arabia into Mesopotamia during the early 1st millennium AD. Both Christianity and Islam had a profound effect on these tribes, and many Tanukh who subsequently migrated into Syria and Lebanon during the 8th and 9th centuries became adherents of the DRUZE sect.

## TATS

A Caucasian people of northeast Azerbaijan, south Dagestan (Russian Federation) and Iran. Under PERSIAN rule from the 4th century AD, most subsequently adopted Shia Islam. Sedentary farmers, they have been almost entirely assimilated into AZERI culture, encouraged by Soviet collectivization and assimilatory policies. In Iran similar assimilation has occurred. Their identity as a distinct people survives mainly in folklore. In 1989 they numbered up to 325,000.

## TA-YUAN

See TOCHARIANS.

## TELUGU or Tenugu or Gentoo or Toulangi

A people of the state of Andhra Pradesh, India, and also the name of their language. For the early history of the Telugu, see ANDHRAS, their ancient Sanskrit name, sometimes still used. The majority of the Telugu are Hindus, though there are some Telugu Christians or Muslims.

The Telugu language is heavily influenced by DRAVIDIAN languages and by other major languages from India's history, including Arabic, Persian, Sanskrit and English. It belongs to the INDO-ARYAN family and has many dialects. As the official language of Andhra Pradesh state, it is now spoken by over 60 million people, and is the second most widely spoken Indian language after HINDI. Over 85% of the population of Andhra Pradesh speaks Telugu, and the language is also used in Bangladesh, Sri Lanka, Singapore, Burma (Myanmar), China and Malaysia.

Since the collapse of the Andhra empire in the 3rd century AD, the Telugu have enjoyed various further periods of prosperity and power. During the 10th and 11th centuries, after Nannaya had translated the Mahabharata into Telugu, the Chalakya dynasty came to power, reuniting the Telugu people. They came under Muslim rule in 1565, then in the 17th century parts of their territories were ceded to the British and French.

In the 19th century, the Telugu were among the early leaders of the Indian nationalist movement, seeking to unite all Telugu-speakers, whether under British or regional Indian rule.

In 1953, after Indian independence, the state of Andhra was created, incorporating the core Telugu territories. In 1956 the neighbouring state of Hyderabad was split and its nine Telugu-speaking regions joined Andhra, forming the the new state of Andhra Pradesh.

## THARU

A people who originally inhabited the lowlands of Nepal and settled in the Terai regions on the Indian border. They number up to 1 million, constituting about 4% of the NEPALESE population. They are Hindus and animists and speak a language called Naja, as well as other dialects such as Prakriti, URDU and Nepalese.

A number of conflicting theories account for Tharu origins in Nepal. One theory dates their arrival from the end of the Indus Valley civilization (see HARAPPANS) in about 1700 BC. Another claims that they are the descendants of the Shakya dynasty who propagated Mahayana Buddhism in Nepal from the late 1st century BC to the early 1st century AD. Yet another thesis argues that the Tharu arrived in Nepal during the Muslim invasion of India between the 12th and 13th centuries AD.

One peculiar characteristic of the Tharu is their immunity to malaria, which enabled them to live in the malarial Terai region untroubled by the outside world until 1950. When malaria was eradicated from the area, however, other Nepalese moved into Tharu lands, and the Tharu became marginalized. They suffered social, economic and physical exploitation because of their lack of contact with modern lifestyles. The majority were forced either to migrate or to work as bonded labourers (*kamaiya*) to landlords on

land that was previously their own, despite the abolition of slavery in 1926.

In the early 1950s the Tharu organized the Backward Society Education (BASE) in an attempt for Tharu equality. They campaigned for minimum wages for the labourers, but the only result was further persecution. In response they protested in the streets and organized strikes. After many promises, the Nepalese government granted freedom to the labourers. However, many were evicted and were forced to set up camps near the jungles and rivers, causing many deaths during the monsoon. Despite further promises, still only around 10% of the Tharu have had their lands returned to them, while around 60% remain in illegal occupation of land that once belonged to them.

## TIBETANS

The majority people of the Himalayan country of Tibet, an autonomous region of China. There are around 2.6 million Tibetans living in Tibet, constituting almost 93% of the entire population. A further 2 million Tibetans live outside the Tibet Autonomous Region (TAR), in China (mainly in Qinghai and Sichuan provinces which neighbour TAR), Bhutan, Nepal and in exile in India and the West. The Tibetans have no single ethnic origin but are mainly MONGOLOID and Turkic (see TURKS). Their language is a member of the Sino-Tibetan family.

Tibetans adhere to a syncretic form of esoteric Mahayana Buddhism, known as Lamaism or Tibetan Buddhism, that incorporates many of the practices from the indigenous Tibetan religion of Bon. Lamaism remains central to modern Tibetans' cultural and national identity, for which reason it has been subject to frequent hostility from the country's Chinese rulers.

The Tibetans were first recorded in the 2nd century BC by CHINESE writers, who called them 'Qiang' (see CH'IANG). At that time they lived on the steppes northeast of China, from where they migrated into modern day Tibet early in the 1st millennium AD. In the 6th century AD the kings of the Yarlung Valley succeeded in uniting much of Tibet. King Songsten Gampo (ruled 630–49) and his successors built a Tibetan empire that extended into Nepal, India and China.

During the 7th century Tibet took control of a vital part of the Silk Route, and in the 8th, under King Trisong Detsen (ruled 755–97), they even sacked the Chinese capital Chang'an (modern day Xian).

During this period Mahayana Buddhism was introduced by Indian monks, such as Padmansambhava, and gained Tibetan royal patronage; to counter the opposition of adherents of Bon, it was even made illegal not to be Buddhist. In the 10th century the Tibetan state collapsed and Buddhism languished for over a century, until it was revived by Indian Buddhist missionaries. Buddhist monasteries became centres of political and spiritual power, ruling the countryside in alliance with local aristocratic families.

In 1239 Tibet was conquered by the Mongols, who ruled the country by appointing the influential Saskya Lama as viceroy. Through these contacts, the Mongols adopted Lamaism themselves. After the fall of the Mongol empire in 1368, Tibet remained under the theocratic rule of the lamas.

The Dalai Lamas (Dalai means 'ocean of knowledge'), whom the majority of Tibetans still recognize as the spiritual and temporal rulers of Tibet came to power in the 16th century. In 1720 Tibet became a Chinese protectorate but the country remained essentially autonomous.

The fall of the Chinese Qing dynasty in the revolution of 1911 allowed the Tibetans to re-assert their independence. Unfortunately for the Tibetans, because of great power rivalries in the region, this was not internationally recognized. In 1950 the Communist Chinese invaded and re-conquered the country.

### Repression and resistance

In 1959 a Tibetan revolt against the Chinese occupation was violently crushed. Around 87,000 Tibetans were killed and the Dalai Lama, with around 100,000 followers, fled to India and established a government in exile at Dharamsala. The Chinese saw Tibet as a backward feudal society but reforms, such as the abolition of serfdom, were offset by attacks on the Tibetan cultural identity and Sinicization. These pressures were at their most intense during the Cultural Revolution (1966–9), when Mandarin was made the official language and most of Tibet's monasteries were looted and demolished.

In 1980 religious activity was permitted once again and a small number of monasteries were re-founded. At the same time, however, the Chinese government adopted a policy of encouraging the immigration of HAN Chinese settlers into Tibet, which, if continued, will eventually turn the Tibetans into an ethnic minority in their

**"** Men which were wont to eate the carkasses of their deceased parents. **"**

**William of Rubruck, 1253, on the Tibetans**

Tibetans

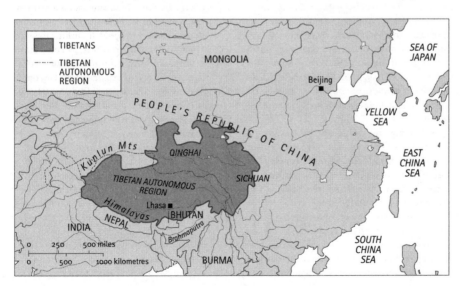

own country. The Tibetans are also suffering increasing economic marginalization; Tibetans rarely find employment in Chinese-owned businesses or government-funded infrastructure projects.

Since 1965 Tibet has been an officially designated an 'autonomous region of the Peoples' Republic of China', but few Tibetans have ever played a role in the regional government, whose autonomy is, in any case, purely nominal. Continuing Tibetan resistance to Chinese rule, led by Buddhist monks and nuns, takes the form of peaceful demonstrations and acts of passive civil disobedience. Resistance continues to be met by violence and it is estimated that from 1950 to the present day at least one-sixth of the Tibetan population have lost their lives under Chinese occupation. In 1989 the current 14th Dalai Lama was awarded the Nobel Peace prize for his unceasing non-violent opposition to the Tibetans' subjugation, but at present the future for his people looks bleak.

> " Everything with the Toda is taken *au sérieux.* "
>
> W.E. Marshall, 1873

## TIMURIDS

A CHAGATAID dynasty of MONGOLS that originated from Kish in modern Uzbekistan and succeeded in building an impressive empire under their leader Timur Lang, or Tamerlane, (1336–1405). At the height of their power, the Timurids controlled parts of India, Iran, Afghanistan and Syria, and had defeated, among others, the Ilkhans, GOLDEN HORDE TARTARS and the Mameluk rulers of Egypt. The aim of the Timurids was the re-establishment of the Mongol empire of Genghis Khan, and their victories were often accompanied by the mass slaughter of local populations, as evidenced at both Delhi and Baghdad.

Following the death of Timur Lang, his empire was divided between his sons, and subsequent succession crises led to further splits and frequent civil war. By 1506 the empire had ceased to exist. Babur, the founder of the MUGHAL dynasty, was of Timurid descent.

Despite their reputation as ferocious conquerors, the Timurids were patrons of the arts, and miniature painting, poetry and historical writing all flourished throughout their empire. In addition, most Timurid rulers patronized building projects, particularly in their capital, Samarkand, to which large numbers of artisans from conquered territories were deported to work. These buildings are particularly noted for their free use of colour.

## TIMURI

See HAZARA.

## TOCHARIANS or Ta-Yuan

See YUE-QI.

## TODA or Ahl

A pastoral people who live in the Nilgiri Hills in Tamil Nadu, southern India. They number around 12,000 and are governed by a tribal elder system. They speak a unique language stemming from DRAVIDIAN.

Toda religion is also unique, founded on veneration of the buffalo and its milk as the life-giving blood of the people; as such their main occupation is herding. During the 20th century some Toda converted to Islam.

## TOFALARS

A southern Siberian people of Irkutsk *oblast* (region), Russian Federation. Traditionally shamanists and nomadic hunters, gatherers and reindeer-herders, they speak a Turkic language (see TURKS). They suffered severe exploitation under RUSSIAN rule from the 17th century. Soviet collectivization, forced settlement and compulsory boarding education largely reduced them to urban wage-earners; as a result, they have become heavily assimilated. In 2002 they numbered about 650.

## TORGUTS

See KALMYKS.

## TOULANGI

See TELUGU.

## TSAKHAR

See CHAHAR.

## TSAKHURS

A Caucasian people of Rutul region, south Dagestan (Russian Federation), and neighbouring Azerbaijan. Herders and skilled artisans who practise Sunni Islam, they speak a North Caucasian language. Under pressure from TURKS and PERSIANS, they sought RUSSIAN help in the 19th century, which resulted in their annexation. Soviet collectivization and assimilatory education policies undermined their traditional culture, but their identity as a people remains strong. In the 1990s, however, this came under threat when the collapse of the USSR left them partitioned between two nations. In 1979 they numbered about 14,000.

## TULU

A people who inhabit Tulu Nadu, an area within Karnataka state, southern India. They speak Tulu, also known as Tal, Thalu, Tullu, Tilu, Thullu and Tuluva Bhasa, one of the five DRAVIDIAN languages of southern India, and one of the oldest. There are approximately 2.5 million Tulu-speakers, concentrated mostly in Tulu Nadu, but also found in Kerala, Maharashtra, Tamil Nadu, Andhra Pradesh and within the rest of Karnataka. The Tulu are mostly Hindus and JAINS. According to legend, the Hindu god Parasurama created Tulu Nadu, which is also called Parusurama Srishti.

The earliest habitation of Tulu Nadu is dated to around 10,000 years ago. Tulu Nadu was previously called Alvakheda, named after the most successful Tulu dynasty, the Alupas or Aluvars, who ruled for 1000 years. Their strength was such that they resisted the rule of King Asoka in the 3rd century AD.

In the 5th century AD the Tulu, previously mainly Jain, were introduced to Sanskrit Hinduism by Brahmins. They remained completely independent until the 14th century, when the TAMIL kings of Vijayanagar seized power. In the 17th century the rule of the Nayaka dynasty was shortlived and in the 18th century the Tulu were incorporated in a Muslim sultanate. In 1801 the BRITISH gained control and established their headquarters in Madras.

In 1956, nine years after Indian independence, the southern Indian regions were divided into separate states and the Tulu-speaking ethnic group became part of Karnataka state.

## TURCOPOLES

A term originally used in the 11th century in the BYZANTINE empire to describe military units formed from the descendants of Turkish mercenaries. In the 12th and 13th centuries the term came to be used in the Crusader states in the Holy Land to describe TURKS who had converted to Christianity and who served as light cavalry in the crusaders' armies.

## TURKMEN

A Central Asian people who were descended from nomadic pastoralists. The Turkmen had migrated by the 16th century, possibly from the Altay Mountains, into an area frequently crossed by Turkic (see TURKS) and other invaders east of the Caspian Sea. Their territory was largely sandy desert, with different clans controlling oases, from which they raided trade caravans and each other. They are Turkic-speaking Muslims noted for their fine carpets and fast Akhal-Teke horses.

Never a unified state, the Turkmen were conquered by the RUSSIANS after a massacre at the fortress of Gök-Tepe in 1881. Major changes only came, however, with Soviet rule from 1920. Collectivization forced them to become sedentary farmers, mainly of cotton. This, coupled with attacks on their religion, provoked resistance, but this was limited to guerrilla warfare and was suppressed by 1936.

The Turkmen remained a rural people, with the growing urban population of their region dominated by outsiders, and there remained little to form the basis of a national identity. In 1989 the Agzybirlik (Unity) political party was formed by social and environmental progressives, but it remained weak, and with the independence of Turkmenistan after the collapse of the USSR, a renamed Communist Party was able to retain control.

Turkmen

With opposition suppressed, poverty spreading and corruption widespread, Turkmenistan is unstable. Indeed, perhaps the elaborate cult of personality around president Sapamurid Niyazov is an attempt to provide a symbol of unity. Turkmenistan does have vast reserves of fossil fuels, but regional instability has prevented their exploitation so far, and bitterness and apathy in the face of desperate poverty seem to be the main response to Niyazov's efforts. In 1995 the Turkmen numbered 4.3 million, with 2.7 million in Turkmenistan and the rest in Turkey, Iran, Afghanistan, Iraq and Syria.

## TURKS

A number of different peoples who are descended from Turkic-speaking tribes but whose exact origins are uncertain. They were first recorded by Chinese sources living in the steppe regions of Central Asia. Today the term 'Turk', together with 'Turkish', is more commonly used to refer to the citizens of the modern republic of Turkey (capital Ankara). In 2002 the population of Turkey stood at approximately 69 million.

By the 7th century AD, nomadic Turkic tribes controlled an extensive empire in Central Asia. During this period they frequently clashed with the Chinese and had perfected light-cavalry

tactics to devastating effect. By the mid-9th century, however, this empire had collapsed, and large numbers of Turks migrated westwards, a pattern that continued into the 10th century. These tribes subsequently came into contact with both the ARAB and BYZANTINE worlds and succeeded in creating an extensive empire in Mesopotamia and Anatolia. Many of the Turkic tribes abandoned nomadism after these victories. From this point until the early 20th century, and despite temporary conquest by the MONGOLS, Turkic dynasties controlled large tracts of western Asia, and even succeeded in extending their territories into Europe. Chief among these were the SELJUKS and OTTOMANS.

### Modern Turkey

In 1918, following the defeat of the Ottoman empire in World War I, attempts were made by the victorious Western powers to dismantle Turkey. This led to the resurgence of Turkish nationalism, which culminated, following a war of independence, in the foundation of the Republic of Turkey in 1923.

The vast majority of the population of modern Turkey are of Turkic descent. A very large minority, however, amounting to about 20% of the total population, are KURDS. They tend to live in the southeast of the country in an area unoffi-

> **"** The Turkmen … have no fixt Residence any where, but Travel with their Families and Cattle from Place to Place, carrying their Wives and Children upon Camels. **"**
>
> T. Smith, 1683

cially referred to as 'Kurdistan'. The Kurds reject Turkish status and have mounted a number of violent campaigns in order to win political and cultural autonomy, most notably during the 1990s. Today they remain determined to win independence, but are attempting to pursue this goal in the political arena. Other minority groups in Turkey include Armenians and Greeks.

### The rise of moderate Islam

The majority of western Turkic peoples were converted to Islam during the 10th century, and today about 80% of the population of Turkey are Sunni Muslim; the vast majority of the remaining 20% are Shi'ites (with many adhering to the Alevi doctrine). Unlike their Islamic neighbours, however, since 1928 the Turks have adopted a secular government, and many abhor Islamic fundamentalism. As a result, Islamic political parties, such as the National Salvation Party and the Virtue Party, who have espoused closer links with the Muslim world, have been subject to judicial censure. Indeed, fear of the success of these parties has often led to the coalition of secular groups who otherwise would have stood at polar opposites of the political spectrum. Support for Islamic parties has risen substantially in recent years, however, and in the 2002 elections the moderate Islamist Justice and Development Party (AKP) were the winners. This success may, in part, be due to the considerable economic problems the Turks have experienced since the 1950s, with high inflation and allegations of corruption leading to considerable social unrest. The army retains a high profile in Turkish political life and has intervened on more than one occasion in order to oust a government in the face of popular discontent.

### Foreign relations

Many Turks favour a more Western outlook, and the republic is looking forward to inclusion in the European Union. Turkey also has a recent tradition of close relations with the USA, particularly in the face of the perceived Soviet threat during the Cold War and the subsequent rise in fundamentalist Islamic terrorism, although the Turkish refusal to allow their country to be used as a launch-pad for a northern offensive against Iraq during the second Gulf War led to a cooling in relations. This generally pro-USA stance is not shared by adherents of left-wing or less moderate Islamic parties.

Since independence, the Turks have not generally enjoyed good relations with the Greeks, especially after the Turks' support for Turkish Cypriots. Turkey has not, however, become prey to the anti-ISRAELI sentiment propagated in many neighbouring Islamic countries.

The vast majority of Turks around the world speak a Turkic language. The official language of the republic of Turkey is Turkish, although about 30 other languages are spoken within the country, most notably Kurdish, Armenian and Arabic; officially the Latin alphabet is used. Close ties with the West have led to the adoption of many aspects of Western culture in Turkey, although longstanding Turkish traditions remain important. Turkish poetry, textiles and metalwork are particularly renowned, and the 20th century has witnessed a renewed nationalistic element in art and literature.

## TUVINS

A southern Siberian people of the Tuvinian autonomous republic, Russian Federation, and of Mongolia. Once under MONGOL rule, the Tuvins formed the theoretically independent republic of Tannu-Tuva from 1921. In fact, Soviet influence was strong, and the republic was annexed by the USSR in 1944.

| Turks: ancient and modern Turkic peoples |
| --- |
| Azeris |
| Cumans |
| Huns |
| Kazakhs |
| Khitan |
| Kyrgyz |
| Tatars |
| Turkmen |
| Uigurs |
| Uzbeks |

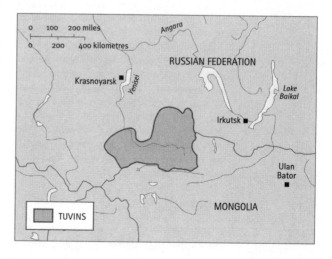

Tuvins

The Tuvins are traditionally nomadic herders and shamanists, though from the 18th century most became Lamaist Buddhists, and they speak a Turkic language. Soviet rule brought collectivization and settlement, though isolation protected much of Tuvin traditional culture from destruction. The Tuvins are best known today for their traditional 'throat singing'. In 1979 they numbered nearly 170,000.

## UBAID CULTURE

A Late Neolithic MESOPOTAMIAN culture that flourished 5500–4000 BC. It extended from the Persian Gulf to the Mediterranean, but was concentrated in southern Mesopotamia. The name is derived from excavations that were carried out at Tell al-Ubaid, which provided significant evidence of the culture.

The Ubaidians were the first people to master the techniques of irrigation in the flood plain between the Euphrates and Tigris rivers. This innovation demanded a concerted community effort and helped lead to the development of the first towns, as village communities joined forces to work the land. These phenomena were further stimulated by the resultant rise in agricultural productivity, particularly following the development of the plough, which allowed larger urban units to be fed. As a result, the precursors to SUMERIAN city-states were founded at sites such as Ur, Eridu, Lagash and Erech.

These settlements have provided evidence of reed and mud-brick houses as well as platform temples with altars, offering tables and decorated walls. These temples later developed into Sumerian platform and ziggurat complexes, and Eridu appears to have been the principal Ubaidian religious site. The Ubaidians also fostered extensive trading links in order to obtain necessary raw materials and produced distinctive painted pottery, copperware and terracotta figures. The Ubaid culture was succeeded by that of the Warka (or Uruk) which saw the flourishing of the Sumerian civilization.

## UDEGHE

A southeast Siberian people of Khabarovsk region, Russian Federation. Similar in culture to the OROKI, with whom RUSSIANS initially grouped them, they were traditionally shamanists and nomadic hunters, gatherers and reindeer-herders, and they speak a Tungus language now nearly extinct. They fell under Russian control from the 19th century, and the 20th century brought a vast influx of Russian settlers, Soviet collectivization, forced settlement and assimilatory education policies alongside the devastation of their environment. From the 1990s attempts were made to recover parts of their traditional culture, but their survival is in doubt. In 1991 they numbered about 1600.

## UIGHURS

A Turkic people (see TURKS), the vast majority (around 8 million) of whom reside in China's Xinjiang Uighur autonomous region. Considerable numbers of Uighurs are also found in Europe, Kazakhstan, Kyrgyzstan, North America, Pakistan and Turkey.

They are first mentioned in Chinese texts of the 3rd century AD. They later formed an alliance with the CHINESE during the 7th century against the Turks and TIBETANS. In 744 the Uighurs succeeded in overrunning Mongolia, but were driven out by the KYRGYZ in 844. Thereafter, they migrated southwest and settled in the Xinjiang region of modern China.

In 1209 they were incorporated into the MONGOL empire. The Mongols subsequently adopted the Uighur script for writing the Mongolian language and also adopted Uighur administrative practices in government posts within China. Since 1759 they have been subject to Chinese domination.

They were Manicheans in religion from 762 to around 1300, but subsequently converted to Islam, and today most adhere to the Sunni doctrine. Traditionally nomads, most Uighurs now live a sedentary lifestyle and inhabit small village communities. In recent years, large-scale HAN Chinese immigration into the Xinjiang region has led to some ethnic tension, and a concomitant dilution of traditional Uighur society and culture.

u

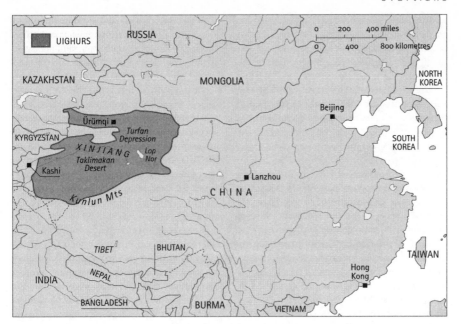

UIGHURS

## ULCHI

A southeastern Siberian people of Khabarovsk region in the Russian Federation. Sedentary hunters, gatherers and mainly fishers, they are shamanists who speak a Tungus language now nearly extinct. They fell under Russian rule from the mid-19th century, and Soviet rule brought collectivization, the concentration of population and new means of subsistence, such as farming and lumbering. Assimilatory education policies and the pollution of their environment led to a severe degradation of their culture and economic dependency. Their survival is in doubt. In 1990 they numbered 3200.

## UNITED ARAB EMIRIANS

See EMIRIANS.

## URARTIANS

The people of the ancient kingdom of Urartu, which was based upon the region around Lake Van (modern Armenia). They succeeded in creating an empire that extended into Turkey and northwestern Iran. The term 'Urartu' is ASSYRIAN for '[Mount] Ararat'; the Urartians themselves referred to their land as 'Biane'. They were closely related to the HURRIANS, and their cultures display many similarities, particularly in the areas of language and religion.

The kingdom of Urartu was created following a number of Assyrian raids during the 13th and 12th centuries BC, which were succeeded by similar ARAMAEAN attacks. Fear of further invasion led to the federation of previously independent Hurrian states and a number of alliances with the Neo-HITTITE city-states, leading to the foundation of a new kingdom. During the 9th and 8th centuries BC, a succession of Urartian monarchs expanded their empire, which, by the mid-8th century BC, bordered that of the Assyrians and presented itself as a serious rival to Assyrian domination in the region.

Urartian hegemony was shortlived, however; they suffered a number of defeats by the Assyrians led by Tiglath-Pileser III and Sargon II, and the latter finally destroyed Urartian power at the Battle of Lake Urmia in 714 BC. Sargon subsequently laid waste to large tracts of Urartian farmland and demolished their irrigation systems. In the same year the Urartian armies were also defeated by the CIMMERIANS and SCYTHIANS, and the kingdom never fully recovered from these calamities. The MEDES also exerted pressure, and the kingdom finally collapsed around 600 BC following migration into the area by the ARMENIANS.

The Urartians were ultimately absorbed by the newcomers, but were known for a time as the 'Chaldians', a term probably derived from the worship of their chief deity, Khaldi; to the Greeks they were known as the 'Alarodians'.

While Assyrian culture heavily influenced the Urartians, they were renowned for their distinctive architectural styles, particularly evident in temple complexes, which influenced later PERSIAN and Greek designs. Some of their fortresses were virtually impregnable and made use of both carved stone and rock-cut features. Carved and inlaid Urartian bronze work is also highly regarded. The first writing system used to express the Urartian language was pictographic, but cuneiform was later adopted under Assyrian influence. The Urartians built a number of towns and cities and were responsible for major engineering feats designed to provide sufficient water for agriculture, such as canals, dams and associated irrigation systems.

## URDUS

A people of India and Pakistan who are unified by their use of the Urdu language. Urdu is the official language of Pakistan, but despite this only 8 million people, or 8% of Pakistan's population, speak it as their first language. The majority of Urdu-speakers reside in India. Urdu means 'camp language' and is intrinsically bound to Islamic identity in Pakistan and India.

The Urdu language is very similar to HINDI, and prior to the Pakistan–India Partition in 1947 the two languages were combined as Hindustani. The main distinctions between Hindi and Urdu had arisen in the 16th century, with the Muslim invasions of India. These brought Arabic and Persian influences into Urdu and immediately served as a symbol of Muslim identity in India. At Partition, a large number of Urdu-speaking Muslims fled from India to the Sindhi region of Pakistan (see SINDHIS), where within a short time rioting broke out between the two communities over cultural differences.

Today Urdu is used in Pakistani political ideology as a means of cultivating nationalistic fervour. Urdu is also taught in the Punjab region as part of the educational curriculum.

## UZBEKS

A central Asian people descended from nomadic pastoralists. In 1996 they numbered about 19.6 million, with 16 million in Uzbekistan and the rest in Afghanistan, China and neighbouring central Asian states. Turkic-speaking (see TURKS) Sunni Muslims, they are noted for their piety, though many men drink alcohol in company. Formed from a merger of tribes of the GOLDEN HORDE TATARS, they are perhaps named for its great leader Öz Beg.

By the end of the 15th century they had migrated from northwest Siberia and conquered the territory stretching south and east from the Aral Sea, including the cities of Bukhara, Khiva and Samarkand, the first of which they endowed with seminaries and mosques of international renown. During the 18th century, however, their empire was broken into separate khanates based on these cities, and these were conquered by RUSSIAN forces 1855–76. Major change, however, came with Soviet rule. Collectivization and settlement were accompanied by industrialization and cotton cultivation. These resulted in environmental degradation, leading to widespread health problems, and to the extermination of much of the Uzbek intelligentsia.

The Uzbeks proved resistant to Russification and in 1989 a non-communist national movement emerged addressing cultural and language issues, a key step in developing a national consciousness. It proved too weak, however, to prevent continued rule by a renamed Communist Party after independence in 1991. Uzbekistan remained essentially a police state with only a façade of democratic institutions: militant Islamic rebels have failed to overturn the government, and there remains systematic violation of human rights. Perhaps to rally support and encourage a developing national identity, the government of this impoverished but populous country has sought status as a regional power, allying with the USA in its so-called 'war on terror'.

> " People have less freedom here than under Brezhnev. "
>
> Unnamed western diplomat on Uzbekistan, 2003

## VAKHS

A Pamir people of the Gorno-Badakhshan autonomous *oblast* (region) in Tajikistan. Their culture and historical experience are very similar to those of the BARTANGS. Sedentary farmers and herders who practise Ismaili Islam, they speak an INDO-IRANIAN language. In 1960 they were estimated at 7000: their present numbers are unknown.

## VEDDAS or Veddahs

The aboriginal inhabitants of Sri Lanka, whose heritage has been traced to the late Palaeolithic period, around 16,000 BC. They are related to the southern Indian DRAVIDIANS. The name Vedda, used only from the 17th century, is Sinhalese, meaning 'hunter'. The Veddas refer to themselves as the *Wanniya-laeto*, meaning 'forest dwellers'. They were originally a cave-dwelling community with a matrilineal society through which they traced themselves back to the mother ancestor, Yaka Princess Kuveni. They practised ancestor worship, animism and shamanism. Because of the SRI LANKAN history of invasions and migrations, the Veddas have become largely assimilated into either SINHALESE or TAMIL cultures. As a result, their language has vanished and, as a separate ethnic group, they are on the verge of extinction.

## WESTERN LIAO

See KHITANS.

## WHITE SHEEP TURKS or Ak Koyunlu

A Turkic tribal confederation (see TURKS) who, between the late 14th and late 15th centuries, controlled an empire that encompassed much of eastern Anatolia and northern Mesopotamia. They were first mentioned by Byzantine sources in 1340: like the closely-related BLACK SHEEP TURKS, their name probably refers to the symbol used on their battle-standard. They were responsible for the defeat of the Black Sheep Turks in 1467–9 and of the TIMURIDS in 1468. They were defeated in turn, however, by the OTTOMANS in

1473, and subsequently lost their Anatolian territories.

The White Sheep Turks were predominantly Sunni Muslims. During the early years of the 16th century they suffered a series of defeats by the Shi'ite Safavid rulers of Persia, and the subsequent loss of their Iranian possessions. The White Sheep Turks were quickly absorbed into the Ottoman and Safavid empires, and by 1510 had ceased to exist as a separate political entity.

## XIONGNU or Hsiung-Nu

A nomadic Turko-MONGOL tribal confederation, the first such alliance to emerge on the Central Asian steppes. They fought a series of guerrilla wars against the CHINESE, to whom they are related, and are first recorded by Chinese sources in the 5th century BC.

The Xiongnu were frequently at war, it was not until the late 1st century AD that the Han Chinese, following a long period of sustained pressure, managed to reduce them to tributary status. One of the results of these campaigns was the division of the confederation into two parts (northern and southern); those quelled by the Chinese were the southern element. The northern Xiongnu inflicted an overwhelming defeat upon the YUE-QI around 170 BC and forced them to migrate westwards. Thereafter the Xiongnu continued to dominate the western steppes until overwhelmed by the Mongol Xianbei (Hsien-Pi) confederation. The Xiongnu continued to be a thorn in the side of the Chinese for another 300 years, however, and from time to time became embroiled in Chinese civil wars. Certainly, they were able to take advantage of such conflicts, and for a time from the late 3rd to the early 4th centuries AD, they controlled northern China. Despite these successes, however, by the late 4th century their confederation had begun to disintegrate, and by the 5th century they disappeared from history.

The Xiongnu spoke a Turkic language, and their culture appears to have been heavily influenced by the Chinese. Grave goods have also highlighted trading connections with the GREEKS and PERSIANS. They were extremely proficient horsemen and mastered the use of the composite bow to devastating effect. It is thought that

> " In the forests of Ceylon are found ... the Veddas or 'hunters', shy wild men who build bough huts, and live on game and wild honey. "
>
> Edward Tylor, 1881

the HUNS were descended from the Xiongnu, as were the TURKS of Central Asia.

## YAGHNABIS

An INDO-IRANIAN people of central Tajikistan. Primarily sedentary farmers, they practise Sunni Islam and speak an Indo-Iranian language. Since the mid-19th century they have become increasingly dispersed and assimilated into the TAJIK culture. The Soviet government encouraged this and even relocated them to a more populous area of Tajikistan in the 1960s. Their language and indeed their survival as a people are uncertain. In 1975 they numbered about 2000.

## YAKUTS

A northeast Siberian people of the republic of Sakha (Yakutia), Russian Federation. The most numerous Siberian people, they were traditionally shamanists and semi-sedentary hunters, gatherers and reindeer- and horse-herders who speak a Turkic language (see TURKS).

Conquered by the RUSSIANS in the 17th century, they were brutally exploited as they were colonized. The influx of immigrants led to severe land thefts, and the Yakuts proved rebellious. Strong assimilatory pressures reached a peak with Soviet collectivization, forced settlement and assimilatory education.

Since the collapse of the USSR they have sought an equitable share of their resources and to reduce Russian influence, despite being a minority in their own republic. In 1990 as part of their declaration of sovereignty they changed the name of Yakutia to Sakha, which is their own self-designation. In 1998 they numbered nearly 400,000, or about one-third of the population of Sakha.

## YAZGULAMIS

A Pamir people of Gorno-Badakhshan autonomous *oblast* (region), Tajikistan. Their culture and historical experience are very similar to those of the BARTANGS. Sedentary farmers and herders who mostly practise Ismaili Islam, they speak an INDO-IRANIAN language. In 1960 they were estimated at up to 2000; their current numbers are unknown.

Yakuts, Yukaghirs

## YEH-LU

See KHITANS.

## YEMENIS

The citizens of the modern Republic of Yemen (capital Sana'a). The population of Yemen stood at about 20 million in 2002, and more than 1 million Yemenis are also believed to live in other countries throughout the world. Although the republic was formed only in 1990, the term 'Yemeni' can be traced back to at least the 13th century. 'Yemen' means 'the Land of the Right Hand' – that is, the land of Mecca.

The area that now comprises the Republic of Yemen has, for over two millennia, been an important trading region between the Far East, Africa and western Asia. The SABAEANS, MINAEANS, QATABANIANS, HADRAMITES, HIMYARITES and ETHIOPIANS all controlled the area at various times during the ancient period. In AD 630 BEDOUIN tribesmen brought the Islamic faith, and for about 200 years Yemen became subject to the caliphate. In the 9th century the ISMAILIS arrived, and at the same time the region reverted to local control, which endured until the arrival of the OTTOMANS and BRITISH in the 16th and 17th centuries respectively. By 1918, the northern Yemenis had secured their independence from Turkey, but it was not until 1967 that the British were forced to relinquish their control over the south, centred on the city of Aden.

The modern republic was formed in 1990 from the amalgamation of the northern Yemen Arab Republic and the southern People's Democratic Republic of Yemen. A democratic republic is rare among Arab states, and since unification there have been tensions within the country, although these have been focused principally on rivalries between adherents of the former republics. Shortly after unification, there was a brief attempt in 1994 to re-found an independent southern state. This was swiftly suppressed, and the southern Yemen Socialist Party was ousted from government.

Some hostility continues to exist: for example, the Socialist Party refused to take part in the 1997 elections. These conflicts are based on the perception by some groups in the south that northern politicians dominate the political arena. Violence accompanied the 1997, 1999 and 2001 electoral campaigns. Much of this discontent has also been generated by economic problems, especially over the last ten years. In 1991, following Yemen's initial support for the IRAQI invasion of Kuwait in 1991, nearly 1 million Yemeni workers were expelled by the SAUDIS, causing severe economic distress, particularly following the 1994 civil war. There has been a concomitant rise in Islamic fundamentalism in the region, and attacks have been staged against US and British targets in Yemen. However, the Yemeni government has supported the US-led 'war on terror' from 2001.

The Yemenis have traditionally defended PALESTINIAN interests in their struggle with the ISRAELIS. They have also had territorial disputes with both the Eritreans and the Saudis.

### Yemeni culture

The vast majority of Yemenis are ARABS, but African, INDONESIAN and INDIAN traits are also much in evidence because of long-standing trading links with these areas. Arabic is the official language, and Islamic Shari'a law is influential in the judicial system. Almost all of the population is Muslim, with 53% Zidi Shi'ites, and 46.9% Shafi Sunnis. There are also small numbers of Ismailis, Christians, Hindus and Jews.

Traditional Yemenite culture remains highly valued, particularly in the areas of dance, poetry and prose. Chewing qat (a stimulant leaf) is an important social activity for men. Tribal links remain strong despite active governmental policies designed to break down such ties in favour of a more national focus. There are considerable cultural differences between the traditionally Ismaili north and Qahtan south, and these have also helped fuel tensions between the two regions of the new republic. MAHRA tribes live along the border with Oman. Most Yemenis do not live in urban areas, and subsistence farming is still a major source of livelihood, particularly in the south. Despite the existence of an oil and petroleum industry, Yemen remains relatively poor compared with most other west Asian countries.

## YUE-QI or Asi or Tocharians

A nomadic INDO-IRANIAN tribal confederation. They were first mentioned, during the 2nd century BC, by the Chinese, whose territory they frequently raided. The Yue-Qi were heavily defeated by migratory XIONGNU around 170 BC, and most were subsequently pushed westward into Bactria, where they founded the KUSHAN empire; those who stayed became known as the Lesser Yue-Qi. The Yue-Qi finally disappeared during the Middle Ages, assimilated by other Turkish (see TURKS) or MONGOL nomad peoples. A number of well preserved mummies of red-haired, fair-skinned people, discovered in the Tarim Basin in western China in the 1990s, are thought to be those of members of the Yue-Qi.

## YUGH

A southeastern Siberian people of Krasnoyarsk region in the Russian Federation. Similar in culture to the KETIS, with whom they were once numbered, they proved unable to withstand the assimilatory pressures of Russian and Soviet rule. They were only recognized as a distinct people in the 1960s, by which time they were already rapidly disappearing. In 1991 they numbered only 15, and only three had any understanding of the Yugh language.

## YUKAGHIRS

A northeastern Siberian people of the republic of Sakha (Yakutia) and the Kamchatka peninsula, Russian Federation. Traditionally shamanists and nomadic hunters, gatherers and reindeer-herders, they speak Yukaghir. Conquered by the RUSSIANS in the 17th century, they were reduced by diseases and exploitation. Under Soviet rule they were collectivized and their traditional culture was degraded by assimilatory education policies, while their territory was devastated by industrial pollution. The CHUKCHIS, YAKUTS and EVENKI assimilated many.

Since the collapse of the USSR they have sought to recover their traditional culture, not least by pressing for re-establishment of the ethnically defined autonomous area they enjoyed in the interwar years. In 1995 they numbered some 1200.

> " The Yukaghirs settled on the banks of the River Anyui, maintain themselves the whole year on the reindeer they kill in spring and autumn. "
>
> C.H. Cottrell, 1842

# East and Southeast Asia and Oceania

# ABORIGINAL PEOPLE

The native ethnic group of Australia, comprising some 500 peoples and languages, all part of a non-AUSTRONESIAN language group with no known links with any outside languages. The Aboriginal language group is divided into 28 families. The largest by far of these language families, Pama-Nyungan, is spoken across seven-eighths of Australia. The remaining 27 families are all confined to the far north and northwest of the continent.

By most estimates the Aboriginal peoples ('Aborigines') have inhabited Australia for up to 60,000 years. There are, however, archaeologists who argue that Australia was first settled 80,000 or more years ago. This suggests that *homo sapiens* peopled the continent very shortly after they appeared in Africa, which would make the Aboriginal people among the oldest branches of humanity. They certainly possess the longest continuously surviving culture on the planet.

Most Aboriginal people originally occupied semi-permanent settlements on the coast, where they fished, hunted and gathered. In the interior they were nomadic hunters and gatherers. They developed the most basic technology, which to European eyes obscured highly complex social organizations in which every member had a full role to perform. Their culture is highly developed and rich in folklore, oral history and art.

Though many Aborigines are now Christian, the basis of their traditional religious beliefs was the 'dreaming', which explains the relationship between the natural and the mythical world. The 'dreaming' was the time when all things were brought into existence and the rules governing human relationships and conduct were laid down by ancestral beings. The spirits of the dead and other spiritual beings are held to occupy the world and to need placating through rituals. Other rituals are required to increase the fertility of the land and for rites of passage for both sexes. Aboriginal peoples believe there is a deep spiritual relationship between themselves and the land: they regard themselves as its guardians, not its owners. They may exploit it but must sustain it, for example by burning vegetation to allow new growth and thus attract game. To lose the land, however, is a monstrous blow.

## The colonial impact

The first BRITISH settlers who arrived as transported convicts in 1788 marked the beginning of a terrible calamity for the Aboriginal people. Although many officials were sympathetic towards them, many Australian settlers dismissed them as savages. Those living on desirable farmlands were simply an inconvenience, and land seizures were often brutal. A number of massacres occurred, the last known being in the Kimberley region of Northern Territory in 1926, after cattle had been killed. Far more Aboriginal people died through European epidemics, some of which were deliberately spread, that killed vast numbers. Within 100 years the Aboriginal population had collapsed from about 1 million to about 60,000.

Land laws were based until 1992 on the principle of *terra nullius*, which stated that the land was empty before Europeans arrived, thus denying Aboriginal people any land rights. In the south, where European settlement was greater, most Aboriginal peoples became fragmented, marginalized, destitute, increasingly urbanized and subject to racist laws and attitudes. In the north, more of them managed to cling to their traditional culture and territories, even if ownership had passed to Europeans. Indeed, they were often little more than slave labourers.

By the 1930s, Australian governments tended to assume that the Aboriginal peoples were heading for extinction, and sought to make the process as painless as possible. Limited services such as health and education were provided, but the practice of separating children from parents, especially those of mixed parentage, continued, giving rise to a traumatized 'stolen generation', who were exploited and stripped of their culture.

In the 1940s, Aboriginal people began to form their own organizations, such as the Aborigines' Progressive Association, which campaigned for better status, cultural protection and civil rights. The 1966 strike by the GURINDJI attracted widespread sympathy, and discriminatory laws began to be repealed. Aboriginal voting rights were confirmed and Aborigines were counted in the census for the first time. In 1992 *terra nullius* was overturned, and land claims could were pursued, though progress was painfully slow. Even in 1995, Aboriginal people

**"** We don't own this land, the land owns us! **"**

An Aboriginal truism

**Aboriginal people**

*The survival of Aboriginal languages is a rough guide to the current distribution of the indigenous peoples in modern Australia, but it also reveals how much of Aboriginal culture has been lost.*

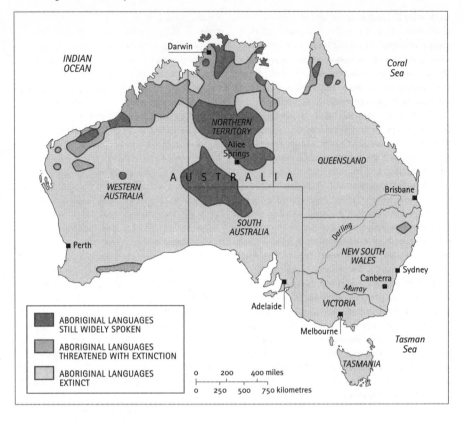

INDIAN OCEAN

Darwin

NORTHERN TERRITORY

Alice Springs

WESTERN AUSTRALIA

A U S T R A L I A

Perth

SOUTH AUSTRALIA

Coral Sea

QUEENSLAND

Brisbane

Darling

NEW SOUTH WALES

Canberra

Sydney

Murray

Adelaide

VICTORIA

Melbourne

Tasman Sea

TASMANIA

ABORIGINAL LANGUAGES STILL WIDELY SPOKEN

ABORIGINAL LANGUAGES THREATENED WITH EXTINCTION

ABORIGINAL LANGUAGES EXTINCT

0    200    400 miles

0    250    500    750 kilometres

a

had a life expectancy 18 years shorter than other Australians and were several times more likely to be unemployed or in prison. A report of the United Nations Commission on Human Rights in 2000 was scathing on issues such as social exclusion, poverty, cultural protection and discrimination. By then the ATSIC (Aboriginal and Torres Strait Islander Commission) had been formed as an elected body to address their needs, and controlled Au$1.1 billion of the federal budget devoted to their affairs. This has promoted welfare provision, economic development and repatriation of ancestral artefacts. With less than half of the federal budget and a leadership troubled by scandals, however, it is still a limited response to a large set of very serious problems.

In 2003 Aboriginal peoples numbered about 300,000, but fewer than 50,000 had any knowledge of their original languages.

# ACEHNESE

An AUSTRONESIAN-speaking people living in the mountainous northwest of Sumatra, Indonesia, where they number around 150,000. Their main centre is the city of Banda Aceh.

The Acehnese were among the first INDONESIANS to adopt Buddhism and Hinduism, between the 5th and 8th centuries AD, and to convert to Islam during the 13th. By the early 16th century an independent sultanate (known as Achin or Atjeh) had been established, which prospered through the region's participation in the international trade in spices. These trading contacts attracted European interest. By the early 17th century much of Indonesia was under DUTCH control, and while the sultanate survived, its rulers were brought under foreign domination. Between 1873 and 1878 the Acehnese fought a major war against the Dutch, who tried to destroy the sultanate in an attempt to gain more direct control over the East Indies. Bloodshed continued into the 20th century and was only halted by the JAPANESE invasion in 1942. Upon INDONESIAN independence in 1949, Aceh was incorporated into the North Sumatra province of the new republic.

The Acehnese are traditionally a fiercely independent people, and many within the area have viewed the distant Java-based government with suspicion – seeing it simply as a new form of foreign domination. Certainly, many Acehnese do not identify themselves as Indonesian. In 1953 the first in a series of rebellions occurred in the region, and this resulted in the government's creation of the Aceh Special District as an attempt at compromise. Nationalists, however, viewed this as unacceptable, and the result was further tension, rebellion, and the creation of the Free Aceh Movement (which now numbers around 3000 members). To date, the Acehnese continue to agitate for independence from Indonesia, and troops are regularly used to quell insurgence. The principal agricultural product of the area is rice, but there are also substantial oil and natural gas deposits in the region, and petroleum and gas are major export industries – a major factor in Jakarta's determination to hold on to the area.

## AETAS or Ayta

A NEGRITO people of Luzon in the Philippines. The Aetas are now mainly farmers, but very small numbers continue to live a traditional hunter-gatherer lifestyle, generally in the mountainous regions of Luzon, and in particular in the Zambales Mountains. The term *aeta*, meaning 'black', is commonly used by lowlanders to describe the Negritos. As well as their own native language, they also speak those of their neighbours, with whom they trade and interact. Traditional religion continues to play an important part in Aeta culture, but many Aeta have also been converted to Christianity.

## AINU

An indigenous people inhabiting the JAPANESE island of Hokkaido and the Russian islands of Kuril and Sakhalin. Their precise ethnic origins

are unknown, but their culture appears to have close SIBERIAN parallels. Ainu means 'human', and they were recorded in Chinese texts during the 6th century; they were not officially recognized by the Japanese until 1997.

The Ainu originally inhabited most of the Japanese archipelago, and their early settlements are identified as belonging to the JOMON CULTURE. From the 6th century AD, however, they are known to have fought a series of wars against the Japanese, conflicts that led to a significant fall in their numbers and their migration into the northern-most islands where most Ainu are now to be found. To the Japanese, they were later known as the *Ezo* ('unwanted'). The Ainu are physically very different from their Japanese neighbours, being generally shorter and thicker-set, with thick wavy hair and blue or grey eyes. The Ainu language is unrelated to Japanese or any other known speech.

Until fairly recently, the Ainu lived a traditional semi-nomadic hunter-gatherer lifestyle. Tribal identity was especially strong, and the social structure was patriarchal. Religious beliefs were centred on the natural world – particularly bear-worship: shamanism and the ritual sacrifice of a bear were prominent features. During the 19th century, however, the Japanese began to settle in large numbers on Hokkaido, and in the course of the 20th century traditional Ainu culture and society were eclipsed by modern Japanese forms.

Until well into the 20th century there had been a tendency among the Japanese to view the Ainu as culturally and socially inferior, and since the 19th century concerted governmental efforts have been made to persuade the Ainu to abandon hunting and to lead a more sedentary, agricultural, lifestyle. These efforts have been to a large degree successful, and many Ainu have been happy to assimilate with the Japanese majority; only a small number still practise their traditional religion or use their native language. Furthermore, because of inter-marriage, of the 24,000 remaining Ainu, very few are considered to be pure Ainu. Today, many live on reservations that attract significant numbers of tourists. As a result, there is a very real danger of the extinction of Ainu culture, although in recent years efforts at a revival have had some success.

The Ainu are still renowned for the quality of their carvings and textile weaving.

## ALEKANO

A native people of Goroka district, Eastern Highland province, Papua New Guinea. Sedentary farmers, they speak an Eastern New Guinea Highlands language that is declining in use. With a tradition of owing nothing to outsiders, whom it was acceptable to kill or rob, they were often involved in wars with their neighbours until the 1950s. Among themselves obligations are clear – when they adopted football from the British their tournaments became a ritual with rules that were intended to ensure a draw. By 2000 they numbered over 23,000, and those near the town of Goroka enjoyed the benefits of electricity and consumer goods. Recently, however, younger members of the community have been willing to sell land to developers, without regard for the economic consequences.

## AMBONESE

A mainly MELANESIAN people of the island of Ambon, Indonesia. Since the early 16th century, the island has been subject to considerable Western influence, first through PORTUGUESE settlement, and later through DUTCH and BRITISH interest. The JAPANESE also occupied Ambon during World War II.

The Ambonese fared relatively well under Dutch rule, and were reluctant – based on both economic and religious considerations – to join newly-independent Indonesia in 1950. Many Ambonese are Christian and were suspicious of the Muslim Java-based INDONESIAN government. Their attempts to found an independent South MOLUCCAN Republic failed, however, following armed Indonesian intervention.

Religiously, the Ambonese remain divided between the northern Muslims, whose numbers have increased rapidly due to immigration, and the southern Christians. The latter group, who prospered economically under the Dutch and were formally the dominant group on the island, still prefer not to consider themselves Indonesian, and religious violence continues to be a problem.

The Ambonese language belongs to the Ambon-Timor group of AUSTRONESIAN languages, but displays Portuguese, Dutch and MALAY-Indonesian influences. The current Ambonese population is about 700,000.

## AMI

An AUSTRONESIAN people who migrated to the island of Taiwan between 4000 BC and AD 1000, probably from the Malay Archipelago. They number around 130,000, and many elements of their culture remain traditional. Shamanism and dream interpretation are important features of their religious practices, and the social structure is matrilineal, with women enjoying equal rights with men. The Ami have also been very influenced by CHINESE culture, however, and many have been assimilated to a significant degree into TAIWANESE society.

The Ami are divided into five cultural-linguistic groups. They all speak a language (Ami) that is related to Malay, though it has no native written form. Many, however, are abandoning this in favour of the majority Mandarin language. The Ami remain a mountain-dwelling agricultural people and are unique among indigenous Taiwanese people in that they produce their own pottery.

## ANAGU

A network of related ABORIGINAL PEOPLES of central Australia, centred on Uluru (Ayers Rock). They include the YANKUNYTJATJARA and PITJANTJARA, the latter of which is dominant. Their close affiliations were strongly reinforced in defence of their sacred sites from the depredations of tourists, and from 1976 they began campaigning to recover Uluru and the equally sacred Kata Tjuta (the Olgas) rock formation. They further cooperate in addressing common social needs and are vehemently opposed to proposed nuclear waste dumping and uranium mining on their lands.

## ANDILYAUGWA

An Australian ABORIGINAL PEOPLE of the coast of the Gulf of Carpentaria, Northern Territory. Traditionally hunters and gatherers of the scrub forest and coast, they speak a non-Pama-Nyungan language. Some have been converted to the Bahai faith. In 1996 they numbered 1240.

## ANNAMESE

See VIETNAMESE.

## ARAKANESE

See RAKHINES.

## ARANDA

An Australian ABORIGINAL PEOPLE of the MacDonnell Ranges and Alice Springs area, Northern Territory. Traditionally hunters and gatherers, they are a relatively numerous people, divided into small sub-groups of about three families ranging over their own areas, generally of about 260 sq. km / 100 sq. miles. They survive in some of the harshest territory in Australia, with temperatures of 40°C / 105°F.

The Aranda speak a Pama-Nyungan language, and in 1994 they were estimated to number about 3000.

## ASMAT or South Papuans

Hunter-gatherers of INDONESIAN New Guinea, who were first contacted only during the 1930s. They speak a South Papuan language. They live in large villages of up to 2000 individuals, at the centre of which is a *yeu* (ceremonial men's house) where all the important village festivals are celebrated.

Traditionally, the Asmat were a cannibalistic headhunting tribe. They are renowned for the quality of their wood-carving, which displays themes drawn from both war and headhunting. Their wood-carving also has a religious significance, as in their creation myth mankind is 'carved' by a Great Creator.

## ATONI

A Proto-Malayan and MELANESIAN people who inhabit the upland areas of western Timor. Their language is Timorese, and they are predomi-

nantly an agricultural people, who use shifting techniques to produce rice and maize. INDIAN influence is noticeable in the Hindu elements of their religious practice, but despite this – and the introduction of Christianity to the region – animism remains strong. The Atoni population numbered around 650,000 in the 1990s.

## AUSTRALIANS

Citizens of the Commonwealth of Australia, combining ABORIGINAL PEOPLES, descendants of BRITISH and IRISH colonial settlers and more recent immigrants of other, increasingly varied, ethnic backgrounds.

The first European settlement was the British penal colony established at Botany Bay in 1788, which tottered on the brink of starvation for 16 years. Free settlers soon followed to develop an agricultural economy. The discovery of gold in the 1850s brought a huge influx of settlers, who rapidly dispossessed or exterminated the Aboriginal population. In 1901 the separate colonies of Western Australia, Northern Territory, Queensland, South Australia, New South Wales, Victoria and Tasmania were brought together into the Commonwealth of Australia, a self-governing dominion of the British empire, which by 1931 was effectively an independent state.

A largely British-based culture, evident from the first settlements, acquired a new, Australian dimension. British sports – cricket, rugby league, rugby union, association football – and Australian-rules football became almost national religions. A culture celebrating masculinity and comradeship or 'mateship' also emerged. Australians see their land as offering immense opportunities; it is sometimes called 'the lucky country', for those who are energetic and prepared to take risks. A distinct Australian version of English, humorously known as 'Strine' after its typical pronunciation of 'Australian', also began to become distinct.

Until the mid-20th century, however, Australians continued to see themselves as essentially transplanted British. In the two World Wars they had no hesitation in supporting the 'mother country', and their soldiers showed a reckless courage that impressed friend and foe alike.

*"The 'Aralta' draw peculiar designs on flat upright rocks. "*

**W.H. Wiltshire, 1891, referring to the Aranda**

*"Brace yerself Sheila! "*

**An Australian seduction (jocular)**

Those World Wars, however, also caused a shift in Australian attitudes. In 1915 the death toll of the Gallipoli campaign and subsequent heavy losses on the Western Front convinced many that British general officers were careless of Australian lives. In 1942 the fall of Singapore to the JAPANESE, again blamed on British officers, showed that the 'mother country' was, in fact, incapable of protecting Australia.

Other changes were also in progress. At the start of the 20th century, CHINESE immigration had prompted a racist 'white Australia' policy, designed to exclude Asians in particular. That policy was finally abandoned in the 1970s due to the need to increase the Australian population. By the 1980s more than 100 nationalities were present in Australia, many from Asia and the Middle East, and a genuinely multicultural nation had emerged, with remarkably little racial tension. Australians do pride themselves on being a tolerant nation (except perhaps in attitudes towards the Aboriginal people). They are also fiercely egalitarian and very down-to-earth in their attitudes and speech. An important aspect of this is a marked lack of natural deference to those in positions of authority – something Australians ascribe to their nation's convict origins.

All these changes transformed Australian attitudes to Britain, now hardly the mother country to many Australians. The 'cultural cringe', by which Australians had deferred to all aspects of British culture, vanished. They consider their own artists, such as Sidney Nolan and Arthur Boyd, and writers such as Thomas Keneally and Peter Carey, to be at least the equal of any British contemporary. A degree of hostility towards the British developed, reflected in the stereotyped caricature of the 'whinging poms': whiners dependent on welfare who lack the courage and enterprise that made Australians what they are. Australians also take enormous delight in defeating the British, and especially the ENGLISH, at any sport. Britain, however, still remains a favourite travel destination, and in a referendum in 1999 a republic was rejected, though not so much out of loyalty to the British monarchy as for a lack of agreement about what should replace it.

In 2003 there were nearly 20 million Australians.

## AUSTRO-ASIATICS

A Southeast Asian ethno-linguistic group. Its early members had, by the early 3rd millennium BC, settled over a large area encompassing much of mainland Southeast Asia. They comprised both hunter-gatherers and rice farmers. In historical times, the range of Austro-Asiatic peoples has been greatly reduced by migrations of Austronesian, Tai and Burmese peoples. Many of the languages spoken in the region today, amounting to over 150 (including some Indian languages), remain Austro-Asiatic, such as Mon-Khmer, NICOBARESE and Munda (see MUNDAS). The Austro-Asiatics may have been closely related to the AUSTRONESIANS.

## AUSTRONESIAN

The largest language family in the world, formerly classified as Malayo-Polynesian (a term now used for a sub-group only), comprising as many as 1200 languages. After INDO-EUROPEAN it is also the most widespread, extending from Madagascar to Taiwan, including the Southeast Asian countries of Thailand, Malaysia, Indonesia, the Philippines and Brunei, and many of the islands of the Central and South Pacific (though not Australia or New Guinea). Austronesian speakers are a minority in Cambodia and Vietnam. Early forms of Austronesian were probably spoken in Taiwan before 4000 BC by people of Mongoloid origin. They were possibly pushed out by newly arriving AUSTRO-ASIATIC peoples from the north.

## AYTA

See AETAS.

## BABA CHINESE or Straits Chinese

A hybrid CHINESE people who reside in Penang, Malacca and Singapore. The Baba Chinese have tended to accept cultural assimilation with the majority MALAY population far more readily than other Chinese groups in the region. As a result, they speak a dialect of Bazaar Malay (known as Baba Malay) and have adopted a number of

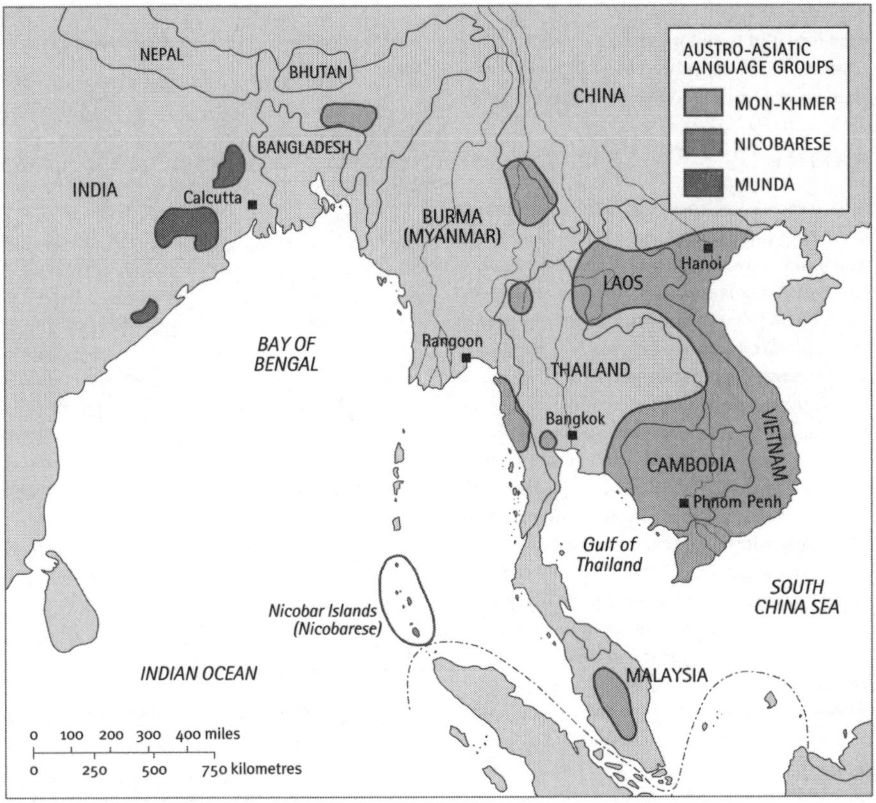
AUSTRO-ASIATIC LANGUAGE GROUPS
MON-KHMER
NICOBARESE
MUNDA
NEPAL
BHUTAN
CHINA
BANGLADESH
INDIA
Calcutta
BURMA (MYANMAR)
Hanoi
LAOS
BAY OF BENGAL
Rangoon
THAILAND
Bangkok
VIETNAM
CAMBODIA
Phnom Penh
Gulf of Thailand
SOUTH CHINA SEA
Nicobar Islands (Nicobarese)
INDIAN OCEAN
MALAYSIA
0 100 200 300 400 miles
0 250 500 750 kilometres

**Austro-Asiatics**

*The wide distribution of Austro-Asiatic languages shows the former extent of Austro-Asiatic settlement in the third millennium BC.*

other aspects of Malay culture, such as dress and cuisine. This cultural diversity is reflected in the number of religions prevalent among the Baba Chinese, including Taoism, Buddhism and Christianity. There are currently around 402,000 Baba Chinese.

## BAHNAR

An AUSTRO-ASIATIC mountain-dwelling people of central Vietnam between Kontum and Ankhe. They remain a fairly isolated agricultural people. They cooperated closely with the FRENCH colonial administration and during the Vietnam War fought against the North Vietnamese. The Bahnar have clashed frequently with the communist VIETNAMESE government in their quest for political autonomy. Their religion is animistic. There were 137,000 Bahnar in 1993.

## BAI

See PAI.

## BAJAU

An AUSTRONESIAN-speaking people who reside principally in the Philippines and Borneo. Some groups are traditionally known as the Sea Gypsies, and the majority of FILIPINO Bajau continue to gain their livelihood by harvesting fish and other marine products. Most live mainly on houseboats. MALAYSIAN Bajau, however, tend to be divided into two groups: those who live by the sea and those who have moved inland and pursue a living centred upon buffalo herding. While many Bajau continue to adhere to traditional animism, large numbers, particularly in Malaysia, are becoming far more culturally assimilated with their neighbours and so have converted to Islam. In the Philippines the Bajau form a part of the Moro group of peoples. Their language is Samal, related to Philippine Bisaya. There were some 20,000 Bajau in the late 1990s.

## BALINESE

An AUSTRONESIAN-speaking people originating from the island of Bali (capital Denpasar), which lies between Java and Lombok in Indonesia. Large numbers of Balinese also live on Lombok. While the majority of the peoples of Indonesia are Muslim, the principal religion of the Balinese is Hinduism, mixed with elements of animism. Bali was conquered by the JAVANESE king Sanjaya in 732 and remained heavily influenced by Eastern Javanese politics and culture; the island was usually ruled by vassal kings and princes. These influences were further consolidated by the influx of many Javanese aristocrats, priests and scholars following the conversion of many Javanese to Islam during the 15th century.

Following the DUTCH annexation of much of Indonesia, the island was essentially left alone and only indirectly administered as part of their empire. Bali did not grow any of the spices prized in Europe, and merely provided mercenaries for the army as well as slaves. From the mid-19th century, however, the Dutch adopted a much more aggressive policy, and Bali was incorporated directly into the Dutch East Indian empire. Following World War II, and independence from the Dutch, Bali became part of the Republic of Indonesia in 1950.

The Balinese culture is essentially Hindu-Javanese; they do not possess a caste system, but social distinctions do exist based upon the Hindu Varna. The Balinese are, mainly, an agricultural people. By the 9th century irrigation was being used on the island to produce the rice crop, and the Balinese now produce large quantities of rice, cane sugar, copra, tobacco, fruits and vegetables. Tourism accounts for a major proportion of Balinese income, and handicrafts are produced locally from wood, tortoiseshell and various metals to sell to tourists. Perhaps owing to the long-term influence of Javanese culture and politics on the islanders, the Balinese have been inclined to accede to their incorporation into the republic of Indonesia and generally accept Indonesian national status. The Balinese population is currently around 2.8 million.

## BATAKS

An ethnically and culturally mixed INDONESIAN people, principally of AUSTRONESIAN descent, who live on the island of Sumatra. Sub-groups include the Toba, Karo, Mandailing, Simalungan and Pakpak. The Batak name is said to derive from 'Si Raja Batak', a mythical hero ancestor figure. Most live in the mountainous region centred on Lake Toba, and they were almost undisturbed by outside influences until the early 19th century. They remain a largely agricultural people with a traditional patrilineal tribal structure. Their native religion is based on animism and ancestor worship, in which women mediums play a prominent role. They developed an indigenous script, based on INDIAN forms, and their religion displays some Hindu influences.

Since the 19th century, however, customary Batak culture has tended to become diluted; large numbers, for example, have abandoned their native religious beliefs in favour of Lutheran Protestantism or of Islam. Moreover, since Indonesian independence, modernization has grown apace in Sumatra, and many Bataks have been culturally and economically assimilated into modern Indonesian society. So, many Bataks now take an active part in the country's government, trade and administration. In addition, the Christianized Bataks display a more Westernized cultural outlook than many of their traditional Batak or Muslim neighbours.

There are currently around 5.7 million Bataks, and while large numbers of them are happy with Indonesian status, the Batak national identity remains strong. Most continue to use the native Batak language in everyday life, although the Indonesian national language is largely used for government, business and commerce. Bataks are linguistically closely related to the Gayo, but also to the MINANGKABAUS and MALAYS.

## BELAITS

See DAYAK.

# BICOL or Bicolanos

A FILIPINO lowland minority AUSTRONESIAN people, who occupy the historical region of Bicolandia. They are an agricultural people, with rice-growing an important source of income, and the vast majority adhere to Roman Catholicism. Many Bicol have been at the forefront of communist agitation against Filipino governments. There were some 3.5 million Bicol in the 1990s.

# BIDAYUHS

See DAYAK.

# BIDJANDJARA

See PITJANTJARA.

# BINANDERE

A native people of Oro province in Papua New Guinea. They numbered 6700 in 1991. Occupying sago swamps and plains, they are fishers and hunters and practise slash-and-burn agriculture. They speak Binanderean and many are Christian, though some still practise their traditional animist religion. They are noted as wood-carvers and potters and have strong oral traditions. The elders transmit oral history and use their knowledge of history, law and precedents to serve as judges, settling all forms of disputes.

# BISAYA or Bisayah or Dusun

A DAYAK people of Borneo, Malaysia. They reside principally in northern Sarawak, although significant numbers are also found in Brunei. They are an agricultural people who, in recent years, have been encouraged to abandon their traditional shifting growing techniques in favour of sedentary production.

The Bisaya speak Murut languages, closely related to Sabah Murut and Duryn. Their religion is a local amalgamation of Islam and animism. It is possible they are related to the BISAYAN and Murut.

# BISAYAN or Visayan

The collective name for the AUSTRONESIAN cultural-linguistic groups of the central Philippines, comprising Cebuan, Lanayan or Hiligaynon, and Samaran.

# BLACK BONE YI

An AUSTRO-ASIATIC people who inhabit the mountainous regions of southwestern China. The Black Bone Yi have remained remarkably unaffected by CHINESE culture. For most of their history they retained a caste-focused social system in which they formed an aristocratic elite who ruled over the lower class White Bone Yi. In YI society, the measure of a Black Bone's importance was directly related to the number of White Bone retainers over whom he acted as master and patron. This social system was eventually ended by Chinese intervention in the 1950s. The Black Bone Yi maintain a highly independent society, however, and continue to use their own Tibeto-Burman language and non-alphabetic writing system.

# BLACK LISU

See LISU.

# BLACK TAI

See TAI.

# BRUNEIANS

The people of the Sultanate of Brunei (capital Bandar Seri Begawan), who numbered 341,000 in 2002. The majority of the population (67%) are MALAY, with significant numbers of CHINESE (15%), INDIANS and indigenous peoples. The term 'Brunei' is derived from 'Borneo'.

Throughout history the region has been subject to a number of disparate cultural influences, notably Chinese, Hindu, Islamic and European. By the 16th century, the sultan controlled all of Borneo, together with some of the Philippine islands; subsequent internecine strife, however, led to the gradual loss of most of this territory, and the growth of foreign influence. By 1888,

> **Bruneians: main ethnic groups**
>
> Belaits
> Bisaya
> Dayak
> Ibans
> Kadazan
> Murut

b

Brunei was a British protectorate, and remained so until independence in 1984. Despite the multi-ethnic composition of the population, Brunei has been comparatively free of internal strife over the last 100 years. Much of this stability has, no doubt, been because of the relatively high per-capita income in the country, which is generated by the export of petroleum and natural gas. A large-scale insurrection occurred in 1962, however, following plans for the unification of Brunei with Malaysia – a policy that was subsequently dropped.

The majority of the population (63%) are Sunni Muslims, and the judicial system is based on Islamic Shari'a law. Most of the Chinese residents, however, are Buddhist, and recent policies to increase Islamic culture have created a degree of tension between the Chinese and Malay population. There are also significant numbers of Christians, and traditional animism is still practised in the remoter parts of the country. The official language of Brunei is Bahasa Malay, although both English and Chinese are widely spoken.

## BUGIS or Buginese

An AUSTRONESIAN people, communities of whom are spread throughout the INDONESIAN archipelago and Malay Peninsula, but who originated in southern Sulawesi (Celebes). Today most are cit-

izens of Indonesia. The Bugis are principally an agricultural and fishing people. They produce mainly irrigated rice and live in regions of high population density. They have also been renowned for centuries for their maritime, trading and boat-building skills.

Prior to the arrival of the DUTCH in the early 17th century, the Bugis comprised a number of disparate warring kingdoms who fought for control of the lucrative spice trade. Following Dutch intervention, they enjoyed a short period of political domination over southern Sulawesi, and this followed a number of successful wars against the MACASSARESE (to whom they are ethnically related), fought with Dutch assistance. Later encroachments by their former allies and renewed conflict with the Macassarese during the 18th century, however, gradually led to the migration of large numbers of Bugis away from the island. By the mid-18th century, Bugis migrants had gained control of, or considerable influence in, a number of important states in the Malay Peninsula and eastern Borneo, including Johore, Selangor, Riau, Kedah and Perak. Although by the early 19th century they no longer dominated many of these areas, Bugis communities are still found in Borneo and Malaysia. Many of these, however, have assimilated with the indigenous populations.

Those Bugis who remained in their homeland retained a considerable degree of local

Bugis

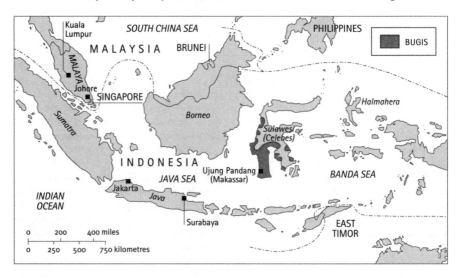

autonomy, but were nominally subject to Dutch rule. Following a brief period of British control (1810–16), Sulawesi reverted to the Dutch, and a major Bugis uprising occurred in 1825. By the mid-19th century the Dutch had determined to subject the island to direct rule, and the Bugis finally lost their independence in 1905.

During World War II Sulawesi was captured by the JAPANESE. A brief period as a member of Dutch Eastern Indonesia (1946–50) was succeeded by the incorporation of the Bugis into the United States of Indonesia (later the Republic of Indonesia) in 1950.

The Bugis have been a mainly Muslim people since the early 17th century, although earlier animist, Buddhist and Hindu influences have left a mark on their cultural development. They are also related to the upland non-Muslim TORADJA. In recent years, Bugis communities have clashed with a number of disparate peoples, often over religious and ethnic differences. In Borneo, Bugis, CHINESE, DAYAK and MALAY populations have all clashed violently with incoming MADURESE migrants. In Western Papua and Eastern Timor, immigrant Bugis traders and shopkeepers have been the focus of PAPUAN and EAST TIMORESE attacks; moreover, violence has also broken out between migrant Bugis in Ambon and Christian AMBONESE.

Generally, the Bugis have tended to accept Indonesian status more readily than other ethnic and religious groups, such as the ACEHNESE, although during the 1950s and 1960s Sulawesi was the scene of Dutch-supported militant anti-government movements. In 1951 many Bugis supported the creation of an Islamic Indonesian state.

There were estimated to be about 3,310,000 Bugis at the end of the 20th century.

# BULO

See STIENG.

# BUNABA

An Australian ABORIGINAL PEOPLE of the east Kimberley area of Western Australia. Nomadic hunters and gatherers, they speak a non-Pama-Nyungan language. They occupied desirable farming land and suffered massacres and land theft at the hands of settlers during the 19th century. Led by their great leader Jandamarra, they fought one of the few sustained wars of resistance by the Aboriginal peoples, in a guerrilla campaign of 1894–7. They were finally brutally defeated, and later generations had to buy back part of their traditional lands simply to have access to them. In 1990 there were up to 100 language speakers, but there were no children among this number. They are at risk of losing their identity as a distinct people.

# BURMESE or Burman

The Burmese are the majority people of the Republic of Burma (the name of which the military government insisted should be spelled 'Myanmar' in 1989, although this has not been widely accepted). They are predominantly a Mongoloid people, descended from Burman tribes who migrated from southern China during the 9th century. As a national rather than an ethnic term, 'Burmese' also describes all the citizens of the republic.

The Burmese have been the dominant people of present-day Burma since the 11th century, when a Burman dynasty centred on the city of Pagan succeeded in defeating the MON and SHAN. Between 1287 and 1301 Burma was subject to Mongol control, but then disintegrated into a number of small rival kingdoms following the collapse of the Mongol empire. Reunification did not re-occur until the expansion of the Burman Toungoo dynasty during the mid-16th century; this unified state survived until the mid-18th century.

In 1752 a new dynasty, centred on Konbaung, gained control of Burma and defeated both the THAIS and RHAKINES. By this period, however, a number of European powers were pursuing their own trading interests in the region, principally the British, Dutch and French. During the 19th century, the Burmese fought a series of unsuccessful wars against the British, triggered initially by a Burman attack on Assamese territory, which culminated in the eventual incorporation of Burma into the BRITISH empire in 1885.

**"** The Burman is a smiling obdurate humanist. **"**

H.G. Wells, 1939

### Colonialism and after

The period of British control and economic exploitation helped evolve a distinct consolidation of Burmese national identity, displayed in the new prose literature of the period, and by the 1930s there was a strong movement for independence. Rebellions occurred in both 1938 and 1939. By 1942, a Burmese Independence Army had been formed; this subsequently worked in league with the JAPANESE invading army in order to oust the British. In 1945, these same units fought alongside the British against their former allies. Britain finally acknowledged Burmese independence in January 1948.

The Burmese are linguistically related to both the CHINESE and TIBETANS, and in 2002 they accounted for 69% of the total population of Burma (which stood at nearly 49 million). Alongside these reside a number of important ethnic minorities, including the SHAN (8.5%), KAREN (6.2%), RAKHINES (4.5%) MON (2.4%), CHIN (2.2%), KACHIN (1.4%), NAGA, PALAUNG and LAWA. Under the British there was significant INDIAN immigration, and many Chinese have also moved into the region.

While many of these minorities have their own state, not all have been content with 'Burmese' status. Many of these peoples fought against the Japanese in 1942, and were suspicious of the Burmese-dominated government, fearing the ultimate loss their tribal identities. Since 1948, major ethnic rebellions have occurred involving the Karen, Shan and Kachin, and these people continue to agitate for independence. Many quote a right of secession incorporated into the constitution of 1947 in their demands for autonomy; examples of groups representing minorities include the Karenni National Progressive Party and the National Democratic Front.

There have also been major insurrections involving the Burmese population over the last 30 years, but these have not been based on religious or ethnic considerations, but rather on dissatisfaction with incumbent political regimes. These political opponents have, however, frequently made common cause with those fighting for ethnic independence.

The vast majority of Burmese adhere to Theravada Buddhism (89.1%); there are also relatively small numbers of Christians and Muslims. Alongside their Buddhist beliefs many Burmese also continue to honour spirits known as *nat*, and these are frequently honoured in separate shrines within Buddhist temple complexes. Most Burmese boys are expected to spend at least some time as novice monks, a rite known as the *Shinpyu*.

The art and architecture of the region has been heavily influenced by Indian forms due to long-standing trade links between the two regions. Over 70% of the population are dependent on agriculture for their livelihood, and rice is the principal crop. Burmese is the official language of the republic, but many of the minority peoples continue to use their own native languages and dialects. The written language is based on Sanskrit, and the Burmese literary tradition dates back to the 12th century.

## CALDOCHE

The people of the Pacific island of New Caledonia who are of European (mostly FRENCH) descent. In 1996 over 68,000, or 37.1% of the population spoke French or patois, indicating Caldoche identity.

The Caldoche first arrived in 1864 when France established a penal colony on the island, and by 1897 some 21,000 convicts had been sent there. Free settlers soon joined them when nickel was discovered. Caldoche land incursions and other abuses brought them into conflict with the native KANAK population, who were defeated in a brief war in 1878. This ethnic violence proved a recurrent problem, and there were serious clashes in 1984–6 between pro-independence Kanaks and the Caldoche who opposed it.

Although the New Caledonian economy is mainly agricultural, the Caldoche culture is in many ways more akin to that of rural USA or Australia than France: for example, rodeos are highly popular.

## CAMBODIANS

The citizens of the modern republic of Cambodia (capital Phnom Penh). In 2002, the population stood at nearly 13.8 million. The ancient Hindu term for the region was Kanbuja, and is from this that 'Cambodia' is derived. Some believe that the area takes its name from a great sage named Cambu Svayambhuva, from whom the early Cambodian kings claimed descent.

The vast majority (over 90%) of the population of Cambodia are ethnic KHMERS, who live alongside small numbers of VIETNAMESE, CHINESE, THAIS and CHAMS. The 'Cambodians', therefore, are essentially synonymous with the Khmer, and the name has been used interchangeably for many years. More recently, however, particularly following Cambodian independence from France in 1953, the term 'Cambodian' has tended to take precedence, especially among foreign commentators. Small numbers of Khmer are also to be found in eastern Thailand and the Mekong Delta in Vietnam.

The history of the modern republic has been one of frequent internecine conflicts, but these have not tended to be centred on ethnic or religious issues, but rather on political agendas. Nevertheless, there has been a long history of Khmer–Vietnamese hostility, and a number of minority groups, principally the Chams, were persecuted by the Khmer Rouge regime (1975–9), as was the Buddhist faith. Until the 1990s the Khmer Rouge still controlled significant portions of the Cambodian–Thai border, and other areas of the country have also been difficult for central governments to control; as a result, the unification of the modern republic has been achieved only recently.

The vast majority of the population adhere to Theravada Buddhism, though there are also small numbers of Mahayana Buddhists, Muslims (mainly among the Chams) and Christians. Khmer–Cambodian national identity is strong. Historically, it has been heavily influenced by INDIAN culture, particularly in early art, architecture, writing and social structure. Traditional Cambodian music and dance play a prominent part in everyday life. Over the last 25 years there has been a concerted effort to revitalize such traditions following the demographic and cultural devastations inflicted by the Khmer Rouge (under whom about 1.5 million Cambodians are thought to have died).

The national language is Khmer, and there have been active policies to eradicate the use of French as a second language.

About 75% of the population continue to rely on agriculture as the principal source of their livelihood, with wet-rice cultivation the principal form. Following the catastrophes that accompanied the Vietnam War and the era of the Khmer Rouge, and despite significant steps towards reconstruction, the Cambodians remain one of the world's poorest peoples.

## CANTONESE

A people of China related to the HAN. Although they speak the Cantonese dialect (also known as Yue), they have been thoroughly assimilated into the culture of the Han majority and consider themselves CHINESE. Most reside in the provinces of Guangdong and Guangxi, especially in the city of Guangzhou (Canton) and in Hong Kong and Macau.

The majority of emigrant Chinese are of Cantonese descent, and throughout the world they have gained a reputation for their business and culinary expertise. The Cantonese were at the forefront of nationalistic, anti-BRITISH sentiment during the events that led to the Second Opium War in the mid-19th century. There are currently more than 70 million Cantonese speakers.

## CAPE YORK ABORIGINAL PEOPLE

See WIK.

## CHAMMOROS

A people of the Oceanic Mariana islands of mixed SPANISH, FILIPINO and MICRONESIAN descent. Originally the Chammoros were MICRONESIANS, who settled the islands around AD 500 and established a farming, fishing and hunting economy. When the Spanish arrived in the 16th century, they misunderstood the Chammoro custom of give-and-take in regard to property, and labelled them thieves. Harsh treatment and the attack on their traditional culture from missionaries soon provoked wars, which, coupled with epidemics, reduced a population of 100,000 to a mere 5000, with few men

C

**Chin:**
**main ethnic**
**sub-groups**

Aimol
Baite
Chiru
Hrangkhol
Thados

remaining. Spanish and Filipino men were brought in to repopulate the islands.

When the USA took the islands in 1898, a strong AMERICAN influence was added to the culture and the Chammoros are now US citizens. They numbered 78,000 in 1997, and are trying to reassert their heritage, with their traditional Austronesian language increasingly taught, and demands being voiced to return to pre-conquest placenames.

## CHAMS

An AUSTRONESIAN minority people who reside principally in Cambodia (the Western Chams) and Vietnam (the Eastern Chams). The Western Chams number around 200,000, the Eastern Chams around 80,000. Both groups are descended from the inhabitants of the kingdom of Champa, which controlled significant areas of the Southeast Asian mainland between the 2nd and 15th centuries. The kingdom was first formed following the disintegration of the Han CHINESE empire, but was not fully unified until the 4th century. Frequently at war – with the Chinese, KHMER, MONGOLS and ANNAMESE – the Champa kingdom was defeated by the Annamese in 1471, and finally eradicated entirely in 1611 by VIETNAMESE Cochin China. Following this defeat many fled west into Khmer territory.

The Chams are known to have been present in modern Vietnam since Neolithic times, and by the 1st millennium AD had established important maritime and trading links with India and China. Certainly, INDIAN influences became an integral part of Cham culture, and much of the art and architecture, as well as their early writing system, displays this inspiration. By AD 400, the Champa kings had also converted to Hinduism, and Siva became the principal deity of the region. In the north, Chinese influences were strong, and many temples also display Khmer influence. These cultural stimuli were later passed on to the Vietnamese, and Indian influences are still visible today. Traditional animism and spirit worship also remain important in the lives of many Chams.

Most Chams today pursue an agricultural lifestyle, although in Vietnam trading is still a major occupation. The Vietnamese Chams have been largely assimilated to the dominant culture, and this has also been the case, but to a lesser degree, in Cambodia. Here, the Chams have formed ethnic ties with the MALAY population, where they are also known as Malay-Chams or Khmer Islam; the latter term is derived from the fact that most have converted to Islam (they follow the Imam San sect). Nevertheless, in Cambodia, the Chams now largely speak the Khmer language. Between 1975 and 1979, the Chams were systematically persecuted by the Khmer Rouge regime, and many continue to live in poverty. In Vietnam, where most Chams are Buddhists, they use the Vietnamese language.

## CHIMBU

See SIMBU.

## CHIN

A group of SINO-TIBETAN-related tribes who inhabit the mountainous border regions between India and Burma. It is possible that they migrated to this area from Tibet or China. The term 'Chin' is an English form of the BURMESE word *khyang*, perhaps meaning 'friend' or 'ally'. The Chin refer to themselves by a number of names, such as Laizo or Mizo. The rugged terrain of their homeland has not ensured their complete isolation from other cultures, and while traditional tribal society and animistic religion remain important, many have been converted to Christianity, or have absorbed Hindu influences. Chin tribes include the Aimol, Baite (or Biete, or Bete), Chiru, Hrangkhol and Thados, and they are related to the Nagas. In 1994 there were about 1.5 million Chin, 900,000 of whom lived in Burma.

The Chin are an agricultural people and speak a Sino-Tibetan language, of which there are over 40 Chin dialects. Hunting is a popular activity, and success carries great social and religious prestige. Some Chin tribes have no social hierarchy, while others possess a stratified society based on wealth. Internecine conflicts have been common throughout Chin history, and they frequently raided the territory of their neighbours. Between the late 19th and mid-20th centuries the Chin were incorporated into the British empire.

# CHINESE

A people of predominantly HAN origin, the vast majority of whom live in the People's Republic of China, though large numbers also reside in countries throughout the world. In 2002, the population of China (capital Beijing) stood at over 1294 million, making it the most populous nation on Earth.

Some Chinese ethnologists have advocated the belief that the Chinese are entirely aboriginal to China, first emerging recognizably in the Yellow River valley. Others argue that Chinese origins can be linked, for example, to the MONGOL peoples of the Central Asian steppes. Either way, there can be little doubt that the Chinese evolved one of the earliest high civilizations in history, one that was the equal of the contemporaneous civilization of Mesopotamia. The LONGSHAN and YANGSHAO cultures initially developed in the region occupied by modern China. The earliest dynasties that can be confirmed historically, however, are those of the Shang (c.1766–1122 BC) and Zhou (1122–256 BC). There are currently over 300 different peoples, speaking 205 registered languages, living within the People's Republic, and the Chinese government recognizes 56 major nationalities. Some of the major examples of these ethnically-based nationalities are isted in the accompanying box. Many of the differences between these groups are linguistic or cultural. China encompasses a very large geographical area, with vastly differing climates and terrains; mountain, desert, tundra and tropics are all represented, with a concomitant variety in ethnic composition. The Han Chinese are the numerically dominant group and currently account for nearly 92% of the total population. The overwhelming majority of Han live in 19 eastern provinces of China, while the western regions are the homeland of many minority groups.

## Assimilation and subjugation

A number of minorities, most notably the Manchus, have assimilated with the majority Han population, and the Manchu language is now all but extinct. Others, however, remain firmly committed to their tribal or national traditions, and the communist government has taken considerable steps to help preserve tribal identities, despite a hiatus during the Cultural Revolution (1966–76) when a number of ethnic minorities were persecuted. These measures have included the establishment of autonomous regions and enclaves, the foundation of schools and the propagation of writing systems, based upon Pinyin, for those minority languages that previously had no form of writing.

As a result of these measures, ethnic tensions are relatively infrequent throughout China, although there are exceptions. Since the annexation of Tibet by China in 1950 and the subsequent persecution of their religion, the Tibetans, for example, remain staunchly committed to winning their political and religious freedom. Much the same is also true of the Muslim Uighurs of western China, although – except during the Cultural Revolution – they have not been religiously persecuted. In recent years, in order to ease urban pressures in eastern China, and also to promote Chinese cultural values, the government has been encouraging Han Chinese to migrate to the western provinces. At present, this policy does not appear to have had a detrimental effect on ethnic relations within these areas, with the exception of Tibet.

China's sheer size and variety of terrain do not make it an easy area to unify. Many of the succession of emperors who have ruled over much of the last 2000 years entrusted provincial administration to local governors and warlords, some of whom became virtually autonomous and caused much internecine strife. It has only been since the arrival of the communist regime in 1949 that a much more centralized governmental, administrative and economic system has been forged. Even now, however, much is left in the hands of local bureaucracies. Despite these difficulties, there can be little doubt that the Chinese have a deep-rooted sense of the antiquity of their own nationhood, and a major factor in the growth of this unity and national identity has been the propagation of their writing system.

There are currently 12 major dialects of the Chinese language (which belongs to the SINO-TIBETAN group), many of them mutually unintel-

**Chinese: main ethnic groups**

Bonyei
Chuang
Han
Hmong
Hui
Kawa
Koreans
Li
Manchus
Mongols
Pai
Puyi
Qinchai
Tai
Tibetans
Tuchia
Tung
Uighur
Yao
Yi

ligible. Mandarin is the most widely spoken and is regarded as the 'standard' dialect, while outside of China, Cantonese is the most prolific. A Chinese writing system has existed for over 3000 years (originally pictographic), but since the 3rd century BC there has been only one officially acknowledged script, and this has undoubtedly helped forged Chinese self-awareness. The Chinese script is now the world's oldest continually used writing system. More recently, the introduction of the romanized Pinyin system has facilitated greater literacy and understanding and has been viewed as an attempt to weld the many disparate peoples of the republic into a united whole.

## National identity

China's generally isolationist stance toward much of the rest of the world has also helped to consolidate the nationalism of the Chinese people. Even those who succeeded in conquering China, such as the Mongols, BRITISH, FRENCH and JAPANESE, were all regarded as inferior and barbaric. Moreover, there was a resurgence of nationalistic feeling during the late 19th and early 20th centuries, exemplified by the Boxer Rebellion (1898), at a time when China was being economically exploited by a number of foreign powers. These nationalistic feelings ultimately led to the foundation of a republic (1912), and were later harnessed by the communists in their drive for political power.

Many Chinese people in other parts of the world retain a strong sense of their national identity, and community feelings remain central to everyday life. Many retain Chinese as their first language and live in 'Chinatowns' that have evolved in many cities throughout the world. This lack of assimilation has often caused them to be viewed as outsiders in their adopted countries and to be subject to racism. The Chinese have gained a reputation as traders in many countries, and some have been the target for discontented groups – for example, during recent rioting among PAPUAN nationalists.

Today, more than half of the population of China claim to have no religious beliefs, and their right to this atheist stance is one of the cornerstones of the communist government's manifesto. Traditionally, however, Confucian philosophy, Buddhism and Taoism have had a deep impact upon the Chinese people, and many continue to adhere to these beliefs. Certainly, since religious tolerance was granted in 1978, many have overtly practised their faith. There are also a small numbers of Chinese Muslims and Christians, and animism continues among some of the more isolated peoples. The nationalistic connections of Tibetan Buddhists continue to contribute to their persecution.

Despite a rigorous policy of industrialization in China since 1949 and the migration of large numbers of people to the towns and cities, a phenomenon caused by considerable rural poverty, the majority of the population (about two-thirds) continue to derive their livelihood from agriculture, with rice and wheat being the principal crops grown. Attempts at economic modernization in recent years have led to an unprecedented boom but also to large-scale unemployment and economic difficulties for many people, which in turn have led to a rise in social tension, criticism of the government and the growth of some opposition groups, such as the Exercise and Meditation Movement. In 1989, for example, the protests begun by students in Tiananmen Square spread quickly to other towns and cities – an indication of widespread urban discontent.

## A more open China?

The Chinese possess one of the oldest cultures in the world, and in many fields their endeavours remain unsurpassed, for example in porcelain production, ivory carving and the art of calligraphy. Today, traditional Chinese culture remains extremely important and has been actively patronized by the communist government. Opera, theatre, music, sport and literature are all very popular and continue to emphasize Chinese national identity. Many operas and works of fiction, for example, focus on national and revolutionary heroes. There has also been a return to traditional forms of Chinese medicine, and these are finding a ready market outside China, notably in the Western world.

Despite regular contact since the 15th century, Chinese culture has been relatively little affected by Western influences, partly because of a xenophobic disdain of 'inferior' races. In recent

> 66 It is in his staying power that the Chinese excels the world. 99

Arthur H. Smith, 1894

years, however, following a relaxation in governmental attitudes, some Western culture is beginning to become popular, particularly in the areas of music and popular fiction. Since 1978, with the reintroduction of some private enterprise, China has also become much more open to Western economic influences and investment. In 2001 China became a member of the World Trade Organization. It is too early to say how this will affect the future of the Chinese people, but at present significant social tensions continue to exist. The recent return of both Hong Kong (1997) and Macao (1999) to Chinese suzerainty has been seen as another step toward achieving total national unity. Recently, closer links have been forged with the TAIWANESE, although China continues to regard the 'errant' island as rightfully part of the People's Republic.

Since 1949, the Chinese have had a number of border disputes with India, and tracts of land between the two countries remain disputed territory. During the 1970s there were also significant tensions between the Chinese and the Russians and Vietnamese. The Chinese were, however, the principal external supporters of the Khmer Rouge (see KHMER) of Cambodia.

In recent years there has been a growth in tension between the Chinese and the USA, sparked most recently by a collision between a US spy plane and a Chinese fighter aircraft, and the ensuing political standoff. These political tensions have, at times, led to the persecution of Chinese populations abroad, most notably following the 1965 Chinese-backed communist uprising against the government of Indonesia and during the Indonesian invasion of East Timor in 1975. As late as the 1990s Chinese publications and the Chinese New Year celebrations were banned in Indonesia, and the Chinese population was again the focus of racial attacks in 1998.

## CHRU or Churu

An AUSTRONESIAN agricultural people who inhabit the mountainous regions of southern Vietnam. Their relative isolation has ensured that they have been little affected by outside cultural influences. Their religion is principally animistic, and they speak a CHAM dialect. The Chru, whose population was estimated as around 15,000 in the late 1990s, are usually counted among the MONTAGNARDS.

## CHUANG

See ZHUANG.

## CHUKCHIS or Chukots

A Siberian people of the Chukchi peninsula in the northern Yakut autonomous republic, Russian Federation (see map, page 584). They call themselves *Iygoravetlyan*, meaning 'real person', and speak a Chukotko-Kamchatkan language.

Traditionally nomadic reindeer herders and more sedentary coastal fishers, the Chukchis are culturally similar to the TLINGIT of Alaska and British Columbia, to whom they are related. From their first encounter with the RUSSIANS in 1649, they and their Koryak allies fought bitterly to protect their freedom against genocidal attacks. The Russians established a series of fortresses on their territory, but they were unable ever to collect any significant tribute from the Chukchis. In 1778 the Russians cut their losses and signed a treaty, their only defeat in the conquest of Siberia. However, the Chukchis were severely weakened by the epidemics brought by alcohol and diseases associated with trade during the 1880s. In 1889 they agreed to pay a token tribute to the tsar.

The major outside impact on the Chukchis came with Soviet collectivization, which destroyed their traditional economy, while compulsory boarding education undermined their traditional culture. At the same time exploitation of mineral resources brought outsiders and pollution. Only at the end of the 20th century did they begin to recover as a people. In 1997 they numbered about 15,000.

## CHUUKESE

See TRUKESE.

## COOK ISLANDERS

See RAROTONGANS.

Chukchis

See page 583.

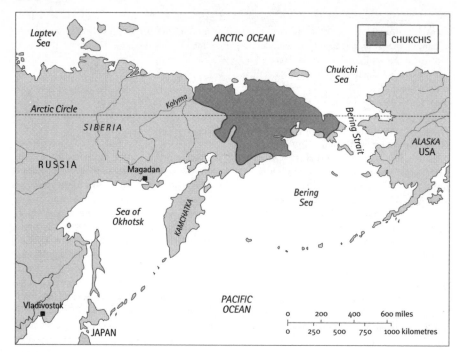

CHUKCHIS

**C**

## CUA

A MONTAGNARD people of Vietnam who speak a dialect of AUSTRO-ASIATIC. The Cua are a farming people who have been little affected by outside cultural influences. They practise animism. In the late 1990s the Cua population was estimated at 27,000.

## DAI

See TAI.

## DAYAK or Dyak

An AUSTRONESIAN group of indigenous and non-Muslim peoples of Borneo (in regions now incorporated into modern Malaysia and Indonesia). Significant numbers also reside in Brunei. Their current population is around 2 million. They comprise numerous different ethnic groups and these are conventionally grouped into larger ethno-linguistic categories, for example Iban, Kayan, Kenyah, Muruts, Ngaju and Punan-Punan.

Traditionally, the Dayak are an agricultural people who utilized slash-and-burn techniques and produced rice as their principal crop. They also hunted and gathered to supplement diets. Established Dayak villages are predominantly situated along rivers, and the communal longhouse is the traditional living space. Indigenous Dayak religion is animism; since the 19th century, however, large numbers have been converted to Christianity or Islam. Village handicrafts include textile dying, wood-carving and iron working.

Historically, there has been frequent intertribal warfare among the various Dayak tribes, with headhunting a common feature of these conflicts. Recent years, however, have witnessed the growth of a form of Dayak national identity in the face of a number of perceived threats to their traditional way of life. The INDONESIAN government, for example, which has tended to view the Dayak as somewhat backward, has actively encouraged the resettlement of large numbers of Muslim MADURESE in the provinces of Western Kalimantan. This policy has been met with considerable hostility among the Dayak, who are

DAYAKS

becoming a minority in their own homeland and fear a loss of their traditional land rights. These tensions have frequently resulted in outbreaks of violence, most notably in 2001, when hundreds of Madurese were killed and thousands forced to flee Borneo altogether. Significant in these attacks was the recurrence of traditional Dayak headhunting. In addition, in MALAYSIAN Borneo, both Muslim migration and the propagation of Islam as the official state religion have led to the alienation of many animistic and Christian Dayak.

Despite these tensions, however, many Dayak, particularly in Malaysia, are becoming assimilated into the society and culture of the MALAY-Muslim majority – in particular the Ibans. Significant numbers are abandoning traditional agricultural lifestyles in favour of employment in modern industries. In addition, sedentary agricultural techniques are also increasingly taking preference over slash-and-burn forms. These changes, of course, are serving to fuel the fears of those Dayak who wish to retain their traditional society and culture.

## DEMON

See SOLORESE.

## DJAMINDJUNGA

An Australian ABORIGINAL PEOPLE of the Victoria River coastal area, Northern Territory. Hunters, farmers and fishers, they speak a non-Pama-Nyungan language. Their sedentary coastal lives made them exposed to settler influences and land theft. In 1990 there were only about 30 native-language speakers left, and the language is nearly extinct. They are at risk of losing their characteristics as a distinct people.

## DJAWI

An Australian ABORIGINAL PEOPLE of the coast and islands around King Sound, Western Australia. Hunters, gatherers and fishers, they have become heavily acculturated by AUSTRALIANS and by other Aboriginal peoples, and in 1981 their language was virtually extinct.

## DJIWARLI

An ABORIGINAL PEOPLE of the Mount Augustus area, Western Australia. Nomadic hunters and gatherers, they have been overwhelmingly acculturated by AUSTRALIANS and other ABORIGINAL PEOPLES, and in 1981 only one surviving person could still speak the non-Pama-Nyungan Djiwarli language.

# DONG

See TUNG.

# DUSUN

See BISAYA.

# DYAK

See DAYAK.

# EAST TIMORESE

The inhabitants of the Republic of East Timor (capital Dili). Considerable numbers of East Timorese are also found in the INDONESIAN province of West Timor and in Australia. In 2002, the population of East Timor was about 779,000. The East Timorese are mainly AUSTRONESIAN-speaking, with some small PAPUAN-speaking groups. Sub-groups include the TETUM (Belu), Makassai and Mambai.

From the late 16th century, East Timor was increasingly subject to PORTUGUESE influence, in particular after the partition of the island between the Portuguese and Dutch in 1859. The late 19th century, however, witnessed a growth in East Timorese nationalism, and a concomitant increase in demands, and agitation, for independence and national self-determination. This was briefly achieved, following a Portuguese withdrawal from the region, in 1975. Almost immediately, however, Eastern Timor was invaded by the Indonesians, who retained control of the area until 1999. This period was marked by frequent rebellion, civil war, resettlement, Muslim immigration, famine, disease and politically motivated executions and massacres. In all it is estimated that one-third of the population died during Indonesian occupation. Independence was finally achieved in 2002.

East Timor has no official religion, but perhaps as many as 75% of the population are Catholics, although traditional animism is still an integral part of the beliefs of the majority of people. The official languages of the East Timorese are Tetum and Portuguese, with English and Bahasa Indonesian used for business and commercial purposes. Owing to the devastations that accompanied the Indonesian occupation and the conflicts leading up to the withdrawal of Indonesian forces, East Timor is one of the world's poorest nations. The vast majority of people rely on agriculture as the principal source of livelihood, with slash-and-burn techniques still in widespread use. Coffee, rice, corn and sweet potatoes are the principal crops, and cattle, buffalo and pigs are also raised. Cotton textiles and basketry are the predominant crafts.

# EASTER ISLANDERS or Rapa Nui

A native people of one of the world's most isolated inhabited islands, now a dependency of Chile. They are of POLYNESIAN descent and arrived around AD 400. New settlers may have arrived from South America around AD 1100, bringing new cultural influences.

In their isolation, The Easter Islanders developed a unique culture. Their carved *Rongorongo* script was the only written language in Oceania. Far more famous are their *moai* – the solemn statues that circle the island's coastlines, whose purpose is unknown. They also practised traditional Polynesian crafts such as wood-carving and tattooing.

Easter Island appears to have had a large population, up to 10,000, at one point, but this proved too large for the island to support. The agricultural practices of the islanders were unsustainable and triggered an environmental collapse that left bare and treeless what had been a lushly forested and vegetated island. Without new sources of wood, the people also lost the ability to make canoes, so could no longer exploit marine food resources. There is evidence, such as increased production of volcanic glass spear heads and the overturning of every *moai*, of internal strife over dwindling resources.

After Europeans first arrived in 1722, their diseases and a slave raid in 1862 reduced an already dwindled population to just 111, and destroyed all but remnants of the traditional Easter Island culture by the end of the 19th century. In 1999 there were 2500 Easter Islanders, but very few have ancestors from the original population.

# EMISHI

See AINU.

# ENGA

A native people of Enga province and Sau island, Papua New Guinea. They speak dialects of Enga, a Trans-New Guinea language, and practise slash-and-burn agriculture in scrub forest and on mountain slopes. Traditional beliefs remain strong, and they blame malevolent ghosts, which must be placated by a sacrifice, usually of a pig, for injuries and illness. They are divided into clans, averaging 350 members, which occasionally raid each other's territory. In the 1990s they numbered over 150,000.

# ERLITOU CULTURE

A former CHINESE culture which flourished between the 20th and mid-17th centuries BC. The culture is named after the site associated with early finds, and is renowned for the high quality of the bronze work produced. The later Erlitou period is perhaps contemporaneous with the early Shang dynasty.

# EZO

See AINU.

# FIJIANS

The native people of the South Pacific island group of Fiji. The islands were initially settled before 1000 BC. Fijians are a mixture of POLYNESIAN and MELANESIAN stock and speak an Austronesian language. They are wide-ranging traders with TONGAN contacts and are also farmers and fishers. Their culture is rich in mythology, oral history, dance and song. They are noted for their fire-walking ceremony and elaborate funerary ceremonies. Their traditional religion required that malevolent spirits be placated, which required widows to be strangled to accompany husbands into the spirit world. From the 1830s Christianization undermined such beliefs and ended cannibalism. It also brought European diseases that killed huge numbers.

BRITISH rule from 1874 changed the ethnic mix of the islands by importing thousands of indentured INDIAN workers. In 1995 there were about 345,000 native Fijians, or 46% of the population. They had become a minority within their own nation and resented Indian economic and political power. In 1987 Fijians launched a coup, intending to reclaim the land, its resources and political power. The flight of thousands of Indians regained a Fijian majority, but international sanctions forced Fiji to adopt a non-discriminatory constitution in 1997, which was overturned temporarily in another coup in 2000. Such political instability seems to have become a permanent feature of Fijian political life.

# FILIPINOS

The citizens of the Republic of the Philippines (capital Manila). Significant numbers of Filipinos are also found throughout the world, principally in the United Arab Emirates and Hong Kong. In 2002 the population of the Philippines stood at over 78.5 million. More specifically, however, the term 'Filipinos' refers to the lowland Christians. The Filipinos are an ethnically mixed people, but the vast majority are descended from AUSTRONESIANS who migrated to the islands from Taiwan, the Malay Peninsula and Indonesia during the second and first millennia BC. There are more than 100 different ethnic/regional Philippine peoples, and these include the Apayao, AETA (Ayta), Bagobo, BAJAU, BICOL, Bisaya, Bontok, Bukidnon, Gaddang, Ibaloy, ILOCANO, Kalinga, Mandaya, Manobo, Subanon, Tausung and Tinggian. There are also two major non-Austronesian minorities of SPANISH and CHINESE descent, many of whom are MESTIZOS. Although the Philippine archipelago consists of over 7000 islands, the vast majority of Filipinos inhabit the regions of Manila, Luzon and Mindanao.

Despite early trading contacts with China, India and western Asia, and subjugation to the INDONESIAN Sri Vijayan kingdom and the Chinese Ming dynasty, it was the arrival of the Spanish, in the early 16th century, that had the most profound cultural influence on the islanders. Indeed, the very expression 'Filipino' is not native, but derived from the Spanish, who

f

named the islands after their king, Philip II. 'Filipino' was originally a term of reference used when describing an individual born in the region, but of Spanish descent. Thereafter, Spanish influence was profound, particularly in the area of religion, with vast numbers converted to Roman Catholicism, a phenomenon that proved to be the first means by which many of the disparate ethnic groups of the region were united. Today, over 80% of islanders are Catholics. Such was the success of these outside influences, that very little of the former Philippine culture remains. What has survived, for example in the area of music, is practised by a very small minority of people. In addition to the Catholic majority, there are also fairly small numbers of Protestants, Muslims, Independent Filipino Christians, Taoists, animists and Buddhists.

**The struggle for unity**

Given the vast number of different ethnic and regional groups throughout the Philippines, political and cultural unification of the islands has not been easy, and regional culture remains important. Filipino nationalism dates back only as far as the 19th century and, until the realization of Filipino independence in 1946, was directed against Spanish, American and Japanese domination. There are about 80 different languages or dialects used by the islanders, and another means towards greater unity has been the propagation of a national language, known as Pilipino, which is based upon that of the TAGALOGS. Nevertheless, only about 55% of Filipinos use this language, and this has resulted in the use of English in schools, business and commerce. More than 90% of Filipinos continue to use their indigenous regional languages.

Many Muslim communities, who tend to be concentrated in the south of the archipelago, were never fully incorporated into the Spanish colony, and these have tended to evolve a very different culture from the Christian majority. Certainly, large numbers – for example the Moro (Muslims of the southern Philippines) and the Magindanao (an ethnic group) – totally reject Filipino status and the rule of the Christian-dominated Manila-based government. As a result, groups such as the Moro Islamic Liberation Front have agitated for many years for the creation of an autonomous Muslim region, and this has often led to violent confrontation.

## GARAWA

An Australian ABORIGINAL PEOPLE of the Borroloola area, near the Gulf of Carpentaria, Northern Territory. Nomadic hunters and gatherers, they occupied territory desirable to sheep farmers, and suffered massacres and land theft in the 1870s and 1880s. Driven into harsher territory to survive, including scrubland and mangrove swamps, they were threatened even here by the pollution of lead and silver mining from the 1890s, which threatened their food supplies and health. They were not above killing the occasional settler to even the score.

In 1981 the Garawa numbered over 200 speakers of their non-Pama-Nyungan language. In the 1980s they began the slow and frustrating process of pursuing a land claim against the territorial government.

## GILBERTESE

See I-KIRIBATI.

## GUMATJ

An Australian ABORIGINAL PEOPLE of the Yirrkala area, Northern Territory. Nomadic hunters, gatherers and fishers in the scrubland and coast of their territory, they speak a Pama-Nyungan language. They are noted for their strong relationship with the crocodile, which they hunt and eat only when preparing for war. At other times they see themselves as the protectors of crocodiles. They also host the annual Garma festival, where a number of Aboriginal peoples assemble for traditional dance, music and song. In 1983 they numbered over 300 language-speakers.

## GUNWINGGU

An Australian ABORIGINAL PEOPLE of Arnhem Land, Northern Territory. Nomadic hunters and gatherers, they speak a non-Pama-Nyungan language. They believe themselves to be descended from the first woman, Waramurungundi, and

**Filipinos: main ethnic groups**

Apayao
Aeta (Ayta)
Bagobo
Bajau
Bicol
Bisaya
Bontok
Bukidnon
Gaddang
Ibaloy
Ilocano
Kalinga
Mandaya
Manobo
Subanon
Tausung
Tinggian

the first man, Wuragag. In 1990 they numbered over 900 but only around 400 were fluent speakers of the Gunwingguan language.

## GURINDJI or Gurinji

An Australian ABORIGINAL PEOPLE of the Tamani Desert, Northern Territory. They are nomadic hunters and gatherers, and speak a Pama-Nyungan language.

In the late 19th century, like many other Aboriginal peoples, they found that the only way to remain on their newly confiscated lands was to work for the cattle-raisers. This was sometimes seen as successful collaboration between settlers and Aboriginal people: the wages were often good and they could remain on their lands without abandoning their nomadic lifestyle. For some, however, particularly the Gurindji, it meant virtual slave labour, no wages, a subsistence diet at best, and flogging if not murder for infraction of rules.

These conditions continued well into the 20th century, and in 1966 the Gurindji went on strike, hoping to improve their abysmal conditions and regain some of their land. They walked off Wave Hill cattle station, owned by the multinational Vestey Corporation, and withstood all threats and blandishments to return. Their strike became a turning point in Australian history when it breached racist barriers and attracted widespread support from the Australian labour movement, not least from the Communist Party. This supplied the financial, political and moral support needed to keep the strike solid until 1973, when their land claim was settled. By such support and by inspiring other Aboriginal peoples to protest their lot, the Gurindji created the modern land-rights movement.

In 1983 there were around 250 fluent Gurindji speakers and up to 400 people who had a partial knowledge of the language.

## HAGEN

A native people of the Hagen district, West Highlands province, Papua New Guinea. Sedentary farmers who grow sweet potatoes, yams and taro by slash-and-burn agriculture, they speak Melpa, an East New Guinea Highlands language. They are noted for their traditional *bilum* costume and their sing-sing ceremonies, involving singing and dancing. Most follow their traditional animist religion, although some are Christian. In 1991 they numbered 130,000.

## HAN

A CHINESE people who constitute 92% of the population of China (see map, page 590). It is generally believed that the Han are of MONGOL origin, but some Chinese historians argue that they are indigenous to China. Such is their domination of Chinese culture that the Chinese word for a person from China translates as 'Man of Han'. The Han take their name from the Han dynasty (206 BC–AD 220). China's second imperial dynasty, the Han established what have come to be regarded as the fundamental characteristics of Chinese civilization, in particular the fusion of Confucian, Daoist and Buddhist teachings that remains influential in modern China.

Population pressure among the Han, who now number over 1 billion people, has forced large numbers to migrate into areas such as the Mongol and Uighur Autonomous Regions (see UIGHURS). These migrations have led to ethnic tensions between Han Chinese and the resident populations who fear an associated loss of land and weakening of their traditional cultures. Today, because of the huge geographic region covered by the Han, there is a considerable amount of linguistic diversity among them.

## HAWAIIANS

A native people of the Central Pacific island group of Hawaii. First settled by the LAPITA CULTURE by 1200 BC, Hawaii was resettled by POLYNESIANS from the Marquesas Islands by AD 400 and became a single nation by 1810 under King Kamehameha the Great. The islands, then the Sandwich Islands, soon became a favoured calling place for whalers and missionaries. The diseases they introduced rapidly reduced the population, which fell in 100 years from 800,000 to 39,000. AMERICAN companies wanting to develop a sugar industry imported great numbers of Asian labourers, conspired to overthrow the monarchy in 1893, and encouraged

> 66 I bin thinkin' longa time about my people not having proper conditions. I bin thinkin' we got no one to help us, no one behind us ... 99
>
> Gurindji leader Lupgua Giari, c. 1966

h

> 66 Hawaiians are too nice – too nice for their own good. It's our culture. 99
>
> Francine Cabacungan, 2001

**Han**

*See page 589.*

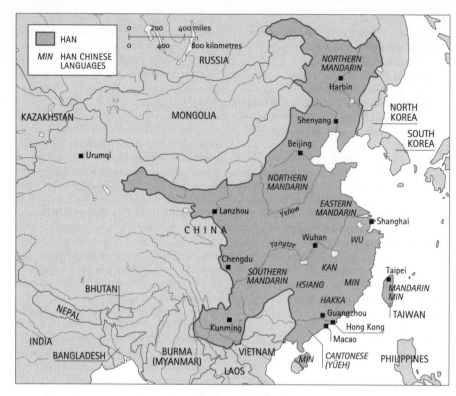

HAN
*MIN* HAN CHINESE LANGUAGES

0    200    400 miles
0    400    800 kilometres

RUSSIA

NORTHERN MANDARIN

Harbin

KAZAKHSTAN

MONGOLIA

Shenyang

NORTH KOREA

SOUTH KOREA

Beijing

■ Urumqi

NORTHERN MANDARIN

■ Lanzhou    Yellow    EASTERN MANDARIN    ■ Shanghai

C H I N A

Wuhan    WU

Yangtze

Chengdu

SOUTHERN MANDARIN    KAN    Taipei

BHUTAN    HSIANG    MIN    MANDARIN MIN

NEPAL    HAKKA    TAIWAN

INDIA    Guangzhou    Hong Kong

Kunming    Macao

BANGLADESH    BURMA (MYANMAR)    VIETNAM    MIN    CANTONESE (YÜEH)    PHILIPPINES

LAOS

**h**

US annexation of Hawaii in 1898. Land alienation was coupled with an intense programme of Americanization; the Hawaiians' native language was banned in schools and traditional religious practices were marginalized or forbidden. Cultural destruction was further enforced by the tourist industry, which invented an entirely superficial and inauthentic culture to present to visitors, brushing aside a true culture that is rich in music, poetry, dance, handicrafts and ritual.

In the 1970s, however, Hawaiians began to reclaim their traditional culture and raise issues of land rights and sovereignty, not least by challenging the authority of American courts. By the 1980s a more radical national movement, in the main led by women, was demanding an end to environmental destruction and cultural misrepresentation, and had also raised the issue of independence. This has been supported by acts of civil disobedience, including refusals to complete tax returns and to recite the pledge of allegiance in schools. Indeed in 1993 there were mass demonstrations and weeks of public mourning to mark the centenary of the overthrow of the monarchy. In 1998 the native Hawaiians numbered 240,000, about 20% of the population of the US state of Hawaii, although only about 9000 could speak the Hawaiian language.

## HEWA

A native people of Southern Highland province, Papua New Guinea. Hunters, gatherers and slash-and-burn farmers, they speak a Sepik-Ramu language. Their traditional religion is still strong and involves constant efforts to appease or deceive malevolent spirits who are so dangerous that no-one may enter the rainforest or sleep alone. Traditional funerary rites are still followed. In 1986 they numbered about 2150.

## HITI

A former native people of Bellona Island, in the Solomon Islands, western Pacific. Little is known of them; they were described as a small, hirsute people by the POLYNESIANS who exterminated them several centuries ago. Caves, burial sites and temples are all that remain, although there were unconfirmed sightings as late as the 1970s.

## HMONG or H'moong or Miao or Meo

A mountain people largely of southwest China, where they number more than 7 million. They are closely related to the YAO. Widely dispersed, they typically live in nucleated villages in tightly-knit communities comprising extended families, which often divide into smaller units on the death of parents. They are patrilineal in kinship organization. Traditionally they have used forest slash-and-burn techniques to cultivate a wide variety of crops, especially rice, corn and opium.

Ancestral Hmong were first recorded living in western Hunan and eastern Guizhou (Kwei-chow) some 2000 years ago, and they subsequently spread into the province of Sichuan, Guangxi Zhuang Autonomous Region, and elsewhere in Indo-China. They are now present in northern Vietnam and Laos, and in northern Thailand, where they are known as H'moong. Largely because of their wide dispersion, marked differences have developed in their culture and language such that up to 80 different groups of Hmong have been identified in China alone. In Vietnam they are also identified according to the predominant colour of their women's costumes, such as the Black Hmong of the high mountains (also known for their musicality and word-play) whose clothing shows their attachment to a deep purple-black indigo. They all speak dialects of Hmong, one of the Hmong-Yao languages of the Chinese-Tibetan family, although many have adopted the language of other ethnic groups among whom they have settled. In religion they venerate ancestral and other spirits and believe in demons whose malevolence is moderated by shamans. They also practise animal sacrifice. The village, operating under a headman, has been the traditional unit of wider social organization,

h

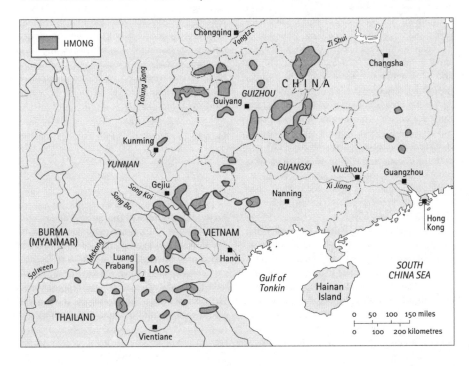

Hmong

certainly in China, and some villages were even grouped together in regions under appointed leaders. In modern states they form part of local government organization. The Hmong have a rich folk culture, especially in song, and a long tradition of metalworking, handicraft and textile work, notably batik.

## HONG KONG CHINESE

The inhabitants of the Special Administrative Region of Hong Kong (capital Victoria). The population at the beginning of the 21st century stood at over 6 million. Controlled by the BRITISH since 1842, the region was finally returned to CHINESE control in 1997. The vast majority of the population (98%) are of Chinese origin, with small minorities, mainly of European or Asian extraction, living among them. Between 1992 and 2000 large numbers of VIETNAMESE refugees were deported back to Vietnam.

Although heavily influenced by Chinese culture, the prolonged exposure of the Hong Kong Chinese to Western influences has made them a very cosmopolitan people, and both Eastern and Western fashions, festivals and entertainments are popular. The majority of Hong Kong Chinese, however, continue to adhere to Buddhist, Taoist and Confucian beliefs, although there are small numbers of Christians, Muslims, Hindus and other believers present within the population – mostly among the minority peoples.

The Special Administrative Region of Hong Kong is among the most economically prosperous in the entire world, possessing a massive industrial, trading and financial base. The vast majority of people (95%) live an urban lifestyle, often in very crowded conditions. Most of the working population is employed in the industrial and commercial sectors, although fishing is also an important activity.

Since 1997, the official language of the Hong Kong Chinese has been Mandarin Chinese, although both Cantonese and English are also widely spoken. While the majority within the Special Administrative Region consider themselves to be ethnically Chinese, there have been some concerns, principally centred on the continuation of various civil and political freedoms, over the resumption of Chinese control.

## HUI

A Muslim people of Turkic origin (see TURKS) whose ancestors migrated into China during the medieval period. Today they number around 9 million, with large numbers concentrated in the Ningxia Hui Autonomous Region and many more scattered throughout China, Tibet and the former Soviet republics of Central Asia. Most live an agricultural lifestyle, and their communities tend to be very close-knit.

Over the centuries, the Hui have become assimilated to HAN culture and society, and many would class themselves as CHINESE. They remain, however, dedicated to their Muslim beliefs, and this has caused some tensions with the Chinese administration. Although they are Chinese-speaking, the Hui retain Arabic for religious purposes.

## HULI

A native people of Southern Highland province, Papua New Guinea. Sedentary farmers and fishers, they speak an East New Guinea Highlands language. As in many Papuan nations, men and women live separate lives. Huli males spend up to two years outside the normal community undergoing initiation into adulthood and constructing *manda tene*, the elaborate ceremonial headdresses, decorated with bird-of-paradise feathers, that mark their new status. In 1991 they numbered about 70,000.

## IBANS

See DAYAK.

## IFUGAO

An IGOROT people of the mountains of northern Luzon in the Philippines, who speak an AUSTRONESIAN language. In the late 20th century they numbered approximately 190,000. The Ifugao are wet-rice farmers who live in small villages, usually of less than a dozen households. Their houses are built of wood and are often carved with elaborate decorations. Using only simple hand tools, the Ifugao have constructed a vast system of irrigated cultivation terraces for

h

rice farming, which often extend for thousands of feet up steep mountainsides. They also grow sweet potatoes and breed pigs and chickens.

Ifugao society is organized into 'kinship circles', which extend as far as third cousins. Feuding between kinship circles was once common, as was headhunting. Disputes between kin groups or individuals can be settled by the arbitration of a mutually agreed go-between with an expert knowledge of traditional law and customs. Ifugao society is hierarchical, with an aristocracy who maintain their prestige by lavish feasts. Ifugao religion is polytheistic. Sacrifices of animals and rice wine are used to invoke the favour of ancestral spirits as well as more than a thousand other deities.

## IGOROT

A group of AUSTRONESIAN peoples of the mountains of northern Luzon in the Philippines. Their name is derived from a TAGALOG word meaning 'mountain people'). Most Igorot live on the higher mountain ridges, above the rain forests which cloak the foothills. The Igorot numbered about 500,000 in the 1990s.

The Igorot languages form a sub-group of the Philippine languages, which belong to the Austronesian family. The Igorot people are divided into ten ethnic groups, each of which has its own language or dialect. The Nabaloi or Ibaloi, Kankanai, Lepanto or northern Kankanai, Bontoc, southern Kalinga, Tinggian and IFUGAO are the true mountain Igorot. They are wet-rice farmers who have laboriously terraced the steep mountainsides to create irrigated paddy fields. The Gaddang, northern Kalinga and Isneg or Apayao live in the lower rain forest areas and are dry rice farmers who practise shifting cultivation, regularly moving to new fields as the fertility of the soil is exhausted. The Igorot maintain their traditional polytheist religions and a belief in ancestral spirits and in the efficacy of animal sacrifice.

## I-KIRIBATI

A native people of a group of Central Pacific atolls (formerly the Gilbert Islands), comprising the Republic of Kiribati. Most of the people are MICRONESIANS, but the islands were also settled by Samoan POLYNESIANS by the 15th century AD, fishers and farmers who spoke an AUSTRONESIAN language. The islands were made a BRITISH protectorate in 1915 and became independent in 1979 (after the Ellice Islands had split off to become Tuvalu; see TUVALUANS), just as valuable phosphate mines were exhausted. The I-Kiribati are known as an egalitarian and democratic nation, which respects human rights. However, they are not self-sufficient in food and are heavily dependent on remittances from workers overseas. The scale of migration from the outer islands to the main island is also a problem. In 2003 they numbered 77,000.

## ILOCANO

A MALAY people who are the third-largest ethnic group among FILIPINOS. They currently number about 8 million in the Philippines, with significant numbers also in Hawaii. They are predominantly agricultural, with rice the main crop. They speak an AUSTRONESIAN language, and the vast majority adhere are Roman Catholics.

Ilocano

# INDONESIANS

The people of the Republic of Indonesia (capital Jakarta). They numbered about 228 million in 2001 – the fourth largest population in the world. Indonesia is a vast archipelago of over 13,000 islands, which together cover a land area of some 1.9 million sq. km / 735,000 sq. miles. Both linguistically and culturally, Indonesia forms a part of Indo-Malaysia, an area that also includes the Malay Peninsular, Malaysian Borneo, Brunei and the Philippines. The population is extremely diverse. There are over 700 different ethnic groups, including the ACEHNESE, BALINESE, BATAKS, BUGIS, JAVANESE, SUNDANESE, MADURESE and TORADJA. This diversity is echoed in the number of languages and dialects spoken in the area, the most prolific being Bahasa Indonesia (the official language), Javanese, English, Dutch, Sundanese, Arabic and Chinese. As a result, the term 'Indonesians' is something of a modern construct, and many within the country would not describe themselves in this way. Indeed, the official language, Bahasa Indonesia, is not originally a true native tongue, but a synthetic form based on the Malay trade dialect, much used during the 19th century, and incorporating elements of Portuguese, Dutch, Chinese, Arabic and Indian. Bahasa was adopted as the national language on the country's independence in 1949, and may be viewed as an attempt to foster unity amongst Indonesia's many ethnic groups.

The first human inhabitant of Indonesia was JAVA MAN, who lived on the island of Java around 800,000 years ago. During the Neolithic period AUSTRONESIAN peoples migrated to the islands from mainland Asia, and it is from these that most modern Indonesians are thought to descend. Most of the population of modern Indonesia still live in the relatively small area encompassing Java, Madura and Bali. By the early centuries AD, wet-rice cultivation had been adopted in a number of regions allowing them to support a growing population, and providing a surplus for trading purposes. India and China were the major importers of goods from the islands, which included cloves and camphor, and, because of these and other links, INDIAN forms heavily influenced Indonesian culture and society (although the caste system was not

adopted). Sanskrit was the first written language used in the area. This development tended to be confined to the coastal areas, and particularly to aristocratic groups; Hinduism and Mahayana Buddhism were also introduced. Between the 7th and 13th centuries a number of rival Indonesian states (both Buddhist and Hindu) had developed into formidable trading powers along the coasts of Sumatra and Java, most notably the Sri Vijaya and Majapahit empires, and between them these dominated commerce with China and India.

Islam was introduced into the islands through trade with India, the MALAY kingdom of Malacca and the ARABS, and by the late 13th century had begun to attract significant numbers of converts. The religion spread swiftly through Sumatra and Java, and today 87% of all Indonesians are Muslim, making the country the world's most populous Muslim nation. Besides Buddhism and Hinduism, other religions practised in the area include Christianity and animism. The period also witnessed a considerable influx of CHINESE migrants to the islands, and over the next few centuries their descendants gradually came to dominate Indonesia's commercial classes.

## Colonized or colonizer?

DUTCH influence is also very noticeable in the area. Drawn by a desire to control the spice trade, the Dutch East India Company, with Dutch military support, gradually gained control of the archipelago. By the late 1600s much of what is now modern Indonesia was under Dutch control. The invaders were responsible for the foundation of Jakarta (known to the Dutch as Batavia), and for the introduction of new crops such as coffee. Never before had any state claimed suzerainty over the whole area, and this may be viewed as the first attempt to unite the various peoples in the area into a single entity – the Netherlands East Indies. In reality much of the region remained only nominally under Dutch control. Only Java and the immediately surrounding area were administered directly; elsewhere peoples were either controlled indirectly, through pliable local rulers, or remained untouched. Even when the Dutch attempted, during the late 19th and early 20th centuries, to

---

**Indonesians: main ethnic groups**

Acehnese
Ambonese
Balinese
Bataks
Bugis
Dayaks
Javanese
Papuans
Sundanese
Madurese
Toradja

pursue a much more aggressive colonial and plantation policy in the region, many areas remained outside their control. Nevertheless, despite increasing calls for independence, particularly from Muslim and communist groups, the Netherlands East Indies remained part of the empire until the JAPANESE invasion in 1942. Following World War II, Indonesian independence was finally recognized in 1949.

With so many ethnic groups populating the islands comprising Indonesia, however, unity has been almost impossible to achieve. Essentially, the concept of the Republic of Indonesia, and of an Indonesian nation, is no more natural than that of the Netherlands East Indies; indeed, the former is simply a new manifestation of the latter. Dutch control was always based on the island of Java, and the government of the state of Indonesia continues at the traditional Dutch capital, now Jakarta. The term 'Indonesian', therefore, may be best applied to the dominant area centred on Java and the Javanese. Certainly, many within the republic would not describe themselves as Indonesian, and have viewed the Java-based government with suspicion. As early as the 1950s there were sporadic outbreaks of violence from anti-government groups based in Muslim Aceh and other parts of Sumatra. This opposition has continued to prosper, as central government has regularly been perceived as unable to deal effectively with many of the social and economic problems facing the country. Organized groups currently in opposition to the government include the Papuan Independent Organization and the Free Aceh Movement.

Further evidence of ethnic divisions within Indonesia is to be found in the reaction to the government's policy of population migration (transmigrasi). Certain areas of the 'inner islands', especially on Java and Madura, have become very overpopulated, and the Indonesian government has attempted to encourage people to resettle in other, less densely populated regions. This policy has, on occasion, led to a violent backlash from peoples in whose homelands the migrants have been settled; for example, DAYAK in Borneo have massacred Madurese immigrants, and Javanese have been attacked by PAPUANS in Irian Jaya. In addition, religion has also played a significant part in

destabilizing the Indonesian state. Some Muslim areas have sought independence, and, as in the case of Aceh, strict Muslim law for their region. In recent years there have also been serious clashes between AMBONESE Christians and Muslims. Since the 1950s, however, the Indonesian government has made serious efforts to foster national unity through the remembrance of the national struggle for independence, the use of Bahasa Indonesia, a national education system and the propagation of a national 'ideology' (pancasila).

## IWAIDJA

An Australian ABORIGINAL PEOPLE of the Coburg Peninsula coast, Northern Territory. Nomadic hunters and gatherers, they speak a non-Austronesian language. Unusually for a coastal-dwelling Aboriginal people, they have managed to retain a considerable degree of their traditional culture, remain on their traditional lands and even have access to traditional food sources, such as long yam, turtle and shellfish. In 1983 there were about 180 language-speakers.

## JAKUN

See ORANG ASLI.

## JAPANESE

The citizens of Japan (capital Tokyo), who numbered over 127.5 million in 2002. Significant numbers also live in the USA, Canada, Brazil and Peru. Today, the Japanese are a very homogeneous people of mostly Mongoloid origins; the only sizeable exception is the AINU. The official language of Japan is Japanese, although English is widely spoken as a second language. Occupied for around 30,000 years, Japan was home to both the JOMON and YAYOI cultures.

Traditional Japanese culture was heavily influenced by the CHINESE and to a lesser extent (through the medium of Buddhism) by the INDIANS. Buddhism was introduced via China in AD 552, for example, and early Japanese art, literature, architecture and administrative practice all bear testimony to Chinese inspiration. The Japanese writing system was also originally

*j*

" [in Japan] old men fly kites while the children look on. "

Sir Rutherford Alcock, 1863, noting an apparent inversion of cultural roles between Japan and Britain derived from the Chinese. Today, although the Japanese have strong indigenous cultural traditions such as the Shinto religion and Sumo wrestling, more than 80% still adhere to the Buddhist faith. Following a period of political and cultural isolationism between the 17th and 19th centuries, the Japanese were also strongly affected by Western political and cultural forms, and these influences are still strong today, especially in the areas of government, education, popular entertainment and clothing. Less than 4% of Japanese people, however, profess to be Christians, and this is perhaps in part because of Christianity's incompatibility with indigenous Shinto beliefs, which are based on polytheism and ancestor worship.

Despite attempts by a number of Japanese dynasties to unite the country politically, either through conquest or the promulgation of national religions, the people of Japan were not significantly united until the 17th century. During the late 19th and early 20th centuries, the notion of Japanese nationalism and imperialism grew at a considerable pace, aided by the high political position attained by a number of high-ranking military personnel. The emperor was advanced as a figurehead for national unity, and during this period the Japanese fought successfully against both the RUSSIANS and Chinese. This nationalist sentiment coincided with a more anti-Western outlook, intensified with the rise of a militarist government in the 1930s, which led directly to the Japanese attack on the US fleet at Pearl Harbor and their entry into World War II in 1941. During this time the Japanese amassed a large, if shortlived, empire that included much of Southeast Asia and a large part of China.

Since the end of World War II, the Japanese have become one of the most economically prosperous people in the world, and corporate loyalty has become deeply embedded within Japanese cultural identity. In many ways, this mirrors the much earlier phenomenon of Japanese feudalistic practice. Around 80% of Japanese people live an urban lifestyle and work in business and industry. Agriculture remains important, however. Rice-growing and fishing are major activities. The Japanese now have close economic and political ties with the Western world, and in particular with the AMERICANS, but this has led at times to outbursts of popular discontent, for example during the 1970s.

## JAVA MAN

A name given to a group of fossils of *homo erectus*, an extinct species of early human, which were discovered at Trinil on the island of Java (in present-day Indonesia) during the late 19th century. Java Man flourished during the middle Pleistocene epoch around 500,000 years ago. Java Man became extinct before the end of the Pleistocene and was not an ancestor of the modern JAVANESE, or any other modern human population.

## JAVANESE

An AUSTRONESIAN people who are the largest ethnic group of the Republic of Indonesia. There are over 76 million Javanese, the vast majority of whom live on the island of Java. The ancestors of the modern Javanese arrived on the island in the Neolithic period, having migrated to the region from mainland Asia. Irrigated rice production was practised in various regions of the island from a relatively early date, and the resulting food surpluses allowed the Javanese to foster trade links with both India and China. As a result, by the early centuries AD, both the INDIANS and CHINESE heavily influenced Javanese culture; for example, both Hinduism and Buddhism were introduced, as was Sanskrit.

Today, almost all Javanese practise Islam, which was introduced during the 15th century. Many, however, would not be considered devout in the strictest sense, as animism, together with Hindu and Buddhist legacies, remain strong. Moreover, large numbers do not observe Islamic dietary requirements or festivals. The Javanese, however, insist upon correct social behaviour, taught to children from a very early age, and their society retains a strict moral code.

Western culture has also had a major impact on Javanese society, particularly PORTUGUESE and DUTCH types. The Dutch have been very influential, and between the 17th and mid-20th centuries Java lay at the centre of the Netherlands East Indies. The Javanese capital, Jakarta (formerly Batavia), for example, was originally a

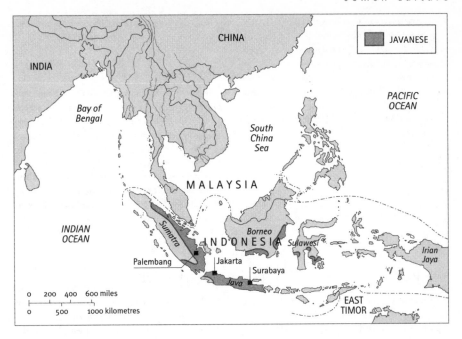

Dutch foundation. The Javanese, however, were at the forefront of the independence movement, and rebelled (unsuccessfully) against the Dutch between 1825 and 1830. Overrun by the JAPANESE during World War II, the Javanese thereafter agitated actively for the end of Dutch political control. They were again leaders in the war of independence (1945–9). Since independence, Javanese politicians have been the dominant force in the political life of Indonesia, and owing to their role, and the fact that the Javanese are the largest ethnic group, they, more than any other people, have considered themselves to be INDONESIAN. Jakarta, the capital of Java, is also the capital of Indonesia. Java is one of the most densely populated regions in the world, and the Indonesian government has actively fostered Javanese migration to other areas of the republic, in particular to Borneo, Sulawesi and Sumatra. This is a policy that has been extremely unpopular among the peoples living in the regions targeted for settlement, and has led to violent clashes between indigenous peoples and the so-called *transmigrasi*.

While the majority of Javanese still live in rural areas and gain their livelihood from farm-ing, large numbers have moved to the expanding Indonesian towns and cities. Many Javanese are still relatively poor by world standards.

## JOMON CULTURE

A Neolithic culture of Japan characterized by the production of pottery with a distinctive corded motif. Indeed, the term *Jomon* translates as 'cord marks', and was applied to the culture by archaeologists during the late 19th century. The Jomon is the first human culture known to have produced pottery, and the earliest examples date from about 11,000 BC. The culture existed throughout Japan from around this date until *c.* 250 BC, although it was more prolific in the east and north. The Jomon were not AINU, but may in fact be early ancestors of the modern JAPANESE.

Originally semi-nomadic hunter-gatherers, they were practising a primitive form of agriculture by around 4000 BC, growing millet and buckwheat and raising cattle. As a result, they tended to pursue a more sedentary lifestyle and resided in traditional Jomon horseshoe-shaped villages of increasing size. These comprised sunken pit dwellings that were situated close to the coast or rivers. By around 300 BC the Jomon were also practising rice cultivation. Bone, stone and clay decorative items have also been found, as have objects of an apparent religious significance, indicating that the Jomon may have worshipped fertility deities. There is little evidence of social stratification in their culture. The Jomon culture was ultimately succeeded by that of the YAYOI.

## JUCHEN

See RUZHEN.

## JUI

See PUYI.

## KACHIN

A tribal hill people numbering around 725,000 concentrated in the heavily forested outlying region of northeast Burma. They are also found in adjoining areas of Yunnan province, China, and in smaller numbers in Arunachal Pradesh and Nagaland in India. The Kachin speak languages of the Tibeto-Burman group, mostly Jinghpaw, but possess a variety of dialects and customs. They are traditionally animists, although a small number in Burma were converted to Christianity through missionary activity. They cultivate cereal crops such as maize, millet, wheat and barley in drier areas, along with beans and cash crops such as tea and the opium poppy. In some locations they also grow rice on irrigated terraces. They are also involved in trade along the valleys in iron, jade, amber, silver and salt, though some of these products have recently declined in importance.

Under BRITISH rule (1885–1948) the Kachin Hills frontier territory was administered separately from most of Burma, and their traditional political and social organization remained largely unchanged, although colonial control put an end to endemic feuding and banditry which provided an additional means of subsistence. Kachin State is one of seven federal divisions comprising modern Burma, although the Kachin have continued to resist central government authority since independence.

*"among the Karadjiri ... the term bugari refers to the period when the ancestor spirits formed the world's physical features and instituted the Law. It also signifies 'dreaming'. "*

M. Charlesworth,
1992

## KADAZAN-DUSUN

See DAYAK.

## KAH SO

See SO.

## KAKDJU

An Australian ABORIGINAL PEOPLE of the Oenpelli area, Northern Territory. Nomadic hunters and gatherers, they have been heavily acculturated by other Aboriginal peoples, and in 1981 a mere six Kakdju spoke their non-Pama-Nyungan language, which may now be extinct. They are in danger of losing their distinct identity.

## KAMILAROI

An Australian ABORIGINAL PEOPLE, of northern New South Wales. Once nomadic hunters and gatherers, they dwelt in dense forest, and like many other Aboriginal peoples practised burning off vegetation to encourage new shoots attractive to their prey. During the 19th century settlers cleared the forest, which largely destroyed the Kamilaroi as a distinct people. In 1997 a single family of three or more still spoke their Pama-Nyungan language.

## KANAK

A MELANESIAN people who are native to New Caledonia, a South Pacific island group. Farmers and fishers, they speak dialects of an AUSTRONESIAN language, and it is debatable if they comprise several sub-groups, or are in fact separate nations given a single collective name.

In 1864 the FRENCH established a penal colony in New Caledonia; the descendants of these convicts became the European ethnic group known as the CALDOCHE, enlarged by free settlers when nickel was discovered. Their abuses and land seizures provoked a guerrilla war in 1878 in which the Kanak were defeated after several months of bloodshed that considerably weakened them. Kanak resentment, however, never died, and in the late 20th century they were clamouring for independence, which once again brought them into violent clashes with the Caldoche. Their political aspirations have yet to be fulfilled. In 1998 negotiations opened between the Kanak and the French government, in which greater respect for Kanak traditions and culture was promised, but a movement towards independence appeared to be stalled. In 1996 they numbered over 78,000 people, or 45% of the New Caledonian population.

## KARADJIRI

An Australian ABORIGINAL PEOPLE of La Grange mission, Roebuck Bay, Western Australia. Occupying the fringe of desert country, they are hunters and gatherers who speak a Pama-Nyungan language. In their creation myth, everything in the world was brought into existence when the first two humans named them. In 1991 only 12 Karadjiri spoke the language, and they are at risk of losing their distinct identity altogether.

## KAREN

A diverse tribal people belonging to southern Burma and forming the third-largest ethnic group in the country, numbering around 2.6 million people. Some live on the THAI side of the mountainous border. They all speak a variety of Tibeto-Burman languages of the SINO-TIBETAN family. A distinction can be made between White Karen (comprising the Pwo and Sgaw groups) and the Red Karen, also known as the KAYAH or Karenni of Kayah State, who have separate Tibeto-Burman languages and identities. The Karen were originally confined mostly to the hills of the southeast of modern Burma by the majority BURMESE, and a mutual aversion remains.

After Lower Burma came under BRITISH colonial control in the 19th century, the Karen began to spread into the richer lowlands around Moulmein and the Irrawaddy delta, especially Bassein. Many exploited their skills as rice growers in the hills to develop new areas of cultivation. Others, who had received a Christian education in the hill missions, found work as health professionals, teachers and administrators or in the colonial police and army. Although many Buddhists and animists remained, an increasing number of Karen adopted Christianity, which further divided them from the majority Burmese.

The long-held desire for a sovereign Karen state was disappointed when Burma became independent in 1948. Despite outstanding service to Britain as anti-Japanese guerrillas, the Karen were subsumed into the new country. They rebelled in 1949 and various groups – who were opposed to the dominant Burmese, distrusted the new Union of Burma and desired greater autonomy – united under the name 'Karen'. The failure of the rebellion was assuaged by the creation of the federal Karen (Kayin) State in 1954, but national aspirations and periodic armed insurgency have continued.

Culturally, the Karen are known for their attractive and relatively plain architecture and accomplished decorative crafts, notably their patterned, brightly coloured textiles.

Karen

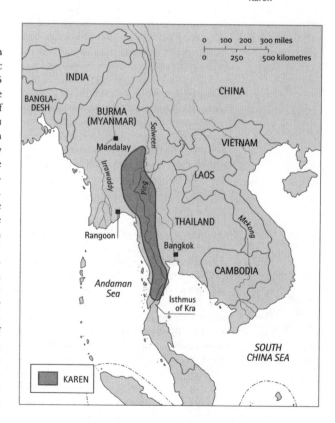

# KARENNI

See KAYAH.

# KAWELKO

A native people of Western Highlands province, Papua New Guinea. They speak Melpa, an East New Guinea Highlands language. They moved from subsistence farming to cash crops (tea and coffee) in the 1960s. They also keep pigs, which are highly prized and eaten only on special occasions, being used more often to pay bride prices or settle blood feuds. The Kawelko are also noted for their gift-giving ceremonies, called *moka*, in which the giving of gifts earns social stature. Their traditional animist religion is still strong. In 1991 they numbered about 2000.

# KAYA

Ancient confederation of tribal peoples who flourished in southwest Korea from before the 3rd century BC, among whom the Karak were dominant (see KOREANS). They were conquered by the more centralized and developed kingdom of Silla in the 6th century AD. Because of their isolated geographical position they developed strong maritime trade and other connections with China across the Yellow Sea and maintained links with related peoples in Japan, who were frequently called upon as allies in the wars with neighbouring powers of Paekche and Silla.

# KAYAH or Karenni or Red Karen

A people of southeastern Burma. They are also known as Red Karen, the name apparently derived from their characteristic red robes. They comprise the Padaung, Zayein, Yinbaw and Bre groups who originate in Kayah State, one of the constituent divisions of Burma, situated north of Karen State on the southern edge of the Shan Plateau. Although linguistically and ethnically KAREN, they are culturally distinct and predominantly Buddhist.

Kayah:
main ethnic
groups

Bre
Padaung
Yinbaw
Zayein

# KAYAN

See DAYAK.

# KAYTETYE

An Australian ABORIGINAL PEOPLE of the Tennant Creek area of Northern Territory. Nomadic hunters and gatherers, they speak a Pama-Nyungan language. Like the WARUMUNGU, they fought white settlers who built a telegraph station on their most sacred dreamtime site, killing cattle to drive them away, and a large number were murdered in reprisal. Losing their ancestral lands, they entered cattle stations to remain near them and to survive. Their fortunes changed at the end of the 20th century. In 1999 they regained an 8-tonne boulder being used as a gravestone for John Flynn (who founded the flying doctor service). This had been removed from a sacred rock formation of Karlu Karlu (the Devil's Marbles), and was returned there. In 2002 they regained title to part of their traditional lands, and Australia's Governor General, as the queen's representative, apologized for the massacres they had suffered, though they have not gained the monument to their dead that they want. In 1983 they numbered about 200.

# KENYAH

See DAYAK.

# KHAMTIS

A people of Burma who speak Khamti, a northern TAI language. Their population is small but widely spread. They appear to originate from the area of Mung Kang in Upper Burma, and following conflicts with the majority BURMESE some migrated to the vicinity of Lakhimpur in British Assam up to the mid-19th century. The languages of Khün in Burma and Northern SHAN are part of the same northern sub-group of Tai. The Khamti people are mainly Buddhist.

# KHMERS

A people of the Mon-Khmer ethno-linguistic group who comprise 90% of the population of

Cambodia and are therefore often referred to as CAMBODIANS or Kampucheans. Sizeable populations also exist in the adjoining border regions of Vietnam to the east, especially in the Mekong delta, and Thailand to the west. The Khmer, or Cambodian, language is part of the AUSTRO-ASIATIC group. It has had a great influence on neighbouring languages and has borrowed liberally from INDO-ARYAN Sanskrit and Buddhist Pali.

### Early history

The origins of the Khmer are obscure. Human occupation of the Cambodian region can be traced to before 4000 BC, and there is no doubt that these original inhabitants have contributed to the ethnic fusion that created the modern-day Khmer, including noticeable similarities in physiognomy, economy and culture. It is suggested that the main body of the ancestral Khmer arrived from the Khorat Plateau in modern-day Thailand in the productive Mekong River delta before 200 BC. There they developed the important kingdom of Funan, which flourished up to the 6th century AD and was heavily influenced by INDIAN culture and the Hindu religion that accompanied strong trading links.

The earliest Sanskrit and Khmer inscriptions using a south Indian script appear around this time. Another major innovation was the development of irrigation, which improved rice production and contributed to the growing power of the Khmer. Funan became the pre-eminent kingdom in the Lower Mekong Valley, centralized and well-organized, but it was just one of many Khmer states of varying size and importance. From the 6th century it was superseded by a rival and more insular kingdom further up the Mekong river in northwest Cambodia commonly known as Chenla (or 'Land-Chenla', distinct from Funan, identified as 'Water-Chenla').

An additional Indo-Malayan cultural influence on the Khmer was exerted around the 8th century AD as a result of the regional domination by the great Malay kingdom of Indonesia and possibly even immigration from Java and Sumatra. The development of a unified Khmer kingdom based on Chenla can be dated from the reign of the Cambodian prince Jayavarman II (790–835), who appears to have asserted

Khmer independence from lingering Indonesian rule. A successor, Yasovarman I (c. 890–910) based the Khmer capital on his new walled city of Yasodharapura in the Tonlé Sap basin, abundant in rice and fish, 240 km / 150 miles northwest of the modern-day capital Phnom Penh. Yasodharapura has become known as Angkor (derived from a Sanskrit word meaning 'city') and represents the high point of medieval Cambodian civilization. Today it is a World Heritage Site of great archaeological importance.

Apart from a brief interlude in the 10th century Angkor remained the capital of the kingdom until its abandonment in 1432, and grew to cover an area of 200 sq. km / 75 sq. miles, incorporating a lavish water supply moved through a sophisticated system of reservoirs, canals and channels. It also boasted magnificent temples of which the largest and most beautifully carved and decorated is Angkor Wat, the funerary temple and astronomical observatory of Suryavarman II (ruled 1113–50) built on a square plinth some 1000 m / 3300 ft on each side. It was dedicated to the Hindu god Vishnu, attesting to the continuing Indian cul-

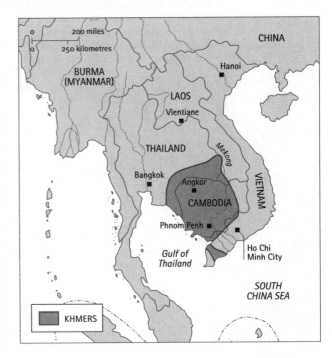

Khmers

tural influence in a society also marked by religious toleration between Hindu, Buddhist and local beliefs. Under Suryavarman's rule Cambodia expanded to its greatest extent, conquering and subduing territories occupied by modern-day south-central Vietnam, Laos and Thailand, including the Burmese Tenasserim coast and the Malay peninsula.

### Decline and renewal

Subsequent political developments contributed to the decline of the Khmer kingdom, particularly at the hands of the formerly subject TAI (Thai and ethnolinguistically-related groups) based on Ayutthaya, or Siam, who were responsible for the sack of Angkor on numerous occasions. The city's abandonment in the 15th century coincided with a mass conversion of the Khmer from Hinduism and Mahayana Buddhism to the more austere Theravada Buddhism practised by the Tai, and which is still common in Cambodia along with ancient animist beliefs and faith in magic. The new centre of the much reduced Khmer state moved south to Lovek in the region of Phnom Penh, but from the 1590s until 1863 when the FRENCH protectorate was established it was given to internal feuding and subject to the power of neighbouring Siam and Vietnam. French control prevented the division

and absorption of Cambodia by its enemies and led to modernization of the country's institutions, infrastructure and agricultural sector in which the majority of the population continues to be employed. With security came a cultural revival, particularly in music, and traditional arts as well as education continued to be encouraged following independence from France in 1953. The cultural and economic development of the Khmer were seriously retarded by more than four decades of warfare and particularly the genocide perpetrated by the communist Khmer Rouge under Pol Pot in the late 1970s.

## KHMER ISLAM

See CHAMS.

## KOREANS

People of the Korean peninsula in East Asia now occupied by the states of North Korea (capital Pyongyang) and South Korea (capital Seoul). Over many centuries ancestral Koreans speaking Tungusic (or Manchu-Tungusic), a branch of the Altaic language family, moved southwards from Siberia and Manchuria and gave rise to the Korean ethnic group and to the modern Korean language. It is now spoken by more than 72 million Koreans (around 50 million in the South) and several million in neighbouring countries and elsewhere. There are differences in script, spelling and vocabulary between prevailing usage in South and North Korea, and since 1945 the latter has been particularly assiduous in removing obvious foreign (Chinese, Japanese and English) influences.

Early Korean state formation led to the emergence of the powerful rival kingdoms in the 1st century BC among which the kingdom of Silla came to predominate. It conquered the KAYA people and its main competitors, Paekche and Koguryo, to create, in the 7th century, a single unified country for the first time. Various divisions and reunifications occurred in subsequent centuries, often with the involvement of the CHINESE, whose influence became a perpetual feature of Korean political development.

Cultural, intellectual and technological development advanced rapidly during the

**Koreans**

period of the Choson (Yi) dynasty (1392–1910), established following the successful rebellion against MONGOL rule. Hamyang (Seoul) became the capital, state administration was reorganized under a hereditary ruling class, and Confucianism officially replaced Buddhism, established since the 4th century AD, at the heart of national life. Printed literature also began to emerge in the early 13th century.

JAPANESE interest in Korea was evident from the unsuccessful invasions of the 1590s, although 19th century rivalry with China led to the annexation of Korea in 1910. Significant emigration took place during this period of Japanese exploitation, which lasted until its defeat in 1945 when the USSR occupied the north of the country and the USA the south. Failure to agree to terms for reunification led communist North Korea – by then supported by China – to invade the South in 1950.

In the ensuing war, which lasted until 1953, around 1.8 million Koreans on both sides died, many civilians became refugees, and the country's infrastructure was almost destroyed. The political stand-off remains and the region is still a source of acute international tension, recently exacerbated by the North's claimed development of nuclear weapons.

Since the 1960s the South Koreans have built an advanced democratic industrial society prospering in foreign trade. North Koreans have been unable to match this success with their centrally planned economy and authoritarian political system. Difficult relations with their former communist-bloc trading partners have exacerbated economic problems. The North has received international aid in recent years, and famine continues to affect a large part of the population. In both countries, rural depopulation and the growth of cities have become features of national life.

**Religion and culture**
In religion and outlook there is a varied pattern of beliefs which overlap to a large extent. Confucianism has few overt followers, but it remains the basis of Korean attitudes, and associated ancestor worship remains common. Buddhism and Christianity are important in the South but little followed in the North, where state-favoured atheism is widespread. Even in South Korea around half the population can be described as non-religious. New religions have emerged, notably the syncretic Chondogyo (established in 1860), a blend of Confucian, Christian, Buddhist and other beliefs, which is stronger in North Korea. Ancient Shamanism and geomancy are still evident. Traditional Korean culture has been strongly influenced by Buddhism, Confucian thought and by Chinese cultural developments uniquely expressed in Korean literature. Freedom of expression in North Korea, however, is still restricted by central authorities who promote traditional art and culture.

## KUBU

See NEGRITOS.

## KUNGGARA

An Australian ABORIGINAL PEOPLE of the Normanton area, Queensland. Nomadic hunters and gatherers who occupied an area that attracted considerable numbers of European settlers, they came under heavy pressure from disease, land dispossession and acculturation. Their Pama-Nyungan language is either nearly or totally extinct. It is questionable whether they still exist as a distinct people.

## KWAIO

A native people of Malatia province, Solomon Islands. Hunters and farmers, they speak a Malayo-Polynesian language. They were once reputedly cannibals who attacked outsiders on sight, but colonial rule had a severe impact, as many were enticed or kidnapped to work in near-slave conditions in Australia between 1871 and 1903. On return they were provided with trade goods, including Snyder rifles. When in 1927 the BRITISH attempted to disarm and tax them, there was a brief, brutally supressed guerrilla war.

Most Kwaio are heavily acculturated and live on the coast, but about 3000 out of nearly 17,000 shun modernization, clinging to traditional beliefs and practices. These include a view

**k**

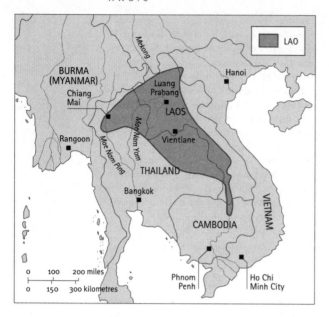

Map legend: **LAO**

BURMA
(MYANMAR)

Chiang
Mai

Luang
Prabang

Hanoi

LAOS

Rangoon

Vientiane

THAILAND

Bangkok

VIETNAM

CAMBODIA

Mekong

Mae Nam Yom

Mae Nam Ping

0    100    200 miles
0    150    300 kilometres

Phnom
Penh

Ho Chi
Minh City

influence (see THAIS) until the extension of FRENCH imperial control in the 19th century. French is still spoken in Laos, although among foreign languages English and Vietnamese have become increasingly common. In the mid-20th century, particularly after World War II, nationalist feeling strengthened and Laos gained independence from France in 1954 in consequence of the wider Indo-Chinese war of liberation. Following a long period of civil conflict the communist Pathet Lao, with strong ties to Vietnam, gained control of the government of the Kingdom of Laos in 1975 and established the Democratic Republic. During this period of political repression as well as continuing economic distress around 10% of the population, including many of the most highly educated, fled to Thailand, where there is still a significant Laotian minority. Since the late 1980s there have been moves towards economic liberalization, but Laos remains a one-party state.

**Hill peoples, commoners and aristocrats**

The Laotian population is linguistically and culturally diverse. From around the 8th century AD the ancestral Lao, a branch of the numerous TAI-speaking peoples of the region, migrated from southern China. The area of modern Laos was thinly populated by tribal peoples, described pejoratively as *Kha* (slaves), who were forced into the mountains, where their descendants still live today. The largest Laotian group is the Lao-Lum, forming 65–70% of the country's population of 5.7 million. They speak Lao (Laotian), the official language, closely related to Thai. Traditionally they were socially fragmented, based on commoner or aristocratic descent.

The fragmented Lao-Theung (Mon-Khmer) people, also descended from indigenous Indo-Chinese peoples and found in adjoining countries, are the second-largest ethnic group in Laos (around 17%). (See also MON.)

The Lao-TAI hill peoples comprise several distinctive groups such as the northern Tai-Neua, and the Tai Deng (Red Tai) and Tai-Dam (Black Tai), named after the favoured colours used in the female attire of those groups. They speak closely related Lao dialects and comprise around 8% of the population. The Lao-Tai generally had elaborate social organizations based on villages,

Laotians

of women as polluting at specific times such as menstruation, childbirth or eating, and belief in ancestor spirits. These traditional Kwaio lack healthcare and other services.

# LAHU

See HMONG.

# LAIZO

See CHIN.

# LAMET

See HMONG.

# LAOTIANS

The inhabitants of Laos, officially known as the Lao People's Democratic Republic (capital Vientiane), in Indo-China. Laotian development as a nation was throughout its history thwarted by powerful neighbours. The first Laotian state was Lan Xang, established in the 14th century as a tributary of the KHMER people of modern Cambodia. It fragmented into three competing kingdoms in 1713 and each fell under Siamese groupings of villages and larger territories led by a hereditary land-owning aristocracy. Other minority peoples known collectively as Lao-Soung have migrated to Laos from neighbouring regions over several centuries and include the YAO (Man) and HMONG (Miao). Most Laotians practise Theravada Buddhism concurrently with the tribal religions followed by about a third of the population. The latter are particularly strong among the hill peoples of Laos. Buddhism has markedly influenced the country's literary tradition (as well as the Laotian language and script) which has also drawn inspiration from the great Hindu epics. Agriculture and forestry remain the primary economic pursuits of most Laotians, and the Mekong river is exploited for its fish resources and hydroelectric production. The Laotians are also known for their varied and skilled crafts.

## LAPITA CULTURE

The culture of the first settlers of island Melanesia. Named after a type of ceramics discovered in New Caledonia, it is believed to have originated in New Guinea. Highly skilled sailors and navigators, these people explored and colonized over vast ocean distances between 2000 and 500 BC, bringing their food crops and animals, alongside a material culture noteworthy for its ceramics and shell jewellery. Descendants of the Lapita people include the POLYNESIANS.

## LARAKIA

An Australian ABORIGINAL PEOPLE of the Darwin area, Northern Territory. Nomadic hunters and gatherers, they spoke a non-Pama-Nyungan language, now nearly, if not completely, extinct. They came into contact with European settlers early in the 19th century, and after massacres were driven from their lands. Few elements of their traditional culture survive, and they have been absorbed by other Aboriginal peoples.

## LAWA or Wa

Peoples who occupy the mountainous area of northern Thailand; but also the related, though distinct, hill-dwelling peoples of eastern Burma

and southwestern Yunnan in China, where they are also known as Va. They speak AUSTRO-ASIATIC Mon-Khmer languages. Ancestral Lawa are thought to have occupied the delta plain of southern Thailand before retreating into the northern hills with the arrival of TAI-speaking people at the start of the 2nd millennium AD. Today they number around 17,000 only and have largely been absorbed into THAI society: the majority speak Thai as their first language, and their ancient animist beliefs are combined with Thai Buddhism. They are sensitive to issues of environmental conservation in the practice of traditional shifting cultivation. In social organization they are matrilineal, village-based and divided into Lua commoners and the more distinguished Kun, who claim royal descent.

## LI or Sai

An agricultural people of Hainan Island, southern China, who number 1.3 million. They describe themselves as *Sai* and are divided into five branches – the Ha, Qi, Meifu, Run and Sai – descended from the Luoyue people, part of the Baiyue of south China, whose ancestors began arriving in Hainan around 3000 years ago. Almost all Li live in the mountainous southern part of the island in the Li-Miao Autonomous Prefecture. They worship ancestor spirits, other local spirits and earth gods, and speak the Li branch of the Sino-Tibetan language family. A Li script was created only as recently as 1957. The Li have the longest known history of textile production in China, notably in silk cotton.

## LISU

The Lisu are an AUSTRO-ASIATIC people related to the YI. The Lisu number around 520,000, most of whom live in mountainous areas of Yunnan in southern China. Other groups live in Burma and northern Thailand. The CHINESE recognize three groups of Lisu: the Black Lisu, the White Lisu, and the Flowery Lisu. The names originally related to the degree of their assimilation to Chinese culture, the Black Lisu being the least Sinicized. The Lisu are a farming people whose staple crops are rice, corn (maize) and buckwheat. The Lisu have a clan-based society.

**Laotians: main ethnic groups**

Lao-Lum
Lao-Soung
Lao-Tai
Lao-Theung

**Li: main ethnic groups**

Ha
Meifu
Qi
Run
Sai

Marriage within a clan is forbidden; men must seek wives from another clan. Lisu religious beliefs are a mixture of animism and ancestor worship.

## LONGSHAN CULTURE or Lung-shan culture

A late Neolithic culture that flourished along the lower Yellow River of China, c. 3000–1500 BC. The culture is named for the Longshan site in Shantung Province, central China.

The Longshan people began making walls and defensive ramparts of rammed earth, and they produced characteristic fine black burnished pottery, usually wheel-turned, together with plentiful grey pottery widely dispersed in China. Tools and weapons were made of highly polished stone, and bone was commonly used for arrowheads. Oracle (animal) bones used for divination began to appear in the succeeding Shang period of the Bronze Age.

## MACASSARESE or Makasarese

One of the main ethnic groups of the western INDONESIAN island of Sulawesi (Celebes). They are related to the Sumatran-coast MALAYS and JAVANESE and speak a language of the extensive AUSTRONESIAN family.

Until the 14th century, Sulawesi formed part of the Buddhist Srivijaya empire of Sumatra and subsequently of the Hindu Javan Majapahit empire whose cultures were strongly influenced by India. In the 16th century control passed to a number of warring states (which gradually adopted Islam, the main religion on the island today), especially to the Macassarese and the closely related Buginese people, who also originated in the southwest peninsula of Macassar. The port-city of the same name (now Ujung Pandang) was an important centre of the spice trade and attracted the DUTCH, who established a settlement at Macassar in 1607 and slowly gained control over the whole island.

The Macassarese, who joined the Republic of Indonesia in 1950, are widely regarded as industrious and energetic, particularly in trade and shipbuilding, but also in a variety of handicrafts and fine work such as jewellery. In the early 1990s the Macassarese numbered 1.6 million.

## MADURESE

An AUSTRONESIAN people originating on the island of Madura (capital Pamekasan), which lies off the eastern coast of Java in Indonesia. Despite living on a relatively arid and infertile island, the Madurese remain an essentially agricultural people whose chief products are cattle, salt, copra, coconut oil and teak timber. The population of Madurese speakers is about 8 million, with the majority living in the eastern portion of the neighbouring island of Java. The Madurese comprise approximately 7.5% of the population of Indonesia, and their language is related to JAVANESE. They are predominantly Sunni Muslims.

The island of Madura and its inhabitants have always been closely connected with, and dominated by, Java, and since independence in 1949 have tended to accept their status as INDONESIANS. In response to problems of overcrowding on Madura since the 1950s, the Indonesian government has been trying to encourage islanders to migrate to other, less densely populated, areas of the republic – a policy known as *transmigrasi*. Unfortunately, this has led to ethnic tension. Over the last few years native Borneo MALAYS and DAYAK have killed hundreds of Madurese immigrants who had settled in Borneo.

## MAILU

A native people of the coast of Central province, Papua New Guinea. Fishers, hunters, farmers and traders, they speak Mailuan, a trans-New Guinea language. Their traditional religion is strong and involves a belief in malevolent spirits that makes them conspicuously afraid of darkness. In 1980 they numbered about 6000.

## MALAYS

A people of Southeast Asia who are concentrated on the Malay Peninsula and neighbouring coasts and islands, especially northern Borneo (including Brunei) and eastern Sumatra. They are most

numerous on the Malay peninsula and the collective name Bumiputra describes the indigenous Malays and the small number of aboriginal people, the ORANG ASLI. The latter mostly follow their ancient traditional religions and speak Semelaic Mon-Khmer languages, with the exception of the Jakun ethnic group who speak archaic Malay.

The Malay are the majority people of the modern state of Malaysia (see MALAYSIANS) and have also migrated to adjoining countries. Some live in the border region of Thailand to the north. Malaysian government development policies since the 1970s have created a modern, urban society out of a country traditionally based on village communities cultivating wet rice and rubber. They speak numerous Malay dialects of the Western or Indonesian branch of AUSTRONESIAN, which are particularly closely related to Sumatran languages, including MINANGKABAU. Malay, thought to be spoken as a first language by around 35 million people, is the official language of Malaysia. Pidgin forms, notably Bazaar Malay, have been commonly used as the *lingua franca* of the coast and also the

commercial world for centuries. Through maritime trade, enterprise and their undoubted seafaring skills, ancestral Malays spread throughout the region from the island of Borneo beginning around the middle of the 1st millennium AD. By this time Malays journeying far to the west had also been the first to discover and colonize the island of Madagascar, where their descendants form the MERINA and Betsileo peoples today. Malay cultural development was influenced by contact with peoples on the edge of their world and maritime intercourse brought a new faith, Islam, widely adopted from the 15th century and disseminated from the Sultanate of Malacca, the region's most important trading state. The earlier Srivijayan name 'Malay' itself came to be identified solely with Muslim Malay-speakers, and the religion remains a centrally important part of Malay identity.

## MALAYSIANS

The people of the Southeast Asian country of Malaysia, which comprises the mainland West, or Malay Peninsular (the location of the capital,

Kuala Lumpur) and a large northern part of the island of Borneo, or East Malaysia. The MALAYS are the dominant community and comprise more than half the population of around 25 million. Although early states existed on the peninsula, notably as the Indian-influenced Buddhist empire of Srivijaya (7th–13th centuries AD) and later Malacca (Melaka), a single unified country emerged only with BRITISH decolonization in 1963. Malaysia was created as a federation of Malaya, Sarawak, Sabah and Singapore, although the last of these opted for independence in 1965.

The Malaysian people are particularly diverse in terms of ethnicity, language and culture. The most important element of the population is the Malay community, which has forged a common identity cemented by the adoption of Islam from the 15th century. Islam superseded Buddhism, Hinduism and local religions, but elements of these remain part of modern Malaysian culture. The Bumiputras (indigenous Malays and aboriginal peoples of the peninsula) form 60% of the population in Malaysia, the remainder comprising immigrant CHINESE, who now dominate trade and retailing, and South Asians. The latter groups were brought into the country during the British colonial period during the 19th and early 20th centuries to provide labour for the rapidly expanding rubber plantations, tin mines and other industrial and transport sectors.

The Chinese form 30% of the population and speak pidgin Baba Malay and their own several languages. They adhere to Chinese philosophical beliefs, religions and regional cultures, as do the smaller communities of INDIANS, PAKISTANIS and SRI LANKANS, who form around 10% of the total population.

The indigenous people of East Malaysia are even more diverse. There are many ethno-linguistic groups other than Malays, notably the Ibans, a DAYAK people of Sarawak, the Bidayuh (Land Dayak), the Melanau and the Kadazan. These are mostly interior hill people who have remained culturally aloof, speak separate AUSTRONESIAN languages and are less likely to be Muslim. Nearly half of Malaysians are non-Muslims, notably Buddhists (around 20%), followers of Chinese and traditional animist beliefs, Hindus and Christians.

The Muslim sultanate of Malacca dominated the Straits of Malacca in the 15th century and became the most important trading centre in Southeast Asia. It also established control over a number of smaller sultanates, islands and coastal territories that can be described as a prototype of the Malaysian state, although it was soon undermined by the Portuguese conquest of 1511 and by their Dutch successors. A fragmentation took place into minor sultanates, and new ones were established, such as Buginese Selangor from the mid-1700s, contributing to a competitive and unstable political environment which also encouraged opportunistic or forced migration around the region.

These upheavals have contributed to the diversity of the Malaysian regions, language, culture and beliefs. Many MINANGKABAU migrated across the Straits from Sumatra to peninsular Malaya in the 17th century and have bequeathed their system of royal election to modern Malaysia, whose head of state, or paramount ruler, is chosen from among the hereditary rulers of the traditional Malay sultanates. A Malay class system lingers from the days of former aristocratic government.

## Modernization and independence

Instability – which led to what was termed Malay 'piracy' by Western countries – and the demands of trade were factors that led to the growing involvement of Britain in local affairs. The British Straits Settlements became the base for pacification and control, ultimately leading to the creation of the colonial territories that formed the basis of modern Malaysia. The Brooke family of 'White Rajahs' exercized personal rule in Sarawak, and the North Borneo Company in modern Sabah, until World War II. Much of the country's infrastructure, administration and economic structure were created during this period, only interrupted by the Japanese occupation.

The national independence movement that emerged strongly in the 1930s was further galvanized by the war, but the process of achieving political freedom exacerbated inter-communal tensions. This contributed to the 12-year communist insurgency perpetuated largely by Chinese guerrillas from 1948. Malaysians were forced to reconcile their divisions, and have been assisted by the impressive economic development that has made the Malaysian economy one of the most successful in Asia. The country has benefited from a high-quality education system and has become a leader in high-technology industries and manufacturing, which have diversified an economy still strong in agriculture, forestry and mining. Modern Western-style cities have emerged, which have added another layer to a distinctive Malaysian culture. Traditional cultural activities remain important to the respective Malaysian communities.

## MANCHU or Man

A people who originate in the Manchuria region of northeast China, known to the CHINESE as the Northeast Provinces. They are descended from early hunter-gathering Tungusic peoples who later pursued rudimentary cultivation and animal husbandry. In the mid-1st millennium BC they were known as the Sushen, later Yilou, whose descendants, the RUZHEN, established a powerful state in Manchuria from the 8th century AD, expanding to include northern China in the 12th century and founding the Jin dynasty. The Jin empire was conquered by the MONGOLS in the 13th century and the Ruzhen returned to their traditional ways. In the 16th century they adopted the name 'Manchu'.

The disparate Manchu ethnic and tribal groups were unified in the late 16th century under Nurhachi, Governor of the Jianzhou Prefecture, who organized the entire population along military lines both for war and for food production. Equestrianism, archery and hunting were important parts of their martial culture. The Ruzhen proceeded to regain control of Manchuria from their Chinese overlords and captured Beijing (Peking) in 1644. They became known as the Manchu people, whose Qing (Ch'ing) imperial dynasty had subdued the rest of China by 1680. The last Qing, or Manchu, emperor was overthrown in 1911.

The Manchu language is part of the Manchu-Tungusic group of the ALTAIC family. Growing intercourse with the Han since the 17th century and a mass migration of Manchu to the Qing imperial court and territories to the south (and the movement of Han farmers to Manchuria) led to many Manchus adopting Mandarin Chinese; the Manchu language is now virtually extinct. Despite imperial policy to preserve a strong Manchu identity, acculturation and intermarriage have eliminated many of the distinctions between Manchu and Han. Traditionally, Manchu men wore long pigtails which were adopted throughout China under the Qing dynasty, a fashion long abandoned.

Ethnic Manchu today number around 10 million. Agriculture remains their chief economic activity and the basis of their way of life, which has traditionally centred on family and clan loyalties. The Manchu believed in many ancestor and nature spirits, whose relationships were mediated by court, village and clan shamans, although Chinese religious beliefs came to predominate.

## MANGARAIA

An Australian ABORIGINAL PEOPLE of the Elsey and Mataranka stations, Northern Territory. Nomadic hunters and gatherers, they speak a non-Pama-Nyungan language related to GUN-WINGGUAN. Their traditional lands were suitable for cattle-rearing, and European settlers organized 'nigger hunts' to murder the Mangharaia. The survivors were forced to work on cattle stations on their own former lands, and suffer brutality, contempt and insults. In 1999, when they regained title to Elsey station and reasserted their identity as a people, they numbered about 50 language-speakers.

## MAORI

The native people of New Zealand. They are a POLYNESIAN people who began to settle New Zealand possibly around AD 900. Their oral tradition tells of the discovery of Aotearoa (the land of the 'long daylight') by the navigator Kupe. Subsequently waves of migrants arrived. Each major *iwi* (tribe) was founded by such migrations, and Maori genealogy is traced back to particular ancestral canoes. Maori legend also speaks of an ancestral homeland, Hawaika. The location of this homeland is a subject of great controversy, but Tahiti (see TAHITIANS) seems

**Maori**

*The distribution of major Maori iwi (tribes) on the eve of European settlement of New Zealand.*

NGA PUHI  **MAORI TRIBES**
c. 1800

TE AUPOURI

PACIFIC OCEAN

TE RARAWA

NGA PUHI

NGATI WHATUA

NGATI TAMATERA

NGATI PAOA

NGATI WHANAUNGA

NORTH ISLAND
(Te Ika a Maui)

WAIKATO

NGATI MARU

NGATI TE RANGI

WHANAUA APANUI

NGATI HAUA

NGATI RAUKAWA

TE ARAWA

WHAKATOHEA

NGATI TAMA

NGATI TOA

TUHOE

NGATI MUTUNGA

NGATI MANIOPOTO

RONGOWHAKAATA

TE ATI AWA

NGATI TUWHARETOA

TARANAKI

NGATI RUANUI

WHANGANUI

NGA RAURU

NGATI APA

RANGITANE

MUAUPOKO

NGATI KAHUNGUNU

NGATI IRA

NGATI APA

RANGITANE

NEW ZEALAND

SOUTH ISLAND
(Te Waka a Maui)

POUTINI

NGAI TAHU

TASMAN SEA

NGATI MAMOE

Stewart Island

0    50    100 miles
0    100    200 kilometres

likely. Their original starting point, and indeed that for all Polynesians, is also much disputed. Recent genetic evidence suggests that they originated in China and migrated via Taiwan, the Philippines and the Pacific islands. This is disputed by those who believe they originated in Indonesia or even Southeast Asia.

They were sedentary traders, hunters, farmers and fishers, and speak Maori, a Malayo-Polynesian language. Their religion recognized a supreme creator god and many lesser spirits. Like other Polynesian peoples, they have a culture rich in song, music, dance, mythology and tattooing. Also like other Polynesians, there was tribal warfare, and defeated enemies could be treated harshly, including being subjected to ritual cannibalism. As the Maori population grew and the competition for resources became fiercer during the 14th century, they developed *pa*, or hilltop fortifications, although wars were fought with battleaxes, clubs and stabbing spears, not projectile weapons. This changed with the arrival of European settlers (*pakeha*) in the early 19th century. These settlers introduced European diseases and muskets, both of which had a catastrophic impact on the Maori. Those tribes with access to muskets attacked their less well-armed neighbours in a series of territorial wars known as the Musket Wars. Epidemics added greatly to the death toll, and by the 1840s a large minority of the Maori population was dead, enslaved or forced to migrate; simultaneously European settlers were arriving in droves.

In 1835, 34 important *ariki* (chiefs) appealed to the BRITISH government for protection from the French. This was formalized in the Treaty of Waitangi (1840), which was intended to ensure permanently friendly relations, but in fact resulted in bitterness and war. There were misunderstandings on both sides concerning concepts of ownership and sovereignty. The Maori agreed to sell lands only to the Crown but often did not accept a change of ownership as being permanent. The extent to which royal authority extended over the Maori was also a subject of acrimony.

Alarm at the scale at which land was passing to settlers led, between 1845 and 1872, to a series of land wars. The Maori proved courageous and resourceful, developed a fearsome reputation as enemies, and indeed won many engagements. Some tribes, however, allied with the British, and as a result retained much of their land and were often rewarded with some of the lands of defeated enemies. In 1858, in an attempt to end internal divisions, several chiefs elected To Wherowhero as king, but his authority was never fully accepted.

British technology and numbers were finally decisive. Defeat brought demoralization, massive land seizures and the reduction of many Maori to landless labour, increasingly urbanized and impoverished. The general degree of land retention, however, remained extremely high in comparison to other colonized lands. The Maori have also had guaranteed representation in New Zealand's parliament since 1867.

Still, in the mid-20th century, with so many Maori conspicuously failing to share the growing affluence of New Zealand, they attempted to negotiate some redress for blatant violations of the Treaty of Waitangi. Although initially rebuffed, a radical protest movement, Nga Tamatoa, became increasingly vocal and attracted widespread sympathy during the 1970s. Some issues, such as language and education, were addressed, and some progress was made over land and sovereignty claims. In 1994, however, the government decided to seek a permanent settlement of all claims, and set a NZ$1 billion limit on its cost. The Maori rejected this settlement, claiming it would set an arbitrary cash value on their suffering and do little for the urban, often unskilled and unemployed majority. In 1995 the Maori numbered about 310,000, of whom up to 70,000 were Maori-speakers.

# MARIANANS

Citizens of the Commonwealth of the Northern Mariana Islands, in North Pacific Oceania. First settled by the CHAMMOROS by AD 500, who were nearly exterminated under SPANISH rule, the islands were repopulated by Spanish and FILIPINO settlers. In 1899 they passed to German rule and in 1914 to JAPANESE control. Under the Japanese, the islands saw large-scale immigration of Asian workers, who swamped the Chammoro population and overwhelmed their culture. In 1944, however, US forces invaded the islands and decimated the Asian population. Under US rule, subsistence agriculture began to give way to industrialization, and American culture was widely adopted by the local people.

Indigenous Chammoros are now trying to reclaim their culture, but the islands remain a cultural fusion. A notorious home for sweatshop labour, the islands attract other Asian and South American influences. In 1976 the Marianans voted to become a US Commonwealth, making them US citizens, although Guam rejected unification. In 2000 they numbered about 50,000, 90% of whom live on the island of Saipan.

# MARIND-ANIM

A PAPUAN people of the southern coast of Irian Jaya (western New Guinea) in Indonesia. They were known for their headhunting expeditions and distinctive sexual practices and were divided into two groups, each with its own mythology and ceremonial responsibilities towards the other. In Marind-anim culture semen was believed to be the source of male growth and both male and female fertility. The frequent ingestion of semen through oral sex was believed to be beneficial to both sexes, increasing their strength and fertility. Boys were assigned a *binahor* 'father' from the other group whose role was regularly to inseminate the boy anally until he reached manhood. The Marind-anim also believed that for a woman to conceive it was necessary for her to copulate not only with her husband but with all of his male blood relatives as well. These practices resulted in high levels of sexually transmitted diseases and consequent infertility and low birth rate. The Marind-anim frequently kidnapped children from neighbouring peoples to make up their numbers. The Dutch colonial government suppressed the sexual practices of the Marind-anim in the 20th century and put a stop to their raiding. The Marind-anim were subsequently converted to Christianity and have now mostly lost their distinctive identity as a people.

# MARQUESANS

A native Central Pacific island people of the Marquesas Islands. Hunters, farmers and fishers, they speak dialects of a POLYNESIAN language. They were once reputedly cannibals who treated prisoners with ferocious cruelty, but missionaries from 1797 and FRENCH rule since 1842 began to break down traditional culture and society. The Europeans also brought diseases that had a catastrophic impact. The population fell from about 90,000 to 2255 in 1926, before climbing to over 7300 by 1988. Once among the best carvers in the Pacific, the Marquesans were celebrated for their *Tiki* statues. Their culture, rich in song, dance and legend, has largely disappeared, but their tradition of tattooing is re-emerging.

# MARRA

An Australian ABORIGINAL PEOPLE of the Roper River area, Northern Territory. Nomadic hunters and gatherers, they speak a non-Pama-Nyungan language. They are one of several Aboriginal peoples who hold the (perhaps once universal) belief that spirit children, the souls of ancestors, inhabit certain locations where they can enter a woman's body and cause pregnancy. They have, however, been heavily acculturated and largely absorbed by other Aboriginal peoples. In 1991 at most 15 of them could speak their language, which is therefore nearly extinct.

# MARSHALL ISLANDERS

The native people of the Marshall Islands, a group of 1225 Pacific islands and reefs. First settled by MICRONESIANS by 500 BC, they are farmers and fishers who speak an AUSTRONESIAN language. Comprising a large number of independent chiefdoms, theirs was a socially stratified society in which chiefs had (and still have) great authority. In the 19th century traders, whalers and missionaries brought Christianity and diseases that rapidly reduced their numbers. The islands were annexed by the Germans in 1885, and passed to JAPANESE rule in 1914. They saw heavy fighting in World War II and became a US Trust Territory. Under AMERICAN rule a number of thermonuclear test explosions, most on Bikini atoll, caused great problems with radioactive contamination, leading to a clamour for independence from 1973. Although independent from 1986, they still remain heavily dependent on US aid. In 1996 they numbered nearly 57,000.

# MASSIM

A MELANESIAN people of the Massim archipelago, Papua New Guinea. Farmers, fishers and noted wood-carvers, they speak an AUSTRONESIAN language. Their traditional animist religion is strong, and missionaries who arrived in 1847 were simply ignored. They are known for their little-understood *kula* tradition, in which gifts of shells or necklaces are passed between partners in different communities, and for the complex

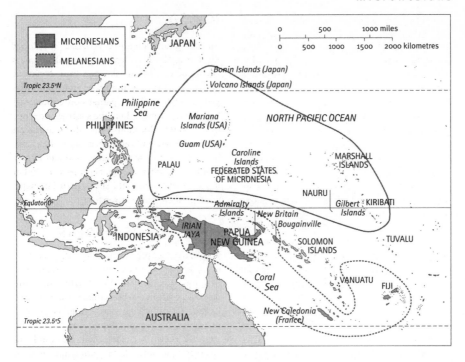

marriage obligations to the spouse's family. In 1998 they numbered 6000.

## MELANAU

See DAYAK.

## MELANESIANS

An ethnic and cultural group that colonized vast stretches of the southwest Pacific. Originating in Southeast Asia, they began colonizing the Pacific islands around 2000 BC. They became culturally, politically and linguistically splintered, speaking about 400 mainly AUSTRONESIAN languages, with many groups speaking completely different languages from their neighbours. In general they were animists, believing in spirits occupying geographical features and in the ghosts of ancestors inhabiting the world, though many are now Christian. Internecine warfare was common, with some groups reputedly practising cannibalism and headhunting. European colonization has left them divided between a number of states, including Papua New Guinea,

the Solomon Islands, Vanuatu and Fiji. In the late 20th century, however, a renewed interest in their common culture developed among an emerging educated elite. Art festivals and cultural centres are reviving traditional ceremonies, dances, music and a strong oral-history tradition. In 1998 there were fewer than 1 million language-speakers, but the total population is uncertain.

## MEO

See HMONG.

## MIAO

See HMONG.

## MICRONESIANS

An ethnic and cultural group that spread over a large swathe of the northwest Pacific. Micronesians began colonizing Pacific islands, probably beginning from the Indonesian islands, around 1500 BC, and became culturally, linguistically and politically splintered. In general they were farmers and fishers who held land communally and held obligations for mutual aid within extended family groups. Their culture included dance, music (including the shell trumpet and nose flute), body-painting and storytelling, much of which has been lost under the influence of missionaries. Traditionally animists, they believed in spirits inhabiting places and natural objects, and practised ancestor-worship. European colonization has left them divided between a number of states, including Kiribati, Nauru and the Federated States of Micronesia. In the Federated States, which became independent from the USA in 1986, there have been great efforts to preserve the traditional culture, including attempts to ban Western dress. Micronesians are also very proud of their heroic seafaring ancestors. In 2003 the population of the Federated States was over 108,000, but the total population is unknown.

## MIDDLE SEPIK

A PAPUAN people of East Sepik province, Papua New Guinea. They are sedentary gardeners and hunters, and the women fish to provide the trade goods to acquire the sago flour that is their staple diet. All of the 25 villages, each with a population in the hundreds, speak dialects of a Sepik-Ramu language, and have a common ancestry. There is, however, a high degree of cultural diversity, and each village specializes in particular artistic forms, ranging from wood-carving to body art. Carved masks, painted and decorated with teeth, shells and feathers, are widely produced, used to ward off evil and to attract benevolent spirits. These masks are stored in the distinctive *Haus Tamberan*, or massively constructed and richly carved spirit house that is found in every village. The Middle Sepik have begun to enter the money economy through marketing their art to the outside world.

## MIN CHIA

See PAI.

## MINANGKABAUS

An INDONESIAN people from the west-central Padang highlands of Sumatra, where they are the dominant group. They are ethnic MALAYS whose AUSTRONESIAN (Malayo-Polynesian) language closely resembles Malay. They are known as Urang Padang ('people of Padang') in this language. The Minankabaus are an enterprising and outward-looking people and have a strong tradition of migration (*merantau*). In the 19th century many moved to British-controlled Malaya to work in mining, and have since become successful smallholders and retail traders, especially in the state of Negeri Sembilan in southwestern West Malaysia. They are also widely dispersed across Indonesia. In Sumatra the Minangkabaus number more than 5 million, and their agricultural matrilineal society is based on strong family and clan ties, although these began to loosen in the late 20th century. Traditionally extended families occupy large wooden longhouses. Their early culture was strongly INDIAN-influenced, and their religion remained Hindu until the king of Minangkabau converted to Islam in the 16th century.

## MIZO

See CHIN.

## MOLUCCANS

The inhabitants of the Moluccan islands of eastern Indonesia, the majority of whom are MALAYS. There are also many minority ethnic groups, including the Alfoers, AMBONESE, Batjan, Makianese, Tanimbarese, Ternatan, Tidorese, Tobelorese and Sawai. The population consists mostly of coastal Malays and interior Alfoers. Islam is the dominant religion, but there is a large Christian minority, and religious violence is common. The population of the Moluccas is around 1.5 million.

## MON or Talaing

A MONGOLOID people who migrated from western China into the area of modern Thailand around the 6th century AD, and from there into the Irrawaddy River delta of southern Burma. In the following three centuries they established a number of kingdoms, notably Dvaravati in west-central Siam, which had an important role in transmitting INDIAN culture to the region and particularly to the KHMERS and the THAIS, who absorbed Dvaravati in the 13th century. In Burma a separate kingdom emerged, based at Thaton, the first mainland state in southeast Asia to adopt Theravada Buddhism, which arrived from Ceylon (Sri Lanka) and southern India. Thaton was conquered by the northern BURMESE in 1057, and its culture and religion were rapidly assimilated. Throughout the region Buddhism was widely adopted along with Indian elements of art and sculpture, Pali writing, scholarship, law and government. In Lower Burma the Mon periodically regained their independence, finally extinguished in 1757 when the Burmese razed their capital at Pegu. Mon are present in Thailand, mostly west of Bangkok, but most of the small remaining population is concentrated in southeastern Burma, where they pursue a predominantly agricultural way of life. They speak Mon, also known as Talaing or Peguan, which is a Mon-Khmer language of the AUSTRO-ASIATIC family, but many Mon now only speak Burman of the majority community. The Mon of Burma number around 1.2 million and have an affinity with the MUNDA of east-central India.

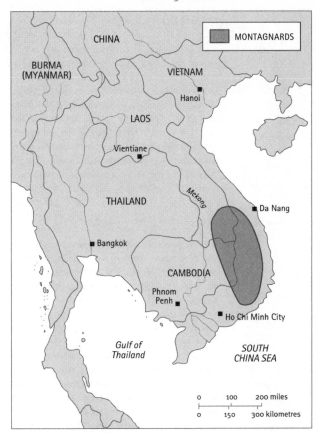

Montagnards

## MONTAGNARDS

The numerous upland peoples of Indochina. The name means 'highlanders' in French and has come to be particularly associated with the mountain-dwellers of the Central Highlands of Vietnam, who number around 1 million. Montagnards, who are ethnically completely different from the Vietnamese, are culturally diverse and strongly attached to their individual identities and traditional ways of life, which have developed in isolation. Their languages also vary widely and include links with AUSTRONESIAN and Mon-Khmer, some of them becoming written languages only with the introduction of the Roman script by French officials and missionaries. There are 30 or so tribes in the Central Highlands, notably the Jarai, Rhade and Bahnar, forming several distinct ethnic groups

who have been struggling either for independence or for greater political autonomy since the dominant Vietnamese first migrated into coastal Indo-China. This impelled the Montagnards to align themselves with the French colonial authorities and in the later 20th century with the USA during the long Vietnam War. State policy towards them has since been suspicious and even hostile.

The Montagnards are traditionally animists with a belief in ancestor spirits, often mediated through shamans, although as many as half have adopted Christianity, which further distinguishes them from the Vietnamese. Typically, Montagnards live in small temporary villages, sometimes in matrilineal kin groups and use shifting cultivation techniques to grow rice, their staple food.

## MORTLOCKESE

A native people of a northwest Pacific island group, now part of the Federated States of Micronesia. Settled by MICRONESIANS after 1500 BC, they were traditionally farmers and fishers who speak a Malayo-Polynesian language. They are considered a gentle nation, although in the past they manufactured *tapuana*, hibiscus-wood masks to ward off evil spirits in battle. They also tend to be more Westernized in dress than other members of the Federated States. In 1999 they numbered over 5900.

## MOTUANS or Motu Koita

A native people of Central province and the Port Moresby area, Papua New Guinea. Often referred to as the Motu Koita (at some time in the past they absorbed another group, the Koita), they are farmers and fishers who speak a Central Papuan language. Their great disadvantage was to dwell in the area in which British colonizers chose to develop a port that would become a national capital. As the land was the resting place of their ancestors and their own security, the concept of selling it was alien. Consequently they were cheated out of much of their land, and now developers are trying to separate them from the rest. The result has given them all the disadvantages of urban life, in slum dwellings, great unemployment, poor health care and high mortality rates, with none of the associated advantages such as economic opportunity. In 2000 they numbered perhaps 50,000.

## MUONG

A minority people in the north of Vietnam who are considered the sole survivors of the aboriginal VIETNAMESE people. They number more than 1.1 million and are located to the southwest of the capital, Hanoi. They speak Muong, part of the Viet-Muong branch of the Mon-Khmer (AUSTRO-ASIATIC) group of languages, distinguished by its lack of CHINESE influence compared with Vietnamese. This reflects their cultural isolation in the mountains of northern Vietnam, where they have exploited the forests, hunted for game, pursued a mixed agricultural way of life and traded with the lowland population. Muong live mostly in patrilineal extended families in village settlements, adhering to their traditional animistic beliefs and maintaining their cultural distinctiveness from the majority Vietnamese who have dominated them for centuries.

## MURNGIN

An Australian ABORIGINAL PEOPLE of Arnhem Land, Northern Territory. Nomadic hunters and gatherers, they speak a non-Pama-Nyungan language. They are one of a number of Aboriginal peoples in which a man is required to observe strict food taboos his wife's first pregnancy. Their numbers are uncertain.

## MYANMARESE

See BURMESE

## NAGOVISI

A native people of Bougainville, Papua New Guinea. Fishers and slash-and-burn farmers who traditionally held the land in common, they speak an East Papuan language. In 1972 gold- and copper-mining began on their territory, and the government permitted mine tailings and noxious waste, including cyanide and heavy metals, to be dumped into the river. By 1987 most marine life was destroyed and the riverbed had risen, in some places by 40 m / 130 ft, causing poisoned groundwater to pollute their land. Demands for massive compensation and for the mine to be closed were ignored, and in 1988 they were at the forefront of the Bougainville Revolutionary Army. They shut down the mine and fought a guerrilla war that was suppressed with great brutality. Although concessions were offered, their survival as a people is in doubt. In 1975 they numbered about 5000, but continued unrest renders subsequent population estimates problematic.

## NAMBIS

See PIPEL BILONG NAMBIS.

> 66 Port Moresby ... is the centre of the Motu tribe .... The Motu make great trading voyages to the Gulf of Papua. 99
>
> A.C. Haddon, 1894, referring to the Motuans

> 66 Our land is being polluted, our water is being polluted, the air we breathe is being polluted with dangerous chemicals that are slowly killing us and destroying our land for future generations. Better that we die fighting than be slowly poisoned. 99
>
> Francis Ona, Nagovisi spokesman, c.1988

## NANGIKURRUNGGURR

An Australian ABORIGINAL PEOPLE of the confluence of the Flora and Daly rivers, Northern Territory. Nomadic hunters and gatherers, they speak a non-AUSTRONESIAN language. In 1988 they numbered just 275 language-speakers.

## NAURUANS

The MICRONESIAN people of the South Pacific island nation of Nauru. With 21 sq. km / 8 sq. miles of land, Nauru is one of the smallest republics in the world. Traditionally farmers, hunters and fishers, they speak a Malayo-Pacific language. In the 19th century European missionaries, diseases and firearms proved catastrophic for them, killing one-third in 40 years and destroying most of the traditional culture. The GERMANS annexed Nauru in 1888 and discovered a vast layer of phosphates covering the island. After World War I the Nauruans came under AUSTRALIAN administration until independence in 1968, and phosphate extraction continued. This provided a very affluent lifestyle, but at a very high cost. The Nauruans imported most of their food and developed a taste for junk food, which caused severe problems with obesity and diabetes. Satellite television made Australian-rules football the new religion. The environmental consequences of phosphate extraction were catastrophic. Around 90% of the island has been denuded of topsoil by open cast mining. With phosphate reserves reaching exhaustion in 2003 and no alternative source of income, Nuaruans look towards the future with great uncertainty. In 1996 they numbered about 11,000, but this figure includes many immigrant workers.

## NEGRITOS

Asian pygmies descended from the original nomadic hunter-gathering peoples of Southeast Asia, whose lifestyles have changed very little. Over many centuries they have also been absorbed by other peoples and are now part of the ancestral make-up of many other peoples of the region. They are dark-skinned, have physical characteristics in common with Negroid peoples and are generally between 147 and 152 cm / 4 ft 10 in and 5 ft in height. They have been pushed into the remoter mountain and forested areas and are still present in New Guinea, the Philippines (see AETAS), Indonesia, the Malay Peninsula (see SEMANG) and the Andaman and Nicobar islands in the Bay of Bengal. They are now culturally and linguistically diverse, retaining a belief in their own gods and spirits supplemented by elements of locally dominant religions. Some, such as the Andamanese (see ANDAMAN ISLANDERS), have been acculturated and lost their tribal identities. Their overall numbers across the region are small and difficult to estimate.

## NEW GUINEA HIGHLANDERS

A linguistic and cultural group of mainly PAPUAN peoples of New Guinea, speaking the Central and Western families of trans-New Guinea languages. Mainly farmers living inland, they have had fewer contacts with the outside world and are more conservative in their views on culture, society and religion than other peoples of New Guinea. They tend to see the more Westernized lowland peoples as untrustworthy. In the province of Irian Jaya, where there is a strong movement for independence from Indonesia, they have their own political movement: Denmak, or the Penis Gourd Peoples Assembly. The gourds commonly used as penis covers among Highlanders symbolizes the future they envisage for Irian Jaya: a male-dominated, traditionalist society, in which political power is kept firmly in the hands of Highland chiefs. In 1997 they numbered nearly 1 million.

## NEW GUINEA LOWLANDERS

An obsolete term formerly used to describe the native inhabitants of lowland New Guinea. The New Guinea lowlanders describe themselves as PIPEL BILONG NAMBIS ('people of the coast'), but this simply refers to where they live and has no overtones of common ethnic identity.

## NEW ZEALANDERS

Citizens of New Zealand combining MAORI, the descendants of colonial settlers and the more

> *"* The Nauruans have never been cannibals, but they had the reputation of being savage warriors. *"*
>
> R.D. Rhone, 1921

**"** Ladies and
Gentlemen,
tomorrow morning
we will be docking
in Wellington,
New Zealand.
Please put your
watches back
35 years. **"**

Jocular (and
clichéd)
announcement
made on a
British cruise liner
c. 1988.

recent immigrants of varied ethnic roots. They
often refer to themselves as 'Kiwis' after the
native flightless bird. New Zealand was first settled by the MAORI from around AD 900.
European settlers began to arrive in the early
19th century, bringing guns and diseases, and
dispossessing many of the Maori in a series of
land wars. Initially regarded as an offshoot of the
AUSTRALIAN settlement, New Zealand was administered by New South Wales from 1814 to 1841.
The Treaty of Waitangi (1840) with the Maori,
however, marked the colony's origin as a separate entity. Sheep farming brought prosperity,
and the first steps towards an industrial economy were established by the end of the 19th
century. New Zealand became a dominion of the
British empire in 1907, and by 1931 was effectively an independent state.

A distinct New Zealand culture developed. As
did Australians, New Zealanders at the beginning of the 20th century tended to see
themselves as transplanted BRITISH. In Britain's
wars of that century, they had no hesitation in
contributing troops, and indeed contributed
more as a percentage of their population than
any other dominion. Attitudes, however, were
changing. They have an enormous passion for
British sports, especially rugby union and
cricket, and the dominant culture was British in
origin. But there were also important Maori
influences, for example in art and music. New
Zealanders also take great pride in their egalitarian ways. Like Australia, this was seen as a
country of enormous opportunity for the adventurous and hard-working. New Zealanders
therefore met the great social changes of the late
19th century boldly. They often led the world in
social reform, establishing social services and
encouraging trade unions in advance of Britain.
They led the world in women's suffrage: women
voted in parliamentary elections in 1893, and in
many areas in local elections in the 1860s. In
1867 the Maori were guaranteed representation
in the New Zealand parliament to seal their
inclusion within the nation.

It was through World War I, however, that a
real nation began to emerge. As with Australians,
New Zealanders resented what they saw as the
waste of their soldiers' lives by incompetent
British generals. The losses in 1915 during the

Gallipoli campaign taught them that the British
were fallible; the 'mother country' ceased to be
idealized and British identification was no
longer such a source of pride. Instead, New
Zealanders perceived their own fallen as heroes,
and the self-image of New Zealand as a 'man's
country' developed. Despite this, New Zealand
has led the world in addressing many issues
related to the rights and roles of women, building on the extension of the franchise. A sense of
nationhood was reinforced with separate representation at the Versailles Treaty negotiations
and in the League of Nations. Most immigration,
however, remained British. In the 1950s British
immigrants outnumbered non-British by over
four to one. Multiculturalism has grown much
more slowly, while a growing gap between rich
and poor now threatens New Zealand's egalitarian traditions, and such issues as Maori
grievances and closer relations with Australia are
proving divisive. Republicanism, however, is
much less of an issue than in Australia. The
Maori, for example, see the Treaty of Waitangi,
made directly with the British Crown, as their
main legal protection. In 2003 there were over
3.9 million New Zealanders.

## NGAANYATJARRA

An Australian ABORIGINAL PEOPLE of the Warbur-
ton Ranges, Western Australia. Nomadic hunters
and gatherers, they speak a Pama-Nyungan language. They were forcibly settled in the 1930s,
and children were forced into boarding education. Their desert isolation, however, protected
their culture better than that of many other Aboriginal peoples. In 1973 they gained control over
their settlement, and in 1990 formed the War-
burton Arts Project to preserve their culture.
They retained control, for example, over their art
and oral traditions. In 2002, after five years of
lobbying, they obtained dominance over a territory twice the size of Switzerland, in order to
further protect their culture and environment. In
1995 they numbered about 1200.

## NGAI TAHU

A MAORI *iwi* (tribe) predominant in South Island,
New Zealand. Maori-speaking sedentary traders,

hunters, farmers and fishers, they trace their descent from the POLYNESIAN migrants who arrived in the 14th century on the canoe known in their oral history as *Takitimu*. During the Musket Wars of the early 19th century, they expanded their territory and conquered the neighbouring Ngati Mamoe, descendants of the same Polynesian migrants, whom they totally assimilated. Subsequently they suffered severe land seizures and spent 150 years seeking redress. In 1998 they achieved a landmark victory in New Zealand legal history when they were awarded NZ$ 170 million in compensation and had part of their lost territory returned. Among the land regained was Mount Cook (the highest in New Zealand). The cash settlement also made them particularly wealthy landowners, and they look towards the future with immense confidence. In 1995 they numbered over 30,000, making them the third-largest Maori people.

## NGAJU

A DAYAK people living mostly in Central Kalimantan Province in southern INDONESIAN Borneo, particularly along the Kayahan and Katingan rivers. They number around 1.5 million. As are the Dayak generally, the Ngaju are an indigenous people of the interior of the island who speak an Indonesian language of the AUSTRONESIAN (Malayo-Polynesian) family and retain their traditional animistic and polytheistic beliefs. Their religion, Kaharingan, is a variant of Hinduism and they are renowned for their elaborate mortuary rituals and erection of wooden memorial statues. They live in traditional longhouse communities and continue to practise shifting cultivation, fish local rivers and exploit forest products. Tribal-warfare headhunting was formerly an important element of the Ngaju, and Dayak, way of life.

## NGAPUHI

A MAORI *iwi* (tribe) of northern North Island, New Zealand. Maori-speaking sedentary traders, hunters, farmers and fishers, they trace their descent to the POLYNESIAN migrants aboard the canoes known in their oral history as *Kurahaupo*

(in the early 12th century) and *Mamari* (in the mid-14th century). They were the first to seize the opportunities offered by the European presence. Their great *ariki* (chief) Hongi Hika visited Britain in 1820 and was feted among the aristocracy. On his return he sold the gifts he had received and bought muskets, bringing a new intensity to the Musket Wars. For the next ten years he led 10,000 warriors against the Ngapuhi's traditional enemies in a war of conquest.

The Ngapuhi had good relations with European settlers and were the first to sign the Treaty of Waitangi (1840). Relations soon soured, however, and their chief Hone Heke became among the first to take up arms against the settlers when he cut down the flagstaff symbolizing British sovereignty at Kororareka. The Ngapuhi were not united in the war; some sought to preserve their land and sovereignty through collaboration with the British. Hone Heke was soon defeated, and large-scale land confiscations soon followed, dispossessing collaborators and resistors alike. The Ngapuhi have, however, retained their cohesion as a tribe, and have largely adhered to their communal traditions. In 1967 they converted an entire football ground in Auckland into a *marae*, or traditional meeting place. In 2003 they numbered 103,000 and are the largest Maori people.

## NGARINMAN

An Australian ABORIGINAL PEOPLE of the Victoria River area, Northern Territory. Hunters and gatherers, and speakers of a non-Pama-Nyungan language, they occupied fertile river territory and appeared to have been more sedentary than most Aboriginal peoples. This land was desirable to cattle-herders, however, and the Ngarinman suffered murderous attacks and dispossession. They did, however, have some very inaccessible terrain in which they could shelter. Later they sought refuge by working on the cattle stations, where some found decent wages and treatment, while others found mistreatment and starvation rations. Indeed some of them participated in the famous Wave Hill strike of 1966 by the GURINDJI. In 1983 they numbered up to 170 language-speakers.

## NGATI RAUKAWA

A MAORI *iwi* (tribe) of southern North Island, New Zealand. Maori-speaking sedentary traders, hunters, farmers and fishers, they trace their descent from the POLYNESIAN migrants who arrived in the mid-14th century aboard the canoe known in the oral history as *Tainui*. In 1819 they joined the great NGATI TOA *ariki* (chief) Te Rauparaha in his war of conquest during the Musket Wars, and migrated south from Waikato to the Manawatu plains, near present day Wellington. Later they invaded and occupied parts of northern South Island. As the number of European settlers grew, this simply made them more vulnerable to illegal land losses. They still pursue redress for this. In 1991 they numbered over 6200.

## NGATI TOA

A MAORI *iwi* (tribe) of southern North Island, New Zealand. They speak Maori, and are sedentary traders, hunters, farmers and fishers, who trace their descent from the POLYNESIAN migrants of the mid-14th century aboard the canoe known in their oral tradition as *Tainui*. Never a large tribe, they enjoyed a period of spectacular success through the military and diplomatic skills of their leaders, notably the great warrior *ariki* (chief) Te Rauparaha. Driven from their lands on the Coromandel coast in the Musket Wars of the early 19th century, Te Rauparaha formed an alliance with a number of tribes, including the NGATI RAUKAWA and later parts of the TE ATI AWA, and led a war of conquest in the south, occupying the Manawatu plains and areas of northern South Island. The alliance broke down in the 1830s when the Te Ati Awa refused to accept Ngati Toa control of Cook Strait. Weakened, they were not able to resist subsequent land seizures, for which they still seek redress. In 2002 they were involved in a dispute with the New Zealand government over fishery allocations. Their traditional culture is internationally celebrated in the *haka* (chant and war dance) known as 'Ka Mate', created by Te Rauparaha and now performed by New Zealand's rugby union team, the All Blacks, before every international game. In 1991 they numbered nearly 1300.

## NGATI TUMATAKOKIRI

A former MAORI *iwi* (tribe) of South Island, New Zealand. Sedentary traders, hunters, farmers and fishers, they spoke Maori. They are noted for attacking Dutch explorer Abel Tasman's crew in 1642 at Massacre Bay. In the early 17th century they expanded from the upper Wanganui River area and conquered much of the northwestern part of the island. They were, however, poorly situated to have access to muskets. In 1810 the better-armed NGATI TOA, led by Te Rauparaha, defeated and slaughtered them in the Battle of Paparoa Ridges. Few survived, and those not enslaved fled. Explorers found a few families in the 1840s living in hiding, but as a tribe they had ceased to exist.

## NGAWUN

An Australian ABORIGINAL PEOPLE of the Flinders River area, Queensland. Nomadic hunters and gatherers, they spoke a Pama-Nyungan language. Occupying land desirable to cattle-herders, they suffered brutal land loss and came under heavy acculturation pressures. By 1981 there was possibly just a single speaker left of a language that was effectively extinct.

## NIUEANS

A native people of the South Pacific island nation of Niue. The island was settled by POLYNESIANS by AD 1000, and the Nieuans were traditionally fishers and farmers, who spoke a Malayo-Polynesian language. While they adopted Christianity in the 19th century and are notably devout, their isolation has enabled much of their traditional culture to survive, including costly coming-of-age ceremonies, during which boys get haircuts and girls pierced ears. Niue became part of a British protectorate in 1900 and was placed under New Zealand administration. Independent in 1974, Niueans remain in free association with New Zealand and are New Zealand citizens. They do face problems of depopulation, with only 2100 people on Niue by 2002; but there are 10,000 people of Niuean descent in New Zealand. They have also managed to arouse the wrath of the US government, which imposed sanctions on Niue in 2001 because it was a tax haven and forced Niue to shut down its 'offshore' banking operations.

## NI-VANUATU

The native people of the western Pacific island group of Vanuatu. The islands were settled by MELANESIANS by 2000 BC. The Ni-Vanuatu currently speak 109 AUSTRONESIAN languages, on 80 islands. Farmers and fishers, they developed a culture rich in music; stone, wood and tree-fern carving; rock- and body-painting; and tattooing. Traditional beliefs are still strong and calamities are attributed to sorcery, while *nimangki*, a gift-giving tradition, is still practised. They are also credited with the invention of bungee jumping.

In the 19th century they were ravaged by European epidemics and by slave-raiding that was not ended until the early 20th century. The islands, called by Europeans the New Hebrides, came under the joint colonial rule of an Anglo-French condominium (locally referred to as a pandemonium). This caused problems in the 1960s with a growing demand for independence. The BRITISH were willing to grant it, but the FRENCH were not, until growing civil unrest led to violence and looting in towns in 1980, pushing them to agree immediate independence as Vanuatu. A secessionist movement based on Santo island launched a rebellion, quickly suppressed with help from Papua New Guinea, making it the only nation in Oceania that did not gain independence peacefully. The Ni-Vanuatu have since experienced a degree of political instability, based on regional religious and political differences between Francophone and Anglophone areas. In 1998 they numbered about 182,000.

## NORFOLK ISLANDERS

A western Pacific island people, descended from the PITCAIRN ISLANDERS. In 1856 the entire population of Pitcairn Island was persuaded to migrate to Norfolk Island, formerly a notoriously brutal penal colony. The ancestors of today's Pitcairn Islanders returned, but most stayed. They were promised self-government, as eugenicists in Britain felt their unique culture deserved preservation. It is noted for its strict morality and its patois based on 18th-century English (the people are descended from the male mutineers from HMS *Bounty* and female Tahitians). In 1896, however, on the pretext that by allowing immigration the Norfolk Islanders were abandoning their culture, their self-government was revoked by AUSTRALIAN authorities. Subsequent Australian influences have undermined the culture of the island to the extent that it was felt necessary to add it to the school curriculum to save it from extinction. Australian political control is, as with its cultural domination, deeply resented.

Some degree of self-government was restored in 1979, but not all that was promised. The Norfolk Islanders have made several appeals to the United Nations over this issue, declaring themselves an indigenous people in 1994, with a distinct culture, language, customs and traditions, and therefore having the right to choose their own destiny. These claims remain unrecognized by the Australian government, which has thus far prevented the UN General Assembly from discussing them. In 2003 the Norfolk Islanders numbered about 1800.

## NORTHERN WEI

See TOBA-WEI.

## NUNG

A people of north Vietnam who now number around 800,000. There are estimated to be more than 120,000 in China and smaller numbers in Laos and Burma. They speak Nung, which is part of the TAI language group. The Nung are an agricultural, village-based people who typically live in thatched houses raised on stilts. They use slash-and-burn techniques to cultivate the valleys and terraces on hillsides producing chiefly rice and corn; they also exploit the upland forests. Cash crops are grown or harvested. They have a strong textile, handicraft and folk-culture tradition and in dress they favour the colour indigo, associated with loyalty and fidelity. Their religion centres mainly on ancestor worship but also includes an eclectic mix of beliefs in spirits and deities, including the Buddhist Kuan-yin,

*"* Before our eyes in the closing stages of the 20th century a bloodless genocide is happening ... The 'old' Norfolk Islanders are dying out, the young are being taught by Australian schoolteachers to view themselves as Australians. But they are not ... They are the descendants of a proud and strong people who were given an island by the British Crown 140 years ago. *"*

Norfolk Island website, 1996

and Confucian thought. The minority Nung feared the communist CHINESE revolution in 1949 and migrated to Indo-China, where they were recruited by the French, later the Americans, to fight local communist-nationalist movements. Towards the end of the 20th century some became 'Boat People' in an attempt to find sanctuary in neighbouring countries and further abroad.

## NYUNGAR

An Australian ABORIGINAL PEOPLE of the Perth area of Western Australia. Nomadic hunters and gatherers, they speak a Pama-Nyungan language. A relatively large people, they resisted the first European incursions under their leader Yagan in 1833. In reply, settlers began a war of extermination, massacring an entire clan at Pinjarra in 1834 and beheading Yagan. His head went on public display in Britain before being donated to a Liverpool museum, which had it buried in a pauper's grave in 1968. In 1997 a delegation of Nyungar went to Liverpool to get the head repatriated. They eventually succeeded, but there was considerable internal acrimony over the best place to bury it.

In 1991 the Nyungar began an annual ceremony to commemorate the Pinjarra massacre, intended to promote inter-communal reconciliation. This has had some success, although racists repeatedly behead a statue erected in Yagan's honour. The Nyungar have also campaigned to protect their sacred places, not least a stretch of the Swan River near Perth, where *warghuls*, energy lines depicted as snakes, reside. In the 1990s they defeated plans to develop the site. Their language recently became extinct, although about 8000 claimed knowledge of a few phrases in 2000.

## OKINAWANS

A native people of the largest of the Ryukyu islands in the East China Sea. Descended from settlers from Southeast Asia and Japan, possibly as early as 30,000 BC, they speak a language related to Japanese. An agricultural and maritime economy developed, and Okinawans traded with the Chinese as early as the 7th cen-

tury AD. Between the 14th and 19th centuries Okinawa was an independent kingdom alternating between JAPANESE and CHINESE domination. Okinawan traders are credited with introducing gunpowder into Japan. In 1879 the Japanese invaded the island; the last king, Tai Sho, was exiled to Tokyo and Okinawa finally became a prefecture of Japan.

Okinawans have a distinct culture, rich in its *eisa* (performing folk art) and art, and a cuisine strongly influenced by Japan. Karate originated in Okinawa. The traditional Okinawan animistic and shamanistic religion, influenced by Shinto, Buddhist and Taoist beliefs, remains strong.

In 1945 US forces stormed Okinawa, a process in which 100,000 (or one-third of the population) died, and until 1972, when it was returned to Japanese sovereignty, it was administered by the USA. Okinawans were allowed to elect their own administration only in 1966. The USA retains several military bases, and this is a source of resentment to Okinawans, especially the descendants of those who once owned the land. There is also resentment of the Japanese government, which is perceived as having failed to protect Okinawan interests from the USA. There is a considerable movement for greater home rule. In 1993 Okinawans numbered over 1.2 million.

## ONABASULU

A PAPUAN people of South Highlands province, Papua New Guinea. Once reputed to be cannibals, they are slash-and-burn farmers on the mountain slopes of their homeland. Longhouse dwellers, they speak a Central and South New Guinea language. They have been noted, among others, for the range of insects they exploit as a food source. More recently they have been struggling to adapt to the changes being introduced by recent oil extraction. In 1998 they numbered about 800.

## ORANG ASLI

The native peoples of the Malay Peninsula. They comprise three groups of peoples: the Jakun, who speak an archaic MALAY language, and the SEMANG and Senoi, who speak various Mon-

> " More than half of the Okinawans dislike Americans, because of their offensive behaviour. "
>
> The Guardian, 1973

Khmer languages. Numbering around 20,000 in the late 20th century, the Jakun are the most numerous of the three groups. The Jakun are a settled farming people, who cultivate rice, sweet potatoes and millet, but also harvest and trade forest products and hunt using blowpipes and poison darts.

The main sub-groups of the Jakun are the Binduanda, Mantera, Orang Kanak, Orang Laut and Orang Ulut. Jakun religion is essentially polytheistic and has an important place for ancestor worship. The Jakun believe that humans have multiple souls; those that inhabit the right side of the body go to an afterlife in the spirit realm but those of the left hand side remain in a restless existence on earth.

The Senoi, numbering around 18,000 in the late 20th century, have a similar way of life to the Jakun. As well as in the Malayan peninsula, they live in scattered groups along the northern coast of Sumatra in Indonesia. The Semang are a NEGRITO people, numbering less than 4000 in the late 20th century, and still maintain a hunting, fishing and gathering way of life, without permanent settlements. The Semang religion is shamanistic. All three peoples are threatened by assimilation to the more numerous Malay peoples and by deforestation, which is destroying their traditional way of life.

## PADZI

See SOLORESE.

## PAI or Bai or Min Chia or Po

A TAI people of the area between the upper Yangtze River and the base of Lake Erhai in Yunnan province in southern China. They number some 1.6 million, comprising an officially recognized national minority. Around 80% live in the Dali Bai Autonomous Prefecture (founded in November 1956) in the Yunnan province, while the remainder are distributed among the provinces of Sichuan, Bijie, Guizhou and Xichang. The language spoken by the Pai people incorporates many Chinese words because of the long contact with the HAN people, but is in fact a sub-dialect of the YI language that stems from the Tibetan-Burmese branch of the Chinese-Tibetan family. Archaeological evidence dates the origins of the Pai to the Neolithic period. Pai religious beliefs are a syncretic blend of Bud-

Pai

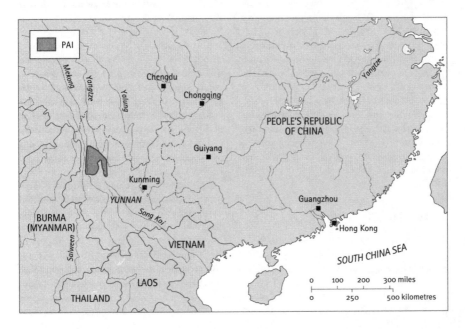

dhism, Taoism and the veneration of local spirits and deities.

The Pai developed close ties with the Han people during the times of the Qin (221–207 BC) and the Han (206 BC–AD 220) dynasties. The close ties with the Han brought many benefits to their main occupation as agriculturalists, and during the Sui (AD 581–618) and Tang (618–907) dynasties agricultural production rose to similar levels to those of the more advanced central regions of China.

During the Tang dynasty the Pai upper classes established close links with the Tang court, and with their backing established the Nanzhao kingdom, whose capital was at Dali. The Nanzhao kingdom lasted for over 300 years, until the MONGOLS conquered it in the 13th century, whereupon the Yuan dynasty established rule. Dali, under the Yuan dynasty, was designated a prefecture of Yunnan province of southwest China. Privileges and official positions were offered to the lords of Dali in order for the Yuan to gain further control over the Pai, resulting in the replacement of the feudal system by the landlord system. However, during the Ming dynasty (1368–1644) the lords' privileges and positions were revoked, and court officials took control of the region, increasing agricultural activity and developing the landlord economy. The Qing dynasty (1644–1911) further suppressed the Pai by appointing more court officials to rule over them. During the mid-1800s, after a number of uprisings against the Qing, the Pai formed the Dali Administration, a political movement promoting their interests.

Economic and social reforms have transformed the Pai region since the communist revolution in 1949, resulting in increased agricultural production and trade. In November 1956 the aforementioned Dali Bai Autonomous Prefecture was founded.

## PAINTED POTTERY CULTURE

See YANGSHAO CULTURE.

## PALAUANS

The native people of the western Pacific island group of Palau. At the edge of Oceania, they are of combined MELANESIAN, FILIPINO and POLYNESIAN descent, and speak a Malayo-Polynesian language. They are farmers and fishers and are mostly Christian, though traditional beliefs still persist. They came under SPANISH rule in the 16th century, were sold to Germany in 1899, occupied by Japan in 1914, and became a US Trust Territory in 1947. All these influences can be seen in their culture, for example in the JAPANESE and American influence in their cuisine. Independence was achieved in 1994, but only after considerable difficulty. The US government demanded a compact of free association, exchanging aid for bases, but could not gain the two-thirds majority required in a referendum. Only after changing the constitution to allow a simple majority vote was it accepted. Many Palauans strongly oppose the continued US presence. There is also growing resentment at a large Asian minority, who comprised 28% of the population of over 19,000 in 2003.

## PALAUNG

An indigenous BURMESE people, best known for their long history of tea production, who live in Burma, the Yunnan province of southwest China, and Thailand. They are also known as Pale, Rama, Ta'ang, Pulei, Shwe, Palay, Palong or Bulai. They live closely with the SHAN peoples and are organized largely in village communities with headmen. The Palaung language is from the Mon-Khmer branch of the AUSTRO-ASIATIC family of languages, and the population of the Palaung is estimated at approximately 240,000. Palaung religious beliefs are a mixture of Shan Buddhism (a form of Theravada Buddhism), folk beliefs and animism. According to Palaung folklore, they are descended from an angel called Roi Ngoen.

During BRITISH colonial rule in the 19th century the Palaung carried significant political power, enough to control the Tawnpeng Kingdom within Burma. However, with the end of colonial rule in 1948, and as a consequence of the Burmese military government, all land ownership rights of the Palaung have been revoked. For about the last 40 years the Palaung State Liberation Army (PSLA) has staged militant resistance against the government. Within Thailand the Palaung are among the newest ethnic groups. Many now live as refugees in Thailand to escape persecution in Burma.

## PALAWA

See TASMANIANS.

## PAPUANS

A linguistic and ethnic group of peoples of Papua New Guinea and the Indonesian province of Irian Jaya (which between them comprise the island of New Guinea), making up 80% of the island's population. They speak mostly trans-New Guinea languages and occupy the interior and south of the island. Thus many are also NEW GUINEA HIGHLANDERS.

Generally farmers and fishers living in small villages, Papuans are mostly Christian, although traditional beliefs remain strong and the fear of sorcery is widespread. They were colonized in the east by Britain, in the west by the Netherlands and in the northeast by Germany. The German and British colonies passed to Australian administration, leaving the Papuans divided between Indonesia and Papua New Guinea, with little in common in politics.

In Bougainville, Papua New Guinea, a separatist rebellion in the 1980s left 20,000 dead. Separatists in Irian Jaya launched a rebellion in the 1960s and claim INDONESIAN security forces have killed 800,000 since then. They are, however, deeply divided in their aims for an independent state. Their numbers are uncertain.

## PEI WEI

See TOBA-WEI.

## PEKING MAN

The name first given to the fossilized remains of a group of 40 hominid individuals who became the defining type specimens of the species of *homo erectus* known as *Sinathropus pekinensis* (Peking Chinese Man).

After two years of excavation, fossils were unearthed in 1929 in a cave in Dragon Bone Hill, near the town Zhoukoudian in the Fanshan district of Beijing (Peking), China, by Canadian anatomy professor David Black. Estimates vary, but it is thought that the fossils date to between 200,000 and 700,000 years ago, in the Palaeolithic period.

Peking Man is the earliest evidence of human habitation in China, although it postdates JAVA MAN. According to skeletal evidence the life-span of Peking Man was very short; 68% died around the age of 14 years old, while less than 4.5% reached or surpassed the age of 50. Peking Man is the earliest human species that is known to have used fire. During World War II it was feared that the fossils would be destroyed, and as a result they were shipped to the USA. They never arrived, however, and they remain missing. Renewed excavations at the same site in 1958 found new specimens.

Peking Man is seen as the ancestor of the modern Chinese by (especially Chinese) anthropologists who favour the multi-regional theory of human evolution, and as an evolutionary dead end by supporters of the single-origin or 'out-of-Africa' theory, which is almost universally accepted by evolutionary anthropologists in the rest of the world.

## PINTUPI-LURITJA

An Australian ABORIGINAL PEOPLE of the Papunya settlement, Northern Territory, and Balgo Hills, Western Australia. Nomadic hunters and gatherers, they speak a Pama-Nyungan language. Their culture originated in the Gibson Desert, but most were rounded up and forced to settle by the federal government in 1962. A group of about 20, however, evaded capture until 1984, making them one of the last groups to be settled. Cultural extinction seemed to be their inevitable fate, but they have a strong tradition of body, shield and spear-thrower painting, and were able to adapt their water-dreaming painting to Western media, such as canvas, and market it commercially. This has received national acclaim and provided a modicum of prosperity. Some have been able to return to their traditional lands, over part of which they gained title in 2003. In 1986 they numbered about 1000.

**"**An unsewered, undrained, garbage-strewn death camp in all but name.**"**

Description of a Pintupi-Luritja settlement in 2000

*p*

## PIPEL BILONG NAMBIS

A loosely connected group of peoples of the New Guinea coastal areas. Their name means 'peoples of the coast', and they share some broad cultural and political aims. They are in general more urban, wage-earning and Westernized than NEW GUINEA HIGHLANDERS, whom they see as backward, if not savage. The limits to their common views can be seen in the province of Irian Jaya, where there is a strong movement for independence from Indonesia. Unlike New Guinea Highlanders, the lowlanders cannot develop a single political movement or a single vision of a independent West Papua. They have formed the Papua Council, but even this umbrella group has difficulty holding together all the groups struggling for independence. In 1997 they numbered over 3.5 million. (See also PAPUANS.)

## PITCAIRN ISLANDERS

The people of Pitcairn Island, an isolated South Pacific island of just 5 sq. km / 2 sq. miles. The first settlers were POLYNESIANS, who appear to have abandoned the island in the 15th century. The modern population is descended from mutineers from HMS *Bounty* and their TAHITIAN wives in 1790. Nine mutineers, six Tahitian men, twelve women and a child landed. They quarrelled, however, and by 1808, when they were found by an American whaler, only one mutineer, 10 women and 23 children survived. They were resettled on Tahiti in 1831, but 65 disliked their new lives and returned.

The island was made a BRITISH colony in 1838. The inhabitants subsisted on agriculture, fishing and trading with passing ships. In 1856 overpopulation threatened and some were resettled to become NORFOLK ISLANDERS. They speak a version of English, with a local idiom, accent and vocabulary, and since 1887 have been Seventh Day Adventists. They eat no pork or fish without scales and abstain from alcohol.

The population reached a maximum of 223 in 1937, but since then has dwindled, with many migrating to New Zealand. Indeed, absentee landowners are a problem. In 2003 the Pitcairn Islanders numbered 44, and the population could soon fall below a viable level. While they are largely self-sufficient in food, the British government has ended subsidies, and essential imports such as energy are difficult to finance. The island could soon be abandoned, or even handed over to French administration.

In 2003 sex offence allegations against 13 men, the bulk of the island's male population, were followed by some guilty verdicts, threatening to undermine the colony.

## PITJANTJARA or Bidjandjara

An Australian ABORIGINAL PEOPLE of South Australia, centred on Uluru (Ayers Rock) and numbered among the ANAGU. Traditionally hunters and gatherers who speak about 50 dialects of a Pama-Nyungan language, they were dispossessed of their land in the 19th century, and their sacred site of Uluru, which they believe has great magical properties, became a tourist attraction. Mining operations further threatened their sacred sites and way of life.

In 1981, however, they gained title to 160,000 sq. km / 62,000 sq. miles of their former lands, including Uluru. This gave them control of public access to the site and some degree of control over mining companies.

Unfortunately the South Australian Supreme Court overturned some of these powers, and while there have been steps to include them in federal law, in 2004 the Pitjantjara were still locked in acrimonious disputes with the state government over land rights. In 1995 there were about 3000 speakers of the Pitjantjara languages.

## PO

See PAI.

## POHNPEIAN

The native people of the northwestern Pacific island group of Pohnpei, now part of the Federated States of Micronesia. The island was settled by MICRONESIANS after 1500 BC, and the Pohnpeian were farmers and fishers who spoke a Malayo-Polynesian language. Culturally similar to other members of the Federated States, they are noted as weavers of fine *pandanus* mats. Once ruled by tyrants, their particularly beautiful

Polynesians

*The Polynesians made some of the greatest of all voyages of exploration and colonization, settling over a huge area of the Pacific.*

island contains the fortress of Nan Madol, and it is unclear how they transported the massive masonry blocks to the site. Traditional values, customs and roles still prevail, though with a young population, nearly half being under 15 years old, there is a great demand for education. In 1993 they numbered 27,700.

## POLYNESIANS

A cultural, ethnic and linguistic group of peoples who colonized vast stretches of the central and southern Pacific. Probably they originated in Asia, and they began expanding, seemingly from Samoa, around 1000 BC, showing a mastery of shipbuilding, sailing and navigation. They were farmers and fishers, and as many of the islands they settled lacked the necessary indigenous plant and animal species to support them, they imported most of the food plants and animals they needed. Culturally they proved conservative, with groups separated by generations still remaining very similar. They had a considerable mythology and worshipped a wide array of gods that needed appeasing. Theirs was a highly stratified society, with chiefs held to be descended

from gods, and with transgressions against their laws often resulting in the severest punishments, reputedly including human sacrifice and (in a few cases) cannibalism. They also held firmly to the concept of *tapu* (taboo), in which a variety of actions was prohibited, and while most Polynesians are now Christian, these have largely been incorporated into their new beliefs. They believed firmly in the supernatural, and had a culture rich in oral history, music, dance and tattooing. Warfare among groups was common.

During the 19th century they were colonized by a number of Western powers, while their population plummeted because of European diseases. The Polynesians speak languages of the Malayo-Polynesian sub-group of the AUSTRONESIAN language family, and their total population today is uncertain. They are currently divided among a number of independent states and dependencies of New Zealand, France, the USA and Chile. They are found in numerous islands and island groups, and include therefore EASTER ISLANDERS, TONGANS, Society Islanders (including TAHITIANS), MARQUESANS, HAWAIIANS and SAMOANS. The MAORI of New Zealand are also Polynesians.

# PUNAN

See DAYAK.

## PUYI or Jui

A TAI-speaking hill people of Guizhou province in southern China. To their east live a closely related Tai people, the TUNG. In the 1990s the Puyi numbered around 2.65 million and the Tung around 2.62 million. As a result of long contact with the CHINESE the Puyi have become very Sinicized in their culture. Traditional beliefs in ancestral spirits survive but some Puyi are now Buddhist or Christian.

## PYU

A people who thrived between the 1st or 2nd and 9th centuries AD in Burma. Some of the earliest BURMESE inscriptions, from around AD 500, allude to them. Records show that the Pyu were among the first settlers in Burma, having migrated from the Tibetan plateau. They spoke a Tibeto-Burman language and were strongly Theravada Buddhist. In Burma the Pyu established the kingdoms of Tagaung, Halingyi, Beikthano, Thayekhittaya (Srikestra) and Hanlin. In the 7th century the capital of the Pyu kingdom was Hanlin; the previous capital, Thayekhittaya, had been sacked and burned by the TAI Nanzhao kingdom of modern Yunnan, southwest China. The capital was moved again to Halingyi in the early 9th century, but in 832 Halingyi was also sacked by the Nanzhao kingdom, leading to the fall of the Pyu and allowing the Mien (BURMESE) peoples to migrate to the central plains. At the height of Pyu power they probably claimed sovereignty over some 18 individual kingdoms. They traded with India and China and even came into contact with the ROMANS between AD 97 and 121.

## RAKHINES or Arakanese

The majority population of the region of Arakan, in modern Burma, and the adjacent area of Bangladesh. Around 2 million Rhakines live in Burma today, comprising 4% of the total population of that country. Rhakines are an ethnically mixed people, descended mainly from the PYU, but also including ARAB and MONGOL elements. They are ethnically related to the CHAKMA and speak a Tibeto-Burmese language generally regarded as a dialect of BURMESE. The Rakhine language is also spoken by the Marma. 'Rakhine' is thought to be derived from Sanskrit *rasha* or Pali *rakssha*, meaning 'monster', possibly because they practised cannibalism before conversion to Buddhism in the 5th century BC.

According to their own legendary traditions, the Rhakines originated in the 3rd millennium BC, but their reliable recorded history begins only after their conversion to Buddhism. Between the 4th and late 18th centuries AD Arakan was generally independent. Arabs migrated into the region during the 7th century, the Mongols invaded in the 13th century and the Portuguese arrived in the 15th century, but it was not until the conquest of the region by Burma in 1784 that Arakan's autonomy was finally lost. Thereafter, as part of Burma, the Rakhines became subject to BRITISH rule, then to JAPANESE domination (1941–5) before the establishment of Burmese independence in 1948.

**Rakhines**

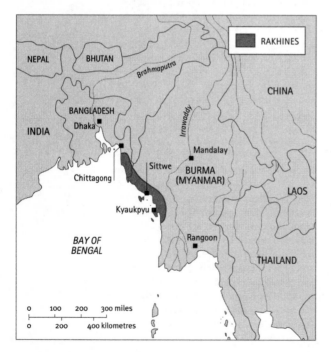

Today the population of Arakan is divided between the majority Rakhines, who are Buddhist, and the Rohingyas, who are Muslims. Over the course of the last 30 years, and in particular in 1991–2, there has been a great deal of tension between these groups, and the Rohingyas have been subject to local and government-backed oppression. Rhakines regard Rohingyas as interlopers who have no right to live in Arakan.

Large numbers of Rohingyas (perhaps as many as 1.5 million) have fled to other countries, principally Bangladesh, and many desire the creation of an independent Muslim state. Although they have supported the present military government in its oppression of the Rohingyas, the Rakhines have themselves been subjected to forced labour and resettlement and many fear assimilation by the Burmese, to whom they are, in many ways, so similar.

## RAMINDJERI

An Australian ABORIGINAL PEOPLE of the Victor Harbour area, South Australia. Living in a fertile area with reliable water supplies, they were sedentary hunters, gatherers and fishers who spoke a Pama-Nyungan language.

Early relations with Europeans were cordial, and whalers employed them as whale spotters and harpooners. But relations soured as they were dispossessed of their lands and drastically reduced by epidemics in the 1830s.They were perhaps saved from total extinction by the Rev. George Taplin, who was appointed to oversee and protect them. He built the first church for Aboriginal peoples.

Survival, however, was bought at the price of the almost complete destruction of their traditional culture. They did, fortunately, manage to retain their identity as a people, and agitated for redress. As a result, in the 1980s academics were trying to revive their extinct language. Kondali, a mosaic whale, was constructed on Kleinings Hill overlooking Victor Harbour to symbolize the reconciliation process.

Hindmarsh Island was returned to them in 1999, perhaps the only land recovered by ABORIGINAL PEOPLES without recourse to the courts. Their numbers today are uncertain.

## RAPA NUI

See EASTER ISLANDERS.

## RAROTONGANS or Cook Islanders

The people of the Cook Islands, a South Pacific island group. Local tradition has it that the MAORI migrated to New Zealand from here. Their culture is closely related to that of the Maori, although they have their own strong arts, crafts and dance traditions. Their traditional religion, including 71 gods and 12 heavens, has disappeared because of the activities of missionaries, but most of the traditional culture remains strong.

A British protectorate from 1888, the islands were administered by New Zealand in 1901 and became self-governing, in free association with New Zealand, in 1965. They became highly concerned in 1995 about the dangers posed by French nuclear testing in the Pacific, and sent a traditional voyaging canoe, the *Te-Au-O-Tonga*, on a 10,000-km / 6000-mile voyage through the French zone around Mururoa atoll to protest against the tests. In 2000 they numbered over 20,000.

## RED KAREN

See KAYAH.

## RED TAI

See TAI.

## RORO

A native people of Central province, Papua New Guinea. Farmers and fishers, they speak an AUSTRONESIAN language.

Their culture is noted for its music, dance, chant and body paint. Traditional beliefs remain strong; for example they reputedly believe that relatives killed unexpectedly will haunt them, and only when the spirit reaches the proper 'place of the dead' will it become a source of help. In 1991 the Roro numbered about 8000.

# RUZHEN or Juchen

A former pastoralist people from eastern Siberia. They spoke a now extinct Tungistic language closely related to MANCHU. In 1124 the Ruzhen conquered the KHITAN state of Liao in northern China and founded the Jin dynasty. Although they were a minority among their mainly HAN Chinese subjects, the Ruzhen maintained their identity by using their own alphabet in official documents and banning CHINESE language, clothing and customs. They disappeared after they were conquered by the MONGOLS in 1234.

# SAI

See LI.

# SAMAL

See BAJAU.

# SAMOANS

The native people of Samoa, a central Pacific island group now divided into two polities. It was originally settled by Polynesians by around 1000 BC. The Samoans established a farming and fishing economy and speak a Polynesian language. Their traditional culture was rich in dance, song, music and tattooing, and marked by a strict code of etiquette and keen sense of propriety. In the 19th century they became notably devout Christians, although they incorporated some traditional beliefs.

Politically fragmented between chiefdoms, they suffered severely when US, British and German interests, vying for influence, armed and advised chiefs they intended to promote as puppets. Supremacy wars raged from 1848, and strife ended only when in 1899 it was agreed to partition the islands between Germany and the USA. In German western Samoa a resistance organization, Mau a Pule, was organized in 1908, and still operated after New Zealand took over administration in 1914. Western Samoa became an independent state in 1964, although universal suffrage was introduced only in 1990, and only chiefs could stand for parliament. The US Navy administered American Samoa until

> *"Very genteel, very songful, very agreeable, very good-looking, chronically spoiling for a fight. "*
>
> Robert Louis Stevenson on the Samoans, 1890

1951, and only chiefs were allowed to vote for an elected governor in 1978. American Samoans became US nationals, but not citizens, and were largely ignored until the 1960s, when a huge drive to modernize the islands began: traditional culture was brushed aside in a wave of Americanization. It survived better in Western Samoa, where traditional songs are still favoured by all ages. In 2003 there were over 68,000 American Samoans and over 178,000 Western Samoans.

# SEA GYPSIES

See BAJAU.

# SEMANG

A people belonging to the ORANG ASLI, or aboriginal groups of Malaysia. They are an indigenous NEGRITO tribal people with populations in the Malay Peninsula. The Semang are among the oldest extant ethnicity in the world today; archaeological evidence dates their heritage to around 30,000 years ago, in the Palaeolithic era. They live as nomadic peoples, traditionally hunter-gatherers, in self-governed tribes and sub-tribes. They use blowpipes to hunt small game. The total population of the Semang is estimated to be approximately 4000–5000. Their language, a dying one, is mostly AUSTRO-ASIATIC, a branch of the Mon-Khmer languages. The name 'Semang' is derived from KHMER, meaning 'debt slave', as in the 19th century the MALAY enslaved many Semang. In religion, the Semang practise magic, shamanism and animism. The Semang still live a traditional life, sheltering in caves and under rocks and leaf-covered overhangs. They are among those peoples most threatened by modern changes in Southeast Asia, such as loss of habitat to logging and agriculture.

# SENOI

See ORANG ASLI.

# SHAN or Shan Tai

The largest ethnic-minority BURMESE people. Their population is between 4 and 4.9 million people, or 10% of the total population. They populate the Shan state of Burma and also live in Thailand, Laos, China, India and northwest Vietnam. Most Shan are Buddhist, although some are Hindu, Muslim or Christian. The Shan language is monosyllabic and belongs to the southwest TAI family that also utilizes words from the Burmese language. Traditional Shan society is ordered into two main classes: commoners (mainly farmers) and nobility. The latter traditionally provided their rulers.

The history of the Shan people is a long and chequered one. Academic speculations place the Shan possibly in the Yunnan province of China 2000 years ago. Between AD 650 and 1253 the Shan were part of the Nanzhao kingdom, known as the Six Tai United States, which included Yunnan and parts of Thailand, Laos and Burma. The Tai peoples of Nanzhao began migrating around the 8th century AD to what is now the Shan state within present-day Burma and other places within the region, such as India. A second wave of migration from the Nanzhao kingdom was precipitated by its conquest by the MONGOLS around 1253. It was during these migrations that the TAI acquired their name. As a result of encounters with the KHMER peoples the Tai became known as the Syam (Siam), which is taken from the Sanskrit word *syana* meaning 'golden' or 'swarthy' (referring to the Tais' skin complexion). In Burma the name Syam became corrupted into Shan. Many Shan still refer to themselves as 'Tai'.

The Shan ruled over their own kingdom, known as the Golden Kingdom, largely without opposition for approximately 600 years. At its peak the Golden Kingdom dominated Burma, and it remained powerful until the 19th century.

The BRITISH arrived in Burma in 1885 and annexed the Golden Kingdom in 1887–9. Under British rule the Shan states still enjoyed great autonomy, with the rulers of the now 30 or so separate states governed by hereditary Shan chieftains. In 1922 most of the separated states joined the Federated Shan State, and as a result enjoyed still greater autonomy.

In 1962 Prime Minister U Nu of Burma was overthrown in a military coup, staged partly for fear that the Shan and other ethnic groups would formally withdraw from Burma. In 1974

the Shan lost most of their autonomy through the Burmese constitution. In 1990 the Shan formed the Shan Nationalistic League of Democracy (SNLD), which won the second-largest number of seats in a national election. However, the military government refused to recognize the poll and as a result harassed many of the SNLD's members.

Over the past 40–50 years there have been a number of Shan resistance movements, some militant, directed towards the government. One of the government's responses has been the forced mass relocation and observation of entire villages in attempts to crush resistance; the largest to date was in 1996–7. Many of the relocated Shan villagers still have not returned to their village homes, and over 50% of these are estimated to have fled to Thailand.

## SHAN BAO

See TAIWANESE ABORIGINALS.

## SIAMESE

See THAIS.

S

Shan

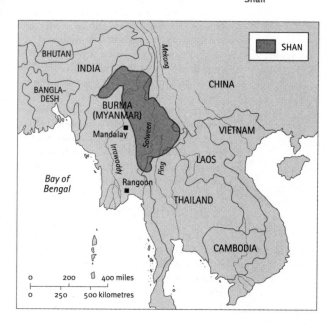

# SIKANESE or Sika

An AUSTRONESIAN people of the Maumere region of Flores in Indonesia's Lesser Sunda Islands. The Sikanese speak a language related to SOLORESE. Their population numbered around 180,000 in the late 20th century. The Sikanese practise shifting slash-and-burn agriculture, cultivating dry rice, maize and cassava. The majority are Roman Catholics, but some elements of traditional religious practices survive; for example, villages are situated around offering stones.

# SIMBU or Chimbu

A PAPUAN people of Simbu province in the Eastern Highlands of Papua New Guinea. Mainly subsistence farmers, they cultivate sweet potatoes and breed pigs and, in recent years, have grown coffee as a cash crop. They speak Chimbu, an East New Guinea Highlands language.

The Simbu had a complex ceremonial system based on the ritual exchange of pigs, shells and feathers. Their system of land allocation within clans ensures that everybody has access to agricultural, forest and forage land, and they will invite relatives to join them to redistribute people to resources as needed.

Traditional religious beliefs have been undermined by the activities of Christian missionaries since their first contacts with Europeans in the 1930s. The Simbu still have a strong belief in witchcraft, however; for example, they are afraid to let blood fall on swampy ground for fear the spirit, or *dingan*, will cause illness. Likewise they are careful to make offerings to ancestors lest their ghosts become angered. Accusations of sorcery are a common cause of disputes between groups. Simbu society remains egalitarian and has no hereditary positions of authority. In 1994 the Simbu numbered about 80,000.

# SINGAPOREANS

The people of the independent city-state of Singapore and the surrounding 59 islets. The Singaporean population of around 4.2 million is almost entirely of immigrant origin, approximately 75% ethnic CHINESE, 14% MALAY, 7.6% INDIAN, and 1.4% others. Reflecting their make-up, the Singaporeans speak four official languages: Mandarin Chinese, Malay, Tamil and English. Their religions are also diverse and include Buddhism, Islam, Hinduism, Confucianism and Christianity. Indeed, because of its ability to display many diverse Asian cultures in a unified manner, Singapore has been dubbed 'Instant Asia'. The Singaporeans are known as a harmonious nation with very little evidence of unrest internally or externally. However, the promotion of Mandarin over other languages, notably in the government's 1996 'Speak Mandarin' campaign, has led to protests by the country's ethnic minorities.

Singapore Island was once known as Tumasik and was inhabited by fishermen and pirates. In the early 13th century it was the trade capital of the Srivijaya empire, until in the 14th century it was taken by the JAVANESE Majapahit Kingdom from the Malay archipelago. A Malay legend states that Singapore gained its name when a Sumatran prince came across a lion – a symbol of good fortune – on Tumasik (from the Javenese *tasek*, meaning 'sea'). He named the island Singapore meaning 'Lion City'.

Between the 15th and 17th centuries Singapore came under the rule of the Malacca empire, the French and the Dutch. In 1819, on the intervention of Sir Stamford Raffles (1781–1826), who recognized its strategic location, Singapore became part of the BRITISH empire – a centre for the spice trade and a major naval base.

Singapore's prosperity attracted migrants from across South and East Asia, especially from China. In 1941 Singapore was taken by the JAPANESE, but in 1946 after the British returned, it was made a Crown Colony.

In 1959 Singapore became autonomous, in 1963 it joined the Malay Federation, in 1965 it became an independent republic, and in 1971 the British withdrew completely. Since independence the Singaporeans have become one of the world's most prosperous people and very influential in the Association of South East Asian Nations. Singaporean governments, which have generally been authoritarian in nature, have encouraged economic individualism and social conformity in equal measure, an approach that seems to suit most Singaporeans.

## SO or So Makon or Kah So or Thro

A people who live along both banks of the Mekong River in Thailand and Laos. They are bilingual, speaking a Mon-Khmer language for most purposes and Lao for social occasions. The word *so* means 'elder brother' in Lao-Thai. There are approximately 55,000 So in Thailand and 102,000 (2.1% of the population) in Laos. Around 70% of So adhere to Theravada Buddhism, although many also practise animism and ancestor worship. It is thought that MON or KHMER tribes were the original ancestors of the So. Around 400 years ago the So were forced from their land by the THAI, after which they settled in their present environment.

## SOLOMON ISLANDERS

The native people of the Solomon Islands, a western Pacific island group. Many of the islands were settled by MELANESIANS around 1000 BC, and the outer islands were later settled by POLYNESIANS. The islands became politically fragmented, with over 70 Malayo-Polynesian languages spoken. The Solomon Islanders were traditionally farmers, fishers and foresters, and most became Christian in the 19th century. Colonized successively by Spain, Germany and Britain, they became independent in 1978.

The biggest problem in the islands has been ethnic tensions exacerbated by economic decline. In 1998 these problems came to a head when resentment on the largest island, Guadalcanal, against settlers from other islands exploded into violence, killing hundreds. As a result the economy collapsed and armed gangs brought anarchy. A peace deal in 2000 failed to rein in the lawlessness, and the government had to appeal for an Australian security force to help stabilize the country. There are secessionist groups in the outer islands, and the Solomon Islands' survival as a nation is in doubt. In 2003 the Solomon Islanders numbered over 509,000.

## SOLORESE or Solor or Solot

An AUSTRONESIAN people of Indonesia's Lesser Sunda Islands (Solor, Adonara, Lomblen and Flores). The Solorese are divided into two groups, the Demon and the Padzi, who have different customs and religious beliefs. Solorese society is organized in clan lineages. Land is owned communally by each clan. The Solorese living in inland areas practise shifting slash-and-burn cultivation of maize and dry rice. Those who live on the coast are more likely to be engaged in trade or fishing. The Solorese originally practised a polytheistic religion but today most are Muslims, except for those who live on Flores, who are Roman Catholics. Their language is related to that of the SIKANESE.

## SOUTH PAPUANS

See ASMAT.

## STIENG or Stieng Budip or Bulo

An indigenous people belonging to the MONTAGNARD tribal peoples who inhabit the highlands and hill areas of eastern Cambodia and western Vietnam. Their language is also called Stieng, a language belonging to the Mon-Khmer language family, and some Stieng are also bilingual, speaking both Stieng and KHMER. There are approximately 3600 Stieng in Cambodia and 48,000–50,000 in Vietnam. The Stieng predominantly practise animism and idolatry, and some are Theravadan Buddhist; very few are Christian. The Stieng are classified as an official ethnic minority in Vietnam. They are closely related to the Jarai, BAHNAR, Koho, Rhade and the Mnong.

## STRAITS CHINESE

See BABA CHINESE.

## SUNDANESE

An AUSTRONESIAN-speaking people inhabiting the modern province of West Java in Indonesia (capital Bandung). INDIAN culture heavily influenced them by the first centuries AD, but they were later converted to Islam during the 15th and 16th centuries. During the 16th and 17th centuries, the region was the centre of the important commercial Sultanate of Bantam, which came to an end with their conquest by the DUTCH. During the 1880s, the Sundanese were at the centre of a mass peasant rebellion against the Dutch, and the area was later subjected to the forced cultivation of coffee. The Sundanese played an important role in the later INDONESIAN independence movement, and, due to their close association with the JAVANESE, have been far more willing than many within the country to identify themselves as Indonesians. In 1990 there were 27 million Sundanese.

## TABGATCH

See TOBA-WEI.

## TAGALOGS

An indigenous people of the Philippines. They were originally a river-centred culture, and their name derives from their own language bearing the same name (part of the AUSTRONESIAN family of languages) and means 'people who live by the river'. The Tagalogs have also been described as one of the most 'civilized' native peoples of the Philippines.

They practise a tribal religion based on their chief deity Bathara, which reveals an INDIAN influence on their religion, as *Bathura Guru* is Sanskrit for 'the highest Gods'. However, because of contact with the West, most notably after the SPANISH colonization in 1571, and the AMERICAN purchase of the Philippines in 1898, the Tagalogs have in part adopted Christianity. (Their religion has been described as folk Christianity.) Because of Western influence the Tagalog language has also incorporated many influences from Spanish and English.

The Tagalogs migrated from Malaya during the second wave of MALAY migration in the 10th–13th centuries AD. They originally settled in Manila, central and southern Luzon, and the islands of Milindero and Marinduque. These areas remain the most concentrated areas populated by the Tagalogs. Over time the Tagalogs have spread out from these centres throughout the Philippines, making them a national ethnic group, at 24 million the second-largest in the Philippines, constituting around 34% of the country's population. In 1937 the Philippine

> **"** Their natural levity hinders them from paying attention long to any one thing. **"**
>
> John Reinhold Foster on the Tahitians, 1778

president, Quezon, selected Tagalog as the national language. In 1958 it was renamed Pilipino, and in 1987, Filipino. There are currently over 20 million FILIPINOS who regard it as their first language. However, these speakers are not to be confused with the native Tagalogs.

## TAHITIANS

The native people of the island of Tahiti in the South Pacific, now part of French Polynesia, an overseas territory of France.

The island was settled by POLYNESIANS around 200 BC, who established a farming and fishing economy and spoke an AUSTRONESIAN language. They were politically fragmented between often warring chiefdoms, until mutineers from HMS *Bounty* in 1789, acting as mercenaries, helped to establish the Pomares dynasty, which in the early 19th century became the rulers of a unified state. By 1842 the FRENCH ruled through a figurehead queen, Pomares IV. Diseases had reduced the Tahitians in number, and missionaries had banned much of their traditional culture, including their religion, the practice of tattooing and dances deemed lascivious. Although they mostly Christian, Tahitians retained some traditional beliefs in, for example, ghosts, or *tupapau*.

In the late 20th century there was renewed interest in their traditional culture, and efforts were made to recover it. At annual *Tuirai* festivals, cultural competitions are held in which once banned dances are very popular. Other dances recount legends, while epic poetry is recited in rhythmic chants. Politically Tahitians have become more active. In 1995 the French resumed testing nuclear weapons on nearby Mururoa atoll, causing rioting on Tahiti and giving rise to an independence movement. Few, however, believe the French will ever meet such demands. In 2003 the Tahitians numbered about 150,000.

## TAI or Dai

A major group of Southeast Asian peoples united by their common Tai language family. The Tai are also related to the speakers of the Sino-Tibetan language family. There are currently approximately 76–80 million Tai people in Southeast Asia, with some 45–55 million in Thailand, 3 million in Laos, 2.8 million in Vietnam, 21.2 million in China and 3.8 million in Burma. Tai are also found in the Assam region of India and in Malaysia. Tai peoples include the THAIS (or Siamese), SHAN, PAI, PUYI, Lu, Nua, ZHUANG and the distinct Lao-Tai tribes of the Black Tai, White Tai, Red Tai and NUNG.

Despite the array of Tai peoples there are three main groups of Tai languages: Northern, Southwestern and Central. The most well-known Tai dialects are Thai and Lao. The vast majority of Tai adhere to Theravada Buddhism, although some practise a syncretic form with indigenous folk and spirit beliefs.

The Tai have a long history in Southeast Asia. Archaeological evidence suggests that the ancient Tai existed in the 6th century BC as valley-dwelling peoples and wet-rice growers, living in dispersed villages that were bound together by principalities and chiefdoms, in the southern part of the Yunnan province of China along the Yangtze River.

In the 6th century AD, with the help of the CHINESE, one Tai tribal ruler named Pi-lo-ko took control of the remaining five states, and thus a largely unified and influential Tai kingdom was established. The kingdom was called the Nanzhao kingdom, also known as 'The Six Tai United States'. The cordial relationship with China did not last long because the Chinese, fearing foreign invasion, attacked Nanzhao several times during the 6th century. Nanzhao was a significant regional power, frequently making war on its southern neighbours.

Such expeditions saw the first waves of Tai migration into Southeast Asia, which established the modern Tai peoples in their present homelands. A second wave of southern migration was forced in 1253 when the MONGOL emperor Kublai Khan conquered the Nanzhao kingdom. As the Tai migrated they encountered, and fought with, many different peoples, such as the KHMER.

It was as a result of encounters with the Khmer that the Tai became known as the Syam (Siam or Siamese), which is taken from the Sanskrit word *syana* meaning 'golden' or 'swarthy' (referring to the Tai skin complexion).

The main direction of Tai migration was south into what is now Thailand. In 1238 the Tai founded the kingdom of Sukhothai in northern Thailand, which expanded into Laos, Siam and Burma. Further migrations from the north strengthened the kingdom and led to the founding of a second Tai kingdom at Ayutthaya, north of present-day Bangkok, in 1315. The foundation of these kingdoms mark the beginnings of the development of the modern Thai identity. Tai peoples still living in their original homeland of Yunnan include the Puyi, Lu, Nua, Pai and Zhuang. For the modern history of the Tai people, see THAIS, SHAN, PAI and NUNG.

## TAIWANESE

The people of the East Asian island of Taiwan, technically the people of the Republic of China (not to be confused with the mainland People's Republic of China). Taiwan is also known as Ilha Formosa, meaning 'beautiful island' in Portuguese (so named by Admiral Andrade who in 1517 was the first European to see it), and Taian, which according to some Chinese scholars is a term that was used by TAIWANESE ABORIGINALS to mean 'foreigner'. The Taiwanese population of 22.3 million largely comprises three main groups: the Taiwanese Aboriginals (1.6–2%), the first wave of chinese immigrants (84%), and the second wave of Chinese immigrants (14%) after 1945. Mandarin Chinese is the official Taiwanese language, and Taiwanese is also widely spoken. Other forms of Chinese and indigenous dialects from the AUSTRONESIAN family are also spoken. The Taiwanese practise a number of religions, ranging from Chinese-influenced Buddhism and Taosim with Confucian ethics to Protestant and Roman Catholic Christianity.

The earliest settlers in Taiwan, besides the Taiwanese Aboriginals, were Chinese from the Hakka, Fujian and Guandong provinces. They arrived as early as the 7th century AD, with Chinese invasions beginning in AD 603. It is the Fujian language that is often referred to as 'Taiwanese'. In the 15th century the eastern Taiwanese came under the control of the JAPANESE. In 1590 the Portuguese occupied Taiwan and introduced Catholicism. The Dutch ruled 1623–60 and introduced Protestant Christianity. In the 18th century Taiwan became part of the

Chinese empire. In 1858 China was forced to sign the Treaty of Tianjin by their victorious British and French opponents in the Opium Wars. Consequently, many ports were opened up on the island, allowing an influx of Christian missionaries. After China's defeat in the Sino-Japanese War in 1895 Taiwan became a province of Japan, which it remained until returned to Chinese rule in 1945.

Following their defeat by the communists in the civil war on the Chinese mainland, the anti-communist Kuomintang (KMT) fled to Taiwan and established a government there in 1949. With US backing the KMT claimed to be the legitimate government of China and occupied the Chinese seat at the UN. The KMT government lost its seat in the UN in 1971, after the USA and other countries finally recognized the communist government of China. Its lack of international recognition notwithstanding, Taiwan has prospered economically and is still considered to be one of the East Asian 'tiger economies'. Despite over 50 years of *de facto* independence, the question of whether there is a Taiwanese national identity is complicated by the island's uncertain political status. Since 1971 a Taiwanese movement for formal independence has grown, but most Taiwanese remain wary, fearing that such a declaration might provoke a Chinese invasion. However, the Taiwanese have no enthusiasm for reunification with China either, even under the 'one state, two systems' scenario offered to Hong Kong.

## TAIWANESE ABORIGINALS
## or Yuanzhumin

The indigenous peoples of the island of Taiwan, where they live predominantly in the highlands and mountainous regions. They traditionally speak one of nine languages belonging to the AUSTRONESIAN family. Until 1994 they were also known as the Shan Bao (Mountain Compatriots), and from this date they have been known as the Yuanzhumin (Aboriginals). As a people they are ethnically and linguistically related to indigenous peoples of the Pacific islands. Aboriginals constitute approximately 1.6–2% of Taiwan's total population of 22.3 million, which is otherwise of CHINESE origin. The majority of

aboriginals now officially adhere to some form of Christianity. The Republic of China officially recognizes 16 separate aboriginal tribal lineages, while more than ten still remain unrecognized.

Archaeological evidence shows that the aboriginals' ancestors arrived in Taiwan at least 3000 years ago. However, the first written documentation of the aboriginals is dated from the 5th century, during the Chinese HAN period.

The Dutch occupation of Taiwan between 1623 and 1660 had a great impact on aboriginal lives. Upon arrival the Dutch befriended many tribal villages and succeeded in uniting many opposing tribes. The Dutch employed them as trade workers, to supply them with deerskins for foreign trading.

Under Chinese rule from 1660, the aboriginals were categorized into plains people and highland/mountain people, and were called savages. Despite the Chinese government's initial promise of recognizing aboriginal land right, taxes were imposed on the aboriginals. Large plainland areas were put up for rent and many aboriginals were forced to sell or move off. As part of a process of assimilation, many aboriginals took Chinese surnames and adopted Chinese religion and Confucian ethics.

By the early 19th century large groups of plains aboriginals, voluntarily or forcedly, had become mountain aboriginals. The Chinese also used the plains aboriginals as middlemen for trading with the mountain aboriginals. Little is known of the mountain aboriginals until the late 19th century when the Treaty of Tianjin (1858) ended the Opium Wars and Christian missionaries arrived in Taiwan and propagated their message to the aboriginals.

Traditional aboriginal life started to draw to a close in 1895 with JAPANESE occupation. The Japanese disallowed the aboriginals any form of contact with the rest of the islanders and even restrained them with military force. In 1910 a formal educational program began in an attempt to enforce a homogeneous Japanese identity on the Taiwanese. By the mid-20th century Japanese customs and culture had largely swamped the aboriginals.

Under the Nationalist Chinese government the aboriginals were renamed Shan Bao. The Chinese too made attempts to assimilate the aboriginals to their own culture. Japanese education was replaced with a formal Chinese version, and Mandarin was introduced as the principal Taiwanese language.

The first aboriginal-rights group emerged in 1984, and the name 'Yuanzhumin' replaced Shan Bao: this was officially recognized in 1994. In 1996 the council of aboriginal affairs was formed to represent the Yuanzhumin in government and to combat growing stigmatization, marginalization and discrimination.

Since the start of the 1990s the Taiwanese government has taken steps, such as introducing aboriginal history into the school curriculum and developing museums and cultural events specifically aimed at aboriginal identity, in an attempt to raise the aboriginal profile and show that the Taiwanese have a distinct identity. Today the aboriginals are officially recognized as an ethnic group.

## TANGU

A native people of Madang province, Papua New Guinea. Farmers, hunters and gatherers, they speak a Sepik-Ramu language. They believe that truth comes through dreams, and the revelation revealed to one of their number led to the practice of ritual sexual intercourse in cemeteries. They are also noted for their slit-gongs, by which they transmit messages. As every person and place has a unique call sign, vast amounts of information can be sent very quickly. In 1993 they numbered about 3000.

## TANNESE

A sub-group of the NI-VANUATU people, found on Tanna island, Vanuatu, in the South Pacific. They share the MELANESIAN culture of other Ni-Vanuatu, but with some variations. They are, for example, noted for their particularly strong *kava*, a soporific drink that is described as a non-addictive narcotic. Women are forbidden to use the drink or even approach during its consumption, once on pain of death. Reputedly cannibals in the past, they carved stone idols to propitiate evil spirits and believed in sorcery.

In the 19th century, when what was then the New Hebrides was ruled by the Anglo-French condominium, British Presbyterian missionaries became determined to end traditional beliefs and such practices as *kava* drinking, wearing penis sheaths, revenge killings and dances such as the spectacular *toka*, the clan alliance dance. The missionaries established a virtual theocracy, punishing absence from church, and they, alongside European plantation owners, became thoroughly detested for their arrogance.

The Tannese reaction, when it began to appear in the 1930s, was somewhat eccentric. They adopted, as did other peoples in the region, the 'cargo cult', but took it rather to extremes. The vast array and quantity of goods (or cargo) delivered to Europeans was seen as a product of magic, and several peoples sought to gain control of this magic for themselves. The Tannese had already shown signs of rejecting the teachings of missionaries in the 1930s, with reported sightings of 'John Frum', a spirit messiah come to lead them back to traditional ways. The arrival, however, of 100,000 US troops in 1941 (many of them AFRICAN AMERICANS) – with an endless supply of cargo – made a strong impression. The Tannese stopped attending church and working on the plantations en masse, killed imported cattle, burned money and began to prepare for the cargo that John Frum, who in their thinking had now been conflated with the US troops, would supply.

Wharfs and airstrips, complete with warehouses and replica radio masts, were built, and ceremonies were performed combining traditional dance with US military drill. Efforts to reason with them were rejected as the deceit of missionaries. The cargo cult eventually abated, but it is still practised in some areas, which is a source of embarrassment to those clinging to traditional beliefs or who have returned to Christianity, and is a sign of divisions among the Tannese. In 1989 they numbered nearly 20,000.

## TARGARI

An Australian ABORIGINAL PEOPLE of the Kennedy Range, Western Australia. Nomadic hunters and gatherers, they speak a Pama-Nyungan language. Acculturation pressures have been very strong, and in 1981 only six people remained who spoke their language, which was thus nearly extinct. They are near to losing their distinct identity.

## TASMANIANS

A former Australian ABORIGINAL PEOPLE, or more likely a group of peoples, of Tasmania. They were nomadic hunters and gatherers and spoke up to five dialects of two related languages, now all extinct. The Tasmanian languages are not clearly related to any other known languages although some linguists believe they have affinities with the Indo-Pacific languages spoken in New Guinea.

The Tasmanians occupied generally desirable lands, and the early inhabitants of the notorious British penal colony found them a considerable nuisance and occasionally massacred them. This casual murder culminated in 1830, when the colonial authorities offered a bounty on captured Tasmanians. This began the Black War, which saw 3000 armed men sweep the island to round them up. The Tasmanians eluded them, but European diseases had a far more disastrous impact. In 1835 the last few dozen known survivors were deported to Flinders Island, where most of them quickly perished of European diseases. This, ironically, was the result of humane intentions.

The island's governor Sir George Arthur (1825–36) and his successor Sir John Franklin (1836–43) were appalled at the way the Tasmanians were being treated, and wanted to segregate them to protect them. In 1876 the last known Tasmanian, Truganini, perished, and against her express wishes and religious beliefs, her body was exhumed and became a museum exhibit. It was only cremated and scattered at sea by ABORIGINAL PEOPLE 100 years later. Even then, it took until 2002 for the Royal College of Surgeons in Britain to agree to repatriate her hair and skin samples.

The extinction of the Tasmanians, however, is not as straightforward an issue as it might seem. There were many people of mixed birth on Tasmania, many from Tasmanian women bought or kidnapped by sealers. Many kept quiet about their heritage for fear of discrimination. In the 1970s, with Aboriginal peoples everywhere resurgent in their pride and assertive in their demands for recognition, the Tasmanian community resurfaced. There were also those of MAORI, WEST INDIAN and Asian heritage on the island who had suffered discrimination, and many of them identified themselves with the Tasmanians. This has given rise to the deeply divisive issue of who should be defined as a Tasmanian. About 6000 people on Tasmania claimed descent from Aboriginal peoples in 2002.

## TE ATI AWA

A MAORI *iwi* (tribe) of eastern and southern North Island, New Zealand. Sedentary traders, farmers, hunters and fishers, they claim descent from the POLYNESIAN migrants who were aboard the *Tokomaru* canoe, and speak Maori.

The Te Ati Awa lived in the Taranaki area, but in 1819 part of the tribe chose to follow the NGATI TOA *ariki* (chief) Te Ruaparaha in his war of conquest and migrated to the Manawatu plains. In the 1830s their refusal to accept Ngati Toa control of Cook Strait did much to weaken Te Ruaparaha's alliance, just when the European settlers were making inroads into Maori lands. Both branches of the Te Ati Awa suffered land seizures, especially in the Taranaki area, where bitter land wars in the 1860s led to enormous confiscations. While some compensation in the form of small allotments of poor-quality land was promised, very little was ever actually awarded.

In 1998 the Te Ati Awa opened negotiations with the New Zealand government over the violations of the promises made in the Treaty of Waitangi (1840) and the illegal land losses they had suffered. This led to a settlement in which they received an official apology, NZ$ 34 million compensation, the return of some land and the option to buy more as it became available, alongside assurances of access to fishing grounds and steps to protect their culture, including changing some place names back to their original Maori. A central claim to Mount Taranaki is still disputed. In 2000 the Te Ati Awa numbered about 13,000.

## TETUM or Tetun or Teto or Teta or Tetung

An indigenous people who were possibly the first inhabitants of East Timor. They traditionally live in the central steppes and currently number over 300,000. The Tetum language is from the AUSTRONESIAN family, and the name Lia-Tetun means 'language of the plains'. The Tetum are said to be the descended from Indo-Malay people who brought INDONESIAN lifestyles to Timor, and the Tetum are also found in Indonesia. The Tetum are traditionally animistic and shamanistic, although because of Portuguese influence growing numbers adhere to Catholicism. In the 14th century the Tetum were synonymous with the Belu tribe, who established the Wehali kingdom that united much of central Timor. During the Wehali period Tetum, as a language, spread throughout Timor. In the 18th century the Tetum language took on many influences from PORTUGUESE, and the Portuguese promoted Tetum as a national language. Today Tetum is the national language of Timor, spoken by over 75% of the population. (See also EAST TIMORESE.)

## THAIS

The indigenous TAI people of the Kingdom of Thailand, where they form approximately 75% of the population. The ethnic Thais are found throughout Thailand but are concentrated mainly in the central region. Minority peoples of Thailand include CHINESE, MALAY, CAMBODIAN, KHMER, VIETNAMESE and BURMESE, as well as other smaller ethnic groups. The Thais speak a language belonging to the SINO-TIBETAN or Tai family. The vast majority of Thais adhere to Theravada Buddhism.

The Thais were not originally indigenous to Thailand. They migrated to the region from what is now the Yunnan province of China during the 6th century AD. Some historians believe that the 'Proto-Thai' were actually Tai-speakers originating in northern Vietnam, who subsequently settled in southwestern China. By AD 650 these people had established the Nanzhao kingdom (known as the Six Tai United States), a Tai kingdom that also included the LAOTIANS and the SHAN. The peoples of Nanzhao began migrating

south in the 8th century, and by around 1000 they were under pressure from the CHINESE. In 1253 the Mongol ruler Kublai Khan destroyed the kingdom, resulting in an increased flow of immigrants into Southeast Asia. From their encounters with the Khmer peoples during and after this migration, the Tais became known as the Syam (Siamese), taken from the Sanskrit word *syana*, meaning 'golden' or 'swarthy' (referring to the Tais' skin complexion). The Thais captured the Khmer site of Sukhothai, which became the capital of the first Siamese kingdom in 1238.

During the reign of the second Sukhothai king, Rama Kamheng (1260–1350), the kingdom expanded to Laos and south Burma, a writing system was formed that became the basis for recording the Thai language, and the codification of Thai Theravada Buddhism was established. Sukhothai began to decline after a rival dynasty established itself at Ayutthaya, near present-day Bangkok, in 1351. The foundation of Ayutthaya is generally regarded as marking the origin of the modern state of Thailand, although even by this time the Thai identity was

> *"The Chinese do the heavy work in Bangkok and the Siamese [Thai] let them – proving the moral superiority of the former and the mental superiority of the latter."*
>
> Crosbie Garstin, 1928

Thais

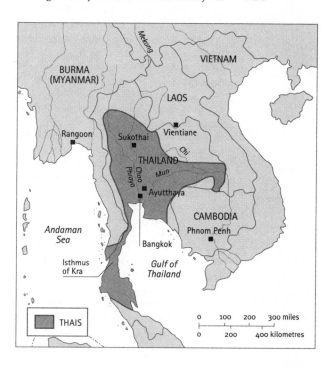

Thais

already established. During the 14th–15th centuries Ayutthaya expanded, taking many Khmer lands, including Angkor, and annexing Sukhothai in 1538. Through their interactions with the Khmer the Siamese assimilated many Khmer customs and words. The 16th century was a period of encounters with the French, Dutch and Portuguese. In 1688, during the reign of King Narai, Siam was closed to the West for fear of French invasion, and this period lasted nearly 150 years. During the 16th century the Burmese invaded Thailand a number of times; their last invasion succeeded in capturing Chiang Mai and destroying Ayutthaya. Eventually, however, the Thais, under the King Naresuan (ruled 1590–1605) succeeded in expelling the Burmese. Subsequently the Siamese capital was moved to Thonburi. In 1782 the Chakkri dynasty, which continues to the present day, came to power. Under kings Rama I (ruled 1782–1809) and Rama II (reigned 1809–24) the Thai kingdom was reorganized to face new Burmese attacks, and the capital was moved to Bangkok. Under the rule of Rama III (ruled 1824–51) trade and cultural influences increased with China and there was expansion into Laotian and Khmer territories. It was with King Rama IV, also known as King Mongkut, that Siam – with the signing of the British Bowring Treaty (1855) and subsequent European and American treaties – once again opened up to the West. He appointed Westerners to the court, and foreign nationals and Christian missionaries began to arrive. The Western influence also brought advancements in medical care and education. Rama V (ruled 1868–1910) continued the cordial Western relations, resulting in the setting up of a civil service and a rail service. Rama VI (ruled 1910–25) established the first compulsory Siamese education.

In 1932 a relatively peaceful coup changed Siam into a constitutional monarchy. As a result, in 1939 Siam changed its name to Thailand, also known as Muang Thai ('Land of the Free'). During World War II Thailand was occupied by JAPANESE forces, and between 1945 and 1948 Thailand briefly changed its name back to Siam. From 1945 there were many unsuccessful coups staged until in 1979 democratic elections were held. Under new rule the Thai people prospered.

In 1991 another military coup was staged, this time successful but shortlived, because in 1992, owing to popular demonstrations, the civil government was restored. In 2000 the Thai Rak Thai ('Thai loves Thai') Party gained power. The constitutional monarchy continues under the rule of Rama IX.

# THO

A Southeast Asian people found principally in northern Vietnam and Guangxi province of southern China, where they number between 1 and 1.25 million people. They speak a Viet-Mon-Khmer language that belongs to the TAI family. They practise an eclectic mix of religions, blending together polytheism with Taoism, Buddhism and animism. They are also known as the Tay, Thu, Keo, Cuoi, Ho, Tay Poong, Dan Lai and Ly Ha.

# THRO

See SO.

# TIWI

An Australian ABORIGINAL PEOPLE of Melville and Bathurst islands on the Northern Territory coast. They were formerly relatively sedentary hunters, gatherers and fishers and speak a non-Austronesian language. Like other Aboriginal peoples, they were much reduced by diseases and land loss in the 19th century. In 1968, however, they were assisted to adopt the clay they traditionally used for their distinctive rock and body art to pottery, and developed highly gifted craftsmen with a more reliable source of income. This allowed them to revive their traditional, very complex *pukumani* funerary ceremony, designed to put the deceased to rest, which had been in decline. In 1995 their Tiwi island council also adopted its own flag. In 1983 they numbered 1500.

# TOBA-WEI or Tabgatch or Toba or Pei Wei or T'o-Pa

A former Turkic-speaking nomadic people (see TURKS) who, in the early centuries AD, lived on the Mongolian steppes close to the northern borders of China. In 386 the Toba, leading a confederation of Turko-MONGOL tribes, defeated the Juan Juan, the Yen and other kingdoms of northern China, and established the Dai dynasty's supremacy in what is now the Shansi province. Shortly afterwards the dynasty changed its name to Wei, after whom the Toba kingdom is usually known as Toba-Wei. Within a relatively short time the kingdom expanded greatly, and the nomadic people largely became sedentary, becoming more and more influenced by CHINESE culture and customs.

Having no traditions of literacy, the Toba-Wei were not well equipped to handle internal affairs, therefore they were forced to opt for Chinese assistance. Chinese culture, legal system and social structure quickly subsumed that of the Toba. A policy of adopting Chinese culture was taken in 495, the result of which was the total disregard of their own heritage and culture. As a result of Chinese influence, the Toba, previously anti-Buddhist, adopted Chinese Mahayana Buddhism and Taoism.

The pro-Chinese policy and its consequences, however, were not welcomed by all. The lower classes of Toba-Wei, the very people who pioneered the kingdom, including the army, lived on the extremities of the kingdom and still clung to Toba culture. In 524 they staged an uprising that resulted in a 10-year civil war. In 528 they assassinated the ruling monarch and the majority of the royal court. In 535 the empire was split into the Eastern and Western Toba-Wei empires, but these quickly disintegrated.

Because of assimilation by the Chinese, the Toba-Wei no longer exist as a separate ethnic group.

## TOLAI

A native people of Gazelle peninsula, New Britain province, Papua New Guinea. The area was settled by MELANESIANS, who arrived perhaps around 2000 BC and established a farming and fishing economy. The Tolai speak an AUSTRONE-SIAN language and were said to be cannibals. Although Christians, they persist with traditional beliefs, such as a fear of *tabaran*, or malevolent spirits inhabiting the rainforest,

which require elaborate rituals to turn aside. They were in the past victimized by a secret society, *Ingeit*, which preyed on their fear of sorcery.

The Tolai occupy the territory in which the city of Rabaul developed, and this exposed them to outside influences to a much greater degree than their neighbours. This has had both negative and positive effects. Under German rule (1884–1914) a considerable portion of their lands were seized for plantations. European influences also had a corrosive effect on society and social controls; this could be seen in 1961 when Tolai youths attacked 'foreigners' working on those plantations. The Europeans have also supplied economic opportunity, however, and the Tolai entered the cash economy, growing coffee for example. Greater disposable wealth has led some to want to change the traditional matrilineal form of inheritance to a patrilineal form. The Tolai have, since independence, come to form the provincial political elite, and so great is their influence that their neighbours have demanded to secede from the province. In 1991 they numbered over 61,000.

## TONGANS

The native people of the nation of Tonga, a South Pacific island group. The first inhabitants were of the LAPITA CULTURE, who arrived around 3000 BC, but around AD 950 they were colonized by POLYNESIANS. Farmers and fishers, the newcomers spoke an AUSTRONESIAN language and established a culture rich in folklore, mythology, music and its famous *lakalaka* dance. The Tongans also have a tradition of gift-giving to new friends and even strangers.

They were an aggressive nation, however, later likened to Vikings for their extended raiding and glorification of war. They encountered Europeans with confidence in the late 18th century, though some outer islands were devastated by whalers. Soon, however, the Tongans were reduced by European diseases, and their culture and society were impacted by missionaries who arrived in 1822. No European power ever seriously tried to colonize them, however, as they seemed to possess few exploitable resources. In 1896 the Tongans persuaded the BRITISH government to establish a protectorate, in which they

*t*

**" The merriest creatures I ever met. "**

James Cook on the Tongans, 1773

retained considerable autonomy, sending an independent force to fight the JAPANESE in World War II. Full sovereignty was restored in 1976. The economy was, however, heavily dependent on remittances from workers overseas. In the 1990s there were calls for political reform of the kingdom following corruption scandals, but the nobility remain firmly in control. Indeed they remain extremely proud of the survival of much of their traditional culture. In 2003 they numbered about 98,000.

## TORADJA or Toraja

A people who come from Tana Toraja (Toraja Land) in the central regions of the INDONESIAN island of Sulewesi (Celebes). Toradja is a fairly recent name used by neighbouring people, the Bugus, which means 'people from the west' or 'people of the interior land'. The population of Tana Toraja is around 380,000, and a further 1 million live outside Tana Toraja and away from the island. They speak a form of Bahasa Indonesia, the Indonesian language that evolved from Bazaar Malay. Some 80% are Christian, 11% Muslim and 9% animist; many also practise elaborate traditional Toradja tribal rituals.

The Toradja are the only predominantly Christian tribe on Sulewesi and live in separate hamlets bound by kinship, family and area ties. They are famed for their unique houses, whose roofs resemble saddles, and for their elaborate rituals. The ancestors of the Toradja are thought to be the proto-MALAY, originating possibly in Indo-China and migrating southwards around 3000 years ago. In the 14th century they inhabited the coastal areas of the island, but owing to invasions they were pushed towards the centre.

## TORRES STRAIT ISLANDERS

A people of the islands between Australia and New Guinea and of parts of Cape York, Queensland, Australia. They are descended from Australian ABORIGINAL PEOPLES, MELANESIANS and POLYNESIANS. The original inhabitants appear to have been Aboriginal peoples who by 2000 BC had been joined by the Melanesians, who established a hunting, fishing, farming and trading economy, which was subsequently enriched by

Polynesian migration. The languages they used have largely disappeared and most now speak Torres Strait Creole, an English-based pidgin.

Their isolation perhaps protected them from the worst excesses of European invasion and settlement in the 19th century. From the 1870s, however, the activities of missionaries began to erode a traditional culture quite distinct from that of other Australian Aboriginal people in its music, dance, lifestyle and religious belief. Pearl fisheries brought JAPANESE, FILIPINO and CHINESE influences that further undermined this culture. The islanders are known to have believed that the cultural objects manufactured by their ancestors had spiritual worth, but little of their pre-Christian religion survives other than a tombstone unveiling ceremony. Politically, they gained the right to elect their own island councils in the 1930s, and in 1992 a court ruling confirmed their ownership of their lands.

With an economy now heavily dependent on fish, they have a high level of welfare dependency and still complain of discrimination. In the late 1990s they numbered over 30,000.

## TROBRIAND ISLANDERS

The MELANESIAN people of the Trobriand Islands of Papua New Guinea. Fishers and farmers (especially of yams, which have a totemic significance in their culture), they speak an AUSTRONESIAN language. They are Christian, but traditional beliefs persist: for example, they fear *mulukwansi*, or witches, and perform magic rituals when on the open sea. They are noted as practical jokers, especially teasing outsiders and, like the MASSIM, practise the *kula* gift-giving tradition. They are also noted for a relaxed attitude to sexual behaviour: intercourse is not believed to cause pregnancy and is encouraged among the young. In 1991 they numbered about 22,000.

## TRUKESE or Chuukese

The native people of the Truk Islands in the western Pacific, now part of the Federated States of Micronesia. Farmers and fishers, they speak a Malayo-Polynesian language and share typical MICRONESIAN cultural characteristics. In 1989 their numbers were estimated at over 38,000.

## TUCHIA or Tujia or Tu Jia Zu

A CHINESE people who live in the Hunan and Hubei provinces of China. The Tuchia language is unique and belongs to the Tibeto-Burman group of the SINO-TIBETAN family. There are approximately 6.4 million Tuchia, but only 20–30,000 converse in their native tongue. The Tuchia call themselves *Bizika*, meaning 'native dwellers'. This is somewhat misleading, as their origin is uncertain. Theories include their descent from the ancient Ba people or from the Wuman, who arrived in the area at the end of the Chinese Tang dynasty (AD 618–907). What is certain, however, is that by around 910 the Tuchia were a distinct ethnic group. During the Ming dynasty (1368–1644) the Tuchia were used as soldiers against JAPANESE pirates. It was only in 1950, however, that the Chinese recognized them as a separate ethnic group. During the 20th century the Tuchia culture was dying out as they became assimilated with the surrounding Chinese peoples and culture. They are now largely indistinguishable from the HAN majority.

## TUNG or Dong or Tung Chia or Tung Ja

An official CHINESE ethnic minority with a population of between 2.7 and 3.1 million Tung language-speakers. They are mostly found in the southern Chinese provinces of Guizhou, southwestern Hunan, northern Guangxi and Hubai, where they live in villages and clans and employ a tribal elder system of authority. The Tung language belongs to the Kan Dai and Kam Sui branches of the sino-tibetan family. The Tung are polytheists, pantheists and animists; however, under HAN influence some have adopted Buddhism. It is thought that the original Tung were migrants from Thailand some 3000 years ago who settled in the Hunan, Guizhou and Guangxi provinces. They were certainly documented in those areas during the Qin dynasty (221–206 BC). In the 1950s a romanized alphabet of the Tung language was made, although the Chinese government has banned it. Most Tung use Chinese ideographic writing.

## TUVALUANS

The native people of the nation of Tuvalu, a western Pacific island group (formerly the Ellice Islands). The islands were settled by POLYNESIANS in the 14th century AD. The Tuvaluans are farmers and fishers and speak an AUSTRONESIAN language. Isolated and lacking natural resources, they were largely ignored until Peruvian slavers began raiding in the 1860s, prompting the BRITISH to annexe them to halt the depredations. Tuvalu became independent in 1978, splitting off from the former Gilbert Islands, home of the I-KIRIBATI. Although the Tuvaluans are deeply devout Christians, their traditional culture and customs remain strong. Music and dance are vital to their celebrations, while society remains stratified and courtesies and customs rule all aspects of life. In 1998 they were the only nation in the world held above reproach on human rights issues.

The great issue to Tuvaluans is the environment. Tuvalu is one of the lowest-lying countries in the world, with no point higher than 4 m / 13 ft above sea level, and there are fears that global warming will drown the entire nation within 50 years. Thus they were outraged in 2000 when US President George W. Bush repudiated the Kyoto protocol on global warming. Fearing the need for eventual evacuation they have persuaded the New Zealand government to accept a quota of their number as refugees, but the Australian government refused. In 2002 they numbered over 8400.

> " As long as Tuvalu is above sea water there will be people staying here. We will not move. "
>
> Premier Saufatu Sopo'aga, 2003

## VANUATUANS

See NI-VANUATU.

## VIETNAMESE or Annamese

The indigenous inhabitants of Vietnam. They are the largest ethnic group, constituting 85–90% of Vietnam's population of 80 million. CHINESE people make up 3%, and the remaining population comprises over 53 ethnic minorities including the KHMER, Muong, CHAM, MEO, TAI, Man and MONTAGNARDS. Vietnamese, also known as Kinh, is the official language; it descends from the Mon-Khmer AUSTRO-ASIATIC

> " They [the Vietnamese] are a very white people, because there it begins to bee cold. "
>
> Monsieur de Monfort, c. 1604

V

family and has Tai and Chinese influences. Other spoken languages include Chinese, English, French, Khmer and tribal dialects. The Vietnamese are diverse religiously, adhering to Mahayana Buddhism (the majority religion), Taoism, Islam, Roman Catholicism, indigenous beliefs and new religious movements. The Vietnamese have a long history littered with conflict. Archaeology suggests that the first Vietnamese were settled many thousands of years ago, as early as Neolithic times, and that the first culture was the Phun-ngyuyen Culture *c*. 2000–1400 BC. Between 500 and 300 BC the Vietnamese, whose name was then the Lac – named after the first Kingdom of Au Lac, lasting 1000 years – inhabited the Red River delta. In the 2nd century BC the CHINESE Qin dynasty (221–206 BC)

invaded. However, when the Qin dynasty collapsed a kingdom named Nan-yue or Nam Viet was built by a rebel commander. This remained independent until 113 BC, when it was conquered by the Chinese HAN dynasty. Under the Han dynasty the Vietnamese were strongly influenced by Chinese culture, but they subsequently developed their own styles, becoming renowned for the quality of their blue and white decorated porcelain. There was resistance to Chinese rule and for a short period (AD 39–43) the Vietnamese were independent under the Trung Sisters. Subsequently, however, the Chinese returned to power and ruled the Vietnamese for the next 900 years. The Chinese knew the region as Annam ('the pacified south') and it is from this that the Vietnamese were often called 'Annamese' by outsiders.

In 939 the Vietnamese finally drove out the Chinese and founded the kingdom of Dai Viet. Powerful dynasties were established during this time, the greatest of which was the Ly dynasty (1010–1225), which defied the forces of Kublai Khan in the 13th century and the Ming dynasty in the 15th century. Under the first king of the Le dynasty the Vietnamese extended their power into Cambodia, shattering the Khmer kingdom in the 16th century, and conquered the CHAMS of southern Vietnam. Following a period of civil war, the Vietnamese were divided into northern and southern states in 1620. In the late 18th century the weakened Le dynasty collapsed and in 1789 the Tay Son brothers re-united Vietnam. The Nguyen dynasty was founded in 1802 by Nguyen Anh, the only surviving member of the Nguyen rulers of the southern state, with FRENCH assistance. The French, however, including Christian missionaries, were treated with suspicion. Many were persecuted or murdered during the 1830s. In response the Nguyen were attacked by Napoleon III in 1858 and 1862, and the French gained control over the south. By 1883 the Vietnamese were under French colonial rule and Vietnam became part of the colony of French Indo-China.

Before, during and after World War II, the Vietnamese resisted colonial rule. The leading figure in the Vietnamese independence movement was Ho Chi Minh, who founded the communist and nationalist Vietminh movement in 1941 while the country was under JAPANESE occupation. On Japan's surrender in 1945, the Vietminh declared independence, but France fought to restore colonial rule. French forces withdrew only in 1954, after their defeat by Vietminh forces at Dien Bien Phu.

The 1954 Geneva accords once again divided Vietnam, with the Vietminh in the north and a US-backed anti-communist military regime in the south. The southern regime lacked popular legitimacy and struggled to control communist insurgents whose aim was to unite the country under the Vietminh government of the north.

In 1965 the USA committed combat troops to support the southern regime. Between 1965 and the 1973 ceasefire around 15% of Vietnamese lost their lives or became wounded during the Vietnam War. The ceasefire and withdrawal of US troops did not stop North Vietnamese ambitions; in 1975 Saigon (now Ho Chi Minh City), the capital of South Vietnam, was captured and the country reunified. Thousands of supporters of the military regime fled abroad, principally to the USA, where they are now a well-established ethnic minority.

After 1975 Vietnam suffered economic and political isolation. This was worsened when the Vietnamese overthrow of the genocidal Khmer Rouge regime in Cambodia provoked a Chinese invasion in 1979. The collapse in 1991 of the USSR, Vietnam's main ally, forced the country into rapprochement with the West. Solid Vietnamese relations with the USA were established in 1994, and in 1999 a framework trade agreement was laid down. Despite much suffering and loss, the Vietnamese nation appears to be rising again, peacefully, into modernity.

## VISAYAN

See BISAYAN.

## WA

See LAWA.

## WAIKATO

A MAORI *iwi* (tribe) of northeast North Island, New Zealand. Sedentary hunters, fishers, traders and farmers, they trace their descent from the POLYNESIAN migrants of the mid-14th century in the *Tainui* canoe, and speak Maori.

Initially a federation of tribes, the Waikato were formed into a single group during the Musket Wars of the early 19th century, when they expanded their territory south and eastwards. Like all other MAORI, they successfully adopted European agriculture and technology very quickly, and had built ten flour mills by 1853. Many Waikato *ariki* (chiefs) refused to accept the Treaty of Waitangi (1840), however, and fiercely resisted settler incursions. It was a Waikato chief, Te Wherowhero, who was elected as King Potatua I by a number of Maori tribes in an attempt to unite their resistance.

As they began to lose the land wars, the Waikato became a centre of the ferocious Hua Hua warrior cult, and on defeat retreated into the 'King Country', shunning all contacts with settlers until the 1880s. As a result they lost a considerable part of their lands. They have, however, been notable in their success in preserving their traditional culture and language.

After long and often acrimonious negotiations with the government, the Waikato agreed in 1994 to a settlement of their grievances, receiving NZ$ 60 million and the return of lands (including the campus of the University of Waikato) and an apology for their mistreatment. In 1996 they numbered nearly 36,000.

## WAILBRI or Walbiri

An Australian ABORIGINAL PEOPLE of the Alice Springs area, Northern Territory. Nomadic hunters and gatherers, they speak a Pama-Nyungan language. They are noted for their spiritual centre of Ngama, where they produced a famous rock painting of a python. Here they performed regular ceremonies to initiate young men, promote the expansion of their people and replenish the landscape and food supplies. Notwithstanding this, their desert lands are harsh, and by the mid-1940s disease and the loss of resources had reduced them to just 600, half of whom had moved away, seeking an easier subsistence. They were at that point forcibly sedentarized at Yuenduma, near Ngama. By 1990 they had grown to 3000 in number.

# WALLIS AND FUTUNA ISLANDERS

A POLYNESIAN people of Wallis and Futuna Islands, two South Pacific island groups. The culture and language of the Futuna islands were strongly influenced by the SAMOANS, while the Wallis islands came under the domination of the TONGANS. They are traditionally subsistence farmers and fishers, and land tenure is still governed by custom and is based on local communities or kinship groups.

From the early 19th century the islands were frequently visited by whalers and traders, bringing European diseases, and they were annexed by the FRENCH in the 1880s. While many traditions remain strong, such as *kava* drinking and *tapa* painting, European and AMERICAN cultural influences are very strong. In 1999 they numbered over 14,000.

# WALMAJARRI

An Australian ABORIGINAL PEOPLE of the Fitzroy River and Lake Gregory areas, Western Australia. Nomadic hunter-gatherers, they speak a Pama-Nyungan language. They initially lived in the Kutjungka area of the Great Sandy Desert, and were contacted only in 1939, by German missionaries, making them one of the last groups to be contacted and to leave the desert. They drifted into cattle stations and were ignored by the government. In 2001, however, they won title to part of their ancestral lands, including their sacred site at Paruka (Lake Gregory), as well as guarantees of some measures to protect their culture. In 1990 they numbered about 1000.

# WARRA

An Australian ABORIGINAL PEOPLE of the coast of Spencer gulf, South Australia. Sedentary hunters, fishers and gatherers, they spoke a Pama-Nyungan language. Occupying territory where considerable numbers of European settlers arrived in the 19th century, they came under considerable pressure through land loss, disease and acculturation. By 1981 there was possibly just a single speaker of the language, and their identity as a distinct people was seriously at risk.

# WARUMUNGU

An Australian ABORIGINAL PEOPLE of the Tennant Creek area, Northern Territory. Nomadic hunters and gatherers who speak a Pama-Nyungan language, they, along with their neighbours, the KAYTETYE, were driven to fight the white settlers when a telegraph station was built on one of their most important dreamtime sites in 1872. After killing cattle to drive off the settlers, large numbers of them were murdered, and they were driven from much of their land. In 1892 a reserve was created for them, but it was repeatedly moved before being terminated by the territorial government in 1962. They entered a land claim, which had taken years to prepare, in 1982. The territorial government had already sold much of the land and fought the legal claim, but by 1994 most of the land had been returned. In 1983 they numbered about 200, and were working hard to preserve their traditional culture.

# WEIPA

An Australian ABORIGINAL PEOPLE of the Cape York peninsula, Queensland. Originally many were part of the WIK grouping of Aboriginal peoples, especially the WIK. They were relatively sedentary hunters, gatherers and fishers, and speakers of Pama-Nyungan languages. They were notable for the great cockleshell mounds built over successive generations during their gathering activities. These mounds are among the largest in the world, and are protected as archaeological relics. Contacts with Europeans became an increasing problem from the 1870s, however, with several Weipa being recruited (or kidnapped) to work for the local fishing industry. Diseases and violence proved disastrous. Two local cattle-herders are reputed to have launched a private war of extermination in the area, killing hundreds. In 1898, with official encouragement, Presbyterians founded a mission at Weipa to protect them. They attempted to introduce handicraft industries, but never had the capital for these to prosper. In 1932 the mission was moved to a more accessible site near Embley River, to which the name Weipa was transferred. In 1951 bauxite was discovered on

Weipa land, and they began to be viewed as an inconvenience by those wishing to extract the ore. State financial support was abruptly halted in 1953, and 96% of their land was arbitrarily transferred to a mining company in 1957. They survived and adopted the name *Napranum*, and in 2001 were counted at 766. In 2002 they began what could prove a very expensive land claim against the state government.

## WHITE TAI

See TAI.

## WIK

A group of associated Australian ABORIGINAL PEOPLES of York peninsula, Queensland. Generally relatively sedentary hunters, fishers and gatherers, they speak Pama-Nyugan languages. They are noted for the great mounds of cockleshells produced by generations of gathering, which are now a protected archaeological site.

By the 1870s they were under intense pressure from the fishing industry, which employed or kidnapped them as labour, and local cattle-herders had begun a campaign of extermination. Some after 1898 joined a Presbyterian mission (see the WEIPA). Others survived as best they could on their former lands, often as virtual slave labour on cattle stations, although on many such stations conditions and wages were reasonable and they could maintain their traditional lifestyle on their traditional lands.

In 1996 they took their grievances against the state government to court, which decided that their title to their traditional lands, which had been leased to cattle-herders, were still valid. This meant that the Wik had the right to share the land, a concept entirely in accordance to the customs of Aboriginal people. The decision, however, provoked outrage and racist abuse from cattle-herders who feared losing their land. In 1981 speakers of eight Wik languages numbered about 1300.

## WOLEAIAN

The native people of Woleai, a western Pacific island group that is now part of Yap state in the Federated States of Micronesia. Farmers and fishers who speak an AUSTRONESIAN language, they share many of the cultural traits of other MICRONESIANS. They suffered severely in World War II, as the JAPANESE felled the main island's trees to make way for an airfield, which was heavily bombed by US forces. Despite this upheaval they are noted for holding firm to traditional ways, with rules forbidding Western dress and no commercial facilities for tourists. About 850 of a total population of about 2000 lived on the islands in 2000. Their greatest demand is for more books to be published in their own language.

## WOPKAIMIN

A PAPUAN people of Ok Tedi region, Western province, Papua New Guinea. Farmers and fishers, they speak a trans-New Guinea language. Their society was founded on kinship groups, and their traditional culture underwent massive dislocation from the mid-1970s, when gold- and copper-mining began on their territory. The mine brought prosperity initially, and they acquired ropes and shotguns to enter the vast Luplupwiutem caves and hunt the bats effectively (quickly hunting Bulmer's fruit bats to extinction). The mine also brought a much-needed clinic. By the 1990s, however, millions of tons of mine tailings and toxic chemicals dumped into their river had destroyed nearly all fish stocks, driven away game and destroyed 1300 sq. km / 500 sq. miles of vegetation. After an international scandal they were offered compensation, but their survival as a people is in doubt. In 2003 they numbered less than 1000.

## WORORA

An Australian ABORIGINAL PEOPLE of Collier Bay, Western Australia. Sedentary hunters, gatherers and fishers, they speak a non-Pama-Nyugan language. In the early 20th century they came under pressure from increasing numbers of settlers, and they settled at a Presbyterian mission at Kunnunya. After 1950 they were forced to move several times by the state government and struggled long and hard to permanently re-occupy their traditional territory. This contained their sacred site at Woongguru, where men would conceive the spirit of a child in a dream. It was also necessary to preserve the hundreds of cave paintings of *wandjinas*, who assisted in the creation of the world and needed to be kept strong. In the early 1980s their cave-painting tradition appeared to be disappearing, but 20 years later there was renewed interest in traditions among the young. In 1981 there were 170 language-speakers.

## WUNAMBAL

An Australian ABORIGINAL PEOPLE of the Kimberley Ranges area of Western Australia. Nomadic hunters and gatherers, they speak a non-Pama-Nyungan language. Their sacred site at Mitchell Falls has long been highly attractive to tourists for their outstanding natural beauty, and also for the sacred rock art of the Wunambal. Indeed tourists have camped on sacred ground, defaced the art and even removed bones from burial grounds.

In 2000 the Wunambal were further enraged when the Western Australian government arbitrarily announced the creation of national parks and conservation sites on their lands, which they saw as land confiscation. Therefore in 2001 they began an ethno-ecology programme to ensure that tourism is properly managed to protect their environment and culture, and to ensure that visitors respect their laws, for example by not swimming in the deep pools where *wungurr* (creator snakes) lived. They have had less success in preserving their language, which, with 20 speakers in 1990, has become nearly extinct.

## YAMATO CULTURE

The name given to the period of Japanese history from AD 250 to 550 during the rule of the Yamato court. Japan is sometimes called Yamato Japan during this period, as it was the Yamato that united Japan for the first time in its history. The Yamato period is also called the Tumulus or Tomb period for the masses of gigantic tombs built for the Yamato elite. By the end of the Yamato reign their rulers referred to themselves as *Temo* or 'Great Kings', who traced their ancestry to divine origin. In religion the Yamato were

Shinto, although later in the period's history Buddhism was introduced.

During the 3rd century AD the Yamato rulers originated in the Yamato region of the southwestern peninsula of Honshu, the main island of Japan. During the early Yamato period they ruled over the majority of the archipelago, and their political and religious centre was Mount Miwa, which they regarded as the habitation of their great Shinto god. The period up until the end of the 4th century was one of expansion and consolidation. The Yamato centre shifted to the Isonokami shrine in Tenri, and their power extended even as far as the Korean peninsula, where they came into contact with the powerful Paekche kingdom. Through such contact with the mainland, Japanese culture was greatly influenced by the CHINESE and KOREANS, and great advances were made in agriculture, technology and social systems. The Chinese script was also adopted.

Early in the 5th century the Yamato expanded westwards into the Osaka region, and Yamato Japan came under more militant rule. Yamato Japan, now united, received Confucian scholars at the royal court in 513; thus started the vast influence of Confucianism in Japan. Similarly, in 552, Buddhism arrived in Japan, overseen by the famous prince Shotuku. It was around this period that the Yamato and Paekche alliance waned and the Japanese aristocracy began to fight against Yamato hegemony. Although the year 550 is regarded as the end of the Yamato culture it was not until 642 that the Soga officially captured the throne and gained power. Over this period of Yamato decline the Soga clan, which Prince Shotuku was from, led a coup against the Yamato rulers. Consequently the introduction of Buddhism and its clash with Shinto can be seen as one of the decisive factors in the Yamato culture's decline.

## YANGSHAO CULTURE

China's first indigenous and fully agriculturally developed farming culture. The culture existed between 5000 and 3000 BC, during the Neolithic period. It is also known as the Painted Pottery Culture, named for its famed painted black, white and red pottery. The first pieces of pottery were unearthed at a village called Yang-shao in Henan province, and it is from this location that the culture derived its name. The culture was centred in the Henan and Shaanxi provinces on the banks of the Yellow River. Yang-shao society was organized as tribal clan communities with two social strata, those of the chiefs and those of the craftsmen and farmers. Homesteads had central dwelling-houses surrounded by groups of about five other buildings. Villages were surrounded by defensive moats, and graveyards were placed outside these. Little is known of Yangshao religious practices.

## YANKUNYTJATJARA

An Australian ABORIGINAL PEOPLE whose territory once ranged from the Musgrave Range to Uluru in central Australia. Traditionally hunters and gatherers, they speak a Pama-Nyungan language and have close affiliations with the PITJANTJARA. Collectively the two peoples are among the ANAGU. The more dominant Pitjantjara did occupy parts of their territory during a drought of the 1930s, but they still closely cooperate in defence of their sacred sites and environment. As the Yankunytjatjara are still suffering the after-effects of BRITISH nuclear tests in the 1950s, with previously unknown health problems including cancer and asthma, they are very much at the forefront of the Irati Wanti ('the poison, leave it') movement opposing nuclear dumping. In 1985 they numbered up to 300 language-speakers

## YANYULA

An Australian ABORIGINAL PEOPLE of Borroloola, Northern Territory, and Doomadgee, Queensland. Nomadic hunters, gatherers and fishers, they speak a Pama-Nyungan language. They are notable for their dugout canoes, which their ancestors are thought to have learned to make from visitors from ancient Indonesia. From about 1880 they came under pressure from settlers. Cattle-herders regularly crossed their territory, destroying food resources and polluting water supplies. In order to survive, they began consuming the crops and stock of settlers, leading to brutal reprisals. They survived through taking often highly exploitative employ-

ment in the cattle industry. In the 1970s they began to pursue land claims, and recovered both the Sir Edward Pellew Islands and land around Robinson River. In 1990 they numbered up to 100, but had several descendants among the GARAWA and MARRA.

## YAO

A mountain-village people of Southeast Asia. They are an official CHINESE minority and are also found in Vietnam, where they are known as the Man, as well as in Laos and Thailand. They number around around 2.13 million and are most numerous in southern China (concentrated in Guangxi Zhuang autonomous province) where they are estimated to number 1.5 million. They all speak closely related SINO-TIBETAN languages and live within villages and clans with 75–100 dwellers under a headsman. Their societies are patrilineal. They are polytheists, animists and ancestor-worshippers. Owing to contact with Arabs, the Yao have been exposed to Islam, which also became influential. Most Yao are migratory farmers practising slash-and-burn cultivation and who also exploit the forested uplands to trade with neighbouring lowlanders. In the CHINESE province of Guangdong (Kwangtung) some even migrated to the lowlands where they cultivate wet rice.

They were known as the 'savage Wuling tribes' 2000 years ago and were found in the Hunan province. They were renamed the Moyoa 200–300 years later. Prior to the foundation of the People's Republic of China in 1949 they were known by 30 differing names; from 1949 onwards their official designated name has been 'Yao'. Historically they have had close contact with the Song, Ming and Qing dynasties, from which their livelihoods, culture and occupations have benefited greatly despite a history littered with rebellion, most notably during 1316–31. However, for a thousand-year period up until 1949, the Yao leaders were used very much as puppet figures for central governmental powers. The Yao played a prominent role in the communist revolution prior to 1949. Since the founding of the People's Republic and the Chinese policy of regional autonomy, the Yao have enjoyed greater autonomy. In 1951 they were granted the

**"** We say 'NO radioactive dumping in our *ngura* – in our country.' It's strictly poison and we don't want it. **"**

Declaration of Irati Wanti, the anti-nuclear dumping movement with the Yankunytjatjara at its forefront.

Yao

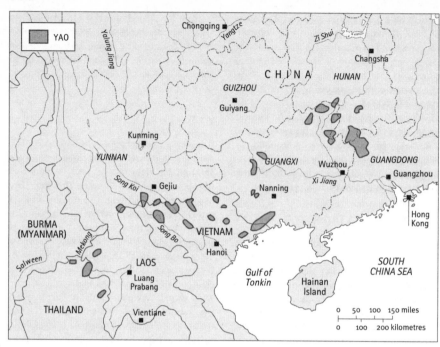

YAO

Longsheng Autonomous County, the first Yao autonomous region. Since then many more have been established, including hundreds of Yao townships. The Yao have also benefited from vastly improved education and healthcare systems. They are closely related to the HMONG.

## YAPESE

The native people of Yap, a western Pacific island group that is now part of the Federated States of Micronesia. Farmers and fishers, they speak an AUSTRONESIAN language and share many of the cultural traits common to MICRONESIANS. The most traditional group in the Federated States, they wear traditional dress and perform the dances that recount entire stories. They are Christian, but traditional beliefs, such as a belief in ghosts, persist. They also use *rai*, the traditional stone money that can measure 4 m / 13 ft in diameter, for special occasions. In 1996 they numbered some 7540

> " They [Yapese] appear to be philosophers in adversity. "
>
> George Keate,
> 1788

## YAYOI CULTURE

A JAPANESE culture from between *c.* 300 BC and *c.* AD 300 that marked a crucial and pivotal point in Japanese history. The beginning of this culture, named after the Yayoi area of Tokyo where the first archaeological evidence of it was unearthed in 1884, developed in the Gobi Desert of northern China. From here these peoples migrated southwards and eastwards to Korea and then on into Japan, arriving in Honshu around 300 BC and spreading throughout Japan.

Their CHINESE and KOREAN influences mixed with the indigenous JOMON culture, resulting in what is said to be the origin of the first distinctively Japanese culture, social structure, religion and language. The immigrants brought to Japan wet-rice cultivation, iron- and bronze-casting technologies, linguistic influences, hierarchical social structures and customs such as burial methods and communal functioning, as well as the origin of the Japanese Shinto religion. The Yayoi had many gods for specific purposes, as in modern Shintoism. During the Yayoi period people lived in *uji* or clans, with the patriarch acting as both leader and priest.

## YERAKAI

A PAPUAN people of Ambunti district, East Sepik province, Papua New Guinea. Farmers and fishers, they speak a Sepik-Ramu language. They are mainly Christian, but traditional beliefs, such as a deep fear of sorcery, are still held. In 2002 they took part in a project, financed by the Dutch government, in growing vanilla as a cash crop, hoping to improve living standards without resorting to logging. In 1981 they numbered 390.

## YI

An indigenous people who live in Sichuan, Yunnan, Guizhou, Guangxi Zhuang, Liangshan Yi, Longlin, Mabian and other provinces of China. They mostly live in the mountainous southwestern regions, although some live in the valleys and flat lands. The total Yi population is over 6.5 million. The Yi are of AUSTRO-ASIATIC origin and speak the Yi language, a Tibetan-Burman member of the SINO-TIBETAN language family. The size of the Yi population means there are a minimum of six dialects and a number of minority related languages including Pai, Lisu, Lahu, Nahsi and Han. The Yi are polytheistic, Taoists and Mahayana Buddhists

The Yi were formerly known as the Lolo (or Luoluo), a name given to them after the fall of the Yuan dynasty in 1368; as the Cuans during the Song dynasty (960–1279); and as the Wumans under the Tang dynasty (618–907). The name Yi actually derives from the Chinese character meaning 'barbarian'.

The ancient Yi are thought to be closely related to the ancient Qiang and Di in western China. Originally Yi society was matrilineal, but around the beginning of the Christian era it became patrilineal. In the 2nd century BC the Yi were a clan people, with a class system, who were centred on the Yunnan and Sichuan provinces, and over the subsequent 500 years they spread to the northwestern Guizhou, northwestern Guangxi and northeastern and southern Yunnan regions. In the 8th century AD the Yi were incorporated into the TAI Nanzhao kingdom and were frequently used as slaves. Upon the collapse of Nanzhao in 937, the Yi became part of the Dali, Luodian and other regimes. However, in the

Yi

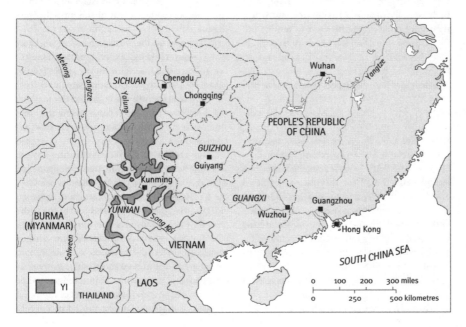

13th century these were conquered by the Yuan (Mongol) dynasty. Under Yuan rule the Yi developed a feudal landlord economy based on a hereditary caste system in which an aristocratic minority, the Black Bone Yi, exploited the lower class White Bone Yi, holding many in slavery.

This system was curtailed by the Chinese communist government in 1949, and several autonomous Yi prefectures were established in 1952–80; the first was the Liangshan Yi Autonomous Prefecture of Sichuan. In 1956 talks began, concluding in 1958, that saw the complete abolition of Yi slavery. Over 690,000 Yi were freed and settled on land confiscated from the former slave owners. Education was also made widely available during the 1950s to all Yi. Since this period, traditional Yi agricultural and farming life has vastly improved in productivity, economy and living standards. Now many Yi live as part of a modern nuclear family.

## YIR-YIRONT

An Australian ABORIGINAL PEOPLE of Cape York peninsula, Queensland. Nomadic hunters and gatherers, they speak a Pama-Nyungan language. Every clan has its own spirit centre, based on a body of water such as a lagoon or creek, where their spirit children are believed to reside until they are sent into a woman's body to be born. In 1991 they had just 15 speakers of a nearly extinct language, most speaking Torres Strait Creole, and their identity as a distinct people was at risk.

## YOLNGU or Yuulngu

A collective name for 16 clans of ABORIGINAL PEOPLES of northeast Arnhem Land, Northern Territory. The Yolngu speak Pama-Nyungan languages. Coastal dwellers, they hunted, gathered and fished, and tended to be more sedentary than other groups. They also had early contacts with traders from modern Indonesia seeking pearl shells, and this influenced their culture, for example by introducing dugout canoes. Sustained contacts with white settlers did not come until the 1930s. Land encroachment was resisted and a number of clans were massacred, while the Yolngu killed in reprisal, including the crew of a

Japanese pearling vessel in 1933. There were calls for a punitive campaign, but instead Methodist missionaries were able to establish a mission at Yirrkala and achieve friendly relations, not least by respecting traditional practices and beliefs. Problems of social exclusion, poor education, substance abuse and official harassment remained (explored only in part in the famous 2001 film *Yolngu Boy*). But in 1963, after the government arbitrarily confiscated land for bauxite mining, they sent a petition to the federal parliament using their traditional artistic medium, bark. This attracted international attention, and did much to establish the modern land-rights movement. They received concessions, including some homeland centres where they can occupy or visit their ancestral lands; but severe social and economic problems persist.

## YUANZHUMIN

See TAIWANESE ABORIGINALS.

## ZHUANG or Chuang

A TAI-related CHINESE minority people, the majority of whom reside in the Guangxi Zhuang Autonomous Region (established 1958). There are over 16 million Zhuang currently living in China.

They were resident in southeastern China by the closing centuries of the 1st millennium BC, when they were overrun by the HAN Chinese. Over the last 2000 years, the Zhuang have lived in close contact with the Han, and the majority of them have been thoroughly assimilated into mainstream Chinese culture and society. Nevertheless, the Chinese government has attempted to preserve the cultural identity of the Zhuang through the creation of an autonomous region and the support of specialist language-teaching. In addition, a romanized alphabet, based on Pinyin, has been introduced to facilitate the transcription of the Zhuang language, which previously had no writing system. Most Zhuang, however, prefer to rely on the Cantonese language for much of their daily lives; as a people, the Zhuang are content with Chinese status. There has been a considerable level of industrial growth in the Autonomous Region over recent

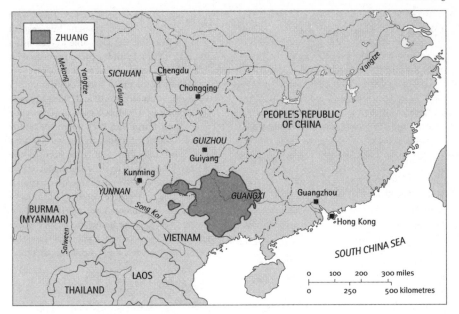

decades, but the majority of Zhuang continue to farm rice as a means of livelihood. Traditional Zhuang religion, still practised by some, is based on animism and magic, and there is tradition- ally far more sexual freedom allowed than is deemed acceptable in most Chinese societies. The Zhuang are related to the LAOTIANS, the PUYI, the SHAN, the THAIS and the TUNG.

# Index of entries

Apalai 27
Apanto 27
Aparni 439
Apolista 27
Apswa 439
Aquitani 288
Arabs 439
Aragonese 288
Arakanese 571
Aramaeans 440
Aranda 571
Arapaho 27
Arára 28
Araucanians 28
Arawak 28
Archaic cultures 28
Archi 288
Argentinians 28
Arikara 29
Arins 441
Armenians 441
Armini 288
Armoricans 288
Aruaki 29
Arubans 29
Arumans 288
Arupai 29
Arverni 288
Aryans 443
Arzawa 443
Asante 167
Asi 443
Asmat 571
Aspero tradition 29
Assamese 443
Assiniboine 30
Asturians 289
Atacameños 30
Aterian culture 169
Ateso 169
Athabaskan 30

Athenians 289
Atoni 571
Atrebates 289
Atseguwa 30
Atsina 30
Attacotti 289
Auaké 30
Aunjetitz culture 290
Aurignacian culture 290
Australians 571
Austrians 290
Austro-Asiatics 572
Austronesian 572
Avars 290
Aymara 31
Ayta 572
Azande 170
Azerbaijanis 445
Azeris 445
Azoreans 291
Aztec 31

# B

Baba Chinese 572
Babylonians 445
Bacairi 31
Bactrians 447
Badagas 447
Badarian culture 170
Baffin Island Eskimo 32
Baggara 170
Bagvalal 291
Bahamians 32
Bahnar 573
Bahrainis 448
Bai 573
Baikots 448
Bajau 573
Baka 170
Bakhtyari 448

Balanta 170
Balearic Islanders 291
Balili 170
Balinese 574
Balkars 291
Balochis 448
Balti 449
Balts 291
Bamana 170
Bamileke 171
Bamum 171
Banana 171
Banas culture 449
Banda 171
Bandjabi 171
Bandkeramik culture 291
Bangladeshis 449
Bangni 449
Banjari 449
Bannock 32
Bantu 171
Banu Asad 449
Bara-Jangar 450
Barbacoa 32
Barbadians 32
Bartangs 450
Bashkirs 292
Basketmaker culture 32
Basmil Turks 450
Basotho 173
Basques 292
Bassa 173
Bastarnae 292
Bataks 574
Batavi 293
Bateke 173
Batoro 173
Bats 450
Batswana 173
Batwa 173
Baulé 173

Malays 606
Malaysians 607
Maldive Islanders 508
Malians 224
Malinke 224
Maliseet 87
Maltese 372
Manchu 609
Mandan 87
Mande 225
Mandingo 225
Mangaraia 609
Manhattan 87
Manipuris 508
Manjako 225
Mannaeans 508
Mansi 508
Manso 87
Manteño 87
Manx 372
Maori 609
Mapuche 88
Maraca culture 88
Marajo culture 88
Marathas 508
Maravi 225
Marchland Poles 373
Marcomanni 373
Mari 373
Marianans 611
Maricopa 88
Marind-Anim 612
Marma 509
Maronites 509
Maroons 88
Marquesans 612
Marra 612
Marshall Islanders 612
Martiniquais 88
Massa 226
Massachusett 89

Massagetae 374
Massim 612
Matabele 226
Mataco 89
Mators 510
Mattaponi 89
Maué 89
Mauritanians 226
Mauritians 226
Mawaca 89
Maya 89
Mayo 91
Mazandaranis 510
Mazovians 374
Mbaka 226
Mbanza 226
Mbaya 91
Mbum 226
Mbundu 227
Mbuti 227
Medes 510
Meherrin 91
Meitheis 511
Melanau 613
Melanesians 613
Mende 227
Menominee 91
Meo 613
Meos 511
Mercians 374
Merina 227
Meroitic culture 227
Meru 227
Mescalero 91
Mesolithic cultures 374
Mesopotamians 511
Messapians 374
Mestizo 91
Métis 92
Mexicans 92
Miami 92

Miao 613
Miccosukee 93
Micmac 94
Micronesians 613
Middle Sepik 614
Midianites 511
Mimbres 94
Min Chia 614
Minaeans 512
Minangkabaus 614
Mingrelians 512
Minnesota Swedes 94
Minoans 375
Mishars 376
Mishmi 512
Mission Indians 94
Mississippian Temple Mound
  culture 94
Missouri 95
Mitanni 512
Miwok 95
Mixe 95
Mixtec 95
Mizo 614
Mizos 513
Moabites 513
Mobile 95
Mochica 95
Mocoví 96
Modoc 96
Moesians 376
Mogollon 96
Moguls 513
Mohave 96
Mohawk 96
Mohegan 97
Mojo 97
Moksha 376
Moldovans 376
Molossians 377
Moluccans 614

St Lucians 121
St Vincentians 122
Sakas 536
Sakha 536
Salinan 122
Salish 122
Salluvii 401
Salvadorans 122
Samal 630
Samaritans 536
Samarran culture 538
Samish 123
Sammarinesi 401
Samnites 401
Samoans 630
Samoyeds 538
San 247
San Augustin culture 123
Sandawe 248
Sanga 248
Sangoan culture 248
Sanpoil 123
Santal 538
Santarém culture 123
Santee 123
São Toméans 248
Saponi 123
Sara 249
Saramaka 124
Sardinians 401
Sarmatians 402
Sarsi 124
Sarwa 249
Sassanians 538
Saudis 538
Sauk 124
Savoyards 402
Saxons 402
Scandinavians 403
Schaghticoke 124
Scordisci 403

Scots 403
Scythians 405
Sea Gypsies 630
Sea Peoples 539
Sechelt 124
Sekani 125
Seleucids 540
Seljuks 540
Selkups 540
Semang 630
Seminole 125
Semites 540
Sene 249
Seneca 125
Senegalese 249
Senoi 630
Senones 406
Senufo 250
Sequani 406
Serbs 406
Seri 125
Serrano 125
Seychelle Islanders 250
Shacriaba 126
Shan Bao 631
Shan 630
Shangane 250
Sharchops 541
Shasta 126
Shawnee 126
Sherpas 541
Shetland Islanders 408
Shilluk 251
Shina 541
Shinnecock 126
Shirazi 251
Shona 251
Shor 541
Shoshone 126
Shuar 127
Shughnis 542

Shuswap 127
Siamese 631
Sibir Tatars 542
Sicani 408
Sicels 408
Sicilians 408
Siena 252
Sierra Leoneans 252
Sihanaka 253
Sikanese 632
Sikhs 542
Siletz 127
Silures 409
Simbu 632
Sinabo 127
Sindhis 543
Singaporeans 632
Sinhalese 544
Sinkyone 127
Sino-Tibetans 545
Siona-Secoya 127
Sioux 128
Siriono 128
Siuslaw 128
Skagit 129
Sklaveni 409
Skokomish 129
Slave 129
Slavs 409
Slovaks 410
Slovenes 410
Smithfield culture 253
Snohomish 129
Snoqualmie 129
So 633
Sobaipuri 130
Solomon Islanders 633
Solorese 633
Solutrean culture 411
Somali 254
Songhai 255